Chisholm's handbook of commercial geography

CHISHOLM'S HANDBOOK OF COMMERCIAL GEOGRAPHY

Entirely rewritten by

Sir Dudley Stamp
CBE, DLit, DSc, LLD, EkonD

Nineteenth Edition revised by
G. Noel Blake and Audrey N. Clark

With maps and diagrams

LONGMAN
LONDON and NEW YORK

Longman Group Limited
Burnt Mill
Harlow
Essex CM20 2JE

Distributed in the United States of America by Longman Inc.,
New York

*Associated companies, branches and representatives throughout
the world*

New editions © L. Dudley Stamp and S. C. Gilmour, 1960, 1962
Eighteenth edition © L. Dudley Stamp, 1966
Nineteenth edition © Geographical Publications Ltd, 1975

First published, 1889
First edition, 1889
Tenth edition, 1925
Eleventh edition, revised and edited by L. Dudley Stamp, 1928
Thirteenth edition, entirely rewritten by L. Dudley Stamp, 1937
Seventeenth edition, revised and edited by L. Dudley Stamp and
S. C. Gilmour, 1962
Eighteenth edition, 1966
Nineteenth edition, revised and edited by G. Noel Blake and
Audrey N. Clark, 1975

ISBN 0 582 48332 8

Library of Congress Catalog Card Number: 60–16277

Printed in Great Britain
by J. W. Arrowsmith Ltd, Bristol

Contents

Contents

Contents

Africa

Contents

Contents

Notes on author and editors

George Goudie Chisholm MA, BSc (Edinburgh), Hon LLD (Edinburgh) 1850–1930

George G. Chisholm spent the first forty-five years of his life in Scotland striving to build up a reputation for geography which would carry it beyond the petty collection of dull facts. His efforts to extend the frontiers of the subject, and his personal insistence on absolute precision resulted in the first publication of his *Handbook* when he was thirty-nine. Six years later his reputation was established by the publication of Longman's *Gazetteer of the World* with its innumerable original references. In 1895 he left Scotland for thirteen years in London as one of the line of distinguished geographers at Birkbeck College. In 1908 he returned to Edinburgh to become the first Lecturer in Geography at the University. Here he began to wield great influence as a lecturer to future teachers, to BCom students (from 1919) and to those taking the new postgraduate Diploma in Geography. He was the Secretary to the Royal Scottish Geographical Society and Examiner to such bodies as the Institute of Bankers. In 1921 his work was recognised by the change of post to that of Reader and two years later, aged seventy-three, he retired and received the highest academic honour of the university, that of Honorary LLD.

In retirement he concentrated on the completion of the major postwar revisions of his *Handbook* and published the ninth and tenth editions before his death in 1930.

Samuel Carter Gilmour 1879–1963

S. Carter Gilmour was born in Lincoln and educated at Bedford School where he developed a lasting enthusiasm for geography. This later developed into a specialisation in geographical journalism and he collaborated with Sir John Scott Keltie (for many years secretary of the Royal Geographical Society and editor of the *Statesman's Year Book*) in a popular series of school readers *Adventures of Exploration*. For some twenty years he was travel editor of *The Field*, and then became editor of Thomas Cook's *Guides*. On the outbreak of the Second World War he joined the staff of the *Crown Colonist* (later the *New Commonwealth*) and was widely read on all commonwealth affairs.

His extensive knowledge of information sources and his meticulous attention to detail made him an ideal collaborator with Professor Stamp in the successive revisions of the fourteenth to the seventeenth editions.

Professor Sir L. Dudley Stamp, CBE, DLit, DSc, LLD, EkonD, 1898–1966

Professor Sir Dudley Stamp was one of the outstanding British geographers. Accepted for King's College, London, at the age of fifteen, he took a first-class honours degree in geology and, after service with the Royal Engineers, returned to the geology staff to take both MSc and DSc by 1921. At the age of twenty-five he was appointed the first professor of geography and geology at the University of Rangoon, and travelled in India, Malaya, China and Japan before returning to the London School of Economics in 1925, where he was Sir Ernest Cassel Reader in Economic Geography for twenty years. In 1945 he was appointed to the Chair in Geography, moving in 1949 to the newly created Chair of Social Geography. At the age of sixty, in 1958 he retired and became Professor Emeritus and Honorary Lecturer.

His great contributions to public service began in 1930 with his increasingly authoritative interest in land use. He initiated the Land Utilisation Survey of Great Britain (an acre by acre mapping of the country which has become a landmark in British geography) and during the Second World War served on the Scott Committee on Rural Land Utilisation and as chief adviser on land use to the Ministry of Agriculture. In 1949 he initiated the extension of his land use work to a world survey; from 1952 to 1956 he was president of the International Geographical Union; and in 1963 he became president of the Royal Geographical Society. He was the official United Kingdom delegate to FAO on food, land use and conservation, and his international reputation was acknowledged by the award of honorary doctorates by many universities at home and overseas. He was knighted in 1965 for services to land use.

Professor Stamp took over the editorship from George Chisholm in 1926 and was responsible for the revision of a further eight editions, including the major review occasioned by the Second World War, in which he was assisted by S. C. Gilmour.

G. Noel Blake, MBE, BSc(Econ)

After the sudden death of Professor Sir Dudley Stamp in 1966, the editorship passed to G. Noel Blake, who studied economics under Hugh Gaitskell and Professor Noel Hall at University College London and geography under Professor Stamp at the London School of Economics from 1932–36. He served with the Royal Air Force during the Second World War and retired with the rank of Air Commodore in 1969. His career was concerned with the organisation of logistic support, and in particular with industrial response to major government contracts for electronic and aerospace equipment. He travelled widely in India, Japan and the Far East; and in the United States and Canada. After four years lecturing at the staff college he was, from 1960–63 concerned with the installation of computers to control the distribution and procurement of equipment. From 1964–69 as Director of Mechanical Transport, and latterly as Director of Movements (RAF) at the Ministry of Defence, he was responsible for major surface and air transportation networks throughout the world.

Audrey N. Clark

Audrey N. Clark, editor and publisher, director of Geographical Publications Limited, a company founded by Sir Dudley Stamp in 1933, has contributed the sections on Europe and Asia. She worked with Sir Dudley Stamp from 1938 until his death, as secretary of The Land Utilisation Survey of Britain, and as his personal and research assistant.

Preface to the nineteenth edition

In the preface to the first edition of his *Handbook of Commercial Geography*, published in August 1889, George G. Chisholm recorded that his aim was to 'impart an intellectual interest to the study of the geographical facts relating to commerce'. He also stressed the importance of such an 'intellectual interest' to success in business and stated that the work was intended for three groups: 'First, teachers who wish to impart additional zest to their lessons in geography from the point of view of commerce; secondly, pupils in the higher schools and colleges that are now devoting increased attention to commercial education; and thirdly, those in commercial life who take a sufficiently intelligent interest in their business to make their private studies bear on their daily pursuits.'

It is a remarkable tribute to the foresight of Chisholm that he judged aright; for each of these three classes his book became a standard work and may justly be claimed a classic. Yet he wrote at a time when university study of the subject was virtually unknown and when school teaching of geography comprised mainly a wearisome repetition of lists of capes and bays, towns and products. In the course of thirty-six years after the first edition he supervised no fewer than twenty-three new editions and reprints, and the book underwent a process of steady growth and evolution. The huge task of incorporating the changes occasioned by the First World War fell to him in his declining years; but after the tenth edition in January 1925 the work of revision was taken over by Professor Stamp (later Professor Sir Dudley Stamp) who rewrote and revised a further eight editions. As editor Sir Dudley Stamp endeavoured to retain as much as possible of the original work, in particular of the history of the development of commerce, in order to 'counteract any tendency for facile correlations based only on the present position'. Sir Dudley's major rewrite, published in 1937, was overtaken almost at once by the turmoil and disruption of the Second World War. *Chisholm's Handbook* went out of print during the war years and the enormous task of rewriting, to incorporate yet again the changes of the aftermath of war, was undertaken in collaboration with S. Carter Gilmour. Successive editions followed rapidly, to keep pace with the continual changes in both political and economic spheres, until the death of Mr Gilmour in 1963 and of Sir Dudley Stamp in 1966.

The need for the successive editions of the *Handbook* has been dictated by the continual changes in world trade since it was first published — in its commodities, in its pattern and in its volume. Its usefulness lies, as the original author so rightly foresaw, in the evergrowing demand for a factual and objective reference work which contains comprehensive information on the commodities of international commerce; the factors affecting their production, distribution and exchange; and a compact regional geography for each of the trading nations of the world. Thus bringing together in a single volume a wide range of information and up-to-date statistics that otherwise could be obtained only by reference to a multitude of source documents in major libraries, in the records of individual firms and trade organisations, and in the growing volume of reports from national and international statistical offices.

The publication of the nineteenth edition again provides the opportunity to widen the scope of the *Handbook*. Chisholm, writing during the peak of Victorian prosperity when Britain's trade (still largely carried by sail) was based on her coal and iron deposits and her colonial empire, naturally concentrated his attention on those commodities which were grown on, or won from, the earth's surface. Commerce today comprises an exchange of merchandise involving an infinitely greater range of 'commodities', including such things as invisible imports and exports, tourism, and manufactured products of great complexity. Clearly such items have their place in so far as geographic factors are material (although the space available in a single volume imposes its own limitations), but within Chisholm's original balance of emphasis. The fact remains that the commodities which bulk largest in world trade are still the raw materials, natural products and foodstuffs. The opportunity has also been taken to bring all statistics as up to date as possible. In this connection it should be noted that the steady advance of both national and international statistical recording (with improvements in standardisation of data classification and in source accuracy) brings its own problems of communication and correlation. With the expanding use of computers and with new printing techniques, the elapsed time between origin and publication will be progressively reduced; but at the time of preparation of this edition the statistics for 1970–72 were in most cases the latest available.

Translation into monetary terms has long provided a convenient common denominator for comparing statistics covering a wide range of different items. Chisholm, even in the 1880s, was already aware of the problems of interpreting such value statistics over a long term. Nonetheless until the Second World War the statistics in the *Handbook* were summarised in terms of the £ sterling, the value of which (by present-day standards) had been comparatively stable since the first edition. This also sufficed universally for, as the first Preface so succinctly puts it, 'a commentary on the *Annual Statement of the Trade of the United Kingdom* . . . forms a nearly complete synopsis of the trade of the world'. Since the Second World War international statistics have been standardised in terms of the United States dollar, which has provided a less stable yardstick. Indeed the changes in the value (purchasing power) of national currencies and in the rates of exchange between countries has been so continuous in the middle of the twentieth century as to make the recording of trends in monetary terms increasingly misleading — or, at best, demanding so many annotations as to dates and rates of change in money values as to be confusing. In this edition therefore value statistics have been limited to those that offer a sound basis for comparison, and quantitative statistics (increasingly dependable as the United Nations statistical services mature) are used elsewhere.

In so wide a field improvements and corrections will always be possible and any suggestions, addressed to the editor care of the publishers, will always be welcomed.

January 1974   GNB
                                                                              ANC

Preface to the first edition

This book is designed to meet a want recognised by all who are interested in adapting our education to the needs of the time.

Since its commencement several works have appeared which seek to accomplish a similar object by methods different from those adopted in the present work. A few words of explanation as to the plan here followed are therefore all the more necessary.

I cannot better explain the aim of the work than by adopting the words of Mr Goschen in the address which he delivered to the students of Aberdeen University on his installation as Lord Rector (31 Jan. 1888). I have endeavoured to impart an 'intellectual interest' to the study of the geographical facts relating to commerce. It will, I imagine, be generally admitted that Mr Goschen has not overrated one whit the importance of this intellectual interest with a view to practical success in business; and it is a consideration by no means to be ignored that in following this road to practical success we give to life one of the elements that make success valuable.

To say that in the present work I have endeavoured after intellectual interest is only another way of saying that it has been my aim to make the book really educational. In writing the work I have had three classes chiefly in view — first, teachers who may wish to impart additional zest to their lessons in geography from the point of view of commerce; secondly, pupils in the higher schools and colleges that are now devoting increased attention to commercial education; and thirdly, those entering on commercial life, who take a sufficiently intelligent interest in their business to make their private studies bear on their daily pursuits.

From what has just been said about the aim of the work, it follows that this book is not to be regarded as a general work of reference on all that may be included under the head of Commercial Geography. It is not a mere repertory of the where and whence of commodities of all kinds. My wish has been to throw light on the vicissitudes of commerce by treating somewhat fully of the trade in the more important commodities, and emphasising the broad features of the trade of different countries, not to encumber the book with a multitude of minute facts. In the selection of details for mention I have sought to single out those which are most significant, and most obviously significant, and it is not so much the details themselves as their significance which it is desirable to impress on the memory.

The general arrangement of the work is shown by the Table of Contents. The sections under the head of Commodities may be regarded as substantially a commentary on the *Annual Statement of the Trade of the United Kingdom with Foreign Countries and British Possessions*, which forms a nearly complete synopsis of the trade of the world. It is this publication that is frequently referred to simply as the 'Annual Statement' or the 'Annual Statement of British Trade'. In drawing up this commentary, a brief sketch of the leading processes of manufacture has been given, for reasons that hardly need to be pointed out. These processes have often, as in the case of iron, an important bearing on the geographical distribution of industry. Moreover, there can be no intelligent interest in trade without an understanding of the reasons why certain commodities are produced and exchanged at all, and in many cases the explanation of this involves the knowledge of manufacturing processes. Take, for instance, the first article entered in the 'Annual Statement' just referred to under the head of both Imports and Exports — 'alkali'. What interest can there be in this article of trade for those who have no knowledge of the relation of 'alkali' to such familiar commodities as glass and soap? It is manifest, too, that the interest of this trade is much heightened when we consider its connection, more or less direct, with the trade in salt, nitrate of soda, sulphur, sulphuric acid, lead, bleaching powder, and other commodities.

This illustration serves to show how closely interconnected are many of the facts belonging to the domain of commercial geography. It is for the sake of bringing this into prominence that the present work has been divided into numbered paragraphs, to facilitate cross-reference. Such references are made by printing the number of the paragraph referred to in bold type. [This system was abandoned in later editions.]

With regard to the arrangement of commodities depending directly or indirectly on climate, under the heads Products of the Temperate Zone, Sub-Tropical and Tropical Products, I need hardly point out that no hard and fast line can be drawn between the different groups. Commodities have been entered under the heading which refers them to the region in which they are produced commercially in greatest quantity, and in which accordingly they are most characteristic; but it must not be inferred that there is any absolute limitation in any case to one climatic zone.

The separate treatment of commodities and countries has involved in some cases a certain amount of repetition, but it must be remembered that the same facts are in effect different when regarded from different points of view. It may here be explained that generally under the head of Commodities only the relative rank of countries as a whole in the production of, or trade in, certain articles is considered, the local distribution of industries in particular countries being reserved for treatment under the head of the countries to which they belong. An exception is made in some cases in which local characteristics are an essential part of the explanation of the predominance of any particular country.

As regards statistics, it will be observed that there has been greater anxiety to make figures instructive than to furnish the latest figures procurable. In a work not designed as a yearbook, the main thing is to make the figures so far as possible comparable with one another. My chief aim in the collection of statistics has been to illustrate tendencies in progress. In the body of the book the statistics given under the head of Commodities are mostly of quantities. In the general tables in the appendix showing the commerce of different countries of the world for certain periods, I have been obliged to use the only common measure available, that of value, with all its defects. It is necessary, however, to warn the reader that in consulting the tables the great defect pointed out in par. 133 [a reference to pp. 13—19 in this edition] ought never to be left out of mind. In making use of these statistics in the body of the book I have endeavoured to do so in such a manner that what may be learned from them on the assumption of uniformity of prices is all the more manifestly true when actual changes in price are taken into account. In order to remove one of the defects attached to the use of values as measures for comparison — namely, the changes in the relative value of gold and silver or inconvertible paper — the tables have all been made to represent as far as possible gold values. In the case of countries in which a gold standard is not in use, the tables have been drawn up on the basis of the average gold value for each year of the actual currency, so far as the information at my disposal allowed. Further explanations on this head are given in notes to the tables themselves.

By adopting this course I do not mean to suggest that a more accurate representation is given of the rise and fall of trade in silver-using countries than would be afforded by tables drawn up on a silver basis. In the case of India, for example, it may be objected that the using of gold instead of silver values gives a wholly inadequate idea of the growth of Indian trade; but that is equally true of England (see the table compiled from the Report by Mr Giffen, cited on p. 482). The course in question has been adopted solely as affording a more accurate comparison between the commerce of different countries.

The plan of giving the average value of imports and exports for periods of five years has been resorted to with the view of showing more clearly the tendencies of commercial development. Such periods seemed long enough to mask what may be called accidental fluctuations from year to year, and at the same time they are short enough to show a number of successive stages in recent years.

The Maps introduced into this volume have been prepared by Mr F. S. Weller, FRGS. In those showing density of population and products, the names of products written in italics are those of the principal exports. The railway maps are intended chiefly to serve two purposes. Those of the parts of Europe where railways are abundant are designed to show the interruption to communication caused by mountain ranges. Those of parts of the world in which railways are still few are intended to show the lines along which traffic is already promoted by this means of communication, and the routes by which it is expected that traffic is most likely to be developed in the future by railway construction. The names of minerals and some other products which may be expected to assist in giving importance to projected railways are frequently added.

With reference to the material I have made use of in compiling the present work, I must in the first place express my indebtedness, direct and indirect, to British merchants and manufacturers. From my inquiries on the subject of commercial geography I certainly have not derived the impression that, if British commerce has in recent years advanced with less rapid strides than that of some other countries, geographical ignorance on the part of the British merchant can be set down as one of the principal causes. Much of my most interesting material has been drawn from mercantile sources. No single periodical has been of more use to me than the London *Chamber of Commerce Journal*. The interesting report of the *Bombay and Lancashire Cotton Spinning Inquiry*, instituted by the Manchester Chamber of Commerce, shows how thoroughly alive British merchants and manufacturers are to the geographical conditions that affect their business.

Among the general works to which I am indebted I owe most to Scherzer's *Wirthschaftliches Leben der Völker*. It is this work that is referred to when 'Scherzer' simply is cited as my authority. I have seldom been able to acknowledge the precise amount of my obligations to this book, and here I can only say in general terms that I owe more to it than would appear from a comparison of this compilation with the work referred to. The work cited by the name of Andree is the *Geographie des Welthandels*, by Karl Andree, revised and completed by Rich. Andree. British and United States Consular Reports, the *Board of Trade Journal*, and the annual supplements to the *Economist* giving a review of the trade of the past year, have all furnished me with important information, and I have also derived much from articles and the numerous valuable notes in the *Scottish Geographical Magazine*, which has devoted special attention to this subject.

I am indebted to various gentlemen practically connected with different industries for their kindness in reading the proofs of the sections relating to these industries. I have also to thank my friend Mr F. W. Rudler, of the Museum of Practical Geology, who has kindly read over the proofs of the section dealing with minerals; but my chief acknowledgements under this head are due to my friend Mr T. Kirkup, author of *An Inquiry into Socialism* &c. It is to him that I owe the original suggestion of the work. He also kindly revised the first plan of the work three years ago, and the text owes innumerable improvement to his careful reading of the proofs of the more important sections. I have also to express my thanks to Mr C. H. Leete, Fellow of the American Geographical and Statistical Society, for suggestions and corrections relating to the section on the United States, and to Mr B. Daydon Jackson, one of the Secretaries of the Linnean Society, for his kindness in verifying the authors of species in the case of the scientific names of plants, which have been mentioned to facilitate identification so as to enable those who have access to a scientific library to obtain further information.

London: July 1889.   GEO. G. CHISHOLM

Note on metric conversion

Metric measurements are incorporated throughout this edition (followed by the UK equivalent) and conversion tables have been included in the appendices. Where statistics indicate an order of magnitude, reasonable approximations have been made. For example, the equivalent for the commonly used yardstick:

'temperature falls $1°$ F for every 300 ft'
is given as:

'temperature falls $0.5°$ C for every 100 m'
rather than the more precise (but less easily remembered) '$0.53°$ C for every 91.44 m'. Or, again, a plateau of an average elevation of '2 700 ft' is given as '820 m' rather than the more precise (but no more helpful) '822.96 m'.

Unless otherwise specified, all 'tons' referred are are 'metric tons'.

Introduction

The great geographical fact on which commerce depends is that different parts of the world yield different products, or furnish the same products under unequally favourable conditions. Hence there are two great results of commerce: the first, to increase the variety of commodities at any particular place; the second, to equalise more or less the opportunities for obtaining any particular commodity in different places between which commerce is carried on. Among the difficulties to be overcome in this transfer we must include all the profits necessarily exacted in the movement of goods from hand to hand (profits of exchange).

The variety of products in different places is due either to original distribution or to artificial production, whether by cultivation or manufacture. The original distribution of basic materials (minerals, oil, forest products, etc.), of economic value is an important matter for consideration in commercial geography, but under this head we must consider, not merely the latitude and longitude of the place of occurrence, but all the varied conditions, local, political, or historical, which help to render the commodities commercially available. In the case of cultivated products, soil and climate are fundamental considerations in determining the variety obtaining at different places; but, again, these are not the sole considerations. Facilities for finding a market, and all the conditions that affect these facilities, have also to be taken into account.

The cost, in labour, of bringing goods from one part of the world to another has been greatly reduced since the time of the earliest commerce of which we can get a glimpse. This has been made possible by the gradual development of the means of transport. As this development has proceeded, the variety of products entering into commerce and obtainable at particular places has constantly increased. In the earliest periods the articles in which commerce was developed, involving the longest and costliest journeys, were necessarily such as were of great value in proportion to their bulk. Such commerce supplied chiefly the luxuries of the rich, and commodities on which a high value was

1

conferred by religion. Records of early Egyptian, Assyrian, and Phoenician trade speak of gold, silver, and precious stones, ebony and fine woods, ivory and inlaid work, incense and perfumes, balsams and gums, apes, peacocks, panther skins, and slaves as the principal gifts of commerce. Indian dyes (indigo) appear to have reached Egypt in the time of the eighteenth dynasty (1700–1475 BC); Baltic amber was probably brought to Assyria in the time of Tiglath-Pileser II (eighth century BC); and Chinese silks are known to have reached the Indus through Afghanistan in the fourth century BC, though probably without anything being known in the country where the goods were bought of the country in which they originated. The silks were no doubt gradually transferred from tribe to tribe on the route, and in this manner they are likely to have occasionally reached the West at a much earlier date.

The early trade in bulky articles such as grain was necessarily confined to regions with good water communications. From an early period in Greek history the necessity for this trade gave peculiar importance to the grain-growing regions on the northern shores of the Black Sea. Rome at the height of its prosperity made Sicily the granary for central Italy, and later grain was also obtained from Egypt, Mauritania, and Spain. Sea carriage within the Mediterranean rendered all these sources of supply easy of access; but where distant land carriage was necessary the prices demanded were such as only the wealthiest could pay. Varro, in the first century BC, mentions citron wood along with gold as among the costliest luxuries at Rome, and about the same date as much as 1 400 000 sesterces (£10 500) was paid for Alexandrian tables made of thya-wood (the wood of *Callitris quadrivalvis*) with ivory feet.

Similarly, during the flourishing period of the trade between Italy and the East at the close of the fifteenth century (before the opening of sea communications) we find that the principal articles of commerce were silk, silk-stuffs and other costly manufactures, spices and drugs. But, in 1560, after the seaway to the East had been fully established, Antwerp attained the summit of its maritime and commercial prosperity, based on such commodities as leather, flax, tallow, salt fish, timber, corn and pulse, and other articles of general consumption. There was also a remarkable choice of costlier articles, such as wrought silks and velvets, cloth of gold and silver, tapestries, dimities of fine sorts, jewels and pearls, dyes and perfumes, drugs and spices.

In Shakespeare's time we know from Shakespeare himself that sugar, currants and dates, rice, mace, nutmegs and ginger, as well as civet and 'medicinable gum', were all familiar in England, while the manufactured products of the time comprised, among others,

> Fine linen, Turkey cushions boss'd with pearl,
> Valance of Venice gold in needle-work.

Many of the articles mentioned, which are now within the reach of everyone, must have been comparatively rare luxuries at the time. Without going beyond Shakespeare we get a hint that rice was dear. 'What will this sister of mine do with rice? But my father hath made her mistress of the feast, and she lays it on.' From other sources we learn the cost of some of the other tropical products mentioned. In 1589 a quarter of an ounce of tobacco cost in England 10*d*. (4p), 1 lb of sugar 20*d*. (8p). The difference in money value between then and now gives little idea of the actual cost, but we find from the same source that a pound of sugar then cost as much as a quarter (28 lb) of veal or mutton.

The contrast between Shakespeare's day and our own is striking in many ways. Tea, coffee, and cocoa, besides other minor but still familiar articles, such as sago and tapioca, have all been added, along with a host of others, to the list of mercantile commodities. The price of tropical products has been so reduced that, for example, tea, sugar, coffee, cocoa, and tobacco are all in common use even in the arctic homes of the Laplanders. In the trade of the world almost universally the articles of greatest aggregate volume have come to be the natural products, raw materials, and manufactured articles in most general use — wheat and rice, meat, butter and cheese, cotton and cottons, wool and woollens, iron and ironware, oil, rubber, etc. We thus see that the increasing variety of commodities entering into commerce is in a great measure an increase in the commoner articles of consumption.

The equalising tendency of commerce has already been incidentally illustrated by the reduction in price of tropical commodities just mentioned. The tendency may be described, first, as one towards stability of prices from year to year, a tendency manifested most conspicuously in the case of those commodities the supply of which in any particular region, apart from commerce, would largely be dependent on the weather. Between 1641 and 1741 the price of wheat per quarter* (8 bushels) in England oscillated between 23*s*. and 76*s*. (£1.15 and £3.80); in the period from 1741 to 1841, between 22*s*. and 129*s*. (£1.10 and £6.45), the highest prices being reached during the period of the Napoleonic wars. But in the period 1842 to 1883 as the New World came into production the limits of oscillation were only 39*s*. and 75*s*. (£1.95 and £3.75), the latter figure being reached during the Crimean War. The early years of the present century again saw very low prices with the abundance of supply from the new lands, but the correlation of today's prices with those of 1883 is less valid than the comparison of 1883 and 1641. After two world wars the changing value of currencies in all countries — including the dollar and the pound — makes direct comparison with the past impossible. Instead of the free functioning of

* One quarter = 8 bushels = 480 lb = 218 kg.

exchange rates, currencies are now managed and controlled. The operation of free trade has been replaced by a complicated system of bulk buying by governments with prices rendered artificial by subsidies and in other ways. Again, there have been barriers between 'hard' and 'soft' currency groups — while Soviet Russia and the lands behind the Iron Curtain are largely isolated from the rest of the world. In these circumstances the interaction of supply and demand is obscured, but the main objective is still to increase the stability of prices.

In a free-trade world, excessive prices in one region are kept down by supplies sent from other regions where the commodity is cheaper. The sending away of the surplus from these latter regions tends to raise their own prices. The reverse of this effect is best demonstrated where communications are very imperfect and commerce consequently limited. Thus in 1885, when Quito, a town high in the Andes could be reached from Guayaquil, the principal port on the coast 320 miles away, only by means of pack-animals, local produce was exceptionally cheap, but imported articles were excessively dear. Beef sold at from 2*d*. to 2½*d*. (1p) a pound, mutton 1½*d*. to 2*d*. (1p), chickens 6*d*. to 7½*d*. (3p) apiece; ordinary labourers received about 6*d*. (3p) a day; carpenters, and other artisans about 1*s*. (5p), finding their own food. On the other hand, dry goods, common cutlery, and crockery cost up to 50 per cent higher than in foreign markets; and common ironware cost fully twice as much. So also in the hills of the Upper Chindwin district in Burma, 1 600 km (1 000 miles) from Rangoon, three chickens could be bought for 1*s*. 4*d*. (7p) in 1925, but the same sum was freely offered by the local inhabitants for an empty wine bottle.

Although the basic tendency of international commerce is towards comparative steadiness in prices, the level towards which the price tends is not the lowest. Merchants sell abroad because they can get a better price than at home. It is their quest after higher prices that reduces the inequality under this head in different parts of the world and, in turn, continually widens the scope of the market.

Hence there follows a third result of the growth of commerce, namely, the development of the resources of different regions to the utmost extent possible under the existing conditions, and with this development a keener and more widespread competition.

But in process of this development it becomes apparent that the equalising tendency of commerce is only a general trend, which is apt to be disturbed from time to time by great variations in price. These disturbances may arise from inventions causing a sudden cheapening in the processes of production, such as the great textile inventions or those which gave rise to the modern methods of steel-making; they may arise from the introduction of cheaper means of transport, and the disturbance due to this cause is felt all the more keenly when the cheaper transport is to regions with cheap production costs; or they may arise from a vast and rapid expansion of the demand for some commodity — which in due course will be overtaken by the resultant upward swing in production.

An historic instance of the disturbance that may be caused by the rapid expansion of the demand for a commodity is seen in the history of the iron trade after 1870, as reflected in the price of pig-iron 'warrants' — i.e. forms of receipt for warehoused goods, the title to which can be transferred by assignment. The average price of these warrants at Glasgow in the years 1869 to 1871 varied between about 53s. (£2.65) and 59s. (£2.95) per ton; in 1872 the average rose to about 102s. (£5.10), in 1873 to 117s. (£5.85), after which it fell steadily to about 54s. (£2.70) in 1877. The sudden rise was due to the fact that, vast as our industry had already become in 1872, it was not yet equal to the demands that were then made on it for further expansion by the laying of railways, and the establishment of numerous factories in America and Germany. The annual increase of railway mileage in America rose steadily from 1 177 miles in 1865 to 7 379 miles in 1871. The annual exports of iron and steel from the United Kingdom to the United States increased correspondingly from 186 000 tons in 1865 to 1 064 000 tons in 1871; those to Germany, Holland, and Belgium increased from 255 000 tons in 1866 to 1 015 000 tons in 1872. But in the subsequent course of iron prices the general equalising tendency of commerce can be detected. The vast demand of 1871 to 1873 led almost immediately to such an increase in the means of producing iron that, when the next great expansion of the demand came about, it was met with ease. From 1877 to 1887 the variations in average annual price of pig-iron warrants at Glasgow were only between 40s. and 54s. 6d. (£2.00 and £2.73).

Inevitably there are hardships attendant on such disturbances, but the resulting improvements are of value to the world in the long run, in so far as they permanently lightening human labour in the production and distribution of the means of satisfying human wants — as transportation costs become cheaper and as production processes become more efficient. But the full advantage of any permanent benefit to mankind from the developments of which we are now speaking is best reaped when every kind of production is carried on in the place that has the greatest natural advantages for the supply of a particular market. By natural advantages are meant a favourable soil and climate, the existence of facilities for communication (external and internal), the existence of valuable minerals in favourable situations, and especially of the materials for making and driving machinery. All these advantages are more or less permanent, although exhaustible resources are now rapidly threatened with modern exploitation techniques. Unfortunately the nations of the world from time to time ignore this simple truth and build up agriculture and industry in less favoured localities behind tariff walls, for social or political reasons.

To natural advantages may be added historical advantages, which are in their nature more temporary. Perhaps the most important of all is a strong and stable government based on principles not hostile to industry. This, it may be observed, is one of those which may be very enduring in fact; while its obverse, the enduring disadvantage of a weak and unstable government is equally true.

With reference to the temporary character of certain advantages for commerce and industry, it is likewise a fact of the greatest moment that the commerce and industry of the world have during the twentieth century been in a transition stage the like of which has never been known before. Communications are being improved, the means of production are being accelerated and cheapened, and developing nations introduced to the latest technological advances with a rapidity hitherto unparalleled. But commerce and industry are still governed by geographical conditions, which accordingly demand the most careful and detailed examination.

The statement just made is often denied as the opposite of the truth, it being contended that geographical conditions are counting for less and less instead of more and more. Those who hold this view point out that where an isthmus stands in man's way he cuts it; a mountain, he bores it. But wide-reaching geographical relations determine which isthmuses to cut, which mountains to pierce, and a close study of the local conditions is made to decide where and how the works had best be carried out. The laying of railways through hilly or mountainous country is dictated by the need to avoid stiff gradients and sharp curves, and similar care is now taken in the alignment of great motor roads. The steepness of the gradient on the west side of the Kicking Horse Pass across the Rocky Mountains ultimately compelled the Canadian Pacific Railway to provide an easier descent at the cost of a lengthened route; while more recently geographical considerations were the major ones in determining how best to transport oil from the Alaskan oilfields, providing the alternatives of ice breaking tankers through the Northwest Passage, a pipeline through the permafrost and across the continent, or by tanker to a shorter pipeline alongside the Panama Canal.

The opening up of the entire world by improved means of communication has led to extensive study of every country where development is possible and has removed many obstacles to development; but the very fact that man is acquiring greater power in dealing with nature delineates more sharply the limit beyond which he cannot pass in his modifications of the original conditions. Nowhere is this clearer than in the creation of oases, where lie side by side 'the desert and the sown'. Irrigation has been greatly extended in many parts of the world, but geographical conditions determine just where it is possible. The tendency towards an ultimate prevalence of geographical conditions in determining the distribution of commerce and industry is, it is true, a tendency to a remote result. The influences which dictate the location of industry are varied and complex in their action, especially in modern times. On this subject the reader is referred to what is said under 'Commercial and industrial towns' on pp. 113—19 and here it is enough to add that the chief means of thwarting the dominant tendency of geographical conditions in commerce and industry is not man's increasing control over nature, but his political action, which, either by tariffs or by other means, may direct the channels of commerce.

The advantages that may be expected to be reaped when the development of commerce has reached its goal are the enjoyment of the greatest possible variety of commodities at all the habitable parts of the earth (that is, the greatest variety possible for each place), and the utmost attainable stability of prices. When the network of commerce is complete in its main lines, when it has only to be gradually extended or made more intricate with the development of population, then the deficiencies in the natural products of one region will be supplied from any surplus that may accrue in other regions. It is true that this will usually take place on condition that the region so supplied has something to give in exchange; but this, once again, depends on comparatively stable prices — for only then can dependable future estimates be made which will justify the development of the means of production to provide this surplus.

Meantime, it cannot be forgotten that commerce is still very far from having reached that goal. What we now see is the greatest haste on all sides to secure such advantages as may offer themselves for the prosecution of commerce and industry, we see an extreme phase of competitive and aggressive commerce as between nation and nation, individual and individual. As it is only with nations that we have here to do, we may now note the principal means by which nations, either directly or indirectly, endeavour to promote their own commerce and industry. There are two basic methods — to restrict competing products or to provide assistance for one's own.

Firstly there are protective tariffs; that is, import duties levied on such a scale as to encourage the production of the goods so taxed in the country itself by the total or partial exclusion of such goods of foreign origin. In so far as such duties may be necessary or may help to establish an industry in a region in which it is fitted by natural advantages to take root , the imposition of duties of this nature tends in the direction of the goal towards which commerce as a whole is moving. But the direct and immediate effect of high tariffs is opposed to the tendency of the changes in progress referred to on p. 5 and especially of the rapid multiplication of means of communication. When efforts are constantly being made to cheapen the supply of commodities it is scarcely credible that those who consume them should consent to have their price raised by an arbitrary barrier, but then the pressure for tariffs comes from producers rather than consumers.

This last remark is made solely from the point of view of commerce, and does not exclude the consideration that there may be other reasons for the imposition of tariffs. The term 'key industries' has been applied to such as are considered essential for the good of the state. In Britain agriculture and certain chemical industries are among those which have been regarded as belonging to this class, although as a country whose economy is so greatly dependent on foreign trade, the erection of tariff barriers (which invite retaliation) must be handled with care.

Secondly there are quotas. These restrict imports, either by value or by volume, to a level considered acceptable to the wellbeing of home production. Quotas normally specify the goods to be accepted from individual nations, and are therefore more selective in their effects than tariffs which are levied regardless of the source of supply. Quotas may also be employed to control the movement of labour or services (for example the percentage of commerce that may be carried by foreign shipping lines); and in the last resort may be entirely prohibitive, as when a country decides that its merchant fleet shall include no foreign-built vessels. Governmental assistance to commerce is usually given in the form of subsidies. These are payments made directly or indirectly on the exportation of goods — and again if it can be proved that a subsidy has served to establish an industry capable afterwards of being maintained on a selfsupporting footing, then a similar plea may be entered in favour of this aid to industry. One of the earlier forms of subsidy was to shipping lines in return for the carriage of mails. Agriculture and the sugar industry are the most important of those which have been affected by subsidies in recent years. Indirect support may also be given by granting long-term credit facilities at specially low interest rates (a major concession in times of rising world interest rates); in rebates on taxes; in assistance for industrial reorganisation (for example, to encourage vertical integration of raw materials/semifinished product/final product into a single trading group); in assisting firms in areas which attract governmental regional aid (shipbuilding in particular is often located in areas depressed by the aftermath of previous prosperity). Even national defence policies may play their part, as with the United States ruling that all coastwise shipping must be carried in American ships (a potent decision, since 'coastwise' includes Alaska and Puerto Rico).

Mention should also be made of export duties. These are less frequently levied as they tend to be limited to those commodities in which the state enjoys an advantage amounting almost to a monopoly. For example, the export duties levied by England in the Middle Ages on certain kinds of raw wool made up the great bulk of the state revenue for centuries. More recent examples are the income derived by the

Middle East oil-producing states from their oil exports — and by India from jute exports. Again, in the last resort the export control may be entirely prohibitive — as, for instance, the occasional prohibition of the export of UK scrap iron (an essential ingredient in steel production) when it is judged that home market needs are of greater importance than the potential export earnings of foreign exchange.

So far as the free flow of commerce is concerned, government interference is the more deplorable for being arbitrary. As already stated, such interference may have many purposes — for example, the maintenance of low food prices, or the protection of newly developing industries, etc. In any event the government will have judged that the greater national interest justifies the course taken. In the short term the original aim may well be achieved, but the long-term effects are less predictable. The increasing interdependence of the trading nations means that the self-interest of one nation must have commercial repercussions on the interests of other nations with which it trades. Free trade encourages the natural growth of these interests, while protectionism generates retaliation. The balance between these two swings from time to time; but eventually all commerce (production, distribution, manufacture and selling) revolves around the interplay of supply and demand.

Lastly, there is the interference of war with its far-reaching effects on industry and commerce. They include immense destruction of life, and so of labour power, at the period of greatest vigour; fluctuation of the birth-rate in the belligerent countries;* destruction of property of all kinds; diversion to various destructive agencies of the labour normally devoted to providing for the future, especially by the creation of transport facilities, the erection of plant, and the manufacture of machinery; the sudden redistribution of capital (where that redistribution takes place within the state, the burdening for years to come of the bulk of the population with payments due to the smaller section of the people who form the state creditors, and, where that redistribution operates between state and state, changes in the relative advantages for production

---

* The following table, based on the United Nations' *Demographic Year Book*, shows the numbers of the live births per 1 000 of the population between 1938 and 1967 in certain countries. After an initial decline early in the war in the case of the European belligerents, the allied rates mounted to a maximum in 1947, but later fell away from that level.

	1938	1941	1943	1945	1947	1950	1955	1963	1967
UK	15.5	14.4	16.6	16.3	20.7	16.1	15.8	18.3	17.5
Germany†	19.7	18.6	16.0	–	16.5	16.2	15.7	18.6	17.2
France	14.9	13.4	15.9	16.5	21.3	21.0	18.5	18.2	16.9
Canada	20.6	22.2	24.0	23.9	28.6	26.8	28.4	24.8	21.2
USA	17.6	18.9	21.5	19.6	25.7	23.5	24.6	21.6	17.9

† Rates to 1943 for Germany as constituted in 1937. Later rates for West Germany only.

and commerce which may prove permanent). There is the loss of markets to a belligerent nation, a loss which may never be recovered as others step in as suppliers and a permanent rearrangement of the channels of commerce results. It is not out of place here to refer also to the mutual hatred and distrust between nations resulting from war, inasmuch as industry and commerce nowadays depend so largely on credit, which implies mutual confidence. This was demonstrated in the isolation of Germany and Japan immediately after the Second World War. An isolation which, incidentally, provided both countries with the time and incentive to concentrate on their immediate problems. Both employed the time to rebuild and modernise their devastated economies so effectively that they had a vastly improved base from which to launch their return to world trading in the late 1950s.

Governments also assist commerce in many ways. They maintain consuls in the principal mercantile towns of foreign countries who are charged with the duty of looking after the interests of subjects of the country represented by them and with furnishing such information as is likely to be of use to trade between the countries. British merchants and manufacturers have not the advantage of being able to consult British consular reports on the Commonwealth countries, but this requirement is met in other ways. All the selfgoverning countries maintain representatives under various titles, who make it their business to disseminate information likely to promote trade between the United Kingdom and the countries which they represent. Trade commissioners are appointed to various countries, including those within the Commonwealth and government export advisory committees cover trading information throughout the world.

The establishment of chambers of commerce, or voluntary associations of merchants in different localities, is now almost universal, and similar chambers are established by merchants in foreign cities where a large amount of business is conducted. These organisations are given cohesion by an Association of British Chambers of Commerce and an International Chamber of Commerce.

Another method of promoting national commerce is the establishment of commercial libraries and museums, and national and international trade fairs. Exhibitions are a kind of temporary commercial museum, and floating exhibitions which convey samples of a country's commodities to distant markets are one of the latest means resorted to in different countries with the view of promoting national commerce. In the United Kingdom the Imperial Institute, founded in 1887 as a national memorial of Queen Victoria's Jubilee, and now rehoused as the Commonwealth Institute, includes a commercial museum of Commonwealth products; and most Commonwealth governments have in their London offices permanent exhibitions of the commercial products of their respective countries. Great exhibitions such as that held at

Wembley in 1924—25 have been of more vital interest than museums. This was also demonstrated by the Great Exhibition of 1851 and again a century later by the Festival of Britain in 1951.

Commercial and technical education are other means of promoting national commerce of great importance. This is recognised by th existence of many professional institutes (such as the Institute of Bankers) which provide educational courses and conduct examinations. Nearly all of them include commercial geography in their requirements.

An inevitable feature of war, especially war on a gigantic scale as in 1914—18 and 1939—45, is the extension of government control of industry and even the direct participation of the government in industry. On the one hand it has to be kept in mind that such success in industry as was achieved by the government during the wars was secured at the expense of the taxpayer, whereas industry must be able normally not merely to maintain itself by its own produce, but also to provide for its own growth. On the other hand, one cannot forget that for a long time the tendency in many parts of the world has been towards a great extension of the share taken by the state in industries of various kinds. The private ownership of railways, for example, is now exceptional. The Canadian government is the owner not only of a large part of the railways in that country but of elevators and steamships; and ships for trading purposes are owned by other governments. Under the Soviet system in the USSR, ownership and control are all-embracing. Before the Suez Canal was nationalised, our own government held many of the shares; during the First World War it became a partner in the Anglo—Iranian Oil Co. (now British Petroleum), and gave financial support to companies manufacturing dyestuffs; between the two wars, marketing boards, quotas and subsidies multiplied; and after the Second World War nationalisation became a main plank of Socialist government policy.

Several of these means of retaining and promoting commerce remind us forcibly of the closeness of the bonds with which commerce is steadily drawing different countries together, and of the complicated action and reaction between different parts of the world to which commerce gives rise. The improvement of machinery, of processes of production, of means of communication, the better organisation of industry, the advancement of education in one country, demand similar advances in other countries. New wheatfields in America necessitate improved systems of agriculture and the advancement of agricultural education in England, and the introduction of better agricultural machinery into Russia. The perfecting of the processes in the refining of beet sugar in Germany demands better organisation among the cane planters of the West Indies and Guyana. The workers and their unions more and more clearly recognise that any advantage secured for themselves in one country must be extended also to other countries. As long ago as 1885 the United States consul for Dundee stated that the longer hours worked in the Calcutta jute mills were believed to be the determining cause of the depression in the jute industry of Dundee; and he added that both employers and employed were consequently anxious that the 10-hours-a-day Factory Act should be extended to India. On the continent of Europe a long agitation in favour of international legislation on this subject led, at least in part, to the establishment of the International Labour Office in Geneva. The power of Japan to compete in world markets has long been linked with low labour costs. But the increasing interaction of world trade is forcing her wage levels upwards, not, incidentally, to the detriment of her trading position since increased capital investment has reduced the impact of labour costs.

It may perhaps be looked on as one of the hopeful features for the future that the importance of the considerations set forth in the preceding paragraph is coming to be more and more clearly recognised, and that the more enlightened among both masters and men are becoming increasingly convinced that it is only by mutual and worldwide cooperation that some of the most perplexing problems of industry can find a solution. 'After all,' said the Rt Hon G. N. Barnes in a speech on the Treaty of Peace Bill in the House of Commons on 21 July 1919, 'hard conditions of life are not due to any conscious cruelty on the part of any class or any individual. They are rather due to fundamental causes which can be removed only by the cooperation of classes.' If one result of the world wars should be that all countries come to realise that the healthiest conditions (in the widest sense of the term) for all engaged in industry were essential to the highest prosperity of the country, and all governments accordingly made it a prime aim to do what in them lay to secure such conditions as a permanency, we should all then be able to acclaim at least one good as issuing from those calamities. The establishment of the Ministry of Health in Britain may be noted in this connection; indeed Chisholm when he first drafted this Introduction more than eighty years ago was foreseeing much that we now take for granted in the 'welfare state' and in the increasing participation by governments in their countries trading activities.

ECONOMIC STATISTICS

One of the chief functions of the study of commercial or economic geography is that it enables us to form reasonable estimates of the future course of commercial development, in so far as that is governed by geographical conditions. Such estimates must, of course, be based on one's knowledge of forces in operation at the present time, and must be recognised as liable to be falsified by discoveries yet to come. The most widely informed have made forecasts which have proved to be utterly wide of the truth, but which could not be called unreasonable at the time. When Adam Smith wrote that 'the small quantity of foreign corn imported, even in times of the greatest scarcity, may satisfy our farmers that they can have nothing to fear from the freest importation' (*Wealth of Nations*, Book IV, Chap. 2), no one could be expected to foresee the ultimate consequences of the inventions of the ingenious young instrument-maker, James Watt, whom Smith had befriended at Glasgow. When Dr P. Colquhoun in his *Wealth of the British Empire* (2nd edn, 1815) demonstrated the utter inutility of the new British colony in Australia, even that can hardly be pronounced unreasonable in the light of the knowledge of the time. Such examples may serve to remind us of the tacit qualifications with which all attempts to forecast the future are to be interpreted, but they should not deter us from making such anticipations as the circumstances allow.

In attempting such forecasts statistical data are unquestionably an important aid. In commercial geography the value of figures is twofold. First, they help to distinguish the important from the unimportant. Second, when we have figures for a series of years they direct attention to changes that have been in progress in the past, and may thus serve to suggest the more fruitful branches of inquiry and help us to estimate with more chance of success their probable future trend. In both ways they serve as a guide to what is most worthy of examination in our special subject. In order that they may illustrate changes in progress it is obvious that the series are likely to be the more instructive if they are comprehensive, if they cover a long period and if they are continuous.

Figures stating values may be very misleading in making comparisons between different periods even in the trade of the same country. With a view to removing this misleading tendency various index numbers, as they are called, have been calculated, and need explanation. For individual commodities the index number expresses the ratio of the average value of a given quantity in a given year, to the average value during the year or period which is taken as the base. This is simple, but such index numbers are not index numbers in the sense that they are calculated to serve as an index of other numbers not definitely known. This is what is aimed at by the general index number, which is based on the average price of many commodities, all articles largely consumed, such as wheat or wine or raw materials. In working out a general index number the commodities may either be regarded as of equal importance, or they may be weighted, i.e. multiplied by a factor which represents their comparative importance.

If then the selected commodities may be taken as illustrative, the general index number serves to show how far values have been affected by some cause or causes having a wide-reaching influence, and the variations in the index numbers for the individual commodities when compared with the general index numbers will be the means of indicating how far some special cause or causes must have affected their fluctuations in value. It should be noted that the basal period is arbitrarily chosen. The old Board of Trade index used 1900. In 1921 the Board of Trade adopted an index number on a new principle; new bases were adopted in 1938, 1947 and 1958. The continual change of the base year partly reflects changes in the value of money and partly changes in the list of 'representative' items.

Whatever be the cause of changes in index numbers, the facts underlying those changes modify the significance of the values given for exports and imports. For example, if we take the average value of imports into the United Kingdom for each of the periods of five years from 1871—75 to 1906—10, we find that there is only one, namely, the period 1886—90, which shows a decline in value as compared with the previous quinquennium — in round numbers £390m. against £400m. But if we apply the Board of Trade index number, base 1900, to these figures the values become changed to £333m. in 1881—85 and £379m. in 1886—90, showing an increase in the latter period of nearly 14 per cent instead of a decrease of about 2.5 per cent. Now with an index number calculated as was the old Board of Trade figure by allotting a weight to each commodity proportional to the average value of annual consumption, this shows that during the latter period considerably more supplies of food and raw materials must have been coming into the country than in the one before. That being so, we may be sure that those increased supplies would find their way into the hands of consumers. Stocks are not held indefinitely in the hope of better prices — perishable goods cannot be. So far as the increased imports, then, were foodstuffs, they must have been a direct benefit to the consumers; so far as they were raw materials, increased supplies must have helped to maintain the demand for labour, for they were imported in order to be used, and manufacturers still found their advantage in using them in spite of the fact that they did not see their way to sell the products at former prices. It is not even a necessary consequence that the lower selling prices of the products meant lower profits to the manufacturers.

These considerations have a special bearing on the trade returns recorded in this volume. During and after the Second World War prices increased greatly, so that imports and exports in 1950, for instance, were as a rule valued at very much more than in 1937, though the actual quantities of the goods imported and exported were often less. The Statistical Office of the United Nations is accordingly introducing an index of quantity in trade, somewhat comparable with a cost of living index.

Further, when the tables of imports and exports are used for making comparisons of the trade of different countries one may be led into error in various ways. First, it is important to remember that returns for the same country do not always refer to the same economic unit. When accessions of territory are gained by a country there is likely to be a change of this nature: similarly when territory is lost. Next, it is to be noted that there is no uniformity in the nature of the total given for the trade of a country whether the commerce referred to be designated general or special. Under the name of general commerce all articles imported and exported are included, but under the head of special commerce only imports for home consumption and exports of home produced goods are supposed to be reckoned. But this is far from being uniformly true. Thus, in the tables of German trade for 1911 raw cotton, caoutchouc, and rice appear among the special exports to the aggregate value of more than £6m., although obviously none of these is a product of Germany, and we cannot tell how great may have been the value of other re-exports when the goods are of such a nature that they may or may not have been German products. In Britain, on the other hand, while no attempt has been made to distinguish goods imported solely for home consumption, a distinction has been made for many years between exports of native origin and manufacture and re-exports of foreign or Commonwealth origin. The distinction between exports and re-exports has often been an arbitrary one, however, particularly with sophisticated products comprised of many components from various sources (both home and foreign). Further, since the value added to re-exported goods in the form of services can exceed the value added by processing to goods of native origin, the distinction has proved to be without economic significance. Advantage was therefore taken of the transfer to the United Nations Standard International Trade Classification in 1970 (see below) to introduce yet another change in statistical practice — and thereafter re-exports have no longer been identified separately.

The British tables are misleading or inadequate on two counts which are difficult to remedy. The general tables are exclusive of what is called transhipment trade, of which a separate statement is made. The transhipment trade is exclusively of articles imported and exported in bond and includes a considerable amount of trade on British account, that is, the import of goods bought by British merchants and resold by them abroad. Secondly, statistics of external commerce usually include the description of the goods exported or imported, the quantities, the countries of origin or destination of the goods, and the value. In the case of many articles, and especially those most largely imported and exported, such as foodstuffs and raw materials, the description presents no difficulty, so that one may make comparisons without fear of being misled. But in many cases it is otherwise, and difficulties in making comparisons for the same country for long periods are constantly being made by tariff changes necessitating different classifications, and even where there are no tariff changes alterations in the classification of goods are often made simply with the view of giving a more satisfactory statement of the facts of commerce. Such periodic changes present difficulties to all countries in the interpretation of statistics. The United Nations Organisation has therefore drawn up a Standard International Trade Classification specifying over 1 300 commodity headings as a first step to the standardisation of trade statistics on an international scale. The Board of Trade adopted this new classification for the presentation of the United Kingdom trade accounts from 1970 onwards.

In England the earliest systematic collection of commercial statistics appears to have been made in 1697. From that time down to 1797, inclusive, the values entered for English commerce and, after the union of the Parliaments in 1707, for that of Great Britain, were official values based on the prices of 1694 and for new articles on the price of the first year of their introduction. The so-called values were, accordingly, not current values, but for each commodity served to give indications of changes in quantity from year to year, although totalled values had little meaning at all. From 1798 in the case of exports declared values were added, not substituted, so that we have the absurdity in Porter's *Progress of the Nation* (1851 edn, p. 356) of two tables giving professedly the same thing, the value to the last pound of exports from the United Kingdom from 1801 to 1849, yet utterly divergent from one another, showing from 1820 onwards a steadily growing excess of official over declared values till in 1849 we have

Official value   £164 539 504
Declared value   £63 596 025.

In the commercial statistics of the Netherlands the use of official values was maintained until the end of 1916. The 'values' in Dutch returns were based on the prices of 1860 or thereabouts. In one case, Peruvian bark, the so-called value was, in a year just before the First World War, some seventy times the true value.

In the case of imports computed values, that is values officially estimated in accordance with what were believed to be the current prices of the time, were introduced and used in Britain till 1870 inclusive, but from 1871 onwards declared values have been entered for imports also. This calls for great caution in extending comparisons of import values further back than 1870. According to British practice import values are those at the port of arrival, that is, include freight but not merchant's profit, export values those at the port of shipment, 'free on board' (fob).

The foregoing points have been made to emphasise the care that must be taken in using statistics — in particular in ensuring that the source, the coverage and the method of calculating value are fully understood. Notes on these items are normally appended to all official tables. The problem of comparing the trade of the countries of the world has been simplified by the conversion of national units of weight and volume into their metric equivalents in all publications of the United Nations Organisation — and has been further facilitated by the introduction of the Standard Trade Classification.

SUBJECTS FOR INVESTIGATION

No student of commercial geography can be unaware how many subjects there are that still await investigation, and in many cases how far the means for obtaining the desired information are lacking. This deficiency is felt in a peculiar degree with regard to the trade, and more particularly the home or internal trade, of our own country, but in all countries one has often to regret that the available data refer to the country as a whole instead of particular regions which it would be useful to investigate. The late Lord Stamp in his important Presidential Address to the Geographical Association in 1937 dealt with the contacts between geography and economic theory. He pleaded for an understanding of economics by geographers and for a greater use of geographical facts and illustrations by economists. He pointed out that five types of geographic—economic studies could be distinguished: (*a*) the simple static, when a presentday geographic fact was explained by an economic fact — really no explanation at all; (*b*) the inductive static, when several such examples were used to formulate a general statement; (*c*) the simple dynamic, when the element of change and the historical factor were introduced; (*d*) the inductive dynamic; and finally (*e*) the formulation of general economic or geographical laws based on a wide study of examples of the fourth class. He held that economic geographers had not yet reached the fifth stage and that an immense field of work remained to be explored.

Some of the suggestions for further investigations which Chisholm listed in earlier editions of this work might well be revived in the light of such a general programme, namely:

How far British influence in different parts of the world has contributed to the growth of the trade of the developing countries.
The conditions of commercially successful and unsuccessful irrigation.
The advantages of rural and urban centres for different kinds of manufacturing industry and the influence of communications networks.
The effect on commerce of the construction of particular railways, pipelines or ports.
The relations of seaports to their hinterlands.
The influence on commerce of the possession by different countries of bulky commodities such as coal, timber, iron ore, crude oil and the like.
The effect of local labour, local supplies of raw material and local markets in the development of manufacturing industries.
The effects of government interference in modifying the influence of natural advantages — or of disadvantages.

Introduction

The gradual conversion of manufacturing industry from the heavy and extractive to the light and 'mobile'.
The interplay between the exhaustion of natural resources and the introduction of alternative materials.

I
General factors affecting the production and distribution of commodities

Climate

Under the head of climate we have to consider here only the main climatic factors affecting the production and distribution of articles of commerce. The commodities whose production is most immediately affected by climatic conditions are those derived from the vegetable kingdom; but those of animal origin, being directly or indirectly dependent on vegetation, are subject to the same influences. It is, however, climate as influencing vegetation, and more particularly as influencing cultivation, or the bestowal of human labour in promoting vegetation, that we have to keep chiefly in view in considering the effect of climate on the production of commodities.

All kinds of vegetation require a certain amount of **heat** and a certain amount of **moisture**. The great source of heat is the sun, and of moisture the ocean, where evaporation is brought about through the heat of the sun. The winds are carriers of both heat and moisture, so that it is essential to study the direction of the prevailing winds in order to understand the distribution of temperature and rainfall over the globe. **Temperature** decreases on the whole from the vicinity of the equator towards the poles, but the rate of decrease is unequal over land and water. Water being more slowly heated and cooled than land, the diminution in temperature towards the poles is more rapid over the ocean than over the land in summer, less rapid in winter. The ocean and other large bodies of water therefore have a moderating effect on the temperature of adjacent lands. This effect is brought about mainly by the agency of the winds, and when considering land temperatures it is more important to study the direction of the prevailing winds than the mere distribution of land and water. Winds depend on local differences in the pressure of the atmosphere. They tend to blow from regions of high pressure to regions of low pressure. Regions of low pressure occur over the warmest parts of the ocean near the equator, and in the interior of the great land masses in summer, when they are most directly exposed to the rays of the sun. Over the ocean the region of high temperature and low pressure forms a belt, towards which winds blow more or less from the north and south. The direction of these winds is, however, modified by the rotation of the earth, in consequence of which these winds, known as the **trade winds**, blow more or less from the east, over some parts of the ocean with such regularity that, in the language of Sir Thomas Browne, 'sailing from Lima to Manilla . . . you may fasten up the rudder and sleep before the wind'. It is important, therefore, to observe and constantly to bear in mind that over a great width of the ocean in low latitudes extending on both sides far beyond the tropics, there is a strong tendency for the winds to blow away from the west sides of the continents and towards the east sides. The position of this wide belt, or rather of the two wide belts separated by an intermediate belt of calms corresponding to that of lowest pressure, is not constant. It moves north and south with the sun, along with the whole system of atmospheric pressures dependent on the height of the sun above the horizon. Wherever and whenever the trade winds blow, however, they have a certain effect on mitigating the temperatures of the regions exposed to them.

Outside of the trade wind region in the northern hemisphere there is normally in the winter months an **area of low pressure** in the North Atlantic to the north of 60° N, and in the North Pacific a similar area more to the south. Towards each of these the winds tend to blow, in consequence of the rotation of the earth, in great anticlockwise spirals. Hence southwesterly, and consequently warm, winds prevail at this season on nearly all the west coasts of Europe and a large part of the west coast of America, while northerly, and hence cold, winds prevail on the opposite coasts, that is, on the east coast of North America, and the east coasts of northern Asia. The contrast between the temperature of these coasts in corresponding latitudes is another great fact constantly to be borne in mind, as well as the fact that the benefit of the relatively high winter temperatures is carried some distance inland by the winds. Warm ocean currents flowing in the same direction as the winds help to maintain their temperature; but it is to be observed that without the winds these currents would have little effect on the temperature over the land. In the summer months the area of low pressure still exists in the North Atlantic, so that southwesterly winds still prevail, though not so strongly on the west European coasts. In the North Pacific during the summer months an area of low pressure can scarcely be said to exist. In the southern hemisphere outside of the trade wind belt the conditions are greatly altered by the fact that the amount of land is very small. It is enough to say that there the prevailing winds throughout the year, at least to the south of 40° S, are westerly. These westerlies blow more constantly over the open oceans of the southern hemisphere than elsewhere and are often referred to as the 'Roaring Forties'.

The influence of the pressure of the air over the land in determining the direction of the prevailing winds is most marked where there are great bodies of land, above all in eastern Asia and in Australia. In the interior of eastern Asia in summer are regions of very low pressure, in winter of very high pressure. Hence, in summer incoming ocean winds, southwesterly, southerly, southeasterly, blow over all the southeast of Asia, including the islands, from the Indian peninsula to about the parallel of 60° N. During the winter land winds, northeasterly, northerly, northwesterly, prevail in the same region. These are the **monsoons**, which have an important effect on temperature as well as on rainfall. The word monsoon is derived from an Arabic word meaning a season, and is still used, in the Indian subcontinent, as meaning the rainy season. The summer winds, though blowing from lower latitudes, do not tend to raise the temperature, because they come from the ocean; but the winter winds being land winds as well as coming from higher latitudes have a marked effect in lowering the temperatures, more particularly in the temperate zone. For this reason also the winter temperatures in the east of Asia are much lower than those in corresponding latitudes in the west of Europe and Africa, a fact of great importance in commercial geography. In Australia similar results are due to the alternation of high and low pressures in the interior, but owing to the difference of hemisphere the seasons and the directions of the winds are reversed.

In consequence of the facts stated with regard to the prevalent winds, there is, in the temperate zones, and more particularly in the **northern hemisphere**, a general lowering of the mean temperature from west to east over the land, due chiefly to an easterly increase in the cold of winter, only partly compensated by an easterly increase in the heat of summer. The increase in the extremes of heat and cold is greater in the broader of the two great land masses, and the lowest temperatures on the earth have been recorded towards the east of Asia, some distance inland, since the sea everywhere has some effect on mitigating extremes of temperature. While the eastern land mass thus exhibits greater cold and greater contrasts of summer and winter temperature in the east of Asia than are presented in the east of America, its western or European portion, being exposed to warmer winds traversing a warmer ocean than those which visit the western coasts of North America in high latitudes, is characterised by a more equable climate and higher winter temperatures than corresponding latitudes on the latter coasts; and, in general, we find that when we compare equal latitudes in the west of America and the west of Europe, the latter continent shows the higher temperatures; but when we make a similar comparison for the east of America and the east of Asia, the higher temperatures are found in America.

These important general facts bear directly on the production and distribution of mercantile commodities, since the northern limits of various cultivated plants the range of which is somewhat rigorously determined by climate, such as the orange and the vine, are further north in Europe than in the west of North America, and further north in the east of North America than in the east of Asia. Again, whereas the whole of the west coast of Norway, extending to beyond 70° N, is at all times free from ice, the northern coasts of the peninsula of Alaska, in about 57° or 58° N, are regularly beset by ice in winter. On the other hand, whereas the eastern coasts of North America are rarely encumbered by ice south of the Gulf of St Lawrence, in about 46° or 47° N, ice is to be seen in the Chinese Gulf of Chihli in lat. 40°. Halifax, in Nova Scotia, in 44½° N, is nearly always open, and thus can serve as a winter port for Canada; while the Soviet seaport of Vladivostok, in the east of Siberia, to the south of 43° N, is closed by ice for about a third of the year. With regard to cultivated plants, however, it must be mentioned that those which are able to profit by long and hot summer days during a very short summer can be grown in higher latitudes in eastern Asia than in eastern North America. Rye, barley, and even cucumbers, can be grown at Yakutsk in eastern Siberia, in 62° N (the same latitude as the mouth of the Yukon in Alaska, and Frederikshaab in Greenland), the barley being sown in the first days of May, and ripening about the middle of July — within two and a half months.

The land surfaces of the **southern hemisphere** are too narrow to exhibit the easterly increase in the extremes of temperature, especially since they do not extent into those latitudes in which that increase is most marked. One noteworthy circumstance regarding the climate of the temperate zone of the southern hemisphere, is that it is generally colder, at least on the land, than in corresponding latitudes of the northern hemisphere; so that the limit of cultivation of various plants is in a lower latitude to the south than to the north of the equator. A glacier descends in Chile to the water's edge in about lat. 46° S, a latitude corresponding to that of the middle of France in the northern hemisphere. In the Australian state of Victoria, the orange is cultivated only in the extreme northwest in a latitude comparable to the latitude of southernmost Spain. In the South Island of New Zealand, which is in latitudes corresponding to those of northern and central Italy, oats is an important crop, as it is in Scotland and Ireland.

As the winds are the carriers of heat and cold it follows that the physical configuration of the land, apart from the direct effect of elevation, may indirectly affect temperature. Mountains, by obstructing winds, in some cases afford protection from cold winds, in others prevent certain districts from getting the benefit of warm ones. Temperature is also greatly modified by evaporation and condensation of water vapour, evaporation always tending to bring about a lowering and condensation a rise of temperature.* Heat is lost during the night by

* The conversion of water into vapour, like the conversion of ice or any other solid into the liquid state, involves the expenditure of heat. That is, heat (in the scientific sense of the term) is used in the conversion, and is not available for raising or main-

radiation, and since there is greatest loss of heat in this way where the atmosphere is dry, clear, and rare, there are great extremes of heat by day and cold by night in the interior of continents, especially at high elevations. Low temperatures prevail at high altitudes, but it is to be remembered that these low temperatures are those of the air. There is no diminution, but the reverse, in the strength of rays of the sun on any body directly exposed to them.

It is important to be clear as to the meaning of the diminution of mean temperature with altitude. This is not a phenomenon observable equally at all times of the day and year. A statement as to the rate of that diminution, usually given as equal to about $0.5°$ C ($1°$ F) for every 100 m (300 ft) of ascent,† expresses the result of averaging differences of temperature in a vertical column of air at different times and in different situations, and in a great many cases it is of much more practical importance to observe that at certain times in certain situations the difference is the other way, the lower temperatures at the bottom, the higher on the upper slopes or even on mountain tops. This will be understood when it is borne in mind that various causes are at work affecting air temperatures. First it should be noted that the air is heated principally not by the direct rays of the sun, but indirectly through the warming of the surface of the earth which then imparts its heat in various ways to the air above. Naturally, therefore, when the surface of the earth is warm, the air is all the warmer the nearer it is to the surface, and this difference is enhanced by what occurs in connection with one of the modes of conveying the heat from the ground to the higher strata of the air, namely, by means of convection currents. The air nearest the ground expands in consequence of its greater heat and so becomes relatively light and rises. But as it rises it becomes subjected to less pressure and expands still more, and this expansion is accompanied by an instantaneous lowering of temperature permeating the whole mass. As long as the air rises and there is no condensation of the water vapour in it into cloud, rain, snow or any other form of water, this cooling goes on at the rate of $0.5°$ C ($1°$ F) for every 55 m (180 ft) of ascent, a figure which does not express an average but states a fact observed with every rise of air, whether by day or night, in summer or in winter. The rate of cooling, however, is checked when any condensation takes place. But if the heating of the air above takes place from the ground upwards, so also in a large measure does the cooling at night. At night every part of a column of air loses heat by radiation upwards into space, and the higher strata lose heat in this way most rapidly on account of the greater rarity and frequently also the greater dryness of the atmosphere. But the ground loses heat in this

taining temperature. Meanwhile, of course, temperature may be maintained, and even raised, by external supplies of heat from the sun.

† The rate is less in winter or at night, more in summer or by day.

way, above all on clear nights, much more rapidly than any part of the air column, and that brings about a more rapid cooling of the air near the ground. The adjacent stratum is cooled by actual contact. The strata immediately above that are cooled by a more rapid radiation of heat downwards to the ground than upwards into space. The result is that at the coldest part of a summer night there is a regular increase of temperature from the ground upwards, a so-called inversion of temperature, at least up to the height of more than 600 m (2 000 ft) above the ground, whereas the diminution of temperature in the same direction at the hottest period of a summer day may be equal to about 1° C (2° F) for every 90 m (300 ft) of ascent, or double the average diminution (cf. p. 25). This inversion of temperature is important in cultivation as it gives rise to the frost pockets mentioned below, so well known to gardeners. Indeed microclimates may occur even within the area of an ordinary garden which profoundly influence the growth of plants.

From this account it will be understood that the lowering of mean temperature with altitude will differ according to the nature of the superficial configuration. Isolated peaks, exposed on account of their isolation to ascending winds from all directions, will show a much more rapid rate of diminution than mountainous country in which a large extent of the solid crust is raised to a high altitude. Where we have an extensive high level tableland, or even high valleys out of reach of ascending winds, air several hundreds of metres above sea level may be as near the ground, that is, as near the heating surface, as air above a plain only a few metres above sea level, and the high ground in this case will be more intensely heated than the low ground by sunrays falling at the same angle on both. In such a case the only circumstances that bring about a lower mean temperature at the higher latitude are the greater rarity and generally also the greater dryness of the atmosphere. These conditions prevent the air from taking up heat as rapidly from the ground by day and favour a more rapid cooling by night. The total lowering of the mean temperature, however, is reduced to a minimum. Hence it is possible to cultivate wheat in western Canada, in the same latitude as Snowdon, at as great a height as the top of Snowdon. At Banff, Alberta, at the height of about 1 400 m (4 600 ft), considerably higher than the top of Ben Nevis, the ordinary English garden flowers such as larkspurs, campanulas, sweet-williams, stocks, pansies, and marigolds flourish even in September, and at the same season at Lake Louise, about 1 740 m (5 700 ft) above sea level, eschscholtzias, asters, and other flowers bloom freely.

The facts just mentioned cannot but suggest that it is difficult to attach any clear meaning to isothermal lines drawn on maps representing land with varied physical configuration, based on observed mean temperatures reduced by a common multiplier to so-called sea-level temperatures, and at any rate will serve to bring home to everyone that in economic geography we have to do not with sea-level temperatures but with the temperatures actually observed, a point emphasised by Professor Herbertson in his well-known paper on 'The thermal regions of the globe'.* The isothermal lines drawn over the sea on two of his maps serve to indicate the great variations of temperature on different coasts in the same latitudes. The map showing, for different regions, the number of months with a mean temperature over 10° C (50° F) indicates how the temperature requirements of vegetation suited to the temperate zone are met, but it must be kept in mind that it does so only very broadly. It is not on mean temperatures even as actually observed that vegetation depends, but upon the actual temperatures experienced within a range that differs for different plants.

Differences in the range of temperature which different plants will stand make it important to observe the conditions in which exceptionally low temperatures are liable to occur on low grounds as compared with higher slopes. As heated air expands and rises so cold air contracts and sinks. In calm weather the air on mountainsides gets cooled by night more rapidly than on the valley bottoms. The radiation upwards is more rapid on account of the greater rarity of the air, and it starts from a lower temperature than at the valley bottom; the air on the slopes becomes so heavy that it flows down the mountain or hillsides to the valley bottom, and there accumulates if there is no adequate outlet for it. Hence it is that, for example, in the choosing of sites for orchards in regions subject to low temperatures, the lie of the ground must be carefully studied. One must see that there is good air drainage, a free way of escape for descending cold air. Above all frost-pockets or hollows in which cold air might accumulate like water in a lake must be avoided. Where mountain valleys, in parts of the world with severe winters, are shut off from the prevailing winds, the mean winter temperature is lower in the valley bottoms than higher up. The celebrated Austrian meteorologist and climatologist, Hann, pointed out that in such valleys in the Alps the human settlements are for that reason found on the hillsides, not in the lower parts of the valleys. For the same reason, in part of the Appalachian mountains cultivation is mainly confined to what is known as the thermal belt, sufficiently high to escape the extreme rigours of winter. It is on the slopes of the hills, not in the valley bottoms, that wheat is grown round Yakutsk and in the upper Angara. In upland pastures sheep frequent the higher grounds at night.

As the ocean is the great source of **moisture**, the further inland a region lies the less chance it has of receiving an ample rainfall, unless there are special conditions favourable to the condensation of water vapour. Water vapour is condensed through the more or less rapid lowering of the temperature, and one of the most frequently operative

* *Geographical Journal*, xl, (1912), 518–32.

causes in bringing about that reduction of temperature is the presence of mountains, obstructing moisture-laden winds, and thus forcing them to ascend and become cooled by expansion. Consequently, regions on the maritime side of mountains often have sufficient rainfall when those on the other side have not. In the tropics there is generally a more marked distinction between rainy and dry seasons than in most parts of the temperate zone. This distinction is most marked in the monsoon regions, in which the winter winds are naturally for the most part dry winds, whereas those of the summer months come heavily charged with moisture and bring about a very high rainfall in the parts more directly exposed to them. In these regions accordingly we have the combination of heat and moisture specially favourable to vegetation, and this characteristic is particularly noticeable in the parts of the monsoon areas belonging to the temperate zone, which are in consequence greatly more productive than regions in the same latitudes elsewhere. The distribution of rainfall throughout the year is illustrated by the graphs on p. 29.

The foregoing account of climatic conditions has been written in terms of what must be called the old meteorology. The newer concept pays less attention to pressure and winds and considers rather the movement of air masses of varying characteristics. The air masses may meet along fronts and such fronts are marked by atmospheric disturbances. In particular the polar front marks the outer limit of the mass of cold heavy air over the polar regions. What has been called the intertropical front, where the air masses associated with the northeast and southeast trades meet, is now referred to rather as a zone of convergence.

Enough has been said to indicate that climatic conditions vary widely from one part of the world to another not only in the amount and season of rainfall, the degree and degree of variability of temperature, but also in many other ways. At the same time identical or almost identical climatic conditions recur in several parts of the world: it may be in equatorial Africa, South America and Indonesia: or it may be (with the seasons reversed) in the South Island of New Zealand and in Scotland. The important conception of 'major climatic regions' was introduced to British geographers long ago by Professor A. J. Herbertson of Oxford. His regions were based on conditions both of temperature and rainfall. The Herbertsonian regions, or modifications of them, are still sometimes used, though greater use is made of the climatic regions devised by the German climatologist, W. Köppen. Köppen's regions are defined with greater rigidity and delimited by arbitrarily chosen temperature limits which sometimes have little corresponding precision on the ground. Another mathematically precise classification introducing the idea of 'precipitation efficiency' rather than actual rainfall was introduced by the American climatologist, C. W. Thornthwaite. On the other hand, the American ecologist,

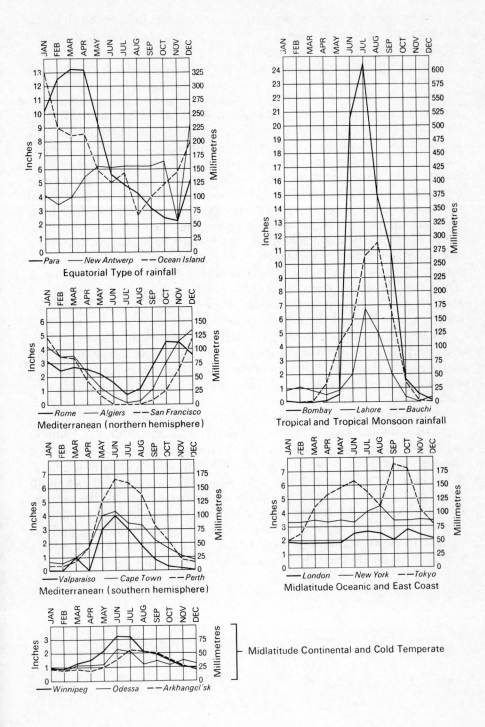

Equatorial Type of rainfall
—Para — New Antwerp — —Ocean Island

Mediterranean (northern hemisphere)
—Rome — Algiers — —San Francisco

Tropical and Tropical Monsoon rainfall
—Bombay — Lahore — —Bauchi

Mediterranean (southern hemisphere)
—Valparaiso — Cape Town — —Perth

Midlatitude Oceanic and East Coast
—London — New York — —Tokyo

Midlatitude Continental and Cold Temperate
—Winnipeg — Odessa — —Arkhangel'sk

F. E. Clements stressed the importance of plants as indices of the whole complex of significant climatic factors so that the observed natural vegetation becomes the best indication of a climatic region.

The importance of the concept of climatic regions in commercial geography is in the applicability of lessons learnt in one part of a given region to all other areas having an identical climate. The climatic conditions of parts of Canada are exactly repeated in Russia, so lessons learnt by scientific experiment in the one area can be applied in the other. If the Canadians are successful in breeding a new type of wheat which will ripen further north and with a shorter summer than existing varieties, the results of these experiments are immediately of great value to the Soviet Union. On the other hand, serious mistakes have often been made in the past in trying to transfer customs or procedure from one part of the world to another where they are not suitable. Thus some of the early English settlers in Ceylon saw no reason why they could not grow the crops which they had grown in England, so they took with them oats and barley and wheat and tried to grow them. When the Pilgrim Fathers went from some of the country districts of England and settled in New England they cleared the forests and built homes and cultivated the ground believing that they had the same soil and climatic conditions as they had left behind them in England. There are many areas where they settled where the soil was very poor, and today much of the land they so laboriously cleared is being abandoned; it is not good enough, and really has never been good enough, for cultivation.

Many important commercial products can be produced only in one type of climate. The rubber tree (*Hevea*) is a native of the climatic region of the Amazon basin of South America where it is always hot and always wet; the rubber tree cannot be grown where there is a long, dry season or where there is a cold season, but it can be grown in all those parts of the world where the climatic conditions are the same as in its own home area. Indeed, nearly all the natural rubber of commerce comes today from gigantic plantations in Malaysia, Indonesia, and Sri Lanka (Ceylon). Plantations were started near Calcutta, but a long dry season there makes the cultivation of *Hevea* impossible.

Climatic regions

Low latitudes

The equatorial regions. The equatorial climate (*Köppen's AA'r*) is found in a belt on either side of the equator, extending roughly between 5° N and 5° S of this line. The characteristic vegetation is tall evergreen forest where it is always wet and always hot so that the forests are never leafless. It might be called also the climate of the hot, wet *selvas* (a local name for the Amazon forests). The temperature is high all the year; there is very little variation between the hottest month and the coolest month, and there is usually only a small difference between day and night. The average for the year is about 25° or 27° C (78° or 80° F), and the range between the hottest and coldest month is usually less than 2.5° C (5° F). Although the atmosphere is always hot and steamy and the temperature is uniformly high, the thermometer very rarely rises above 38° C (100° F) and frequently does not rise above 32° C (90° F); on the other hand, it does not as a rule fall much below 21° C (70° F). In the interior of the great forests there is little movement of the air, the climate is very tiring, but in situations near the sea or on islands it is often very pleasant, for the land and sea breezes give a welcome movement of the air, a cooling sea breeze by day and a land breeze by night. The rain falls at all seasons of the year and there is no dry season except in relative amount. In the early part of the day bright sunshine causes much evaporation and an upward current in the atmosphere; the ascending moisture-laden air becomes cooled and clouds form during the afternoon. The convectional rain which follows is often accompanied by thunder and falls in torrential downpours, usually of short duration. By the evening the sky is clear again. There are usually two seasons in the year which are wetter than the rest; in most cases the rains are at their maximum a short while after the period when the sun is shining vertically. Typical of the equatorial lands is the belt of calms or doldrums where there is no marked wind or wind direction. Island stations have light and variable breezes but some regions near the equator are influenced by the trade winds or monsoon winds which are typically developed further to the north or further to the south. The equatorial region is nearly everywhere one of heavy rainfall, about 2 000 mm (80 in) of rain a year being typical. There are three main areas: the Amazon basin of South America; the Congo basin of Central Africa; the islands of southeastern Asia and the neighbouring parts of the mainland, including Malaysia.

In high plateaus near the equator the temperature is very much lower and the 'Ecuador type' of climate is found, typically on the high plateau of Ecuador at an elevation of 2 500 to 3 000 m (8 000 to 10 000 ft). Here the average temperature is only 13° C (55° F), and this had been described as the 'land of eternal spring'.

There is a fierce struggle in the forest, not for moisture of which there is an abundance, but for air and light. Giant trees, nearly all having tall unbranched bolls with a crown of leaves at the top, form a close mass often so thick that little sunlight reaches the ground. Many of the trees are of hardwood species and there are two major difficulties in exploiting these forests. One is the great variety of trees, so that the extraction of particular types of timber is extremely difficult. The other is the character of the timber itself, usually hard and costly to work though often forming magnificent 'cabinet' wood. Some towns such as Manaus in the heart of the equatorial forests of South America actually import softer, more easily worked building timber from North America. The struggle for light and air results in the existence of large numbers of woody climbers; the trees by which these have climbed may afterwards decay, leaving the climber hanging from the branches of neighbouring trees and the coils forming tangled masses on the ground. This is one reason why the equatorial forests are so difficult to penetrate. Many smaller plants, including orchids and ferns, find a foothold in the higher branches of the trees (growing there as epiphytes) and thus reach the light. In the denser forests the ground may be almost clear of vegetation except decaying matter, but in open forests there is a luxuriant growth of broadleaved herbs. In the denser forests the animal life is almost restricted to the treetops and all groups of animals can exhibit members especially adapted to this particular habitat. Where man is concerned the equatorial climate has been well described as a good servant but a bad master. In the dense forests of South America and much of the Congo the climate is still the master, and the forests are sparsely inhabited. On the other hand Malaysia and Java are densely populated. The forests there have given place to plantations of rubber, oil palm, tea and coffee. For the white man, too, these are far from being the unhealthiest or most uncomfortable parts of the world. The disagreeable aspect of the equatorial climate is the absence of variety.

The tropical regions and the tropical monsoon regions (Köppen's Awg).
The word 'tropical' is commonly used in such a loose way that it

conveys little more than the idea of heat, but geographers have assigned a more precise meaning to the word tropical as applied to the tropical climate. The tropical and tropical monsoon climates are found typically within the tropics on either side of the equatorial belt, that is, beyond 5° N or S of the Equator. In contrast to the equatorial regions there is a marked difference between the temperatures of the hot and cool seasons of the year. Near the equatorial belt or in maritime situations where the rainfall is heavy, the difference of temperature may be small, but in other parts there is frequently as much as 17° or 22° C (30° or 40° F) between the hottest and the coldest months. The difference between day and night temperatures is correspondingly large.

The tropical regions lie between the equatorial forests on the one side and the hot deserts on the other. From the point of view of rainfall there is a gradation from 2 000 mm (80 in) a year or more on the forest edge to 380 mm (15 in) on the other edge; at some of the wettest stations in the tropical belt the rainfall may be as much as 5 000 mm (200 in) a year. There is, however, a distinctly dry and distinctly wet season, and it is usually possible to distinguish between (*a*) a cool dry season followed by (*b*) a hot dry season, when the land becomes greatly heated and the highest temperatures are recorded, and (*c*) the rainy season.

With the coming of the rain begins a lowering of temperature, but the rain comes in the hot season of the year, while the cooler months are practically rainless. This season of intensive rainfall favours the growth of grass, but where there is sufficient moisture to give a constant underground supply trees also flourish. Thus in tropical and tropical monsoon lands four belts of vegetation may be distinguished. (*a*) Near the equatorial belt, provided the rainfall is sufficiently heavy, there is forest differing but little from that of the equatorial belt. (*b*) Where the rainfall drops below about 1 500 or 2 000 mm (60 or 80 in) this passes into a forest in which the trees are deciduous, losing their leaves or having a resting period during the heat of the year. The forests of Burma and parts of India famous for their teak, sal and other timbers belong to this region, as do many of the forests of West Africa. (*c*) Then comes the characteristic grassland of so much of Africa, the great stretches of grassland with occasional trees, or savanna. In India, where it is too dry for the growth of monsoon forest, its place is taken by rather a scrubby kind of woodland with a limited amount of grass. (*d*) Towards the desert areas the vegetation becomes poorer and poorer, the trees are replaced by spiny bushes and the grass is found only in sparse tufts.

In the drier parts the reliability of the rainfall from one year to another is a serious matter. Some years the fall is sufficient to ensure good crops, whilst in other years a poor rainfall results in famine conditions.

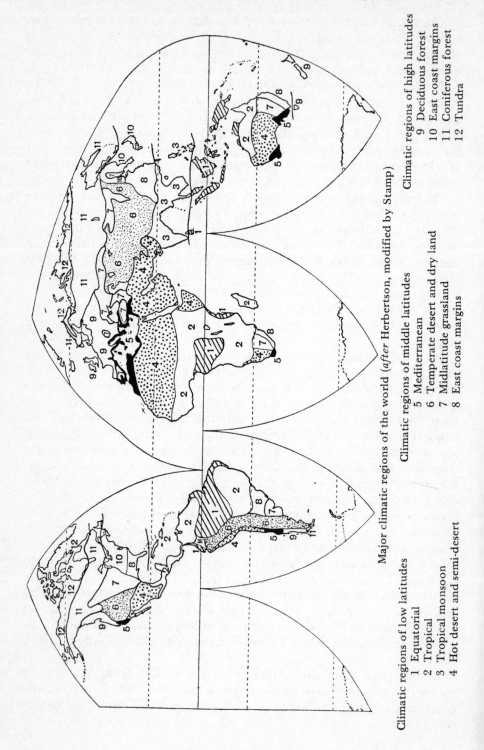

Major climatic regions of the world (*after* Herbertson, modified by Stamp)

Climatic regions of low latitudes
1 Equatorial
2 Tropical
3 Tropical monsoon
4 Hot desert and semi-desert

Climatic regions of middle latitudes
5 Mediterranean
6 Temperate desert and dry land
7 Midlatitude grassland
8 East coast margins

Climatic regions of high latitudes
9 Deciduous forest
10 East coast margins
11 Coniferous forest
12 Tundra

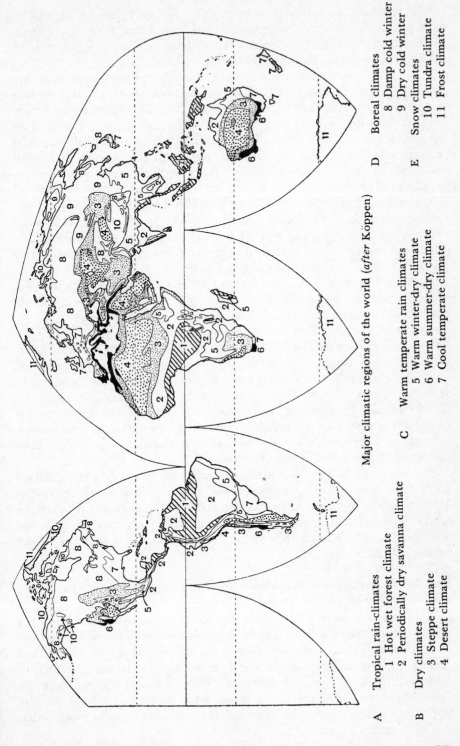

Climatic regions

Major climatic regions of the world (*after* Köppen)

A Tropical rain-climates
   1 Hot wet forest climate
   2 Periodically dry savanna climate

B Dry climates
   3 Steppe climate
   4 Desert climate

C Warm temperate rain climates
   5 Warm winter-dry climate
   6 Warm summer-dry climate
   7 Cool temperate climate

D Boreal climates
   8 Damp cold winter
   9 Dry cold winter

E Snow climates
   10 Tundra climate
   11 Frost climate

35

The animals are of two main groups: the swift-footed, vegetable-eating animals such as the antelope and giraffe that take refuge from their enemies in flight; the carnivores such as the lion and the leopard which prey upon the members of the first group.

Man in the savanna is primarily a hunter; just as the grassland is able to support vast numbers of grass-eating animals, so man is able to rear great herds of cattle and becomes a pastoralist. The natural grass which flourishes in the savanna may be replaced by the cereal grasses and so man becomes an agriculturist. The more important crops of the tropical regions, like the occupations of man, vary with the amount of rainfall and the degree of development. India and Bangladesh afford an example of a very densely populated region and Africa or parts of South America of the more sparsely populated tracts.

In areas with more than 2 000 mm (80 in) of rain a year rice is the staple food of the people and almost the only crop, as in Bangladesh. The main danger is not a lack of water but one of flooding: protective works are often necessary to prevent floods.

In areas between 1 000 and 2 000 mm (40 and 80 in) of rain a year rice is again an important food crop, largely replaced by maize in Africa, while sugarcane and oilseeds are other important crops.

In areas between 500 and 1 000 mm (20 and 40 in) of rain (dry belts) the land is normally covered with scrubland, thorn forest or grassland; different types of millet or Guinea corn are the staple grains of the people as in all the warmer parts of the Indian subcontinent and in tropical Africa, though in regions such as the northern zone of the Indian subcontinent wheat and barley may be grown as winter crops. Sesamum and various oilseeds are cultivated and cotton is a characteristic crop. There is always the danger that the rain may be less than average and that famine may thereby result.

In the tropical regions cattle are reared in numbers and in Africa sometimes form virtually a measure of wealth of individuals or groups. Unfortunately quantity rather than quality is the criterion adopted. In many parts of Africa the destructive tsetse fly is very much in evidence and limits cattle rearing. Sheep may be important, as they are in the Indian subcontinent.

The hot desert regions (Köppen's BW) lie on the poleward side of the regions with a tropical or tropical monsoon climate. They are confined to high pressure belts where the currents of air are descending and the winds blow outwards so that there are no moisture-laden winds coming in from the ocean. They are mainly on the western side of the land masses because on the eastern side a certain amount of rain is caused in these latitudes by the trade winds. In the hot desert regions there are few clouds and the sun pours down with unmitigated force on the unprotected soil, while the absence of cloud also permits rapid radiation of heat and the nights are often very cold. There is thus a big contrast between day and night and between the hot season, when the sun is vertically overhead, and the cold season. There is further little or no rain to exercise a cooling influence on the temperature; many of the deserts are low-lying so that there is not even altitude to temper the heat of summer, with the result that the highest temperatures of the world are recorded in these regions. Thus, El Golea in the Sahara has an average temperature of 34° C (93° F) in July, whereas in January its average is only 4° C (39° F), about the same as London for the same month. Jacobabad, in Sind (Pakistan), has one of the highest recorded average temperatures in the world for the month of July – 37° C (98° F). On the margins of the desert nearest the equator the desert proper fades into semidesert as soon as the rainfall reaches 225 to 250 mm (9 to 10 in) a year; this in turn passes gradually into the grasslands of tropical regions. On these margins of the deserts such rain as does fall comes mainly in the same season as it does in the tropical lands, that is to say, in the early summer. On the poleward margins, on the other hand, the desert fades gradually into Mediterranean scrubland where the rain comes in winter. Cairo with 33 mm (1.3 in) of rain a year is an example of this type. The largest deserts occur in the northern hemisphere, for the simple reason that the land masses there are broader. The Sahara stretches almost continuously from the Atlantic to the Red Sea and then eastwards over Asia to the borders of Baluchistan and the desert of the Indian subcontinent. North America has the deserts of the Mexican and United States borders, South America the Peruvian and north Chilean deserts that occupy the area between the Andes and the Pacific Ocean. In South Africa the Kalahari, while not a true desert, stretches right to the Atlantic Ocean, and in Australia a large area has a rainfall of less than 250 mm (10 in) a year, the great dry heart of the continent.

There are few deserts where absolutely nothing grows; over much larger areas there is some vegetation, often sufficient to support at least some animal life. The plants have various means of storing water; some have very long roots which go down to great depths and so find water, others have special stems and leaves in which water can be stored, while many are provided with spines and thorns to prevent their being readily eaten by animals. Of special importance are the fertile areas or oases occupying hollows where an underground supply of water comes sufficiently near the surface to be accessible to vegetation. Some oases may consist merely of a clump of trees surrounding a pool or well, where the typical tree is the date palm, but other and more important oases are areas of several hundred square kilometres and may support a big population as in the heart of Arabia.

The sparse population of the deserts falls into three groups: (*a*) the wanderers who move about from place to place, in the old days with camels, or for shorter journeys with mules, and act as carriers of goods from one desert margin to another, or at other times formed bands of nomadic robbers; (*b*) the settled people of the oases who devote themselves to growing grain; rearing cattle, sheep, goats, horses and camels, and the cultivation of such desert plants as the date palm — to this group belong many of the Arabs; (*c*) the settled population of miners and oil workers, attracted by mineral deposits independently of climatic conditions, as for example in the nitrate fields of northern Chile, the minerals of Western Australia or the oilfields of the northern Sahara and the Persian Gulf.

In the desert regions some interesting influences of climatic conditions on man can be traced. The desert has often produced people with a philosophical outlook, such as the ancient Egyptians and the Arabs, learned in mathematics and astronomy. Over long periods the inhabitants of oases may live peacefully and happily, but the effect of a dry year, or especially a succession of dry years, or the failure of the underground water supply, is to drive the inhabitants abroad in search of other means of sustenance. Many racial migrations due to these factors may be traced in the pages of history: the arrival of the Shepherd Kings in Egypt, the wanderings of Abraham which led him to the Promised Land.

On the whole deserts have acted as barriers to civilisation and to the movement of human beings. The Sahara generally still separates ethnic and cultural groups, for through the centuries it has been more difficult to cross than even the open ocean.

Middle latitudes

Outside the tropics there is usually a considerable difference between the western and eastern margins of the great continental masses. On the western margins the Mediterranean type of climate passes inland with decreasing moisture to midlatitude desert regions, or in certain areas to grasslands, the so-called temperate grasslands which are characteristically found in the interiors of continental masses. On the eastern margins again is another type of climate.

The Mediterranean regions (Köppen's CSa). One of the most distinctive and best known of all the climatic types is that known as the Mediterranean, which is characteristic of the lands surrounding the Mediterranean Sea. Like the hot deserts which border them on the side nearer the equator, these regions are hot and dry in the summer, with outblowing winds: in winter, however, they come under the influence of the westerly wind belt and enjoy moist, mild winters. This is the typical winter rain climate, contrasted with the typical summer rain climate of the tropical or tropical monsoon lands, but the Mediterranean regions are outside the tropics and so on an average are cooler. Sunshine is a typical attribute of Mediterranean lands: almost cloudless skies in summer, and even in winter fewer clouds than would be expected.

The Mediterranean climate is restricted to the western sides of the continents, roughly between latitudes 30° and 45°. The largest area is that found round the Mediterranean Sea, while others occur in North America (parts of California), South America (central Chile), South Africa (southwestern Cape Province), and Australia (southwest of Western Australia, South Australia, and part of Victoria). Here during the hot summer the trade winds in all cases are blowing offshore. A typical Mediterranean climate could not exist on the eastern side of a continent where the trade winds blow from the ocean and are moisture-laden. Within the Mediterranean region there is considerable variation in the details of the climate especially round the large Mediterranean Sea. Eastwards the winters tend to be colder, but the coldest month has usually an average temperature of over 5° C (40° F), while in the more typical parts of Mediterranean lands the coldest month has a temperature of over 10° C (50° F). The summers are both hot and dry with a mean temperature of over 21° C (70° F), in many areas of over 27° C (80° F). The rainfall varies but is usually small, between 250 and 1 000 mm (10 and 40 in) a year in typical cases; on mountains with exposed situations it may be much higher.

The climate does not favour shallow-rooted herbs and grasses which require light showers during the spring and early season when they are growing; it favours, on the other hand, deep-rooted trees and shrubs which are able to withstand the long dry summer. Many of the trees have small leathery leaves or leaves with a coating of wax to retain moisture, others, such as the olive, have leaves covered with fine silky hairs, all devices designed to prevent excessive loss of moisture through transpiration in the hot summer. Some of the plants, such as the vine, have exceptionally long roots. In those regions where forests occur, even forest trees are specially protected; the thick bark of the cork oak of Portugal is an example of this. The dry summer conditions of Mediterranean lands are ideal for the ripening of fruit; typical are the citrus fruits (oranges, lemons, and grapefruit), together with a great variety of fruits from trees which lose their leaves in the winter, such as peach, pear, apricot, and apple as well as the olive, almond, fig, mulberry, and vine. Of grain certain types of wheat and barley grow well, having been adapted by man to the climatic conditions. Deficiency of rainfall is often a serious drawback, and irrigation has played a large part in many Mediterranean regions. The Mediterranean lands have harboured many of the great civilisations of the world, Greece and Rome, Crete and Carthage.

The midlatitude desert regions (Köppen's BWk). The middle latitude deserts cover enormous areas in the heart of the land mass of Eurasia and considerable tracts of the heart of North America, but in South America they are represented only by the Patagonian Desert. In the northern hemisphere they occupy flat areas cut off from the ocean by mountain barriers and by distance. In general the midlatitude deserts are characterised by wide ranges of temperature and a very low rainfall. Generally, too, they form large areas of high pressure with great masses of cold air in winter and areas of low pressure with inblowing winds in summer. The scanty rainfall occurs mainly in the summer except in those regions which border the Mediterranean countries, for example Iran.

Elevation and latitude permit of a subdivision of midlatitude deserts into several types. The *Tibet type* occurs on the high plateaus of Central Asia, over 3 400 m (11 000 ft), and in Bolivia in South America, again over 3 400 m (11 000 ft). Many parts of the Bolivian plateau are almost too well watered to be described as desert. The *Iran type*, characterised by the enclosed plateau of Iran, forms a transition to the hot desert type. Similar areas occur in North America round Salt Lake City. The *Gobi or Mongolian type* occurs at lower elevations further away from the equator.

Midlatitude grassland regions (Köppen's BSk). The midlatitude grassland regions are also called the temperate grasslands or the temperate continental regions, but the word 'temperate' is an unfortunate one because it is in these regions that great contrasts are found between summer and winter.

There are great tracts in the heart of the land mass of North America and the land mass of Eurasia which are far removed from the moderating influence of the sea. There are no cooling sea breezes to counteract the extreme heat of summer, nor are there warm ocean currents and pleasantly westerly winds to mitigate the extreme cold of winter. When the land becomes heated in spring, low pressure areas form and air masses from the ocean come sufficiently laden with moisture to bring a moderate rainfall. This rainfall comes mainly in the spring and summer, and affords conditions more suitable to grass than to trees. So in these regions are found the great midlatitude grasslands of the world: the prairies of North America, the steppes of southern Europe and southern Siberia. The winters are very long and very severe, the summers short but hot. Average temperatures below −18° C (0° F) are common in winter, but the three hottest months usually have temperatures over 16° C (60° F) and frequently over 21° C (70° F). In the southern hemisphere the land masses are so much narrower that the extreme continental type does not occur. In South America, however, the pampas, cut off by the high Andes from the westerly winds of the South Pacific, enjoy a comparable though much more moderate climate. In South

Africa grassland is found on the surface of the lofty South African plateau. Here temperatures are much higher, snow being a rarity, and the existence of the grasslands is due largely to elevation. The Murray–Darling basin in Australia has also a modified continental grassland climate.

The grass is usually lower and less coarse than in the tropical grasslands, and the rolling plains are usually treeless. The contrast between the tender green of the spring, the brown, dried-up wastes of late summer, and the boundless sheet of snow in winter is characteristic of these regions of the northern hemisphere. The animals, as in the Tropical Grasslands, are divided into grass-eaters, swift of foot to escape from their enemies, and the carnivores, amongst which man must really be classed.

Primitive man, as a native of the grasslands, was primarily a hunter, as were the Red Indians of the prairies. The second stage in human development came with the domestication of such animals as the sheep and goat, the ox and the horse. At this stage pastoral industries become of supreme importance, and man is nomadic, wandering about with his flocks and herds in search of fresh pastures. Droughts and a consequent shortage of pasture have repeatedly led, throughout history, to great movements of these nomadic peoples and raids on the settled population of surrounding lands. It is interesting to note that in the grasslands of the southern hemisphere the rearing of sheep is still a major industry, as in Australia, South Africa, and parts of Argentina. In Canada and the USSR the extremes of winter cold are too severe for sheep rearing to be really successful; but a climate so favourable to native grasses has naturally proved favourable to those grasses which man has helped to perfect as the main cereals. These grasslands have become the world's granaries, from which the deficiencies of the industrial countries are made up. Except in South Africa, where maize is the leading cereal, wheat is the crop of first importance in international commerce, followed by barley, oats, and rye. The prairies, the pampas, the veld of South Africa, and the downland of Australia are already well tilled; but there are still areas to be developed in Soviet Asia. One large area of rather dry grassland remains undeveloped in Mongolia and China (Manchuria), where settlement is penetrating gradually along the fringes.

In the grasslands of the southern hemisphere, particularly in Argentina and Uruguay, cattle rearing is important; but there is a distinct tendency for 'bread' to oust 'meat' in the competition for these lands. There are no longer the numerous huge ranches that formerly existed; they are being broken up, and wheat-farming becomes of greater importance. Hence the need for finding new lands for meat production, and the utilisation of the Tropical Grasslands.

East coast margins (Köppen's CW). On the eastern side of the land masses in the same latitudes as the Mediterranean lands of the western side there are regions which in temperature are roughly comparable, but where the rainfall comes mainly in summer. These regions are sometimes called the warm temperate regions, but actually again the word 'temperate' is not very appropriate because of the contrasts which are often found between summer and winter. Nor is there one actual type of climate; any one of the particular regions has its own particular features. The areas are the southeastern states (the cotton lands) of the United States of America, the greater part of China, the southeastern coastlands of Australia, and of South Africa, and the region of Uruguay and southeastern Brazil in South America. The southeastern United States have a well distributed moderate rainfall throughout the year, usually with a maximum in the latter part of the summer, when the rain-bearing winds from the ocean flow in towards the low pressure areas created by the heat in the interior of the continent. The economy of this region used to be almost entirely bound up in the production of cotton. Central and northern China form part of the great 'monsoon' region of Asia. The climate differs from that of the Indian subcontinent and southern China in the coldness of the winters. The rainfall, like that of the Indian subcontinent, is due to the development of a low pressure centre, towards which rain-bearing winds from the ocean blow. While the Indian subcontinent is protected from the cold winds in winter by the Himalayas, China is not so fortunate. Bitterly cold winds blow outwards from the heart of Asia towards the sea throughout most of the winter, bringing the temperature over much of the country down to freezing point or below. The temperature of Peking, in the same latitude as Sardinia, is well below freezing in January. Snow falls commonly over the greater part of central and northern China. The summers, however, are both hot and wet, favouring the growth of rice in the south, whereas millet and wheat are the principal grains further north. Cotton is a leading crop in central China.

In the three continents of the southern hemisphere, climatic conditions in the three corresponding regions are somewhat similar (Eastralian type of Eastern Australia). The rainfall is well distributed throughout the year, with a summer maximum derived mainly from the trade winds. But the southern continents are not broad enough to develop large high pressure centres in winter with cold out-blowing winds, so the southern regions are much more temperate and have much milder winters.

Though the natural vegetation varies from country to country high forest is typical: evergreen where the rainfall is sufficiently well distributed. These rain forests often exhibit a luxuriance of growth rivalling the equatorial forests, but they are more open. Palms and tree ferns are noteworthy in many areas. In the Gulf States there are both broad-leaved and coniferous forests; from the latter the well-known pitch pine is obtained. China has been extensively cleared of her natural vegetation, so that it is very difficult to know what was the original forest cover. It should be mentioned that Japan has this type of climate, but in her case the conditions are modified by the position of the country as an archipelago.

Sufficient has been said to indicate that these regions are eminently suited to human occupation and development. The valleys of central China, with their rice, cotton, tea, and silk, resemble monsoon India and Bangladesh, or rather exceed it, in their density of population, and include the most densely populated agricultural tracts of the whole world. The density may be upward of 1 150 to the sq km (3 000 to the sq mile) − 1 150 people who find their sustenance throughout the year from the small tract of land afforded by 1 sq km. The Gulf States of America are a storehouse of cotton with the maize belt immediately to the north. The eastern coastal strip of Australia and the warm coastal belt of Natal have both attracted relatively large populations. There are considerable untouched forest areas, however, in the interior of South America − untouched largely because they are swampy and unhealthy.

High latitudes

The cool temperate oceanic regions (Köppen's Cf). On the western margins of the continents on the poleward side of Mediterranean lands are regions which lie constantly in the belt of the variable westerly winds − once called the 'anti-trades' − and so are under the influence of cool, rain-bearing winds from the ocean the whole year. The two characteristics, small range of temperature between summer and winter and a well-distributed rainfall throughout the year, are at once obvious. The westerly winds do not blow as steadily as the trade winds, but rather as a succession of eddies and whirls: cyclones and anticyclones. Residents in northwestern Europe know well the prime importance of the cyclones and anticyclones in determining local weather conditions. The largest area having this type of climate is northwestern Europe, but British Columbia and the northwestern United States form another important area. In the southern hemisphere there is a small tract in southern Chile, but no part of Africa lies sufficiently far south, whilst in Australasia only Tasmania and New Zealand (especially the South Island) are typical. In Europe, owing to the drift of warm water, the North Atlantic drift, which is the continuation of the Gulf Stream, the mild winters characterising this type of climate extend exceptionally far north, there being no land barriers. Conditions are most truly oceanic, that is the annual range is least, near the western coasts. The winters become steadily colder as one goes eastwards and the summers slightly warmer; so it is customary in Europe to distinguish two subdivisions:

the northwest European type, where the average temperature of the coldest month is above freezing — averaging about 4° C (40° F); and the central European type, where the average temperature of the coldest month is about or below freezing. The rainfall is well distributed throughout the year, but the total amount varies somewhat widely. In the west the mountains are the wettest part, the plains, lying to the east of the mountain ranges, are the driest. Some parts of the British Isles have a rainfall of over 2 000 mm (80 in), as in the Lake District, whilst in the east of England the rainfall drops to little over 500 mm (20 in), and is as low as 450 mm (18 in) in eastern Germany.

This so-called cool temperate climate is the natural home of the temperate deciduous forests. The delicately tissued leaves are easily injured by winter frosts, and the trees have made the winter their resting period. The very name of the 'fall' of the year, though replaced in England by the less descriptive 'autumn', is indicative of the marked nature of the phenomenon of leaf fall. Many of the trees of these forests (see p. 236) yield valuable hardwoods, more easily worked than the timbers of equatorial lands, but hard relatively to the softwood timbers of the coniferous forests. Well-known examples are the oak, elm, maple, beech, and birch. Deciduous forests formerly covered most of northwestern and central Europe, only interrupted by highlands clothed with evergreen forests or by tracts of moorland and heathland. In North America the mixture of several species of evergreen conifers, usually predominant, gives the forests a somewhat different aspect.

It has been said that the cool temperate climate is the one perhaps most favourable to the development of the human race. It is sufficiently cold to necessitate physical work for the maintaining of bodily warmth in winter, but the summers are never so hot as to make outdoor work unpleasant. Many of the industrial countries of western Europe are situated in this region. Over the greater part of Europe the natural vegetation, the forest, has been cut down to make room for agricultural, pastoral and industrial development. All the important temperate cereals (wheat, barley, oats and rye) flourish, at any rate in the drier parts, with maize in the warmer parts. The natural fruits include apples, pears and other deciduous fruits. In the drier regions sheep flourish on the hill pastures; in the wetter areas the grass grows richly and affords excellent pasture for cattle. The corresponding area in North America is equally suited for development except that much of British Columbia is too mountainous for settlement; and in the deep valleys which separate the mountain ranges the rainfall is often extremely low, some parts receiving no more than about 125 mm (5 in) a year. The mild winters of such places as Vancouver form a pleasant and interesting contrast to the severe winters of the prairies of the heart of Canada. New Zealand forms an interesting example of modern development in the southern hemisphere of this type of climate. Only Chile's area, with too great a rainfall and too great an extent of mountainous country, remains undeveloped.

East coast margins (Köppen's DW). The eastern margins of the great land masses are far colder in winter than the corresponding western margins. Many of the ports, for example Montreal and Vladivostok, are icebound, though the summers are hotter than in corresponding latitudes on the west coasts. In the northeastern United States, the Maritime Provinces and the St Lawrence valley of Canada, there is a well-distributed rainfall which permits of dairy and arable farming. The corresponding region in Asia, in China in the area formerly known as Manchuria, is a region where the monsoon winds still play their part, so it is the summers which are hot and moist, the winters extremely cold and almost rainless. The land masses of the southern hemisphere are not sufficiently broad for this type of climate to be developed.

The forests which normally clothe the two regions of the northern hemisphere are of mixed deciduous and coniferous species. The industrial development of those portions of the United States which fall in this tract and of the corresponding parts of Canada is such that they are no longer selfsupporting in the matter of foodstuffs. The same intensive development has not yet taken place in the Asian regions; indeed, Manchuria is a tract as yet relatively undeveloped. It is obvious from the results attained with this type of climate in America, that there are vast possibilities in the future for Manchuria.

The cold temperate or sub-Arctic regions (Köppen's Dfc). Stretching across the northern hemisphere as a broad belt is a region whose average temperature is low and where the greater part of the somewhat scanty precipitation is in the form of snow. The natural vegetation is everywhere of the evergreen, coniferous forest type. The really distinguishing feature is the shortness of the summer, which is insufficiently long for the ripening of cereals. A little oats and barley are grown, but the region is beyond the economic limit for the cultivation of wheat. In most typical stations only one month rises above 16° C (60° F), and in many cases the annual average is below 5° C (40° F). In certain parts near the ocean the range of temperature between summer and winter may be comparatively small, but in the heart of northern Asia there is actually a range of over 38° C (100° F), the greatest in the world. A similar type of climate occurs on mountain ranges throughout Europe and North America. In the southern hemisphere only the extreme south of South America and the mountains of New Zealand have a climate sufficiently cold to belong to this type. Where agriculture is so little favoured, natural vegetation remains important. The peculiar structure of the thick-skinned resinous leaves afford adequate protection both against cold and excessive loss of moisture. The finest tree growth is in the warmer southern parts of the sub-Arctic belt; northwards the trees become scattered and smaller or grow but slowly. Thus it takes fifty or sixty years for timber forests to regenerate in the southern margins, but up to 200 years in the poleward tracts. The coniferous forests, or taïga, are the world's great storehouse of softwood timber, such as pine, fir, and deal. The great belt of forest stretching across North America is the most important in the world; in Europe there are the forests of Scandinavia and northern Russia, whilst the same type reappears in the hills and mountains of northwestern and central Europe. Across the north of Asia, that is in Siberia, the forested areas are largely inaccessible and suffer from the peculiar physical conditions of the land. The great rivers there flow northwards towards the frozen Arctic Ocean, and are themselves frozen throughout the winter. In the spring the upper courses in the warm south melt, whilst the central and lower courses are still icebound, with the result that floodwaters spread far and wide over the flat country and turn the taïga into a vast forested morass. This is reflected in the poor condition of much of the timber.

Plans are in hand to divert the upper courses of the Tobal and Irtysh (which flow into the River Ob) so that they flow south towards the Aral Sea and Tashkent areas. This will provide much needed irrigation for the cotton crops of central Asia, and will assist in draining the marshlands and improving the quality of the timber.

The sparsely inhabited and less accessible regions of the coniferous forests are occupied mainly, before development, by hunters and trappers, for the animals of the northern forests are protected from the cold by thick fur. The main fur-producing tracts are round Hudson Bay in Canada, and in the forest regions of Siberia. In the economy of a civilised world, logging and timber-working industries take first place in these tracts, the production of wood pulp for paper being not the least important of the uses of coniferous wood. The trees are felled during the winter, dragged or taken by truck over the slippery snow to the watercourses, and floated down the rivers when the snows melt. Accessibility, the presence of streams suitable for floating, and the existence of water power, later hydroelectric power, for sawmills and pulping mills are the factors influencing development. By far the most important areas are along the southern fringes of the forest in eastern Canada and in the countries of northern Europe. The influence of the abundance of easily worked wood is illustrated by the traditional dwellings in the forested regions, from the rough log cabins of the Canadian woodsmen, the timber-workers of Finland and northern Russia, to the elaborate wooden chalets of the Swiss mountain forests.

The softwood forests of the smaller countries of Europe have been worked so long that it is difficult to maintain an output of timber and wood pulp, and certainly almost impossible to increase that output.

The only two countries in the world which still have very large reserves of softwood are Canada and the USSR.

The cold desert or tundra regions (Köppen's E and F). Within the Arctic Circle the winters are very long and very cold; there are at least some days on which the sun never appears and the summers are very short though warm. Though for certain periods the sun never sets, it never rises far above the horizon. It is too cold for forest; the natural vegetation is moss and lichen, with stunted bushes and small trees near the forest limit. Agriculture is practically impossible, for the ground is frozen for three-quarters of the year. The short hot summer does, however, sometimes produce an amazingly prolific growth of grass and herbs, which can take advantage of the continuous sunshine of mid-summer; hence the introduction of the name 'Arctic prairies', substituted in Canada for the old term 'barren lands', which scarcely does justice to the region. One of the great problems is the permanently frozen subsoil or permafrost.

Though they are at present almost uninhabited, there are future possibilities for the development of these lands, both for the breeding of reindeer or caribou, and through the continual prospecting for new sources of minerals and oil.

Canadian—United States weather stations have been established in the Arctic archipelago north of the Canadian mainland, where the tundra lands pass into regions of permanent ice and snow. The plateau of Greenland represents the ultimate development of the extreme type of cold desert climate. To this the Antarctic continent corresponds in the southern hemisphere.

Highland regions

In ascending a mountain in the tropics we may be said to pass through, in a very broad and general sense, the main vegetation regions as from the equator polewards. Thus the tropical forests and grasslands give place upwards, very frequently, to a belt of hardwood trees, then to a belt of conifers above which come the alpine pastures which are the counterpart of the Arctic pastures just described. There are other differences which are due to the effect of elevation and the consequent rarefaction of the atmosphere. From the point of view of commercial geography it is important to remember that, in a mountainous country, a wider variety of products can be grown than might otherwise be possible; thus on plateau regions in the tropics it is possible to cultivate crops which are otherwise only grown in temperate latitudes — as, for example, on the plateau of Kenya.

Population in most parts of the tropics is relatively scanty, and commercial crops are grown mainly on plantations. Many of these plantations are on hill slopes presenting combinations of soil and climate not to be found elsewhere. While the temperature is more moderate than on the low grounds, it has all the uniformity characteristics of the tropics, and the slopes of tropical mountains exposed to warm ocean winds enjoy frequent and copious supplies of rain, combined with the advantage of excellent drainage, so that there is little fear of the roots of crops or trees suffering from excess of moisture. The only danger to be guarded against is the possibility of the soil being washed away from the roots at the same time. Indeed, soil erosion is an ever-present problem.

For Europeans residence on tropical hills is perhaps healthier than residence on the low grounds in the same latitudes; but even at the elevation at which coffee is grown, a tropical climate is for them neither entirely healthy nor agreeable. The enervating effects of the heat and moisture render them unfit for work such as they could engage in with comfort in more temperate regions; and notwithstanding the uniformity of the temperature as indicated by the thermometer, the unpleasant sense of heat often alternates with an equally unpleasant sense of cold, for the excessive moisture of the atmosphere renders one sensitive to variations of temperature which would scarcely be felt in a drier climate. Humboldt mentions in one place that he and his companions, after a short residence in the torrid zone, found that their senses had become so easily affected by the slightest change of temperature that on one occasion they could not sleep for the cold even when they discovered, to their astonishment, that the thermometer indicated a temperature of 22° C (71° F). Sir Dudley Stamp reported similar experiences in Burma and elsewhere; after residence in Rangoon with average temperatures of 28° C (80° F), night temperatures of 10° C (50° F) in the hills produced the feeling of intense and penetrating cold. An African traveller mentions that on the Senegal one could not expose oneself in the open air after sunset to a slight lowering of temperature without feeling the sensation of decided cold. In central Africa, within 10° of the equator, certain Africans keep themselves warm at night by spreading the mats that form their bedding on hollow clay benches heated by fires or glowing charcoal inside, just as is done in China.

In the highland regions of the temperate zones not only is the temperature on the whole lower than within the tropics, but the variations in temperature are generally greater. As far as the more productive parts of the earth are concerned, it is chiefly in the temperate zones that frosts occur, and water vapour is precipitated as snow. A snow covering of longer or shorter duration is a regular annual occurrence in higher latitudes (from about 40° or 46° N, according to the locality), except in those western tracts which are exposed to the warm winds from the southwest. The deepest snows in cultivated regions are those which occur in the eastern provinces of Canada, where snow lies on the ground to a depth of from 1—1.5 m (3—5 ft). Both snow and frost may be regarded, on the one hand, as interruptions to field labour. Frost also interrupts communications by closing navigable rivers, and snow by blocking railways and roads. On the other hand, snow favours timber transport and sledge travelling, and aeroplanes fitted with skis have overcome some of the difficulties of winter travel. To the peoples of northern Siberia the aeroplane became a commonplace even before they had seen a motorcar. In regions of scanty rainfall snow is in many parts of the world extremely important as a natural store of moisture for summer use, especially on mountain slopes, and all the more if forests are present to prevent its removal by gravitation. Elsewhere this store may result in injury by flood. Both snow and frost, moreover, must be recognised as beneficial to the soil, and hence favourable to cultivation. Snow, being a bad conductor of heat (owing to the large proportion of occluded air), protects the underlying soil from the rigorous temperatures in the air above and, on melting, saturates the ground with moisture, which brings vegetation rapidly forward. Frost, again, by freezing and expanding the water in every pore of the soil which it reaches, pulverises the soil and thus enables the coming vegetation to send its rootlets to a great depth, to obtain the greater nourishment.

Underground water supplies and temperatures

Underground water circulation and underground temperatures both depend more or less on climate, and can influence man directly or indirectly in the same way as climatic conditions. Everywhere at a greater or less depth water is present, saturating loose earth to the exclusion of air. The upper surface of this water-saturated layer, the level of which is indicated by the surface of water in wells, is known as the watertable, and its depth below the surface is determined by the amount and mode of precipitation and the rate of evaporation. The amount of water that penetrates to a sufficient depth to feed this layer varies according as the precipitation is in the form of fine or heavy rain, or of snow or hail, and according as the melting of snow or hail takes place when the ground underneath is frozen or not. The circulation of this underground water depends on the porosity of the rock and the slope of the water-bearing strata, which may differ greatly from the surface slope. It is from this underground water that springs are derived. In many places matters dissolved in the upper layers of soil are carried down a short depth to form a hard layer known as hardpan, which the roots of plants do not penetrate at all, or only with difficulty. Where the soil lies horizontally this hardpan may form vast underground sheets, such as those known in the Landes of southwestern France as *alios*, in the plains of northern Germany as *Ortsteine*.

49

Surface temperatures penetrate only to a slight depth. Daily variations in temperature cease to be observable at a depth of about a metre, and even the yearly variations are perceptible at the most to a depth of 25—30 m (80—100 ft). The depth at which they can be detected is least in the tropics, about 7 m (20 ft) where the annual range of the surface temperatures is least, and greatest in the interior of the continents, where the range is widest. Below the level of this layer of constant temperature the temperature underground steadily increases at a rate that varies somewhat with different circumstances, among which the conductivity of the rocks is prominent, but is calculated to be on the average about 0.5° C (1° F) for every 18 m (60 ft) depth. This causes variations in the temperature of spring water, that coming from the greatest depth having the highest temperature, and generally, therefore, the greatest abundance and variety of mineral content. Most medicinal springs are hot springs. As the layer of constant temperature is shallow in the tropics the spring water there is never refreshingly cool but always at temperatures of from 20—22° C (68°—72° F). On the other hand, in Iceland, where there are low equable temperatures and there is consequently a layer of constant temperature near the freezing-point close to the surface, the spring waters are so cold that instead of being allowed to irrigate the fields they have to be carefully led away from them, as their effect would be disastrous. The increase of temperature with depth below the surface has a great effect in mining operations and in tunnelling under high mountains. Men cannot work for any considerable time in dry air when the temperature is above 49° C (120° F), or in moist air when it is above 41° C (105° F), or even less. Now at Edinburgh a temperature of 41° might be expected at a depth of less than 1 070 m (3 500 ft), one of 49° at about 1 330 m (4 350 ft). This latter depth is one that is commonly attained by many mine workings (although there are mines over 2 320 m (7 600 ft) in depth in South Africa), but it is only by the most careful ventilation that the working of such mines is practicable. In the moist air of the Alpine tunnels great difficulty was met with in carrying on the work even at temperatures of 32° C (90° F), and the piercing of the Simplon tunnel would have been impracticable but for the cooling due to the expansion of the compressed air which was used to drive the boring tools.

The soil and its treatment

The soil exercises an influence on vegetation in various ways. In the first place, it supplies a portion of the food of plants. It also supplies substances which may not themselves be converted into vegetable tissue, but which serve to carry the foodstuffs from one part of the plant to another, or to effect the necessary changes in these foodstuffs to enable them to be absorbed by the plant. And, thirdly, the nature of the soil affects the life of the plant by the effect it has upon the temperature of the roots, or other parts of the plant embedded in the ground; for some soils are more readily heated than others, and more readily give up their heat to bodies in contact with them.

Soils differ from one another, physically and chemically. Physically, soils differ in the condition of their particles. They may be coarse or fine, porous or compact. Other things being equal the fine loam or silt soils are more fertile, in that they supply food more plentifully than coarse soils. All the food which plants derive from the soil enters the small rootlets dissolved in moisture, and the finer the earthy particles the more easily are the necessary substances dissolved. This is one reason why the soil of deltas is usually remarkable for its fertility, for such soils are made up of the finer sediment carried along by a river. When, however, the mineral particles become so small as to be ultra-microscopic (clays) the soils take on quite a different character and become tenacious and nonporous.

The advantages or disadvantages of porous soils as compared with those which are compact and tenacious vary according to circumstances. One advantage porous soils nearly always have: they are light and easily worked by plough or spade. They are also easily permeated by water, and thus readily permit rain to sink into them, instead of running off the surface. Equally they favour the rise of moisture from great depths, by capillary action (the action by which liquid diffuses itself through a lump of sugar). This may be an advantage for certain plants or in certain climates, but a disadvantage for other plants and in other climates. It is an advantage in climates in which showers are frequent and the atmosphere moist during the growing season. It is a disadvantage in climates of an opposite character, where it is important for plant life that the moisture in the soil should be retained within reach of the roots, that is, that it should neither sink away to a great depth, nor rise up too rapidly and evaporate. In moist climates porous soils are generally, by virtue of the superior dryness of their superficial layers, more easily warmed than heavy and compact soils. Hence light porous soils are generally described as dry and warm, and those of the opposite kind, like clays, as wet and cold. Soils may be so compact as to prevent the access of air to the roots and hence infertile from that cause.

So great are the natural differences in respect of chemical composition that, to take wheat as an illustration, the soil of one region may yield a crop of 35 or even 45 quintals per hectare (50 or even 70 bushels per acre), whereas that of another yields, with a climate equally favourable, no more than 5 or 10 quintals (12 or 15 bushels), or perhaps even less. The composition of the soil often varies very greatly from local causes within limited areas; but there are, on the other hand, many wide regions noted for being covered with a soil either characteristically rich or characteristically poor. Everywhere, it ought to be mentioned, the soil is due to the crumbling away of solid rock under atmospheric weathering (which varies according to the climate) more or less modified by the vegetable, and even the animal, life that comes to occupy it. Large deltas are generally remarkable for their fertility, not only in consequence of their physical nature as mentioned above, but also because they contain ingredients derived from the whole basin of the river by which they are formed, and hence are likely to contain all the constituents which a variety of plants require as food. For a similar reason, great alluvial plains like those of the Ganga and the Po are generally remarkable for their fertility, and so also are the beds of former lakes, such as the basin of the Red River of the north, in the United States and Canada.

Organic matter, or humus the product of decay of vegetable matter, mixed with earthy (mineral) constituents, produces a soil of great fertility, rich in plant food. A wet soil, however, hinders the intermixture of the vegetable remains with the earthy particles and causes the formation of what is called acid humus, of which peaty soils are the most familiar example. The moisture of such soils is not readily taken in by the plant tissues, and hence those soils support only a special kind of vegetation of a dry woody habit like heaths. In some places humus is formed abundantly in tropical forests, where vegetation is continuous and the accumulation of vegetable waste proportionately great. But it is not readily formed in all tropical forests. If the climate has long dry spells and the forests are rather open, the falling leaves dry up, get hard and crisp, and are easily broken by the wind, so that their elements are dispersed in the form of gases. To this cause is ascribed, in a great measure, the infertility of a large part of Brazil. Where there is a regular winter accumulation of snow, this covering has, among other important effects, that of burying the fallen vegetable matter and saturating it with moisture so as to favour the formation of vegetable mould. The action of earthworms in promoting the formation of a soil rich in this ingredient, by covering the surface deposits with layers of earth brought up from beneath, has been made a matter of almost universal knowledge by the well-known work of Darwin.*

Many lavas or rocks originally poured out from the interior of the earth in a liquid state decompose into a soil of exceeding richness. Soils of this kind form some of the most fertile tracts, not only in Java and Japan, Campania and eastern Sicily, and other regions where there are volcanoes still active, but in many regions where there have been no volcanoes within historic times. Among the latter are soils covering considerable areas in Hungary, and the much more extensive tract which forms a large part of the wheat-growing area of Oregon and Washington in the United States, the tract occupying both sides of the Columbia River, where the soil results from the decomposition of a broad basaltic plateau; also the coffee soils of São Paulo in southern Brazil, due to the disintegration of diabase rocks rich in potash and other fertilising ingredients. In some cases, so rapid is the decomposition of lava, that some of the vineyards on the slopes of Mount Vesuvius occupy lava fields which came into existence within the nineteenth century.

Among other soils noted for their fertility occupying extensive areas in different parts of the world may be mentioned the black soil (chernozem or black earth) of southern Russia and central Asia, the yellow loessic soil of northern China, and the black cotton soil of the Indian plateau, which last differs from all the others previously mentioned in being very stiff and heavy, and owes a large part of its fertility to its being so peculiarly suited to the character of the climate where it is found, in that it is very retentive of moisture.

The soils known as laterites, being of a colour and having a porous nature like red bricks (Lat. *later*, a brick), are characteristic of tropical and subtropical climates and are produced by the decomposition of

* It is singular that the anticipation of Darwin's observation in a book so popular as Gilbert White's *Natural History of Selborne* should, apparently, be so little known, and that Darwin himself should have forgotten White's remark. The passage referred to occurs in Let. LXXVII (edn of Capt. T. Brown, 1833: Let. XXXV in the edn of E. T. Bennett, revised by J. E. Harting, 1875), where we read: 'Earthworms, though in appearance a small and despicable link in the chain of Nature, yet, if lost, would make a lamentable chasm. For . . . worms seem to be the great promoters of vegetation . . . by boring, perforating, and loosening the soil, and rendering it pervious to rains and the fibres of plants, by drawing straws and stalks of leaves into it; and, most of all, by throwing up such infinite numbers of lumps of earth, called wormcasts, which, being their excrement, is a fine manure for grain and grass.'

rocks under the influence of rapid changes in temperature, and the alternation of wet and dry seasons. They owe their red colour to the presence of iron, and when fully formed iron and alumina remain as the chief constituents. The lime, potash, and magnesia which may have been contained in the rocks from which they are formed all disappear, and in the high temperatures of the tropics even the silica gets dissolved and washed away, frequently being redeposited as a cementing substance in underlying sands. When the process is thus carried out to its full extent such soils are almost worthless. This takes place only in exposed situations where the rainfall is very high, but the term laterite is loosely applied to many red earths in which the solvent action has not gone so far, and which, accordingly, vary in their properties, some being fertile, others not. If the term is applied generally to the red earths of the tropics, then laterites have been estimated to cover 49 per cent of the area of Africa, 43 per cent of that of South America, and 18 per cent of that of Asia. But this estimate includes under the head of laterites the red soil which is found to be particularly favourable to the coffee tree on the slopes of the mountains of eastern Brazil, south of Rio de Janeiro. In many parts of Africa the infertility which characterises this soil is due rather to its physical than to its chemical characters. The solution of the silica has proceeded only so far as to coat the particles of earth with a thin glaze, giving rise to a soil so porous that the rain runs through it readily and the soil dries up with remarkable rapidity, unless refreshed with frequent showers.

The soil of arid regions is in some cases chemically very rich, so that when water is supplied the ground is exceptionally productive. For this there are two reasons. The soil is largely windborne, and being collected from wide areas is likely, as in the case of the soils of river deltas, to possess a great variety of ingredients. Second, such vegetation as grows naturally in those regions produces an exceptional root growth, and those parts of a plant are always richest in nitrogen. Hence, though the soil may be comparatively poor in humus because of the scantiness of the vegetation, its nitrogen content is not necessarily correspondingly feeble, and may be considerably in excess of that found in humid areas.

In other arid or drier parts of the earth the soil is frequently highly infertile, and even poisonous to vegetation, from the excess of salts found on the surface, due to the fact that the moisture which does penetrate beneath the ground dissolves the salts in the earth, and then, rising up again and evaporating, leaves the salts behind as an incrustation. Vast areas of this description are found in the interior of Asia and southeastern Europe, of Australia and South America, while smaller tracts of the same nature exist here and there as patches amongst the fertile regions of California and the Canadian prairies, where they are known as 'alkali spots'. The formation of such salt incrustations is one of the risks attending irrigation in arid areas.

It will be clear from the above account that soils depend very largely on climatic conditions; indeed, the great soil groups of the world correspond largely with the great climatic regions. This generalisation was first appreciated in Russia by Glinka and the many soil scientists or pedologists who followed him. Within a major soil group local variations depend largely on the characters of the underlying rocks. This is notably the case in a cool, moist climate such as Britain where many of the soils are 'aclimatic'. Soil science has made much progress in recent years and one method of study widely followed is that of the soil profile. Many soils, traced from the surface downwards, exhibit a surface horizon of leaching (the A horizon), a lower horizon of secondary enrichment (the B horizon), and a lowest horizon of slightly altered parent rock (the C horizon). These three horizons are particularly well seen in the ash-grey soils or podsols of northern latitudes, soils of the northern coniferous forests, often lacking in fertility owing to the extensive leaching from the surface layers.

Preservation of the properties of the soil. However rich a soil may be by nature, sooner or later its fertility will be impaired by cultivation unless means are taken to prevent this deterioration. Substances that serve as the food of one crop are removed when that crop is carried away and consumed elsewhere, and as the same kind of plant always requires the same kind of food, the fertility of a soil is in general reduced very rapidly when the same crop is grown repeatedly on the same land, and when nothing is done to restore the ingredients that are thus removed. Under a careful system of cultivation two plans are adopted to counteract this tendency of the soil to lose its fertility. One is to vary the crops that are cultivated in succession on the same piece of ground, which spares the land in two ways. First, since different plants withdraw from the soil different substances as food, or at least varying proportions of the same substances, a crop requiring chiefly one kind of food is made to follow a crop which requires chiefly another kind. Secondly, it is not always necessary to remove from the ground the whole of the cultivated plant, and the parts of the plant not required may be returned to the ground, and help to restore to it some of the ingredients required not only by this crop but by crops of other kinds.

Obviously this is an imperfect method, and the only way to maintain permanently the fertility of the soil is to restore by fertilisers the ingredients that are withdrawn by successive crops. But here it must be noted that the quantity of matter to be returned to the ground is small in comparison with that which is carried away as produce of the soil, even though the plant food contained in the manure is generally a small proportion of the bulk of the manure itself. It has been found by experiments made in England in the cultivation of wheat that the use of 90 kg (200 lb) of a particular kind of fertiliser made a difference of nearly 270 kg (600 lb) in the weight of the yield, as compared with that from a similar piece of land that had borne wheat without fertiliser nine times in succession.

Small as the total proportion of plant food derived from the soil is, the constituents of such food are very varied; but the three essentials to plant growth most likely to be lacking in cultivated soils are nitrogen, phosphoric acid, and potash; hence fertilisers containing these substances are important articles of commerce. All three are contained in animal refuse of various kinds, and these are generally convenient manures to apply to the ground where mixed farming (part crop-growing and part cattle-raising) is carried on. It has long been known that leguminous crops such as clover, lucerne, beans, peas, and lentils require no nitrogenous manures and even serve to replenish the soil with soluble nitrogen for subsequent crops, but an important stimulus to the cultivation of such crops for use as green manure was given by the discovery in the 1880s that this was due to the fact that bacteria present in nodules on their roots and rootlets served as the means of fixing nitrogen derived from the air. Commercial fertilisers are available in various compounds. Nitrates, phosphates, and potassic salts, or mixtures of these, are artificially prepared and contain the essential ingredients along with others, while natural compounds are found in deposits of greater or less abundance in various parts of the earth and are worked as minerals, though they may be to a large extent of vegetable or animal origin. Fertilisers therefore enter into world trade to the amount of millions of tons annually; in 1956—57 the world's demand for nitrogen compounds amounted to 6.5m. tons, phosphates 7.3m. and potash 6.2m.; in 1967—68 the figures were 22.5m., 16.4 and 14.0m. tons respectively.

The bones of animals variously treated have long been used as artificial fertilisers. Being to a large extent composed of phosphate of lime, they are of great value not only on account of the phosphoric acid and nitrogen they contain, but also because of the lime itself, which by neutralising the acidity of the soil helps to bring about certain chemical changes which make the plant foods in the soil available to the vegetation. Since all the elements which a plant derives from the soil enter the rootlets in a state of solution, no constituent of plant food is of any use to the plant unless it be first dissolved. For use as fertiliser, bones are in some cases merely ground into a coarse meal, in other cases steamed so as to remove most of the nitrogen but to leave a high proportion of phosphorus, and in yet other cases treated for the same purpose with sulphuric acid so as to produce what are known commercially as super-phosphates, although in this branch of manufacture mineral phosphates are mainly used. Since 1886 a fine meal or flour obtained by grinding basic slag, which contains from 30—35 per cent of phosphate of lime, has become more and more used as a phosphatic manure. For many years there was an enormous trade in the export of Chilean nitrate (sodium nitrate) from the desert regions of northern Chile. The mineral phosphate (guano) derived from the droppings of birds is a product of many tropical islands and mineral phosphates are mined elsewhere. All these mineral fertilisers have severe competitors in the artificial fertilisers produced by industry.

Notwithstanding the manifest advantages of the adequate use of fertilisers in maintaining the value of the soil, their employment in sufficient quantity to ensure the preservation of a high degree of fertility can still be extended. Where the population is sparse land is cheap, and the cultivator usually finds it more profitable to derive as large crops as he can from the ground without fertilisers, and to begin to cultivate new ground when the first shows signs of being exhausted. Moreover, where the population is scanty, there are fewer opportunities of obtaining animal manure, which in regions possessing a dense population is the kind most readily available. The eastern states of the United States, which were those first cultivated, were in the beginning cultivated without manure, and as these lands became partly exhausted, others further west became the chief regions of agricultural production; as the population from the development of commerce and industry thickened in the eastern states, so the use of fertilisers became more and more general.

Cultivation which involves the use of a greater and greater extent of land, is known as extensive cultivation, as opposed to intensive cultivation, which consists in putting more into the land to get more out of it; and the furtherance of the latter system — that is, the increasing use of fertilisers — is always a sign of advancing agriculture and industry in general. The great yields of wheat in the countries of western Europe are due to the practice of this system.

Reference has already been made incidentally to the loss of soil where the crops are grown on hill slopes. Such loss is apt to occur wherever there is sloping ground, and especially where the crop does not cover the soils completely. Where grasses, including the ordinary European cereals, are grown the loss from this cause is not rapid, and may be made good by the natural formation of new soil; but it is otherwise with such crops as maize, tobacco, and so on which have considerable intervals between the individual plants. This loss is all the more serious if the climate is arid and the soil loose and powdery. From time to time soil erosion has been a major problem in the United States. Great tracts of once fertile land have been robbed of their soil by dust storms; the rapid runoff of rainwater unhindered by vegetation has, at the same time, resulted in disastrous floods. The Soil Erosion Service of the Federal Government has developed preventive measures such as forming long mounds, known as magnum terraces, at right angles to the direction of slope so as to arrest the flow of soil-bearing water. The grassing of exposed slopes is another preventive measure. In Africa also soil erosion is a very serious problem. In general, in all parts of the world, the tendency is for the higher parts of ground to become impoverished by erosion. The lower parts are correspondingly enriched where there is no tendency to an excess of moisture. The most productive parts of sloping ground are for the most part those just above the lowest level, one reason for the prevalence of agricultural villages at the base of hills in many parts of the world.

Irrigation. As fertilisers are the means of correcting deficiencies in the soil, whether these be original or the result of exhaustion, so irrigation is the means of remedying of the deficiency of moisture. The ease with which this remedy can be applied varies greatly according to circumstances. Nowhere is it easier than on the land adjoining those rivers which regularly overflow their banks, like the Nile, the Tigris, and Euphrates or, in past times, the Ganga. In such cases all that is necessary is to provide canals and sluices by means of which the flow of water over the surface of the land may be to some extent regulated; and it is likewise a fact of the highest importance that the irrigation of land so situated is not only exceptionally easy, but also of exceptional value. For a river when in flood is always most highly charged with fertilising sediment; so rich is this in the valley of the Nile, for example, that wherever 'red water' can be supplied there is no need for manure. Formerly in the Ganga valley, again, embankments were in few places required to restrain its inundations, for the alluvial silt which it spilled over its banks year by year afforded to the fields a top dressing of inexhaustible fertility. If one crop were drowned by the flood, the cultivator calculated that his second crop would abundantly requite him. But the most urgent need of water is in those dry seasons when the river floods are deficient, and the policy in the Indian subcontinent for many years has been the replacement of inundation channels by perennial canals. The usual system now is to build a dam across the river, often in an upper part of its course, and then to lead canals from the artificial lake so created. Branch canals lead from these, and then distributaries, all controlled, conduct the water to the fields. Spare water seeps back gradually into the river course.

In other cases, various more or less costly methods have to be employed to render water available. Water may be raised by buckets from wells or rivers. Large tanks (these may be of concrete, as on the banana plantations of the Canary Islands, and should not be confused with the so-called tanks of the Indian subcontinent which are small lakes made by damming a stream) may be constructed to store the superfluous waters of one season or period against the deficiencies of another.

In some places the structure of the country is such that when holes are dug in the ground to a certain depth water rises freely to the surface, often with great force. Such artesian wells have been sunk in many regions where the rainfall is deficient. Large areas, as of Australia, formerly wholly or nearly barren, have been made more productive. Usually artesian water is too highly charged with mineral salts to be suitable for irrigation, but it is excellent for watering stock.

Irrigation water can be much more profitably used in agriculture than an equal quantity of rain. It can be preserved in tanks till the exact period at which it is needed. It is thus kept from sinking into the ground to a great depth, and so becoming lost to vegetation, as happens to much of the rain that falls on the earth where the soil is highly porous. At the same time it suffers infinitely less loss than generally diffused moisture through evaporation, a matter of peculiar importance in those bright and warm regions where irrigation is specially required. For crops of great value it is even sometimes found of advantage to distribute the water to the fields entirely by underground pipes, as in Israel. By the adoption of this method evaporation is almost wholly prevented. It is often difficult to teach the cultivator in arid regions that too much moisture can be injurious to his crops: there is actually an optimum quantity which if exceeded results not only in waste of precious water but also in a decrease in production.

It will be seen that though irrigation is almost always costly, the advantages derived from it are correspondingly great. They are: (*a*) The supply of water by irrigation is more certain and regular than that by rain even in regions where the rainfall is generally plentiful, and that of itself increases crop production. (*b*) Irrigation water is often more or less rich in fertilising ingredients; in the Indian subcontinent, as a general rule, irrigation doubles the weight of crops off the same land. (*c*) Irrigation by flooding is sometimes of service in washing away noxious constituents from the soil. (*d*) Irrigation often enables valuable crops to be grown in place of inferior ones. (*e*) It renders cultivation possible in some cases during the whole period of the year for which the temperature is sufficient. In southern California, as well as in western Arizona, crops may be started at whatever season suits the convenience of the grower, except two months in the year, and this holds true for market gardens as far north as San Francisco; in some areas five cuts of alfalfa may be taken off the same field in a single season. In Algeria three crops of potatoes may be grown in succession in one season on irrigated land. It naturally follows that the density of population in irrigated regions often reaches a very high level. In the irrigated portion of the Spanish province of Murcia, for example, the density is nearly 660 to the sq km (1 700 to the sq mile), as compared with 67 per sq km (167 per sq mile) for the average of Spain generally.

It is one of the chief advantages of terrace cultivation (that is, the cutting of hill slopes into terraced fields rising steplike above one another) that fields so made are irrigated with great facility. Hence this mode of laying out fields is largely practised in the warmer parts of the world, and in some cases a marvellous amount of labour is spent on them. Describing the ascent from Hodeida to Sana in Yemen, Major-General Haig wrote:

> The whole mountain side, for a height of 6 000 feet, was terraced from top to bottom. The crops had all been removed; only some lines of coffee trees here and there were to be seen, but everywhere above, below, and all around, these endless flights of terrace walls met the eye. One can hardly conceive the enormous amount of labour, toil, and perseverance which these represent. The terrace walls are usually from five to eight feet in height, but towards the top of the mountain they are much higher, being sometimes as much as fifteen and eighteen feet. They are built entirely of rough stone laid without mortar. I reckoned on average that each wall retains a terrace not more than twice its own height in width. So steep, in fact, is the mountain, that the zigzag continues almost the whole way to the top.

Typical of many parts of monsoon lands in Sri Lanka, Java, China, and Japan are the irrigated terraces for rice cultivation.

The extension of irrigation works in many of the drier parts of the world — Egypt, Iraq, India, Pakistan, Turkestan, the United States, Canada, Australia and South Africa — has been a special feature of modern development. But irrigation after all is confined to limited areas, and many arid or semi-arid areas must rely on what is called **dry farming**. By this is meant the treating of the land in such a way as to conserve the moisture it contains, the essential thing being to prepare the surface in the form of a mulch. This term is applied to any covering of the surface that tends to resist capillary action and protect the moist earth underneath against the direct rays of the sun. Even stones spread thickly over the ground may serve as a mulch, and in the drier parts of the Mediterranean region stony tracts are regularly sown which in a moist, cool climate like that of the British Isles no one would think of cultivating. In gardening operations mulches are made with leaves, manure, straw and similar materials which, though very effective as mulches, have the drawback of preventing the continual stirring of the land and consequently the aeration of the ground underneath. But this continual stirring itself provides an excellent mulch in the form of a dry powdery surface soil, and it is by the frequent use of the plough, harrow and other implements of tillage that dry farming is generally carried on. In loose light soils this treatment is supplemented by the use of an implement known as the subsurface packer to consolidate the earth underneath the surface and so retard capillary action. Dry farming has long been practised in the drier parts of the Indian subcontinent, southern USSR and in the arid regions of the United States, Canada and

Australia. It is particularly of value in all regions near the economic margin for farming, notably in South Africa — though the danger of sudden wind and rain storms makes soil erosion an ever-present threat.

Labour

The influence of labour on production varies with the quantity required and the quality available. In such industries as coalmining the quantity required to produce a certain value has long been high — more or less two-thirds of the total cost. The pattern now is changing. In the United Kingdom in 1960 when 47 per cent of the total output was produced by machinery, wages accounted for 48s. (£2.40) out of a total cost per ton of 84s. 5d. (£4.22) — 57 per cent. In 1969 when mechanisation accounted for 92 per cent of the total output, wages amounted to 49s. 3d. (£2.46) out of a total cost per ton of 104s. 1d. (£5.20) — 47 per cent. Such reduction in the wages component of production costs is typical of the increased mechanisation of manufacturing processes. The traditional methods of production were labour intensive; but where the increased utilisation of machinery is feasible the emphasis gradually changes to a capital intensive system where the quantity of labour tends to fall — and its quality to rise. The labour force in the United Kingdom coalmines fell from 570 000 to 305 000 between 1961 and 1970 and during this time mechanisation of output rose from 47 to 92 per cent. But real and money wages for those still employed rose steadily; whilst the labour force was reduced by 46 per cent, the total wage bill fell only by 10 per cent.

The quantity of labour available can be discussed statistically. For example, the distribution of labour between the major economic activities of each nation provides a guide to the type of economy and the comparative degree of economic growth, from the basic subsistence industries of agriculture and fishing through mining, manufacturing and commerce to the service industries (retailing, hotels, tourism) that accompany a high standard of living. The distribution of the economically active population of the United Kingdom over the last 100 years is shown in Table 1, with comparative statistics for six other western nations and Japan. The figures for Japan show a pattern of continued emphasis on agriculture at the expense of expansion of the service industries; but with a high percentage enjoyed in commerce and transport.

Table 1 — Distribution of labour between major economic activities

| Year | Agriculture and fishing | Percentage distribution | | |
		Mining manufacturing and construction	Trade transport and communications	Service industries
United Kingdom				
1851	22	43	16	19
1901	9	46	21	23
1951	5	49	22	24
1970	2	48	19	31
Other western nations (1970)				
Portugal	43	29	12	16
Finland	22	35	22	21
France	13	37	26	24
West Germany	8	48	21	23
Belgium	4	43	25	28
USA	4	31	30	35
Japan (1970)	18	27	37	18

On the other hand the quality (or efficiency) of labour is less easy to measure. It varies between countries, between trades and between districts. Current wages give some indication, but the bargaining which decides the market value of labour in a free society takes place amid many extraneous influences. Government legislation on working conditions, the comparative strength of employer and employee organisations, the mobility of labour (both between locations and between trades) and many other factors all cause short-term deviations from the long-term trend towards equality of wages for equal efficiency under equal conditions. A more generalised measure of quality is provided by an analysis of various broad industrial groups by the 'value added' to the total product in relation to the labour force employed. This tends to measure quality by the amount of product produced per head. We find that in the United Kingdom in 1968, petroleum, petrochemicals and manmade fibres (all capital intensive industries with high volume production and technically skilled labour) had the highest 'value added' for each employee. While the construction trades and clothing (i.e. labour intensive with lower production rates) showed the lowest added value, with food-processing, engineering and printing/publishing falling in between.

As with all other aspects of commerce, the part played by labour has changed greatly over the last 100 years. Chisholm could, as recently as 1887, preface his discussion of labour in the first edition with:

Human labour may be broadly divided into slave, or forced, and free labour, the latter being that which is now generally employed in the production of commercial commodities. There are, however, great diversities in the money wages of free labourers in different parts of the world. The highest wages are those paid in 'new' countries such as the United States and Canada, Australia, Uruguay and the Argentine Republic; the lowest are paid in tropical countries, and in particular in those regions in which there is an exceedingly dense population dependent mainly on agriculture.

Although the reference to slave labour belongs to the nineteenth century, the differences between the efficiency of labour in different countries still hold good. Geographical factors such as climate still affect housing, clothing and fuel requirements; climate and cultural traditions are still reflected in differing societies and in differing standards of living; so that all discussion of comparative wages on an international basis should be made in the context of the local costs of living. But although there are still great differences in the condition and reimbursement of labour around the world (currently epitomised by comparing the developed with the developing countries) the other major change since the 1880s has been the slow but persistent trend to improve standards of living and to some reduction in the disparity of wages between countries. Unskilled labour is still poorly rewarded in South America, Africa and southeast Asia but the universal availability of fertilisers, of machinery and of technology, together with improved communications is gradually leavening the differences. Japan's success in the international market can no longer be explained away by a simple reference to the low standard of living and low wages of her labour force. During 1969, for instance, money wages in the United States and the United Kingdom rose by 7.5 per cent (a rise of some 2 per cent in terms of real wages, i.e. after adjustment for the falling value of money); in Japan there was a 16.5 per cent increase in money wages (a rise of 10.9 per cent in real wages). During the same year the average increase in real wages in the developed countries was 4.2 per cent; in the developing countries it was 6.8 per cent.

The conditions under which labour is employed and the wages paid are largely influenced in a free society by government legislation and the bargaining powers of employers' and employees' organisations. In the United Kingdom the Factory Acts of the mid-nineteenth century limited the working hours for women and children. The provisions in those Acts that expressly applied to adult male workers were only such as were intended to secure health and safety. Since the First World War, however, there has been a general limitation of the number of hours' work for men. The employment of the young is now limited in Great Britain under the Education Acts, culminating in the Act of 1944 which provided for raising the school-leaving age in 1947 to fifteen (sixteen in 1972—73) and for at least part-time education to sixteen (later eighteen). The Employers' Liability Act of 1897 rendered employers liable in certain cases for injuries sustained by persons in their employment, whether there may have been any contributory negligence on the part of the injured or not. This was developed until in 1946 compensation for industrial accidents became a contributory social service extending to all persons employed under contract, without limit of income. There is similar legislation in many other European countries. In Switzerland the limitation of hours expressly applied to men as well as women and in Germany the Imperial Industrial Code empowered the Imperial government to limit the hours for men and women alike where excessive hours were deemed injurious to health. The former German Empire was the pioneer in the insurance of workmen against illness (under an Act of 1883), against accidents (1884), and in providing for old-age pensions, beginning at the age of seventy (1889). In the United Kingdom old-age pensions, beginning at the same age, were introduced in 1908, and later measures led to the National Insurance Act of 1946 which consolidated existing schemes of insurance against sickness, unemployment, and old age. Such insurance was made compulsory and universal. Relief for the married worker was provided in 1945 by family allowances in the form of a weekly grant for each child after the first. In the United States labour legislation has long been a matter reserved to the individual states, but under the Roosevelt administration of 1933—45 the Federal government formulated a series of codes for the major industries and in 1966 the Social Security Act introduced medical care for those over sixty-five.

The outstanding feature of labour relations in all the western industrial countries during the twentieth century has been the growth of the power of organised labour. The trade unions, like the craft guilds and trade associations before them, are also concerned with health, safety and working conditions, but their chief aims are generally the increase of wages and the reduction of working hours. The pattern and the power of the trade unions, and the legal framework within which they negotiate, vary greatly between countries. In the United Kingdom the national tradition has been one of free collective bargaining, with state intervention to lay down minimum wages in industries where the unions are weak. Unlike Belgium (with two major unions representing 65 per cent of the working population) or the United States (with 190 major unions representing 26 per cent of the working population), there were no less than 570 unions in the United Kingdom in 1970 (representing some 11m. or 44 per cent of the 25.5m. working population). Because of this fragmented union structure, there are usually several unions involved when collective negotiations are undertaken with employers' associations. As the economy becomes more complex, with increasing specialisation and interdependence of industry, so the strength of the unions increases and their ultimate power (the withdrawal of labour) carries greater weight. Where such strike action threatens the national interest, certain countries (the United States, Canada, Denmark, etc.) impose legal restrictions of varying effectiveness in an attempt to minimise the interference with the free flow of commerce; but the ultimate sanction to excessive wage demands lies in the threat of resultant business failure, trade recession and increased unemployment, a threat which carries diminished impact in an expanding economy or where state aid to the unemployed affects the issue.

This ability of freely organised labour to ensure that its rewards are forced as high as is economically acceptable is, historically, a recent development and is not to be found in centrally controlled societies such as those of the USSR and China. The early editions of this *Handbook* referred to many examples where labour had little chance to affect its conditions of work or its remuneration. In the 1880s, for instance, slavery was still a cause for concern in parts of Africa and southeast Asia, having only recently been suppressed in the United States, Egypt, the West Indies and Brazil. Indentured coolie labour on tropical and subtropical plantations, immigrant labour contracted for railway construction in the United States, and virtual serfdom in Latin America, Russia and India were other areas where labour had little power and few privileges. Where labour was plentiful and poorly organised it was traditionally exploited; but industrialisation and the great growth of social legislation has given labour the opportunity steadily to improve its position in an increasingly mechanised commercial world.

Machinery and power

The other great change in the conditions of production in manufacturing industry since the Industrial Revolution has been the introduction of machinery. Even the cast-iron ploughshare is an invention little more than 180 years old (it was patented by Ransomes of Ipswich in 1785) and it did not come into general use in the United States until the early nineteenth century. Since then the mechanisation of industrial processes has increased steadily in all countries, but with the greatest growth in the more advanced nations, much of whose income is now dependent upon the manufacture of yet more machinery. By the middle of the twentieth century world trade in machinery was second only to that of foodstuffs in importance, with three-quarters of all exports going to the already developed nations and one-quarter to the developing countries. Since the Second World War the traditional part played by powered machinery in supplementing the physical work of labour has been extended by the introduction of computers to supplement the repetitive mental work. This development in turn makes possible yet a further advance: the combination of computer and mechanised processing to provide the fully automatic production line with minimal labour requirements.

The use of machinery is in some cases dependent more or less on physical conditions, in others on the supply and attitude of labour. The extensive employment of agricultural machinery for instance is influenced largely by surface features, great level plains being obviously peculiarly favourable to its use. Even where the superficial configuration presents no great obstacles to its use the climate may prove a hindrance, soft wet soils being unsuitable or at least difficult for heavy machines. In coalmining the thicker and more continuous seams are better adapted for coal-cutting machinery. This is one reason why, in the early years of the present century, the use of such machinery increased much more rapidly in the United States than in the United Kingdom. In the States, the seams of bituminous coal worked are only such as can be worked easily; whereas in the United Kingdom, with its older industry, most of the easily worked seams in the older mines have been worked out. It is in the newer, larger and deeper collieries of this country that coal-cutting machinery has since been making up lost ground.* Where labour is very abundant and cheap the use of machinery may not be economic. Thus, in the countries of the Far East the proportion of machinery to the number of employees is still small, and it has on occasion been found economically advantageous to replace expensive machinery with low-priced hand machinery. The employment of machinery even where it would be economic is still, as in the past, sometimes retarded by the opposition of the workers. In rapidly developing new countries or regions this hindrance is less marked, and that is another reason why coal-cutting and many other machines, even when invented in this and other old countries, have first been generally adopted in the United States. The attitude of the workers in old countries is at least understandable. Their first thought with regard to machinery is apt to be that it is a means of displacing labour and so reducing its price; and though in the long run the effect of machinery may be to ease the burden of labour and improve the standard of living, its immediate effect is often to inflict hardship on some.

The growing use of machinery has necessarily been accompanied by a great extension in the use of power. As with machinery, the production and use of power is concentrated in the major industrial nations; of the world output of 5 222 500m. kWh in 1971, no less than one-third was produced by the United States and over 80 per cent was used by only eight nations. Direct wind and water power was used during the early days of the Industrial Revolution. Such power cannot be distributed and early industry was therefore located alongside the source of power; even today this explains the location of certain long-established industries, such as textiles, in many parts of the world. Throughout the greater part of the nineteenth century, coal-driven steam engines were the main source of industrial power. Factories often required numbers of such engines, each with its own attendants and continually kept ready for work, even when there was no work to do. Against this background the introduction of electricity was a great advance since it could

* Percentage of coal cut by machinery:

	1900	1913	1924	1938	1948	1955	1961	1970
USA	24.9	50.7	69.5	87.5	90.7	93.0	93.5	94.0
UK	1.5	8.6	19.0	29.0	36.0	40.0	48.0	92.0

The marked increase in the percentage in both countries is notable, but the figures are not strictly comparable, because of the different methods of mining and statistical analysis. The rapid rise in the UK percentage between 1955 and 1970 has been accompanied by the closure of nearly 600 of the less efficient pits.

† USA, 1 717 521m. kWh; USSR, 800 360m.; Japan, 385 612m.; UK, 256 098m.; West Germany, 259 631m.; Canada, 216 472m.; France, 148 998m.; Italy, 124 860m.

be generated at large installations located where power sources could be most economically harnessed. Coal, oil, natural gas, water and nuclear power (as well as the sun and the tides) are all used for the generation of electricity, the balance between the various sources differing in different countries. Coal is in general still the major source, particularly in the United Kingdom and the United States, with the added advantage that the lower grades can be used. Oil is the next most important source, with nuclear power and water power as the sources for the future as the fossil fuels (coal, oil and its accompanying gas) become exhausted. In certain mountainous areas hydroelectric power is already of great importance. All of Norway's, and 97 per cent of Switzerland's, electrical power comes from this source, while it is the main source of supply in various regions such as the Columbia River basin (Rocky Mountains), Churchill Falls (Labrador) and the Parana River (Uruguay/ Brazil). Hydroelectric power is particularly important as a source of cheap power where great quantities are required, such as in the smelting of aluminium ores, production of wood pulp and other processes requiring extremely high temperatures. For such industries the adequate supply of cheap power is a major factor in their location. The location of the power stations themselves is largely influenced by the power source. Hydroelectric installations must be located on their water supply; coal-fired stations can be situated where coal can be delivered economically (i.e. coal supply is only one factor); oil and gas fired stations can be located for marketing reasons, since their power sources can be cheaply conveyed to them by pipeline; nuclear stations are even more footloose, but have tended in the early days of development to be located near ample supplies of cooling water; all have the overriding advantage that their power can be distributed to consumers over considerable distances. In the United Kingdom, for instance, the distribution grid totalled no less than 520 000 km (323 000 circuit miles) in 1970. Even more important for the future will be the nuclear (atomic) stations which will provide electricity completely independent of the traditional sources of power, and will make power available locally for the development of desert, Arctic, or even undersea regions.

Devastating agents

War is the great disturber of production and commerce; but there are disturbing agents which are more or less normal though not regular in their action. These may be classed under three heads — physical destroying agents, the most important of which are directly or indirectly due to climatic conditions; destructive forms of life, whether vegetable or animal and the activity of man.

Physical agents

Among the physical destroying agents we may mention first, **frost,** from which most tropical and subtropical plants, such as coffee, tobacco, cotton, suffer greatly when they happen to be exposed to it. In certain regions, and especially in those which have a climate at once warm and arid, **hail** is destructive to both crops and fruit. Reference is hardly needed to the destructiveness of **violent winds** at sea, but it may be noted that the main devastation is wrought on land by the hurricanes of the North Atlantic, north of 10½° N off the West Indies and Florida; the typhoons of the South China Sea, principally between the south coast of China and Taiwan; the cyclones of the Indian Ocean, and especially the Bay of Bengal, and above all the tornadoes of North America, where such storms reach furthest north and furthest into the interior of the land. These violent storms occur mainly at the change of the monsoons — from April to June, and from September to November in the Indian Ocean; in spring and autumn elsewhere. Loss of life can be minimised by tracking and predicting the course of these violent winds, but little can be done to avoid their devastation of property and of produce.

To certain crops, and especially those which depend on the amount of blossom that comes to maturity, such as fruit trees, cotton, coffee, and so on, great damage is often caused by unseasonable winds of less violence; but more destructive on a large scale than any of the agents yet named is **drought.** The regions liable to suffer most heavily from this cause are those which lie on the borderline between regions of sufficient rainfall and those in which the rainfall is too scanty to allow cultivation without irrigation, but in which the rainfall, though sufficient in most years, is apt from time to time to fail. In the densely peopled regions of the Indian subcontinent and China situated in such 'famine zones', the failure of rain has often caused the loss of millions of human lives. Perennial irrigation and the improvement of communications have mitigated but not removed the dangers. In the less populous regions in the interior of South America, Africa and in Australia, the destruction caused in this way is confined to sheep and cattle and other livestock. Despite the protection afforded by artesian wells and storage reservoirs, after the great drought of 1914 the number of sheep in Queensland dropped from 23.1m. to 15.9m. in 1915.

Great destruction is sometimes wrought by **floods** on the banks of such rivers as the Hwang Ho, Mississippi, and the Ganga, or even the Danube and some of its more important tributaries; also on low-lying lands in the neighbourhood of the sea. Stupendous embankments have been constructed along the Ganga in Lower Bengal to guard against this danger, but these restrain without altogether preventing the excesses of the inundations; and the same may be said regarding the similar works that have been executed in the United States and the Hungarian plains, on the banks of the rivers above named. Among the more memorable excesses of the sea may be mentioned that by which the greater part of the land converted into the Zuyder Zee, some 5 200 sq km (2 000 sq miles) now largely reclaimed, was submerged in successive inundations in the twelfth to fourteenth centuries, and that by which an area of about 7 750 sq km (3 000 sq miles) at the head of the Bay of Bengal was overwhelmed and many thousands of people lost their lives, during cyclones in November 1876 and November 1970.

Volcanic outbursts and earthquakes, though fortunately comparatively rare occurrences in their more awful forms, may also be mentioned as physical agents which occasionally produce widespread destruction. The Japanese earthquake of September 1923 resulted in the death of nearly 100 000 people, inclusive of those who perished in the fires which followed.

Animal and vegetable agents

The living destructive agents are probably on the whole more injurious than the physical agents above mentioned, inasmuch as many of them are extremely persistent, being difficult to extirpate, and renewing their attacks on particular crops or on various forms of vegetation, animals, and man year after year. The mere enumeration of such destroyers would fill a volume, and whole volumes have been devoted to individual pests. Here we can only allude to a few of the more important.

The **vegetable pests** consist mainly of minute fungi which affect various parts of a plant and indicate their presence by the discoloration they produce. Such are the fungi producing the diseases known as rust in cereals and mildew on the vine and many other plants, each subject to attack by its own fungus. Another is the fungus (*Hemileia vastatrix*) which almost completely destroyed the cultivation of the coffee tree in Ceylon. International cooperation and research, coordinated by the United Nations' agencies is steadily reducing the impact of these diseases and although not eliminated they are increasingly being contained.

Of **animal pests**, the most destructive, on the whole, are insects. Among these may be mentioned locusts, different species of which infest treeless regions in both the Old World and the New. Since biblical times they have invaded cultivated fields, where they arrive flying in thick solid masses, filling the air, darkening the sun, forming an immense unbroken cloud which may take more than an hour to pass. When they settle they consume every green thing to be seen, the working of their jaws meanwhile causing a sound which can be heard at a great distance. Systematic campaigns using aircraft and insecticides have now almost eliminated the threat of this particular plague, and sustained international cooperation should maintain control in the future.

Among insects destructive to particular objects of cultivation may be mentioned the Hessian fly (*Cecidomyia destructor*, Say), which attacks wheat and barley, and proved peculiarly destructive in various parts of the United States, so as to lead to the abandonment, for a time at least, of wheat cultivation in certain districts; the Colorado beetle, which wrought great ravages among the potatoes in the United States in many years subsequent to 1861; the phylloxera, which for a time put an end to the cultivation of the vine in several Departments in France; the boll-weevils and boll-worms (moth caterpillars), which for many years have done enormous damage to the cotton crops of the United States and Egypt. Other insects, such as the tsetse fly, are the carriers of disease to domestic animals, as well as to human beings.

Among destructive animals of a higher type there are the sea lampreys which invaded the Great Lakes of North America in 1936 and within twenty years reduced the trout catch from 15m. lb to a few hundred lb per year. A still more serious plague, both in Australia and in New Zealand, grew out of the introduction of the rabbit, the multiplication of which in some instances compelled squatters to abandon their sheepruns, and cultivators their holdings, and caused different Australian governments to expend hundreds of thousands of pounds in efforts to extirpate it, or rather to keep it down. Then the disease myxomatosis virtually exterminated the rabbit. Rats proved equally destructive among the sugarcanes of Jamaica. The mongoose, a small but fierce carnivorous animal, introduced into that island with great success to destroy the rats, later became almost as great a pest itself through its raids on domestic poultry. In many of these cases the most serious results have accrued where man by the introduction of plants or animals from other localities has upset the local 'balance of nature'. But in the parts of Argentina that have a similar climate to the pastoral regions of Australia, the native vizcacha, an animal with similar habits to those of the rabbit, is quite as destructive, and has likewise been the object of all sorts of devices to compass its extermination.

Minute organisms are the causes of many diseases in man which have a serious effect on production in the regions where they are prevalent, and it is fortunate that in recent years remarkable progress has been made in the knowledge enabling man to combat those diseases. Some of these organisms are conveyed to man by insects. Malaria, yellow fever, sleeping sickness, and elephantiasis all belong to this class. Malaria is almost confined to those areas in which the mean temperature exceeds 15° C (60° F) for the summer months, and on the whole it increases in virulence towards the equator. It is set up in man by a microscopic organism introduced into the human system by mosquitoes belonging to the genus *Anopheles*, and in consequence of this discovery the disease has been extirpated in many places in which it was formerly rife. Two methods are adopted in fighting against the disease. One is to destroy the mosquito, which is done when the insect is in the larval state. In that stage it lives in water, and where the water which might rear the larvae cannot be drained away, a thin film of oil on its surface will prevent the larvae from breathing. Spraying from the air with DDT has also given excellent results, but this potent chemical compound has a great disadvantage. It does not readily decompose and may harm animal life other than the noxious pests for which it was intended. Its use is banned or discouraged in many countries. The other method is to destroy the animal parasites in the human body by appropriate drugs. Where spraying and prophylactic drugs can be applied universally to a restricted area, malaria can be eliminated; but the exercise of such control to continental areas presents great problems and has yet to be accomplished.

In Cuba and in Panama, the war against yellow fever was waged with such success by Colonel W. C. Gorgas, a United States doctor, that it has now been exterminated. The insect carrier in this case was the *Stegomyia fasciata*, and the immediate excitant a microscopic spiro-chaete. In Africa the carrier is the mosquito *Aëdes aegypti*, and although these are sporadic epidemics it should now be possible to contain any serious outbreak. More stubborn is the resistance offered by sleeping sickness, a disease known to have been endemic in Africa for hundreds of years. From time to time it appears to break out as a scourge, and has carried off thousands in Uganda, the Congo region, and other parts of central Africa. It is due to an internal parasite

(*Trypanosoma*) for which the tsetse fly acts as receptionist, host and transmitter. The main species of the fly are *Glossina palpalis*, carrier of *Trypanosoma gambiense*, and *Glossina morsitans*, carrier of *Trypanosoma rhodesiense*. The former is the better known; it was responsible for the deadly epidemic of sleeping sickness in Uganda around the end of the last century when between 200 000 and 300 000 were killed within a few years. This tsetse fly, *G. palpalis*, which is almost exclusively the carrier of *T. gambiense* from man to man, is confined to the immediate vicinity of expanses of water — a limitation of habitat very helpful to anti-sleeping sickness measures. *G. morsitans* has a much wider range and serves as the intermediate host of *T. rhodesiense* not only between man and man but between animals, and also between man and animals. With modern drugs the disease is no longer a menace, but many out of reach of medical services still die each year. *Nagana*, the animal disease analogous to sleeping sickness, is even more deadly than its human counterpart, and there are vast tracts of Africa which are practically banned to domestic livestock and mixed farming because of the prevalence of tsetse fly. Large sums of government money have been and are being spent on research and experimental remedies, including drugs, bush clearance, spraying insecticides from the air, and the reduction of game animals. Land can be reclaimed from the tsetse fly by such methods, but it must be sufficiently productive to repay the heavy cost.

Elephantiasis, of which the leading symptom is a swelling of the skin and the adjacent cellular tissue, is prevalent on the coasts of West Africa, India, southern China, the South Sea Islands and Brazil. Due to a filaria or microscopic worm carried by a group of the genus *Culex*, it has so far baffled efforts for its extirpation.

Other diseases sometimes appearing as widespread epidemics include plague, which is of two types, the bubonic, characterised by a swelling of the glands, and the lung form. Both are due to bacteria, of which the carriers are rat-fleas. There is no limit to its geographical range. The Black Death of 1348—49, which was of the lung type, raged in the high valleys of the Alps as much as on the plains, in Greenland as much as in Italy. It is diffused along the lines of commercial intercourse, but fortunately modern sanitary regulations are sufficient to cope with it, at least in the temperate zones. Cholera was long endemic from Bombay to southern China, but more particularly in Lower Bengal, and occasionally spreads like the plague along the lines of human intercourse. Again and again the great annual religious concourse at Hardwar, where the Ganga enters on the plains of India, has been the source of an outbreak which has spread far and wide, and in the latter years of last century with a rapidity which corresponded to the improvement in the means of communication. An epidemic which started there in March 1892 reached St Petersburg in less than five months, and before the end of August reached New York. With air travel the disease can now be carried around the world in a matter of days; but international cooperation and modern medicine make it possible to contain the sporadic outbreaks which still occur. Improved sanitary conditions have almost extirpated in Europe the once nearly universal disease of leprosy, another disease due to bacillus infection. The disease still has a grip on southeast Asia, also on central Africa, notably in the great river basins. Taken in time, it can now be cured, provided doctors and drugs are made available, and provided those who suffer from the disease will present themselves for treatment. Scurvy, which at one time took so heavy a toll on seamen — on his pioneer voyage to India and back in 1497–99 Vasco da Gama lost 100 out of a crew of 160 — was eliminated after the discovery of the means of warding off the disease by a diet of fresh fruit and vegetables. Of recent years influenza has taken a toll of human life comparable with the plagues of the Middle Ages. Indeed it is one of the serious aspects of modern life that as man's medical skill conquers one disease after another, others arise (rapidly disseminated by modern communications and aggravated by the growing density of urban population) which were previously either little known or were mild in their attacks.

Man

Lastly, man himself is proving in the twentieth century to be a devastating agent whose actions can be as deleterious as any of the natural phenomena so far discussed. Apart, again, from two major wars which for the first time have affected the whole world, man's general capabilities are now such that they can affect the balance of nature. Man has long been a devastating agent but his depredations have hitherto been only of regional significance. The tribal burning of forest to provide food gardens left behind exhausted plots fit only for scrub; the share cropper of the middle west of the United States moved on and left behind the dust bowl; but now the rise in world population (particularly of urban population), the pressures for improved standards of living and the growth of technological skills all combine to make possible a far greater impact on the environment. The known reserves of capital resources (coal, oil, minerals, etc.) are vast, but consumption is rising rapidly and they are irreplaceable. It has been estimated, for instance, that in the United States nearly two-thirds of all the coal consumed has been burned since 1920, and nearly two-thirds of all the oil and gas consumed has been burned since 1940. Alternative sources of power may be developed but the traditional ones will slowly become more costly to mine. The renewable resources of sea and forest have already reached the point in some areas where supplies can be assured only by rationed consumption and planned replenishment. The pollution of air and water by the great urban and industrial concentrations poses further problems, as do the unforeseen effects of the whole-sale employment of chemicals, since man himself is at the top of a food pyramid which begins with small organisms affected by such effluents. Fortunately there has been timely recognition of these serious potential threats of devastation. Since they stem from man's activities it should be possible for man to control them before they get out of hand, even if that control does impose additional costs on production and distribution.

II
Circumstances connected with the exchange of commodities

Transport

Transport methods vary considerably from country to country, and from region to region, being dependent upon a number of geographical and historical factors; they may be conveniently grouped into eight categories.
1. Human porterage, including wheeled vehicles moved by human labour.
2. Animals, used (*a*) as beasts of burden; (*b*) for draught purposes.
3. Roads and motor vehicles.
4. Railroads, including light trackways.
5. Ropeways and cableways.
6. Inland water transport.
7. Ocean transport.
8. Air transport.

Human porterage

In central Africa, in various parts of southeastern Asia, and even in densely peopled districts of China, some movement of goods overland still takes place by means of human porters, or by wheeled vehicles drawn or pushed by men. Prodigious loads were sometimes carried under exceedingly difficult climatic and topographical conditions, as in the tea traffic between southwest China and Tibet, where the normal load per man was 90 kg (200 lb), and two mountain passes more than 2 200 m (7 000 ft) above the level of the starting-place had to be scaled; about 190 km (120 miles) were covered in some twenty days. The wheelbarrow is still in use in northern China, where every centimetre of the land is so precious that the narrowest possible roads are used, such as will accommodate a wheelbarrow but not a two- or four-wheeled cart. In Korea the labourers still carry heavy loads on A-frames.

Animals

Except in the most highly industrialised countries animal transport is still of some importance, especially in rural districts, though in general mechanisation of transport is tending more and more to displace animals. In most European countries, and in those which have been influenced by Europeans, by far the most serviceable animal is the **horse**, used as a draught beast, but in central and eastern Europe the **ox** was of greater importance — perhaps a comment on the greater velocity of life in the West, the horse being valued for its speed, the ox for its strong, steady, if rather leisurely, pull. In southern Europe, and the regions round the Mediterranean generally, the **ass**, which thrives better than the horse on the scanty herbage, is an animal of much more consequence than in the rest of Europe, and hence is more cared for and of finer aspect and better qualities; in the mountainous parts of those regions the **mule** is preferred to both, on account of its sure-footedness and endurance, and its power of thriving on coarse browsing.

In the most populous parts of Asia and in southern Africa various breeds of oxen are the principal beasts of burden; next to these, in Asia, come **buffaloes**, horses being for the most part neither numerous nor of good quality.

Among animals of regional importance, **reindeer** are used in northern Asia, Europe, and North America, notably to draw sledges over the snow-covered ground; **dogs** are also employed, as by the Eskimos, for the same purpose. In the mountainous parts of central Asia a peculiar species of ox, known as the **yak**, which is found both wild and domesticated is used as the mule is used in southern Europe. In some parts of the same region **goats** and **sheep** may carry light burdens, and goat-carts used to be seen in the Alpine region of Europe. In the Andes of South America, the **llama** is the principal beast of burden. The Asian **elephant,** which is found from the south of the Himalayas to the borders of China, and in the large tropical islands from Ceylon to Sumatra and Borneo, is invaluable as a beast of burden throughout that region, wherever there are no proper roads. Where roads do exist, it does not accomplish so much work in proportion to the amount of food which it consumes as the ox, or buffalo, but it can make its way across marshes and through forests which could not be traversed by any of the other animals mentioned. Throughout India, the catching of wild elephants for training is under government supervision; the chief area is now in Burma, where the animals are used mainly for timber haulage in the forests. The African elephant is rarely trained for labour, though it was so by the ancients (for example the Carthaginians), and, in northeastern Africa, down to the Middle Ages.

The **camel**, in desert and semidesert regions, is even more indispensable as a beast of burden than is the elephant amid forest and marsh. Provided with one or two humps of fat which serve as reserves of nutriment, and with its stomach lined with hundreds of small cells capable of holding water, a camel when well fed and supplied with water at starting can accomplish immense journeys on the most meagre fare, and almost without drink. By no other animal is so much merchandise carried over long distances. Until the recent advance of the motorcar and the aeroplane, it was the sole means of commerce between the oases of northern Africa, as well as between the North African coast and the fertile territories of the Sudan, and it is still largely employed in western Asia. It was introduced into Australia, and was used on exploratory journeys, but has been replaced now by the motorcar. Camels were seldom used singly, but in caravans, often consisting of several hundreds, not only for the sake of carrying a large quantity and variety of merchandise, but also for the sake of having a sufficiently large body of men to defend the caravan against marauders.

The simplest method of using animals for transport is to employ them as beasts of burden, like the pack-horses which formerly carried most of Britain's internal trade; but this method is far from being the most efficient. An immense advantage is gained by employing the beasts to draw wheeled carts. One animal, broadly speaking, can pull at least four times as much as it can carry. Even in roadless and trackless country, teams of oxen, as in South Africa and in Argentina, are employed to haul agricultural produce in strongly built wagons. For the most part, however, the use of wheeled vehicles involves the making of roads.

Roads

The development of road vehicles and the rapid progress of new methods of transport during the present century, have involved vast changes in the technique of road construction. Roads that were adequate in foundation, surface, and width for the meagre traffic of horsedrawn carts 100 years ago are almost useless for modern highspeed motor traffic. Until comparatively recent times most roads have been dependent upon locally obtained raw materials for their construction; consequently, in clay areas, where natural road-metal is absent, communication was apt to be difficult in winter because of mud, and unpleasant in summer on account of dust. This is still to a large extent true of considerable areas of the earth's surface, such as parts of the Hungarian Plain, western Siberia, and the plains of Australia and Argentina. There are many well known descriptions of eighteenth-century English roads running across the clay belts of this country to be found in the works of travellers such as Defoe and Young. Heavy lumbering carts with their numerous horses cut the roads into deep ruts, and the laying of stones only served to make progress more dangerous and uncomfortable for travellers on horseback or in wheeled vehicles. Under such conditions it is not surprising that Edinburgh was ten to twelve days' coach journey from London, Exeter four days, Birmingham two days, and so on. It is true that the formation of the

Turnpike Trusts, which devoted part of the toll money collected from vehicles to the maintenance and improvement of the road surface, helped to improve many of the main roads of Britain, but little real advancement was possible until scientific principles, which had been almost dormant since the building of the Roman roads, were introduced into road construction. The two names most deservedly famous in this connection are those of Telford and Macadam, two Scots working in the early part of the nineteenth century.

Telford's method consisted of laying a foundation of solid stone blocks and covering this with a layer of small broken stone, thicker in the middle than at the sides so as to produce a camber which, with the provision of adequate ditches on each side, would effectively drain the road. Macadam's system was based on the principle that if a road is made of suitable material and is well drained it can be laid on the natural subsoil without the intervention of Telford's costly stone pavement. His roads were made of a sheet of broken stone of uniform size, each piece about 3–5 cm in diameter, the road being cambered to throw off surface water. He found that such a sheet of broken stone, after rolling by traffic, became firmly bound together as an impermeable mass, and so resisted the ravages of water. Limestone, which yields a fine powder when pieces are ground together, was found to be the most suitable rock; rainwater and this powder formed a natural cement.

Both Telford's and Macadam's roads were effective so long as horse-drawn wagons and iron-tyred wheels formed the bulk of the traffic, but when the perfection of the internal combustion engine permitted the development of the motorcar, they became inadequate. A rubber-tyred wheel, caused to rotate by an engine, exercises a disruptive effect on a road surface composed of small stones, especially during wet weather, when the rubber acts as a sucker and pulls out any loose stones; in dry weather the dust raised by the passage of swiftly moving vehicles rapidly becomes an intolerable nuisance, as it does in those parts of the world where the motorcar has preceded the construction of suitable road surfaces. A motor road requires a cohesive surface prepared either by the use of concrete, as in America, or, as is more commonly the case in Britain, by employing tarmacadam — broken stones sealed with tar or bitumen. The use of tar on roads was one of the first remedies for the problem of dust; the tar also acts as a waterproof coating and so delays the decay of the road through the penetration of water and the disruptive action of frost.

Many varieties of stone can be used for the purpose of road-making, but limestones and close-grained igneous rocks, such as basalt, are the most reliable. Coarse-grained rocks, such as granite, do not make good macadam because the large individual crystals tend to crack; granites were, however, successfully employed in rectangular blocks called 'setts', especially in industrial districts where much heavy traffic had to use the roads. The unequal weathering of the constituent crystals kept the surface slightly rough, and so suitable for horse traffic. Blast-furnace slag, crushed into pieces and tarred, is also much used for macadam in districts where it is produced. Stone chips are also commonly used as a surfacing material for tarred roads.

The world total of motorcars and commercial vehicles in use in 1972 was 271.8m. Passenger cars totalled 214.5m., 57.29m. were commercial vehicles. The United States had far and away the largest number — 116.8m., forming over 43 per cent of the total. Cars alone in the United States were 96.5m. roughly one for every 2.1 of the population. West Germany came second with over 15m. cars (one in four of the population) and approximately 1 075 700 commercial vehicles. In comparison with prewar figures (1938) the United States total of cars and commercial vehicles showed an increase of over 300 per cent. The increase in the world total was still more: over 400 per cent. It is significant that while the number of cars declined during the war years in Europe, Asia, and Africa, the number of commercial vehicles everywhere increased. Under the stimulus of both world wars, the building of lorries (trucks) has grown by leaps and bounds, and both in the 'old' and in the 'new' countries this type of vehicle now plays an important part in everyday life. In the United Kingdom and in the United States the motor lorry, by providing cheap and fairly rapid door-to-door transport of mixed loads, has made great inroads into the traffic formerly carried by rail and canal; in countries less well covered by a rail net, and in countries, such as the 'pioneer belts' of Africa and elsewhere, where railways have not been established, this vehicle has been essential in promoting economic development. Rough roads that will carry a lorry are far more cheaply and quickly constructed, and much less trouble to maintain, than are railways. The use of six wheels instead of four, and the mounting of vehicles on 'caterpillars', are devices that have been developed to overcome the difficulty of rough pioneer roads and of movement in polar regions.

The manufacture of motor vehicles is now a major international industry, with United Kingdom exports alone totalling £1 000m. per year. Until 1967 the output of North America was greater than that of the rest of the world; but in 1968 when the United States and Canada produced nearly 10m. vehicles the combined total of the rest of the world moved ahead with over 11m. vehicles (West Germany with 3.6m. and Japan with 2m. taking second and third place after the USA).

Railways

The difficulty of hauling large quantities of bulky commodities over the ordinary country roads in the days before Telford and Macadam was responsible for the growth, in the eighteenth century, of numerous 'railways' in the coalmining and iron-working districts of Britain; especially where the clay soil provided an indifferent foundation and where gradients down to the rivers were steep. Even the Romans had laid stone tracks for their wagon-wheels; it was a short step from this to the laying of timber baulks covered with iron plates (hence the term 'plate-layer', still employed on British railways for track maintenance men) and so to actual iron rails, flanged to keep the wheels from slipping off. Transfer the flanges from the rails to the wheels, and the idea of the modern railroad is complete. Between 1801 and 1825 no fewer than twenty-nine 'iron railways' were built in Britain, mainly in connection with collieries, ironworks, or canals, horses being used to haul the wagons. The coincidence of this period with that of the development of the steam locomotive produced the railways we know today. James Watt began building stationary steam engines on a commercial scale in 1775, and between 1801 and 1825 such men as Trevithick, Hedley and Stephenson were responsible for applying Watt's invention to the problem of locomotion. The first steam railway for general purposes was that between Stockton and Darlington (designed to give an outlet to the Tees for the coal from Witton Park in Durham), opened in 1825. The Liverpool and Manchester line followed in 1830. In 1831 the first passenger train ran on the American continent, from Albany to Schenectady in the state of New York; and in 1835 the first railway on the mainland of Europe was opened, between Brussels and Malines.

Topographical controls of railway routes are more obvious than those affecting roads. The problem of the railway builder lies midway between those of the road engineer and the canal builder. High speed express train working becomes difficult when frequent gradients steeper than about 1:100 are encountered — though it is possible to work trains by the normal method up gradients of 1:22, as on the Kicking Horse Pass line through the Rockies. It has been estimated that the cost of working a given trainload over a kilometre of track on a gradient of 1:50 is twice that of working the same train over a kilometre on the level. Hence the most elementary factor in geography — the relief of the land — is of great importance in controlling the routes which the lines take.

The superiority of railways for the movement of bulk freight justified vast expenditure to make routes for the lines where the features of the country did not afford them. Railway tunnels from 11—20 km (7—12 miles) long have been driven through the Alps, and in the Andes heights of over 4 800 m (15 800 ft) are reached by railways in Bolivia and Peru. In mountainous countries, special types of railways have made their appearance; notably rack-railways, in which the locomotive can use the rack or toothed rail on steep sections (even on gradients as steep as 1:2) and on level tracks can proceed in the ordinary manner. The first mountain rack-railway was that up Mount Washington in New

Hampshire, USA, completed in 1868. Since that date numerous examples have been built in various parts of the world, especially in Switzerland. Many such railways have been built for purely tourist purposes, such as the Snowdon Mountain railway, but one European main line, the connection from the Adriatic coast to Serajevo, employs the system in its ascent of the Dinaric Alps, and so also do several main lines in South America, as from Arica to La Paz.

Mountains are not the only obstacles to continuity of railway lines. In order to extend the facilities for communication by rail without break of bulk, wide stretches of sea and lake are crossed by train ferries: specially constructed vessels with rails laid on their decks, carrying whole trains. The channel separating Denmark from Sweden has long been overcome in this manner; for years a goods train ferry has been in operation between England and the Continent *via* Harwich, and in 1936 the first passenger ferry service between London and Paris was opened *via* Dover—Dunkerque. A channel tunnel to serve the same purpose has long been planned.

The development of a railway network may take two quite different forms, according to whether the country is an undeveloped or a long-settled region. In a virgin area, like the Canadian prairies 100 years ago, large-scale settlement was impossible owing to lack of means of communication. Thus, until the completion of the Canadian Pacific Railway in 1885, western Canada was practically uninhabited, and settlement closely followed the first lines of railway. In such a case the railway developed the country; even today little wheat is grown in areas remote from a railway. In the same way the railway lines of the Argentine pampa, and of the Middle West of the United States, have provided a basis for settlement. Quite different is the state of affairs in an already developed country such as Britain. Here the railway routes were dependent on pre-existing conditions — the distribution of population, the position of towns and industries, and the existence of developed natural resources, such as minerals and harbours. The initial function of the railway in such conditions is that of connecting places which are already important. The railways stimulated the industries of the regions they served, and this growth encouraged the construction of further rail connections. Junction points began to attract population and industry, and at certain junctions new towns sprang up, such as Crewe and Swindon. The railways, too, helped to foster the growth of their seaport terminals, and in several cases were responsible for the entire construction of new ports, such as Southampton and Immingham.

A railway locomotive must haul the trucks containing the load as well as the load, but it is only the load on which freight is earned. Hence it is desirable to have a railway wagon reasonably light in proportion to the paying load. Large wagons present this advantage, but it is not everywhere that convenient loads for large wagons and long heavy trains are available. The idea of reducing transport expenses by the adoption of larger wagons originated in the grain-growing regions of the northwest of the United States. Much has been said on the advantage of introducing large railway wagons into Great Britain, but the problem where wheat is grown in enormous quantities and mostly transported to one or two great markets, is entirely different from that of collecting produce in forty or fifty counties and redistributing it in 10 000 towns and villages. In America it has been found profitable in some cases to use 50-ton steel trucks, nowhere more advantageously than on the lines connecting Pittsburgh with the lake ports, where the trucks can be filled in one direction with iron ore, and in the other with coal. There it was estimated that the substitution of these trucks for the older 30-ton wooden ones effected a saving of 315 tons deadweight on a 1 500-ton train.

On the continent of Europe trucks are employed which are smaller than those in ordinary use in America, but larger than most of those in Britain, where the normal size is 12–13 tons. Though the British and continental track gauges are the same, the original British structure gauge (based on the size of a load of hay, and governing the dimensions of tunnels, etc.) does not admit of the use of the wider continental rolling stock. After nationalisation, the British Transport Commission, which became operative on 1 January 1948, adopted 16-ton all-steel trucks as the standard of replacement for mineral wagons. In the early days of railway construction several gauges were used, but since the abolition of the GWR broad gauge (5 ft 6 in) in Britain in 1892, all main lines have been on the standard gauge of 4 ft 8½ in. This is also the gauge of continental Europe (except Spain and Russia), and of North America. Several countries, notably Australia (which is tackling the problem), Argentina, and India, suffer from a mixture of gauges.

A number of locomotives in the world are still steam driven, but they are giving way to those powered by diesel engines or electrical motors. Those in the United Kingdom have been progressively replaced since the Second World War. All suburban (the network of southeast England is the largest in the world) and main-line locomotives are now powered by electricity, either by a third rail, overhead cable, or by a diesel-engined locomotive.

About 1870 began the extensive development of **tramways** as urban passenger carriers in Britain. Nearly all the original tramways were private enterprises and the vehicles were horsedrawn. In 1882 an Act was passed enabling local authorities to purchase any electrical installation at the end of twenty-one years without making any allowance for goodwill. In 1888 the period was increased to forty-two years, but the influence on investors remained. In 1928–29 there were 221 tramway undertakings and 3 900 km (2 420 miles) of track in Britain, and the number of tramcars was over 14 000. By 1938 the length of track was down to 1 900 km (1 183 miles) and the number of tramcars was under 9 000. By 1966 all had gone. This decline marked the lead taken by British towns in rejecting trams in favour of the more flexible motor omnibuses. The tramway rails were removed but in some areas the overhead electrical installation was used to drive 'trolley buses'. These in turn have been discarded because of their inability to manoeuvre away from their source of power, and urban passenger movement is dominated in the United Kingdom and the United States by the privately owned automobile, supplemented in the larger cities by motor omnibuses and underground electric railways. How long this pattern will last will depend on the ability of the cities to control the impact of the ever-growing car population, and on the development of economic alternative methods of public transport, such as overhead monorails, etc.

Ropeways and cableways*

For general transport duties and especially for industrial waste disposal, ropeways are of great advantage. The main feature is that the loads are suspended from an overhead rope or ropes and are carried clear of ground conditions. There are two systems — the Monocable for duties up to 150 tons per hour, and the Bicable for duties up to 500 tons per hour with individual loads of up to 5 tons. With the Monocable system an endless haulage rope runs over sheaves mounted on trestles and serves both to support and to transport the load. The Bicable system uses a fixed carrying rope and a light haulage rope to move the cars which run on the track rope. Bicable ropeways can be entirely automatic in action and angles can be introduced on the line at any point. The ability to transport materials over obstacles which either forbid alternative transport to cause excessive detours is one of the major features of ropeway practice.

A cableway is a specialised version of a ropeway and serves both to lift and traverse a load. Because of the very long spans which are possible and the high speed of operation, cableways are universally used for dam construction and in mountainous areas. Loads may be up to 30 tons.

Inland water transport

Water carriage has, within the last 100 years, undergone as great a revolution as land carriage. The use of boats on rivers, both for down- and up-stream navigation, must have been one of the earliest of human inventions, and in some parts of the world, as in Russia and the valley

* With acknowledgements to the chairman of the Aerial Ropeway Association.

of the Ganga, the want of roads was to a large extent long made up for by the abundance of navigable rivers. Rivers, however, flow where nature has dictated rather than where man would wish; and although atomic power now makes the redirection of rivers feasible, physical conditions strictly limit the alternatives that are possible. Railways have the advantage over rivers of speed and choice of destinations, and these advantages in most cases more than compensate the disadvantage of dearer haulage. A railway generally has a great advantage over a river even on a parallel course. A waterway is of no use unless there are places on it where goods may be landed and lifted, but good navigable rivers are apt to flow for long stretches through marshy and unstable country without landing places. This character greatly diminishes the value of the Po as a waterway, and the Mississippi flows in places for kilometre after kilometre without the possibility of discharging goods, where the parallel lines of railway have numerous stations. The utility of a river as a waterway is, moreover, affected by the weather to a much greater extent than are railways. Nearly all rivers are subject to great variations in level. The St Lawrence is an exception, as the steadiness of its flow in the open-water season is maintained by the chain of great lakes of which it is the outlet, but it is a unique exception. Hence traffic on most rivers is apt to be stopped or impeded by high and low water, and where the winter is severe there is a regular stoppage of traffic through ice. Nevertheless, large rivers on which steamers can be used still form important means of communication, and especially in countries not yet fully opened to modern commerce. The best of such rivers have one great advantage over railways, that it is easier on them to transport great quantities at one time. A train load of more than 7 000 tons − considerably less in the United Kingdom − may be regarded as something quite exceptional, but on the Rhine, for instance, it is easy to exceed that in barge-trains. If they served no other purpose they would still be of commercial value as tending to keep down rates on competing lines of railway.

Navigable canals are another means of transport, and they also have had their importance diminished by the introduction of railways, though in some regions they have played a very important part in the development of commerce. Level regions are naturally those most suitable for canals, and in such, one of the chief uses of rivers is to feed navigable canals, as in more mountainous districts one of the chief uses of rivers is to afford water-power. The most important canals of modern times, however, are the **ship-canals** connecting different seas or inland cities to the oceans − such as the Manchester−Liverpool Ship Canal, the Houston−Galveston Canal, and the St Lawrence−Great Lakes system which makes it possible for oceangoing vessels to sail over 2 400 km (nearly 1 500 miles) into the interior of North America.

The three paragraphs which follow have been retained for their historical interest from earlier editions of the *Handbook*:

Somewhat delusive expectations of economy in transport from the use of inland water carriage are sometimes entertained. These are all based on the admittedly low cost of mere haulage at a slow rate. It is estimated that on an ordinary good wagon road a single horse-power will drag about 3 000 lb at the rate of 3 ft per second (approximately $1\frac{1}{3}$ tons at two miles an hour); on a railway about 30 000 lb ($13\frac{1}{3}$ tons) at the same rate; in water up to as much as 200 000 lb (90 tons). But in making inferences from this general fact it should be borne in mind (1) that the cost of increasing the rate of speed is much greater by water than by land; (2) that the average rate of transport on canals is greatly reduced by the delays at locks; (3) that the economy of water transport is greatly reduced by the fact that even canals do not afford the same facilities as railways for conveying goods over the face of the country without break of bulk; (4) that canals are in most cases of too small dimensions for modern requirements; and (5) that the maintenance of an adequate supply of water in canals may be difficult and expensive.

With regard to the first of these points it is noteworthy that some of the earliest experiments with steamboats were made with the view of increasing the speed and economy of transport on canals. Since the screw propeller was introduced, these experiments have been renewed with greater success, seeing that its use is not so likely to injure the canal banks. To prevent destruction of the banks, mechanical propulsion is prohibited on some canals, including a few of those of Britain. In other cases concrete banks have been made. A few attempts have been made to increase the speed by the use of locomotives on the canal banks. This mode of traction was tried on the Forth and Clyde Canal in 1839, steam locomotives being used. More recently electric motors running on rails on the banks have been employed both in France (on the Burgundy Canal) and Belgium (on the Charleroi Canal); but in the latter case the experiment has been abandoned. This method is, however, used in taking vessels through the locks of the Panama Canal. Electric propulsion with the aid of overhead wires has been tried with success on a section of the Staffordshire and Worcestershire Canal. The current consumption, with a load of 33 tons, was found to be one unit per mile; the cost, at 1*d.* per unit, 0.03*d.* per ton-mile.

In view of the importance of the second consideration above mentioned, the map (p. 360) of the English waterways has been drawn up so as to show the numbers of locks. The delays due to this cause have given rise to various projects for economising time in surmounting differences of level in inland navigations. Hydraulic and pneumatic lifts are employed. In 1875, an hydraulic lift, with a lifting power of 100 tons, working through a height of 50 ft, was completed to connect the Weaver navigation at Anderton, in Cheshire, with the Trent and Mersey Canal. It has since been rebuilt and electrified, with two single tanks. A more complicated structure, with a capacity of nearly 600 tons and a somewhat higher range of working, was completed in 1899 on the Dortmund–Ems Canal at Henrichenburg not far from Dortmund. Inclined planes have been employed from a very remote date in China. In April 1910 the Grand Junction Canal substituted inclined planes for the flight of ten locks which formerly overcame a height of 75 ft at Foxton in Leicestershire. The boats ascended and descended inclined planes simultaneously in wet docks which moved up and down on rails, a stationary steam-engine effecting the lift. By this means two boats were moved up and down simultaneously in 12 min, while formerly 1 hour and 20 min was required for passing a couple of boats in either direction. The Foxton lift was closed in November 1910, as there was not enough traffic to warrant the cost of working it.

The difficulty of intercommunication by inland waterways without break of bulk arises from the fact that it is not practicable to construct canals in as many directions as railways, and the full advantage of such intercommunication, even where it is possible, can in many cases not be enjoyed, owing to the inevitable differences in canal dimensions. The larger the waterways the greater is the economy in the transport, but the construction of large canals is in many cases quite impracticable, in many others not economically practicable.

Ocean transport

Marine navigation is the mode of transport which presents the greatest combination of advantages. Besides the advantage of cheap haulage for low speeds offered by navigable water generally, the ocean offers a free road traversable in all directions, one on which it is possible to increase almost indefinitely the size of vessels, the size being limited mainly by accommodation available at ports and partly by the dimensions of such canals as Suez and Panama. These advantages far outweigh a somewhat greater risk of loss at sea than on land from storms and other causes. It is in this mode of transport that the most important developments have taken place in modern times. These developments, which affect the size of the vessels employed, the range and precision of navigation, and the power used for propulsion, have gone hand in hand with a great expansion of international seaborne trade. The world total of cargoes loaded for export in 1937 was 490m. metric tons; in 1957 it was 960m. and in 1967 1 750m. With an estimated growth rate of 6 per cent each year it could reach 2 800m. by 1975 and 3 500m. by 1980, approximately half of which will be crude oil and petroleum.

The navigation of the sea in small boats for trade purposes is, however, not yet quite extinct. The islanders of the Pacific Ocean and the Eastern Archipelago undertake short voyages in a great variety of craft, in which they go far out of sight of land, but such adventurous enterprises unaided by the modern appliances for navigation are the exception. In ancient times the Phoenicians were the most adventurous seamen, at least in European waters. About 1000 BC their vessels traversed the entire Mediterranean, and even went beyond the Pillars of Hercules (Strait of Gibraltar), and as far as the Scilly Isles; and about the beginning of the sixth century BC Phoenician seamen in the employment of Pharaoh Necho, King of Egypt, are credited with having made a voyage round Africa. But their expeditions were mainly coasting voyages. Writers of the first century AD mention as something recent the discovery of the use that could be made of the monsoon winds in sailing from the mouth of the Red Sea to India at one period of the year and back at another. It is at least certain that a trade of this nature was regularly organised within that century, though even these voyages were probably not wholly on the high seas. Before the close of the Middle Ages, however, vessels sailed with the monsoons from the east coast of Africa direct to India and Ceylon.

In modern times ocean navigation has been greatly facilitated by the use of the mariner's compass. This instrument was known to the Chinese at a much earlier date than in Europe where it is reported towards the close of the twelfth century. Since then it has undergone a long series of improvements, especially in the nineteenth century, when the increasing use of iron in shipbuilding rendered it necessary to devise methods for neutralising the disturbing effects of that metal on the compass needle. It was not till sailors became accustomed to this instrument that they became bolder in their ventures. So it was not until 1492 that Columbus discovered America, and Vasco de Gama the seaway to India (1497–98) — a discovery hardly less important in the history of commerce, on account of the effect it had on the fortunes of the great trading centres of Italy and southern Germany.

Improved chronometers, which are as indispensable as a compass for determining a precise course on the high seas, date only from 1736, following John Harrison's invention of the compensation pendulum.

Steam navigation, by which so great a revolution was effected in sea carriage, originated, like steam railways, in the nineteenth century. The patent for the first steamboat which proved a success was taken out in 1801 by Symington, and a boat constructed on this patent had a few trials on the Forth and Clyde Canal. The first really successful steamboat voyage was that made in 1807 from New York to Albany on the Hudson by a vessel constructed by Fulton, who had worked independently on the problem of steam navigation since 1803. In 1819 a ship crossed the Atlantic using steam as an auxiliary, and in 1838 two ships, sailing about the same time from Cork and Bristol respectively, made the first commercially successful steam voyages across the Atlantic. In 1820 the first iron vessel made a voyage from London to Paris, and in 1832 an iron vessel, the *Elburkah*, made the voyage from Liverpool to the Niger.

It was not until the middle of the last century that steamers began rapidly to displace sailing vessels, and in the 1860s iron came to be more and more substituted for wood as the building material. The invention of mild steel made it possible to use steel in place of iron, and this material was first used in the Cunard liner *Servia* in 1881. The great advantages of steel vessels over wooden ones was their greater strength, endurance, and lightness in proportion to the load. Wooden vessels seldom lasted for more than twelve to fifteen years, whereas the life of a steel vessel may exceed forty years. The weight of a wooden ship was nearly as great as that of its cargo, whereas a steel vessel can carry a load of from two to four times its own weight; river and lake steamers, which are not so strongly built, carry an even larger proportion. Early in the present century, motor ships were introduced as an alternative to steamships, and an oil tanker registered in 1911, the *Volcanus*, was the first ship to be driven by a diesel oil engine running on the heavy crude oil which is a distinguishing feature of that type of motor vessel. As we shall see presently, motor and diesel ships have since found increasing favour, though steamers (largely oil-burning) still constitute nearly half of the world's shipping tonnage.

Here may be noted the meaning of tonnage. Cargo tonnage is taken to be the weight of cargo carried, expressed in long tons (2 240 lb) metric tons (2 204.6 lb) or short tons (2 000 lb). By volume 42 cu ft of cargo (1.19 cu m) is normally reckoned as equivalent to 1 shipping ton. Gross tonnage is a space measurement 100 cu ft (2.83 cu m) being reckoned as 1 ton (1 000 kg); it is the capacity of the permanently enclosed space between the frame of the vessel and the deck, together with any closed-in space above the deck. Net registered tonnage is also a space measurement, but from the gross tonnage is deducted the space occupied by engines, gear, crew's quarters, and officers' quarters; it therefore represents, the space available for cargo and passengers – as in gross tonnage, 100 cu ft (2.83 cu m) are reckoned as 1 ton (1 000 kg). Displacement tonnage refers to the weight of water actually displaced by the vessel when fully laden; it is really the weight of the vessel and its contents when fully laden. Deadweight tonnage is the total weight of cargo, fuel, and passengers. It is the total load carried when loaded to maximum loadline and is usually given in long tons. As a rough conversion for a mixed fleet of tankers and cargo vessels, gross registered tons plus 50 per cent equals deadweight tons; for 'giant' tankers the dwt.

(deadweight) tonnage may be 120 per cent higher than gross. The United States space conversion for mixed cargo is 40 cu ft (1.13 cu m) to 1 shipping ton — as against the UK figure of 42 cu ft (1.19 cu m).

There has been a steady increase in the size and speed of vessels. The ships in which the great voyages of discovery were made in the fifteenth and sixteenth centuries were, according to our standard, very small. The largest of the three caravels with which Columbus discovered the New World was of only 100 tons burden (cargo tonnage). But let us not be misled by such figures as to the average dimensions of the merchant vessels of the period. Small vessels were often purposely chosen for voyages of discovery, as being better fitted for the exploration of unknown coasts. This is still true in Antarctic exploration. Even in the twelfth century, an average-sized merchantman in the Mediterranean appears to have had accommodation below deck for about 250 tons of cargo, besides a considerable cargo above deck.

The largest ships of the 1930s and 1940s were the great passenger liners. In 1939 two of over 80 000 gross tons were regularly crossing the Atlantic, and a third was nearing completion. The first of these, the French *Normandie* (83 423 tons), launched in 1935, set up a new record for the transatlantic crossing, with an average speed of over 30 knots per hour, but in 1938, the British *Queen Mary* (81 237 tons) made the crossing at 31.69 knots. The third and largest, the British *Queen Elizabeth* (83 673 tons), saw her first service as a troopship in the Second World War, and the other two mammoths were among the many great merchant ships used for that purpose. All three survived the war, but soon afterwards the *Normandie* was destroyed by fire in New York harbour and the *'Queens'* were taken out of service in the 1960s.

In 1952 the 'Blue Riband' was captured by a smaller but more heavily powered vessel, the *United States*, built not only for passenger and cargo traffic but for possible war service. With a tonnage of only 53 329, she crossed the Atlantic on her maiden voyage at the average speed of 35.59 knots, covering the 2 942 nautical miles between the Ambrose Light vessel and Bishop Rock in 3 days, 10 hours, and 40 min. On the return voyage the speed averaged just over 36 knots.

The short era of the giant passenger liner was ended by the growth of air travel in the 1950s and 1960s. Of the 393 vessels of over 50 000 gross tons in 1970, 316 were oil tankers, seventy-five were bulk carriers and only two were passenger liners; ninety-eight of the oil tankers were over 100 000 tons, with deliveries planned for just under 500 000 ton vessels in the mid-1970s. Table 2 shows the world and commonwealth shipping totals from 1900 to 1970. The figures are the numbers of ships, with millions of gross tons shown in brackets (sailing ships did not warrant recording after 1940).

It will be noted: (*a*) that the number of sailing ships (and their very limited tonnage) is significant as recently as 1900; (*b*) that the average

Table 2 — Shipping totals, 1900–1970

Shipping	*1900*	*1913*	*1939*	*1950*	*1960*	*1970*
World total						
1 Steam and motor	27 610	30 514	31 186	30 852	36 311	52 444
	(28.9)	(47.0)	(69.4)	(84.6)	(129.7)	(227.5)
2 Sailing vessels	11 712	6 617	1 423	—	—	—
(included in total)	(6.5)	(3.9)	(0.9)			
Commonwealth						
1 Steam and motor	10 838	11 287	9 488	8 690	7 896	7 369
	(14.2)	(20.4)	(21.2)	(22.1)	(25.8)	(36.3)
2 Sailing vessels	2 908	1 278	511	—	—	—
(included in total)	(2.1)	(0.6)	(0.2)			

tonnage of steam and motor vessels has risen progressively from 1 400 tons in 1900 to over 4 000 tons in 1970; (*c*) that the British fleet, while falling by some 2 500 vessels (from nearly half to less than one-seventh of the world total), has increased its tonnage by 250 per cent; and (*d*) that the gross tonnage of the world fleet has almost doubled between 1960 and 1970. The major fleets of the world in 1970 are shown in Table 3.

Table 3 — Major fleets, 1970 (in millions of gross tons, number of vessels in brackets)

Total fleets		*Oil tankers*		*Ore and bulk carriers*	
Liberia	33.3 (1 869)	Liberia	19.3 (711)	Liberia	10.1 (534)
Japan	27.0 (8 402)	UK	12.0 (604)	Japan	7.9 (339)
UK	25.8 (3 822)	Japan	9.2 (1 373)	Norway	6.9 (326)
Norway	19.3 (2 808)	Norway	8.8 (373)	UK	3.8 (213)
USA	18.5* (2 983)	USA	4.7 (359)	Greece	2.2 (124)
USSR	14.8 (5 924)	Greece	3.8 (253)		
Greece	10.9 (1 850)	France	3.5 (133)		
Total	227.5 (52 444)		86.1 (6 103)		46.6 (2 528)

* The US fleet includes some 6.5m. gross tons in the reserve fleet.

The oil tankers account for 37 per cent of the total 1970 fleet, and the ore and bulk carriers for 20 per cent. In 1961 the UK had the largest fleet of oil tankers (7.3m. tons) followed by Liberia (7m.), but since then the economic advantages offered by the Liberian 'flag of convenience' have become of even greater significance as tankers have increased in size and cost. In 1967 there were 118 vessels of 50 000 tons and upwards in the world's fleets — 105 were tankers; by 1970 there were 393 vessels and no less than 316 were tankers, a growth of

300 per cent in three years. Japan is rapidly becoming the dominant civil maritime power. Of the total of 4.8m. tons constructed in 1969, Japan built 1 500 000 tons, followed by UK with 600 000 tons; West Germany with 460 000 tons and Denmark with 450 000 tons. Outstanding orders in early 1970 clearly indicate the future trend. The Japanese order book stood at 20.6m. tons, followed by Sweden with 5.6m. tons and UK with 4.7m. tons.

Along with the increase in numbers and in size of vessels there has been an increase in their speed, and improvements in the construction of marine engines have brought about this extra speed with economy of fuel. One of the most important of these improvements was the invention of the triple-expansion marine engine, in which the steam is passed in succession into three cylinders, so as to act on three pistons and utilise its expansive force to the utmost. By such improvements the consumption of fuel had in 1897 been reduced since the early days of steam navigation from between 5 and 7 lb to about 2 lb per indicated horse power per hour. In recent years the steam turbine has been applied almost universally in marine engines. In such engines the steam, instead of acting on opposite sides of a piston reciprocally, is made to impinge continuously on a series of blades fixed to a revolving drum. Here also may be noted the increasing use of oil fuel and diesel oil engines in ocean steamers, and of petrol motors on inland waterways, as well as barges drawn by tugs at sea. In June 1920 two of the largest ocean liners were equipped for the use of oil fuel, for though oil was dearer than coal it presented the great advantages at sea of reduced bunkering space (little more than half that required for coal), the reduction of the crew by about 50 per cent in consequence of no stokers being needed, and a great reduction of the time required for replenishing the fuel supply.

Except during the Second World War there has been a steadily increasing proportion of motor ships to steamers. In 1929 the tonnage of motor ships building in the world was more than half of the total vessels under construction. In 1939 motor ships represented nearly a quarter (24 per cent) of the world's total tonnage, but during the war the proportion of motor ships dropped to 20 per cent, and that of sailing ships to 1 per cent, while the proportion of steamers rose to 79 per cent. This was due to the large numbers of steamers (burning oil fuel) built in the United States during the war. The increase in motor ships continued after the war until in 1970 they accounted for 66 per cent of the total tonnage — the figures being steamships (reciprocating and turbine) 7 959 vessels totalling 82m. gross tons, and motor ships (diesel and diesel-electric) 44 485 vessels totalling 145.4m. tons. It will be noted that the larger vessels tend to be oil-burning steamships, i.e. only 13 per cent of the ships account for 34 per cent of the tonnage. Among the larger ships, the oil tankers, the figures were: steamships

48.9m. tons (1 670 ships) as against motor ships 37.1m. tons (4 433 ships).

One consequence of the increase in the size and speed of ships has been the increase in the size and depth of the harbours belonging to the great seaports, or the establishment of outer ports for the accommodation of vessels unable to reach older ports. Countries which have deep and capacious natural harbours, or such as require least outlay to adapt them to the requirements of the present day, are therefore at an advantage in the competition for maritime trade.

Another less obvious but very important consequence has been the increase in the safety of sea voyages. This has been brought about in two ways. First, the large steamers are much less liable to be wrecked by storms than the smaller vessels of past days. Second, as Chisholm pointed out, it was the introduction of steamers that swept pirates from the sea. People who are acquainted with only present conditions cannot but be astonished on learning of the losses that formerly took place on ocean voyages. Of the eighty-six ships sent to the East by the English East India Company in the first twenty-one years of its existence (1601–21) only thirty-six returned with cargoes, the others having been captured, lost, or become worn out. In the ten years 1590 to 1599, thirty-three large carracks left India for Europe, but of these only sixteen reached Lisbon. On the route from India to Japan at that time we are told that of nine starting on the three years' enterprise, only four might be expected to return. The average life of a carrack is given as apparently about three years. Heavy as were these initial losses it was possible, only a few decades later, to take out a marine insurance policy from Macassar (Makasar, Celebes) to London at a rate of 5 per cent. This is the rate quoted in a Lloyd's policy dated February 1656. It is the oldest marine insurance policy in the United Kingdom and is a forerunner of the invisible exports (broadly, payments for services) which play an important part in the United Kingdom balance of payments today.

Ocean trade routes

The route by which goods are conveyed by sea to their ultimate destination depends not only on the relative situations of the place of origin and destination, but on many circumstances, some connected with the nature of the commodities, some with the type of vessel used.

To understand how the nature of the commodities carried affects the route, two important considerations must be borne in mind. First, the transfer of goods from one vehicle (whether ship, railway wagon, or truck) to another adds to the cost of movement. It is therefore an advantage to convey goods directly from the port which serves the districts where they are obtained to that which serves the district in which they are ultimately sold. But, second, it is cheapest to convey goods in the largest possible vessels, provided those vessels can be filled. This frequently makes it cheaper to incur extra costs in unloading and reloading (handling expenses), and send goods first in smaller quantities to a great port, from which they are sent in large vessels to another great port, from which again they may be sent by sea to some other port nearer their final destination. Bulky goods such as coal, timber, ores and clays, are most likely to be carried direct, for the quantity of such goods that may be required in a small district may be enough to fill a larger or smaller ship, and thus bring about the greatest possible saving in handling. That is why so many small British and Irish seaports import timber directly from abroad, why small ports in Cornwall and Devon send off entire cargoes of china and other clay; and why formerly so many British ports sometimes exported coal in small vessels and so many small foreign ports received British coal. Such bulky commodities as these are often useful as return or ballast cargoes, helping to reduce the freight charge in one direction by forming the whole or part of a cargo in the opposite direction. The former importance of coal to British commerce in this way has often been emphasised, but salt, cement, clays, and even bricks also aid British commerce in the same way. China clay sometimes serves as a return cargo from England even to the United States. Though in value bricks form an absolutely insignificant article of export from the United Kingdom, the weight of bricks annually exported before the First World War was probably one-fourth or one-fifth of the weight of cotton piece goods exported. Similarly it was return cargoes of wood pulp and other timber products that favoured the temporary rise after that war of an export trade in coal from the United States to Sweden.

On the other hand, the economy of carrying in large ships explains why much of the tea, coffee, spices and other commodities sent from the East to the United Kingdom come first to London in ships largely filled with bulky commodities. Of all these commodities much greater quantities are used in London itself than in any other centre of the country; but great quantities are also sent away by rail from London, and great quantities by sea to both British and foreign ports for which London acts as an entrepôt. The daily shipping reports show how many ships come to the large ports laden with 'general cargoes', that is, cargoes composed of many kinds of goods brought together to get the advantage of carriage in large ships. Naturally, most 'liners' which run to definite schedules, on definite routes, carry general cargoes. 'Tramps', on the other hand, tend to specialise in bulk cargoes. It is obvious that the advantage of carrying in large ships will be the greater the longer the distance that goods are so carried. This is why the eastern goods mentioned come chiefly to London in the first instance, and also the reason why the bulk of Australasian and Cape wool imported into

England comes first to London, even though not a pound of it is worked up there, but all has to be sent away either to Bradford or some other town.

Economy of transport is a secondary consideration in the case of perishable goods, such as fresh meat, vegetables, fruit and flowers, butter and eggs; or goods of high value in proportion to their bulk, such as mails or valuable manufactured goods. These are taken by the quickest routes in spite of the increased cost per mile, and may often be transfered from land to sea or air if necessary, for the sake of speed.

Now that ocean routes depend so largely on economic factors, it is of interest to record how winds and currents formerly were of paramount importance. A sailing vessel taking the outward route from the English Channel to New Zealand kept well to the east of the Azores so as not to have southwesterlies as headwinds and so as to get the benefit of the northeast trades as soon as possible. After crossing the belt of calms and variable winds the vessel made for the coast of South America, at first at right angles to the southeast trades, and afterwards, from about 21° S, getting the benefit of the winds that circulate in the 'horse latitudes' of the South Atlantic. These winds, blowing, in the west of the area referred to, from about 20° to 30° or 35° S, parallel to the coast of South America, ultimately brought the vessel to the 'roaring forties', which carried her steadily eastwards south of the Cape of Good Hope and Tasmania to New Zealand. On the homeward voyage the same winds carried the vessel south of Cape Horn, after which the vessel stood well out to sea and sailed northward through the middle of the Atlantic more or less obliquely to both trade winds and, keeping well to the west of the Azores, had a good chance of favourable winds — the prevailing southwesterlies — up the Strait of Dover.

Steamer routes are almost independent of winds and currents. Where practicable, the shortest route from port to port is taken, and that is a route following an arc of a great circle of the earth, in other words, a circle of which the centre of the earth is the centre. Hence, where the route is from north to south a meridian is followed, but where the route is from east to west it is only on the equator that the route lies along a parallel of latitude. The further north an east to west route lies in the northern hemisphere the more will the shortest route curve towards the north from the parallel connecting places at the ends of the route. In the northern hemisphere, if the route is to a port lying northeast of the starting point, the great circle route will be represented on a map drawn on Mercator's projection* by a curved line lying to the northwest of the straight line connecting the starting point with the

---

* Mercator's is the only projection on which all directions referred to points of the compass are shown by straight lines. That is why this projection is nearly always used for marine charts.

destination. It is only on a globe that great circle routes can be at once seen and measured. This is done by means of a flexible strip of brass called a quadrant, marked in degrees of the earth's equator according to the scale of the globe for which it is constructed. Each degree (approximately 69 statute miles) represents 60 nautical miles,* the unit in which ocean distances are usually stated.

To take great circle courses, however, is not always practicable. The relations of sea and land may prevent it, and so also may the character of the climate. For example, the great circle route from Cape Town to Wellington, New Zealand, goes to the south of the Antarctic Circle, and for that reason a more northerly though longer route is preferred. Among frequented ocean routes those in which great circle sailing causes the most marked deviation from the parallels of latitude are those of the North Pacific, where very wide stretches of ocean have to be crossed between the ports of North America and those of eastern Asia. Yokohama is south of San Francisco, yet a steamer sailing for Yokohama from San Francisco (37.45° N) begins by sailing northwestwards, and describes a curve which rises to about 48° N. In the narrower waters of the North Atlantic the curve of the east—west great circle routes to the north of the parallels is not so striking, especially since Newfoundland obstructs the great circle from the south of Ireland to all American ports north of Cape Hatteras. The trend of the coastline south of that cape is along the line of a great circle passing thence to the south of Ireland, and so it follows that the routes to all American ports between Nova Scotia and the Gulf of Mexico are almost identical from about the meridian of 60° W (i.e. just west of Newfoundland) eastwards to the English Channel. This is accordingly the busiest of the ocean trade routes and lanes are prescribed for the sake of safety, varying according to the period of the year.

In some cases the route is modified by the position of refuelling bases. Next to the North Atlantic route, the most frequented, until it was closed in 1967, was through the Suez Canal, which was the meeting-place of all European and North Atlantic lines to East Africa and the Far East, and most of those to Australia and New Zealand. The part from the Strait of Gibraltar to the mouth of the Gulf of Aden is common to most of the lines following these routes. On this section the chief fuelling stations are Gibraltar, Marseille, Algiers, Port Said, and Aden. These fuelling stations are also great entrepôts. At Gibraltar and Port Said many goods are landed by vessels entering the Mediterranean from the west or east respectively for ports of the Mediterranean or the Black Sea. Aden is a place at which goods for East Africa can be dropped and picked up by steamers belonging to eastern Asiatic and Australasian lines. Colombo is the fuelling station and entrepôt where the lines that pass south of Australia diverge from the Far Eastern

* One nautical mile = 1.1508 statute miles = 1.852 km.

route. Singapore is the chief fuelling station and entrepôt, and Djakarta a minor but still important port, for vessels going further east, and at one or other of these the lines diverge that go north of Australia. The main route to the east continues on to Hong Kong, Shanghai, Nagasaki, and Yokohama, all great fuelling stations and to two great entrepôts, Hong Kong for southern China, and (until the Communist regime) Shanghai for the Yangtze valley and northern China. Important branch lines run from Singapore to the ports of Thailand and Vietnam, and to Manila in the Philippine Islands.

In the North Atlantic Ocean, Las Palmas, Tenerife and Madeira are important ports of call both on the route to Cape Town and on the route to all the South American ports south of Cape St Roque, at the eastern shoulder of the continent. St Vincent, one of the Cape Verde Islands, is also a well-known fuelling base for ships trading with South America. Norfolk, on the coast of Virginia, a place of shipment of the excellent steam coal of the Pocahontas coalfield, distant about 650 km (400 miles) by rail, was frequently visited for coal by vessels returning from the Gulf of Mexico to the English Channel or the Irish Sea; and after the opening of the Panama Canal the adjacent port of Newport News became a great coaling place on that route. St Thomas, one of the American Virgin Islands, and St Lucia, one of the Windward Islands (Commonwealth), are fuelling stations in the West Indies too, visited on routes from North to South America or from Europe to Central and northern South America.

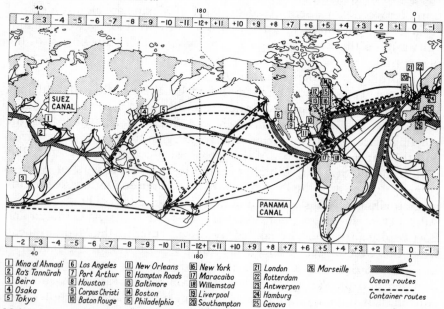

1 Mina al Ahmadi	6 Los Angeles	11 New Orleans	16 New York	21 London	26 Marseille
2 Ra's Tannūrah	7 Port Arthur	12 Hampton Roads	17 Maracaibo	22 Rotterdam	
3 Beira	8 Houston	13 Baltimore	18 Willemstad	23 Antwerpen	Ocean routes
4 Osaka	9 Corpus Christi	14 Boston	19 Liverpool	24 Hamburg	
5 Tokyo	10 Baton Rouge	15 Philadelphia	20 Southampton	25 Genova	Container routes

Main ocean trade routes and principal ports.

Standard time zones are shown on the north and south margins of the map.

In the South Atlantic the chief coaling and oiling stations are Cape Town and Buenos Aires. On the American seaboard of the Pacific the great fuelling station between San Francisco and Concepción Bay (Chile), where coalmines exist close to the sea, is Balbao, at the entrance to the Panama Canal. Honolulu is a fuelling base on the routes from western North America to Australia and New Zealand, and Durban rose to importance on the Indian Ocean, drawing coal supplies from the Natal coalfields.

In 1965, some 1 700m. tons of cargo were carried on the world's ocean routes, as against 500m. tons in 1949 and 1 000m. in 1960. It is estimated that the total will rise to 2 800m. tons by 1975 and 3 500m. tons by 1980, partly as the result of the increasing numbers of bulk carriers (oil and mineral) in the world's fleets and partly as the result of increased average speed which gives shorter round-trip timings. The North Atlantic routes are by far the busiest, followed by the routes from Europe to Central and South America. The closure of the Suez Canal in 1967 changed the pattern of shipping routes overnight and forced all vessels to use the route around the Cape of Good Hope. This route was already becoming more important because hundreds of the largest tankers were too big for the Canal or, at best could pass through only in ballast or if partly laden. The resultant increase in voyage times was greatest for the Red Sea ports and Aden, but the difference decreases rapidly as voyages lengthen — so that the journey from Japan or New Zealand to the United Kingdom around the Cape is little longer than the journey through the Suez Canal.

Aviation

The most striking development in twentieth-century transport has been the coming of the aeroplane. The English Channel was first crossed by a heavier-than-air machine in 1910. Both aeroplanes and airships developed rapidly, but the airship did not long survive. The German type, the Zeppelin, named after its designer Count Zeppelin, met with some success in civil transport, but British and American experiments were abandoned after repeated disasters, and German interest also practically ceased in 1937 when the latest Zeppelin burst into flames in New Jersey after a transatlantic flight. On the other hand, heavier-than-air machines became an increasingly important factor in modern transport. Between the two great wars the world was covered by a network of regular air services, transoceanic and transcontinental as well as national. British, Dutch, French, Belgian and American companies were prominent in developing long-distance routes. When the Second World War broke out the principal British Company, Imperial Airways, was operating regular services, mostly with flying boats, linking up with the Middle East, India, Burma, Siam, Singapore, Hong Kong and Australia,

Table 4 — Aircraft performance 1930s to 1980s

Decade	Speed (mph)	Range (miles)	Passenger capacity
1930	160	750	30
1940	300	4 000	70
1950	500	4 800	80
1960	575	6 000	145
1970	625	4 500	350*
1980	1 500	4 500	150†

* In addition, the Boeing 747 can carry 24 tons of cargo.
† The supersonic aircraft of the 1980s will provide fast travel to complement the mass travel offered by the new giant aircraft of the 1970s.

as well as with central, west and South Africa. In 1940 Imperial Airways was merged with British Airways into a single government-owned but independently managed corporation, known as British Overseas Airways Corporation (BOAC). This was employed in the war in maintaining lines of communication, opening new routes, and transporting military personnel, supplies, urgent dispatches and so on; its aircraft flew over 57m. miles on war service, and carried nearly 300 000 passengers and 250 000 tons of cargo and mail.

Since the Second World War all aspects of aviation have developed rapidly, in speed and size of aircraft, in the capacity of the world's airlines, and in the completion of a universal network of air routes. Table 4 shows, in generalised terms, the improved performance of typical aircraft in each decade since the 1930s. Throughout the 1960s the number of passengers travelling by air increased at a rate of some 12 per cent each year. Across the North Atlantic, for instance, 36 per cent travelled by air in 1953. By 1963 the figure was 78 per cent and still rising. In 1969 the world's airlines carried 289m. passengers and it is estimated that this figure could well double by 1975, and double again by 1980. Aviation is now by far the prime means of passenger movement on international routes.

Air transport, like ocean transport, requires both routes and ports. Since two-thirds of the earth's surface is covered by water, some 85 per cent of the international air routes are over the seas; but the speed with which international frontiers are crossed and the increasing congestion of the air routes have dictated the need for rapid and detailed international agreements on the standardisation of communication links, navigational aids, airport facilities and so on. Such standardisation is obviously essential for flight safety when an aircraft crossing the Atlantic in a few hours must pass through several different national control zones; or on a flight from London via Moscow to Tokyo, when 10 000 km (6 220 miles) are covered in 14½ hours flying time. As with

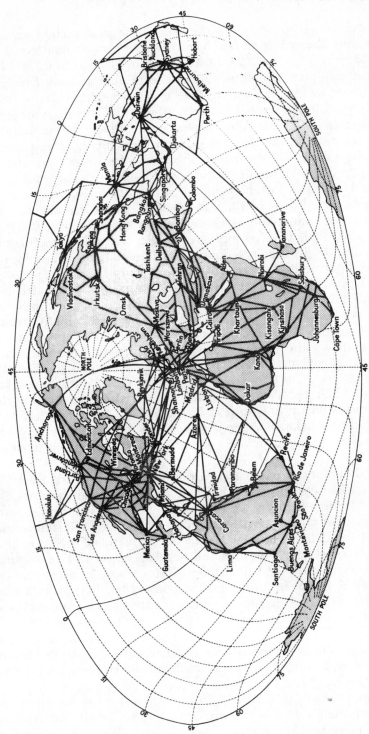

Main air routes of the world

103

ocean travel, the air routes follow the lines of the great circle. They are, of course, not diverted by surface barriers and are largely unaffected by climatic barriers. Flying at 12 000 to 18 000 m (40 000 to 60 000 ft), land masses and arctic conditions do not force aircraft away from the shortest routes as they do shipping. On the other hand, since movement by air is essentially movement between urban areas, and since the great bulk of the traffic is between the few great urban centres, there is greater congestion on the air lanes than on the shipping lanes, particularly in the vicinity of the larger airports, with aircraft arriving as frequently as two each minute at peak periods. The aircraft has therefore played a major part in fostering international cooperation. An international conference in Chicago in 1944 paved the way for the formation of the International Civil Aviation Organisation (ICAO) in 1947. By 1957 there were seventy-one member states. The chief task of the Organisation is the introduction of international rules in the interests of safety and of the orderly development of civil flying.

In the United Kingdom the Civil Aviation Act of 1946 created two new corporations: British European Airways (BEA) and British South American Airways; but in 1949 the latter was merged in BOAC, which in addition to the long-distance commonwealth services is responsible for the routes to the United States pioneered during the war. Each corporation is government-owned, with its own board of directors appointed by the Minister of Civil Aviation, who has the right to say what routes shall be flown. BEA and BOAC were linked under the British Airways Board on 1 April 1972 and as British Airways they now operate the main scheduled services; but private companies may run charter services, and some private companies are operating scheduled air services.

The total number of passengers carried was 15m. in 1961. By 1973 the numbers had risen to 43m., handled at forty-six main airports, 91 per cent of those passengers were handled by the twelve major airports and no less than 60 per cent passed through London (Heathrow and Gatwick). Of the 20m. who were leaving on international flights, no less than 75 per cent passed through the London Airports. These figures should be compared with the United States whose passenger movements totalled 162m. in 1969, no less than 146m. being on internal flights. With extensive territory, widely scattered urban centres and freedom from political barriers, the United States leads the world in air transport facilities. Over half of all the passengers travelling by air and 70 per cent of the air freight of the world are carried by United States airlines, and over three-quarters of each are movements on internal flights within the United States.

Although primarily a passenger-carrying vehicle, the aircraft is of growing importance in the movement of freight. Small and valuable items, including mail, have always been carried along with passengers (c.f. the important contribution made to ocean freighting by the passenger liners which also run to fixed schedules) but the 1960s have shown a rapid expansion of air freighting with an annual growth of over 20 per cent and a matching increase in the number of aircraft employed solely for cargo carrying. Loads of 30 to 40 tons are commonplace, up to a maximum of 140 tons which can be carried by the United States' giant C5 freighter. Such loads are small in shipping terms, but the speed of air movement adds greatly to the capacity available. Nonetheless the total weight of cargo moved by air is very small when compared with the weight moved by sea and by pipelines. Air cargo tends to be limited to perishable, high value and low density items which can support the higher cost of carriage by air. By value, however, the part played by air movement is more important. In 1973, for instance, London Airport (Heathrow) was, in terms of value of goods cleared, the third largest port in the United Kingdom (after the sea ports of London and Liverpool). Goods cleared totalled £2 111m., nearly 17 per cent of total UK exports. London is the fourth largest air cargo airport in the world, after New York (John Kennedy), Chicago (O'Hara) and Los Angeles International, these three airports reflecting once again the predominance in world air traffic of internal air movement within the United States. The giant passenger aircraft of the 1970s are also available as cargo carriers, and their increased size makes air movement possible for a far wider range of high value items, e.g. cars, computers, machine tools, etc. The increased use of prepacked cargo containers, supplemented by surface delivery arrangements to and from the airport, will also make for movement direct from point of origin to destination without intermediate handling — an important consideration generally, but especially in the air freighting of flowers, fruit and vegetables. Bulk movement of low value items is never likely to be made by air, except in very special circumstances. The lighter nature of air freight is shown by the average loading density which is assessed at 500 kg per 2.83 cu m (100 sq ft), as against the 1 000 kg per 2.83 cu m in shipping movement.

Apart from its importance in the field of transport, the aircraft (and the aerospace industry) plays an important part in the economy of the highly industrialised nations. The industry demands highly skilled labour and advanced technology. These are reflected in the costs of the end product. The cost of Rolls-Royce engines, for instance, has risen from 1953 (the Dart) at £7 000, through 1964 (the Spey) at £65 000 to 1970 (The RB-211) at £250 000; and of these costs, 5 per cent only is the cost of raw materials. Each new generation of aircraft brings further advances in techniques which can be applied to many other industries; advances in structures and structure testing, in metallurgy, electronics, glass, fuels and food preparation. Development into space has furnished satellites which, orbiting permanently in the same position relative to the earth's surface, will provide worldwide facilities for communications (sound and vision), weather forecasting (vital to the tracking of typhoons, cyclones, etc.), navigational aids of universal applicability, and aircraft control. Satellites can also bring a new dimension to mapping, crop control and exploration of the earth's resources.

Handling

The liberalisation of tariff restrictions since the Second World War has been accompanied by a rapid growth in world trade; in particular in industrial goods between the highly industrialised nations and, to an unprecedented degree, in the bulk movement of commodities such as fuels and minerals. This bulk movement of comparatively low value items emphasises the importance of what has long been a major component in the cost of transportation − the cost of handling, i.e. the loading and unloading of goods and their transfer between one means of transport and another. As transportation becomes more efficient, so the costs of handling become more significant. For instance, it has been calculated that a ton of coal can be carried 1 600 km (1 000 miles), on the Great Lakes between Buffalo and Duluth for about the cost of shovelling it from the sidewalk into the purchaser's cellar. Handling costs can be reduced by reducing the number of times goods must be transferred, by aggregating goods into the largest mass possible, and by mechanising the handling processes.

Before the opening of the Panama Canal goods sent from a factory in New York to a customer in Ecuador had to be loaded and unloaded ten times; with the opening of the Canal this was reduced to four times. Similarly changes of gauge between railway systems make extra handling necessary. Improved and standardised means of transport have steadily reduced charges during the twentieth century, but the more recent improvements have been in the handling methods themselves. As the carrying capacity of railway wagons, ships and aeroplanes has increased, so handling techniques must be developed to speed the loading and unloading processes so that the turn-round time (the non-productive time) of the transport vehicle can be reduced to a minimum. The railways are still the largest carriers of bulk by land, although pipelines have already replaced them for specific products, such as the bulk movement of natural gas. In Canada, for instance, mile-long coal and ore trains carry 10 000 tons at a time, and with automatic rotary dumpers the contents of each wagon can be tipped into a ship's hold in 30 sec, without disengaging the couplings. Apart from the movement of minerals in bulk from mine to port or consumer, the railways can also offer a fast main line link between major termini for mixed goods delivered to them in bulk, that is in containers (see below). In the United Kingdom this system offers an overnight trunkline service moving some 500 000 20-ton containers a year with distribution to destination by road, the whole operation being limited to the movement of a single container to load and unload each wagon or truck. Across Canada and Siberia such a system could offer a rail bridge to the Far East. Containers shipped from Europe to Japan could arrive in twenty-five days using Canadian railways between Halifax and Vancouver — as against thirty-five days by sea through the Panama Canal, and forty-five days round the Cape of Good Hope. But as double handling would be involved at both ends of the rail link the cost would be 50 per cent greater than direct movement by sea. The Trans—Siberian rail bridge offers great saving of time, although yet further handling is involved where the USSR broad gauge railway meets the European standard gauge. The railway track (in gauge, gradient and curves) places finite limitations on the sizes of wagons and the speed of trains. At sea, however, the growth of bulk carrying vehicles has been of far greater magnitude.

In 1970 60 per cent of the world's gross tonnage was accounted for by bulk carriers — of oil, minerals or containers. The giant oil tankers epitomise the advantages of bulk movement combined with mechanised handling. Loaded and unloaded by pumps and pipelines, their increasing size is accompanied by decreasing size of crew and reduced cost per gallon of oil carried. The operating costs of a 50 000 ton tanker with a crew of sixty-two has been given as $4.91 per ton of crude oil. For a 170 000 ton tanker the figure is $2.54, and for a 250 000 tonner with a crew of thirty-six — $2.26. Other bulk carriers are designed for single cargoes, such as the iron ore carriers; or for alternative cargoes such as the OBO (oil, bulk, ore) which offer a versatile capacity for return loads, e.g. oil from Middle East to Australia, iron ore from Australia to Japan, steel from Japan to Middle East. All these giant ships demand major capital investment in new ports, dry docks, and loading facilities — as for example at Port Hedland in Western Australia where a 72 000 ton iron ore carrier can be loaded within twenty-four hours.

The major improvement in handling facilities in the 1960s has been the development of containers. These are in effect large 'boxes' made of steel or aluminium alloy in an agreed pattern of sizes to assist in standardisation of ships' holds, dock handling and road transport facilities throughout the world. A wide range of general cargo commodities that require to be moved from a single point of origin to a single destination can be loaded into a container, locked and moved successively by road, rail and sea with the minimum of handling and the maximum of security. Against the obvious advantages must be set the problems of collecting together the goods to fill the containers (typical size 20 ft x 8 ft x 8 ft, carrying 20 tons), and the administrative problems of insurance and customs clearance for single containers carrying mixed loads to mixed (ultimate) destinations. Again, capital outlay is considerable — on special ships, dockside cranes, container hoists, etc., but the savings are also considerable. Canadian Pacific Railways, for instance, replaced eleven conventional cargo ships with 850 000 tons a year capacity by four container ships which offered a total of 2m. tons a year capacity. This increased capacity coming partly from the faster speed of the new ships, but mainly from reduced time of turn-round in port, the container ship being loaded in forty-eight hours as against ten days for normal mixed cargo. Similarly on the United Kingdom to Australia route, nine new container ships will replace some eighty to ninety conventional cargo lines — a container ship spending only 10 per cent of its life in port as against the general cargo liner's 50 per cent. It has been calculated that the average dock worker handling mixed cargo with slings, pallets, etc., could clear 25 freight tons in a week; with containerised cargo he can clear 500 tons a week, entailing far less physical effort. On the other hand, of course, the containers themselves must be loaded ('stuffed') and this is still largely a labour-intensive operation carried out at container depots (or individual factories where justified) where goods are aggregated into container loads by destinations, and packed with care to ensure minimum damage on voyage. The loaded container reduces pilferage and loss in transit to a minimum, and deterioration of contents on voyage can be avoided by use of special containers with controlled internal environment, e.g. insulated, refrigerated, protected against magnetic interference, etc. Lastly, to be efficient, container ships require twoway traffic. Since a great variety of products can be carried, this requirement can be met between the industrialised nations, and in the 1970s all the main shipping routes of the world will offer container services as the special port handling facilities become available. In 1970 the world total of container ships was 1.9m. gross tons, and it is estimated that it will be 14m. gross tons by 1980, replacing some 800 to 1 000 conventional cargo ships.

Handling facilities for movement of goods by road and air are also improving. Trucks carrying 30 to 40 tons compete successfully with the railways for movement of containers up to distances of 160 km (100 miles), and over greater distances when they need not be offloaded for short sea voyages, e.g. when the loaded vehicle can roll straight on to the ferry and then roll off to complete its delivery journey. Handling of freight by air in the 1970s will be facilitated by the introduction of wide-beam cargo airliners and a corresponding increase in the use of air containers — lightweight and contoured to fit the aircraft. Even the simple assembly of loads on to pallets (flat loading platforms which, with their load, can be handled mechanically) represents a 50 per cent saving over handling and stacking of individual items. Aircraft containers share with surface containers the further advantage that the individual packing of commodities carried can be less robust than would otherwise be necessary, and for movement by air this is an important reduction of uneconomic payload.

The other major postwar handling development has been the great extension of pipelines to carry crude oil, petroleum and chemical products, natural and liquid gas, and solids such as coal and chalk in the form of slurries. Grain can also be handled like a liquid and piped mechanically. Pipelines have long been used for carrying water and sewage, and the transmission of electric power by transmission lines is a similar handling principle. Modern pipelines cover great distances and have great capacity. Most of the oil pipelines are 1 067 mm (42 in) in diameter, while there are plans for 2 540 mm (100 in) trunk pipelines for gas in USSR. Pipelines of 3 200 km (2 000 miles) and more are in use, for example, supplying Canadian natural gas from Alberta to California, and Texan oil to the northeastern United States. The gas and oil pipelines of the United States provide the most extensive network of any country, but construction is in hand in all countries. In 1969, for instance, a further 42 000 km (26 000 miles) was added to the world's pipelines, and lines are continually being built to bring remote resources to seaports, e.g. oil from the northern slopes of Alaska, or when feasible straight to the consumers, for example Siberian gas to Europe.

Communications

Another essential prerequisite for the efficient exchange of commodities is an adequate system of communication. The growth of commerce that followed the Industrial Revolution gave rise to the need for a reliable means for transferring information, and this was met by the development of cheap postage. The penny post was introduced in the United Kingdom in 1840, and though two world wars have increased the nominal postage rates, they are little if any more in relation to the value of money then and now. The International Postal Union owed its foundation to a conference held at Berne in 1874. The practical use of the electric telegraph dates only from 1846 and the first message through a submarine cable (between the South Foreland and the coast of France) was sent on 13 November 1851. In 1866 the first successful submarine cable was laid across the Atlantic Ocean and with the completion of the cable from Vancouver by way of Fanning, Fiji, and Norfolk Islands to New Zealand and Australia in 1902, all the oceans have their opposite sides connected by this means. Communication by wireless telegraphy on the Marconi system was established between the Lizard, in Cornwall, and the Isle of Wight, a distance of 320 km (200 miles), in January 1901, and in 1907 regular communication by the same means was established between Clifden, County Galway, Ireland, and Glace Bay, Nova Scotia. The telephone first became known in its present form at the Philadelphia Exhibition in 1876. Since 1914 rapid progress has been made with wireless telephony, and by 1919 this was associated with direction-finding apparatus, making it possible for ships to ascertain their positions at sea by taking bearings on shore wireless stations.

The first wireless conversation between London and the United States was held on 15 January 1923. Regular telephonic communication was established early in 1927. It would be difficult to exaggerate the importance of broadcasting information and news by wireless, which is now general. The effect is most marked in the less accessible portions of regions like Australia where individual farms may be separated by a score of kilometres and formerly received a newspaper perhaps once a week or once a month, but are now in instantaneous receipt of news from the great centres. A still more recent development in wireless is the beam system whereby messages, instead of being broadcast, can be projected in a definite direction. The beam system was used between England and Canada in 1926. Major improvements have continued. By cable many messages can be sent simultaneously or many conversations held over a single wire. Satellites in orbit round the earth are used for reflecting radio waves and in 1968—69 a worldwide communications network came into use for both sound and vision.

These successive improvements in communication facilities have all been aimed at increasing the capacity of the relaying system and the speed with which messages can be passed. However, the growth of trade since the Second World War has resulted in a growth of administrative communications that in certain areas can no longer be handled efficiently by manual means. It is therefore timely that the wartime advances made in electronics have provided the basis for the latest development in communications: the introduction of electronic data (information) processing machines, i.e. the computers. Originally (1945—55) employed to speed the solution of mathematical calculations, computers have developed rapidly (1960—70) to take over routine office work and to control intricate industrial flow processes, such as petrochemicals, machinery, etc. Rapid advances in technology have resulted in great capacity becoming available at steadily reduced costs. For example, the handling of a batch of information that would have cost £125 by manual means in 1950 could be cleared by a computer for 11*d.* in 1960 and, by a later model, for less than 1p in 1970, the time taken having fallen from a matter of hours to a few seconds. This ability to handle a great mass of information has resulted in the need to speed communications so that ample data is available to employ the computer effectively. This improvement in data transmission means that information can be made available which is up to date within a matter of minutes on such diverse subjects as airline and hotel reservations, air freight opportunities, market states and prices, stock exchange prices, meteorological data, banking services, etc. Most of these are available on a national scale in 1970 and plans are in hand to extend them internationally in the near future. Communications have therefore come to full maturity — if one contrasts the merchant venturer who launched his argosy and had to wait six months or more to find out what he had purchased, with the modern importer who should shortly be able to receive information on quality, quantity and price in real time, that is as each of these factors varies in the world trade markets.

Commercial and industrial towns

Clearly there are certain places in which it is most convenient for the exchange of commodities to take place. These are great business centres, commercial towns; and the situation of those towns in many cases shows that there are special conveniences for exchange that have favoured their rise and growth. All towns are more or less centres of exchange. Whatever else they may be, they are places where stores of goods in common request are kept, so that the inhabitants of the district around may be able to supply their needs.

The special advantages leading to the growth of great business centres may be of very various kinds. The mere fact that a town lies about the middle of a densely peopled district is likely to make it the most convenient place of exchange for the products of that district and for articles brought from more distant parts. So, too, towns situated where a number of roads converge are likely to grow into more important business centres. Since roads from level country will naturally converge towards passes which lead over hills or mountains, towns are apt to arise, in such situations, at the meeting of hill and plain. In like manner, many towns have grown up at spots where there was a convenient crossing-place over a river by ford or bridge; and many others exist at the confluence of navigable rivers, at the head of navigation, at marked bends on rivers, or where the superficial configuration leads to the convergence of numerous railways, as at Chicago, Toronto, Winnipeg, or Atlanta.

Business towns likewise spring up in many situations in which the circumstances necessitate a change in the mode of carriage. Of this class of towns, seaports are the most numerous examples. Where goods have to be transferred from any mode of land carriage to ships, there must necessarily be a town to accommodate those engaged in this transfer. Hence it is that so many of the large towns of the world are seaports, the relative importance of which depends chiefly on the productiveness and accessibility of the regions served by them, or, in a single word, of their hinterlands, and the facilities which they afford to shipping.

The term hinterland is one that may be used with reference both to a

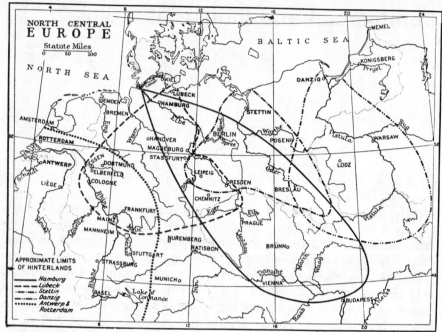

Hinterlands of some European ports.

This map has been retained on account of its historic interest. Proposed by Chisholm, it is an early example of the concept of hinterlands.

single seaport and to a seaboard on which there are several seaports, and may be defined as the land which lies behind a seaport or a seaboard and supplies the bulk of the exports, and in which are distributed the bulk of the imports of that seaport or seaboard. The necessity for the first clause in this definition arises from the way in which the outline of the land sometimes determines the port with which an inland region communicates in its relations with different parts of the world. Thus the West Riding of Yorkshire may be included in the hinterland of Liverpool for Irish and even for much transatlantic trade, but for North Sea trade it obviously belongs to the hinterland of Hull, Goole, or Grimsby. The Elbe basin forms the chief part of the hinterland of Hamburg in relation to all North Sea and oceanic traffic, but is included in that of Lübeck in relation to the Baltic. Toulouse belongs to the hinterland of Bordeaux for all traffic except that of the Mediterranean, for which it would make use of Sète or even of Marseille.

The word, which is of German origin, was introduced into English about 1884, in connection with the discussions that arose on the occupation of parts of the West African coast. It came at once into general use from the fact of its meeting an obvious requirement. A later extension of hinterland has been to include the land tributary to an urban centre, independently of whether that urban centre is a port.

From some of the examples given, it will be observed that the hinterlands of different ports may overlap even in relation to the same seas. This arises from the influence on a seaport of shipping facilities and facilities for communication with the hinterland. The hinterlands of Hull and Goole to a large extent coincide, but where the economy of transport effected by the use of large ships is the chief consideration, Hull will be preferred on account of the superior facilities there afforded, but where smaller vessels serve, Goole may have the preference in consequence of being nearer the hinterland. The trade of Québec may encroach on the hinterland of Montréal, but its distance from that hinterland will prevent it from doing so except in the case of such traffic as is greatly promoted by rapidity of transit, such as passenger traffic and traffic in the more perishable or more valuable and less bulky commodities. Trade rivalries and the nature of the internal means of communication also affect the competition of ports in the same hinterland, as in the case of Grimsby and Hull. Lastly, it should be pointed out that the extent and importance of a hinterland may be greatly increased by improvements in the means of internal communication, by improvements in the port itself, and particularly by adjustment of inland freight rates.

The necessity for change in the mode of carriage also helps to explain why many towns are situated, or were founded, at the highest point to which rivers could be navigated, or could be ascended by vessels of a certain size; many where a rapid hinders, or a fall prevents, further navigation. To one or other such points goods are, or were formerly, conveyed by boats, and a town sprang up where they were landed. Other towns on navigable rivers are situated where there is a sudden change in the direction of the stream, because at that point goods had to be landed which were not intended to follow the new direction taken by the river. Even where the navigation of rivers has ceased to be important, the study of navigable rivers has a permanent place in economic geography on account of their having determined the original sites of towns, although subsequent growth may be due to other causes, and to the provision of other means of communication. It has been said by Moulton that the location of every city of importance in the eastern part of the United States, with the single exception of Indianapolis, was determined by the influence of water transport.

Many large towns have sprung up where there is abundance of coal, or coal and iron, or oil, or extensive waterpower, the mainsprings of modern industry; and all such towns are more or less business centres. Yet they are often far from being business centres in proportion to the extent of their production. Where numerous manufacturing towns exist on a great coalfield the business of exchange may be centred in one of them that is not pre-eminently itself a manufacturing town. The great magnitude of the business of exchange in such a region is adverse to the

115

carrying on of manufacturers in its business centre, for the cost of land, owing to the requirements of merchants and others for offices, etc., becomes so great that it is too expensive to erect large factories. Hence it is that Manchester, in which, according to the estimate for a local manufacturer, is sold probably three-quarters of the cotton yarn spun, and even a larger proportion of the cotton cloth woven in the United Kingdom, is less of a manufacturing town than many of the smaller towns round about.

What has just been said makes it clear that a variety of influences must be kept in mind as affecting the localisation of industry. These work in combination, in some cases one or two of them having the chief efficacy, in others another group, and unfortunately neither individually nor in association is it possible to measure them. The main localising influences may be considered under the heads of the market, the labour supply, the cost of land, the situation of raw material, the nature and situation of the sources of power, the value of the commodities produced in relation to the cost of their production, governmental influence, and finally the supply of capital.

In connection with influences coming under any of the heads enumerated, two general facts are worthy of note. First, the psychological action of the sense of opportunity as a stimulus to exertion can hardly be exaggerated. 'What is wanted,' says Bertrand Russell, 'in order to keep men full of vitality is opportunity, not only security.' Marshall remarked 'that a man's energies are at their best when he is emerging from poverty and distress into the command of great opportunities'. It is the great function of capital to create opportunities, but economic development is likely to be most rapid where opportunities are easiest to turn to account.

The second general fact is that greater economies can usually be effected where it is profitable to work on a large scale. It is obvious that the profitableness of large-scale operations must depend on the adequacy of the market, which again is governed by various conditions as (a) the number of people in the market; (b) the purchasing power of the people; (c) the nature of the commodity for which a market is sought — cheap goods for mass distribution or more valuable commodities for limited distribution; (d) facilities for transport as enlarging the range of the market. Here it may be noted that the aim of a preferential tariff is to preserve a home market for the favoured industry. Where the protection afforded is absolute, the whole country embraced by the tariff forms a local market for the protected industry.

As to labour, its affect on the location of industry will depend on (a) the proportion of labour costs to the cost of the finished product, (b) wage differences between different regions, (c) the skills available — in this case the pool of labour provided in an established industrial region is a major factor, and (d) the local mobility of labour. The cost of land is another consideration; the higher prices of the already developed urban area being offset by the accompanying advantages of a local market and of a wide range of supporting industries, services, transport facilities, etc. The supply of capital is, with labour, the second major factor in production. Here again it is more likely to be forthcoming in the short term in a developed area with its existing banking and financing services.

The cost of transportation, both of raw materials and of the finished product, has long been a major consideration in the location of heavy industries, as have the sources of power and the location of the raw materials themselves. Coal in particular has traditionally played a major part in promoting the growth of industrial towns. If the mines are large and numerous in one locality, the population of miners with their dependants and the shopkeepers required to supply their wants will form a considerable town; and this population is generally increased by the industries to which the presence of the coal gives rise. It is evident, however, from a consideration of the facts of industrial distribution in different parts of the world, that the influence of coal in attracting industries to the coalfields varies in different circumstances. The major coalfields of England and Scotland, of Germany, Belgium, and the north of France have all become seats of varied industry, but in the United States, the greatest coal-producing country in the world, most of the manufacturing towns lie hundreds of kilometres away from the mines, even when the power which they used was mainly derived from coal; and some of the leading textile manufacturing towns of both Germany and France are also at a great distance from the mines.

To understand the very powerful influence coal has had in attracting manufacturers to the place of its production, one must bear in mind that the influence exerted by raw materials is dependant on the percentage of the raw material that enters into the final product. A raw material which enters wholly into the manufactured product without leaving any waste can have little effect in planting an industry where the raw material is found, unless, of course, the intrinsic value of a heavy or bulky raw material is extremely small. Conversely, a raw material of which a large proportion is waste, e.g. copper ore with a copper content of 2–5 per cent, tends to attract the industry making use of it, or at least those stages of the industry which are necessary to get rid of the great bulk of the waste. Hence it is that pulp and paper are made in the neighbourhood of the forests from which the timber is obtained as 60 per cent of the pulp-wood is waste; sugar is generally locally manufactured at least to the stage of 'raw' sugar; coconut kernels are dried into copra; cacao beans extracted and dried; metallic ores partially refined on the spot into mattes, and so on. Now when coal is used as fuel no part of the coal enters into the finished product, so that the cost of carriage is an extra which would be wholly saved if

117

the industry could be carried on where the coal is produced; an extra which is all the more serious on account of the great bulk of coal in proportion to its value. The tendency of coal to localise industries from this cause has of course been greatly lessened by the *indirect* use of the coal to generate electricity which has minimal transportation costs. As a striking illustration of the way in which other considerations may combine to localise an industry away from the coal, even where coal is used in large amount, one may take brick-making as carried on, on a very large scale at Peterborough, England. The raw materials are clay, water, and coal. Neither the water nor the coal enters into the final product, but the clay does so wholly, yet the industry is carried on where the clay, not the coal, is found, brickfields cover a great extent of ground, and it would probably be difficult to find land as cheap on the coalfields as that where the clay lies, and, what is more important, to carry the clay to any coalfield would be carrying it further away from the great market for the bricks, namely London.

On p. 259 estimates are given of the percentage use of coal for different purposes in the United Kingdom and the United States between the two world wars, and in Germany before 1914. A large proportion was consumed in the metal industries, in the blast-furnaces and in the making of mild steel and ingot iron; hence it is natural that these industries should be specially attracted to the coalfields. It is these industries that form the chief exception to the general rule in the United States that the manufacturing towns are not on the coalfields. Even in the smelting of iron it sometimes happens that the ore is carried to the coal. In other cases so little of the ore enters into the raw iron that there is less waste of haulage in bringing the coal to the ore, especially if the limestone, another material required in smelting as a flux, no part of which enters into the product, is more conveniently accessible from the ore deposits. In yet other cases the advantage of using the means of transport in both directions, instead of having in one direction empty railway wagons or ships in ballast, leads to a reciprocal trade with a smelting industry at both ends. Sometimes again all three raw materials are collected at some convenient point in relation to the transport of the materials, the labour supply, and the means of distribution of the product, as at Middlesbrough in England, and Buffalo, Cleveland, south Chicago, Gary, and Duluth on the Great Lakes of America.

Among finished articles using steel as the raw material without waste, rails and structural steel in particular may be mentioned as manufactured extensively where the steel is produced, but this is because these industries benefit by large-scale organisation as well as through the economy arising from using the steel before it has lost the heat given to it in the process of manufacture. Still, the increase in bulk in structural steel adds so much to its cost of transport that it may also be found advantageous to carry on this industry near tidewater or even near a very large market, in spite of the local lack of both coal and iron. The bulkier the final product and the more skilled labour counts for in its production, the less powerful is coal as a factor in determining the seat of an industry, and in such cases the tendency is for the industry to be carried on in the vicinity of the principal market or markets. It is for these reasons that the manufacture of agricultural implements grew up largely in agricultural districts, as in the east of England and the north-west of America. The large areas required for the plant in these industries, and indeed for many modern industrial plants with their 'horizontal' layout, are another reason for their deserting the more crowded industrial centres. This trend to become less directly dependant on the source of power is assisted by the transmission of electricity from central generating stations; and by the ease with which oil and gas can be piped to new generating stations sited far from the sources of their fuel supplies.

Where the advantage of local coal is the main cause or one of the main causes of establishing industries employing a good deal of labour, other industries to which cheap coal is not of such vital importance may be set up in the same places to take advantage of the labour supply thus afforded. The contiguity of various industries favours all of them in so far as it facilitates the shifting of the workers from industry to industry, or at least from one branch of an industry to another, according to the vicissitudes of trade. Further, light industries using female labour often grow up side by side with heavy industries using male labour, or in other areas where the male labour is employed, for example in ports.

All the circumstances mentioned above are manifestly subject to change, and so contribute to fluctuations in industry and commerce. Markets may become more valuable through increase in population or the development of resources previously unused, by improvement in the means of transport, and in other ways. The supply of labour, both skilled and unskilled, may be changed by migration, that of skilled labour locally increased by education and experience. Capital, where scanty and dear in proportion to the undeveloped resources, may be cheapened by local accumulation, by increase in security, or by increasing knowledge in the investing countries of the security actually afforded. In the case of primary raw produce an important distinction must be made between those products which are completely or economically exhaustible, such as minerals and natural fertilisers worked like minerals, and those which can be reproduced indefinitely; and again, among the latter, between those which can be reproduced annually or even several times in a season (such as clover, alfalfa, etc.), and those which can be reproduced only at intervals of years, such as timber and pulp wood trees.

As already indicated, the prosperity and relative importance of towns at the present day are in many instances due to other circumstances than those which determined their original situation and favoured their early growth. The very fact that a town exists and has attained a moderate size makes it a more or less convenient centre of exchange, and hence may make it worth while to increase its facilities for this purpose. Growing up in the first place, it may be, at a point to which roads naturally converged, it became of sufficient importance to have new roads made from it. In turn railways have been made to towns because the towns already existed; and now the prosperity of the town is determined by the railways. The importance of such natural advantages as have been indicated in the foregoing pages is still to be seen in situations where towns grow up in new countries. In the older countries geographical inertia or geographical momentum are significant in that industrial regions have a tendency to be self-perpetuating — new industries bringing additional labour which in turn creates an enlarged market for further growth.

Commercial countries

The facilities for exchange that have given certain towns a high degree of importance as business centres have also given particular countries a commanding position in the commerce of the world. The comparative importance of these trading countries has changed through the years, as has the pattern of commodities which have formed the basis of world trade. In the Middle Ages the most valuable commerce was between eastern Asia and Europe; and as long as this was carried on through western Asia or by the Red Sea, Italy had peculiar advantages for securing the bulk of it. The ships of Genoa and Venice visited all the coasts of the Mediterranean, the Black Sea, and western Europe, and commerce with the heart of Europe was carried on by way of the Alpine passes. Before the close of the fifteenth century some of the land routes for commerce with the East had already been closed through political events, but the discovery of the seaway to India round the Cape of Good Hope gave the most serious blow to the eastern trade of the Italian cities. In 1504 the galleys of Alexandria returned in February to Venice empty — a thing that had never been seen before, and in March those from Beirut were likewise found to be empty. The chronicle reporting this is continued till 1512, and speaks constantly of the scarcity of spices in Venice; in 1506 it is specially noted that at a fair in that year the Germans had bought very little. Meanwhile eastern commodities were now to be purchased at Lisbon, but soon the towns of Flanders and Holland (Antwerp and Rotterdam) secured the bulk of the commerce with central Europe.

Then began the long period during which the flow of trade has been dominated by the west European nations. In the seventeenth and eighteenth centuries the lead was taken by those with overseas possession, in particular the British, French, Dutch and Spanish empires. After the eighteenth century, as the influence of the Industrial Revolution became more widespread and as the New World became more populous and wealthier, so worldwide commerce began to gather momentum. The colonising powers of Europe took an even greater lead as they developed into manufacturing nations, with the British Isles

121

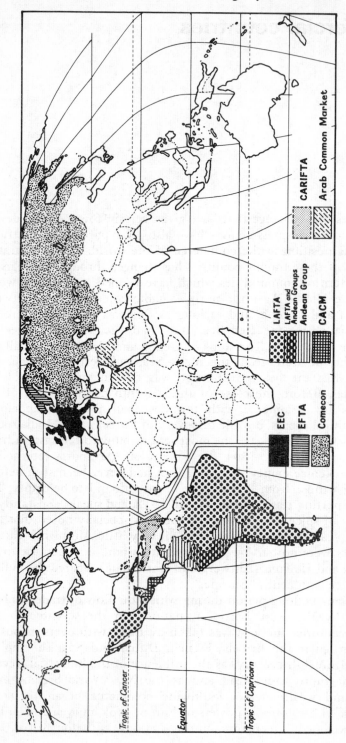

World map of economic groups, 1974

enjoying advantages of resources, industry and traditions of world trading which were to make them predominant. The two world wars of the twentieth century have changed the pattern again and the leading commercial countries of the mid-century are the United States (and Canada), west Europe and Japan — all, it will be noted, with major industrial areas in the temperate zone. The United States, with great resources and great capital wealth, owes much of her leadership to the firm base of an extensive home market. It is a measure of her pre-eminence that she dominates world trade while still consuming nearly 90 per cent of her total production internally. It is also noteworthy that West Germany and Japan, the two nations which suffered the heaviest material losses of the Second World War, are among the leading commercial countries of the 1970s, a position largely made possible by the postwar development of their industries, employing new tools and the latest techniques. They could therefore enter into world trading with the minimum of outdated capital investment — an important con-sideration for industrial nations when some three-fifths of the world's trade is in manufactured articles and machinery.

The pattern of world trade is increasingly that of mass produced items seeking mass markets. The major commercial countries of the future will therefore tend to be those with great resources of produc-tivity and capital, and a sufficiently stable political system to reap the benefits of such assets. Only the United States, the USSR and China offer nation states of requisite size and potential to emerge as leaders; but physical features, and national and political characteristics will also affect their roles in international commerce. Meanwhile the rest of the commercial countries — developed and developing, producers and suppliers — tend increasingly to join together in trading groups to provide a community with greater prospects than could be achieved by the individuals trading separately.

Major economic groupings, 1974. (*Caption to map on p. 122.*)

European Economic Community (EEC) members: Belgium, France, West Germany, Italy, Luxembourg, Netherlands, United Kingdom, Irish Republic, Denmark, Kenya, Uganda, Tanzania, Madagascar and eighteen other African states are associates of the EEC.

European Free Trade Area (EFTA) members: Austria, Iceland, Norway, Portugal, Sweden, Switzerland. Finland is an associate member.

Comecon members: Bulgaria, Czechoslovakia, East Germany, Hungary, Poland, Romania, USSR, Mongolia, Cuba. Yugoslavia is associated, but with limited participation. China, North Korea and North Vietnam are observers. Albania joined in 1949, resigned in 1961.

Latin American Free Trade Association (LAFTA) members: Argentina, Brazil, Chile, Mexico, Paraguay, Peru, Uruguay. Colombia, Ecuador and Venezuela are associated by treaty. LAFTA has two subgroups: the Andean Group, comprising Bolivia, Chile, Colombia, Ecuador and Peru (Venezuela, initially active in the establishment, has not yet signed the agreement); and the River Plate Basin Association, comprising Argentina, Brazil, Paraguay and Uruguay.

Central American Common Market (CACM) members: Costa Rica, El Salvador, Guatemala, Honduras, Nicaragua.

Caribbean Free Trade Association (CARIFTA) members: Antigua, Barbados, Guyana, Dominica, Grenada, Montserrat, St Kitts—Nevis—Anguilla, St Lucia, St Vincent, Trinidad, Tobago, Jamaica.

Arab Common Market is open to all members of the Arab League; so far only Iraq, Jordan, Syria and Egypt have signed the agreement.

Language and instruments of exchange

Language

The language of commerce, when carried on between peoples speaking different tongues, has long been of a very mongrel character. In the days when Italian trade was predominant in the Levant there arose in all the coasts of that region a trade language, the basis of which was a corrupt Italian, but which borrowed numerous words from the local dialects in different places. This language is known as the *lingua franca*, and is still spoken in some eastern Mediterranean towns. The dominant languages of commerce have all begotten corrupt forms of speech of a similar nature. In Chinese ports a mongrel kind of English was spoken, known as 'pidgin' English (*pidgin* being the Chinese pronunciation or corruption of *business*). A 'negro English' used to be spoken in many places on the west coast of Africa, another kind of corrupt English in New Guinea. Arabic is spoken with many corruptions, and much admixture of words derived from other languages throughout the Muslim world. The language of the mixed Arab and Bantu peoples in tropical East Africa known as Swahili, is the common medium of intercourse throughout that region, as well as among some people of the Congo basin; and the Hausa language acts as a sort of *lingua franca* over practically all Africa north of the equator and west of the Nile valley. Hindustani, a dialect of Hindi, has become the *lingua franca* over northern India and has been carried by Indian seamen (lascars) and Indian traders to most of the great ports of the world. Spanish is the prevailing language of the New World south of the United States, except in the Guianas and Brazil. The wide predominance of Spanish commerce in former days is still seen in the survival of a few Spanish words in more than one *lingua franca*, of which English or some other language forms the basis. More and more, however, with the increase of rapid communication, the commercial languages are becoming restricted to those of Europe and North America. The United Nations Organisation confirmed this trend in 1945 with the decision that its working languages, i.e. the languages for international reports and statistics, could be limited to English and French. In General Assembly affairs these are supplemented by Spanish and Russian, and the official languages recognised are these four together with Chinese and Arabic (1973). English is now the universal language for certain specific areas, such as air traffic control and satellite communications; while the electronic technology that has produced the computer has also introduced the ultimate in universal language — the transfer of all information by means of the two digits (0 and 1) of the binary system.

Instruments of exchange

Indispensable to trade on a great scale is the existence of some common measure of value. Such a common measure is money, the use of which made obsolete the old system of barter, that is, the exchange of articles that are intended for other purposes than media of exchange. In the old trapping days of the Hudson's Bay Company, at the time when beaver skins were of great value in Europe, a trade gun would buy from the Indians as many beaver skins as could be piled up on each side of it. Coloured beads, which were worn as ornaments, were another very common means of purchase. But the need for some agreed common measure of value soon comes to be felt, and hence some article of exchange in very general use is adopted as a standard with which the other articles of barter are compared. The articles that have been used as money in different parts of the world are very various. Of all non-metallic kinds of money, that which came into most extensive use was the cowrie-shell (*Cypraea moneta*), which was used in the trade of Africa, southern Asia, and the islands of the Pacific. The home of this shell is the Pacific and Indian Oceans, and shiploads of it were conveyed from the Maldive Islands, the Philippines, and other island groups to the European ports carrying on trade with the African tribes among which it circulated. In Uganda, in 1800, a single cowrie-shell worth 1/800th of a rupee had definite purchasing value, and when a hut tax of Rs 3 was imposed as recently as 1900, cowries came pouring in by the million. At the other extreme, the island of Yap, in the western Carolines, not only had shell money but hoarded communal wealth in the form of large millstones of aragonite (a form of carbonate of lime) measuring up to 6 m (18 ft) in circumference and weighing up to 3 tons. In ancient Mexico the currency of the country consisted of 'bits of tin stamped with a character like a T; bags of cacao, the value of which was regulated by their size; and, lastly, quills filled with gold-dust'. Even on the Atlantic coast of the United States it was stated, as recently as 1888, that oysters were used as money in a certain district on Chesapeake Bay, an oyster forming the regular subscription of a daily newspaper.

Of all forms of money the most convenient are paper notes and metallic coins, and the printing of notes and coining of metals are in all countries a prerogative of the government. Coins are seldom made of any one metal, and for convenience of manufacture various alloys are used. The value of a coin today seldom depends on the amount of fine metal which the coin contains. Coined money is of two sorts, which may be called standard money and token money. In the former the fine metal used is the standard metal of the country — that is, the metal which ultimately fixes the value of all the coins used in the country. In order that any particular metal should form a perfect standard, the metal in question must be received for coinage in unlimited quantities by the state, the coins made with that metal must be made unlimited legal tender; that is to say, payment in such coins must be declared to be a valid discharge of any debt, however large, whilst there must also be freedom to melt and export the coins. If gold, therefore, is the standard metal of any country, any mining company can take as much gold as it raises to the mint of that country, and receive in exchange the same quantity of gold in the form of coin, with a small reduction, it may be, for the expense of coining. In these circumstances, it is obvious that the value of the gold is represented exactly by the value of the equivalent coin, and the value of the coin will rise and fall with the value of the gold.

It is otherwise with token money. The value of fine metal in such money is fixed by law. Metal is not received in unlimited quantity for coinage at the mint; and as the money made with it is merely token money, it is not made legal tender except in payment of certain specified sums. In the United Kingdom the standard money (sovereigns and half-sovereigns) was withdrawn from circulation during the First World War. Gold remained the standard until abandoned in September 1931, but the greater part of the circulation since the First World War has consisted of full-legal tender paper notes; and this is true of most countries. Where silver or copper coins are token money, they represent in face value a greater value, and sometimes a much greater value, than that of their fine metal content. If otherwise there would be a natural tendency to melt the coins for the sake of the metal they contained.

Everybody is familiar with the fact of variations in the price of commodities. Now in gold standard countries there would be not only variations in the value of commodities in relation to gold, but also in that of gold in relation to them. In countries not on the gold standard, such as Britain, it is, of course, natural to refer to values in 'sterling' or in the case of the United States to US dollars. Where there has been a change of prices in one direction (whether a rise or fall) of all or nearly all commodities, it will be right to say absolutely that, whatever the cause may have been, there has been a change in the value of money. When distant dates are compared (intervals of a generation, or of centuries, for example) it is nearly always found that such a change in value has occurred. It is therefore important to bear in mind that, whereas statistics in which values are expressed in the same standard coin afford a more or less satisfactory means of comparing different countries at the same period, they are far from being satisfactory as a means of comparing the commerce of the same country at widely different dates. The sum of £5m. considered in respect of 'purchasing power' was very different in (say) 1880 from the same sum in 1920, and the difference was still greater after the Second World War. These considerations make it extremely difficult to compare prewar and post-war trade and resort is often had to the *weights* of the chief commodities.

Money in the form of coin is used only to a very limited extent, whether the parties belong to the same country or to different countries. The equivalent of coin in paper is the more usual mode of payment in the case of all but small transactions, and the proportion of debts discharged in this way is generally greater in proportion to the commercial development of the country. Whatever the form of a paper circulation may be, its efficiency as a perfect substitute for coins depends on the fact of the holder of the paper being able to obtain the equivalent in coin whenever he wishes it. In payments made within the bounds of any particular country, the most usual substitutes are bank notes and cheques. Bank notes are promises of a bank to pay; in England only the Bank of England can issue them. Cheques are order to a bank to pay, made by persons who have money to their credit in the banks on which the orders are made. In large transactions, payment is very often made in the form of a bill of exchange, which is a demand upon a merchant to pay at a certain date a certain sum of money for goods which he has received. Such a demand is usually presented to the merchant on whom it is drawn for his acceptance, which he signifies by his signature, and when accepted by him it becomes a valid claim against him and a negotiable document.

Bills of exchange are used in settling debts between persons belonging to different countries, because they are a cheaper method of doing so than using coins for the purpose. If gold coin or bullion were sent, the cost of its carriage would have to be paid for; it would have to be insured, and other expenses would have to be incurred. It is therefore a cheaper method for a merchant who has a claim against him in another country to send over an equivalent claim which somebody else may have on someone in that country. He buys that claim in the form of a bill of exchange, and the price which he has to pay for it varies according to circumstances. It varies according to the credit of the person or persons who accept responsibility for the bill, according to the date at which it becomes due (being obviously of less value if payable three months after date than if payable at sight); and even with the 'best' bills — that is, those secured in the most satisfactory way by the credit of the responsible parties — it varies according to the state of trade between different countries. When the bills procurable in one country, A, payable by importers in another country, B, are greater in value than those available in B and payable by importers in A (which is equivalent to saying when A has exported to B a greater value than B to A), then A will have more bills than are necessary to meet the claims of B. Those holding such bills in A will, accordingly, be unable to get as good a price for bills as those in B who hold bills on A. They will be glad to sell them at as good a price as they can get, for they run the risk of being unable to find a customer for them, and hence being obliged to bear the expense of having coin sent over to them in discharge of their claims. Holders of bills in B which are payable in A, on the other hand, will find that there is a great demand for their bills on the part of persons who fear lest they may have to bear the expense of sending coin over in discharge of their debts, and the holders will ask as high a price as they can exact.

Enough has been said to make three facts of importance manifest; first, that the rate of exchange for the equivalents of the same coins may be different in one country from what it is in the other (which, in fact, it usually is); second, that there may be differences in the rate of exchange between countries having the same standard coin (as England and Australia); and third, that in normal circumstances the extreme limit of fluctuation in the rate of exchange for bills payable at sight, above or below the exact equivalent of the coinage of the one country in the coinage of the other, must be the cost of transmitting the coin itself.

Much that is said in the preceding paragraphs is no longer applicable all over the world because of varying degrees of currency control adopted by most countries, especially during and since the Second World War.

III
Commodities

Commodities dependent directly or indirectly on climate

Temperate zone products

Wheat

This, the most valuable of all the grains of temperate climates, has been cultivated from the remotest antiquity. Remains belonging to the Neolithic period, or New Stone Age, show that at that time, long before the beginning of written history, as many as five different varieties of wheat were already in cultivation. The crop early acquired an important place in all parts of the temperate zone in the Old World where the climate was favourable, and gradually extended its domain at the expense of other crops which in certain regions were more easily grown but yielded a less valuable grain. Though in the New World wheat, like most other grain crops, was unknown in the time of Columbus, its cultivation has since spread there to such an extent that the United States and Canada are now among the world's largest producers. In Australia also this grain is in general cultivation, and there are few parts of the world with a suitable climate and a sufficient population where wheat is unknown.

A crop so valuable, so widespread, and so long in cultivation could not fail to exhibit a great number of **varieties** and to show the result of continued research for improved quality. The varieties of wheat culti-vated at the present day yield larger grains than those of the ancient lake-dwellings. The number of varieties now grown is probably in a literal sense countless, as new ones are constantly being produced. Very often, as in the case of other cultivated plants, these varieties manifest strong local preferences, and only flourish in particular regions. The seeds of English wheat fail in the Indian subcontinent; on the other hand, the wheat-growing region of northern India and Pakistan, in which the crop has to ripen during the cool season before the advent of the scorching heats of summer, has developed varieties of wheat which ripen in a shorter period than those of colder climates, but which will not grow in England. It is still more important that varieties have been developed which ripen in the short summers of the Canadian northwest

131

and Siberia. Not only does the behaviour of the crop under cultivation thus vary in different regions, but there is also a difference in the composition of the grain derived from crops grown in different parts of the world.

The best soil for the cultivation of wheat is one in which clay predominates, but which is not too stiff and heavy. As regards climate, wheat demands a higher temperature than any of the ordinary cereals of the temperate zone except maize, so that its northern limit lies to the south of those of oats, rye, and barley. Further details of soil and climate best adapted for wheat are given in the following extracts from the report in the Tenth Census of the United States.

As regards soils, we may say in a general way that light clays and heavy loams are the best for wheat. On the one hand, very heavy clays often produce good crops, both as to yield and as to quality; and, on the other hand, the lighter soils may yield a good quality — it is simply smaller in quantity. The best crops, however, come from moderately stiff soils, but any fertile soil will produce good wheat if all the other conditions are favourable. Good wheat-lands agree in this: that they are sufficiently rolling for natural drainage, are at the same time level enough to admit of the use of field machinery, and are easily tilled, admitting the use of light field implements in their tillage, and thus allowing of a very large production of grain in proportion to the amount of human labour employed.

It was because of the cost of ploughing clay land (requiring a three-horse plough in place of the usual one- or two-horse) that heavy soils went out of cultivation in England before the use of tractors again altered the position.

For commercial as well as agricultural success, climate is an all-controlling condition. Wheat is normally a winter annual. For a good crop the seed must germinate and the young plant grow during the cool and moist part of the year, which season determines the ultimate density of growth on the ground, and consequently mostly determines the yield. It ripens in the warmer and drier parts of the year, which season more largely determines the quality, plumpness, and colour of the grain. In climates with winters so cold that all vegetable growth is suspended, we have two distinct classes of varieties, known respectively as spring and winter wheats [i.e. wheats sown in spring and in winter]. . . . In California, and in similar climates, as in Egypt, this distinction does not exist in respect to their cultivation, although the varieties partake more of the character of winter wheats than of spring, both in their mode of growth and in the character of the flour made from them. But in all climates, and whatever variety may be grown, the crop must be sown and have its early growth in a cool part of the year. Wheat branches ['tillers'] only at the ground, and produces no more heads than stalks, and it only sends out these branches early in its growth or during cool weather, and when the growth is comparatively slow. A cool, prolonged, and rather wet spring is therefore best for the ultimate yield of the crop, a warm, rather dry, rapidly growing, and early spring diminishes the yield; there are then fewer stalks, and the heads are fewer.

It is thus clear why the great mid-continent grasslands of the world (see pp. 40—1), with their spring rains, favour wheat cultivation.

In a country of cold winters, for good crops it is better that the ground be continuously covered with snow. Bare ground, freezing and thawing, now exposed to cold and dry winds, and now to warm sunshine, is exceedingly destructive to wheat. It 'winterkills' in two ways: it may be frozen to death by cold, dry winds, or, as is more often the case, particularly in soils rich in vegetable matter, it 'heaves out', and by the alternate freezing and thawing of the surface soil the roots are lifted out of the soil and the young plant perishes.

A little before the time of harvest, some moisture is required to 'swell the grain'.

The quality of the grain is largely determined by the climate, a hot, dry, and sunny harvest-time being best for wheat of the first grade. The wheat of sunny climates — those of California, Egypt, Northern Africa, and similar countries — has always ranked high for quality. The particularly bright character of American grain depends upon the climate rather than upon the soil. The sunny climate of the whole United States south and west of New England is favourable for this, and from the time of the first settlement of the colonies the bright colour of American grain as compared with that of Northern Europe, particularly that of Great Britain, has been remarked.

Table 5 shows the average yields of wheat in hundreds of kilograms per hectare in selected countries in 1967 and 1971. A bushel of wheat weighs 27.2 kg (60 lb), and 2 000 kg per hectare (20 quintals per hectare) is approximately 30 bushels per acre.

Yields fluctuate from year to year according to favourable or adverse conditions for the crops, but the general improvement in wheat yields in the period 1967—71 is in large measure due to the use of improved strains of seed, the greater use of fertilisers, and in many instances to improved farming techniques. This applies particularly to India.

The countries standing highest in the list are mostly those with a dense population and an intensive system of agriculture that has been undergoing continuous improvement for generations, countries accordingly in

Commodities

Table 5 — Average wheat yields in selected countries, 1967, 1971

Country	100 kg/hectare 1967	1971	Country	100 kg/hectare 1967	1971
Netherlands	47.9	49.5	USSR	11.6	14.1
Denmark	46.5	48.4	India	8.9	13.0
United Kingdom	41.8	44.0	Australia	8.3	11.8
New Zealand	37.3	33.6	Algeria	6.3	7.1
France	36.3	38.6			
Egypt	24.6	27.7	World	13.4	15.8
United States	17.4	22.8	Europe	26.0	28.5
Canada	13.2	18.3	N. America*	16.0	21.5
Argentina	12.6	13.9	Africa	8.2	10.1
Turkey	12.5	14.0	Asia (excluding Chinese People's Republic)	9.9	11.7

Source: *Food and Agriculture Production Yearbook*, 1971

* In the FAO statistical table for wheat North America comprises Canada, the United States, Mexico, as well as Guatemala and Honduras. Geographers usually include the last two countries in Central America. The average wheat yield of North America comprising only Canada, the United States and Mexico was 19.2 in 1967, 22.6 in 1971 (100 kg per hectare).

which fertilisers are cheap relative to the value of the land. Countries which farm extensively on rich soils brought under cultivation more recently have medium yields. Some cases of an exceptionally low yield are worthy of special notice as illustrating the effects of different causes. In Australia generally the low out-turn is to be ascribed mainly to the climate, which has a scanty rainfall, and so is unfavourable to the tillering of the wheat and the filling of the ear, though it is warm and sunny, which is highly favourable to the quality of grain. In recent years great improvements in yield have been effected. In South Australia the average yield was 8 quintals per hectare (13.5 bushels per acre) in the decade 1943—53; during part of last century it was about 3.4 quintals (5 bushels). In the USSR the low average of the out-turns was in part due to the methods of cultivation, for the soil on which much of the Soviet wheat is grown is one of the best in the world. A large part of the wheat-growing area of the Soviet Union may, however, like that of Victoria and of South Australia, be described as lying on the margin of adequate rainfall, so that the yield varies greatly with the amount of the rainfall; the same is true of such areas as the western prairies of Canada and adjoining parts of the United States. In the years 1914—54 the yield of wheat in Victoria varied from a minimum of 1 quintal to a maximum of 15 q., in New South Wales from a minimum of 2 q. to a maximum of 14 q. per acre. In Manitoba the average yield in 1900 was less than 6 q., in 1901 more than 17 quintals per hectare. These may be compared with the returns for Tasmania and New Zealand, in which the rainfall is more ample, and in which the extreme yields in 1914–64 were respectively 6* and 18, and 15† and 34 quintals. In Argentina several causes combine to bring about a low average yield. In some years droughts destroy the crops (especially in the west of the wheat-growing area), in other years floods, in others frosts (especially in the south), in others locusts (especially in the north). Hence here also there are great variations in the calculated yield. In 1896–97 it was estimated at about 3.4 quintals per hectare (5 bushels per acre), as against 12 in 1938–39, 8 in 1941–42, 12 in 1953.

The superiority of wheat as a food grain for man lies in the quality of the bread made from the flour, which is generally regarded as more palatable than bread made from other grains, even though these may be little, it at all, inferior to wheat in nutritive properties. This superiority is so generally recognised that it is difficult to realise that wheaten bread was a rarity even in some parts of England less than 200 years ago. It is still a rarity over a large part of the world though it is now coming more and more into use. Europe, while constantly increasing its consumption of wheat relative to population, has long been dependent on supplies from elsewhere, and the international commerce in wheat and wheat flour exceeds that in all other grains. The great wheat-importing countries are those of the west of Europe, in which manu-facturing industry is so highly advanced that there is a relatively large population dependent on supplies from abroad; and the United Kingdom stands at the head of the list, so that an account of the British wheat trade will serve to give a general view of the wheat supply of the whole world.

Early in the eighteenth century England could supply all her own wants in wheat, and in good years could even spare more than a quarter of a million bushels for export. It was only towards the close of the century, after the great development of the cotton manufacture had begun, that the import of grain became a regular necessity. The amount imported continued on the whole to increase, notwithstanding the existence of import duties, which were generally fixed on a scale which imposed higher duties as the price of wheat fell. In those days the chief supplies for the United Kingdom were from France and the continent of Europe. From 1 February 1849, a uniform import duty of 1s. per quarter was established, and on 1 June 1869 even this was abolished, both wheat and flour being admitted into this country from that date duty free.‡ Meanwhile the dependence of the British Isles on foreign wheat continued to grow, and the sources of supply became more

---

* In 1939–40; the lowest on record. Usually not less than double.
† The lowest yield on record from 1868 to 1949 was 12 quintals in 1897–98.
‡ A duty of 3d. per cwt on wheat, 5d. on flour, was levied in 1902–03.

widespread. It has been estimated that shortly after the middle of the nineteenth century the United Kingdom produced on an average between 70 and 80 per cent of all the wheat consumed in the country. The proportion fell steadily to less than 20 per cent in 1930—34. From 1935 it rose to nearly 25 per cent, home production being stimulated by the overthrow of the almost traditional British free trade policy by the National Government in 1932, and the institution of a wheat quota. Since the Second World War, the United Kingdom has again become more self-sufficient, with some 50 per cent of wheat and flour consumed coming from home production in the 1960s.

Table 6 presents some of the most important facts relating to the British import trade in wheat since 1881. Up to 1900 the figures relate to the quantities *shipped* from each country; thereafter they are limited to the quantities *consigned* from each country — i.e. to supplies originating in each country.

Table 6 — **Imports of wheat into the United Kingdom** (including wheat flour in equivalent weight of grain)*

Countries of supply	Average annual supplies in percentages of total									
	1881–1885	1891–1895	1896–1900	1911–1913	1927–1929	1930–1932	1936–1938	1948–1950	1958–1960	1972–1973
United States:										
Atlantic ports	35.4	41.6	49.7	–	–	–	–	–	–	–
Pacific ports	18.1	10.5	9.9	–	–	–	–	–	–	–
Total US	53.5	52.1	59.6	24.6	25.0	12.0	6.1	5.9	12.9	13.4
Argentina	–	8.0	8.4	13.7	25.3	15.9	7.1	0.7	7.5	–
Canada	3.5	5.1	7.8	20.5	32.5	31.4	41.1	76.7	55.0	38.6
USSR	11.7	14.3	9.6	9.0	0.7	13.7	5.4	–	2.9	–
India	12.3	9.5	4.3	18.1	1.8	1.0	4.2	–	–	–
Australasia	5.2	3.0	1.7	10.9	11.9	18.3	26.6	15.5	11.1	6.3
Austria–Hungary	2.6	1.5	1.5	0.1	0.1	–	–	–	–	–
Germany	5.5	1.0	1.3	0.6	1.1	2.1	0.3	0.1	–	–
Others	5.7	5.5	5.8	2.5	1.6	5.6	9.2	1.1	10.6†	41.7‡
	100.0	100.0	100.0	100.0	100.0	100.0	100.0	100.0	100.0	100.0
	Average annual in millions of tons									
Total	3.8	4.8	4.8	5.9	6.0	6.2	5.0	4.9	4.8	3.8

* For purposes of conversion, the United Nations Food and Agriculture Organisation reckons that wheat yields 75 per cent of its weight in flour. Grain of all kinds may be shipped either bagged or in bulk; by the latter method about 12 per cent more weight can be carried and the cost of the bags is saved. Bulk transport is facilitated by the use of elevators.
† Nearly half from France.
‡ 34.6 per cent from France and Netherlands.

These vast imports early led to a lowering of the British price of wheat, the mean of the yearly averages of the price of the imperial quarter (8 bushels) sinking from 54*s*. 6*d*. (£2.73) in 1871–75 to 22*s*. 10*d*. (£1.14) in 1894. This led to a rapid contraction in the area devoted to wheat, which in 1860 occupied about 1.6m. hectares (4m. acres) in the United Kingdom, and in 1895 under 0.61m. hectares (1.5m. acres). During the First World War efforts were made to increase the home production, but in postwar years acreage and production dropped again, in 1931 reaching a new low level of 0.49m. hectares (1.25m. acres). Under the strict government control practised in the Second World War it reached nearly 1.4m. hectares (3.5m. acres) (1943). This high level was not maintained, but in 1965–66 the figure was still over 1m. hectares (2.5m. acres).

If we now look at the **sources of supply** as shown in Table 6, we see that in the last quinquennium of the nineteenth century more than 75 per cent of the total supply was shipped from the United States, Canada, and Argentina, the United States alone shipping just under 60 per cent of the total. After 1900 the more exact system of assigning imports to the countries of supply reduced the lead of the United States; and the further decline, as the twentieth century advanced, in the American share of the total was due at least in part to the increase in home consumption as the United States developed into a great manufacturing country. Canada and Argentina, on the other hand, gained in importance as sources of wheat supply to Britain, and Australia also became an important contributor. In Argentina, which first appeared in the British import tables as a source of wheat in 1883, the expansion was due to the opening up of a new region of virgin soil. Its share of the British imports of wheat was very erratic before the Second World War, and in the three years 1936–38 Canada and Australasia provided, on an average, over two-thirds of the total. During the war years Canada strengthened her already predominant position, and Australia and Argentina, though far behind, were other important sources of supply; while at the close the United States came more to the fore again. In 1952 Canada supplied 72 per cent of the United Kingdom imports of wheat and flour (reckoned in terms of wheat), and in 1960 just on half. The United States, Australia, France and Argentina — in varying order in good and bad years — are the other chief contributors, and the USSR was also an appreciable source of supply in some years.

This limitation of British wheat imports to practically three of four countries was the result of war and the aftermath of war. The prewar sources of supply covered a wide range of countries, including not only those listed in the foregoing table, but many others, notably Romania and France. The inclusion of France as a regular and considerable contributor is an example of the intricacies of modern trade, for in the prewar quinquennium, as in some postwar years, France did not grow enough wheat for home requirements, her imports being greater than her exports.

Despite the many contributories, normally, to Britain's wheat supplies, it remains broadly true that she has long been dependent on North America and Australia; and the prospects of supplies from these sources are of vital importance. Apart from political and financial considerations, which do not come within the scope of this work, the outlook is reassuring. Canadian experience is in many ways typical of the course of development, and a brief resumé will give an idea of the problems not only there but in the 'newer' lands generally.

Wheat-growing in Canada, though not confined to the Prairie Provinces, had its birth there, as a modern industry of world importance, following the building of the Canadian Pacific Railway in the 1880s. Grain crops, with wheat always in the forefront of the picture, were the mainstay of the pioneer settlers who flocked into the prairies, and farming was subject to the advantages and disadvantages of pioneer enterprise. The soil was virgin and fertile; land was abundant and cheap; the right type of settler might hope for a free grant of a quarter section (65 hectares: 160 acres — a quarter of a square mile). Big 'bonanza' farms of, say, 2 000 hectares (5 000 acres) played a part in the development; but the typical farm was the holding of 65 hectares (160 acres), owned by the man who worked it with the help of his family and went all out to make it a success. Adverse factors were the 'extensive' as opposed to the 'intensive' type of farming, careless cultivation, and the tendency to crop the land year after year without observing a proper rotation or making good the loss of fertility. This 'wheat-mining', as it came to be called, meant low yields and threatened at one time a serious position in the Prairie Provinces through soil exhaustion. There was also the proverbial danger of having all or most of one's eggs in one basket. Happily, remedial measures were adopted, including mixed farming, more thorough cultivation, measures to preserve soil fertility, and the development by scientific research of strains of wheat resistant to rust, drought, and other menaces. In the short-term there must always be fluctuations of crop yield, but in the long view, production is seen as a gradually mounting switchback. Local consumption naturally has increased with the spread of manufacturing industry and the growth of population, but by far the greater part of the production is exported. The very large share of Britain's imports of wheat supplied by Canada has already been noted; yet it is only a fraction of the Canadian production of wheat. In 1947, when the wheat and flour imported into Britain from Canada amounted to over 2.3m. metric tons, the Canadian wheat crop was about 10m. metric tons, while in 1952 it reached the record total of 15m. metric tons. In 1961 it was down to 7.7m.; in 1965 up to 17.6m.; in 1971 down to 14.4m.

The United States has been affected by more and greater changes than Canada has yet experienced. In 1870 more than half the population who were gainfully employed were engaged in agriculture; in 1970, the proportion was one in twenty-five. Improvident farming has led to heavy loss of soil fertility and extensive soil erosion. But in the States, as in Canada, remedial measures have been adopted and recent years have seen record wheat crops, more than enough for home needs, vast as these have become. In 1947 a bumper crop of 34.6m. metric tons was harvested, of which over a third was exported, and in 1967 the harvest was 41.4m. Development has reached a different stage from that in Canada. In 1950 the United States had 5 382 162 farms, but by 1968 this had fallen to 3 059 000. Some 90 per cent of all farms are owner-occupied, and nearly 30 per cent are small family farms of less than 20 hectares (50 acres) with little, if any, hired labour. Although mechanisation and business methods are increasingly applied, in 1967 some 16 per cent only were large industrial units with annual sales in excess of $20 000. These farms, however, produced 70 per cent of the total value of all farm products. In 1920 the average farm size was 60 hectares (150 acres). In 1968 it was 149 hectares (370 acres); while 350 000 farms were 200 hectares (500 acres) and above. The number of very large units is slowly increasing and over 70 000 farms are 800 hectares (2 000 acres) or larger.

In both Canada and the United States the wheat industry exemplifies modern methods of production, handling and transport. A considerable quantity of the wheat exported from Canada, Australia, and the United States is in the form of flour. Sometimes reasons other than industrial policy call for prior manufacture. Hungarian millers are noted for the superb quality of their flour, not only because of the excellence of their wheat, their machinery and their methods, but because of the dry climate. Flour of equal quality cannot be made in the moist climate of Britain even from the same wheat treated by the same processes. Climatic conditions also determined the popularity of Indian wheats in Italy and other Mediterranean countries in former days; these hard Indian wheats yield the most suitable flour for macaroni and vermicelli.

India's share (using the name India in its old sense) in bringing down the price of English wheat in the closing decades of the last century was due, not to the opening up of vast new lands, as in North America, but to the cheapness of labour in old and populous countries. The climate of those regions in which wheat cultivation is chiefly pursued — the Punjab, the former North-West Province, and former United Provinces — is on the whole as favourable to the growth of wheat as the climate of the United States wheatlands, though in the Indian subcontinent insufficient rainfall often necessitates irrigation. The Indian crop is now grown for home consumption. In most years there is little or no surplus but in good years India is now self-sufficient; and Pakistan's increased production has considerably reduced the quantity of wheat she imports.

World production in 1971 was 343m. metric tons, more than eight times the estimated total in 1883–84. In 1956 as much as 30 per cent of the total was credited to the USSR, and over 10 per cent to continental China. In 1971 the USSR again headed the list with 27 per cent of the estimated world production; Asia (excluding China) had 15 per cent, Europe 23 per cent, and Canada and the United States together 17 per cent, accounting for 82 per cent of the total, leaving South America (chiefly Argentina), Oceania (chiefly Australia), and Africa (chiefly North Africa), to supply the comparatively small balance. It was estimated that China's output contributed over 9 per cent.

The following table, the particulars of which, except in the case of North America, are mainly derived from Scherzer, shows that there is not a month in the year in which a wheat harvest does not take place in some part of the world.

Table 7 — Wheat: harvest months

January	Australia, New Zealand, Argentina, Chile.
February	Indian subcontinent.
March	Indian subcontinent, Upper Egypt.
April	Mexico, Cuba, Lower Egypt, Syria, Iran, Turkey.
May	Morocco, Algeria and Tunisia; the northern parts of Turkey, China, Japan, Texas, Florida.
June	The Mediterranean peninsulas and the south of France; California, Oregon, Utah, and the greater part of central and eastern United States territory south of 40°; Afghanistan, Japan.
July	France, Hungary, southern USSR, the northern parts of the United States of America, Ontario, and Québec.
August	England, Belgium, the Netherlands and Germany; the Prairie Provinces of Canada.
September	Scotland, Sweden, Norway, USSR.
October	Finland, northern USSR.
November	Peru, South Africa.
December	Burma, South Australia.

Future production will be affected by recent development of new strains of wheat which have an annual yield two to three times greater than the existing varieties. These new varieties demand careful seed propagation and this will largely control their rate of distribution. Seed production itself has always been a major subsidiary industry; for example, Argentina with a wheat production of between 5 and 7m. tons consumes some 680 000 tons of seed grain a year. The new varieties also require more fertilisers and a more rigorous irrigation and pest control if their full potential is to be realised — factors which demand the introduction of a more intensive type of cultivation than is currently practised universally. Wheat will, however, continue to be the most valuable of the grains as the new varieties will add to the production capability of the existing wheatlands, and will make wheat-growing less uncertain in hitherto marginal conditions. This in turn will affect the pattern of world trade as the traditional importers become increasingly self-sufficient.

Maize or corn

Maize or corn is the only grain crop which was introduced into the Old World from the New, and it owes the name of Indian corn, by which it is sometimes known in England, to the fact that it was the only cereal cultivated to any extent by the American Indians before the arrival of Europeans. It weighs nearly as heavily as wheat, 25.4 kg (56 lb) to the bushel, against wheat's 27.2 kg (60 lb), and is usually a more prolific crop. World yield in 1971 (including China and USSR) averaged 27 300 kg per hectare against the average yield of wheat, 15 800 kg per hectare. The average yield of maize in the period 1948—52 was 15 800 kg per hectare, of wheat 9 900 kg per hectare. The pronounced increase in the maize yield is mainly due to the use of new strains of seed. Maize cultivation spread rapidly in the tropical and some of the warm temperate parts of the Old World when it became known there, but much more rapidly in Africa, and even in the east of Asia, than in Europe, which had a less suitable climate for its cultivation. In England, for example, the summer is not sufficiently long, warm, and sunny. The ideal climate for this grain is one with a summer 4½ to 7 months long, without frost, the middle portion hot both day and night, sunny skies, sufficient rains to supply the demands of a rapidly growing and luxuriant crop, falling at such intervals as best to provide sufficient moisture without ever making the soil actually wet. It is thus essentially a summer crop, and one that requires summer rains (or irrigation), though not very heavy and frequent rains. It is therefore unsuited to those countries which, like California, Chile, and most of those round the Mediterranean, though admirably adapted for the growth of wheat, are characterised by summers of remarkable dryness. In Europe therefore it is grown in the central and eastern parts: Italy, Hungary, Yugoslavia, Romania, and parts of the USSR. The new hybrid strains, with short stalks, ripen quickly and have extended the area possible for maize cultivation; but the crop still flourishes in Europe only in those countries where the greater part of the rainfall of the year occurs in summer, and where the summers are at the same time remarkably sunny. The same characteristics render the climate of a great part of the United States eminently suited to this crop, which is the principal crop of the country; so that when a native of the United States speaks of 'corn' simply, it is always maize that he means, just as an Englishman means by the same word wheat. World production has more than doubled over the last twenty years and the United States grows nearly 46 per cent of the present crop of some 308m. tons; China is the second largest producer with a crop estimated to exceed 40m. tons. In

Brazil, South Africa and Mexico it is the leading cereal crop, while in Argentina it is almost as important as wheat. The principal use of maize is as feed for cattle and pigs – the grain, meal and young juicy plants all being used. In the United States Corn Belt the bulk never leaves the farm on which it is grown, save 'on the hoof'.

The quantity and value of the maize imported into the United Kingdom (chiefly for the feeding of cattle and pigs) are next to those of wheat among grain crops. Down to the end of the last century more than half the import was usually derived from the United States, which was followed by Romania. Then Argentina came to the front, and for a time before the Second World War supplied 90 per cent of the imports, which amounted to over 3.5m. tons. After the war imports did not reach half that quantity till 1958; supplies from Argentina, though still important, lost their commanding position, and the United States regained its pre-eminence. In 1973 the imports of maize into the United Kingdom amounted to 3.3m. tons, of which the United States supplied 1.7m. South Africa nearly 0.20m., and Argentina only 0.07m. In 1962, imports had been up to 4.6m. tons. Supplies from all countries are very variable; maize is an outstanding example of the kaleidoscopic nature of the changes of world sources of supply and of the increasing importance of cereals in meat production.

In the British Isles maize is used as human food only to a very limited extent, and chiefly in the form of 'cornflour'; but in many of the countries in which it forms a staple crop it is used as human food in various forms. In the United States specially grown 'sweet corn' forms a favourite vegetable, and a preparation known as hominy – a kind of porridge made from coarsely ground maize – is locally used. 'Corn on the cob' started to become popular in Britain in the 1930s. In Mexico maize is still, as it always has been, the principal food of the people, being coarsely ground at home and made into flat pancakes called tortillas, which are eaten warm. The polenta, which forms part of the food of the inhabitants of Italy, except in the extreme south, is generally made from maize meal; and so too is the mamaliga of the Romanians. In Transcaucasia the heads of maize are cooked under the name of kukurus. Maize is a staple food grain in nearly all the damper parts of Africa; and in South Africa 'mealies', as the corn cobs are called, and mealie meal enter considerably into the diet. Various kinds of beer and spirits (including much whisky in America) are also made from maize, now used to some extent even by English beer brewers.

Oats

This crop can be cultivated with advantage over a wider range in latitude and on a greater variety of soils than wheat, but the climate best suited to it is one that is moister and has cooler summers than that best adapted for the latter crop. Such climates produce grain of better quality for all the purposes for which oats are grown, and produce a much greater weight of grain per bushel, the variations in this respect being much greater than in the case of wheat. Whereas wheat does not often weigh much more or much less than 27.2 kg (60 lb) per bushel, oats may vary between 12 and 22 kg (26 and 50 lb) per bushel (FAO average, 14.9 kg: 33 lb). This is all the more important since there are also great variations in the amount of meal yielded by oats, only the best qualities yielding as much as half their weight. Being more easily grown than wheat, the crops of oats formerly exceeded the crops of wheat in a number of European countries, though not along the Mediterranean coast, where the summers are not suited to oats. The largest crops are grown in the United States, USSR, Canada, Poland, West Germany, France and China. As recently as 1950, a greater weight of oats than of wheat was grown in the United Kingdom, but latterly the position has been reversed. By 1971 the crop of oats was nearly 1.4m. tons, against 4.8m. tons of wheat. In the United Kingdom, Scotland with its cool summers and Northern Ireland with its damp conditions took the lead in the production of oats. The quantity of oats imported into the United Kingdom is but a small fraction of the imports of wheat and flour; in 1946—47 Canada was the chief source of supply, in 1948—49 Australia, in 1950 USSR, in 1955 Canada and Australia; while in 1956 there was a UK net export. World production is 50—58m. tons from 30m. hectares (74m. acres). About half the area is divided between the United States and USSR.

In countries where this grain is grown, it generally forms a part of the food of the people. In Scotland it constituted, in the shape of oatmeal porridge, oat-cakes and other forms, the chief food of the people as late as the end of the eighteenth century; but it is mainly for horses that oats are grown (hence the recent decrease, in line with the worldwide decline in numbers of work-horses), this grain being proved by experience to be the best for that purpose. In ancient times the grain was not much grown — no doubt in consequence of its unsuitability for the climate of the countries round the Mediterranean, where the civilised nations of antiquity had their seats. It is not mentioned in the Bible, but it was cultivated in a small way in Italy, as food for horses, as early as the beginning of the Christian era. In central Europe it was a grain of much greater antiquity, for it is found among the remains of the lake dwellings of Switzerland, but not among remains of as great age as those which include wheat and barley.

Barley

This is in several respects a highly remarkable crop. By some writers it is believed to be the most ancient of cultivated grains. Several varieties of it (including two of that kind which is known in England as bere or bigg, having six instead of two rows of grain in the ear) have been found

143

among Neolithic remains. Its range in climate is wider than that of any other cereal, cultivation having led to the development of some coarse varieties which ripen their grain within a shorter period than the hardiest varieties of oats. Hence, of all cereals it is that which reaches furthest north in latitude, and highest up on the mountain slopes. In Norway it is cultivated even in 70° N. On the other hand, it flourishes well in any soil and under any climate that is suited for wheat, and it is in such climates that the best barley is grown. Thus it happens that it is the associate of oats in the northern countries of Europe, which are on the whole too cold for wheat, and the associate of wheat in the southern countries of Europe and the other countries round the Mediterranean, which are too dry in summer for maize, but where the barley, like the wheat, is of excellent quality. In the United States this pattern is repeated and the largest proportion of barley is grown in North Dakota and in California, which, like the Mediterranean countries, has a climate unsuited both for maize (except on irrigated land) and for oats.

Barley appears to have been the chief bread grain of the ancient Hebrews, Greeks, and Romans; it was the most productive of the cereals suited to the Mediterranean climate, the yield of grain being similar to that of wheat. In 1965 the world average was 15.2 quintals per hectare (27 bushels per acre) − a bushel of barley being 22.7 kg (50 lb); this is about 14 per cent more in weight than the average yield of wheat. In 1971 the world yield was 18 500 kg per hectare, production totalling 152.4m. tons from 82.2m. hectares (203m. acres). Comparable average figures for the period 1948−52 were 59.3m. tons from 52.4m. hectares (129.5m. acres).

Barley-bread was once common in Scotland, and is still used to some extent in Japan, India and Scandinavia; but nowadays barley is principally grown for cattle-feed and for beer made from malt, barley grain which has been allowed to sprout and then been killed. It is for this purpose that the best grain is imported into Britain; and for the same reason it is a very important crop in Germany and the other beer-drinking countries of Europe. In Scotland and Ireland considerable quantities are used in the making of whisky. About a third of the world supply of some 150m. tons is grown in Europe, and nearly a quarter in the USSR. About 16 per cent is grown in the United States and Canada. Imports into the United Kingdom are only a fraction of the wheat and flour imports. They come mainly from Canada and Australia, but quantities fluctuate greatly. The barley grown in Turkey, not great in amount, is noted for its high quality.

Rye

This is the least familiar of all the grain crops grown in the British Isles, but there used to be no other cereal except wheat cultivated so largely on the mainland of Europe as a bread grain. It is grown on a smaller scale (world production only 31m. tons in 1971, and declining) than the cereals previously considered, and nearly 39 per cent of the total is credited to the USSR. Of all the bread plants it flourishes on the poorest soil and in the most inhospitable climates, though the optimum conditions are similar to those for wheat. It was a great boon to the vast tract stretching from Holland, through northern Germany, into central Russia, which is mainly covered by a poor, sandy soil. Throughout that region it was the prevailing bread grain. In the United Kingdom, where grown at all, it serves chiefly as a fodder crop, for which purpose it is useful in the south of England in the period between the exhaustion of the supplies of root crops and the maturing of clover and lucerne. In the United States the use of the grain in the making of bread has diminished, as the immigrants from northern and eastern Europe turned to wheaten bread in place of the nourishing but sour rye bread of the old lands; but rye whisky is popular and so is wheaten bread flavoured with rye. The straw, which is largely used for packing and making certain kinds of paper and pasteboard, is a valuable part of the crop.

Buckwheat

This is a grain crop almost unknown to the agriculture of the United Kingdom, but of importance in some parts of the world. It does not belong, like the grain crops already mentioned, to the great family of the grasses, but is an ally of some of our common weeds, such as snake-weed and persicaria, and a more distant ally of the common dock or sorrel. It is a native of eastern Asia, and was introduced into Europe only at a late period. Its French name, *sarrasin*, appears to indicate that in that country it first became known through the Saracens or Arabs. The grain is said to be very nutritious, and the crop has these recommendations, that it can be grown with hardly any cultivation on the poorest soils, especially, like rye, on very light, sandy soils, and that its sowing time is late (in the United States from May to the middle of August), which often allows of its being sown to replace another crop that has failed. But against these advantages there are to be placed the great disadvantages that its yield is uncertain, and that the very ease with which it can be grown encourages slovenly habits of cultivation. Ninety per cent of the worlds' annual production of 1m. tons is grown in the USSR and there are small crops in France, Poland and Japan.

Pulses

This is a general term rather vaguely used for certain pod fruits, that is, fruits (in the botanical sense of that word) having large seeds enclosed in a long seed vessel, the most familiar examples being peas and beans. The vegetable forms which have this kind of fruit are extremely numerous, and comprise lofty trees as well as tender plants; but the term pulse is confined to such as supply seeds or pods capable of being used for food by men or cattle. For the most part, the pulses of commerce are derived from green plants often weak-stemmed, but we may include under this head the fruit of two trees, the carob, or locust, and the mezquite.

The chief pulses of commerce are common peas and beans, chick-peas, and soya beans. **Peas** are those suited to the colder climate, and are largely cultivated everywhere in the less warm parts of the temperate zone, though not confined to these parts. Many varieties of the **common bean** (*Phaseolus vulgaris*, Linn.) are cultivated, some suited to one climate, some to another; some grown solely as food for horses and cattle, others eaten by man. The largest imports of beans into this country are from the warmer parts of the temperate zone. The land under beans in Great Britain and under peas is considerably less than in the later part of the nineteenth century. A distinction is made between 'field peas' and those grown in market gardens for immediate human consumption or for freezing, drying or canning for human food. The United Kingdom production of 450 000 tons of peas a year is second only to the USA (1.3m. tons), and the sales of frozen peas now account for 25 per cent of all sales of frozen food in the UK. **Chick-peas** (*Cicer arietinum*, Linn.) are an important product and article of trade in India and Pakistan, where they are known as **gram**, and 85 per cent of the world's crop is grown. In Spain they are one of the chief articles of diet, and from Spain have become known in the former Spanish colonies of Central and South America. In warm countries, where butcher-meat is little consumed, this and other pulses are an almost essential part of the regular diet, since they supply elements of food (especially protein) not contained in sufficient quantity in grain and fruits.

It is for the same reason that **soya beans** are largely consumed in the Far East. The plant is indigenous to eastern Asia, and it is widely cultivated there; before the Second World War China and Manchuria, were credited respectively with a half and a third of the then world production of 12m. tons. China found her market within her own borders, but Manchuria did a big export trade with other Far Eastern countries, and early in the present century extended her exports to Europe. In the prewar quinquennium 1934–38 she provided 90 per cent of world exports of soya beans totalling 2.25m. tons. Cultivation of this bean has spread rapidly in North America and now the giants in production are the United States and China. The United States production has increased from 15.5m. tons in 1958 to 31.8m. in 1971 — more than half the world total of 48.2m. tons, and more than double China's production of 11.5m. tons. Apart from direct human consumption, the soya bean is useful for cattle food and for its oil content, and the United Kingdom imports the soya bean in all three forms.

The **groundnut** or earth-nut (*Arachis hypogaea*, Linn.) is so called because the pod ripens underground. It is popularly known here and in the United States as the monkey-nut or peanut. Though cultivated chiefly as an oilseed (see p. 224) it is also largely used as a fodder plant and, increasingly, as human food. It is of remarkably wide range in latitude, being grown from the heart of the tropics to as far north as 37° in the United States, the northern limits of the cotton plants; and it thrives in very poor sandy soils. World production in 1971 (in shell) was over 18.4m. tons, India providing nearly a third, China nearly 15 per cent, Nigeria 6 per cent and the United States over 7 per cent.

Among other pulses of more or less importance in agriculture and commerce are **lentils, vetches,** and **lupins,** with world production of some 1m., 2m., and 0.75m. tons per year respectively. All these are cultivated for their pods in southern Europe and the Mediterranean region generally; lentils also in India. Lentils are celebrated for the nutritious character of their seeds (with a high protein content) and the meal derived from them is the basis of many invalid and other patent foods advertised under various names. In central and western Europe vetches and lupins are cultivated solely for use as green fodder, lupins being a crop of special importance in certain localities, from its being adapted to very light, sandy soils. In common with nearly all members of the pea and bean family, these crops enrich the soil; bacteria occupying nodules on the roots are able to 'fix' atmospheric nitrogen and convert it into nitrates available as plant food.

The long flat dried pod of the **carob tree** sold under the name of locust beans, and sometimes called St John's Bread, from the fact of its being supposed by some to be the locusts stated in the New Testament to have been eaten by St John the Baptist in the wilderness, is the fruit of a tree (*Ceratonia siliqua*, Linn.) belonging to the Mediterranean generally, but especially abundant on the island of Cyprus. The pods, and locust bean flour and gum are exported by the Mediterranean islands and are used in food preparation and for cattle fodder. So rich are the Cyprus carob pods in sugar that a sweet juice can be extracted from them capable of being used in preserving fruits, as well as for the other purposes to which sugar is applied. Imports to the United Kingdom in 1969 were some 35 000 tons. **Mezquite** is the name of several species of American trees of the genus *Prosopis*, producing a sweet pod something like that of the carob tree. The most widely distributed species (*Prosopis dulcis*, Kunth), to which the Spaniards gave the name of the carob (algarrobo), after the similar tree of their own country, has pods nearly 1 metre in length; but this is rather a tropical tree than a tree of the temperate zone. The species to which the name mezquite is given in North America (*P. juliflora*, DC, and *P. pubescens*,

Benth.) have smaller pods, which, as well as the beans contained in them, are much relished by cattle. They thrive in the north of Mexico and in the United States from Texas to California.

Potato

This important plant is one of the gifts of the New World to the Old. The cultivated species, which is known to botanists as *Solanum tuberosum*, Linn., and is a member of the same genus as our common weed the woody nightshade, is a native of the high and dry regions of the Andes from Chile to Venezuela. Its introduction into almost every other country of the world has proved of immense importance on account of its extreme productiveness, its easy cultivation, and its remarkable powers of acclimatisation. Varieties of this plant are capable of cultivation from the tropics to the furthest limits of agriculture, even beyond the polar limit of barley. There is much uncertainty as to the date of its introduction into Europe. It is believed to have been known in Spain in the first half of the sixteenth century, and is commonly said to have been introduced into Ireland by Sir Walter Raleigh from Virginia in 1586. Sir Walter Raleigh did not introduce any plant from Virginia about that time, though colonists originally settled in America by him may have done so. In any case, the plant first known in England as the potato was the batatas or sweet potato.

Whatever the date of introduction, it was long before the potato proved acceptable in most European countries. In Ireland it was earlier cultivated than in Great Britain. In England its cultivation did not become general till the eighteenth century, and it was only in the latter half of that century that it came to be widely grown in Germany, where the autocratic powers of Frederick II of Prussia had to be exercised to secure its introduction into the sandy districts of Pomerania and Silesia. Now Poland and East and West Germany are normally the biggest European producers outside the USSR. Other leading European producers are France, and the United Kingdom. The world crop in 1971 totalled 306.4m. tons (the annual average in the period 1948–52 was 247.6m. tons) to which the USSR contributed 92.3m. tons, and Europe as a whole 134.7m. tons. China's output is probably about 27m. tons. Because of the bulkiness of potatoes compared with their value, foreign trade is mainly with nearby countries. The United Kingdom grows most of the potatoes it requires, but imports early new potatoes which come on to the market before the homegrown; in 1963 it took over 431 000 tons valued at £17.5m. and in 1970, 303 000 tons valued at £18.7m. In the Channel Islands the cultivation of early new potatoes is a staple industry, especially in Jersey. Other sources of supply are France, Spain, and the Canary Islands. On the other hand, the United Kingdom exported 60 200 tons of seed potatoes in 1969, valued at £1.9m. In continental Europe considerable quantities are used in the manufacture of alcohol (almost entirely for industrial purposes) and starch.

One great objection to the cultivation of the potato is its liability to disease, which in some years, as in 1845—46 in Ireland, has caused great distress in countries depending mainly on this crop. Great progress has, however, been made with disease-resisting varieties.

Other vegetables

Amongst other vegetables of the temperate zones which enter considerably into international trade may be mentioned onions and tomatoes. Onions are imported into Britain from (mostly) Spain, the Netherlands, Egypt, and Chile — in quantity a steady supply of 220 000 and 230 000 tons, valued at some £9m. against a home production of 90 000 tons. Tomatoes, likewise a fairly constant import, smaller in quantity but of much greater value than onions, are nearly all imported from the Canary Islands (two-thirds), Netherlands and Spain. In 1970 they amounted to 108 000 tons, valued at £28m. Other vegetables — turnips, mangolds, parsnips, etc. — are mostly of too little value to justify the expense of distant transport, and are chiefly produced at home. In 1963 the area under turnips, swedes and mangolds in the United Kingdom was less than two-thirds of the area under potatoes, but the weight of production was considerably greater. Cauliflowers, carrots, cucumbers and lettuce are also largely homegrown, but air transport and out of season deliveries make importation an economic proposition. Some £3m. worth of each were imported in 1969 in quantities ranging from 11 000 tons of lettuce to 42 000 tons of carrots.

Fruits of the temperate zone, including nuts and edible seeds

Despite a normal apple crop of 600 000 tons in the United Kingdom, postwar imports have ranged up to nearly 300 000 tons, and though this is not much more than half the prewar import, the value has more than quadrupled (£32.5m.). Before the war Canada was sending 40 per cent of the imports, the other chief suppliers being Australia and the United States. Postwar trade conditions have greatly reduced the imports from both Canada and the States. Australia now head the list, followed in varying order, dependent on the year's harvests, by South Africa, France and Italy, New Zealand, Canada and the States. Other imports include pears (over £5m.), plums, apricots, and cherries; also canned and bottled fruits. But the bulk of the fruit trade of the United Kingdom is in fruits which cannot be grown at home, from lands with a Mediterranean climate or from the tropics. The principal temperate zone fruits of this nature are the citrus fruits (oranges, grapefruit and lemons), grapes, currants and raisins, figs, melons, almonds and other edible nuts, chiefly walnuts and chestnuts.

The **orange** (*Citrus aurantium*, Risso) is believed to be a native of China, where the tree is still cultivated with great care in the southern half of the country. From China it had already spread to other parts of southern Asia before the discovery of the seaway from Europe, and from some part of southern Asia it was introduced into Europe by the Portuguese in 1548. It is now cultivated in several varieties in a great many places in tropical and subtropical countries. Its northern limit in North America extends in the west to about lat. 37° N, in the east to about 31½° N; the bulk of the production is from California and Florida. In Europe its northern limit rises in western Portugal to about 40° N, and then, except in the valley of Andalusia, merely skirting the coast of the Iberian Peninsula, ascends to its highest, about 44° N, in the northwest of Italy. In Asia it begins in the west about latitude 37° (1½° S of Izmir), and sinks in the east to about 34°. In the southern hemisphere, the limit is about 37° S.

The other species of the citrus genus of commercial importance are the **lemon** (*C. limonum*, Risso), the smaller-fruited **lime** (*C. limetta*, Risso), and the large thick-rinded **citron** (*C. medica*, Risso). The last species was the first to be introduced into Europe (not long after the beginning of the Christian era), and owes its specific Latin name to the fact that it was known to the Romans as a tree abundant in Media (the tract on the southeast of the Caucasus). All the species appear to be native in India. A hardier species of the genus is the kumquat (mandarin) of Japan (*C. japonica*, Thunb.), which is grafted on a wild stock that remains uninjured by frost. It yields a small fruit resembling the orange in flavour, though slightly bitter. Since the First World War the larger fruited **grapefruit** has become of commercial importance, and is largely cultivated in California, Florida, the West Indies, South Africa, and Israel.

It may give some idea of the magnitude of the trade in citrus fruits that in 1973 the import of oranges alone — which are approached among other fruits only by bananas (£28.3m.) in the value of their imports — reached 468 000 tons valued at £34.7m. Grapefruit, lemons, and other citrus fruits added £16m. to the value, bringing the citrus total to 625 000 tons valued at £51m. with a further £26m. imported as fruit juice and £3.8m. as tinned fruit.

Formerly almost the entire quantity of oranges and lemons imported into the United Kingdom was derived from Spain and Italy — the lemons more particularly from Sicily. The supplies were only available during one season of the year. Now oranges are available throughout the year from one or other of the chief exporting countries, the main suppliers to this country being Israel, South Africa, Spain, Morocco, and Cyprus. Of old, the Maltese, Jaffa, Azores (St Michael), and West Indian oranges were the most celebrated, the last being considered by some to surpass those of all other places, but the export is small and many varieties have been perfected in the newer countries. In India the oranges of Nagpur and the Khasi Hills have a high reputation, in Argentina those of Tucuman. **Limes** are grown for export, and for the making of lime-juice, more abundantly in the West Indies (chiefly in Dominica, also in Montserrat) than in any other part of the world.

Figs can be cultivated in the Mediterranean region over a somewhat wider range than the orange, the tree which produces this fruit not being so sensitive as the orange to frost. Large quantities are grown for export in Algeria, also in the eastern part of the Mediterranean, and above all in Turkey, in the district lying to the north of those to which the orange is confined. The valley round Izmir (Smyrna), which carries on no orange cultivation, produces figs of peculiarly fine quality. Greece also produces excellent figs, both on the islands and the mainland; and so also does southern Italy. The necessity of cheap labour for packing the figs, which are exported almost exclusively as a dry fruit, is no doubt an obstacle to the cultivation of the fig, especially in those regions which are suitable also for the more valuable orange. The **apricot** is said to be to Syria what the fig was to Smyrna and Ephesus. The improvement in methods of drying and, above all, the growth of canning have made this fruit, as well as the **peach**, of great importance also in the newer 'Mediterranean' lands of California, South Africa, and Australia. Imports of apricots were valued at £0.3m. and peaches at £3.7m. in 1969.

Grapes are of course produced wherever the vine is grown, but they are exported as a fruit chiefly from those districts which do not produce a grape suitable for wine-making. Large quantities of table grapes are grown in this country, and elsewhere beyond the limit of regular vine culture, in greenhouses. They are imported chiefly from South Africa, also from the Netherlands, Belgium, Italy, Greece, and Spain. **Raisins** and **currants** are dried grapes. Raisins are imported into this country chiefly from Australia, Turkey, Greece, and the United States. **Sultana raisins** are made from a seedless grape largely cultivated in Turkey and on some of the adjacent islands including Cyprus. **Currants** are the dried form of a still smaller seedless grape obtained from a variety of vine which appears to be one of the most exacting of all plants as regards soil and climate, and one that exhibits in the most marked manner the effect of local influences. The currant vine is almost confined to Greece, and currants together with sultanas were formerly the most valuable export of that country. They now hold second place to tobacco. Even in Greece its domain is limited, and however carefully the vine may be cultivated, it is impossible to get equally good fruit in all the districts in which it is grown. The smallest, but sweetest and best flavoured currants are grown on the islands; on the mainland the best qualities are grown only at the head and on the south shore of the Gulf of Corinth. It was on this gulf, in the neighbourhood of the town of

Corinth, of which the name currant is a corruption, that this variety of the vine was first cultivated on the Greek mainland. Between the two world wars output was carefully restricted, but competition arose from certain of the 'newer' countries (e.g. Australia) where currants (and likewise sultanas) are now successfully produced. In 1969, 110 000 tons of currants, sultanas and raisins were imported into the United Kingdom, with a total value of £15.5m.

Almonds, walnuts, and **chestnuts,** all, it would appear, originally products of the interior of Asia Minor (Turkey), in the neighbourhood of the Black Sea, have spread far west, and more or less north. Almonds are imported into Britain (£5.5m. in 1969) from Italy, Portugal, Spain, Morocco and Iran; they are largely produced also in France. Walnuts (£2m. in 1969) and chestnuts, which have penetrated further into the heart of Europe, are imported into this country from France and Spain. Among other southern fruits of slight importance in commerce are the **prickly pear,** the black-spotted pear-shaped fruit of a cactus, introduced into southern Europe from the drier parts of tropical America; the **black mulberry,** the **pomegranate,** and the **pistachio nut. Avocado** or **alligator pears,** the fruit of a West Indian tree, grown in Israel and elsewhere have become popular.

Wine

From a geographical point of view, and more particularly, as will appear further on, from the standpoint of commercial geography, the vine is one of the most interesting of all economic plants. Its original home seems to have been somewhere in western Asia or the southeast of Europe. According to Hehn, the region from which it spread is the luxuriant country to the south of the Caspian Sea, part of the ancient Media. 'There in the woods the vine, thick as a man's arm, still climbs into the loftiest trees, hanging in wreaths from summit to summit.'* But it appears to be indigenous as far east as Afghanistan and as far west as the Carpathians.†

How early the must, or juice of the grape, was converted into wine we know from the Hebrew scriptures; and the virtues of this product in process of time caused the spread of vine culture wherever civilisation advanced along the shores of the Mediterranean, as well as eastwards, through the drier parts of Asia. By Europeans the vine of the Old World was introduced into America, where, however, there are native species (*Vitis labrusca*, L., etc.), now cultivated for wine. The spread of vine

* Hehn's *Wanderings of Plants and Animals,* p. 73 (Eng. edn).
† Remains of vine-leaves have been found in prehistoric tuffs at Montpellier and elsewhere in the south of France, and grape-pips round the lake-dwellings of Switzerland, while fossil relics both of the vine and fig (*Ficus carica*) have been found in the Quaternary travertine of Miliana in Algeria.

cultivation is still going on, and the vine is rapidly extending over the whole domain suitable to it throughout the world.

The limits set to its cultivation by climate are somewhat rigorous; for though there are many varieties of the vine, as of all cultivated plants, there are none adapted — like some varieties of maize, for example — to a comparatively short summer. A moderately high temperature, extending far into the autumn, is essential to the maturing of the grape, so as to make it fit for wine-making. In Europe, a mean temperature of about 15° C (60° F) in the month of September is one of the conditions of successful cultivation; and this determines the northern limit of the vine as a wine plant in both the Old World and the New. In western Europe, where the temperature is subject to moderating influences both in summer and in winter, the northern limit is in about 47½° N, a little to the north of the mouth of the Loire, but it gradually rises eastward as the summers get warmer, until in the western part of Poland it reaches its highest latitude anywhere in the world, about 52½ or 53° N. As we go still further east the summer in equal latitudes gets shorter though warmer, and hence the September temperature declines. Consequently, the wine limit gradually sinks to the region of Rostov, where it is further south than in the west of France. The extremely sunny character of southeastern Russia causes it, however, once more to rise a degree or two, but it again sinks in Asia to about 40° or 41°. The corresponding limit on the American continent has a similar form. It begins in California about 37° N, rises to above 42° N in the Canadian province of Ontario (owing partly to the moderating influence on climate exerted by the Great Lakes), but declines again slightly in the United States. In the southern hemisphere the limit is about 40° S.

But while the range of cultivation of the vine is thus limited on the north and south, the habit of the plant gives it one great advantage within those limits. The roots of the vine stock penetrate the soil to a great depth; and this fact, besides placing the roots beyond the reach of frost, which is important in those regions in which a summer of sufficient length is succeeded by a winter of great severity (as in some parts of Russia and central Asia), enables it to draw on deep stores of moisture, and thus to flourish without irrigation even in those parts of the Mediterranean in which the summers are nearly rainless and almost all other vegetation is then at a standstill.

Lastly, it is to be noted that the limits above described are not fixed solely by climate. They are fixed partly by commerce. They are not the limits within which the vine can grow and yield grapes whose juice can be made into wine, but the limits within which wine of tolerable quality can be produced — that is, wine sufficiently good to have a commercial value. In former times the vine was cultivated as a wine plant in the valley of the Severn, and in several of the southern counties of England, as well as north of its present limits on the mainland of

Europe, but the advance of commerce bringing better wines from more favoured regions has caused vine growing to be given up in those places.

The amount and quality of the wine obtainable from grapes vary greatly. In the first place, the fruit is affected by differences in the soil and climate. A sunny climate without excess of rainfall is most suitable, hence it is often grown, especially in the more northerly districts, on hill slopes exposed to the sun, the slope favouring the draining away of superfluous moisture. The excess of summer rains prevents the cultivation of the vine for wine-making in monsoon countries such as India and China. The best soil for the vine is one both warm and retentive of moisture — that is, one that retains enough moisture without being wet; and it is the combination of these characters that makes chalky and other limestone soils so suitable for viticulture. Secondly, the preparation of wine of high quality is an industry that demands skill and experience, and consequently is practised mainly where the industry is of long standing, and where there is sufficient capital and labour. Thirdly, the vine is subject to many diseases, some of which have at times greatly reduced, and occasionally almost extinguished, the wine industry in certain districts. A fungus (*Oïdium Tuckeri*, Berk.) after the middle of the nineteenth century committed extensive ravages in the Mediterranean region and among the vineyards of Madeira. Since about 1863 the vines of France and many other countries have suffered even more severely from an insect enemy, the well-known phylloxera, which reached Madeira in 1878 and took ten years to extirpate there. In France alone upwards of 0.5m. hectares of vineyards were reported to be infected by the disease due to this insect in 1885, and more than 1m. had already been destroyed.

France and Italy lead the world in production of wine, but it is necessary to go back to 1875 for the maximum area, 2.4m. hectares (6m. acres) on which the vine was cultivated in France. In the next ten years, 1876—85, production averaged 43m. hectolitres (946m. gallons) — less than half the output in 1875. Following the phylloxera ravages, which reached their height about 1890, many vineyards were replanted with American vines, which are less liable to the attacks of the insect. By 1902 the area under vines had fallen to less than 1.8m. hectares (4.5m. acres), but the vines were stronger, and in normal years much more productive, relatively to area. In the first quinquennium of the century, production averaged 51m. hectolitres (1 122m. gallons), and though it suffered a sharp setback during the First World War, afterwards it advanced again till in 1934—38, when the area had further fallen to less than 1.6m. ha (4m. acres) production averaged 63m. hectolitres (1 380m. gallons). Averages do not tell all the story. Vintages are always very variable, being much affected by the weather as well as by disease and pests. In France the yield ranges between 11 to over 35 hectolitres per hectare (100 to over 300 gallons per acre).

The effects of the Second World War were much the same as the First. Countries overrun by war could not maintain their output of wine, while countries outside the field of conflict increased theirs; after the war the former mostly recovered the lost ground, while some of the latter had difficulty in retaining their gains. Table 8 shows the output of the main producing countries. In the case of the countries which were not overrun by war, it should be noted that the high level of their output was reached during the war, not in 1945, when world production in general was at a low ebb. Spain, for instance, had an output of 21.4m. hectolitres (470m. gallons) in 1943: Portugal 14.5m. hectolitres (319m. gallons) in 1944. The 1959 figures show the full measure of postwar recovery up to that year. World production was greater than in 1938, and nearly all the leading countries – France, Italy, Spain, South Africa, Argentina – exceeded their prewar output. On the other hand Algeria illustrated what has been said about annual crop fluctuations, while several other countries, though exceeding their prewar figures, had appreciably lower productions than in some of the intervening years.

Table 8 – Annual production of wine, in million hectolitres*

Country	1938	1959	1967	1971
Europe				
Italy	41.8	66.4	75.0	65.0
France	60.0	60.3	61.6	61.3
Spain	16.0	17.0	23.6	24.5
USSR	6.4	7.3	17.8	29.0
Portugal	10.9	9.0	8.7	8.2
Romania	6.0	6.0	6.8	7.7
West Germany	2.3	4.3	5.6	5.5
Yugoslavia	4.7	4.6	5.2	6.0
Hungary	3.1	4.6	4.8	4.5
Greece	4.7	3.8	3.8	4.8
Bulgaria	1.8	1.8	3.4	4.3
Africa				
Algeria	21.5	18.6	6.8	8.2
South Africa	1.5	3.0	4.2	5.8
Morocco	0.8	2.8	3.3	1.1
The Americas				
Argentina	9.3	13.3	28.2	21.0
USA	5.5	10.5	11.4	14.0
Chile	3.6	3.6	4.7	5.3
Brazil	0.8	1.5	1.9	2.3
Australia	0.9	1.5	1.7	3.0
World total	205.1	243.4	284.7	289.7

* 1 hectolitre = 22 gallons; 10 hectolitres = 220 gallons = 1 ton.

Europe's share of the wine produced is falling – 62 per cent in 1966 against 85 per cent before the First World War. South Africa and the Americas have a growing share, reaching 21 per cent in 1966.

France still takes the first place as regards the quality of its wine production. Its most celebrated wines – such as the **clarets** or Bordeaux wines, from the best vineyards of the basin of the Gironde; **champagne**, grown on the chalk hills of the old province of that name; and **burgundy**, named from another old province – are among the best of wines. The last named is grown at its best on the 'golden' slopes of the Côte d'Or, where that range looks down on the warm valley of the Saône.

The export trade in French wines is large and valuable. Until the ravages of the phylloxera began there was only a trifling import to set against this large export, but since 1880 French imports of wine have exceeded the exports. In 1938 imports were 16.3m. hectolitres (358m. gallons), exports 1m. hectolitres (22m. gallons). But the quantities vary greatly from year to year. In 1958 imports were 19.8m. hectolitres against exports of 1.3m. hectolitres, yet in 1969 the figures were 6.8m. and 4.8m. respectively. There is not the same disparity in value, the imported wine being chiefly an inferior commodity from Algeria (declining since Algeria became independent of France), Italy and the northeast of Spain. The explanation of this two-way trade is twofold. First, the fixed habits of the people lead to a larger consumption of wine per head in France than in any other country; second, France retains the reputation which it has long had in foreign countries, especially in England, for its light wines.

In quantity Algeria leads the world as an exporter of wine, providing nearly half of the total exports of some 23m. hectolitres (500m. gallons). Then comes France (4.75m. hectolitres: 100m. gallons), Portugal, Spain, Italy and Morocco, each with a usual export of some 2.4m. hectolitres (50m. gallons). Tunisia (about 1.6m. hectolitres: 30m. gallons) is a little behind, while Yugoslavia exports some 0.5 to 0.75m. hectolitres (10 to 15m. gallons).

Of the **wines of Italy**, though some were celebrated in classical times, only a few are favoured by connoisseurs; one of the best known is Chianti. Some of the **Spanish wines** have long been in high repute, especially in England, the most noted being those strong southern wines which take the name of **sherry** (formerly sherris) from the town of Jerez de la Frontera, near Cadiz, in which district the best sherry is still produced as it was in the days of Falstaff. A greater quantity of wine, however, is produced in the northeast of Spain, for example, in the provinces of Barcelona and Zaragoza. The wines of **Portugal** are, except the light wines near Lisbon for local consumption, chiefly grown in the basin of the Douro, and that which is exported is shipped at Porto. In England these wines are known as port; indeed, by law, the name 'port' may not be used except for these wines. Of the wines of central Europe the most celebrated are those of **Hungary** (especially Tokay). **West Germany**, though low in the list of wine-producing countries in respect of the quantity of its output, is noted for the fine quality of the vintage of some of its valleys, and above all those of the warm valleys of the middle Rhine and its tributary streams, the Mosel and the Neckar. These German white wines, except those from the valley of the Mosel, are known as hock (probably from the village of Hochheim) and are generally light wines with a lower alcoholic content than those of France and Italy.

In the **United States** the cultivation of the vine is becoming increasingly important, especially in **California**. During the prohibition period, manufacture of wine was forbidden and thousands of acres of wine grapes were destroyed. The repeal of prohibition in 1934 gave a new impetus to vine cultivation, and by 1967 the area under grapes was 250 000 hectares (620 000 acres), producing 3.9m. tons of grapes. Sales of fresh grapes are large and although California produces 90 per cent of the crop only 30 per cent of these go to produce wine — almost all for home consumption.

In **Algeria** the spread of vine culture since 1878, when it was in its infancy, has been very rapid. The vine was introduced into what is now the Cape Province of **South Africa** in 1653, soon after the arrival of the first European settlers. The part of South Africa where the first settlements were made has a climate very similar to that best adapted to the vine in Europe, and there it has proved very productive. Considerable quantities of the fruit are used as table grapes or converted into raisins. The production of wine has increased and, in addition to home consumption, wines of the hock, claret, and burgundy types are exported to England. A proportion of the grapes is also used in making brandy and other spirits, but the production under this head has greatly declined. There are several government vineyards where research is carried out. The **Australian** production of wine is increasing and several wines, especially of the burgundy and port types, have found favour in the home market. South Australia, Victoria, and New South Wales are the chief states in which the vine is grown.

The **British trade in wine** is affected by the existence of a customs duty which varies according to the proportion of spirit contained in the wine. Of the British import 78 per cent is from Spain, France, and Portugal. About 3 per cent of the wine imported is re-exported, being sent to all parts of the world. The quantity of wine consumed in the United Kingdom steadily declined from 2.7 litres (0.6 gallons) per head in 1876 to 1.35 litres (0.3 gallons) in 1886 (the minimum till 1900). Since 1955 owing partly to the prohibitive taxes on spirits and relative increase in price of beer consumption per head has doubled (over 2.25 litres in 1964). For comparison in France the consumption in 1876 was rather more than 135 litres (30 gallons) per head and it has exceeded 180 litres (40 gallons).

Hops

The hop vine is a slender-stemmed, twining and climbing plant culti-vated for the sake of its clusters of small greenish flowers, used as a seasoning for beer, to which they impart a bitter flavour. In cultivation it is allowed to twine round upright poles, cords or wires. In the United Kingdom only the female flowers are used in beer-production; in conti-nental Europe male flowers are used. About 66 per cent of the world production is grown in four countries. In 1967 the United States grew 22 500 tons, Germany 24 000 tons (nearly all in West Germany), the United Kingdom 11 200 tons, and Czechoslovakia 7 300 tons – a total of 65 000 out of a world crop of 96 200 tons.

The obstacle to further extension of home production lies in the fact that hops are a very exhausting crop, requiring to be grown only on the richest soil. In England, the crop is mainly grown in the Weald of Kent, where large numbers of hop-pickers, drawn from east London, used to combine work with a summer holiday. In recent years hop-picking has been largely mechanised, and comparatively few workers are required to operate the mechanical contrivances employed. Next to Kent, the principal county producing this crop is Hereford. It is not grown at all in the northern counties. Besides being grown only on rich soil, the crop in England is highly fertilised so that the average yield compares well with the yield elsewhere.

In Germany hops are chiefly grown in Bavaria, especially in the division of Middle Franconia. Before the Second World War this crop extended very rapidly in Alsace-Lorraine. In Czechoslovakia the chief hop-growing area is the Czech or Bohemian plateau around the famous beer-brewing centre of Plzn or Pilsen. The hop as a cultivated plant was introduced into England from Belgium (Flanders) only in 1525.

Beet

This is the common name for several varieties of a widely cultivated species of plants (*Beta vulgaris*, Linn.). They have large broad leaves and long taproots, and it is principally for the sake of the latter that they have been introduced into agriculture. One variety is grown in this country, under the German name of **mangold** or mangel-wurzel, as food for cattle, like the turnip. Requiring a hotter and drier climate than this latter crop, it is mostly grown in southern and eastern parts of England, and, being sensitive to frost, it is not grown in those parts of the island in which the summers are short or the situation too exposed.

Another, and now a much more important variety, the sugar beet, became in the course of the nineteenth century the great rival of the sugarcane in the production of sugar. This variety is now cultivated over a very large area that has steadily grown in central Europe, stretching from France, through the Netherlands, Belgium, West and East Germany, Czechoslovakia and Poland to Romania and southwestern USSR (the Ukraine). Under the protection of high duties sugar is extracted and refined in the United States from beets grown in many states in the north and west, and there are now hardly any parts of the world with a suitable climate in which sugar beet is not cultivated. The area under cultivation and the total production doubled between 1953 and 1965, from 4.2m. to 8.1m. hectares (10.4m. to 20m. acres) are from 91.1m. to 199.8m. tons. World production increased to 238m. tons in 1971, with 34 per cent grown in the USSR. See the sugar industry, p. 208.

Flax

Flax is a plant remarkable for the variety of useful products which it yields, as well as the variety of uses to which these products can be put, and hence is well called by botanists *Linum usitatissimum*, Linn. The fibre of the bast, or inner bark of the stem, which is tall and slender like that of the cereals, is from 20 to upwards of 127 cm (8 to 50 in) in length. This fibre is itself called flax, and from the earliest times has been spun and woven into a fabric known as **linen** (from the Latin name of the plant). Manufactured flax fibres have been found in Neolithic remains. The seed (linseed) yields an oil largely used in making paints and, in its greatest purity, varnish. The crushed cake that remains after pressing out the oil is an excellent food for cattle. Also the seeds, when ground, afford linseed-meal, which is used medicinally. The tow, composed of the shorter fibres of the flax, not used for weaving, is spun into twine and cords, and linen rags furnish one of the best materials for paper-making.

Flax is grown through a wide range of climate. It thrives in Europe and in the colder parts of USSR where fibre production is more important, and in the United States, Canada and Argentina where seed production is more important. The USSR, USA, Argentina, India, and Canada produce 80 to 90 per cent of the 2.5 to 3.5m. tons of linseed produced in the world annually, while the USSR alone provides two-thirds of the 0.5 to 0.75m. tons of the world supply of flax fibre. The USSR and India have some 3m. and 2m. hectares (7.4 and 5m. acres) under flax, Canada, the USA and Argentina each around 1m. hectares (2.4m. acres).

The crop is much dependent on weather conditions. Its chief commercial value in any given area derives from either the fibre or the seed. Where, as in India and Argentina, the plant produces the best seed for oil, the fibre is nearly valueless; and where the fibre is good, as in

USSR, the seed is of less value, though in that country flax is grown both for the oil and the fibre. Far more crops are grown for linseed than for fibre. The total area, at its peak in 1956, was more than 9.7m. hectares (24m. acres), the peak area cultivated for fibre was estimated at 2m. hectares (5m. acres). Though the flax plant is adapted to extremes of climate, the best fibres flourish in a temperate climate, such as that of Europe. Belgium, especially, is noted for the quality of its flax. Flax of excellent quality was grown in considerable amount in the northeast of Ireland, and throughout the island it was a culture of great antiquity. Cultivation has now almost ceased.

The soil best suited for the growth of flax for the fibre is one that is tolerably firm and moist. This latter circumstance is what renders the flat surface of the plains of Europe and the USSR so well suited for its growth. But there are other conditions besides soil and climate which have an important influence on the extent of flax cultivation. Flax is one of those crops which require the employment of a good deal of labour before the fibre is ready for the factory. In the first place, instead of being cut like grain, flax has to be pulled up by the roots. Next, if it has been allowed to seed, it must be rippled – deprived of its seed-vessels by means of an iron comb. After that the straw has to be retted, that is, steeped in water to rot the soft tissue but leave the fibre and the woody core. The quality of the fibre depends largely on this operation, for which the water should be soft and stagnant or nearly stagnant. Finally the straw is scutched with revolving blades, to remove the woody core of the fibre.

It is the labour required for these processes that chiefly prevents the cultivation of flax in England and Scotland. Both before and during the Second World War efforts were made to extent its cultivation in Britain, but with little commercial success, though the plant is quite suited to the climate. The quantity imported of flax alone has varied little from 40 000 tons in 1938 to 43 500 tons in 1963, the value going up from £3.4m. to £7.7m. Since 1963 the growing use of manmade fibres has reduced these imports. By 1973 they had fallen to 25 000 tons, valued at £7.0m.

Lawns and **cambrics** are among the special fabrics made from flax. The latter is named from the French town of Cambrai, where the manufacture is still carried on. The traditional canvas of sailmakers was made from hemp fibre; it is now made chiefly from flax or cotton where manmade fibres are not used.

Hemp (*Cannabis sativa*, Linn.)

Hemp is a plant the bast of which yields a fibre similar to that of flax, only coarser and stronger. It is used chiefly (in England almost solely) for ropes and cordage; the fabric woven from it, which takes the name of canvas, from the Latin name of the plant, was principally used in making sails. The finer kinds of fibre are used in making a cloth similar to linen, and hemp yarn, like linen yarn, can be combined with other yarns in weaving. Like flax, true (soft) hemp is adapted to a wide range of climate; but the soil and climate best suited to it when grown for the fibre are similar to those required for flax, and the mode of cultivation and after-treatment of flax are likewise suitable for hemp. The USSR with an annual output of 100 000 tons produces nearly 30 per cent of the world total of hemp, and is the biggest producer. Italy has the reputation of growing the finest quality, and until recently was also the second largest producer, but its output has declined with falling prices, and India now ranks second with Yugoslavia third. In the United Kingdom hemp is now rarely seen.

The term 'hemp' is also applied to a number of other fibres, some tropical, some extratropical, adapted to the same uses as the true hemp fibre. By far the most important of these are two tropical products, manila hemp and sisal (pp. 214, 805). Other tropical 'hemp' products are sunn hemp and Deccan hemp (pp. 215, 630). Sunn hemp is grown more for its derivative stimulants than for its fibres. Among plants belonging to temperate climates, the so-called **New Zealand flax** (*Phormium tenax*, Fort.) is much better suited to the purposes of hemp fibre than to those of flax fibre; it is, indeed, sometimes called New Zealand hemp, but its ordinary name now is **phormium**. The fibre is derived from the leaves, which are long and narrow like those of the yellow iris. The plant grows abundantly in New Zealand and is easily cultivated. It thrives on inferior boggy soil, almost useless for other purposes, and it has been grown in several of the southwestern counties of Scotland. The use of the fibre in manufactures is impeded by the difficulty in freeing the gum content. Exports of phormium fibre from New Zealand reached a maximum of 27 877 tons in 1905. Since then production has declined. In 1940 eighteen mills processed 29 872 tons of leaves, and produced 3 613 tons of dressed fibre and 443 tons of tow. In 1966 production was 5 000 tons.

Of the other fibre-yielding products of the temperate zone, the most important is **esparto**, or, as it is called in North Africa, **alfa**. These are the commercial names of various grasses (chiefly *Stipa tenacissima*, Linn., but also *Lygeum spartum*, Loefl., and *Ampelodesma tenax*, Linn.), derived from northern Africa (Algeria and Tunisia) and southern Spain, and used chiefly in paper-making. In Spain esparto fibres are also employed in making ropes and cordage as well as in plaiting, and in Tunisia it is processed to cellulose. Imports of esparto into the United Kingdom in the five years 1934—38 averaged 313 671 tons. In the post-war years a maximum of 389 000 tons valued at £15m. was reached in 1951. In the next five years, 1952—56, the average dropped to 274 000 tons and by 1960, the import was 230 000 tons, valued at £3.4m. By

161

1970, wood pulp was the main raw material for paper-making and esparto imports (mainly for high grade papers) were down to 41 000 tons, valued at £37 000.

Wool

Wool is the name given to a kind of hair found in greater or less quantity on almost all mammals, on a few of which it forms the principal covering of the body. From ordinary hair it is distinguished by two important properties. First, while a hair is almost smooth on the outside, each fibre in wool is covered with minute overlapping scales, the edges of which are turned in one direction like slates on a roof. These scales are so minute that they cannot be discerned by the naked eye or by the touch, unless a woollen fibre be drawn between the fingers in the direction opposite to that in which the edges of the scales are set. Second, each fibre of wool is finely crimped or curled, so that when drawn out it becomes greatly lengthened, returning again to its original length when the strain is removed. It is the spring due to this curl which imparts to woollen fabrics that elasticity which distinguishes them from those made from cotton, linen, and other fibres. Another distinguishing property of wool is its power of felting — that is, of becoming matted into a kind of cloth without weaving, but merely by rolling or beating.

The **domestic sheep** furnishes by far the largest proportion of the wool of commerce. Several different species of wild sheep produce quantities of winter wool. But no wild species of sheep possesses the well-known woolly fleece which is one of the principal products of the domestic sheep. When the sheep was first domesticated it is impossible to say. Egyptian monuments record that the Egyptians owned domestic sheep at a very remote period, though there are no pictures of this animal so old as some of those of the horse and ox.

In countries suited for rearing it, the sheep is now the most numerous of domesticated animals, and in most of these it is chiefly for the sake of the fleece that it is reared. The climate best adapted to the sheep as a wool-producer is one that is comparatively dry and equable, or at any rate free from extremes of cold. The grassy tracts of the Mediterranean countries are accordingly peculiarly favourable, and it was in that region that the **merino** sheep, the variety which now produces fine wool in all parts of the world in which it thrives, originated. This variety, which is characterised by its dense and soft fleece, with a fine but strong and very curly fibre, was first known in northern Africa, and was thence introduced into Spain about the middle of the fourteenth century. In Spain, which even in Roman times was renowned for the excellence of its fleeces, the variety was still further improved by careful rearing. In the seventeenth century the finest cloths of western

Europe were all made from Spanish wool, and Spain retained its reputation for wool till long after that period. The merino sheep was introduced into Saxony towards the middle of the eighteenth century and later into Prussia and Bohemia; each in turn becoming noted for the quality of their wool production.

In the Middle Ages wool was by far the most valuable of the English exports. It is still an important agricultural export* of the United Kingdom, though for many years the production of British wool gradually declined, from an annual average of 72 300 metric tons (159m. lb) (greasy basis) in 1871–75 to 50 000 tons (111m. lb) in 1934–38. Exports were better maintained during this period; until shortly before the First World War they increased considerably, and though not increasing at the same rate in later years they continued to form a growing percentage of the diminishing production. The decline during the Second World War, and the subsequent climb up, are shown in Table 9. The figures for production are on a greasy basis (i.e., for wool in its natural condition). The export figures in the table are for home-grown wool only.

Table 9 – Production and export of British (home-grown) raw wool

| | Production | | Export | | Percentage |
Year	'000 metric ton	Year	'000 metric ton		exported
1937–38	47.3	1938	13.7		29
1943–44	41.0	1944	1.5		1
1947–48	34.1	1948	4.7		14
1954–55	50.0	1955	13.2		26
1959–60	58.2	1960	18.7		32
1962–63	58.2	1963	26.7		46
1971–72	48.0	1972	11.0		23

Note: 1 metric ton = 2 204.6 lb.

Estimates of the production of raw wool in the leading wool countries of the world, at different periods of the present century, together with estimates of the world totals and of the number of sheep are given in Table 10.

The recording of wool production on a greasy basis greatly modifies the value of the figures for comparative purposes. The wool on the sheep includes a proportion of grease and dirt which may vary between 40 and 65 per cent of the total weight and which must be removed before the wool is ready for use. Each fibre has a natural covering of grease, which is known as the yolk, and which on the living animal has the important property of preventing the wool from becoming felted.

* To the value of £70m. in 1973.

Table 10 — Wool production and sheep population in leading wool countries

Country	Production of wool (greasy) in '000 metric tons				Sheep in millions	
	1909–13	1934–38	1962	1971	1962	1971
Australia	318	452	757	869	158	169
USSR	105	100	367	424	137	139
New Zealand	90	136	282	322	49	59
Argentina	163	171	185	189	47	41
South Africa	72	114	146	113	38	38
USA	143	205	136	82	31	18
Uruguay	71	52	68	54	22	19
UK	61	50	58	48	29	27
World	1 449	1 722	2 585	2 675	998	1 065

The wool may be scoured before export, although this practice is apt to result in the felting of the wool when packed in bales for long voyages; more frequently the fleece is washed to get rid of the dirt, the yolk being retained. Very often the wool is exported in its natural condition; United Kingdom exports in 1973 for instance, were 11 100 tons greasy or cold water washed and 15 500 tons 'scoured'. The amount of clean wool, that is, the amount of fibre available for manufacturing purposes, thus varies greatly according to the difference of practice in this respect.

Merino and crossbred wools provide just over three-quarters of the total supply of raw wool on the market, while carpet wools make up the balance. The predominant position of Australia among the world sources of supply stands out clearly in the table. Merino sheep were introduced into Australia about the close of the eighteenth century, and produced a wool unequalled for softness and lustre, unlike the original merino, which was very long in staple. As the merino sheep yields very poor meat, the growth of the trade in frozen lamb and mutton has led to the rearing of increasing numbers of sheep crossed with English breeds, yielding better meat and producing a different variety of wool. Crossbreds require plentiful pasture with a good rainfall, whereas merino sheep, though badly affected by drought, thrive best on light pastures with light rainfall.

Next to Australia for wool, though far below it, is the Soviet Union; New Zealand comes third, with crossbreds as the mainstay of its production. The United States, which had the second largest output before the Second World War, has since lost ground both actually and relatively, and now imports from Australia, Argentina and New Zealand, with some finer grades from the United Kingdom; approximately half the imports are carpet wools. The rearing of merinos has been established in South Africa since about 1812, but the wool is neither so fine nor so long in the staple as that of Australia; until the outbreak of war in 1939 the chief markets for it were in continental Europe (France, Germany and Belgium). It is the most valuable single export from South Africa apart from gold.

For Australian, New Zealand, and the best South African wool the chief market is the United Kingdom, which derives from the Commonwealth and River Plate area the great bulk of the wool needed for home manufacturers. Of the 150 800 metric tons imported in 1973, 70 200 tons were divided 40:60 between Australia and New Zealand, 17 900 tons came from Argentina and Uruguay, and 15 700 tons come from South Africa. Now, as before the war, the different branches of the British woollen industry make use of far more imported than home-grown wool; and of the total quantity of imported wool (including that which is re-exported) that of Australasian origin has averaged 60 per cent or over for nearly 100 years. As in Australia, large numbers of crossbred sheep have come to be reared in recent years in Argentina. A great deal of the best blood of British breeds has been introduced into the country, and the crossbred wool of that country is now unsurpassed. But approximately half of the United Kingdom's 1970 imports were still of top quality merino.

In the latter part of last century London was almost the sole market for Australian wool, but now the bulk of the wool is sold by auction in the chief Australian capitals. One result of this is that a large proportion of the wool from that part of the world is now sent direct to New York, the principal continental ports and, increasingly, to Japan. Normally between 80 and 90 per cent of the wool grown in Australia is sold in the local market prior to export.

The United Kingdom also draws quantities of raw wool from China, Pakistan and India (whence the wool obtained is generally of poor quality, used chiefly for making carpets or blankets), France, Chile, the Falkland Islands and the Irish Republic.

Other wools. The principal animals besides the sheep yielding materials for the woollen manufacture are the **goat**, the **alpaca** and **vicuña**, and the **camel**. The fibre derived from all of these is more nearly allied to wool than to hair, though there are gradual transitions between the properties of the one and the other.

Of the varieties of goat, those most famous for their wool are the **Angora goat** and the **Cashmere** (Kashmir) **goat**. The former is a native of the steppes of the interior of Turkey, and its wool, known as **mohair**, is remarkable for its length, fineness, softness, and silky appearance. The goat has been introduced with great success into **South Africa,** and mohair has long been an important export of the Republic of South Africa. The **Cashmere goat** is the animal that furnishes most of the material for the costly Cashmere shawls, so called from having been first made in the kingdom of Cashmere or Kashmir. The material used in the manufacture is not the ordinary covering of the goat, but a fine downy under-covering which grows in winter on this and other animals (such as the yak) belonging to the higher slopes of the Himalayas. The **alpaca** is an animal closely allied to the llama, and, like it, a native of the lofty plateaus of the Andes. It has long been domesticated for the sake of its wool, which is remarkably soft and elastic. The wool of the **vicuña**, another ally of the llama and alpaca, is of even more value than that of the latter animal, but, since the vicuña is found only at elevations above 4 000 m (13 000 ft), it is not domesticated and the supply of wool from this source is consequently small and decreasing. Imports of these various wools into the United Kingdom in 1970 were: alpaca, vicuña and llama 370 tons, camel's hair 380 tons, and cashmere 1 400 tons, to a total value of £2.7m.

Camel's hair, formerly used chiefly for making painters' brushes, is now employed in the manufacture of coarse shawls, carpets, blankets, and other fabrics, the yarn made from it being usually mixed with other yarns. A fine and light-coloured camel-hair was imported from China, a coarser and darker-coloured kind from the USSR, and as this latter kind was very strong and did not readily stretch it was largely used in making belting for machinery.

Woollen manufactures

In point of antiquity the origin of the spinning and weaving of wool belongs to the same remote period as that of cotton and linen. In point of extent the woollen industry is, in temperate countries at least, equal to that of the cotton industry, although the output of woollen fabrics is much smaller.* In temperate and cold countries, in which close-fitting garments are worn, wool is a most suitable material for clothing, not only because it is a bad conductor of heat (due largely to the amount of air occluded), but also because moisture is less readily absorbed by the woollen fibre, and perspiration more readily passes through woollen tissues than through tissues of another kind. Where, as in the tropics and warm countries generally, clothes are worn more loosely, this circumstance is of less consequence.

The treatment of wool in manufactures is in many respects like that of cotton, but some differences require notice. First of all the wool has to be thoroughly freed from the yolk or natural grease which invests it, since that would prevent it from taking the dyes, and otherwise inter-

---

* World fabric production is recorded partly in metres, partly in square metres, and partly in metric tons. In 1965 those countries recording in metres reported production (in million metres) as: cotton fabrics 24 000; rayon/acetate 4 200; wool 700; silk 0.1.

fere with the processes which it has to undergo. Dyeing may follow, and then the fibres may be oiled artificially to make them more easily workable. The nature of the next steps depends on the use to which the wool is to be put, or more particularly on the kind of yarn that is to be made from it. Formerly all long-stapled wools were combed, or so treated that the fibres were laid as nearly as possible parallel to one another, and were then spun into a kind of yarn known as worsted, which is used in knitting and the weaving of fabrics. All short-stapled wools, on the other hand, were carded and spun much in the same way as cotton, and the yarns so made were the only ones capable of being used in making milled or fulled cloths, in which advantage is taken of the felting property in wool to thicken and shrink the cloth after weaving, and afterwards to raise the nap of the cloth mechanically in such a way that, in the most highly finished fabrics, a uniform surface is presented without any appearance of the intercrossing of fibres that takes place in weaving. Wool was therefore formerly divided into (*a*) combing, (*b*) carding or clothing wool. Machines have been invented capable of combing wools having a staple as short as 25 mm (1 in), and, on the other hand, wools with a staple of as much as 12.7 cm (5 in) long may be used in making milled cloth. Wools are still divided into combing and carding or clothing wools, but the former term is no longer synonymous with long-stapled, or the latter with short-stapled wools, and the distinction as between wools is no longer so absolute as it once was. But the distinction between worsted yarns and carded or clothing yarns still holds good, and it is to the industry concerned with the latter that the term 'woollen manufacture' is specially applied.

Among the principal varieties of woollen cloth in the special sense of the term are: (*a*) broadcloths, so called from the great width of the web, the finest quality of cloth; (*b*) cashmeres, a fine thin twilled fabric, much used for ladies' dresses; (*c*) tweeds, a fabric of looser texture than broadcloth and less highly milled, first and still mostly made in Galashiels and other towns belonging to the Tweed basin, chiefly used for clothing; (*d*) doeskin, a strong twilled cloth also used for men's clothing. Blankets and flannels also belong to the woollen manufacture in the special sense of the term.

The name worsted is said to be derived from the parish of Worstead in Norfolk, where a colony of Flemish weavers, who are credited with having introduced the manufacture of worsted into England, settled in the twelfth century. Merinos and serges are among the chief kinds of worsted fabrics made entirely of sheep's wool, but such fabrics are the exception, as worsted yarn is increasingly mixed with yarns made from other materials. The fibres now chiefly used for mixing are the numerous manmade fibres. Hosiery and knitwear form a separate industry and so does the making of carpets. The best carpets (Turkey, Brussels, Axminster, Wilton, etc.) are made on a ground of jute, hemp or rubber, only a few entirely of wool. Handmade carpets are still produced in Iran and other eastern countries.

Mention should also be made of shoddy. This is yarn (and the material made from that yarn) spun from fibres which have been shredded from woollen rags. This produced an inferior cloth but made good use of the woollen waste of the United Kingdom and gave rise to a considerable import trade in rags. The introduction of manmade fibres has now greatly reduced shoddy production, but the trade is an early example of an increasingly important feature of modern industry: the recovery of scrap for use as raw material.

In the Middle Ages woollen manufactures attained their highest development in Flanders, which had the advantage of being within easy reach of abundant supplies of wool, especially from England, and being able to send its manufactured products to the best markets by sea, river and land. In the middle of the twelfth century Flemish woollens were already worn in France and Germany. A writer of the thirteenth century says that all the world was clothed in English wool wrought in Flanders. It was from Flanders that English kings at different times introduced artisans into England with the view of improving the woollen manufactures of their country. Towards the close of the eleventh century this was done by William the Conqueror; it was again done by Edward III, in the first half of the fourteenth century, and again by Henry VII towards the close of the fifteenth.

England had already begun to export considerable quantities of woollen cloth in the sixteenth century, but the cloth was mostly undressed and undyed, these finishing processes being performed in Holland as late as 1650. Early in the following century the woollen industry of England had risen to such importance that woollen manufactures formed upwards of 40 per cent of the value of the exports, and about 1780 this industry is spoken of as having 'long been the glory of England and the envy of other nations'. Soon after that it began to share in the improvements brought about in the cotton industry by the introduction of machinery, but as the leading industrial countries of the world all produced quantities of woollen goods, the British woollen industry (in the wide sense of the term) never acquired the predominance that was to be attained by the British cotton manufactures. In 1921 the factories engaged in woollen, worsted, and shoddy manufactures in the United Kingdom employed about 237 000 persons, considerably less than half the number in the cotton industry. Nearly half of these were employed in the woollen (including shoddy) factories, the remainder in the worsted. At the Census of Production, 1949, the woollen and worsted industry employed 179 000 operatives; cotton, spinning and weaving 257 000.* Native English wools are best

* Later figures are not comparable because of the increasing inter-mixture of manmade fibres with wool.

adapted for the worsted industry, which helps to account for the fact that it is in this branch that England has long had a special reputation, as shown by the export trade in woollen and worsted yarns; through all the fluctuations of the past 100 years, worsted yarns have been an easy first until the late 1960s when the position was reversed.

Table 11 — Woollen and worsted yarns: UK exports in '000 metric tons

Average of years	Woollen yarn	Worsted yarn	Alpaca and mohair yarn
1862—66	0.7	12.7	0.7
1906—10	1.2	25.2	7.4
1926—30	3.0	17.2	3.5
1936—38	3.0	11.7	1.5
1945	0.7	2.9	0.2
1952—56	2.3	8.2	1.0
1960—64	4.5	8.2	1.7
1973	10.5	4.0	—

Exports of combed wool, made up into bundles known as tops, increased from 3 000 tons (6.4m. lb) in 1890 to over 22 700 tons (50m. lb) before the Second World War, and though at the end of the war they were down to 7 300 tons (16m. lb), they rose steadily to 43 600 tons (96m. lb) in 1963. In 1969 they were 26 100 tons (57m. lb) valued at £26m. In 1973, 21 000 tons valued at £38m.

Table 12 — Woollen and worsted woven fabrics: UK exports in millions of square metres

Average of years	Woollen fabrics	Worsted fabrics
1857—61	21	112
1901—05	47	86
1911—13	84	59
1921—25	108	53
1931—35	52	27
1936—38	60	32
1945	23	11
1951—55	54	29
1960	49	26
1973	36	18

The exports of worsted yarn have long been greater than those of woollen yarn; but their steady reduction is a reflection of the increasing competition of alternative yarns from manmade fibres and of the increasing independance of traditional export markets. On the other hand, as Table 12 shows, exports of woollen cloth have been greater than those of worsted cloth throughout the twentieth century.

Silk

Next to wool, silk is the most important of animal products used in weaving. The great bulk of the silk of commerce is derived from the **silkworm**, which is the caterpillar stage of a kind of moth, whose food consists of the leaves of the white mulberry (*Morus alba*, L.). It is hence called *Bombyx mori*, or the mulberry bombyx. In the body of the silkworm the substance that becomes the silk fibre exists in the form of two jelly-like masses, which harden on exposure to the air. When the 'worm' is about to pass into the chrysalis stage, it sends out this substance by two minute openings at the head, and the two streams, at once uniting, form an extremely fine thread, which the worm coils round itself to form a cocoon. From the cocoons the silk of commerce is directly obtained, but the thread of a single cocoon is much too fine for use in spinning and the threads from several cocoons must be united, individual threads being sufficiently adhesive to make this an easy matter. For the finest qualities of silk yarn, the product of five to seven cocoons is used; for coarser qualities, the product of eleven, or even twenty.

After being reeled off from the cocoons the silk is made up into hanks, and in this condition forms the raw silk of commerce. The outer husks of the cocoon and a part of the silk in the interior are incapable of being reeled off, and in addition, numerous fragments of thread remain as refuse after the process of reeling. These are exported from silk-producing countries under the names of husks, knubs, and waste, and can be manufactured into silk fabrics. Cocoons also are exported, but generally in comparatively small quantity; for since 45 kg (100 lb) of cocoons yield only about 4.1 kg (9 lb) of raw silk; it is obvious that the carriage of the silk is more economical than cocoons.

Since mulberry leaves form the principal food of the silkworm, the animal can be reared in all climates in which the mulberry thrives. Silkworms are usually reared under cover, the trees being stripped of their leaves in order to supply them with food, and the animals can thus be protected from the weather. The range of climate suitable for silkworm rearing is consequently a wide one. Still, the character of the climate is very important. The health and productiveness of the caterpillars are greatly affected by the temperature, and as the rearing of the insect from the egg to the formation of the cocoon is completed within seven weeks in spring, there are great fluctuations in the amount of raw silk produced, according as the weather is genial or not. In Japan the 'autumn crop' free from the vagaries of spring is now more important than the spring crop. But the geographical distribution of raw silk production does not depend solely on climate. This industry is almost confined to Asia and Europe, notwithstanding that there are many regions elsewhere in which the climate is suitable. The limitation in the range of production arises from the nature of the labour connected with the industry. The tending of the silkworms previous to the spinning of the cocoons, and the subsequent operations necessary to prepare the raw silk for the market, demand not only a considerable amount of labour, but also the utmost carefulness and delicacy on the part of those employed. Silkworm-rearing is therefore generally confined to those parts of the world where labour is abundant and has inherited from previous generations a capacity for watchfulness and delicate manipulation.

Chinese legend ascribes to Si-ling-she the honour of having discovered the art of spinning and weaving silk about 2700 BC. The rearing of the silkworm is generally distributed over **China**, but is principally carried on in the middle provinces (about latitude 30° to 35° N), and in the southern province of Kwangtung. In addition to the produce of the carefully reared and tended mulberry moth, there is a large amount of silk obtained in China from the wild moth. It used to be reckoned that about one-quarter of the total production and one-tenth of the export came under the head of **wild and coarse silk**. With no estimate of home consumption, it is difficult to assess China's present position among silk-producing countries, but its exports have been left far behind by those of **Japan**, which easily dominates world trade in silk. The production of raw silk in Japan was subject to greater fluctuations than in China, a natural consequence of its more northerly latitude and greater liability to cold springs, until the development of the autumn crop. The Japanese have readily adopted European inventions and the bulk of the silk is reeled not by hand but in steam filatures. There has been similar development in China, at least as regards the export trade. Whereas in 1894 China's exports of filature silk were only about 5 per cent of her exports of hand-reeled silk, midway between the two world wars most if not all of the exports were filature silk.

In **India** the rearing of the mulberry silkworm appears to have been introduced as early as the sixth century, but the industry is far from having attained the importance which it possesses in China and Japan. The mulberry was chiefly cultivated in Bengal, where the East India Company made special efforts to foster the production of silk as far back as 1767, and Bengal silk became an important article of export. Nowadays Mysore provides a large proportion of India's output of cocoons and considerable quantities of silk are obtained from 'wild' moths, in Assam, the old Central Provinces, and west Bengal. The general name of tussore silk is given to their produce, and most of the silk so called is distinguished by its natural fawn colour. Imports, however, now more than balance exports.

Hong Kong is an active centre of the silk trade and Korea maintains a sizeable export to the United States, but elsewhere conditions are often irregular. Imports have dwindled in Burma and are irregular in Iran and

Iraq, but Iran still exports from the strip between the Elburz Mountains and the Caspian. The silkworm industry also survives in Turkey, Lebanon, and Syria.

In the early days of the Roman Empire silk was used as a material for garments worn by the rich, and before the commencement of the Christian era the raw material had been imported into Italy for weaving. But it was not till the sixth century AD that Europe was able to make a beginning with the rearing of silkworms. Justinian, who was at that time emperor of the East, and his consort Theodora, encouraged the new branch of agriculture, of which **Greece**, and more particularly the Peloponnesus, became the principal seat. The peninsula just named is said to have obtained its modern name of Morea from the Greek word for a mulberry-tree. Silkworms were also introduced by the Arabs into **Sicily** and **Spain**, and during the Arab (Moorish) domination in southern Spain the production of silk was very extensively pursued. It is still carried on in Murcia and Valencia in Spain, in various parts of Greece, and in other parts of the Balkan Peninsula; but in the five years 1934–38 the total estimated production of all these regions, measured by the weight of cocoons produced, was only about one-fifth of that of **Italy**, which provided 80 per cent of the silk produced in Europe. In Italy the silk-producing region is not now the island into which the silkworm was first introduced, but the great plains of the north, Lombardy, Piedmont, and Venetia, in many parts of which the long rows of mulberry-trees, stripped bare of their leaves in summer, are a spectacular reminder of the nature of the industry pursued there.

Nowadays **France** ranks below Italy, Greece and Bulgaria in the weight of cocoons it produces, though in the middle of the nineteenth century its production of silk — chiefly associated with the Rhône valley — exceeded the Italian production. In 1856 the business of silkworm-rearing in France began to be adversely affected by the outbreak of disease among the worms; and the ravages of this disease, which at a later date spread to Italy, Spain, Greece, and even the silk countries of the Far East, were such as to bring down the silk production in France in 1876 to less than a tenth of what it was in 1853. After 1876 matters improved when Pasteur discovered a method for controlling the spread of the disease. Local silk production is now supplemented by imports from Italy.

World production of raw silk in 1938 (exports only in the case of China) was estimated at 56 000 tons (123m. lb). Japan, Italy and China supplied four-fifths of the exports; the United States, France the United Kingdom and Japan were the leading importers. Faced with the competition of rayon fabrics and, later, nylon hosiery, the output of raw silk had been declining for some years, and the Second World War had a disastrous effect on the industry. Mulberry trees had to give place to food crops and by the end of the war the annual output had dropped to 11 000 tons (24m. lb) — one-fifth of the 1938 figure. Since the war there has been some revival. The International Silk Association estimated production in 1969 at 39 000 tons (86m. lb). Japan provided 53 per cent of the total (usually about three-quarters is machine-reeled, the rest hand-reeled). China was credited with 9 000 tons (22 per cent) and Korea with 2 400 tons (7 per cent). In Italy, as in India, despite extensive government aid, great difficulty has been experienced in maintaining the industry against the high costs of production in relation to world prices.

World exports of raw silk, which before the war approached 35 000 tons a year, were down to 5 500 tons at the end of the war. For some years, as production rose exports also rose, but then came a setback. By 1969 exports from the chief producing countries were down to less than 2 500 tons; Korea being the major exporter having taken over that role from Japan which had become a net importer.

The United States in 1938 took 84 per cent of Japan's export of raw silk, in 1958 only 33 per cent of the much smaller quantity available. By 1969 imports from Japan were negligible, Italy and Korea providing 75 per cent of the total which had fallen from 25 000 tons in 1938 to less than 1 000 tons in 1969. China, apart from her markets in the Soviet Union and eastern Europe, has an outlet to the free world through Hong Kong.

Silk manufactures

The continuous silk thread as it is wound from the cocoon does not require to go through the processes necessary in spinning wool, cotton, and other fibres. The making of true silk yarn is known as **throwing**, and consists merely in giving the thread a slight twist, which enables it to combine better with other threads. The processes undergone by silk waste to convert it into yarn are essentially the same as those adopted in spinning other fibres and the yarn so made is distinguished as spun silk.

Of the fabrics made from silk, the chief are satins and velvets. The former being woven so that almost the only threads appearing on the outer or 'right' side of the tissue are weft threads, which present a uniform glossy surface; the latter are woven so that the outer surface presents a short soft pile, made by passing the warp threads over fine wires, which are afterwards drawn out. The loops then remaining are either left as they are, in which case the tissue is called pile velvet, or cut to form cut velvet. This fabric is now imitated in cotton, nylon and mixed tissues.

Though Italy was one of the earliest seats of the silk manufacture in Europe, and though during the Middle Ages this branch of industry developed to a high pitch in Venezia, Lucca, Genova, Bologna, and other Italian towns; though, too, that country, as we have seen, stands far ahead of all others in Europe in the production of the raw material, in the manufacture of silk fabrics it ranks far behind France, and its silk is exported largely in the form of thrown silk. The higher branches of the silk industry are now, however, more important than at the end of the last century as silk increasingly becomes a luxury product.

In silk manufactures France now surpasses all other countries in Europe. The centre of the industry in France is Lyon, and the history of the industry offers interesting illustrations of the influence of political events, of inventions, and of fashion on the prosperity of manufactures, and the commerce depending upon manufactures. The silk industry of Lyon began to flourish after the capture of Milano by Francis I of France in 1515, that monarch having then induced several silk artisans of Milano to settle in Lyon. Encouraged at a later date by Henry VI, and favoured by the extension of silkworm-rearing in the Rhône valley, the industry rapidly rose to a position of great importance. The first blow inflicted on it was the persecution by later French kings of the Huguenots, or French protestants — a persecution which drove many of the French silk-workers out of France, and sowed the seeds of the industry in many other parts of Europe, even in Russia. From this blow, however, the French industry revived, and about the beginning of the nineteenth century it received great impetus from the invention in Lyon of the celebrated apparatus named, after its inventor, the Jacquard loom for the weaving of figured patterns. Originally invented for making rich silks with intricate woven patterns, this apparatus has since been applied to the weaving of other fabrics (linen, etc.). When the sewing-machine and mass production came into general use, fashions of ladies' dresses became more elaborate and more changeable, so that there was less demand for the fine and costly but lasting tissues which used to be the glory of the French looms. Silks of an inferior and less durable quality, and mixed fabrics having the appearance of silk, were introduced; and since the looms of Germany and Switzerland were more speedily adapted to meet this new taste, the French industry suffered greatly. Subsequently the French manufacturers adapted themselves to the new requirements of the trade, but by then the competition of the cheap Japanese silks has beaten all producers. Moreover since the First World War the great competitor has been artificial silk, or rayon, a name which in British trade parlance formerly covered all manmade fibres. None the less, with the rising standard of living throughout the world there is still a market for real silk as well as the competitive synthetic fibres.

In the **United Kingdom** silk manufacture is not so highly developed as the other branches of the textile industries. The British Isles have not the advantage, like the chief silk-manufacturing countries of the Continent, of being able to produce any of the raw material and when the duty on silks in this country was abolished under the treaty with France in 1860, British manufacturers found themselves completely beaten, even in the home market, by those of France. On the other hand, in the years between the two world wars the silk industry, hand in hand with rayon manufactures, made great strides in the United Kingdom. The chief centre of silk manufacture and of certain styles of rayon is the district embracing Macclesfield (Cheshire) and Leek (Staffordshire). Lancashire and Yorkshire are also known for their rayon fabrics, the spinning of silk waste, and the weaving of 'spun' or schappe silk.

Silk manufacture advanced rapidly in the United States, under the protection of a high duty, though the production there of spun silk practically ceased. The chief seat of the manufacture is Paterson, in New Jersey, within 24 km (15 miles) of New York. The great Japanese industry is associated especially with the heart of the country; production and spinning are carried on in the numerous small basins, weaving is especially important at Kanazawa, and Kobe and Yokohama are the great commercial centres and ports. Although the revival of sericulture and of silk manufacture play a not inconsiderable part in the postwar economic recovery of Japan, the position in 1964 was thus described in an official Japanese publication:

> The development of new products such as nylon and other synthetic fibres has prevented the industry from ever regaining its prewar importance. Sericulture is carried on much as in prewar days, mainly by womenfolk. Sericulture techniques, however, have been improved, silkworms often being raised collectively so as to economise on labour. Formerly reeling was carried out by individual farming households but today cocoons are sent to drying houses and reeling mills.

Between 1930 and 1961 mulberry-growing land dropped from 1 765 000 acres to 410 000; farmers from 2 216 000 to 629 000; cocoon production from 399 500 tons to 115 300. Three-quarters of the raw silk is retained for use in home factories; exports are down to less than a quarter of the production of 20 515 tons in 1971. World production of silk in 1971 was 40 268 tons; of cocoons 339 255 tons.

Silk and silk products were given considerable prominence in the early editions of this work, but their greatly reduced importance in world trade no longer justifies such extensive treatment. None the less, much original material has been retained as a reminder of the changing pattern of commodities which have featured in world trade over the last 100 years. Silk has always been a comparatively expensive article and the total value of the silk trade was therefore far greater when world trade was but a small fraction of what it is today. As a labour-intensive luxury item it could neither expand to take part in the greatly increased demand which accompanied the growth in purchasing power of the industrialised nations, nor could it compete with the capital-intensive, mass produced manmade substitutes. It remains a luxury item, but is now insignificant in commercial value when viewed against the bulk production and bulk exchange of alternative textile materials (see footnote on p. 166).

Subtropical products

Cotton

Cotton consists of the hairs of a fluffy tuft which envelopes the seeds of the cotton plant. When the seed vessel has opened, the tuft swells to the size of an apple, and remains firmly held by the withered parts of the seed pod long enough for the cotton to be easily picked. Of all the products of a subtropical climate cotton is among the most important, and its importance dates back to the earliest times of which there is any record. The first mention of it is found in Indian books written more than 800 years before the Christian era. The first European writer who is known to have mentioned it is Herodotus, who wrote in the fifth century BC, and speaks of a tree which he knew by repute as growing in India, and bearing instead of fruit a wool like that of sheep.* The wide spread of the plant in prehistoric times is even more remarkable. While most of the chief cereals, along with flax and hemp, were introduced from the Old World into the New, and the New World gave to the Old maize, tobacco, and the potato, cotton was found by the earliest explorers, from Columbus to Cook, growing almost everywhere in the area in which it is now found.

At the present day its cultivation is almost universal in tropical and subtropical regions, but it is in the latter that it attains its widest extent. The United States, Egypt, Mexico, Turkey and Brazil, are the most important countries of production so far as international commerce is concerned; the USSR, India, Pakistan and China are large producers of cotton for home consumption, and occasional factors in the export trade. In all these countries except India and Brazil the districts where cotton is chiefly grown lie outside the tropics, and in India the cotton districts though mainly tropical, are generally at least 300 m (1 000 ft) above sea level. Its northern limit in the New World is about 37° N; in the Old World it is largely grown in Turkmenskaya to the north of 40° and even, in Sinkiang (Chinese Turkestan), in the oasis of Turfan between 42° and 43° N, but this is below sea level.

The world area under cotton reached a peak in 1937–38, with an estimated total of 38m. hectares (93m. acres), yielding 8 200 metric

* One cotton plant, probably *Gossypium arboreum*, was certainly known at a very remote date in Egypt.

tons (18 000m. lb) – half the production being provided by the United States, and three-quarters of the remainder by India, the Soviet Union, China and Egypt. During the Second World War the growing importance of food production led to a big decline in the acreage devoted to cotton, which reached a low level of under 22m. hectares (54m. acres) at the end of the war, with a low level production of 4 500 tons (10 000m. lb) (1945–46). With the removal of United States restrictions of the area planted and the extension of cultivation in other countries, the area under cotton in the world continued to increase and stocks to accumulate. By 1965 production reached 11 700 tons (25 700m. lb) from 35m. hectares (86m. acres) and has apparently stabilised at this high level.

The cotton plant is not everywhere precisely the same. The genus *Gossypium*, contains several species which differ in size, in the colour of their flowers, and, what is most important from a commercial point of view, in the length, strength, and fineness of the fibre forming the tufts. All the cultivated varieties are now believed to be reducible to three species – *G. herbaceum*, Linn., and *G. arboreum*, Linn., natives of the Old World, and *G. barbadense*, Linn., a native of the New World.

The species now most widely cultivated, both in the Old World and the New, is *G. herbaceum* (the *G. hirsutum*, Linn., the species to which the ordinary American 'uplands' cotton used to be referred, is now regarded as a variety of that species). It grows to the height of about 1.25 to 1.5 m (4 to 5 ft) and produces soft and silky fibres of moderate length, that is, from 22 to 33 mm (0.9 to 1.3 in) long. It is a native of India, Indo–China, and the Eastern Archipelago, and has been introduced into all other parts of the world with a suitable climate – into the United States some time in the latter part of the eighteenth century. There it succeeds better than in its original home, yielding an average fibre of about 25 mm (1 in) in length. The best of all cotton, however, is that derived from *G. barbadense*, and known as **sea island cotton**, from the fact that in the United States it was first cultivated on the string of flat islands which line the coast of Georgia and South Carolina. The fibres are both fine and strong, and their length may be as much as 63 mm (2.5 in), though the mean length is some 44 mm (1.6 in). If allowed to grow on from year to year this species of cotton may attain a height of 4.5 to 6 m (15 to 20 ft); but being, like other species of cotton, cultivated mostly as an annual, it is seldom allowed to grow to a greater height than 1 m (3 ft). This species appears to thrive best in slightly saline conditions, and to require a greater amount of moisture and a longer period to mature than the ordinary species. It has been almost eliminated in the United States by the boll weevil but has been successfully introduced into the Leeward Islands, Egypt, Tahiti, the Fiji Islands, and Queensland. A tree cotton known as **caravonica cotton**, said to be a hybrid between Sea Island and rough

Peruvian cotton, has been grown for a number of years in tropical Queensland, and has been introduced into other parts of the tropics. Its fibre is of long staple, strong and moderately rough, and as the plant has to be resown only every eight or nine years, its cultivation is recommended by the small amount of labour involved.

As regards climate, all the species of cotton plant require a long summer free from frost, with a moderate but not excessive amount of moisture. The cotton plant grows well in a dry warm soil, but it will put up with considerable differences in soil under diverse climatic conditions. It is peculiarly sensitive to frost; and as it generally requires about seven months or 200 frostless days to yield a paying crop, this fact alone has a great influence on the extent of its cultivation. Very equable, warm, but not excessive temperatures, especially during the period of vigorous growth, appear to be those most favourable to the plant, and plenty of bright sunshine is essential to the production of fibre of good quality.

The United States has long been the world's largest producer. The potential cotton-growing area lies south of 37° N, which is approximately the line of 200 frost free days, and east of 100° W beyond which the rainfall is too low, although irrigation makes cultivation possible in marginal areas where soil conditions are otherwise suitable. The total area of this 'cotton belt' is some 18m. hectares (450m. acres) but the area where the cotton plant is grown has changed appreciably over the last 100 years. Before the war of 1861—65, South Carolina and Georgia produced 75 per cent of the total crop; but by 1969 they produced only 4 per cent. In the interval the main cropping area had moved steadily westward, first to the rich alluvium of the Mississippi valley and then to the plains of Texas. This changing pattern was occasioned by the exhaustion of the land from overcropping in the older areas, and from the depredations of the boll weevil. This pest entered the cotton belt from Mexico in 1892 and spread rapidly northwards and eastwards causing severe losses for many years, almost eliminating the sea island strain in the eastern areas. Apart from the use of pesticides, the boll weevil has been largely contained by the introduction of strains of cotton which developed earlier and in dryer conditions. This in turn made it possible for crops to be grown increasingly on the rich lands towards the west of the belt. The focus of production now lies beyond the Mississippi, with Arkansas, Texas, Arizona and California producing 65 per cent of the total crop in 1969.

The area under cotton has also varied considerably for, as a cash crop, cotton is as sensitive to economic factors as it is to climatic limitations. From 1880 to 1900 the area under cultivation rose from 5.2m. to 10m. hectares (13m. to 25m. acres) as the great home market of the United States began to develop. It continued to rise to a peak in 1926 of 19m. hectares (46m. acres) with a yield of over 4m. tons. Since then both area and total crop have fallen, partly as the result of the need to grow food crops during the Second World War; partly because of the growing competition from manmade fibres, either as substitutes or as mixtures in the finished fabric; and partly because of the changing commercial importance of cotton as the traditional markets of the developing countries become increasingly independent. As a result the United States' share of world production fell from 30 per cent in 1956 to some 20 per cent in 1968, and government controls over the area to be planted have reduced the fields to some 5 to 6m. hectares (12 to 15m. acres) in the late 1960s with a production of between 2m. and 3.5m. tons. The crop yield has steadily increased since the Second World War however. In the 1950s it ranged between 240 and 330 kg per hectare (220 to 300 lb per acre), but by 1970 it had reached 560 kg per hectare (500 lb per acre). This was achieved by (*a*) the increased application of fertilisers; (*b*) the ability, with such limited acreage, to grow crops in the optimum growing areas; and (*c*) the increased use of machinery for planting, tending and harvesting the crop.

As the world's largest cotton producer, a position now shared with the USSR, the United States has also been the largest producer of cotton seed. The seed is a byproduct of the first of the manufacturing processes (ginning) by which the cotton fibre (lint) is separated from the seed in preparation for spinning into yarn. The cotton seed is crushed to produce both an edible oil, for cooking, margarine, etc., and a meal or oilcake, which can be used as a fertiliser or as cattle feed. In 1968 the harvest of 4 000 tons of cotton seed produced 700 tons of oil and 1 800 tons of meal, almost all of which was consumed in the United States.

In **India** and **Pakistan** cotton is dependent on the rains of the southwest monsoon. The main production areas are on the peninsular plateau behind the Western Ghats, where the total rainfall is often in some parts rather scanty, and on the alluvium of the upper Indus and Ganga in the Punjab and Uttar Pradesh where the rainfall is even scantier but where there are extensive areas under irrigation. The chief cotton-growing regions of India differ from those of the United States in having the higher temperatures in early summer and apparently in having a smaller proportion of bright weather. On the tableland of India the scantiness of the rainfall is made up for by the peculiar character of the black cotton-soil. It is derived from the decomposition of the basaltic rocks which cover so large a portion of the peninsular. It is of great fertility, and is said to have borne crops for thousands of years. In one respect this soil agrees with the best soils of the American cotton region, namely in the presence of lime. But its main value in so dry a climate is its remarkable tenacity of moisture. Instead of allowing the rain to sink away like the best cotton-soils of America, it becomes during the rains a tenacious mud. In dry weather the whole surface of the ground where this soil occurs becomes seamed with interramifying cracks, between which the soil forms hard lumps, but these lumps still retain water imprisoned in their spongy cells. Hence, wherever this soil prevails irrigation is not required for cotton culture.

The average yield is less in India than in Pakistan, and in both is less than in the United States. In 1971 the United States yield was nearly 500 kg per hectare (445 lb per acre); Pakistan 300 kg per hectare (270 lb per acre) and India 110 kg per hectare (98 lb per acre). The staple of Indian cotton is generally short, from about 13 to 20 mm (0.5 to 0.9 in), as against 25 mm (1 in) or more for the ordinary American cottons, and this renders it unsuitable for many of the branches of the manufacture carried on in Lancashire. During the present century, the quality of Indian cotton generally has been greatly improved, and there has been considerable extension of the area under cotton, especially through irrigation in the north as well as in the old Central Provinces. About 1906 a variety of cotton known as Cambodia cotton was introduced from Indo—China and has proved well suited to the red soils east of the Cardamom Hills when irrigated and heavily fertilised. The cotton is similar to the medium staple American cotton and yields over 225 kg per hectare (200 lb per acre). The long staple American cottons are grown in the irrigated lands of northern India and Pakistan (Punjab and Uttar Pradesh), and grow best when specially bred for local conditions.

In **Egypt** cotton cultivation is necessarily confined to the areas of perennial irrigation. The rich soil gives a higher average return than the United States; from 1963 to 1965 the yield averaged 680 kg per hectare (610 lb per acre) and by 1971 had reached 780 kg per hectare (nearly 700 lb per acre). The staple is from 30 to 38 mm (1.2 to 1.5 in) and the cotton is the best grown on a large scale; before the Second World War it fetched 50 per cent more than the average of American cotton and twice that of Indian. After the war Egyptian still headed the price list of cotton in large supply, but though in July 1947 it was treble the prewar price, both American and Indian approached it more nearly in value than before the war. Much of the production has been of the sakel or sakellaridis type with a staple of 33 to 48 mm (1.3 to 1.8 in) and of recent years even better types have been introduced. This high quality is no doubt to be ascribed to the fertility of the soil, and to climatic conditions. The skies are mostly bright, and the temperature rises and falls during the period of growth with remarkable regularity to make the Nile delta an ideal growing area.

Egyptian cotton has also been tried in Texas, but though the temperature curves of some parts of Texas (as at San Antonio) are close to those of Cairo, in those parts the climate is not equally bright and dry. On a small scale Egyptian cotton has been grown under irrigation with fair success at Phoenix, Arizona, and in a few other parts of the arid region in the southwest of the United States, but less than 1 per cent of the crop is of this type.

Cotton is a striking example of the changes which time often brings in the world pattern of an important commodity, as regards its sources of supply and commercial distribution. During the period 1786–90 the British West Indies furnished more than 70 per cent, the Mediterranean countries 20 per cent, and Brazil about 8 per cent of the imports of raw cotton into the United Kingdom; the share of the United States and India together was under 1 per cent, and Egypt contributed nothing at all. A hundred years later, in 1886–88, when the import had increased seventyfold, from about 11 400 tons to 800 000 tons (25m. lb to 1 750m. lb), the share of the United States had risen to 75 per cent, that of India to 12 per cent and that of Egypt to 9.5 per cent, while the share of Brazil had sunk to 2.75 per cent, and that of the British West Indies to insignificance. Fifty years later still, before the Second World War, the average annual import of raw cotton into the United Kingdom in the quinquennium 1934–38 was down to 631 000 tons (1 390m. lb), and the United States' share of the smaller total had dropped to 41 per cent; but Egypt's share was up to 20 per cent, and India's was 14 per cent, these three countries between them supplying 75 per cent of the total. Brazil had come to the fore again, with an average of 8 per cent, and Peru supplied 6 per cent, the balance of 11 per cent being provided mostly by the Anglo–Egyptian Sudan (5 per cent) and by British African colonies and protectorates. The British Cotton-Growing Association (founded at the beginning of the century) and the Empire Cotton-Growing Corporation (incorporated in 1921 with a government grant of £1m. and the right to levy funds on the industry) encouraged cotton-growing in colonial territories, with some positive increase in production but little percentage addition to normal world supplies. Apart from the Sudan (now independent), where the Gezira irrigation scheme has been a great success, cotton-growing has improved steadily in Pakistan and Uganda.

The initial decline in world production due to the Second World War was naturally reflected in the movement of trade. In 1947 the imports of raw cotton into the United Kingdom were down to 325 000 tons (714m. lb) – little more than half the prewar average. In 1949–51 they increased to over 455 000 tons (1 000m. lb) a year, but then came a prolonged slump. Already the dollar exchange problem had been limiting British purchases; in the three years 1949–51 the import of American cotton had fallen from 40 to 30 to 22 per cent of the total imports. With world production rising to surplus levels, the United States government, pledged to support local agriculture, bought and stocked cotton from the farmers at uneconomic prices by world standards. Manmade fibres became increasingly important and India, Hong Kong, and other territories formerly a market for British cotton goods began manufacturing more and more for their own needs; and in some cases exporting cotton goods to Britain. In 1972–73 imports of raw cotton averaged only 171 000 tons (376m. lb). The leading sources of supply were Colombia, Turkey, the United States, Sudan, Brazil, the USSR and Pakistan; with the United States providing less than 7 per cent and Egypt only 2 per cent.

Cotton is exported in bales of cleaned cotton, that is, cotton-lint freed from its seed by a process called ginning. It is an interesting fact, illustrative of the variety of circumstances that affect the development of commerce, that the early extension of cotton production in the United States was due to the invention of an improved ginning process. Previously the separation of the seed was done by hand, a process which demanded the cheapest available labour; and in 1792 so little was it thought probable that the United States could ever contemplate the export of cotton in quantity that, in negotiating a treaty with Great Britain in that year, the United States ambassador agreed to a provision (struck out, however, by the senate) which forbade the export of cotton from the United States to this country. In 1793 the invention of the saw-gin by Eli Whitney made it possible to process a bale in a matter of minutes instead of weeks and imparted such a stimulus to the cultivation of cotton in the United States that the country rapidly became the chief source of supply of raw cotton in the world. The growth of cotton in India and Egypt received a great impetus from the scarcity of the raw material due to the civil war in America in 1861–65, and the effects were permanent in both countries.

Inventions by which the process of manufacturing cotton were cheapened have likewise been among the chief causes that contributed to the vast development of the commerce in this commodity in various forms; and it is a fact of great consequence in the history of British commerce that all the more important of these inventions originated in England.

Cotton manufactures

The Arabs are said to have introduced the cultivation of cotton into Spain in the eighth century and by the middle of the following century cotton manufactures on a considerable scale were carried on in the Moorish towns of Cordoba, Granada, and Seville. It is no doubt to this fact that cotton owes its name, which is of Arabic origin. Augsburg is known to have exported cotton fabrics of its own manufacture in the fourteenth century. The first recorded importation of cotton into England was in 1298, for the making of candlewicks (a manufacture of much greater relative importance in days when candles were the chief means of artificial lighting). In 1352 we find the first mention of Manchester cottons, but the fabrics so called were not what we know as cottons. Even as late as the seventeenth century a coarse kind of woollen cloth, a web of frieze, was known as cotton. Later the term appears to have been applied to mixtures of wool and cotton, or linen and cotton. That true cotton was used in Lancashire about 1640 appears from the fact that about that date there is mention of Manchester cotton buyers in the Levant. The use of cotton in manufactures extended very slowly. Between 1697 and 1749 the import of the raw material into England remained almost stationary, and there can be no doubt that the manufacture of cotton goods on the Continent was greater than in England. A change was brought about by the inventions that took place in England towards the end of the eighteenth century, and revolutionised first the cotton industry, and ultimately textile industries of all kinds.

Without entering into details, some of the major inventions are worth noting. The spinning jenny of Hargreaves, invented in 1764, patented in 1770, was the first machine by which more than two yarns could be spun at once. Arkwright's water-frame (so called because soon after its invention water was used as a motive power in driving it) was an improved device for the same purpose, patented in 1769. In its improved form it is known as the throstle. Crompton's mule, a sort of cross between the jenny and the throstle, constructed in 1779, was a much better contrivance than either, and is a machine still used for the spinning of weft yarns. These three machines changed in a great measure the condition of the cotton industry in Great Britain. The spinning-jenny could be used in domestic spinning, and the chief effect of its invention was that the old spinning-wheel was thrown away into lumber-rooms, and the jenny adopted in its place, with the result of greatly increasing the output of yarn in each family. Arkwright's machine, however, was more suitable for working in large factories; and factories began to multiply when, in 1785, it was declared that Arkwright had no claim to the patents he had obtained, so that anyone might adopt the inventions patented in his name. The result was that, whereas in the old days of the spinning-wheel the weaver might have to spend the morning going to half a dozen cottages to obtain yarn enough to employ him for the rest of the day, now so much yarn was produced that the supply greatly exceeded the demand; the handloom weavers could not use it all.

The next step was the invention of the first powerloom by Edmund Cartwright, a clergyman having little knowledge of mechanics, and none of weaving. His first machine was patented in 1785, and an improved form in 1787; but even this second form had to be improved by further inventions before it could be made capable of weaving cloth as rapidly and cheaply as a handloom.

Later a new spinning-machine known as the ring spinning frame was invented. It was first put in operation in the United States about 1832, but not until much later was it applied with success in the United

Kingdom, where, however, it rapidly grew in favour for the production of warp. In all machines improvements in detail are almost uninterrupted, and all processes conducted by machinery were greatly accelerated by the introduction of steam power to drive the machines. This was first applied in the cotton industry at Papplewick in 1785. In the case of spinning, the result of the change since the time of the early inventions is illustrated by the following facts. When the hand wheel was still in use it required six or eight spinners to keep a weaver employed, and the earnings of a family amounted to only a few shillings a week. Even the mule was first employed as a domestic machine, and the earnings of a family in spinning were raised in some cases to as much as £6 per week. Before the close of the eighteenth century the cost in wages of the production of a pound of yarn of medium fineness was reduced to less than a halfpenny.

All these inventions were extensively applied in England a considerable time before they were introduced on the continent of Europe. In applying them England was peculiarly favoured by its abundance of coal and iron, and its admirable situation for commerce. Moreover, the wars which raged on the Continent from about the time when these inventions began to take effect down to 1815 interfered with the development of industry on the Continent much more than in Great Britain. The consequence was that England became pre-eminently the seat of the cotton industry, and by 1801 manufactured more cotton than the entire continent of Europe. The value of cotton goods exported from Britain was officially estimated in 1785 at less than £1m.: in 1815 it was estimated at upwards of £22m., and though, in accordance with what is mentioned on p. 127, it must be remembered that these estimates gave no satisfactory indication of growth in value, they do indicate a very remarkable growth in quantity. After that the volume of the British cotton industry, as indicated by the quantity of raw cotton entered for consumption in the United Kingdom, went on increasing with but slight fluctuations until the present century (see p. 181). In all the quinquennial periods from 1831–35 to 1906–10 there were only two in which there was a decline as compared with the previous periods, the only considerable decline being in the period of the American civil war 1861–65. On the average about four-fifths of the quantity of cotton manufactured in the United Kingdom was exported. So far as external trade is concerned, this country rapidly acquired and for long retained an unquestioned predominance in the cotton industry, in spite of the fact that we were wholly dependent on imported raw material — a predominance that was never approached in the woollen industry, even when we had almost a monopoly of one of the most prized varieties of the raw material.

The reasons for this predominance may be attributed partly to the special natural advantages Britain possessed for the industry; partly to the general causes favouring concentration of an industry developed on a very large scale; but still more perhaps to the fact that this is an industry well suited to turn to account the country's great advantages for maritime trade. Cotton goods were (and still are) consumed in all parts of the world. From any one centre of production most of the markets must be reached from the seaboard, and for such markets no country had advantages equal to those enjoyed by Britain and a free trade policy greatly assisted in turning these advantages to account.

A decline set in after the First World War. In 1913 cotton piece goods exported from the United Kingdom were valued at nearly £98m.; by 1938 the figure had fallen to £32m. In 1945 the quantity exported was only 40 per cent of the prewar figure, though the value had fallen no more than 10 per cent. The 1951 figures afforded a more striking illustration of the change in relative values brought about by the war and its aftermath. The quantity of cotton piece goods exported was 75 per cent of the quantity in 1938, but the value had gone up from £32m. to £132m. As many as fifteen countries within the Commonwealth took piece goods to the value of over £1m., ranging up to £26m. in the case of Australia. The difficulties which beset the cotton trade after 1951 (see p. 181) were reflected not only in the imports of raw cotton but also in the exports of cotton piece goods. In the five years 1952–56 the value of such exports dropped steadily till in 1956 it was only £61m. – less than half the 1951 figure. By 1970 the total was down to £24m. with only £7.6m. going to the Commonwealth – less than £1.6m. each to Australia and New Zealand.

During the long development of the British cotton industry there have been great changes in the destination of its products. In 1820 the continent of Europe received more than half the total quantity of cotton fabrics exported from Great Britain, the United States received nearly one-tenth, and eastern Asia little more than one-twentieth; in 1880 the continent of Europe received scarcely one-twelfth, the United States less than one-fiftieth, and eastern Asia (chiefly British India) more than one-half of the whole. In 1969, one-third went to Africa, one-fifth to Europe and little more than a token quantity to India. Of yarn Great Britain supplied large quantities to the continent of Europe; the proportion of the total export declined from above 95 per cent in 1820 to 48 per cent in 1891, but it rose to 67 per cent before the First World War and was about the same before the Second World War. By 1969 it had fallen to 30 per cent. Eastern Asia, which in 1820 received no appreciable quantity of British yarn, received in 1891 33 per cent of the amount exported, though the proportion afterwards declined to 16.5 per cent before the First World War and less than 1 per cent before the Second World War largely as a result of Japanese competition.

Such facts point to a rapid growth of the industry in many countries, and, so far as the United States is concerned, Table 13, which shows the

Table 13 — **Disposal of United States cotton crop (percentage)**

Year	United States	United Kingdom	Others
1831	17	58	25
1861	20	52	28
1891	33	38	29
1911	40	26	34
1916	55	22	23
1931	45	10	45
1941—45	87	3	10
1969	76	1	23

changing pattern of distribution of the cotton crop, makes it clear that an increasing proportion of America's output of raw cotton is consumed at home. Foreign competition is not merely a matter of recent years. Although the decline of British supremacy was hastened by the First World War, it had become inevitable. Foreign competitors were at first engaged in the easier task of conquering their home markets, and only later began to compete more keenly in world markets. India, Japan, and China have all entered the field as competitors in the machine cotton industry. The growth of cotton-spinning in the southern states of the Union, as well as in India and Japan, is peculiarly instructive. In the southern states the number of cotton spindles increased from 1.2m. to 4.8m. between 1887 and 1900; in India from 2.9m. to 4.9m. between 1890 and 1901; in Japan from 325 000 in 1892 to about 1m. in 1897. By 1965 there were 15.8m. in India while Japan's total increased from 2.4m. in 1914 to 7m. in 1930 and 12.7m. in 1965. In China the number of spindles in 1965 was estimated at 12m. In the case of the cotton industry of India and the United States the question of tariff hardly affects the matter. Till 1922 cotton yarns were admitted into India duty free, yet, in spite of dear coal, cotton spinning by machinery has continued to grow from its inception. The first mill was started in 1851. The geographical advantages of local supplies of raw material, abundant labour, and a local market have been decisive. Japan had a 5 per cent duty on imported yarns, and has, besides the local market, the advantage of local supplies of coal to counterbalance the necessity of importing the great bulk of its raw material. In the export trade its competition was almost worldwide before the Second World War, and now already that branch of Japanese trade has shown vigorous revival. In the United States the southern industry competes chiefly with that of the north, against which it enjoys no protection. Again the pre-ponderating advantages are geographical. The growth of the industry, particularly in India and Japan, greatly affected the industry of Lancashire, which had to turn its attention more and more to the higher (finer) counts of yarn, and the

Table 14 — Mill consumption of raw materials, 1939—68 (in metric tons)

Year	Raw cotton	Manmade fibres*		World total
		Artificial	*Synthetic*	*(million tons)*
1939	2 200 000			2.20
1950	5 940 000		—	5.94
1951	7 327 980		—	7.33
1952	7 185 640		—	7.18
1953	7 669 200		—	7.67
1954	7 840 360		437 386†	8.28
1955	7 855 546		494 111	8.35
1956	8 588 140		552 597	9.14
1957	9 336 360		556 097	9.89
1959	9 833 826		1 024 588	10.86
1960	10 170 666		1 111 267	11.28
1961	10 420 956		1 155 926	11.57
1962	10 344 500		1 286 464	11.63
1963	10 623 389		1 366 883	11.99
1964	10 984 889	1 397 021	439 218	12.82
1965	11 203 656	1 691 039	699 970	13.59
1966	11 742 088	1 173 480	917 893	14.39
1967	11 769 646	1 323 881	740 559	13.89
1968	11 829 428	1 430 749	996 609	14.35

Source: By courtesy of the International Federation of Cotton and Allied Textile Industries
* Artificial (cellulosic) and synthetic (non-cellulosic) fibres
† Data not available for previous years

production of a greater proportion of woven goods for the Eastern markets. It was the increased production of finer yarns in the United Kingdom that led to the increase noted on p. 185 in the proportion of British yarns sent to the mainland of Europe, and this was why the number of cotton-spinning spindles in Great Britain remained greater than in all the rest of Europe combined till after the First World War. A similar change has been brought about in the northern seats of the American industry by the development of the southern. But in neither case did the change stop here. Both India and the southern states of the Union began to manufacture the finer yarns in greater and greater quantity. In 1900—01 more than 20 per cent of the weight of yarns produced in India was of the finer types. By 1918—19 under the stimulus of the scarcity of supplies from Lancashire during the First World War this had risen to 35 per cent. A steadily increasing quantity of woven goods has also been produced by mills in India. Likewise in the southeast of the United States and in Japan, a steadily increasing proportion of spindles has been devoted to the higher counts. Mule spindles, formerly necessary for the production of the finer counts of

Table 15 — Comparison of mill consumption in major areas between 1954 and 1968 (in million metric tons)

Area	Raw cotton		Manmade fibres	
	1954	*1968*	*1954*	*1968*
Europe	2.709	3.634	0.259	0.803
North America	2.036	2.119	0.152	0.710
Asia and Oceania	2.604	5.184	0.015	0.807
South America	0.393	0.531	0.008	0.066
Africa	0.097	0.362	0.003	0.041

cotton yarn, declined in 1950—65 from 23m. to 1m., while ring spindles increased from 100m. to 130m. Improved ring spindles now meet all needs at lower labour costs.

In the spinning of raw cotton into yarn by the ordinary processes there is about 1 lb lost as waste in every 6 lb of raw cotton, and there is further loss in the manufacture of cotton cloth. For some time this waste has been treated in large quantities on the continent of Europe in such a manner as to make it available for the spinning of either pure or mixed yarns, and this industry has also been introduced into the United Kingdom. Cotton waste is also largely exported for wiping and polishing.

Tobacco

The tobacco of commerce is obtained from the prepared leaves of several species of a genus of plants known as *Nicotiana*, and now cultivated in almost all parts that have a warm enough summer. The leaf contains nicotine, which acts as a stimulant and narcotic, but which, being an active poison, is capable of exercising most injurious effects if swallowed. Besides being used as a luxury, tobacco is used to a small extent in medicine, and as a sheep-wash for the destruction of insects which infect the fleece. The species of tobacco most usually cultivated is the *N. tabacum*, Linn., which grows to the height of from 1.2 to 1.8 m (4 to 6 ft), and produces several clusters of white or pink flowers.

The tobacco plants are all natives of America, and the use of the leaf in smoking was widespread in that continent at the time of its discovery in 1492. The practice was quickly adopted by the European discoverers and introduced into Europe, where, notwithstanding the prohibitions and denunciations of Popes and crowned heads, it spread rapidly. In Europe the plant is said to have been first cultivated in Holland in 1615, but it soon extended to other countries. Increasing usage induced governments to encourage cultivation for the sake of raising a revenue from it. In Great Britain the cultivation of tobacco was forbidden at an early date for the sake of encouraging it in Virginia, where it became an important article of commerce almost immediately after the foundation of the colony. In Ireland the cultivation of the plant was allowed till the reign of William IV, when an Act was passed prohibiting it there also, for the sake of convenience in raising revenue; in both England and Ireland prohibition was continued till 1886, when cultivation of the plant was again allowed under certain conditions which were further relaxed in 1910.

Like maize, barley and potatoes, tobacco is adapted to very diverse conditions. It can be grown anywhere in the tropics, and has been cultivated with success even in Scotland. The limitation of its range arises principally from the necessity of protecting it during growth against frost. This is particularly necessary in the early stages, when a single white frost is enough to spoil the whole crop, and is one reason for the usual practice of sowing the seed in small beds, for these seed-beds can be sheltered from frost by being covered. Adaptable as tobacco is to a great variety of conditions, it exhibits in a peculiar degree the effect of this diversity in the differences of the characteristic qualities of the product. The tobacco obtained from a variety of the plant adapted to one soil and climate is widely different from that obtained from a variety adapted to a different soil and climate. These diversities are well illustrated within the wide area of the United States, where the chief tobacco states are North Carolina, Kentucky, South Carolina, Virginia and Tennessee.

Table 16 — Tobacco: production and exports in '000 metric tons

Country	Average 1934–38 Crop*	Average 1934–38 Export†	1959 Crop	1959 Export	1967 Crop	1967 Export	1971 Crop	1971 Export
USA	600	200	815	210	893	259	774	215
China	630	15	422	42	850	65 (est.)	811	n.a.
India‡	500	21	267	39	353	55	362	48
USSR	225	4	190	96	260	140 (est.)	262	n.a.
Brazil	94	31	144	29	243	45	245	55
Japan	64	4	130	5	209	6	150	—
Turkey	55	32	121	67	182	92	155	84
Pakistan‡	—	—	100	—	178	10	150	3
Bulgaria	134	24	99	62	118	77	120	58¶
Greece	57	44	80	55	102	88	88	59
Indonesia	104	48	77	15	95	14	75	6
Rhodesia §	20	15	111	80	94	90	62	n.a.
World total	2 950	—	3 690	—	4 923	—	4 566	—

* Wet weight.
† Dry weight.
‡ India includes Pakistan for 1934–38.
§ Includes Malawi (Nyasaland) in 1934–38 and 1959.
¶ 1970. Tobacco manufactures provided an additional 45 000 tons.
n.a. Not available.

The total world area under tobacco was estimated in 1971 to be a little over 4m. hectares (10m. acres), producing over 4.6m. tons; the annual average for the period 1948–52 was 2.8m. tons from nearly 3m. hectares (7.4m. acres).

World production is rising slowly, with more rapid increases among the smaller producing countries. It will be seen that some of the chief producing countries play only a minor part in the tobacco trade of the world. The United States leads in respect of both production and exports. It not only outstrips China and India, the other two outstanding sources of world production, but it supplies from a quarter to a third of the tobacco entering into international trade. On the other hand, China and India export comparatively little, whereas some of the minor producing countries are world-famous for their products. Cuba and Jamaica have gained a reputation for cigars, and Sumatra and British North Borneo vie with one another in producing the best cigar wrappers, a fact due partly to soil and climate, partly to care in treatment. Hungary enjoys the reputation of producing the best European-grown tobacco. In recent years Africa has come to the fore as a minor but increasing source of supply, the chief producing areas being south and south central Africa; in Rhodesia and Malawi tobacco is a main agricultural product for export, and the combined crop is half the total production in Africa.

Crops have been grown from time to time in the United Kingdom, but commercially they are negligible. West Germany and the United Kingdom import more tobacco than any other country, mostly for home consumption. All but a small percentage is unmanufactured, higher duty being charged on manufactured tobacco. Before the Second World War the imports of unmanufactured tobacco to the UK amounted (1938) to 157 000 tons (345m. lb), of which 75 per cent came from the USA. In 1946 the quantity was up to 197 000 tons (433m. lb), with the United States supplying 85 per cent. Currency restrictions, especially in connection with dollar imports, reduced the total and in 1960 imports were 166 000 tons (365m. lb) valued at £102m. In 1973 they were 149 000 tons (328m. lb) valued at £137m., with the United States supplying 38 per cent.

Before the Second World War, Germany was the second biggest importer of unmanufactured tobacco, and the Netherlands third, the Dutch imports being largely for manufacture into cigars for export (over 20m. cigars were exported in each of the years 1938 and 1939). After the war German imports ceased for a time and Dutch imports were greatly reduced (partly because of the troubled conditions in the Netherlands East Indies, which had been a chief source of supply); with the remarkable result that the United States, the world's largest producer and exporter of tobacco, became in 1945 and 1946 the biggest importer after the United Kingdom, though very far behind (annual imports about 36 000 tons — chiefly oriental leaf from Turkey and Greece for blending, and cigar leaf from Cuba and Puerto Rico). By 1954 the old order was restored: Germany (97 000 tons: 80 per cent Federal) was again the leading importer after the United Kingdom, followed by the United States (70 000 tons), the Netherlands (34 000 tons), and France (30 000 tons).

Opium

Opium is the hardened juice of a cultivated species of poppy called *Papaver somniferum*, Linn., a variety of the wild species *P. setigerum*, DC, a native of the shores of the Mediterranean. There is reason to believe that the cultivated form has existed in India for a period not far short of 3 000 years. The juice is contained in the seed vessel, the wall of which is scratched so as to allow it to exude. It then hardens, and is picked off. Opium is chiefly used as a stimulant or narcotic, and is either swallowed in small quantities or smoked (by itself or in prepared mixtures), or taken in the form of certain preparations made from it. Of these the most important are laudanum, which is made by soaking opium in spirits of wine, and solutions of morphia, which is the narcotic principle of opium.

Formerly, India was the country in which opium was chiefly grown as an article of foreign commerce, and its cultivation in British India was made a monopoly of the government, which once derived from it an annual revenue of about £10m. It was grown in the Ganga valley, round Patna and Varanasi (Benaras), and on a fertile tableland further west, corresponding to the old kingdom of Malwa. Towards the end of 1906 edicts were issued by the government of China for the suppression of the use and cultivation of opium in that country within ten years, and in 1911 the government of India agreed to bring the export entirely to an end in 1917 or earlier, if proof was given of the absence of native-grown opium in China. There is now no ordinary trade in opium between India and China. In 1923 the government of India adopted the certificate system recommended by the League of Nations, whereby any export of opium must be covered by a certificate from the government of the importing country, approving the consignment as being needed for legitimate purposes. Also, in 1926, the government of India undertook to reduce the export of opium to Far Eastern countries by 10 per cent per annum until it was extinguished. As a result of these various measures, the area under cultivation for opium in India dropped from 248 000 to 1 900 hectares (615 000 to 4 700 acres) between 1906 and 1939. During the Second World War, official demands for opium for medical and scientific purposes sent the acreage up again, and by 1962 it was 45 000 hectares (111 000 acres), from which 185 000 licensed cultivators produced 969 tons of raw opium. The poppy is cultivated under licence by international agreement and all the crop is bought by the central government, which maintains an opium factory in Uttar Pradesh (the former United Provinces).

Outside China and India, opium is chiefly consumed in Muslim countries, where it still has some use as a substitute for wine and alcoholic liquors. Iran and Turkey are the principal countries of western Asia in which this drug is cultivated, and in both it forms an article of export. In quality the product of Turkey surpasses that of any other part of the world. In the countries of western Europe opium is chiefly used in medicine, and the English supply is mainly derived from what used to be known as the Asia Minor section of Turkey (Izmir). United Kingdom imports in 1973 were 214 metric tons valued at £2.4m.

According to a report issued in 1948 by the Permanent Central Opium Board, which functions under the United Nations, world production of raw opium in 1936 — the latest year to which a world total was assigned — was 3 761 metric tons. Of this, all but 10 per cent was accounted for by China (1 612 tons), Iran (1 347 tons), and Turkey (426 tons). Production was mainly for home consumption; world exports were returned as only 400 tons.

Tea

Tea is the name given to the dried leaves of one or more shrubs or trees allied to the camellia. The mild stimulant in tea, caffeine, is identical with that found in the two commodities next considered, coffee and cocoa. These three commodities likewise agree in requiring for their cultivation at least warm summers with frequent rains, although they differ greatly in the degree of cold they will stand. They also agree in requiring more or less cheap labour to prepare them for market, and this necessity in many cases excludes them from regions where the climate is suitable. Lastly, they agree in being derived from trees which take a certain number of years to come into profitable bearing, and this has an effect on the fluctuations of prices of these commodities, and hence indirectly on their geographical distribution. The fluctuations in price have been striking in the case of coffee and cocoa and one cause is to be found in the long period of waiting for returns. High prices are likely to stimulate the laying out of plantations. When these plantations come into bearing there is likely to be an oversupply, leading to a fall of prices that tends to throw out of cultivation the plantations in those parts of the world that are least favourably situated. Tea has not suffered similar fluctuations and the area under cultivation has steadily expanded in India, and in Ceylon, but the increasing production of these two parts of the world told severely on China, which lacked modern methods of transport, and only by slow degrees and to a very limited extent introduced modern machinery for preparing the leaf. In

1881 China's exports of tea were about 136 000 tons (300m. lb) a year; before the end of the century they had dropped by nearly a third. The decline continued into the present century, accelerated by the disturbed conditions in China, and in the quinquennium before the Second World War the exports by sea — by far the greater part of the exports — averaged only 41 000 tons (90m. lb). During the war they dropped still lower. China may now be producing more tea than any other country, but both area and production can only be estimated.

Considering the extensive consumption of tea, coffee and cocoa one may well be struck by the comparatively small areas required for their production. J. C. Willis in his *Agriculture in the Tropics* (1914), estimated the world crop area at about 2m. hectares (7 800 sq miles) — little more than the area of Wales. Now the area in Brazil alone, representing perhaps half of the world total, is over 4m. hectares. In the five prewar years 1934–38, the annual production averaged about 2.2m. tons, which also seems comparatively small for the world supply, in view of the fact that it was less than half the weight of wheat and flour which the United Kingdom alone imported annually. Willis's estimate for cacao was 240 000 tons (in 1911) from 728 000 hectares (2 800 sq miles) — the area of the West Riding of Yorkshire. Since then the production of all three crops has increased greatly, but the total area is still comparatively small. World production in 1971 was: coffee beans 4.9m. tons, cacao beans 1.5m. tons and tea 1.3m. tons. The area for tea totalled some 1.3m. hectares (5 000 sq miles) — still less than the size of Yorkshire.

The tea plant comes into full bearing in the fifth year. It grows to a height of 2.5 m (8 ft) if required for seed, but is generally pruned to a low bush to encourage leaf production and assist plucking. One variety, which grows wild in Assam, and is by some regarded as the stock from which all other tea plants are derived, attains the dimensions of a tree. The name of the plant and its product is Chinese, but even in China the plant is said to have been unknown till the middle of the fourth century and did not come into general use in that country till four or five centuries later. The first European who is known to have mentioned it is the traveller Pinto, who visited Canton in 1544. As late as 1664, the English East India Company, when it wished to make a present of some tea to the king of England, had to buy a small quantity from the Dutch, and when it was first imported into England, in 1665, it was sold at the rate of £3 per lb.

Tea is one of the hardiest of all subtropical plants. Severe frosts, such as it is exposed to in northern China, check its growth and diminish its yield, but do not kill it. The plant is thus suited for a wide range of climate, but the best is one which is warm, moist, and equable throughout the year. Like the cotton plant the tea shrub requires regular supplies of moisture during the summer months, but is easily injured by an excess of moisture settling about its roots, so that the ground on which it is grown ought to have good drainage. All these conditions are best obtained on the slopes of mountains within the tropics or in subtropical regions, and it is in such situations that tea is chiefly grown up to an elevation which varies with the latitude. The soil best suited to the tea plant is virgin forest soil, a light, rich, friable loam containing a good supply of vegetable mould or humus, or of organic matter in some other form; such soils are most readily obtained in the situation just described. The presence of iron either in the soil or subsoil is desirable, and hence reddish soils are preferred. It is noteworthy that, unlike cotton, tea is chiefly grown, in the principal producing countries, on soils remarkably poor in lime.

The successful cultivation of the tea plant depends not merely on soil and climate. In its preparation for the market, tea demands much hand treatment, so that it can be profitably grown as a marketable commodity only in those parts of the world which, besides other suitable conditions, have plenty of cheap labour. It is for this reason that India, Bangladesh, Ceylon, China, Indonesia and Japan are the principal countries of its production.

In China the first crop of leaves is gathered at the end of the third year, but care has to be taken not to exhaust the plant by stripping it too closely. Three pickings are made each year and as the best leaves are the young ones, the earliest gathering is the best. Women and children are mainly employed in this work. Having been first dried in the sun, the leaves are then crushed to extract the moisture. This done, they are heaped up and allowed to heat for some hours, until they have become a reddish-brown colour. They are next rolled up by hand, and are afterwards again exposed to the sun or slowly baked over charcoal fires. The object of the rolling is to mass the leaf into a state conducive to rapid fermentation. This is brought about by warming the leaf for an hour or so, and has the effect of reducing the proportion of tannin in the leaf from 12 to about 5 per cent. The leaves in this form are known as 'black tea'. In the preparation of 'green tea' there is no fermenting process, but the leaves are merely roasted in an iron pan, and then rolled a little, these operations being repeated several times in succession and the tea finally dried off. Tea is also prepared in China in the form of bricks and tablets for convenience of land transport by porters or pack-animals. The ordinary brick tea is made only of the refuse of the tea prepared by ordinary methods — inferior tea leaves, stalks, and tea dust. But the finest tea dust can be compressed by steam machinery into tablets of tea of excellent quality. A kind of tea known as 'flat tea' is prepared in Japan from unrolled leaves picked from bushes that have been partly blanched by being grown in the dark for two or three weeks before picking.

The introduction of tea cultivation into the Indian subcontinent was due to government incentive. Experimental plantations were started by the Indian government on the hills of Assam, and at different points on the southern slopes of the Himalayas, between 1834 and 1849, and a grant of land was made by the government to the first private tea company formed in India, in 1839. It is only since 1851, however, that tea-planting in India has been a marked success. During the intervening century the area under cultivation has increased to over 345 000 hectares (850 000 acres) (including Bangladesh), with nearly 37 000 hectares (91 000 acres) more in Pakistan. Assam alone harvests some 170 000 hectares (420 000 acres) — nearly half the total area of Indian tea plantations. Tea is also extensively grown at various points on the Himalayan slopes, in Bengal, in Uttar Pradesh, and even in the Punjab; also on the Nilgiri Hills in southern India (and to a very small extent in Lower Burma). In northern India the limit in height of profitable cultivation is mostly about 1 070 m (3 500 ft) above sea level, but on the Nilgiris the best elevation is from 1 460 to 1 710 m (4 800 to 5 600 ft).

There are three main varieties cultivated in the Indian subcontinent: the Chinese plant, which yields a comparatively weak tea, and furnishes a small yield; the native tea of Assam; and a cross between the two, which last is most in demand among the planters. The method of cultivating and preparing the tea is much the same as in China, except that the bushes while bearing (that is, during the southern monsoon, March to November) are picked about once every ten days, and that the rolling is performed by machinery. The average yield varies greatly in different localities, but improved methods of cultivation have brought about a long-continued and marked general increase. In 1882 the average for the whole of India was under 336 kg per hectare (300 lb per acre). By 1934–38, the yield per acre averaged close on 560 kg per hectare (500 lb per acre) and by 1965 the yields per acre had nearly doubled to 1 000 kg (890 lb per acre). Even before the war, world production was so high that a number of countries, including India, Ceylon, and the Netherlands East Indies, entered into an International Tea Agreement to regulate exports, and achieve stability of prices and trading conditions. The United Kingdom has always taken the great bulk of India's exports of tea, which before the war amounted to about 159 000 tons and increased to 208 000 tons in 1970, out of a total estimated production of 420 000 tons.

About 1880 the cultivation of tea in Ceylon began to extend with extraordinary rapidity in consequence of the failure of the coffee plantations. The soil and climate have been found to be admirably suited to the shrub, which has yielded an average of 900 kg per hectare (800 lb per acre). Abundant labour, no longer required on the abandoned coffee plantations, has afforded the means of preparing the product for the market at the smallest possible cost. Leaf-rolling machinery is in general use, and all the operations up to the export stage are performed on the estates. In 1883, for the first time, Ceylon's exports of tea exceeded 450 tons (1m. lb), and so rapid was the growth of the plantation industry that by the end of the century they had risen to nearly 68 000 tons (150m. lb). During the present century, production − nearly all for export − has risen to 212 000 tons (466m. lb) (1970). A third or more of the tea exported is shipped to the United Kingdom.

The production of tea in Indonesia made great strides after the first plantation was made in Java in 1827. Before the Second World War the output was about three-quarters of that of Ceylon. Over 80 per cent of the total was grown on plantations managed by Europeans or Chinese, the remainder being grown by the native population on small holdings. The most important area is between 305 and 1 370 m (1 000 and 4 500 ft) above sea level in western Java, and the output both there and in Sumatra was increasing until first the Japanese occupation, and then the destruction following on revolutionary disturbances, caused a serious setback to the industry and for the time being practically put a stop to commercial dealings. There has since been a steady revival of production to 78 000 tons (171m. lb) in 1967, 70 000 tons in 1970 − about one-third of Sri Lanka's (Ceylon's) production.

The cultivation of the tea plant is said to have been introduced into Japan and Korea early in the ninth century AD, and before the Second World War Japan had a tea export trade surpassed only by India and Ceylon, Java (Indonesia) and China. Here too the war led to a great falling off both in production and in exports, but a steady recovery increased production in 1970 to 91 000 tons (200m. lb) − well above the prewar level. Japan tea is mostly prepared as green leaf (the leaf being simply steamed, rolled and fire-dried). Almost the whole of the export is taken by the United States.

The great bulk of the world's tea (78 per cent) is produced by the five countries just considered − India, Sri Lanka, China, Japan and Indonesia. The total world production in 1971 was reckoned at 1.3m. tons (2 961m. lb), of which India and Sri Lanka provided 51 per cent, Japan and Indonesia 14 per cent, and China 13 per cent.

The cultivation of tea has been developed in many other countries, but it will be seen that all told their supplies are relatively small. Chief among them are the Commonwealth territories of east and central Africa, providing some 3 per cent of the total, mostly from Kenya and Malawi, with Pakistan providing a further 3 per cent. Mozambique provides nearly 1 per cent, and Taiwan over 2 per cent, leaving only percentage fragments for other countries. The USSR is extending its acreage in Transcaucasia and is already a considerable source of supply with an estimated 67 800 tons in 1971. The high price of labour in the United States generally makes tea an unprofitable crop as a marketable commodity, but it has been grown for home use on a small scale on

Table 17 — Tea consumption, 1960

| Country | kg | lb | Country | kg | lb | Country | kg | lb |
	per head			per head			per head	
United Kingdom	4.4	9.6	Ceylon	1.5	3.4	Egypt	0.75	1.7
Irish Republic	3.5	7.6	Canada (1959)	1.1	2.6	Japan	0.75	1.7
New Zealand	3.0	6.7	Morocco	1.1	2.4	USA	0.3	0.6
Australia	2.7	6.0	Netherlands	0.8	1.8			

many of the farms in the southern states and in California.

Before the Second World War the exports of tea from the chief exporting countries totalled over 410 000 tons (900m. lb), and after dropping during the war by about one-third they increased again to 590 000 tons (1 300m. lb) in 1967. Imports into the United Kingdom amount to nearly half the world trade. Although during the war individuals were rationed and purchase by merchants in open market gave place to bulk purchase by Government, the war increased rather than diminished the popularity of tea as a beverage in the United Kingdom. The estimated consumption per head of the population dropped of necessity from 4.2 kg (9.3 lb) in 1938 to 3.2 kg (7 lb) in 1943, but rose steadily and (after derationing in 1952) to 4.4 kg (9.6 lb) in 1960 — the highest figure for any country. This involved an import of over 227 000 tons (500m. lb).

The estimated per caput consumption in 1960, in the principal tea-drinking countries outside China, is shown in Table 17.

Though consumption in the United States is only 280 g (10 oz) per head, the States import more tea than any other country outside the United Kingdom.

Tropical products

Coffee

The coffee of commerce consists of the seeds (the 'beans') of several species of trees or shrubs, chiefly of *Coffea arabica*, Linn., which if left to itself grows to the height of 7 to 9 m (23 to 30 ft), but in cultivation is kept down to the height of some 2.4 m (8 ft) in order to facilitate the gathering of the fruit. The seeds are enclosed in dark cherry-red pulpy berries, each of which usually contains two. The tree comes into full bearing in six years, and remains profitable for from thirty to forty years, after which the soil is worn out. The best soil for the coffee tree, as in the case of tea, is virgin forest land rich in vegetable remains, the accumulations of past ages. A warm and moist climate is required for it, but the heat must not be excessive. An almost ideal climate for coffee is found in Yemen, the home of the original Mocha coffee. Here, winter and summer alike, a thick mist ascends every morning from the low grounds on the coast to the slopes on which the coffee is grown. About midday the plantations themselves become enveloped in mist, which lasts till after the greatest heat of the day, and then disappears. So regular is this occurrence that in certain places there are scarcely twenty days in the year on which the mist fails to rise. By night, on the other hand, the air ascending from the hot plains helps to prevent an excessive lowering of the temperature, so that we have, as it were, a hothouse culture with natural self-regulating arrangements. Elsewhere coffee trees, at least when young, must be cultivated either under cover or under the shelter of trees. Bananas and erythrinas are frequently grown for this purpose, and in Brazil a tall, coarse pea, which enriches the ground when it dies, is often planted. On the other hand, the coffee tree cannot stand continued frost; and though it has to endure occasional frost in Paraguay, in most coffee-growing countries the mean temperature of the coldest month is above 11° C (52° F), and the mean minimum temperature about 6° C (42.5° F). On this account its range in latitude is more limited than that of tea. Coffee, indeed, is not grown to any great extent outside of the tropics, although the most important place of production, the coffee region of Brazil, lies just beside the southern limit of the tropical zone.

Even within the tropics, the cultivation of coffee is generally restricted to comparatively limited areas; the reason of which is that coffee is a product grown mainly as a commercial product, that is, for consumption outside of the regions in which it is produced, and demands a large amount of labour in preparing it for the market.

The preparation of the coffee beans consists in their separation from their coverings and the processes of drying and 'curing'. In making the finest kinds of coffee the berries are first pulped, or stripped of the outer pulpy covering, in a machine specially devised for the purpose. The curing process which then follows consists in exposing the beans to the sun for six or eight days; and as the beans after being pulped are extremely sensitive to injury from rain or dew, great care must be taken during this stage to protect them from these influences. When cured the beans are, in most coffee districts, sent to coffee-works erected in the larger towns or the seaports to be hulled or peeled — that is, divested of the outer skin in which the beans are still wrapped. Before being bagged for shipment the beans are winnowed, graded, and sorted, the sorting being not only according to quality but also according to size, since beans of the same size can be more equally roasted before being ground.

The use of coffee as a beverage appears to have been very limited till within the last 200 or 300 years. The oldest work regarding the origin of the practice is an Arabic manuscript of 1587; and from this it would appear that the original home of the coffee tree is in the southern parts of the highlands of Ethiopia (Abyssinia), where it is undoubtedly a native. Thence it was introduced into southwestern Arabia, and through the Arabs it became known to Europeans. It is to this fact that the tree owes its specific name of *arabica*, while the generic name, and the ordinary name of the plant and its product, is derived from that which was given to it by the Arabs, and this again is possibly derived from Kaffa, the name of one of the highland districts of Abyssinia whence the tree was originally brought. The introduction of coffee into Arabia must have taken place at least as early as the eleventh century, but even in the middle of the sixteenth century the beverage was still unknown at Constantinople. About a century later still (in 1652) the first coffee-houses were started in London, and these soon became favourite resorts of the wits and men of letters of the time; but in England the drinking of coffee was gradually given up to a large extent in favour of tea, which was introduced even more recently. In the United States and Europe, on the other hand, coffee has come more and more into favour. The order of leading countries as coffee-drinkers was modified by the Second World War. While consumption per head of the population increased in some cases, in others the impact of the war led to a big decline. Table 18 shows the consumption per head in 1958 and 1971 in the major coffee-importing countries.

Table 18 – Coffee consumption, 1958 and 1971 (kg per head per annum)

Country	1958	1971	Country	1958	1971
USA	7.2	6.2	Netherlands	3.9	6.5
Sweden	8.3	13.0	Switzerland	3.6	5.9
Belgium	5.2	7.4	Germany, W.	3.0	5.0
France	4.2	5.1	Italy	1.7	3.3
Canada	3.9	4.2	UK	0.8	2.1

The United States stands in much the same commercial relation to coffee as the United Kingdom does to tea. Not only are its people among the biggest coffee-drinkers, but it imports more coffee than all the other coffee-importing countries put together. It is interesting to note that in 1946 the United States consumption of coffee rose to 8.8 kg (19.4 lb) per head against the United Kingdom consumption of 4 kg (8.8 lb) of tea per head; this corresponds roughly with the comparative amounts of coffee and tea needed to prepare equal quantities of the two beverages.

The coffee-growing countries of the world fall into three main groups: South and Central America, the dominant factor in world supply; India and Indonesia, more important in the past than in the present; East and West Africa, young and growing sources of supply in Ethiopia and the former European colonies. In all, the area under coffee before the Second World War was estimated at over 4.9m.

hectares (12m. acres) and production at about 2.2m. tons. Exports in the prewar quinquennium averaged about 1.6m. tons, of which Latin America provided over 80 per cent, and Brazil alone over 50 per cent. Acreage, production and exports all declined during the war, especially in Brazil and Venezuela. In other countries the position kept fairly stable, and in Brazil production has been creeping up again and surpassing its prewar output; while exports have regained their prewar level in nearly all countries, and in some have gone far beyond it.

Though subject to big fluctuations, Brazil has played a dominant part in world production and export of coffee for over a century past. The coffee tree was introduced into northern Brazil early in the eighteenth century, but not till about fifty years later into the region where it has since flourished so well. The coffee-producing region in Brazil lies between about 21° and 24° S, and is divided into two zones, one of which is traversed by a system of railways connected with Rio de Janeiro, and the other by a system connected more directly with the more southerly seaport of Santos. The coffee-growing area is, in general, the plateau with rich volcanic soils sheltered behind the coast range at a height of 180 to 760 m (600 to 2 500 ft) above sea level. In 1906–07, a year of very high production, Brazil furnished 80 per cent of the world's total. In 1917 the area under coffee in Brazil had grown to 1.8m. hectares (4.5m. acres), and in later years it nearly doubled that acreage. The result was overproduction, and in 1931 the Brazilian government placed the sale of coffee under federal control. To bring supplies down to demand, large quantities of coffee were destroyed — 78m. bags over a period of fourteen years.* These restrictive practices, while helping to maintain prices, encouraged other countries to increase their output, and in 1937 Brazil reversed her policy; but the Second World War brought wider control through an Inter-American Coffee Convention, to which the United States was a signatory. The area under coffee in Brazil dropped from over 3.4m. hectares (8.5m. acres) before the war to about 2.2m. hectares (5.5m. acres), and production from 1.4m. tons to under 0.5m. tons. The decline was not due wholly to the war; planters were relying less on coffee, and yields suffered from a succession of bad seasons.

In general, the war benefited the coffee-planting industry. Adverse weather conditions were not confined to Brazil, and with smaller crops and increased consumption in the United States, the prewar surplus stocks were gradually reduced. At the end of the war, a Pan-American Coffee Conference recommended the removal of all restrictions and controls. Production in Brazil was soon up again to over 1.05m. tons, with exports around 1m. tons, dropping to 0.65m. in 1954 as the old

---

* The Brazilian bag of coffee weights 60 kg (132 lb), or about seventeen bags to the ton, so that the quantity of coffee destroyed was over 4.5m. tons.

troubles recurred; but in 1959–60 the area had increased again to 4m. hectares (9.8m. acres) and production jumped to 2.6m. tons, or well over half the estimated world crop of 4.5m. tons, while exports were around 1m. tons — more than 40 per cent of the world total. In 1971 production was 1.8m. of a world total of 5.2m. and exports were still in excess of 1m. tons.

No other country comes anywhere near Brazil as a producer of coffee, but the other countries of Latin America together provide much of the balance of the world's supply. Colombia is easily second, producing 661 000 tons and exporting 360 000 tons in 1971. El Salvador, Guatemala and Mexico each export about 100 000 tons. In quality, no coffee surpasses that of the district of Alta Vera Paz, in northern Guatemala. The Blue Mountain coffee of Jamaica is also famous.

Before the war, the Dutch East Indies (now Indonesia) ranked next to Colombia, with annual exports of 50 000 to 100 000 tons. The Japanese occupation of the islands and the postwar revolution almost killed the trade for the time being, but there was a recovery to eighth largest producer by 1971 to 180 000 tons. The introduction of the coffee tree into Java dates from 1650, when it was carried by the Dutch from Arabia. Plantations are generally at a height of from 600 to 1 200 m (2 000 to 4 000 ft) above sea level. Formerly about two-thirds of the coffee in Java (Djawa) was grown on government plantations, but now private plantations provide 80 per cent. Coffee in Java suffered from disease, as did coffee in Ceylon, but the replacement of *Coffea arabica* by the disease-resisting but lower quality Liberian coffee (*C. liberica* or *C. robusta*) enabled the industry to recover in Java. In Ceylon, as previously noted, the industry practically died out and was replaced by tea planting.

The cultivation of coffee in India is said to have been introduced about two centuries ago by a pilgrim on his return from Mecca; but it was only after 1840 that it spread with any great rapidity. The coffee plantations are mainly in Mysore and Madras on the eastern, and therefore more sheltered, slopes of the Western Ghats, to the south of about 15° N. The most desirable elevation on these mountains is from 760 to 1 060 m (2 500 to 3 500 ft) above sea level. The tree is also cultivated on much lower ground further east, but it is nowhere grown with success in northern India. At no time has production or export been more than a very small percentage of world supply, and in the early decades of the present century the proportion declined to less than 1 per cent. In the quinquennium before the Second World War, the area under coffee averaged 73 000 hectares (185 000 acres) and the production 16 000 tons. Both area and production were well maintained during the war, and in 1945–46 the crop was over 25 000 tons. Later, production dropped again, but recovered from under 25 000 tons in the early 1950s to 108 000 tons in 1971.

In Africa, coffee-growing made considerable strides both before and during the Second World War. Since the war production has increased steadily. Kenya coffee (*arabica*) early gained a high reputation on the London market, and though during the war more pressing needs, coupled with a series of dry seasons, led to a drop in Kenya's exports, this was followed by an all round increase in East Africa's production. In Uganda, the biggest coffee grower and exporter in the Commonwealth in 1971, the output rose from around 35 000 tons in the early 1950s to 204 000 in 1971; in Tanzania production went up from 15 000 tons to over 64 000; and in Kenya from about 12 500 tons to 59 000. Other leading sources of supply in Africa are the Ivory Coast (240 000 tons in 1971), Angola (210 000), Ethiopia (215 000), Malagasy Republic (65 500), and Zaire (72 000). Africa's total production in 1971 was 1.3m. tons approximately a quarter of the world total of 4.9m. tons.

Cacao

Cacao, or cocoa, is the product of an American tree *Theobroma cacao*, L., not to be confounded with the coconut palm or the coca shrub. The tree comes into full bearing in twelve years (in favoured regions earlier) and continues to yield good returns for about thirty years, after which the yield begins to decline although the tree may live for eighty years. Cocoa enters into commerce as 'beans', which are the seeds contained, to the number of 50 to 150, in a red or green fleshy fruit some 20 cm (8 in) in length. These beans or seeds are composed to the amount of half their weight of a fat known as cocoa butter, which has the valuable property of never becoming rancid, however long it is kept. Being rather difficult of digestion, however, this fat is removed in preparing cocoa for drinking, but a proportion is added (along with sugar and milk) in the manufacture of chocolate.

Before entering into commerce the beans have, like those of coffee, to undergo preliminary treatment, and the quality of the product depends greatly on the care bestowed on the necessary processes. The first process is one for setting up fermentation, which removes the pulp of the fruit, destroys the power of germination in the seeds, and prevents mustiness. The best beans are fermented for a period of five or seven days, either in wooden 'sweat boxes' or by placing them in a heap along with plantain or other green leaves — a process during which so much heat is developed that the hand cannot be held in the heap. Later the beans are dried, and are then ready for shipment. When roasted and split, or broken, they form 'cocoa nibs'. Cocoa manufacture takes place almost entirely in the importing countries.

The cocoa tree must be grown where there is little or no wind, which would break the heavy seed vessels. It succeeds best under a higher temperature than coffee, and requires a great deal of moisture and a considerable depth of soil — much greater than that necessary for sugar. It therefore generally grows nearer the equator than coffee, and mostly on low grounds being confined to an area within 15° to 20° of the equator. Like coffee, it is liable to suffer from direct exposure to the rays of the sun, and is mostly grown under the shade of other trees. During the present century the main area of production has shifted from tropical America to West Africa. In Ghana (the former Gold Coast), cocoa has had a meteoric rise from nearly zero to easily the largest crop of cocoa in the world; and in Nigeria also the crop has become important, despite pests and diseases, notably 'swollen shoot', the drastic remedy for which is to cut out the diseased trees.

Between the two world wars, consumption in Europe and North America (largely in the form of chocolate as a confection) nearly trebled. World exports of cocoa increased from some 250 000 tons in 1913 to 736 000 tons in 1939 some 80 per cent of total production. West Africa provided over two-thirds of the latter total, the Gold Coast contributing 38 per cent, Nigeria 16 per cent, French West Africa (mainly the Ivory Coast) 7 per cent, the French mandated territories in the Cameroons and Togoland 5 per cent, and the islands of Fernando Poó (Spanish) and São Tomé and Principe (Portuguese) 3 per cent. On the other side of the Atlantic, Brazil, with 18 per cent, ranked next to the Gold Coast as a source of supply, while the Dominican Republic (4 per cent), Ecuador and Venezuela (4 per cent), and Trinidad and Grenada (1.5 per cent) made up the exports from Latin America and the Caribbean to well over a quarter of the world total.

Most of West Africa's exports are classed as 'ordinary', and most of the supplies from the other side of the Atlantic as 'fine' these being the two recognised grades of cocoa in the industry.

World production and exports, though reduced by the Second World War, soon recovered from the setback, production increasing from under 0.75m. tons in 1957–58 to over 1.5m. tons in 1971, while exports rose from 619 000 tons in 1955 to over 1.1m. tons in 1971. Analysis of the exports according to source of supply gave much the same results in 1964 as in 1939 (see above). West Africa still accounted for nearly three-quarters of the total, but the incidence of swollen shoot disease has led to some marked changes in main areas of production. Its spread has been checked not only by cutting out diseased trees but by diligent spraying of the remainder. In 1952 over 15m. trees had been destroyed in Ghana alone, by 1955 over 40m. Helped by spraying, however, Ghana had a record crop of 433 000 tons in 1960–61 and over 411 000 tons in 1971.

Rice

Rice (*Oriza sativa*) or padi is another cultivated grass and is the characteristic grain crop of the plains in the monsoon area of the tropical and subtropical parts of southeastern Asia. There are many varieties of this crop, some of which require very different conditions from others; those which are most abundantly produced not only demand a high summer temperature, but have to be grown in fields capable of being flooded at certain stages of their growth; and it is these conditions which are afforded in the great river deltas and low-lying seaboard tracts subject to inundation during the summer rains of the area referred to. The fields in which the rice is grown are embanked to retain the water as long as may be needed, and where not sufficiently level by nature are carefully terraced by man; and if the rains or the overflow of rivers are not sufficient to inundate the fields, the necessary water must be furnished by irrigation. The amount of flooding required varies at different stages of growth. While the seedlings are in an early stage of growth, 50 mm (2 in) of water are ample; but when the stem is strong, high floods are almost unable to drown it. During flooding growth is astonishingly rapid, as much as 23 cm (9 in) having been known to be added to the height of the stalk in twenty-four hours. From the highly peculiar conditions in which rice grows, it follows that where grown at all it is grown to the exclusion of almost every other crop; and outside of the regions above indicated, the cultivation of rice is for the most part locally restricted to small areas, presenting exceptional facilities for artificial inundation. There are, indeed, hundreds of varieties of rice, including many known as upland or hill rice, which thrive on a drier soil, in India and Pakistan even at an altitude of 2 440 m (8 000 ft).

The great number of different varieties has been perpetuated by tradition and by the comparative isolation of the many cropping areas. There are two main classes (*japonica*) the upland rice with a generally high fertiliser response and the swamp or lowland rice (*indica*) well adapted to tropical conditions with two or more crops a year. The great advance of the 1960s has been the development of new strains to combine the best features of both types and produce new varieties which yield up to 200 per cent more than the older types. They have the disadvantage of requiring a plentiful application of fertiliser and a very carefully controlled supply of water. Rice yield per hectare is nearly twice that of wheat, and total production in 1971 was 307m. tons against 343m. tons of wheat. This was produced from some 135m. hectares (333m. acres) as against 217m. hectares (536m. acres) producing wheat.

Rice forms the staple food grain of nearly half the human race, and exceeds all other grain crops in volume and is approximately equal to wheat in weight. No other tropical grain yields so large an amount of food from a given area of land; and hence the lowlands of Asia adapted to this crop are the most densely peopled parts of the continent. Japan (at least until recently), the Philippine Islands, parts of Indonesia and southeast Asia are lands within whose borders the great bulk of the entire population live mainly on rice. In the Indian subcontinent and China there are certain regions, and these in many cases the most populous, where rice is likewise the mainstay of the inhabitants.

Relatively to this vast consumption, rice does not enter very largely into the commerce of the world. The great countries of Asia for the most part supply their own needs as regards this commodity within their own borders, and the trade in rice is principally a home trade i.e. the exchanged local surpluses. The density of population in most of the great rice-producing regions of the world allows little surplus for Europe and America. Ninety per cent of the world's crop is grown in Asia and in 1971 total production of rice (paddy) was 307.4m. tons. China 104m.; India 66.5m.; Pakistan 18m.; Japan 14.1m.; and Indonesia 18.5m. together produced some 72 per cent. Thirty-six per cent of the crop is grown within the tropics and another 60 per cent between 20° and 30° from the equator. Brazil (6.6m. tons) and the United States (3.8m. tons) are the largest producers outside Asia, while there is considerable production in Iran, Italy, Colombia and Mexico. World exports have traditionally come from Burma, Thailand and Vietnam (Indo–China) — comparatively small countries which are less densely populated and in the main rice-growing region. Growing self-sufficiency from recently increased yields has affected the pattern of world trade, and the United States and Thailand are now the major exporters. The United Kingdom imported 140 000 tons of rice in 1973 valued at £19m. — as against 93 000 tons in 1960 valued at £4m.

Rough rice (paddy) is rice still in the husk after threshing and produces an average 20 per cent husks, 10 per cent bran, 65 per cent whole and broken kernels, and 5 per cent dirt and waste. The husks, the outer covering, have little food value and a high silicon content and are used as fuel and in the rice mills and for the fabrication of building materials, insulating boards, etc. The rice bran is the outer skin and the germs which are removed from the kernels by milling; it contains most of the vitamins and protein and has a high food value. Rice oil (for cooking, cosmetics, etc.) is extracted from the bran and the resultant meal, with the addition of molasses, makes nutritive cattle cake. Apart from direct use as food, rice can be used to produce wine, rice starch and rice flour. Rice straw is used in the manufacture of hats, mats, strawboards and can be used as a mulch for other crops.

Traditionally demanding a great deal of labour for planting, tending and harvesting, rice can be grown successfully under mechanised conditions — particularly when appropriate strains are sown with short, strong straw which is firm enough to remain upright for harvesting and brittle enough to be harvested efficiently.

Millets

This name is given to several grain crops, the most important of which are tropical. The two kinds most largely grown are the Great Millet (*Sorghum vulgare*, Pers.) and the Spiked Millet (*Pennisetum typhoideum*, Rich.). They are both among the leading crops of India and form the staple food grains of the drier regions of both India and China. Great Millet is also largely grown in Africa under the name of durra. It is sometimes known as Guinea corn. Neither product enters largely into the commerce of the world. A species of sorghum is widely cultivated in the United States and elsewhere for green fodder. The so-called millets of the temperate zone, including *Setaria italica*, Beauv., agree only on yielding grain of a small size.

Minor farinaceous products

Tapioca is derived from the long tubers of the manioc plant (*Manihot utilissima*), a native of Brazil, but now largely cultivated in the tropics of South America and Africa. The tubers, before being subjected to heat and pressure, are highly poisonous, but the meal, a granular substance derived from them and known as tapioca or cassava, according as it is the result of one or other mode of treatment, is wholesome but low in protein content. This meal forms a staple article of food in Brazil and in many parts of tropical Africa, but it enters little into world trade, being consumed entirely where it is grown. Since the tubers do not deteriorate if left in the ground for one or two years, and since they are immune to locust attack, cassava can provide a useful food reserve. World production has nearly doubled between 1948 and 1971 — from 48m. tons to 92.2m. tons.

Sago is obtained from the pith of the sago palm (*Metroxylon Sagu*), largely cultivated in freshwater swamps in southeast Asia. It is self-seeding and so easy is the cultivation of the palm, a single family is able to tend a plantation of 400 trees. When mature the palms are cut down and the pith is processed into a granular form. This is imported into Europe, mainly from Malaysia and Indonesia, and is used in food preparations.

Arrowroot is derived from starchy, edible roots but the true arrowroot is obtained from the rhizome *Maranta arundinacea*, L., a native of tropical America. The main source of supply is the West Indian island, St Vincent. Other kinds are produced in India and elsewhere, but are mainly of local importance. All share the properties of producing a fine starch which is easily digested.

Yams

Yams are thick tubers of several species of *Dioscorea* which send up long slender annual twining stems. The tubers vary in weight from 0.5 to 45 kg (1 to 100 lb) according to the species. When cooked the tubers acquire a mild taste like that of a potato and form the secondary food in many parts of the tropics — although in the wetter parts of West Africa and the South Sea Islands consumption is so high as to make them the staple food. They should not be confused with the **Sweet Potatoes** (*Ipomoea Batatas*) also grown in tropical and warm temperate lands and eaten in the same way as potatoes. World production of yams and sweet potatoes is about half that of potatoes — 148m. tons as against 306m. tons.

Sugarcane

The sugarcane belongs botanically, like the cereals, to the family of the grasses, but its seed or grain is commercially of no value, and the plant is cultivated solely for the sake of the juice which is found in its stem, and which yields sugar. It is a tall plant, growing to the height of from 3 to 4.5 m (10 to 15 ft), and some of the stalks attain a thickness of over 38 mm (1.5 in). Every year these stalks are cut down just before flowering, but the root stock is perennial and continues to throw up fresh shoots every year. The yield declines slowly after the first two or three crops and the usual rule is to renew the plants after five years. The range of the sugarcane in latitude is wider than that of coffee, but not so wide as that of tea. In the northern hemisphere it is grown successfully to the north of latitude 37° in the south of Spain, and in the southern hemisphere, in Natal and New South Wales, to about latitude 30° S. A moist soil being required for sugarcane, the situation in which it is grown is very different from that of tea or coffee, but with too much moisture the juice will be watery.

Originally a product of eastern Asia, the sugarcane was made known in the West by the Arabs, who appear to have introduced it first into Egypt, then in the ninth century into the Mediterranean islands, and later into Spain, the only part of Europe where it still flourishes. Today it is cultivated in all tropical and many subtropical countries. The largest producer of cane sugar for export is Cuba. In the prewar quinquennium 1934—38 its average annual production was given in the United Nations (FAO) returns as over 2.6m. tons — one-sixth of the world total of 16.2m. tons of refined centrifugal cane sugar. The FAO postwar returns are based on the weight of raw sugar, which is rather more (in the ratio 100:92) than the weight of refined sugar; but the outstanding fact is the increase in both the area cultivated; and production of sugarcane. The prewar area harvested was over 4m. hectares (10m. acres); in 1958—59 it was nearly 6.5m. hectares (16m. acres) and in 1971 it was 11m. hectares (27m. acres). Prewar production of cane sugar reached 15m. tons; in 1958—59 it was over 26m. tons and in 1971 it was nearly 42m. tons. In addition there has been an increase in the output of non-centrifugal sugar (mostly village-made Indian gur) from about 4.5m. to 11.3m. tons.

These figures do not show fully the increase since 1934—38. Such indeed was the profusion of supplies that it was difficult to find markets for them all. Elaborate schemes to regulate exports and prices were negotiated, and Cuba cut down her production of 7.1m. tons of cane sugar in 1951—52 to 4.5m. tons in 1954—55. By 1971 it was up again to 4.5m. tons, but was less than in 1951—52. Brazil, whose area under sugarcane and whose production of cane was greater than that of Cuba, was the second largest producer of cane sugar in 1971 (5.4m. tons). India, with a production of 3.4m. tons of centrifugal cane sugar, was also credited with 7m. tons of gur. Other countries producing 1m. tons of centrifugal cane sugar in 1971 were Australia (2.8m.), Mexico (2.5m.), Philippines (2.1m.), and South Africa (1.7m.).

As in production, so in the sugar export trade, Cuba dominates the world. Despite her internal troubles, she averages some 5m. tons a year (a third of the world total). Australia, Brazil and the Philippines export some 1m. tons a year, followed by Taiwan, the Dominican Republic and Mauritius each of whom export in excess of 0.5m. tons.

The sugar industry

Sugar, now regarded as a necessity of life in almost all parts of the world, was unknown to the classical nations of antiquity. Even about 400 years ago refined sugar, in the form of loaf sugar, was still unknown. The invention of the process is ascribed to a Venetian about the end of the fifteenth or beginning of the sixteenth century. As late as the beginning of the eighteenth century the total amount of sugar consumed annually in Europe is estimated to have been about 50 000 tons. Now the United Kingdom alone consumes over 3m. tons, besides molasses and glucose (a kind of sugar derived from the starch of maize or potatoes, and used as a sweetener in jam-making, in brewing, as an invalid food, and for many other purposes).

Down to the nineteenth century the sugarcane was almost the sole source of supply of the sugar consumed in Europe. Since then sugar beet has become a formidable rival. The presence of sugar in beetroot was discovered by a Berlin apothecary named Marggraf, as far back as 1747. Before the close of the same century another Berlin chemist, named Achard, devised a method of extracting the sugar from beet; but the first attempts to do this were not commercially successful. At a later date great improvements were introduced in the method of extraction by the French Comte de Chaptal, and after 1820 the making of beet sugar became firmly established in various countries in Europe. As time went on, production increased until in 1913 the world's supply was derived almost equally from the two sources. The beet-growing countries were severely affected by the First World War, and since then cane sugar has become predominant. Of the total world production of some 73m. tons in 1971, approximately 42m. tons came from cane and over 30m. tons from beet.

In comparing the two 'raw materials', the advantages on the side of sugarcane are easy culture in tropical and subtropical climates where labour is at its cheapest; natural richness in sugar ; and a perennial root stock. Beet suffers under the disadvantage of requiring intensive cultivation (more especially plentiful supplies of potash), of requiring to be replanted year by year, and of being grown where labour is relatively dear. On the other hand, as a result of modern selection, a given weight of sugar beet is now actually richer in sugar than a corresponding weight of cane — in 1967, for instance, 508m. tons of sugarcane produced 38m. tons of sugar and 235m. tons of sugar beet produced 28m. tons of sugar. Beet has the advantage of being grown where population is dense, and where accordingly the market is close at hand both for the raw material used in the refineries and also for the manufactured product. It has the further important advantage of yielding byproducts of much higher value than are obtained from the sugarcane. The canes after being deprived of their sugary juice are chiefly used for fuel; but the beet-pulp, besides being a useful fertiliser, especially as returning potash to the ground, is a valuable food for cattle, a circumstance of special importance in thickly peopled countries.

The sugar beet industry enjoys further advantages in the methods and machinery used for extracting sugar from the beet. The roots containing the sugar are first treated in one of two ways, either of which extracts from their substance a larger proportion of the juice contained in them than is usually derived from the sugarcanes. One method is to subject them to the action of powerful presses; a better method is that known as the diffusion process, the invention of a German named Robert, but improved and first made practically useful in France (by Charles, and afterwards by Peret of Roye). By this process the juice is dissolved out of the sliced beet root by hot water. The after-treatment of the beet juice differs in some respects from that of cane juice, but is in the main similar. The improvements in the cultivation and treatment of sugar beet are such that whereas in 1836—37 18 tons of beet were required to produce 1 ton of raw sugar, now the world average is only 8 tons (see p. 210).

In the case of the sugarcane, the stems of the plant are crushed between rollers which still leave in the cane a considerable proportion of the juice. The juice that is pressed out is boiled and otherwise treated, part of the substance then forming the crystals of sugar, while the remainder flows away in the form of a syrup known as molasses. From the country of production cane sugar is usually exported in an unrefined condition, called raw sugar, and the raw sugar is further treated and refined by the importing countries, more syrup flowing away during these further processes.

An indication of the comparative yields of sugar from cane and beet is provided by the *Production Yearbook* issued by the Food and Agriculture Organisation of the United Nations. According to the original data, world production of sugar beet in the prewar quinquennium 1934—38 averaged 75m. metric tons a year and world production of beet sugar 9.5m. tons. Provided that no substantial part of the beet was used for other purposes, about 8 tons of it was needed to produce 1 ton of sugar. In the same years world production of sugarcane averaged 168m. tons, and of cane sugar 16.5m. tons (about 10 tons of cane to 1 ton of sugar). Postwar revision of the 1934—38 returns increased the divergence, and analysis of the 1971 returns shows averages of 13.4 tons of sugarcane and 8.4 tons of sugar beet per ton of sugar. These are world averages and necessarily include a number of estimated yields. Australia, for instance, produces 1 ton of sugar from 6.3 tons of sugarcane, while the UK produces 1 ton of sugar from 6 tons of sugar beet.

During the present century scientific research has led to improvements in growing and extracting cane sugar as well as beet sugar, and the Commonwealth Economic Committee, in a postwar survey of plantation crops, asserts that cane sugar can usually be produced more cheaply than beet sugar, which would have difficulty in competing with it without the support of subsidies or protective tariffs. This support has long been given, not only in countries whose traditional economic policy is protectionist, but in the United Kingdom. Sugar beet is grown chiefly in Europe, and especially in East and West Germany, France, Italy, Poland, Czechoslovakia, the UK, and other highly industrialised countries, which favoured it with the double object of ensuring home supplies of sugar and encouraging agricultural industry. National support has been supplemented by elaborate international agreements, affecting both beet sugar and cane sugar, and aiming at the control of production and prices in face of supplies tending to overtake demand.

As already stated, the production of beet sugar increased until in 1913 world supplies rivalled those of cane sugar. Between the two world wars cane sugar regained the predominance. Of the world production of some 25m. tons of centrifugal sugar in the years immediately preceding the Second World War, cane sugar accounted for about 60 per cent. During the war, world production declined to about 20m. tons, the decline of beet sugar in the war-ravaged countries of Europe being especially marked. But there was rapid recovery in the years following the close of hostilities — more rapid in the case of cane than of beet — and by 1948—49 total production had regained the prewar level. By 1962 world production of raw sugar had reached 52m. tons — over double the prewar total — and by 1971 it was 72m. tons. The United Kingdom production of sugar from homegrown sugar beet was some 1m. tons in 1973. Imports that year totalled 2.1m. tons over 80 per cent of which came from Commonwealth sources.

Besides the two great sugar-producing plants, sugar is obtained in greater or less quantity from various other sources. In the eastern parts of Canada and in the northeastern states of the USA, sugar is obtained from the sweet sap which flows out on tapping the trunk of various species of maple and above all the sugar-maple (*Acer saccharinum*, Linn.). From this source is obtained a very small proportion of the native grown sugar of the United States, but one which has a special use as a sweetmeat or as syrup. In tropical countries sugar is similarly obtained from various species of palms: in India from the wild date palm, the Palmyra palm, the coconut palm, the toddy palm, and the sago palm; and in Malaysia and Indonesia from the sugar palm.

Cinchona

Cinchona is the name of a Linnaean genus of tropical trees, several species of which yield a bark highly prized in medicine, formerly as a sovereign remedy for the malarial fevers incident to tropical climates. The bark yields extracts, the best known of which is quinine. Compounds from these extracts are also used. The species of Cinchona are all natives of the eastern slopes of the Andes, from about 7° N to 22° S, occupying, generally in scattered groups, a belt of from about 900 to 3 000 m (3 000 to 10 000 ft) above sea level, a belt in which they are exposed to copious rains, enjoy a tolerably constant temperature, and plenty of sunshine. The species most valued for their bark include *Cinchona succirubra*, Pav. yielding the red bark of commerce; *C. calisaya*, Wedd., and *C. ledgeriana*, Moens, yielding the more valuable yellow bark; and *C. officinalis*, L. They flourish best within 8° or 10° of the equator at from 1 200 to 2 200 m (4 000 to 7 000 ft) above sea level, where the mean temperature is from about 13° to 21° C (55° to 70° F). Further from the equator they are confined to a lower elevation.

The great value of this bark led to numerous attempts to introduce the trees into other parts of the world. Originally, the region from which it was introduced into Europe belonged entirely to the domain of the old Empire of Peru, and subsequently to the Spanish viceroyalty of Peru; and hence it became known by the name of Peruvian bark. After the establishment of the various South American republics, that of Colombia furnished the chief supply. The first attempts to introduce the tree into tropical parts of Asia were made by the Dutch. The first tree was introduced into Djawa (Java) in 1852, and a few years later the cultivation of the cinchona was a successful government industry on that island. To India the tree was brought direct from South America by Clements Markham in 1860. A government cinchona plantation was

211

soon after established on the Nilgiri Hills, and a second was afterwards set going in Darjeeling, in latitude 27° on one of the rainiest parts of the Himalayan range.

But it was the Ceylon plantations which first greatly affected the international commerce in this bark and its price. Down to about 1880, Colombia remained the chief source of supply for the London market; but so rapidly was cinchona cultivation extended in Ceylon that the British imports of the bark from that country increased from 67.5 tons in 1881 to over 1 043 tons in 1886. Later the Colombian supply dwindled to insignificance, and the supplies from Ceylon and India also fell away, partly on account of disease and partly because prices ceased to be remunerative. Before the Second World War, the supreme source of supply was Djawa (Java), which in some years provided over 90 per cent of the world total. A large proportion of the United Kingdom import was in the form of quinine and quinine salts from the Netherlands, the imports of cinchona bark being only a fraction of what had been received from Ceylon in 1886. With Djawa and the Netherlands both in enemy occupation during the Second World War cinchona and quinine were in very short supply and substitutes were developed. Both then and for a time after the close of hostilities, the United Kingdom was dependent on spasmodic imports from different sources, including not only South America but Central America, Zaire (the Belgian Congo), and (in 1946) South Africa and Malaysia (British Malaya). In 1947, imports were up to the prewar level in quantity, amounting to 145 tons of bark and over 10 tons of quinine and quinine salt. Since then they have fluctuated considerably and they are increasingly affected by the use of alternative drugs, such as mepacrine, which are now used in the prophylaxis and treatment of malaria.

Tropical vegetable fibres

Of these the most important soft fibre (apart from cotton) is **jute**, which is derived from the bast chiefly of two species of a genus of plants known as *Corchorus*. These are slender-stemmed annuals, from about 3.6 m (12 ft) high. The cultivation of the plant is almost confined to Bengal (in Bangladesh), especially in the Ganga delta. Here the annual production exceeds 2m. tons. China grows some 400 000 tons; no other country more than a few thousand. But India and Thailand supply close on 0.5m. tons of allied fibres (kenaf, mesta, etc.). In Bengal jute grows in every variety of soil, but by preference on the alluvial sandbanks thrown up by rivers, for which situation it is peculiarly adapted by the fact that, except in the early stages of growth, it can stand heavy flooding without injury. The fibre, which is extracted from the stem by various processes, including that of retting, has long been woven on handlooms into gunny cloth — 'the brown paper of the wholesale trade' as it has been called. Wherever and however made, the cloth is almost universally used as sacking for agricultural produce; although manmade fibres (polypropylene) are replacing it in some uses and the bulk handling of grain has lessened the demand to some extent, jute still plays an essential part in world trade.

Till about 1835 the use of this material in weaving was almost confined to India; then it began to be imported into Dundee, where it was largely used in spinning and weaving of hessian canvas and other fabrics principally used for sacking in the developing international grain trade. For a time Dundee was the only seat of jute factories, but the industry later spread to other towns of the United Kingdom (especially to such as were also engaged in the linen industry), and factories were established on the Continent and in India itself. The Indian factories are almost all confined to the immediate neighbourhood of Calcutta, jute being the Bengal industry which rivals that of cotton in Bombay. Complications followed the partition of India. The jute-growing lands of eastern Bengal, forming about 75 per cent of the area then under jute in Bengal, passed to East Pakistan, which developed an export trade through Chittagong, whereas nearly all the factories, as well as the traditional port of export (Calcutta), were in India proper. While the two countries were one, all the supplies of raw jute naturally went to the neighbourhood of Calcutta. The interposition of a frontier created a barrier which, in the absence of a spirit of cooperation between the two governments, revolutionised the course of trade and industry locally. Some compromise became necessary between India and Pakistan, but each tried to become more selfcontained in respect of jute; India sought to increase its output of raw material to feed its mills, while Pakistan set about building new mills to utilise its supplies. Formerly, as stated, the Pakistan area under jute greatly exceeded the Indian, but the total is now more evenly divided. Joint production, before partition, reached a peak of 2.35m. tons in 1940. In later years it fluctuated between 3 and 3.5m. tons, with Pakistan usually but not always in the lead. A complication is the difference between the official and commercial estimates of production, and governmental involvement with production and exports of both countries. At the end of 1971 East Pakistan seceded from the Republic of Pakistan to become the independent sovereign nation state of Bangladesh, which accordingly has all the jute-growing areas and the jute mills formerly benefiting Pakistan within its boundaries.

The industry is one of the first importance, commercially, to both India and Bangladesh. India, concerned for her jute mills, prohibited the export of raw jute in 1950, and also took the biggest share of Pakistan's exports of raw jute. Pakistan's next best customer was the United Kingdom, which in 1968 imported 115 000 tons of raw jute, valued at £14m., and 45 000 tons of jute manufactures valued at £8m.,

213

the raw material coming almost wholly from Pakistan, and the manufactures mostly from India. In both cases the quantities were much below the prewar figures.* Next to India and the United Kingdom, the best customers for raw jute are Japan, Belgium, France, West Germany and the United States. The largest buyers of jute manufactures (yarn, woven fabrics, and sacks) are USA, Argentina, Australia and the UK.

Jute spinners have been experimenting with synthetic fibres, with promising results in replacing the jute bales used for shipping wool and in the manufacture of ropes, twines and the backing material for tufted carpets. Jute yarn, either alone or in combination with other yarns, is also employed in the manufacture of various other fabrics, such as carpets, furniture-coverings, and curtains.

Next in importance to jute among tropical hard fibres in European commerce is **abaca** or **Manila hemp**, so called from the chief place of export. It is obtained from the long leaves of *Musa textilis*, Nees, a plant belonging to the same genus as the banana and plantain, found wild on the Moluccas and Philippine Islands, and cultivated almost exclusively on the latter. Along with constant humidity and a high but fairly regular rainfall it needs a well-drained soil, and is often put on steep mountainsides. The fibre is from 1.8 to 2.8 m (6 to 9 ft) in length, and is separated from the leaf by hand labour or by mechanical strippers. Though more difficult to work and more brittle than hemp fibre, it is made into ropes of great tenacity and endurance, and it is largely exported for that purpose. The finer fibres are woven by the people of the Philippine Islands into delicate tissues, and in Europe they are likewise used (often in combination with silk) in making curtains, coverings for furniture, and other fabrics. Ninety per cent of the world production of some 110 000 tons comes from the Philippines, but future commerce will be affected by the growing substitution of manmade fibres.

In eastern countries (India, China, Japan, and the Eastern Archipelago) fibres derived from the bast chiefly of two varieties of *Boehmeria nivea*, Hook., a species of plants belonging to the nettle family, have been used from the earliest times in spinning and weaving. The fibres, known in India as **rhea**, in the Malay Islands as **ramie**, and to Europeans by the name of **China grass**, are pre-eminent amongst vegetable fibres for strength, fineness, and lustre, and produce an almost silky-looking fabric, called China cloth or grass cloth, which in China is very generally used for the making of summer clothing. Its various qualities render it fit for making all sorts of woven fabrics, from the coarsest to the finest — sail-cloth, table-linen, 'alpaca', velvet, and even lace and cambric. The chief obstacle to its use at present is its high price, arising from the difficulty with which the fibre is separated. The

* In 1973 UK imports from Bangladesh were 72 100 tons of raw jute, valued at £10m. and 111m. sq. yd. of jute manufactures valued at £7m.

fibres are attached to the core of the stem of the plant and to one another by a gummy substance which cannot be removed by the ordinary process of retting and has to be abstracted by treatment with chemicals. When examined under the microscope the individual fibres are seen to be interrupted at intervals by enlarged nodes, making the fibres difficult to work.

Since about 1880 a hard fibre known as **sisal** has been largely used (first in America) for the making of binder twine. It is derived from the fleshy leaves of various species of Agave, but chiefly the *Agave rigida*, Mill., a native of Yucatan, which has been widely introduced into other parts of the tropics with a similar climate, notably East Africa — where Tanzania (Tanganyika) is now the world's largest producer — and Brazil. Even before the Second World War the production and exports of sisal exceeded those of Manila hemp, and during the war, when the Philippines were in Japanese hands, and afterwards, sisal went further ahead, till in 1971 world production totalled 605 000 tons, 70 per cent coming from Tanzania and Brazil.

Of other tropical or subtropical fibre plants none has, as yet, attained any considerable place in international commerce. One of them, a leguminous or pod-bearing plant, *Crotalaria juncea*, Linn., yields from its bast the **sunn hemp** (kenaf) of India, not unlike jute; production — not all for fibre — in 1971 was 254 000 tons. In the same country the *Hibiscus cannabinus*, Linn., a member of the same family as the cotton plant, is cultivated especially in the north, for its fibre, which is also obtained from the bast, and is known as **Deccan** or **gambo-hemp**. Several trees belonging to the same family furnish a soft silky wool, which, like the true cotton, is an investment of the seeds, but which, being too short for spinning, is used for stuffing cushions and other similar purposes. These are known as **silk cotton trees,** and the most important are *Bombax Ceiba*, Linn., a native of tropical America, *Bombax malabaricum*, DC., a native of India, and *Eriodendron anfractuosum*, DC., a native of India and the Eastern Archipelago, whence the Dutch introduced the product into commerce under the name of **kapok** or **vegetable down**. Thailand has become the biggest exporter, and on account of kapok's extreme buoyancy it was used in making life-jackets.

The fibres of the leaves of the screw-pine, *Pandanus odoratissimus*, Linn., a native of southern Asia, Madagascar, and the islands of the Pacific, enter into commerce under the name of **vicua,** or **vacoua,** as a material for coarse sacking. Those from the outside of the stem of the palm, known to botanists as *Attalea funifera*, Mart., are exported from Brazil, under the name of **piassava,** as a material for brushes and brooms. Under the same name the fibres of *Raphia vinifera* are exported from West Africa. The ubiquitous coconut palm furnishes, among its numerous other products, the fibre called **coir**, which is commercially by far the most important of all these minor fibres. The fibre forms a thick matting on the outside of the nut, and after separation and treatment is exported as material for brooms and brushes, doormats, staircarpets, and other purposes. In 1959 Ceylon exported 80 000 tons of fibre, and India 75 000 tons of manufactures. All these fibres face increasing competition from manmade substitutes.

Tropical fruits

Oranges, limes, dates, and some other fruits are imported into the United Kingdom and the temperate zone more or less from the tropics, although the supply from within the tropics is in most cases less than the supply from without. Bananas and pineapples are the main tropical fruits which enter into world trade. The trade in **bananas** has grown with improvements in transportation and cold storage methods. They are the product of the large plant known to botanists as *Musa sapientum*, L., and its varieties, including a hardy dwarf variety known as *M. Cavendishii* or *chinensis*, suitable for cultivation in the temperate zone, and now largely cultivated in the Canary Islands. All the varieties require high temperatures, a great deal of moisture, and a deep soil. When these conditions are satisfied they are grown almost universally in the tropics. South and Central America (notably Brazil, Ecuador, Venezuela and Colombia), the West Indies, Canaries and West Africa are the principal parts of the world in which cultivation is carried on extensively as a plantation industry. The United States, the United Kingdom, and certain European countries are the principal markets. The trade has grown to enormous proportions since the construction of special cold storage cargo vessels where the bananas can be kept at the exact temperature of 11° C (52° F). The bananas grow in 'hands', of twelve to sixteen fingers along a main stem forming a 'bunch'. The average 'bunch' is over 120 bananas, each plant yielding one bunch weighing some 20 to 23 kg (45 to 50 lb). Other species of Musa, including *M. paradisiaca*, L., which yields the plantain, are also grown to a large extent in the tropics as food, but do not enter into world commerce. The name plantain is, however, loosely used in many parts of the world as practically synonymous with banana. World production has risen steadily from 13m. tons in 1950 to 28m. tons in 1971 — almost 60 per cent coming from Central and South America.

The import into the United Kingdom increased from about 14 000 tons in 1900 to upwards of 305 000 tons in 1938. For three years during the Second World War, 1942–44, the importation of bananas into the United Kingdom was prohibited, and later the Ministry of Food bought all supplies till private trading was again allowed in 1953. In 1973 imports were 302 000 tons valued at £28m. Almost all came from the British West Indies. The United States imports from South America and Europe largely from West Africa.

Rubber

Rubber was formerly known as caoutchouc or india-rubber. The first is a South American name from the country of its origin. Columbus, on his second voyage (1493), noted it as being used in Haiti for the making of balls. Torquemada mentions in 1615 that it was then derived from a Mexican tree, and used by the Spaniards to waterproof their cloaks. The Portuguese found it in use at an early date in Brazil for the making of syringes (whence its Portuguese name of *seringa*). But the substance and its uses first became generally known in Europe through a paper read to the French Academy by La Condamine in 1736. For more than eighty years after that almost its sole use in Europe was for the purpose which the second name suggests, namely the rubbing out of pencil marks. At the present time it would be difficult to measure the minute fraction of the consumption of rubber that use represents. The 'india' prefix indicates the source from which the chief supplies of the material were then obtained. The first important extension of the use of rubber was due to the invention in 1823 by Mackintosh of the waterproof fabric named after him. A still greater extension followed when Goodyear in America in 1842, and independently Hancock in England in 1843, discovered the method of destroying the stickiness and of hardening caoutchouc by treating it with sulphur. This is known as the process of **vulcanising**. A small proportion of sulphur (5 to 7 per cent) incorporated with the rubber makes a compound adapted for a great variety of mechanical purposes. A larger percentage (39 to 84 per cent) makes the equally familiar hard black compound known as ebonite. What above all has stimulated the modern growth of the rubber industry has been the twentieth-century development of motoring and aviation. The great bulk of world consumption of rubber is absorbed by the manufacture of tyres and tubes.

Rubber is the coagulated latex or juice derived from a variety of trees, all tropical. To prevent putrefaction the coagulation must be effected within about twenty-four hours of the collection of the juice. For many years the largest supply was obtained from trees of the allied genera *Hevea* and *Micrandra*, growing wild in the Amazon valley, in Brazil, Bolivia, and Peru, not in clumps, but widely scattered amongst a great variety of other trees, as is usual in well-watered parts of the tropics. The species from which most was obtained is the *H. brasiliensis*, Müll.-Arg. (*Siphonia elastica*, Pers.). Rubber from all these trees was known from the place of export as **Pará rubber**. The trees yielding the best juice are those growing on tracts of land which are annually flooded. Those growing where the roots are always submerged yield too watery a juice, and those that grow on higher ground beyond the reach of floods a juice too viscid. Rains are occasionally plentiful in its habitat, but the region is exposed to prolonged periods of drought. In

Central America and the northern parts of South America, an inferior caoutchouc is obtained from *Castilloa elastica*, Cerv. In India, rubber has been obtained from a species of fig, *Ficus elastica*, Roxb. (Assam rubber); in Borneo, from a species of Willughbeia; in other parts of the Eastern Archipelago, from *Urceola elastica*, Roxb.; in Africa, principally from various species of twining plants belonging to the genus Landolphia, but also, in Lagos and other parts of West Africa, from *Funtumia elastica* (= *Kickxia elastica*, Preuss). All the species mentioned are trees, most of them confined to latitudes well within the tropics, the only exception being the *Ficus elastica*, which grows in a part of India with a characteristic tropical climate.

Owing to the practice of 'robber economy' (whereby the rubber-bearing trees were ruthlessly cut down in order to obtain instantly the maximum yield and were thereby killed), wild rubber has come to form a very small percentage of the world's supply. The bulk is now obtained through the produce of regular plantations, in which it is possible by careful tapping to obtain a steady supply of juice from the same trees for many years in succession, and to effect other economies not practicable by the old mode of collection. Experiments began to be made with Brazilian rubber trees as far back as 1876 and 1877. Through the authorities of Kew Gardens trees were introduced into suitable parts of the tropics in both the Old World and the New. At first the progress of rubber planting was slow. The *Hevea* rubber tree takes ten years to mature, and at the end of the last century it was still considered doubtful whether plantations with expensive European company management would pay. But the foresight was justified and by 1913 nearly half the total production of 101 000 tons was plantation rubber. In 1923 the total production was estimated at 410 000 tons, more than 90 per cent being plantation rubber.

Before the Second World War, in the five years 1934–38, total production averaged just on 1m. tons a year, of which only about 2 per cent was wild rubber, coming mostly from Brazil. All but a still smaller percentage of the plantation rubber was produced in Asia, more than three-quarters of it in Malaysia (Malaya) (43 per cent) and Indonesia (36 per cent), while Ceylon, Thailand and Vietnam (Indo–China) between them furnished another 15 per cent. In the early stages of the war, production was intensified; in 1940 it amounted to over 1 400 000 tons. World totals for the later years of the war are not available, owing to the Japanese occupation of the principal rubber-growing countries; but in 1942 Ceylon's production reached 116 000 tons (nearly double the prewar average), and in tropical Africa it rose to 40 000 tons (over five times the prewar average). The production of wild rubber also increased — from 20 000 tons (prewar average) to nearly 50 000 tons.

This increased production could not make up for the loss to the world at large of the main supplies of rubber. To meet the shortage, synthetic rubber was manufactured on a large scale in the United States, and both the quality and the price of the manufactured article made it a formidable rival to the natural product. Before the war, world output of the synthetic product was estimated at 68 000 tons; in 1944 it was over 900 000 tons. To ensure maintenance of the new industry for possible future need, it was made obligatory in the United States to include a certain percentage of synthetic rubber in any rubber content of manufactured articles; but it was not until 1962–63 that production of synthetic rubber exceeded the output of natural rubber – when the consumption of both was in the region of 2.2m. tons. The effect on the plantation industry was all the more marked because, before the Second World War, the United States bought about half the total world supply of rubber, the other half being absorbed mostly in Europe (the United Kingdom 15 per cent), Japan and Canada. The limitation of the United States market for plantation rubber naturally had a depressing effect on prices, and that at a time when the rehabilitation of the industry in the Far East involved largely increased costs. Before the war rubber fetched from 7*d.* to 8*d.* (3p) per lb on the London market; when the market was freed from control after the war, the price was 9*d.* (4p) per lb, rising later to 1*s.* (5p). Happily the damage suffered by the plantations during the Japanese occupation was much less than had been feared; production made a rapid recovery, and the postwar problem was not one of shortage but of surpluses, both of natural and synthetic. The Korean War and the rearmament programmes of the great powers transformed this situation, and new demands sent up the price to 2*s.* 9*d.* (14p) per lb in 1950 and 4*s.* 3*d.* (21p) per lb in 1951, only to decline heavily again in the following year, when demand eased off.

These postwar developments serve to illustrate the varied conditions which have been experienced from time to time in marketing the supplies of plantation rubber. From the early years of the present century, with supplies increasing by leaps and bounds, while demand also increased widely but erratically, there were periods of under-production and overproduction, of booms and slumps, with the latter predominating. In 1909–10 the British import price rose to nearly £30 per cwt (over 5*s.* (25p) per lb); in 1913 it had fallen to £13 per cwt (just under 2*s.* 4*d.* (12p) per lb). Another boom after the First World War was followed by another slump. Overproduction was averted by restricting output in the British rubber-growing countries. Later the restriction was removed, and in 1931 the price of rubber fell to less than 2½*d.* (1p) per lb. An International Agreement to regulate both production and export came into force in 1934, but it could not be carried out during the war, and though in the United Kingdom the Ministry of Supply was the sole importer of rubber from 1941 to 1946, free marketing was permitted again in 1947.

The price fluctuations which make rubber such a speculative asset soon developed again. Rubber is particularly sensitive to the winds of change. The effect of the Korean War has already been noted. The threat of a recession in 1956 caused prices to drop between January and May from 3s. to 1s. 9d. (15p to 9p) per lb, only to be followed in December, when the Suez crisis threatened a shortage by a rise to 2s. 10d. (14p). Since then production and consumption have steadily increased, with prices falling gradually. In 1971 world production of natural rubber was reckoned at over 3m. metric tons, of which Malaysia supplied 1.3m. tons, taking the lead from Indonesia which had been the largest source of supply for some years. Next, but at a considerable distance, came Thailand and Ceylon. These four countries provided 86 per cent of the world production. Malaysia and Indonesia supplying 72 per cent.

The United States and British governments established strategic stockpiles from which supplies can be released to relieve shortages and reduce prices as and when necessary. Also there are regular and growing supplies of synthetic rubber, of which the market absorbs 3.5m. tons a year. As the quality approximates increasingly to that of the natural product, synthetic rubber is becoming a formidable rival. The production of synthetic is extending in western Europe and in the United States; but there is room for both products in meeting the ever-growing demands of transportation, and natural rubber may hope to hold its own.

Gutta-percha is the hardened juice of several other tropical trees of the family of *Sapotaceae*. The chief supply in this case comes from Indonesia. Formerly *Dichopis Gutta*, Benth., furnished the bulk of the supply, but this tree was so ruthlessly destroyed in obtaining the juice that it was almost exterminated and the genus *Payena*, especially *Payena Leerii*, Kurz, now contributes most of the product. Gutta-percha is used for many of the same purposes as rubber and is capable in many respects of the same treatment. Mixed with carbon, it can be vulcanised like rubber, and with the addition of sulphur, either to the soft or hard state. The former practice of destroying the trees to get the juice has now largely been given up. They may be tapped and preserved like rubber trees. Another variety of gutta-percha, known as **balata,** is obtained from South America, mainly Guyana and is the product of another member of the *Sapotaceae*, the bullet tree *Mimusops balata*, Crueg. With the increasing use of rubber from *Hevea brasiliensis* the use of other types has decreased.

Products of various climates

Vegetable oils, oilseeds and oilcake

Almost all vegetable oils are extracted from the fruit or seed. The plants supplying oil vary widely in their character, ranging from small herbs to tall trees. Almost all of them belong to warm countries, that is to say, either to tropical lands or the warmer parts of the temperate zone, or if they are not confined to these regions, are there of most importance for their oil. Oil has been extracted on a commercial scale from forty or more trees and plants. The most important commercially are the coconut palm, the oil palm, groundnuts, linseed, soya beans, and cottonseed, which furnish 90 per cent of the international trade in vegetable oils. Other important sources are the olive, rapeseed, sesame and sunflower seed, castor, tung, and perilla.

Two of the chief uses of almost all vegetable oils, except drying oils such as linseed oil, are the manufacture of soap and the manufacture of margarine. Some vegetable oils, such as olive oil, groundnut, corn, poppy, sesame, and cotton oil, are largely used as table oils for cooking, preserving, etc.; others, including rape, cotton and olive, were used for lighting, though for this purpose they have largely been replaced by mineral oils; others, such as rape, hemp, and palm oil, are employed in lubricating machinery; others are used in medicine and perfumery; others in making candles; others, known as drying oils in mixing colours for painting, as well as in various manufactures. The output of inedible industrial oils is generally greater than the edible.

Olive oil, though not the most important commercially, is the finest of the edible oils. The first crushing gives the highest grade oil for culinary and medicinal purposes. The residue yields, by solvent methods, oil for soap-making and other industries. In the first ten years after the Second World War, the production of olive oil in the main producing countries averaged 890 000 tons, representing, at the usual rate of extraction, nearly 6m. tons of olives. In addition, the world crop includes a considerable quantity of olives grown for direct consumption; in California, for instance, table olives are grown in at least the same quantity as olives for oil. Normally, light and heavy crops alternate, as in consequence do the supplies of oil, which in the postwar decade ranged from less than 0.5m. tons to well over 1m. tons.

The olive is a slow-growing tree, small in size and taking fifteen to twenty years to reach maturity. It lives to a great age and was originally a native of the Mediterranean region being suited to a warm temperate climate (dry summers) rather than a subtropical one. The site best suited to it is that which has a dry and gravelly limestone soil, and is well sheltered. These needs are met in many parts of the Mediterranean region (including Portugal), throughout which (except in Egypt) the tree is highly characteristic. Indeed, it may be fitly taken as marking both in altitude and in latitude and longitude the limits of this type of climate in different parts of the world, the tree having now been introduced wherever that type of climate prevails. In Spain there are extensive forests of it on the southern slopes of the Sierra Morena and in the upper part of the Guadalquivir valley, east-northeast of Cordova. In Italy its principal seats are Apulia, the western seaboard of Calabria, Tuscany, and the west side of the Gulf of Genova. In France the area (the lower part of the Rhône valley) devoted to it is very small. In comparatively recent years Tunisia with Sfax as its chief port, has become an important source of supply. There, on the estates producing the best quality, it is planted in the ratio of only about sixteen to the hectare, whereas in Spain and Italy the ratio is as much as 125 to 275 to the hectare.

In the Black Sea region the distribution of the olive illustrates in an interesting manner the influence of climate. The tree is absent from the south of the USSR, except on the southern slopes of the mountains in the Crimea, which afford the necessary protection against cold northerly winds. In the north of Turkey along the south shore of the Black Sea the olive thrives admirably along the whole coast from Trabzon to Samsun, and in ancient times extended to Sinope; that is, it occupies or once occupied the whole of that part of the coast looking northeastwards and participating in the shelter afforded by the Caucasus Mountains. It is excluded, however, from that part of the coast which looks northwestwards and is liable to be swept by cold winds from southern Russia.

The olive tree is grown in many other parts of the world, but in none of them is olive oil a product of outstanding importance. In 1971 Spain and Italy together produced 60 per cent of the world output of 1.4m. tons of oil; Greece, Portugal, Turkey and Tunisia together produced 28 per cent, leaving only 12 per cent for the combined contribution of all other countries, principally Morocco, Syria and Algeria.

In most countries, production both of olives and of olive oil is largely for home consumption. The chief importing countries ouside Europe have been the United States and the South and Central American republics, especially Brazil, but increasing production of other edible oils in South America has affected this trade adversely. During the Second World War the United Kingdom imports of olive oil almost disappeared, and during the 1970s the average was only 3 000 tons as against the prewar average of 10 000 tons.

Cottonseed oil has given economic value to a byproduct of the cotton-growing industry long treated as waste. The seed is costly to market, but the setting up of crushing plants in the producing countries has revolutionised the position. In the United States, 1 ton of cotton-seed yields 17 per cent cottonseed oil and 47 per cent cottonseed meal. World exports of cottonseed in 1938 totalled 716 000 tons; in the six years 1954—59 they averaged less than half that quantity. In 1938 world exports of cottonseed oil were 60 000 tons; in 1954—59 they averaged 268 000 tons, and in both 1955 and 1956 exceeded 320 000 tons, nearly all from the USA. By 1968 however, home consumption had increased and this, along with reduced production, had cut US exports by 90 per cent. World output of cottonseed (mostly in the United States, USSR, China, and India) is some 20m. tons, and the oil content 3.2m. tons. The oil is largely used as a substitute for olive oil as a cooking and salad oil, and in the manufacture of margarine. It faces competition from lower priced soya bean oil and animal fats.

In 1959 just on 85 per cent of the seed exported came from the Sudan, Nigeria, Syria and Nicaragua, while the United States supplied over 83 per cent of the oil exported. United Kingdom imports of this oil were limited by the restrictions on dollar trade, and seed is not so readily available as in the past; countries like Uganda, with crushing plant, prefer to extract the oil themselves. But the United Kingdom is still a large importer of available seed, and the refining of the oil has become a great industry at Hull. Besides the refined oil the seed yields much oil that is mixed with beef products to form compound lard, and the inferior kinds are used in the making of soap and candles. The refuse cake or meal is used as a cattle-food and as a fertiliser, and the hulls can be used without any other feed to fatten the cattle. In 1973 the United Kingdom imported no cottonseed but 26 000 tons of cottonseed oil, and 165 000 tons of cottonseed cake and meal.

Linseed, as already noted (p. 159), is another name for flax seed; it yields 34 per cent of oil, and is the product for which the flax plant is most widely cultivated. World production in 1970 exceeded 4.1m. tons, but in 1971 it reached only 2.8m. tons. The USA, USSR, Argentina and India are the main producing countries. Fully half the total production enters international trade. The United States head the list of individual importing countries, but collectively the United Kingdom and other countries of western Europe absorb the greater part of the available supplies.

As in the case of cottonseed, there has been a big switchover in trade from linseed to oil. Between 1938 and 1959, world exports of linseed dropped from 1.6m. tons to 633 000 tons, while the exports of linseed oil rose from 105 000 to 280 000 tons. Argentina, which now exports little or no seed, provided over 76 per cent of the world exports of linseed oil in 1959; India, which has also stopped exporting seed, provided another 7 per cent, and Uruguay nearly 6 per cent. The United States also provided over a third of the seed on the export market. In the United Kingdom, imports of linseed fell from 276 000 tons in 1938 to 58 000 tons in 1973, while imports of linseed oil rose from 18 700 tons to 25 000 tons.

The property of drying on exposure to the air, which gives linseed oil its special importance in making paints and varnishes, adapts it for many other uses. When treated with sulphur it forms linoleum and in composition with various fabrics, and in particular mixed with ground cork, it is used for floor coverings.

Groundnuts, or peanuts (see p. 147) contain an oil which is largely used for margarine. They constitute one of the biggest world crops of oil seeds, covering (1971) over 18.8m. hectares (nearly 49m. acres) and yielding about 18.5m. tons of unshelled nuts. India and China supply half; the United States, former French Africa, and Nigeria a fifth — some 1m. tons each. The unshelled nuts yield about 32 per cent of oil, and the shelled nuts about 45 per cent. The best oil is expressed from the unshelled nuts, but usually the nuts are shelled before export, to save freight, the shelled nuts being about 70 per cent of the weight unshelled.

In 1938, out of a world crop of 8m. tons, unshelled weight, 2.1m. tons were exported as nuts and (likewise from the countries of production) 55 000 tons of oil. India supplied over half the total, and West Africa most of the balance. During the war production kept remarkably steady, but exports dropped to about a third of the prewar level before rising in 1954–55 to about a half. Groundnuts are not only used to express oil; they are good to eat for man and beast, and in the general shortage of foodstuffs they were used increasingly for that purpose. In 1946 India, the world's largest producer, restricted the export of groundnuts, and since that year Nigeria has headed the list of exporting countries. In 1959, out of exports of 1.25m. tons of nuts, Nigeria provided 497 000 tons (1969, 525 000 tons) and Sénégal and Mali 283 000 tons. In 1969 Sénégal exported only 97 000 tons and Mali 6 000 tons. There has been a big increase in local production of oil, of which over 0.25m. tons were exported from Africa and Asia in 1959, mostly from Sénégal and Mali (113 000 tons), Nigeria (48 000 tons), India (44 000 tons), and China (25 000 tons). Europe takes the bulk of these exports, both the groundnuts and the oil going mostly to Britain and the Continent. United Kingdom imports in 1973 were 74 000 tons of groundnuts (69 000 tons unshelled) and 73 000 tons of groundnut oil.

Soya beans have a low oil content — about 17 per cent. The oil has long been used for cooking in China, and with the discovery early in the present century of methods of ridding it of a rancid flavour it began to be used in the West in the manufacture of compound lard and margarine. It is also widely used in industry for the manufacture of soap, paints and plastics. The quantities coming on to the world market declined between the two world wars — from an annual average of 200 000 tons of oil in 1924–28 to 125 000 tons in 1934–38. Manchuria contributed about 60 per cent of the total, and when that country was shut off by the Second World War, Europe received very little. A compensating factor has been a big development of the United States crop of soya beans. In 1971 of a world crop of over 48m. tons the States produced 31.8m. tons of soya beans, considerably more than the crop in China (11.5m. tons). United Kingdom imports in 1973 were

767 000 tons of soya beans and 13 000 tons of soya bean oil.

Two palm trees yield large supplies of oil: the **coconut palm** and the **oil palm**. The coconut palm flourishes in the coastal belts of tropical countries, especially around the shores of the Indian Ocean and in the western Pacific. Before the Second World War, **coconut oil** constituted one-quarter of the vegetable oils and one-fifth of all oils and fats entering international trade. It is expressed from copra, the dried flesh of the coconut, the yield being as much as 63 per cent of oil suitable for soap and margarine. The prewar production of copra averaged 2.5m. tons a year, and exports took the form of both copra and oil. In 1938, an average year, copra itself entered into world trade to the extent of 1.5m. tons (oil potential 1m. tons), and oil expressed from copra was exported to the amount of 0.33m. tons. Until the 1939–45 war upset world economy, the Dutch East Indies, the Philippines and Malaya supplied about three-quarters of the copra exported; exports of oil came chiefly from the Philippines, Ceylon and Malaya. The trade in both copra and oil was widely distributed, the biggest share going to the United States. During the war, with so many of the chief sources of supply in Japanese occupation, world trade dwindled to small proportions, but by 1955 it was back at its prewar level, a decrease in the exports from Malaya and Indonesia being balanced by a notable increase in the exports from the Philippines. World production of copra reached 3m. tons a year throughout the 1960s (3.7m. tons in 1971), United Kingdom imports in 1973 being 38 000 tons of copra and 47 000 tons of coconut oil.

The **oil palm**, or Guinea oil palm (*Eloeis guineensis*, Jacq.), is indigenous to West Africa between 10° N and 10° S. Since the First World War it has also been widely cultivated in West Indonesia and Malaysia. Its fruit yields two distinct oils — **palm oil**, which is expressed from the pericarp or fibrous matter surrounding the kernel, and **palm kernel oil**, which is crushed from the hard kernel. The pericarp yields a very varied percentage of oil, which is usually expressed locally and exported for use chiefly in soap-making and the tinplate industry, though also used to some extent for edible fats. Palm kernels yield about 47 per cent of oil and are usually exported whole, the oil being extracted in the importing country; it resembles coconut oil and is used for making margarine and soap.

Before the Second World War the exports of palm oil rose to 0.5m. tons, of which southeast Asia supplied over half and West Africa nearly half, with the Dutch East Indies and Nigeria as the two outstanding sources of supply, and the United Kingdom and United States as the chief importing countries. Exports of palm kernels totalled over 2.75m. tons, of which the Dutch East Indies and Malaysia supplied only a small part, the great bulk coming from West Africa, with Nigeria as the dominant contributor (nearly half) and Europe (particularly Germany) as the supreme market. Apart from southeast Asia, supplies were fairly well maintained during the war, and later the exports of palm oil increased, averaging nearly 600 000 tons in 1954–59. Whereas in 1938 the Dutch East Indies headed the list, after the war (as Indonesia) they failed to recover and Nigeria took the lead with 33 per cent of the total, the Belgian Congo (now Zaire) coming second and Indonesia third. There was a change, too, in distribution, for while the United Kingdom continued to rank as the chief importer of palm oil, the United States took only 5 per cent. The exports of palm kernels also increased (to over 0.75m. tons), with Nigeria supplying more than half and the United Kingdom taking from 40 to 60 per cent. By 1971 world output of palm oil reached nearly 2m. tons, Nigeria and Malaysia each contributing 500 000 tons. In 1971 world output of palm kernel oil totalled 1.17m. tons. Nigeria's output was 310 000 tons, Brazil's 185 000, Zaire's 130 000 and Malaysia's 102 200. In 1973 United Kingdom imported 240 000 tons of palm oil and 34 000 tons of palm nuts and kernels.

Rapeseed, which comprises various species of the Brassicas (Cabbage) family, including the summer variety known as colza, is one of the most widely grown oilseeds, especially in eastern Asia. It yields 35 per cent of a lubricating oil, which is also widely used for edible purposes, and during the war it more than held its own among world crops, the cultivated area increasing from 6.5 to 8.1m. hectares (16 to 20m. acres), and production from 4m. to 5m. tons — most of it grown in China (over 60 per cent), India (25 per cent) and Japan. Commercially it takes a minor place among oilseeds, under 10 per cent of the production entering into world trade whether as seed or oil. Prewar exports of seed amounted to about 100 000 tons, and of oil to 25 000 tons (equivalent to about 75 000 tons of seed). Since the war, world output has tended to increase steadily, reaching 7.8m. tons in 1971. Exports of seed increased (less regularly) from 40 000 tons to 215 000 tons, and of oil from 16 900 tons to 41 000 tons (equivalent to 125 000 tons of seed). India is the largest producer, followed by China, Poland and France. Canada has become a major exporter, growing rape as an alternative crop in the wheat areas.

The sesame seed of commerce includes till, gingelly, and benniseed, all of which yield a high percentage (45 per cent) of edible oil favoured in tropical diets and for confectionery. Like rapeseed, it is widely grown for home consumption, chiefly in eastern Asia, and does not enter largely into international trade. China and India had far and away the biggest share of the prewar production of 1.5 to 1.75m. tons, and produce the bulk (50 per cent) of the 1.5m. tons grown in postwar years. Compared with other oilseeds, sesame is a low-yielding crop and the area under cultivation has increased little over the last fifty years. Prominent among secondary sources of supply are Sudan, Mexico, and

Burma. The comparatively small exports (6 per cent) are provided by and distributed among many countries.

Sunflower seed. The USSR is the dominant factor in the production of this seed, but crop yields determine the contribution to international trade. In 1938 the USSR had 3.2m. hectares (8m. acres) under crop out of a world total of 4m. hectares (10m. acres), and produced over 2m. tons of seed out of a world total of 2.75m. tons. In 1971 the Soviet acreage was estimated at 4.8m. hectares (11.8m. acres) and the production at 5.7m. tons. World acreage and production had increased still faster — to 8.6m. hectares (21.2m. acres) and 9.6m. tons. In Argentina the area under sunflower in 1950 had jumped up to over 1.6m. hectares (4m. acres), yielding over 1m. tons; but acreage and crops both declined again, partly because of adverse seasons and partly because of politico—economic conditions. Argentina still ranks next to the USSR, but the 1950 record has not been repeated. Trade in seed, as distinct from the oil, is everywhere small. Like groundnuts, sunflower seed is used locally for food. It yields about 25 per cent of oil, the best grades being suitable for foodstuffs, others for soap, paint and lubricating. As with most other oilseeds, the residual oil cake is a valuable cattle-food.

Tung oil, or Chinese wood oil, has a reputation for unique drying properties, which give it value in the manufacture of paints (restricted by the increased use of water-based paints) and varnishes, linoleum and oilcloth, and have led to its cultivation outside China. The oil is expressed from the fruits of the tung tree, which have a commercial yield of about 16 per cent. Chinese production of the oil is down to an estimated 90 000 tons a year (1970) compared with an annual production of 120 000 tons before the Second World War (of which nearly 80 000 tons were exported). China's chief customer was the United States, which itself has a variable production dependent on seasonal conditions. In 1966 and 1967 the output was 11 300 tons; in 1968 it was down to 2 300 tons and in 1970 only 2 000 tons. The only other considerable producer is Argentina (around 14 300 tons in 1970), but Paraguay, Brazil, and Malawi (Nyasaland) have a small output. In 1959—69 United Kingdom imports ranged from 11 000 tons to 6 000 tons.

Another vegetable oil with drying properties, useful for varnishes, etc., is derived from **perilla seed**, the commercial rate of extraction being about 37 per cent. Perilla, a plant akin to peppermint and spearmint, is mostly grown in eastern Asia, especially China (Manchuria), where cultivation spread rapidly before the Second World War and covered some 162 000 hectares (400 000 acres), yielding nearly three-quarters of the average world production of 170 000 tons. The Manchurian crop was grown largely for export, and in the years immediately before the war it provided for overseas markets an average of 64 000 tons of seed and 14 000 tons of oil. The seed went to Japan and thence, as oil, to the United States. Production since the war seems to have declined, and there are little signs of the revival of trade in its wider aspects.

Babassu kernels, derived from a palm tree growing wild in Brazil, are as rich in oil as copra (63 per cent) and the oil is not unlike coconut oil. They are extremely hard, and the difficulty of cracking them has hindered their use. Prewar production of the kernels averaged 40 000 tons, and postwar harvests have increased. In 1959–60 they were estimated at over 90 000 tons. The potential production is enormous, but the present output is practically all absorbed by home industry.

Poppy seed is a byproduct of the white or opium poppy of Asia and a major product of the black poppy, which is grown in Europe for edible and industrial use. It yields over 40 per cent of oil. Europe's annual production of the seed before the Second World War, about 50 000 tons, is now only half that quantity. Only small quantities enter into international trade. They are mainly European in origin and are imported by the United States and West Germany.

Oilcake is a general name for the masses of crushed seeds that remain after the oil has been pressed out of them, and it is now very largely used in the feeding of cattle, which it fattens very rapidly; frequently also as a fertiliser. It is chiefly derived from linseed, rapeseed and cottonseed, but also from coconut, in which form it is known as **poonac.**

Essential oils. Essential oils are volatile, aromatic substances, usually but not always liquid, obtained from various grasses, plants, trees and shrubs. They are mainly used in perfumery, particularly the manufacture of soap, medicine, dental preparations, disinfectants, and for flavouring confectionary. The most important of these oils, forming a class by themselves, are the turpentine oils. World production before the Second World War amounted to 150 000 tons a year as compared with 10 000 tons of all other essential oils. **Spirit of turpentine** is obtained by distillation from the resin of various firs, pines and other cone-bearing trees. It is very largely used to dissolve resins, and in the making of paints and varnishes, as well as for cleaning. Among other essential oils are the citrus oils (from the peel of sweet and bitter oranges, lemons, grapefruit and limes); many varieties of flower oils such as attar of roses, jasmin oil and geranium oil; peppermint oil, citronella, cinnamon leaf and cinnamon bark oils; and camphor. There are many others, making up a valuable total, though not amounting to a great deal in weight. Exclusive of spirits of turpentine, the imports of essential oils into the United Kingdom in 1973 were valued at £26m. Individually the most valuable items were lemon oil, £3.6m.; peppermint, £2.3m.; orange oils, £450 000; and citronella, £810 000.

The United States is the chief source of supply of **grapefruit** and **sweet orange oils** (bergamot) **peppermint** and **spearmint** (the latter now largely used in canning peas); and it shares with Sicily the main production of **lemon oil**. The postwar dollar problem led to a movement to increase production in the Commonwealth, particularly East Africa, the West Indies, and Mauritius and Seychelles. **Lime oil** is already produced mainly in the Commonwealth (West Indies and West Africa), and Ceylon is the source of **cinnamon bark oil** and **cinnamon leaf oil**, both of which, especially the latter, are also produced in the Seychelles. **Clove oil** comes from the islands of Zanzibar and Pemba, and Kenya is producing appreciable quantities of **geranium oil** and **cedarwood oil**. Southern India, France and the French Community, and Indonesia also figure prominently in the supply of various essential oils. **Camphor** is mainly derived from a species of cinnamon (*Cinnamonum camphora*) which grows in Japan, Taiwan (where it is a government monopoly), central China and West Malaysia; it is extracted by distillation from the wood and leaves.

Small quantities of certain essential oils are produced in the United Kingdom, particularly **lavender**. English lavender is among the finest in the world and is used in the making of the highest quality perfumes.

Waxes

The waxes of commerce are of animal, vegetable and mineral origin. Under the last head comes **paraffin wax**. Waxes of animal and vegetable origin are not a very big factor in British trade. Imports into the United Kingdom in 1973 were 4 000 tons, valued at about £1m. Beeswax, with which **honey** may be considered, is an almost universal product. In Italy its use in connection with Catholic ceremonies has led to a considerable import, and in Europe generally the production of both honey and wax is less than the consumption. The deficiency is made good in part by the bees of the New World — another case of reciprocal benefits, for the honey bee was introduced into the New World by the Spaniards. Before the upset of war and currency difficulties, Canada and the West Indies, the United States and Central America supplied much of the honey imported into the United Kingdom, while Australia and New Zealand were also leading contributors; by 1950 Australia was supplying more than three-quarters of the total, with the West Indies, Argentina and Chile well behind. In 1969 total imports were 15 000 tons. On the other hand the beeswax imported into the United Kingdom (700 tons in 1973) came, and continues to come, mostly from equatorial Africa, principally East Africa.

The chief vegetable waxes entering into world trade are **carnauba** and **candelilla**. Carnauba wax is found mainly in the form of a glutinous powder on the leaves of the carnauba or wax palm (*Copernicia cerifera*, Mart.); it is an important export from Brazil, the only country which supplies it in commercial quantities. Carnauba wax is in great demand

and the price is high, but attempts to produce it synthetically have had little success. It is mostly used in making polishes, floor waxes and carbon paper. The high price of carnauba wax has increased the consumption of candelilla, which is found as a coating on a weed (*Pedilanthus pavonis*) growing mostly in Mexico but also in southern Texas. It is used for dressing leather, for furniture and shoe polishes, and as a substitute for beeswax and carnauba.

Less important, commercially, are **Japanese wax**, obtained from the berries of certain sumac trees (chiefly *Rhus succedanea* Linn.) grown in Japan and China; and **myrtle wax**, which comes from a North American shrub (*Myrica cerifera*, Linn.) and is used in the manufacture of varnishes. The wax obtained from the **wax-palm of the Andes**, and the **insect white wax** of China, are both important in internal trade, but are not exported.

Gums and resins

Resin is a general name for a variety of substances which are all originally fluids in the tissues of plants. They solidify and are all more or less clear or translucent though generally with a tinge of colour. They are all inflammable and insoluble in water, but generally are soluble in organic solvents and essential oils such as turpentine. As a rule they exude in a fluid state from the trunks and branches of trees, but sometimes they are found in cavities inside the trees or in the ground where the trees have grown. **Gums** resemble resins in appearance and origin, but are soluble or swell in water, and are insoluble in alcohol and essential oils.

Imports of these gums and resins into the United Kingdom in 1938 amounted to nearly 100 000 tons, valued at close on £2m., and in 1973 to nearly 13 000 tons valued at over £5.5m. The largest and most valuable of the imports in each of these years was **rosin** (colophony); in quantity it accounted for well over three-quarters of the total, and in value more than half. It is used in the making of paper, soap, varnishes and printing inks, and for many other familiar purposes. Rosin is obtained by distilling turpentine, and is the substance left after the oil of turpentine has been separated. Both are produced mainly in the United States, and that country supplies nearly half the United Kingdom imports of rosin. Substantial amounts are produced in China, France and Portugal, and these countries are also a source of United Kingdom imports.

The other resins of commerce are mainly used in the making of varnishes and lacquers and for burning of incense. One of the best known among the imports into the United Kingdom is **copal** (*Copaifera copallifera*), frequently known as gum copal. It is obtained from both the Old World and the New, but the Zaire Republic dominates the market, with medium grade supplies. East Africa produces a small quantity of high quality copal. United Kingdom imports of all types of copal in 1969 amounted to under 1 500 tons compared with over 10 000 tons prewar — a reflection of the substitution of synthetic materials.

One of the more valuable resins imported into the United Kingdom is lac. The quantity in 1973 (1 800 tons) was half that of 1969, but its value was more than doubled to £1.3m. Lac is entered in the trade returns under three names — sticklac, seedlac, and shellac. The resin is secreted by the lac insect (*Tachardia lacca*), parasitic on a number of host trees. The main source of supply is India (chiefly in Bihar and Orissa and the former Central Provinces, now Madhya Pradesh), with much smaller production in Thailand and Vietnam. The twigs of the tree encrusted with the resin form **sticklac**; when the resin is separated from the wood and washed free from lac dye, etc., it appears in the form of grains known as **seedlac**; and when it is melted and strained and made into thin irregular sheets it is called **shellac**. Lac in its various forms is used in making varnishes, lacquers, sealing wax and in the electrical industry.

Gum arabic is largely imported into the United Kingdom for use in the confectionary trade (which absorbs 60 per cent of the total), in pharmacy, as an adhesive for postage stamps, and in high-class stationery. Poorer grades are used in the lustring of silk, crêpe, etc., as 'dressings' for fabrics, in calico printing, and in making matches. Among numerous other uses, it enters into the making of fine colours and lithographic ink. Imports in 1973 were nearly 6 000 tons valued at more than £1.8m. Gum arabic is derived from various species of *Acacia* growing in different parts of the world. The best kind is imported into Europe, mostly from the dry regions of northern Africa and the Sudan. It is derived mainly from *Acacia senegal* (or *Acacia verek*, Ait.), a tree found throughout the region south of the Sahara, between Sénégal and the Nile. An allied species is found in the arid portion of India immediately to the northwest of the Deccan Peninsula. The trade in gum from the Sénégal region is in French hands, and that particular gum is imported into other countries mainly from France. Another species of the gum, *Acacia drepanolibium*, is found in Tanzania, where it forms about 95 per cent of the production. Nigeria also produces gum arabic on a commercial scale.

Gum tragacanth is more expensive and is imported in smaller quantities than gum arabic — in 1973 just over 310 tons valued at nearly £750 000. It is used in calico printing as a vehicle for applying discharges (chemical agents for removing colour), and for pharmaceutical and other purposes. It is not found in the countries of the Commonwealth, but is the product of several species of *Astragulus* (milk vetches), a thorny herb or shrub found in the countries around and beyond the Mediterranean; Iran is the main source of the United Kingdom imports.

Two other gums are **Karaya**, which comes mainly from India and is a product of a number of *Sterculia* species; and **Kauri** gum, the resin of the New Zealand pine, which is a species of Dammara (*D. australis*, Lamb). Neither is now of great trade value. Karaya gum found some favour in the United States, where it was used in the manufacture of sauces and ice-cream. The United Kingdom imported 440 tons of it in 1950. Kauri gum, the finest of all resins for varnishes, is now scarce. Not only have the New Zealand pine forests been much reduced, but the gum from the living tree is of minor value. The best Kauri gum is a fossil product dug in lumps from the site of ancient forests, now forming the Fern Country of the North Island; and this ground has been pretty well worked over. Imports into the United Kingdom declined from 2 000 tons in 1934 to 650 tons in 1950. The industry may now be considered dead.

Other gums and resins entering into commerce include **dammar**, the product of a cone-bearing tree (*Dammara orientalis*, Lamb.) which grows in the Malay Archipelago; **sandarach**, the product of another cone-bearing tree found in North and South Africa, Australia and North America; **mastix**, the product of a species of Pistacia found above all on the island of Chios; and **amber**, the product of an extinct conifer, found mainly on the Baltic coast of Prussia and used largely for ornamental purposes, especially in China. Of the resins burnt as incense, the most important are true **frankincense**, the product of various species of tree belonging to the genus Boswellia; **myrrh**, the product of a species of Balsamodendron; and **bensoin**, derived from the bark of *Styrax bensoin*. This last is also used medicinally.

Spices, stimulants and condiments

The most important spices are all products of the torrid zone — principally pepper, ginger, cloves and mace. Imports of all four and of other spices into the United Kingdom in 1938 were about 8 000 tons valued at £340 000, and in 1973 about 16 500 tons valued at £6.6m.

Peppercorns and **black** and **white pepper**, which make up the great bulk of the pepper of commerce, are all derived from one species, a twining and climbing plant, *Piper nigrum*, Linn., largely cultivated in southern India and the Malay Archipelago. Its spice is the most generally used of all spices and has long been the most important in world trade. The peppercorns are the whole berries, and black and white pepper the result of grinding them; for white pepper the peppercorns are first deprived of their outer skin by steeping them in water for several days. Nearly the whole of the pepper imported into this country comes from the Malay Peninsula, but more than half of this import is the product of Indonesia, Sarawak and Thailand, collected at Singapore. Another species (*P. longum*, Linn.) produces **long pepper**, which is the dried unripe fruit of that shrub; **cubebs** are the berries of another species (*P. cubeba*, Linn.); and a fourth species, the **betel** (*P. betel*, Linn.), furnishes the leaves which are used along with areca nut and other ingredients to compose the favourite stimulant chewing mixture of the people of India. **Cayenne pepper** is the product of a totally different plant, being the ground pods of different species of Capsicum, one of which has smaller pods which are used whole under the name of **chillies**. Originally natives of South America, they are now grown in tropical countries in the Old World as well as the New, and even in the warmer parts of the temperate zone, as in Spain and Hungary. Before the Second World War the United Kingdom was the great market for all kinds of peppers, and re-exported usually from one-third to two-thirds of her imports, but during the war, when the Japanese occupation of the principal countries of supply led to a world pepper famine, this re-export trade disappeared. After a fluctuating revival, re-exports of spices in 1969 were under 700 tons, valued at £350 000.

Ginger is the dried root-stock of a plant (*Zingiber officinale*, Rosc.) native to southeastern Asia, but now largely cultivated also in the West Indies and in West Africa. It is widely grown in tropical countries for local consumption, being used in cookery for flavouring and as an important ingredient in curry powders. Almost all British imports are from Jamaica, Sierra Leone and Nigeria, to a total of 2 500 tons in 1973, valued at £781 000. Before the war there was an even larger import of ginger preserved in syrup as a confection, and this came mostly from Hong Kong and China.

Cloves are the flower buds of *Eugenia caryophyllata*, Linn., dried before opening. Zanzibar's two islands, Zanzibar and Pemba, particularly the latter, provide the bulk of the world supply. They have about 3.5m. clove trees, yielding exports of 9 000 tons in 1959, 12 000 tons in 1960. Local industry includes the distillation of clove oils, and the clove tree has been the main factor in the economy of Zanzibar. A serious outbreak of the 'Sudden Death' disease affected production in the late 1940s and the 1950s, but its onslaught has subsided, and there are now estimated to be 4m. trees. The value of their products, the cloves and clove oil, forms nearly 50 per cent of the total exports of Zanzibar and Pemba. Secondary sources of supply are Malagasy (Madagascar) and the Moluccas — or Spice Islands — the latter being the original home of the clove tree.

Mace is closely associated with **nutmegs**. Both come from the same tree, *Myristica fragrans*, Willd.; nutmegs are the kernel of the fruit and mace the investment (aril) of that kernel. This tree also came originally from the Moluccas (still the chief source of supply), but has been introduced into Grenada in the West Indies. Indonesia produces the better nutmegs, and the West Indies the better mace; the former are used mainly for flavouring sweet dishes and the latter for flavouring sauces and ketchups.

Among other spices, the **cinnamon** of the shops comes from two different trees, consisting in both cases of the bark (ground or unground) of the smaller twigs. The dearer and better product is derived from the *Cinnamomum zeylanicum*, Nees., or Ceylon cinnamon, and is distinguished in commerce as **true cinnamon**, though it was not discovered till the thirteenth century. The cinnamon of the ancients was the **cassia lignea** of commerce, the product of *Cinnamomum loureirii*, Linn. The Ceylon cinnamon is very exacting as to soil and climate, and much of it has been replaced by coconuts. The Seychelles are an important source of supply, also of cinnamon oil. The tree is grown in the Malay Archipelago, and has been introduced into the West Indies and South America. The cassia lignea is much more widespread, growing wild (as well as cultivated) in the tropical and subtropical parts of both the Old and the New World. China is one source of supplies.

Kola nuts which contain caffeine and are largely used as a stimulant in tropical Africa, are derived from various species of the Cola tree, particularly *Cola acuminata*, Schott and End. This tree has also been introduced into the New World. The **coca** shrub (*Erythroxylum coca*, Lam., and other species) is native to tropical South America on the eastern side of the Andes. Ever since the discovery of those regions its leaves have been known to impart, when chewed, an extraordinary power of enduring fatigue; they now enter into commerce as the source of the alkaloid cocaine.

Most of the other spices come from the West Indies, the most important being pimento: the unripe dried berries of *Pimenta dioica*. Popular names for it are **pimento** and **all-spice** — this last from its mixed flavour of cinnamon, cloves, and nutmeg. Among the minor spices in European trade may be mentioned **cardamoms** (*Elettaria cardomomum*), the most valuable of all Indian condiments; they are grown to such an extent on the mountains of southern India that the range forming the background of the new state of Kerala has been named Cardamom Hills. They are also grown in Central America and Guatemala; and are used in curry powders and for flavouring confectionary and certain liqueurs. **Vanilla** (*Vanilla planifolia*) is the pod of a twining orchid originally belonging to Mexico and South America, but long since introduced into the tropics of the Old World, notably the islands of Malagasy, Réunion, Mauritius, Seychelles, and Ceylon, which now rival Mexico in the production of this commodity. **Cummin**, the seed of a plant (*Cuminum syminum*) native to the upper Nile regions, but introduced at an early stage into southern and eastern Asia is a culinary spice in curry powders. It now plays little part in European commerce. **Star-anise**, the seeds of a tree (*Illicium verum*, Hook. f.) in south China, is imported into Europe as a flavouring for spirits. Oil of anise is also obtained from **aniseed**, the seed of a herb of the hemlock family (*Pimpinella anisum*), long established in Europe and North America. It is used in medicines, in flavouring beverages, and has given its name to the liqueur 'Anisette'. The chief spices and condiments grown in Europe are **fennel, caraway, coriander,** and **mustard.**

Dyestuffs from the vegetable kingdom

Vegetable dyes have been largely replaced in modern industry by dyes made from mineral and coal-tar products. Dye woods are the heart-wood of certain trees, chiefly grown in tropical countries. **Logwood,** a wood of a dark red colour yielding an extract which is used in dyeing blue, brown, and black, comes from *Haematoxylon campechianum*, Linn., a lofty tree very abundant in the Mexican province of Yucatan, but mainly exported from the West Indies and Belize (British Honduras). The other principal dyewood is **fustic,** a wood yielding a yellow colouring-matter, used in combination with other materials to produce dyes of different colours. It is the product of *Morus tinctoria*, Don., and is exported mainly from Nicaragua under the name of **mora-wood.**

Other dyestuffs of vegetable origin are either parts of herbs from which dyes may be extracted, or extracts used in dyeing, whether derived from herbs or from the wood of trees. The fine blue dye, **indigo,** is obtained chiefly from a shrub *Indigofera tinctoria*, Linn., a native of the tropical parts of southeastern Asia, and of South America and Egypt. Commercially its place has been largely taken by the synthetic **indigotin.** Also of former rather than present importance are madder and safflower. Madder is variously known as **madder, madder-root, garancine,** and **munjeet;** garancine being the colouring principle extracted from the madder plant, and munjeet being the Indian madder (*Rubia cordifolia*, Linn.). The European madder, *Rubia tinctorum*, Linn., used to be the principal source of certain red and yellow dyes. Other red and yellow dyes were obtained from the flower-heads of the **safflower** (*Carthamus tinctorius*, Linn.).

Cochineal, a red colouring matter, is obtained from the dried bodies of an insect (*Dactylopius coccus*, Costa), allied to the insect which yields the lac of India (p. 231) and to the kermes insect, which lives on the kermes oak in the Mediterranean region and yields another red dye, the 'scarlet' of the Bible. Cochineal is still imported from the Canary Islands, where the various species of the Napolea plant upon which the insect feeds are largely grown for the sake of this product. Also imported from the Canary Islands, as well as from tropical Africa and tropical America, is a lichen (*Roccella tinctoria*, DC.) from which two dyes are obtained. One of these, a blue dye, is **litmus**, the colouring for the well-known litmus paper used as a test for acids, which change the colour from blue to red. Another dye used for chemical tests is **turmeric**, an extract from the underground stem of *Curcuna tinctoria*, Roxb., an oriental plant. **Gamboge**, the hardened sap of another tree belonging to southeast Asia, is, like turmeric, a yellow dye; both are used in making coloured varnishes.

Timber

The timbers of commerce are usually classified as 'softwoods' (derived from coniferous trees – Gymnosperms), and 'hardwoods' (derived from deciduous and evergreen broadleaved trees – Angiosperms). For the most part the two classes consist of relatively 'soft' and 'hard' timbers, but the distinction is botanical and there are notable exceptions to the applicability of the two terms, some of the softest and lightest known timbers being technically 'hardwoods'.

Timber is, for the most part, exported on a large scale only where there are exceptional facilities for water transport. Most of the timbers of commerce are **softwoods** obtained mainly from **firs** and **pines**. They are in general use for building purposes; also enormous quantities of pulpwood are consumed in the manufacture of woodpulp for newsprint. Canada, Brazil and the USSR are the only countries now having a large reserve of 'natural' softwood, but the USA and many countries of Europe have a steady output from plantations. Two-thirds of the world's production of timber comes from the northern forests, mainly softwoods, which stretch across Europe, the USSR, and North America; one-third is from the tropical forests, mainly hardwoods, which stretch across Africa, southeast Asia, and Central and South America. The proportion of softwood timber which finds its way into international trade is still greater – something like 90 per cent; and the balance of commercial timbers is made up mostly of temperate hardwoods. Although there are vast reserves of tropical hardwoods, they provide at present only a small percentage of the world's trade in timbers. They include beautiful cabinet woods, but the trees in tropical forests are very mixed, and it is difficult to extract one particular type.

Trade in softwoods. The chief softwood exporting countries are Finland, Sweden, Canada and the USSR; the USA both exports and imports, especially from Canada, and on balance is a net importer. No total figure for the quantity of timber imported into the United Kingdom can readily be given.

Before metrication the trade returns quoted wood and timber imports in several measures of quantity: standards, piled cubic fathoms, cubic feet and tons. No attempt is made to estimate a common denominator, and the figures here put forward in an endeavour to sum up the position do not claim to be impeccable. Softwoods are mostly calculated in standards, and are listed as hewn, or sawn, or planed, or boxboards, as the case may be; the great bulk arrive sawn. Sleepers of all kinds are also recorded in standards, but roundwood logs of pine, spruce, etc., are reckoned in piled cubic fathoms, as also are pitprops. Hardwoods are measured in cubic feet. There are various measures for a standard of timber; one of the commonest, the Petrograd standard, is equivalent to 165 cu ft (4.68 cu m). It is not the largest, and its adoption for conversion purposes in connection with United Kingdom imports will not give an exaggerated idea of the quantity. A piled cubic fathom is 216 cu ft (6.16 cu m). If these rates be applied for purposes of conversion on a rough and ready basis, with due recognition of the possibilities of error, the sum total of the imports of timber into the United Kingdom in 1938 is found to have been about 550m. cu ft (15.6 cu m), while in 1956, though the imports were considerably more than in some of the intervening years, the total was still only about 356m. cu ft (10.1m. cu m). By 1969 the total was some 405m. cu ft (11.6m. cu m), while wood pulp imports had increased steadily to 2.6m. tons.

If figures for the total imports by quantity are difficult of precise assessment there is no doubt about the increase in value. In 1938 the value of all imports of wood and timber was returned as under £43m.; in 1956 it was £160m.; and in 1960 it was £186m. By 1973 it had risen to £457m. − to which might be added £202m. for wood pulp and £98m. for newsprint. If all wood and wood products are included the total import bill in 1973 was over £765m. − the fourth largest item. Home produced timber accounted from some 10 per cent of the total consumption. By the end of the century, new planting will increase home production threefold; but increased demand will still limit supplies to 12 or 15 per cent of the total.

Hardwoods. Analysis of the hardwood imports is particularly instructive as showing the effect of the postwar dollar shortage in changing the avenues of trade. Before the Second World War, the United Kingdom imports of hardwoods averaged (1934–38) nearly 46m. cu ft (1.3m. cu m) a year, of which the United States and Canada supplied 55 per cent, British Colonies 6 per cent, and the rest of the world 39 per cent. In 1956 these imports, which had followed a switchback course in the interval, falling or rising considerably, were less than 40m. cu ft (1.1m. cu m), of which the United States and Canada supplied under 10 per cent, while other Commonwealth countries (principally in West Africa) had jumped up to over 50 per cent. In 1973 imports were 48m. cu ft, Canada and the United States supplied less than 5 per cent while West Africa (Ivory Coast, Ghana and Nigeria) supplied 45 per cent.

Among the temperate hardwoods, **oak** is normally a large export both from North America and from central Europe. Elm, beech, walnut, and maple are among the other important timber trees of the temperate zone, and the spotted wood of the New England sugar-maple, known as bird's-eye maple, is highly esteemed for cabinet work. Prominent among tropical hardwoods is **mahogany**, the wood of *Swietenia mahogoni*, L., a large tree belonging to tropical America, including the West Indies. The best quality is obtained from Cuba. When grown on marshy ground, like most of that of Belize (British Honduras), the timber is comparatively soft. Under the name of mahogany various red cabinet woods are now largely imported from West Africa. **Teak** is of the highest value for shipbuilding and in construction generally, being as hard and durable as oak, and having at the same time this advantage over oak, that while the latter timber is said to promote rust, teak contains an oil which tends to preserve iron by preventing rust. It is widespread in Burma, which used to be the world's largest exporter of teak; but it also thrives in Thailand and other parts of southeast Asia with a moderate rainfall of between 1 000 and 2 000 mm (40 and 80 in). As the wood when full of sap is heavier than water the tree has to be killed, by cutting off a ring of the bark, if it must be floated down stream. **Ebony** is a name given to the wood of various trees. The hardest, blackest, and most valuable kind is the product of *Diospyros ebenum*, Koe., a native of India. **Rosewood** is another name given to several different kinds of timber, the best being derived from various species of *Caesalpinia*; the best of all, it is said, from *Caesalpinia brasiliensis*, Sw. The term **cedar** is applied to a number of trees whose wood is thought to resemble that of the true cedar of Lebanon in colour or appearance or both. The cedar of Lebanon furnishes none of the timber of commerce. The **white cedar** is derived from *Juniperus oxycedrus*, L., *Cupressus thyoides*, L., and other trees; the **red cedar** (used in making pencils) from *Juniperus virginiana*, L., and *J. bermudiana*, L. Most of the cedarwood of commerce comes from the West Indies and Central America. Red woods derived from two gigantic species of *Eucalyptus* — **jarrah**, or *Eucalyptus marginata*, and **karri**, or *E. diversicolor* — are imported to the United Kingdom from Western Australia for the manufacture of floor blocks, furniture, and other purposes. The wood of the jarrah is also very useful in making piles to be sunk in water, as it has remarkable durability in water both salt and fresh. They both grow in restricted areas in the southwest of the state.

The world demand for timber is increasing — slowly for building purposes where steel, concrete and other materials are increasingly employed, but rapidly for paper making. World production of paper and newsprint rose from 40 to 128m. tons between 1957 and 1971. With increasing literacy and an increasing world population, it is estimated that by 1985 the demand will call for 75 per cent more wood for paper making than was used in 1967. Timber is a renewable resource, but the natural forests can no longer meet more than a fraction of such a demand and extensive plantations will be required. Should supply lag behind and prices rise, then substitute plastic materials may be increasingly employed for paper making.

Furs

The fur trade deals in the skins of a variety of animals differing greatly in size and value. The regions from which the furs are collected are almost exclusively the temperate and cold parts of the world, the finest sorts being all from the colder regions. Most of the furs come, therefore, from the northern hemisphere, where there is the greatest area of land in high latitudes; and most are handled by a few traditional markets. The furs from North America are collected, at the New York market, but in still greater quantity reach the London market, which also receives supplies from the southern hemisphere as well as from Europe. The furs of Siberia and northern Russia are principally collected at Gor'kiy. Another major market was Leipzig, which owed its importance to its central situation, not only as regards the source of supply, but as regards the region in which furs are mostly worn, fur garments being more in demand in central and eastern Europe than in western Europe, where the winters are relatively mild. United Kingdom imports of furs and fur clothing were valued at £4.3m. in 1973.

To enumerate all the animals that contribute a share to the fur trade would be to mention nearly all the land mammals belonging to the colder parts of the earth, as well as a good many of those belonging to more temperate regions, and several marine mammals. Among those which supply the greatest number of skins to the trade are **squirrels**, **rabbits**, **musk-rats** (a kind of beaver belonging to North America), **coypus** (a beaverlike animal whose skins are imported, under the name of nutria skins, mainly from the region round the River Plate in South America), and **seals**. Before the Second World War, rabbit skins were imported into the United Kingdom alone in numbers up to 26m. in one year, undressed (mostly from Australia and New Zealand), and 10m. dressed (mostly from Belgium). Among the mammals which yield the furs of greatest value are the **sable** (from the USSR), **mink** (from North America), the **stoat** or **ermine** (from Europe and Asia), the **sea otter** (from the west coast of North America), the **black** or **silver fox**, the **lamb** (karakul) and the true **fur seal**. The coat of the blubber seal is of but little value, and the true fur seal, which yields the valuable sealskin of commerce, is a species belonging to a group distinguished from other seals by the possession of external ears. This species is obtained chiefly on the Pribilov Islands, two small islands in Bering Sea, where they come annually to breed. Under the regulations of the government of the United States only limited numbers may be killed there every year. The species is also hunted by Canadian sealers in Bering Sea and the North Pacific.

The fur trade of British North America was for a long time the monopoly of the Hudson's Bay Company, founded in 1670. Two hundred years later the company sold its rights to the Dominion of Canada, though still retaining certain stations and a portion of the land. Now there are several other fur companies operating in the same region. The fur trade of the USSR has been from the first to some extent in the hands of the government. An important development in the fur trade in the present century has been the farming of certain fur-bearing animals. In Canada, for instance, mink, chinchilla, fox and nutria (coypu) are bred on fur farms. This method of production makes it possible to supply undamaged skins in peak condition. In 1966—67 Canadian wild-life pelts were valued at $12m. (mainly beaver, musk rat, squirrel and fox) while pelts from farms were valued at $22.6m. (mink providing 98 per cent). Rising costs and general concern for the future of the wild life of the world, have encouraged the increased use of manmade simulated furs.

Meat

Not very long ago considerable quantities of the meat supply of the United Kingdom were obtained from the larger domestic animals imported alive; Eire still supplies annually over 500 000 cattle, sheep and lambs, of the total value of £40m. to £60m. By far the largest supplies of fresh meat are now imported chilled or frozen. This process was first tried, with more or less success, about 1875 in America in the chilling of beef, a process by which the meat is cooled to a temperature of only $-1.5°$ C (29° to 30° F), and is not hardened. Both beef and mutton are also carried in large quantities frozen at temperatures of from $-12°$ to $-9°$ C (10° to 15° F), in which case they have to be thawed out before being ready for consumption. The principal market for these products has always been the United Kingdom. If it had not been for these supplies it is probable that the cost of living would have been greatly enhanced in this country, and a more or less serious check given to the development of our manufactures.

The chief sources of frozen meat are Argentina, New Zealand, and Australia. Chilled beef comes mainly from Argentina. Chilling preserves the quality better than freezing, but the geographical factor comes into play; from the greater distance of Australia and New Zealand meat carries best when frozen. The trade in frozen mutton began in earnest in 1881. In that year the import first exceeded 10 000 carcases (all from Australia). Before the First World War the mutton and lamb carcases imported (1913) had increased in number to some 13m., and the total import of chilled or frozen beef and mutton was over 700 000 tons. Before the Second World War the total had further increased to over 950 000 tons, with an import value of some £43m. Beef provided nearly two-thirds of the whole in quantity, but little more than half the value. Including meat imported in other forms, it was estimated that the imported supplies constituted 40 per cent of the total consumption of meat in the United Kingdom.

The Second World War was responsible for many changes in the production and distribution of meat supplies, and postwar currency difficulties, involving continued government controls, prevented any early return to normal trade conditions. In 1960 imports of chilled and frozen beef and mutton were still below the prewar total, reaching 740 000 tons; but the import value had more than trebled, amounting to £145m. The imports of frozen beef (350 000 tons) were less than the imports of chilled or frozen mutton and lamb (375 000 tons), but the values were almost identical — beef £72m., mutton and lamb £73.5m. Only one or two outstanding features in a kaleidoscopic situation can be noted. During the war the saving of shipping space was especially important, so chilled beef was replaced by frozen beef, which could be packed more closely; and boned and boneless beef and veal, which formed less than 10 per cent of the prewar imports of beef and veal into the United Kingdom, increased to over 70 per cent in 1942, dropping back again to just under 20 per cent in 1973.

The first half of the twentieth century saw other than war changes. Early in the century the biggest supply of meat to this country came from the United States in the form of beef and live cattle, but before the Second World War the supply from that source was very small, and the United States itself had become an importer of Canadian, Australian and South American meat. It is noteworthy that the modern development of Argentina's livestock and meat industry has been accompanied by the restriction of ranching and the extension of arable farming, much of the meat being produced on the relatively small farms, where fodder is grown to fatten the cattle. Normally Argentina leads easily in the supply of beef to the United Kingdom, and New Zealand in the supply of mutton and lamb, with Australia taking second place in both categories, though liable to severe setbacks on account of drought. The Irish Republic is also an important source of beef and veal.

Other forms of meat — canned products; bacon, hams and pork; poultry, rabbits, etc. — make a bigger addition to the total than is perhaps commonly realised. In 1938 they added 600 000 tons to the 950 000 tons already quoted for chilled and frozen beef and mutton, and more than doubled the value, bringing the total for meat imports to over £90m. In 1973 they more than doubled both the quantity and the total value, raising the grand total of £726m. It will be noted that despite the big increase in value, the quantity of the total meat imports in 1973 (1.3m. tons) was barely equal to the total in 1938 (1.55m.). In 1973 imports were roughly a quarter each of beef, mutton and lamb, bacon, and other. The 1960s were marked by intensive production of beef at home (especially barley-fed) and a vast expansion in poultry. As a result the United Kingdom became self-sufficient for almost all poultry consumed, some 90 per cent of pork and 70 per cent of beef, and 40 per cent of mutton and bacon. From 1950 to 1970 the number of poultry (chickens, turkeys, etc.) increased from 88m. to 118m. some 40m. being broiler chickens for the table. During the same period the cattle population increased from 10 to 12m.

Pork, bacon, hams and lard for the British market were all formerly derived mainly from the United States, but now little pork is imported and most of the bacon and other products come from Denmark, Poland and the Netherlands.

Meat is a major source of the proteins which are essential for a healthy diet, but supplies are unevenly distributed throughout the world. Although the numbers of animals have been rising steadily between 1950 and 1970 (cattle from 780 to 1 080m., sheep from 770 to 1 040m., pigs from 295 to 650m.) the increased consumption of meat has largely occurred in the developed countries, i.e. those with the higher standard of living. It has been estimated, for instance, that the annual consumption of animal protein in the European community is equal to that of tropical Africa, Latin America and the Near East combined. In spite of the considerable increase in cattle, the majority are used as a source of dairy products or as draught animals — Asia with over 280m. head is seriously deficient in meat supplies. There may be some improvement as the new strains of cereals provide larger crops with surpluses for conversion to protein via cattle food (the traditional wheat surpluses of Argentina are already so employed). Poultry are an important source in that they adapt easily to different climates and are a relatively quick method of producing meat. Pigs also are more adaptable to tropical conditions than cattle or sheep, and efficiently convert feedstuffs to food. The tropical grasslands, particularly those of east and south Central Africa, have been the subject of optimistic forecasts of new sources of meat supply on the grand scale. In the past, any such hopes have been overshadowed by the prevalence of the tsetse fly, which infests cattle with *nagana*, the fatal animal disease corresponding to sleeping sickness in man, with the result that cattle are still practically barred from vast areas of equatorial Africa. The use of Antrycide, one of many drugs under experiment, combined with attacks on the habitat of the fly through bush clearing, aerial spraying, etc., holds out hope that areas hitherto denied to stock can, with reasonable pre-cautions, now be opened up; but the end of the war against tsetse and trypanosomiasis is not yet in sight and other sources of protein must be sought.

Miscellaneous products, chiefly of animal origin

There is a large world trade in **eggs**, for which the United Kingdom was easily the best market before the Second World War. It imported about 3 000m. a year; or, at the rate of 16 000 eggs to the ton (the rate adopted by the United Nations Food and Agricultural Organisation), about 187 000 tons — half the world total of eggs entering international trade. Moreover, the United Kingdom imported a considerable, though much smaller, quantity of eggs not in shell — mostly liquid or frozen, and only to a very small extent dried. It is significant of the demands for transport during the war that while the imports of eggs in shell and of frozen or liquid shelled eggs fell away greatly, the imports of dried eggs increased enormously. Now both world production and trade in eggs in the shell are greater than ever, the increase being especially marked in home production. In the United Kingdom this was always greater than the import, and after the war it went on increasing till in 1956 it exceeded the prewar production and imports combined. Imports declined steadily, and though still large (460m. in 1956) were less than West Germany's imports (3 500m.) and Italy (645m.). In 1973, UK imports of eggs in shell were only 273m. over 90 per cent coming from EEC.

World production of eggs in 1971 was over 408 000m. The United States was the largest producer with 71 500m. followed by USSR, Japan and the United Kingdom with 41 000m., 32 000m., and 14 700m. respectively. These figures are estimates since statistics of the individually owned flocks of poultry in the world are difficult to obtain; they are, however, a true reflection of the comparative impor-tance of commercially produced eggs.

Imports of **butter** into the United Kingdom before the war amounted to close on 500 000 tons. Cold storage has made possible worldwide supplies, and while Denmark supplied nearly a quarter of the total, New Zealand sent more than a quarter and Australia one-fifth. During the war, New Zealand and Australia supplied nearly all the greatly reduced imports, and in 1973 they provided one-half of the 330 000 tons imported, while Denmark supplied one-quarter. A formidable rival of butter is **margarine**, made from animal fats, vegetable oils, or a mixture of both, and flavoured with lactic acid ferments so as to be almost indistinguishable in taste from butter. After the war the annual con-sumption of margarine per head in the United Kingdom exceeded the consumption of butter until 1957. Imports of margarine have never approached the imports of butter. Before the Second World War they increased to over 5 000 tons (mostly from the Netherlands), dropped to a very low level during the war and were only 500 tons in 1973. Annual consumption per head was 12.1 lb of margarine and 19.5 lb of butter. Home production of margarine is about 320 000 tons as against some 50 000 tons of butter.

Cheese was formerly supplied largely by Canada, but before the Second World War New Zealand was supplying more than half the United Kingdom imports of 150 000 tons, while Canada sent nearly a quarter, and Australia and the Netherlands usually between 5 and 10 per cent apiece. A cool summer climate is a favourable condition in the cheese-making districts of both New Zealand and Canada (chiefly Québec). During the war, cheese was notable for being imported in even larger quantities than in peace, reaching a peak of over 300 000 tons in 1942. In 1956, imports were nearly 135 000 tons. New Zealand supplied two-thirds, Australia nearly a tenth, but supplies from Canada and the United States were limited by the shortage of dollars. In 1968 imports were still some 135 000 tons (£62m.) with 36 per cent coming from New Zealand and 56 per cent coming from the Irish Republic, the Netherlands and Denmark.

Fresh milk is mainly only an article of local trade; but **condensed milk,** made by evaporating milk with sugar or other ingredients, was imported before the war to the amount of 80 000 tons, chiefly from the Netherlands and Denmark, Canada and New Zealand, while imports of milk powder brought the combined total to 100 000 tons. During the war years, the United States became the chief source of supply, and both condensed milk and milk powder were imported in much larger quantities. In postwar years, home supplies increased and dollar shortage cut imports. In 1973 the imports of both preserved and powdered milk totalled over 55 000 tons, mostly from the Irish Republic, Denmark and the Netherlands. Some extension of world trade in fresh milk may follow the development of heat treatment processes which give several months of shelf-life without refrigeration.

Ghee, or butter clarified by boiling, is an article of commerce in India and neighbouring countries. **Koumiss,** the fermented milk of mares, is a favourite drink among certain nomadic tribes in central Asia, and in the USSR. An imitation koumiss is made in other countries from asses' and cows' milk.

Of animal products not used as food the most important are **hides** and **skins** which enter largely into world trade both in the raw state and as leather at various stages of manufacture (see p. 300). Hides are preserved for and during transport either by being steeped in brine or by some process of drying. They are known respectively as 'wet' and 'dry'. The annual import of 'wet' cattle hides into the United Kingdom before the Second World War averaged about 50 000 tons, and of 'dry' hides about 25 000 tons, both supplied by a worldwide range of countries, headed in the case of 'wet' hides by Argentina and in the case of 'dry' hides by Australia and the Union of South Africa. Imports of sheep and lamb skins averaged well over 25 000 tons, mostly from New Zealand, Australia and South Africa. Goat skins, mostly 'dry' and mostly from India, with British East Africa and Nigeria as the other chief sources of supply, were imported to the average annual number of nearly 10m. skins.

During the war and the early postwar years the import of 'wet' hides was not only maintained but largely increased — in some years the supplies from Argentina alone were as great as the prewar total. In 1947 the import reached a peak of nearly 100 000 tons, but it reverted in 1951–56 to the prewar standard of around 50 000 tons. The import of 'dry' hides declined in the later war years, and after a temporary recovery averaged only about 12 000 tons. Both Australia and South Africa dropped low in the list and were replaced as the chief British sources of supply by Kenya, Tanzania, and Nigeria, where much attention has been given to improved methods of drying, with great benefit to the quality of the hides. During the war, the import of sheep and lamb skins also fell below the prewar average, but later recovered, with New Zealand, Australia and South Africa still the main contributories. Goat skins were likewise affected, and supplies from India, Pakistan and Africa fluctuated considerably after the war, the sequence of the individual countries as sources of supply varying from year to year. 'Wet' goat skins disappeared from the United Kingdom trade returns after 1941, only 'dry' goat skins being imported. In 1973 the import of hides and skins totalled 76 000 tons (£42m.). Cattle hides coming mainly from the Irish Republic, the Commonwealth and western Europe. Imports from Argentina were negligible, her main exports going to the Soviet bloc and Italy. Sheep and lamb skins totalled 15 000 tons and came mainly from Australia, USA and South Africa.

Of other animal products, **bones** are used in making a great variety of articles, and bone-ash enters into the manufacture of pottery. Bones are used also in making glue, and, being largely composed of phosphate of lime, in making fertiliser. The United Kingdom imports of bone and bone-meal amount to around 5 000 tons a year.

Ivory is the dentine or tooth substance forming the tusks of elephants, hippopotamuses, walruses, narwhals, and other animals. **Elephant ivory** is distinguished by its lozenge-shaped curvilinear markings. **Hippopotamus ivory** is denser and harder than that of the elephant, and of a superior and more enduring whiteness, but the solid pieces of this kind of ivory are all small, so that it can be used only in making small articles. **Walrus ivory** is inferior to that of the hippopotamus, and that of the narwhal is coarse and of little value. The total annual consumption of ivory in Europe, the United States, British

India, China, and Japan was estimated towards the end of the last century at, in round figures, 1 100 tons valued at £1m., the biggest consumer being the United Kingdom (350 tons). Almost all of it was elephant ivory (1 000 tons), three-quarters coming from Africa, the rest chiefly from the East Indies. The remains of the Siberian mammoth, which had supplied ivory to China for seven centuries, continued to yield a little. With the reduction of big game in Africa and measures for its preservation, trade in ivory has since declined. The annual imports into the United Kingdom before the Second World War were 100 tons or less, and during the war they almost disappeared. Plastic materials provide substitutes for most commercial uses.

Under the name of **vegetable ivory** are imported the seeds of two palms, *Phytelephas macrocarpa* (Ecuador, Peru and Colombia) and *Hyphaene thebaica* (the Dum palm of the Sudan and other parts of North Africa). The seeds, known in the former case as corozo nuts, have only a fraction of the value of true ivory, and were used for making buttons and toys until they, too, were replaced by plastics.

Among animal products of minor commercial value, **horns** and **hoofs** were imported into the United Kingdom chiefly for making combs, buttons and knife handles; **horsehair** as a stuffing for upholstery; **cowhair** to make felt for roofing and for boilers and pipes of steam engines. The United States is the leading country of supply. Between 1 000 and 2 000 tons (some £5m.) of **pigs' bristles** are imported annually for making brushes. **Feathers**, mostly for bedding, are imported in slightly larger quantities, but surprisingly are much less valuable (some £750 000). They come from a worldwide range of countries, with Eire heading the list. Trade in ornamental feathers is largely dependent on the vagaries of fashion. In 1913 South Africa's exports of ostrich feathers reached a peak of 450 tons valued at nearly £3m.; in 1914, on the outbreak of war, the bottom dropped out of the market, and the fashion was never revived. The number of domesticated ostriches in South Africa dropped from 750 000 before the First World War to 40 000 before the Second World War, and in 1943 exports of ostrich feathers ebbed to 8 tons, valued at £13 000. Since 1960 they are no longer separately listed in the British monthly trade returns.

Sponges consist of a horny internal skeleton of marine animals whose living portion consists of a coating of slime, which has to be removed before the sponge becomes an article of commerce. The animals yielding the best sponges live at a depth of only 4 to 6 m (13 to 20 ft), and hence, when not covered by seaweeds, can easily be seen from the surface. The sponges are generally obtained by divers, but a submarine vessel from which the fishers can seize the sponges by means of specially constructed tongs and deposit them in a basket on the bowsprit has been devised. The best sponges are all obtained from the eastern half of the Mediterranean Sea, from the Gulf of Gabès in the east of Tunisia to the coast of Syria. In this area is also included the Dalmation coast of the Adriatic as a sponge-yielding region. The fisheries are carried on mainly by Greeks, Sicilians, Arabs, and Dalmatians, and are best organised by the Greeks, who make the longest voyages in search of sponges and have their headquarters on the little island of Kalimnos, off the coast of Turkey. Outside the Mediterranean the only important source of sponges is off the shores of the Bahamas, Cuba, and Florida, where the sponges are all of inferior quality. Most commercial sponges are now synthetic.

Tallow and **stearine** (stearine is the harder ingredient in tallow) are most largely imported from Australasia (especially New Zealand) and the cattle countries of South America (especially Argentina). Stearine is used principally in the manufacture of soap, tallow in the making of candles. Total imports in 1973 were some 15 000 tons (£2.8m.). **Isinglass**, which is the finest form of gelatine, used in confectionery and in the arts, as well as for clarifying wine and beer, is obtained from the sound or swim-bladder of various kinds of fish, and is imported into this country chiefly from India, Brazil and (prewar) Japan. In the USSR it is largely made from the sound of the sturgeon, and in the United States from other species of sturgeon which abound in American rivers; but neither of these countries supplies much of this commodity to the United Kingdom. The thicker and less refined kinds of gelatine, including **glue** and **size,** do not enter largely into foreign commerce, but are made in large quantities from native and imported hides and bones for boiling. Leather which is not made by tanning can also be used in the manufacture of glue; but not tanned leather, for the chemical action of the tannin or tannic acid destroys the gelatine.

The more important **animal oils** of commerce are the produce of the **whale** and **seal fisheries**. One, called **train oil**, is derived from the blubber or coat of fat which invests these animals under the skin. Originally this kind was mainly obtained from the **Greenland whale** (baleen) in the seas off the west coast of Greenland and the northern coasts of Norway, and in the Arctic Ocean generally to the north of Norway and Iceland; but whaling in these waters had largely ceased before the First World War. The seal fisheries off Labrador and Newfoundland, and in the Gulf of St Lawrence, were and still are prosecuted in ships specially equipped for the purpose.

When the northern whale fisheries showed signs of exhaustion Norwegians and others actively prosecuted whale fisheries in the south Atlantic Ocean, both off the coast of South Africa and South America (especially round the Falkland Islands), in the Ross Sea of Antarctica and in the North Pacific, now these in turn are becoming exhausted. The former Dundee whale and seal fisheries are extinct, and so are those of New Bedford, Massachusetts. By international agreement the catch is now being limited to save all whales from rapid extinction.

Although only Japan, the USSR and Norway now have major whaling fleets, the techniques of hunting and killing are so efficient that it has been necessary to prohibit catching of the blue and humpback whales. Similarly, agreed quota limitations have been placed on the fin, sperm and sei whale catches which reduce by two-thirds the annual catch of over 60 000 whales during the 1960s. In 1971 the United States decided that the future of the species was endangered, and halted all commercial whaling. **Sperm oil** is derived from the cachalot, or sperm whale, which contains immense quantities of oil in a cavity in its enormous head. The **sperm whale** being found in almost all parts of the ocean, this kind of oil was imported from many parts of the world. Train oil was used principally for margarine, but sperm oil, a finer and more valuable kind, yields in cold weather a kind of waxy body called **spermaceti**, which, mixed with a little beeswax, is used in the making of candles and by itself in the making of cold cream, salves, etc. A finer kind of train oil than that derived from the baleen whale is obtained in large quantities from the **bottle-nose whale** (*Hyperoodon rostratus*). The sperm whale yields another valuable product, namely **ambergris**, which was largely used in perfumery, and is sometimes found in the body of the animal, sometimes floating on the surface of the water. It is a result of disease. The world production of whale and sperm oil has fallen steadily from 490 000 tons in 1958 to 191 800 tons in 1971 to 151 400 tons in 1972 − partly as a result of reducing catches and partly as a result of increasing use of many substitute oils.

Of true fish oils, the most important is cod-liver oil, which is largely made in Great Britain from oil first processed aboard modern trawlers. Canada, Iceland and Norway also turn out considerable quantities from the great cod fisheries of those countries. Another important fish oil is halibut-liver oil, and a true fish oil is made from the menhaden (*Brevoortia*); see p. 251. The oil is chiefly used in leather-dressing, but also in rope-making and painting. Other animals oils are derived from tallow, lard, bone fat, etc. From the **dugong**, a kind of oil capable of being used for the same purpose as cod-liver oil, as well as in cooking, has been extracted in Queensland.

The following are among the animal products which, though of commercial value, either do not enter into the foreign commerce of the British Isles or are too small an item to be separately enumerated in the trade returns. **Coral** is the name given to the skeleton of a whole group of marine animals; but the red or pink coral, the skeleton of *Corallium rubrum*, used in the making of trinkets and other ornaments, is the only one of note. The coral industry is specially an Italian one, and its chief seat is Torre del Greco, at the base of Mount Vesuvius, in the Bay of Naples. Formerly the chief supplies of coral were obtained by diving in the Bay of Naples, as many as 500 boats having often set out from Torre del Greco; but the industry has lost much of its importance. The coral banks both in this bay and to the south of Sardinia have been largely exhausted, and the banks along the coasts of Algeria, Tunis and Tripoli are now more productive. **Coral** is also obtained on the coast of Catalonia; round the Cape Verde Islands; in the Adriatic, especially on the east coast; and in other places. A considerable quantity of coral was formerly exported directly or indirectly to China, where it was used in the official dress of the mandarins.

Pearls and **mother-of-pearl** are derived from various shells, especially of the oyster family, belonging principally to tropical seas. The mother-of-pearl is the internal part of the shell, and pearls are secretions of the same kind of matter round some small parasite or particle of foreign matter which acts as an irritant. Among the most noted pearl fishery banks are those in the Persian Gulf, in the Gulf of Mannar (Ceylon), in the Sulu Archipelago, in the neighbourhood of the Moluccas and the Aru Islands, in Torres Strait and along the northwest coast of Australia, at Tahiti, and in the Gulf of California. By providing a suitable irritant inside the shell of the oysters, the Japanese have succeeded in producing cultured pearls, practically indistinguishable from those formed without an artificial stimulus. Pearls are also obtained from various river shells, especially *Unio margaritifera*, which is met with in many European rivers, including some of those of Scotland and the north of Ireland.

Parchment, the skin of sheep, and **vellum**, that of calf, prepared for writing on, no longer have the value that belonged to them before the invention of paper, but are still manufactured for use in formal documents and in book-binding. The so-called **catgut** consists of the dried and twisted intestines of sheep and other animals. It is used in making the strings of musical instruments, racket-cords, and cords used by clock-makers, polishers, etc. The intestines of larger animals serve to make **gold-beater's skin**.

The **nests** of a certain kind of swift (*Collocalia esculenta*), which breeds in caves at various places in the Eastern Archipelago, are looked upon as a delicacy in China, where they are imported in millions annually. The nests are entirely made from a peculiar saliva secreted by the bird.

Fisheries

With the oceans covering 70 per cent of the earth's surface, fisheries have, since the dawn of civilisation, held a high place in the world's economy. As a source of food supply they have grown in importance with the growth of communications. In Britain, the fishpond was prominent in monastic days, but with the coming of the railway era a century ago, sea fish began to find their way to the remotest country districts.

Two main lines of advance may be distinguished in the modern industrial development of world fisheries. The more obvious is the taking of fish for immediate human consumption, as in the British trawl fishery, most of whose catch — usually kept on ice at sea — goes into consumption within forty-eight hours of being landed, not least widely through the agency of 30 000 fried fish shops. In contrast with this are such fisheries as the California pilchard fishery and the Peruvian anchoveta fishery, from which the catches in the past have served primarily as raw material for extensive meal and oil plants. The meal provides animal feed, the oil is used by margarine factories.

The Food and Agriculture Organisation of the United Nations estimated that in 1970 the world catch of fish (including freshwater fish) was over 69.3m. metric tons — a record figure to date but increasing annually. The six leading countries each contributed over 2m. tons and together provided over 40m. tons, or over half the world catch. Peru headed the list with 12.6m. tons; then came Japan, 9.3m., USSR, 7.3m., China, possibly 5.8m., Norway (including Spitsbergen), 3m., USA, 2.7m.; India 1.7m.

Eight other countries each had catches of 1m. and 1.6m. tons, bringing the sum total up to three-quarters of the whole. These countries were Thailand 1.6m. tons, South Africa 1.5m., Spain, 1.49m., Canada, 1.38m., Indonesia, 1.25m., Denmark, 1.23m., Chile, 1.16m., UK 1.09m. tons. All the continents with the exception of Africa reported more fish caught in 1970 than in 1969.

One of the most valuable fishing grounds in the world is the chain of submerged plateaus or 'banks' in the North Atlantic, off the coasts of

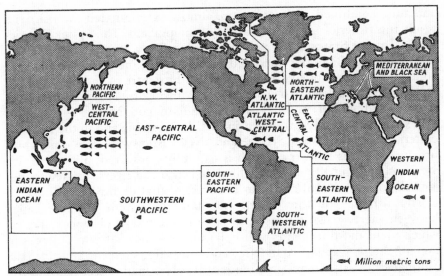

Major fishing grounds of the world. World catch in 1971 was 69.3m. tons

Canada (Newfoundland, Labrador, Québec, and the Maritime Provinces), the New England States, and the French islands of St Pierre and Miquelon. They attracted the attention of the early explorers who visited America and have been extensively fished since the sixteenth century. Although they have been eclipsed by the Pacific Coast fisheries (including Alaska), those of the New England States, notably Massachusetts and Maine, are still very important. The principal fish caught are cod, mackerel, hake, herring, rosefish, haddock, pollack, whiting and flounders. Others include the menhaden (*Brevoortia*) and the alewife (*Pomolobus*), which somewhat resemble the shad and are caught in immense quantities off the eastern coast of the United States from Connecticut to the Carolinas.

On the Pacific Coast the specialities of the fishing industry are the catching and canning of pilchard, salmon and tuna (tunny) for export. In recent years both the size of the pack of tuna and its value have rivalled the size and value of the salmon pack. The salmon fishing industry is chiefly pursued in the States on the Columbia River (Oregon) and the Sacramento (California); in British Columbia on the Fraser, Skeena, and Naas Rivers, as well as several inlets; and, in recent years above all, in the rivers and creeks of Alaska. The sardine, mackerel, herring and halibut fisheries are also important commercially. Notable, as an example of the value of scientific control, is the restriction of the Pacific halibut fishery, which, instead of reducing the yield, is actually increasing it. The chief products of the lake fisheries of the United States were whitefish (*Coregonus*), trout, 'Lake herring' (*Leucichthys*), and sturgeon. The Great Lakes were ruthlessly exploited and this, combined with pollution, almost exterminated the fish; as a result the fisheries are now relatively unimportant. The oyster fisheries of the United States are of very great value. They are chiefly carried on in Chesapeake Bay, Maryland and Virginia being the states most largely concerned in the industry, and Baltimore the centre of the trade.

The Canadian fisheries yield, in order of weight, chiefly herring, cod, salmon, and halibut; in order of value, salmon, cod, herring and halibut. The salmon is mainly produced in British Columbia and in the rivers of eastern Canada. Nova Scotia and New Brunswick are important provinces in this industry, which is carefully conserved; billions of fish are hatched annually and later liberated into the rivers. In Newfoundland the production of cod is far in excess of that of any other fish.

The fisheries of the United Kingdom underwent a great change between the two world wars. The inshore and middle distance fisheries, which yield the finer kinds of fish, became secondary to the fisheries in far northern waters, round Iceland and Spitsbergen and off the Murmansk Coast, where large modern trawlers made great hauls of the less favoured food fishes, principally cod. After the Second World War it was estimated (1949) that 58 per cent of the fish landed in Britain came from these northern waters. The round voyage takes between three and four weeks — seven days each way, out and home, and ten days on the fishing grounds — a period of absence which gave rise to various problems affecting the landing of the fish in fresh condition. An answer was found in the quick-freezing of fish at sea, and the length of voyage for 'factory ships' no longer matters. The fish are prepared at sea into fish fillets, fish fingers, etc.

The areas open to British fishing fleets off the coasts of Norway have been restricted by a postwar judgment of the International Court at The Hague, in favour of a Norwegian claim that the three-mile limit of its national waters should extend not from the shores of big inlets but from straight lines drawn between the points of entrance. Later Iceland has claimed and was accorded the right, in a dispute with Britain, to extend the area around its coasts in which all trawlers (including Icelandic) are forbidden to operate, on the ground that certain waters are being overfished. Indeed the tendency in recent years has been to extend the limit of territorial waters so far as fisheries and their control are concerned, and the whole problem has been enlarged with the undersea exploration for oil and natural gas. The whole North Sea is now divided up between the riparian nations, but the wider problem of delimiting territorial waters universally has still to be resolved.

Icelandic and other northern fisheries are pursued chiefly from Hull and Grimsby. The waters of the North Sea are much richer in food fishes than the other waters of the British Isles, and the five leading fishing ports — Grimsby, Hull, Aberdeen, Great Yarmouth, and Lowestoft — are all on the east coast, the former important place taken by the last two being due to a great concourse of Scottish drifters which used to join the local boats at the time of the autumn herring fishing. The importance of Great Yarmouth and Lowestoft as fishing ports declined as the herring catch diminished. The value of the fish caught in Irish waters is relatively small, and when the Irish herring fisheries were of notable importance before and after the First World War, the main production was by drifters from Scotland and England.

The English fisheries are more miscellaneous than the Scottish; they include herring and mackerel, pilchards and sprats among fish caught near the surface, and plaice, soles, haddock, cod and turbot among the demersal or bottom-frequenting fish, whereas in the Scottish fisheries the herring is without a rival, haddock and cod coming next. Pilchards, which are the mature form of the true sardine, are a speciality of the Cornish coasts, and though they are no longer caught in the old large numbers, research has shown them to be more abundant than the present unimportant inshore fishery would seem to indicate. Besides the fishing ports already mentioned, Fleetwood, North Shields and Milford were important in England and Wales, and Wick, Lerwick, Fraserburgh, Peterhead, Stornoway and Leith in Scotland. Aberdeen is the greatest trawling centre north of the Humber. The great market is Billingsgate, in London. Oysters are largely produced at Whitstable on the north coast of Kent, and at Colchester near the mouth of the Colne, in Essex. Salmon fishing in Scottish, Irish, and some English rivers is largely 'preserved' for sport and is a source of considerable wealth. There is also a valuable commercial salmon fishery, though industrial development along the banks of salmon rivers like the Tyne and the Tees has by pollution destroyed once important salmon fisheries.

The principal Norwegian fisheries are those of cod and herring. The cod fisheries are carried on chiefly when the fish come in early spring to the spawning areas round the Lofoten Isles; to a lesser degree the fishery concerns itself with feeding cod on the Finmarken coast. The cod are mostly salted for export, but filleted fresh fish, frozen, are taking a place in world markets. The herring fisheries are mainly in the neighbourhood of Bergen. Fish canning, especially of brisling, or sprats, is important, and between the two world wars Norway built up an enormous export industry in canned fish of many varieties.

Important features of the French fisheries apart from cod, herring, and the other main food fish, are sardines, lobsters, and oysters. The sardine and anchovy fisheries are carried on mainly on the Mediterranean coast. The market for the Provence fisheries is Beaucaire on the Rhône, east of Nîmes. On the Atlantic side the chief seats of sardine-packing are Bordeaux and Le Mans. Sardines and anchovies are likewise caught and prepared for export on the coasts of Spain, Portugal and Italy. Oysters are produced mainly on the coasts of Brittany and other parts of the Atlantic seaboard further south. Since about 1856 artificial oyster-breeding has been pursued in France with great success, chiefly in the basin of Arcachon (to the south of the Gironde), and in the bay of Morbihan (on the south coast of Brittany).

Apart from the sardine and anchovy the only important food fish of the Mediterranean waters is the tunny. This fish (*Thunnus thynnus*) is a relative of the mackerel (*Scomber scomber*); it attains a length of some 4 m (13 ft), and a weight of some 450 kg (1 000 lb). It appears in shoals in the beginning of summer, especially off the coasts of Sicily, Sardinia, and southern France. The fishery is carried on chiefly on the coasts of Sicily and Sardinia, which are visited by many fishermen, foreign as well as Italian, during the fishing season. On the Atlantic coast the white-fleshed tunny (*Alalorga*) is important for the canning industry.

The USSR has very important sea fisheries, and in recent years has been the second or third biggest producer of salmon; the fishery concessions on Asian rivers, chiefly to the Japanese, were important. Its river and lake fisheries, particularly in the Caspian, are also noted for their sturgeon; caviare, or the roe of the sturgeon prepared as a delicacy, is one of the most important fishery products.

As regards Asia, mention has already been made of the magnitude of the Far Eastern fisheries. Sardines, herrings, and bonitos (a large fish of the genus *Sarda*) rank high among the products of the Japanese fisheries, which also include, in the Yellow, East and South China Seas, one of the greatest demersal or ground fisheries in the world. The Philippines fishery is substantial, and, in general, fisheries play an important part in the economy and diet of the peoples of southeast Asia. In another category is trepang, a kind of sea cucumber (the French *bêche-de-mer*), which is extensively fished for the Chinese market along all the coasts of the Eastern Archipelago and Northern Australia.

The foreign commerce in fish is by no means proportional to the size of the fisheries, most kinds of fish being produced mainly for markets near at hand. Formerly herrings were the chief fish exported from Britain. Before the First World War nearly five-sixths of the British catch was exported, but the industry has never fully recovered from the loss of markets in 1914—18. Before the Second World War the annual landings of herrings in the United Kingdom were about 250 000 tons — less than half the pre-1914 catch. Increased landings of other fish kept the total up to about 1m. tons a year, of which 200 000 tons or more were exported. Within their narrower limits herrings were still the main export of fish, and for a time this was true after the Second World War. Both in 1950 and 1951 about two-thirds of the exports both of fresh fish and of cured fish were herring, and so were four-fifths or more of the canned fish exported, West Germany being the chief market.

In other respects the Second World War brought about big changes, alike in the export and in the import trade of the United Kingdom in fish. Exports dropped heavily. In 1938 they amounted, all told, to 219 000 tons (fresh or frozen fish 54 000 tons, cured or salted 160 000 tons, canned 5 000 tons). In 1951 the total was under 59 000 tons — little more than a quarter of the prewar figure; and by 1961 it was down to 38 000 tons. The decline was especially marked in the export of herrings, and was intensified by a shortage of supplies, affecting the home market as well as the export trade. The exceptionally low figures for 1961 were in part due to adverse weather conditions. It was in the previous year that the new trend manifested itself: in that year exports of fresh or frozen fish first exceeded those of salted or dried. In 1969 the total exports were up to 78 000 tons (fresh or frozen 51 000 tons, cured or salted 20 000 tons, canned 7 000 tons).

Imports have not been affected to the same extent. In 1938 they totalled 186 000 tons (109 000 tons fresh or simply preserved, 77 000 tons canned) and in 1951 were about the same, after having risen in the interval to 300 000 tons — a commentary on the shortage of meat. In 1953 they were down to 110 000 tons, but increased again to over 235 000 tons in 1968 (153 000 tons fresh or simply preserved, 82 000 tons canned). Cod, plaice, haddock and herrings were the chief supplies. Norway, Denmark and Japan were the chief supplying countries.

Very different has been the experience of the imports of canned fish. As shown by the figures already quoted, the prewar imports of canned fish were over 40 per cent of the total. About three-quarters of these canned imports consisted of salmon, which was easily the most valuable item in the whole of the import trade in fish. Practically all the canned salmon came from Canada, the United States, the USSR, and Japan. For the time being the war knocked out the last-named country as a source of supply, and difficulties developed in the trade with the USSR, while restrictions on dollar expenditure reduced trade with Canada and the United States. In the early 1950s the import of canned salmon dropped from its prewar level of nearly 60 000 tons to between 5 000 and 10 000 tons; but in 1956 it increased to nearly 20 000 tons, and reached over 23 000 tons in 1973. Throughout these postwar years, the value of the canned salmon imported has been one of the biggest items in the account for imported fish. It figured for £21.4m. in 1960 when the total import of canned fish was valued at £31m. The main items, apart from salmon, were crab (£2.1m.), pilchards (£1.6m.) and sardines (£1.6m.). Though more in weight than the canned fish imported, the imports of fresh or lightly preserved fish are much less valuable — £58m. in 1973 against £73m. for canned (of which salmon, again, accounted for £35m.).

Apart from the United Kingdom, the great markets for Norway's cod fish are the same as those for the dried and cured cod fish which make up the bulk of the export from Newfoundland, namely Spain, Portugal, and Italy, Roman Catholic countries in which there is still a very large consumption of fish. St John's in Newfoundland, Bergen in Norway, and Bordeaux in France are the centres of this trade. Dried and cured cod are also sent to the West Indies and South America.

The deep sea fisheries of Germany grew rapidly after the last decade of last century, largely in consequence of state encouragement, exemplified by the provision of fishery harbours, such as those of Wesermunde, Cuxhaven, and Hamburg-Altona; by the freeing of fishing boats from harbour and pilotage dues; and in other ways. There were great developments in the trawl fishery for herrings, and a new drifter fleet was built up under the policy of self-sufficiency. Since the Second World War, West Germany has taken steps substantially to redevelop her herring fisheries.

Recent years have been marked by a great development in tropical fisheries. Fish is a valuable source of protein and the Japanese — among the largest fish eaters in the world — have long relied on this source. The rise in Indian production is due in part to the introduction of modern equipment (including facilities for freezing), in part to the improved facilities for distribution by road with fast lorries. Similarly in West Africa fish is now sent far inland by road. The fisheries of Peru and of South Africa are other examples of recent expansion in tropical and subtropical seas. The Peruvian catch rising from 960 000 tons in 1958 to 12.6m. tons in 1970.

The world catch has risen steadily from 32.8m. tons in 1958 to 69.3m. tons in 1970, and it is estimated that demand will rise to 107m. tons by 1985. So great an increase will require careful international conservation, particularly in the relatively restricted waters of the four main traditional fishing grounds; the east and west coasts of North America, and the seas off northwest Europe and around Japan. Modern fishing techniques can speedily threaten commercial extinction. This has already happened with the blue whale, and the Atlantic salmon and even the great reserves of tuna, cod, and herring could be in danger. As a source of rich protein food, the world's supply of fish is a self-renewing resource of great abundance from plankton up — provided always that the pattern of sea life is not unbalanced, and provided that it is not overcropped. Fish farming, encouraged by the Food and Agriculture Organisation, will undoubtedly contribute considerably to supplies in the future. It is already significant in Japan, the USSR and Denmark; and the great lakes created by the new large dams in the major rivers in Africa are also providing a suitable habitat for fish rearing.

Mineral products

Coal

Coal consists of vegetable matter which has been buried and sealed up out of contact with the air in past ages, and has then undergone a series of chemical changes, the general result of which is the elimination of a large proportion of hydrogen and oxygen and an increase in the relative proportion of carbon in the remaining substance. In pure woody fibre the proportion of carbon present is little more than half, whereas in ordinary **bituminous coal** it may amount to from 85 to upwards of 88 per cent. The substance known as **lignite**, or brown coal, consists of vegetable matter which, being younger, is much less altered than is ordinary coal, and contains a smaller relative amount of carbon, say 70 per cent. In certain situations, the process of removing hydrogen and oxygen has gone further than in the formation of bituminous coal, and as much as 94 per cent of carbon may be present. There is then formed a kind of coal called **anthracite**, which is lustrous on the surface, does not soil the fingers, is difficult to light, burns with little or no flame, but produces an intense heat when it does burn. **Coke**, an artificial product made by heating bituminous coal in closed vessels or ovens, and removing the more volatile constituents, contains as high a proportion of carbon as anthracite, but the product acquires in the process a highly porous or vesicular structure along with hardness and density. It is these properties that make it so valuable in the blast-furnace, its hardness enabling it to resist crushing by pressure, and its porosity presenting a greater amount of surface to the action of heated air. Formerly the removal of the volatile constituents was effected by carbonising the coal in beehive ovens, which produced excellent coke but did not conserve the gases which were given off, and destroyed such valuable constituents as tar, benzol, and ammonia. These ovens have now been replaced by others which separate and conserve all the byproducts.

Supplies of coke are derived from three main sources. (1) In the manufacture of gas for lighting and heating, gasworks produce large quantities of coke which are mostly used for domestic purposes as fuel for hot-water boilers, closed stoves, and central heating. The coal is carbonised in various types of retort, both horizontal and continuous vertical, the latter producing a more reactive and hence more suitable coke for domestic uses. (2) The collieries manufacture for sale to industrialists a harder and more lumpy kind of coke, used almost exclusively for blast furnaces and metallurgical purposes. The 'ovens' for making this quality of coke are large vertical chambers, each of which may contain as much as 10 tons. (3) In recent years there has been a marked tendency for steelworks to build their own batteries of coke ovens, with double benefit: they can select for carbonisation coal which will yield a coke of the particular quality they require, and the ovens can be heated — in part at any rate — by blast furnace gas, thus releasing the high-grade coke oven gas for the steel furnaces and other purposes at the works. In 1937 the quantity of coal carbonised was over 41m. tons, divided almost equally between gasworks and other producers; and the resulting quantity of coke and breeze was 27m. tons. There was little variation in these figures during the war years, 1939—45; afterwards the quantity increased slightly to 32.5m. tons in 1959, followed by a steady drop, so that in 1963 the production of coke was 25.2m. tons, and in 1971, 17m. tons.

It is known that coal was worked at several places in Roman Britain, but it seems to have been little used in Anglo-Saxon times. The first proper coalmines are said to have been opened at the close of the twelfth century (1198) in Belgium, and it is long before we hear of a trade in Newcastle coal. In 1615 that trade employed 400 vessels in distributing coal over England. In 1660 the total coal production of England was estimated at less than 2.25m. tons, or about two-fifths of a ton per head. At the beginning of the nineteenth century, after the invention of the steam-engine and its application to spinning machinery, but before the invention of steamboats, as well as before the introduction of railways, and before coal gas came into general use for lighting, the production of coal in England is estimated to have been 10m. tons, equal to about five-eighths of a ton per head for the estimated population of the United Kingdom. The vast increase in the use of coal between 1880 and the First World War was due chiefly to the requirements of modern factories, railways and steamers, blast furnaces, gasworks, and electrical installations.

The Royal Commission on the Coal Industry (1925) gave figures showing the approximate consumption of coal in the United Kingdom in 1924,* and these have made it possible to draw up a table (Table 19) showing a percentage analysis of the total, along with more or less corresponding figures for Germany in 1913 (taken from or based on those given in W. A. Bone's *Coal and its Scientific Uses*, pp. 478, 479)

* Report of the Royal Commission on the Coal Industry (Cd 2600, HMSO, 1926, p. 11).

Table 19 — Percentage comparative consumption of coal: 1913—24

	United Kingdom (1924)	Germany (1913)	United States (1923)
Domestic	12.9	9.1	12.8
Electric power	3.0	2.9	6.8
Industrial/coke	} 26.8	{ 23.4	15.6
Factories		14.1	21.5
Iron/steel	5.4	10.0	5.6
Railways	5.1	9.3	28.8
Bunker coal	7.2	5.3	1.6
Collieries	6.3	3.5	2.4
Agriculture	—	4.0	—
Gas	6.3	5.3	1.0
Miners free coal	2.5	—	—
Export	24.5	13.1	3.9
	100.0	100.0	100.0

and the United States in 1923.* So far as these figures correspond with one another the most striking differences were under the heads of export, railways, and bunker coal, and are significant of geographical differences between the three countries. Long before 1914, the British export of coal had been expanding at a more rapid rate than the production, and in 1913 the coal† exported from the United Kingdom was 78m. tons, 26.7 per cent of the total production of 290m. tons. This heading is one indication of the same geographical advantage as is revealed also by the high proportion of bunker coal used in the United Kingdom, while the high proportion of coal used on the railways in the United States is equally significant of the enormous land area and internal land trade in that country.

Table 20 — Percentage comparative consumption of coal: 1968

	United Kingdom	United States
Electric power	45	56
Domestic	13	2
Coke	15	17
Industry	14	14
Gas	4	1
Others	7	4
Export	2	6
	100	100

* The Mineral Industry, 1925, p. 149 (bituminous coals only).
† Inclusive of coke, cinders, and patent fuel.

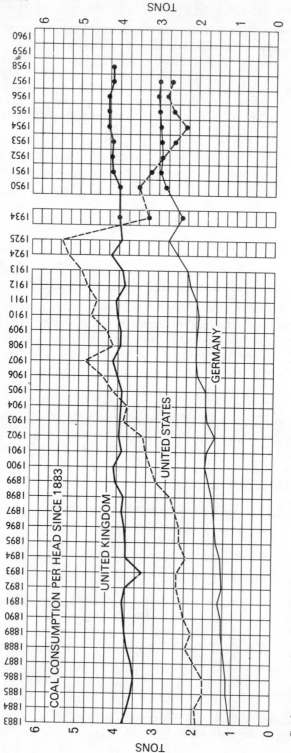

Coal consumption since 1883.

The figures for Germany after 1945 refer to West Germany only.

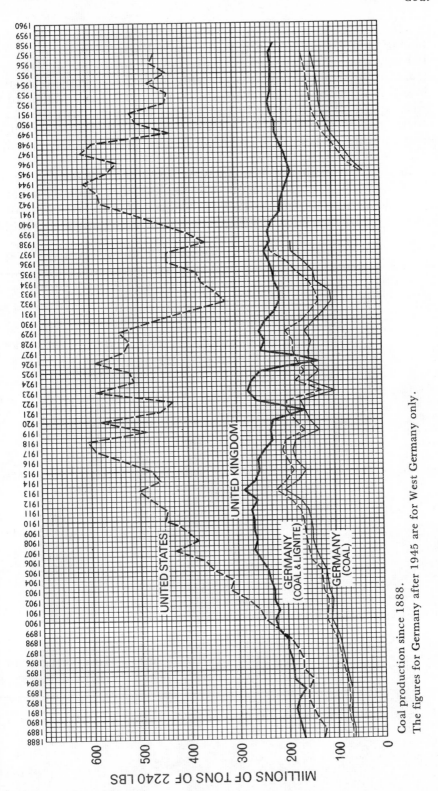

Coal production since 1888.

The figures for Germany after 1945 are for West Germany only.

The year 1913 marked the climax of the prosperity of the coal-mining industry in Great Britain. During the war years 1914—18 the industry was under government control; export prices rose so high that much of the export trade was lost and foreign fields were stimulated into active development. In 1920 the output had fallen to 230m. tons and exports to 44m. tons, 19 per cent of the output. A gradual recovery followed, only to be succeeded by the disastrous year 1926 when, owing to labour troubles, production fell to 126m. tons and exports to 21m. tons.

In 1937 the royalty rights in British mines were nationalised at a cost of £66 450 000. Production in that year reached 240m. tons and exports 43m. tons. But in 1939 any hopes of early recovery were dashed by the Second World War. The output of saleable coal declined

Table 21 — Reserves and production of anthracite and bituminous coal

Country	Estimated reserves thousand millions of tons (anthracite and bituminous coal only)	Annual production of anthracite and bituminous coal in millions of tons					
		1906—10 (average)	1935	1945	1962	1967	1971
United Kingdom	16	261.7	222.3	182.8	200.6	174.8	147.1
Australia	16	9.3	10.9	12.8	24.9	35.2	48.9
Canada	61	9.7	8.7	10.5	7.3	8.5	13.7
India	} 106	11.5	23.6	29.2	{ 61.4	68.2	70.2
Pakistan*					—	—	—
New Zealand	1	1.9	0.8	1.0	0.8	0.6	0.7
South Africa	72	5.2	13.4	23.2	41.3	49.3	58.7
Austria	0.002 }	} 14.8	{ 0.2	0.1	0.1	—	0.1
Hungary	1 }		{ 0.9	0.7	2.7	4.4	5.0
Czechoslovakia	12	—	10.7	11.5	27.1	25.9	28.7
Poland	46	—	28.1	26.0	109.6	123.8	145.5
Netherlands	2.4	—	11.7	5.0	11.6	8.0	9.0
Belgium	1.8	23.3	26.1	15.6	21.2	16.4	10.9
France	2.8	35.6	47.2	32.8	52.4	47.6	33.0
West Germany	70 }	} 142.6	140.7	40.6	{ 142.0	112.3	111.0
East Germany	0.05 }				{ 2.8	2.4	5.4
Spain	8	3.6	6.9	10.6	13.9	12.6	10.7
China	1 011	—	12.0	25.0	382.0	420.0	390.0
Japan	19	14.3	37.2	22.0	54.4	47.5	33.4
USSR	4 122	24.6	93.7	160.0	386.4	414.1	441.4
United States	1 100	405.9	378.0	562.4	395.6	481.2	503.1
World total	6 700	1 250	1 072	1 150	1 987	1 920	2 128

Source:
Survey of Energy Resources, 1968, World Power Conference.
* Before the secession of Bangladesh.

to 174m. tons in 1945, and for some years after fighting ceased not only were home supplies severely rationed but the export trade in coal was almost suspended, with disastrous effects on the national economy. Coal used to provide one-tenth of the total exports in value and four-fifths in volume. In the words of the Royal Commission (1925): 'By furnishing outward cargo for a large amount of shipping it cheapens freights for the imports.'

Tables 19 and 20 show the change in the conditions between UK and USA in the 1920s and the 1950s. At the outset the British export of coal, despite the First World War, was still large. After the Second World War Britain was struggling to produce enough coal for home consumption, the trouble being shortage not of coal but of miners.

Out-of-date conditions in some of the mines and discontent among the miners were both limiting factors in production. In the hope of meeting the need, the coalmining industry was nationalised in 1947. Wages were increased, hours of work reduced, and a five-day week was established, while schemes for improving the equipment of the mines were put in hand. Production in 1947 fell just short of the government 'target' of 200m. tons, and in 1948 a beginning was made with the revival of the export trade. Later, the restrictions on home consumption were withdrawn, but there was no great revival of either home trade or exports and by 1970 production had fallen to 140m. tons and exports to 4m. tons. Cheap imported oil and, later, natural gas, presented a new and, in many ways, a more convenient fuel and source of power.

There have been many speculations as to the future of the coal supply of the world as a whole and of particular countries. The vast extent and content of the known coalfields of the world as shown in the first column of figures set out in Table 21 removes, indeed, any fear of the using up of the coal supply of the world to the remote future. With regard to the coal supply of any particular country* or region it must be borne in mind that however ample the reserves, they will be mined only so long as it is economically feasible. As to the future of coal production where large deposits of coal still remain to be extracted, it is difficult to prophesy as the conditions which determine whether a coalfield is worked are numerous and variable. Much depends

---

* The second Royal Commission on the Coal Supplies of the United Kingdom estimated the total quantity of available coal in the United Kingdom in seams of 1 ft in thickness and upwards, down to a depth of 4 000 ft, at 100 915m. tons in proved coalfields, and 39 483m. tons in unproved coalfields — a total of 140 398m. tons. The figures provided for the 1968 World Power Conference Survey, based on seams of 30 cm (11.8 in) and upwards, down to a depth of 1 200 m (3 900 ft), were 12 227m. tons in measured reserves and 3 280m. tons in unproved reserves (a total of 15 501m. tons), indicating the great variation that occurs in estimating reserves of unworked mineral deposits.

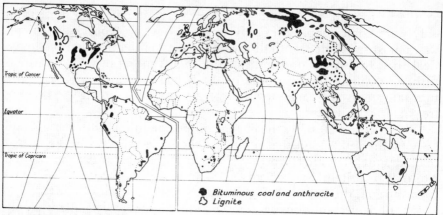

World distribution of coal

on the quality of the coal, the situation of the coalfield and the ease with which the region can be supplied with coal from elsewhere or with power from other sources. As hydroelectric power is a competing source, it should be mentioned that where there is plant for continuous development of power by this means one British horsepower hour (= 500 foot-pounds = 746 watts) is equivalent to the consumption of 0.9 kg (2 lb) of coal. With continuous working, therefore, on 300 days in the year, a horsepower year would be equivalent to the consumption of over 6 tons in that time. Thus, for example, Canada's developed water power resources represented a saving of coal of 160m. tons per annum in 1967.

The chief geographical considerations in connection with coal, apart from its distribution and the accessibility of the seams, arise from the cost of carriage. When coal is made dear by difficulties of transport there is every inducement to make the best provision practicable to secure its efficiency. This was done traditionally by locating industry near to the coalfields, but even greater efficiency is achieved by transferring its energy as electrical power, and the higher transport costs become the greater is the inducement to resort to this method of utilising fuel. This has been well illustrated in Britain with the development of the electricity grid. Many of the early generators were either on the coalfields, i.e. the electricity was pithead carboelectricity, or were situated where they could easily receive bulk supplies of coal. In 1938, 93 per cent of the energy consumed to produce electricity came from coal; by 1968 it was under 50 per cent as oil and nuclear power provided alternative sources.

Lignite, as the name indicates, is a woody kind of coal, sometimes of a brown colour; in Germany it is known as brown coal (*Braunkohle*). It is produced mostly in East Germany (more than one-third of world supply), and largely also in other central or eastern European countries, in Australia and New Zealand, and in Canada and the United States. World production is upwards of 760m. tons. Its heating value in proportion to that of true coal is reckoned in Germany to be about 5:7, but its price is only about half that of coal, which limits its range of transport. Most of the German supply is used for making briquettes, a favourite form of fuel for both industrial and domestic purposes. There is obviously a great advantage in using lignite where mined to generate electricity. Thus Melbourne is supplied with electricity from the Morwell lignite deposits.

The great bulk of the coal produced is used within the countries which mine it; this is particularly true of lignite. Of the total production of some 2 640m. tons (1 920m. coal: 720m. lignite) in 1967 only some 160m. tons entered into world commerce. Trade was concerned largely with the movement of better quality coal and coking coal for industrial uses. The United States, Poland, the USSR, West Germany and Australia being the main net exporters; and Japan, Canada, East Germany, Italy, France and Denmark net importers. Coal was the energy source of the Industrial Revolution which produced the industrialised nations of the developed world. Petroleum, natural gas and nuclear power now provide competing and alternative energy sources. Modern industrial development, and in particular that of the developing world, is not therefore so dependent upon the traditional base of adequate coal resources.

Petroleum and its products, with other allied substances

Petroleum, which means rock-oil, is a general name given to oils which flow freely or are pumped from holes bored in the earth. From the crude oil as it issues from the earth numerous products having a great variety of uses are made by distillation and other processes, these products differing from one another in weight and fluidity, as well as in other properties. The names given to these products are variously used in different places, which is the source of a great deal of confusion. The name 'kerosene' is generally given to a light oil which is used in lamps for illumination. Kerosene is also employed as fuel for domestic heating, in some tractors, and in gas turbine engines. Heavier kinds of oil are used for many other purposes, such as heating and providing power for heavy diesel engines, or as lubricants in all kinds of machinery. The development of the internal combustion engine made gasoline or petrol the most important product of petroleum for very many years, and it is only recently that the heavier oils have begun in some countries to rival it in importance. In the process of distillation the various products that make up petroleum are separated out, petrol being among the lightest and fuel oil one of the heaviest. Crude oils vary in their contents of petrol and other products; on an average they

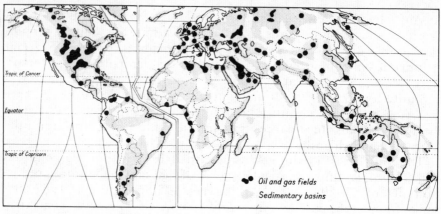

World distribution of hydrocarbon resources, 1972.
Notice that all the oil and natural gas resources discovered to date lie in the sedimentary basins of the earth's crust.

contain about 20 per cent of petrol, and as world requirements of petrol are very high (amounting to nearer 40 per cent than 20 per cent of all petroleum products) the yield is commonly increased by processes such as 'cracking', whereby the heavier fractions are split chemically into petrol on the one hand and very heavy oils on the other.

Apart from the main products of petroleum there are many others important to modern life. The end products obtained from the distillation of mineral oil include bitumen or asphalt and paraffin wax. Some petroleum derivatives have medicinal uses; and a vast range of products, obtained from the lighter fractions of petroleum, form the raw materials for the petrochemical industry, which manufactures plastics, synthetic fibres, detergents, and many other household and industrial products.

Products similar to those obtained from petroleum can also be produced by processing oils obtained from shales. The shale-oil industry has long been established in the midland valley of Scotland, but of recent years has suffered from the exhaustion of the richer shales (which yielded as much as 80 gallons per ton of shale) and the competition of the more cheaply produced crude oils. There are vast deposits of oil shale in many parts of the world which will be worked when a rise in crude oil prices or the invention of more efficient retorting processes renders their exploitation economically possible. A pilot production line has already been started on the Athabasca tar sands of Alberta in Canada. Low-grade coals may also be used, and indeed coals of all types, so that the countries which are rich in coal deposits but poor in mineral oil have turned their attention to the production of oil from coal. This can be effected by several processes, including low temperature carbonisation (converting coal into a smokeless fuel and an oil

266

byproduct) and high temperature carbonisation (yielding coke and liquid products, including benzole). Other methods of obtaining oil from coal include the hydrogenation process, which gives a large yield of petrol but at very considerable cost. Large works for the hydrogenation of coal were established before the Second World War at Billingham-on-Tees, but the process is now carried out with a creosote pitch mixture. In America, experiments have also been made to develop the Fisher Tropsch process, extensively used in Germany during the war.

None of these processes is economical compared with the production of refined products from petroleum, and since the Second World War many countries with little or no crude oil production of their own have set up large-scale refineries to deal with imported crude oil. In 1938 refining capacity in the United Kingdom was 1.9m. tons; by 1960 it was 49.25m. tons; and by 1973 it was 141m. tons. Additional imports of certain petroleum products were still necessary, even in 1972, but there was a surplus of others which were available for export.

The petroleum industry on a great scale is entirely modern. Its growth is due to the abundance of the supplies discovered in certain regions, the great utility of its products, the ease with which oil can be extracted from the earth and transported over long distances in pipes or in ships built to carry oil in bulk, and its relative cheapness. Petroleum was known to the ancients, being mentioned by Herodotus, Plutarch, and Pliny; but the development of the industry has taken place since the oilfields of the United States began to be worked only 100 years ago and its great expansion has taken place since the end of the Second World War.

Table 22 shows the rapid increase in world production during the present century. In the second decade a succession of new fields was discovered in the States, where production increased from 34m. metric tons in 1913 to 100m. metric tons in 1923. Since then many new oilfields have been discovered in many parts of the world, and the known reserves are sufficient to meet world needs for some decades. But oil, like all minerals, is a wasting asset, and the total quantity available would appear to be much less than that of coal.

The following notes on the chief producing countries are given with due reserve. Development of new areas is rapid, and even though older areas tend to increase their production, their position in relation to other countries may decline. Between 1938 and 1970 the United States more than trebled her output, but her share of world production fell from 61 per cent to 20 per cent.

United States. In the United States the productive oilfields lie in groups in several areas. The first extensive development took place in the eastern states, where a great oil region about 260 km (160 miles) in

Commodities

Table 22 — World production of crude oil and natural gasoline in million metric tons

1900	20	1940	300	1958	937
1905	30	1941	313	1959	1 012
1910	45	1942	293	1960	1 089
1915	59	1943	317	1961	1 120
1920	95	1944	358	1962	1 258
1925	146	1945	368	1963	1 347
1928	188	1946	391	1964	1 450
1929	211	1947	432	1965	1 520
1930	200	1948	489	1966	1 640
1931	189	1949	488	1967	1 760
1932	180	1950	540	1968	1 996
1933	198	1951	609	1969	2 148
1934	208	1952	640	1970	2 330
1935	227	1953	678	1971	2 486
1936	247	1954	709	1972	2 605
1937	287	1955	800	1973	2 848
1938	281	1956	869		
1939	291	1957	913		

Table 23 — Output of chief petroleum producing countries*

New World	Million metric tons			Old World	Million metric tons		
	1938	1963	1973		1938	1963	1973
USA	170.7	393.3	518.4	USSR	34.1	206.0	421.2
Venezuela	28.1	169.4	175.5	Iran	10.4	76.9	292.6
Canada	0.9	37.0	102.2	Saudi Arabia	0.1	86.4	364.1
Mexico	5.5	16.4	26.7	Libya	—	24.0	103.8
Argentina	2.4	14.0	21.9	Kuwait	—	100.8	137.6
Colombia	3.1	8.5	9.8	Iraq	4.4	60.4	96.1
Brazil	—	5.1	8.7	Nigeria	—	3.9	101.8
Trinidad	2.6	7.0	8.7	Algeria	—	26.0	48.8
				Indonesia	7.4	23.6	66.7
Others	2.2	5.0	17.8	Neutral Zone	—	16.4	27.9
				Qatar	—	10.0	26.8
				Oman	—	—	14.6
				Egypt	0.2	5.5	13.7
				Romania	6.9	12.0	14.3
				China	—	12.0	50.0
				West Germany	—	7.6	6.6
				India	—	—	7.3
				Brunei/Sarawak	0.9	4.2	15.3
				Gabon/Congo	—	—	9.0
				Others	1.1	9.8	140.4
Totals	215.5	656.3	889.7		65.5	690.7	1 958.6
Percentages	77%	49%	31%		23%	51%	69%

* Output in individual countries is often expressed in barrels. The relation between barrels and tons varies in different countries, ranging between seven barrels and a little over to the ton according to the density of the product. A barrel contains 35 Imperial gallons: 42 US gallons: 1.59 hectolitres.

length, and 65 km (40 miles) broad in the middle, stretches from south-west to northeast through the western parts of the states of Pennsyl-vania and New York. Oil was observed on the surface of the ground within this region as far back as 1819, but the first company for utilising the oil was formed in 1853, and at first the only method of collecting the oil was by spreading cloths over the ground to soak it up. The first well drilled for the express purpose of obtaining oil was completed in 1859. There are now around 320 000 km (200 000 miles) of oil pipelines in the United States, most of which carry oil from individual oilfields to the great refineries, though some are used to transport the refined products to the centres of consumption.

In 1885 95 per cent of the United States crude oil came from the Pennsylvanian fields. Since then the proportion has steadily diminished. Another group of fields lies to the south of the Great Lakes, in the states of Illinois, Indiana, and Ohio. The Mid-continent Fields lie in the states of Kansas and Oklahoma. The Gulf Coast Fields, as the name implies, lie near the coast of the Gulf of Mexico in the states of Texas and Louisiana.

The oilfields of the southern part of the state of California have also proved very remarkable. Located round Los Angeles, they are largely the cause of the rapid rise of that town. California became the foremost producing state of America and was noted for its remarkable series of 'giant producers'. Before the Second World War a decline set in, and Texas and Oklahoma went ahead of California; but since then Oklahoma has gone back. Table 24 lists states producing over 2m. tons of crude oil in 1968. Total production in 1972 was 532m. tons.

Despite the enormous increase in output in the United States, home demand has actually caught up on supply and while there is still considerable export trade, largely in motor fuel and lubricants, there is a still bigger import trade — chiefly in crude petroleum and residual fuel oils. On balance, the United States, the world's largest producer of petroleum, is a net importer.

Table 24 — **Production of crude oil in the USA, 1968**

State	Million metric tons	State	Million metric tons
Texas	162	Mississippi	8
Louisiana	117	Montana	7
California	54	Colorado	5
Oklahoma	32	Utah	3
Wyoming	20	Arkansas	3
New Mexico	17	Michigan	2
Kansas	14	Other states	59
Illinois	8		
		Total USA	511

Canada. Canada's chief oilfields are in Alberta. There have been notable developments, especially around Edmonton, as the result of discoveries in and since 1947. By 1960 Canada's production was over 27m. metric tons, and two years previously Alberta alone had 8 550 wells yielding over two-thirds of the Canadian output. Already pipelines were taking oil eastwards to the Great Lakes and westwards across the Rockies to Vancouver in British Columbia. Simultaneously there was a big development of plans for utilising Alberta's abundant supplies of natural gas, from which can be extracted petrochemical products (butane, ethane, propane, etc.) now in great demand. Apart from Alberta's outstanding contribution to Canada's production of oil, the balance of the Canadian output is provided by the other Prairie Provinces, British Columbia, the North West Territories, Ontario and New Brunswick.

Mexico for long occupied second place amongst oil producers; in 1921 its output formed 29 per cent of the world's total. Legislation and the disturbed state of the country interfered with the industry. Many of the wells became exhausted and no comparable new supplies were found. In other countries new fields were being tapped. As a result, for some years Mexico has produced under 1.25 per cent of the world's total, though with the growth of that total Mexico's actual output has shown steady development. The main fields lie near the coast, in the neighbourhood of Tampico.

South America. After the First World War South America became a prime factor in oil supply, thanks mainly to Venezuela, which has become the world's fifth producer. Its oilfields lie in two main areas: in the west, around the shallow Gulf of Maracaibo, where production started, and in eastern Venezuela, Argentina, Colombia, Trinidad and Brazil are next in rank, though their combined output is only a fraction of that of Venezuela. Lower in the scale are Peru, Chile, Ecuador, and Bolivia; but the combined output of these last three was only 1 per cent of the total output in South America.

The USSR as a whole is second to USA in present output, and has great potentialities. The Transcaucasian oilfields belong to a larger region, extending from the Crimea along both sides of the Caucasus, and along the northern frontier of Persia to Merv and Sarakhs in the southeast. There are two small districts, one near the Caspian Sea, and one near the Black Sea, both on the south side of the Caucasus Mountains, in which the supply of oil in this region is peculiarly abundant. By far the richer of the two is the district around Baku, on the Caspian, where inflammable oils have been known to exist from a very remote period, though it was not till the latter part of the nineteenth century that their working was taken in hand in earnest. In 1900 a pipeline over

225 km (140 miles) long was opened from Baku to Mikhailovo, near the eastern end of the Suram tunnel, and this line was afterwards continued to Batum. Petroleum is produced also in other parts of Transcaucasia, abundantly in the Grozny and Maikop districts of Cis-Caucasia and offshore in the Caspian Sea. Notable too are the Volga-Ural (the 'Second Baku') oilfields, believed to be providing nearly two-thirds of the country's total output of oil, and the new Siberian ('Third Baku') fields between Tyumen—Tomsk and near Novosibirsk.

Europe outside Russia. Oil has long been worked in fields on the outer slopes of the Carpathian Mountains, with Romania as the country of largest output. Other European countries where oil production is established include West Germany, France, Italy, the Netherlands, Austria, Hungary and Yugoslavia, with smaller quantities from Albania, Bulgaria, Poland and Czechoslovakia. Over the past half-century there have been repeated endeavours to locate oil in the United Kingdom. During the First World War a small production was established at Hardstoft in Derbyshire — no longer being operated — but more important discoveries occurred in the Eakring area of Nottinghamshire in 1939. From this area the UK obtained an extremely small output of petroleum (about 100 000 tons a year, against a consumption of 90m. tons), other contributions coming from Formby in Lancashire and from two other fields in Nottinghamshire — Plungar and Egmanton — which are comparatively recent discoveries. The spectacular discoveries of oil and vast quantities of natural gas in the northern coastlands of the Netherlands not only altered fundamentally the economy of that country but led to intensive exploration over the bed of the North Sea by Britain and other neighbouring countries. Both oil and gas have been discovered and the great bulk of UK requirements can be met from this source during the last quarter of the twentieth century.

Asia. Burma maintained an output of 1m. tons a year before the Second World War; afterwards it dropped to about 10 000 tons, now it is up again to 1m. tons. There are significant fields in the Punjab (Pakistan) and Assam (India). Indonesia, as the Netherlands East Indies, yielded large supplies before the Second World War (up to 7m. tons and more in a year), and though production dropped to a few hundred thousand tons in the postwar troubles, it is now over 65m. tons. In North Borneo, Sarawak, and Brunei, there was a notable postwar development. There are closely associated oilfields in Sarawak and Brunei, which have long yielded useful supplies. For some years after the war Brunei was the leading source of supply in the Commonwealth, and though it no longer occupies anything like that position it still produces over 15m. tons.

A very important field was worked in Iran during the first half of the twentieth century by the Anglo-Iranian Oil Company, in which the British government, in 1914, acquired a majority of the ordinary shares. In the spring of 1951, while proposals to increase the share of the profits payable to Iran were being negotiated, the government nationalised the industry and repudiated the concession to the oil company. In the absence of an amicable settlement, exports of oil from Iran ceased, the company withdrew from the country, and in the autumn of 1952 the Iranian government broke off diplomatic relations with the United Kingdom. They were resumed a year later and the oil industry was restarted on an international basis in 1954. Production increased rapidly, and was soon greater than before the trouble. In 1950 it had reached 32m. tons; in 1957 it was 35m., and by 1973 it was over 292m. tons.

Important though supplies from Iran have become, there are two other major producers in the region: the sheikhdom of Kuwait, at the head of the Persian Gulf, and the kingdom of Saudi Arabia, comprising most of the Arabian Peninsula. The respective outputs of these two countries in 1973 were 137m. and 364m. tons.

Iraq, north of Arabia, has also increased production since the war, though operations were temporarily disrupted by the closing of the Suez Canal and the damage done to Iraq's pipelines to the Mediterranean. At that time Iraq had three pipelines from Kirkuk, the chief centre of supply, to the Mediterranean — two to the port of Tripoli, in the Lebanon, and one to Banias, on the Syrian coast. In 1956 Iraq was the third largest producer in the Middle East, with an output of 30m. tons, but in the following year it was overtaken by Iran. Its own output in 1973 was nearly 96m. tons.

The fields of Kuwait and Saudi Arabia are along the shores of the Persian Gulf and oil has been discovered in quantity in the sheikhdom of Qatar (1973 output 26.8m. tons), in the Neutral Zone (28m. tons) between Kuwait and Saudi Arabia, on Bahrain Island (3.4m. tons), and above all in the Trucial States — with Abu Dhabi producing 63m. tons in 1973. Underwater production in the Persian Gulf was begun off the coast of Saudi Arabia in 1957.

Other countries. In Africa, oil is produced in Egypt. Vast reserves have also been located and are being developed in the Sahara. Libya with an annual production in 1973 of 103m. tons is a major source of supply, while production from Nigeria, Algeria and Angola is increasing. In Australia the search for oil has met with success (Moonie in Queensland). Japan is a minor producer in Asia and there are new fields in the heart of China.

Demand and reserves. Since the end of the Second World War the demand for oil products has increased fivefold. Almost half of the total production is exported and oil has become the largest single item of international commerce. The geographic separation of the regions of production and the regions of consumption, and the rapidly changing pattern of world energy consumption, have made it an item which features in the trading accounts of almost every country. Energy consumption was estimated by the Institute of Petroleum (the various items being converted to metric tons coal equivalents, e.g. oil 1 ton = 1.5 ton coal; hydroelectric power 1 000 kW = 0.125 ton coal) in 1948 as: coal 62 per cent; oil 26 per cent; natural gas 10 per cent; hydro/nuclear 2 per cent. In 1973 the comparable figures were: oil 54 per cent; coal 18.9 per cent; natural gas 18.9 per cent; hydro/nuclear 8.2 per cent. It is probable that in Japan and western Europe the figure for oil is nearer 60 per cent, while in the developing countries of Africa and South America — short of coal and introducing industry with the latest techniques — it could well be over 65 per cent. Alongside the growth in world consumption from 532m. tons in 1950 to 2 765m. tons in 1973 there has been equal pressure for the discovery and exploitation of new reserves. Proven resources in 1947 were estimated as 9 500m. tons. By 1960 they were up to 40 800m. tons, and by 1973 to 86 560m.; with estimates of a possible finite maximum of some 350 000m. Since energy consumption could well treble by the end of the twentieth century, and since not all the potential reserves will prove to be workable, the eventual exhaustion of this non-renewable energy source is likely to occur long before the exhaustion of the coal reserves.

Asphalt or mineral pitch is a solid or nearly solid substance which results from the evaporation of the lighter fractions of natural oil or the thickening of petroleum through the absorption of oxygen, and is hence met with in nature either as a superficial layer above deposits of petroleum exposed to the air, or as a substance entirely occupying the place of such deposits so exposed. It is largely used for surfacing roads and sidewalks. The chief source of supply is Trinidad's famous Pitch Lake. Argentina, the United States and Switzerland also have deposits.

Natural gas

Formerly a waste product burnt at the oilfields, natural gas will supply nearly 20 per cent of the world's power sources during the 1970s. As a fuel it has the advantages of minimal pollution effects and ease of distribution. Overland transportation in bulk has been made possible by the rapid construction of pipelines. The 107 cm (42 in) diameter pipes used for petroleum can be used (along with smaller sizes) for the gas network; but gas can also be transported by plastic pipes, and experiments are in hand to construct gas 'trunklines' with pipes of up to 254 cm (100 in) in diameter. Transport by sea is economically feasible only in liquid form. This requires special tankers with insulated containers to carry the gas at temperatures of −160° C (−260° F). At higher temperatures the liquid re-gasifies. In liquid form, a 37 000 ton tanker can carry gas equivalent to a 120 000 ton crude oil tanker.

The increasing importance of this readily available byproduct of the petroleum industry is reflected in the extensive pipeline networks of North America (gas is piped from Alberta to California, and from Texas to New England), the USSR and Europe; and in the increasing international trade in liquid gas. The United States imports from Venezuela and North Africa; western Europe from North Africa; and Japan from the Persian Gulf states, Brunei and Alaska. Great quantities of gas are still burnt off at the Middle East oilfields, and its eventual entry into world trade depends on the economies of transportation. Meanwhile each new oilfield brings its supply of natural gas. In Europe the North Sea fields, and those of the Netherlands and France are sources of supply, while increased supplies will be brought to Italy, Austria and even West Germany as the USSR constructs major pipeline links with the west Siberian oilfields.

Gold and silver

Tables 25 and 26 show the world production of gold and silver and the output in leading countries in 1912, 1938, 1967, 1970 − that is, before the First World War, before the Second World War, and in recent years. In both cases (gold and silver), countries are shown in descending order of production in 1967. In the Second World War the mining of gold and silver, unlike the production of petroleum, came to be of secondary importance. Since the war the demand for artistic and industrial uses has increased steadily. For the last fifty years, the biggest factor in the world's supply of gold has been South Africa, mainly the Transvaal, which in 1955 provided 85 per cent of a total of 482 000 kg (14.6m. troy ounces) for the whole Union. In 1898, the year before the Boer War, the value of the gold produced in the Transvaal was £16m. After increasing steadily year by year from 1902 till 1912, when it amounted to £38.7m., the value of South Africa's gold production began to decline, and in 1922 it had dropped to £29.8m. A rapid rise followed and the value reached £44.2m. in 1929. During the Second World War it increased to over £60m. (both in 1941 and in 1942), but in 1949 it was down again to £49.7m. This was at the standard of very nearly 85s. per ounce fine, applied to an output of 386 000 kg (11.7m. troy ounces); but at the price realised in 1955 the market value of the gold produced in that year was £182.7m. In 1959 the realised value was £250m. and by 1967 it was over £450m.

Gold generally occurs either in alluvial deposits (into which it has been washed by the degradation of the rocks from which the deposits

Table 25 — World production of gold (in thousands of kilograms*)

Country	1912	1938	1967	1970
South Africa	310.6	401.3	943.4	1 000.4
USSR†	35.3	174.9	328.1	195.0
Canada	20.1	156.1	92.1	72.7
USA	149.2	140.9	49.3	56.4
Australia	76.6	52.8	25.2	19.3
Ghana	13.0	22.4	23.7	21.9
Rhodesia	22.8	27.1	17.1	15.6
Philippines	–	29.7	15.6	18.7
World total	744.2	1 240.8	1 573.1	1 480.0

* 1 troy oz = 480 grains = 31.1 grams = 0.03 kg.
  1 kg = 32 troy oz.
† Estimates only.

Table 26 — World production of silver (in thousands of metric tons)

Country	1912	1938	1967	1970
Mexico	2.46	2.67	1.25	1.33
Canada	1.04	0.73	1.16	1.38
Peru	0.27	0.68	1.12	1.22
USA	2.11	2.04	0.99	1.37
USSR	0.01	0.23	0.80	1.15
Germany*	0.16	0.23	0.66	0.91
Australia	0.45	0.51	0.62	0.81
Japan	0.16	0.36	0.34	0.92
World total	7.40	8.84	7.20	10.57

* East and West Germany combined.

are derived) or in quartz-veins in a free state. Often it is associated with various metallic sulphides, chiefly iron and copper pyrites, either in quartz-veins or in other forms in which these ores occur, so that it can either be mined directly or obtained as a byproduct of other metals. From quartz-veins and other hard rocks gold has to be obtained by stamping or crushing, a process involving more expensive machinery than is used in digging for alluvial gold; but quartz-veins are sometimes capable of being profitably worked to a depth of 600 m (2 000 ft) or more. The famous 'banket' of the Witwatersrand from which the bulk of the Transvaal gold is obtained is a hard quartz-ore conglomerate of Pre-Cambrian age, in which the gold is so finely disseminated as to be invisible to the naked eye.

Gold has two outstanding characteristics: it is indestructible and as a traditional measure of wealth it has long been connected with money.

Most of the gold that has been mined by man is therefore still available and can be continually re-used (except in so far as the cost of reprocessing is greater than the value of gold recovered). Nonetheless the demand for industrial and artistic purposes has risen sharply since the Second World War. The International Monetary Fund estimated that the world demand tripled between 1958 and 1967. In March 1968 major fluctuations in the market value finally resulted in an international decision to divorce private transactions in gold from the official monetary transactions. The managed national currencies are therefore no longer tied directly to gold, although it still retains its value as an ultimate means of payment in international transactions. There are now two recognised gold prices: the fixed official price for monetary transactions between central banks ($35 an ounce 1968–70), and the floating price dictated by supply and demand in the commercial market.

Silver ores generally occur in veins, or irregular deposits. But silver-lead ore sometimes occurs in great quantity in large 'pockets' or cavities in limestone rocks, which are very productive for a time, but are soon exhausted. It is from such chambers that the greater part of the silver of the United States was obtained after the discovery of the famous Comstock lode in Nevada in 1859. New discoveries have maintained the output and the leading states are Idaho, Utah, Arizona, Montana, and Colorado — all Rocky Mountain states. Some two-thirds of the production of North America is now derived from the desilverisation of ores worked for other metals, principally lead and copper. It is by the desilverisation of copper ore (at Mansfeld in the Harz) that a large proportion of the silver of Germany is produced.

The United States absorbs half of the world's consumption of silver. Twenty per cent is used for coinage and 80 per cent for industrial purposes. The industrial distribution indicates the current uses for this precious metal: 30 per cent to photographic materials; 22 per cent to electrical and electronic products; 18 per cent to tableware; 14 per cent to electro-plating and jewellery; 13 per cent to solders and catalysts, and 1 per cent each to mirrors and medical uses.

Lead

The consumption of this metal greatly increased during the nineteenth century in consequence of its use for the smaller gas and water pipes now largely replaced by copper), roofing, and in various branches of manufacturing industry, as in lining the chambers used in making sulphuric acid. The high position formerly taken by the United Kingdom in the lead industry has been altered by the fact that lead ores are now generally treated in the countries in which they are produced, so that the former large import of lead ores (39 000 tons in 1973) is now replaced by that of lead or lead alloys (236 000 tons in 1973), chiefly from Australia and Canada. In 1971 world production of lead ore was 3.5m. tons and the chief producing countries in order of importance were USSR, USA, Australia, Canada, Mexico, Peru, Yugoslavia and China.

There are various industries subsidiary to that in lead. The most important of these is the extraction of silver, a small proportion of which is nearly always contained in galena, the chief lead ore, a sulphide of lead. Sulphide of zinc is also associated with galena; and lead, silver and zinc are frequently produced in the same mines. White lead, which is very largely used in making painters' colours and in making the glaze on earthenware, is a carbonate of lead or a compound of lead and carbonic acid. Litharge is a lead oxide or compound of lead and oxygen, and is a yellowish substance used in making the glaze on earthenware and for other purposes. One form of this is called massicot, and from it is made by heating another compound called red lead or minium, which contains a greater proportion of oxygen, and is largely used in the making of flint glass and porcelain, as well as in making red paint.

World consumption of lead was estimated in 1970 as some 3.8m. tons; 2.9m. tons being primary lead, i.e. melted from lead ore, and 900 000 tons being secondary lead, i.e. recovered from scrap, remelted or recovered in alloys. In the United States (353 000 tons: 503 000 tons), the United Kingdom (66 000 tons: 126 000 tons) and West Germany (136 000 tons: 191 000 tons), the production of primary lead (given first in the above figures) was smaller than the production of secondary lead in 1967. Such dependence on secondary sources is becoming increasingly important in modern metallurgical industries as world prices make recovery more profitable, for example, for steel, aluminium, copper, zinc, etc. The current consumption of lead in the United States is some 35 per cent to batteries; 20 per cent to petrol as additives for internal combustion performance (likely to be reduced as antipollution measures require decreased lead content); 6 per cent to red lead and litharge and 5 per cent to cable covering and solders.

Copper

This metal is found in many if not in most countries of the world, sometimes pure (the native copper occasionally forming huge masses), more frequently in the form of ores, which vary greatly in richness. In 1867 Chile, the northern half of which is intersected in every direction by veins of copper, contributed two-thirds of the entire copper production of the world; but owing to the discovery of rich deposits of copper in other regions less remote from the great markets of the world, its share of the total copper production has been greatly reduced. In 1880 it still stood first in the list of copper producing countries, but the United States has since taken the lead and now supplies about a fifth (1 400m. tons in 1969) of the world production of 5 940m. tons. The USSR and Zambia are close rivals for second place, their production in 1969 being respectively 900 000 tons, and 720 000, while Chile produced 669 000 tons. If the South Central Africa copper belt be regarded as a whole, extending from Zambia over the Zaire border into Katanga, it rivals the United States as the largest source of world supply. In 1969 with Zaire (Congo, Kinshasa) providing 357 000 tons, the combined output of the area was over 1 020 000 tons. The only other outstanding source of supply is Canada — 506 000 tons in 1969. In that year the half-dozen countries mentioned were responsible for 80 per cent of the total world production which has doubled between 1950 and 1970, and in 1971 reached 6 425m. tons.

The production of copper ores from the mines of the United Kingdom is now unimportant. A certain quantity (220 tons in 1973) of ore is imported from Canada and there is a large import of copper (507 000 tons in 1973) which has undergone some preliminary treatment. This is converted into pure copper, chiefly at Swansea. It figures in the trade returns as 'Unwrought copper, including rough copper of 94 per cent copper content or over', and is divided into 'Electrolytic and other refined' and 'Blister or rough'. The former and larger class of unwrought copper is supplied by Canada and the United States, Zambia and Zaire, and Chile. Other unwrought copper comes almost entirely from Zambia and Chile.

Being an excellent conductor of electricity, copper is extensively used in making telegraph wires for underground communication and marine cables. Apart from the electronic and electrical industry the chief uses of copper are in making pipes, brewers' and distillers' plant, in shipbuilding, the making of plates for the printing of textiles, and in the dye industries. Copper is one of the ingredients in the two alloys known as **bronze** and **brass**, the former composed of copper and tin (a very hard compound), and the latter of copper and zinc. Copper is, in short, a key industrial metal.

The consumption of copper has increased at 4 per cent per year since the Second World War, and during the 1960s the price fluctuated greatly, from £230 a ton in 1963 to £750 in 1970; but up to £1 400 by 1974. Temporary interruptions to supply, great differences in the copper content of ores and in mining costs between the producers, the introduction of new recovery techniques which made the working of lower grade ones feasible, a large potential supply of scrap which could provide up to 40 per cent of the copper coming on to the market: all these factors made it difficult to stabilise supply and demand. The resultant market fluctuations encouraged research into substitutes; and the hope of further price rises encouraged the opening-up of new production areas in Australia, New Guinea and Iran. World demand is still expanding and the figures of consumption per head indicate that it will continue to do so as nations become more industrialised. Estimated consumption in 1970 was: India/China 0.25 kg per head, South America 0.5 kg per head, USSR 3.5 kg per head and USA 6.8 kg per head.

Zinc

This metal was first known in Europe only as an import from China and India, where it had long been employed in the manufacture of brass. The principal ores are zincspar or calamine, a carbonate of zinc, and zinc blende or sulphide or zinc, both impure, and the methods of treating them were discovered in Europe only in the eighteenth century. Belgium, Germany and Poland led the way in zinc production from ores before the Second World War; but since then the United States, USSR, Japan and Canada have become the major producers. World production of zinc ores, reckoned in terms of their metal content, totals some 5.5m. tons a year, and to this total Canada, USSR, Australia and the United States contribute around 2.8m. tons. The hub of the United States mining has shifted from the Ozarks and New Jersey to the Mountain States. Canada's contribution has exceeded that of the United States since 1964 and USSR, Australia, Peru, and Japan have expanding outputs.

The United States is now a net importer of zinc ore and in 1969 lay fourth in world production of zinc with some 0.5m. tons in 1969 out of a world total of nearly 5.5m. tons — an increasing proportion of which is zinc produced from secondary (scrap, etc.) sources. Canada, Australia and Mexico are major exporters. Imports into the United Kingdom (like of those of lead and copper) show a preponderance of refined zinc over zinc ore; 226 000 tons as against 141 000 tons in 1973. Zinc is largely used with other metals to form zinc-based alloys, for galvanising iron sheets, and for brass products. Aluminium and plastics are increasingly employed as substitutes for some of the traditional uses. World price soared in the 1970s to over £850 a ton.

Tin

The tin mines and other tin deposits of Cornwall and the adjacent parts of Devonshire, which supplied the Phoenicians with tin 3 000 years ago, continued to be almost the sole source of supply of this metal until the end of the seventeenth century. The region is still the only significant place of production in Europe, but supplies from other parts of the world are now of overwhelming importance. In the years 1938—53 the annual production of tin ore in Great Britain, in terms of tin content, declined from 2 000 tons to under 1 000 tons, whereas world production in 1938 was 164 000 tons, and intensified production early in the Second World War brought the total in 1941 up to 241 000 tons. Nearly two-thirds of the world production came from southeast Asia, Malaysia alone supplying nearly 50 per cent. There was a big drop in production during the Japanese occupation of southeast Asia, and after the war the difficulty of securing new machinery (dredgers, etc.), coupled with the unrest in the Far East, made recovery a slow process. In 1962 world production was returned as 169 000 tons; Malaysia contributed 34 per cent, Indonesia 11 per cent, and with 8 per cent from Thailand, southeast Asia was again providing nearly 60 per cent. World production in 1971 was some 236 000 tons to which Malaysia contributed 32 per cent, Bolivia nearly 13 per cent, USSR an estimated 11.5 per cent, Thailand 9.1 per cent, China an estimated 8.4 per cent and Indonesia nearly 8.3 per cent. Bolivia is of outstanding importance. Before the war it made a good third to Malaysia and the Netherlands East Indies, with exports of 25 000 tons in 1938; and during the war it became the leading country of supply, a position it retained up to 1947, with annual exports of 30 000 to 40 000 tons. In 1957, with world production at 180 000 tons, it still rivalled Indonesia, both having exports of nearly 28 000 tons.

When prices declined, the International Tin Council imposed restrictions on exports, and in 1959 world production was down to 141 000 tons. The restrictions were removed in 1960; with rising demand prices soared and new sources of supply became an urgent need. In Africa Nigeria and Zaire are considerable sources. Under Belgian rule the latter provided about 15 000 tons a year. In 1971 6 500 tons were produced. In the same year the output from Nigeria was 7 300 tons. China is credited with 20 000 tons, Australia with 9 400 tons.

To a large extent Malaysia, Indonesia and Zaire have developed their own smelting industries, but tin is also extracted in the United Kingdom and the United States, both of which import quantities of ore.

Tin ore is met with either in veins (or lodes) in the rock, or in alluvial deposits. The former is called mine tin, the latter stream tin. The stream tin, being generally near the surface, is naturally the easier to obtain where it is abundant; and it is the abundance of such deposits in Malaysia that makes that part of the world such an important source of supply at the present day. Most of the tin ore of the world is the oxide, cassiterite, which being both heavy and stable, tends to be found concentrated at the base of gravel and can easily be separated by washing from the lighter constituents. Tin is mostly exported in the metallic state or as a concentrate for further refinement. It is largely used to cover sheets of iron or steel with a coating as a protection against rust, and thus to form tin-plates. Some 45 per cent of the world's tin is used for this purpose; another 20 per cent is used for solders, and some 15 per cent for metal alloys. World production of tin is fairly stable around 230 000 tons, increase in demand being offset by substitutes and improved techniques (such as tin-plating by electrolysis instead of hot-dipping) which reduce the requirement.

Mercury or quicksilver

Mercury, the only metal fluid at ordinary temperatures, has long been principally obtained in Europe from the Spanish mines of Almaden in the Sierra Morena, which were worked even under the Romans. In 1942, at the height of the Second World War, Spain supplied 75 per cent of the mercury imported into the United Kingdom, and in the following year 100 per cent. Other sources of supply include the Amiata mines in Tuscany (Italy), and the Idria mines in Carniola (formerly part of Austria—Hungary; in the possession of Italy between the two world wars; now held by Yugoslavia). While Italy had the Idria mines, her production of mercury marched with that of Spain, and even without them she has usually produced more than Spain. In 1969, however, Spain produced 2 200 tons against Italy's 1 847, the two providing nearly half the world supply of 9 440 tons. It is estimated that the USSR is now the world's third largest producer, with a probable output of 1 620 tons in 1969. After Europe, America leads (1 010 tons in 1969). In the middle of the last century, the New Almaden mines were opened in California (Santa Clara Co.) and were followed by the New Idria mines (San Benito Co.). Large quantities of mercury are produced in the United States, and at the close of the Second World War her production vied with that of Spain and Italy, as also did Mexico's, each of these four countries having an output in 1944 of some 1 200 tons. Canada has large reserves which she also developed as a war measure, but since then production has been small and erratic as has the production of the USA and Mexico.

The uses of mercury are various. In its pure state it is employed in the making of scientific instruments. Combined with other metals, it forms amalgams which are soft and easily fusible. An amalgam of mercury and tin was once largely used in the silvering of mirrors, but is now generally replaced by electro-deposits of silver. Silver and gold were extracted by employing mercury to form amalgams with them, and a large amount of mercury was employed for this purpose in the extensive silver mines of California and Nevada, near the chief seat of the United States production of quicksilver. The main industrial use is in the electrolytic preparation of chlorine and caustic soda, while increasing quantities are used for pharmaceutical purposes and in mildew-proof paints. In its major uses it has no substitutes as yet.

Iron and steel

The uses of iron are too numerous to specify, and for the most part too familiar to need specifying. No other metal is produced in such abundance or over so large an area of the world. As Chisholm wrote in the first edition: 'At the present day, indeed, none but the most backward tribes in a few out-of-the-way islands and corners are unacquainted with its working.' Its use in the past goes back to a remote antiquity. The iron implement brought to light in 1837 by J. R. Hill walled up in one side of the Great Pyramid of Giza carries us back over 5 000 years. The explanation of the rarity of ancient iron implements as compared with those of bronze is found in the fact that under the influence of air and moisture iron rusts so rapidly that its preservation is possible only under very exceptional conditions. So liable is it to disappear that, of all the numerous articles of iron that must have existed in ancient Egypt, the remnants that have been discovered do not weigh in all more than a few pounds, and this in a country with a dry climate specially suited to the preservation of such articles. The discoverers of the New World stated that the inhabitants of the parts at which they first touched, the West Indies and Darien, were unacquainted with iron, and their statements have frequently been taken to apply to the whole of America, including the civilised empires of Mexico and Peru. But against this there is the express testimony of several contemporaries of the first explorers — testimony from which it appears that the working of iron was practised before the arrival of the Spaniards in various parts of the American continent.

But ancient and widespread as the iron industry is, its rapid growth in modern times, and in particular since the close of the eighteenth century, is an astonishing fact, or would be so if we did not bear in mind the other great developments in industry and commerce within that period. In 1740 the whole production of iron in England is estimated to have been only about 18 000 tons; even in 1796, after the introduction of spinning machinery, only 125 000 tons. The enormous growth since then is the result of the vast demand for iron, converted into steel, in machinery, railways, shipbuilding, and the making of bridges and other structures. Iron is, in fact, the second of the two great material factors which form the basis of modern industry and commerce on a large scale, fuel being the other. The history of iron in many of its details is of singular interest, not only as showing how the volume of iron production has been raised to its present pitch, but also because some of the facts in that history have had an important effect on the geographical distribution of the industry.

Iron, like so many other metals, is not found native in nature but has to be extracted from ores, which exist in abundance throughout the world and which vary greatly in their richness and purity. The ores have to be smelted or reduced to a metallic condition by heat and chemical action, and the iron then sinks to the bottom of the furnace and is run off into moulds. This is what is called **pig iron** or **cast iron**, and is never pure. It contains a considerable proportion of carbon, of which pure charcoal is one of the forms; sometimes it contains substances much more injurious to its quality, the most prejudicial being **sulphur** and **phosphorus**. Even the carbon is injurious to some extent as it renders cast iron brittle. It is for this reason that, by driving out almost all the carbon, cast iron is converted into **wrought** or **malleable iron**, which does not harden greatly when cooled suddenly. This is usually effected by a process called puddling, which consists in remelting the cast iron on the hearth of a furnace, and stirring it when molten so that the carbon can escape and be burnt in the intensely heated air of the furnace. As the carbon escapes the iron is brought away in large lumps, and afterwards hammered into rude slabs called blooms, and rolled out to form bars, sheets, etc. In this form of iron there remains an admixture of slag or 'cinder'. The process of driving out the carbon was improved by the invention in 1784 of the reverberatory furnace, in which the charge of iron is placed in a separate chamber from the fuel and thus protected from the carburising action due to the combustion. This invention was due to Henry Cort in England, who in the previous year had introduced grooved rollers in rolling-mills for the production of bars of definite shapes.

The material so formed is very tenacious and tolerably hard, but for some purposes not sufficiently hard. For the making of most machinery, construction equipment, and cutlery of all sorts, a kind of iron is required which, besides being very tenacious, must also be flexible, elastic, and very hard; and for these and other purposes iron is converted into **steel**, which is nothing else than a form of iron containing a small proportion of carbon. The term steel is now confined to products which contain between 0.3 and 2.2 per cent carbon, enough to make them harden greatly when cooled suddenly, but not enough to prevent them from being usefully malleable. Special steels are produced by the addition of small quantities of chromium, nickel, titanium, etc.

The history of the iron industry consists in a gradual series of improvements in the methods by which all these processes are carried on. Only a few of the great steps in advance can here be mentioned. In many cases, the most important improvements, associated with the names of certain inventors, are only slight modifications of methods which in the course of the gradual development of this industry had been previously suggested; modifications, however, which were just what was needed to make the methods practically useful.

In ancient times, when the methods of working iron were primitive, good iron could be made only from the best ores, and hence districts containing ores of fine quality had the principal trade in iron. During the early history of Greece certain tribes inhabiting the northern slopes of the tableland of Asia Minor, to the west of Trebizond, among others the Chalybes, seem to have carried on a large trade in iron for this reason, and from them the Greeks derived their word *Chalups* for hard iron or steel. To the Romans were known many deposits of iron ore, including the rich ores of Bilbao, in the north of Spain. Remains of Roman ironworks are found in various parts of Great Britain, but so imperfect were their methods of smelting, so small a proportion of the iron was removed from the ore, that the slag or refuse material from the smelting furnaces of the Forest of Dean, in Gloucestershire, supplied ore for the furnaces of that region for a period of between 200 and 300 years in the seventeenth and eighteenth centuries.

Down to the late eighteenth century, one reason of the limited and costly production of iron was that wood or charcoal was the only fuel used in smelting; and this fact had an important effect both on the geographical distribution of the iron industry, and on the countryside in which that industry was long pursued. Iron could be smelted only in the neighbourhood of forests, and in process of time forests were cleared in feeding the furnaces. The forest from which the Weald takes its name perished in supplying fuel to the iron furnaces of Kent and Sussex, the last of which was blown out early in the nineteenth century. An English Parliamentary report of the year 1719 makes strong complaint of the devastations wrought by the ironworks in the counties of Warwick, Stafford, Worcester, Hereford, Monmouth, Gloucester and Salop. About twenty years later the English import of foreign iron was computed at about 20 000 tons annually – 10 per cent more than the home production. The greater abundance of wood was one important reason why the iron industry of Germany was greater than that of England in the earlier part of the eighteenth century.

Coal was first used with practical success in the smelting of iron by Dud Dudley (son of Lord Dudley) in 1619, but the practice was then followed only by himself, and the knowledge of it died with him. The use of coal in the form of coke was introduced by the Darbys of Coalbrookdale early in the eighteenth century, but the process was kept a secret by them, and it was not till after the middle of that century that it became generally known. Some coals, such as the splint coal of the Glasgow district, are capable of being used in the blast furnace even without being made into coke. Though the use of coke or coal is a great advance, such fuel does not make so pure an iron as charcoal, inasmuch as it usually contains sulphur and other impurities.

Besides coke or other fuel, it is necessary in the case of most kinds of iron ore to put into the smelting or blast furnace along with the ore a quantity of flux to facilitate the reduction. The material so employed is generally limestone or lime; and consequently facilities for obtaining this mineral form an important geographical factor affecting the location of the iron industry. For some kinds of ore, such as red hematite which contains 55—70 per cent of iron, this is not always required. Most kinds of ore, too, require to be roasted previously to being put in the blast furnace — an operated performed to reduce the bulk of the ore and at the same time to remove by burning most of the sulphur and other substances that can be volatilised. For red hermatite, again, this operation is considered unnecessary.

After the introduction of coal and coke in smelting, the next great step in the economising of fuel was the invention of hot-blast, that is, the practice of heating the air used in blowing the smelting furnaces to a high temperature before introducing it into the furnace. This invention, due to J. B. Neilson of Glasgow, was first applied in 1828. In 1832 more saving was effected (first in Germany) by using the waste gases of the furnace to heat the blast. About 1870, in the best constructed furnaces the blast had a temperature of only about 425° C (800° F), but afterwards it was sometimes raised to as high as 890° C (1 650° F). Such high temperatures were, however, found to be rapidly destructive to 'pipe stoves' of the old type, and these were consequently superseded by a new type of furnace in which the blast is usually maintained between 480° and 650° C (900° and 1 200° F). Blast furnaces have also been enlarged and improved in construction. In 1880 an outturn of 115 tons of iron per day was exceptionally large; now the normal output of an average furnace is up to 500 tons a day. Once a modern blast furnace is shut down it takes two months to restart it, or, if a new lining and hearth are required, about four months. The consumption of coal has been steadily reduced. In 1796 6 tons of coal were required to produce 1 ton of iron, 2 tons of coal (1.25 of coke) sufficed in 1900, and 0.6 tons of coke in 1970.

There are now many methods of producing **cast steel** on a large scale, and three of these are sufficiently widely practised to have a geographical interest. The first, introduced before 1860, is that which is associated with the name of Sir Henry Bessemer, being employed in the production of what is called Bessemer steel, although the method practised in most of the great iron countries involves an important improvement introduced by R. F. Mushet. By the Bessemer process molten pig-iron is poured into a vessel known as a converter lined with a highly refractory material, usually ganister, so arranged that cold air can be blown through the molten mass, burning away both the carbon and the silicon entirely. The due proportion of carbon is afterwards added and mixed with the fused metal by a repetition of the blowing. As originally devised, this process was found to be unsatisfactory except in the case of a few ores. The resulting product was very brittle, and Mushet's improvement consisted in adding the carbon in a compound containing manganese, which serves to correct the fault. The compounds employed are spiegeleisen and ferromanganese, which are made from certain iron ores rich in manganese, such as are found in Spain, the Siegerland district in Germany, Greece, Sweden, and elsewhere. When the iron ore used contains a sufficient amount of manganese, the use of spiegeleisen or ferromanganese is not necessary. The amount of iron that may be converted into steel in a single converter at one time by this process varies according to the capacity of the converter. A common size is the 12–15 ton Bessemer converter.

Another process, known as the Siemens-Martin or open-hearth process, differs from the Bessemer process only in that the operations are performed in a different kind of furnace, in which the air employed to remove the carbon plays over the molten metal instead of being blown through it. Some such furnaces even as early as 1902 had a capacity of as much as 100 tons. A common capacity is 50 to 80 tons.

Even with the improvement of Mushet these two processes are not applicable to all kinds of pig iron. Neither of them removes phosphorus if the pig iron contains it, and steel is rendered brittle by even a very slight proportion of this ingredient. In the best tool steel it is considered that the proportion of phosphorus should not exceed 1 part in 5 000, in bridge steel 1 in 2 000, and in rail steel 1 in 1 000, and with the increasing weight and speed of trains railway engineers became more exacting in this respect. The processes for making steel and ingot iron on a large scale can accordingly be applied in their original form only to iron made from ores in which phosphorus is not contained, or is present only in a very small amount indeed. Such ores are known comprehensively as Bessemer ores. In the Old World, the only ore from which iron of this quality can be made in large quantity is the hematite, which occurs in the northwest of England, in northern and southern Spain, in Greece, Sweden and Algeria, and on the island of Elba. So long, therefore, as no process was known for making cast steel on a large scale so as to overcome the above-mentioned drawback, the geographical distribution of these ores was obviously greatly in favour of the English iron and steel industry, for not only did England herself possess stores of the valuable ore in the most convenient situation, but ores from Italy, Spain, and Algeria could be landed after a sea voyage close beside the blast furnaces of Newport and Middlesbrough, whereas on the continent a railway journey, or at least a transhipment to river or canal boats, was in most cases necessary to bring them to the districts where the iron industry was pursued.

It was accordingly a discovery of the highest importance for the future distribution of the iron and steel industry when a method was devised by which phosphorus could be removed from the pig iron in the process of converting it into steel. A practicable method of doing this was invented by Mr Thomas and Mr Gilchrist of Middlesbrough, in association with others. The method consists in using for the lining of an ordinary Bessemer converter a composition which, while serving the other purposes of the lining, has a chemical action which will remove any phosphorus that may be present in the iron poured into the converter. Lime is mixed with the lining to serve as a 'base', with which the phosphorus, quitting the iron, may combine; and the process is hence known as the basic process. If the proportion of phosphorus be too great to be removed by that means alone, additional lime is added in the converter along with the metal. This process was first practically applied in 1879, and besides making the ores extracted round Middlesbrough (the Cleveland ores) for the first time available for the manufacture of mild steel or ingot iron, it enabled the mainland of Europe to compete with the United Kingdom in the iron industry more keenly than hitherto.

The basic process was first applied in the United States in 1890, but has since then made rapid progress. In the United Kingdom it was not so largely adopted as on the Continent and in the United States, the reason probably being that it was not so conveniently applied to the open-hearth as to the Bessemer method of making steel. Open-hearth plates were preferred by shipbuilders, who were major users of British steel. Later processes have, however, been devised for facilitating the manufacture of basic steel — in particular the basic oxygen process. By this process some 250 to 300 tons of steel can be produced every 45 minutes, as against 10 hours by the open-hearth method. In the United States and United Kingdom some 35 to 40 per cent of the output was produced by this method in 1969. As use of the open-hearth declines the proportion could rise to 85 per cent by 1980. The last Bessemer converter in the UK was closed in 1974.

Other changes in production techniques in the mid-twentieth century are concerned with the enrichment of the iron ore, the use of alternatives to coke as the main fuel, and the development of the flow method, rather than the traditional batch method of production. It is typical of the industry today that high grade ore and coking coal are conveyed great distances to the producers, in preference to the use of local supplies of inferior quality. This in turn requires giant ore carriers of 100 000 tons and over, adequate port facilities, and steelworks within reasonable distance of the coast. To minimise waste in transport, the richer ores are carried, and partial processing on the ore fields is increasingly producing prereduced ores such as 'Himet' and sponge iron with iron contents of over 90 per cent. By adding other minerals such as nickel it is possible to produce enriched ores which can be fed straight to the steel process. The study of alternative fuels is occasioned by the fact that although the coal reserves of the world are immense, those of good coking coal are not. The lower quality coals do not make good coke as they burn inefficiently and produce excessive slag. There are therefore experimental furnaces in North America and Europe employing oil, gas, natural liquid gas, powdered ('fluidised') coal and electricity in the search for the most efficient alternative — either to replace coke or to reduce still further the quantity required per ton of steel. The electrical furnaces offer advantages for ferro-alloys, high grade and special steels, particularly those using a high proportion of scrap as their raw material. In 1970 in the United States some 12 per cent of the steel output was produced by electric furnaces. Where there is ample hydroelectric power, as in Scandinavia, electric furnaces are also used for producing pig iron. All these developments tend to bring greater returns as the size of the plant increases. The optimum steel works of the future could well be an integrated plant, i.e. with a production line flow from raw material to finished product, on a single site with an output of some 10m. tons of steel a year.

In recent years various compounds of steel with other metals have been made for special purposes, increasingly with the use of the electric furnace. One of these is **nickel steel**, which contains from 3 to 3.5 per cent of nickel, and about 0.25 per cent of carbon, and is much tougher and stronger than ordinary steel, and yet extremely ductile. **Manganese steel**, which contains from 12 to 14 per cent of manganese and 1.5 per cent of carbon, has extraordinary tenacity, but appears to be too expensive a product for ordinary use. This largely arises from its extreme and irreducible hardness, which necessitates it being cut by special instead of the ordinary tools. **Chrome steel** contains about 2 per cent of chromium and 0.8 per cent of carbon. When suddenly cooled it is not only extremely hard but highly elastic. **Stainless steel**, contains about 13 per cent of chromium and other metals, according to the special type required. It resists corrosion, is non-toxic, and has many industrial uses. What is known as **high-speed steel** is an alloy containing in its best varieties between 5 and 6 per cent of chromium and about 18 per cent of tungsten, with less than 1 per cent carbon. It remains hard at a temperature of even 400° C (760° F), and is used in the manufacture of turning lathes, a process in which great friction develops very high temperatures. Where lightness as well as great hardness and power of resisting shock is important, as in the steel used in some parts of automobiles, a small quantity of vanadium is now frequently combined with chromium. Steel containing both nickel and chromium is used in aircraft production, and many other compounds are specially manufactured for specific industrial uses.

From the nature of the **iron industry** it follows that it is mostly developed in those countries which stand first in commerce and manufacturing industry generally. As a strategic industry it attracts government controls and protection, and is often the first industry to be developed in newly industrialised nations. The consumption of iron and steel is relatively high in three main areas; transportation, in the construction of railways, bridges, ships, automobiles, etc.; construction, in the building of harbours, factories, etc.; and in constructing machinery.

Table 27 — **Production of iron ore*** (in million tons)

Country	1913	1929	1948	1960	1967	1971
USSR	—	7.7	16.2	61.4	90.3	110.3
USA	61.9	73.0	50.8	47.8	50.3	48.8
Canada	—	—	1.4	10.7	23.4	27.0
Sweden	7.3	11.2	8.2	13.0	17.6	21.6
France	21.5	49.9	7.5	21.7	16.0	17.1
Australia	—	—	1.3	2.8	12.3	39.6
United Kingdom	16.0	13.2	3.9	4.7	3.6	2.9
World total	135.0	161.0	103.5	232.2	339.8	428.7

* Figures for 1913 and 1929 refer to total iron ore produced; figures for 1948 onward are for iron content of all ore produced.

The United Kingdom, which led the world in the production of iron ore till near the end of the nineteenth century, is now seventeenth in the world production list. The United States, which began to outstrip the United Kingdom in 1889 and went ahead by erratic leaps and bounds, reaching an annual output of over 100m. tons both during the Second World War (in 1942 and 1943) and was surpassed in production by the USSR in 1958. Sweden has increased production steadily, while prominent new competitors are China (whose estimated output jumped from 3m. tons in 1950 to 24.2m. tons in 1971), Canada and Australia.

Table 28 — **Annual production of pig iron and ferro-alloys**

Country	Million tons					Percentages				
	1913	1938	1962	1967	1971	1913	1938	1962	1967	1971
USA	28.1	29.1	61.4	81.2	75.7	39	32	24	24	17
USSR	4.0	14.5	55.3	74.8	89.3	6	16	21	21	20
Japan	—	0.5	18.5	41.0	74.6	—	—	7	12	17
West Germany	17.3	16.2	24.5	27.5	30.2	24	18	9	8	7
France	4.8	6.6	14.2	15.9	18.7	7	7	6	5	5
UK	9.7	7.7	13.9	15.4	15.4	14	8	5	4.5	4
Total of above six countries	63.9	74.6	180.6	255.8	303.9	90	81	72	75	70
World total	71.0	91.5	267.3	356.8	437.1			100		

The production of pig iron has also fluctuated considerably in the leading countries, but throughout the years covered by the table over-leaf, the United States held the lead until recent years. Germany, formerly second, has twice suffered setback through her defeat in world wars, and West Germany now ranks fourth, first place having been

Table 29 — Annual production of crude steel (ingots and castings) in million tons

Country	1913	1938	1944	1946	1962	1969	1971
USA	31.3	28.3	80.0	59.5	89.2	128	109
USSR	–	17.5	–	11.8	76.3	110	121
Japan	–	–	–	1.7	27.5	86	86
West Germany	17.3	22.3	18.0	2.7	32.6	45	40
UK	7.7	10.4	12.1	12.7	20.8	28	24
France	4.6	6.0	3.0	4.3	17.2	20	23
Total of above six countries	60.9	84.5	113.1	92.7	263.6	417	403
Percentage of total	81	79	76	86	74	79	75
Total world production	75.4	107.6	148.0	107.7	360.7	530	575

taken by the USSR, and third place by Japan. In recent years Britain and France have had much the same output (between 16 and 18m. tons). Both have been overtaken by China (not listed in Table 27) but with an estimated 27m. tons in 1971.

The figures for production of crude steel (ingots and castings) in Table 29 show that in 1969 the United States still headed the list and the USSR was second. Japan had risen rapidly to third place having quadrupled her output between 1960 and 1970. The 'big six' countries listed produce about 80 per cent of the world's iron and steel, but many countries have now entered the ranks of producers. Each of the following made more than 10m. tons of steel in 1971: Canada, Italy, Czechoslovakia, Poland, China and Belgium. Sweden's manufacture of iron and steel is favoured by plentiful supplies of hydroelectric power, but her production absorbs only a small part of her output of iron ores, which are excellent and much in demand for export.

The iron and steel industry is so important to the economic development of industrialised nations that it is universally subject to varying degrees of government interest. This varies from full control over the home industry, through tariffs, quotas and export credits to active participation in ensuring an adequate supply of raw materials. The markets for the finished products are also seldom completely free. For example, the industry was greatly assisted in Germany and the United States (as well as in other countries) by protective tariffs securing so far as possible the home market. The extent and importance of the market so secured should be noted, for within its own borders the United States offers the largest (the wealthiest, though not the most populous) free trade market in the world for the products of this as of most other industries, and pre-1913 Germany (the German Customs Union) was one of the largest on the mainland of Europe.

Table 30 — Estimated reserves of iron ore

Country	Actual reserves (millions of tons)		Potential reserves (millions of tons)	
	Ore	Iron content	Ore	Iron content
Europe	12 032	4 733	41 029	12 085 + considerable
America	9 855	5 154	81 822	40 731 + enormous
Australia	136	74	69	37 + considerable
Asia	260	156	457	283 + enormous
Africa	125	75	Many thousand	Many thousand
	22 408	10 192	> 123 377	> 53 136 + enormous

The great markets for steel products are, however, the industrial countries. Machinery of all types and transportation equipment account for some 30 per cent by value of all world trade in the mid-twentieth century, and the growing world population will ensure that the demand continues. The greatly increased consumption of iron in recent years has aroused apprehensions as to the possible exhaustion of the supply. These apprehensions were being expressed as long ago as the Eleventh International Geological Congress held at Stockholm in 1910. The results given in the summary of the returns by Professor Hjalmar Sjögren at that time are admittedly to be regarded as only very rough estimates, but they are here reproduced (Table 30) for comparison with the position in 1970. The reserves are classed as actual and potential, according as they refer to areas then actually worked, or areas containing ores that might become available through new discoveries or improved recovery techniques.

As the present annual production of pig iron is well over 350m. tons, and that of steel has reached 550m. tons, it might appear that the 'actual' reserves would not suffice for many years. Since the date of this survey vast new deposits have been located in many parts of the world, for example in the USSR, South America, eastern Canada, Australia and Africa. Known reserves now total no less than 248 000m. tons and potential reserves another 205 000m. As with coal, the reserves are plentiful and are greatly augmented by re-cycled iron and steel.

Salt

This product, so universally used and so widely distributed, is more an article of local production in almost all countries than an article of international commerce. It is obtained both from deposits on the land (rock salt and brine pits) and by the evaporation of sea water. World production is estimated at 133m. tons, of which China is credited with

15m. tons, while the United States output is over 40m. tons. The United Kingdom and West Germany each produce about 8.5m. tons, France, Canada, and India each about 5m., Italy 3 to 4m., Mexico over 3m. tons. Except for China, these are all exporters of salt, as are also the Netherlands, Poland, Romania, Egypt, Tunisia, Aden, Mexico, the West Indies, Taiwan and Thailand. Exceptionally, the list in 1959 was headed by Canada, with exports of over 1m. tons. The United Kingdom has the largest consumption of salt per head, due largely to the use of this mineral in the chemical industry. **Natron** is a low grade, naturally-occurring mineral salt found in the Sahara regions and in Mexico; it is used in the chemical industry.

Other minerals

Antinomy, employed to give hardness to softer metals in various alloys, more particularly in the making of type metal, bell metal, and Britannia metal; also used for making antimonial lead for storage batteries, for pigments and for fire-proofing. Consumption has increased steadily to a total of 65 600 tons of ore (antimony content) in 1969. South Africa (18 000 tons) is the main source, followed by Bolivia and China.

Manganese, an indispensable constituent of certain compounds of great importance in the making of steel. One of its ores, known as the black oxide of manganese or pyrolusite, is also largely used in the manufacture of bleaching powder, and as a decoloriser in glass-making. The annual production of manganese ore (in metal content) rose to 7.3m. tons in 1969. The USSR provided 2.3m. tons, South Africa 1m., Brazil over 900 000 tons, Gabon, India and Australia each around 500 000 tons. These countries supply 6m. tons or 83 per cent of the total. The ore is largely exported by the minor contributors, and very largely imported by the United States; the United Kingdom, Japan, France, West Germany, Norway, and Poland are also large importers. Manganese ores are found in Merioneth and elsewhere in Great Britain, but production is negligible. In the United States considerable supplies of manganese ores are worked, chiefly in Minnesota, Montana, and New Mexico. The metal manganese is used in various alloys. With copper it produces a very tenacious kind of bronze; with copper and zinc, sometimes with the addition of a little iron and nickel, a substance resembling nickel. Total production reached 8.2m. tons in 1971.

Chromium, a metal occurring in nature chiefly in the form of chromate of iron or chrome iron ore, is an important constituent in stainless steel-making. It is also used in the manufacture of bichromate of potash, from which various pigments are derived. Chromium plating has largely replaced nickel plating as it gives a bright metallic surface, which is stainless and does not tarnish. World production of chrome ore was 2.53m. tons in 1969, the main sources being USSR (710 000 tons), South Africa (539 000 tons), Turkey (260 000 tons) Albania (172 000 tons, estimate) and the Philippines (168 000 tons). Chromium-cobalt alloys, sometimes with the addition of tungsten or molybdenum, are used under the name of stellite in the making of high-speed cutting tools containing no iron.

Molybdenum is a refractory metal belonging to the tungsten and uranium group. Some 80 per cent is used in the manufacture of special steels, and the balance in high-temperature alloys and chemical applications. It is in more ample supply than other steel additives such as tungsten, titanium, vanadium, etc. With a world production of 73 820 tons in 1969. Some 60 per cent was produced by the United States (45 000 tons), Canada (13 740 tons), USSR, Chile and Peru. United Kingdom imports in 1973 were 11 000 tons valued at £10m.

Vanadium is extracted from the ore petronite and, as one of the hardest metals, is added to high-grade steels such as those used in tool making to improve toughness and strength. Some 85 per cent of the total production goes to steel manufacture, the balance is used in non-ferrous alloys and as a catalyst in chemical manufacure, e.g. of sulphuric acid. World production of the ore has risen steadily from 970 tons (vanadium content) in 1948 to 11 500 tons in 1971. Main suppliers are the United States (50 per cent), South and Southwest Africa, and Finland.

Titanium belongs to the carbon, silicon group of metals. The chief ores are ilmenite and rutile, and are mined largely in the United States, Canada, Australia, and Norway. As with the other 'new' metals which have increased in industrial importance since the Second World War, its main use is in the manufacture of high grade steels — particularly for the aircraft and aerospace industry. It is also used as a pigment in paints and dyestuffs. The United Kingdom import of ore, mainly ilmenite, was some 410 000 tons valued at £7.9m. in 1973. Imports of titanium oxide were mainly for paints.

Arsenic is another metal chiefly used, not by itself but in its compounds. Derived as a byproduct of copper refining it is manufactured in the United States, Germany, England, and elsewhere for use in the manufacture of weed-killers and insecticides, and in the preparation of green pigments and wood preservatives.

Bismuth, chiefly used as a catalyst to give increased fusibility to various metallic alloys, and in making certain colouring matters. The ore is produced, often as a byproduct of lead refining, mainly in Peru, Japan, Mexico, Bolivia and Canada.

Platinum, a rare metal, but indispensable in the chemical arts on account of its resistance to heat and acids, which renders it the best material for making crucibles and vessels required for certain purposes. Over 90 per cent goes to industrial uses (electrical, chemical, glass making and as a catalyst in petroleum refining) and only some 5 per cent to jewellery and decorative purposes. World production was 100 000 kg (3.3m. troy ounces) in 1968, two-thirds from USSR and the balance mainly from South Africa and Canada. Large reserves have recently been found in Australia.

Nickel, formerly produced in Germany, is now mainly produced in Ontario in Canada, nearly half of the world's supply being obtained in the Sudbury district. Increased production from Australia and New Caledonia combined with that of the USSR will shortly reduce the Canadian proportion to one-third. Forty per cent of total supply is used in stainless steel-making, and the rest for special alloys and plating. World production was 692 000 tons of ore in 1971.

Cobalt, in one of its forms, is found associated with nickel, and as such it is chiefly used in high-temperature alloys, in the arts, in the form of the oxide as a blue colouring matter for pottery and glass; smalt (finely ground glass coloured with this oxide) is used in colouring paper, etc. Zaire supplies nearly half of the annual world production of some 23 000 tons.

Aluminium is a metal valuable for its lightness, its resistance to the action of air even in the presence of moisture, and the excellence of its alloys, especially aluminium—magnesium (Duralumin). Aluminium is now sometimes used for the transmission of electrical currents, giving nearly twice the carrying power of copper. The metal is made from two compounds found in nature: cryolite, obtained from the west coast of Greenland, and now of minor importance; and bauxite, mined in large quantities in many countries. The bauxite ore is refined to form alumina and this enriched ore is then smelted to produce aluminium. Some 4 tons of bauxite produce 2 tons of alumina and 1 ton of aluminium. The world production of 3.9m. tons of bauxite in 1938 increased during the Second World War to 13.4m. tons in 1943; and by 1971 it had reached nearly 64m. tons. Though Jamaica did not begin to produce bauxite till 1952, that country headed the list with over 12m. tons. Other leading producers were Australia (12m.), Surinam (6.7m.), USSR (4.4m.), Guyana (4.3m.) and France (3.1m.).

The metal is extracted by means of an electric furnace. Very high temperature being required, aluminium factories are usually erected where hydroelectric power is available, as at Niagara Falls, on the Saguenay River in Canada, in Norway, on the Pacific coast of North

America, and at Kinlochleven in the Scottish Highlands. Increasingly however new smelters are being erected nearer to the industrial markets. World production of aluminium in 1971 was 10m. tons, mainly in the United States (3.6m. tons).

Aluminium production has increased sixfold since the Second World War. As one of the new light metals its main uses are in transportation (car and aircraft manufacture: lightweight containers), in the construction industry, and in the electrical and consumer durable industries. It is increasingly employed in alloys which are made specifically for new industrial techniques. Large deposits of bauxite in Australia, Guinea and Jamaica, together with extensive reprocessing of scrap, should ensure supplies for several hundred years.

Tungsten or *Wolfram*, which has considerable importance in the production of high-speed steel and high-temperature alloys, was mined in Cornwall, but is now obtained mainly in China and USSR (nearly half of the world's production of 46 510 tons in 1971) and to a less extent in Korea, the United States, Bolivia, Australia and Portugal.

Sulphur, used in making sulphuric acid, in vulcanising and as a remedy for certain vine diseases. It is exported as elemental sulphur occurring in a free state, chiefly from the United States and Mexico, and, as a constituent of iron and cupreous pyrites, chiefly from Spain, Portugal, Cyprus, and Norway. The great bulk of the world production of native sulphur comes from the United States (chiefly Texas; balance from Louisiana, Mexico and the USSR). The United States also has a large production of sulphur derived from pyrites (chiefly Tennessee) and, as a byproduct, from petroleum refineries and gas plants.

Mineral fertilisers. Among these the most important are: (*a*) **potash**. Germany (East and West) and France have long been the chief contributors, producing 57 per cent of the world's supply of 9m. tons in 1960. By 1971 production was 19.8m. tons with USSR and Canada as the major producers. (*b*) **nitrate of soda**, and other nitrogenous fertilisers. Practically the entire supply of natural nitrates (about 1.25m. tons) used to come from northern Chile, in the form of nitrate of soda. At the time of the First World War this Chilean natural product constituted the bulk of the world's supply of nitrogen compounds, but it is now only a fraction of the total, owing to the increase of manufactured nitrogen compounds, amounting to upwards of 20m. tons, which are widely used as artificial fertilisers, including those produced by hydroelectric power in Norway and elsewhere by the fixation of atmospheric nitrogen. (*c*) **phosphate of lime**, from the phosphate-rock (85m. tons in 1971), found most abundantly in the United States (Florida and Tennessee); in the USSR, Morocco and Tunisia; and in various islands in the Pacific and Indian Oceans, notably Nauru, and Christmas Islands. (*d*) **guano**, consisting of the droppings of birds accumulated through the ages in regions where there is little or no rain to wash away the deposits. It is worked as a mineral, and may be described as an earthy nitrate or combined nitrate and phosphate rock — a subdivision of group (*c*). The classic example of guano deposits on a large scale is their occurrence in the Lobos Islands, off the coast of Peru, which produced 57 000 tons in 1967 in spite of increasing competition from chemical fertilisers.

Borax, a compound of boracic acid and soda, found in many parts of the world with a very dry climate, such as the states of California and Nevada in the United States, the western strip of Peru and Chile, Tibet and Turkey, and also manufactured from boracic acid obtained by concentration from springs in the south of Tuscany. It has very varied uses in the arts. Among the most important are its employment in the making of enamel and glazes for pottery, and in the making of certain kinds of glass, the borax serving to some extent as a substitute for silica. It is also used for softening water.

Nitrate of potash (*saltpetre*). See pp. 308—11.

Graphite or *plumbago*, popularly known as 'black lead', a substance familiar from its domestic uses and its use in the making of lead pencils, but also very largely employed in making crucibles and type metal and for other purposes. Formerly the best kind was obtained from Borrowdale in Cumberland, but the chief source of supply is now Korea. Other sources include Mexico, Malagasy, Sri Lanka and Japan. In Europe graphite is produced in Austria, Germany, Norway, Italy and Czechoslovakia. The United States has some supplies. World output is some 350 000 tons, and imports into the United Kingdom some 10 000 tons a year.

Lithographic stone is known to occur in various places, but the best stones are all obtained from the quarries of Solenhofen in the neighbourhood of Donauwörth in Bavaria. Now largely superseded by zinc plates and photographic processes.

Grinding and polishing substances. (*a*) **Buhrstones** are the stones used in the old kind of corn-mills, now superseded by steel rollers. The best specimens of this kind of stone are obtained in the Paris basin. (*b*) **Grindstones** were formerly produced at Newcastle, at Wickersley (near Sheffield), and elsewhere in England; at various places on the Bay of Fundy in Canada; and in Ohio and Michigan in the United States, now almost entirely superseded. (*c*) **Infusorial earth**, or tropoli powder, is a fine siliceous earth used in polishing metals, glass, etc., and also in the manufacture of dynamite, found not only in Tripoli, from which it takes one of its names, but more abundantly in Germany, on the Lüneburg Heath, between the Elbe and the Aller, and also in Scotland, France, Maryland (US), and elsewhere.

Gypsum is a sulphate of lime and is often deposited in the drying up of salt lakes. It is produced most abundantly in the United States, Canada, Great Britain, France, and Spain. It is used in the manufacture of Plaster of Paris and other plasters.

Clays. Vast quantities of clay are used in the manufacture of bricks, roofing tiles, sanitary ware and other purposes. It is a plastic material composed of silica and silicates of aluminium with small quantities of iron, potash, etc. The world tendency is towards large-scale works. The two special types of clay which have high unit value are china-clay and fire-clay. (*a*) Among producers of **china-clay**, the United States closely heads the list, and is followed by Great Britain. In Britain the clay occurs in large pockets in the granite masses of Cornwall and Devon and annual exports are some 2m. tons valued at £25m. Besides being used in the making of porcelain it is employed in the making of paper and as an inert filler in many products. (*b*) **Fire-clay** is used in making fire-resisting bricks, crucibles, etc. In Great Britain the deposits chiefly worked are those found in certain coalfields (south Staffordshire, Glamorgan, Durham).

Asbestos is a fibrous, non-inflammable mineral found in igneous rocks and has a great variety of uses — for the making of fireproof curtains, as a packing for cylinders, and as a heat insulating covering for boilers and pipes, for making fireproof paint, wall decorations, clothing for furnacemen and others. World production in 1971 was 4.8m. tons, much of which was derived from Canada south of the St Lawrence. The other half was provided almost entirely by the USSR, South Africa, Rhodesia, China, the United States, and Brazil. United Kingdom imports of 180 000 tons came almost exclusively from Canada, South Africa and Swaziland.

Ganister, a fine hard pure sandstone derived from the Lower Coal Measures, used for lining furnaces, is obtained for British use chiefly from the neighbourhood of Sheffield.

Fluorspar is chiefly produced in Mexico, China, the USSR, Germany, the United States, and Italy. In 1962 these six countries produced, in quantities ranging from 300 000 tons down to 150 000 tons, nearly 75 per cent of the world output of 1.6m. tons. Four secondary sources of supply — France, Spain, the United Kingdom (mainly Derbyshire), and South Africa — made up another 20 per cent of the total. Fluorspar is used in lead smelting and in the making of ferrosilicon and ferro-manganese.

Slate is less used than formerly for roofing but the waste, when finely powdered, is used in the making of bricks of great density and strength.

Building stones. Building stones are widely quarried for local use but some have special characters which give them an international reputation. Amongst the latter are certain fine-grained limestones which split equally well in any direction and hence are called 'freestones'. The freestones or oolitic limestones of Bath and Portland in Britain are famous. Certain granites are also important, and there is a considerable trade in marbles. United Kingdom imports of marble and granite are some 15 000 tons each, while exports of stone (and sand) are in excess of 2m. tons.

Road metal. A stone suitable for use as a road metal must be tough, must not be splintery, and must not when broken give much dust. Provided these qualities are present, local material is used. Various igneous rocks, especially basalts, are particularly good.

Cement and lime. The burning of limestone for lime is an important industry but even greater is the manufacture of Portland cement from impure earthy limestones or from limestone mixed with mud or clay. The manufacture is more and more concentrated in large units. With the development all over the world of building in reinforced concrete there has been a vast expansion in the production and use of cement. World production doubling to over 500m. tons between 1957 and 1970. USSR, USA and Japan are the largest producers. As with road metal transport costs are high and where suitable raw materials are available there is a corresponding advantage in local production. But it is difficult to avoid the production of much dust so that cement-making has to be classed as an industry with noxious characters where local residential and agricultural land is concerned.

Sand and gravel. The use of concrete involves also the need for vast quantities of sand and gravel. Since gravel is most easily worked in the superficial deposits marking the terraces or flood plains of rivers there is a danger of large areas of good agricultural land being destroyed in the process of working. Shingle from sea and lake shores is extensively used. Building in concrete blocks and other forms of artificial stone has proved a strong rival to the use of natural stone.

Radium and uranium are metallic chemicals extracted from pitch-blende, uranium oxide. Radium was formerly the valued constituent with medical and photographic uses, but the developments which have followed the production of the atomic bomb have made uranium far more important commercially. The military requirement and the expansion of enrichment techniques gave rise to a rapid growth in demand immediately after the war. This was followed by a slowing down of production and the closing of some mines while research and development of civil uses for nuclear power went ahead. This industry makes heavy demands on advanced technological skills and development was slow during the 1960s, but as the number of nuclear-powered electricity stations increases so the demand for uranium will increase. With an estimated world reserve of 1m. tons of uranium oxide, production in 1971 was some 25 500 tons, with 60 per cent coming from the main suppliers: the United States, Canada and South Africa. Large and rich deposits have been found in Australia and production will commence in the late 1970s as the new power stations come into operation. In 1969 less than 3 per cent of the total electricity generated was from nuclear powered stations — some 24 000 MW. Under present plans this figure should increase tenfold by the end of the century to provide some 30 per cent of all power generated.

Manufactured articles in which various materials are used

Leather

Leather consists of the skins of animals prepared in various ways. Its manufacture has given rise to an extensive commerce in articles of different kinds: first, in the hides and skins which form the raw material (see p. 244); second, in the substances used in treating this raw material; and third, in the manufactured product — leather, and articles made from leather.

Tanning is the principal process in converting hides into leather. It consists in saturating the hides, after preliminary cleaning and dressing, with a solution which alters the chemical character of the constituents of the hide, and renders it firm and durable. Traditionally this solution was derived from some vegetable substance, the bark or some other portion of a tree or other plant, which yielded tannin, or tannic acid, a very powerful astringent. Substances containing tannin exist in the native vegetation of almost all parts of the world, and the discovery of the art of making leather appears to have been made independently in many different regions at a very early date. The processes of tanning are represented on the older Egyptian monuments, and the North American Indians knew how to make a pliant and excellent leather before the European discovery of America. On the other hand the art was unknown throughout a large part of central Africa south of the Sudan.

Till just over 100 years ago, oak bark was the agent almost exclusively used for tanning in Great Britain; now it is only one of fifty or more competitors, chiefly extracts of wattle bark and quebracho, and myrobalans; though other barks and bark extracts including gambier, sumach, valonia and divi-divi are also notable tanning agents. In 1959 the United Kingdom imports of myrobalans, and of extracts for tanning (quebracho, wattle bark, etc.) amounted to 43 000 tons valued at £2.2m. In 1960 the figures were down to 38 000 tons valued at £1.7m., and in 1973 to 12 000 tons valued at £1.3m. Extracts now predominate: a result of the growing tendency to engage in the partial manufacture of raw materials in the country of origin, both to save freight and to promote local industry.

Barks include different kinds of oak bark, larch bark and others found in Britain and elsewhere in the northern hemisphere; also mangrove bark from tropical and subtropical regions. **Wattle bark and extract** come chiefly from Natal, with Kenya as a more recent source of supply. In Natal the wattle bark is derived from various species of acacia, the best being that of the *Acacia pycnantha*, Benth., or black wattle (introduced from Australia), a bark that yields nearly a third of its weight of tannin. Both in the United States and in Canada hemlock spruce bark is one of the principal tanning agents. Bark from the native oak is still used for the best leather, as it is in Canada, but supplies are becoming very scarce and are mostly confined to the southern Appalachian region. Chestnut trees were formerly the third most important source of tannin in the United States, but supplies have dwindled almost to nothing, because most of the trees have died of chestnut blight. There is a considerable import of tanning agents into the States.

Myrobalans are imported chiefly from India. They are the fruits mainly of two species of trees of the genus *Terminalia*, abundant in Indian forests, and are the principal substances used in India for tanning.

Quebracho, from Argentina and Paraguay, is used for the rapid tanning of cheap leather. It is an extract from the wood of a tree, *Aspidosperma Quebracho*, Schlect., native to the forests of the Parana—Paraguay basin, and is exported in very large quantities, especially to the United States. Soaring prices after the Second World War led to a decline in the demand, but there has since been a recovery.

Gambier is extracted from the leaves of a shrub (*Uncaria Gambier*, Roxb.), belonging botanically to the Cinchona family, a native of the Malay Peninsula and the Eastern Archipelago. It is also used in dyeing, and in China is much used for chewing, along with betelnut. Having the tannin concentrated by the process of extraction, 1 ton of gambier will go as far as 6 tons of oak bark in tanning. **Sumach** consists of the powdered leaves and young twigs chiefly of one species of shrub (*Rhus coriaria*, L.), and is imported from the Mediterranean, above all from Sicily, where the best quality is cultivated. **Valonia** is the name given to the acorn-cups of a species of oak which grows in Turkey, used in dyeing as well as tanning. Of other vegetable substances used for tanning the best known perhaps is **divi-divi**, which consists of the twisted pods of a leguminous tree known as *Caesalpinia coriaria*, Willd., a native of South America.

Attempts to tan with mineral substances were made for about 100 years before the successful development of 'chrome tanning' with compounds of chromium. Most of the light leathers now produced are tanned by means of chromium salts.

For certain purposes skins are made into leather without tanning. A soft flexible kind of leather suitable for gloves, etc., is made by a process called tawing, in which alum and other salts are the principal substances employed. **Wash-leather,** or chamois leather, is made by working oil into the cleaned skins. **Morocco leather** when genuine is made from goatskin, is always coloured on one side, and on that side has the well-known roughened surface imparted to it by means of a stamp, generally of boxwood. It takes its name from the country, Morocco, through which it was first introduced into Europe having been manufactured in northern Nigeria. It was introduced by the Moors into Spain, where Cordova and other Moorish cities acquired celebrity in connection with this product, so that the name of cordova leather or cordwain came to be applied as a general term for Spanish goatskin leather. About the middle of the eighteenth century the manufacture was introduced into Alsace, and since then it has been carried to all other industrial countries. For centuries Spain supplied fancy leathers to all Europe. Russian leather is distinguished by its peculiar odour, which is so disagreeable to insects that the presence of a few books in this leather in a bookcase is said to be enough to preserve the other volumes from their attacks. The odour is due either to the leather being tanned with the bark of the Russian birch, or to its being treated with a kind of oil made from the bark and roots of that tree.

The European countries in which the manufacture of articles from leather is most highly developed are Germany, France, and the United Kingdom. West Germany is especially noted for its coloured leathers. France stands pre-eminent in its glove manufacture and is also noted for its lacquered or patent leather, a product first made in that country about the middle of the eighteenth century. Of the British exports of leather manufactures, the most important are boots and shoes — nearly 4.5m. pairs valued at £1.5m. in 1938; over 7m. pairs, wholly or mainly of leather, valued at £11m. in 1960; and 16m. pairs in 1973 valued at £35.5m. — a reflection of increased costs and the fall in the value of money. Imports are also considerable. The United States also has a large industry in leather, but, as with many other countries, manmade substitutes are increasingly important.

Paper

The history of paper-making is of peculiar interest. The ancients used parchment and papyrus rolls, the latter being made from the thin inner skins found at the bottom of the stems of a rush which grows in the Nile delta. The process was laborious and the rolls were costly, yet Egypt carried on a large and lucrative trade in them, and vast thickets of papyrus grew where now are fields of cotton, maize, rice, etc.

The art of paper-making originated in China about AD 105. The inventor, Tsai Lun, became the god of the paper-makers. From China the art spread into central Asia and is known to have been established at Samarkand early in the eighth century AD, when the town was in the hands of the Arabs. They introduced it into Spain, and it is known that linen rags were being used for the purpose of paper-making before the close of the twelfth century. It was probably for this reason that a small district situated south of Valencia in Spain, which had been celebrated in Roman times for its flax, was equally celebrated in the twelfth century for the excellence of its paper, which was widely exported.

The art of paper-making was first established in England in 1490 when the first British paper-maker set up a mill in Hertford. During the sixteenth century a paper-mill was erected at Dartford, in Kent, which county is still noted for its paper-making. Paper was first manufactured by hand with rags as raw material. The industry was, however, revolutionised by the invention in 1798 of the first mechanical paper-making machine by a Frenchman called Robert. His machine was further developed in England by the mechanic, Bryan Donkin, and the growth of the mechanical process of paper-making led to the search for ample and continuous supplies of fresh raw materials. With the coming of the Industrial Revolution during which intense development of industry was compressed into a short period of time it was urgent that greatly increased supplies of paper should be made available, and this need hastened the development of paper-making machines. These early machines were slow and cumbersome but they turned out paper at a much faster rate than the old hand craftsmen. Paper was no longer a luxury and as more became available and more people learned to write, more wanted to send letters to friends. In those days there were no such things as envelopes, private letters were just folded and tucked in so that anyone could read them. In 1839 the Treasury offered a prize for the best sealed cover in which to send letters and this was won by a William Mulready with an elaborate design made of paper. One result was the introduction of the penny post in 1840.

Paper-making machines have two main functions: (a) to receive a mixture of beaten pulp, with about ninety-nine times its weight of water, and to intermesh the fibres; (b) to remove the water stage by stage, so that the intermeshed fibres are left as a dry sheet. This is done by carrying the pulp on a continuous wire mesh in the first stage, and then, after a great deal of water has drained away, drying the formed paper over heated cylinders in the second stage. The chief raw material is wood pulp. It far exceeds all others, and can be either in a mechanical processed form (i.e. simply ground from the log and cooked), which is suitable for low-grade papers such as newsprint; or in other chemically processed forms from which various types of paper are made, many dependent on a specific type of pulp for the usage to which the paper will be put.

Supplies of wood pulp for paper-making (derived from spruce, fir, poplar, etc.) come largely from the rigorous Northern climate, the main centres being in Scandinavia, North America, USSR and Newfoundland. In these centres trees are cut, pulled into streams and rivers, and floated down to the pulping plants, which are often adjacent to the actual paper-mill. In recent years attempts have been made to extend the habitat of certain trees which are indigenous to northern countries, but which grow more prolifically in temperate climates. Advantage is being taken of the more rapid growing qualities of such trees in a temperate climate by establishing new paper-mills in, for instance, India, New Zealand, Tasmania, and the southern USA. New methods of pulp preparation promise to make it possible to use a wide range of woods, including oak and ash and many 'local' timbers, such as eucalyptus. Additional new raw materials are now being brought into use, such as 'bagasse' (a residual product of sugarcane), bamboo, and straw; and the industry is continually experimenting with other raw materials which seem promising. Reprocessed waste paper is also an important raw material — increasingly so as the cost of wood pulp rises. Bagasse and bamboo are particularly indicative of a modern trend in the siting of paper-mills; this is to take the mill to the raw material rather than to transport the pulp to the mill.

Esparto grass, which is grown in large quantities in North Africa, is used for fine-grade writing and printing papers. The mills using this raw material have, to a marked extent, established themselves in the Central Lowlands of Scotland and approximately 20 000 tons of esparto pulp are imported yearly. Linen rags, cotton and other vegetable fibrous materials, which were the sole raw materials of the paper-making industry before the Industrial Revolution, are now used only for various specialised purposes, and are also mixed with other materials.

Since the 1960s, plastics have gained ground in competition with paper — both in a continuous sheet form and as a raw material (in the form of fibres) for the conventional paper-making processes. Plastics offer a range of textured surfaces, can be treated to accept printing ink and are inherently stable and free from deterioration. They are also resistant to water and grease, and are difficult to tear. They are increasingly used for wrapping purposes and as an alternative for high-gloss, coated papers.

Estimates of the consumption of paper *per capita* per annum in different countries vary greatly. The United States easily heads the list as regards the consumption of newsprint. According to the *Statistical Yearbook* of the United Nations, the *per capita* consumption in 1972 was nearly 44.7 kg, against 28.5 kg in the United Kingdom, 18.5 kg in West Germany, and 11.2 kg in France. Australia and New Zealand each had a bigger *per capita* consumption of newsprint than the United Kingdom. On the other hand the number of new book titles published in 1972 was highest in the USA (81 124) followed by the USSR (80 555), UK (33 109) and West Germany (40 354). Other estimates credit the United States with a total *per capita* consumption of paper and paper products of 270 kg per year.

The United States and Canada are the giants of the paper-making trade. In 1959 the United States made 40 per cent and Canada 18 per cent of the estimated world production of 54m. tons of wood pulp for paper-making. In 1971 the percentages were approximately the same, but total production had risen to 103m. tons. Secondary but still large producers of wood pulp were Sweden, Finland, USSR, Japan, West Germany, Norway and France, each with an output of over 1m. tons — ranging from 7.9m. tons in Sweden to 1.5m. tons in France.

The United States also leads in the production of paper (43.3m. tons against Japan's 10.9m. tons in 1971). Canada provides the biggest share of the world's output of newsprint (7.6m. tons out of 20.9m. tons, against the United States 2.9m. tons), but the United States not only import most of Canada's production, but use enormous supplies of pulp for the manufacture (37.7m. tons) of the better kinds of paper. The United Kingdom, with a production of 3.7m. tons of paper, is close to France (3.8m. tons) in the list of the smaller paper-manufacturing countries, following the USSR and West Germany (over 5m. tons). Finland, Italy, Sweden and China produce over 3m. tons.

The paper industry of the United Kingdom is almost entirely dependent on imports for its raw material. In 1973 wood pulp and waste (2.6m. tons) valued at £201m., and paper and paper products (3.6m. tons) valued at £402m. gave an import bill of £603m. which was only partially offset by £130m. of exports, mainly paper. United Kingdom production of some 500 000 tons of wood pulp provided a small percentage of raw material used, although waste paper (1.8m. tons) made a major contribution to reducing imports. Sixty-five per cent of the wood pulp and 53 per cent of the paper imported came from Sweden, Finland and Norway with a trend towards increased paper imports. In 1954 imported paper met 25 per cent of the total consumption, by 1969 the figure was 34 per cent (mainly newsprint). This reflects the increased processing of the wood pulp by the producer countries. Faced with increasing competition in newsprint and the lower grades of paper, the industry is increasingly concerned with special and quality papers, disposable tissues, paper clothing, and light card and board for packaging.

Earthenware and porcelain

The simplest form of manufactured article made from earth, or rather from clay, is a brick dried in the sun. This was one of the earliest human inventions, and bricks of this kind are still made in Egypt and other parts of the Old World where fuel is scarce and sun heat by day is constant; also in those parts of the New World which have a similar climate, where they are known by the Spanish name of adobes. It was but a small step to the burning of bricks by artificial heat. The potter's wheel, by means of which mere steadiness of hand enables a workman to mould moist clay into a perfectly round form, is likewise an invention of great simplicity and great antiquity, though unknown, like every other form of wheel, in the New World before the time of Columbus. The method of glazing pottery is a less obvious discovery, and must have been due, like a host of other inventions, to some fortunate accident. The oldest specimens of earthenware are unglazed. Yet the art of glazing was known to the ancient Assyrians, Egyptians, and Etruscans, all of whom were noted among the nations of antiquity for their pottery. Improvements in the potter's art were made by the Arabs during the period of their highest civilisation. By them the making of painted earthenware with a finely glazed or enamelled surface seems to have been practised before it was known to any European people. But the finest of all kinds of earthenware, the kind known as porcelain, was originally a Chinese invention, referred by Chinese chroniclers to the time of a dynasty which reigned in China from the second century BC to the first AD. In Europe this earthenware was unknown till the thirteenth century, and does not seem to have become widely known till it was introduced by the Portuguese about 1500, which accounts for the fact that the name porcelain (together with its equivalents in other European languages) is of Portuguese origin. It was 200 years later before the art of making porcelain became known in Europe, where it was discovered independently. An inferior kind of porcelain was made at St Cloud in 1695, but the true or hard porcelain, as it is called, was first made about 1709 by a German alchemist, Böttcher, who discovered it to be the product of a mixture of sand with kaolin or china clay, a fine kind of clay resulting from weakening or alteration of granite. A porcelain factory was set up at Meissen, in Saxony, and efforts were made to keep the art secret, but it gradually spread and is now carried on in all countries with a highly developed manufacturing industry. In central Europe, it is largely concentrated in Bavaria and Czechoslovakia.

For the manufacture of ordinary pottery many kinds of clay will suffice if free from iron, which causes the clay to fuse during baking. Other ingredients are also used, such as burnt and powdered flint and phosphate of lime, the latter often in the form of bone-ash. The decorations on ordinary pottery may be painted on the unglazed ware, and afterwards protected by a glaze composed of various ingredients fused together by a second baking. The glaze on porcelain is a thin coating of glass and the painting may also be done on the glaze with pigments of finely powdered coloured glass, after which the articles are again put into a kiln to be fired. An unglazed kind of earthenware known as terra cotta is moulded into statuary and other ornamental articles, and unglazed pottery is extensively used in the south of Europe, in Africa and Asia.

In England the manufacture of earthenware remained in a backward condition till after the middle of the eighteenth century. Its chief seat was Burslem, in north Staffordshire, a place well suited for this manufacture because of the great variety of clays and the abundance of coal in the vicinity. Among the clays of this district (the Potteries) is a great abundance of the coarse clay used in making the saggars or seggars in which the earthenware is baked. Thanks to the presence of these two heavy materials, coal and coarse clay, the district continues to be the centre of the English manufacture of earthenware and porcelain. The finer kinds of kaolin are obtained (in the British Isles) solely in Cornwall and Devon, but it is cheaper to send this china clay to the Potteries than to bring the coal and coarse clay to Devon and Cornwall.

The first great improvements in English pottery were due to Wedgwood, who was born at Burslem in 1730, and potteries were among the earliest of the new style factories of the Industrial Revolution. Besides the products of the Potteries, in the local sense of that word, England is noted for its ornamental stoneware (the hardest and heaviest kind of earthenware) made in London (Lambeth), and for the great development in the use of glazed tile — in bathrooms, etc. In 1936—38, exports of 'Pottery and other shaped and fired clay products' (as the Board of Trade then classified all such goods) averaged £4m., and imports £1.3m. After the war the United Nations introduced a Standard International Trade Classification, and the entry in the British returns became 'Pottery articles commonly used for domestic purposes' — a less comprehensive grouping, comprising mainly earthenware, china and porcelain. Even so the exports in 1960 were valued at £14.1m. Glazed tiles provided £2.7m. more. The Commonwealth (especially Canada and Australia) and the United States provided the best markets. Imports in 1960 were valued at between £1m. and £2m. In 1973 exports had risen to £15.2m., with glazed tiles another £5m. Imports were £10m.; but exports for all types from the pottery industry were over £42m.

Germany and France have long been important centres of manufacture. It was a tradition of the former German Federal rulers to encourage the art. Prussia, Bavaria, Saxony, all had their royal 'Porzellan—Manufakturen', mostly supported by bounties. In Saxony, Meissen (northwest of Dresden and the true home of 'Dresden china') vied with Sèvres, near Paris, in producing the most beautiful coloured porcelains known. Now they have lost some of their pre-eminence and English porcelain ranks with the best. Since the Second World War the historic Meissen mark — the crossed swords — has been replaced by the Soviet Star.

In the United States the home industry developed rapidly under the protection of high import duties. In the East, China is still noted for its porcelain, and so is Japan. Normally, China still exports a considerable quantity of fine chinaware; Japan has developed a big trade in both cheap and fine china. Hardly any other branch of industry has so many names relating to the geography and history of the art. In English, porcelain is very commonly known by the appropriate name of chinaware, and kaolin as china clay. The name **majolica** was given by the Italians to painted and enamelled earthenware which they appear first to have become acquainted with as a product of the island of Majorca, and the name has been adapted into English. **Faience** is a name for the same kind of ware derived from the Italian town of Faenza, where it was first made in Italy. **Delft** is the name of another kind of painted and enamelled ware first made at the town of that name in the Netherlands, and painted blocks of this kind of ware are generally known as Dutch tiles.

Glass

Glass is made by melting together various ingredients, of which silica is the only one that enters into the composition of all kinds of glass. Silica is one of the most widely diffused substances in nature, and is found in various forms, quartz (the main constituent of most sands) and flint being the most familiar. Sands are usually impure, discoloured, it may be, by iron, or mixed with lime or other ingredients; but sometimes they consist of nothing but silica, and such pure sand or sandstones afford the best material for glass-making. In England various deposits of sand, at King's Lynn in Norfolk, at Hastings, and Leighton Buzzard, have in turn been noted for the excellence of the material which they afforded for glass-making. In France the most famous deposits are the sandstones of Fontainebleau. The United States possess exceptionally fine glass sands in the west of Massachusetts and elsewhere.

Along with silica there is always fused in the making of glass some alkaline substance, either soda or potash. Glass made solely from soda is perishable, and in the making of most kinds of modern glass, lime is added. Soda is chiefly used in the forms of carbonate of soda and sulphate of soda, which are largely manufactured for the purpose; but for some of the commoner sorts of glass, as bottle-glass, common salt is sometimes used. Potash is generally used in the form of carbonate of potash (the pearl-ash of commerce), sometimes in that of nitrate of potash or saltpetre. The glass made from potash is the freest from any tinge of colour, but that made from carbonate of soda, besides being nearly colourless, is easier to work in the state of partial fusion in which glass is usually treated. For ordinary purposes, accordingly, this substance is preferred. Potash is used either with or without lime in the manufacture of some of the best kinds of glass, such as Bohemian glass and English flint glass (crystal). In making this last kind of glass, lead (generally in the form of red lead) is used instead of lime, rendering the glass softer and more fusible and lustrous. The use of lead is an English invention of the eighteenth century. Besides these ingredients various others are used for special purposes, as to remove colours* which some impurities in the materials employed in making the glass might impart, or to give colours desired to coloured glass. In the making of bottle-glass, the colour of which is an unimportant consideration, very varied ingredients may be employed. In Germany some kinds of rock, such as basalts, trachytes, and granites, which contain a certain quantity of soda and potash along with from 65 to 75 per cent of silica, and are easily fusible, have been employed with success in glass-making.

After the fusion of the materials glass is worked at a high temperature in a soft and somewhat pasty condition, and it is frequently reheated. The implement chiefly used is the blowpipe, by means of which balls of the glass paste are blown out into hollow forms. To make bottles and similar articles, almost all that is necessary is to blow the glass in moulds of the proper shape. When flat sheets are required, different methods are employed. By the old method a ball of blown glass was twirled round and round without blowing till it spread out flat except at the middle (the bull's eye). By another it is blown and twirled into a long cylinder, which is then cut on one side longitudinally and laid flat. Only the best kind of glass, made from the most carefully selected materials, is capable of being rolled out into sheets by means of steel rollers. Glass so made is called plate-glass. Since the 1960s all types of flat glass throughout the world are increasingly produced by the British patented float-glass process which makes possible the continuous production of flat glass in a wide range of thicknesses. Flint-glass is the kind best adapted for being cut and engraved in the cold state.

The invention of glass took place in prehistoric times. It was known at a very early period in Egypt, but the oldest piece of transparent white glass of which the date is known is a vase found among the ruins of Nineveh and now preserved in the British Museum. It has inscribed upon it the name of Sargon, an Assyrian king who reigned about the close of the eighth century BC. In ancient times the Egyptians and Phoenicians were the two peoples most noted for their glass-making, for which both Egypt and Phoenicia supplied excellent sand, the former near Alexandria, the latter in the bed of the small river Belus (now the Na'aman), which enters the sea near Akko (Acre). The alkali in Egypt

---

* For this purpose manganese is chiefly used, but when in excess this substance itself imparts an amethyst hue to the glass.

was obtained from the natron (soda) lakes situated to the west of the delta. In Italy the making of glass does not seem to have been practised till about the beginning of the Christian era, and there is no positive evidence of window glass having been used there before the third century AD. In modern times the Venetians acquired celebrity for the beauty of their glass manufactures; the art began to be practised there soon after the foundation of the city. Belgium, which has local supplies of sand as well as coal, and manufactures soda compounds form imported materials, is the headquarters of window glass manufacture in Europe, and also makes excellent mirror glass. Czechoslovakia has also a large glass industry.

The glass industry of the late nineteenth century was labour intensive with many small firms producing glass by batch methods. The modern industry is dominated by one or two large firms in each country. It is capital intensive and highly automated with large continuous process plants for manufacturing, coating, polishing and rolling. The product has many industrial uses, the largest being flat glass (for domestic and construction uses) and glass containers which together account for 60 per cent of the United Kingdom output. Other products are safety and laminated glass for automobiles, domestic glass (both hand-finished and mass-produced), laboratory and scientific glassware, glass for lenses (optical and ophthalmic), and glass fibre for insulation and incorporation into other materials such as plastics, rubber, etc. Technical development is concerned with improved transparency and the development of compound products with ceramics and metals. The United Kingdom has long been a net importer of glass, but since the Second World War has been a net exporter. Imports of glass and glassware of all types in 1973 were valued at £24m., and exports at £39m., to which must be added nearly £9m. in fees from other countries using the float-glass process under licence.

Soap

Soap as a commercial product is a chemical compound resulting from the action of soda or potash on various fatty or oily substances, and hence, besides being an important commodity (unknown to the ancients), it is also the cause of a large trade in the various fats and oils that enter into its composition, as well as in the alkalis mentioned. Hard soaps are those made with soda; soft, those made with potash. Glycerine is a byproduct of the soap manufacture. The fatty substances principally used in the manufacture of soap in the United Kingdom are tallow, coconut oil, cottonseed oil, palm oil, and other vegetable oils. In the south of Europe the staple ingredient of this nature is olive oil, along with which are used, in addition to those just mentioned, groundnut oil, oil of sesame, and many others (see pp. 221–7). Even the grease from sheep's wool can be employed in this industry to form a lanolin based soap.

Chemical industries

The chemical industry is concerned with a very wide range of products: gases, liquids and solids. The majority are derived from, and are employed in, other manufacturing processes. Chemical products are used in almost every modern industrial process. The industry has developed dramatically over the last 100 years from small-scale exploitation of laboratory chemical experiments to great national and international companies characterised by large-scale automated processing plants, high capital investment and high volume output.

The many products of the industry include chemical fertilisers (see p. 295), inorganic and organic chemicals, gases and explosives. The inorganic include basic chemical materials such as alkalis, salt, chlorine, sulphuric and other acids, mineral pigments, silicates, pesticides, etc. The organic include the products of the hydrocarbons (coal, petroleum and natural gas) such as synthetic fibres, synthetic rubber, plastics, resins, detergents, pharmaceutical products, etc. Since it is essential to most other industries, the chemical industry has expanded greatly since the Second World War, particularly in the highly industrialised countries of North America, western Europe and Japan, which together produce 75 per cent of the total world output of chemicals. World exports were valued at $4 710m. in 1955; $14 000m. in 1967; and $20 600m. in 1970 — 40 per cent coming from western Europe. The greatest expansion has been in petrochemicals, i.e. products (including plastics) derived from petroleum and natural gas. World output, excluding the Soviet countries, rose from 50 000 tons in 1940 to 50m. tons in 1970. Output could reach 500m. tons by the end of the century, and it is probable that the consumption of plastics will exceed that of iron and steel in the not far distant future as synthetic materials and products increasingly replace traditional materials over a very wide range of personal, domestic, constructional and industrial uses. How universal is this replacement of natural commodities by manmade materials is demonstrated by a simple formula for hair lotion. That prepared for James II was largely orange and rosewater with cloves, honey, nutmegs and vanilla pods distilled in brandy, and perfumed with musk and ambergris. The modern formula is largely alcohol with lactic acid, ricinoleyl alcohol, hexachlorophene, cholesteral and d-Panthenol.

With so wide a range of products, only a few can be noticed here.

Potash, is an alkali used in manufacturing glass and soap, as well as a number of other chemical industries, but its main use is as a fertiliser (p. 295). It was formerly made by the burning of vegetable matter, and the chief exporting countries were Canada, Russia, and other timber-producing countries. In France it was made from the grease of wool, which was largely a waste product. After the discovery of the great deposits of potassium salts in central Germany, however, that country became the main source of supply. Subsequently, deposits were discovered in the south of Alsace and in the northeast of Spain, near Cardona and Sceria. During 1914–18, efforts were made in various countries to extract it from different raw materials, as from minerals containing felspar. In the United States a variety of glauconite, occurring in a narrow strip in the states of Delaware and New Jersey, proved a source, and large deposits are now worked near Carlsbad to make the United States one of the largest producers although still a net importer.

Sulphuric acid is employed in a great many industrial operations and is probably the most important single product of the chemical industry. It is chiefly made from nitrate of soda and sulphur or iron pyrites, a compound of iron (often with more or less copper) and sulphur. The sulphur or iron pyrites is burned, and the resulting vapour acted upon (in leaden chambers) by nitric acid vapours obtained from the nitrate of soda, which is heated along with the very acid (sulphuric) which the subsequent operations are intended to produce. Nitrate of potash (saltpetre) may be used instead of nitrate of soda, cheapness being the ground for preference. In more recent processes of manufacture, cheaper for the preparation of the very strong acids required in many industries, the nitrates are replaced by platinum, which acts as a catalyst on the dioxide of sulphur. World production of sulphuric acid is dominated by the United States which produces some 25m. tons annually.

Bleaching powder. Hydrochloric acid obtained in the first stage of the manufacture of carbonate of soda is used in the manufacture of bleaching powder, which is a compound of chlorine and lime. Manganese, in the form of the black oxide of manganese, is employed to free the chlorine from the hydrochloric acid, and the chlorine is then passed into chambers containing powdered slaked lime. The end product is used for bleaching in many industries and as a disinfectant.

Sulphate of ammonia, a valuable nitrogenous fertiliser, is one of the byproducts of the distillation of coal, of the shale-oil industry, and of aluminium manufacture (see also below). Another byproduct is *coal tar*, at one time applied to the same purposes as wood tar (preserving ropes, timber, etc.), and in the making of dyes of almost every hue. The first dye made from coal tar was named mauve. It was discovered accidentally in 1856 by Dr W. H. Perkin, and was applied industrially in the celebrated dye-works of Messrs Pullar at Perth. Other shades were soon discovered. At first this branch of industry was mainly carried on in Great Britain, the country most abundantly supplied with the raw material; later the chief seat of the industry was transferred to Germany, which became the dominant factor in world production and trade, while Great Britain was content to supply a large proportion of the raw materials. All that was altered by the First World War; probably no other industry had its geographical distribution so radically changed by that war. The materials used in the production of dyestuffs from coal tar are largely the same as those used in the manufacture of high explosives, and were recognised to be of vital national importance. In 1921 an Act of Parliament prohibited for ten years the import of synthetic organic dyestuffs and their raw materials into the United Kingdom, except under licence of the Board of Trade. Still more rigorous protective measures were adopted in the United States.

The result was a complete reversal of the trade position. In the United Kingdom the imports of synthetic organic dyestuffs, which amounted to nearly 18 000 tons in 1913, dropped to little over 2 000 tons in 1938, but in 1973 15 500 tons. On the other hand, the exports of finished dyestuffs obtained from coal tar increased from under 2 500 tons in 1913 to nearly 4 000 tons in 1938, and in 1973 had soared to 42 000 tons, valued at over £69m. In the United States the value of the imports of coal tar dyestuffs dropped from $7m. in 1913 to $5m. in 1938, and $2.75m. in 1948. Home production increased enormously, but such were the demands of the home market that up to the Second World War there was little if any development of the export trade, which remained almost negligible. In 1948, however, after the Second World War, the United States exported coal tar dyestuffs to the value of over $63m. ($22.9m. in 1955).

Alum, which is largely used in the sizing of paper, dyeing, calico-printing, painting and the preparation of colours, the tawing of leather and other industries, is prepared by several processes from clay or slate. In former days it was relatively much more important in the dyeing industry than now, having a very prominent place in the commerce of the Middle Ages.

Carbide. After 1892 an important industry sprang up as a result of the discovery in that year (almost simultaneously by Wilson in America and Moisan in France) that the carbide of calcium is formed when lime and carbon are fused together in an electric furnace. It then became possible to manufacture cheaply the powerful illuminant acetylene gas, a compound of carbon and hydrogen which is formed by the action of water on calcium carbide. Norway and Switzerland engaged in production and export, and large supplies were produced in the United States, France, Italy and Austria. The use of acetylene gas as an illuminant has declined but it is widely used for welding.

313

Rayon and nylon. Until the beginning of the present century the textile industry depended on fibres of natural origin. Since then new fibres have been produced by chemico-mechanical processes. In many characteristics these 'manmade fibres', as they are comprehensively called, are superior to the natural fibres, and their manufacture has developed rapidly into a major industry. Since 1925 their world production has exceeded the production of silk, and since 1948 it has exceeded the world production of wool.

Because of their surface characteristics the new fibres were known for many years as artificial silk. In the retail trade this description gave rise to opportunities for misrepresentation and occasioned so much trouble that concerted action on a world scale was taken by the manufacturers to introduce a new name — rayon. In the United Kingdom the Textile Institute and the British Rayon Federation at first accepted 'rayon' as an inclusive term covering all textile fibres not of natural origin. In many other countries the term was understood in this sense, but in the United States the definition was limited, officially by the Department of Commerce as well as industrially, to manufactured fibres of cellulose origin. The great bulk of early manufactures of manmade fibres were of cellulose origin, the principal raw material being wood pulp or cotton linters physically and chemically changed to produce the fibres. But there is also a wide range of synthetic fibres from a coal or petroleum base in which the fibres are built up from chemical or mineral constituents.

Whatever the raw material, the essential feature of manufacture is to prepare from it a high viscosity fluid by solution in an aqueous medium or a volatile organic solvent, or by melting. The fluid is made to flow through orifices and then solidified by chemical action (wet spinning), or by evaporation of the solvent (dry spinning), or by cooling (melt spinning). The filaments thus formed are drawn together and collected parallel or twisted together, to produce a yarn known as continuous filament yarn. Alternatively staple fibres can be made by cutting the filaments into regular lengths and spinning them, according to fineness, on appropriate spindles. Typical examples are viscose rayon (wet spinning), cellulose acetate rayon (dry spinning), and nylon (melt spinning).

The distinction between fibres of cellulose and noncellulose origin is now widely observed, and two main groups of manmade fibres are recognised, each with many subdivisions. The rayon group has long been the larger and includes viscose and acetate together with fibres produced from protein bases such as casein. All the fibres in this category are made from natural polymers. The nylon group comprises wholly synthetic fibres, made from chemical substances derived chiefly from coal and oil and is expanding rapidly. It includes such trade names as Orlon, Terylene, Dacron, etc.

By the 1970s the world production of cellulose fibres, which had been expanding slowly to some 3.5m. tons a year (1.4m. tons continuous filament and 2.1m. tons staple fibres), was surpassed by the synthetic fibres which totalled over 4m. tons in 1969—70. The United States being the largest producer followed by Japan, USSR, West Germany, the United Kingdom and Italy. Apart from clothing and household textiles, the main uses are in the manufacture of tyres of all types and, increasingly, in new bonded materials.

Oxygen, etc. Included in the chemical industry is the commercial manufacture on a large scale of oxygen, nitrogen and nitrogen compounds, acetylene, carbon dioxide, and hydrogen. Oxygen is largely manufactured for the iron and steel industry, engineering and medical purposes. Nitrogen is obtained from the air for the production of various nitrogen compounds used as fertilisers and is directly combined with hydrogen to form ammonia. As an inert gas it is increasingly used to purge empty petrol tanks, and as a freezing medium in the frozen foods industry. Hydrogen is largely manufactured to harden oils for the preparation of margarine and to enable low grade oils to be used in the manufacture of soaps. It was required in large quantities in the process of hydrogenation, whereby coal, or a substitute, was turned into oil. Argon and acetylene are used extensively in welding processes: propane and butane are used as fuels and also for process work in clay, glass and the food industries: helium, used for producing controlled atmospheres for scientific purposes and as a lifting medium for lighter-than-air craft, is used as a cooling agent in nuclear reactors: carbon dioxide is used in carbonating beverages and in welding.

As with the rest of the chemical industry, gas production since the Second World War has grown with the industries it serves, and is dominated by a few large companies using bulk production methods. Major recent developments have been the manufacture of gases in bulk tonnages (in particular of oxygen to meet the growing demands of the new basic oxygen process of steel-making), and improvements in insulation techniques. The latter has made possible the exploitation of the cyrogenic (very low temperature) properties of gases for converting them to a liquid state. Nitrogen, for instance, liquifies at $-196°$ C ($-320°$ F). Helium when transported under pressure as a gas, requires 200 kg of steel container for every kilogram of gas shipped, but in a super-insulated container it can be shipped in bulk as a liquid at minimum cost. Bulk distribution of gases in liquid form therefore becomes possible by rail, road and pipeline to meet the growing demands of industry.

IV
Regional Geography

Europe

Climate. Europe, the smallest of the continents, is, taken as a whole, the most densely peopled. Its situation and outline are particularly favourable to its climate. The whole area, except a small fraction in the north, lies within the temperate zone, and the great irregularity of its outline causes it to enjoy in a higher degree than any other continent the mitigating effects of the sea on extremes of heat and cold. Its westerly situation is of even greater importance in this respect; and its southern peninsulas have a peculiarly warm and equable climate, not only in consequence of the moderating effect of the Mediterranean Sea on the temperature, but also because these peninsulas are to a large extent protected from cold northerly winds by mountain barriers on the north.

In temperate Europe there is the same increase in extremes of temperature from west to east as in other parts of the north temperate zone, and this is true to a certain extent even of the countries belonging to the Mediterranean region. Besides these peninsulas, or the greater part of them, nearly the whole of France and the British Isles, and the whole of Belgium and the Netherlands, are outside the area in which the mean daily temperature sinks below freezing point for at least one month in the year. On the other hand, the area in which the mean daily temperature is above 10° C (50° F) for at least eight months in the year is confined almost to the Mediterranean region, although it includes also the west of France from about the Loire southwards. In the east of Russia the area in which there is at least one month with a mean daily temperature above 20° C (68° F) extends as far north as the latitude of the Orkney Islands.

By far the greater part of the area of Europe has a sufficient rainfall for cultivation, so that south of the region in which the temperature puts a limit on agriculture almost the whole of the lowland area, and even, in the far south, land at the height of between 600 and 900 m (2 000 and 3 000 ft) is capable of being tilled. The deficiency of rainfall discourages the pursuit of agriculture chiefly in the southeast of Russia and in the interior of Spain. But though the rainfall is thus generally

319

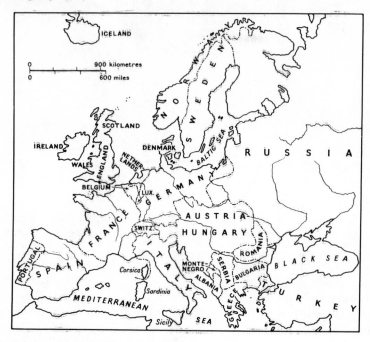

Europe: political, 1913

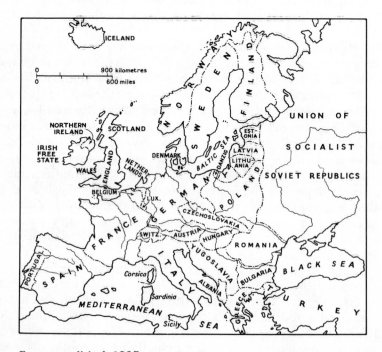

Europe: political, 1937

Europe: political, 1973

distributed, and occurs everywhere more or less all the year round, it is most abundant at different places during different seasons. The west, and above all the northwest, is the region in which autumn rains prevail, the east that in which there is a predominance of summer rain, but it is really only in the Mediterranean peninsulas that there is a marked deficiency of rain during any particular season. There the rains are chiefly winter rains, and the middle of summer is remarkable for its drought, to the south of about 40° N almost rainless. These winter rains are apt to be very violent and are blamed for the denudation of large areas, especially in the neighbourhood of some of the most populous sites of antiquity, where the needs of the population caused the mountain slopes to be stripped of their woods. It is thus clear that Europe embraces a number of the climatic regions described on pp. 38—47.

The **Mediterranean** type is found in those lands round the Mediterranean Sea, but in the eastern Mediterranean there is a marked increase in winter cold and summer heat. The **northwest European** type is found as far east as Denmark and East Germany where, with at least one month below freezing, it gives place to the **central European** type and then in central Russia to the **eastern European** type. In southern European USSR (with an outlier in the Hungarian Plain) is the **Mid-continent grassland** type of great extremes and with a rainfall mainly in spring. This fades into a **temperate desert** around the Caspian Sea. In

321

northern European USSR, Sweden, and Norway is the **cold temperate** type fading northwards into the **tundra**.

Many of the cultivated trees and plants now thoroughly characteristic of certain parts of Europe are known or appear to have been introduced into that continent within historic times. The olive, the cypress, and the laurel, the evergreens now so characteristic of the Mediterranean peninsulas, and so well adapted to stand the dry summers of that region, seem all to be of Asian origin, though introduced at a very early date. Of Oriental origin also is alfalfa or lucerne, the equally characteristic fodder plant of that region, the deeprooted ally of the clover which survives the driest summers, and hence has been introduced into many other parts of the world with a climate similar to the Mediterranean. From Asia also came the fig, mulberry, almond, walnut, chestnut, and apricot, all before the birth of Christ. The mulberry of the ancients, however, was the black mulberry, the sycamine of the Greeks, the white mulberry being a much later arrival from the East. From Asia likewise came at various dates, mostly after the beginning of the Christian Era, rice, cotton, and several members of the orange genus (citrons, lemons, and oranges proper). After the discovery of America by Columbus, agaves and cacti, potatoes, maize, and tobacco were added to the vegetation and agriculture of this continent.

The chief cereals of Europe seem to have been cultivated there in prehistoric times; wheat and barley, as well as two kinds of millet, are proved by remains found beside the lake dwellings of Switzerland to have been cultivated in the later Stone Age. Many common cultivated plants, including cabbages, peas, vetches, parsley, and onions would seem, on the evidence of language, to have been introduced into central and northern Europe from Italy.

At the present day Europe is to a larger extent a manufacturing region than any other continent, but the predominance of manufactures is characteristic only of certain countries. Even before the Second World War manufactured goods provided half or more of the value of exports of native origin from the United Kingdom, France, Belgium, Germany, Switzerland, Italy, and Czechoslovakia. In some other European countries the chief exports are still products of the soil, the forest, or the sea, but usually partially manufactured or prepared. One of the most important facts in the commercial history of the continent within the last 100 years is the extent to which agriculture has been affected by the rapid development of commerce in grain with many parts of the world in which wheat and other crops are produced under exceptionally favourable conditions.

Inland waterways. The countries of northern Europe are separated from those of Mediterranean Europe by a great barrier of mountains: the

Pyrenees, Alps, Carpathians and their associated smaller ranges and plateaus. Consequently the natural gaps through these mountains have always been of utmost importance as affording routeways, and even the difficult passes of the Alps have assumed a special significance. Broadly speaking, the climate of northern Europe with its well distributed rainfall is such as to afford a constant supply of water to the rivers, and this factor, combined with the generally level character of the north European plain, has led to an extensive use of waterways as highways of commerce. The rivers have been improved, in some cases canalised, and linked by canals so that the waterways are still significant in France, Belgium, the Netherlands, East and West Germany, Poland, and the USSR. On the other hand, the rivers of the Mediterranean lands, partly because of the seasonal character of the rainfall, are of less importance. The one great river, the Rhône, which flows into the Mediterranean from the north, has afforded a valley routeway of special note. Unfortunately the great river of central Europe, the Danube, flows into the enclosed Black Sea, and loses thereby much of its value as a commercial highway.

The Danube itself is an important international waterway but it suffers various disadvantages. Its usefulness was restricted by the cataracts and steepsided gorge at the Iron Gates between Orsova and Turnu Severin which limited the size of barges passing through, until the 1970s. A series of locks now permits convoys of nine 2 000-ton barges with their shepherding tugs to pass through this formerly hazardous stretch of the river. Some reaches of the Danube are subject to freezing for about two months in the year; and there are few towns along its marshy banks below Budapest. Yet another factor which has limited traffic were political restrictions, the outcome of two world wars.

The most important of the inland waterways in Europe is the Rhine, and next in importance, in respect of volume of traffic, are the waterways connecting northern France and western Belgium. Before the Second World War the Rhine and Marne canal carried large quantities of coal in both directions and some thousands of tons of iron ore from France into Germany. Two of the great European canals are in Germany: the Dortmund–Ems Canal, connecting the Rhine with Dortmund and the port of Emden in West Germany; and the Mittelland Canal, completed in 1938, connecting three rivers, the Ems, Weser and Elbe. The Kiel Canal, connecting the mouth of the River Elbe on the North Sea with the Baltic port of Kiel, enables ships to cross from the Baltic to the North Sea without going round Jutland. Before the Second World War the tonnage carried was equal to two-thirds of that carried on the Panama Canal.

Czechoslovakia, though an inland state, has a direct water outlet to the North Sea through the Elbe, which rises in Bohemia and is navigable below its junction with the Moldau, north of Prague. In Poland the Wisla (Vistula) and its tributaries are navigable.

Various projects for connections along routes that offer the prospect of heavy, bulky traffic suited to inland waterways have been or are being carried out, e.g. on the Neckar and the Moselle. But in general waterways are decreasingly used, though the Soviet Union in particular has been active in linking her main rivers constructing the White Sea Canal to afford a direct link between the Baltic Sea via Leningrad) and the White Sea. Other important links — including the 102 km (63 mile) canal, opened in 1952, which connects the Volga and the Don — combine with the White Sea Canal and the natural waterways of the country to provide inter-communication between the White, Baltic, Caspian, Azov and Black Seas.

Routes linking Britain with continental Europe. The surface routes between Britain and the Continent are of course interrupted by the sea. The ports on the shortest sea routes are Dover and Folkestone, connecting England with France by Calais and Boulogne respectively. The Dover—Calais route is shortest of all, being only 40 km (22 nautical miles) as against 46 km (25 nautical miles) on the Folkestone—Boulogne route, but Boulogne has the advantage of being 44 km (27 statute miles) nearer Paris. Dover also connects with Ostend 126 km (68 nautical miles) and with Dunkerque. Other important ports are Harwich, from which British Rail runs a service to the Hook of Holland (the outlying port of Rotterdam; 187 km: 101 nautical miles), and Esbjerg in Denmark (666 km: 360 nautical miles); Newhaven to Dieppe (140 km: 76 nautical miles) for Paris; and Southampton to Le Havre (226 km: 122 nautical miles) and St Malo. There are also routes from Tilbury, Leith, Newcastle, and Hull to the Continent. Car ferry services and container traffic are of growing importance on many of these routes.

Railways. Fortunately the railways of Europe, except in the USSR and the Iberian peninsula, are on the same gauge throughout, thus permitting transcontinental through running. The gauge is the same as in Britain (4 ft 8½ in), though most continental rolling stock cannot be used in this country owing to the narrowness of tunnels and bridges.

Paris is the great focus for the routes touching the coast of France at all the ports from Calais to Le Havre. The distance by rail from Calais to Paris, via Boulogne and Amiens, is 300 km (186 miles), and from Le Havre to Paris, via Rouen, 227 km (141 miles). The influence of topography on railway routes is well seen in the main line to the Mediterranean, which runs down the Rhône valley east of the Central Plateau, and the main line to Spain, which runs west of that same plateau. The Pyrenees long formed a barrier to railway communication between France and Spain and until 1912 no railway actually crossed the chain, the links between the two countries being round the eastern and western ends. The stupendous engineering feats necessary to surmount the obstacles afforded by the Alps will receive attention under the countries concerned.

The Nord Express from Paris to Stockholm passes through the north of West Germany to Hamburg, into Denmark and on to Copenhagen, crossing the Great Belt by train ferry (50 km: 31 miles). From Copenhagen another train ferry (32 km: 20 miles) connects with Malmö in south Sweden, whence the journey is continued overland to Stockholm. A variant of this route which has been opened up since the Second World War and is of growing importance is now followed by the Italian—Scandinavian (Rome—Stockholm) Express. Instead of continuing to Hamburg it branches off at Hanover and runs to the north coast of West Germany at Grossenbrode, whence a train ferry connects with Gedser, the southernmost point of Denmark, on the island of Falster. In 1963 this ferry was diverted to the new ports of Puttgarden (Germany) and Rödby (Denmark), with a sea crossing of only fifty minutes, as against three hours from Gedser to Grossenbrode. Gedser is also connected by train ferry with Warnemünde, in East Germany, but this service is used more for freight than for passenger traffic.

Among many other important through services it must suffice here to indicate the main transcontinental routes, leading eastwards to the USSR, southeast to Istanbul, and into Asia. The Orient Express runs from Paris up the Marne valley, along the route of the Marne—Rhine Canal past Nancy, across the north of the Vosges to Strasbourg, where it crosses the Rhine, then northwards along the base of the Black Forest, and eastwards to the Neckar valley. At Stuttgart the route forks. One branch goes east and north, via Nürnberg to Prague. The other goes east and south to Ulm, on the Danube, thence via München and Salzburg to Linz, where it rejoins the Danube. It continues down the valley of the Danube to Vienna.

The Arlberg—Orient Express, starting from Paris, crosses northeastern France and northern Switzerland, via Basle and Zürich, into Austria; tunnels under the Arlberg Pass, and after touching Innsbruck, Salzburg, and Linz, continues via Vienna to Budapest and Bucarest.

The Ostend—Vienna Express crosses Belgium and Germany via Brussels, Köln, and the Rhine valley to Frankfurt-am-Main and Nürnberg, and runs into the Danube valley, reaching Vienna by way of Passau and Linz.

A more direct route to Belgrade and beyond is that of the Simplon—Orient Express, which runs from Calais via Paris and Lausanne to Milan, across northern Italy via Venice to Trieste, and through Yugoslavia down the Sava valley to its junction with the Danube at Belgrade, thence to Nis, Thessaloniki (Salonica) and Athens, with a branch to Istanbul (until 1961). Another connection with Greece and Turkey is provided by the Tauern Express, which starts at Ostend and follows the route of the Ostend–Vienna Express to Köln, then the Rhine and Neckar valleys to Stuttgart, continuing via Ulm, München, Salzburg and the Tauern and Karawanken tunnels to join the route of the Simplon–Orient Express at Ljubljana.

Asian connections. From Haydarpasa, on the Asian side of the Bosporus opposite to Istanbul, the Turkish Railways continue on the standard gauge. The Taurus Express winds its way to the Taurus range down to Adana in the Cilician plains, mounts over the Amanus range to Fevzipasa, continues eastwards across the Euphrates to Mosul, on the Tigris, and descends the Tigris valley to Baghdad. Thence a metre-gauge line crosses to the Euphrates valley and follows it to the Persian Gulf at Basra. A connection has been made recently between the standard gauge railways of Turkey and Iran. It incorporates a train ferry across Lake Van, thereby avoiding the difficulty of engineering a line through the mountains which border the lake.

South from Fevzipasa a connecting service runs via Aleppo and Homs to Tripoli and Beirut, traversing a military railway, built by the British during the Second World War and now operated by the Syrian and Lebanese Railways. The section beyond Beirut to Haifa is not in use. From Haifa there is in normal times a through service to Egypt, but this is at present interrupted by the lack of cooperation between Israel and the Arab world; the Israeli terminal is Beersheba and the Egyptian terminal Rafa. The railway from Gaza to Cairo crosses the Suez Canal by a swing bridge a few kilometres south of Kantara. There is in fact through railway connection between Europe, Asia and Africa, except for the crossing of the Bosporus from Istanbul to Haydarpasa, which could be made by train ferry.

The other great railway link with Asia is the Trans–Siberian line. On the European side the natural connecting route is via Berlin and Moscow. The Soviet gauge is 5 ft but by the use of changeable bogies Soviet Union trains can be run over the general European system. At the other end, railway developments in China made it possible, in 1936, to travel by rail from Calais to Canton. Through traffic was further facilitated in 1957, by the opening of a mile-long railway bridge and highway for road traffic across the Yangtse, linking Hankow, Hanyang, and Wu-han.

Road and air routes. The road network of Europe continues to expand, with even bigger and better highways for fast and heavy traffic. A system of European through routes (numbered E1, E2, etc.) has been laid down. All large European cities are linked by regular air services, and air services are especially important in the USSR where distance is a major factor. Air services link Moscow with Iran as well as with the Far

East. The colonial powers — Britain, France, Belgium, the Netherlands and Portugal — early developed air routes to their Asian and/or African territories which formed the basis for the present air routes; and transatlantic air services put Europe in regular communication with both North and South America.

Economic cooperation. In 1957, under the Treaty of Rome, six of the countries of western Europe — France, West Germany, the Netherlands, Belgium, Luxembourg and Italy — entered into a treaty to form a European Economic Community (the 'Common Market'), a free trade area. Discussions on its possible extension to include the United Kingdom in a form which would safeguard British trade relations within the Commonwealth did not meet with success before the treaty came into force in 1959.

In March 1958 a new European Assembly to serve as the parliamentary body for the European Economic Community in three institutions — the Common Market, the Coal and Steel Community (see p. 391), and Euratom — was inaugurated at Strasbourg in the Maison de L'Europe.

After the Treaty of Rome had been consummated, without Britain, a European Free Trade Association (EFTA) was negotiated in 1959 between the United Kingdom, Denmark, Norway, Sweden, Switzerland, Austria, and Portugal (the Seven). Two years later Finland was associated with EFTA, but negotiations for Britain's entry into the Common Market broke down.

Eventually, on 22 January 1972, the United Kingdom, Ireland, Denmark and Norway signed the Treaty of Accession to the Common Market and Euratom, thereby joining the EEC from 1 January 1973; and documents on accession to the Coal and Steel Community. In September 1972 the majority of the Norwegian people, in a referendum, voted against joining the EEC. For political reasons, of which one of the main was the preservation of neutrality, Austria, Sweden and Switzerland remain outside the EEC.

In eastern Europe the Council for Mutual Economic Assistance (Comecon) was formed in 1949 by Bulgaria, Czechoslovakia, Hungary, Poland, Romania and the USSR at a conference held in Moscow, later to be joined by Albania and East Germany. In 1962 Albania resigned and in the same year Mongolia joined.

The British Isles

The British Isles lie in the northwest of Europe, between the parallels of 50° and 60° N: the fiftieth parallel of latitude runs a little to the north of Lizard Point in Cornwall and the Scilly Isles, and the sixtieth through the southern end of the mainland of Shetland. The meridian of 0° passes, of course, through London (Greenwich) whilst longitude 10° W passes through the western peninsulas of Ireland.

Prior to 1922 the British Isles formed the United Kingdom of Great Britain and Ireland. In that year twenty-six of the thirty-two counties of Ireland became the Irish Free State (later the Irish Republic) so that the term United Kingdom became applicable to the United Kingdom of Great Britain and Northern Ireland.

The surface of England and Wales. Within the British Isles, England has by far the greatest proportion of the surface available for production or purposes subsidiary to production. According to the most recent agricultural returns, more than 70 per cent of the entire area of land and water was under crops or grass or lying fallow, and when it is considered that about 7 per cent of the surface was occupied by woods, and that a large area is taken up by towns, factories, roads, and railways, it will be seen that the area occupied by unproductive hill and moorland is comparatively small − about 10 per cent. The comparable figures for Japan are interesting: they show less than 20 per cent under crops and grass, and over 65 per cent forest and mountain.

The hills and mountains of England are chiefly in the north and west. Indeed Britain can be divided roughly into two halves, 'highland Britain' and 'lowland Britain'. Highland Britain occupies the north and west; lowland Britain the south and east. The Cheviot Hills with their broad spurs, and the tablelands of the Pennines, which run from north to south from the Scottish border into the heart of Derbyshire, cover a considerable extent of ground, and are fit, so far as agriculture is concerned, for little else than sheep pastures; in these districts the population is even now very sparse. Other extensive tracts with a relief too hilly or a soil too poor for intensive agriculture include the Lake District and the moorlands of Devon and Cornwall as well as certain tracts in lowland Britain such as the Yorkshire moors and parts of the chalk hills and downs: Salisbury Plain and the Marlborough Downs in Wiltshire, and the Chiltern Hills. In addition, there are considerable tracts of light, hungry soil or sandy areas such as the Bagshot area southwest of London, the New Forest of Hampshire, and the 'Breckland' of Norfolk and Suffolk.

The upland masses of the Pennines, the Lake District, and the southwest were hindrances in the construction of roads and railways. In the southeast, roads and railways out of London seek the gaps through the Chilterns or the North Downs, but otherwise physical features in the south and midlands rarely present insuperable difficulties to the development of a road and rail network.

In Wales the proportion of hilly and mountainous country is much greater than in England, and the area of land under crops or grass or in bare fallow is rather less than 54 per cent against 30 per cent occupied by moorland and rough pasture. The ranges of the Welsh hills are, however, short, and there are many openings allowing an easy passage for railways and roads.

The surface of Scotland. Scotland is the highland area of the UK; its northern half has hills and mountains so closely packed together that even now there are few roads leading through the narrow and sparsely peopled valleys between them. Of the surface of Scotland less than one-quarter is under crops or grass or in bare fallow, and the greater part of the land suitable for cropping is confined to the central lowlands, an area roughly definable as bounded by two parallel lines, one stretching from Stonehaven in Kincardineshire to the Firth of Clyde opposite Greenock, the other from Dunbar in Haddingtonshire to the southern part of the Ayrshire coast. This is the great coalfield area of Scotland, which gave rise to most of its manufacturing industry. It is this region which has at all periods of Scottish history been the most densely peopled part of the country. It now contains a greater proportion of the population than ever for new industrial growth (petrochemicals and integrated iron and steel works), which is taking advantage of the existing services of the area, is still strictly contained by the topographical limits of the region.

Climate. The mildness and equability of the climate of the British Isles as a whole have already been explained and illustrated (p. 43). The special advantages of the climate of the British Isles with regard to production are that it is favourable to active exertion throughout the day all the year, and even for the most part stimulates to active exertion; that the mildness of the winter causes little or no interruption to field labour in any of the parts best suited to agriculture, and its comparative freedom from heavy snowfalls causes little interruption to communication; and that it is seldom unfavourable to domesticated animals. For the sake of comparison with other countries it is well to remember that the average annual rainfall at Greenwich (in one of the drier parts of Great Britain) is about 630 mm (25 in), and that while the average mean temperature of the hottest month at Greenwich is 17.5° C (63.5° F), at Edinburgh 14.7° C (58.5° F), that of the coldest month is about the same at both places, 3.9° C (39° F). In general it may be said that the drier parts of Britain — the east — with an annual rainfall of 750 mm (30 in) or less favour arable farming and the ripening of crops; the midland regions and lowlands of the west with between 750 and 1500 mm (30 and 60 in) a year are more suited to grassland farming, for crops are liable to suffer from too much moisture inducing rust diseases. It is only in the highland areas of western Britain that rainfall or humidity conditions can be described as approaching the excessive and so render farming difficult. The distinction thus made between eastern and western regions is important as affecting legislation designed to encourage British agriculture.

The length of the shortest day (sunlight) varies from about 5½ hours in the extreme north to eight hours in the extreme south. In the more thickly peopled region of Scotland the shortest day in the year is about 6½ hours in length (in the latitude of Dundee). It is to be remembered also that the shortness of the day is to some extent compensated in the high latitudes to which the islands belong by the length of the twilight.

Agriculture. In the Middle Ages Britain produced a surplus of agricultural produce and both corn and wool were exported. Home agriculture flourished during the Napoleonic Wars after which, despite temporary setbacks, it continued to flourish until the peak was reached in the 1860s and 70s. Then, the Corn Laws repealed, began the great expansion of agricultural production in the new lands of the United States, Canada, Argentina, and Australia. Cheap food flowed into Britain as payment for manufactured exports and for services rendered. Farming in Britain became a neglected industry. The whole pattern of farming and with it the face of the countryside changed. Farmers economised in labour by turning over from ploughland to grass: acreage under crops, especially cereal crops, decreased accordingly, whilst that under permanent pasture expanded. Marginal and poor land was abandoned and so the area of rough grazings steadily expanded. Industry and housing cut steadily into the farmland. During the First World War the submarine menace threatened food supplies and there was a temporary rise in ploughland and output, especially in 1918, but in general the trend continued to 1938. In that year the threat of war resulted in a change: with the outbreak of war in 1939 enormous energy was put into the farming industry and home production. Because of the demand for airfields the total land available for farming in 1943 — a peak of wartime production — was actually less than in 1938; Table 31 shows the remarkable changes. Ploughland was increased by nearly 50 per cent, wheat and barley areas almost doubled. As a result home food supply was increased from a little over 35 per cent of consumption to about 55 per cent. The former reliance on imported feeding stuffs for animals gave place to the home production of all but a small fraction of the 10m. tons previously imported. Indeed each farmer was required to grow his own to avoid a burden on internal transport.

When the Second World War ended the necessity for maximum home food production remained so that foreign currency could be conserved for the purchase of vital raw materials. The sale of Britain's overseas investments to pay for the war meant that there was no longer an automatic flow of foodstuffs and raw materials as interest which there had been previously.

The revolution in British agriculture was accomplished with the help

Table 31 — Agricultural land use: Great Britain* and Northern Ireland
(figures in thousands)

	1938	1943	1957	1960	1970	
Total land area (*acres*)	59 533	59 533	59 558	59 541	59 533	24 112 ha
Crops and grass (*acres*)	31 755	31 058	31 030	30 860	27 951	11 304 ha
Arable land (*acres*)	12 957	18 728	17 524	18 051	17 800	6 920 ha
Permanent grass (*acres*)	18 798	12 330	13 502	12 809	12 200	4 941 ha
Wheat (*acres*)	1 928	3 464	2 113	2 102	2 495	1 009 ha
Barley (*acres*)	988	1 786	2 622	3 372	5 542	2 242 ha
Oats (*acres*)	2 395	3 680	2 348	1 974	929	376 ha
Sugar beet (*acres*)	336	417	430	436	463	187 ha
Temporary grass (*acres*)	3 968	4 219	6 246	6 786	5 700	2 307 ha
Rough grazings (*acres*)	16 589	17 119	16 827	18 299	17 180	6 957 ha
Cattle total	8 762	9 259	10 881	11 771	12 581	
Cows in milk	2 800	2 910	3 331	3 451	5 309	
Sheep	26 775	20 383	24 796	27 871	26 080	
Pigs	4 383	1 829	5 974	5 724	8 049	
Poultry	74 246	50 729	94 868	103 005	139 513	
Horses for agriculture	748	693	123	66	–	
Tractors	–	117	502†	505‡	–	
Wheat harvest (tons)	1 965	3 447	2 683	2 992	4 108	
Barley harvest (tons)	904	1 645	2 957	4 241	7 378	
Oats harvest (tons)	1 992	3 064	2 145	2 058	1 214	
Sugar beet (tons)	2 191	3 760	4 539	7 215	6 311	

* Including Isle of Man.
† 1956.
‡ 1959.

of mechanisation. The 'average' farm worked as a full-time holding in Britain is about 40 hectares (99 or 100 acres); where rough grazing is included it is reckoned as 4 ha (10 acres) equivalent to 0.4 ha (1 acre) of permanent pasture. There are about 420 000 'farms' in England, Wales, and Scotland, but many of these are small part-time holdings and the number of full-time farmers is estimated to be about 300 000, while some 50 000 are part-time farmers. Broadly every farmer has at least one tractor and various other mechanical farm implements. Britain can claim to be the most highly mechanised farming country in the world and the percentage of the total labour force engaged in agriculture (under 3 per cent) is the second lowest in the world, only Kuwait being lower with 1 per cent. The crop yields and the stocking of land by animals is very high: Britain ranks a little below Denmark, the Netherlands and Belgium in this respect.

The British climate is more suited to grass and fodder crops than to wheat production, so that home production has tended to concentrate on milk, in which the British Isles is self-sufficient, and on dairy produce, leaving a large proportion of the wheat for bread to be imported. The total import of wheat between 1913 and 1935 ranged from 4.8 (1918) to 6.6m. tons (1931). This was cut to an import of

2.8m. in 1944 at the height of the war, and to an average of 4m. tons in 1946–50. In 1973 it was 3.7m.

There have been some notable changes in the cultivation of grain crops in the British Isles since the 1960s. The area under wheat has remained relatively stable with a small increase in 1970, but that devoted to barley has soared at the expense of oats. Barley is now the leading cereal except in northwest Scotland and western Ireland. New strains of short-strawed barley can be grown in areas formerly devoted to oats; they give higher yields than oats, provide good stock feed (especially for pigs); and the shortness of the stem makes them eminently suitable for mechanised harvesting.

The other important move has been towards intensive rearing of poultry and of pigs in enclosed and totally controlled environments. One effect has been to make the United Kingdom self-sufficient in poultry and eggs, formerly imported in quantity.

The growth of the sugar beet industry in this country is of special interest. Experimentally sugar beet had been cultivated on a small scale in various parts of England before the First World War. In 1911 experiments were made at the instance of the Development Commissioners at seven stations scattered over the south, southeast, and midlands of England, and as the result of those experiments the Commissioners regarded it as proved that beet giving yields equalling, if not exceeding, those obtained on the Continent could be grown in England. A factory was built at Cantley, near Norwich, in 1912 but largely with Dutch capital. The industry was not established when war broke out and the factory was closed. After the war assistance was given by the removal of the excise duty in 1922. In the Budget of 1924–25 the import duty on sugar was reduced from 105p to 58p (21s. to 11s. 8d.) per 0.05 ton (per cwt) and the government subsequently agreed to grant a subsidy of 97p (19s. 6d.) per 0.05 ton (per cwt) on homemade sugar (for the first four years, thence forward being gradually reduced) but with an excise duty of 49p (9s. 9d.), thus giving a subsidy to the industry of 107p (21s. 5d.) per 0.05 ton (per cwt). By 1931 there were seventeen factories in operation in England and Scotland and the output for 1930–31 was 422 700 tons, against 291 500 in the preceding season or 50 000 in 1925–26. The subsidy was due to cease in 1935 but the industry, though of great value to the farmers in East Anglia, was unable to carry on without some measure of protection. With continued subsidy the area under beet rose to 136 000 ha (336 000 acres) in 1938 and continued to expand during and after the Second World War to over 160 000 ha (400 000 acres). In 1953 there was a record crop of 5.27m. tons. After further fluctuations, the crop leaped up again in 1960 to 7.21m. tons. Production is affected both by the season and the prevalence of disease (virus yellows), which reduces both volume and sugar content. The processing plant is essentially attached to country districts. Where considerably more than 80 per cent of the raw material is a waste product of the sugar manufactured, but is a valuable cattle food and land fertiliser, the advantage of having the sugar factories close to the beetfields is obvious. The factory industry is essentially a seasonal one, being carried on only for three or four months during the winter, after the beet harvest. It is accordingly one that provides employment in rural areas at a period when agricultural employment is slack, and is at the same time an aid in maintaining the labour supply for those districts all the year round. The production of sugar beet in 1970 was 6.3m. tons.

Geographical factors influencing the growth of Britain's prosperity and trade. Until about 1900 the foreign commerce of the British Isles exceeded in value that of any other country in the world; per head it was greater than that of most other countries in which there was a population of high density. The export trade fell behind that of the United States from 1900 to 1931 absolutely, but not per head. This shows that for foreign commerce the British Isles must have certain advantages of one kind or another, and we must therefore consider what these advantages are. First the advantages and the disadvantages under which the country laboured until the First World War will be enumerated. Secondly those which require elucidation will be examined and notice taken of the ways in which there have been changes since 1913 in the influence of the factors concerned. It should be noted, however, that in this enumeration the sole point of view is the immediate interest of commerce. Chisholm wrote that it was not intended to hint that all the so-called advantages and disadvantages were necessarily to be regarded as such with reference to the wellbeing of the people, and he drew up the following lists.

The advantages were:
1. A favourable climate.
2. The abundance of coal and iron and some other raw materials, especially raw materials leaving much waste.
3. The efficiency of British labour.
4. The fact that nearly all the great mechanical inventions by which industry was revolutionised originated in this country, which thus got the start of other countries in their application.
5. The abundance of capital.
6. The concentration of population in industrial regions, facilitating the organisation of industry, including the minutest subdivision of labour.
7. The completeness of the internal communications.
8. The nearness of the coast on all sides.
9. The numerous seaports.

10. The geographical position.
11. The magnitude of the shipping.
12. The extent of the British colonial and other possessions.
13. The extent to which the English language spread over the globe.
14. The long establishment of commercial relations with the best markets of the world.
15. The free trade policy that prevailed in this country for more than seventy years.

The disadvantages that have to be placed on the other side are:

1. The deficiency of large water power, essential in some branches of industry.
2. The high cost of land arising from the density of population and the great development of industry, a disadvantage necessarily experienced most in the great centres of industry.
3. The higher rate of wages long paid in Great Britain compared with those paid by its chief rivals in manufacturing industry.
4. The government and selfimposed restrictions on labour.
5. The backward state of education, and especially of technical and commercial education, which existed in the United Kingdom compared with the point reached in this respect by some of its rivals at least until 1900 or even 1914.
6. The irrational spelling of the English language.
7. The want of a decimal coinage and system of weights and measures.
8. The high tariffs of many countries of the world while Britain still followed a free trade policy.
9. Currency restrictions imposed in many countries of the world.

It scarcely needs to be pointed out that these advantages and disadvantages listed are not in the order of their importance. Of the advantages, those from 1 to 6 are such as affect the production of articles of commerce, and the remainder, those which pertain to their distribution; and of the former, Nos 1 and 2 may be reckoned as natural advantages, Nos 4, 5, and 6 advantages mainly due to historical causes. No. 3, the efficiency of the British artisan, is largely an historical advantage, due to the acquired skill resulting from the experience of generations and from familiarity with a gradual and constant series of improvements in industrial operations.

With regard to climatic advantage it is unnecessary to say more. But in relation to the second advantage, wealth in coal and iron, it should be pointed out that the strength of these assets lay not only in their abundance but also in the fact that important supplies of both occurred in close proximity and near to seaports. Accordingly early industrialisation developed on the coalfields where there was an ample supply of power as well as the raw materials, coal and iron, needed for the manufacture of machinery. Supplies of limestone and ganister, the other minerals of importance in the iron industry, were never a problem because they are abundant in Britain, occurring in association, either with coal or with iron ore.

At a later stage, with the advent of electricity, thermal power stations using local coal were built on the coalfields, meeting the needs of the nearby industry and of the dense population which had grown up.

In a consideration of the coalfields it should be noticed that the coalfield of Durham and Northumberland is bisected by the estuary of the Tyne, to which belong the seaports which first had major trade in coal; that it is in immediate proximity to Sunderland and various lesser ports; and that its southern end is close to the iron ores of Cleveland. The coalfield of Cumberland includes the seaports of Maryport, Whitehaven and Workington, lying close to the iron ores of south Cumberland and of north Lancashire, once a rich source of iron. The South Wales coalfield gave rise to a vast iron industry because it possessed rich beds of ironstone, now unworked: less refractory ores are now imported and the industry has migrated to the coast. The North Staffordshire coalfield also had an appreciable output of iron ore. In Scotland the coal-

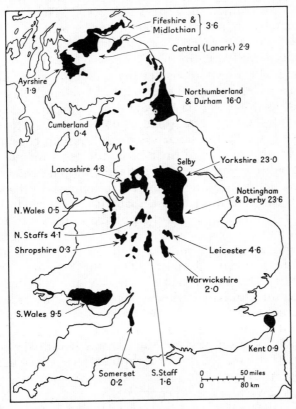

The coalfields of Great Britain and their production in 1968 expressed as a percentage of the total national output

fields are likewise close to the sea and similarly were once rich in iron ore. In the west the Ayrshire coalfield extends to the ports of Troon and Ardrossan; in the Clyde basin the coalfield spreads below the port of Glasgow; and the ports of Grangemouth, Alloa, Burntisland, Dysart, Leith and others are either on or near the coalfields further east. The western coalfield supplied large quantities of splint coal which could be used directly in the smelting of iron ores. The blackband ironstone once plentiful in parts of these coalfields (as in Ayrshire and the Clyde Basin) yielded a very fine quality of wrought iron which was much used in shipbuilding until the development of cheap steel. The ironstone was in the main so rich in carbonaceous matter that the expense for fuel in the operations preliminary to smelting was considerably reduced.

With the exhaustion of the iron ores of the coalfields the only ores at present used are the Jurassic ores of Cleveland, Frodingham, South Lincolnshire and Northamptonshire, containing from 20 to 35 per cent iron, worked opencast near the outcrop, which are suitable for modern steelworks. The hematic ores of Cumberland and Llanharry, richer in iron and containing very little phosphorus, form the only true Bessemer ores obtained in Britain, and are still worked. The United Kingdom depends mainly on imports of concentrated or pelletised iron ore from West Africa, Canada, Sweden, Norway, Brazil, Venezuela, and to some extent from the USSR and Spain.

British coalfields extend considerably under the cover of later rocks and there is little fear of the exhaustion of coal. Reserves, which include seams of 30 cm (1 ft) and upwards in thickness in depth down to 1 200 m (4 000 ft), total some 200 000 tons, sufficient for the country's needs for 800 years at the present rate of consumption. The difficulties which faced the British coal industry after the First World War were mainly due to two causes: the diminution of the export trade and the uneconomic working of the older collieries in the long-worked parts of the coalfields. Most British coalfields today can be divided into two halves: the older, shallower half, partly worked out and operated by old small units, if at all; and the newer, deeper half recently opened up and operated by large modern units. Examples of this twofold division can be found in Durham and in the Yorkshire—Nottingham-shire coalfields. This led first to schemes for the voluntary, or if that failed, compulsory 'rationalisation' of the industry by grouping of col-lieries. Later nationalisation of coal resources followed, and finally the nationalisation of the industry itself under the National Coal Board in 1946. Competition from oil and the Second World War combined to kill the export trade; the present problem is to produce the right qualities of coal for domestic needs at a price competitive with impor-ted oil, natural gas and nuclear energy.

The fourth, fifth, sixth, and seventh of the advantages listed require no special elucidation, though it may be pointed out that (5) and (6), the abundance of capital, and the advanced organisation of industry, are in part a consequence of (4), that is, of the United Kingdom having got the start of other countries in modern mechanical appliances; but this again is subject to a qualification pointed out below (p. 339). Following the Second World War Britain faced the disadvantage of having factories equipped with out-of-date machinery, expensive to replace or too valuable to scrap. With regard to the eighth advantage, the nearness of the coast on both sides, it is hardly necessary to explain how this may place a manufacturing region within easy reach of many more markets than are accessible to one that has outlets only in one direction. The precise nature of this advantage can be illustrated by some of the trade of some of our seaports. Though Lancashire, on the west side of the Pennine Upland, was for long the great seat of cotton manufactures, Hull frequently exported nearly as great a value of cotton yarn as Liverpool; Hull and Grimsby together much more than Liverpool; the eastern ports of Great Britain collectively exported more of that yarn than the western ports. The reason for this was that continental nations such as Germany and France which were then among our chief customers for cotton yarn, were more easily reached from the east side. Woollen manufactures, again, are mainly carried on to the east of the Pennines, but the woven fabrics are much more largely exported from Liverpool than from any other port, though woollen yarns are exported thence only to a limited extent. The abundance of seaports, the ninth advantage enables the advantages just illustrated to be implemented; it is an advantage also in another way, in the extent of the accommodation it provides for shipping. In the British Isles there are more than twenty seaports with a natural depth of at least 8 m (25 ft) at high water, and most of these are situated in the vicinity of the great industrial areas. In view of the increasing size of the shipping of the present day this large number of deep harbours, or harbours which, having soft bottoms, can easily be dredged, is a matter of special importance to the commerce of this country.

The tenth advantage named, the geographical position of the British Isles, is of great moment in more ways than one. In the first place, the Channel has been a natural bulwark of the highest value. For long it enabled the kingdom to place its chief reliance for defence on the Navy and later the Air Force, a much less heavy drain upon the working population than the vast armies which continental nations were obliged to train and keep on foot. Secondly, it is of great importance to British commerce that the islands occupy a somewhat central position among the principal trading nations at the present day. It was of no significance that America lay to the west, until America began to rear a population which entered world trade. In view of the three advantages specially considered in the last two paragraphs, it may safely be asserted that the British Isles have in the aggregate greater advantages than any other area of equal extent for reaching all those parts of the world which are most conveniently reached from the seaboard. The effects of this with respect to the distribution of British products will be understood readily enough from the illustration already given of the advantage of having seaports on different sides; and its influence on trade in foreign goods is considered below. The central position of Britain is similarly advantageous to air services.

The advantages accruing to British commerce from the extent of the Commonwealth are in a large measure indirect. The fact that throughout the Commonwealth the English language is the language of commerce is important. Since 1887 many Commonwealth conferences have been held to discuss among other matters the interests of trade. The self-governing dominions and one-time colonies have given preference in one form or other to imports from the mother country. In this policy Canada was the pioneer in 1898; South Africa and New Zealand followed in 1903, and Australia in 1908. The granting of a preferential tariff to the members of the Commonwealth, generally on a reciprocal basis, is now usual among all members.

In order to realise the importance of the language factor one has only to think of the rapid increase of an English-speaking population, not only in the Commonwealth but also in the United States. In the past century English-speaking peoples have increased more rapidly than the population of the world as a whole; and English is spoken by more people in the world than any other language with the exception of Chinese.

Of the economic disadvantages of the country mentioned above the deficiency of water power is, in view of the great wealth in conveniently situated coal, a disadvantage chiefly in relation to those industries which demand the very high temperatures possible in electric furnaces. Such industries have, it may be noted, developed the water power resources as at Kinlochleven and near Fort William. Elsewhere, in North Wales, in southern Scotland, and latterly in the northwest Highlands and the Grampians, water power is harnessed and electricity generated, the works being connected with the national grid system. The total possible annual saving of coal by the use of water power in the United Kingdom has been estimated at a few million tons at the most and only a small fraction of the electricity generated is derived from water power. A water power scheme was prepared in 1920 by the Ministry of Transport. It was proposed to construct a concrete barrage, serving as a bridge for railway and motor traffic, across the Severn estuary near the tunnel, where the channel is 4 km (2.5 miles) wide. By means of a series of sluices and turbines the tides would be harnessed to develop over 500 000 horsepower during a ten-hour day, with a peak load capacity of over 1m. horsepower. Such an installation would, it is claimed, supply the industries of the Midlands and South Wales, with a permanent supply of cheap electric power. Although a decision was reached after the Second World War to proceed with the road bridge, the power scheme was shelved. Britain has also developed nuclear power stations mainly in remote areas round the coasts.

The second disadvantage, the high cost of land, may be regarded as an inevitable result of the development of industries. The third, the higher rate of wages, if considered by itself, cannot but be looked upon as a disadvantage in the struggle for cheapness into which the competition for foreign commerce in a large measure resolves itself; but it must not be forgotten that in considering the cost of labour the relative efficiency of labour has always to be taken into account. With the raising of standards of living in the world, the consequent rise in real wages, and international agreements on labour conditions, world differences are disappearing.

The state of technical and commercial education in Britain was until a few years ago a more serious disadvantage than it is now.

The want of a decimal coinage and system of weights and measures for long considered an impediment in business transactions is being rectified. Decimal currency was introduced in 1971, and a fully metricated system of weights and measure should be in operation by 1975.

In the earlier editions of his *Handbook of Commercial Geography* Chisholm developed gradually his concepts of the advantages and disadvantages of Britain in the development of international trade. Sir Halford Mackinder in his classic work *Britain and the British Seas*, first published early in the present century, likewise laid much emphasis on the importance of Britain's physical location on the earth's surface. In many ways, however, the discussion is now more of historical than of current interest. It is true that the advent of the air age has again underlined Britain's favourable location, but the position which emerged after the Second World War presented many new features. One is the shortage of land: only 24.1m. hectares (59m. acres) in the whole of England, Wales and Scotland of land of all types to serve the many needs of about 55m. people. The expansion of industry, housing and the needs of recreation, transport and defence have all cut into and are continuing to absorb food-producing land, hence the development of national land use planning. Also, many countries which were once Britain's eager customers for manufactured goods are making their own, competing with us in world markets and even exporting to us. The struggle is to maintain quality and efficiency, often in face of tariff barriers and currency restrictions unknown to an earlier age.

Population. Since the first edition of this work was published in 1889 there have been eight censuses of the United Kingdom, and Table 32 shows the intercensal increase or decrease of the population *per cent per annum* in the main divisions of the kingdom. In the last line is

Table 32*a* — Intercensal increase or decrease of UK population per cent per year

Country	1881–91	1891–1901	1901–11	1911–21	1921–31	1931–51	1951–61	1961
England	1.10	1.14	0.98	0.45	0.60	0.51	0.54	0.5
Wales	1.20	1.32	1.85	0.91	−0.24	0.01	0.16	0.9
Scotland	0.75	1.06	0.63	0.25	−0.08	0.26	0.24	0.1
Great Britain	1.06	1.14	0.99	0.46	0.47	0.45	0.48	0.5
Northern Ireland	−0.54	0.01	0.11	0.06	−0.12	0.51	0.39	0.6
United Kingdom (as now constituted)	1.00	1.10	0.96	0.44	0.45	0.45	0.48	0.4
United States	*1890*	*1900*	*1910*	*1920*	*1930*	*1940*	*1960*	*197*
census increases (%)	25.5	20.7	21.0	14.9	16.1	7.2 *1950* 14.5	18.5	13.2

shown for comparison the *decennial percentage* increases in the population of the United States. Note that there was no British census in 1941, so that the column for 1931—51 covers twenty years. Census populations in 1971: England 45.8m., Wales 2.7m., Scotland 5.2m., Northern Ireland 1.5m.

Table 32*a* shows the general trend of the population. The pre-1914 moderate increase in Britain (with an absolute decline in Ireland) gave place to a slight increase in Britain as a whole but an absolute decline in Scotland and Wales. This was rural depopulation, and the actual or relative decline applied to rural counties of England as well. The increase was mainly in the main manufacturing belt of Britain — an area stretching from Manchester to London which had more than 57 per cent of the people of the country.

The changes in the period 1931—51 show an increase in all parts of the United Kingdom. This is in part due to an influx of political refugees from continental Europe, notably Poles and Austrians. The decline in Wales was checked; even the absolute decline in the Irish Republic was reversed.

Although there has been, since the end of the Second World War, emigration to Canada, Australia, New Zealand, Rhodesia and elsewhere, there has at the same time been an influx of Commonwealth immigrants from the crowded and poverty stricken parts of the West Indies, such as Jamaica, and from West Africa. Many young Pakistanis have also come to Britain.

Urbanisation of population. In common with most countries of the world Britain has continued to show rural depopulation and urban expansion. Official figures of 'rural population' refer to persons living in rural districts which may in fact include towns of considerable size. Persons living in farms, scattered rural habitations, and in villages in fact

ble 32b — Population changes in counties and conurbations in Great Britain, intercensal period 1961–71

County	Change, per cent per year 1961–71	Population 1971, thousands	County	Change, per cent per year 1961–71	Population 1971, thousands
ffolk, W.	2.48	165	Yorkshire, N. Riding	0.88	726
untingdon			Devon	0.88	898
and Peterborough	2.44	203	Westmorland	0.81	73
rkshire	2.36	637	Nottinghamshire	0.78	976
xfordshire	2.12	382	Gloucestershire	0.72	1 077
sex	2.09	1 358	Denbighshire	0.62	185
dfordshire	1.95	464	Herefordshire	0.57	139
uckinghamshire	1.95	588	Pembrokeshire	0.50	99
ssex, W.	1.81	492	Derbyshire	0.46	885
orthamptonshire	1.64	469	Monmouthshire	0.39	462
ertfordshire	1.61	925	Warwickshire	0.32	2 082
intshire	1.59	176	Yorkshire, E. Riding	0.31	543
ampshire	1.59	1 565	Yorkshire, W. Riding	0.28	3 785
utland	1.57	27	Lincolnshire	—	—
ent	1.56	1 399	(Holland)	0.23	106
nglesey	1.46	60	Cardiganshire	0.23	55
orset	1.44	362	Glamorgan	0.23	1 259
iltshire	1.41	487	Caernarvonshire	0.11	123
ight, Isle of	1.35	110	Durham	0.05	1 410
merset	1.32	683	Lancashire	−0.02	5 118
ropshire	1.25	337	Cumberland	−0.07	292
eicestershire	1.24	772	Radnorshire	−0.10	18
heshire	1.23	1 546	Montgomeryshire	−0.24	43
ssex, E.	1.17	748	Northumberland	−0.31	796
orcestershire	1.07	693	Carmarthenshire	−0.33	163
ffolk, E.	1.07	381	Brecon	−0.33	53
ornwall and			Merionethshire	−0.81	35
Isles of Scilly	1.07	382			
urrey	1.02	1 003	*Conurbation*		
incolnshire			West Yorkshire	0.14	1 728
(Lindsey)*	0.97	471	West Midlands	−0.03	2 372
taffordshire	0.96	1 858	South East		
orfolk	0.96	618	Lancashire	−0.14	2 393
incolnshire			Central Clydeside	−0.42	1 728
(Kesteven)*	0.91	233	Tyneside	−0.60	805
ambridgeshire			Greater London	−0.70	7 452
and Isle of Ely	0.89	303	Merseyside	−0.88	1 267

Excluding Lincoln County Borough.

341

number only about 10 per cent of the population, including the 3 per cent actually engaged in farming. As farming has become more efficient through mechanisation and in other ways, the same output is possible with a smaller labour force. The result is rural depopulation except in those areas which appeal to retired people, or to towndwellers in search of a weekend cottage, or to those who work in towns but prefer to live in rural surroundings and travel some distance to work. But of the 154 towns with a population exceeding 50 000 in 1971, ninety-five had continued growth in the intercensal period 1961–71. It was realised before 1939 that the growth of Greater London and Greater Birmingham constituted a threat to efficient organisation and the dispersal rendered imperative by bombing during the Second World War is now regarded as a proper objective of planned location of industry. Manufacturers were encouraged to go to the areas, usually the older or peripheral industrial areas, scheduled for development; and New Towns were, and continue to be developed to encourage movement away from urban areas which are regarded as having grown too large.

British industries. The local distribution of British manufacturing industries presents many points of interest, some pure geographical, some historical. The textile industry in the United Kingdom no longer plays a significant part in the economy, but the geographical factors which influenced its location are interesting for historical reasons. The *cotton industry* came to be almost wholly confined to a few localities in the west of Great Britain: in England the spinning and weaving of cotton almost restricted to the west side of the Pennine Upland, mainly · to that part of Lancashire which lies to the south of the Ribble; in Scotland, to Glasgow and other manufacturing towns in the west. The reasons were, initially, geographical. In the Middle Ages the local supply of wool from the Pennine sheep gave encouragement to a crofter's industry of spinning and weaving. The local soft waters were suitable for scouring and dyeing and later the water power from swift streams was used. Liverpool grew as a port with the 'trade triangle' (p. 373) and the new textile material cotton was naturally introduced here to a community already skilled in the processes of spinning and weaving. The humid climate of the western side of the Pennines proved peculiarly favourable, whilst with the coming of the industrial revolution there was coal present in abundance. Both for the spinning and weaving of cotton a moist climate is desirable, and in districts where the manufacture is carried on, dry weather, and especially cold and dry weather, adds considerably to the expense of the operations; for where the air is too dry the yarn is liable to become brittle through losing its natural moisture, and all the more likely is this to result when, as on cold days, the temperature of the spinning 'mill' or weaving 'shed' is much above the temperature of the air outside. The failure of cotton factories started in other parts of England was attributed in some cases to no other factor. Even the shelter of a hill against dry east winds was considered a matter of high pecuniary value. Modern factories, equipped with humidifiers, can afford to ignore such factors once so important. Soft water for dyeing and other operations remains, however, an important factor.

In England the town most closely associated with the cotton industry is Manchester. This is one of those towns which owed their original importance in a large measure to the fact of their lying in a plain just on the border of hill country, a position which, as already explained, naturally leads to the convergence of roads from many parts of the plain as well as from one or more valleys among the hills. It is natural to find that a town has been situated in this position from a very early date. Manchester (the ancient Mancunium) was already in existence in the time of the Romans, and in the early part of the fourteenth century it became known as a manufacturing town through the settlement of Flemings here. But the first materials of its textile manufactures were wool, a local product, and linen yarn obtained from Ireland. It is uncertain when cotton was added to these, and though Manchester 'cottons' were spoken of even in the fourteenth century, it was not till long after that pure cotton fabrics were made there, or anywhere else in England. Since the great inventions of the eighteenth century Manchester developed with the cotton industry, the trade in cotton goods and yarns having always been centred there. In 1774 Manchester and Salford together had a population of little more than 27 000; at the census of 1801 the joint population of the two townships had risen to 84 000. In 1891 the population within a radius of 19 km (12 miles) of Manchester Exchange was upwards of 1 600 000, in 1921 it was over 2 200 000 and in 1931, 2 300 000. In 1951 the census returns gave the population of the conurbation as 2 421 000 — little change in 1971. In the course of time Manchester has become the commercial and business centre of the group rather than the chief manufacturing town.

Among the surrounding towns once mainly engaged in the cotton industry are Oldham, Bolton, Bury, Rochdale, and other towns which have enriched the bleak Lancashire moorlands to the north and east of Manchester; Stockport and Hyde in Cheshire to the south, and Glossop in a Derbyshire valley southeast of Manchester: all situated on the great coalfield west of the Pennine Upland. Further north are Preston, Blackburn, Accrington, and Burnley, all Lancashire towns, the last three likewise situated on the same coalfield. Oldham and Bolton are the towns most noted for cotton spinning mills, the former being engaged chiefly in the production of medium yarns, the latter of the 'higher counts'. The northern towns of Burnley, Blackburn, Preston, Nelson, and Accrington, all situated along the route of the railway from Preston to

Skipton, led in cotton-weaving. All these towns are on the northern margin of Rossendale Fells, a spur of the Pennine Upland, some at a level of about 150 m (500 ft). Wigan, though once a cotton manufacturing town, was notable chiefly as the principal centre of the coal trade in Lancashire. In 1900 there were no fewer than thirty-five towns in South Lancashire and the parts immediately adjoining which had at least 100 000 spindles engaged in this industry, Oldham heading the list with nearly 12m. and Bolton following with 5m. In the heyday of the cotton industry, in 1914 the number of spindles belonging to the Oldham federation was 19m., that of Bolton, 9m. In face of the competition of Japan, India and many other countries, and competition from manmade fibres the relative and actual importance of the cotton industry has declined. Many mills have been converted to other manufactures, others have closed. In 1939 there were 1 600 cotton mills in Lancashire; in 1968 there were only 635, and the number continues to dwindle. Between one-third and one-half of the output is now entirely or partly concerned with manmade fibres. It is no exaggeration to say that the textile industry of Lancashire is now more closely allied to the chemical industry than to the natural product, cotton.

For its supplies of raw cotton the great cotton manufacturing region of England was once dependent on the port of Liverpool, but later a very considerable quantity of cotton was imported direct into Manchester by the Manchester Ship Canal, which was constructed between 1887 and 1893 and opened for traffic on New Year's Day, 1894. It extends from Eastham on the south side of the Mersey to the heart of Manchester, has a total length of 57 km (35.5 miles), and a minimum depth of 8.5 m (28 ft). The bottom width of the canal at the full depth is, with a few exceptions, 36.5 m (120 ft), which is sufficient for quite large ships to pass one another, at the bend at Runcorn the width has been increased to nearly 54 m (175 ft). The entrance locks at Eastham have been supplemented by the Queen Elizabeth II Dock — the largest oil dock in the country — opened in January 1954, with accommodation for four 30 000 DWT tankers and the new jetty at Tranmere for larger vessels. Tankers of up to 18 000 DWT regularly navigate the canal as far as Stanlow Oil Docks, and ships of up to 12 500 DWT go as far as the Terminal Docks in Manchester.

The port is provided with graving docks, large grain elevators, oil tanks, cold storage accommodation, and other modern equipment. Throughout its length the canal traverses part of the busiest industrial region of England. At the Manchester end the industrial development at Trafford Park has diversified industries. There are iron and steel works at Irlam, several at Runcorn, and the great Stanlow oil refining and petrochemical complex near the western end. In 1894 the total value of the trade of the port (imports and exports) was £6.9m. (about 40 per cent imports), in 1929 it amounted to £69.5m. (90 per cent imports),

Table 33 — Some imports and exports at the ports of Liverpool and Manchester, 1893–1957, comparing the quantities of the various commodities in percentages of the total trade of the United Kingdom in such commodities

Commodity		1893	1894	1906	1912	1935	1951	1957
Imports								
Raw cotton	L	92.3	90.5	77.7	79.3	65.7	65.6	75.9
	M	—	1.6	16.6	16.6	33.4	28.5	23.2
Paper-making	L	10.8	10.4	3.0	1.8	0.6	3.2	2.0
materials	M	—	4.1	14.3	10.9	9.7	12.2	17.6
Wood, sawn and	L	9.2	8.2	6.6	8.4	26.3	27.4	12.6
hewn	M	—	1.2	5.6	5.2	4.5	1.9	4.2
Manganese ore	L	—	—	20.6	20.3	21.3	41.6	46.2
	M	—	—	7.3	10.3	6.0	1.7	11.4
Petroleum	L	22.4	19.9	9.9	8.3	6.9	4.3	1.8
	M	—	0.3	12.1	9.8	13.0	13.4	17.9
Wheat	L	28.9	25.3	25.6	23.0	19.0	19.7	17.5
	M	—	0.1	5.3	7.8	10.2	6.4	9.0
Maize	L	25.0	24.9	22.9	17.7	25.7	23.9	18.5
	M	—	0.1	2.4	2.4	4.1	4.0	10.2
Bacon and hams	L	63.3	61.7	51.4	34.9	10.5	0.2	2.8
	M	—	—	1.9	1.2	1.9	0.5	1.8
Exports								
Cotton fabrics	L	75.9	73.2	69.0	66.2	67.8	67.3	58.9
	M	—	3.6	9.1	12.3	7.2	4.2	8.3
Cotton yarn	L	39.4	35.7	34.2	31.2	34.9	43.9	58.5
	M	—	17.2	22.2	25.2	15.5	9.9	11.1
Woollen and	L	48.2	40.3	57.2	32.1	37.4	35.5	34.0
worsted fabrics	M	—	0.5	2.6	3.5	4.0	7.5	7.3
Machinery, etc.	L	34.3	31.2	32.4	32.9	38.8	38.1	31.0
	M	—	2.1	5.1	5.6	3.9	4.3	3.8

in 1951 to £361m. (75 per cent imports), and in 1956 to £408m. (over half imports). In respect of the value of its trade Manchester ranks fourth among UK ports, imports outweighing exports. The total capital expenditure on the canal down to the end of 1913 was nearly £17m., and the first dividend on the preference stock belonging to the Corporation of Manchester (2.5 per cent) was paid in 1915.

The growth of the port of Manchester is particularly interesting historically: some details are given in Table 33. Much of the trade attracted to Manchester is destined in fact to the many factories now extended along the length of the canal.

It will be observed that petroleum, an article of comparatively small value in proportion to its bulk, is the commodity in which the trade of Manchester and the canal has grown most rapidly to the prejudice of that of Liverpool. In paper-making materials we have another bulky article. In relation to it we have to consider the situation of the mills, and with reference to that again the situation of the streams supplying the water and that of the consumers of the product. Raw cotton was for long the most valuable of the articles imported at Manchester. The growth of that import as compared with the corresponding import at Liverpool was for a considerable period steady, though slow, showing the difficulty of displacing an old market requiring a high degree of organisation. The hold which Liverpool retained on the export trade of cotton fabrics is not surprising if the widespread distribution of the markets for these products is considered, and the relations of the chief weaving towns to the ports of Liverpool and Manchester respectively. Among later developments, all illustrative of the influence of an enormous consuming population in the immediate neighbourhood, may be mentioned the import trade in frozen meat, wool, and tea. The first large cargo of wool from Australasia reached the port in July 1916, and large provision was later made for this trade.

At a distance from the Manchester district the only large town in which cotton manufactures formed the staple industry is Nottingham on the Trent, in which certain branches of the manufacture, that of cotton hosiery, and the making of machinemade net and lace, the latter less important than formerly, have their chief seat.

In Scotland the only town specially associated with cotton manufacturing is Paisley, with a manufacture of cotton thread.

The area of the West Riding coalfield which enjoys the pure, soft or lime-free water which flows from the Millstone Grit uplands is for the *woollen industry* of Great Britain much what Lancashire is for the cotton industry, though this section of the textile manufactures of the country is not so restricted in its range as the other. The principal centre of the trade of this region is Leeds, which occupies a situation geographically very similar to that of Manchester: just off the Pennines, a business centre with a surrounding ring of manufacturing towns.

Leeds stands on the Aire amidst the gently undulating country that lies between the broad flat Vale of York and the narrow dales on the west. It thus has free communication with the north, east and southeast, and on the west it commands two principal lines of communication, one by the valleys of the Calder and Colne to Manchester and South Lancashire, the other by the valley of the Aire to mid-Lancashire. Like Manchester, it is a very old seat of trade and manufacturing industry. It is described by Camden (1607) as 'much enriched by the woollen manufacture', and nowadays, while still retaining its importance in the woollen trade, it has added to that many other important industries. It is the commercial centre of the woollen trade rather than a manufacturing centre. Besides being the chief centre of the wholesale clothing trade in the country, it has footwear and metal industries (especially copper).

The narrow dales of Yorkshire to the west of Leeds are filled with large or small manufacturing towns once wholly engaged in the woollen industry. In some of them its origin belongs to as remote a date as in Leeds itself, these dales 'well supplied with water, fuel, and cheap provisions', and surrounded by sheep pastures yielding a fine lustrous wool, having been among the localities to which the woollen industry migrated at the close of the Middle Ages, when the expense of living hindered its prosperity on more ancient seats nearer London. In Wakefield and Halifax as well as in Leeds foreign artisans were settled by Henry VII in 1489, and a generation later Halifax was already noted for its products in this branch of manufacture. When modern machinery was introduced the abundance of coal in the region served to stimulate the industry in those valleys still further, and many of the towns now engaged in the manufacture date their rise only from that period.

At the present day the centre of all branches of the worsted manufacture is Bradford, which is situated in a small basin among the hills to the west of Leeds and a little to the south of the Aire. Here the primary advantage seems to have been abundance of pure water suitable for the scouring of the wool, an advantage which the corporation of the town took care to preserve as the industry increased. The worsted industry is another of those industries in which the abundance of capital is of great importance. The combing of the wool is a highly specialised industry involving the use of complicated machinery, but employing mainly female labour. Accordingly, to be carried on economically it must be on a large scale. Bradford likewise had large silk, velvet, and plush mills (in which the raw material used was schappe or spun silk), and close beside it on the Aire itself is the model town of Saltaire once famed for alpaca. Halifax in the Calder valley still specialises in light worsted fabrics, and carpets but also has brass and wire industries. Huddersfield on the Colne, a tributary of the Calder though not even mentioned by Camden, is pre-eminent in the manufacture of high-class woollens and worsteds and in pattern design. Other industries include dyestuffs and vehicle building. Dewsbury and Batley manufacture heavier fabrics, including blankets and shoddy and make textile machinery. Wakefield, Barnsley, Keighley, Morley, Heckmondwike, and many others in this area are engaged in some branch of the woollen industry. Even on the west side of the Pennine Upland there are some towns that still carry on their old woollen manufactures, mainly felts, basic to the slipper industry, flannels and blankets. Rochdale has flannel mills, and Bury, Ashton, and Glossop all manufacture woollens of some kind; Denton and Stockport have felt factories.

The district in the west of England that early became known for its 'cloths' as distinguished from the 'stuffs', for which the bulk of English wool was best adapted, still retains something of its renown in connection

347

with this manufacture, and especially for the making of broadcloth. In some of the towns in which the industry was formerly pursued it has died out, but it still flourishes at Stroud in Gloucestershire and in the Stroud valley generally, and survives at Witney (blankets), Trowbridge (woollens and worsteds), Wilton and Axminster (carpets) and to a small degree in Frome, Wellington and Ashburton.

In the north it is interesting to note that Kendal still retains something of the industry for which it was already known before the close of the fourteenth century; but in the east of England, where numerous towns were once noted for their woollen or worsted goods, even Norwich the cultural centre with footwear, food processing, engineering and many other industries has lost its textile industries.

In Leicester, a manufacturing town throughout its history, the woollen and worsted industries arose from the extension of hosiery manufactures. The Leicestershire breed of sheep yields one of the finest wools for the making of worsted yarn; and there was the advantage of the nearby coalfield. The making of lace and elastic webbing was added to the textile industries. Kidderminster in Worcestershire was for long celebrated for its carpets; but it should be noted that the so-called Kidderminster carpets are made chiefly in Scotland and the Yorkshire woollen districts.

In Scotland abundant soft water and the widespread rearing of sheep led to a scattered woollen industry, of which a few significant remnants remain. Woollen manufactures were once the staple industry of certain towns in the basin of the Tweed: Hawick (now devoted to hosiery), Jedburgh, Galashiels from which the industry spread to Selkirk, and Innerleithen. They came to specialise in a cloth appropriately known as tweed, a name derived not from the river but from the misspelling of 'twill' or 'tweel'. Tweed is now produced in other parts of Scotland and in Yorkshire. Carpets and other woollen goods are made in the Glasgow–Paisley, Ayr–Kilmarnock districts. On the steep south slopes of the Ochil Hills the woollen industry still has centres at Alva, Alloa and Tillicoultry. Finally mention must be made of the handloom production, now mainly from machine-spun yarn, of the famous Harris homespun tweeds in the Hebrides; and the domestic knitwear industry in the Shetlands.

The leading textile industry of Northern Ireland was *linen*. The United Kingdom still has about one-third of the world's flax spindles and Ulster is the most important linen manufacturing region in the British Isles. The manufacture is now almost restricted to Belfast and the surrounding district. It first received a stimulus in this area, especially at Lisburn on the Lagan above Belfast, at the end of the seventeenth century through the settlement of Huguenot families after the revocation of the Edict of Nantes. The excellence of the spring water in the Belfast area was important in bleaching, and the linens produced have always been of the highest quality. For the finest linens flax was, and is, imported from Belgium, which also now supplies linen yarn. Before 1914 the bulk of the flax was imported from Latvia, Estonia, northwest Russia as well as from Holland. The USSR still provides a certain amount. In Scotland the chief centres of linen manufacture are Kirkcaldy, Dunfermline and Dundee; in Dundee it is chiefly the coarser linens that are produced. Most of the linen yarn used is now obtained from Belfast. This branch of industry has been carried on in Scotland mainly north of the Firth of Tay since the eighteenth century, and its predominance there may perhaps be ascribed to the fact that the local ports are the first reached by ships rounding the north of Denmark from the flax-growing lands bordering the Baltic. Dunfermline in the west of Fife has been producing damask tablelinens since the early part of the eighteenth century. About one-third of the output of the linen industry is exported, mostly to North America, the United States taking a third of total exports. West Germany and Italy take most of the yarn.

Jute yarns and fabrics, including hessian and sacking, are still manufactured at Dundee, where the industry first developed in the United Kingdom. Jute is widely used in carpet-making, and in the linoleum industry, the centre of which is Kirkcaldy. The raw material comes almost entirely from Bangladesh. Bulk handling of grain and the use of plastic materials have cut severely into the trade.

The *silk* industry of the British Isles is almost confined to England and is still pursued to a small extent, despite competition from manmade fibres, mainly in Macclesfield. It reached its peak in the first half of the nineteenth century, for long a widespread domestic industry, but by then firmly established on an organised commercial basis in Derbyshire and the neighbouring parts of Staffordshire and Cheshire, where the streams furnished pure water, an important requirement. Macclesfield and Congleton in Cheshire, Leek in north Staffordshire, Derby, Ilkeston and Chesterfield in Derbyshire were all important silk fabric producing towns. In general the mechanised silk fabric industry developed at locations on the outskirts of the main textile manufacturing areas. Refugee Huguenots in the seventeenth century brought their skills to Coventry, where a flourishing manufacture of ribbons soon developed, and to London, where the manufacture of silk was for long carried on in Spitalfields and Bethnal Green.

All these natural raw materials of the textile industry, cotton, wool, flax, jute, silk, once so important to the economy of the United Kingdom face competition from *manmade fibres* of cellulosic and noncellulosic origin. Experimental work on 'artificial' fibres in Britain dates from 1850, but it was only after the Second World War that the great upsurge in production came, especially of such noncellulosic fibres as nylon. The manmade fibre industry is part chemical part textile, and it is impossible to generalise on the geographical influences at work in its location. The most notable factories are at present at Wilton, on Teesside, at Grimsby, and in Northern Ireland; and to a less degree in South Wales, at Manningtree in Essex, and at Tiverton in Devon. The home market absorbs much of their great output of manmade fibres, but there is a rising export of synthetic fabrics and of synthetic yarn which compensates, in small measure, for the diminishing exports of other textiles. Textiles no longer dominate as the major export from the United Kingdom; their place has been taken by metals, manufactures therefrom and engineering products.

Iron smelting is one of Britain's most ancient industries: the precise date of its origin is unknown, but it certainly antedates the Christian era by more than 500 years. Most of the iron ore now used in the iron and steel industry in the British Isles is imported, although domestic Jurassic ores still provide a useful resource (see p. 336). The basic demands of an iron and steel industry are simple: a supply of iron ore, a supply of fuel, and a market for the produce: the industry cannot exist unless at least one of these needs is either near at hand or easily accessible. At various times the location of the main centres of the industry in Britain have shifted in response to the exhaustion of local iron ore resources, changes in processing techniques involving the favouring of one type of ore or another, or improved transportation routes. There are also many iron and steel plants which continue to operate in locations where the advantageous geographical factors which initially gave rise to the choice of site have ceased to operate, illustrating 'industrial momentum' or 'geographical inertia'. A very full exposition of the history and the present situation in respect of the iron smelting and iron and steel industries will be found in L. Dudley Stamp and S. H. Beaver, *The British Isles*, sixth edition (Longman, 1971), and a shorter account in L. Dudley Stamp, *A Commercial Geography*, ninth edition (Longman, 1973).

Iron ore smelting today is carried out (*a*) at locations in the fields of the low-grade Jurassic ores (such as Scunthorpe and Corby); (*b*) at ports or waterside locations convenient for the processing of imported ores (Middlesbrough and Workington, both of which initially had the advantage of nearby ore supplies; at Cardiff, available coking coal being an original advantage; and at Dagenham); and (*c*) on some coalfields where the original advantages were the local supplies of Coal Measure ironstone and suitable fuel (such as at Consett, Ilkeston, Coatbridge, Bilston, Stoke-on-Trent). It is especially those which fall in the last group which provide examples of industrial momentum.

The locational demands of the *steel-making* industry differ from those of iron smelting. Steelworks may be (*a*) adjacent to smelting works, leading to the integrated works which now dominate in Britain (for example Motherwell (Ravenscraig), Consett, Middlesbrough,

Scunthorpe, Corby, Rotherham, Margam, Newport, Cardiff, Ebbw Vale, Port Talbot, Shotton, Irlam and Workington: notice the predominance of coastal locations); (*b*) close to the market; (*c*) in an engineering district where the works provide a ready supply of scrap as well as a market for the output of the steelworks, an example of perpetual motion (for example at Wednesbury and Motherwell). Scotland particularly is making full use of LD converters and electric furnaces, and the hotstrip mill at Ravenscraig provides large quantities of sheet steel for the motor vehicle industry.

An example of the way in which the iron and steel industry has adapted to change is illustrated at Teesside. Middlesbrough, on the south side of the Tees, owes its rise to a bed of iron ore, previously discovered in the valley of the Esk near Whitby, being traced in 1850 to the vicinity of the present town. The location of Middlesbrough, convenient for obtaining supplies of fine coking coal from southwest Durham and of limestone from outcrops within 65 km (40 miles) to the northwest, and well served by railways, presented all the conditions for the establishment of a great iron industry. All that was necessary to make it a great seaport was the dredging of the estuary of the Tees to a depth sufficient to admit large vessels and to create a harbour protected from the waves of the North Sea. Both these objectives were achieved, the latter by the construction of a breakwater composed partly of the scoriae from neighbouring blast furnaces. When the acid steel process was introduced Middlesbrough, at its waterside location, was well placed to receive the necessary high-grade Spanish iron ores; and transport costs were economic because the ore carriers were laden with coal from the coalfield nearby for their return voyage. The flat land of the estuary provided room for the industry to expand. Foreign competition in the iron and steel industry followed the First World War, necessitating the modernisation of plant and the rationalisation of the Teesside branch of the industry in all its aspects. The number of blast furnaces was reduced. Since the Second World War a new ore terminal has been built to accommodate bulk ore carriers of 100 000 tons bringing supplies of iron ore from West Africa, the Americas and Sweden to the new fully integrated works. The coastal location of Teesside, combined with the availability of flat land needed for modern iron and steel plant and the good lines of communication with the domestic industrial market are now the most advantageous geographical factors which encourage the development of the iron and steel industry in the Middlesbrough area.

In connection with the manufacture of articles made from iron, two towns in England are specially noteworthy: Birmingham and Sheffield. Both became engaged in the working of metals at a very early date, and both have grown to a large size through the prosecution of such industries down to the present day.

Birmingham lies almost exactly in the middle of the low plateau between the Rivers Trent, Severn, and Avon. The surrounding forests, together with abundance of iron ore in the neighbourhood, seem to have determined the form of the industry which grew up here. The smiths of Birmingham are mentioned as early as 1538. Under the name of Bremicham the town is described by Camden in 1607 as 'swarming with inhabitants, and echoing with the noise of anvils'. In 1727 its iron and hardware manufactures were estimated to employ or support upwards of 50 000 people. The local iron ore is no longer used; the 'Black Country' is no longer a country of blast furnaces belching forth smoke by day and lighting the sky with a lurid glare by night. But the heavy iron and steel industries have given rise to a great variety of metal manufactures especially of articles of small size. Birmingham and the whole of the adjoining parts of south Staffordshire, Worcestershire, and Warwickshire are crowded with large and small towns, Wolverhampton, Walsall, Wednesbury, West Bromwich, Dudley, the inhabitants of which are all mainly engaged in similar occupations — the making of all kinds of articles in metal as well as other goods especially associated with the supply of food and domestic articles to the dense local population. All kinds of domestic ironmongery as well as needles and pins are produced in this district, but motorcar components, engines and machinery are the major manufactures, and motor vehicle assembly the major enterprise. Bromsgrove, Redditch, and Stourbridge in Worcestershire belong to the same group of towns in respect of the nature of the industry which they carry on. Redditch and West Bromwich for example supply springs for the car assembly works, Birmingham steel tubes.

In those regions where there are heavy industries relying on male labour there results a surplus of female labour. Consequently light industries tend to become established in the same areas to absorb this female labour. The food industries of Birmingham (e.g. chocolate at Bournville) may be noted in this connection.

Sheffield lies at a junction of valleys in the extreme south of Yorkshire. In the neighbourhood there were supplies of coal and iron, as well as water power and excellent grindstones, long used in the making of cutlery, fine cutting tools and the best tool steel. A great stimulus was given to this industry by the discovery in 1740 by Huntsman, a Sheffield cutler, of the improved method of making cementation or crucible steel. But with the introduction of the Bessemer process of steel-making in 1858 Sheffield became the seat of steel industries on a much larger scale, making ships' plates, armourplates, crankshafts and axles, ordnance, and all kinds of steel castings and forgings. For the finest work it has for years imported the high grade iron ore from Sweden. Local water power is no longer used, nor are the grindstones; there is no local iron ore but the momentum remains, and Sheffield continues to make special steels. Despite its inland situation it has the advantage of accumulated plant and steel, and continues to contribute 60 per cent of the national output of alloy steel.

Industrialisation in Britain has progressed over so many years that it is no exaggeration to say that there are now very few sizeable towns which lack either a foundry or a factory which makes use of iron and steel. British engineering towns fall into distinct types: (*a*) those which developed near supplies of coal and iron, such as the towns of the coalfields, where the type of engineering depends on local factors; (*b*) those away from the resources of coal and iron which grew from a local specific demand for certain iron products, such as agricultural implements; (*c*) those which developed as a result of the coming of the railways; (*d*) those which have arisen on account of a large available pool of labour.

It is impossible in a book of this length to detail the **engineering** activities in Britain but the regional classification of engineering provinces as listed in Stamp and Beaver, *The British Isles* (sixth edition) gives a very broad general guide; only the more important items are mentioned:

Manchester and south Lancashire. Textile machinery, constructional engineering, engines and locomotives, and electrical apparatus. The heavy machine tool trade is the greatest in the country. After Manchester and its suburbs the chief engineering towns are Blackburn, Bolton, Preston and Oldham.

Yorkshire, Nottinghamshire and Derbyshire coalfield. Textile machinery (West Riding), heavy engineering, locomotives (Leeds, Huddersfield, Wakefield), machine tools, drilling and boring machinery, hydraulic apparatus, constructional steelwork; all employing iron and steel from Middlesbrough, Scunthorpe and Sheffield; the special trades of Sheffield; and the miscellaneous industries of Derbyshire and Nottinghamshire.

The northeast coast. Marine and locomotive engines on Tyneside; ship plates, rails and constructional steelwork on Teesside.

The Scottish Lowlands. Marine engineering, constructional engineering, heavy machinery, locomotives, heavy electrical engineering; machine tools, mining equipment, hydraulic engineering machinery, sugar-making machinery; cast iron articles; sewing machines.

The 'Black Country' and Birmingham. Heavy foundry and forge work, constructional engineering; hardware, hollow-ware, railway rolling stock, springs, chains, tubes.

The smaller Midland coalfields and adjacent areas. In North Staffordshire miscellaneous foundry products and machinery for pottery industry; locomotive building, heavy electrical engineering, reinforced concrete engineering at Stafford; farm machinery (Uttoxeter). In Warwickshire and Leicestershire miscellaneous iron and steel industries producing components for the motor assembly and aircraft industries; castings, forgings, tools (Coventry); heating and ventilating plant, machinery for hosiery and footwear trades, stone-crushing machinery (Leicester); electrical apparatus and machinery (Rugby and Loughborough).

Southeastern Britain. Scattered miscellaneous machinery industries and foundry products, especially agricultural and excavating machinery and locomotives; excavating machinery (Lincoln); dredges (Gainsborough); cranes, excavators, railway goods and electric road vehicles (Ipswich); boilers and gas engines (Colchester); petrol-driven farm machinery, road rollers (Grantham); pumps, oil engines, electrical gear (Bedford); motor assembly, ball bearings, refrigerating plant (Luton); specialised motor vehicles (Guildford); oil engines (Yeovil); motor assembly (Oxford); multifarious engineering trades of London, the largest employer of engineering labour in Britain, where electrical and motor trades are particularly important.

The *motor vehicle assembly* industry deserves special mention because its influence is so farreaching and its products figure largely in exports from the United Kingdom. In the main it developed in towns where the bicycle industry was already entrenched: Oxford and Coventry are the supreme examples. The innumerable components entering the assembly plant come from a wide range of industries, and initially there was a tendency for motor works to be opened in areas with an established tradition of engineering, capable of supplying skilled labour (for example Dagenham near London). In areas of industrial decline motor works can provide employment if there are good supply routes: the establishment of the industry on Merseyside (Ford at Halewood, Vauxhall at Hooton, Leyland—BMC at Speke near Liverpool) and in Scotland (Rootes at the new town of Linwood, southwest of Glasgow, BMC at Bathgate) was due to government policy to encourage manufacturing in Development Areas. In Britain the making of panel steel car bodies is separate from the assembly plants, and is concentrated in Llanelli, Swindon and Wolverhampton, the sheet steel being provided by Port Talbot. Nearly all the components, including tyres, are supplied mainly by West Midland towns: the Lucas works at Birmingham provide most of the electrical equipment, Leamington Spa most of the clutches, chromium plated fittings are made in the towns of the old 'Black Country', wheels in Wellington (Salop), Bilston, Darlaston and Coventry.

The products of the engineering industries (motor vehicles, aircraft, engines, power plant, switchgear; machinery of all kinds including textile machinery, office machinery and earth movers; finished steel, and electrical equipment) now dominate United Kingdom exports, having taken over the contribution formerly made by textiles.

Metalliferous mining in Britain of the copper of Cornwall and Anglesey, the lead of Derby, Durham, Cumberland and Dumfries, the manganese ore of Merioneth and Caernarvon, the tin of Cornwall, and the zinc of Cumberland, Derby, Flint and Dumfries, is almost dead. In 1860 Swansea could claim to be the world's chief copper smelting centre, with an industry which had been flourishing in the age of Elizabeth I, at that time based on Cornish and Devonshire ores. Today the greater part of the metalliferous materials imported to the United Kingdom is in the form of crude metal, already smelted and sometimes partly refined although some ores and concentrates (for example zinc and bauxite) are still brought in for smelting at the old centres such as Swansea, Liverpool, Bristol. More commonly these old coastal centres, as well as ports such as London and Manchester, work up the imported metal sheets, wires and so on for local industry. London's surplus of raw imports is sent to the West Midlands and to South Wales.

The extraction of *alumina* from *bauxite* takes place at Burntisland, and at Newport, South Wales. The next process, the reduction of the alumina to *aluminium*, requires much electricity; hence its location at sites near hydroelectric power stations, with a ready supply of low cost power, such as in the Scottish Highlands at Fort William and Kinlochleven. In 1968 the government approved the proposal for three new smelters, away from traditional locations: at Lynemouth on the Northumberland coast, supplied with electric power from a coal-fired power station in order to boost coalmining; at Invergordon on the Moray Firth, supplied with power from the national grid as well as by hydroelectric power from the Highlands; and at Holyhead, also served by the national grid, which will ultimately be fed by the nuclear power station nearby at Wylfa. As far as aluminium manufacturing is concerned the foundry industry is linked with motor vehicle production, especially in Coventry and Birmingham; rolling and wire drawing are carried out in southwest Lancashire (Warrington, Prescot, St Helens); Rogerstone, near Newport, has a large rolling mill and there are other plants in South Wales, notably at Swansea and Resolven. The hollow-ware factories are concentrated at Birmingham, making successors to the old cast-iron articles previously produced.

Imported *lead* is mainly manufactured at the receiving ports: London, Newcastle, Manchester, Bristol (Avonmouth), Glasgow; *zinc* at the same ports, but also at Swansea and, above all, Birmingham. Much of the bar *tin* imported is used in the important tinplate industry of South Wales, but there is smelting at Bootle and at Northfleet on the Thames.

The smelting and refining of the imported part-smelted *copper* (matte) continues in the areas once devoted to the ore smelting: southwest Lancashire (Widnes) and South Wales (Swansea and Port Talbot). Copper is second only to iron in its usefulness in industry, and is especially vital to the electrical and machine-making branches. Consequently copper manufactures are closely packed in the great engineering cities: Manchester, Glasgow, London, Birmingham, Liverpool, Sheffield, the engineering towns in the West Riding, southeast Lancashire and Tyneside. Birmingham dominates the *brass* trade, which faces serious competition from stainless steel and plastic materials. *Bronze* manufactures are linked to the engineering and motor industries at Manchester, Coventry and Glasgow, but again Birmingham dominates, as it does in the working up of *precious metals*, taking the lead in this case over London and Sheffield.

The making of **earthenware and porcelain** is another industry which involves a great consumption of fuel, and hence became established in this country mainly in coal-yielding districts. It is explained elsewhere (p. 307) why the making of the greatest variety of earthenware has come to be carried on mainly at Stoke-on-Trent in north Staffordshire, a county borough in which are now incorporated the former 'pottery' towns of Burslem, Tunstall, Hanley, Fenton, and Longton, as well as Stoke. Worcester and Derby have long been noted for their porcelain. Stourbridge makes a very hard kind of stoneware from fireclay found in the neighbourhood.

Glass making developed chiefly on or close to the coalfields, as at St Helens in Lancashire, where there are excellent glass making sands, at Birmingham, at Dudley and Stourbridge in Worcestershire, at South Shields, at Glasgow; glass bottle manufacturing at Castleford, Doncaster, Rotherham, and other places in Yorkshire. As common salt is the chief material used in the making of 'alkali', itself the basis of the **chemical industry**, the rise of the latter is closely associated with the chief salt-yielding districts of England. Of these the most important was long in Cheshire, with the towns of Northwich, Middlewich, Winsford, and Sandbach, Droitwich and Bromsgrove in Worcestershire. More recently the great focus is formed by the towns on both sides of the Tees (Billingham, Haverton and Port Clarence in Durham, Middlesbrough in Yorkshire). There are other works in north Lancashire (at Preesall, near Fleetwood, and on Walney Island), at Stafford, and elsewhere. The other seats of the chemical works of the country are Widnes, at the head of the estuary of the Mersey, on the Lancashire side, and Flint, both near the Cheshire salt district; and works of the same kind exist on the south Durham salt district, at South Shields, also at St Helens and Swansea. The manufacture of dyestuffs which sprang up after the cutting off of German supplies in the First World War has its principal seats on waterways: on the Thames, on the Mersey and the Manchester Ship Canal, at and near Huddersfield, at Grangemouth on the Firth of Forth. The geographical distribution of the chemical industries has been profoundly influenced by the amalgamation of all the chief producers as the Imperial Chemical Industries, Limited, one of whose main centres is the town of Billingham-on-Tees. The chemical industries have been described as the 'most married' of all the industries, since their products — dyes, bleaching agents, acids, and so on — are required by a great variety of other industries; hence the emphasis on transport.

Ardeer, near Irvine, one of the most important early centres in the country for the manufacture of explosives, is on a site deliberately chosen on a sandy foreshore, because while near a seaport the sand-dunes afforded a natural isolation for the different works of this dangerous industry. There are other sites of a similar type, many developed during the Second World War. The works at Ardeer, part of the ICI 'empire', are now concerned with more peaceful production: chemical products such as dyestuffs, and silicon polymers, used as water repellents or where a chemically resistant plastic is needed.

A few of the British industries in which a cheap supply of coal was initially of less importance than other requirements may now be noticed.

One of the locational factors of the **paper making** industry is a plentiful supply of water, preferably pure. It is especially important that it should be free from traces of iron. Formerly this industry was mostly carried on in districts with pure streams at locations not far from large towns. The towns provided raw materials in the shape of rags and wastepaper and satisfactorily sizeable markets for the output of the paper mills. The vast quantities of cheap bulky materials such as wood pulp now used in the industry favour its localisation at or near seaports well placed for the sale of its products, a situation of which the large Sittingbourne and other Thamesside or Medwayside works form a good illustration, with the vast London market nearby. From the first introduction of paper-making into Britain the chief sites of the industry have lain in north Kent, in the Dartford—Gravesend and the Maidstone—Medway areas, with the advantage of the pure streamwater from the Chalk. It is now the chief newsprint-producing area. Similarly the pure water from the Millstone Grit and the availability of textile rags favoured locations in Lancashire and adjacent parts of Cheshire and Derbyshire, Radcliffe and Bury now being leading centres. In Scotland Edinburgh has a tradition of producing fine quality paper of great variety, finding an outlet in the local printing and stationery trades, apart from exports; and there are paper mills in the Central Lowlands, Glasgow producing quantities of newsprint. Aberdeen is another centre. There are many old centres of paper-making, inland in Britain, producing specialised types: banknote paper on the flanks of the Mendips near Wells; fine writing paper and blotting paper at mills in the Chilterns such as Apsley and Loudwater; fine transfer paper for the pottery industry at Cheddleton, near Leek; paper for packaging for the food industry at Watchet, in Somerset. Today there are more paper converting mills in Britain than paper making establishments, producing board, boxes and so on for manufacturing industries; these are especially located in the Midlands.

Chair making developed as a speciality of the beechgrowing districts of the Chiltern Hills where, before 1914, the industry employed 50 000 families. Some districts specialised in seats, others in legs and other small parts, the components being assembled in High Wycombe. High Wycombe progressed to become a major **furniture producing** town. It has in fact been suggested that it is unique in the world in that furniture manufacture is the single dominant economic activity: the industry is more normally associated with other miscellaneous industries in large industrial areas. In Britain much furniture is made in the London area, particularly along the River Lea from Bow, through Leyton, Tottenham, Edmonton to Enfield; and at Barnet, Watford and Letchworth. This concentration of the industry on the capital is typical of other northwest European countries.

A newer and most important industry is the **refining of petroleum**, naturally carried on near, but usually not at, the leading ports. As long ago as 1920 oil refineries were built at Skewen (Llandarcy) near Swansea, connected by pipeline through which crude petroleum was pumped in and the refined products returned to the docks for shipment. Similarly large works were established down the lower Thames at Shellhaven, along the Manchester Ship Canal, at Stanlow, at Grangemouth, at Heysham. After the Second World War the largest refineries in Europe were completed at Fawley on Southampton Water in 1952, and other very large works were built along the south bank of the lower Thames on the Isle of Grain. The giant bulk tankers which came into service in the 1950s require deep water. Milford Haven, formerly a small fishing port, has been developed as a major oil terminal, capable of taking tankers of 250 000 tons; the refineries have an output of over 10m. tons a year. The water at Grangemouth on the estuary of the Forth is too shallow to take large tankers, so an oil terminal has been built at Finnart on Loch Long where there is deep water, and a pipeline carries the crude petroleum eastwards to the Grangemouth refineries. Stanlow is served by new docks at Eastham and at Tranmere on the Mersey estuary. The newest refineries, which owe their location to deep water approaches, are on the south bank of the Humber estuary (Killingholme), and on reclaimed land at Belfast harbour.

An important and fast expanding ancillary of the oil refining industry, based on its byproducts, is the **petrochemical industry** to which it gives rise. Plastic materials, manmade fibres and detergents are just a few of the products of petrochemicals. To illustrate the speed of growth, the output of plastics quadrupled between 1938 and 1948;

and the output of 620 000 tons in 1961 had doubled by 1968.

The making of **footwear** is the leading industry in Northampton and Mansfield, is among those of Leicester and Stafford; and is carried on to a greater or less extent in many other large towns. The making of high quality shoes in Norwich is the main survival of the old textile industry. Until recently **gloves** were made at many small towns in agricultural districts where labour was cheap, as at Worcester, Hereford, Woodstock, Taunton and Yeovil in Somerset, Torrington in Devonshire, and Chester. Proximity to a market is the main locational factor governing the **clothing industry**, although a local supply of raw materials influences location, as illustrated by the clothing output of Leeds which specialises in garments of wool cloth, or of Manchester with its production of clothing made of light materials, such as cotton and manmade fabrics. The clothing industry is especially concentrated in the Greater London area, as well as in other conurbations where there is a vast pool of labour and a big ready market.

Transport and communication. The high grounds of England interfere comparatively little with communications. They have been overcome by rail and road but before the railway era, when **water transport** was so important, they were more serious obstacles. Britain is less suited to the construction of canals than are France and Germany; the surface is not mountainous but is sufficiently hilly to require a large number of locks. In relation to internal communication the most important of the former navigable rivers were the Ouse (Yorkshire), Trent, and Mersey, the Thames and the Severn with their tributaries. The Ouse is navigable for barges throughout its length, and its most important tributaries are navigable likewise or have been canalised.

Three lines of canals were laid across the Pennines, linking Hull and Goole on the east with Liverpool and Manchester on the west. Of these only the Leeds and Liverpool Canal is now in use; it ascends the valley of the Aire via Leeds and Skipton, crosses the watershed at a height of 145 m (477 ft), and descends on the Lancashire side via Burnley and Blackburn to Liverpool. Another line of canals ascended the Calder via Wakefield and Sowerby Bridge, to descend by Rochdale to Manchester, where it connected with the Bridgewater Canal. The Rochdale Canal, which formed part of this route, is now closed to navigation. The third canal, joining Manchester with the Calder and Hebble Navigation via Ashton and Huddersfield, formed a more direct communication between the opposite sides of the Pennine Upland, but rose to a greater height, 220 m (656 ft). The crossing at this altitude was effected by piercing the Standedge Tunnel, more than 5 km (3 miles) in length. The Huddersfield Narrow Canal which formed part of the route was closed to navigation in 1944.

In lowland England the Trent, the Mersey, the Thames, and the

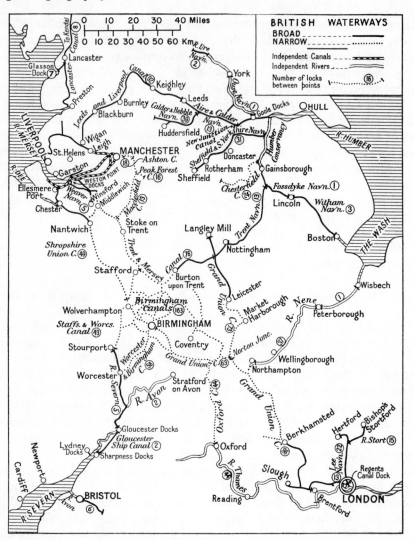

Navigable waterways of England and Wales

Severn are all interconnected by inland waterways, natural or artificial. The Trent itself is navigable for small seagoing steamers as high as Gainsborough and since 1952 has been improved to take 200-ton barges to Nottingham; the Thames can take vessels of 200 tons as high as Hampton; and the Severn, vessels drawing 2 m (6 ft) as high as Stourport. The Gloucester Ship Canal, which connects Gloucester with the estuary of the 'sandy-bottomed Severn', enables vessels drawing more than 3 m (10 ft) to ascend to that town.

The canals of England are mainly works of the latter part of the eighteenth century and the early part of the nineteenth. The Bridgewater Canal, constructed under the direction of James Brindley, was completed in its eastern section (from the Earl, afterwards the Duke, of Bridgewater's coalmines at Worsley to Manchester) about the end of 1761, but was not connected with the Mersey until 1776. At the period when they were made canals were of very high importance for the development of English industry and commerce: with the development of railways their value steadily diminished. Some are still not without importance for the carriage of heavy and bulky commodities, but even in the carriage of coal they are unable to compete with railways except where the conditions are exceptionally favourable to this mode of transport. The railway companies gradually acquired many of the British canals but the National Coal Board abandoned the use of water transport in 1967; and many of the canals built to serve the coalfields have fallen into disuse and have been closed. The Grand Union Canal uniting London with the Midlands, has been improved and is partly provided with concrete banks. Beyond the northern limits of the map the River Tees is navigable (draught about 2 m: 6 ft) for 30 km (19 miles) below Yarm, and the River Tyne for 30 km (19 miles) from the sea.

The British Transport Commission operated three canals in Scotland. The Forth and Clyde Canal enabled small vessels to pass from Grange-mouth on the Firth of Forth to Bowling on the Firth of Clyde, but is now disused. A ship canal with a minimum depth of 4 m (14 ft) was constructed through the Great Glen Valley, which connects Loch Linnhe and the Moray Firth and divides the Highlands of Scotland into two sections. This, the Caledonian Canal, is noteworthy as a work of engineering, but was never much used for the purpose for which it was designed, to allow seagoing ships of moderate size to avoid the stormy passage through the Pentland Firth. The short Crinan Canal allows small steamers to pass from the Clyde to the west of Argyllshire without passing round the Mull of Kintyre.

Apart from these Scottish canals, the control of over 3 200 km (2 000 miles) of inland waterways in England and Wales passed to the British Transport Commission under the Transport Act of 1947. It later became the British Waterways Board. The chief 'independent' water-ways were the Thames and the Bridgewater Canal, the latter being under the Manchester Ship Canal Co. The Board's inland waterways in England and Wales were divided into three groups (see map, p. 360):

I.   542 km (336 miles) of river and broad navigation carrying 75 per cent of the total traffic, selected for development at an estimated cost of £5.5m.

II.   1 600 km (994 miles) of waterways, mainly narrow canals, for continued use as before.

III.   1 240 km (771 miles) with insufficient commercial prospects to warrant retention for navigation, but with other possible uses.

By 1958 some 435 km (270 miles) of the waterways in Group III had been statutorily closed to navigation. On the other hand, work had been begun on the development of the waterways in Group I. In February 1959 the government announced its decision to set up an Inland Waterways Redevelopment Advisory Committee for two years, to promote schemes for redeveloping Group III canals on amenity lines in conjunction with the National Trust as well as to include in this connection possible proposals for Group II canals.

British Waterways traffic totalled 12m. tons in 1953 and 9m. in 1963 and the decline continues, accelerated by the fact that the National Coal Board discontinued water transport in 1967. Some 20 per cent of the waterways carry 90 per cent of the traffic, and the main remaining waterways are the River Trent below Nottingham, the Air and Calder, the Sheffield and South Yorkshire, the Calder and Hebble, the Fossdyke, the River Weaver, the Berkeley Canal, the River Lee below Enfield, and the southern end of the Grand Union Canal below Uxbridge. There is a proposal to use the Grand Union below Berkhamsted for container traffic, to relieve road congestion, linked to the M1 motorway. The greater part of the canal system is now of small commercial use, but it has great potential value for amenity purposes, such as boating, cruising and fishing; and parts are valuable for water supplies or drainage.

What has been said regarding the construction of canals implies that in **railway** construction the obstacles presented by the physical features of the country were of still less consequence relatively to the much higher value of the new means of transit. In view of the distribution of industry, the most serious hindrances to railway communication are those presented by the Pennine Upland and those on the routes connecting the most populous parts of England with the most populous parts of Scotland. Manchester and Sheffield are connected by a line passing through the Woodhead tunnel, which attains an altitude of over 3 000 m (1 000 ft). On the northern routes the chief connection between Lancashire and the valley of the Eden is by way of Shap Fell, where the summit level of the rails on the main west coast route to Scotland is 280 m (916 ft) above sea level; that between the West Riding of Yorkshire and the same valley reaches between the headwaters of the Ribble and Lune a height of 380 m (1 250 ft). The next high crossings on the northern routes are all in Scotland. In Glamorgan and Monmouthshire serious hindrances to communication are presented by the high ridges separating the populous coalmining valleys in the west, more than one railway having to climb to an altitude of more than 365 m (1 200 ft) within a short distance, involving gradients up to 1 in 45. Obstructions to communication presented by water have been overcome by low level railway or road tunnels at the mouths of the Severn and the Mersey, and under the Thames at several places in

London. The Severn railway tunnel, below Chepstow, the longest in the British Isles, is 7.2 km (4.5 miles) long. It was opened in 1886. A proposal to tunnel the Humber, thwarted by an adverse vote of a Committee of the House of Lords in 1873, was revived in 1907, but did not materialise. The proposal for a road bridge was given high priority in the post-1945 programme, second only to the road bridge over the Severn near the line of the tunnel. Under the Mersey tunnels for local rail traffic connect Liverpool and Birkenhead. At the time of its opening in 1934 the Mersey road tunnel was the longest underwater road tunnel in the world. At London main railway lines cross the Thames by bridges; the London underground railway serves local passenger traffic.

The Scottish railways are most closely laid in the Midland Valley, and through the valleys of the Southern Uplands wind railways connecting with the lowlands on the other side and with England. The lowest of all these routes, forming the shortest connection with England, is that by the east coast (the main east coast route), which has nowhere to rise as much as 150 m (500 ft) above sea level. The next route, on the west, has first to climb to above 275 m (900 ft) between Edinburgh and Melrose, and then to about 300 m (1 000 ft) in crossing in a tunnel a spur of the Cheviots between Hawick and Liddisdale, where the main line descends to the Solway, and a branch passes eastwards to the head of the valley of the North Tyne. A still more westerly route (the main west coast line) connects both Edinburgh and Glasgow with Carlisle, reaching between the valleys of the Clyde and the Annan an altitude of about 315 m (1 028 ft). By winding far to the west, through Kilmarnock, a fourth line effects a crossing at a little more than 180 m (600 ft) in height in passing from the valley of the Ayr to that of the Nith. The chief obstructions to communications offered by water in Scotland are overcome by means of two of the most remarkable railway bridges in the world at the time of their building, the Tay Bridge at Dundee, for many years the longest in the world, 3 286 m (3 593 yards), or a little more than 3 km (2 miles), opened in 1887, and the Forth Bridge at Queensferry, a few kilometres above Edinburgh, 2 528 m (2 765 yards), or more than 2 km (1.5 miles) long, opened in 1890.

Under the Railways Act of 1921 (effective 1923) all the main railways of Great Britain were united into four groups with a view to economy of management. The groups were the Southern Railway, the Great Western Railway, the London, Midland and Scottish Railway, and the London and North Eastern Railway. Under the Socialist government which came into power in 1945 the railways were nationalised as British Railways, organised into six regions. One region comprises Scotland, the others correspond roughly with the former companies, with the LNER divided into an Eastern and a Northeastern. Nationalisation came into effect on 1 January 1948.

Plans for the electrification of railways had before the First World War been adopted by the main companies, especially for London suburban lines. On the Southern Railway nearly all the suburban lines were electrified in the interwar period and the main lines as far as Eastbourne, Hastings, Brighton, and Portsmouth. The southern region of British Railways has now the largest electrified suburban network in the world, and has adopted the third rail system. By contrast the London Midland has been reorganised with overhead electrification; Western region relies on diesels. The last scheduled steam-hauled train ran in June 1968.

During the First World War train ferries operated between Richborough and Calais, and Southampton and Dieppe. The Richborough installation passed into private hands and on 11 October 1921 the first commercial train conveyed by ferry, bringing about 300 tons of fruit from the south of France, arrived in Britain. On 24 April 1924 a goods train ferry from Harwich to Zeebrugge was formally opened, but it was the Southern Railway which in 1936 inaugurated a through sleeping-car service for passengers to Paris by train ferry from Dover to Dunkerque. Schemes for a Channel tunnel across the Strait of Dover are being considered.

As in other industrially developed countries the railways in Britain faced losses in competition with road services (which now, in 1972, carry over 60 per cent of internal freight, and probably over 90 per cent of passengers). Dr Beeching was asked by British Rail to study the financial position and to suggest solutions to the problem of the uneconomic railway system. His report, published in April 1963, proposed the drastic reduction of railways by one-third and the closing of 4 000 stations. This curtailment of services was not made, but the lines were cut from 30 617 km (19 025 miles) to 21 067 km (13 721 miles) and the number of stations from 5 474 to 2 888 between 1956 and 1966; and a further 1 209 km (751 miles) of line were closed in 1967–68. Freight services were reorganised: express freightliner trains were introduced, linked to road haulage, with fully mechanised freight handling; freight depots were reduced in number and the land thus released used for other purposes. A current plan for the railways (1972) involves further rationalisation. It is suggested that of the proposed reduced basic network of 17 700 km (11 000 miles) some lines should be commercially viable while others should be subsidised on social grounds.

Road transport, which has so severely hit the railways, has been considered seriously in Britain only since the Second World War. A few desultory attempts were made in the 1920s and 1930s at cutting 'arterial' roads to serve the largest urban centres, but the first Motorway (express highway) was not opened until 1958. The Motorway programme is now progressing steadily, and other trunk routes are being 'improved'. The Firth of Forth road bridge was opened in 1964, the

Tay and Severn bridges in 1966. New tunnels have speeded traffic: a companion to that already existing at Blackwall under the Thames; a second one under the Mersey; another under the Tyne. The map of the Motorway system in fact closely resembles that of the rationalised railway network.

Congestion of roads in urban areas is being tackled by oneway traffic systems and restrictions on parking; and, more drastically, by the building of urban motorways which are immensely costly owing to high land prices and the expense of constructing viaducts, cuttings and tunnels through built-up areas. Between 1960 and 1970 the number of driving licences held in the United Kingdom increased from 11.7 to 17.52m.; in the same period the number of private cars more than doubled; and it was estimated in 1970 that 53 per cent of all households in Britain had the regular use of a car.

Pipelines have progressed from their traditional role as carriers of water and of town gas. They now transfer crude oil, petroleum products, feedstock for the petrochemical industry as well as natural gas from the North Sea fields across Britain; and chalk slurry from quarries in the Chiltern Hills is pumped by pipeline to cement works in Rugby.

Britain is too small for internal **airways** to be of very great advantage. Nevertheless domestic air traffic in both freight and passengers has grown considerably since 1952. International air traffic is of ever-increasing importance; ocean liners particularly could not compete with air services, and the quantity of air freight carried is growing rapidly, with the increase in size of aircraft and the use of containers especially designed to fit them. London airport (Heathrow) is now, in terms of value of its trade, the third most important port in the United Kingdom, after the seaports of London and Liverpool. The car ferries from various airports to the Continent are well used at holiday periods, two connecting the south coast direct with Switzerland. Britain is connected with all parts of the world by the main international airlines, concentrated in the main on the London airports of Heathrow and, to a less extent, of Gatwick, but Manchester and Prestwick (for Glasgow) are extensively used as ports of call. Plans have been drawn up for a third London airport to be located, after lengthy consideration, at Foulness. Currently (1974) they have been shelved in favour of building-up minor airports to meet the greater traffic of the late 1970s.

Seaports. As already stressed on p. 337 the abundance of seaports has been a vital factor in the growth of UK overseas trade. On the average of the period 1908–12 the ten seaports, London, Liverpool, Hull, Manchester, Harwich, Southampton, Bristol, Glasgow, Leith, and Grimsby, received nearly 83 per cent of the total value of the imports of the United Kingdom, and despatched nearly 85 per cent by value of all the exports. In 1968 the order, by value of the trade, was London,

Liverpool, Hull, Manchester, Southampton, Glasgow, Harwich, Bristol, Dover and Folkestone, Grimsby, Tyne ports, ports of Northern Ireland, and Goole. The first two of the seaports handled over half of the total imports and exports although Liverpool's share is declining.

London still stands first in rank among British seaports, as it always has done. During the years 1909–13 it received 33 per cent of the imports in value and despatched 25 per cent of the ports, and these proportions have steadily increased since the First World War, except for the obvious setback of the Second World War. The situation at the head of ocean navigation on a river which allows ocean vessels to ascend into the interior and which has its mouth directly opposite another great estuary, that of the Scheldt, and nearly opposite the mouth of the Rhine, gives it a commanding position for continental trade. It is these two circumstances which determined its early growth, and hence indirectly made it the capital of the country, a position which favoured its further increase in population and wealth more and more as the British Empire extended. It thus became ultimately the greatest import market in the world, a fact which of necessity greatly promoted its entrepôt and transhipment trade, especially since so much of that trade, on the export side, is carried on with the neighbouring continental countries. More than 40 per cent of that characteristic trade of the United Kingdom is carried on at this port. The enormous local market of Greater London with a population of over 7m., together with the facilities for redistribution by both land and sea, have made London the main port, not only for such eastern products as tea and spices, but also for coffee and cocoa; and it is no doubt the latter circumstance, the ease of redistribution as well as collection, that was the determining factor in making London the chief centre for Australian trade. Increasing difficulty was felt in meeting the requirements of the enormous shipping of this port, and the complaints of shippers led in 1908 to the passing of the Act placing the whole port, defined as extending from the tidal limit of the river at Teddington Lock to a line joining Havengore Creek in Essex to Warden Point in the Isle of Sheppey, under the control of a single authority, the Port of London Authority. The PLA acquired not only all the docks of importance, but also the warehouses belonging to them. It provided for the establishment and maintenance of a 4 m (14 ft) channel at low water up to London Bridge, and one of 9 m (30 ft) in depth with a minimum width of 180 m (600 ft) up to the Albert Docks opposite Woolwich. The Tilbury Docks, opened in 1886, were the deepest docks of the port, 11.6 m (38 ft); and they had 22 ha (54.5 acres) of waterspace; the docks were extended, a new lock opened at Tilbury in 1929 with a length of 305 m (1 000 ft) and width of 33.5 m (110 ft). Facilities for the efficient handling of large containers have been added at Tilbury, to make it one of the best equipped ports in the world. Many of the smaller PLA docks upriver, however, have wharves and warehouses unsuited to the character of today's trade and have been closed, the land so released being developed for other purposes. Nevertheless London remains pre-eminently the leading port, handling the greatest entrepôt trade of the United Kingdom.

Liverpool rose to a high rank among the seaports of the world only within the last 250 years. Early in the eighteenth century it was a small place; its chief trade was with Ireland, and in that trade it had rivals in Preston and Chester, which were equally well suited for the small ships then in use. Its importance rose with the growth of the American trade and with the development of the cotton, woollen, and other manufactures of its hinterland, which may be said to include the whole of the industrial area from the Ribble to the north of Warwickshire and even, for the bulk of ocean traffic, that lying to the east of the Pennine upland in the West Riding of Yorkshire. The inadequacy of the ports at the mouths of the Ribble, Dee, and even the Severn, prevented them from offering any serious rivalry. Since 1894, however, its hinterland has been invaded by the port of Manchester. The port of Liverpool includes the docks on the Cheshire side of the Mersey at Birkenhead, as well as the Garston docks on the Lancashire side, formerly belonging to the London, Midland and Scottish Railway Company, which built train marshalling sidings. The port is under the control of the Mersey Docks and Harbour Board, constituted in 1857. A sandbank at the mouth of the Mersey, which formerly prevented the entrance of large vessels at low tide, has been dredged to allow large vessels to enter or leave the port at dead low water. Birkenhead–Wallasey, since the completion of the rail and road tunnels under the Mersey, may be fairly regarded as forming geographically part of Liverpool.

By value Liverpool's share of total trade has declined considerably since 1948, reflecting the greater trade now handled by ports on the east and south coasts as a result of Britain's growing trade with the Continent. Liverpool was for long second to London as the leading entrepôt port. Measured by tonnage handled this is true now only if Milford Haven, with its great import of crude and export of refined petroleum, is excluded.

Hull, lying on the east, the continental side of Britain, is one of the older ports of England, though its antiquity does not reach back to Roman times. It is said to have been founded by King Edward I, who here encouraged the building of a town, which was called King's Town. Hence the full name of the town, Kingston-upon-Hull, Hull being properly the name of the small river which enters the Humber on the north bank at the site of the town. Unfortunately the Humber cuts off Hull from links with the heavily industrialised area in the south. A road–rail bridge was considered for many years but finally it was decided that a road bridge should be built. It will have a single span of some 1 400 m (4 600 ft) and should be open in 1976. It will probably be used more by regional than national traffic, most of the latter operating between Hull and points to the west; but it will contribute greatly to the cohesion of Humberside, a fast-expanding industrial region. The ancient and large trade in fish is still maintained in Hull which is well situated to supply the northern Midlands, but not so convenient for London and the southern Midlands for which, especially London, Grimsby on the Lincolnshire coast has greater advantages. For the same reason its wool imports destined for Yorkshire increased at the expense of London. Thus the import of raw wool at Hull in 1913 was 48m. lb (less than 10 per cent of that of London), in 1920, 70m. lb (nearly 14 per cent of London), in 1929, 148m. lb (over 38 per cent of London), but the proportion has since fallen. The leading import of Hull is, in normal years, wheat; but the port resembles London in the very general nature of the cargoes handled. Many of the imports are offloaded into lighters for water carriage into the hinterland. It has also a large trade in oilseeds, a trade favoured by the large adjacent markets for oilcake on the one hand, and for the oils and oil products in the manufacturing districts. There is a considerable import of foodstuffs, especially bacon and butter from Denmark; and Hull is equally conveniently situated for the imports of timber from northwest Europe. Exports from the hinterland are destined for the Continent: vehicles, textile machinery, iron and steel products and a wide range of manufactured goods, chemicals, wool and wool yarn and so on. On the south bank of the Humber are the ports of Grimsby, pre-eminently a fishing port, and of Immingham, a short distance to the north, which has been specially equipped for the export of coal and large iron and steel castings. It has an important oil refinery at Killingholme, and serves the chemical and fertiliser industries. Goole, the third of the Humber ports, owes its importance chiefly to the shipment of coal brought by the Aire and Calder navigation and development by the former London, Midland and Scottish Railway. Again trade is mainly with continental ports.

Glasgow, surpassed by Southampton in tonnage of shipping and also in value of imports and exports, has had a history in many ways similar to that of Liverpool. It rose into importance only with the development of the New World and modern manufacturing industry, and the accommodation that it affords for mercantile shipping has had to be provided artificially to even a greater extent than that in the Mersey. Its first lucrative transoceanic trade was with the southern plantations of North America and the West Indies, whence tobacco and sugar, then relatively more valuable than they are now, were imported. The trade began as a smuggling trade even before the union of the English and Scottish Parliaments, but so flourished afterwards that Glasgow beat all its English rivals in the tobacco trade. The tobacco was brought from the plantations under the regulations then in force first to Britain. Most was intended for export to the Continent, and the overland transport from

Irvine, which was then the port of Glasgow, to an eastern port (Bo'ness) was shorter than that between any other western and eastern ports. The Clyde was then but a small river. Less than 200 years ago it was still fordable 19 km (12 miles) below Glasgow. Then came the industrialisation which made coal and iron all-important, and the fact that these minerals are found together in the immediate vicinity of Glasgow made it economic to convert the river into a channel of the sea so that it could bear on its waters the ships of all nations, and of the deepest draught.

Glasgow grew as a great manufacturing town with a wide variety of industries, shipbuilding and marine engineering being especially important. It is unlike most British ports in that the value of exports passing through slightly exceeds that of imports. The former include whisky, machinery, transport equipment and manufactured goods from central Scotland. The imports include foodstuffs such as wheat, maize and butter, as well as tobacco; crude petroleum at Finnart, sent by pipeline to the Grangemouth refineries; and iron ore, received at a special quay with a direct rail link to the Ravenscraig iron and steel works. The Ravenscraig iron and steel works will benefit when an iron ore terminal, now being built at Hunterston on the Ayrshire coast is opened. Hunterston has the advantage of a natural deepwater harbour capable of taking 350 000-ton bulk carriers without dredging; it also has a gas-cooled nuclear power station, and it seems likely that a considerable industrial complex could develop in this area in the future.

Southampton, the chief commercial port on the south coast, usually lying fifth in respect of tonnage as well as in value of trade, has a long history. A Roman station stood on the tongue of land between the Itchen and the Test where the town is now situated. By 1450 it ranked third among British ports. Docks were built in 1842, which in 1891 were acquired by the London and South Western Railway Company, later part of the Southern Railway. They passed in 1948 to the British Transport Commission and eventually to the British Transport Docks Board.

Southampton has been endowed with great natural advantages: considerable depth of water, a relatively small tidal range, and a double high tide which gives high water for two hours twice during twenty-four hours, combined with a short ebb. Dredging is easily accomplished and has ensured that the docks can accommodate large vessels; there are deepwater quays, and newer facilities deal with mechanised handling of container traffic. Land has been reclaimed behind the New Docks and quays, where there is a flourishing industrial estate. There are dry docks for servicing and shipyards where naval and commercial vessels are built.

In the heyday of the ocean liners thirty of the world's main shipping companies ran passenger services from Southampton to all parts of the world. Because of its situation it was a regular port of call for vessels plying to and from northern Europe to the Americas and elsewhere. Southampton remains Britain's leading passenger port, for some 50 per cent of all sea passengers to and from the United Kingdom pass through it. As a cargo port its imports include large quantities of meat; fruit from the West Indies, South Africa and Europe; timber from the Baltic; grain from North America and Australia; and coastal cargoes from Scotland and Northern Ireland. Crude petroleum for the refinery at Fawley figures largely in imports, and the consequent refined products in exports. Within 160 km (100 miles) radius of Southampton there is a population of some 16m. and the port is connected by fast road, rail and freightliner services with the Midland industrial region. Exports therefore include every type of manufactured article, including motor vehicles.

With Southampton may be contrasted the ports which have passenger services to the Continent: Harwich which serves the Hook of Holland and Flushing in the Netherlands and Esbjerg in Denmark; Dover linked to France (Calais and Dunkerque) and Belgium (Ostend); Folkestone to France (Boulogne); Newhaven to Dieppe. More freight traffic passes through Dover and Harwich (which also have car ferry services) than through the others, Harwich especially handling much container traffic, in growing quantity.

Bristol is the only western seaport of note in the early commerce of England. Owing to the shallowness of the upper part of the estuary of the Severn it served as an outlet not only for the populous region immediately to the east of it but also for the Severn valley. After European settlement in the New World it was one of the first seaports to secure a large share of the trade in tobacco and sugar. Links with Spain and France early laid the foundation of today's wine trade. Bristol's port development was retarded by the inadequacy of the Avon to meet the requirements of large ships; the Corporation of the City of Bristol therefore built large deepwater docks near the mouth of the Avon, at Avonmouth, included in the port of Bristol. With its established links with the West Indies Avonmouth soon became, and maintains its position as, the premier banana port of Britain. Other imports provide raw materials for the Severnside metallurgical and chemical factories (zinc concentrates, aluminium and chemicals), and are increasing. Exports are small and include paper, chemicals, metals and machinery. Manufactures in Bristol (tobacco, chocolate and soap) are associated with its traditional trade. There is a new industrial complex developing at Severnside.

The ports of South Wales grew in response to the developing coal trade in the nineteenth century. The coal export trade has declined but Cardiff and Newport now function as iron ore importing centres, the former for the dockside plant at Cardiff, the latter for the steel works at

Ebbw Vale and at Llanwern. Both ports export iron and steel products. Barry handles coastal oil traffic, and bananas. Swansea imports crude oil for the refinery at Llandarcy, as well as nickel matte and zinc concentrates for its own metal works. Tinplate and anthracite are exported. Port Talbot specialises in the import of iron ore. More significant however is the import of crude oil at Milford Haven, for its refineries.

Most of the other British ports, serving limited hinterlands, handle a relatively small export trade and import mainly foodstuffs and some raw materials for local use. In eastern Scotland Leith serves the Edinburgh area, exporting whisky and the manufactured goods of the Central Lowlands (machinery, textile manufactures, and so on). The port at Burntisland receives bauxite for the aluminium plant; Dundee continues to import jute, jute fabrics and flax; Aberdeen is still an important fishing port and imports wood pulp and other raw materials for its paper industry. In northeast England the River Tyne from Newcastle to Gateshead forms a great sheltered harbour, closely linked with the Scandinavian trade with passenger and freight services (roll-on, roll-off ferries) to Bergen and Oslo. The traditional coal of Newcastle is now of little significance, and has given way to exports of machinery, ships, and manufactured goods, including textiles from Lancashire and Yorkshire. Imports include iron ore (taken by special train to Consett), petroleum products, nonferrous ores, timber, ships engines made abroad, and the usual foodstuffs (bacon, butter, wheat).

Middlesbrough on the Tees estuary has already been mentioned as accommodating iron ore and crude petroleum bulk carriers bringing raw materials for its local plants. The export products of the large-scale Teesside chemical works now exceed in value the exports of iron and steel.

British foreign trade. In early times and throughout the Middle Ages the great feature of English trade was the export of raw materials and the import of manufactured articles. By far the most important of the exported raw materials was wool, but it was only one of several, the export duties levied on which furnished a large part of the revenue of the Crown. With the obvious intention of facilitating the collection of this revenue the regulation of this trade was attempted in the reign of Edward I, and the trade was more definitely organised by an ordinance of Edward III in 1353. Therein the only staple commodities enumerated are wool, wool-fells (that is, sheepskins with the wool on), leather or hides, and tin, but on other occasions lead, cheese, butter, alum, tallow, and worsted are also mentioned, the last, however, very seldom. The ordinance decreed that all these commodities should when exported be taken exclusively to certain English, Welsh and Irish ports, the 'staple ports', where the duties were collected. The English ports included all those of any consideration on the east coast except

Berwick-upon-Tweed; Southampton and Exeter on the south coast, and Bristol on the west. The reason for the exception of Berwick-upon-Tweed from the list of English ports probably was that if it had been included under the regulations of the staple, English wool would have been smuggled across the Scottish Border and exported from some Scottish port. Sometimes Newcastle also was omitted from the staple towns. Carmarthen was the sole staple port for Wales. In Ireland there were four: Dublin, Waterford, Cork, and Drogheda. No external staple port was mentioned, although there had been a staple abroad at various ports in the Low Countries at previous dates, and subsequently it was again found convenient to fix upon some external port as the one place beyond the seas to which all staple commodities should first be sent. From near the end of the fourteenth century till 1558 Calais was the sole external staple, but when the English lost Calais in that year the staple was transferred to Bruges. The trade in the staple commodities was mainly, but for one reason or another not at all times solely, in the hands of a privileged body known as the Staplers, who had a court of their own at Calais. The Staplers were mostly foreigners, and indeed several ordinances, including that of 1353, absolutely prohibited the trade in staple commodities to Englishmen, these being liable to smaller dues than foreigners. The loss that the revenue thereby incurred was one that the kings could not always afford, and one that was occasionally more than made good by the granting of special licences to Englishmen to engage in the staple trade even when there was a general prohibition. Such licences were of course obtained only on conditions that were advantageous to the Crown. Among the foreigners engaged in the staple trade of England were many Italians, but members of the Hanseatic League were still more conspicuous. The merchants belonging to this league had gained special privileges in the foreign trade of England before the close of the thirteenth century. In what was known as the Steelyard in London on the Thames, a site now partly occupied by Cannon Street Station, they has a well-protected residence with warehouses, and they had similar residences at some other English ports. Their privileges were for the most part maintained till 1598, when they were finally withdrawn by Queen Elizabeth.

Long before this the trade of native English merchants had been growing through the efforts of an organised company known as the Merchant Adventurers. The name of 'adventurers' was given to those who traded in commodities not embraced by the regulations of the staple. English grain and honey could thus be freely exported to Norway and other parts in which such commodities found a market; but as English manufactures grew these became the most valuable commodities outside of the staple. Woollens accordingly came to be the chief wares whose sale abroad was pushed by the adventurers. When this body became a regularly organised society is uncertain, but in 1404 a charter was conferred on it by Henry IV, and shortly after the company was enabled to establish its headquarters at Antwerp. Other charters were subsequently conferred on it, and it grew to be an extremely influential body in the sixteenth and seventeenth centuries. Its headquarters were ultimately transferred to Hamburg, on which account it became known as the Hamburgh Company, but though its chief seat was thus abroad the membership was absolutely restricted to Englishmen. In later days its special domain was all that part of the North Sea coast which lies between the Strait of Dover and the north of Denmark.

The Merchant Adventurers became the model for several other merchant companies, which claimed, if they did not always enjoy, monopolies of trade elsewhere. Sebastian Cabot, who with his father John Cabot had made the first voyage from England to America in the search for a northwest passage to India in 1497, lived long enough to suggest to the Merchant Adventurers in the middle of the following century a voyage in search of a northeast passage to the same destination. The voyage was actually made in 1553 under Willoughby and Chancellor and led to the discovery of a route to the White Sea and the mouth of the Northern Dvina. In the same year a company known as the Muscovy Company received a charter conferring upon its privileges in the trade with Russia and Persia. In 1579 the Eastland Company obtained its first charter conferring privileges in connection with Scandinavian and Baltic trade. Afterwards the Levant or Turkey, the East India, and the Africa or Guinea Companies, as well as the Hudson's Bay Company, were successively founded. The most important of these for the future of England was the East India Company, which obtained its first charter on the last day of 1600, and subsequently to the implicit annulment in the Declaration of Rights in 1689 of all royal monopolies of trade, had a monopoly of the Eastern trade expressly conferred upon it by Parliament. This monopoly was retained for India till 1813 and for China till 1833. By this date the Company had become a great territorial power, and from 1833 it was little else.

Meanwhile the nature of English trade had completely changed. English manufactures had long been the principal exports. Throughout the eighteenth century woollens were the most important of these, and so jealously was any rivalry in this trade regarded that every effort was made to check the rise of a similar industry in Ireland. In the course of the eighteenth century cotton goods came to acquire more importance. They were among the goods of the notorious 'Triangular Trade'. Bristol and other merchants carried manufactures from England to West Africa to be exchanged for slaves who were taken to the West Indies to be sold, whence the ships returned home with cargoes of sugar and other tropical produce. This was a highly lucrative trade not prevented until 1 January 1808, when the slave trade was made illegal. At last the revolution in industry gained such momentum that it created a new era not merely for English commerce but for the commerce of the world. In England the effect was the rapid rise of cotton manufactures to the first place among exports. Later the practice of conferring royal charters on trading companies was revived. Between 1880 and 1890 such charters were granted to the British North Borneo Company, the British South Africa Company, the Royal Niger Company and the Imperial British East Africa Company. These charters have since been withdrawn and the companies themselves have disappeared.

We may now examine the salient features of British foreign trade in the twentieth century. First we note the high place which bulky articles have taken both in import and export trade: among the imports timber, grain and ores; and among the early exports, coal. To appreciate the importance of this fact one must compare the values of the commodities with the values per ton, in order to understand how, for example, iron ores though low in order of value among imports, must take a quite different place in an enumeration of imports according to quantity. Very bulky in proportion to value is coal, which in respect of quantity was for many years by far the most important of British exports.

The export trade in coal was formerly one of peculiar importance to Great Britain, especially until the First World War. In 1913, for example, a total approaching 100m. tons of coal was exported or sent away in bunkers, and a large amount of our shipping was employed in the carriage outwards of this one commodity. On the assumption that 4 register tons of shipping would be required to convey 9 tons weight of coal, this represents over 40m. register tons of shipping. In 1898 coal was estimated to make up 86 per cent of the total weight of British exports. The indirect importance of this traffic to the commerce of the United Kingdom was that the ships that went out laden with coal were ready to bring back cargoes of foreign goods at low freights.

Coal and coke were chiefly exported from fields near the sea: from Cardiff, Newport, and Swansea, the outlets of the South Wales coalfield, and the Tyne ports (Newcastle and North and South Shields), Sunderland, and Hartlepool, the outlets of the Northumberland and Durham coalfields, and from various ports on the Firth of Forth. The excellence of the so-called smokeless (that is nearly smokeless) coal furnished by the eastern part of the South Wales coalfield as fuel for steam engines caused Cardiff to outstrip Newcastle in the export of coal to foreign countries; but Newcastle and Sunderland ranked first among the ports which supplied coal in coasting vessels for domestic use, their convenient situation for the supply of London being much in their favour. The actually smokeless coal known as anthracite is produced only in the western part of the South Wales field. The diminution in the demand for Cardiff steam coal accounted for the depression in the coal trade of South Wales and emphasised the need for alternative industries.

Both the production and export of British coal reached their highest totals in 1913 just before the outbreak of the First World War. Naturally shipments were interrupted by the exigencies of that war and by the submarine menace, and the old markets were never fully recovered. Much of the world's shipping, both British and foreign, naval and mercantile, changed to oil fuel so that British bunker coal was in smaller demand and less was sent to the world's coaling depôts; many countries formerly buying coal were compelled to develop their own resources. In the 1920s there was much unemployment among miners in South Wales and Durham. Subsequently there was some improvement until in 1939 war again disrupted the whole industry. Britain nationalised first her coal resources and later her whole coal industry; mines were modernised to the extent that from 1946 more than 75 per cent of the coal was cut mechanically. During the Second World War young men had to go into the armed services and the average age of miners rose to thirty-nine in 1942–47 compared with thirty-six in 1937. After the war young men did not take to mining and a new difficulty arose. Britain has considerable reserves and had many customers, especially in Europe, anxious to buy at least 50m. tons a year, but could not get enough labour to satisfy home needs, and thus became an importer of coal, drawing supplies from America. The British miner remembering the unemployment of the 1920s was unwilling to accept the use of Italian or other immigrant labour. Until 1958 the domestic consumer was still rationed but surplus stocks of small coal, difficult to use, had accumulated. Later, overproduction again became a problem as oil increasingly replaced coal.

When we reflect that all Britain's external trade as well as much of her internal trade was formerly necessarily carried on by sea, it is obvious that this is one important cause that must tend to promote British shipping. When we also consider local advantages for the building of steel ships and their engines and the large proportion of maritime population, the great and long-continued importance of British shipping is not surprising. But times change: the United Kingdom shipbuilding industry, which for so long led the world, has declined, and in recent years has come third to Japan and West Germany in output of gross tonnage. Ships therefore no longer hold the position they once did in exports.

The position regarding shipping is complicated by the fact that registration under a certain flag does not prove that the shipping is all owned by subjects of the nation to which that flag belongs. A high proportion of the world's tonnage is registered under 'flags of convenience', in Panama and Liberia, for example, where laws are relatively relaxed and taxation is low. Much shipping under foreign flags is owned by British subjects; on the other hand some foreign capital is invested in

British ships, and loans to foreign countries issued in the United Kingdom are not all held by residents in the United Kingdom but may and often do include large sums lent by foreigners.

In many ways the pattern of British shipping has changed since the end of the Second World War. The few ocean liners that remain afloat are mostly concerned with holiday cruising; passenger traffic goes by air; a large proportion of freight is handled by freightliners on regular schedules and less by tramp or charter tonnage. A high proportion of British, as of world, tonnage is represented by tankers, including some of the largest vessels afloat, specifically constructed to carry only one commodity.

Before the Second World War Britain had a flourishing entrepôt trade. A geographically central position among trading nations was a contributory factor, but there were two others, equally important. One was (and is) the onesided character of British industries. So large a proportion of British exports consist of manufactured goods that the country is necessarily dependent on imports of foodstuffs and raw materials. The large trade with all parts of the world which developed over the centuries led to the employment of a vast amount of shipping, providing at the same time conveniences for an entrepôt and transhipment trade. The second factor favouring this trade was the number and the situation of seaports.

The entrepôt trade suffered severely from the destruction in the port of London during the Second World War. It recovered, dominates trade at London's seaport and airport, and is important at Liverpool and Southampton. Its monetary value continues to rise, but expressed in value relative to the export trade it is declining. The principal items entering the entrepôt trade statistics are rubber, wool, raw fur skins, tea, coffee, spices, tobacco and nonferrous metals, more than half of which are destined for western Europe.

A feature of United Kingdom trade has long been the large excess of the value of imports over exports. The balance is maintained by invisible exports, that is, economic services, rendered to other countries for which those who render such services are entitled to be paid. The most important of these were overseas investments and loans, and earnings of British shipping on foreign or Commonwealth account. Large sums of money were also earned by Britain by banking and insurance and, up to the outbreak of the Second World War, London remained the banking centre of the world.

The Second World War resulted in the sale of many of Britain's overseas investments, the loss of large numbers of merchant vessels, and the passing of financial world leadership to New York. Instead of invisible exports — in return for which there was an automatic inflow of foodstuffs and raw materials — equal to a third of the total imports and ranging in the years 1913 to 1938 from a low of £255m. in 1932 to a high of £595m. in 1920, Britain found herself in 1945 having to pay her way by selling exports to the value of imports needed. American aid, a recovery in such invisible exports as tourism and shipping helped to adjust the balance; but the export drive remained paramount in national economy. The home market had to be starved, many articles being reserved for export. It has since been the aim of successive governments to try to achieve a favourable balance of trade.

Even allowing for increased output of food by British farmers — up to 55 per cent of the total consumed — foodstuffs remain dominant among imports. Wheat, flour, and meat are essentials. Other main features are shown in Tables 34 to 37.

The pattern of export trade has changed radically. With the diminution in importance of the one raw material formerly exported in quantity, coal, the proportion of manufactured goods has risen but the dominant position once occupied by cotton manufactures has disappeared. The long continued export of iron and steel manufactures is a remarkable illustration of the commercial advantages of Britain especially when we consider the relative advance of other countries in the conditions favouring the initial stages of the industry. In 1886–90 the United States took about three-quarters of the value of the tinned plates exported from Britain; now the import of tinned plates into that country is comparatively small. This is typical of the changes wrought in British trade as, one after another, her former customers have developed their own manufacturing industries. Iron and steel were among those comparatively bulky commodities that helped to cheapen the carriage of more valuable ones.

Now the emphasis is on manufactures for which the native iron and steel industry provides a basis: machinery of all kinds, vehicles including ships, locomotives, motorcars and aircraft. That Britain has not lagged behind in technological development is seen in the export of a range of chemicals, manmade fibres and electrical apparatus.

As to destinations of exports we may note that the maximum percentage to India was in 1886–90, after which it remained comparatively steady for a long period, but with a marked drop after the First World War. Exports to the Commonwealth as a whole remained between 30 and 40 per cent from 1880 to 1913, but began a steady rise above 40 per cent after the First World War. The highest percentage to the United States was in 1871–75 but when United States home manufactures were established it soon declined.

The destination of British exports following the Second World War shows a steady diminution in the flow of British goods to the Commonwealth, especially in the 1960s, falling to some 22 per cent of total exports in 1969. At the same time there was growth in exports to the EEC countries (France, West Germany, Netherlands, Belgium, Luxembourg, Italy) and to the other members of EFTA (Austria, Portugal,

Table 34 — United Kingdom imports

Commodity	Percentages of total value					
	1924	*1926–30*	*1931–35*	*1938*	*1960*	*1971*
Raw materials	*31.4*	*28.3*	*24.5**	*27.0*	*34.0*	*35.8*
Raw cotton	9.5	6.0	4.6	3.2	1.6	0.5
Raw wool	5.5	4.7	4.9	4.6	3.3	0.6
Wood and wood pulp	4.0	4.8	5.5	6.4	6.8	3.7
Petroleum and products	—	3.6	4.2	} 3.3 {	10.6	12.1
Oil-seeds and nuts	4.1	1.4	1.5		1.2	0.4
Rubber	0.8	1.7	0.9	1.3	1.7	0.5
Hides, skins and furs	1.7	2.2	2.1	2.0	1.1	0.7
Zinc, lead, tin, copper, iron and other ores	1.8	2.4	1.8	3.0	3.7	5.3
Foodstuffs	*44.7*	*44.1*	*49.5**	*46.8*	*33.9*	*21.0*
Meat	8.2	9.5	12.2		{ 7.6	4.7
Fresh beef and mutton	4.1	4.0	5.5	} 9.9	3.2	2.0
Bacon and hams	3.5	4.4	4.5		2.6	1.3
Animals	1.7	1.1	1.2	1.0	0.7	0.7
Grain and flour	9.5	8.3	8.7	8.1	4.8	5.5
Wheat	5.4	5.0	4.1	4.2	2.3	1.4
Maize	1.3	1.1	1.5	1.9	1.4	0.9
Wheat meal and flour	0.7	0.6	0.5	0.4	0.3	2.9
Butter	4.3	4.2	5.2	5.5	2.7	1.6
Tea	3.2	3.1	3.6	3.3	2.6	1.0
Sugar	3.5	2.0	} 2.0	2.1	1.6	1.0
Raw	—	1.6				
Refined	—	0.4				
Fresh fruit and nuts	2.5	2.9	4.0	4.1	2.1	1.7
Eggs	1.5	1.4	1.2	1.7	0.2	0.2
Cheese	1.1	1.2	1.1	1.1	0.7	0.6
Tobacco	1.2	1.4	1.7	2.5	2.3	1.1
Manufactures	*23.4*	*26.9*	*24.8**	*25.4†*	*31.8*	*43.2*
Silk yarns and manufrs.	2.0	1.2	0.6	0.5	—‡	—
Wool yarns and manufrs.	} 1.2 {	0.9	0.6	0.4	0.2	—
Apparel		1.6	1.3	0.9	0.9	1.8
Cotton yarns and manufactures	0.7	0.8	0.5	0.3	1.5	0.7
Iron and steel manufrs.	1.7	2.3	1.5	1.6	2.3	1.5
Machinery	0.8	1.4	1.6	2.3	5.6	13.0
Leather manufactures	1.1	1.2	1.1	0.7	0.3	0.4
Chemicals	1.2	1.3	1.0	1.5	3.9	5.8
Paper and cardboard	—	1.5	1.8	1.6	1.9	2.6
Annual total in £millions	1 279.8	1 184.5	745.5	919.5	4 556.4	9 976.5

* Classes for 1931–34 only.

† Includes 'non-ferrous metals and manufactures', amounting to 4.4 per cent of all imports; and oils, fats and resins, manufactured' (chiefly refined petroleum), amounting to 4.8 per cent.

‡ Less than 0.1 per cent.

Table 35 — United Kingdom domestic exports

Commodity	Percentages of total value					
	1924	*1926–30*	*1931–35*	*1938*	*1960*	*1971*
Raw materials	*13.3*	*9.9*	*11.9*[1]	*12.1*	*7.3*[4]	*2.9*
Coal and coke	9.8	6.4	8.7	8.0	0.8	0.2
Foods	*7.0*	*7.6*	*8.0*[1]	*7.6*	*5.6*[5]	*5.6*
Fish	1.1	1.1	1.1	0.8	0.2	—
Spirits	1.5	1.3	1.6	2.4	2.0	2.7
Manufactures	*77.4*	*79.8*	*76.3*[1]	*77.5*	*84.9*	*91.5*
Cotton manufactures	24.9	19.2	15.3	⎫		0.3
Yarn	3.5	3.0	2.7	⎬ 10.5	1.8[6]	0.3
Thread	0.9	0.9	1.1	⎭		—
Iron and steel	9.3	8.3	6.9	8.8	6.1	4.4
Machinery	5.6	7.4	8.3	12.1	20.1[7]	28.3
Electrical goods	1.3	1.8	1.9	2.9	6.6[8]	7.4
Automobiles	0.8	2.4[2]	3.3[2]	⎫	⎰ 11.8[9]	10.8
Railway vehicles	1.0	1.4	0.6	⎬ 9.6[3]	⎨ 0.6	—
New ships	0.7	1.8	1.1	⎭	⎱ 1.5	0.6
Wool manufactures	8.5	7.2	6.9	⎫		
Tissues	5.2	4.6	3.8	⎬ 5.7	2.9[10]	0.7
Yarn	2.0	1.5	1.6	⎮		
Tops	0.8	0.7	0.8	⎭		
Silk and art silk	0.3	1.4	1.3	1.2	0.9[11]	0.8
Linen yarn and manufrs.	1.7	1.4	1.5	1.3	0.4	—
Apparel (including boots and hats)	3.8	3.7	3.0	2.2	1.3	1.8
Paper and cardboard	1.2	1.4	1.6	1.5	1.2	1.0
Rubber manufactures	0.3	1.3	1.4	0.3	1.2	1.1
Earthenware and glass	1.6	1.9	2.0	2.0	1.0	0.6
Leather manufactures	1.5	1.1	0.9	0.8	0.7	0.6
Chemicals	3.2	3.5	4.7	4.7	9.0	9.6
Annual total in £millions	795.4	677.2	389.5	471.4	3 536.0	9 314.0

[1] Classes are for 1931–34 only.
[2] Includes cars and other road vehicles and parts.
[3] Vehicles, including locomotives, ships and aircraft.
[4] With the decline in the export of coal, the main items in the exports of raw materials in 1960 were petroleum and products (2.9 per cent) and wool (2 per cent).
[5] Refined sugar (0.5 per cent) was the biggest item next to spirits in the exports of 'Food, beverages and tobacco' in 1960 but was only just above tobacco (0.5 per cent).
[6] Cotton yarns and woven fabrics.
[7] Non-electric.
[8] Electrical machinery.
[9] All road vehicles mechanically propelled, and parts thereof. Aircraft provided another 1.7 per cent.
[10] Woollen and worsted yarns and woven fabrics, and miscellaneous textile manufactures of wool.
[11] All artificial silk — i.e. synthetic fibre yarns and woven fabrics. Silk goods proper, only a fraction of 0.1 per cent.

Table 36 — UK imports from various countries

Countries of origin	Percentages of total value					
	1924	*1926—30*	*1931—35*	*1938*	*1963*	*1971*
United States	18.5	16.3	11.6	12.8	10.3	10.8
Argentina	6.2	6.1	6.4	4.2	1.8	0.6
Germany	2.9	5.6	4.9	3.3	4.3†	6.5†
India and Pakistan	6.2	5.1	5.0	5.4	3.5‡	1.4‡
France	5.3	4.9	3.3	2.6	3.2	4.4
Denmark	3.8	4.6	5.2	4.1	3.4	3.0
Australia	4.6	4.4	6.6	7.8	4.3	2.8
Canada	5.2	4.4	6.2	8.8*	7.6	6.3
Irish Republic	4.0	3.8	3.2	2.5	3.2	4.0
Netherlands	3.3	3.8	3.3	3.2	4.3	5.0
New Zealand	3.8	3.9	5.1	5.1	3.6	2.3
Belgium	2.8	3.0	2.5	2.0	1.8	2.0
USSR	1.5	2.2	2.8	2.1	1.9§	1.1
Sweden	1.6	2.0	2.3	2.7	3.4¶	4.0
Commonwealth	*30.2*	*27.1*	*33.5*	*36.9*	*32.1*	*18.9*
Foreign countries	*69.8*	*72.9*	*66.5*	*63.1*	*67.9#*	*81.1*

* Including Newfoundland.
† West Germany.
‡ 1963: India 2.9, Pakistan 0.6. 1971: India 1.1, Pakistan 0.3.
§ Exports to USSR 1.4.
¶ Exports to Sweden 4.1.
\# Imports from Persian Gulf states, 1963, 3.8.

Table 37 — UK exports to various countries

Countries of destination	1924	1926—30	1931—35	1938	1963	1971
India and Pakistan	11.3	11.2	8.8	7.2	4.4*	1.9*
Australia	7.8	7.2	5.6	8.1	5.8	3.8
United States	6.6	6.3	5.0	4.3	8.3	11.4
Irish Republic	5.3	5.5	6.2	4.4	3.6	5.3
Germany	5.4	5.1	4.3	4.4	5.1†	5.6†
Canada	3.5	4.6	4.8	5.0*	4.2	3.7
South Africa	3.8	4.2	6.2	8.4	4.8‡	4.2‡
Argentina	3.4	4.0	3.4	4.1	0.6	0.6
France	5.2	3.9	5.0	3.2	4.4	4.2
Netherlands	3.1	3.1	3.2	2.8	4.0	4.3
Belgium	2.8	2.9	2.5	1.7	2.5	3.6
New Zealand	2.6	2.7	2.8	4.1	2.8	1.5
Italy	2.2	2.0	2.3	—	4.0§	2.6
Commonwealth	*41.7*	*45.6*	*45.7*	*44.6*	*37.9*	*18.3*
Foreign countries	*58.3*	*54.4*	*54.3*	*55.4*	*72.1*	*81.7*

* 1963: India 3.4, Pakistan 1.0. 1971: India 1.4, Pakistan 0.5.
† West Germany.
‡ 1963: UK imports from South Africa 2.4. 1971, 1.8.
§ 1963: UK imports from Italy 2.3. 1971, 2.8.

In 1963 of the total foreign trade, 35.1 per cent was with the sterling area; 17.9 per cent with the European Common Market; in 1971 20.7 per cent was with EEC countries.

Norway, Sweden, Denmark, Switzerland, Finland), the two groups together in 1969 accounting for nearly 35 per cent of the total; and exports to the United States took an upturn, for some 7.5 per cent of the total in 1961 to 12.3 per cent in 1969. With Britain's entry into the European Common Market it would seem likely that the trend towards increasing trade with other European countries will continue.

Northern Ireland

Comprising that portion of Ireland which has not severed its constitutional link with Great Britain, Northern Ireland forms with Britain the United Kingdom. It includes half a dozen counties and the boroughs of Belfast and Londonderry, and was established in 1920 with an area of 12 574.7 sq km (5 461.9 sq miles) and a population of 1 258 000. In 1971 the preliminary census return showed a population of 1 525 187, about 40 per cent of whom are classified as rural, 30 per cent actually living in the open countryside. Belfast (400 000) and Londonderry (56 000) are the main urban settlements and support most of the industry. Of the total area about 1.8 per cent is devoted to woods and plantations, 34.2 per cent to rough grazing, 25 per cent to permanent pastures, 30 per cent to arable farming. In 1970 the grain crops cultivated were barley 54 630 ha (135 000 acres), oats 23 350 ha (57 700 acres), and some wheat; potatoes account for 18 900 ha (46 700 acres), fruit for 2 954 ha (7 300 acres). Stock raising (cattle, sheep and pigs) and dairying are leading activities; poultry numbered some 13m. in 1970.

Industry first developed in the Belfast region with the textile industry. Belfast has the advantage of a good natural harbour, shipyards were established early, and the area remains the principal manufacturing region. The shipyards now are among the most up-to-date in the world; and the textile industry, although still using its traditional raw material, linen, has extended its scope to include manmade fibres. The textile and clothing industry together employ nearly 25 per cent of the manufacturing labour force. In recent years the government has encouraged diversification of industry by grants towards capital investment, and the manufacturing industry now includes aircraft works, factories producing electronic equipment, motor vehicle components, textile and other machinery; food processing is also a major enterprise. The principal imports are machinery and transport equipment, metals and manufactures, textiles, tobacco and manufactures, cereals and preparations, chemicals, petroleum and products, coal, fruit and vegetables, paper and manufactures, clothing and footwear. Exports comprise textiles, which have a considerable lead over machinery, clothing and footwear, meat and meat preparations, transport equipment, dairy produce, eggs and live animals. In recent years some 75 per cent of imports originated from Britain or came through Britain from foreign countries; less than 10 per cent came from the Irish Republic. Over 85 per cent of exports were destined for Britain or for foreign countries via Britain; 6 per cent were exported to the Irish Republic.

Northern Ireland has good links with Britain by sea and air. All services are busy carrying passengers and freight. The container transport traffic is fast increasing; and Belfast airport is being enlarged to bring it up to international standards.

The Republic of Ireland (Poblacht Na h-Éireann)

The Irish Republic was first proclaimed by the Free State leaders in 1916 but it was not until 1925 that the boundary between Northern Ireland and the Republic was fixed by an agreement which both accepted in conjunction with the British government.

The Republic comprises twenty-six counties with a land area of 68 900 sq km (26 600 sq miles) divided among the provinces of Leinster, Munster, Connacht and Ulster. The population has remained stable for many years: 2 972 802 in 1926; 2 953 265 in 1946; 2 960 593 in 1951; 2 884 002 in 1966; the census in 1971 recorded 2 971 230. Yet in 1841 the population of all Ireland was recorded as 8 175 000. The great famine which began in 1845 resulted in many deaths and precipitated mass migration to North America. Emigration remains an important factor in the economy of the Irish Republic. Many men leave to work in the building industry and on farms in Britain, and the women to nurse or to undertake domestic work or similar occupations. The Republic's income is therefore supplemented by remittances from emigrants to their families at home.

Surface, climate, land use and farming. Ireland can be described very broadly as comprising a central plain surrounded by a rim of high ground. Although much of the central plain is flat it is broken here and there by sandy hills and higher hills of old rock. It is deeply covered with boulder clay and other glacial debris left by retreating icesheets. Rain falling on to it has difficulty in escaping, so that lakes, bogs and wet boggy moorland result. The surrounding high rim of old rocks is irregular and much broken: arms of the sea penetrate it deeply in the northwest and southwest, giving deepwater approaches to the coast.

The sluggish streams which drain the central plain flow into the main river, the Shannon, the longest river in the British Isles; and where the river plunges over the rim at Killaloe a hydroelectric power station has been built. There are similar stations on the Rivers Liffey, Lee and Erne. Ireland makes full use of hydroelectric power potential because she lacks coal; peat supplies the fuel for another power station in Co. Kildare.

Lying in the path of the westerly winds from the Atlantic Ireland has a mild damp climate, with many days of fine drizzle, and high humidity. Snow and frost are comparatively rare in the south and west, but periods of sunshine and warm weather are insufficient to ripen crops except in the southeast.

In the Irish Republic therefore conditions are more suitable for stock farming than for the cultivation of crops. Of the land area, under one-sixth is devoted to crops, over one-half to permanent grass, and forest and woodland cover a negligible area. Beef cattle are reared on the central plain, some being sent alive for fattening in England, others being destined for the dairy farms which lie in the southwest. The race-horses and hunters for which Ireland is renowned are also bred on the central plain, especially near Dublin; and sheep are reared on the hilly rim especially on the hills of the west and east. The fertile valleys of the southwest support a flourishing dairy industry, organised on a coopera-tive basis. There is a large production of butter, and the skim milk is fed to pigs, reared particularly for bacon. Poultry abound.

Oats are grown to the limit of cultivation in the south and east; potatoes wherever possible; and on a low comparatively dry sunny plateau in the granite Wicklow mountains barley is harvested to supply the Guinness breweries of Dublin. Barley also thrives in favourable areas in the south, between the high land and the sea, where wheat can also be grown, but in a more restricted area towards the southeast.

Communications, population, manufactures and trade. Canals link the navigable waterways, but are no longer used. The railways make use of the gaps in the hills and avoid the boggy areas, converging on Dublin and on Belfast in Northern Ireland. As yet there are no motorways in the Republic. Ferry services to and from Britain are well used, the mail being sent from Dún Laoghaire, the outport of Dublin, to Holyhead in Anglesey. Shannon Airport is an important trans-Atlantic air terminal, and there are frequent flights to Britain and continental Europe.

The main urban areas are Dublin (650 000) which, with its outport Dún Laoghaire, now supports over 849 000 people; Cork with its surrounding area 130 000; Limerick 60 000; Waterford 30 000. To-gether these concentrations represent a very high percentage of the total population, and apart from these areas the Irish Republic is essentially rural and agricultural. In an attempt to stem a too rapid flow from the countryside to these major towns much attention is being paid to agricultural improvement and to agricultural education.

The Republic lacks any useful mineral resources, including coal, so the light industry which is being developed, especially at Dublin and Cork, has progressed with the availability of electric power. The factories are particularly concerned with the processing of food (meat-canning, brewing and so on), the textile, clothing and rug-making

Table 38 — Irish Republic: general imports and special exports

Commodity	Percentages of total value					
	1924	1926–30	1931–35	1938	1957	1971
General imports						
Livestock	–	–	1.9	2.0	0.34 §	0.17
Horses	–	2.1	1.5	1.9	0.28	0.05
Foodstuffs	–	–	30.7	29.2	14.5	9.5
Wheat and wheat products	10.8	10.2	7.6	7.5	1.9	3.09
Maize and maize products	6.4	5.6	4.4	5.5	0.2	0.9
Tea	3.8	4.1	4.1	4.0	3.4	0.7
Sugar	3.7	2.3	1.6	0.7	1.0	0.6
Bacon	2.8	2.9	0.8	0.2	–	–
Oilcake and fodder	2.2	2.0	1.2	0.8	0.6	1.1
Raw materials	–	–	19.6	17.1	–	24.34
Coal	6.4	5.6	6.5	8.0	4.9	1.25
Chemicals, drugs and paints	1.4	2.0	2.7	2.7	4.8	9.35
Petroleum	1.7	1.9	2.1	2.8	9.5	7.7
Manufactures	–	–	47.6	49.4	–	56.6
Apparel	6.4	7.3	5.5	2.3	0.9	2.0
Cotton yarns and manufactures	3.0	3.2	3.9	3.7	2.0	0.8
Woollen yarns and manufactures	2.3	2.6	3.1	3.0	1.1	0.6
Other textiles	–	2.1	3.1	3.2	7.5	3.3
Iron and manufactures	3.5	3.7	4.5	5.5	3.9	3.1
Other metals and manufactures	–	1.5	2.5	1.6	1.8	1.4
Machinery	1.6	3.0	3.7	7.5	8.8	25.76
Vehicles and parts	3.4	4.2	4.1	4.4	9.0	9.0
Paper and cardboard	1.6	1.9	3.0	3.0	3.3	2.6
Boots and shoes	3.0	2.4	2.4	–‡	–‡	0.4
Selected countries of supply						
United Kingdom	81.1	77.4	69.6	50.5	57.1	49.5
United States	5.4	7.3	4.4	11.4	5.7	8.6
Germany	1.1	3.0	4.0	3.6	4.1 ¶	7.3
Argentina	3.3	4.0	3.2	3.4	0.4	0.7
Canada	2.1	1.7	2.5	3.7	2.0	1.3
Belgium	–	–	2.3	2.7	2.0	1.3
Total value in £million	64.5	58.6	40.6	41.4	184.8	764.6
Special exports						
Livestock	–	–	45.1	49.5	39.6 #	13.0
Cattle	35.7	30.0	30.8	40.0	36.0	11.1
Horses	–	5.3	5.1	6.2	2.8	1.5
Pigs	2.4	4.8	3.2	0.9	–	–
Sheep	3.5	3.1	2.4	2.0	0.8	–
Foodstuffs	–	–	43.4	41.3	31.0	33.3
Stout, beer, ale	11.9	11.2	18.6	9.2	4.5	2.1
Butter	8.3	9.7	6.9	9.0	3.6	2.8
Eggs	6.4	6.8	5.9	4.9	0.2	0.02
Bacon	6.5	5.6	5.0†	9.2	2.7	1.7
Fresh pork	2.0	2.8	2.5	0.5	0.2	1.2
Poultry (dead)	1.7	1.6	2.0	1.8	1.7	–
Raw materials	–	–	4.4	5.2	–	10.08*
Manufactures	–	6.6	0.0	3.7	–	30.8
Textiles (including apparel)	–	2.2	1.9	0.1	8.8	9.56
Chief receiving countries						
United Kingdom	98.1	95.4	94.4	92.5	78.5	65.7
United States	0.5	0.5	0.8	0.5	3.1	11.7
Total value in £million	44.4	43.6	23.4	23.9	127.0	534.0

industries, and the making of boots and shoes. There are steel works on an island in Cork harbour, and an oil refinery nearby at Whitegate.

In addition to the remittances sent home by emigrants, tourism is an important invisible export. The main exports are linked with food: live animals, poultry, eggs, bacon, dairy produce and alcoholic beverages. The chief imports are food for the people, feed for the animals, crude oil and petroleum products, textile fibres, chemicals, machinery and a wide variety of manufactured goods. Most of the trade is with Britain, the two countries having a free-trade agreement; and it passes through the main port, Dublin and its outport, Dún Laoghaire. The many small ports have a declining coastal traffic. An important development in the 1960s was the creation of a deep water oil terminal in the southwest, near Whiddy Island in Bantry Bay which, it is anticipated, will accommodate the largest oil tankers. They anchor in the deep water offshore; the oil is piped ashore to storage tanks, to be piped in turn to smaller tankers destined for shipment to Milford Haven and to refineries in continental Europe unable to provide port facilities for the giant tankers. Also in the southwest is Valentia Island, from which submarine cables cross the floor of the Atlantic to North America.

France

France (551 600 sq km: 213 000 sq miles) is over twice the size of Britain but the population is lower; it has however increased in recent years: 1954 census 42.8m.; 1968 census 49.8.; 1973 estimate 52m.

Surface. The greater part of northern France comprises gently rolling land or broken hilly country which offers little hindrance to communication. Lofty mountains, the Pyrénées 3 350 m (11 000 ft) and the Alps (up to 4 500 m: 15 000 ft), form the land frontier on the south and southeast; and in the east are the lower ranges of the French Jura and the Vosges. The chief highlands within the French frontier are those of the Massif Central, the Central Plateau, which lies south of centre, averaging from 750 m to 900 m (2 500 to 3 000 ft. On the east they are bordered by the Cevennes which sink abruptly down to the

---

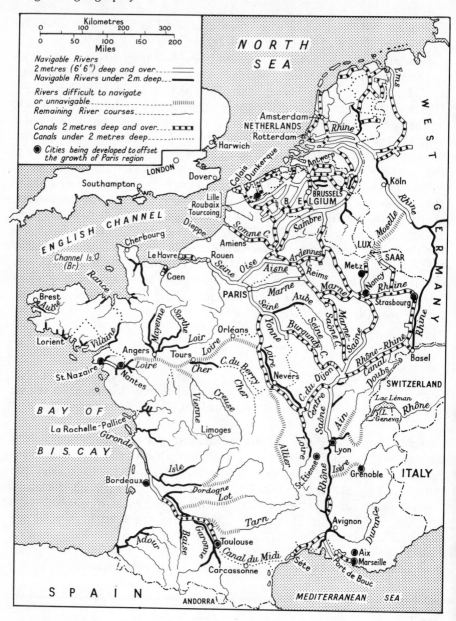

Inland waterways of France, and the principal navigable waterways of Belgium and the Netherlands; and the *métropoles d'équilibre* in France (see p. 392)

Rhône valley; further west they are crowned by the remains of the old volcanoes (the *puys*) of Auvergne; and they are traversed by profound river valleys opening to the north and west. The climate of the Massif Central is bleak and the soil unproductive but some of the valleys have fertile soils derived from volcanic dust blown thither by the prevailing southwest winds from the mountains of Auvergne, notably near Clermont-Ferrand. The level tract between the Adour and the Garonne in the southwest, embracing the maritime dunes of the Landes, contains even less fertile land than the Central Plateau and here, as in the Central Plateau region, the population is scanty. The mass of ancient rock in Brittany, in northwest France, corresponds in character to the mass which forms Devon and Cornwall in the British Isles, and gives rise to similar landscape and land use.

Rivers and internal navigation. France has a considerable length of navigable waterways which are still important to trade. The Seine (with its tributaries, the Oise, Marne, Aube and Yonne), the Loire, Dordogne and Garonne, and the Saône, the chief tributary of the Rhône, as well as minor rivers, flow through plains and valleys presenting few obstructions to navigation for the greater part of their courses. Even the sandbanks and other obstructions in the impetuous Rhône have been, or are being, overcome in the course of work for hydroelectric power stations which involve the cutting of deviation canals; and the Rhine, which forms part of the eastern frontier, is one of the great waterways of Europe. The value of the natural waterways is shown by the canal connections between them, especially in northeastern France, where flat country favoured canal building and where, because of the needs of industry, there is a large amount of traffic in goods of low value in proportion to their bulk and/or weight. Even today one-tenth of the long distance transport in France is by waterway. The major waterways still in use are shown on the map on p. 386, and of these the Seine and its links with the north are the most used, connecting Paris with the industrial area of the northern coalfield and with the Channel ports, and providing means for the carriage of coal, coke, and pig iron for the iron and steel industry as well as limestone, cement, sand and oil. An indication of the importance attached to waterways is provided by the Moselle Canal, built as recently as 1964, having been discussed as early as Roman times. The Moselle Canal, which is a northern continuation of the waterway serving Nancy and Metz, takes up to 1 500-ton motor barges and is of great benefit to the Lorraine iron and steel industry. The improved Saône–Rhône navigation can also accommodate large barges, carrying phosphates, sulphur, cement and salt as well as refined petroleum products. It is possible that in future the usefulness of inland water transport in France may be diminished as coal fuel is replaced by natural gas and by oil, both transferred by pipeline; but for the present the inland waterways play an active part in France's economy and ensure that Paris, Strasbourg, Lyon and Lille are major inland ports.

Climate. France has all the advantages of a westerly maritime situation together with a more southerly latitude than that of the British Isles. Consequently she has (*a*) a tract of Mediterranean climate along the Mediterranean shores and in the lower part of the Rhône valley where typical Mediterranean products may be grown; (*b*) a large stretch of country in the north which has a climate comparable with that of southeastern England but with rather drier and colder winters, favourable for the ripening of cereals; and (*c*) a large tract of country in the west, milder and damper than the last. In winter, when there is high pressure in the Paris basin and low pressure in the Gulf of Lyons, a violent cold northerly wind, the *mistral*, is liable to blow in the Mediterranean climatic region west of the Rhône, and to affect the early crops in the Rhône valley. The Riviera towns which developed as winter resorts (for example Cannes and Nice) are therefore those which are protected by spurs of the Maritime Alps or by distance from the treacherous air currents of the Rhône valley.

Crops. The fertility of the land of France is indicated in that of its total area 32 per cent is cultivated; 25 per cent is under pasture; 2.5 per cent nourishes the vine; over 23 per cent supports forest; only 16 per cent is uncultivated. Agriculture in France is very much more important than in most other west European countries.

Wheat is the most important cereal crop: France is second to the USSR as Europe's largest wheat producer but has only about one-tenth of the Soviet output, and yields are lower than those in Britain. There is a surplus for export which France sells in the Common Market: despite mechanisation her production costs are high and her wheat prices uncompetitive in world markets. Production of barley is 70 per cent of that of wheat: most is used for animal feed, some for malting. These two grain crops are grown in the most favoured arable areas, in the Paris and Aquitaine basins and in the Rhine and Rhône—Saône valleys. Maize is grown, mainly for fodder, in the south of Aquitaine and Alsace. Its popularity is increasing with the advent of new short-stalked varieties and it now occupies an area nearly half of that devoted to barley. Oats are grown in the west in areas too damp for wheat and barley: the area is about three-quarters of that of maize. In the south a small quantity of rice is produced in the Rhône delta.

France was an early producer of sugar beet and the crop exceeds that of potatoes. Both are grown in rotation with cereal crops, especially in the Paris basin.

A plant of great value in France is of course the vine. It is often not appreciated how small is the area under her highly productive vineyards: 2.5 per cent of the total land area. They are mainly in the southern two-thirds of the country, but vines are cultivated further north, producing special wines, among which champagne should be mentioned. France used to import large quantities of *vin ordinaire* from

Algeria, but when that country became independent the supply declined and home production has accordingly increased.

The varied climates of France are well illustrated in the range of her fruits, from the cider apples of Normandy, the apples, cherries and similar fruits of the Paris basin, to the olive (and the flowers cultivated for the manufacture of perfume) of the Mediterranean zone, and the grapes, peaches and apricots of the Aquitaine basin. Market gardening is a profitable enterprise, and particular attention is paid to the production of early vegetables, *les primeurs*. In the Rhône valley the early crops have to be protected from the *mistral*. There is an interesting development on the south coast, in the Languedoc, until recently one of the poorest areas of France. This region is being irrigated by water from the Rhône to produce a rich vegetable and fruit growing area with associated canneries. Communications will be improved by a motorway and the swampy coastal area reclaimed and developed for residents and for tourism.

Animals. Cattle rearing is widespread in France except in the Mediterranean area and in the southwest. The Paris basin, with its cereal and fodder rotation crops, is a notable fattening area. Dairy cattle thrive in the valleys of the Alps, the Vosges and the Jura, in the damp areas of the northwest, and in part of the Massif Central where they spend the summer on the upper pastures and the winter in the valleys. The production of butter is high, so is that of cheese, and pigs are fed on the skimmed milk. The consumption of milk in France, once low, is rising. Sheep are reared for wool and meat in the drier mixed farming areas, and notably in part of the Massif Central, the outer Pyrenees and in the southern Alps. Their milk, and that of goats, is also used for cheesemaking. Pigs are ubiquitous, being reared on small farms and near the dairy farms; and poultry appear in all agricultural areas.

Even from this brief generalised account of French agriculture it will be apparent that France's agricultural output is considerable. She is almost self-sufficient and has a surplus for export. A large proportion of her population — 18 per cent of the labour force — is engaged in agriculture, compared with under 3 per cent in Britain. One of the reasons for this is that, lacking extensive coal resources in the nineteenth century, there was not a drift of rural population to burgeoning industrial areas based on coal, as there was in Britain. The only important coalfield was on the frontier in the far north and it had little effect on the rest of the country. Nor has France developed any vast industrial areas in the heart of the country since then. There are many small farms, in part the result of the Napoleonic law which decreed that all sons should inherit equal shares of their father's estate. Many farms use much manpower because they are undermechanised. There is a sharp contrast in farm management between north and south. On the whole farming in the north, with the benefit of good soils and favourable climates is mechanised, progressive and economic, especially in the Paris Basin where large farm units are common. South of central France the soils are poorer, the climate dry and new techniques not so readily accepted by small farmers who hold strongly to traditional methods.

On average therefore the cost of agricultural production in France is high despite the efficiency of her northern farms. This is a matter of contention with her neighbours in the EEC who could buy cheaper produce from other sources; and it contributes to the high cost of living in France.

Fisheries have already been covered (see p. 253). As in the British fishing industry large trawlers with electronic aids sail even further for their catch. On the west coast generally many small fishing ports have declined because they lack good communications inland; but Boulogne in the north has prospered with good harbour facilities and rail communications to a large market. Many trout and salmon are caught in France's innumerable rivers and streams, and fish cultivation in ponds is common. Fish landed on the Mediterranean coast is eaten locally. Consumption of fish in France is slowly growing, whereas in Britain it is declining.

Minerals and power resources. In general France is not very richly endowed with minerals, even *coal*. There is one large coalfield, that of northern France, which is probably connected under the Strait of Dover with the East Kent coalfield. It stretches beyond the French borders right across Belgium as the Belgian coalfield, and like that field suffers from intense folding of the rocks, resulting in dangerous mining conditions in the presence of water and gas. The only other coalfield of any moment is the Lorraine field, an extension of the Saar coalfield. This has thick deep coalseams, but highly mechanised techniques are used in its exploitation; and this relatively small but productive field provides one-quarter of France's coal. France did not acquire this field until the realignment of her frontier with Germany in 1919. All the other fields are small basins pinched in among the ancient rocks of the plateau. Those at St Etienne and Le Creusot had the advantage of iron ore occurring in the same locality. For strategic reasons they were safer than the coal areas in France's frontiers, and so it was here that the armaments industry grew. Mining costs are high, however, and at present this area contributes only about one-fifth to total coal production.

From 1919 to 1935 France had the advantage of working the Saar coalfield as part of reparations following the First World War. It was returned to Germany as a result of a plebiscite of Saarlanders. After the Second World War it again featured in war reparations and once more, in 1945, came under French control; but in 1956, as the result of a Franco–German agreement, it passed back to West Germany.

It is clear that France's major coal resources are on her northern frontiers; and that at the time of the industrial revolution, in the age of coal and steam in the nineteenth century, France (without the benefits of the Lorraine and Saar coalfields) had inadequate and inconveniently sited coal resources. She had to import large amounts of coal, most of it coming from Britain. The only area with an adequate home supply was the northern coalfield and it was only here that any considerable development took place.

On account of this lack of coal France turned her attention at an early stage to hydroelectric power. Small hydroelectric power stations in the Alps and the Pyrénées were operating long before 1900; but again these schemes did not touch central France. This area had to wait until the 1930s when big hydroelectric schemes were initiated which dammed the rivers rising in the Massif Central, to provide power for the grid. Industry was not attracted to the area because, hampered by inadequate communication, it could not compete with industry more favourably sited on the international valley routeways. In these valley areas there were elaborate schemes harnessing the Rhine, and later the Rhône waters. The Rhône scheme incorporates France's first nuclear power station at Marcoule. Hydroelectric power now supplies 40 per cent of France's output of electricity, and coal supplies about one-half of her energy needs.

On the Rance estuary in Brittany the strength of the tide has been harnessed to generate power, the first station of its kind in the world. It is hoped the area will develop industrially.

There are small oilfields near Paris; at Pechelbronn, north of Strasbourg; and, more important, at Parentis in the Landes, southwest France. The production of these fields is insufficient to meet her needs and France imports much crude oil from the Middle East and Saharan fields, to be refined at the port of entry or distributed by pipeline.

More important at present than her oilfields are France's reserves of natural gas at Lacq, in the foothills of the Pyrénées, where production has grown steadily since 1958, the purified gas being distributed by pipeline. The field may, it is thought, be exhausted by 1983. Natural gas also reaches France through Belgium by pipeline; and liquid gas is imported from North Africa.

France has now however good reserves of *iron ore*, especially in the Lorraine field, restored to France in 1919. Except for a small area in the north lying in Luxembourg, the French gained the whole area but not, unfortunately, the much needed coking coal to smelt the iron ore: this stayed in German hands. France had to wait until the inauguration of the European Iron and Steel Community before she had free access to these valuable West German coal resources. The Lorraine iron is low grade, comparable with the British ores now being worked in the Midlands. The phosphoric content is high. Some of the ore is smelted locally, some sent to the Northern coalfield for the iron and steel industry. There are also reserves of iron ore at Caen in Normandy.

Of other minerals France has large deposits of *potash salts* near Mulhouse in Alsace (also regained after the First World War); high quality *bauxite* at Les Baux south of Avignon (which gave its name to this ore of aluminium); *salt* (important for the chemicals industry) at Nancy, along the edge of the Jura mountains, and in south Aquitaine (it is also obtained by evaporation along the Mediterranean and Biscay coasts); and *sulphur*. France is now one of the world's largest producers of sulphur, obtained as a result of the necessary purification of the natural gas at Lacq.

Population and industry. France suffered calamitous losses of man-power in the First World War, but her population started to grow after the Second World War, increased by a steady flow of immigrants, for whom France has always been an attraction. The most densely popu-lated areas are in the Paris region, the northern and eastern industrial areas, at the ports, and along the Riviera coast. There are few really large towns: in 1969 only forty-nine urban centres in France had a population over 100 000 (compared with ninety-three in the United Kingdom), and most of these, apart from Paris and Lyon, are on the periphery, in line with the coalfields and industry. The Paris region for long has dominated France and suffers increasing pressure of popula-tion and industry. To relieve Paris itself six satellite towns are to be built, one row of three to the north of the capital, one row to the southwest; so that the Paris region will develop in an east—west linear way along the Seine and the Marne. To reduce pressure on the region further, industrialists are being urged to go to other towns to *métropole d'équilibre* — in the provinces: to Roubaix—Tourcoing in the north; Thionville—Nancy in Lorraine in the east; Strasbourg in Alsace; Lyon—St Etienne in the Rhône valley; the Languedoc and Marseille area in the south; Toulouse in Midi-Pyrénées; Bordeaux in Aquitaine; and Nantes—St Nazaire on the coast of the Loire country.

The agricultural population is widely and fairly evenly distributed because of advantageous soil and climatic conditions over most of the country. There is a concentration in some river valleys and, naturally, a lack of population in the poorer agricultural areas.

France has never developed as a great industrial power. She lacked the early impetus of coal-based industry, but is much better placed in the present era of oil, natural gas and electricity. She can either import power resources or use home supplies. Her main industries are manu-facturing: engineering (motor vehicles, tyres, tractors, electronic equip-ment), chemicals, textiles, and food processing, a minor, but growing industry. The main old heavy industries (coalmining, iron and steel) on the northern coalfield and the early chemical and metallurgical industries using hydroelectric power developed in the mountains, particularly in the east, are all peripheral. The eastern industries had the advantage of navigable waterways in addition to hydroelectric power. It is in these two areas and in the Paris Basin that industry is still concentrated; but this situation may change in the future because new industries may develop in areas served by oil and natural gas pipelines, with which France is well supplied. It should be noticed however that the *métropoles d'équilibre* still maintain the peripheral character of France's development.

The old northern coalfield area prospers in some parts, declines in others. This is the region with the highest rate of population increase and there are problems of overcrowding and unemployment in an old industrial area dependent on a contracting coal industry. In some ways it resembles a development area in Britain. Industry is still strongly based on coalmining; iron and steel, chemicals, gas and electricity, all produced by coal; and textiles; but attempts are being made at diversification. An example is the plant being built near Bruay en Artois to produce automatic gearboxes. The main coalmining towns are now Béthune, Lens and Douai. Iron ore is imported for the iron and steel industry from the Lorraine ore field and better quality iron ore is imported from Sweden. The textile industry is a large employer of women. It grew up in Flanders, making use in turn of handspun local wool or flax, later coal for power, now electricity, with cotton and synthetic fibres (produced locally) augmenting the wool and flax. The medieval towns of Roubaix and Tourcoing specialise in cotton, linen, wool and worsted textiles, and carpets. The linen is still spun in the nearby major textile town, Lille, which manufactures cotton textiles. Already connected by motorway with Paris Lille is destined to become the point of convergence of new motorways to Dunkerque, from Valenciennes (with nearby steel mills, now connected by oil pipeline to the terminal at Le Havre), from Brussels, and from Gent. Dunkerque has become an important coastal site for the iron and steel industry of the European Economic Community; it receives iron ore imported from West Africa at its up-to-date plant, and the furnaces are oilfired. The new oil terminal can accommodate large tankers; and over 10 000 ha (25 000 acres) have been set aside near the harbour for new industrial development. Metallurgical, shipbuilding and engineering works are active; and there are plans to locate an aluminium smelter on the newly designated industrial area. The Dunkerque—Calais area has excellent communications with Britain, with northern France, and hence with the other countries of the Common Market. There is no doubt that it and the declining northern region have great potential for growth now that Britain has become a full member of the Common Market.

Steel and tinplate are produced by the most modern methods in the area of the Lorraine iron orefield, especially south of Metz, where the ore is calcareous and therefore self-fluxing. In Nancy textiles are produced, as well as chemicals based on the locally available salt. There is a small declining textile area in Alsace, which originally used the power and the soft water of the Vosges rivers.

Other textile centres are Troyes on the Seine, upstream from Paris, which specialises in knitwear of cotton and manmade fibres; Rouen, once the lowest bridging point on the Seine, at first working with local wool, later cotton imported from the New World (which also sent wheat and coffee); and the newcomer, Dunkerque, making use of synthetic materials at the point of import. Some manmade fibres are products of the petrochemical industry which can be established wherever an oil supply is available. Textile factories using manmade fibres are therefore widely dispersed, a trend which will no doubt continue; it is in the north of France that the concentration on natural fibres persists.

Paris, the capital city, administrative and commercial centre, with a rapidly growing population (8.2m. estimated in 1970 in the continuously built-up area) is the centre of the other major industrial area. Like London it is the focus of routes of communication and similarly its great market is a magnet attracting manufacturers who have inaugurated such industries as metallurgical, chemical, motor works (Renault and Citroen), food processing and countless consumer goods factories in the Paris area. Industrial licensing has been introduced to curb this industrial influx and industrial development is being encouraged in the planned New Towns. The city itself has always been a great tourist attraction.

There is vigorous industrial development in the Rhône–Alps region on the east of France, centred on Lyon. Lyon itself is a Roman settlement, situated at the confluence of the Rhône and Saône rivers; an old commercial and banking city, long famous for silk manufactures. Initially raw silk produced locally was used, to be replaced by imported silk (now a minor fibre, but still important), later augmented by artificial silk, followed by manmade fibres produced locally. Textile manufacturing fostered the making of textile machinery which led in turn to rail and truck manufacture, then to the electronics industry, and hardware. The silk mills also needed dyes: early vegetable dyes were replaced by chemical dyestuffs, which encouraged the growth of the chemical industry in the area. The chemical industry now produces manmade fibres, pharmaceuticals, pesticides, paints and so on, in addition to dyes. Lyon is admirably placed in relation to road, rail and river traffic, oil and gas pipelines and hydroelectric power, with a plentiful supply of water for the chemical industry and labour readily available: very many emigrants from North Africa have settled in the area.

In the past industrial development at Lyon was based on coal supplied from St Etienne nearby. The coalmines have however been steadily closing for some time, and the last is due to shut down in 1975. The miners have at the same time been retrained and the closure of the pits has been balanced by the opening of steelworks specialising in high grade products, such as motor vehicle and bicycle components, and small arms. Ribbons and elastic the traditional products of St Etienne, continue.

The third major town of the region is Grenoble, showing the most startling expansion: a fourfold increase in population since the end of the Second World War, necessitating overspill into a New Town, Echirolles. Pioneers of hydroelectric power laboured in Grenoble and the city retains its links with the past in the production of plant for hydroelectric power stations, hydraulic equipment, barrages, as well as power shovels, ski-lifts, cable cars; while it looks to the future in experimenting with the aerotrain, a railway hovercraft. The Centre for Nuclear Studies is in the University. At present Grenoble suffers from a lack of good routes; it would benefit greatly if the long promised autoroute linking Lyon with Geneva were built, and if the old idea of linking the North Sea and the Mediterranean by waterway, capable of taking 1 300 ton barges, were realised.

To the south Marseille is situated on firm ground to the east of the Rhône delta, avoiding the river's shifting sandy channels. There was a settlement nearby in the days of ancient Greece, and the fortunes of Marseille have waxed and waned with the fluctuating Mediterranean trade. It faded when the New World was opened up to Europeans, to give an emphasis on trans-Atlantic trade; it recovered, when the Suez Canal was opened, as a major port on the western Europe, India and the Far East route. It is well served by road, rail, waterway and air services and is now an outlet not only for France but for much of northern Europe as well. It has a fine rock-girt harbour but is hemmed in by mountains, so that port facilities are being extended at Fos sur Mer to handle bulk cargoes and containers. Crude oil is easily the leading import handled, piped from the terminal, Lavéra, as far as the Rhineland. Other imports are foodstuffs and tropical products such as rubber; local fruit and wine appear among exports, and there is some entrepôt trade. The Marseille area is growing industrially, especially bordering the Etang de Berre, with new oil refineries and associated chemical works. There are the usual port industries: making of soap and margarine (formerly based on local olive oil, now on tropical oilseeds), processing of oilseeds, sugar refining. Its importance in relation to the Rhône—Saône developments to the north and the vitalising of the Languedoc in the west is obvious.

In the Massif Central local fruit used to be used for jam making and local milk for chocolate in Clermont-Ferrand; but a son of Clermont-

Ferrand married an heiress of Mackintosh, of waterproof garment fame, in the early nineteenth century, and the result of this union and imported formula was ultimately the establishment of the Michelin tyre factory; there is also a motorworks. Another traditional industry, the making of fine porcelain, has long been carried on and continues at Limoges, where there is a supply of local clays weathered from the granite.

The gap town of Toulouse has been revivified with engineering, chemical, aircraft and electronics works; at Lacq the chemical industry associated with the exploitation of local natural gas has already been noted.

Many of France's ports are also major industrial centres: the Channel ports which serve Paris (Dieppe, Boulogne, Calais and Dunkerque, of which the last two have the fastest and the last the greatest industrial growth), linked to Britain by car ferry, roll-on, roll-off ferries and air services; the Paris outport, Le Havre (founded in 1509) on the Seine estuary, with its important oil terminals; and Cherbourg, port-of-call on the trans-Atlantic route. To the east the river port of Strasbourg on the Rhine, linked by canal with both Paris and the Rhône basins, receives oil by pipeline from Lavéra; and with easy access to the Paris industrial region and the nearby German markets was a fast developing industrial area in the 1960s. It is the seat of the Council of Europe and of the European Parliament but, surprisingly, is not served by a conveniently close international airport.

To the east of Marseille, Toulon is a naval station and port. On the west coast the port of Bordeaux has served the great wine-growing area since early times. It had a significant trade with America and the West Indies when France had colonies in that area, and with West Africa, but the trade has declined. There is little industry in the hinterland, the population is static, and Bordeaux is not well placed to serve the European Economic Community. Crude oil figures among the imports, for the refineries of the Garonne estuary which also process a supply from the Parentis field; paper is made from local timber, cement from nearby limestone; fungicides and fertilisers (notably superphosphate from imported Moroccan phosphate) are produced, destined for the agricultural hinterland, particularly the vineyards. Tropical foods are imported from West Africa and the West Indies (groundnuts, sugar, rum, coffee, cocoa) and processed locally; but the area Bordeaux serves, Aquitaine, is not a progressive one, and development is slow. The port has however been designated a *métropole d'équilibre*: a Ford plant for the manufacture of automatic gearboxes, electronics factories, new refineries, petrochemical works, a fine new airport and buildings for the annual international trade fair, the modernisation of port facilities, a suspension bridge across the Garonne, a long-term project for a new town at Le Verdon — all are planned and the first three in the list are already in production. Government aid is generous and it is hoped that other manufacturing industry will be attracted to the area.

Further north St Nazaire and Nantes are also *métropoles d'équilibre*. St Nazaire has a long-standing shipbuilding tradition, and metallurgical and petrochemical plants are being set up in the area; light industry is being encouraged. In Brittany a deepwater port has been built at Roscoff for the shipment of produce from the dominantly agricultural hinterland; and another at Brest, the famous naval station, which already has major ship repair yards. This port will be able to take tankers of up to 200 000 tons; the new refinery will have a capacity of some 3 to 4m. tons. An electronics plant is already established. Inland other industry is being set up: electronics and motor works (Citroen) at Rennes; Michelin tyre factory at Vannes; motor works (Renault) at Lorient. Brittany also has high hopes of trade with Britain in her agricultural produce, now that Britain is in the Common Market.

Communications. France has well-developed internal communications. The Romans laid their usual excellent roads, centring on Lyon; and Napoleon I produced a masterplan with Paris as the focus of main roads and the principal towns as minor focal points. The railway and canal building took place mainly between 1830 and 1848. With her early development of hydroelectric power France was early in the field of electrified railways: electric trains were running in the early years of this century. There was great devastation of rolling stock, lines and installations in the Second World War, but France speedily reconstructed her railways and now has one of the fastest modern long-distance rail systems in the world. There are proposals to expand the existing trunk road system. International air links are well used, the Paris airports handling most of the traffic.

Table 39 — Towns with a population exceeding 200 000

	(1968 census)		*(1968 census)*
Paris	8 197 000	Grenoble	332 000
Lyon	1 075 000	St Etienne	331 000
Marseille	964 000	Lens	326 000
Lille	881 000	Nancy	258 000
Bordeaux	555 000	Le Havre	247 000
Toulouse	440 000	Valenciennes	224 000
Nantes	393 000	Cannes	213 000
Nice	393 000	Douai	205 000
Rouen	370 000	Clermont-	
Toulon	340 000	Ferrand	205 000
Strasbourg	335 000	Tours	202 000

Table 40 — France Overseas

	Year of acquisition	Status 1 January 1970
Asia		
India (Pondicherry, Karikal, Mahé, Yananon)	1674	Part of India
Tonking ⎫	1884 ⎫	
Annam ⎬ Vietnam	1884 ⎬	Independent Vietnam 1949, 1954
Cochin–China ⎭	1862 ⎭	
Cambodia	1863	Khmer Rep. Ind. 1953
Laos	1893	Independent 1949
Africa		
Morocco, French Zone	1912	Independent 1956
Algeria	1830–1902	Independent 1962
Tunisia	1881	Independent 1956
Sénégal ⎫	1627–1889	Independent Republic* 1960
French Sudan ⎮	1893	Independent Republic* (Mali) 1960
Guinea ⎮ French	1843	Independent 1958
Ivory Coast ⎬ West	1843	Independent Republic* 1960
Dahomey ⎮ Africa	1893	Independent Republic* 1960
Mauritania ⎮	1893	Independent Republic* 1960
Niger ⎮	1912	Independent Republic* 1960
Upper Volta ⎭	1919	Independent Republic* 1960
Equatorial Africa	1884	Ind. Republics* (Central African Republic, Congo Republic (Brazzaville), Gabon and Chad)
Cameroun (trusteeship)	1919	Independent Republic 1960
Togo (trusteeship)	1919	Independent Republic 1960
Réunion	1643	French department
Madagascar	1643–1896	Independent Rep.* (Malagasy) 1960
Comoro Archipelago	1843	French territory
French Somaliland	1864	French territory of the Afars and the Issas
America		
St Pierre and Miquelon	1635	French territory
Guadeloupe and dependencies	1634	French department
Martinique	1635	French department
Guiana	1626	French department
Oceania		
New Caledonia	1854–1887	French territory
French Polynesia	1841–1881	French territory
Wallis and Fatuna	1842	French territory
New Hebrides	1906	Anglo–French
Condominium		Condominium
Antarctic territories	1772, 1949–50	French territory

* These independent republics retain their links with the Communauté.

Foreign trade. France does not rank among the leaders in foreign trade. Imports usually exceed exports by a small amount and her earnings from invisible exports (apart from tourism, particularly important on the Mediterranean coast and in the mountains) are negligible. She exports machinery, including transport machinery and cars, but imports about two-thirds as much (tractors, electrical machinery and motor vehicles); exports manufactures, mostly of iron and steel and non-ferrous metals, and imports more in the same category. Chemicals are the next export of importance, followed by fabrics and yarns (of which imports are half as much). She exports food products such as cereals, dairy produce, wine, fruit and vegetables; but imports two-thirds as much in meat, fruit and vegetables, coffee and other foods. Crude oil is imported in increasing quantities; and a little coal.

Most trading is with the European Economic Community countries, especially West Germany, followed by Belgium–Luxembourg, Italy and the Netherlands. The rest is with the United States, United Kingdom, Algeria, Syria and Switzerland and with countries of the Communauté Française, or with countries that were formerly colonies and now have 'special links' with the Communauté. There were always close cultural ties between France and the countries she administered and the imprint of the French way of life continues in them, especially in the use of French as the second language. Imports of primary products from her former West African colonies are declining as industry develops in these countries and home-processing grows; but old trading ties remain to some extent, notably with Algeria.

Monaco

The tiny principality of Monaco on the Mediterranean shores near the Franco–Italian border has over 24 000 people in 149 ha (368 acres). It is an interesting example of a country living entirely on tourism.

Belgium

The surface of Belgium is made up, in the west and north, of low flat plains, partly below sea level, succeeded by low undulating land which rises in the southeast to a tableland (the Ardennes) intersected by deep river valleys. Between these two main physical regions, the lowlands and the highlands, lies the long narrow coalfield. The plains afford admirable facilities for inland navigation by both river and canal.

The area, 30 510 sq km (11 780 sq miles) is one-eighth that of Britain, the population (1969 est. 9.6m.) over one-sixth. The high density of over 310 per sq km (774 per sq mile) is fairly evenly distributed. Only the Province of Luxembourg, in the southeast, on the tableland of the Ardennes, has a density of population low enough to be compared with that of an English county such as Hereford. Another district of low but rising density is the Campine, on the northeast, a sandy plain, formerly heathy or marshy, but now partly reclaimed, and rapidly becoming an industrial region centred around a relatively new coalfield. This high density of population overall is due, as in England, both to advanced agriculture and to the great development of manufacturing industries. Two languages are spoken by the bulk of the population: Flemish (virtually Dutch) by those living north of a line drawn from the south of the province of West Flanders to the north of that of Liège, French (Walloon) by those south of the line.

About 50 per cent of the land is cultivated and of that 53 per cent is under crops, the remainder under pasture; forests and woodland occupy 22 per cent of the total land area, and lie mainly in the Ardennes. The chief grain crops are wheat, barley, oats, rye; rootcrops are sugar beet, potatoes, and beet for fodder. Industrial crops such as tobacco, flax, hops and chicory are highly characteristic of some areas, particularly Flanders, Flax is mainly grown in the basin of the Lys, a tributary of the Escaut (Scheldt) and the excellent linen obtained from it has long been held to be due to the remarkably soft water of that river, which is well suited to cleansing and retting the fibre. The centre of this trade is Courtrai.

At the last agricultural census of Belgium 36 per cent of the surface in cultivation was worked by owner-occupiers. Small farm ownership is even more general than small property ownership, most of the farms having an area of between 1 and 20 ha (2.5 and 50 acres). Only 5.3 per cent of the total labour force is engaged in agriculture, but productivity is exceptionally high, due not so much to natural land fertility (except in the rich polders or embanked areas reclaimed from the sea) but to centuries of careful tillage and manuring. Most farms are mixed, raising livestock and growing crops, but there is great expansion in horticulture and market-gardening to supply ever-growing urban markets at home and in the other countries of the EEC. In particular there is an important market-gardening area southeast of Brussels. The numbers of cattle have been steadily rising in recent years, and there has been a very vigorous increase in the numbers of pigs reared.

The principal mineral wealth of Belgium is coal. The coalfields fall into two main divisions. The more extensive occupies the valleys which intersect the Belgian plateau from the eastern frontier near Aachen (Aix-la-Chapelle) to about the middle of the Franco–Belgian frontier, the chief valleys being those of the Sambre and that part of the Meuse valley which continues the line of the valley of the Sambre. Geologically this strip is formed by a series of carboniferous strata lying on the northwestern margin of a Devonian plateau which extends eastwards into West Germany. The main mining activities centre on Mons (the Borinage district), Charleroi, Liège and the areas between. Production has steadily declined in this coalfield since the contraction of the industry. The other main coalfield area is in the Campine, in the Flemish-speaking area. It ranges westwards from Dutch Limburg to near Antwerpen through a length of about 80 km (50 miles) with a width of about 11 to 20 km (7 to 12 miles). Production began in 1917 and has grown steadily so that this field now contributes one-third of Belgium's coal output. The chief mining centre is Genck. Much of the coal is 'long flame', suitable for use in glass and pottery making.

Belgium's coal production averaged 29m. tons in 1936–38; in 1962 it was 21.2m. tons; and by 1970 it had dropped to about 13m. tons. As a fuel it is being replaced by oil and natural gas, the latter being imported from the Netherlands by pipeline. Hydroelectric power is not so significant, but may develop in future. A nuclear power station is operating at Chooze, and two more are planned, at Tihange and Doel.

Belgium has no other minerals of significance: former deposits of zinc have been exhausted; deposits of lead are negligible. Despite this there is a well established non-ferrous metal industry, based on imported ores.

The Belgian (and Luxembourg) iron ores are part of the Jurassic iron ore field of Lorraine. Excellent glass sands are found especially in the Campine and around Charleroi. There are brick and pottery clays, notably around Boom, on the Rupel, between Brussels and Antwerpen, and various stone quarries.

Manufactures are numerous and varied in this highly industrialised and urbanised country. Steel production is the leading industry and production *per capita* is one of the highest in the world. The industry is forward-looking and adapting to the newest techniques. It grew up on the coalfield of the Sambre–Meuse valleys and, supplied by iron ore from Lorraine and Luxembourg, is still concentrated in the region of La Louvière, Charleroi, Hainaut and Liège, with its suburb of Seraing. The situation of Liège is highly characteristic of the towns in the east. It was known to the Romans as *Lugdumum Batavorum*, and during the whole of its history it has been an important trade centre, for centuries famous for the manufacture of firearms. It lies, like Namur, Vervier, Huy and other important towns in the east of Belgium, in a narrow valley of the southeastern plateau, but at an important nodal point. At Liège the valley of the Meuse begins to open out so as to afford free communication in various directions towards the west and north; the valley of the Ourthe which here joins the Meuse opens a way to the south through Belgian Luxembourg; and the valley of the Vesdre which joins the Ourthe just above its confluence with the Meuse leads eastwards by way of Vervier and Aix-la-Chapelle into West Germany. The position of Liège may be compared with that of Manchester or Leeds. The industries of the town and the surrounding neighbourhood now include machinery and mechanical engineering, chemicals, glass making non-ferrous metals, rubber and textile manufactures. There are two large steelworks in the Belgian Province of Luxembourg which adjoins the northern limit of the iron ore deposits of the Duchy; and away to the northwest at Gent there is a new mill producing special steels. The western region of the old coalfield, the Mons–La Louviere–Charleroi area, supports diversified heavy industry similar to that of the Liège area; and there is more in the Antwerpen—Brussels area, although here it is intermingled with light industry. This district has the benefit of the Antwerpen—Brussels—Charleroi Canal for the carriage of raw materials and finished products. The new large integrated iron and steel works at Zelgate, on flat land with ample room for expansion, are also served by waterway: the Gent—Terneuzen Canal.

Apart from being the capital, cultural centre and focus of routeways, Greater Brussels is an important industrial area, with a car assembly plant, food processing and brewing, paper and printing, chemical, pharmaceutical, electrical goods, clothing and jewellery manufactures, together with machinery and mechanical engineering. This latter industry flourishes too in the towns to the west; and petrochemicals are produced at the ports of Antwerpen, Flushing and Oostende.

The other old industry of Belgium, the textile production of Flanders, has adapted to new techniques and materials. Initially based on local wool it used in turn the linen from local flax, imported cotton in the nineteenth century, and now manmade fibres. Verviers is still famous for its woollens, and Courtrai and Tournai are other old-established renowned centres; Gent, well served by waterways, is again coming to the fore, not only as a textile town, but as one producing chemicals and non-ferrous metals, electrical goods, with oil refining as a major industrial factor.

The Campine is one of Belgium's fastest developing areas, with zinc and copper-refining, chemicals, glass-making (using local sands) and brick-making, as well as the explosives industry which was set up because of the relative isolation of the area. There is a car assembly plant, and light industries are being attracted to this coalfield region.

Belgium is small and there were no physical barriers to hinder the development of her excellent communications network. The country is well served by its numerous waterways, electrified railways and roads which, for example, link the port of Antwerpen via the German auto-bahn to areas as far distant as south Germany. The shallow, shelving sandy coast made port development difficult, but Zeebrugge is the outport for Brugge which caters for passengers and car traffic from the United Kingdom, as does Oostende. Antwerpen is the major port and focus of canals (although the waterways leading to it pass through Netherlands territory) and is famous for the diamond-cutting industry. Three-quarters of a million people now live here, finding employment also in shipbuilding, car assembly plants and in factories making electrical goods, photographic materials, in the food-processing and brewing industries and in oil-refining; in fact, the usual port industries.

An important factor in the advancement of Belgian commerce is the economic union of the Low Countries now in force. Belgium and the Grand Duchy of Luxembourg entered into such a union in between the

Table 41 — Belgium: population of major towns

	1970 estimate, city only
Brussels	164 000 (1 071 194 with suburbs)
Antwerpen (Anvers)	226 570
Gent (Gand)	149 265
Liège (Luik)	147 277

two world wars, and in 1944 they signed an agreement with the Netherlands government to work out an economic union of the three countries. From their names has been coined the popular designation Benelux (Be-ne-lux). As a first step their customs tariffs were unified in 1947, and customs duties on the trade between them were abolished, though import licensing remained. A treaty confirming Benelux economic union was signed at The Hague by the prime ministers of all three countries on 3 February 1958; and the Benelux countries were founder members of the European Economic Community.

Belgium enters energetically into world trade. At one time she used to enjoy the rich resources of her dependent territories in Africa, the former Belgian Congo, now selfgoverning Zaire. Apart from coal, clay, sand and stone the country lacks raw materials, which are necessarily imported. Her industrious population exports steel, mechanical engineering products (machinery and machine tools), textiles, nonferrous metals, chemicals, foodstuffs, totalling about 40 per cent of the country's industrial output, one of the highest proportions in the world. This great export is necessary to pay for the import of industrial (mechanical engineering) equipment, foodstuffs, crude oil, textiles, chemicals and diamonds. Most of her trade is within the European Economic Community, especially with France and West Germany, and with the United States. Her economic success is due to the great skill of her industrious people, the ready introduction and acceptance of new techniques and plant, and the speed of the diversification of her industry as her urban centres grow.

Grand Duchy of Luxembourg

Luxembourg, with a population of about 340 000 in 1970, covers about 2 590 sq km (1 000 sq miles) to the southeast of Belgium. Its present boundaries and political independence date only from 1839.

After the First World War a referendum showed a large majority in favour of economic union with France, but the magnates of the French iron and steel industry, fearing the competition of the cheaper labour

403

of Luxembourg, protested against this proposal so strongly that it was abandoned in favour of the alternative: economic union with Belgium. This was negotiated for a period of fifty years, dating from 1 May 1922, when the customs barrier between the two countries was withdrawn. Full economic union followed in 1935. The Second World War brought about a further development, Luxembourg becoming, as from 1 January 1948, a member of the Benelux (Belgium–Netherlands–Luxembourg) Customs Union, designed to promote, by stages, the complete economic unity of the three countries – a consummation reached by treaty in 1958 (see p. 403). It has also joined the European Coal and Steel Community (Schuman Plan) and the European Common Market.

This small country is a land of forested mountains in the north, the Oesling (similar to the Belgian Ardennes) where rivers are dammed for hydroelectric power, as in the Ardennes. The land is too steep for cultivation but there is small-scale dairying in the valleys. The population is sparse. To the south of this region lies Gutland, the aptly named lowlands: an agricultural area where crops of oats, potatoes and wheat are raised and where the vine is grown, a land of small nucleated villages. Great reserves of iron ore lie in the south, worked for centuries, forming Luxembourg's prime asset on which Belgium's heavy industry is also dependent. Iron and steel manufacture is of great import to the Duchy: the output of steel *per capita* is the highest in the world, Esch-sur-Alzette being the main centre.

Luxembourg City (79 000), the capital, was initially a strategically well sited fortress town, and has grown into a commercial and industrial centre, with engineering, chemicals, printing, clothing and food processing works.

It is indicative of the close trade links between Luxembourg and Belgium that in the *Yearbook of International Trade Statistics* of United Nations the two countries are inextricably united in the published statistics.

The Netherlands

The kingdom of the Netherlands, lying to the north of Belgium, is an industrial, agricultural and commercial country. A little larger than Belgium it is no less densely populated, with a land area of over 33 780 sq km (13 040 sq miles) and over 13m. inhabitants in 1970.

The country falls naturally into two divisions, an eastern and a western. The eastern part adjoins the plains of northern Germany and is similar in character. There are considerable stretches of barren, sandy soil still covered with heathlands or afforested with coniferous trees, as in the north German plain, with some swampy areas (fen) where there are peat bogs. Only a limited amount of land can be cultivated in this area, and long ago the Dutch realised its limited capabilities. In order to find occupations for the population small textile towns were deliberately developed there, concerned originally with the spinning and weaving of flax, later of cotton.

The western half, or rather two-thirds, may be regarded as more characteristic of the Netherlands. It is largely the great delta of the River Rhine and associated flat alluvial land. A large proportion lies below sea level and has been reclaimed from the sea, a fine example of the ingenuity and the engineering skill of the Dutch. The low-lying lands were early surrounded by irregular dykes, drainage being effected by wind-driven pumps. Holland became famous for these picturesque windmills, now regarded more as relics of interest to industrial archaeologists. The drainage work goes on, but the pumps, at one time steam driven, are now electrically powered; and the fields of the drained polders (reclaimed land) are neatly rectangular and regular, with farmsteads regularly placed, easily distinguished from the older reclaimed areas. Generally speaking lands reclaimed from marine areas are sandy and produce light soils, eminently suited to the growing of vegetables, bulbs, and a considerable variety of crops. Land reclaimed from riverine deposits produces heavier soils more suited to grass; and it is on these soils that the Dutch rear their famous dairy cattle upon which their dairying industry is based. Some of the farms are large, some small, but everywhere on the polderlands crop yields are high; and pigs are fed on the skimmed milk from the dairying industry. Alkmaar and Edam are famous cheese markets, Haarlem and Hillegom are bulb centres.

In one of the most ambitious reclamation schemes a dam was built across what was then the Zuyder Zee, thereby creating a lake, the Ijsselmeer, the reclaimed land on its margins now supporting well-planned settlements and roads. Another great scheme at present in hand is the Delta Plan. It involves building dams across the mouths of the Rhine and Maas (Meuse) rivers north and east of Vlissingen (Flushing) to Rotterdam. This will result in a freshwater lake and although the prime aim of the scheme is to solve problems of flooding in the area, it will also rid the soil of salt and make additional polderlands for farming, estimated between 10 000 to 14 000 ha (25 000 to 30 000 acres). Rotterdam and Antwerpen in Belgium will be linked by canal, to add to the already widespread network of waterways in the Netherlands.

The only coal in the country is in the southeast, where the Limburg (the Campine) coalfield stretches under the frontier with Belgium. It supplied over 13m. tons in 1938; by 1969 output had been reduced to 5.5m., and production will soon be terminated completely. Coal as a fuel is being replaced by natural gas and by oil. The natural gas from the Netherlands sector of the North Sea resources is piped to the old coalfield and other industrial areas in the Netherlands, as well as to France, Belgium and West Germany. There is research into the use of natural gas in the enrichment of uranium for the production of nuclear power, and two gas centrifuge factories for this purpose have been set up at Almerio. Almost on the German border, at Coevorden and Schoonebeck, there is the richest oilfield in northwest Europe. The output of another field, between Delft and 's Gravenhage (The Hague) has only half its production. The Netherlands have another mineral asset in the saltmines at Hengelo and Delfzije, with a rising production.

The population in the Netherlands is dense, and it has a high rate of increase: about 13.7 per thousand. The total in 1972 was 13.4m., giving a density to the square kilometre of 398, compared with about 228 in the United Kingdom. It is a predominantly urban society: there are over twenty towns with a population exceeding 100 000, the greatest concentration being in Groningen and Randstad Holland. The latter is a ring of towns: Amsterdam, Haarlem, Leiden, 's Gravenhage, Rotterdam and Utrecht, interspersed with agricultural land especially devoted to market gardening and glasshouse cultivation, containing within it a central area of agricultural land which supplies the food needs of the urban ring.

Manufacturing industries are carried on in most towns. Raw materials have to be imported, and industry in the Netherlands is based on skilled engineering at which the Dutch excel. Heavy industry on the Limburg (Campine) coalfield is declining, to be replaced by chemical and plastics industries; but it continues at the major ports or where water transport is readily available, such as Utrecht, where there are steel works, railway works, and factories producing other heavy machinery.

Eindhoven, to which Belgians commute, is a town specialising in electrical goods and car manufactures; and the textile industry still flourishes in Tilburg and Breda, based on cotton, wool and manmade fibres. But it is Randstad which is the magnet, the major developing area. Here, at Rotterdam, is Europort, equalling New York in volume of trade, one of the largest outlets of the European Economic Community, serving entropôt trade for the Ruhr and the Rhine as far away as Basel in Switzerland. It has port facilities for large tankers, container ships and storage. It supports the familiar port industries: refineries, petrochemicals, metals, plastics, food and tobacco processing. Compared with it other ports along this coast fade into insignificance, although the Hoek-van-Holland (the Hook of Holland) still serves as a 'packet station' for passengers from the United Kingdom, and Ijmuiden is an important fishing port. Ijmuiden also has a large integrated iron and steel works, relying like Dunkerque, on waterborne raw materials. The other large port, Amsterdam (the Venice of the North) is the commercial capital, and the centre of shipbuilding and of the diamond-cutting industry; communication in Amsterdam is still largely carried on by water. Although it is not the capital of the Netherlands, the residential city 's Gravenhage (The Hague) is the seat of the Court and

Table 42 — The Netherland: major urban agglomerations 1971

Rotterdam	1 066 177	Groningen	204 767
Amsterdam (capital)	1 035 999	Dordrecht	171 841
's Gravenhage	710 528	Geleen-Sittard	169 579
Utrecht	459 470	's Hertogenbosch	169 013
Eindhoven	341 068	Leiden	164 751
Arnhem	274 384	Breda	159 535
Heerlen-Kerkrade	264 911	Maastricht	144 317
Haarlem	239 249	Velsen-Beverwijk	137 884
Enschede-Hengelo	233 125	Zaandam	130 967
Nijmegen	206 277	Apeldoorn	126 100
Tilburg	205 606	Hilversum	114 862

of Dutch legislature, as well as of the International Court of Justice.

Although the Dutch fight an unceasing battle with water, they make good use of it. The industrial centres of Amsterdam and Rotterdam are the foci of waterways from northern France, Belgium and of course the Rhinelands. The length of river and canal navigation in the Netherlands is double that of the railways. Railways are not so important, but over half have been electrified; and the new motorways act as routeways serving Europe.

With their long association with the sea, the Dutch have always been a great seafaring nation, with fishing and merchant fleets; and like the British they were colonisers, particularly in the East Indies, in South America and in the West Indies. The influence of this can be seen in the preparation of tobacco and of foodstuffs in the home country, such as chocolate and margarine, using raw materials from overseas colonies. These colonies are now independent, with the exception of Surinam in South America and the Netherlands Antilles in the West Indies, with whom trading continues. In addition to her merchant fleet the Netherlands have an equally efficient international airline, KLM.

Much of the trade of the country is in goods in transit, so the same items appear in both import and export statistics: for example petroleum products, chemicals, textiles, iron and steel, machinery and transport equipment, electrical equipment, miscellaneous manufactured goods; but one-fifth of exports from the Netherlands is in the form of food and dairy produce, and she imports more oilseeds, wood and metalliferous ores than is exported. Most of her trade is with Belgium and Luxembourg, West Germany, the United States, the United Kingdom and Israel, the latter taking diamonds for polishing; and a small amount with her former and present overseas possessions.

Germany

Before considering separately the political units of West and East Germany which emerged after the Second World War, it will be useful to study, in a general manner, their common political and physical backgrounds. Before the Second World War, Germany had an area of about 471 400 sq km (182 000 sq miles) and a population of 69m. After the war, the northern part of East Prussia was taken over by the USSR and the territories east of the Oder and Neisse rivers, including the ports of Stettin (Szczecin) and Swinemünde (Swinoujscie), were placed under Polish administration pending a definite settlement by peace treaty. The rest of Germany was divided into four Occupation Zones, administered by the United States, the United Kingdom, France, and the Soviet Union.

In 1949 the territories of the American, British and French Zones, comprising nearly 248 600 sq km (96 000 sq miles) and with a population a little larger than that of Britain were united to form the Federal Republic of Germany (commonly known as West Germany), with Bonn as the seat of government. In the same year the German Democratic Republic (East Germany) was constituted in the Soviet Zone (about 108 200 sq km: 41 700 sq miles).

Berlin constituted a separate territory of over 880 sq km (340 sq miles) forming an enclave in the Soviet Zone. It was divided into four sectors (British, American, French and Russian), falling into two groups — East Berlin (the Soviet sector) (403 sq km: 156 sq miles) and West Berlin (the sectors of the three Western Powers) (480 sq km: 185 sq miles).

In May 1955, the Western Powers restored the sovereign independence of West Germany and admitted it to Western postwar pacts.

In September 1961 the USSR announced its intention to transfer its functions in Berlin to the Democratic Republic. The refusal by the three Western Powers to do the same, and the subsequent closure by the Russians of the frontier between East and West Berlin to stop the growing flow of emigrants, led to an international crisis. Discussions on the future of Berlin and East Germany continue.

Political development. After the disintegration of the Holy Roman Empire (*Erstes Reich*) in 1806 Germany emerged from the Napoleonic wars as a curious medley of thirty-nine independent states: thirty-five monarchies and four republican free cities. They formed the loose 'German Federation' (*Deutscher Bund*), as constituted by the Vienna Congress of 1815. Trade and economics were at a low ebb, and the countries of the federation were hemmed in from all sides by internal and external customs and excise tariffs, so that a crop failure caused by abnormally bad weather conditions in 1816 brought about a famine in the following winter. From then onward a gradual lifting of the internal barriers resulted in the economic, and with it the political, unification of Germany. The first step in this direction was the abolition of all internal duties within the kingdom of Prussia, effective from 1 January

1819. As Prussia comprised about one-third of the territory of the German Federation, it formed an economic unit which was bound to affect the economies of the adjacent states. Trade found transportation cheaper on Prussian territory, and began to prefer the Prussian means of communication. The south German states of Bavaria and Württemberg sought to counterbalance this development by forming a Southern Union (*Süddeutscher Zollverein*) in 1828, while in the same year the Grand-Duchy of Hesse-Darmstadt entered a union with Prussia (*Norddeutscher Zollverein*); these two unions, by mutual agreement, then brought their fiscal systems into harmony.

The beginning of modern Germany dates from 1 January 1834 when the two unions merged in the *Deutscher Zollverein*, and were joined by Saxony and the Thuringian states. Thus the greater part of the German states enjoyed economic union, and the other states had to join sooner or later if they did not want to incur serious economic isolation. Of the larger states, Baden joined in 1835, Nassau and the free city of Frankfurt in 1836, Hanover in 1851, and Schleswig-Holstein in 1866, while Austria stood aside. The incompatibility of Prussian and Austrian interests was responsible for the dissolution of the 'German Federation' of 1815 and the formation in 1866, under Prussian auspices, of the smaller 'North German Confederation' without Austria. Out of this confederation grew, after the Franco–Prussian War of 1870–71, the German Empire (*Zweites Reich*), a federal monarchy. But the economic borders did not yet coincide with the political. The Free Cities of Hamburg and Bremen did not join the Customs Union until 1888, whereas Luxembourg, while politically independent and neutralised under the Treaty of London of 1866, was part of it until 1922, when it entered an economic union with Belgium. In 1891 two Austrian communities in the Alps, accessible only from Bavaria, were incorporated in the Customs Union. On the other hand, two very small villages on the Swiss border, the free ports of Hamburg and Bremen, and the island of Heligoland remained outside the Union. After the First World War Germany lost the territory she had gained overseas, in Africa and elsewhere; considerable areas of former German territory which became part of resuscitated Poland; the large tract of Alsace-Lorraine, returned to France; and, as an economic compensation for war losses, the Saar territory which was made part of the French economic system for fifteen years. It was reunited with Germany by plebiscite supervised by the League of Nations in 1935; again passed under French control for a time after the Second World War; but was returned to West Germany in 1956. The third empire (*Drittes Reich*), under Adolf Hitler, lasted only from 1933 to 1945, and from 1939 onwards was engaged in the Second World War.

The economic body was dismembered at the end of the Second World War, as already noted. The partition into four occupation zones resulted, for a time, in the stagnation of economic life. The federation of the British, French, and American Zones as a single political unit (West Germany, a Federation of eleven Länder) relieved the situation to some extent; but West Germany and East Germany are separated by the borders of the occupation division and by the political commitments and trade alliances which have developed. West Germany, with the capital at Bonn and a parliamentary constitution identifies herself with the West and is a member of the European Economic Community; East Germany, with the capital in East Berlin and a Communist state, looks to the East and is a member of Comecon. East Germany, the German Democratic Republic, is not officially recognised as a separate nation by all other countries; but for the purposes of commercial geography, taking into account her economic allegiances, East Germany will be treated as a political unit in this book.

Surface features. Taking East and West Germany as a geographical entity, Germany may be said to consist of three distinct parts: the northern lowlands, the central mountains, and the southern plateaus and basins. The north German lowlands, bordering on the North and Baltic Seas, comprise vast plains little above sea level near the North Sea, and low hills further inland or near the Baltic coast, where the country was covered by the great ice drift. Each stage in the retreat of the ice was marked by the formation of a great east–west depression, cut out by the masses of water melting from the ice sheet and flowing parallel to its edge. These primeval valleys (*Urstromtäler*), only partly used by presentday rivers, form the basis of the well developed system of inland waterways in northern Germany.

The soils of northern Germany vary greatly in quality and economic value. The most fertile are the soils of the reclaimed lowlands along the North Sea coast, consisting of clay and loam, and the loess soils which cover a continuous strip of land, widening from west to east, at the foot of the central German mountains, from the region of the lower Rhine in the west to Breslau and Oppeln in Silesia (now Poland) in the east. The primeval valleys consist of sandy soil which in places is blown together into sand dunes and mostly covered by vast pine forests. In the northwest, large peat bogs form a bleak and desolate landscape, but even here land reclamation has gone a long way towards improving the countryside.

The central German mountains rise rather abruptly, and form a region distinct from both the lowlands in the north and the plateaus and basins in the south. They stretch from the Belgian and Luxembourg borders in the west to the Czechoslovak frontier in the east, where they give way to the mountains flanking the Bohemian basin. The rock formations vary from granites, basalts, and metamorphic schists to limestones, sandstones, and coal beds. The northern front of the mountains does not form a straight line, but is broken by three deep indentations or bays. Thus the Rhenish Bay penetrates deeply into the Rhenish Massif, the Westphalian Bay between the Rhenish Massif and the Weser Mountains, and the Thuringian Bay between the Harz Mountains and the Thuringian Forest. On the other hand, the Teutoburg Forest and the Harz jut far out into the northern lowlands. Within this mountain belt a variety of plateaus and rounded hills, of basins, rift valleys, and river gorges is to be found; the heights are covered with forests (from which many places derive their names) or heaths, and the basins provide the cultivable land.

The southern front of the mountain belt is in places clearly marked by fault lines (Hunsrück, Taunus, Thuringian Forest), in places obliterated by transverse faulting or cut by rivers. Here are the great gaps through which northern and southern Germany are connected by rail, road, river, and canal.

Southern Germany is composed of numerous plateaus and basins suspended between the high mountain ridges of the Black Forest 1 400 m (4 500 ft) in the southwest and the Bohemian Forest 1 350 m (4 400 ft) in the east. The great rift valley of the Upper Rhine cuts southern Germany into two unequal parts, so that the country rises in steps from a point near Mainz to the southwest and southeast respectively. These steps are marked by long escarpments, such as the Haardt Mountains and the Saar escarpment to the west of the Rhine, Odenwald, Steigerwald, and the Alb plateaus to the east. South of the Danube, between the Lake of Constance and the River Inn, another landscape begins — the Alpine Foreland. High plateaus, mostly above 450 m (1 500 ft), are covered by glacial deposits, such as gravel beds, loams, and loess. The southern parts of the plateaus are covered by glacial drift, which forms a blanket over high hills, encircles some large and numerous small lakes, and at last melts into the foothills of the Alps, of which only a small strip falls within the German frontier.

Inland waterways. With one exception, all German rivers flow to the northwest: the Danube, rising from the Black Forest, flows eastward. The Rhine is the only Alpine river to reach the North Sea; its valley therefore is the only natural waterway through the central mountains and is of supreme importance to the economic life of West Germany. Besides the Rhine, three other large rivers, Ems (draining only West German territory), Weser (of which the upper reaches flow through East Germany, the lower through West), and Elbe (navigable for much of its long course, rising in Czechoslovakia, flowing across East Germany and about 100 km (62 miles) of West German territory before reaching the West German port, Hamburg, the lowest bridging point), flow into the North Sea; and a fourth, the Oder (now mostly assigned to Poland), flows into the Baltic. They form big estuaries, at the head

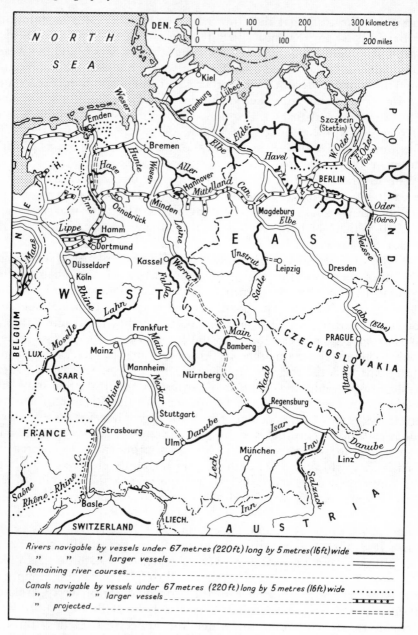

Inland waterways of East and West Germany

of each of which, but still within the tidal range, has grown up a large seaport — respectively Emden, Bremen, Hamburg, and Stettin, the last now included in Poland as Szczecin.

By far the most important river, judged both by length and volume of water, is the Rhine. The navigable stretch of the Rhine between the Swiss frontier, where it enters Germany, and the Dutch frontier, where it leaves, extends to 708 km (440 miles). Its tributary system drains 23 per cent of the territory of the two Germanies. By its long and winding tributaries — the Mosel (with the Saar), the Main, the Neckar — a vast hinterland is made accessible by water. Next in importance comes the Elbe with a tributary system draining 21 per cent of German lands and a navigable stretch of 775 km (480 miles) between Hamburg and the Czechoslovak frontier. The Weser is navigable for 470 km (290 miles), without its principal tributaries, the Fulda and the Werra; the Oder for 800 km (500 miles); the Danube between Regensburg and Passau for 240 km (150 miles).

These natural waterways are connected by a well-planned system of canals, most of them in the north German lowlands, where the primeval valleys favoured the construction of canals. Thus the Upper Rhine region was connected by water with the far distant industrial district of Upper Silesia. Berlin, in the centre of this vast net, had physically at least equal access to the coal of Silesia and of the Ruhr and Saar, to Baltic as well as to North Sea ports. Only the Danube system lacks connection by a practicable canal with the Rhine system, the Ludwig Canal being obsolete. The Rhine–Main–Danube Canal, planned in the year 1921, has been under discussion from time to time, and the greater portion of the 690 km (425 mile) stretch between the Rhine and the Danube has been constructed. Further building, canalisation and straightening still continue. Associated with the locks along this new waterway will be hydroelectric power stations; sixteen of the projected forty-five were already in operation in 1951. Designed to replace the old Ludwig Canal, this new route will not only provide a cheap waterway between the agricultural regions of Bavaria and the manufacturing districts on the Rhine, but will connect West Germany with the Danubian countries and the Black Sea.

The total length of inland waterways in German lands before the Second World War was about 11 270 km (7 000 miles), of which those of economic importance accounted for 7 780 km (4 830 miles). On these waterways 5 375 self-propelled craft and 12 500 barges carried a total freight of over 150m. metric tons a year (foreign craft excluded). The three inland ports with the biggest traffic were Duisburg-Ruhrort (West Germany), at the junction of the Rhine and the Ruhr, the most important inland port in Europe, with a total of 17m. tons in 1936; Hamburg (West Germany: river port only), with 9m. tons; and Berlin, with 8.5m. tons. In 1969 the Federal Republic of West Germany had in use 4 353 km (2 792 miles) of navigable rivers and canals, with an inland waterways fleet of 4.6m. tons, carrying 233.8m. tons of freight.

West Germany has the benefit of Rhine navigation which up to Mannheim far excels that of all other German waterways. No other

European river has so large a population gathered in large towns on its banks, a fact peculiarly favourable to water traffic. From the Netherlands frontier as far as Strasbourg the Rhine has been so improved that barges of 2 000 tons can ascend to that port. Extensive harbour accommodation has been provided at Duisburg-Ruhrort, the port of the Ruhr basin; at Düsseldorf, the port of the southern part of the great manufacturing district of West Germany; at Köln, Mannheim, Ludwigshafen, and other ports on the Rhine. Above Strasbourg, 1 500-ton barges can ascend as far as Basel during more than half the year. Much of the Rhine traffic is directed to and from the German North Sea ports through canals, but West Germany's trade links with the EEC make the port of Rotterdam at the mouth of the Rhine, in the Netherlands, of greater value to her.

German waterways were greatly improved when the Mittelland Canal, with its branches to the industrial districts of Osnabrück, Hildesheim, Hannover, and Watenstedt-Salzgitter was completed in 1938. Running east to west it linked Berlin with the industrial Ruhr, but is now of course cut by the political boundary. A great many waterways have been adapted to take barges of 1 000-tons capacity. Apart from the big rivers, waterways which have been brought up to this standard include the Berlin—Stettin Canal; the Saale as far as Halle, whence an extension to Leipzig is planned; the Main, on which 1 000-ton barges now ascend beyond Würzburg; and the Neckar up to Heilbronn, while a 1 000-ton canal as far as Stuttgart has been under construction.

The Kiel Canal (*Nord-Ostsee Kanal*), completed in 1895, serves seaborne traffic exclusively. It crosses Schleswig Holstein from the North Sea (mouth of the Elbe) to the Baltic (Kiel Bay), and is 97 km (61 miles) long, with a surface width of 103 m (338 ft) and a depth of 12 m (37 ft). It has only two locks, one at either end, and can take vessels up to 315 m ((1 033 ft) long and 40 m (130 ft) wide, with a draught of 9 m (31 ft); but it is chiefly used by small vessels passing between the North Sea and the Baltic, as it enables them to avoid the lengthy passage round the north of Denmark. The saving in distance from the mouth of the Elbe is 383 km (237 miles), and there is a greater or less saving from or to all North Sea ports south of the Tyne. Before the Second World War, the net tonnage of the shipping passing through the canal had increased, after various ups and downs, to 22.6m. (1938). After the war the tonnage was 9.4m. in 1947, increasing to 36.1m. in 1959. The small average size of the vessels using the canal is shown by the numbers compared with the tonnage. In 1938 the number of vessels was 53 530 and the average net tonnage 420, while in 1959 the number was 73 443 and the average net tonnage 492.

Climate and agriculture (prior to the outbreak of the Second World

War). Generally, Germany suffers from too hard a climate to rank as one of the world's prime agricultural areas, despite the general suitability of soils. North Germany reaches up to latitude 55° N (the latitude of Newcastle), and though south Germany extends to below the 48th parallel (on a level with the Loire valley), this advantage is more than balanced by the high average elevation in the south. Nor, wherever favourable conditions may be found, does superiority of climate always coincide with superiority of soil. The higher latitude of the north results in lower mean temperatures during the whole of the year; the easterly situation leads to more intensive climatic conditions and an increase from west to east in the duration of the period of frost. Only in the rift valley section of the Rhine (the long and narrow plains between Mainz and Basel) and the valleys of the Mosel, Main, and Neckar, are there seven months in the year with a mean daily temperature above 10° C (50° F); and only in the Upper Rhine plain is there one month with a mean daily temperature of 20° C (68° F) or more. In East Prussia (now assigned to the USSR and Poland) a mean daily temperature below freezing point may be experienced for three months on end. Most of the land suitable for agriculture has an annual precipitation of between 500 and 700 mm (20 and 28 in). In general the climate suits forestry and grassland, and arable crops which do not need great warmth.

It follows that success in agricultural production is due less to natural conditions than to intensive cultivation. Much has been done in this way to overcome the climatic drawbacks, and a wide variety of crops was (and is) grown. Of the total surface in 1936, 61 per cent was cultivated land (two-thirds of its arable and one-third grassland), 27.5 per cent was forest, and 11 per cent consisted of public domains, water, or uncultivable land. The development of agriculture in German lands has always been carefully fostered. It enjoyed a high degree of tariff protection against low cost extensive production from abroad. Scientific research, beginning more than a century ago, and university training (*Landwirtschaftliche Hochschulen*) in all parts of the country spread progressive thinking and scientific methods of farming. Thus the idea and practice of fertilising were developed, and German agriculture enabled to meet about 80 per cent of the demands of the ever-growing population. Great pains were taken to close even this 'food gap', in order to free the foreign trade budget from a heavy burden, but without notable success. Between 1932 and 1937 the use of fertilisers rose considerably: of nitrates by 162 per cent, of lime by 114.5 per cent, of phosphates by 153 per cent, of potash salts by 152 per cent. The average yields of the several crops were among the highest in Europe, absolutely as well as in relation to the acreage.

Rye used to be the typical grain in central, northern, and eastern Europe. Less exacting than some cereal crops as to quality of soil and mean temperatures, and more resistant to frost, it is very suitable for lighter soils and higher altitudes. In German lands it covered 4.5m. ha (11.25m. acres); the total crop yielded 7.5m. tons in 1928. The area was less than at the end of the last century and has continued to decrease. The area under wheat by comparison remained steady, facilitated by the introduction of breeds adapted to the climate as well as by improved cultivation. In the first three decades of the present century the average yield of wheat increased from 30 to 32 bushels per acre, which was nearly twice the average for the United States or Canada, and still exceeds their presentday averages.

Among root crops the most widely cultivated was potatoes, which in 1935 covered about ten times as great an area in Germany as in Great Britain. From 2.8m. ha (7m. acres) production amounted to about 43m. tons. Potatoes played an important part both as human and animal (hog fattening) food, and in industry. They were grown everywhere, but prefer the lighter types of soil. The other important root crop, sugar beet, gives large yields on heavy rich soils and has been grown on much of the loess belt in central or northern Germany, from the Lower Rhine to Silesia. In south Germany, sugar beet was extensively grown in the Upper Rhine valley and in the Main and Neckar regions. Between 1928 and 1936 it covered nearly 400 000 ha (1m. acres), yielding 12m. tons a year.

Vine cultivation reaches its most northerly boundary in the world in Germany; the area covered by vineyards (73 000 ha: 180 000 acres) in the sheltered valleys of the Mosel, Saar, Rhine, Main, Neckar, and on the shores of the Lake of Constance, was only about one-twentieth of the area so occupied in France. But the white 'hocks' of Germany stand in a class of their own. In the same regions orchards abounded (101 200 ha: 250 000 acres), and limited quantities of tobacco (32 885 tons from 13 152 ha: 32 500 acres in 1936) and hops (10 100 tons from 10 120 ha: 25 000 acres) are also grown. The area under hops decreased to less than one-half between 1910 and 1936, but the average yield was more than doubled, so that the production remained constant.

Mineral deposits. The greatest mineral asset of German lands is bituminous coal. Coal beds are found along the northern fringe of the central mountains, from Aachen to Upper Silesia (the latter now in Poland), and in basins within them, namely, the Saar, Zwickau-Chemnitz (Saxony), and Waldenburg (Silesia) basins. Many of these are still worked. Their productiveness varies greatly. Reserves in the Ruhr basin are estimated at 55 000m. metric tons, or nearly 70 per cent of the total; second in importance is the Saar basin, with 9 205m. tons; third, Germany's prewar part of the Upper Silesian coalfield (now Polish), with 4 000m. tons. Until 1945 the Upper Silesian coalfield was divided between Germany, Poland, and Czechoslovakia; as a whole it is probably the biggest continuous coalfield in Europe. The Saxony field is now controlled by East Germany. Some coalfields in Germany are not yet exploited, and the total reserves in the areas named are estimated at 80 500m. tons.

The output of bituminous coal in Germany (including Austria) in 1938 was 184m. tons, 135m. tons being raised in the territory which now constitutes West Germany. In 1947 the output of both East and West Germany (the four zones of occupation) was 83m. tons, of which the great bulk (70m. tons) was produced in the three Western Zones. By 1964 the output in West Germany had reached over 142m. tons, to fall to under 112m. tons in 1969 with the contraction of the industry.

Lignite deposits are on almost as large a scale. Here East Germany is dominant, i.e. Thuringia, Saxony, and southern Brandenburg, with five large fields; but the biggest continuous lignite-field is west of the Lower Rhine near Köln. Lignite serves as fuel for domestic use and in factories and thermoelectric power stations; also as a basis for coal hydration. While bituminous coal and anthracite are mined from pits, lignite is worked in open quarries and is cheaper than coal. Total reserves are estimated at 56 750m. metric tons, and production throughout Germany and Austria in 1938 was about 190m. tons. Production in the four zones of postwar Germany in 1959 reached 303.4m. tons, of which East Germany provided over two-thirds (211.4m. tons), while West Germany's output was 92m. tons, or considerably more than in 1938. In 1969 East Germany produced nearly 255m. tons, West Germany over 107m.

The production of coal-tar dyes made Germany pre-eminent in the sphere of industrial chemistry. The most important step in the history of this industry was the artificial production of alizarin from anthracene by two German chemists in 1868, and from that date the technical production of dyestuffs was almost exclusively in German hands till 1914. The leading works manufacture not only their own semi-raw materials, but also such subsidiary products as are the speciality of the heavy chemical industry: sulphuric acid, nitric acid, soda, caustic soda, and so on. They require large quantities of raw materials, and are all situated on great waterways — at Ludwigshafen, opposite Mannheim, seat of the celebrated Badische Anilin- und Sodafabrik; Leverkusen on the right bank of the Rhine below Köln (Bayer Works); Frankfurt-Höchst on the Main (Höchster Farbwerke); Merseburg near Halle on the Saale (Leuna Works); Berlin. These works, each of them a large combination of production units, and many smaller ones throughout Germany were united in the super-trust of the famous IG Farben-Industrie until 1948.

Germany's petroleum deposits, though small in relation to world production, are deserving of mention. They are divided into two groups. The first, which has been known for some decades, lies on a semicircle with a 30 km (20 mile) radius north and east of Hannover, the main field being at Nienhagen. The oil wells are bound tectonically to the salt dome structures underground. The known reserves have been estimated at about 2m. tons, and there seems little prospect of any substantial increase on this figure. Three more fields near Hamburg, Wilhelmshaven, and Heide in Holstein are inconsiderable and after long and fruitless search for other sources of supply it was concluded that petroleum in Germany was confined to salt domes. This was proved to be erroneous in 1940–42, when the comparatively big fields north of Bentheim, in the Emsland near the Netherlands frontier, were found. The new supplies were associated with simple anticlines of the cretaceous Teutoburg Forest sandstones, which by faulting hand sunk 400 to 850 m (1 300 to 2 800 ft) below the surface. In all it is estimated that the Federal Republic has oil reserves totalling 47m. tons. A second valuable product is the natural gas of Bentheim, with known reserves of 892m. cu m (31 500m. cu ft) and further probable reserves of 215m. cu m (7 600m. cu ft). The production of crude oil before the war, in the area which is now part of West Germany, was a little over 0.5m. tons. This was exceeded in the postwar years; in 1959 the output was 5m. tons, and in 1973 it was nearly 7m. tons.

German deposits of salts are practically inexhaustible. Rock salt is found in all parts of central, southwest, and north Germany, and is only vaguely estimated at about 10b. tons. Potash salts, for the first time found free in nature, which were formerly dug up and thrown away as waste (*Abraum*) in the course of getting rock salt, are now known to be the more valuable of the two. These 'waste' salts (*Abraumsalze*) became the basis of the German chemical industry and reserves are estimated at about 20 000m. tons. Rock salt production in 1936 was 2.4m. tons, potash 4.7m. tons. In 1959 the production of potash in West Germany was nearly 17.1m. tons; in 1969 it was over 20m. tons in West Germany, in East Germany 2.3m. tons.

From the salts, in their natural state, carbonate of potash is extracted and used in soap-making, dyeing, bleaching, glass-making, calico-printing, pigment-making, pottery, and so on. The mineral salt kainite, or sulphate of potassium, which contains also a certain proportion of magnesium salts, is used as a fertiliser and for other purposes. Other layers in the saltbeds yield nitrate of potassium, for the making of explosives, glass-making, and preservatives; various compounds used in photography, such as cyanide, bromide, and iodide of potassium; and a great variety of other substances. With the Alsace field, Germany held a monopoly of potash salts in world trade till 1918.

In contrast with the abundance of mineral wealth the German lands are poor in metallic ores. Iron ores are found in many parts of the northwest and south, but they are of inferior quality. The whole reserves are estimated at 720m. tons, but of these only half can be exploited under normal economic conditions. The production in 1936 was 7.5m. tons of ores with an iron content of 2.25m. tons. More than four-fifths of the ores came from districts now included in West Germany, and these alone in 1959 yielded over 17.7m. tons of iron ores, with an iron content of 4.7m. tons. Output in West Germany had fallen to 7.5m. tons, and in East Germany to 900 000 tons in 1969.

Copper ores are mined in only one formation, in the southeastern foothills of the Harz Mountains; the metal content of the Federal ore production in 1960 was only 1 750 tons, but that of East Germany was estimated at 20 000 tons. The metal content of the Federal lead ore produced (1960) was 49 000 tons, and of Federal zinc ore 85 000 tons.

Radium ores (pitchblende) in the Erzgebirge extend from the Czechoslovakian side of the ridge, near Joachimsthal, northwards into Saxony. Here, in East Germany, in the neighbourhood of Annaberg and Aue, uranium mines employing 40—50 000 men are being worked under Soviet direction.

Railways. Traffic facilities on land are numerous and well developed. Before the Second World War Germany had nearly 70 000 km (43 000 miles) of railway, mostly of standard gauge, or rather more than Great Britain in proportion to area, and considerably more in proportion to population. After the war, in 1959, the length of railways of the Federal Republic (West Germany) was 36 530 km (22 700 miles), which agreed fairly closely, both actually and relatively, with that of Britain. The most impressive traffic scene is along the Middle Rhine gorge between Bonn and Bingen, where a double-track railway line and a high road are packed between the river bank and the steep cliffs on either side of the gorge. In the rift valley section of the Rhine, between Frankfurt and Karlsruhe, three or even four main lines run parallel to the river and are crossed by numerous lines which converge on the bridges over the Rhine.

On the whole, surface difficulties are not excessive. The northern plains and lowlands offer hardly any obstructions, apart from the big rivers with areas liable to temporary flooding. The connections between north and south are facilitated by the Rhine valley, the Hessian Depressions (a succession of basins and river valleys amidst mountainous regions between Frankfurt and Kassel), and the Leine valley further north. In south Germany, the Upper Rhine presents an ideal traffic lane right through from Frankfurt to Basel in Switzerland; and the basins and high plateaus of Württemberg and Bavaria provide good communications in every direction. Serious obstacles to railway traffic are offered only by the Black Forest, which has only two lines crossing its ridge at high altitudes, and by the mountainous wooded country along the frontier with Czechoslovakia. On the southwest borders of

419

Bohemia, only four lines cross the Bohemian Forest (*Böhmer Wald*) in a distance of 200 km (125 miles): one at Cheb (*Eger*) in the north; the second at Fürth, in the centre; the third skirting the highest peak, Mount Arber (1 340 m: 4 400 ft); and the fourth starting from Passau, on the Austrian frontier. Of these the last two lines are merely of local importance.

The Thuringian Forest, which extends the Bohemian Forest northwestwards into Germany, has long been avoided by railways. The first lines between Bavaria and Thuringia—Saxony rounded either its northwestern tip near Eisenach, or, at the other extremity, the east side of the Vogtland plateau. Since then, three more main lines have been constructed across this mountain ridge. One of them crosses it through a tunnel (3 km: 2 miles long) near Oberhof, the other two keep above ground by steep ascents on both flanks and several long viaducts. Another serious obstacle is the Erzgebirge, along the northwest borders of Bohemia; for a distance of more than 65 km (40 miles) no railway crosses this tract.

Many international lines crossed Germany, from western to eastern Europe or from Scandinavia to Italy. The lines from France, Belgium, or the Netherlands to Poland and the Soviet Union were laid via Köln—Hannover—Berlin—Warsaw or Riga—Leningrad, or Leipzig—Breslau—Cracow; from northwestern Europe to the Balkans through southern Germany via Stuttgart—München. Traffic with Italy is served by three routes. One, following the Rhine up to Basel, and on through the Gotthard or Simplon Tunnels, was in sharp competition with the French Channel ports — Paris—Simplon or Mont Cenis routes. Another connects Scandinavia and the most populous parts of Germany with Italy across Tyrol and the Brenner Pass. The third, leading through Bohemia or the Moravian Gate and connecting eastern Germany with Trieste via Vienna and the Semmering Pass, has been affected by traffic restrictions and political tensions since 1918.

Roads. In 1937 Germany had 215 000 km (134 000 miles) of roads, more than half of them over 5 m (15 ft) wide. A new development in the prewar years was the building of highways reserved for motor traffic (*Autobahnen*). Work on these roads was begun in 1933; over 1 500 km (985 miles) had been completed in 1937, and when work on them was stopped by the outbreak of war in 1939 their length was 5 070 km (3 150 miles). They formed a triangle between Berlin, München, and Köln with extensions from Berlin to Stettin (Poland), Frankfurt an der Oder and Breslau Wroclaw, now in Poland), and from München to Salzburg (Austria). Detached lines connected Königsberg (USSR) with Elbing (Poland) and Lübeck with Hamburg and Bremen. A central line between Dresden and the Ruhr district was partly completed.

The present situation of communications in West and in East Germany are discussed in the following pages, which are concerned with the commercial geography of the divided Germany as it exists in the early 1970s.

West Germany

West Germany lies mainly on the north European plain but stretches so far south that it includes much of the mountainous country of central Europe. On the plain the political boundaries are naturally ill-defined: topographically there is little to mark the boundary between West and East Germany. In the west too the boundary between West Germany and Belgium and the Netherlands is to a considerable extent artificial; the frontier with France for a long distance follows the River Rhine. The North Sea coast is relatively short but is a great asset as the outlet of three main rivers, the Elbe, and Weser and the Ems. The frontier with Denmark is short, and to complete the boundary is the coast of the Baltic Sea. This is of no great value for it is shallow and fringed with lagoons (*haffs*) which become ice-blocked in winter.

Nearly 61m. people live on the 248 548 sq km (95 695 sq miles) of West Germany (including West Berlin), the average annual rate of increase (outside West Berlin) being 1.2 per cent, the same as Metropolitan France, in the years 1958—66. The present annual rate of increase in both countries is lower.

West Germany therefore covers the three physical divisions outlined on p. 410 and, as noted on p. 411, has the benefit of valuable navigable inland waterways, especially the Rhine.

Minerals and power resources. In mineral resources the bituminous coal of the Saar and of the Ruhr, an area which takes its name from a small river, a tributary of the Rhine, which flows through the coalfield, lies within West German boundaries. There are also considerable reserves of brown coal in Rhineland, Helmstedt, Bavaria and Hesse, much less valuable than hard coal but easily worked by machinery in large opencast mines.

West Germany has the good fortune to possess the oil resources under the north German lowland. The most productive fields are in Lower Saxony (in the Emsland) and near Hannover. There are six main areas producing natural gas: four lie between the Elbe and the Weser, others in the Ems estuary (most productive) between the Weser and the Ems. There are other natural gasfields in the upper Rhine valley and in the foothills of the Alps, in an area east of München to the Austrian frontier. Production from all these fields is rising rapidly but is insufficient to meet the increasing demand, so gas is brought in by pipeline from the Netherlands.

Although the great iron ore deposits of the Lorraine field were lost to Germany when the area was returned to France in 1919, West Germany has other reserves of iron ore which, in extent, are some of the biggest in Europe: in Lower Saxony, around Salzgitter in Siegerland and the Lahn—Dill area. Unfortunately the iron content is low and these domestic supplies face competition from imported high grade ores of which about one-third comes from Sweden.

Within the European Economic Community West Germany is the largest producer of lead and zinc from her technically advanced mines; and in recent years her output met 50 per cent of the needs of her lead and 75 per cent of the requirements of her zinc foundries. There are also small copper resources.

The other mineral endowments of West Germany, economically significant, are potash and rock-salts. Potash deposits in Alsace were lost to France in 1919; and in 1945 the other main deposits, as Stassfurt, came under the control of East Germany, together with the salt in the area. Despite these setbacks output of both these resources from West Germany is between three and five times that of East Germany. In West Germany the workings have been mechanised to a high degree and uneconomic mines closed down.

As a source of power coal faces competition from natural gas and oil. There has been rationalisation of the mines, many pits have closed, others have merged their activities; and mechanisation and efficient technology have advanced the output per manshift so that it is now the highest in western Europe. In 1969 the Ruhr contributed 81 per cent, the Saar 11 per cent, the Aachen district 6 per cent, Lower Saxony 2 per cent of total hard coal production. Eighty-four per cent of the exports are destined for EEC countries, mainly France. On the whole output is slowly declining, but it has been suggested that there might be a future slight increase in the use of coal in power stations.

Brown coal, with a high water content (up to 60 per cent) is heavy and uneconomic to transport, but it has the virtues of being easily worked and of being cheaply made into briquettes. In 1969 Rhineland produced 85 per cent of the total brown coal output (and 90 per cent of the briquettes), the Helmstedt area contributed 6 per cent, Bavaria 4.5 per cent, Hesse 4.3 per cent. Very little is exported. Twenty-five per cent of brown coal is processed at factories near the pits; and over half the output of unprocessed brown coal is used in electric power stations situation in the vicinity of the deposits.

The output of natural gas soared quickly from 51m. cu m in 1950 to 2 800m. cu m in 1966, and is still rising, distributed by a spreading network of pipelines. Even in North Rhine—Westphalia, the stronghold of gas produced from coal, natural gas is a serious competitor.

The use of crude oil as a source of power is growing. The oil-refining capacity in West Germany is considerable; in 1969 40 per cent of the refineries were in the Rhine—Ruhr, 20 per cent in Hamburg, Bremen and Schleswig—Holstein, 17 per cent in southwest Germany, 14 per cent in Bavaria, 10 per cent in Lower Saxony (notice the predominance of waterside sites processing imported crude oil). Although, as has been noted, West Germany has a useful steady home production of crude oil (0.2 per cent of the world total in 1973) most crude oil is imported, about 75 per cent of it coming from Arab states.

Hydroelectric power has not been greatly developed, having been overshadowed by the brown coal resources. In 1967 the sources of power in the generation of electricity were brown coal, 26 per cent; hard coal 46 per cent; oil 10 per cent; hydroelectric power 8 per cent; wood and peat 4 per cent; natural gas 2 per cent, nuclear power 1 per cent. It is anticipated that there will be a significant rise in the use of nuclear power and that it will supply one-third of the total source requirement of the electric power industry by 1980.

Climate. The climate of Germanic lands has already been covered on p. 415, but it should be noted that amongst the hills and valleys of the south of West Germany there are great variations in climate and the aspect of the individual valley or mountain slope is significant. Thus on some it is warm enough for the cultivation of the vine. One of the most favoured tracts is the famous Rhine rift valley itself.

Vegetation and agriculture. The higher hills and mountains of West Germany are naturally clothed with forest and the valuable softwood timber of these areas is an important asset to the country. About 29 per cent of the whole country is forested, an immense amount of afforestation having been carried out on the poor sandy soils of the northern plain.

In 1969 over one-third of the total land area of West Germany was recorded as arable land, one-quarter as pasture (excluding the area of West Berlin). Therefore the agriculture of the country tends to a cropland economy rather than to one based on permanent pasture. The hay crop is important; and it is a reflection of the poor quality of the soils and the climate of northern Germany that rye and oats are widely grown. Wheat and barley, demanding better soil and climatic conditions, are mainly crops of the southern half of West Germany where there are fertile soils as the lowlands rise to the uplands. The enormous area under potatoes is evidence of the use which has been made of tracts of indifferent soil in the north. Although the area devoted to it is slowly decreasing, sugar beet is another great commercial crop. There are market gardens near most large towns and the sheltered rift valley section of the Rhine, with fertile soils, produces tobacco, vegetables and fruit (especially grapes) as well as wheat, barley and maize. The gorge section of the Rhine, and the Mosel valley, are noted for their vineyards, the grapes producing fine hocks.

West Germany has limited stretches of the type of moorland pasture which in Britain supports numbers of sheep. The West German sheep population in 1969—70 numbered 840 700 (1 100 in West Berlin); and there were 14.3m. cattle (2 000 in West Berlin). The dairy cows numbered 6.6m., with nearly 5.9m. in milk, none being recorded in West Berlin. Large numbers of pigs are reared; 19.3m. and an additional 11 000 in West Berlin. The chickens were estimated to be over 96m.

Agriculture is changing rapidly in West Germany as in other northwestern European countries. Until 1871 the German states were self-sufficient in food production; but on unification and the immediate growth of industry there was inevitably a drift from rural areas to those where industry was arising. Agricultural land passed out of German hands as a result of the First World War reparations in 1919; but even more serious for agriculture was the partition of Germany into East and West after the Second World War and the loss of agricultural land to Poland. West Germany has the benefit of the industrial areas of the west, but the most productive agricultural land, farmed in large units, which had provided much of the food for the industrial workers in the West, became Polish or East German territory. For historical reasons there is a great difference in the agricultural systems of East and West Germany. By 1871 the long-settled West had evolved into a land cultivated by many small farmers, but the 'newly colonised' East was farmed in large estates, controlled by Junkers, who might justifiably be described as fuedal lords. In general the land they farmed was no more fertile than that of the West, but they had capital to invest in new farming techniques, they were efficient managers, and they were quick to seize the opportunities in supplying food for the industrial West. West Germany in 1945 faced the loss of these highly organised productive large farms, and the problems of her own less specialised small farm units. There was also a big and growing population to feed. In 1955 the 'Green Plan' was introduced, which aimed at creating greater farming efficiency, particularly by the consolidation of dispersed farm holdings; and by better management and mechanisation of farms it was hoped to raise crop yields. The Plan has proved most successful in the northern half of Germany, but in the south there are still many small peasant farms, lacking farm machinery, where labour is underemployed, and the costs of production are consequently high. As in other prosperous industrialised societies food consumption habits are changing: more fruit, vegetables, poultry and dairy produce, but less potatoes and grain are eaten.

In fisheries Germany used to share to a considerable extent in fishing the North Sea. With the decline of fish stocks in this area, especially the herring, West Germany like other northwest European countries has been compelled to send her fishing-fleet further and further away. Large vessels and factory ships are in use, but the catches are insufficient for domestic needs and for the continuous employment of fish processing plant. Quantities of fish are therefore imported, especially herring; and a small amount of fresh and frozen fish is exported.

Population and industry. Although West Germany has, for northwest Europe, a fair proportion of her population working on the land (about 6 per cent of the total population, or 8 per cent of the labour force in 1971) most people live in towns. The total population was estimated to be about 59.8m. in 1972 excluding the 2.1m. in West Berlin. There were fifty-six other towns with a population of over 100 000 and nearly four out of five people live in towns with over 2 000 people. Bonn, the capital houses only about 300 000. The largest urban centres are, apart from West Berlin, Hamburg (1.8m.) and München (1.3m.) and the greatest urban concentration is in the Ruhr area, in North Rhine–Westphalia. The density of population is generally fairly high in the prosperous northern farming area along the North Sea coast, with its many small ports, where land has been reclaimed.

About the same time as the Anglo-Saxon invasion of Britain German lands were being overrun by similar peoples sweeping southwards. They ultimately clashed with, and held, the Romans who were pushing northwards, thereby contributing to the downfall of Roman power. The Franks were the strongest of these northern invaders and became the dominant group. For centuries the course of the Elbe–Saale rivers was the eastern boundary of German lands, on the other side of which were the Slav peoples. Ultimately the Germans crossed the Elbe–Saale line, colonising the area to the east between the twelfth and fourteenth centuries.

Settlement to the west of the Elbe had time to develop slowly, with a pattern of farmholdings and villages similar to that in southern England; but when the Germans invaded Slav territory east of the Elbe they colonised the land quickly, carving it into large geometrically tidy estates. It is the Elbe divide which today forms part of the boundary between East and West Germany, each with its different political system.

By the Middle Ages trade routeways across Europe were well worn from south to north through Alpine passes, along the waterways and valleys to the North Sea; from east to west across the great plain of northern Europe. Where routes met, towns inevitably developed — nodal towns. In the east there was less movement; Berlin came to be the capital of Prussia purely by the arbitrary choice of its royal rulers.

At the time of the industrial revolution Germany was still a collection of separate states, but with natural navigable waterways and some established railways. On unification in 1871, with 64 per cent of her population still living in rural areas, her upsurge as an industrial power was immediate. The old towns, such as Hamburg, Köln, Frankfurt and

München, well served by ancient routeways, by the railways, and by electricity, became industrial centres. The widely distributed and easily worked brown coal, feeding the electricity generating stations, contributed to the successful growth of these dispersed sites; and, easily processed into briquettes, it met the domestic needs of the growing towns. This invaluable, dispersed source of power left free the great coal resources of the Ruhr, to be used *in situ*. Accordingly it was only in the Ruhr that there was industrial concentration on a coalfield comparable with that on British coalfields.

Germany in 1871 had all the prerequisites for an industrial nation: a stimulating climate, a country well placed for trading with the great advantage of good lines of communication already available, especially navigable waterways; coal, brown coal, iron ore and other mineral resources; and above all intelligent and industrious workers, quick to learn new skills. The population figures leapt up between 1871 and 1914 as Germany's industrial growth burst on the world. In particular her application of scientific and technical knowledge was unsurpassed.

In medieval times wool, flax and silk were woven in what is now known as the Ruhr area; and there were iron workings using local ores and charcoal from the forests for smelting. As in Switzerland French Huguenots fleeing from their homeland helped to transform the hand-weaving of textiles by introducing their manufacturing methods. By 1850 the Ruhr coalfield was being mined efficiently, and about the same time Alfred Krupp had what was then the novel idea of gathering together under a single holding company not only the many separate companies involved in making components necessary for the assembly of a particular product, but the delivery of the finished article to the consumer.

The heavy industry which developed in the Ruhr, based on local excellent coking coal and iron ore, had the inestimable gift of the Rhine, navigable by small oceangoing vessels from the North Sea, for the transport of bulky, heavy goods; and the region's pre-eminence was advanced in 1899 when the Dortmund—Ems Canal was cut. This permitted goods to pass entirely through German territory to the North Sea, aided in 1914 by the completion of another link, the Rhine—Herne Canal. The German canals were cut at a later date than those in Britain and were consequently built to accommodate motorised vessels, unlike their British counterparts. There was already a fairly dense agricultural population farming the fertile Ruhr area, and with this labour supply near at hand the Ruhr industrial area extended in time far beyond the limit of the coalfield, in the province of North Rhine—Westphalia. From it today pours forth over 80 per cent of the hard coal, two-thirds of the iron and steel (using imported high grade Swedish iron ore) and 40 per cent of the refined oil production in West Germany. Over 10m.

people live in the towns of this vast workshop, concerned with engineering, railway rolling stock, steel structures, iron and tin goods, hardware, tools, glass and ceramics, furniture, textile, clothing and leather goods. The important chemical industry now uses oil as a rich additional source of raw material. The output of iron and steel in West Germany is the highest in Europe after the USSR.

Essen (engineering), Dortmund, Düsseldorf (shipyards for building barges and other Rhine vessels) and Duisberg (a great inland port) are main steel towns, Solingen in the extreme south producing specialised steels and cutlery. The towns of the northern area are more concerned with coalmining, which faces competition from oil and gas brought in by pipeline, and is declining. In the south of the Ruhr region the cotton and woollen mills of Wuppertal continue the long established textile industry originally promoted there by abundant waterpower. A number of the Ruhr towns — Gelsenkirchen for example — have major chemical industries still based on the byproducts of coal distillation, but the greatest concentration of chemical works is between Düsseldorf and Köln, especially at Wesseling, where both coal and oil are the base materials.

Köln (848 352, 1970 census) is a cathedral city on the Rhine, founded in Roman times at the convergence of routes, but now also a port with typical port industries, including oil refining, petrochemicals and fertilisers, leather and clothing, and food processing activities. The agricultural machinery produced finds a ready market nearby; and Köln is of course famous for its scent. It is a major cultural and commercial centre and almost overshadows the capital, Bonn, which lies further south up the Rhine. Bonn holds a strategic position at the northern end of the gorge section of the Rhine, but as already mentioned is quite a small town of only some 274 500 people (1970 census), known in West Germany as the 'village capital'.

To the west of the Rhine is a detached industrial area round Aachen at the eastern end of the Franco—Belgian coalfield. Near this bank too are the textile towns of Krefeld, long famous for its silk textiles, and Mönchen-Gladbach and Rheydt, which produce cotton and wool textiles in addition to housing clothing factories and works producing textile machinery — the common association of industries evolving from an initial weaving activity.

Further south, again drawn to the navigable Rhine, is another highly productive area, the region of the Rhine—Main. Where the River Main meets the Rhine the town of Mainz grew up at the confluence, famous for its machinery and leather industries. The Opel motor vehicle works are nearby at Rüsselsheim. Frankfurt am Main is one of West Germany's great banking and manufacturing centres, noted for machinery, precision instruments, electrical goods, brewing and chemicals. Crossing the river again, the Saar coalfield, west of the

Rhine, is another heavy industry area, producing about one-sixth of West Germany's total iron and steel production.

The twin city of Mannheim—Ludwigshaffen grew up at the junction of the River Neckar with the Rhine, producing agricultural machinery for the surrounding farmland, the port for the Rhine—Main industrial area.

To the south there is another great industrial concentration in the province of Baden—Württemberg. At Stuttgart motor vehicles are made in the Daimler works, and nearby at Sindelfingen is the Mercedes plant. The advent of railways encouraged the growth of the many varied manufacturing industries in Baden—Württemberg; but in the absence of coal and other raw materials the concentration is naturally on the production of goods of high value needing little raw materials. Clothing, textiles, leather goods, clocks and watches, machine tools, of all descriptions, photographic equipment, optical instruments, glass and ceramics, iron and tin goods, hardware, medical and orthopaedic goods all come under this category, and all are produced in the small industrial centres of the middle Neckar with Stuttgart at its heart.

Away to the east Nürnberg in Bavaria retains its old tradition of making toys, musical instruments and jewellery, and has also developed newer manufactures, including machinery, motor cars and bicycles. Würzburg and Schweinfurt are engineering towns, the latter specialising in ballbearings. The site of München, the prosperous capital of the province, was another personal choice of a royal master of a province. It stands in a nodal position on the north—south route leading to the Brenner Pass. It is the largest city in the south, a busy commercial and industrial centre with electrical, textile and brewing industries (using local barley and hops), as well as works producing rolling stock for the railway, drawing on hydroelectric power provided by the harnessing of local rivers. In the south too are the sawmills, as well as a flourishing dairy industry.

Another town producing rolling stock is Kassel, in the north of the province of Hesse. Newer industrial development lies to its north, in Lower Saxony, especially in the area southeast of Hannover, centred on Salzgitter. Local low grade iron ore from the Harz Foreland field, the presence of brown coal, and salt, and later the discovery of an underlying oilfield have all contributed to the rapid and extensive growth of industry, served by excellent communications. The area is crossed from east to west by the Mittelland Canal, by the railway and by the autobahn linking the Ruhr with Berlin; while nearer to Hannover is the north—south autobahn linking Hamburg with Frankfurt. The vast Volkswagen motor vehicle works were sited at Braunschweig (Brunswick) in 1937 on the strength of these good lines of communication. There are also engineering and food processing factories as well as workshops producing optical instruments in the area. Agricultural machinery is made in Hannover to meet the needs of the local farmers, as well as engineering machinery, chemicals, paper, textiles and rubber.

On partition at the end of the Second World War Hamburg, the port on the Elbe and the lowest bridging point, found itself in an uncomfortable situation. Not only was it devastated by war, it had lost its natural hinterland to East Germany. It has recovered its former function as a shipbuilding centre, and has the usual port industries, handling and processing the import of raw materials such as oil, tobacco, margarine. The Elbe estuary is shallow, another limiting factor, and Cuxhaven on the southern shore of the estuary on the North Sea coast acts as an outport for Hamburg. To improve the city's communications with the great industrial areas of West Germany a new canal is being cut to link the port with the vital Mittelland Canal.

Bremen on the River Weser (with an outport at Bremerhaven) is another port which suffered much war damage. Well served by links of communication it has now emerged as a large-scale integrated coastal steelworks town in the European Coal and Steel Community, as well as continuing its traditional port functions, shipbuilding, the handling of imports of oilseeds, cereals, tobacco, cotton and raw materials for industry, food processing, oil refining and associated industries. The third port is Emden, on the River Ems, with similar activities, the outlet for the industrial Rhine. West Berlin, isolated in the east, had established electrical engineering and the manufacture of railway rolling stock as its major industries, but they have declined since partition.

West German industry, with financial help under the Marshall Plan, made an astonishingly swift recovery after the Second World War. Today West Germany is one of the world's great industrial powers, with a gross national product in 1973 of 926 200m. DM compared with 98 000m. DM in 1950. Of the total production of the European Coal and Steel Community in 1973 West Germany supplied 38 per cent of the coal and 33 per cent of the crude steel. She is the largest consumer of power in Europe, ahead of the United Kingdom.

Communications. The contribution made by navigable waterways in the rise of Germany as an industrial power cannot be overemphasised. They still play a major role in the communications system of West Germany, carrying nearly a third of the goods traffic. Within the last 100 years many canals were cut and the course of the Rhine improved so that it is navigable by 1 500 ton barges from its delta in the Netherlands as far south as Basel in Switzerland. Both roads and railways developed from the medieval trade routeways, maintaining the same pattern and converging on the old towns which grew up at the intersections of routes. The railway system has some electrified lines, and on routes not yet electrified the trains are drawn by diesel locomotives; special railroad cars cater for the growing container traffic; but the railways are losing trade to the roads. The building of the famous Autobahn network began in the 1930s and is being extended today so that eventually high speed international motorways will link the Netherlands, Belgium, West Germany, Switzerland and Austria. In 1970 the total length of classified roads in West Germany was 135 000 km (84 000 miles) including 4 110 km (2 554 miles) of Autobahn, 32 205 km (20 000 miles) of highways; and 65 358 km (40 600 miles) of first class country roads. Motor vehicles licensed in 1970 numbered 16.7m., and of these nearly 14m. were passenger cars, 1.1m. were lorries. The partition of Germany into East and West has cut the number of west–east routes and there are very few crossing-points at the border. As a result communications in West Germany have developed a pronounced north–south emphasis.

West Germany is well served by air, with a major international airport at Frankfurt am Main.

Hamburg and Bremen handle much of West Germany's seaborne trade, but as the state becomes more involved with western Europe particularly with the countries of the European Economic Community, Hamburg is out on a limb to the east. More and more of the goods traffic of West Germany is therefore handled by Rotterdam, the great delta port of the Rhine in the Netherlands. It can be assumed that this trade will continue and Rotterdam will ultimately become West Germany's major outlet port.

Foreign trade. The foreign trade of West Germany includes the import of oil, raw materials for her industries, foodstuffs and machinery; and it includes the export of machinery and vehicles, manufactured goods, chemicals (especially fertilisers), iron and steel. The relatively small amount of foodstuffs imported reflects how admirably West German farmers have increased their output to compensate for the loss of the most productive farmland in the east. As the leading industrial state in the European Economic Community West Germany's foreign trade is primarily concerned with the exchange of manufactured goods with the other countries of western Europe, but she also has a useful exchange of goods with the United States of America.

Table 43 – **West Germany: towns with population exceeding 400 000**
     (1969 estimate)

Berlin (West)	2 134 250	Dortmund	648 900
Hamburg	1 817 000	Stuttgart	628 400
München	1 326 300	Bremen	607 200
Köln	866 300	Hannover	517 800
Essen	696 900	Nürnberg	477 100
Düsseldorf	680 800	Duisburg	457 900
Frankfurt am Main	660 400	Wuppertal	414 000

There are a further forty-three towns which, with suburbs, have a population exceeding 100 000.

East Germany

The emergence of East Germany (the German Democratic Republic: Deutsche Demokratische Republik) as a separate state in 1949 has been covered on p. 410.

It is less than half the size of West Germany, covering only 108 174 sq km (41 722 sq miles) with a total population estimated in 1969 to be 17m. (including East Berlin), compared with the 61m. in West Germany. It has been pointed out (p. 425) that in general the frontier between East and West Germany, particularly along the River Elbe, almost coincides with the historical divide between the Slav and Germanic peoples. In the south East Germany is bordered by West Germany and Czechoslovakia, and her eastern neighbour is Poland. In 1950 the East German and Polish governments agreed that the Rivers Oder—Neisse should form the boundary between their two countries, the west bank being East German territory. This arrangement added considerably to Poland's land in the west. The shallow coast of the Baltic Sea completes the boundary of East Germany in the north.

Minerals and power. Nearly the whole of East Germany lies on the north European plain, with its varied soils; and especially in the north and in the Berlin area there are innumerable swamps and lakes. The River Elbe, navigable for all its length, rises in Czechoslovakia and flows from southeast to northwest across East Germany to its outlet at Hamburg (West Germany). Towards the south the land rises to the uplands of the aptly named Erzgebirge (the Ore Mountains) where deposits of silver are nearly exhausted, but which yield other valuable minerals: uranium, cobalt, bismuth, arsenic, antimony. Underlying the northern flanks is East Germany's only bituminous coalfield, also nearing exhaustion, with only a small output. This lack of hard coal is counterbalanced by an abundance of brown coal. East Germany has the largest output of brown coal in the world and, as in West Germany, it is much used in electricity power stations sited near the deposits; or it is made into briquettes for domestic and factory use. East Germany lacks adequate resources of iron ore, but has other valuable mineral assets: rich deposits of potash and salt near Stassfurt and Halle, copper and uranium on the margins of the Harz Mountains, the latter at Wernigorde.

Despite the vast resources of brown coal other fuel for power is imported: coal from Silesia (where the rich coalfield was formerly part of the German Reich and is now Polish) and from the Donbass basin in the USSR, and crude oil by pipeline also from the East. The widespread distribution of brown coal has on the whole discouraged the development of hydroelectric power, but the upper course of the River Saale has been dammed for this purpose.

Agriculture. Although East Germany does not extend into such southern latitudes as West Germany it has the advantages of warm continental summers and a rainfall generally averaging about 500 mm (20 in) annually: ideal growing conditions for appropriate crops in areas with fertile soils. Over one-third of the total land area is forested — mixed deciduous and coniferous trees on the northern plain, mainly coniferous in the mountains. Nearly one-fifth of the land is permanent grassland, but over half the total land area is arable, producing wheat, rye, barley, oats, potatoes and sugar beet.

Apart from some good soils along the coastal strip of Mecklenburg, the poor sandy soils of the north European plain in East Germany do not provide good farmland; but the Junker landowners made good use of the tracts where heavier clay occurred in Mecklenburg. Their mixed farms combined the production of high yields of rye and potatoes with the rearing of cattle, sheep, pigs and horses. This same output continues today, under new management, but horses are not so important and much sugar beet is grown. In 1945 these vast Junker estates (some of which occupied as much as 20 000 ha: 50 000 acres) were either divided up and distributed to the formerly landless peasantry, who later agreed to collectivisation, or organised as state farms.

As in West Germany, the really fertile land lies in the southern half of the country, particularly in the Saale basin. Cereals and sugar beet are the main crops, apple and plum orchards delight the eye in Thuringen, Erfurt is renowned for its plant nurseries, and hops are grown at Naumberg. Sheep graze the grassy slopes of the Erzgebirge.

Population and industry. After 1945 and until the erection of the Berlin Wall, which cut off East Berlin from West Berlin, there was a steady migration of people from East Germany to West. It has been estimated that 3.5m. people trekked westwards, and although many no doubt moved for political reasons, they were but following the traditional current of emigration from the predominantly rural east to the industrial west, dating from the nineteenth century. This had the affect of adding to West Germany's problem of feeding her growing population, heightened by the loss of the eastern farmland; and it led to the building of the Berlin Wall in 1961, the last route by which East Germans were able to leave their country. In the years 1952–66 the population statistics for East Germany were either declining or static, but since 1966 there has been a very slow rise to the estimated figure for 1971, 17m. (including East Berlin with just over 1m. people). In 1967 it was estimated that nearly 20 per cent of the people were engaged in agriculture (or 19 per cent of the labour force).

East German towns either grew up to serve the needs of surrounding farmland, or at the convergence of routes. The largest urban concentrations today are East Berlin (1m.), Leipzig (585 000), Dresden

(501 000) and there are eight other towns with a population of over 100 000.

Berlin was once a small fishing town on a sandy island amidst lakes and forests. Chosen by the Electors of Brandenburg as their capital, 400 years later in 1871 it became the capital of the German Reich because of its position: central in the northern lowlands then occupied by Germany, on the north–south route from the Baltic to the Mediterranean, and on the west–east route across the great plain. Its industries developed rapidly and by 1939 its contribution to industry was second to that of the Ruhr. The emphasis was on electrical engineering, clothing, food processing, printing and engineering manufactures. It was also a commercial, banking and cultural centre. East Berlin is now the seat of government of East Germany and continues its function as an industrial centre concerned with the production of machinery, electrical equipment, cables and printing.

Apart from Berlin and Rostock, the Baltic port, most of the people of East Germany live in the southern half of the country. Partition left East Germany as a primarily agricultural country, and great efforts have been made since to build up industry to redress the balance, relying on home supplies of raw materials. Steelworks have been built at the new town of Eisenhüttenstadt (formerly Stalinstadt), south of Frankfurt-an-der-Oder, linked by canal to Berlin; and at Calbe on the River Saale, just above its junction with the River Elbe. It had been intended that these plants should rely on brown coal, but instead coking coal is imported from other Comecon countries for the processing of the iron ore imported from Sweden and the Soviet Union.

The brown coal is of immense use in the potash and salt industries near Stassfurt and Halle. The area is also supplied with crude oil by pipeline from the Soviet Union. Fertilisers are produced in enormous quantities for the hungry lands of the Comecon countries, and other plants produce synthetic rubber and fabrics, dyes, photographic and electrical equipment.

Silver was mined in the Erzgebirge in the Middle Ages to be worked by local silversmiths, but the silver has long since been exhausted and its place taken in the economy by the purely functional uranium. The old textile industry, based on wool from sheep grazing the gentle slopes, continues in a slightly different form; cotton at Zwickau, and cotton, synthetic fibres, linen and jute have replaced raw wool in the mills at Karlmarxstadt (formerly Chemnitz); and textile machinery is an additional production in both towns. Karlmarxstadt has progressed further, to the production of motor vehicles. The traditional woollen textile industry continues in the area around Gera, to the northwest of Zwickau. Further northwest the fertile land of Thuringen lacks the raw materials necessary for industry, but nevertheless manufacturing is carried on in various towns: Erfurt, producing electrical goods and specialising in engineering; Eisenach with vehicle works; Jena, famous for its production of fine glass for optical instruments. Raw materials have to be imported and the emphasis, as in the south of West Germany, is on the production of valuable goods requiring plentiful skilled labour, but little bulky raw materials.

Agricultural machinery is made to supply the needs of the fertile surrounding farmland at Leipzig and Magdeburg, both nodal towns (that is at the convergence of routes). Meissen and Dresden are renowned for their production of ceramics, but Dresden has other industries: engineering, machinery, optical instruments and other light industry. Leipzig has especial interest. It stands at the crossing point of routeways, and at the crossroads of cultures. It was natural that publishing and printing should grow up at this centre of intellectual exchange, and it became the focus of these activities in the German Reich of 1871 to 1945. This glory has faded but it retains its other main function, as a trading centre, particularly of the fur trade of continental Europe; and the annual Leipzig Fair first held in the twelfth century, is one of the world's traditional showcases. Local industries include printing machinery manufacture.

On the Baltic coast tourist resorts have grown up under the East German regime. There are shipyards at Wismar and Stralsund but the main port is Rostock which receives iron ore imports from Sweden, and not only serves East Germany but handles the marine traffic of Czechoslovakia. Its port facilities are being reconstructed and extended, and it is served with crude oil by pipeline from the Soviet Union.

Communications were greatly disrupted in East Germany as a result of partition and the cutting of the formerly important routes to the West. Berlin is the main route centre, at the convergence of railways and roads, connected to Dresden and Leipzig and the industrial area of Halle. East Germany has the advantage of navigable waterways (especially the Rivers Elbe, Saale and Oder) but much of the goods traffic is carried by rail, some of which is electrified. Roads have not been greatly extended since the construction of Autobahn before the Second World War, but a motorway has been planned to connect Rostock with Berlin. Compared with the number in western Europe there are few car owners in East Germany, but the number is increasing. In 1969 motor vehicles comprised 1 039 299 passenger cars, 209 783 lorries and 2 790 000 motor cycles.

The leading East German imports are iron ore, plates and sheets of steel, motor cars and tyres, wheat and other foodstuffs, cigarettes. Exports include electric motors, brown coal briquettes, and gas; small quantities of a variety of manufactured goods, including watches and clocks, spectacles, photographic equipment (especially films), stockings. Nearly all East Germany's trade is with other east European

Table 44 — East Germany: towns with population exceeding 100 000 (1970)

Berlin (East), district (capital)	1 085 450	Halle	257 300
		Rostock	198 400
Leipzig	584 365	Erfurt	196 000
Dresden	501 500	Zwickau	127 000
Karlmarxstadt	299 372	Gera	111 300
Magdeburg	270 700	Potsdam	111 100

countries. Russian is taught in the schools as the first foreign language, and as time passes the possibility of East and West Germany reuniting seems remote.

Poland

Since the tenth century the Poles have had a culture quite distinct from that of the peoples in neighbouring states, but their fortunes have fluctuated greatly and between 1795 and 1919 a Polish nation state as such did not exist. The Grand Duchy of Warsaw had a brief life from 1807 to 1815, and the Republic of Kracow flowered for a little longer, from 1815 to 1846, but at other times the Polish lands were divided between Russia, Germany and Austria. It was not until 1919, after the First World War, that an independent Republic of Poland was declared, lying on the north European plain between the Baltic Sea and the Carpathian mountains.

Poland suffered widespread destruction in the Second World War: many of her towns were razed to the ground, and some 22 per cent of her population died. At the end of the war the USSR occupied a large area of Polish territory in the east (up to the 'Curzon line'), including the Pripet Marshes and the ancient city of L'vov. To compensate for this loss Poland moved her western boundary further west, to the line of the Odra (Oder) — Neisse rivers, thereby acquiring former German territory and the major part of the Upper Silesian coalfield. In the north the Free City of Danzig became a Polish port (and known as Gdańsk), and Poland at last thus controlled the natural outlet of the Wisla basin, together with a long Baltic Sea coast and another major port, Szczecin (formerly Stettin, when in German hands). The area of Poland is now 312 700 sq km (120 633 sq miles) comparable with that of the United Kingdom.

This westward shift presented problems. It has been estimated that about 6m. Germans moved out of the former German territory on the west, leaving the area seriously underpopulated. It was resettled by some 2m. Poles who were displaced in the east by the realignment of the USSR frontier, by people from the overpopulated centre and south-east of Poland, and by expatriates returning to the homeland after the war; but Poland was underpopulated at a time when she was most in need of a big labour force for reconstruction.

Materially the westward move was no great disadvantage. In the east good agricultural and forest lands were lost, but farmland of greater fertility was acquired in the west, particularly in Silesia. Carpathian oil and deposits of potash were lost to the USSR, to be more than compensated for by the valuable Upper Silesian coalfield, together with factories and industrial equipment abandoned by the Germans in Silesia. The youthfulness of the population resettled in the 'new' western areas produced a high rate of increase and an adaptable supply of labour for industry. The frontier realignment in the north gave Poland a great navigable river, the Odra (Oder) with a canal link to the Upper Silesian coalfield, as well as major ports.

The land was devastated by war, but Poland had the raw materials and the will to develop industrially, with a limited amount of fertile food-productive land in support. The population of 24m. in 1946 had increased to 30m. by 1961 (the 1970 estimate was over 32.4m.). In 1969 there were 10.33m. Poles living abroad, 6.5m. in the USA, 1.4m. in the USSR, 145 000 in the UK. By 1950 Poland had achieved such a degree of reconstruction that she was able to launch a plan for the mechanisation and upgrading of agriculture; and a full-scale programme of industrialisation with the emphasis on heavy industry, as in other Comecon countries.

Regions. The country may be divided into four regions which stretch across the land. In the north the Baltic zone bordering the sea is marked by many lakes that fill hollows blocked by moraines. The land is on the whole low-lying, the soils vary but are generally of poor quality. There are patches of forest in the sandy areas, meadows on the land which will hold more water; and arable crops are grown on the heavy boulder clay areas. Cereals and root crops, especially potatoes, are cultivated, sheep and cattle graze the delta lands of the Wisla (Vistula), but this Baltic zone is primarily a dairying region. There is little settlement along the shallow coast of the Baltic Sea, with its *haffs* and sand spits: the only towns of any size are the ports of Szczecin on the Odra and Gdańsk on the Wisla. The Masurian area in the east of the Baltic heights, of little use to the farmer, is exceptionally beautiful and one of the delights of holidaymakers in Poland. Both coniferous and deciduous trees fringe innumerable lakes of every shape and size.

South of the Baltic zone the great central plain is mainly agricultural, with soils ranging from the most infertile to the very finest. Great forests contrast with dry heathlands and considerable marshes; but there are wide stretches of rolling farmland, with rye, oats, barley, sugar beet, flax and fodder crops grown for dairy cattle and pigs. The land is often ploughed in long strips. Many of the large estates west of the Wisla formerly farmed by Germans are now highly mechanised state farms where, with the increasing use of fertilisers, crop yields are rising. East of the Wisla sand and gravels support forests and crops of rye, potatoes and flax. There are deposits of iron ore at Leczyca, and widespread areas of brown coal west of the Wisla. Rock salt is exploited near Lódź.

Further south the land rises to a region of low plateaus and basins, built up partly of chalk, with islands of older rock protruding; the whole is covered with a mantle of fertile loess, except for a sandy heath-covered tract in northern Silesia. The soils of the remainder of Silesia are fertile loams, producing high yields of rye, wheat, sugar beet and potatoes. This is the area of Poland's mineral wealth, the vast Upper Silesian coalfield. It has been estimated that the coal reserves underly 5 180 sq km (2 000 sq miles), most of it within Polish boundaries. The local iron ore has been worked out, but deposits of lead and zinc remain. Further deposits of good coking coal lie in Sudety and there are copper reserves in Lower Silesia.

To the south lie the forested mountains of the Sudety, the lowland area of the Moravian Gate, and the forested Carpathian mountains, where transhumance is practised and the valleys cultivated. It is an area of great scenic beauty and attracts many tourists. There are oil and natural gas reserves in the southeast, and salt is mined in the Carpathian foreland.

Two great rivers drain Poland, flowing from south to north. In the west, the Odra, which rises in Czechoslovakia, forms the boundary with East Germany, the frontier running down the centre of the river. The Wisla drains small areas of the USSR and Czechoslovakia, but, like the Odra, it is mainly a Polish river. Both are liable to flood in their courses over the flat Polish plain; both are now contained by an elaborate system of levées, but the flood danger remains in the spring when the snow melts and at the time of maximum summer rainfall.

Climate. Climatically Poland is a transition area, ranging from the northwest European climate, with its mild, moist, maritime characteristics, to east European, with extremes of temperature. The all-important length of growing season decreases eastwards with the rise in the number of days with frost. The Baltic coastlands experience the least frost, but more rain than central Poland, which at its heart has a low precipitation of under 500 mm (19.5 in). Precipitation is highest in the mountains of the south and southwest. Most rain falls in summer in Poland, and in winter precipitation takes the form of snow. Despite the generally low rainfall humidity is high, on account of the constant cloud cover.

Population, agriculture and industry. Poland, for long a basically agricultural country, is becoming increasingly urbanised with the expansion of industry. In the 1920s fewer than 26 per cent of the population were classified as town dwellers; now the figure is nearer 50 per cent, and it can be assumed that this urbanisation will continue. A very large proportion of the population is young (65 per cent under thirty-five in 1968), and women far outnumber men in the older age groups. The youthfulness is undoubtedly affecting Poland's industrial growth. However 35 per cent of the population (42 per cent of the labour force) still work on the land, of which about 50 per cent is arable, and 20 per cent under forest. By far the greatest number of agricultural workers are small farmers cultivating their own land which may not exceed 50 ha (124 acres), the average holding being 5 ha (about 12 acres); others work on state or cooperative farms; or at the state 'machine and tractor centres' from which small farmers borrow equipment. Collectivisation proved unpopular and has been abandoned. Of 19.6m. ha (48.5m. acres) of agricultural land in 1969, 16.4m. ha (43m. acres) was in private hands; 2.8m. ha (6.8m. acres) in state farms; 0.3m. ha (0.7m. acres) in cooperatives. The main crops sown are rye (over 4m. ha: 9m. acres in 1969 in the centre and north), potatoes (2.7m. ha: 6.7m. acres grown for fodder and as an industrial crop as well as for human consumption); much smaller but increasing quantities of wheat (nearly 2m. ha: 5m. acres in the south), oats (1.4m. ha: 3.5m. acres on acid soils), barley (decreasing — 0.7m. ha: 1.7m. acres for brewing, grown mainly in the south and southeast), and small quantities of maize in the warmth of the south. In industrial crops sugar beet easily leads, followed by flax and hemp. The location of sugar beet is often fixed by the presence of processing factories. There is scope for further mechanisation and greater use of fertilisers.

Most farms have a horse for ploughing, a cow or two, pigs and poultry, but there is no really large-scale cattle rearing. The main dairying region lies in the north; sheep find pasture on the mountain slopes in the south. In 1969 there were over 11m. cattle (6.3m. cows), over 14m. pigs, 3.3m. sheep, over 2.5m. horses (mostly working farmhorses), and 85.5m. head of poultry.

To serve the needs of the agricultural population many small market towns developed, especially on the Central Plain. Some retain their original function, others have added new manufacturing industries to their activities. For example at Poznań (46 000) on the River Warta, a tributary of the Odra, factories produce agricultural machinery and chemical fertilisers, as well as processing agricultural produce in flour mills and breweries. A new industrial area is being developed at Konin Inowroclaw where there are deep deposits of rock salt; aluminium will be produced, as well as chemicals from brown coal, the latter supplying fuel for the thermal electricity plant. Bydgoszcz (279 000) an ancient town at the junction of the River Wisla and the canal connecting to the River Noteć, has developed engineering works and a chemical industry producing pharmaceuticals in addition to its old timber industry. Plock, served by the oil pipeline from the USSR also has a new industry: petrochemicals, based on the oil refineries. The whole of the valley of the middle Wisla is developing rapidly; industry is flourishing, with market gardens and dairying to feed the growing urban population. There are many ancient settlements, and catering for tourists is an expanding industry.

Warsaw (Warszawa), the capital, with nearly 1.3m. people, occupies a site on firm ground above the floodplain of the Wisla. Completely devastated in the Second World War, the old area of the city has been rebuilt, faithfully reproduced with the help of paintings and prints, an exact copy of the architectural splendour which was destroyed. Outside the ancient walls modern flats and wide roads provide a sharp contrast. Warsaw performs the functions characteristic of capital cities: it is the cultural, commercial and administrative centre of Poland, but it is an industrial city too, with textile, machinery and pharmaceutical works as well as new plant producing high grade steel in the suburbs to the north.

There are few towns of any great size in the Central Plain east of the Wisla. Bialystok (163 000) has an old textile industry, now using thermoelectric power, and newer engineering activities, but the main centre of Poland's textile industry is Lódź (751 000), southwest of Warsaw. German businessmen built textile mills in Lódź in the nineteenth century when the town was within the Russian sphere of influence, thereby avoiding tariffs on their woollen and cotton cloths. The town now has clothing manufactures, as does Radom (154 000) to the southeast.

Other areas famous for a long standing textile industry, initially wool-based, are the Sudety (where mill towns used to use water power from the mountain streams, and now use coal) and the region of the Upper Silesian coalfield. Textiles lead in production in light industry in Poland, other long established activities being food-processing and the manufacture of ceramics and glass. A newer development is the making of cement, which has naturally flourished since the Second World War with so much building being carried on.

By far the most important industrial and mining growth area is the Upper Silesian coalfield, with its resources of bituminous coal. It provides the main source of fuel, indeed these reserves combined with the widespread brown coal resources used in thermoelectric power stations have discouraged the development of hydroelectric power production, except on a few small rivers in the Sudety and in the Carpathian Mountains.

Only the Ruhr has greater coal reserves than Upper Silesia; but iron ore resources in Poland are inadequate for industrial needs, and much high grade ore is imported from Krivoy Rog in the USSR. The iron and steel industry is located at old centres such as Chorzów (151 000) in the Upper Silesian region, where out-of-date equipment has been rebuilt and modernised, and new plant installed at such centres as Częstochowa and Nowa Huta. Heavy mechanical equipment is made in Upper Silesia as well as light mechanical and electrical goods, transport equipment, steel constructions and bridges. There is little production of agricultural machinery because this is made in the areas of good agricultural land to the north; but there is a considerable output of chemicals for fertilisers, paints and varnishes, as well as a high production of zinc, which is mined locally.

The Sudety also has its share of heavy industry. Much of the coal is converted to coke needed by the metallurgical industry of Upper Silesia; and the recently discovered great reserves of copper will bring further industry to the area.

Another region with an output of metallurgical goods is centred on Ostrowiec and Starachowice southwest of Lublin; and at the confluence of the San and Wisla rivers there are good deposits of sulphur, a key industrial mineral.

As a result of agreements within Comecon, shipbuilding has been stimulated at the ports of Gdańsk and Szczecin on the shallow Baltic coast, far from ideal for harbours. Gdańsk (364 000) lies on the Wisla delta and can accommodate only relatively small vessels. Szczecin (337 000) was largely destroyed in the Second World War and has been rebuilt. Its factories produce metallurgical goods, and like Gdańsk it has the characteristic port industry of food processing. With the third Baltic port, Gdynia (190 000), these two ports act as bases for Poland's merchant marine, which is considerably larger than that of any other Comecon country outside the USSR.

Communications. The three ports are served by rail but the fragmentation of Poland in the nineteenth century militated against the construction of an efficient rail network. Tsarist Russia used a different gauge from the other occupying powers, and the Russians looked upon railways as an instrument of strategy for their army. They laid straight lines to the major urban centres, but frequently built the station at some distance from the town as a defence precaution. The Germans constructed a good system in the part they occupied; but the Austrians were not interested in the development of Poland and did little in the area under their control. Since 1918 the Polish state has been trying to rationalise this disorderly system. Lines now focus on Warsaw and link the city with the major urban and industrial areas, and Upper Silesia is particularly well served by an intricate and much used network, the routes to Gdańsk and Gdynia in particular carrying coal. Some lines, such as that from Warsaw to Katowice (303 000) in the Upper Silesian industrial region, are electrified, but steam locomotives are still in use.

Most freight is carried by rail: the road network, which in general follows a pattern similar to the railways, caters more for passengers.

Although the main rivers are described as navigable, only the Odra is used to any great extent. Linked by the Gliwice canal to the Upper Silesian industrial area, it is used for the import of heavy, bulky goods, especially iron ore, brought upstream from Szczecin; and for the export of coal. The mature course of the lower Wisla has the encumbrances of shifting sandy banks and an uneven flow, although it is linked by the Bydgoszcz Canal with the River Noteć. There is an imaginative scheme, not yet far advanced, which will join the Wisla and the Bug rivers with the Soviet River Dnepr, so that iron ore from the Soviet Union can be waterborne to the new plant at Nowa Huta; and another, which is still on the drawing board, to link the upper Odra, Wisla and Morava to the Danube.

Poland has a national international airline, and an international airport at Okecie (Warsaw), which also serves domestic routes.

Trade. The foreign trade of Poland shows the pattern of an emerging industrial nation. Imports of iron ore are easily the largest, followed by crude and refined oil, natural gas, machinery (including tractors), metallurgical machinery and pig iron for her industry, as well as ships and boats, fertilisers and cotton from the USSR and consumer goods. The import of primary foodstuffs is slightly rising (wheat and barley, rice, fruits and vegetables). Coal is by far the most important export, destined for Austria, Hungary, the Balkan countries and Italy; pipes and steel plates, trailers for cars and tractors, cement and coke are other industrial exports; meat and meat products lead in agricultural produce. Despite the domestic need of feeding the growing industrial population, Poland still has agricultural surplus for export (butter, eggs, poultry and bacon), but the quantity is slowly declining.

Most trading is with Comecon countries, especially the USSR, East Germany and Czechoslovakia. Outside the group there is a useful exchange of goods with the United Kingdom, some with Italy and Austria; and there is worldwide trading on a very small scale.

The first volume of the United Nations *Yearbook of International Trade Statistics* which included Poland was the yearbook for 1955. Imports and exports for five postwar years were recorded mostly by weight in metric tons. The main items in 1949, 1955 and 1969 are shown in Table 45.

In *International Trade Statistics* for 1956 the tables of Polish imports and exports by weight were replaced by tables giving the value of commodity groups in US dollars. Total imports in 1955 were valued at $931.8m., and in 1956 at $912.1m. In both years 'raw materials and materials for production' accounted for more than half the total, the figure for 1956 being $496.8m. In 1956 also another quarter of the

Table 45 – Poland: imports and exports

Special imports: metric tons

Commodity	1949	1955	1969
Wheat	164 630	739 310	1m.
Rye	—	414 763	63 900¶
Fertilisers	804 060	1 085 343	3.8m.¶
Raw cotton	93 344	95 200	156 400¶
Raw wool	15 454	16 300	17 100¶
Iron ore	1.6m.	4.4m.	11.6m.
Petroleum: Crude	91 508	544 900 ⎫	8.9m.
Products	254 775	885 700 ⎭	
Eggs	199m.*	344m.*	326.8m.*¶

Special exports: metric tons

Commodity	1949	1955	1969
Beet sugar	184 472	272 000	132 000¶
Cotton fabrics	50.5m.†	57.5m.†	143.8m.†¶
Coal	26m.	24m.	26.4m.
Cement	506 595	673 700	58 000
Roll mill products	162 500	247 532	
Ships	9.2m.‡	36.5m.§	421 000 dwt
Lignite			4.3m.
Coke			2.3m.

* Number.
† Metres.
‡ Roubles.
§ US dollars.
¶ 1968.

imports was provided by 'machinery and transport equipment' ($229.6m.), while 'agricultural consumer goods' ($126.5m.) and 'consumer goods of industrial origin' ($59.2m.) made up the balance. Comparisons with 1968 statistics are difficult, because by then the value of trade was expressed in zlotys. Imports in that year totalled 11 412m. zlotys, of which iron ore and products represented about 1 000m., cotton and wool 560m. zlotys, and crude petroleum and petroleum products over 7m.

On the export side in 1956 'raw materials and materials for production' ($627.8m.) constituted nearly two-thirds of the total ($934.6m.), the chief items being coal and coke ($425.1m.) and iron, steel and zinc ($111.4m.). Machinery and transport equipment ($139.9m.) included road transport ($54.4m.), ships and boats ($37.9m.), and machine tools ($7m.). Completing the export total were two other groups – agricultural consumer goods ($115.1m.) and consumer goods of industrial origin ($87.8m.) – corresponding with the classification of the imports. Exports in 1968 were valued at 11 431m. zlotys, coal and lignite totalling 1 200m. meat and meat products (including bacon) 581m., rolled iron and steel products 553m. zlotys.

In both the 1955 and the 1956 *Yearbooks*, the analysis of imports and exports according to the countries of supply and countries of destination was by percentages of the total values already quoted. Imports in 1956 came chiefly from the USSR (27 per cent), East Germany 14.8, Czechoslovakia 10.0, West Germany 6.2, China 3.9, Australia 3.8, UK 3.6, France 3.5 – these eight countries accounting for nearly three-quarters of the total. Much the same countries took much the same proportion of Poland's exports, namely, USSR 28.2 per cent, East Germany 10.5, UK 8.3, Czechoslovakia 7.7, West Germany 5.6, China 5.3, Finland 3.5, France 3.2. In 1968 the USSR supplied over 36.3 per cent of imports and took 36.4 per cent of exports; East Germany provided 11 per cent of imports, received 8 per cent of exports; Czechoslovakia 8 per cent of imports, 8 per cent of exports.

Table 46 – Poland: towns with population exceeding 200 000 (1970 census)

Warsaw (capital)	1 308 000	Gdańsk (Danzig)	364 000
Lódź	762 000	Szczecin (Stettin)	337 000
Kraków	583 000	Katowice	303 000
Wroclaw (Breslau)	523 000	Bydgoszcz	281 000
Poznań	469 000	Lublin	236 000

There are fourteen more towns with a population exceeding 100 000.

Switzerland

The federal republic of Switzerland (Schweiz, Suisse, Svizzera) can justifiably claim to be the oldest democracy in Europe, tracing its history back to a defensive grouping of cantons round Lake Luzern in 1291. The Swiss have used the advantages of their geographical location, protected by mountains in the heart of Europe, to maintain an armed neutrality since the end of the Napoleonic Wars, and the land has never been devastated by warfare. This stability has attracted international banks, and other international organisations: the United Nations Organisation, the International Red Cross, the International Labour Office, and the World Health Organisation have offices in Genève; and the headquarters of the World Postal Union and the International Telecommunications Union are in Bern. In pursuance of this strict neutrality and sturdy independence, Switzerland is not even a member of the United Nations Organisation, nor of the European Economic Community; but she joined the loosely-knit European Free Trade Association.

The Swiss have been ready to give sanctuary to refugees from more troubled parts of Europe, among them the French Protestants (the Huguenots) who fled from their homeland in the eighteenth century, and the French who left Alsace in 1871 when Germany took possession of that territory, as well as those fleeing from the regime of Nazi Germany and, latterly, those leaving eastern for western Europe. The influx of these peoples has been a great benefit to Switzerland. They brought capital with them in many cases, but even more important, they brought their skills. The French especially were export clock and watchmakers and silk weavers.

There are four official languages in Switzerland. In the north, centre and west about 75 per cent of the people speak German; 20 per cent speak French in the west; Italian is spoken by 4 per cent in the south; and in the Alps, in Graubünden, an interesting old tongue, Romansch, lives on. It is derived from Latin and is spoken by 1 per cent of the population. Despite these linguistic differences there is unity in the country. The Swiss are good linguists and many speak English in addition to two or three of the major languages of their republic.

Switzerland is particularly interesting because here more than in any other country man has turned every aspect of a difficult environment to his advantage. Lacking raw materials, but with abundant hydroelectric power, combined with the precision skills and hard work of her people, Switzerland in the last century has become one of the most highly industrialised countries in Europe, with a concentration on the manufacture of high quality, valuable goods of little bulk.

Surface. Landlocked in the heart of Europe Switzerland has frontiers with Germany, France, Italy and Austria. It is about the same size as Scotland (41 288 sq km: 15 941 sq miles) with a population of 6.27m. at the 1971 census.

A land of mountains and lakes at a high altitude, Switzerland falls physically into three parts. The southern region (about 60 per cent of the land area) forms part of the main chain of the Alps, 'young' fold mountains which exhibit the effects of ice erosion and shattering by frost in their jagged peaks. In the north is a small strip of the Jura Mountains (about 10 per cent of the land area), which are lower than the Alps but present a barrier through which the Rivers Rhône, Aare and Rhine have carved their valleys. Lying between these mountainous areas is a long, narrow plateau, where nearly three-quarters of the people live: the more hospitable Mittelland, or Swiss Foreland, stretching from Lake Léman (Geneva) to Bodensee (Lake Constance). Even this lower area is about 457 m (1 500 ft) above sea level, and it is by no means flat: glaciation has made it a region of low hills and flat bottomed valleys.

Minerals. Switzerland has little mineral wealth. There are some small deposits of iron ore in the Jura and near Sargans and manganese ore at Herznach (Aargan), no longer worked. Salt is mined in Bex (Vaud) and in Schweizerhalle, Rheinfelden and Ryburg; but there are neither coal nor oil resources.

Climate. The high altitude of Switzerland has a profound affect on climate, which has both a mountain and a Mediterranean regime, and in such a mountainous land there are many small local variations. Bitterly cold winds sometimes sweep down the mountain slopes, causing sudden squalls on the lakes. The *mistral*, which blows at times down the lower Rhône valley or across the Riviera and causes storms in the Gulf du Lion, is of this type. At other times air which is forced down the mountainside is warmed by compression and forms the famous *föhn* wind, which is warm and dry and melts the snow in late winter and spring. In winter snow covers much of the land, the high altitude creating low temperatures, but at the same time a high pressure system stabilises over the Alps to give days of brilliant sunshine, so admirable for winter sports. Conditions are equally agreeable for tourists in summer, when a comparatively low rainfall and blue skies combine to make the mountain scenery equally attractive. On the plateau, the Mittelland, at a lower altitude the summers are warm with a well distributed rainfall; but winters are cold and cloudy, and there is often fog. This is due to temperature inversion when warm air floats over the cold air below. Fogs occur in the mountains too when the heavy cold air flows down the valleysides like water, again creating temperature inversion.

Agriculture. Little remains of the natural vegetation, but the Swiss have made good use of the mountain slopes for forestry. Of the total land area nearly 25 per cent is under forest, 45 per cent is grassland and 10 per cent arable; but even this high proportion of afforested land is insufficient to meet the country's need for timber and wood has to be imported. The best stands of tall timber are on the high north slopes of the Alps which stay longest in shadow. With increasing altitude, above the treeline, are the alpine pastures, a carpet of flowers when the snow melts, and these in turn give way to bare rock, supporting a true Alpine vegetation of 'rock' plants.

Nearly 10 per cent of the working population of Switzerland are engaged in agriculture. In the high Alps forestry and dairying are the main agricultural occupations. Transhumance (*Sömmerung*) is still practised: the cattle are taken up the valleysides to the alpine pastures in summer and are brought down to the valley bottom to be stall-fed in winter. Bringing the milk down from great heights is both difficult and expensive. Many people have drifted away from these rural areas to seek work in industry, and in order to economise on the already scarce labour, milk pipelines have been laid, connected to dairies in the valleys below. A hay crop is hastily gathered from the mountainsides in autumn as the herds return to their winter quarters. Small crops of rye and potatoes are snatched in the short growing season in the Alps; but in the south, in Ticino, maize and tobacco are cultivated in the warm sunshine. Some of the inhabitants in the high Alps migrate to the Rhône valley to help with the grape harvest.

In the Jura Mountains in the north forestry and the rearing of cattle and horses are the principal agricultural pursuits. There is a little arable land and vines are tended in the warm south-facing slopes of the outer valleys.

It is the plateau, the Mittelland, that is the most intensively farmed and productive agricultural area, and the main dairying region. The climate and terrain favour the growth of lush grass, which is carefully sown and cherished. The café-au-lait coloured Swiss cows, so amiable to foreign visitors in late summer, are not allowed to munch at the pasture indiscriminately. They are stall-fed for most of the year and only allowed out in the field after the meadows have been mown in September. The growing season is short, cultivation intensive. The area devoted to cereals is diminishing as grain is increasingly imported; sugar beet and vegetables are grown and, where conditions permit, tobacco. The sunny slope of Lake Léman, the northwest of Lake Neuchâtel, and Ticino in the south all support vines. In the upper Rhône valley the hot dry summers permit the cultivation of strawberries, tomatoes, apricots and peaches for local town markets, but they have to compete with cheaper Italian imports which are available at the same time.

No space is wasted on hedges in the Mittelland, and the utmost use is made of every scrap of land which might support vegetation. Orchards (producing apples, pears, cherries, plums) line the roadsides, and where slopes are too steep for cultivation they are planted with conifers.

There is little large-scale farming in Switzerland, and nearly all the farms are small family units. Mechanisation is virtually impossible on the alpine slopes and even in Mittelland conditions do not encourage the use of large-scale machinery.

Industry. In addition to being the area predominant in agriculture, Mittelland is the home of most of the people, who live in scattered picturesque small towns and villages. Two-thirds of the towns with a population of over 10 000 are located in this area; and the population is enlarged by people who drift from the Alps to seek employment in a less demanding environment, as well as Italians (including Sicilians) and others from overpopulated Mediterranean lands. Some people live permanently in the high Alps, engaged in agriculture, or catering to the needs of tourists. In the Jura Mountains it is the valleys which are most densely populated, where industry has been established. The great economic value of the mountains, however, is that their streams and rivers are the source of Switzerland's abundant and all-important hydro-electric power supply upon which her industries depend. Because the supply of hydroelectric power is so widespread, industry in Switzerland is dispersed, unlike countries where industry developed on or near coal-fields.

In Mittelland the dairy industry, the processing of milk and cheese is important and widespread, and so is the making of chocolate, and of sugar from sugar beet. Greater Zürich (674 000) is the largest growing conurbation on the plateau, with new towns clustering round the old centre. It is a commercial, banking and university city, at the convergence of railways from south and east. Italian refugees in the sixteenth century inaugurated the silk industry, and the factories of Zürich have since progressed to the making of textile machinery, machine tools, and to metallurgy and heavy engineering, as well as cotton textiles, leather goods and chemicals. At St Gallen the production of cotton textiles and embroideries has developed from the old hand industries established with the help of French refugees in the eighteenth century. In the triangle formed by St Gallen, Luzern (textiles and metallurgy) and Basel there are many small textile-producing and engineering centres, including Winterthur. Basel (213 400 in the city, 373 000 in the conurbation), an engineering, textile, chemical and big commercial centre, is the chief town and second city of Switzerland. Its history as a route and defence town dates back to Roman times. It lies on the German frontier at the head of the plain of the middle Rhine, the focus of road, rail and air routes, a port where vessels of the Swiss merchant marine, created in 1941, are registered. Most important of all, Basel is the head of Rhine navigation. Forty per cent of Switzerland's trade is carried by the Rhine, imports exceeding exports. Basel receives oil by a branch line of the main oil pipeline from Marseille (Lavéra) to Strasbourg. Local industries include pharmaceuticals, dyestuffs for the textile industry, food processing, engineering, clock and watchmaking. Bern (city 162 400, 260 600 conurbation) is the Federal capital, a university, publishing and printing city, with manufactures of textiles and watches. To the southwest photographic equipment and typewriters are made in Yverdon; while Neuchâtel is a business centre where watches, clocks and jewellery are manufactured, as well as chocolate. Lausanne (city 138 000, 219 200 conurbation), a city with chocolate and brewing industries, is a favourite tourist centre. The cosmopolitan city of Genève (city 173 600, conurbation 321 000) at the western end of the plateau, is the centre of several international organisations. It has a situation of great beauty, where the River Rhône leaves Lake Léman, so is well placed in relation to Marseille. Its factories produce watches and clocks, jewellery, optical instruments, machine tools and textile machinery. Printing and publishing are other notable occupations.

The valley towns of the Jura have specialised in making clocks and watches since the beginning of the eighteenth century. Access to Basel and the Rhine is achieved by three tunnels (Botzberg, Upper and Lower Hauenstein) which link Basel to the Aare valley. Cement is made in Aarau and Otten. Bauxite is imported by rail up the Rhône valley from the south of France to Chippis in Valais, where use is made of hydro-electric power for its processing into alumina. The alumina is sent to Neuhausen, where it is transformed into aluminium.

In the Alps concentration is on tourism and on hydroelectric power schemes. There is another oil pipeline in the south, which brings oil from the Italian port of Savona to Aigle, in Valais.

The prosperity of Switzerland's manufacturing industries depends on the ready availability of hydroelectric power, the easy import of limited quantities of raw materials (particularly along the Rhine), a high degree of specialisation in producing precision goods of top quality, and a skilled, reliable labour force. Switzerland's skilled engineers and technicians are much in demand overseas, especially in the aircraft and electronic industries.

The Swiss excel too as restaurateurs and hôteliers, and catering for tourists plays a vital part in her economy. At the time of the 1965 census the working population totalled 2.9m. and of these over 152 000 Swiss nationals were employed in catering, assisted by innumerable immigrant helpers. Visitors are attracted not only by the glorious scenery but by excellent hotels and communications.

Communications. Great obstacles had to be surmounted to effect communication between the midland tracts and various parts of the more sparsely peopled regions, and also with the neighbouring countries in the east and south. Not till the nineteenth century was there any carriage road across the Alps, the first being that made by Napoleon across the Simplon in 1805 for the passage of his 'cannon' from the valley of the Upper Rhône to the banks of Lake Maggiore in Italy. Now Switzerland's efficient electrified rail system and good roads penetrate the Alps by tunnels as well as passes; and new roads are being built across Mittelland which already has access north to the Rhine, northeast to Germany, and southwest, via the Rhône, to the industrially developing Rhône—Saône valley.

The St Gotthard road, for long the most important of all on account of the direct communication which it establishes between the most populous parts of Italy (with Milano as the chief centre), Switzerland, and Germany, was largely superseded by the railway which pierces the St Gotthard group in a tunnel nearly 16 km (10 miles) in length (completed in 1882). By means of this railway the continental ports on the North Sea are brought to within a distance of three days for goods traffic from ports on the Mediterranean.

Till 1903 the St Gotthard was the only one of the great Alpine tunnels constructed within Swiss territory, but in that year a tunnel nearly 7 km (4.33 miles) long was opened under the Albula Pass, leading from Coire to the Engadine, and in 1906 another nearly 20 km (12.25 miles) long under the Simplon (Brig to Iselle); also a second Simplon tunnel, begun in 1912, was opened in 1921. The Simplon tunnel has much easier gradients in its approaches than either the St Gotthard or the Mont Cenis tunnel. The highest point is only about 700 m (2 300 ft) above sea level (325 m: 1 070 ft above Lake Léman — the Lake of Genève), while the summit of the St Gotthard tunnel is 1 155 m (3 785 ft) above sea level (715 m: 2 350 ft above Lake Lucerne). Via the Simplon the distance between Milano and Paris is 835 km (519 miles), as compared with 900 km (559 miles) by the St Gotthard route. The Simplon route to northern France is greatly shortened by the Lötschberg tunnel (1913), which pierces the Bernese Alps for 14.5 km (9 miles) and brings Berne directly on to the main route. Road tunnels under Mont Blanc (linking France with Genève) and the Great St Bernard Pass (linking Torino with Lausanne) were completed in 1964—65.

The lines of communication both within Switzerland and externally are so good that Antwerpen and Rotterdam, Le Havre, Marseille and Genova should all be considered as outports.

Overseas trade. Switzerland imports a little coal, increasing quantities of oil, food (including cereals and cocoa), textile yarns, chemicals, iron and steel, non-ferrous metals, fertilisers, machinery and transport equipment. Her main exports are textiles (especially silk, rayon and man-made fibres), embroideries, clocks and watches (which may in the future have to face competition from Japan), jewellery, scientific and

Table 47 – **Switzerland: population of chief towns (and conurbations)**
(1970 census)

Zürich	422 600 (675 100)	Lausanne	137 400 (219 200)
Basel	212 900 (373 400)	Winterthur	92 700 (105 600)
Genève	173 600 (321 100)	St Gallen	80 900
Bern (capital)	162 400 (259 200)	Luzern	69 900 (148 900)

precision instruments, dairy produce (including condensed milk and cheese), confectionary, chemicals (including medicinal and pharmaceutical products). Tourism is a major 'invisible export', but in addition Switzerland has substantial capital available for investment and loan overseas, and this, combined with her prosperous manufacturing industries, makes her economic situation very strong. West Germany provides most imports and takes most exports. Switzerland's other major trading partners are France, Italy, the United States and the United Kingdom.

Austria

After the break-up of the Austro–Hungarian Empire in the First World War, Austria survived as a separate republic till 1938, when it was absorbed by Germany and became part of the Third Reich. In the Second World War, Allied armies liberated the country by May 1945; the Republic was re-established under a National Assembly and divided into four occupation zones, administered by the USSR, the United States, the United Kingdom, and France, with the Allied Council in general control. Vienna was also split into four sectors. In May 1955, the occupying powers restored Austrian independence, agreed to withdraw their forces, and recognised the principle of Austrian neutrality similar to that of the Swiss.

Austria is a country of some 84 000 sq km (32 000 sq miles), slightly larger than Scotland, supporting a population of 7.5m. It is largely mountainous, being occupied in the south by the eastward extension of the Alps, but comprising to the north a section of the Danube basin, the Danube itself flowing across the country from west to east; and thirdly, north of the Danube, there is a region of hills along the Czechoslovak border.

The influence of physical features and of climate is reflected in the use of the land. Over 38 per cent is forested, whilst less than half (even including alpine pastures) is under agriculture. The area devoted to wheat (286 000 ha: 707 000 acres) is slowly declining, while the barley (274 000 ha: 677 000 acres) and rye (147 000: 364 000 acres) areas are slightly growing; but oats (102 000 ha: 252 000 acres) and potatoes (113 000 ha: 280 000 acres) are gradually diminishing. The statistics refer to 1969–70.

In the mountains the utmost use is made of the tiny fields perched high on the hillsides for the production of hay, which has to be cut by hand, and for feed crops for cattle, which numbered over 2.4m. in 1970. The emphasis is on the dairy industry; but forestry is important and the timber crop generally amounts to some 10.5m. cu m annually. The mountain streams have been harnessed to supply hydroelectric power. In the south, in the valley of the Drava which penetrates the mountains, there is an important area of fertile land round Klagenfurt, where cereals, fodder crops and pasture are carefully tended, and where fruit from the orchards and vineyards ripens in the warm summer sun. As in Switzerland, the Alps play an important part in tourism in Austria, especially for wintersports.

The Danube valley, like the Mittelland of Switzerland, may be said to be the most important area of the country and the most densely populated. Wheat, sugar beet, potatoes and other vegetables are grown, market gardening is a major activity, and vines produce good quality grapes on the hilly margins.

Much of the area north of the Danube has been cleared and is devoted to pasture and the growing of rye and potatoes, which do not object to the poor soil and rather bleak climate; but forests still remain, and vines grow on the hillsides in the east.

Farm units are small, but they are becoming increasingly mechanised. By careful farming methods, including the widespread use of fertilisers, maximum production is obtained, so that Austria is now almost self-sufficient in food.

The mountain belt yields the chief minerals: lignite, iron ore, lead, zinc, copper and manganese ores, graphite, and salt. Bituminous coal is almost non-existent, but lignite abounds among the more recent Tertiary rocks in the east of the Alps, and especially in the Styrian valley of Kainach, which opens from the west into that of the Mur below Graz; there is an annual production of some 3 to 4m. tons. The chief iron ore workings are in northern Styria, at Eisenerz (*Eisen*, iron; *Erz*, ore), on the north side of the Erzberg (Ore Mountain), and at Vordernberg, on the south side of the mountain. Here the Erzberg is almost one entire mass of an iron carbonate, and the ore, which has been mined for 2 000 years, is obtained from open quarries. More valuable kinds of iron ore (limonite and siderite) are obtained from the Hüttenberg Erzberg, in the northeast of the neighbouring province of Carinthia. In 1969 the production of iron ore was 3.9m. tons; of pig iron 2.8m. tons; of crude steel, nearly 4m. tons; rolled steel 2.76m. tons.

The working of iron and steel in all forms is chiefly carried on at two places, Steyr in Oberösterreich (Upper Austria), which is in direct railway communication, chiefly by way of the valley of the Enns, with Eisenerz; and Donawitz, close to Leoben, at the mouth of the valley leading from the Mur up to Vordernberg. Graz, in southern Steiermark (Styria), in a small extension of the Mur valley, and Klagenfurt, the nearest important town to the iron region of Kärnten (Carinthia), of which province it is the capital, both carry on iron works along with other industries.

Salt is abundant in the Salzkammergut, in the southwest of Upper Austria, at Hall in the northern Tirol (below Innsbruck), and at Hallein in Salzburg, above the town of Salzburg. Extensive deposits of china clay have been found halfway between Linz and Passau. Austrian graphite is noted for its fine quality, and is found in sufficient quantity to make Austria one of the chief sources of world supply. Before the Second World War, and up to 1944 production averaged 20 000 tons a year; then it almost stopped, but by 1964 had soared to over 102 000, to plummet again to only 26 000 in 1969. There are less important, but still valuable, deposits of antimony, gypsum and quartz. More important is the oilfield in the Zistersdorf area, near Vienna, with a rising production of oil and natural gas. These oil resources are known, however, to be limited, and Austria faces the need for increasing oil imports.

Nearly 23 per cent of the working population are engaged in agriculture, but nearly 47 per cent work in the manufacturing industries. There are five towns with a population exceeding 100 000 and the largest is Vienna, the capital, the one large city left to Austria at the division of the old empire. Before the First World War Vienna had a population of over 2m.; it is now 1.6m. Standing at the base of and partly upon the foothills of the Alps at the east end of the narrow valley through which the Danube flows after leaving West Germany, it is so situated as to cause all traffic between the Hungarian plain and southern Germany to converge on it; and the value of this position is enhanced by the comparatively easy routes to the Adriatic. One of the oldest trans-Alpine railways, completed in 1854, runs from Vienna south-southwest under the Semmering Pass to Bruck, from which one route leads to Venice, another to Trieste. Today Vienna is served not only by Austria's rail network, by by good roads, and an international airport. In December 1970 nearly 1 196 600 passenger cars and 121 000 lorries were registered.

The opulence of the Austro–Hungarian Empire is exemplified in the baroque architecture of this once most luxurious city. But it is more than a city attractive to tourists: it is a centre of commerce and of banking, where factories produce clothes, furniture, pianos, vehicles, textiles, glassware and high quality luxury goods of many types, including leather; and where there are engineering works. It is the dominant urbanised area of Austria. The other main cities, all equally attractive to tourists, also share in manufacturing. Graz (250 000) uses the iron ore and brown coal for its metallurgical industry, timber from the forests for its paper mills, and produces textiles. Linz (204 000) is a nodal bridge town on the Danube, below which the river flows swiftly to Vienna (the Danube is a rich source of hydroelectric power). Linz has heavy industry (using home-produced iron ore and coal imported from the Ruhr), as well as chemical works. There are also iron and steel works at Steiermark, Leoben and Bruck. Salzburg, associated with music festivals and music schools, is another famous tourist centre, as is Innsbruck, again a route centre, with communications to the Brenner Pass and the Engadine. A highway of outstanding historic and commercial importance linking Austria with Italy runs from Innsbruck to Verona via the Brenner Pass on the frontier between the two countries. This route was used in the ancient trade in Etruscan bronzes and earthenware and Baltic amber, and was selected by the Romans for one of their trans-Alpine roads. A carriage road was made across it in 1772, and a railway which crossed the pass instead of passing under it through a tunnel was completed in 1867.

The leading items in Austria's list of imports are chemical products, machinery (for construction and industry), electrical machinery, motor cars, coal, coke and briquettes; yarns and threads for textiles, and iron and steel share equal proportions. Her principal exports are iron and steel, machinery (for construction and industry), wood, electrical machinery, chemical products, paper and cardboard, and garments. There is also surplus hydroelectric power for export to Italy and West Germany. Tourism is the paramount invisible export. Most of her trade is carried on with West Germany and Italy, followed by Switzerland and the United Kingdom.

Her geographical location makes Austria very vulnerable, and like Switzerland she has established a state of neutrality, internationally agreed in December 1955, which allowed her to join EFTA but not the EEC. In recent years she has accepted refugees from eastern Europe, many of whom have settled and augmented the labour force. New industries are developing, and receipts from tourism are rising. As long as conditions in Europe remain politically stable it would seem that Austria could look hopefully to a prosperous future, her manufacturing industries based on home resources of raw materials and power, the import of limited quantities of raw materials and the expenditure of much labour.

Table 48 — Austria: population of main towns
(1968 estimate)

Vienna (capital)	1 642 000
Graz	253 000
Linz	206 000
Salzburg	120 000
Innsbruck	113 000

Czechoslovakia

The Republic of Czechoslovakia was established in 1918 from the former crownlands of Bohemia and Moravia, the greater part of Austrian Silesia, and the mountainous or hilly tract of northern Hungary. In 1938, as a result of the Munich Agreement, large areas were apportioned to Germany, Hungary and Poland. In the following year German forces occupied Bohemia and Moravia, and Hungary moved into Carpathian Ruthenia, leaving the self-declared State of Slovakia alone in central Europe. After the Second World War the pre-1938 frontiers of Czechoslovakia were restored, except in respect of Carpathian Ruthenia, which was transferred to the Soviet Union. Within the restored frontiers, the People's Democratic Republic was declared in 1948.

Agriculture. A long narrow country, nowhere more than 290 km (180 miles) wide Czechoslovakia has, after all these changes, an area of close on 130 000 sq km (50 000 sq miles), about the size of England; and a population officially estimated in 1971 at 14.6m. Much of the area is mountainous or hilly, but 40 per cent is classified as arable, over 13 per cent is pasture and permanent meadow, while over 35 per cent is clothed with forest. The forests are carefully managed and replanted when timber is felled. Before the Second World War over 3.2m. ha (over 8m. acres) of cropland were devoted to cereals, an area which has subsequently declined. Since 1948 the wheat area has slightly increased, so that the crop occupied 1m. ha (2.47m. acres) in 1970; the area of barley is also rising slightly and covered 800 000 ha (nearly 2m. acres); and that of oats is declining, so that only 375 000 ha (927 000 acres) were sown in 1970. The area of sugar beet in the same year was 181 000 ha (445 000 acres), of potatoes 338 000 ha (835 000 acres) both showing a decline since 1948.

Cattle are the mainstay of the livestock industry. The meadows and pastures, permanent and temporary, carry about 4.2m. cattle (1969—70) as well as 977 000 sheep, 318 000 goats and over 5m. pigs. Cows are reported to number over 4m. and the dairy industry is well developed. There are over 31m. head of poultry; but despite all this farming activity Czechoslovakia is far from being selfsupporting in food. Of cereals, wheat is imported.

The richest agricultural district is in the northwest, towards the north of the Czech plateau (Bohemia), drained by the Labe (Elbe) and its left-bank tributary, the Eger. Here are grown not only cereals but sugar beet, hops, the vine, tobacco, flax and hemp. Sugar beet is also largely cultivated in the valley of the Morava; and in 1970—71 over 750 000 tons of raw sugar was produced. There has not been a spectacular rise in agricultural production since 1950 because Czechoslovakian farming has long been efficient and productive. There has however been a concentration on industrial crops, particularly sugar beet, potatoes for distilling, hops and barley for brewing, flax for textiles. There is scope for greater mechanisation in the harvesting of sugar beet, a crop which otherwise requires much labour.

Minerals and power. The western part of the state is also the richest in minerals. The main deposits of coal lie to the west and south of Praha (Prague), those of lignite immediately to the south of the Erzgebirge (Ore Mountains). True coal is also mined in the Cieszyn (Tesin) district, adjoining Polish Silesia. Total output in 1971 was 29m. tons of bituminous coal, 85m. tons of brown coal and lignite. Output of iron ore, found near Praha, totalled 1.57m. tons.

To provide power for industrial plant today a good deal of Czechoslovakia's vast reserves of brown coal is used in thermal power stations. The uranium at Jáchymov, and many mountain streams, could provide power but have not yet been exploited, the former being under Soviet control. Hydroelectric power supplies only 15 per cent of electricity. In the main the stations are on the Váh River in Slovakia, on the River Vlatava above Praha at Slapy, and on the streams of the northern mountains. There are natural gas resources near the lignite deposits in the valley of the Morava River. Oil from the USSR is piped to Bratislava (272 000) a medieval fortress town, now an important river port on the Danube, which has oil refineries, chemical and food processing works. Other refineries are at Pardubice and Kolin.

Industry. Clearly Czechoslovakia has the natural endowment for a prosperous industrial economy with a good balance of agricultural and mineral resources. Bohemia and Moravia trace their industrial roots back to the nineteenth century when the fertile farmlands were densely populated and provided an excellent pool of labour for the iron works, which at first used water power, later lignite and coal. After 1918 the iron and steel industry, and mechanical industries continued to grow and Czechoslovakia became one of the most technically advanced industrial nations in Europe.

Most towns in Czechoslovakia lie in the foothills of the northern Erzgebirge (where they have grown from market towns or from mining settlements), in the foothills of the Sudeten Mountains, in the industrial region of Ostrava, in the Moravian plain, and in the mining area west of Praha. Praha, the capital, is a million city, an ancient settlement, a nodal town on the River Vltava, central in the Bohemian diamond. It has metallurgical and machinery works based on pig iron from the Kladno coalfield, produces locomotives and agricultural machinery and implements, and supports food processing factories, using imported as well as local produce, glass, textile and glove factories.

More progress has been made in heavy than in light industry. High quality steel is produced in the Bohemian works west of Praha, but the most important area is around Ostrava (262 000) where there is an integrated plant at Kuncice as well as steel and rolling mills in the locality. There is another new integrated plant at Kosice in Slovakia, based on local ore and fuel from Moravia. The chemical industry prospers along the valley of the Labe (Elbe) and makes use of river transport for heavy, bulky materials. It is based on brown coal and its products include fertilisers and synthetic fibres.

The old handicraft occupations of the mountain people in Bohemia have developed into the manufacture of goods of high value and little bulk: ceramics, glass (including optical glass), jewellery, textiles. The textile industry was originally based on local wool, flax and water power. Cotton from North America, imported via Hamburg, later became the main fibre, and remains so today, but it is provided by the USSR and by Egypt. The linen industry, using local supplies of flax but boosted by imports, also flourishes. A small crop of hemp supplies the relatively limited manufacture of hemp and jute fabrics and carpets. The high quality glass industry suffered the loss of skilled German workers after the Second World War. Glass and textile manufactures (wool and cotton) are being developed in the highlands of Slovakia, new ventures for this area. Mills using wool from local sheep are expanding, particularly in the valley of the Váh.

The spinning of wool is still carried on in Brno (335 000), despite the fact that the local sheep which used to supply the wool have been replaced by cattle. Brno, the second largest town in Czechoslovakia, grew up where the route from the capital across the Moravian heights met the northeast route across the plain to Silesia. A major industrial town, it manufactures tractors and processes foodstuffs.

Nearly all Czechoslovak towns have clothing factories and Gottwaldov has developed a rubber industry to supply its famous Bata boot and shoe factory, the largest in the world. Factories concerned with food-processing are generally located in the area of the growing crops: in north Bohemia (sugar-refining in the Labe and Ohre valleys), in Moravia and in the Danubian (Hungarian) plain. Plzen leads in breweries (but is also a centre of mechanical engineering), followed by České Budejovice and Praha. The timber of the mountain regions is used for building, furniture-making and the manufacture of cellulose and paper; and the establishment of new timber works is being especially encouraged in Slovakia.

Communications. The country has a good network of communications. Efficient rail transport, partly electrified, carries 90 per cent of freight; the road network has been developed largely since the Second World War. The Danube, Vltava and Labe carry a certain amount of freight. A proposal to cut a canal which would connect the Odra in Poland (near Kozle), through the Ostrava industrial region and the Moravian Gate to the River Morava and hence to the Danube has been discussed for a long time. It would greatly benefit heavy industry, for iron ore could be imported from Poland and coal could be exported from the Ostrava area via the Danube to Hungary and Romania.

The Adriatic ports of Yugoslavia provide Czechoslovakia with facilities for her foreign trade. Unfortunately the principal port, Hamburg on the North Sea coast (on the navigable Elbe (Labe in Czechoslovakia)) was lost to Czechoslovakia when Germany was divided after the Second World War. Hamburg passed to West Germany and as far as eastern European countries are concerned some of its former port functions are now undertaken by Rostock, in East Germany.

Trade. The pattern of Czechoslovakia's growing foreign trade is one of imports of foodstuffs and industrial raw materials, exports of manufactured goods. The imports of foodstuffs for consumption and for processing and the imports of raw materials of vegetable and animal origin have remained almost stationary since 1963; fuels, minerals and metals, chemicals and building materials show a slight rise, but the import of machinery and equipment and consumer goods a much greater increase. Of exports machinery and equipment shows the greatest growth, consumer goods the least. Most trading is with other Comecon countries, the USSR being in the lead; outside the group West Germany, the United Kingdom and Yugoslavia have a fair amount of trade with Czechoslovakia, who also conducts a worldwide trade on a very small scale.

Table 49 – Czechoslovakia: towns with population exceeding 70 000 in 1968

Praha (Prague)	1 034 000	Olomouc	78 000
Brno	335 000	Havirov	78 000
Bratislava	281 000	Karviná	74 000
Ostrava	272 000	Ceské Budejovice	73 000
Plzen	144 000	Usti nad Labem	73 000
Kosice	117 000	Liberec	71 000

Hungary

The total area of Hungary is a little over 93 000 sq km (36 000 sq miles) and the natural resources and geographical conditions which govern its development remain much the same as in the early part of the century; but the plans for using them have been revolutionised. The ancient kingdom, which nominally reverted to that character under a regency between the two world wars, has given place to the Hungarian People's Republic, with its policy of state ownership. Large estates were taken over and distributed as small holdings, now amalgamated in collective agriculture. By 1969 2 678 collectives farmed 5.9m. ha (14.6m. acres) of the total area of agricultural land (8.4m. ha: 20.7m. acres); state farms occupied 1m. ha (2.47m. acres) and 546 000 ha (1.35m. acres) remained in private hands. A five-year plan which came into operation in 1950 aimed at changing Hungary into an industrialised country in which agriculture would play an important but subordinate part. Under an agreement with the USSR for economic cooperation between the two countries several mixed companies were established to develop minerals, oil and gas, shipping and air transport.

With its small area and a population of some 10.3m. (1970) Hungary is a little larger than Ireland and twice as densely populated. Over 90 per cent of the population are Magyars. In 1946 a mutual exchange of their Slovak and Magyar populations was arranged between Hungary and its northern neighbour, Czechoslovakia, and the transfer was carried out during the following years. Many Germans were expelled. The Hungarian language is akin to Finnish or Estonian and quite unlike the tongues spoken in lands surrounding Hungary.

Hungary comprises the extensive plains of the middle Danube and its tributary, the Tisza. The Danube, flowing from the west, forms part of the northern boundary and then, turning south, bisects the country. The banks of the Danube as it crosses the plain are marshy or lined with thickets of willow, affording few sites for settlement; but in the north it cuts its way through low hills which provided a natural defence and a bridging point. Here, on firm ground overlooking the river, the capital, Budapest, grew up. Northwest of the hilly ridge is a small fertile plain devoted to grain, and fodder crops, with orchards in the foothills; the Little Alföld (lowland). The hill and plateau region of middle Hungary includes volcanic hills northeast of the Danube and the ridge of the Bakony Forest on the southwest. The southward-facing slopes favour vine cultivation, providing grapes for Tokay, the celebrated Hungarian wine. The large lake, Balaton, provides considerable quantities of fish as well as being an attraction to tourists. To the southeast the land is fertile: oats are grown on the hills, barley on the heavier soils; but this is a region with growing mining and manufacturing activities.

The Great Alföld. The third and largest region of Hungary is the plain, the Great Alföld, the *puszta* or Hungarian steppe country. Cut off from a moderating oceanic influence by mountains, it experiences extremes of continental conditions. The plain is now mostly under the plough, the rivers have been regulated, trees have been planted, especially *Robinia pseudacacia*, which prepared the way for other vegetation. The cattle which once grazed the plain are now stall-fed on collective farms;

and the new farming system has encouraged the increase of market gardening in order to feed the expanding urban population. Melons, sweet peppers and tobacco flourish. Pigs and geese abound. Maize and wheat are the most widely grown grains; rye is the crop of the less favoured sandy soils, and some oats are cultivated. The sandy area between the Danube and the Tisza, around Kecskemét, produces excellent peaches, apricots, grapes and other fruit. East of the Tisza land is being reclaimed for pasture and for potato production, and it supports a small amount of paddy. Sugar beet is a crop of the upper Tisza valleys, and sunflowers of the northeast.

Of the total area of Hungary 55 per cent is classified as arable, 14 per cent as permanent meadows and pasture, 16 per cent forest. Agriculture prospers, with rapidly growing mechanisation and improved husbandry.

Mineral resources and industries. On the whole Hungary's mineral resources are insufficient for the needs of her developing industries. Brown coal and lignite deposits in the northern hill and plateau region are briquetted to supply local power stations, engineering and chemical plant, especially at Tatabanya. Limestone and cement manufacture supply local building needs in the Budapest area. There are also small reserves of iron ore, non-ferrous metals, silver and kaolin in this northern region. Local oil is refined at Zalaegerszeg in the Bakony forest area, with a production of bitumen. Oil and natural gas are also exploited at several locations on the Great Alföld, especially in the central Danube valley, and oil is produced in the Zala area west of Lake Balaton. Despite all this output the supply of oil is inadequate, and oil is imported by the Friendship Pipeline from the USSR. It is fed to Hungary's largest refinery and power station at Szazhalombatta, south of Budapest. Natural gas is likewise imported, from Romania. Thermal stations supply power, but Hungary will benefit greatly when the projected hydroelectric power scheme at Vác on the Danube bend is finished.

Of other minerals the most important is bauxite, on the margin of the Bakony Forest, northeast of Lake Balaton. Aluminium is produced at Szekésfehérvar and the new town of Várpalota. Bituminous coal and natural gas occur at Pécs, a medieval town which has added food-processing and engineering industries to its traditional leather and timber manufacturing activities. In this region a new town has grown up at Komlo, timber is processed at Mohács, and textiles continue to be made at Kaposvar.

Even the Great Alföld is being industrialised. South of Budapest is the new iron and steel town of Dunaujváros, with its modern integrated plant dependent on imported raw materials: coal from Czechoslovakia and Poland, iron ore from the USSR. Smaller iron and steel works are located at Györ in the northwest and at Ozd in the northeast.

459

Budapest lies on both banks of the Danube: the old fortress town, Buda, is mainly residential, while Pest, on the east bank, has developed on flat land, suitable for the growing number of factories, where railways and roads converge. Transport equipment, heavy electrical equipment and manufactures based on the products of agriculture or designed to serve the needs of agriculture are made.

Where manufacturing industries have been established in the small towns of the Great Alföld they are on the whole based on local agricultural production, or on textiles, chemicals (for fertilisers) and agricultural equipment. Debrecen is a large centre specialising in the manufacture of precision and quality products. The industrialisation programme is more concerned with heavy than with light industry, food processing apart. At present 80 per cent of the iron ore and 75 per cent of the fuel have to be imported, much of it being transported by Danube barge. The Tisza is also navigable for a good length of its course in Hungary. The Adriatic ports of Yugoslavia handle much of Hungary's seaborne trade.

Exports. In 1969 about 25 per cent of Hungary's production was exported, the volume of trade having increased and the pattern considerably changed since 1949. With increasing urbanisation there is no longer such a large surplus of agricultural produce available for export; instead manufacturing industries contribute more to the economy than agriculture, providing goods for the home market and for export. In volume the export of manufactured goods now exceeds that of agricultural products, although cereals, fruit, wine, eggs and poultry continue to be exported to the USSR and to Czechoslovakia. Refrigerated vehicles are used for the transport of perishable commodities and a good deal is sent by air. Bauxite and alumina are important among exports. Of imports raw materials for industry are rising to meet the demands of Hungary's expanding industry. Most trading is with Comecon countries, especially the USSR, but trade with countries outside the group, such as Japan, shows growth.

Table 50 — Hungary: towns, with suburbs, with population
exceeding 100 000 in 1970

Greater Budapest	1 940 000
Miskolc	173 000
Debrecen	155 000
Pécs	145 000
Szeged	119 000

Yugoslavia

The Federal People's Republic of Yugoslavia came into existence in 1945, a few months after the close of the Second World War, and replaced the monarchy which had existed since the establishment of the state in 1918. It was a federation of six republics — Serbia (with the autonomous territories of Vojvodina and Kosovo-Metochia), Croatia, Slovenija, Bosnia and Herzegovina, Makedonija (Macedonia), and Montenegro. To these were added, by cession from Italy in the 1947 Peace Treaty, most of the Italian province of Venezia Giulia (the province comprising the Italian territories in the northeast corner of the Adriatic) and Zara. In the absence of agreement about Trieste, the Peace Treaty constituted a 'Free Territory' of 738 sq km (285 sq miles) around the port, and this Territory was divided into two zones: a Northern Zone of 223 sq km (86 sq miles) (pop. 300 000, mostly Italian) including Trieste, under British and US military control till 1954, when it was handed back to Italy; and a Southern Zone of 515 sq km (199 sq miles) (pop. 100 000, mostly Slovene), administered by Yugoslavia, whose position was confirmed by the 1954 settlement, which slightly adjusted the joint boundary in her favour.

The Constitution of 1963 changed the name of the country to the Socialist Federal Republic of Yugoslavia.

Covering 256 000 sq km (99 000 sq miles), with an estimated population of 20.6m. (1971), Yugoslavia is a little larger than the United Kingdom and supports about a third as many people. The Republic embraces kindred but not homogeneous races, and three languages are officially recognised: Serbo-Croat (which is generally spoken), Slovene, and Macedonian. Printing adds to the differences. In Serb and Macedonian, books and newspapers appear in Cyrillic characters slightly different from Russian and Bulgarian, while Croat and Slovene are in Latin characters.

Physical characteristics. In the northwest and west, Yugoslavia is mainly mountainous. The northwest is traversed by the southeastern ranges of the Alpine system, with an east—west trend; the west by the ranges of the Dinaric Alps, which trend from the northwest to the southeast. The chains of the Dinaric Alps are composed of limestones, including in places steep and rugged dolomitic summits; to the west, younger limestones form the region known as the karst or carso, an area presenting large expanses of naked grey rock with patches of soil of varying depth, generally thin, only in isolated hollows. In spite of the heavy rainfall, the karst region is without surface water, except where it emerges in springs from the base of characteristically fissured cliffs. These features extend into western Bosnia (central Yugoslavia), but the northeast of that province is composed of a gently undulating, fruitful, densely peopled hill country, sinking gradually to level plains traversed by the Danube and some of its large tributaries. The southeast of the country is mountainous, but with fertile valleys and basins.

Land use and agriculture. More than half the country (14.6m. ha: 38.3m. acres), is classed as arable and pasture land. Another third (8.8m. ha: 21.7m. acres), is covered with forests; and the remainder (about 2m. ha: 5m. acres), is made up of built-on areas, and waste land. The arable land (8.2m. ha: 20.3m. acres) is mostly devoted to cereals; wheat (1.8m. ha: 4.5m. acres) and maize (2.3m. ha: 5.7m. acres) alone account for half of it. Wheat produces a crop of 4.8m. tons in a good year, while maize, to which the climate is better suited, has a crop of 7.8m. tons. Rye, barley, and oats are grown on a much smaller scale. Potatoes, from 330 000 ha (815 000 acres) in 1970 produced a crop of 3m. tons – considerably more than before 1939. In general in the last fifteen years there have been notable developments in several important though secondary crops. The area under sugar beet is about 96 000 ha (237 000 acres). Sunflowers are grown for seed on 200 000 ha (494 000 acres); cotton was grown on 11 000 ha (27 000 acres) in 1970; tobacco occupied 54 000 ha (133 000 acres). Olives are a very variable crop, ranging in production since 1948 from 28 000 to 7 000 tons and yielding from 4 000 to 2 000 tons of oil. Fruit trees, especially plums, abound, especially in Serbia; and the vine is cultivated largely on slopes with a favourable exposure, chiefly in the northeast, on both sides of the Danube. Grapes must indeed be reckoned among the major crops of Yugoslavia; they are grown on over 100 000 ha (250 000 acres) and in good years production exceeds 1.5m. tons. Wine, especially a Reisling, is exported.

North of the Danube the loess-covered plains of the Vojvodina are in summer an almost unbroken expanse of maize and wheat. West of the Danube the surface, while still offering much arable land, rises towards Zagreb, and still further west (in Slovenija) arable land is found only in isolated basins, that of Ljubljana covering an area 40 km by 10 km (25 by 6 miles) being especially important.

Cattle totalled over 5m. in 1970, reared largely in Alpine districts; horses (over 1m.) chiefly in the Vojvodina; and pigs (over 5.5m.) in all the most populous parts of the country. Sheep (9m.) and goats (160 000) are most numerous in the karst region. The number of goats has been wisely steadily reduced since 1948. Their habit of indiscriminately devouring all within their reach was greatly damaging to vegetation especially to young trees.

Forests are most extensive in the Alps of Slovenija and in Bosnia. Dalmatia, the maritime tract of the country, has all the products of a Mediterranean region, with laurel thickets, groves of pines and cypresses, and the typical Mediterranean fruits and vegetables (especially olives, figs, grapes).

Minerals and industries. There is a wide range of scattered mineral deposits in this mainly mountainous country, and Yugoslavia is making good use of them in her progression from a predominantly agricultural to an industrial and manufacturing country. There is but little good quality coal, but a vast potential for hydroelectric power. The harnessing of the Danube in its turbulent course through the narrows of the Iron Gate, a joint venture with Romania, is a big step towards its exploitation. The amount of power to be produced annually is 11 000m. kW. Output of bituminous coal was 861 000 tons in 1969, but the large deposits of brown coal yielded nearly 30m. tons. Most are in Kosov (which also has chrome deposits), and are used partly for the production of electricity. Copper is mined at Bor (east Serbia) and at Majdanpek, output reaching 8.7m. tons in 1969. High grade iron ore is mined at Ljubija (north Bosnia) and at Vares (east Bosnia), lower grades at Tajmiste and Demi Hisar in Makedonija (total output in 1969: 2.7m. tons). There are useful deposits of lead and zinc ore to the south of Beograd and northwest of Ljubljana (3m. tons produced in 1969); salt (146 000 tons, 1969) in the northeast of Bosnia; and bauxite in Istria (output 2.1m. tons in 1969). Manganese, antimony, chrome, pyrites, and some gold and silver are also worked. There is a mercury mine at Idrija in Slovenija, regained from Italy in 1945. Oil deposits and natural gas in Slavonia and Vojvodina are insufficient for the needs of Yugoslavia's industries. Oil production in 1973 was 3.4m. tons.

Yugoslavia is pursuing a policy of industrialisation but there is not so much concentration on the development of heavy industry as exists in other countries with a centrally controlled economy. There is much assembly and processing and the chemical industry is producing plastics, pharmaceuticals, petrochemicals, synthetic fibres and detergents as well as the fertilisers required for the upgrading of agriculture, although engineering, including electrical engineering, and shipbuilding, engage a high proportion of the labour force. Industry is widely scattered, partly on account of its development in the old centres of handicrafts, isolated in the past by difficulties of communication, and partly on account of its growth near the widespread reserves of raw materials. Industry is now being directed to new areas sometimes for political or strategic reasons, sometimes, as in the south, to bring work to previously underdeveloped areas.

In the north where the Alps penetrate Slovenija, and the climate is continental, cattle-rearing on the pastures and timber-working are leading occupations. The former gave rise to leather manufacturing, still flourishing today together with another traditional industry: textile manufacture. These long-established enterprises have been joined by the iron and steel industry and by the manufacture of heavy machinery, especially electrical, notably in the main town, Ljubljana (258 000) and at the iron and steel centre of Maribor. This is the most prosperous area of Yugoslavia, long settled, with a good pool of trained labour, access to markets and good lines of communication. Further south the karst area bordering the Adriatic coast presents a barrier to communication between the coastlands and the interior, but with great difficulty a road has been engineered from Trieste in Italy to Cetinje in the south of Yugoslavia. New port facilities are being developed at Ploce to handle bulk cargoes of iron ore and coal; and Ploce will be linked by rail to Sarajevo to serve the industry of central Bosnia. From the port of Bar in Montenegro another railway is being laid to connect with Beograd. Rijeka is the main port, rapidly expanding with oil-refining and ship-building works, as is Split, the second port, with large cement works nearby. Volkswagen cars are assembled in Split under licence, and there are other engineering and chemical works at both ports. Aluminium is produced at Split, based on local deposits of bauxite and hydroelectric power from nearby rivers; and there are iron and steel works. The old market town of Mostar in the karst region supports a wide range of new industries: timber, food, cotton and tobacco processing, textiles and engineering. The new town of Titograd produces aluminium, and Niksic has steel industry.

East of the karst region Bosnia, which used to be a timber exporting area, now specialises in timber processing, the products including cellulose and paper. Brown coal and salt have given rise to iron and steel manufacturing, metallurgical and chemical industries in the Sarajevo basin. Sarajevo, with its advantageous central location, supports timber processing and engineering factories; and new industries are developing in the Sava valley, with the factory workers keeping small family farms in production on the fertile land.

To the northeast, between Beograd and Zagreb, the valleys merge into the most productive agricultural land, the Yugoslav sector of the Hungarian (Pannonian) plain. Oil underlies the area north and south of Sisak, which supports oil-refining and iron and steel industry. The main town, Zagreb, is spreading along the banks of the Sava, with heavy electrical engineering industry; and Beograd (Belgrade) the capital, a long-established fortress town at the convergence of river, road and rail, is now a growing commercial and industrial area, forming with satellite towns the largest conurbation in Yugoslavia, with engineering and electrical assembly plant, and major chemical and iron and steel industries. In the mountainous land south of Beograd Nis is a nodal centre, with engineering, textile and tobacco manufactures. The Skoplje region lies in the earthquake belt, but is being developed industrially with iron and steel, metallurgical, engineering, chemical, textile, food and tobacco industries. The vast deposits of brown coal underlying Kosovo-Polje are being exploited. The outlet port for the area is Thessaloniki in Greece.

Communications. In addition to the improvement in communications between the Adriatic coastlands and the interior a highway has been engineered from Ljubljana to the Greek border, taking advantage of the valleys of the Sava, Moravo and Vardar, and running through Zagreb, Brod, and Beograd; and roads across the mountains are being improved wherever possible. The Danube is in theory navigable through the whole of its Yugoslav course, if the difficulties of ice in winter, floods in spring and autumn and low water in late summer and early autumn are discounted. The Iron Gate hydroelectric project has eliminated a section of the rapids: the dam upstream above Orsova has provided smoother water in the upstream gorges.

Trade. Despite the industrial expansion, which includes the assembly of motor vehicles under licence at Kragujevac (Fiat), Koper (Citroen), Novo Mesto (BLMC), and Split (Volkswagen), to remedy the lack of home-produced vehicles, the Republic will need to import machinery and equipment for industry for some time. At the same time she will not doubt try to avoid the cost of importing food and fertilisers, both of which can be home-produced.

At present the value of the exports is about 80 to 85 per cent of the value of imports, the balance being redressed by tourism, which is particularly important in the Adriatic coastlands, and by the remittances sent home by the host of Yugoslavs working in West Germany, Austria, France and Sweden. The main exports comprise semifinished manufactures: food, alcoholic beverages and tobacco, machinery and transport equipment. The principal imports are machinery and transport equipment (growing); semifinished goods, raw materials (declining); chemicals (which may decline as home production increases); and a diminishing amount of food. The pattern is different from the position before the Second World War, when exports were mainly raw foodstuffs and the raw materials from the mines; processed products are now pre-eminent.

At present Yogoslavia has an adverse trade balance with west European countries, where her food exports come up against the barrier of the agricultural policy of the EEC, but a favourable balance with the Comecon group. Most trading is with West Germany, Italy and the USSR, some with the United States.

Table 51 — Yugoslavia: population of main towns (and conurbations), 1971 census

Beograd (capital)	770 140	(1 204 270)	Split	151 900 (184 000)
Zagreb	566 000	(602 050)	Novi Sad	141 700 (214 050)
Sarajevo	244 000	(292 250)	Rijeka	132 900 (160 630)
Skoplje	312 000	(387 900)	Maribor	97 200 (172 200)
Ljubljana	173 500	(257 650)		

Romania

The frontiers of Romania have undergone many changes during the present century. Established as a monarchy during the nineteenth century from the principalities of Wallachia and Moldavia, with the Dobruja added later, it was considerably enlarged at the end of the First World War by the addition of Bessarabia from Russia, the Bukovina from Austria, and Transylvania and other territories from Hungary. In 1940 the Soviet Union claimed Bessarabia and Northern Bukovina, an area of 50 505 sq km (19 500 sq miles), supporting a population of 3.5m. In the same year, Southern Dobruja (7 770 sq km: 3 000 sq miles) passed to Bulgaria, and 45 325 sq km (17 500 sq miles) of Transylvania to Hungary. As a result of the Second World War Romania recovered the territory yielded to Hungary, but not the territories yielded to Russia and Bulgaria. As delineated by the Peace Treaty of 1947, its frontiers enclose an area of over 237 500 sq km (91 700 sq miles) with a population in 1970, of 20.25m., so that its approximates in both size and population to its neighbour Yugoslavia.

In 1947 the monarchy was overthrown and the People's Republic of Romania proclaimed; under the constitution of 1965 it was renamed and became a Social Republic. The economy is centrally controlled.

Physical features. Physically the country is divided by a great arc of mountains. An arm of the Carpathians, coming from the north and striking south-southeast, links on to the Transylvanian Alps, which swing round to the west. These Alps, rising to over 2 450 m (8 000 ft), are composed mainly of ancient crystalline rocks with steep slopes, clothed with oak, beech and spruce, but the Carpathians are of softer rocks, largely denuded of forest and usually lower in elevation. Brasov (formerly Stalin) stands almost in the angle of the two arms. Within the arc is the Transylvanian Basin, hilly, and in parts over 915 m (3 000 ft) high, but with many broad valleys and cultivated plains between the forested and vineyard-covered slopes. Around this core of high land, Romania is composed mainly of plains, draining to the Danube (which forms most of the country's southern frontier), and to its leftbank tributaries, The Tisza and the Siretul. The climate is subject to extremes of heat and cold, with liability to summer droughts, making the crop yields rather variable.

Agriculture. More than half the country is classed as arable and pasture land (arable over 10.5m. ha: 25m. acres; pasture 4.4m. ha: nearly 11m. acres), and more than a quarter (6.3m. ha: 15.6m. acres) is forested. There remain nearly 2.5m. ha (6.2m. acres) which are unproductive — built-on areas, and waste land. The arable land is mostly under wheat (2.3m. ha: 5.7m. acres) and maize (3.2m. ha: 7.9m. acres). They are grown chiefly on the plains of Moldavia and Wallachia, in the east and south of Romania, especially on the large square fields of the collective farms which have replaced the small strip fields of the former individual holdings.

Next to maize and wheat, the most extensively grown crops are sunflowers, cotton, tobacco, soya beans and a wide variety of fruits (plums and grapes being important). Sugar beet, beans and pumpkins are added to production as the plain curves northwards. Inland from the Black Sea coast an area of high land in Dobruja has, with the aid of fertilisers and improved farming techniques, been coaxed into producing relatively low yields of wheat, flax and tobacco, and is ablaze with sunflowers at harvest time. Sheep graze the pastures of this region. On the western boundary of Romania the eastern margin of the Hungarian (Pannonian) plain, with its fertile soils, yields good crops of wheat, maize, sugar beet, tobacco and fodder crops, the latter to feed the numerous cattle. The rearing of pigs and geese is widespread. Total livestock in Romania in 1970 numbered 13.8m. sheep, over 5m. cattle, 2.2m. dairy cows, nearly 6m. pigs, and 686 000 horses.

Minerals and power resources. Paramount among the country's mineral resources is petroleum, the reserves being the largest in Europe outside the Soviet Union. The oil occurs in a belt varying between 30 and 65 km (18 and 40 miles) wide on the eastern margin of the Carpathians and forms part of the deposits which extend into south Poland. Ploieşti is the main centre, where oil has been tapped since the mid-nineteenth century; others are Argeş, Oltenia and Bacau. Refineries on the Bacau field as well as those at Braşov and Rîmnicu-Sarat are linked by pipeline to the ports of Giurgiu, Galati and Constanţa. About half the production of crude oil is exported.

Romania has vast natural gas resources also, in the Transylvanian Basin, enclosed within the arm of the Carpathians, comprising exceptionally pure methane. The gas is piped to Hungary as well as to Romanian towns along the frontier with Hungary; pipelines cross the Carpathians to Moldavia, and to Bucharest, the capital.

Brown coal and lignite resources are widespread, the southern Carpathians, which also provide some bituminous coking coal, being the most important area. In the foothills northwest of Bucharest brown coal and lignite are briquetted for thermal electricity generating stations. With these good fuel supplies Romania has not felt the need to develop hydroelectric power, although some small plants have been built in the Transylvanian Alps and in the southern foothills in the west and southwest; and a larger station on the Bistriţa River in the East Carpathians to serve an area which lacks other power resources. The most ambitious hydroelectric power project in Romania to date has been that, built in conjunction with Yugoslavia, of the great Danube scheme at the Iron Gate.

There are low grade iron ore and manganese resources in the west,

467

which have given rise to the iron and steel industries of Hunedoara and Reşita, although the latter is dependent on additional imported iron ore. There is chrome ore near the Iron Gate; bauxite from the Hungarian plain is processed at Oradea to provide alumina for the smelter at Slatine; and there are good salt reserves, especially at Slanic.

Industry and communications. In Romania's industrialisation programme the emphasis has been on heavy industry. The widespread and long-established textile manufacturing industry grows slowly from its roots in Transylvania where the availability of water power was once the governing locational factor. Industry has been sited in the Bacau area to bring work to an underdeveloped area: local supplies of oil and lignite have provided the raw materials for the thriving petrochemical industry. The Bucuresti area is also making good use of local supplies of raw materials, and supports engineering, machinery, food processing, oil refining, rubber manufacture and clothing industries.

The principal Danube ports, Braila and Galati, also support major industries. Separated by only 21 km (13 miles) they owe their close proximity to the fact that they were once rivals, one in Wallachia, the other in Moldavia. Both towns have chemical works, and timber processing for the production of cellulose and paper. Galati has a new integrated iron and steel works, at present using imported iron ore and coal brought in from the west, but this fuel may ultimately be superseded by oil or natural gas. The old market towns of the foothills house factories based on local raw materials, and produce fertilisers and chemicals, paper, and electrical manufactures.

Constanţa, the Romanian port on the Black Sea, serves also as an outlet for Czechoslovakia and Hungary. It has the usual port industries of shipbuilding, engineering and food processing, but textile manufacturing as well. The handling of the oil trade is accommodated by the manmade harbour. Constanţa has the advantage of being completely icefree, whereas the Danube ports suffer from the fact that the Danube freezes for some forty days in the year. Transport inland from Constanţa bypasses the lowest stretches of the river which are shallow and fringed with swamps: it passes along the Sulina channel through the delta to reach Galati and Braila where merchandise is transferred to barges for shipment upstream. Much of Romanian trade is seaborne, but imports are brought down by barge along the Danube from Czechoslovakia and Hungary to Giurgiu, which has a new road and rail bridge.

Efforts are being made to improve the communications network, especially those serving the capital, Bucharest, which is now connected across the Walachian plain with Craiova, an engineering and textile centre. A good road now links Oradea in Transylvania to Braşov to Bucharest to Constanţa.

The Danube constitutes an important line of communication from the sea along the southern borders of Romania and the northern borders of Bulgaria, and upwards into Yugoslavia, Hungary, Czechoslovakia, Austria, and southern Germany. Owing to its international importance, navigation on the river was for nearly a century regulated by a Commission of European Powers, which between the two world wars sponsored extensive improvements to the river channel. The Second World War brought a disputed situation. Previously the United Kingdom and France, with Romania, had played a prominent part in the Commission. At a conference in 1948 the Soviet representative introduced a convention restricting the rights of navigation and excluding the Wester Powers from the Commission. This was approved by a majority, composed of eastern European states, and traffic dwindled greatly. The Danubian states have since reached agreements regulating their own traffic.

Trade. There had been a marked change in the pattern of Romania's foreign trade since 1950. Exports of raw materials have declined, exports of manufactured goods and of industrial consumer goods have increased. At the same time there has been a significant decline in imports of the latter category; and a sharp rise in imports of machinery and equipment needed for the industrialisation plan. Imports of raw materials for industry, such as iron ore, coking coal and metallurgical coke from the USSR will probably continue to rise while Romania continues with the policy of concentration on heavy industry. Most trading is with the Soviet Union and other members of the Comecon group, although there is growing trade with West Germany, Italy, France and the United Kingdom.

Table 52 — Romania: towns with population exceeding 100 000 (1970)

Bucharest (capital)	1 475 000	Constanţa	172 470
Cluj	202 720	Ploieşti	163 000
Timişoara	192 600	Braila	151 650
Iaşi	183 800	Oradea	137 600
Braşov	182 100	Arad	137 200
Galati	179 200	Sibiu	120 000
Craiova	175 500		

Norway

Norway and Sweden, which were under one king from 1814 to 1905, are two separate kingdoms occupying the Scandinavian peninsula. Norway, the smaller of the two, comprises the western part of the peninsula — a stretch of country 1 770 km (1 100 miles) long and nowhere more than 400 km (250 miles) wide. With an area of nearly

324 000 sq km (125 250 sq miles), roughly equal to that of the British Isles, it supports a population of over 3.8m. Fjords and lakes account for nearly 15 550 sq km (6 000 sq miles) of the total.

The greater part of Scandinavia is made up of a high tableland furrowed by deep and narrow valleys, the highest parts lying towards the western side, particularly in the southwest of the peninsula in southern Norway, where the Jotunheim attains over 2 440 m (8 000 ft). This high plateau reaches the west coast, and is there cut into by the remarkably deep, steepsided inlets of the sea known as fjords, which give Norway its characteristic coastal scenery. Only at the heads of these fjords, and in a few of the deep inland valleys, notably those behind Oslofjord, is there any cultivable land. The high plateau top presents a desolate aspect, almost the only vegetation being that of a tundra, with heaths, mosses, and lichens. Even the latitudinal advantage of south Norway over the north is effectively cancelled out by the higher elevation. Below the barren plateau top and above the level of the forests are broad stretches of grassland, used as summer pasturage for the cattle kept in the valleys below.

Agriculture. Seventy-five per cent of the land area (23m. ha: 57m. acres) is classed as either waste or built-on, 27 per cent is covered with forest. Only just over 3 per cent (994 000 ha: 2.45m. acres) is available for farming. Nominally 843 000 ha (2m. acres) rank as arable land and only 151 000 ha (373 000 acres) as permanent meadows and pastures; but much of the arable land consists of temporary meadows.

Barley is the most widely grown cereal occupying 185 000 ha (458 000 acres) in 1970. Wheat has declined in importance since 1950 and is now sown on only 4 000 ha (9 880 acres); oats now cover only 57 000 ha (140 000 acres). The 445 500 ha (1.1m. acres) of hay produce a crop of some 2.5m. tons; and the 35 000 ha (87 000 acres) of potatoes usually yield about 800 000 tons annually. There were in 1970 nearly 980 000 cattle, 465 000 cows in milk, 1.8m. sheep, over 640 000 pigs, 85 000 goats and over 5m. head of poultry. Fur farming (mink, blue and silver fox) is increasingly popular and profitable. The north of Norway is very sparsely populated, and the scanty population along the coast are served only by sea. Inland the mountainous land is the home of the Lapps, whose herds of reindeer manage to subsist on the sparse natural vegetation.

Forests. The forests of Norway are a great source of wealth. Roughly three-quarters of the forested area is under pine and fir, timbers valuable on account of their hardness and durability: the short summers ensure that the annual rings are close together. Little is exported nowadays as timber, but vast amounts are consumed in the production of wood pulp and newsprint for export.

470

The rivers of Norway are too rapid and broken to be of much use for navigation. Most of them are short; the longest is the Glomma (565 km: 350 miles), entering Oslofjord, and there are about half a dozen others between 160 and 320 km (100 and 200 miles) long. Some of the larger valleys are used by railways linking the east and west sides of the peninsula, the most southerly being a line from Oslo to Bergen over the Hardangerfjeld, and the most northerly a line from Narvik, on the Ofotfjord, to the Swedish iron ore port of Lulea, near the head of the Baltic. The main function of the latter route is to carry ore from the Swedish mines to the sea during the winter months, when the Baltic ports are frozen up. The total railway mileage for the country is only 4 475 km (2 780 miles).

Hydroelectric power. To a country with no coal and as yet only potential oil resources in the North Sea, the rapid rivers and lofty waterfalls are of enormous value as a source of industrial power. At the beginning of 1960, hydroelectric power was being developed to the extent of 3.68m. kW, and this was only about one-fifth of the potential. The total production of electricity in 1968 (99.8 per cent hydroelectric) was 59 701m. kWh. The largest consumers are the electrochemical and electrometallurgical industries, engaged in electrical smelting (particularly of imported aluminium ores), the manufacture of calcium carbide and of ferrosilicon; and the production of nitrates from liquid nitrogen. Other large consumers are the pulp and paper industries. Electrification of the railways is going forward, and there are very few homes without electricity. Oil production reached 1.6m. tons in the early 1970s.

Minerals. The country's mineral wealth is not impressive in extent or amount. Chief of the ores mined are iron ore at Bodö, Mo, and Kirkenes on the Arctic coast, and pyrites. In 1969 the production of iron ore and titaniferrous concentrates was over 4.3m. tons; pyrites yielded 766 000 tons. Deposits of copper having a metal content of some 14 100 tons are mined annually at Röros, in the Glomma valley, and concentrates of zinc and lead, silver, and molybdenum are produced in smaller quantities. Granite and other stones are quarried for export.

Fishing and other industries. The limited resources of the land encourage Norwegians to turn to the sea. Per head of population Norway has the highest tonnage in the world, but the ships are engaged mostly in carrying goods for other nations, illustrating the lack of natural resources in Norway. Fishing is a leading industry. From the sheltered fjords and islands boats set out in the spring for cod fishing off the north coast and the Lofoten Islands. The chief cod fishing ports are Tromsö and Hammerfest, situated in the extreme north, but with harbours kept open all the year round by the warm waters of the North Atlantic Drift. Centres of the herring fisheries are further south: Bergen, Trondheim, and Stavanger. In addition to freezing at sea, the drying, salting and preparation of the fish is a major occupation in many of the ports, and the products comprise an important export. Brisling are caught off the southern shores and canned at Bergen and Stavanger. Altogether about 3m. tons of fish are landed annually, valued at some 1 000 kroner. Norwegian whalers used to play a leading part in whaling in the Antarctic, some factory ships being equipped to carry out the whole process of oil extraction and the preparation of bone meal and fertilisers from the refuse; but this activity has been curtailed by international agreement.

About 16 per cent of the population are engaged in agriculture, including market gardening and forestry, but over 55 per cent are engaged in mining, building and manufacturing industries. The abundance of hydroelectric power has led to the growth of industries specialising in goods of high value and low bulk which can be sited wherever convenient: near to transport routes, to a labour supply, to the source of power. The old-established industries are concerned chiefly with using timber, fish and dairy produce as raw materials, the pulp and paper works being located mainly in the south on the rivers and harbours. The newer manufacturing industries have grown up in the lowlands round Oslo and the area bordering the Skaggerak. The electro-smelting and electrochemical works lie on the banks of the Glomma River, and it is at Glomfjord that the electrochemical industry is particularly concerned with the extraction of nitrogen from the air for the manufacture of fertilisers, calcium nitrate, nitric acid and other derivatives of nitrogen, including explosives. Along the Atlantic seaboard Stavanger has fish canneries, dealing especially with brisling, while Bergen, the centre of the textile industry, is the main fishing and ship-yard port. At Mo in Nordland the local iron ore feeds the iron and steel plant. Narvik, with about 12 000 inhabitants, is the outlet port for Swedish iron ore mined at Norrbotten, to which it is connected by rail. Oslo, the capital, had the greatest proportion of the 3.9m. people living in Norway in 1970: it housed 481 000 people. It owes its importance to its situation in the principal area of lowland where valleys converge and to its command of the Glomma route leading to Trondheim, the ancient cultural centre, which lies in the district of the best farmland on the Atlantic coast. It also has the benefit of a rail link with the more closely populated part of Sweden, the south. Only two other settlements have populations exceeding 100 000: Bergen (113 000) and Trondheim (128 000).

Trade. Since the end of the Second World War Norway has greatly increased her output and export of manufactures, but exports represented on average only 70 per cent of imports in value in 1967—69; in the future oil should redress the balance. The main exports include pulp and paper, food products, base metals and manufactured metal goods, machinery and transport equipment (especially ships). Imports cover a wide range: machinery, transport equipment (especially ships and boats), chemicals, petroleum and crude oil, food products, and a variety of manufactured goods. Norway became a member of the European Free Trade Association, and signed the Treaty of Accession to the European Economic Community in 1972. At present most of her trade is carried on with West Germany, Sweden (who supply most of the imports), the United Kingdom, the United States, and Denmark.

Table 53 — Norway: population of main towns (1971)

Oslo (capital)	481 200
Trondheim	127 700
Bergen	113 500
Stavanger	82 080

Outlying territories. **Svalbard** is Norway's name for her Arctic dependency, comprising the Spitsbergen Archipelago and many other small islands lying between 74° and 81° N and 10° and 35° E. The total land area is 62 000 sq km (24 000 sq miles). Though the climate is modified by the Gulf Stream and the southwest coasts can be approached from the sea throughout the year, the islands are covered with glaciers and snow and agriculturally the whole area is classed as waste. In past centuries a centre for whaling, the Archipelago became significant when coal was discovered early in the twentieth century. The islands were assigned to Norway by the League of Nations in 1920 and occupied in 1925. During the Second World War the mines were dismantled and the mining camps evacuated, but they were reoccupied after the war.

There are six permanent mining establishments, three Norwegian and three Soviet; the number of Norwegian workers is about 1 000, of Soviet citizens about 2 000. The coal includes both steam coal and house coal, and nearly 700 000 tons of coal are exported annually. Other minerals known to exist are magnetite and other iron ores, copper, lead, bituminous shales, and coloured marbles; but they are not widely worked. Prospecting for oil is in progress. Seals, foxes, and polar bears are hunted. The islands house meteorological and radio stations as well as a telemetry station which supplies satellite data to the European Space Research Organisation; and a permanent research station was inaugurated at Ny-Ålesund in 1968.

Jan Mayen Island, about 480 km (300 miles) north-northeast of Iceland, has an area of 380 sq km (147 sq miles) and rises to over 2 280 m (7 500 ft). Norway set up a meteorological station in 1921 and annexed the island in 1929. It is visited from time to time by fishermen, whalers, and seal hunters.

Sweden

The kingdom of Sweden covers the eastern and larger part of the Scandinavian peninsula, which it shares with Norway. It has a total area of 448 000 sq km (173 000 sq miles), of which the great lakes in the south such as Vänern and Vättern and other inland waterways account for 39 000 sq km (15 000 sq miles). The country, though rising to over 1 800 m (6 000 ft) in places, is generally less rugged and broken than the Norwegian landscape. From the crests near the frontier, the slopes towards the Baltic Sea are long and gradual, terminating in broad coastal plains crossed by many swift-flowing parallel rivers; the fjord type of coastline, so typical of the Norwegian shores of the peninsula, is completely lacking in Sweden.

Land use and agriculture. In the southern part of the country the mountains give way to low-lying fertile land, where the great manufacturing regions and the country's best farming land are found. Agricultural conditions are at their best in Scania, the extreme southern peninsula of Sweden, where soils and general economy are very similar to those of Denmark. On this comparatively small area, which is the most densely peopled part of the country, grain and sugar beet are grown and herds of dairy cattle, pigs and poultry are kept.

Though nearly twice the size of Great Britain, Sweden supported in 1970 only some 8m. people, one-seventh of Britain's population. Wasteland and built-on areas, account for some 40 per cent of the whole country, and 50 per cent is under forest, one of the main sources of wealth in the country. There remains less than 10 per cent (3.4m. ha: 8.5m. acres) which is productive land agriculturally. This is officially divided into arable (3m. ha: 7.5m. acres) and permanent meadows and pastures (394 000 ha: 973 000 acres); but much of the arable consists of temporary meadows. Livestock are less numerous than might be expected: in 1970 cattle numbered only 2m., considerably fewer than in either the Netherlands or Denmark, both with far less pastoral country. There were 816 000 cows in milk. Sheep were 350 000 (compare Norway's 1.8m.). There were 2.1m. pigs, and 66 000 horses. Great crops of hay are harvested. A considerable area of meadowland is devoted to this use, and in a good year the crop exceeds 3.5m. tons.

Nearly half of the arable land is devoted to cereals. Barley is the most popular, occupying 587 000 ha (1.4m. acres), followed by oats (489 000 ha: 1.2m. acres), wheat (263 000 ha: 650 000 acres), rye (77 000 ha: 190 000 acres), and mixed grain (69 000 ha: 170 000 acres). Sweden is one of the few countries in the world growing mixed grain on a large scale. Heavier crops than any but hay are potatoes (1.5m. tons from 59 000 ha: 146 000 acres) and sugar beet (1.47m. tons from 40 000 ha: 99 000 acres).

Fisheries are only a minor industry. Since the herring migrated from the Baltic, the catch has declined greatly, the chief fishing grounds being now on the other side of Sweden, off the coasts north of Göteborg. In 1969 the catch in these waters was valued at 204m. kroner.

Minerals and power. Mining has always been one of the leading industries. Sweden has valuable mineral resources especially of iron ore which occurs in two major localities: in the far north (Swedish Lapland), and to the northwest of Stockholm. The northern deposits, some of the most important and most easily worked deposits of iron ore in Europe, are mined at Gällivare–Malmberget and, about 95 km (60 miles) further north, Kiruna. They all contain a high percentage of iron, mostly over 60 per cent, in some cases 68 or 69 per cent, but while some contain as little as 0.05 per cent phosphorus, the phosphorus content is generally high, from 0.6 to 3.5 per cent. During the summer months these ores are exported from the Swedish port of Luleå at the head of the Gulf of Bothnia; but in winter, when this outlet is frozen up, the ores are carried by one of the most northerly railways in the world to the Norwegian port of Narvik, which is open all the year round.

Phosphoric iron ores are also produced in great quantities in south-central Sweden, south of the Vester (West) Dal River, where Grängesberg, about 225 km (140 miles) northwest of Stockholm, is the centre of a district containing more than 500 mines. The historic seat of the mineral industries of Sweden is further east, on both sides of the lower Dal, which flows into the southern end of the Gulf of Bothnia near Gävle. To the southeast of Gävle, about 110 km (70 miles) north of Stockholm, are the well known magnetic mines of Dannemora. In this district there is an abundance of iron ore low in phosphorus content, and suited for the manufacture of first-class steel. In 1971, iron ore mined in Sweden totalled 21.6m. tons, of which 19.7m. tons were exported.

Coal is mined on a very small scale: under 22 000 tons a year. More important are copper (112 200 tons in 1969), mined since medieval times around Falun, 30 km (20 miles) east of the confluence of the East and West Dal; zinc (160 700 tons in 1969); lead (107 800 tons) and manganese (8 800 tons). Some arsenic, gold and sulphur pyrites are also worked. Large quantities of paving stone are produced from Swedish quarries. The shales in southern Sweden, containing oil and uranium, are not at present worked, nor are the ores basic to the aluminium industry.

The production of electricity from water power is of prime importance to Swedish industrial development, there being no oil and very little coal in the country. In 1971 the production was over 66 000m. kWh, 72 per cent of it hydroelectric. Nearly all the economically exploitable water power is now harnessed, and Sweden is turning attention to nuclear power stations.

Industry. Based on iron smelting and associated metallurgical processes, Sweden has developed industries producing machinery and equipment of a highly specialised nature. Some of these products are the result, directly or indirectly, of Swedish inventions such as cream separators, ball bearings, and lighthouse lanterns. Various types of electrical machinery are also produced. A porcelain and glass industry turns out products of high reputation.

Sweden's great timber resources have given rise to industries based on this raw material with the growing availability of electric power. Sawn and planed timber, plywood, wood pulp, newsprint and other forms of paper, and minor products, including matches, comprise some 15 per cent of the total value of manufacturing, and supply not only the home market but provide valuable exports.

The manufacturing towns of Sweden are situated in the southern part of the country, particularly in the trough containing lakes Vänern and Vättern (Mälaren) and the many associated smaller lakes. Stockholm, the capital city, a cultural, industrial and commercial centre, grew up on and around a small island in the narrow channel which connects Lake Vättern with the Baltic: a crossing place for road and rail on the east coast route. It has much light industry, such as stone, glass, cement and brick manufactures, and printing, and is connected across the lowland to the icefree port of Göteborg. Stockhom itself is hampered by ice in winter. The Göta Canal uses the lakes in its east-west traverse of Sweden. From Göteborg on the Skaggerak to Stockholm on the Baltic is 558 km (347 miles) of which only 90 km (56 miles) is actually canal, interrupted by sixty-five locks. Göteborg, at the mouth of the Göta River, is Sweden's principal port, open all the year round. Norrköping on the Baltic coast has textile industries, notably woollens. Jönköping, at the southern end of Lake Vättern, is the centre of the Swedish match industry. Eskilstuna, behind Stockholm, has hardware and cutlery industries which have earned it comparison with Sheffield. Facing Köbenhavn in Denmark, across the Sound, is Malmö, which handles much of the local dairy produce as well as specialising in the making of transport equipment, leather and rubber goods. Other leading ports include Gävle on the Baltic, Hälsingborg, and Halmstad. Around Karlstad and Gävle and in the area between there are iron and steel works as well as engineering factories.

Living standards. It is estimated that over 77 per cent of the population live in towns. Habitation of the country districts ranges from the thickly peopled farmlands of Scania to the sparsely settled northern regions, with their brief summers and long cold winters. The Lapp people who inhabit these northern regions subsist mainly by fishing and by their herds of reindeer, which supply them with meat, milk, and skins for clothing.

Sweden enjoys one of the highest standards of living in the world. Measured statistically by the gross national product, number of car owners, telephones and so on, and by the value of real wages (that is wages in relation to consumer prices) the Swedish people have the highest standard of living in Europe.

Trade. Sweden's entry among the exporters of manufactured goods is relatively recent, if the products of her timber industry are excluded: it was in the First World War that she began to export more manufactured goods than were imported. The main exports now are still forest products, but include machinery (especially electrical and electronic), instruments, base metals and their products, transport equipment and iron ore, dairy produce and food, including processed food, illustrating the diversification of industry at which Sweden now aims. Main imports are machinery and instruments, crude oil and petroleum, agricultural and food products, chemicals, base metals and metal manufactures, textiles and clothes and a host of small manufactured articles in small quantities. Most trading is carried on with the United Kingdom, West Germany, the United States, Norway, the Netherlands, Denmark and France; in general Sweden trades a little more with the countries of the European Free Trade Association, as a group, than with those of the European Economic Community, as a group.

Table 54 – Sweden: towns with population exceeding 55 000 in 1970

Stockholm (capital – conurbation)	1 300 000	Södertälje	76 000
Göteborg (conurbation)	640 000	Borås	74 600
Malmö (with Lund and Trelleborg)		Karlstad	72 500
(conurbation)	421 000	Sundsvall	65 000
Uppsala	127 500	Skellefteå	62 000
Västeras	116 700	Ornsköldsvik	60 500
Norrköping	115 800	Växjö	59 000
Örebro	115 700	Luleå	59 000
Jönköping	107 800	Umeå	56 200
Linköping	104 700	Lund	56 000
Hälsingborg	100 600	Solna	55 600
Eskilstuna	94 000	Kristianstad	55 400
Gävle	84 600		

Sweden maintains a strict armed neutrality which has not however been internationally confirmed or guaranteed. As a country dependent on foreign trade she is naturally in favour of free trade and has played an active part in the General Agreement on Tariffs and Trade (GATT). Since the Organisation for European Economic Cooperation came into being in 1947–48 Sweden has pressed the case for a European free trade area without political commitments, in line with her own desire for neutrality. With this political aspect in mind it was inevitable that Sweden should join EFTA rather than the EEC.

Denmark

Denmark is a kingdom comprising primarily the greater part (northern two-thirds) of the peninsula of Jylland (Jutland), which thrusts from the north coast of West Germany towards Norway and Sweden, together with some 500 islands lying between Jylland and the west coast of Sweden. The islands have an area of over 13 000 sq km (5 000 sq miles) and Danish Jutland (in which northern Slesvig was reincorporated after the First World War) contains over 28 000 sq km (11 000 sq miles); so that Denmark as a whole (43 069 sq km: 16 629 sq miles) is about half the size of Ireland. It is more densely populated, Denmark having a population of 4 950 048 in 1971.

Though only about 100 of the islands are inhabited, they carry a larger population than the mainland territory, and, commercially, the sea is less of a dividing factor than might be thought. Comparatively narrow channels separate the two largest islands, Sjelland (Zealand) and Fyn (Funen) from one another and from the mainland on either side. A road and rail bridge under 3 km (2 miles) long connects Jylland with Fyn. The Store Baelt (Great Belt) between Fyn and Sjelland, 14 km (9 miles) wide at its narrowest is crossed by train ferry. Two train ferries connect the east coast of Sjelland with Sweden across the Sound, one from Köbenhavn to Malmö (25 km: 16 miles), the other from Helsingör to Hälsingborg, where the Sound is only about 5 km (3 miles) across. Road and rail bridges also link Sjelland with Falster Island and Falster with the island of Lolland; and there was a train ferry service between Falster and Grossenbrode, in West Germany.

Agriculture and fishing. These transport facilities have been an essential part of the policy on which Denmark embarked in the nineteenth century. Faced with a growing population she began an intensive development of her agricultural resources, and of dairy farming in particular. Farms are small, the law forbidding amalgamation of small properties into large estates; grass crops for the livestock are included in the crop rotations and grazed straight off the fields. Farming communities are highly organised on cooperative lines, while marketing schemes

478

ensure that all produce is sold. The result is a country with a large surplus of foodstuffs for export, of a quality whose reputation is known throughout the world and jealously guarded.

Physically Denmark is well suited to this agricultural development: soils over a large part of the country are of glacial origin and fertile; the climate is mild, with a good rainfall; the highest elevation is 172 m (564 ft). Western Jylland is bounded by sand dunes and shallow lagoons, and inland the surface tends to be marshy and infertile, but even here planting of grasses and drainage have aided reclamation. According to the latest returns of the United Nations Food and Agricultural Organisation, about 844 000 ha (2m. acres) (20 per cent) of the total land area is classed as waste or built on, while forested land accounts for another 472 000 ha (1.16m. acres) (11 per cent); but there remain practically three-quarters of the whole (2.9m. ha: 7m. acres) available for farming. Of this area only 10 per cent is classed as permanent pastures, the rest being arable land or land under tree crops. By far the most extensive crops are cereals (over 1.7m. ha: 4.2m. acres), chiefly barley (approaching 5m. tons from over 1.3m. ha: 3.2m. acres in 1970). Oats, mixed grain, rye and wheat occupy very much smaller areas, but give high yields. Noteworthy also, especially in its bearing on the dairying industry, is the scale on which root crops are grown. Apart from potatoes, averaging a total crop of 900 000 tons from 39 000 ha (96 000 acres), root crops are grown on nearly 280 000 ha (690 000 acres) and yield over 12m. tons. They include 2m. tons of sugar beet from 52 000 ha (128 000 acres), yielding 308 000 tons of raw sugar, as well as much larger quantities of residue material, of great value as a fertiliser and cattle food.

Livestock in 1970 included over 2.8m. cattle, 1.2m. dairy cows, over 8m. pigs, 87 000 sheep and 40 000 horses.

Taken as a whole Danish farming is probably the most progressive and technically advanced in the world at the present time. A slowly diminishing labour force (14 per cent of the total population of about 5m., or 15 per cent of the labour force) maintains an increasing production from highly mechanised farms. Nearly all the farmers are owner—occupiers and although there were in 1967 4 792 farms with an area of 60 ha (150 acres) or more, most are small farms (97 976 have between 10 and 60 ha 25 to 150 acres; 56 531 have under 10 ha: 25 acres). Tentative steps have been taken to amalgamate some of the small holdings to form larger, more economic units.

Denmark is a leading sea-faring nation, with an active fishing fleet operating particularly in the North Sea, the Skaggerak and the Kattegat, the herring, plaice and cod being landed at the main fishing ports: Esbjerg, Skagen, Hirtshals and Thyboron. There is fish farming in the shallow Limfjorden, where plaice especially are hatched and reared. Fresh fish and fish products are exported.

Industry. There are small reserves of brown coal and peat, but Denmark lacks resources of coal, water power, iron ore and other metallic minerals. Where the underlying rocks penetrate the glacial drift of the surface, chalk and lime are accessible, and the granite rocks of the island of Bornholm yield china clay for the famous Köbenhavn porcelain.

With an abundance of electric power imported by cable from Sweden, Denmark makes industrial use of all the raw materials she possesses: agricultural produce, fish, china clay and chalk, timber. Iron ore is imported for the flourishing iron and steel industry, which specialises in the production of agricultural machines and the machinery required in transport, refrigeration and processing of food products. There is much activity in the making of alcoholic beverages, processing of tobacco; and in furniture, textile and clothing, fine porcelain, chemicals, electrical and electronic components, plastics and pharmaceuticals, paper and cement manufactures.

Forty per cent of industry, measured in manpower, is concentrated in the area of the capital and chief port, Köbenhavn, which lies in a dominating position on Sjaelland at the gateway to the Baltic. Odense, the port on the island of Fyn, is a shipbuilding centre, making the diesel engines for ships for which Denmark is world-famous. Esbjerg, the only important harbour on the west coast, is the chief port for the Danish export trade to Britain, and the terminus of a regular steamship service to and from Harwich.

Trade. The Danes have been notably adept at changing their exports to meet market demands. In the 1920s exports of agricultural produce represented 80 per cent of total exports, industrial products 20 per cent. By the 1970s agricultural produce accounted for under 40 per cent of the whole, industrial products over 60 per cent; and these trends continue at an increasing speed. With overproduction of dairy produce in Europe it is probable that Danish agriculture in the future will concentrate on stock-rearing, with an outlet for her meat and meat products in West Germany and Italy; but it is her industrial exports, which include chemicals, textiles and clothing, machinery and instruments and a host of small manufactured goods of high quality, which are more important now to her economy. Imports, which exceed exports in value, are in the main raw materials for industry and food-stuffs and fertilisers for agriculture: refined and crude oil, chemicals, iron and steel, machinery and transport equipment. Most trading is with West Germany, Sweden, the UK, the USA, Norway, Italy and other EEC countries. In the years 1965–67 70 per cent of the agricultural production was destined for the United Kingdom.

It has always been the policy of Denmark to support free trade, which led her to join the European Free Trade Association and not the

European Economic Community. In 1972 however she signed the Treaty of Accession to the EEC.

Table 55 — Denmark: towns with population exceeding 40 000 in 1971

Kobenhavn (Copenhagen)	1 378 000	Aalborg	100 000
Aarhus	188 000	Esbjerg	56 000
Odense	133 000	Randers	43 000

Outlying territories. The **Faeroes** (Old Norse, *Faer-öer*, Sheep Islands), a group of islands between Scotland and Iceland, are equal in size to the Shetlands. Area, 1 399 sq km (540 sq miles), with heights up to 650 m (2 800 ft); population (1970) 38 527. Capital, Thorshaven. The climate is mild, and potatoes and turnips normally do well, but barley, which is also grown, does not always ripen. Sheep farming and fishing (with formerly whaling) are the mainstay of the islanders. Fish, fresh, frozen, salted and dried, are the chief exports; also exported are sheepskins, wool and hosiery. By popular vote, the islands remain linked with Denmark, but have enjoyed a measure of home rule since 1948. They joined EFTA in 1968.

Greenland. See under North America (p. 759).

Iceland

For over 500 years, from 1381 to 1918, Iceland formed part of the Danish kingdom. In 1918 it was declared an independent state, sharing the same king as Denmark, but formulating its own internal policy. In 1944, as a result of a plebiscite, the island finally severed all ties with Denmark and was declared a republic.

Iceland lies immediately south of the Arctic Circle, which it touches at the tip of its north coast. With an area of 103 000 sq km (40 000 sq miles), the island is larger by one-quarter than the whole of Ireland; its population was over 204 000 in 1970. Nearly 60 per cent live in the area of the capital, Reykjavik. It is a volcanic island. About one-fifth of the surface is classed as productive land, mainly in the form of permanent meadows and grazing grounds near the coast and along the lower courses of the rivers. The rest is a waste of high plateaux and mountains, rising in the southeast to over 2 100 m (7 000 ft) and partly covered by great ice sheets, the largest of which is the Vatna Jökull. Active volcanoes include the famous Mount Hecla (1 525 m: 5 000 ft), and geysers and hot lakes are characteristic features. The waters of the hot springs are used for domestic and greenhouse heating and for swimming pools.

Some of the volcanic soils are very fertile, but the land cultivated is

481

under 2.3m. ha (5.4m. acres). About 330 000 tons of hay, cultivated and uncultivated, are harvested; 5 500 tons of potatoes, and some 500 tons of turnips. Livestock include 780 000 sheep, 53 000 cattle and about 34 000 horses.

The warm waters of the North Atlantic Drift keep the southern coast free from ice in most winters; and where these warm waters meet the cold from the Arctic an ideal spawning ground for cod and herring is created. Fish and fish products are the mainstay of Iceland's economy and lead her jealously to guard, and if possible to extend, her exclusive fishing rights, at present (1972) fixed at 20 km (12 miles) from Icelandic shores.

Fishing is the island's principal industry, although there is small-scale production of textiles and leather. The full potential of hydroelectric power has not yet been exploited.

The chief port and capital of the republic is Reykjavik, with a population of 81 500 (1970). It has an airport with regular services at home and abroad. There are no railways.

Fish, fish meal, fish oil and sheepskins are the chief exports; petroleum and its products, animal feed, cereals, fishing nets, motor vehicles and wood the major imports. Most manufactured goods have to be imported, and imports much exceed exports. Most trading is with the USA and the United Kingdom, followed by West Germany and Denmark.

Finland

The Second World War, in which Finland fought against the Soviet Union, led to revolutionary changes in her agrarian and industrial economy. Defeated in the war, she had to cede to the USSR a large tract in the southeast, made up of Finnish Karelia with the north and west shores of Ladozhskoya Ozero (Lake Ladoga); part of the north coast of the Gulf of Finland, including the port of Vyborg, and the strip of territory linking her on the northeast with the Arctic Ocean, including the icefree port of Pechenga (Petsamo). Finally, Finland had to lease to the USSR for use as a military base a headland (Porkkala) within artillery range of the Finnish capital Helsinki (Helsingfors), and commanding the entrance to the Gulf of Finland. The USSR renounced its rights to the naval base at Porkkala—Udd in 1955, and by the end of January 1956 had withdrawn its forces from Finnish territory.

The cessions cost Finland nearly 52 000 sq km (20 000 sq miles) of territory, but left her with 337 000 sq km (130 sq miles), including the Ahvenanmaa (Åland Islands; 1 481 sq km (570 sq miles) population 21 600), which are of international importance because of their position in the mouth of the Gulf of Bothnia, between Finland and Sweden. The mainland territory, larger than the whole of the British

sles, but supporting only 4.7m. people, lies between the Gulf of
Finland on the south and the Gulf of Bothnia on the west, and reaches
north beyond the Arctic Circle to the 70th parallel: an extreme length
from south to north of 11 265 km (700 miles) and an extreme width of
640 km (400 miles). The great majority of the population is of Finnish
stock, but there is an influential Swedish element which in former days
was dominant.

Popularly known as the Land of a Thousand Lakes (the actual
number is more like 10 000, mainly in the south), Finland is nearly
one-tenth water; a still larger area consists of swamps, partially covered
with trees, while dry forest covers nearly half the total area. The
Finnish name of the country, Suomi, means 'Land of fens and lakes'. In
general the surface is fairly flat and of no great elevation. Mostly under
180 m (600 ft), broken here and there by higher patches. Along the
USSR frontier and in the far north the general level is up to 455 m
(1 500 ft), while in the extreme northwest, where Norway, Sweden,
and Finland draw together, heights of over 1 220 m (4 000 ft) are
found. Running back from the coast are postglacial plains with fertile
clay soils, but these are liable to frost even in August, and for the most
part Finland is not well suited to agriculture. Geologically it is related
to the Scandinavian peninsula, consisting mainly of granite, gneiss, and
glacial formations, its multitudinous lakes filling hollows formed by ice-
pressure in past ages. As a rule, the gravel soil formed by glaciation is
not favourable to heavy crops; but it is admirably suited to the large
vertical roots of the pine trees or the long creeping roots thrown out by
firs. Among deciduous trees the birch is the most common. Forest
covers 70 per cent of the total area.

There is no coal, but in the north, at Kolari, almost on the border
with Sweden, lies Finland's main mineral resource: iron ore. Uranium is
known to exist but is not exploited. The copper mines near Lake
Juojärvi are the source of Finland's second most important mineral. In
1969 output of iron concentrates and pellets amounted to 662 000
tons, of copper concentrates 33 135 tons, of zinc 70 845 tons.

The growing period is very short, and only 9 per cent of the total
land area is cultivated. Cereals and potatoes account for nearly half and
land cropped for hay just under one-third. Apart from hay, potatoes are
the heaviest crop (over 1m. tons), though occupying less ground than
cereals. Oats provide over 1m. tons from over 483 000 ha (1m. acres),
while barley, wheat and rye, occupying 646 000 ha (1.6m. acres)
provide about 1.5m. tons of grain. In 1970 sheep numbered only
188 600 but there were some 983 800 cattle and about 89 000 cows in
milk. The dairy industry has long been highly developed. Pigs and
poultry are kept for domestic consumption; surplus eggs are exported.
Market gardening, especially under glass, is expanding rapidly. The
largest mink farm in the world is at Oy Keppo Ab, the food for the

mink being imported. Lapps tend their large herds of reindeer, which roam the northern hills.

Two special factors in Finland's postwar situation led to radical changes in her economy. She had to provide Russia with industrial products to the value of 300m. gold dollars, as reparations, spread over eight years from 1944; and she had to accommodate some 425 000 refugees from the ceded or leased territories. The first claim was met by industrial expansion, particularly in shipbuilding and the heavy engineering and metal industries, which were developed to supplement forest products. Nearly 200 000 of the refugees had been engaged in industry or trade and it was comparatively easy to find work for them in the enforced industrial boom. Farms and farm workers were a different proposition. They and their families came flooding into the republic to the number of nearly 250 000. To meet this need, farm lands in Finland were redistributed. Large properties were bought or expropriated and split up; others were compulsorily reduced in size. About 80 per cent of the farms now have a maximum of 10 ha (25 acres) of arable land.

Industrial development took on a permanent character; the USSR undertook to provide a market for Finnish manufactures on an ordinary commercial basis, after the expiry of the reparations period. Meanwhile, Finland's normal export trade revived. At first she could do little more than meet the reparation claims, but as she recovered strength after the war, these were exceeded by exports to western Europe of her main source of economic wealth: timber and other forest products.

Emigration from Finland has been a constant feature: between 1880 and 1910 it is estimated that some 160 000 sailed for the United States and Canada, and more joined the stream in the 1920s and 1930s. Since the end of the Second World War more than 250 000 Finns have left the country to settle abroad, mostly in Sweden but also in Australia: a very high proportion of a small population.

Finland has a big advantage in her intricate system of lakes and connecting rivers and canals, which greatly facilitate the inland transport of timber to her saw mills and pulp mills, and to shipping points on the coast. The length of navigable waterways is some 6 600 km (4 100 miles), while waterways along which timber rafts can be floated extend to nearly seven times that distance. In addition there are 5 722 km (3 560 miles) of 5 ft-gauge railway, of which all but 38 km (25 miles) are state owned. Communications are hampered by terrain and by climate, especially in autumn when the ice is forming and in the spring when it is breaking up, for at these times neither boats nor sledges can be used. Roads and ferry services connect Finland with Sweden and West Germany and there are road connections with Norway and the USSR. The rail connection with Sweden in the north suffers from the difference in rail gauge between Finland and Sweden. The rail link with Leningrad in the USSR is more useful, but most of Finland's trade is carried by sea, aided by icebreakers, a specialised (and export) product of her shipyards.

Home of seafaring people, Finland had a large fleet of tramp steamers before the Second World War. During the war she lost nearly half, and the best of the remainder were handed over to the USSR as part of the reparations. At the end of 1969, Finland had 508 merchant vessels of 1 242 300 gross tons.

Timber from the extensive forests is the prime source of Finland's wealth, providing the pine, spruce and birch for the crude timber, cellulose and paper industries; aspen for matches; and the raw material for the prefabrication of wooden houses as well as the manufacture of such products as cardboard, wallboard, and hardboard. The area most concerned with wood processing is in the basin of the Kymi River, Kemi being the major 'wood' town.

Finland's other natural resources of raw materials — iron ore and copper — are used in the metal manufacturing and machinery industries, providing equipment for forestry and agriculture: farm machinery, dairy plant, machinery for wood working, transport equipment, tools. The export of manufactured goods, of ceramic and stone as well as of metal, is growing, and in recent years has exceeded in value the export of timber and timber products. Rubber tyres have to be imported, but Finland is nearly self-sufficient in other rubber goods, in textiles and clothing, and in leather goods: a reflection of her expanding manufacturing activities.

Table 56 — Finland: estimated population of major towns in 1970

Helsinki	800 000	Espoo	97 000
Turku	220 000	Lahti	89 000
Tampere	220 000	Oulu	83 000

The main towns are nearly all ports and many of them are ship-building centres. The capital, Helsinki, is also the principal port. It lies on a fine harbour and though hampered by ice in winter can usually be kept open by icebreakers. The main manufacturing town, Tampere is one of the few important inland centres, situated on the shores of a lake. It has a large textile industry, using hydroelectric power generated from rapids which flow through the town. Turku is the old capital on the southwest coast. It has timber and wood pulp industries and, with the ports of Pori, Vaasa and Oulu, all on the Gulf of Bothnia, handles the timber export trade and the import of foodstuffs and other goods. Lahti, in the southern coastal plain is a fast-developing well-planned town, a centre of the furniture industry.

The main exports are timber and timber products, machinery and metal products, with a declining export of agricultural produce. Shipping services are significant as an invisible export, and income from tourism is gradually rising. In imports there is growth in the raw materials for industry, petroleum and its products, and consumer goods of all kinds. Most trading is with West Germany, the United Kingdom, the USSR (with whom Finland has tariff agreements), Sweden and the United States. Until 1970 the trade with the countries of EFTA, of which Finland is an Associate Member, was greater than that with the countries of the EEC, largely on account of trade with the United Kingdom.

Spain

Spain shares with Portugal possession of the Iberian Peninsula, which is about two and a half times the size of Britain with only about 80 per cent of the population. Spain has by far the larger share: 85 per cent of the area and nearly 80 per cent of the people. Continental Spain with the Balearic and Canary Islands covers nearly 505 000 sq km (195 000 sq miles) and supports over 33.8m. people. The density of population is highest round the coasts; large areas of the interior are very sparsely settled. This factor is explained partly by the character of the surface and the resulting poor communications, partly by the dry climate. South of the Pyrenees, which form the frontier with France, and the mountains at the back of the north coast, the greater part of the country is occupied by a tableland, the Meseta, in the main between 610 and 915 m (2 000 and 3 000 ft) above sea level. It is bordered everywhere except in the west by mountains and steep slopes, making railway construction difficult and costly; while the scanty population and restricted natural resources of large areas hold out little prospect of remunerative returns from schemes for development.

To add to the difficulties, strategic considerations and national aloofness led to the Spanish railways being built on gauges other than the standard European gauge (4 ft 8½ in), so that through traffic with the outside world is impeded; not only have passengers to change trains at the French frontier, but goods have to be unloaded and loaded again. The same difficulty is not experienced at the Portuguese frontier, the principal Portuguese railways being on the same broad gauge as their neighbour's. As might be expected from the natural conditions, Spain's railway mileage is comparatively small: 17 458 km (10 885 miles) of which two-thirds are of 5 ft 6 in gauge, while most of the rest are of metre gauge (3 ft 3.37 in). Electrified lines totalled 3 811 km (2 368 miles) in 1971. Routes over the plateau converge on Madrid or on local centres such as Salamanca and Valladolid; coastal lines converge on the leading ports: Barcelona, Valencia, Bilbao, and Cádiz.

The rivers of the peninsula, though of considerable length, add little o the means of communication. They are for the most part too much obstructed by shallows and rapids to be navigable for any great distance, and as their beds lie mostly in deep valleys below the level of the tableland, they cannot advantageously be connected by canals. All the main rivers except the Ebro flow westwards to the Atlantic, and often the lower, navigable stretches are within Portuguese territory. The Guadalquivir is the most important Spanish river as regards navigation; its volume is reasonably constant, being maintained in winter by rain, in summer by melting snows of the Sierra Nevada, the lofty range that borders its basin on the south. Oceangoing steamers can reach Sevilla, 112 km (70 miles) from the sea, while strings of barges can go up to Córdoba, more than as far again. The only navigable river on the Mediterranean side is the Ebro, which allows small craft to ascend as high as Logroño, though seagoing vessels do not go beyond Tortosa, about 40 km (25 miles) from the sea. The lower course of the river can be used by seagoing vessels only during high water, and a small canal has been cut to the sea from Amposta, above the delta, so that vessels may enter and leave at any time. Running parallel to the Ebro from Tudela to Zaragoza, a distance of about 96 km (60 miles), is a small canal, interesting as being, in part at least, one of the oldest canals in Europe: its construction was ordered in 1529, though most of it actually dates from the eighteenth century or later.

The climate of the interior is also unfavourable to any great density of population. Over the greater part, the total rainfall is under 500 mm (20 in) a year, though the northern and northwestern coasts receive a considerably higher fall, distributed throughout the year. Elsewhere, such little rain as there is occurs in winter, and the height of summer is a period of extreme drought, especially in the southern half of the peninsula. Summer temperatures are high, and the whole peninsula, except for a comparatively small area in the northwest, has at least eight months with a mean daily temperature of 10° C (50° F) or more. Thus the most thinly peopled plateau areas are those of great heat and drought, in many places with only a thin soil cover bearing little vegetation beyond a few tough grasses, herbs, and shrubs. Snow is rare, though winter temperatures on the plateau are low.

Agriculture. One advantage of the long hot summer is that valuable crops can be grown in quick succession, wherever water is available for irrigation. In particular, the waters of the Ebro are being increasingly used in this way, and its almost desert-like natural basin is being turned into an agricultural region. Irrigation schemes dating back to the Moors, or even to the Romans, have made famous the *huertas* (horticultural lands) of Valencia and Murcia, the *huerta* of Elche, and the *vega* (agricultural plain) of Granada. A distinction is usually made between the *vegas*, which yield only one crop a year, and the *huertas*, which yield

487

two or more. By the construction of dams and artificial lakes, the production of hydroelectric power is associated with the irrigation works.

Despite the arid climate of the interior. Spain is predominantly a farming country, especially on the pastoral side. According to the United Nations FAO *Production Yearbook* over 22 per cent of the total area is classed as forested land, nearly 31 per cent as permanent meadows and pastures and over 40 per cent is under arable or tree crops. Over 6.5 per cent is built on or waste.

Among the larger livestock sheep are far the most numerous: 18.7m. in 1970, cattle numbered 4.3m., horses 285 000, asses 386 000, mules 566 000, pigs 6.9m., goats 2.6m. Cereals occupied 7.3m. ha (18.0 acres), olives about 2m. ha (5m. acres), and vineyards 1.6m. ha (4m. acres).

In southern Spain, vegetables and fruit are the chief crops on the irrigated land, along with rice and maize. The principal maize areas, however, are in the wetter parts of the country (the northwest), where maize is a staple foodstuff. In Spain as a whole, wheat and barley are both more productive. Wheat will grow on the more fertile soils of the plateau, particularly around Valladolid, and altogether it accounts for about half the total area under cereals, occupying over 3.6m. ha (nearly 9m. acres) yielding as a rule over 4m. tons. Barley occupies about 2m. ha (nearly 5m. acres) and yields some 3m. tons.

Despite some falling off in production, Spain vies with Italy as the world's leading olive country. The trees are grown on the slopes behind the Mediterranean coastal plains, mainly for the oil extracted from the fruit. The yield is about one-fifth of the weight of the fruit. The refined oil is a valuable export.

Oranges are an even more valuable factor in Spanish foreign trade. They are grown chiefly in the Mediterranean provinces of Valencia and Castellon, and though the area devoted to them is relatively small, the crop averages in weight 70 per cent of the olive crop before the extraction of oil, and has a very much larger export value.

Figs, pomegranates, and bananas are also among the sub-tropical fruits grown in Spain. Large quantities of wine are made, notably sherry, which came first from Spain (see p. 156). Other products include esparto grass and the cork oak, which has to stand for thirty years before it yields good cork. It then gives increasingly better cork at subsequent strippings, at intervals of about ten years, till the tree is perhaps 150 years old.

Minerals. The mineral wealth of Spain is very abundant, and has been renowned for ages, though even yet it is far from being fully developed. Iron ore exists in quantity in the Basque provinces, and in the province of Viscaya. Bilbao, the port from which the ore is dispatched, is one of the most important iron ore exporting ports in Europe. Santander and Murcia provinces also rank high in iron ore production, while large quantities are also mined in the province of Almeria and near Sevilla, and smaller quantities in Málaga and in Lugo (northwest Spain, not far from La Coruña). All these deposits furnish quantities of ore rich in iron (for the most part from 48 to 60 per cent), and sufficiently free from phosphorus to be used in the manufacture of steel by the Bessemer process. Many of the Cartagena mines have a poor iron content, but on the other hand they are mostly rich in manganese, and their phosphorus content is uniformly low. The deposits worked near Teruel in eastern Spain and exported from the port of Sagunto, while rich in iron, have a rather high proportion of phosphorus: from 0.06 to 0.39 per cent. The Viscaya deposits, which have been worked since ancient times, are apparently the nearest to exhaustion. Other parts of Spain such as Leon possess ores of lower quality which may come to be of importance. In 1971 3.6m. tons of iron ore were produced much of it being used in Spain's growing industrial plants. There are already three integrated steel works at coastal locations: at Avilés in Asturia, at Sestao near Bilbao, at Veriña near the port of Gijón. A fourth, very large complex with L. D. converters is planned to complement a small existing steel works at Sagunto on the coast north of Valencia. It has been estimated that 80 per cent of Spain's steel is consumed in the area bounded by Sabtander–Valencia–Madrid and the French frontier, within 400 km (250 miles) of Sagunto, and the existence of this large market influenced the choice of site.

Much the highest mineral production is bituminous coal (about 8 to 9m. tons a year), the principal mines being in Asturias, in the northeast. A special railway runs from the mines to the exporting and distributing centre of Gijón; it is estimated that the potential reserves are far higher than figures of actual production would show. Anthracite and lignite are also worked, and each yields annually around 2m. tons. Copper ores are mined at Rio Tinto, in the southwest, and lead and silver at Linares, to the south of the Sierra Morena. Large mercury deposits are worked at Almadén. Other minerals include phosphoric salts, zinc, tin, sulphur, manganese, and salt. Oil occurs to the north of Burgos.

Industry and trade. The situation of the chief seats of Spanish manu-facturing industries has been determined more by conveniences for commerce than by local supplies of coal and iron. Electric power is being increasingly used in industry, the installed capacity being 14m. kW in 1968, 8.5m. kW being hydroelectric. The metallurgical industry, based on Spanish iron and coal, is concentrated on the north coast, where water-power from the Cantabrian Mountains is now used for smelting. Bilbao is the centre of the iron industries, and also of the iron export trade. Principal industrial areas of the south are centred on the ports of Sevilla, Málaga, and Cartagena; Barcelona is the centre of the Catalonian textile industry, which produces both woollen and cotton goods. Esparto grass is the basis of paper manufacture, while Valencia and Murcia have silk industries, for which large numbers of silkworms are reared.

Over 1m. tons of fish are caught annually off the Spanish coasts, mostly sardines, tunny, and cod. A large amount is canned.

Since the overthrow of the Spanish monarchy, and the establishment of the present state in 1939, industrial and commercial concerns have been subjected to multiple regulations in the interests of labour and social welfare. A state body, *Instituto Nacional de Industria*, was established in 1941 to promote projects too big for private enterprise. Another state body, *Instituto de Colonizacion*, has been put in charge of land organisation.

Spain has many good ports to handle her foreign trade. The largest is Barcelona, with a fine sheltered harbour. Among others on the Mediterranean coast are Valencia, Alicante, Cartagena, and Málaga. On the Atlantic side of the Strait of Gibraltar, Cádiz has a good harbour and shares the trade of southwest Spain with Sevilla, on the Guadalquivir. On the north coast Bilbao is of prime importance, and other ports include San Sebastian, Santander, Gijón, and La Coruña. Madrid, the capital, almost in the centre of the country, has a variety of industries, and is of first importance as a road and rail centre.

Spain is not a great trading nation. In recent years imports have averaged in value 2.5 times the value of exports. The main exports are food and live animals, fresh fruits and nuts, mechanical and transport equipment, and manufactures of metals, textiles, leather, wood. Main imports are food and raw materials, which equal in value exports of the same commodities; greater in value are the imports of raw materials for industries, chemicals and metalliferous ores. There are also large imports of crude and refined oil and petroleum products. The largest item is the import of machinery and transport equipment, which includes textile machinery, and ships and boats. Most trade is carried on with the United States, East and West Germany, the United Kingdom, Italy and Argentina.

Tourism. The most notable feature of the Spanish economy since 1950 is the rapid expansion of tourism. Coastal resorts of the Mediterranean are especially popular, and the profits earned from tourism have been invested in the development of hotels and in the road network. As a result the Mediterranean coast now has many modern buildings and some good roads.

The Balearic Islands, ranging from 80 to 320 km (50 to 200 miles) off the east coast of Spain, rise above the Mediterranean from submarine plateaus. Four well-known islands, Mallorca (Majorca), Menorca (Minorca), Ibiza, Formentera, and seven islets, have a total area of 5 000 sq km (2 000 sq miles) and a population approaching 500 000, the whole forming a province of Spain (Baleares). The islands produce wheat, fruit, and olives; fruit and wine are exported, with a little iron from Menorca; coal, timber, fertilisers, and foodstuffs are imported. The capital, Palma (209 000), on Majorca, has a regular steamship service with Barcelona (240 km: 150 miles). The principal towns of the other islands are Mahón on Menorca and Ibiza on the island of the same name. There has been here, as on the coasts of Spain, a huge increase in tourism, aided by good air services.

Table 57 — Spain: towns with registered population exceeding 120 000 in 1969

Madrid	3 000 000	Granada	170 000
Barcelona	1 760 000	Alicante	163 000
Valencia	624 000	San Sebastián	162 000
Sevilla	622 000	Gijón	153 000
Zaragoza	439 000	Jérez de la Frontera	150 000
Bilbao	400 000	Badalona	150 000
Málaga	351 000	Sabadell	150 000
Murcia	275 000	Cartagena	148 000
Las Palmas	263 000	Oviedo	143 000
Córdoba	231 000	Santander	143 000
Hospitalet	217 000	Cádiz	138 000
Valladolid	211 000	Pamplona	138 000
La Coruña	194 000	Tarrasa	131 000
Vigo	191 000	Salamanca	121 000
Santa Cruz de Tenerife	181 000		

See also Canary Islands, p. 752.

Portugal

Portugal comprises the western coast plains of the Iberian peninsula and is traversed by several large rivers which, though rising in the Spanish mountains and having the greater part of their courses in that country, become navigable only in Portuguese territory. This factor, together with the greater rainfall of Portugal, more evenly spread over the seasons than the scanty fall of the Spanish interior, has led to more intensive agricultural development and to a heavier density of population than is found in the greater part of Spain. With an area of 91 640 sq km (35 000 sq miles) including islands, and a population of 8.6m., Portugal occupies between one-sixth and one-seventh of the Iberian peninsula and supports between a fourth and a fifth of the total population.

More than one-quarter of continental Portugal is under forest, mostly pine and oak; and of this area more than 24 per cent, 758 000 ha

(1.8m. acres), is covered with cork oak. Portugal provides the bulk of the world's cork supplies, and cork (raw or manufactured) is her second most valuable export.

Agricultural and pastoral industry in general yield comparatively little for export. Nearly all the land is capable of production; less than 5 per cent of Portugal, is waste or built on. But three times that area is classed as 'potentially productive but unused'. There remain 4.4m. ha (10.8m. acres) of arable land and 530 000 ha (1.3m. acres) of pasture. The mild, moist climate of northern Portugal is favourable to livestock and dairy farming, while the summer rainfall favours maize. Traditional farming techniques are used and crop yields are low. The production of cereals is normally insufficient for home requirements. Wheat is grown on 575 000 ha (1.4m. acres), yielding about 0.5 to 0.75m. tons; maize on 406 000 ha (over 1m. acres) and yields about 590 000 tons, over 1m. tons of potatoes are produced from rather more than 104 000 ha (257 000 acres).

The wines of Portugal, notably her speciality, port, takes pride of place among the exports. Olive oil is much lower in the scale and varies greatly. Rice for home consumption is grown on swamp lands, notably in the province of Estremadura on the flats of the lower Tejo in the province of Beira further north, and in the southern provinces of Algarve and Alantejo.

As regards livestock, it was estimated in 1970 that sheep numbered nearly 6.2m., cattle over 1m., goats 550 000, and pigs 1.4m.; and there were 79 000 horses, 139 000 mules, 200 000 asses.

Fishing is one of the most important industries, the chief catch being sardines. The bulk of the catch is tinned and forms the fourth major export but far less valuable than wine, cork, and pulpwood which precede it. Centres of the industry are Matozinhos, in the neighbourhood of Porto; Setúbal, south of Lisboa; and Portimao and Olhao, on the south coast.

There is considerable mineral wealth, as yet not fully exploited. Electric power is being developed. Coal output in 1969 was nearly 425 000 tons, cupriferous pyrites 0.5m. tons, cement over 2m. tons. Minor quantities of other minerals include a small but valuable export of wolframite. An important industry is the manufacture of cotton piece goods for which raw cotton is imported.

Social progress. In the last thirty years Portugal has made great progress in many ways. Cities and towns have been replanned, with modern drainage systems, and good roads have replaced dusty tracks. Educational facilities have been increased and a drive made against illiteracy. Health insurance and other welfare schemes have been started, but the position of the workers is still precarious; a bad season can cause great unemployment in agriculture, and the same applies to the fishing industry. The rapid growth in tourism has had great impact: hotels and villas have mushroomed along the coasts, especially in the south, and catering for tourists is now a major industry.

Communications. The capital of the republic and its principal port is Lisboa (Lisbon), on the north shore of the Tejo estuary. The valley of the Tejo marks the division between the wetter, more prosperous northern part of Portugal, and the drier, less productive south. Lisboa is the focus of routes from all over the country and has a large passenger traffic, being the nearest European port to South America. The trade of northern Portugal passes through Porto, on the River Douro, or through the modern port of Leixoes, just outside the river estuary, which has the advantage of easier approach, deeper water, and excellent facilities for handling goods. Lisboa, with a population of 802 230 (1 034 141 in the metropolitan area) at the census recorded in December 1970, and Porto with 303 424 (693 170) at the same date, are the only two large cities. After them there is a big drop to the next largest, Coimbra, Nova de Gaia and Setúbal, each with under 50 000.

Trade. The value of Portugal's exports has been two-thirds that of imports in recent years. Wine, cork, pulpwood, food and live animals (including pre-eminently fish, fish preparations, fruit and vegetables and their preparations), tobacco, and manufactured goods (especially textiles) figure among the exports; imports include food and live animals, raw materials (especially for textiles), crude and refined oil, chemicals, iron and steel; and among the manufactured goods imported the greatest in value are machinery and transport equipment, followed by other goods made of iron and steel, textiles and precious stones. Most of the trade of Portugal is with West Germany, the United Kingdom, Angola (a dependent territory in west Africa), the United States, France and the other countries of the European Economic Community.

Overseas territories. The African territories of Angola, Moçambique and Guinea-Bissau became independent in 1974—75. Overseas territories are now the Cape Verde Islands and São Tomé e Principe, islands off the African shores. The Azores, three groups of islands in mid-Atlantic, and Madeira are also administered as parts of Portugal. There is also the tiny Portuguese territory of Macao in China, at the mouth of the Canton River, into which emigrant Chinese pour, to make it one of the most densely populated areas in the world. The eastern part of Timor, in the Malay Archipelago, also remains Portuguese. With the exception of Macao these overseas territories provide the home country with some primary products.

Gibraltar

Gibraltar, dominated by its famous Rock, occupies a narrow peninsula less than 4.8 km long by less than 1.5 km wide (3 by 1 miles), extending southwards from the southwest coast of Spain, with which it is connected by a sandy isthmus about 1.5 km (nearly 1 mile) long and 0.8 km (½ mile) wide, rising only a little above sea level. The population, most of Genoese, Portuguese and Maltese descent, numbered some 27 000 in 1970.

The Rock, which rises to a height of 425 m (1 396 ft), descends almost sheer to the sea on its eastern side, and the town is huddled on the western slopes, overlooking a huge natural harbour. Large sections of the Rock have been covered with concrete off which rainwater drains into storage tanks, so that the strongly fortified peninsula has an independent water supply.

Gibraltar was ceded to Great Britain by the Treaty of Utrecht in 1713, after it had been seized in 1704 during the War of the Spanish Succession. In a referendum held on 10 September 1967 the Gibraltarians voted to retain their link with the United Kingdom, and the Rock thus remains a British overseas territory. It has strategic importance as a naval and air base at the gateway to the Mediterranean. Tourism is of increasing importance to the economy of Gibraltar, which has no land suitable for agriculture or other primary industries, but which has a small production of manufactures such as clothing, tobacco, watches, in addition to its all-important entrepôt trade and its port facilities for the provisioning of visiting shipping. It is a free port.

Italy

The Republic of Italy, established in 1946 after the Second World War, differs very slightly in area from the prewar kingdom. Before the war Italy had an area of 310 000 sq km (120 000 sq miles); she was left with 300 000 sq km (116 000 sq miles), a territory nearly a third larger than Great Britain. Her population, 47m. at the 1951 census, was then slightly less than Britain's 49m. At the census of October—November 1961 Italy's population was 50.5m. against Britain's 51.35m.; the 1971 census population was 53.7m.

Under the Peace Treaty of 1947 Italy ceded four Alpine frontier districts to France, a considerably larger territory to Yugoslavia, including the port of Fiume (now combined with the Yugoslav port of Susak and renamed Rijeka), the Dodecanese Archipelago to Greece, and a small island to Albania. An enclave based upon Trieste was made a Free Territory (p. 461) and divided into two zones in the military occupation of Britain and the USA (Zone A) and Yugoslavia (Zone B).

Under a *de facto* arrangement in 1954, Zone A (207 sq km: 81 sq miles) was handed over to Italy, under promise to maintain Trieste as a Free Port, while Yugoslavia retained Zone B (562 sq km: 217 sq miles), with boundary adjustments in her favour.

Though Italy's territorial losses were relatively small, the effects of the war on her industrial and financial economy were of a very different character. The exchange rate of the lira, which in 1939 stood at 85 lire to the £, rocketed to 1 750 to the £, and in 1956 her special imports (i.e. for home consumption) and special exports (i.e. of home produce) were each valued in the United Nations *Yearbook on International Trade* at between 1 and 2m. m. lire. Their analysis is still a guide to the commercial resources and needs of the country. Imports were nearly half as much again as exports, with a value of 1 980 698m. lire, or, at the postwar rate of exchange already quoted, £1 132m. Food cost nearly 15 per cent, much of it for meat, wheat and maize. Fuel (coal, coke and petroleum) accounted for 20 per cent, and half as much again (30 per cent) was spent on inedible raw materials for industry, chiefly cotton and wool. Together these imports made up about two-thirds of the whole, leaving over one-quarter for manufactures, with iron and steel, copper, and machinery as the predominant items.

On the other hand, manufactured goods provided the greater part (56 per cent) of the exports, which were valued at 1 347 982m. lire (£770m.). Textile yarn and thread and textile fabrics (13 per cent), and machinery and transport equipment (21 per cent) constituted a third of the total. Food contributed 20 per cent of the exports, fruit and nuts alone providing half of the amount, with vegetables and rice as other leading items. Petroleum and products added another 8 per cent to the export total.

Physical features and agriculture. Geographical factors exert considerable influence in Italy. Structurally and climatically the country falls into two distinct regions, the northern plain and Alpine foothills, and the peninsula. The northern plain, tipped eastwards and drained to the Adriatic by the River Po and its tributaries, is shut in on the north and west by the great Alpine ranges, which cut Italy off from central Europe; and on the south by the Apennines, curving round from the western end of the Alps to traverse the length of the peninsula. In the natural trough between the two ranges, the plain has been built up by the collection of sediment, a process which is still going on, for the Po carries to the Adriatic every year sediment which is extending the coast eastwards. Adria, now 20 km (13 miles) inland, was in Roman times an important port. Large tributaries from the Alps — the Dora Riparia, Dora Baltea, Ticino, Adda, and Chiese — have pushed the main river over to the southern side of its great plain. Dykes have been built to check flooding of the slow-moving, sediment-laden river, and its waters are used extensively for irrigation, for though there is a good summer rainfall, summer temperatures are high and many crops need irrigation. Winter is very cold in the plain, the Apennines cutting off the northern part of the country from the Mediterranean influences, and so subjecting it to the more extreme continental type of climate.

In spite of this, the fertile soil, summer rain and abundant water render the Lombardy plain the most productive part of Italy. Small farms are the rule, often less than 1.5 ha (3 acres), and traditional farming techniques are still in use in some localities, though much is being done by the government to sponsor mechanical farming methods, proper crop rotation and the use of improved seed strains and artificial fertilisers. Hay is an important crop; wheat and maize are also grown, and in the irrigated areas rice. Cattle raised on the rich meadows have a high milk yield, from which has arisen a large cheese-making industry; Gorgonzola, Parmesan, and Stracchino cheese are all made here. Flax and hemp are also grown, and the rearing of silkworms is an important occupation; mulberry trees are grown specially for their leaves, on which the young worms are fed.

The Italian peninsula can be said to begin at the foothills of the Appennines along the southern edge of the plain, this demarcation being very clearly followed by the straight, 265 km (165 mile) long railway from Rimini on the Adriatic coast to Piacenza on the Po. From the western end of the Alps the Apennines swing across the peninsula to Ancona, enclosing the hilly country of Tuscany and the Campania on the west, then continue through the peninsula into Calabria (the 'toe' of Italy) and on into Sicily. With the exception of the Tevere (Tiber) (400 km: 250 miles) in Tuscany, and the Arno (250 km: 155 miles), rivers are short and flow directly to the sea from both sides of the range. The climate of the peninsula is typical of all Mediterranean countries: dry, hot summers, and mild, wet winters.

On the west coast of the peninsula there are four large plains among the hills of Tuscany and Campania: those of the Arno, the Ombrone, the lower Tevere, and that behind Napoli. The Arno plain, with Firenze (Florence) at its head, has been drained, irrigated, and cultivated extensively, though farms are too small and often too poor to provide more than their own needs in foodstuffs. Wheat and grass crops are grown, with olives and the vine, and some of Italy's best known agricultural products come from this region: Chianti wine, Lucca olive oil, and Livorno (Leghorn) straw. The Ombrone valley, formerly a marshy and malarial region, has been reclaimed and is resettled agriculturally. The plain of the lower Tevere, with Roma as its centre, is also a reclaimed marsh region, where farms and irrigation works have now been established. The city itself is built on hills overlooking the surrounding plain. The plain of Napoli, the most densely settled part of Italy, is very intensively cultivated. With highly fertile soil and an almost subtropical climate it produces wheat and maize, oranges, lemons, olives, hemp, vegetables, and the vine.

The mountains themselves are largely given over to sheep grazing, though large chestnut forests flourish on the lower parts.

Sicily, separated from the 'toe' of Italy by the narrow Strait of Messina, has a good winter rainfall, and in places a highly fertile soil. Citrus fruits are grown on the coastal lowlands, with vines and olives; wheat is the chief crop in the interior, where sheep are also kept. Not much smaller — a fourth instead of a third as large again as Wales — is the island of Sardinia, over 160 km (100 miles) from the west coast of Italy, but only 11 km (7 miles) south of Corsica. It is largely mountainous, barren and poverty-stricken, but supports 2m. sheep on rough hill pastures and has a considerable area under wheat. Its mineral resources are varied and extensive.

More than nine-tenths of Italy is occupied by farmlands and forests. Woods alone cover over 6.1m. ha (15m. acres), and pasture and rough grazing land over 5.2m. ha (13m. acres). The area devoted to cultivated crops is 15m. ha (37m. acres) of which cereals occupy about 6m. ha (14.8m. acres). Wheat is by far the largest crop; it is grown on about 4.1m. ha (10m. acres) and yields a harvest of from 8.5 to 9.8m. tons. Yet even this large crop is not enough for home consumption, and imports of wheat, while naturally varying with the season, have averaged over 1m. tons in recent years. A noted feature of the home production is a hard wheat grown in Apulia, especially suitable for making pasta. Maize, the second largest though much smaller cereal crop, covers over 1m. ha (2.5m. acres) and produces some 4.8m. tons. Other cereal crops, oats, barley and rye are cultivated in the hill country, but on a much smaller scale.

Vines are grown on 1.5m. ha (3.7m. acres). In 1970 the production of wines amounted to some 6.5m. tons and there is a considerable export. Olive trees produced over 2.4m. tons of fruit in 1970, yielding over 420 000 tons of oil. Citrus fruits, chiefly oranges and lemons, grow profusely and in 1970 yielded a crop of over 1.5m. tons. Sugar beet is prolific, and in recent years the area under protection has been increased to 290 000 ha (716 000 acres), yielding over 10.6m. tons in 1970. Chemical fertilisers are widely used, especially super-phosphate.

Livestock included 8.1m. sheep, 9.5m. cattle, 9.2m. pigs, 293 000 donkeys, 188 000 mules, and 296 000 horses in 1970.

After the Second World War and the formation of the republic laws have been passed providing for the expropriation of large estates and their subdivision into peasant holdings. The area involved is some 800 000 ha (1.9m. acres) and by 1962 nearly 635 000 ha (1.6m. acres) had been distributed to small farmers.

Minerals and power. Italy is not well supplied with mineral wealth and needs large mineral imports to meet her industrial requirements. The combined output of iron pyrites and iron ore amount to about 1.2m. tons. With the aid of domestic and imported scrap and home-produced pig iron some 8.7m. tons of cast iron ingots and over 17.4m. tons of raw steel were produced in 1971, while rolled iron totalled nearly 13.4m. tons. About 2m. tons of coal and similar fuels are produced annually and the deficiency is partly made good by the use of hydro-electric power, which has been and is being largely developed. The total electric power generated in 1971 was 124 900m. kWh, 38 per cent of which was hydroelectric. Most of the supply is generated in northern Italy, though the south provides a considerable share, especially in winter when the stations in the Alpine foothills are hampered by lower water levels. The output of petroleum from the Cortemaggiore field is comparatively trifling, but reserves in Sicily are promising and contributed the major part of the 1.2m. tons produced in 1973. Methane was discovered in the Po valley in 1949 and also in the south but its contribution to power resources is not great.

The only minerals producing any notable surplus for export are sulphur and mercury. Italy vies with Spain as the world's chief producer and exporter of mercury. Since the Second World War she has produced about 1.8m. tons a year. Sulphur rock, mined in Sicily in the neighbourhood of Caltanissetta, Girgenti, and Catania produces nearly 500 000 tons of crude sulphur a year, and is Italy's most important mineral product from the point of view of international trade. The potential supplies are vast.

Lead and zinc are mined in Sardinia, bauxite in the Abruzzi. Building and decorative stones are a valuable asset; the celebrated marbles of Carrara and Massa come from the Apuan Hills north of Pisa.

Industry. Industry in Italy is concentrated mainly in the northern plain, and owes its modern development largely to hydroelectric power. In the forefront are textile manufactures. There are nearly 1 000 cotton factories with some 4.4m. spindles, and about 810 factories for combing or spinning or weaving wool. Their products are important items of the export trade, and so are artificial and synthetic fibres and pure silk. The production of manmade fibres has increased very rapidly and in 1969 was over 432 000 tons. Silk culture is practised all over Italy, though mainly in the north. Nearly 845 000 spindles are engaged in the industry, and though production has declined, the output of raw silk in 1969 was over 499 tons.

Iron and steel industries are widespread, the chief old centres being Milano, Savona (west of Genova), Terni (between Perugia and Roma), which has the benefit of the River Nera; and the Isle of Elba, where locally mined iron ores are smelted on the spot. The newer integrated iron and steelworks are at waterside locations, fed by great quantities of scrap and by West African ores: at Piombino (north of Roma), Bagnoli (Napoli), Cornigliano (Genova) and Taranto (in the south). A great chemical industry has grown up, utilising Italian sulphur, borax and other raw materials in the manufacture of sulphuric acid (over 5m. tons a year), fertilisers, and other chemicals. Motorcars are another important manufacture, both for the home market and for export.

Italy has one of the largest capacities for oil refining in Europe and, like the iron ore and scrap, crude oil is imported to be refined at waterside locations (including Genova, Venezia, Ravenna, La Spezia, Livorno, Napoli, Bari and Augusta). The port of Taranto is being enlarged to take tankers exceeding 200 000 tons. Natural gas is also imported, from Libya; and an agreement has been signed with the USSR whereby the Soviet Union will send Italy natural gas by pipeline via Austria. Promising gasfields has been identified underlying the Adriatic and there is also the possibility of natural gas imports from Algeria to meet Italy's fuel requirements.

Manufacturing industries of a traditional nature continue: Venetian glass and Murano lace have long been famous, as have the fine earthenware, mosaics and art products of Firenze; many Italian towns are famed for their sculpture in marble and alabaster. Milano is the chief seat of Italian cutlery manufacture; Tuscany has long been famous for straw plaiting; and there is a flourishing and widespread leather industry.

Italy has many large cities which enjoy worldwide renown for their associations with history and art, but are less widely recognised as centres of industry. Roma, Milano, Napoli and Torino have each over 1m. inhabitants. Roma with over 2m. inhabitants, the largest as well as the capital city, owes its pre-eminence more perhaps to historical than to geographical circumstances; but its situation is not without geographical advantages. It lies about midway between the north and the south of the republic, on the chief river of the peninsula. It has the usual variety of industries associated with capital cities: food preparation, furniture and clothing, luxury goods, etc. Ostia, on a former mouth of the Tevere (Tiber), was the oldtime port; now Civitavecchia, further to the north, handles most of the seaborne traffic. Milano, next to Roma in size and the chief business centre in Italy, became a great seat of trade at a very early date, chiefly in consequence of its central position in one of the most fertile parts of the northern plain and the development of hydroelectric power. Routes over the Alps converged there by way of the shores of Lakes Maggiore and Como, and this advantage was increased later by the St Gotthard and Simplon railways. Napoli, apart from its fine harbour and maritime trade, has such abundance of labour that it has become the seat of various manufactures, including textiles, for which otherwise it offers no particular advantage, food-processing, sugar-refining, soap-making.

Among other large cities, taken in order from north to south, Torino, at the head of navigation on the Po, and at the junction of the Mont Cenis route with the railways of the plain of Lombardy, has iron and steel industries, and notable motorcar and aircraft works. The two great ports of northern Italy, established as such in the Middle Ages and maintaining that position today, are Genova and Venezia (Venice). The canals of Venezia are not only the home of the gondola. Deepwater channels give access to a commercial harbour and there are steel works and an oil refinery as well as other industry at Porto Marghera on the mainland. On the opposite side of Italy, Genova's fine natural harbour, though backed by the Apennines, has easy access to the northern plain through the Bochetta Pass, which lies behind the town. Firenze, chief town of Tuscany, is an important route centre between the Arno plain and northern Italy. It became a great trade centre at an early date, and later developed many banking interests. It was as a wealthy city that it attracted the painters, musicians, and other artists who brought it fame.

Besides those already mentioned, important ports along the west coast include Spezia and Livorno; along the east coast, Ancona, Bari, and Taranto. Reggio, in the 'toe' of Italy, looks across Messina Strait to Sicily, where the largest ports are Palermo (an industrial centre), Catania, Messina, and Siracusa with oil refining and associated petrochemical manufactures.

In all the towns and cities in Italy traditional skilled craftmanship survives, and many workers are employed in small units, making pottery, glass, furniture and leather goods, and in tailoring.

The south of the peninsula, *il Mezzogiorno*, with its poverty-stricken land and people, still bound by old traditions, contrasts sharply with the dominant, vigorous, progressive industrial north. Workers from the south who swell the northern labour force put great pressure on housing and other services in that already overcrowded region. There is official encouragement for industry to set up new plant in the south, including Sicily. A motorway network has been planned to make the south more accessible; houses have been built near new plant. Among the giants Fiat (motorcars), Pirelli (rubber manufactures), Alfa-Romeo (motorcars, at Napoli) have all agreed to open new factories; and smaller enterprises in the manufacturing industries (such as mechanical and electrical engineering, metallurgical, food processing, clothing and paper-making factories) find the possibilities of this 'new' land promising. Labour is cheaper than in the north and transport costs are not excessive if the products are standardised and there is a known stable market.

Trade. The value of imports exceeds that of Italy's exports, and the balance is redressed by invisible earnings from tourism and from the remittances sent home by Italians living overseas. The lack of raw materials is reflected in imports, which include timber, crude oil, iron and steel; and much machinery is imported for growing industries, as well as chemicals, vehicles and instruments. Home supplies of food are insufficient and grain, fish, meat and animals are imported, together with some dairy produce and eggs. Manufactures naturally figure prominently in the exports. The traditional items of cotton goods, raw silk and wool, have been overtaken by clothing and footwear. Tools and machinery are the leading exports, followed by vehicles, chemicals and refined oil, all indicating the importance of labour in Italy's economy. Fruit and vegetables make a useful contribution.

Table 58 — Italy: towns with more than 150 000 registered inhabitants in 1970

Roma (capital)	2 778 900	Messina	274 740
Milano	1 713 540	Verona	262 000
Napoli	1 278 000	Padova	228 900
Torino	1 190 700	Cagliari	225 800
Genova	842 000	Taranto	223 400
Palermo	663 000	Brescia	209 700
Bologna	493 000	Livorno	175 300
Firenze	460 600	Parma	174 550
Catania	414 600	Modena	170 450
Venezia	368 000	Reggio	167 100
Bari	356 300	Ferrara	156 000
Trieste	277 200	Salerno	152 800

Malta

Malta holds a key position in the heart of the Mediterranean, 97 km (60 miles) south of Sicily and three times that distance from the north African coast. It became British territory early in the nineteenth century, and won high renown by its successful resistance to enemy attacks in the Second World War, thereby gaining both the George Cross award, and responsible government.

In 1955 a round table conference on the future of Malta advocated its integration in the United Kingdom, with three Maltese members in the British House of Commons and regular British financial assistance, foreshadowed at some £4—5m. a year. These proposals were approved in principle by the British government and accepted in Malta by a large majority at a referendum in February 1956. Owing partly to Malta's increasing financial demands and partly to a change in British naval policy affecting the volume of employment in the dockyard at Valetta, negotiations to implement the scheme of integration proved abortive. The British government arranged to hand over the dockyard to a ship-repairing company, and to assist financially in providing continued employment for Maltese workers no longer needed by the Admiralty;

but the Maltese government, objecting to the transfer, refused to cooperate and finally resigned in April 1958. The Governor took over control, and the British government introduced an interim form of government by council. Grants of up to £29m. during the next five years were promised towards Malta's financial needs, including support for the dockyard under its new management, which was granted a ninety-nine year lease from the end of March. Malta became fully independent on 21 September 1964 and set about building up an economy based on industry, commerce and tourism in place of the former unbalanced economy, essentially concentrated on the servicing of military installations.

Malta comprises the island of that name (246 sq km: 95 sq miles), the neighbouring island of Gozo (67 sq km: 26 sq miles), and little Comino (2.5 sq km: 1 sq mile), a total area of 316 sq km (122 sq miles) which is about one-sixth smaller than the Isle of Wight. On the other hand the estimated population of over 322 187 (1970) is more than three times that of the Isle of Wight. Some 14 600 ha (36 100 acres) is classed as cultivated, and this is divided into over 12 000 holdings averaging 1 to 1.5 ha (3 to 4 acres). Wheat and barley are the chief cereals, and large quantities of potatoes, tomatoes and other vegetables, grapes and other fruit are grown. Among livestock in 1969 there were over 23 000 pigs, 20 000 goats, 9 800 cattle, 9 000 sheep, 1 700 donkeys, 1 500 horses and 1 100 mules, in addition to 729 000 poultry and 45 600 rabbits.

Malta itself consists of a low plateau descending to a southeastern plain. The capital, Valetta, with its great harbour and dockyard, is well situated in the northeast coast; it has a population of 15 550 (1969), and with suburbs some 60 000. Various light industries are carried on, and electricity is widely installed. A new power station, linked to plant which produces fresh water, is already operating and is to be extended.

Food, raw materials, industrial equipment and consumer goods have to be imported, and in recent years the value of imports has been four times that of exports. Earnings from tourism are growing but cannot alone solve the problem of the island's unbalanced economy. Most trading is with the United Kingdom, Italy and France.

Bulgaria

The People's Republic of Bulgaria was established in 1946 in place of the monarchy. Extending southward from the lower Danube (except in the Dobruja), and westward from the Black Sea coast, it is midway in size (111 000 sq km: 43 000 sq miles) between Ireland and England, and has a population of nearly 8.5m. (1971). A treaty of cooperation with the Soviet Union was entered into in 1948, renewed (for twenty years) in 1967.

The country is predominantly agricultural, even though much of its surface is mountainous. The northern plains, sloping down to the Danube on the north, are broken by irregular tablelands covered by clay and loess soils over a calcareous subsoil. The general appearance is somewhat arid, but this is a great grain-growing region, producing over half the country's wheat and maize. Only in the valleys and depressions are trees and pasture found, the higher land between being windswept and open. The Balkan Mountains, forming the southern rim of the Danube plains, are generally forested, the higher slopes serving as summer pastures for sheep. In the valleys and clearings the more hardy cereals (barley, rye, buckwheat) and potatoes are grown, varied with fruit and fine pasture land. South again, the basin of the Maritsa is characterised by numerous isolated depressions, where cold air is apt to accumulate in winter, forming frost pockets, so that the more delicate fruit trees are forced up to the slopes with a good exposure and a good air drainage. A great part of the fertile Maritsa valley is devoted to horticulture under polythene or glass. Wheat and maize, sugar beet, sunflowers, tobacco, vines and fruit are grown here, while around Kazanlik, in the tributary valley of the Tundzha, the roses are grown from which the famous rose oil, attar of roses, is produced. The Rhodope Mountains provide hill pasture for sheep and goats in the southwest and forested areas in the west.

Nearly 50 per cent of the total area of the country is classed as cultivated and 30 per cent as forest land. Between a third and a half of the cultivated area is devoted to wheat and maize, the area under wheat being roughly one and a half times that of maize. Other cultivation covers sugar beet, sunflowers, some cotton, tobacco, grapes (for wine and table), and the production of silkworm cocoons. Livestock numbered 9.2m. sheep, 350 000 goats, 1.2m. cattle, 1.9m. pigs, 182 000 horses and 299 000 asses in 1970.

After the Second World War land was redistributed and farming organised on a cooperative and collective basis. In 1970 there were 795 cooperatives and 159 state farms.

Bulgaria has considerable mineral wealth, notably good coal and lignite deposits. Production in 1968 was 21.7m. tons of hard coal and over 26m. tons of lignite. Bauxite, iron ore, lead, zinc, copper, manganese and salt are also mined. Oil has been located and developed: production in 1969 amounted to 225 000 tons. The main refineries are at Burgas and at Dolni Dubnik, with a combined capacity of 12m. tons. Thermoelectric and hydroelectric power has been developed, and with the help of the USSR a nuclear power station is being built at Kozlodni, which should be in production in 1974.

In manufacturing the emphasis has been on the production of farm machinery and implements to serve the needs of this primarily agricultural country. Food processing is a growing industry, as are textile, metallurgical and chemical manufactures, especially in the area around Sofiya, the capital. Sofiya, in the far west of Bulgaria, at the northern end of the Rhodope Mountains, lies at an elevation of nearly 550 m (1 800 ft), and is subject to considerable extremes of summer heat and winter cold. It is an important route focus and the centre of a plain (ringed round by mountains), producing rose oil, tobacco, and sugar beet. The country's principal lignite field lies to the southeast of the city. The second main town, Plovdiv, is a textile centre but also specialises in food-processing. Metallurgical works, shipyards and chemical plant which includes fertilisers amongst its products have been developed near the sheltered port of Varna, as well as cement works nearby, to bring work to the area. Ruse on the Danube is an expanding port, an important link on the Sofiya—Bucuresti route. Many tourist resorts are growing up along the coast of the Black Sea.

Bulgaria's role with Comecon is primarily that of a supplier of fruit and market garden produce, both fresh and processed. If highspeed communications could be improved with central and west Europe there is no doubt her export trade to the west could be greatly increased. Crude oil is at present transported up the Danube by barge, but there is a possibility that a pipeline may be laid in the future, an easier and cheaper means of conveying the oil. Oil is one of the main imports, in company with ferrous metals and agricultural machinery. Nearly all trading is within Comecon, especially with the USSR; outside the group most trade is with West Germany and Italy, but on a very small scale.

Table 59 — Bulgaria: towns with registered population exceeding 80 000 in 1970

Sofiya	868 200	Burgas	131 700
Plovdiv	247 500	Stara Zagora	109 100
Varna	219 000	Pleven	89 800
Ruse	149 600		

Greece

Following its foundation in 1830 the Greek monarchy suffered many vicissitudes, including a period between the two world wars when it was superseded by a republic. After a revolution in 1967 the king moved abroad and his duties in Greece were performed by a regent. In 1973, as a result of a referendum, a Republic was declared. Territorial accretions have doubled the 1830 area. Greece is now 132 000 sq km (51 000 sq miles) (almost exactly the area of England), with a population at the 1971 census of 8.7m. Overrun by enemy troops in the Second World War, and torn by civil strife, Greece had its internal economy so deranged that production for some years was less than before the war, especially in the case of minerals; but recent years have seen a marked recovery.

Three-quarters of the kingdom is mainland, and the other quarter is made up by the numerous islands around the coasts, by Crete, and by the Dodecanese (these last having been ceded by Italy to Greece in 1947). The greater part of the country is mountainous, the only considerable plains being in the valleys of the River Piniós in Thessaly, the Rivers Vardar, Strimón (Struma), and Meriç (Maritsa) at the head of the Aegean Sea; and between Pátrai (Patras) and Pyrgos on the northwest coast of the Pelopónnises, the southern peninsula of Greece, which is all but cut off from the rest of the mainland by the Korinthiakós Kólpos (Gulf of Corinth), the natural severance being completed artificially by the Kórinthos (Corinth) Ship Canal across the narrow connecting isthmus.

Agriculture. Over 21 per cent of the land is classed as arable, nearly 40 per cent as pastoral and nearly 20 per cent as forested; but in practise the area that can be put to profitable use is limited by the mountainous terrain, the hot dry climate, and the porous limestone which predominates in the mountainous regions. Much of the cultivable land has poor soil which is subject to erosion, inadequately fed with fertilisers and yields meagre crops. Despite these restrictions, over half the working population is engaged in agricultural pursuits. The dry summers favour wheat, which is by far the largest crop: 2m. tons from 1.1m. ha (2.7m. acres). Maize, barley and oats, in descending order are considerable though much smaller crops; a very little rye and rice are grown.

The most numerous livestock are sheep (7.7m. in 1970) and goats (4m.). Cattle number only 1m.: the summers are too hot and dry for much larger numbers. There are only 440 000 pigs, while horses number 260 000, mules 196 000 and asses 396 000. The home supply of meat and dairy produce is thus inadequate and has to be supplemented by imports.

The most important commercial crops are tobacco and the currant vine. Tobacco-growing is an expensive but very profitable enterprise. It has expanded greatly since the Second World War and is grown on over 106 000 ha (262 000 acres) yielding around 99 000 tons. Most of this is exported and usually provides about 21 per cent of all exports by value. Over 1.7m. tons of grapes are grown, and dried fruits (currants, sultanas and figs) provide about 8 per cent of exports by value. Another 8 per cent is contributed by raw cotton, which is also largely used locally in a well-established textile industry. Until recently all the cotton grown in the country was absorbed by the local industry; then the crop began to exceed local requirements and now it provides one of the leading exports. Other export crops include olives, wine and oranges. A small quantity of a rather more exotic primary product, sponges, is exported.

Minerals and power. Greece has varied mineral wealth but is handicapped by her poverty in fuel. She has lignite, and by 1970 had raised the output to 9m. tons, but the quality is poor. Other minerals include iron ore of good quality (300 000 tons produced in 1967); pyrites (104 000 tons); manganese (73 600 tons); and chromite (42 000 tons). Bauxite has also come to the fore, with a production and export of nearly 2.8m. tons in 1971. Output of sulphur was 225 000 tons in 1964. There are also deposits of zinc, lead, silver, emery, antimony, nickel and magnesite, but they contribute little as yet to the economy. Oil occurs at Kleisoura but production is low. Hydroelectric power schemes linked with irrigation projects are in hand; at present most electricity is provided by thermal power stations.

Industry. Outside the cities industrial development is small, and mainly confined to the preparation of agricultural produce, such as wine-making, currant-drying, extraction of olive oil, and to small textile and chemical works. The large industries are almost entirely concentrated in the Athínai (Athens) area, the capital having grown up where the north—south land routes crowd together across the Isthmus of Kórinthos into the Pelopónnisos. New works have given the city an adequate water supply for the first time. Piraiévs (Piraeus), the port for Athens, is the principal outlet for the country's trade, and has a number of industries concerned with food preparation, engineering and textiles. It includes a fiscal Free Zone of 181 sq km (70 sq miles). The newer industries of the capital include engineering, chemicals, cement works and oil-refining.

The government is fully aware of the high degree of rural overpopulation (53 per cent of the labour force were engaged in agriculture in 1967) and of the need to industrialise and diversify the economy. At present most industrial workers are engaged in textile manufacture and construction work, especially in building accommodation for tourists, for the income from tourism in Greece is great.

Communications. Thessalonki (Salonika) at the head of the gulf of Thermaikós is the port for northern Greece and Yugoslavia, and the terminus of routes from central and eastern Europe via the Vardar valley. There is a Free Zone of over 536 sq km (207 sq miles), and also a smaller Yugoslav Free Zone of 94 sq km (36 sq miles), important in connection with efforts to develop trade between Greece and its northern neighbour. Other ports include Pátrai (Patras) near the entrance to the Gulf of Kórinthos, which exports most of the currant crop; Vólos on the east coast; Kaválla, at the head of the Aegean Sea; and Kérkira (Corfu) on the island of that name, off the northwest coast. The famous Kórinthos has long been in ruins, after repeated earthquakes. The modern town is between 5 and 6 km (3 to 4 miles) to the northeast and about 3 km (2 miles) from the western end of the Kórinthos Canal; it is quite small. The canal is about 6 km (nearly 4 miles) long, has a surface width of 25 m (80 ft), and is navigable by vessels drawing up to 8 m (26 ft). It was wrecked during the Second World War but has since been rebuilt and reopened. Greece also suffered heavy losses in her large merchant fleet. Owing to the difficult terrain much of her trade, domestic and overseas, has always been carried by sea rather than by rail. Nearly three-quarters of the 1939 tonnage was lost, but these losses have been restored and the Greek merchant fleet contributes considerably to the economy today. The railways, also largely destroyed in the war, have likewise been renewed. They have a length of over 2 500 km (1 550 miles). Roads, many of them earth roads, have a length of some 3 900 km (2 450 miles).

Trade. Exports mainly comprise processed agricultural products: food (especially dried fruits), tobacco, textiles, all of which face fierce competition in world markets. The very small export of copper, and aluminium manufactured goods contributes little. The value of the commodities imported in 1967 was two and a half times that of the value of exports, and included a wide range of raw materials and products, including wood, crude oil, textile fibres, chemicals, machinery and transport equipment. Remittances sent home by Greek emigrants and receipts from tourism help to redress the imbalance.

Most trade is carried on with West Germany, the United States, the United Kingdom, Italy, France, the Benelux countries and the USSR.

Kriti (Crete). Situated to the southeast of the mainland, some 320 km (200 miles) from Piraiévs, Kriti is a long narrow island lying east–west with a mountain chain stretching its entire length. Its area is about 8 330 sq km (3 217 sq miles) and it has a population approaching 500 000. Agricultural and pastoral industry is the economic mainstay of the island, which raises fruits, olives, and grain, and provides pasture for sheep and goats. There are three principal harbours, all on the north coast: Khania (Canea), Iráklion (Candia) and Réthimnon. The south coast is steep and harbourless.

The Sporadhes (Dodecanese) ('Twelve Islands'), situated off the south-west coast of Turkey, came under Greek influence and were so named in the ninth century AD. Later they came under Turkish rule, passed to the Italians in their war with Turkey in 1912, and to Greece (the population being largely Greek) after the Second World War. In modern usage the term includes fourteen islands, the largest and most important being Rhodos (Rhodes), not one of the original twelve, but famous in the Aegean from even earlier days (the Colossus of Rhodes was one of the seven wonders of the ancient world), and afterwards the home of the Knights of St John of Jerusalem.

The islands cover 2 660 sq km (1 028 sq miles) and have a population of over 123 000. They are subject to earthquakes. Next to Rhodos, the most important are Léros and Kos (Cos). They embrace fertile tracts, intensively cultivated, and produce for export fruit and vegetables, grain and wine, cotton and silk. Two of the islands Kálimnos and Simi, are centres of the sponge-fishing industry in the eastern Mediterranean.

Table 60 – Greece: population registered in principal towns, 1971 census

Athens (capital)	1 853 000	(Athens and Piraus area 2 373 515)
Kavala	140 751	
Thessaloniki	29 447	(conurbation) 703 350
Patrai	110 632	

Albania

The Republic of Albania, declared as such in 1946 after the formal deposition, *in absentia*, of the king, who had fled the country in 1939 when it was occupied by Italy, comprises over 28 700 sq km (11 000 sq miles). It is mostly a wild mountainous land on the eastern shore of the Adriatic, in area about half as large again as Wales. Elections in 1945 brought a Communist government into power. Both the United Kingdom and the United States broke off diplomatic relations with Albania in 1946 and vetoed her admission to the United Nations; she was however admitted in 1955. The USSR broke off diplomatic relations with Albania in 1961.

The population of some 2m. (1970 estimate) is mainly engaged in agriculture and animal husbandry, especially the latter. Before the Second World War field crops were reckoned to form about 6 per cent of the total area and were limited to the coastal plains. About the same area was devoted to other forms of cultivation and cattle and sheep grazing accounted for a further 30 per cent, leaving well over half the total area covered either with forests or with swamps and other waste land. It was estimated that livestock included 1.5m. sheep, nearly 1m. goats and 330 000 cattle. In 1967 the area of arable land was nearly 17 per cent, the principal crops being maize and wheat, potatoes, sugar beet, fruits (including grapes), tobacco, olives, and some rice. Permanent grass occupied about 24 per cent and forests accounted for over 43 per cent of the total area. Livestock in 1970 numbered 435 000 cattle, 163 000 cows in milk, 150 000 pigs, 1.6m. sheep, 1.3m. goats, 42 000 horses, 23 000 mules and 62 000 asses.

The mineral wealth is potentially good, but has only recently been exploited: hematite and copper in the Pukë area, west of Shkodër; chromium at Kukës, Krumë and Pogradec; and large reserves of bitumen at Selenicë northeast of Vlonë. Crude oil is tapped at Qytet Stalin. All this development is as yet on a very small scale.

The capital, Tiranë, which has some modern buildings is the only town of any size (169 000); it lies in the heart of one of the most fertile plains. The port of Durrës now has an artificial harbour. Shkodër at the southern end of Lake Shkodër is also a port, but is over 40 km (25 miles) from the sea. The rugged peaks and gorges of the limestone mountains in the interior make communication very difficult and mule tracks are still in use. The roads and bridges built between the two world wars when Albania was an Italian colony help to ease the problem a little, but it was not until recently that any attempt was made to construct railways. In 1947 a railway was built between Durrës and Peqin, continued to Elbasan in 1950; in 1948 Durrës was also connected by rail with Tiranë. There are plans to link the mining centres to the capital by rail.

Chemical and engineering plants are being built with financial aid from the People's Republic of China, with whom most trade is carried on, and with whom Albania is politically in sympathy. Machinery and equipment, iron and steel, coke and other fuels form the major imports; major exports comprise wine, vegetables and fruits, tobacco (raw) and cigarettes, some plywood, cotton and blister copper — all in small quantities.

Union of Soviet Socialist Republics*

During the 100 years which preceded the First World War the Russian Empire had steadily expanded from Europe right across the north of Asia to the Pacific coast, and southwards to the mountainous borders of Afghanistan and Persia, so as to include what is now Soviet Turkestan. After the overthrow of the Tsarist regime in March 1917 came the Bolshevik revolution. In the subsequent settlement Finland became independent, the three small Baltic states of Estonia, Latvia, and Lithuania were carved out of what was formerly the Russian Empire and a further tract of country on the western margin became part of the new state of Poland. But there remained an area of over 21.4m. sq km (8.25m. sq miles) with a population approaching 107m. With the frontier adjustments which followed the Second World War, which included the absorption of a strip of Finland, the whole of Estonia, Latvia, and Lithuania as well as large sections of Poland and Romania, the area was increased to 22.4m. sq km (8.65m. sq miles) with a population which was reported in 1941 as 193m., as 200.2m. at

* The term Soviet Union or Union of Soviet Socialist Republics (USSR) is used where the reference is to the whole area. Where Russia or Russian is employed it refers specifically to the Russian Soviet Federal Socialist Republic, which comprises three-quarters of the whole.

the 1956 census, and as 241.7m. at the 1970 census; 1972 estimate: 246.3m. Like the continental United States, the USSR is a continuous mass of land, but has an area three times as large; over 8 050 km (5 000 miles) from east to west, and in places nearly 4 830 km (3 000 miles) from the borders of the Arctic Ocean in the north to the southern frontier. The Union stretches from west to east over more than 170 degrees of longitude and from north to south through more than 45 degrees of latitude, which is half the distance between the pole and the equator. It is ten days' continuous journey in one train from Moscow to Vladivostok; it is three days' continuous journey from Moscow to the southern frontier, and nearly two days' journey from Moscow to the northern shores. There are no overseas possessions, but the USSR has a great sphere of influence, especially in eastern Europe.

If we look at the position of the Soviet Union on the globe we notice at once that not only is the whole in the northern hemisphere, but even the southernmost part does not reach the tropics. The USSR lies entirely in midlatitudes in the so-called Temperate Zone and in the Arctic Zone; no part of the country is tropical. Soviet Central Asia, it is true, has extremely hot summers, and given irrigation can grow tropical and subtropical crops, hence the great importance of this area to the USSR as a whole. Because it does not possess land in equatorial or tropical latitudes one might say that the USSR could never be economically selfsufficient; on the other hand, with its enormous home resources, its great compact mass of land and the nature of its frontiers, which do not encourage foreign trade, the Soviet Union is peculiarly designed to be by nature a self-contained unit.

On the north it is bounded by the Arctic Ocean, along which it has a very long coastline, but nearly all this is icebound in the winter and a sea passage along the northern coast is only possible for two or three weeks in the middle of summer, if at all. Similarly, the very remote Pacific coast of the Soviet Union, in the Far East, is icebound in winter. Across Asia the Soviet Union borders the northeast region of China, the area which used to be known as Manchuria, the desert wastes of Mongolia and the heart of Asia, with their ramparts of mountains. In the south the Soviet Union is bounded by the mountain rampart of Afghanistan, Iran, and Turkey; its coastline along the Black Sea is valuable, but this is an inland sea, the entrance to which is controlled by Turkey at the Bosporus and the Çanakkale Bogazi (Dardanelles). On the west the Soviet Union is bordered by Romania, Czechoslovakia, and Poland. Since the absorption of Estonia, Latvia and Lithuania it has a long coastline along the Baltic but this is, of course, only an enclosed sea. It is only in the extreme northwestern corner of this vast country, in the Arctic coast near Murmansk, now in direct railway connection with Leningrad and Moscow, that the Soviet Union has outlet to an ocean open throughout the year.

Physical features. In the broadest possible way nearly the whole of the Soviet Union is one vast, incredibly extensive plain; only in the far northeast, or as one approaches the mountainous southeastern and southern borders, does this cease to be true. Although the scenery changes from boggy Arctic wastes through great forests of firs and other conifers to the rolling grain lands and then to the sandy uninhabited deserts, a journey in almost any direction across the Soviet Union can scarcely be described as other than monotonous. The country, however, falls into the following major divisions:

1. *The east European plain* or the Russian Platform, occupying practically the whole of European USSR from the Arctic Ocean to the Chernoye More (Black Sea), to the Bol'shoy Kavkaz (the Caucasus) and the Kaspiskoy More (Caspian Sea). Two-thirds of this great area lie within the basin of the River Volga, which is the longest river in Europe yet with its source in the Valdayskaya Vozvyshennost' (the Valdai Hills), less than 230 m (750 ft) above sea level.

2. *The Caucasus and Transcaucasia.* In the southern part of east Europe, stretching as a rampart between the Black and the Caspian Seas, is the great line of the Caucasus Mountains, rising in places to over 3 000 m (10 000 ft) and in E'brus to 5 600 m (18 470 ft). The Caucasus form such a barrier that they are still uncrossed by railway and for long were crossed by only one motor road. The two railways find their way round either end of the mountain chain. The three small countries of Georgia, Armenia, and Azerbaydzhan lie beyond the Caucasus (Transcaucasia) and are now separate socialist republics within the Union. A detached western extension of the Caucasus Mountains passes through the mountainous peninsula of the Krym (Crimea).

3. *The West Siberian lowlands.* This tract of very low, flat country, with large areas liable to spring floods, which forms the western part of Siberia is separated from Russia in Europe only by the low rise of the Uralski Khrebet (Urals), which can scarcely be called mountains and offer little or no barrier to communications, though the highest points do exceed 1 500 m (5 000 ft).

4. *Eastern Siberia,* east of the River Lena, is on the whole a low plateau.

5. *The far east,* a very remote region of the USSR, differs from the remainder in that it consists of a succession of mountain chains, some of them still scarcely explored in detail.

6. *Soviet Central Asia,* east of the Caspian Sea, consists on the whole of a great desert basin bordered by mountains on the south and east, amongst which are well-watered and populous valleys, and rising in the north to a low, undulating steppeland which separates Soviet Central Asia from Siberia.

Such a land of extensive rolling plains is naturally a land of large, slow, meandering rivers; but the Soviet Union is not very fortunate in

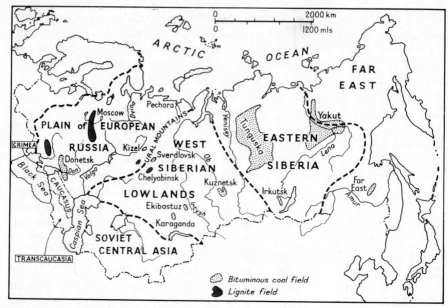

USSR: physical regions and coalfields

its rivers. Siberia is drained almost entirely to the Arctic Ocean in the north by the Ob, the Yenisey, and the Lena, and only in the far east do the Amur and its tributaries flow to the open Pacific; thus the Siberian rivers lead to the frozen Arctic and their lower courses are frozen for many months of the year. Similarly in the northern part of European Russia, the Pechora and the Dvina drain to the Arctic. Soviet Central Asia is a land of inland drainage, and so too is all that huge territory drained by the Volga into the Caspian Sea. Those valuable rivers the Don and the Dnepr drain to the Black Sea, and so does the Dnestr, formerly the boundary between the Ukraine and Romania. Despite the fact that they are all frozen for many months of the year, the Soviet Union makes considerable use of her rivers, and reference will be made to the waterways in a later section.

From the point of view of railway and road construction, the rivers form the principal obstructions to through communication across this great plain and necessitate numerous and very long bridges.

Minerals. The Soviet Union vies with the United States in the richness and variety of its mineral resources.

The Russian Platform or *the plain of east Europe* consists of an underlying block of very ancient rocks which has resisted later earth-building or mountain-building movements, and instead has been subjected to movements of elevation and depression. In times of depression it has been covered by the sea or by large bodies of fresh water

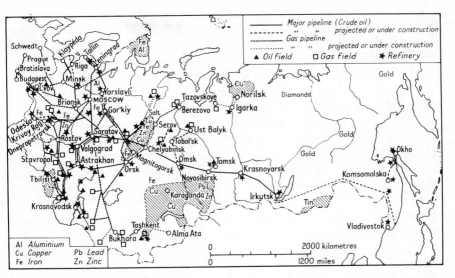

USSR: minerals, natural gas and oil

The major mineral-bearing areas are indicated by diagonal ruling

which have left on its surface deposits today remaining as horizontal beds or beds but very slightly folded. In places, particularly along the north, the ancient rocks of the underlying block crop out, but over the central and southern regions they are covered by the later deposits. Fortunately the later deposits include coalfields in places, so that the European part of the Soviet Union has three great coal basins. There is one in the extreme northeast in the Arctic region — the Pechora Field, now worked in Vorkuta; there is one consisting of brown coal lying to the south of Moscow and known as the Moscow or Tula basin; the third, and by far the most important, is the one known as the Donbass or Donetskiy basin in the south, not far from the Black Sea. Natural gas occurs to the east of the great coalfield; and oil and gas to the north-west in the Ukraine.

Associated with the very ancient rocks which are exposed in the north, are the minerals now being exploited in the Kola peninsula: iron, nickel, copper, apatite from which phosphates for fertilisers are made, nephelite for the production of aluminium, and many of the rare metals used in the production of specialised steel. In the south, at Krivoi Rog near the Black Sea, there are enormous deposits of iron ore, so that USSR leads the world in its production of iron ore (110.3m. tons in 1971) and is equal to the United States, in steel (120.5m. tons). All northern European Russia was covered during the Ice Age by a great icesheet which, on melting, left a hummocky drift-covered surface. Some of the hollows are now occupied by lakes, others by marshy tracts or bogs, some of which are yielding peat. Further south ridges of sand, gravel, and boulders run across the country and mark successive stages in the retreat of the ice sheet and are actually terminal moraines. Beyond this, over central and southern Russia and the Ukraine, are vast tracts which are covered by windborne deposits laid down by the very cold winds of the glacial period and which are the dustlike loess. It is because of the existence of this fertile soil that so much of the area is rich agricultural land.

The *Caucasus* is a typical folded mountain chain, with old rocks exposed in the centre yielding their quota of metallic minerals, including lead and zinc in the north, iron, manganese, copper, and aluminium ores on the southern flanks. Similar minerals are yielded along the southern border of Transcaucasia. On the flanks of the Caucasus are the famous oilfields which were in production before the First World War. The most important are to the south of the mountains, around the eastern end, near Baku, but another field is also worked near Tbilisi. An important field on the northern flanks is Groznyy; there are others near Maikop and under the Caspian. The Soviet Union lies second among the world producers of oil (71m. tons in 1955; 206m. tons in 1963 and 421m. tons in 1973), following the United States.

Although the *Urals*, topographically, form only a low divide, the old rocks break the surface and the tract in the centre is highly mineralised, rich in precious and semiprecious stones and ores. Among the many deposits of iron ore the most remarkable is the enormous Magnet Mountain, near which in the interwar years the great iron and steel town of Magnitogorsk was built. Other mineral deposits in the Urals include those of copper, chromium, manganese, nickel, gold, platinum and bauxite, and many rare metals needed in the production of specialised steels: tungsten, molybdenum, titanium and others. Just as on the flanks of the Caucasus there occur the great oilfields of southern Russia, so later discoveries showed that a line of oilfields exists on the flanks of the Urals; oil and natural gas have now been discovered at intervals almost from the Arctic Ocean to the Caspian Sea. The 'second Baku field' (with associated natural gas) of the central Urals together with the Emba Field on the Caspian north shore yielded as much oil in 1956 as the Old Baku. The 'second Baku' oilfield is now the most productive field in the Soviet Union, linked by pipelines to the major industrial centres in east and west. On the Siberian flank there is an important coalfield, whilst in the north there is one of the largest deposits of potash salts yet known in the world. Ordinary salt is important in the area below sea level north of the Caspian Sea (and also in the Krym (Crimea)) and is obtained from brine lakes.

The *plain of west Siberia* is essentially a low-lying area, formerly a gulf of the sea, now filled up with partly marine and partly land deposits. Vast reserves of oil underlie an area at the confluence of the Rivers Ob and Irtysh; and under the Yamal peninsula in the north there lies what may prove to be the largest deposit of natural gas in the world. There is iron ore in the southwest; and on the southeastern margin of the plain of west Siberia is the great coalfield of the Kuznetsk basin or Kuzbass, now developing as a major industrial region. There is another great coalfield at Karaganda in Kazakhstan in the south, an area also rich in copper, which extends along the shores of Lake Balkhash.

The plateau of *central Siberia*, averaging some 600 m (2 000 ft) in height, consists of a great mass of ancient rock. In places these ancient rocks yield metallic minerals. There are the famous gold deposits of the Lena basin and diamonds in the north, copper and nickel to the northwest, tin on the southern border. On the flanks of the old plateau and covering part of the surface, coalfields with almost horizontal seams are known to exist; still largely underdeveloped, there is the Tunguska coal basin on the west, the Lena basin on the east. Better known are the fields on the south, the Minusinsk basin and the Irkutsk basin and the Kansk basin, all of which have large reserves of coal.

The *far northeast* may still be described as a little known area. Structurally it is complicated, and it is possible that it may yield important mineral deposits. Gold has been discovered in several places, whilst in the south there are two coal basins; in the island of Sakhalin and in Kamchatka there is oil.

Soviet Central Asia, consisting of a central plain with a surround of complex, highly folded mountains, is proving to be an important mineral-bearing area. There are coal basins (including the large Karaganda basin), oil is now important (Ferghana Field), whilst in the ancient rocks there are gold, copper, lead, tin, and zinc.

Even from this very brief note on the distribution of some of the main mineral resources in the USSR it will be appreciated that the reserves exist in unsurpassed volume. It has been estimated that the coal resources, for example, form one-fifth of the world's known reserves; and the Soviet Union lies third to the USA and China in production. The USSR leads the world in output of iron ore, potash, chrome ore, magnesite, manganese ore. She lies second in the world league for diamonds, gold, lignite, natural gas, nickel ore, tungsten ore and zinc, second only to the United States in crude oil, copper and phosphate rock. She is the world's third largest producer of diamonds, nickel ore, mercury, molybdenum, lead ore and salt; fifth in silver; and since 1955 has begun to use her vast resources of natural gas.

Climate. The Soviet Union constitutes the heart of a vast land mass, *Eurasia.* This fact supplies the key to the climatic conditions. This great expanse of land becomes intensely cold in winter, so that the coldest known spot of the earth's surface is in the heart of Soviet Asia; there the lowest temperatures recorded on the earth's surface have been found, e.g. −70° C (−94.6° F) at Verkhoyansk. Extremely severe winter conditions are found everywhere in the north and centre, improving slightly towards the south and particularly towards the southwest in Europe; even so, nearly all parts of the country have an average temperature below freezing-point for the month of January. No part is as fortunate climatically in this respect as the whole of the British Isles; only Transcaucasia and the Iran—Afghan borders have temperatures above freezing in January.

In summer, on the other hand, the whole of the enormous land mass becomes intensely hot; temperatures of over 32° C (90° F) are sometimes recorded even within the Arctic Circle. The deserts of Soviet Central Asia suffer the most intense heat, but the whole country may be described as hot. Only the Arctic coastlands have cool summers.

In winter the great mass of cold, heavy air which rests over the whole area results in a high pressure centre from which there are outblowing winds. Contrary to popular belief the snowfall in winter is comparatively light, rarely exceeding 90 cm (3 ft). It is in the spring when the high pressure area gives place to a low pressure area that inblowing winds from the ocean bring their quota of rainfall. Most parts of the USSR in Europe and the fertile belt of Siberia thus enjoy light, spring rains ideal for grain, followed by the heat of summer. The southwest is the region in which both temperature and precipitation are most favourable to production. Eastwards, around the Caspian Sea and in Soviet Central Asia the rainfall drops below 200 mm (8 in) and desert conditions prevail.

Soils and natural vegetation. The Russians have been pioneers in the study of the soil. They realised that the formation of soil does not depend so much on the character of the underlying rock as on the character of the climate. The great soil belts of the country correspond with climatic conditions and run across the country from east to west, and constitute the natural regions of the country. From north to south the following may be distinguished:

1. *The tundra belt and the tundra soils.* Here the cold in winter is such that the subsoil is permanently frozen; the heat of summer is insufficient to do more than melt the moisture in the surface layers, with the result that in summer the surface of the ground is swampy and the soils boggy. This region is beyond the northern limits of the growth of trees and the ground is covered with tundra vegetation, of mosses and lichens, including the famous reindeer moss, though for a short period there may be rich growth of grass and flowering plants.

2. *The belt of coniferous or softwood forests*, with podsol (ash-coloured) soils. The USSR has by far the largest reserves of untouched forest lands of soft timber in the world, and the coniferous forest stretches as an enormous belt from the Finnish border right across the country to the Pacific Ocean, as far south, roughly, as the latitude of

Leningrad. The great difficulty is one of access to the forests. Only the more easily reached parts have been seriously worked so far. Unfortunately for the Soviet Union the rivers which can be used for floating timber, at least for a few months in the summer, drain towards the Arctic Ocean. There has however been a great increase in the exploitation of timber, even in the more distant forests, and the timber 'ship caravans' of the Arctic Ocean are now piloted by icebreakers and by aeroplanes which study the weather conditions. The industry has made the Arctic coast of growing importance. Chief sawmill centres are Arkhangel'sk for the north; and Volgograd for timber floated down the Volga. The total cut represents only a few per cent of the annual increment by natural growth. In 1971 the USSR lead the world in lumber production. The soils of the forest are light ashen in colour, hence the Russian name podsol; and they are poor in plant food. Thus when the forest is cleared that land is not very valuable for cultivation even when the climate would permit agricultural development. There are also large stretches of boggy soil and tracts of peat.

3. *The deciduous or mixed forest belt of European USSR* consists partly of coniferous trees and partly of deciduous trees which lose their leaves in winter. Here the soils are rather better and much of the land has been cleared.

4. *The black earth belt or wooded steppe.* The natural vegetation of this belt was a rich grassland with scattered trees. The soil consists of loess very dark in colour because of the large quantity of vegetable matter, and is a soil called *chernozem* which is extremely fertile. As a result this is the great grain-growing belt of southern Russia, the Ukraine, and Siberia, and most of the natural vegetation has been replaced by vast fields of grain.

5. *The chestnut-brown soils and the steppelands (grassland).* This is land formerly covered with grass rather poorer than in the belt just described, and where the soils, though good, are not quite so rich. This today is also a grain-growing region, but not of the same remarkable fertility as the black earth belt.

6. *The grey desert soils and the saline soils* are those characteristic of the drier regions of the Soviet Union around the Caspian Sea and of Soviet Central Asia. Here in some areas there is very poor grassland formerly inhabited by nomadic stock rearers with their flocks and herds. In the drier parts little grows, and settlement is possible only where water is available for irrigation. This is, however, an important part of the Soviet Union because it is the warmest; and here, on irrigated land, tropical and subtropical crops can be grown.

7. *The Mediterranean zone.* Along the southern border of the Krym (Crimean) peninsula there is a very small, sheltered tract of land where the USSR can grow some, at least, of the Mediterranean products.

8. *The subtropical zone* is the hot wet lowland of western Trans-caucasia where rice, tea and citrus fruits are grown.

Animal life. Wild animals retreat as man encroaches on their territories and even before the First World War the Tsarist government feared the extermination of the rich and varied wild life by hunters. The Soviet government has shooting and trapping well under control and has established large nature reserves for the protection of native species, into which non-indigenous species of animals have been introduced. The USSR is the home of many valuable fur-bearing animals: mink, marten, musk rat, skunk, otter, silver fox, and squirrel and many others, which provide skins for the fur trade. Some are feral in the forests, others are reared on fur farms; but trading in furs no longer plays a very important part in the economy of the USSR.

In the north herds of reindeer supply milk, meat and other products.

The rivers and the seas surrounding the USSR abound with fish. It forms a considerable part of the diet in the north; and is the basis of the important fish-processing and canning industry. Sakhalin in the Far East is important for its fisheries, and Nikolayevsk is a notable fishing centre on the Pacific coast. The River Volga is famous for its sturgeon, the roes of which yield caviare. In 1970 the fish catch amounted to nearly 7.3m. tons, to place the USSR third, her usual position, among the world's leading fishing nations.

The people of the Soviet Union. The Soviet Union stretches from Europe right across Asia. In the same way the people are essentially Euro—Asian. Much of the failure of western Europe and America to appreciate the true state of affairs in the Soviet Union today is due to a fundamental lack of understanding of the peoples of the Union. In the first place they are extraordinarily varied and include many different racial stocks; nearly three-quarters of the whole are Slavs. About AD 1230 the Mongolians overran Rus (which term covers Russia and the Ukraine in medieval times). For nearly 250 years Rus remained a tribute-paying vassal of the Mongolian state known as Orda and the defence of western Europe against the Mongols and Turks fell to Poland and Hungary.

Various Turkic and other tribes are today the principal inhabitants of central Asia; they penetrated there and to the Volga basin in medieval times where they remain in considerable colonies. It was Poland and Austria who protected the rest of Europe from these invasions and we may almost say that the material progress of western Europe for some five or six centuries was made possible by this protection. Russia's activity against Turkey was strong and successful in the eighteenth and nineteenth centuries. In wars against the Ottoman Empire the southern Ukraine, Crimea, and Transcaucasia were captured.

The heart of Slav Russia was Moscow, but feudal Russia, as far as the ruling class was concerned, appreciated the civilisation of western Europe and Tsar Peter the Great in 1700 established its capital at St Petersburg, now Leningrad, where communication by sea with western Europe was possible. Imperialist Russia had designs on the conquest of much of Asia, and looked on the far eastern coast with Vladivostok and Manchuria as their ultimate outpost in that direction. The first Russian conquest beyond the Urals was made in 1581 under a Cossack leader called Yermak. The expedition was primarily in the interest of a family of Russian fur traders, but it received the sanction of the Russian Government, and politically was merely a continuation of the process of expansion by which the grand princes of Moscow gradually drove back or subjugated the Tartar invaders of the thirteenth century. The immediate result of the first invasion of Yermak was the fall of the Tartar capital, Sibir on the Irtysh, about 16 km (10 miles) above the present Tobol'sk, which was founded soon after. Small parties of Cossacks, living the life of backwoodsmen, gradually pushed eastwards along the rivers, and in little more than fifty years after the conquest of Sibir a blockhouse was erected (1632) on the present site of Yakutsk on the Lena. Before the close of that century the Russians had come in contact with the Chinese on the Amur, but a pause of about 150 years took place in their eastern expansion, after they had in 1689, in the Treaty of Nerchinsk, relinquished all claim to the Amur. Further expansion in this direction took place during the Crimean War, and in 1858 the Chinese agreed in the Treaty of Aigun to recognise the Amur and Usuri and a line drawn from the head of the Usuri southwards to Korea as the Russian frontier. In the latter part of the nineteenth century the frontier was pushed further and further so as to include what is now Soviet Central Asia, and with the completion of the Trans—Siberian railway in 1903 Moscow was placed in direct communication with its far eastern possessions. But the prestige of the country received a severe setback on its defeat in the Russo—Japanese War of 1904—05. In the early nineteenth century Siberia was virtually an uninhabited tract, despite the inherent fertility of much of its area. Its severe winters gained it a notoriety which was heightened by its use as a place of exile for criminals. But all who resisted the existing regime were also liable to exile; many of the most progressive elements of the country who resisted political intolerance preferred to make their way to a new country and so went to Siberia as voluntary exiles. The virility of these political exiles was largely responsible for the amazing growth of settlement, agriculture, and urban life in Siberia, where the rapid growth of such centres as Novosibirsk from about 5 000 in 1897 to 750 000 in little over half a century suggests a comparison with the pioneers who for the same reasons set out to conquer the middle west of America.

The militaristic and imperialistic organisation which persisted until the Revolution of 1917 was very largely the result of the long history of strife. A great gulf separated the peasants from the ruling classes. There were the Cossacks who were the Ukrainians and Russians liable to military service and in return received arms and money grants from the government and also a reservation of considerable stretches of land; they might be described as mercenaries, employed as the advance guard of colonisation or conquest, and as the militaristic police force throughout the country. There were serfs, and serfdom was not abolished until 1861; even after that it was quite common for slaves to be sold in the far eastern markets. Down to 1861 the majority of the peasants were serfs attached to the properties of landowners. In that year they were emancipated in a sense, and portions of the landowners' estates were set apart for them, the government paying compensation which was to be repaid by the peasants by instalments. For this repayment, however, not the individual peasants but the *mir* or village commune was made responsible, and the *mir* as a whole had control of the peasants' land. The land was allotted to individuals in scattered parcels so as to give all an equal chance of getting land of equal quality on the whole, and redivisions of the land took place at intervals of years varying in length in different parts of the country. No member of the *mir* was allowed to leave it at his own free will. By a law of 1906, however, the peasant was made a really free man. He could demand his share of the land in one piece, and buy out his neighbour if opportunity offered. Greater agricultural enterprise was being shown by the more capable. Improved agricultural machinery and implements were being more largely bought and improved methods of farming were being adopted. On the other hand, peasants whose holdings were too small were selling them and becoming labourers. Ultimately these would have been absorbed no doubt by the demands of manufacturing industry. The congestion in the agricultural districts where the land was excessively subdivided was being relieved to some extent by migration to the more thinly peopled tracts in the southeast as well as to Siberia. Formerly emigration to Siberia was allowed only to villagers, but emigration thither from the towns was permitted from the beginning of 1914.

The imperial military organisation which persisted until the revolution of 1917 was largely the result of a long history of strife. A great gulf separated peasant workers from the ruling classes, and even in 1917 the life of the agricultural worker resembled that of the agricultural peasant of England in the Middle Ages. The Soviet regime had to win over this vast mass of illiterate people to the philosophy of Marx, Engels and Lenin, a people made fearful and stubborn by centuries of oppression, and accordingly suspicious of authority, reluctant to adopt new techniques. Unification and industrialisation had to succeed at whatever cost, at speed, and the Soviet regime pushed forward its programme with relentless determination and devotion to doctrine. At times the demands of the Five Year Plans, and the rule of some of its leaders, have undoubtedly brought much hardship and misery; but the country has hurtled from the Middle Ages to the technology of the mid-twentieth century at breakneck speed, to become a leading world power. The extent and effectiveness of industrialisation were clearly shown by the victorious outcome of the struggle with Germany in the Second World War; and by the advanced technology of space research in the USSR today.

The distribution of population. In 1939 the population of the Soviet Union was nearly 170.6m.: at the census taken in 1897 the population of the same area was only a little over 106m. Within the extended post-war limits of the USSR the population in April 1959, as estimated officially, numbered 201 500 000. The 1970 census shows 241.7m. Moscow had a population of 7m. and Leningrad of 3.9m.; there are 223 towns with a population of over 100 000 and the rural population numbered 105.7m., the urban 136m. The rural population is densest along the famous Black Earth belt stretching from the borders of Romania across the Urals into Siberia. Along this belt, too, are the great towns of Siberia such as Chelyabinsk, Omsk and Novosibirsk. To the north and south of this population tends to decrease, but with large urban nuclei in the industrial regions which will be described later.

Occupations of the people. Imperial Russia was essentially an agricultural country with a limited development of industry concentrated almost entirely in two regions: the immediate neighbourhood of Leningrad; and the central tract with its centre at Moscow, together with outlying industrial regions on the Donbass coalfield in the south and associated with oil in the neighbourhood of Baku.

Among the great objectives of the First Five Year Plan (1928–32), the Second Five Year Plan (1933–37), and the succeeding plans, have been not only the industrialisation of the Union to make the country a selfsufficient economic unit, but also the redistribution of industry in such a way as to locate the great industrial enterprises where power (coal, oil, water power, or peat) are available or where there is an abundant supply of raw material, particularly heavy and bulky raw material, e.g. iron ore; and also to employ to the full labour resources in different parts of the country. The result has been, in the first place, the development of local industries to supply local markets, a requirement very important in a country of such vast distances as the Soviet Union. In Tsarist times raw cotton was sent some 3 225 km (2 000 miles) from Soviet Central Asia to Moscow and back again as finished cloth; this was obviously an absurdity, hence the establishment of industry in Soviet Central Asia itself for the supply of local markets.

This scattering of industry proved of immense value in the Second

World War when the Germans overran European Russia as far east as the gates of Leningrad, Moscow, and what was then Stalingrad (now Volgograd).

Agriculture. Forty-five per cent of the whole of the Soviet Union is occupied by forest, 18.5 per cent by pasture, non-agricultural land 25.5 per cent, arable land 10.5 per cent; but the area of the country is so vast that this 10.5 per cent of arable land represents 233m. ha (576m. acres).

By careful land management, the widespread use of home-produced fertilisers, the planting of shelter belts of trees in exposed areas, by irrigation, by drainage of swampy areas, by ploughing virgin lands, by the use of improved seeds and by mechanisation of farm work, the extent of agricultural land has been increased, and much higher yields than used to be possible are produced. In 1970 there were 4.1m. tractors and 605 000 combine harvesters; and helicopters are widely used in agriculture and forestry. The 4m. ha of land irrigated in 1913 had by 1967 extended to 11.3m. ha; and areas previously considered hostile to wheat, for example, now produce good crops. The wheat area in 1945–52 was 42.6m. ha (105m. acres), producing 35.7m. tons. In 1970 65.6m. ha (162m. acres) produced 94m. tons. Other grain areas in 1970 were: barley 21.5m. ha (58m. acres), rye 11m. ha (27m. acres), oats 8.5m. ha (21m. acres) and maize 4.6m. ha (11.4m. acres). Compared with those of western Europe the yields are low, but the physical conditions in the two areas are not comparable: the Russians have the disadvantages of a generally harsh environment. In the same period, 1945–70, the output and yield of potatoes has risen from a slightly decreased area. Sugar beet is especially important as an industrial crop, with a rising production and yield.

The considerable increase in agricultural production has been achieved despite the adverse physical conditions with which the people of the Soviet Union have to contend. The northerly situation of the USSR, with so much of the land covered by permafrost, the extremes of the continental climate, the short growing season, the vast areas of inherently infertile soils and others low in fertility, the extremes of poor drainage over the wide stretch of the lowlands and the prevalence of arid conditions elsewhere, are limiting physical factors controlling agriculture.

The bulk of the cultivated land is now in either state or collective farms. Only about 0.5 per cent of farms lack an electricity supply; and all are highly mechanised. On a collective the worker retains his own house and a plot of land for his own use. In some crops (potatoes, vegetables, meat, milk and eggs) the total output from these private plots tends to be greater than that from the collectives. Between 1953 and 1970 the number of collective farms was reduced; many of the smaller ones were amalgamated, others became state farms, especially where they adjoined industrial areas. In 1953 there were 93 000 collectives and 4 857 state farms; in 1970 the numbers were 34 700 collectives, 14 310 state farms. The state farms (on which labour is employed, as in a factory) were initially intended as research and training stations, or as farms producing specialised crops, models to be copied by neighbouring farms. They have proved to be more useful and controllable than the collectives and their numbers have therefore grown at the expense of the collectives. The average area of a state farm is about 30 000 ha (75 000 acres), but the largest is 202 340 ha (500 000 acres).

The growth of agricultural production is keeping pace with the food needs of the increasing population; and special attention is given to industrial crops (cotton, flax, oilseeds, rubber-yielding shrubs, potatoes for alcohol, as well as to fodder crops which are indirectly industrial crops in that they feed the stock which will yield wool and leather, as well as meat). The aim is to make each region, as well as the country as a whole, as self-sufficient as possible.

The numbers of livestock reared in the last twenty years have risen. In 1951–52 cattle numbered nearly 56m. (including 24m. dairy cows), pigs nearly 20m., sheep 76.8m., poultry (chicken, geese, ducks) nearly 370m. By 1970 there were over 95m. cattle (with over 41m. dairy cows), pigs numbered 56m., sheep 130.6m., poultry 566m. To generalise, cattle-rearing areas coincide with natural grassland; and the land acquired in the west after the Second World War is especially favourable for cattle. Most dairy cattle and pigs (traditionally fed on skimmed milk and potatoes) are to be found in the cleared forest areas, and near urb.n centres. The great cattle area of the Ukraine produces about one-quarter of all the meat and one-fifth of all the milk consumed in the Soviet Union. Poultry are prevalent in the grain producing areas; and reindeer maintain their precarious life in the permafrost zone, the herds being especially numerous between the River Ob and the Kola peninsula.

The great area of grain cultivation is the Black Earth belt. Here the crops are wheat (spring wheat, where the winters are too severe for autumn sowing) and barley. On the warmer southern side of the wheat belt maize becomes the main or leading crop; on the cooler northern side the place of wheat is taken by oats and rye. North of the latitude of Leningrad climate places a limit on the cultivation of many crops, and although barley takes advantage of the long summer days and will ripen within the Arctic Circle, an important crop in these northern regions is oats.

The climate over the major part of the USSR is unfavourable to fruit, so much attention is being given to the southern lands with a view to increasing fruit and vegetable production there. The range of vegetables in most of the Soviet Union is very limited. The main vegetable-growing areas are in the west and southwest; and there is expanding production near the big towns. The vine ripens in the warm lands of the Sea of Azov—Black Sea area, in the Krym (Crimea), in Moldavia and the Ukraine, the last two areas producing a good quantity of wine. Tea, the national drink, is a very important crop in Gruziya (Georgia) and in Azerbaydzhan.

Industry. Industrialisation began quite early in Russia, helped by the labour force created in the 1860s by the abolition of serfdom. Now the mechanisation of industry and the installation of automatic remote control is being pushed forward. Industry is developed near the source of raw materials or of power, to economise on transport costs.

There is no lack of power resources. It has been estimated that Soviet coal reserves, for example, would be sufficient at the present rate of consumption to supply the whole world for over 1 000 years; but the use of coal declines in the USSR, as in other industrial countries, as it gives way to oil and natural gas, with which the Soviet Union is also richly endowed. All three fuels, as well as brown coal and peat, are used in thermal electric power stations. For example, the Moscow and Ural stations use brown coal, those at Leningrad and Gor'kiy use peat, the stations in the Caucasus use oil, for obvious reasons.

In general the rivers of the USSR are unsuitable for the generation of hydroelectric power in their long courses across the great expanse of plain and plateau, freezing in winter; but where hydroelectric installations are feasible the output is prodigious, and in many cases they have been incorporated in navigation, irrigation and flood control schemes. There are many small stations, too numerous to mention; the largest are at Dneproges, at Kuybyshev and at Bratsk. The main waters used are those of the Dnepr, the Volga (where evaporation is a problem), the many streams of the Caucasus (which have long been used), the Yenisey basin (Bratsk is on the River Angara) where Oz Baykal forms a natural reservior, the Ob basin (especially at Novosibirsk) and the Lena basin (which has enormous potential). At Nurek, on the Amu Dar'ya in the mountains of Soviet Central Asia a high dam is being built which will not only be instrumental in creating power, but will ensure water for the irrigation of over 100 000 ha (240 000 acres). Another is under construction in the Syr Dar'ya basin, at Toktogul.

With these abundant power resources there has been little need for the USSR to develop nuclear power stations. However three are now in operation: at Obninsk (Kaluga region), at Novo-Voronezh, and at Beloyarsk. At Shevenko, on the Caspian Sea, is another nuclear power station which not only supplies electricity but desalinates seawater for this flourishing new small oil town in the desert. Another, small, nuclear installation is being built at Bilibino in the far northeast of

Siberia to serve the gold and tin mines; and others at Kirovsk, and at Novy Uzen on the Caspian shore.

The Soviet Union is also experimenting in the harnessing of tidal power. A station is in operation at Murmansk and another is planned for the Mezenskaya Guba near Mezen'.

All these resources of power give a total production which puts the Soviet Union second to the USA in output; and in manufactured gas leads the world. There is therefore plenty of surplus power available, a contributory factor which led to the setting up of 'Mir' in the 1960s, the unified power grid which serves Comecon countries, and to which the USSR is the major contributor.

Industry in Tsarist times was located mainly in the west, especially in the Moscow area and around Leningrad. On the whole it was based on textile manufacture, with the use of flax, cotton and to a less extent wool and silk; iron goods were also produced in the Moscow—Tula area as long ago as the seventeenth century, based on bog iron ore and charcoal made from the trees of the area. The iron and steel industry developed in the eastern Ukraine and in the adjoining province of Rostov; heavy engineering followed in the nineteenth century, with shipbuilding and the manufacture of railway rolling stock, again still in the west. The chemical industry is a much newer phenomenon, developed under the Soviet regime.

At the outbreak of the Second World War nearly all the principal industrial development was still in the west; and it was the west that suffered most, not only from the devastation by German attack, but by the 'scorched earth' policy of the Soviet people as they drew back, leaving behind nothing of any use to the Germans. The expansion of industry and agriculture in the east thus became vitally important to the war effort of the USSR and there was an immediate upsurge of industry in the relative security of the Urals and centres further east. When the war ended the colossal task of rebuilding and developing new industries was begun, in addition to the rehousing of the people and to the restoration of the farmland.

By 1967 the eastern regions (the Urals, Siberia, Far East and Soviet Central Asia) were producing 51 per cent of the coal, 34 per cent of the oil, 37 per cent of the pig iron, 40 per cent of the steel and 40 per cent of the electric power of the USSR and the industrial expansion of these areas is by no means complete.

1. *The central region around Moscow.* In Imperial Russia, this region produced something like half of all the manufactured goods produced in the country. Today the importance of its output is no less, but relative to the output of the whole country it is less significant. Moscow itself is the centre, to the south is Tula, to the north we find Kalinin, Yaroslavl, and Ivanovo, whilst to the east is Gor'kiy. The whole region used to draw its coal from the far south, the Donbass basin; much more

extensive use is now being made of the rather poor brown coal or lignite of the Moscow or Tula basin. The whole area was linked together in an electricity grid under the Second Five Year Plan. It is a region associated primarily with the cotton industry and with textiles generally and the manufacture of clothing, together with various metal workings and machinery manufacture; and chemical and miscellaneous industries. In Moscow there are factories producing motor vehicles, electric locomotives and other power equipment, and machine tools; Gor'kiy has one of the biggest motor vehicle factories in the USSR, while its other factories produce machine tools, and its shipyards river vessels. Yaroslavl and Kalinin are milling towns, the grain arriving by water. Timber is collected near Kalinin to be sent by rail to the north-west for the manufacture of paper from the pulp. Yaroslavl has a newer industry: it is here that synthetic rubber is made from alcohol derived from potatoes and from petroleum brought in by pipeline from the south. The rubber is used in tyre production for the region's motor vehicle industry. The factories of Kostroma specialise in the manu-facture of rolling stock for the railways, especially diesel locomotives; Kineshma makes car parts; there are factories in Vladimir supplying instruments for cars and tractors; and Ivanovo makes the textile machinery for Moscow. There are innumerable other smaller towns, each with its own type of industry. Chemicals are a newer develop-ment: the industry is growing rapidly, and it is in this region that manmade fibres are made for local use.

The iron and steel needed for all this industrial activity is supplied by the integrated works at Lipetsk and from plant at Tula, Gor'kiy and other centres. The iron ore is drawn mainly from the recently opened Kursk field, and it is considered worth while to use coking coal from the Donbass despite the expense of transport. In fact this region lacks the raw materials necessary for industry: on the whole the concentra-tion of industry has developed as a result of a large available pool of skilled labour and not on the strength of available raw materials. Moscow, the capital, has always attracted people: it is the great cultural and administrative centre, famous for its wide boulevards, its magnifi-cent ancient buildings, its massive new architecture.

2. *Leningrad*. The Leningrad region, like the Moscow region, lacks local resources of coal and iron ore. It has however the advantage of its sea-board situation and it is well served by hydroelectric power. The ship-building industry is important and specialises in building icebreakers and timber ships. The first nuclear-powered icebreaker, the *Lenin*, was built here. There is a manufacture of miscellaneous high quality machinery, especially power equipment, a limited textile industry, but an important clothing industry.

Iron and steel is provided by the plant at Cherepovets, which draws on coal from the Donbass, despite high transport costs on such a long haul, and from the Pechora coalfield, the iron ore coming from the Kolskiy Poluostrov (Kola peninsula). Leningrad also produces super-phosphates; and the natural gas supply forms the basis of a highly productive chemical industry. As in Moscow, industry has grown in the Leningrad region because of the pool of labour. Under Peter the Great, Petersburg (Leningrad) was the capital city of Russia, and although it has lost this administrative function, it is still the second city of the Soviet Union.

3. *The Ukraine–Don region.* This area covers the fine rich Donbass coalfield, also one of the great iron ore yielding regions, and in addition spreads over the fertile Black Earth region of the Ukraine. It provides nearly half the iron and steel used in the USSR. Krivoy Rog has the largest iron ore deposit with manganese at Nikopol. The region round the ironfield and eastwards on the coalfield forms the centre of iron and steel production, with the towns of Zaporozhye, Dnepropetrovsk, Donetsk and Zhdanov. There are numerous secondary industries which utilise the iron and steel, such as the manufacture of agricultural imple-ments for use in the fertile belt by which the territory is surrounded. Important centres are Kharkov and Rostov. Innumerable factories process local agricultural material; thus there are sugar mills, flour mills, factories producing fats and oils from oilseeds, such as those of sun-flowers, and tanning mills. Kiev, on the Dnepr, has long been the centre of Ukrainian sugar refining and has important leather manufactures.

The Donbass itself supports a major industrial complex of metal works, chemical works, coalmines and engineering plant, well supplied by electricity from the Dnepr power stations. The present Plan lays down that textile factories should be brought to the Ukraine–Don area to provide work for the female population.

4. *The Ural region* is a newer industrial region than the Ukraine–Don, and is the second main producer of iron and steel. The Urals have long been famous as a storehouse of mineral wealth in the USSR, notable for their great reserves of iron ore. Coking coal is absent but the available lignite is used in the generation of electricity. In the early eighteenth century charcoal and the local iron ore provided pig iron. In the 1930s coking coal from the Kuzbass (Kuznetsk) mines to the east was brought by rail to the furnaces of the 'Magnet Mountain' (Magnitogorsk) in the Urals, the trucks returning laden with the iron ore which the Kuzbass lacked: a mutually convenient arrangement which established an iron and steel industry at each centre. This exchange continues, but the building of a rail route to Karaganda, nearer to the Ural region, means that coal from this important field is also at the disposal of the Urals blast furnaces; there are also plans to draw the great coal resources of Ekibastuz, northeast of Karaganda, into the association. There are countless integrated plants in the Urals, apart from those at Magnito-gorsk, in the area stretching from Serov in the north to Troitsk, some

near the sites of the old charcoal furnaces. As the high grade iron ores of the Urals are worked out the supply is supplemented by deposits conveniently situated along the railway connecting Karaganda and Magnitogorsk.

The southern Urals and Karaganda have one great disadvantage: they lack a good water supply. Water had to be brought nearly 805 km (500 miles) by aqueduct from the River Irtysh to Karaganda.

The development of the Urals as an industrial region was hastened by the loss of the Donbass in the Second World War. The vast iron and steel plant fed the mushrooming industries of the towns; mechanical engineering, chemicals, synthetic rubber manufacturing, the atomic industry, the provision of more thermal electric power stations became of paramount importance. All these activities have continued, as well as the traditional metallurgical industries. There are innumerable centres pouring forth the products of their engineering plant, but two major ones should be noted: Chelyabinsk with a great output of mechanical engineering; and Sverdlovsk which also has mechanical engineering plant as well as manufactures of electrical equipment, and the vast complex known as Ural–Mashzavod which is the biggest producer of industrial equipment in the USSR. The works at a smaller centre, Nizhni Tagil, produce rolling stock for the railways.

5. *The Kuznetsk coalfield,* The Kuzbass, is another enormous iron and steel area. It lies east of the largest industrial town in Siberia, Novosibirsk, an important industrial centre well served by rail. The Kuzbass is part of the 'third metallurgical base' of the Soviet Union. This industrial region uses coal from the Kuzbass and from the Karaganda field, lignite from the Yenisey basin, hydroelectric power from the Siberian rivers, and the iron ore deposits which lie so fortunately close to the Trans–Siberian railway.

There is an important integrated iron and steel plant at Novokuznetsk, which is a leading centre of the chemical industry. Chemicals are also important at Novosibirsk, at Kemerovo and at Topki. Tomsk, on a branchline of the Trans–Siberian railway, has been rather left behind by all this industrial activity in the other towns of the region, but (with Anzhero–Sudzhensk, Belovo and Prokopyevsk) has engineering works. The building of the Trans–Siberian railway opened up this area, which is now served by oil pipeline; agriculture has been extended to feed the growing population.

Further along the railway is an even newer industrial centre, Krasnoyarsk, with up-to-date electric steel mills, served by hydroelectric power, as well as an aluminium smelter, shipyards, timber yards and wood-processing plant. There is a certain amount of light industry too, including a factory making television sets.

There are iron ore deposits on each side of the lower Angara and along the upper Lena, all depending on Kuzbass coal; but with advanced methods of ore concentration it seems likely that the ore will be sent to the Kuzbass for smelting in preference to the development of steel plants at the location of the iron ore.

6. *Other industrial centres.* There are other farflung steel centres: in Central Asia, near Tashkent; on the Kura River south of Tbilisi (where locomotives and pipes for the oil industry are made); and far away to the east, at Komsomolsk on the River Amur.

There are other lesser industrial areas which should be noticed: the Kolskiy Poluostrov (Kola peninsula), associated with timber working and the exploitation of minerals; Transcaucasia, with the industrial region round Tblisi in Gruzinskaya (Georgia) based on oil and metallic minerals, where the production of fruit and vegetables and the canning industry as well as the production of wine are leading occupations; and what may seem to be the surprising industrial development of Soviet Central Asia, almost entirely dependent on the control of the water supply and on the railways. From the terminus at Krasnovodsk, a rapidly expanding town on the shore of the Caspian Sea, timber and machinery can be imported via the River Volga, and oil from the Baku oilfield. In return raw cotton and tobacco can be exported by the same route to the upper Volga basin. The railways to the north and east connect the oasis cities of Soviet Central Asia with the colder northern lands, thus an exchange of the cereals and timber of these lands for the subtropical produce of Soviet Central Asia is possible. Modern irrigation techniques have transformed the landscape and the life of this arid area. Cotton is the main crop, and a wide variety of fruits is grown, as well as tobacco and food grains, including rice. The area is rich in minerals, which form the basis of the growing mining and chemical industries; and it is here, at Baykonyr, that the space research scientists of the Soviet Union work. The development of this generally arid region is one of the most significant activities in the Soviet Union at the present time.

Irkutsk, near Oz Baykal (Lake Baykal), also deserves special mention. It lies in a forested highland area, important for furs, timber, mining and agriculture in the valleys; and at Bratsk, on the Angara, the abundant hydroelectric power is used in the production of cellulose from timber. Northwest Russia and the Baltic republics are also engaged in processing local conifers for cellulose and paper manufacture. The Baltic republics make use of local hardwoods in their furniture industry, while structural timber is provided by the woodyards of Arkhangel'sk, Onega and Petrozavodsk.

Of other industries, the nonferrous metal industry is so widespread it is impossible to give it adequate coverage in a short space. In general the smelting plants are near the location of the ore if sufficient water and fuel resources are available.

The early chemical industry developed in the area of the Donbass, in the Moscow region (based on brown coal) and in the Urals. Mineral fertilisers have long been produced in the Donbass and in the Moscow regions, in the west Ukraine and in the Baltic republics in order to supply the nearby agricultural lands. An area rich in potassium salts was acquired in the western Ukraine when the Soviet Union extended its boundary westwards after the Second World War. Potassium salts are also mined in the upper Kama valley in the Ural region; nitrogenous fertiliser is produced from sulphuric acid on the Donbass; the output of phosphoric fertilisers is important in the Kolskiy Poulostrov (Kola) from the apatite deposits; and in Soviet Central Asia the super-phosphate works provide fertiliser for the cotton lands. There are other deposits of phosphates fortunately near Aktyubinsk in the newly ploughed 'virgin lands'.

The Soviet Union was first in the field in making synthetic rubber. She lacks a supply of natural latex, a product of the equatorial zone. There are synthetic rubber works at Yaroslavl, Voronezh, Yefromov and Kazan, another near Baku and more in Armenia, using a variety of raw materials as a basis, but in the main alcohol derived from potatoes, or petroleum.

Agricultural machinery is made wherever possible in the areas where it is needed. An interesting development has been the establishment of such factories in Soviet Central Asia where mechanical equipment is made for the cotton lands, and machinery for processing the local crop of cottonseed for oil.

The Soviet Union is not well endowed with building stone, and the cement industry is of vital importance. There are two main sources of raw materials: the limestones of the banks of the Volga above Saratov, and the marls of the Black Sea slopes of the Caucasus Mountains. Her resources of stone for road metal are poor over much of the country.

7. *Other inland towns.* Among the chief inland towns besides those already mentioned are Kazan, Kuybyshev (Samara), at the east end of a loop of the Volga, where the river is pushed eastwards by a limestone barrier, long important for its river and eastern land trade, now of importance as situated at the angle of bifurcation of the old southern route of the Trans—Siberian railway and the line to Orenburg (Chkalov) and Turkestan; Saratov, lower down, on the Volga, a centre of the culti-vation and manufacture of tobacco; Volgograd (Stalingrad) on the Volga; Kharkov, a centre of trade and industry in the Ukraine; Kyev, capital of the Ukraine; Orenburg (Chkalov), on the Ural, the old starting-point of caravans to the east and southeast before the construc-tion of the railway; Orsk at the southern end of the Urals. In Siberia, all on the railway, are Omsk, Krasnoyarsk, and Chita.

Before the Revolution large periodic fairs were characteristic of the inland, and even to some extent of the foreign, trade of Russia. The great fairs of Nizhniy Novgorod (now Gor'kiy), the most important of which was held annually in August, were international, Asia and Europe there exchanging products. Irbit, east of the Urals, northwest of Tyumen, was the seat of fairs of great importance to the Siberian fur trade.

Of Soviet towns formerly important but now decayed, two should be mentioned: Novgorod, once the centre of a great trade in furs and other commodities; and the old Tartar capital of Sarai. Novgorod, situated on the Volkhov just below its exit from Lake Ilmen, was for hundreds of years, till it was conquered by the Moscow Tsars in 1478, the seat of a principality which probably owed its independence, and in a large measure also its commerce, to the safety it enjoyed amid the marshes by which it was surrounded. By the Volkhov, Lake Ladoga, and the Neva it carried on an active commerce with the Baltic long before Leningrad existed. At one time its population is estimated to have exceeded 100 000, later it dwindled to a quarter of that number. Sarai has completely passed away.

Communications. The enormous size of the Soviet Union and the development of the east with its great industrial oases set in vast seas of uncultivated, unpeopled land renders the question of communications one of the utmost importance. The severity of the climate and the marshy character of a large part of the surface together with the want of road-making material (both stone and wood being entirely absent throughout large areas in the south) long stood in the way of the construction of roads. For half the year the substitute for roads, is, as usual in such regions, tracks formed by the repeated passage of wheeled vehicles which are apt to be rendered scarcely passable by bad weather. The length of paved roads was only 24 000 km (15 000 miles) in 1913; by 1941 there were 1.5m. km (nearly 1m. miles) of constructed roads and some 143 000 km (89 000 miles) were capable of carrying motor traffic; by 1969 the length of motor roads had grown to 483 200 km (300 000 miles). It is aimed to link the major towns by all-weather highways. Most progress has so far been made in the west, centred on Moscow. Roads link the Trans–Siberian railway to some Siberian towns; and some roads have been engineered in the difficult terrain of the Caucasus and Pamirs. Despite all this activity relatively little merchandise is as yet carried by road.

The rivers form natural routeways but they are winding and often shallow, and frequently do not flow in the direction required by traffic: there is no natural routeway from west to east. The river courses in the west however have been improved and linked by canal. Nearly 145 000 km (90 000 miles) of inland waterway are now classed as navigable.

From Kalinin, the head of steam navigation on the Volga, the direct distance from the mouth of the river is less than 1 450 km (900 miles), the distance by river is about 2 650 km (1 650 miles). Before the introduction of steam navigation, so slow was the rate of progress that it was a matter of months to accomplish the distance between Kalinin and Astrakhan. Even after steam navigation was introduced the average rate of speed of the post and passenger steamers downstream was only about 22.5 km (14 miles) an hour, upstream about 18.5 km (11.5 miles); so that if these rates were steadily kept up through the whole route, about five days would be consumed in the passage between these two places in descending the river, about six days in ascending. The time taken by a tug in drawing a train of cargo-boats must of course be much longer.

Further, no Soviet river port is on an average free from ice for more than ten months in the year. Kherson, at the mouth of the Dnepr, in the latitude of La Rochelle in France, has, on an average, only 280 days in the year icefree; Astrakhan', in about the same latitude, only 264 days. Rybinsk, now the great reservoir on the upper Volga filled in 1941, has only 219 days icefree, Leningrad 218, and Arkhangel'sk, at the mouth of the Northern Dvina, only 177 days or less than half the year.

On the Dnepr, the principal waterway to the Black Sea, rocky rapids impeded the navigation for a distance of 37 km (23 miles) on that part of the river which flows from north to south in the great bend which the stream makes to the east. Though artificial channels were constructed as early as 1853 to avoid these rapids, navigation was little improved till the construction of the great power works under the Bolshevik regime (the Dneprosges Dam, the largest in Europe till 1954). Rapids also impede the navigation of the Dnestr and Bug, and, above Leningrad, the important Neva navigation. The navigation of the Volga is liable to be obstructed by sandbanks which accumulate rapidly where any impediment occurs in the way of the current. There are other drawbacks still. The Volga, which with its tributaries affords more than 11 250 km (7 000 miles) of inland navigation, does not furnish any direct connection with the ocean. Goods intended for the sea were landed at Stalingrad (the former Tsaritsin now Volgograd) at the point where the river turns southeastwards to the Caspian, and were transferred by rail to the Don, a river that can be navigated only by steamers of very shallow draught; now a canal connects the two — reaching the Volga at Volgograd. The Northern Dvina, a fine deep river, flows through a sparsely peopled region, but in one respect it may be regarded as all the more important on that account as a natural waterway, since only by such means was it possible to develop in such a region an export trade in timber and timber products, flax, and other commodities, such as its waters carry.

Even before the First World War many thousands of river vessels were constantly moving between the Neva and the Volga. Many of these were of more than 1 000 tons burden, but even on the larger river vessels of considerable size could be used only during the spring floods. Still, it was significant of the backward state of commerce in Russia generally that the total volume of traffic on the waterways remained comparatively small. The total quantity of goods transported on Russian rivers increased from 23.3 to 44.8m. tons in 1894 to 1910.

Under the First and Second Five Year Plans much progress was made with canal construction. The great Baltic–White Sea Canal now links Leningrad with the northern ocean; the Neva navigation is linked with that of the Volga and with Moscow. The eighteenth-century Mariinsky plan for a canal network has been completed, furnishing a waterway from Leningrad to Rybinsk on the upper Volga, and reducing freight transit from 18 to 2½ days. The Volga–Don Shipping Canal which was opened in 1952 profoundly affected water communication. It provided a deep channel from Kalach to Rostov capable of carrying large vessels; and it effectively linked the White, Baltic, Caspian, Azov and Black Seas. In southern Turkmenistan a canal now crosses the Kara-Kum Desert, from Bussag on the Amu-Darya to Archnan, and has transformed agriculture in its passage. It supplies water for cotton, fruit and vineyards, as well as for livestock; and will eventually be extended to the Caspian. Work is in progress on other waterways, one of which is the Baltic–Volga waterway, to link Klaipeda on the Baltic to Kahovka on the Dnepr. Waters of two northward flowing rivers, the Pechora and the Vychegda, which embouche into the White Sea, are being diverted south to the Volga. Another great irrigation canal project involves bringing water to north Crimea from the Dnepr, at Kahovka. Part of an irrigation canal project in central Kazakhstan, between Irtysh and Karaganda, has already been completed.

In 1913 the inland waterways turnover of goods was 28 900m. in ton-km; in 1969 it was 160 000m. In the same years freight carried was 35.1m. tons and 332.7m. respectively.

Freight carried by water is far less than that carried by rail or road. Indeed in 1969 66 per cent of all goods traffic and 50 per cent of all passenger traffic went by rail. This is notwithstanding over 145 000 km (90 000 miles) of inland waterways (1969) classed as navigable compared with 134 600 km (83 700 miles) of railway.

The extent of water communication in Russia helped to delay the laying of railways. Down to the close of the Crimean War there were only four railway lines in the country. The principal difficulties in the way of railway construction presented by the physical features have been due to the rivers, many of which have required long bridges. The ascent of the Uralski Khrebet (Ural Mountains) is so gradual that on the older line between Perm, at the head of steamboat navigation on the Kama, and Tyumen in Siberia it is scarcely perceptible. On the southern line also the gradients are easy. This line, running from Kuybyshev by Ufa and Zlatoust, is now continued eastwards to join the Trans–Siberian railway. Its steepest gradient is only 1 in 100, and a short tunnel hereabouts is the only tunnel on the entire route between the Baltic and Irkutsk. A railway to the harbour of Murmansk on the Murman coast in the northwest, which is kept icefree all the year round by warm water drifted northward by southwesterly winds, was opened during the First World War.

The railway network is very open compared with that in western Europe. This obviously accentuates the importance of developing local centres of manufacture so as to avoid the enormous distances of transport of the goods, and the importance of developing easy and rapid means of communication by road or by air.

The old roadway into Siberia, followed by so many thousands of hapless exiles, was the trakt, but the most important means of communication in Siberia is now formed by the Trans–Siberian railway. The first stone of the railway was laid at Vladivostok on 19 May 1891, by the Grand Duke Nicholas, afterwards Tsar Nicholas II, and the line then begun was ultimately continued northwards to Khabarovsk on the Amur. The westernmost section, Chelyabinsk to the Ob, was opened in December 1895, and the next section to Irkutsk was opened in the summer of 1898. Originally it was intended that the line should follow the valley of the Amur down to Khabarovsk; but the difficulties of construction in the easternmost section of this route, together with the small prospect of economic development in that region, led with the consent of China to the change of route through Manchuria. The line was continued eastwards through Chita to the head of navigation of the Shilka; but the direct railway to the seaboard was made to run southeastwards from Chita to Harbin in Manchuria, and from Harbin south to Port Arthur and Dairen, and east to Nikolskoye on the Vladivostok–Khabarovsk line. The line was completed before the end of 1902, except for a break at Lake Baykal. For some time trains were carried across Lake Baykal in large ferryboats, but before the end of 1904 the very difficult section round the south end of Lake Baykal was completed. The total length of the railway from Chelyabinsk to Vladivostok is 6 279.6 km (3 902 miles), to Port Arthur from Leningrad, 9 466 km (5 882 miles). In recent years the whole line has been double tracked, and in 1936, with the completion of the Hankow–Canton railway, it became possible to travel from Calais to Canton by railway. In western Siberia the railway gradients are naturally easy, nowhere as far as the Ob exceeding 1 in 135. Further east they rise to 1 in 66, and additional difficulties were presented by the numerous rivers to be crossed. The Yablonoïÿe Mountains east of Lake Baykal are crossed at the height of about 1 030 m (3 400 ft).

After the construction of the Trans–Siberian railway there was a rapid immigration into Siberia from Russia, and a considerable development of trade westwards. In western Siberia the settlers were allotted free grants of 17 ha (40 acres) of land and were exempted from taxes for three years. In 1895 the number of immigrants exceeded 100 000, and in several subsequent years it exceeded 200 000. In 1908 the number of immigrants exceeded 758 000, a number more than twice as great as the highest number of immigrants into Canada up to that date, but after that date there was a decline. The railway naturally attracted to it a great deal of the trade with Russia in Chinese tea and silks, and the railway also carried large quantities of Siberian furs to Europe. Locally there developed also a large trade in grain, principally wheat, animals, meat, hides, tallow, wool, and dead game, but the principal export trade was in butter. The trade in butter, carried in refrigerator cars, was developed with remarkable rapidity by the opening of the Siberian railway, and this commodity reached Europe before 1914 from much greater distances than wheat — apparently as far east as the Minusinsk district or about 4 800 km (3 000 miles) from the Baltic. The total quantity of Siberian butter exported in 1898 was about 2 500 tons, while in 1912—13 the amount received thence by the United Kingdom alone was about 27 000 tons. This trade was largely in British and Danish hands.

The Trans—Siberian Express now runs from Moscow to Peking; a 'short-cut' to Peking was opened up in 1956 by the railway across Outer Mongolia through Ulan Bator. From Moscow to Peking or Manchuria takes about a week; hence numerous air services.

The chief towns of Siberia show the influence of the railway. At the census of 1897 the only two with a population above 50 000 were Tomsk, capital of western, and Irkutsk, capital of eastern Siberia. Kiakhta, on the Siberian frontier opposite the Mongolian town of Maimachin, was formerly the centre of a large caravan trade with China, importing brick tea and exporting furs and other Siberian products. Before the First World War Siberian towns were growing with great rapidity, especially those situated at points where navigable rivers are crossed by the Trans—Siberian railway. At the beginning of the century Novo-Nikolaievsk was only a small collection of huts; in 1914 it had a population of 85 000. Now known as Novosibirsk, it had over 1.1m. people in 1970. Tomsk and Yeniseisk doubled their populations between 1902 and 1912. Even more remarkable has been more recent growth. In 1926 only three Siberian towns had a population of over 100 000, by 1933 this had increased to seven, Omsk, Novosibirsk, Vladivostok, Irkutsk, Tomsk, Krasnoyarsk, and Barnaul, of which the first four and the largest are all on the Trans—Siberian. By 1955 a least twenty-five towns east of the Ural crest had populations exceeding 100 000.

The inadequacy of road transport makes the railway system the lifeline of Soviet industry. By the end of 1969 66 per cent of freight and 50 per cent of passenger traffic were carried by rail. (This makes an interesting comparison with the 1913 figures, when the railways carried 57 per cent of freight and 91 per cent of passengers.) Over 70 per cent of the locomotives are diesel or electric; even the immensely long Trans—Siberian railway is electrified, and the days of the steam locomotives are numbered. No more are being built in the USSR. The total length of rail track was in 1970 about 135 000 km (83 900 miles) compared with 58 500 km (36 350 miles) in 1913.

The vast spread of the Soviet Union and the difficulties of transport make the development of selfsufficient industrial areas of supreme importance. They also give impetus to the advance of air transport. Regular air routes which covered a mere 48 280 km (30 000 miles) in 1938 had grown to over 691 000 km (429 000 miles) by 1970. All the major industrial regions are served by air, and Moscow is a refuelling point on several international air routes. The Soviet international airline carries a considerable number of passengers: 82.5m. in 1972.

Seaports. The principal seaport on the Baltic is Leningrad, with Kronstadt. Till the middle of 1885 Kronstadt was the port of Leningrad for all large shipping, but a canal was then opened through the shallow end of the gulf to Leningrad, and from that very year the great bulk of the shipping was transferred to Leningrad. The harbour of Tallinn, the capital and leading port of Estonia, was also deepened and extended, and developed into a great cotton-port, importing large quantities of this material direct from the United States. Riga, the capital and chief port of the Latvian SSR has long been an important outlet to the Baltic. Former German ports are Kaliningrad (Konisgberg) and Klaypeda (Memel).

On the Black Sea, the chief port is Odessa, the harbour of which being on the sea itself (east of Dnestr) is not so likely to be closed by ice as the river ports. The shipping both of the port of Nikolayev, on the Bug, and Kherson, on the Dnepr, has to cross the Ochakov Bar, which, however, has been deepened by dredging; both these ports, which were more conveniently situated than Odessa for the grain exports of southwestern Russia, grew rapidly, to the prejudice of Odessa. Among the minor Black Sea ports are Kaffa, or Fyedosiya, and Kerch, the last of which had at one time a good deal of business in lightening ships before crossing the bar at the Straits of Kerch or Yenikale. The channel across this bar has been deepened and another entrance to the Azovskoye More (Sea of Azov) has been made by piercing the isthmus of Perekop at the north of the Krym (Crimea). Sevastopol after 1899 became solely a naval port. Nearby the sheltered southeastern shores of the Krym, with an almost Mediterranean climate, have developed numerous resorts, such as Yalta. The chief ports on the Azovskoye More are Taganrog, Azov, Rostov, Osipenko (Berdiansk) and Zhdanov (Mariupol), this last being the port of the Donbass coalfield. At the eastern end of the Sea, oil is received at Batum by pipeline from Baku.

Astrakhan, the chief Caspian seaport, is the centre of the important fisheries of the Caspian Sea and the Volga (sturgeon, etc.). Important fisheries are open all the year round on the Murman coast, to the north-west of the White Sea, and on the Kanin peninsula to the northeast. Murmansk is open through the year and has large timber exports, though many small timber ports along the northern Russian and Siberian coasts were opened during the Second Five Year Plan (1933–37). The Soviet Union is giving a good deal of attention to the northern sea route. Accurate weather forecasting and atomic powered icebreakers lessen some of the hazards, but the sudden unpredictable icing-up of the channel will probably always make the route an uncertain one. It becomes more important as the timber of the Siberian forests is exploited. Igarka, a port on the Yenisey 640 km (400 miles) from the open sea, handles timber floated down river, and has expanded considerably in recent years. Exports from the Far East, handled through Vladivostok, are limited.

The peoples of the Soviet Union have always been land rather than seafaring peoples: but with the emergence of the USSR as a world power after the Second World War her navy and her merchant fleet have gained in stature, active, for example, on the trade route with Cuba.

Foreign trade. Since the inauguration of Soviet rule the USSR has concentrated on building up her home resources and on the industrialisation of the country. To achieve rapid industrial growth it was necessary at first to continue the Tsarist policy of paying for the services of foreign exports and importing essential machinery as well as manufactured goods from foreign countries. The export of Russian primary produce paid the bills for the imports. The Russia of pre-1914 exported quantities of timber, flax, grain and other agricultural produce. By the 1930s foodstuffs represented only about an eighth, animal products, fish and furs another eighth; timber represented over 15 per cent and oil also held a high place. More than two-thirds of the imports were machinery, including electrical machinery, followed by cotton, wool and rubber. Imports came very largely from Germany, the United Kingdom and the United States. *The Statesman's Yearbook 1971–72* records that the imports of raw materials between 1913 and 1967 declined from 50.8 per cent to 24.6 per cent, of machinery and equipment imports increased from 16.6 per cent to 37.5 per cent; and imports of manufactured consumer goods increased from 10.3 per cent to 19.0 per cent. The exports for recent average years show the leading part played by machinery, iron and steel, petroleum and natural gas. Among other important export items are paper, raw cotton, vegetable oil, motor vehicles and tractors, clocks and watches: a list notably different from that of 1925. The USSR is no longer a producer and exporter of primary produce, and its exports present a balance of raw materials and manufactures.

Most trade is carried on with the other member countries of Comecon, especially East Germany, Poland and Czechoslovakia, to whom the USSR supplies a considerable amount of electric power in addition to the oil and gas carried by pipeline; the USSR is very much the dominant partner in the group. The Soviet Union also carries on a small steady trade with countries outside Comecon, including the United Kingdom.

Table 61 — USSR: towns with over 500 000 inhabitants, 1971

Moscow	7 172 000	Perm	863 000
Leningrad	4 002 000	Omsk	850 000
Kiyev	1 693 000	Volgograd	834 000
Tashkent	1 424 000	Rostov-on-Don	808 000
Baku	1 292 000	Ufa	796 000
Kharkov	1 248 000	Yerevan	791 000
Gor'kiy	1 189 000	Saratov	773 000
Novosibirsk	1 180 000	Riga	743 000
Kuybyshev	1 069 000	Alma-Ata	753 000
Sverdlovsk	1 048 000	Voronezh	676 000
Minsk	955 000	Zaporozhye	676 000
Odessa	913 000	Krasnoyarsk	666 000
Tbilisi	907 000	Krivoi Rog	581 000
Donetsk	891 000	L'vov	564 000
Chelyabinsk	891 000	Karaganda	530 000
Kazan	885 000	Yaroslavl	527 000
Dniepropetrovsk	882 000		

Asia

Population. Asia is the largest and most populous of the continents, but not the most densely populated, in which respect, like all the other continents, it has to yield pride of place to Europe. No exact comparison is possible between Europe and Asia, because there is no hard and fast boundary between them; they merge in the Soviet Union, which constitutes more than half of Europe and more than a third of Asia. If the dividing line between the continents be taken as following broadly the course of the Ural Mountains from north to south and thence the Ural River to the Caspian Sea, Asia may be assigned an area of 42.7m. sq km (16.5m. sq miles) and Europe 11.1m. sq km (4.3m. sq miles), with respective populations in 1970 of over 1 300m. (more than half the world total) and 550m. On this basis the average density of population in Asia per sq km is over 30 (80 to the sq mile) against 50 (130 to the sq mile) in Europe. In Asia, especially, the population is very unequally distributed — extremely sparse in the north, centre, and southwest, while round the south and east coasts are some of the most densely populated areas in the world. In that region, India, Pakistan, Bangladesh, Indonesia, the Indochinese peninsula, China and Japan, with an aggregate area practically the same as that of Europe, support nearly twice as many people over 90 per sq km, or on average (240 to the sq mile); leaving some 300m. people spread over the remaining 31m. sq km (12.25m. sq miles), an average of about 9.5 per sq km (25 to the sq mile).

Climate. The explanation of this difference in the distribution of the population is to be found mainly in differences of climate; and these differences, again, are due to situation and superficial configuration. The vast size and the shape of the continent necessarily have the effect of placing the central areas at a great distance from the sea, the chief source of moisture; but it is to be noted that the existence of another continent continuous with it in the west, and a third lying to the southwest, has an important bearing on the climate of Asia. The European continent receives, to the loss of Asia, the bulk of the moisture brought about by southwest winds from the North Atlantic Ocean, and the continent of Africa has a detrimental effect on the Asian rainfall in two ways. First, being situated in latitudes in which there is great rarefaction of the air on the land, and consequently a strong indraught of air from the sea, it diminishes the influx of sea air into the neighbouring parts of Asia. Secondly, it prevents such sea-winds as do blow over the southwest of Asia from being as heavily charged with moisture as they otherwise would be. Hence it is that the monsoons begin, we may say, to the east of the Indus, and hence, too, that these seasonal winds are so all-important in relation to the climate and production of Asia.

The superficial configuration of the continent intensifies the contrast between southeastern and central Asia. The Himalayas, the loftiest mountain range in the world, arrest the summer monsoons of India. North of these mountains, the tableland of Tibet, varying from about 3 000 to 5 500 m (10 000 to 18 000 ft) in height, spreads out northwards to the Astin (Altyn) Tagh and Nan Shan Mountains, and on the east and southeast breaks up into numerous mountain ranges, which also help to prevent the southern monsoon from reaching the heart of the continent. Still more effectively deprived of this essential of life are the lower tablelands in the north-central part of the continent varying from about 610 m (2 200 ft) to upwards of 1 200 m (4 000 ft) in height, and extending to the mountains on the borders of Siberia.

Outside the monsoon region there is probably only about one-tenth of this section of the continent, in which the total rainfall of the year amounts to as much as 400 mm (16 in). The areas in which that amount is exceeded lie chiefly in the parts traversed by mountains in the southwest (western Iran, Caucasia, Armenia, and Turkey in Asia) and in Siberia, in the middle and upper parts of the basin of the Yenisey, and in the basin of the Ob from about latitude 56° to 62° N.

In the drier parts of the continent there are indications that at one time the climate was moister than it is at present, and in some of these districts the population was in consequence more numerous. How far such changes may be taken to indicate a more or less continuous process of desiccation is very uncertain.

Trade routes. The monsoon region in the southeast of Asia has, from the very dawn of history, been a populous and productive part of the continent, and its commodities have been all the more valued in Europe from being the products of a warmer climate, and hence of a different nature from those native to the west. Indian spices, drugs and dyes, and Chinese silks, together with precious stones, have been eagerly sought after by European merchants since the time of the Romans; and some of them found their way to the Mediterranean even in early biblical times (Genesis, 37: 25). The favourite routes by which these commodities were exchanged for European goods varied at different periods. In large part the rise and fall of empires determined the predominant direction of trade, now by way of the Red Sea and Egypt, now by the Persian Gulf and Persia to the eastern borders of the Mediterranean, now by more northern routes and round the Caspian to the Black Sea; from China through Indian ports, or from China across the deserts of central Asia; no route ever used exclusively, but with a recurring tendency to favour the Persian Gulf and the Red Sea. For centuries, indeed, it was a case of ringing the changes on these routes and other variants, as dictated by circumstances. Then, at the end of the fifteenth century, came Vasco de Gama's revolutionary discovery of the seaway to India, which as the years went on, struck a devastating blow at the overland trade. Nearly four more centuries passed before, with the opening of the Suez Canal in 1869, the Red Sea again became the favoured route for traffic between Europe and Asia, this time with the addition of Australasia as a further goal. In the present century, not only have the Red Sea and the Persian Gulf both been linked by railway with the European network, but China has been placed in railway communication with northern Europe by the Trans—Siberian route. Further, valuable freight as well as passengers are now flown swiftly over routes where, in earlier ages, caravans of camels and other beasts of burden pursued their slow and toilsome way.

Political changes. A development of the period following the Second World War was the renunciation by the west European powers of their sovereign rights in their Asian empires, through the grant of selfgovernment to the constituent countries. Britain's former Indian Empire is now composed of four states — India, defined as a republic which remains a full member of the Commonwealth; Pakistan, also a republic but outside the Commonwealth, Bangladesh another Commonwealth republic; and Burma, which was separated from India before the Second World War and afterwards elected for full independence outside the Commonwealth. Ceylon, Malaysia and Singapore have become independent states within the Commonwealth. French Indo—China has become independent: Vietnam, Khmer (Cambodia), and Laos, whose future is still in the melting-pot (p. 611). The Netherlands East Indies, initially without Dutch New Guinea, now rank as the Republik Indonesia Serikat — the United States of Indonesia — an independent state, at first within the framework of the Netherlands Union but contracting out of the Union in 1954.

While these changes were taking place in the Orient, independent states were being established in western Asia, in the territories at the eastern end of the Mediterranean, where Turkey held sway before the First World War and where Britain and France exercised mandates in between the two world wars. Syria and Lebanon became independent states during the Second World War, and that part of Palestine colonised by Jews proclaimed itself an independent state under the name of Israel soon after the war — in 1948 when Britain yielded up the mandate granted by the old League of Nations.

In the Far East, a Japan shorn of outlying territories emerged from the Second World War under military occupation, mainly by American troops, until 1952, when a peace treaty was signed and diplomatic relations were restored. Another major change has been the establishment of Communist rule in China. In many parts of Asia political unrest and the problems created by the pressure of population on resources militate against economic development; but over most of Asia it is the physical features, the climate and the soil, which still play a major part in controlling human activity.

Cyprus

Cyprus, the third largest island in the Mediterranean, lying in the angle between Syria (95 km: 60 miles to the east) and Turkey (64 km: 40 miles to the north), has an area of 9 250 sq km (3 570 sq miles) (nearly half the size of Wales) and an estimated population in 1970 of 633 000. Formerly a Turkish possession, it passed by agreement under British control in 1878, the Sultan retaining nominal sovereignty. The island was formally annexed by Great Britain in 1914 on the outbreak of war with Turkey. Less than one-fifth of the population speak Turkish and are Muslims; over four-fifths are Greek-speaking; many speak English. In the 1950s terrorist campaigns for and against union with Greece (Enosis) led to much violent unrest in defiance of the government, involving emergency measures within the island and diplomatic negotiations with both Greece and Turkey. In February 1959 Britain concluded an agreement with the other two countries and with representatives of the Greek and Turkish communities in Cyprus, establishing in the island a republic of unique character. Britain retained sovereignty over two areas forming British bases, one on the east coast near Larnaca, the other on the south coast near Limassol. It was agreed that a Council of Ministers and a House of Representatives should be constituted on the basis of 70 per cent Greeks and 30 per cent Turks. In addition separate communal chambers, Greek and Turkish, were to have the right to impose taxes and other levies on their respective communities. Neither Enosis nor partition of the island was to be allowed. Elections were in 1960, and in 1961 the House of Representatives voted for admission to the Commonwealth, a request granted forthwith by the Commonwealth Prime Ministers Conference. Clashes between Greek and Turkish Cypriots in 1963 led to a UN peace force being sent to the island. A truce ensued and in 1965 the UN assembly requested other states not to interfere in the internal affairs of Cyprus. Talks between Turkish and Greek Cypriots initiated in 1968 in order to resolve the island's political problems have yet, in 1974, to be concluded.

Shaped like a bill-hook, with the handle extending to the northeast, the island has along the whole of the 160 km (100 mile) northern coast, a mountain range with peaks rising to over 1 000 m (3 000 ft), and in the southwest a broader mass of mountains, culminating in Mount Troödos (Olympus) with a height of 1 950 m (6 406 ft), high enough to permit winter sports and to serve as the summer seat of government. Between the two ranges stretches a great plain, the Mesaoria, given over to farming and having in the centre the capital, Nicosia. Nearly half the total area of the island is classed as arable land; nearly a fifth is forested, only a tenth ranks as pastoral, the rest is built on or waste. Farming is the basis of the island's economy. Fully a third of the working population get their living from the land, and there are nearly 50 000 independent small farmers. Rainfall, mostly in winter, ranges from 355 mm (14 in) in the Mesaoria to 1 000 mm (40 in) among the mountains, and is mostly normally adequate for crops, with the aid of irrigation; but seasons vary a good deal, droughts are not uncommon, and yields fluctuate greatly. Cereal crops in 1970 were wheat, 54 000 ha (133 500 acres), 49 000 tons; barley, 55 000 ha (136 000 acres) 50 000 tons. Fruits and vegetables were the other main crops, grapes yielding 203 000 tons from 39 000 ha (96 000 acres); citrus fruits (oranges, grapefruit and lemons) 170 000 tons; and potatoes 150 000 tons from 30 000 ha (12 000 acres). Cotton, olives (for oil) and tobacco are other crops of a smaller and uncertain scale. There is a steady export trade in locust beans, the horn-like pods of the carob tree.

Because of the scorching summers, there are no good all-the-year-round pastures, and the most numerous livestock are sheep (435 000) and goats (360 000), of which over 500 000 find rough grazing and supply their owners with milk and cheese. Both the goats and their owners did extensive damage to the forests in the past and their activities are now limited. There are nearly 90 000 pigs and over 3.5m. head of poultry.

The forests, though sadly depleted, contain much valuable timber, which is now carefully conserved. A Forestry College, opened in 1951 among the pine forests of the Troödos range, is an important training centre for the entire Middle East.

The mineral resources of Cyprus are of ancient renown; the name 'copper' is derived from *cyprium aes* (Cyprus metal). Since the Second World War there has been a striking revival of the mining industry in the Troödos Mountains, and its products — chiefly cupreous concentrates and pyrites, iron pyrites, asbestos, chrome iron ore, and gypsum — provide nearly one-third of the island's exports; in 1970 mineral exports were valued at £14m.

The narrow gauge railway which crossed the Mesaoria from the port of Famagusta to Nicosia in 1905 was closed at the end of 1951, and Cyprus is now without railway transport. There is a good road system, comprising over 8 000 km (5 000 miles) nearly half of which are paved; main roads constitute nearly a third of the total.

After several years of planning, an Electricity Authority for Cyprus was set up in 1952. A power station was constructed at Dekhelia, in the Larnaca district, and existing electricity undertakings in Nicosia, Limassol, and other leading centres were acquired. Despite the disturbed conditions in later years, so great were the demands on the Authority both for lighting and for irrigation pumps, that the number of units generated increased from 26m. in 1953 to 272m. in 1963. Since independence there has been much investment in the building of dams and the provision of water supplies. There is no heavy industry but a wide range of light manufacturing industries is being developed.

Development has not been confined to material conditions. An intensive campaign against malaria resulted in 1949 in the complete eradication of the malaria-bearing mosquito.

Nicosia, the capital, is also the largest town; it has a population of 115 000, including suburbs. After it comes Limassol, 51 500, on the south coast; Famagusta, 42 500, on the east coast; Larnaca, 21 400, on the southeast coast (1970 estimate). Famagusta is the chief port, and has been steadily improved. Limassol and Larnaca are little more than open roadsteads. There is an international airport at Nicosia.

Imports have long been in excess of exports, thanks to British expenditure on development and welfare and defence. In 1970, imports valued at over £98m. were over 50 per cent manufactures, including machinery; over 10 per cent foodstuffs; and over 12 per cent petroleum and its products and gas (natural and manufactured). Fruit, vegetables and wine dominate in exports.

In 1970 the United Kingdom provided most of the imports and took most of the exports. Other imports were contributed by Italy, West Germany, France, the United States, and many other countries in small quantities. Apart from Britain most exports were consigned to West Germany, Italy, the USSR, the Netherlands and Spain.

Turkey

The ancient sultanate of Turkey, whose ruler was also caliph, or head of the Islam religion, lost much territory in the First World War and was proclaimed a republic in 1923 by vote of a National Assembly. The caliphate was abolished, Western dress introduced, the Roman alphabet adopted, and the capital removed from Stamboul or Istanbul (formerly Constantinople) to Ankara, in the heart of Turkey in Asia.

Turkey belongs, geographically, almost wholly to Asia. Of its present area of 780 576 sq km (301 302 sq miles) only 23 721 sq km (9 153 sq miles) falls on the European side of the Bosporus, the Sea of Marmara and the Dardanelles, while the remainder, comprising the whole of Turkey in Asia (Asia Minor) lies to the eastward of that intercontinental boundary.

Asian Turkey has a long seaboard, extending along the southern shores of the Black Sea, both shores of the Sea of Marmara, the eastern shores of the Aegean and the northern shores of the eastern end of the Mediterranean. On the landward side Turkey borders on the Soviet Union (Georgia and Armenia), Iran, Iraq and Syria. Within these confines is the Anatolian tableland, with a basic height of about 900 m (3 000 ft), skirted by fertile valleys and plains but itself mainly arid and carrying numerous mountain groups and ranges, culminating on its eastern borders in Mount Ararat, rising to over 5 000 m (17 000 ft). Behind the Mediterranean coast the Taurus range towers to over 3 000 m (10 000 ft), broken by the famous gorge known as the Cilician Gate, giving access to the interior from the plains of Tarsus and Adana. Many large lakes are scattered over the plateau, the largest, Lake Van, near the eastern border, having an area of 3 755 sq km (450 sq miles). Rivers are fairly numerous and some are of considerable length, but in general they are not suitable for navigation. They include the upper reaches of the Euphrates. Despite the unfavourable character of the country there is a network of nearly 8 000 km (5 000 miles) of railways, mostly of standard gauge (4 ft 8½ in). Roads cover nearly 59 000 km (36 000 miles) but under 24 per cent are hard surfaced. A bridge carrying traffic across the Bosporus at Istanbul was opened in 1973.

Over three times the size of the United Kingdom, Turkey had in 1970 a census population of 35.6m.

Agriculture. Some 80 per cent of the people live in rural areas and farming is the outstanding industry, though the government aims at developing manufactures. Over 33 per cent of the land area is classed as permanent meadows and pastures; another 32 per cent ranks as arable land; nearly 23 per cent is covered with forests, leaving nearly 8 per cent for built on areas and waste. There are great numbers of livestock: in 1970 over 36m. sheep, 20m. goats (about a quarter of them mohair), 13m. cattle, 1.9m. donkeys, 1m. horses, 290 000 mules, 42 000 camels and over 1m. buffaloes.

Of the 25.2m. ha (62m. acres) of arable land over 1.6m. ha (4m. acres) are occupied by gardens and orchards and 13m. ha (over 32m. acres) are under cereal and other crops, the balance lying fallow. Wheat is the most extensive crop and is grown mainly on the Anatolian plateau; in general advanced techniques are not applied and the average yield is low; but modern machinery is being introduced and the total yield is sufficient for home needs except in very bad years. In 1970, an average year, wheat was grown on over 8.5m. ha (21m. acres) and yielded over 10m. tons. Barley is grown on over 2.5m. ha (6.1m. acres), maize on 660 000 ha (1.6m. acres), rye on 600 000 ha (1.5m. acres), and oats on about 330 000 ha (815 000 acres).

Apart from cereals, grapes are the most extensively cultivated crop (838 000 ha: over 2m. acres), but others, on a smaller scale, are numerous and valuable. Cotton and tobacco are specially important. Tobacco, for long a valuable export, is grown in both European and Asian Turkey; in 1970 it yielded 146 000 tons, the chief centre being Samsun, on the Black Sea coast. Cotton made rapid strides after the Second World War and in 1950–51 for the first time it displaced tobacco as the leading export; production in 1970 exceeded 400 000 tons, mostly in the plains around Adana; Izmir (Smyrna) is also a notable centre of production.

The forested areas are mostly on the slopes between the coastal region and the Anatolian plateau. They include valuable timbers, but have suffered much from the depredations both of man and of goats. A 1937 law to nationalise the forests and prohibit wood-cutting aroused strong opposition, but the forest area is now carefully managed and amounts to nearly 18.3m. ha (45m. acres).

Mineral resources and industry. Mineral resources are considerable and are being developed. Over 8m. tons of coal and lignite are produced annually at Zonguldak on the Black Sea coast, over 660 000 tons of chrome ore and over 2m. tons of iron ore. Turkey lies third (after the USSR and South Africa) as one of the chief sources of supply of chrome; the ore is the principal item among the mineral exports, which otherwise are a trifling factor in the export trade, though efforts are being made to increase them. There is exploration for oil, which is already being produced in Garzan and Raman. The state took over the Zonguldak coalmines and is modernising both the mines and the port in pursuance of its policy of industrial development. In the past this policy has been combined with the nationalisation of public utilities, especially the iron and steel and textile industries, mining and forestry; but later, following a change of government, there was a tendency to stress the advantages of private enterprise. Manufacturing industries are being encouraged, and steelworks are operating at Karabük, Iskenderum and Eregli, using home-produced raw materials. Other manufacturing is at present mainly confined to textiles (wool, cotton and some silk), cement, paper and some small consumer goods.

Trade. Whatever developments the future may hold, Turkey's foreign trade is still that of an agricultural and pastoral country, and many economic difficulties beset a modernising policy. Principal exports in recent years have been cotton, fruits, tobacco and minerals; imports

have been machinery and transport equipment, iron and steel, pharmaceuticals, and petroleum and its products. Earnings from tourism are
growing. Aided by the United States, imports exceed exports. Most
trade is with the United States, West Germany and the UK.

The principal ports are Istanbul, which, though no longer the capital,
is by far the largest city, and Izmir (Smyrna), which has a fine natural
harbour, preserved from silting by diverting westwards the mouth of
the Gediz Chai (Hermus). Ankara, the capital (inland), comes between
the two in size.

Table 62 — Turkey: population of leading cities, census 1970

Istanbul	2 247 600	Erzurum	134 660
Ankara (capital)	1 208 800	Samsun	134 270
Izmir	520 690	Sivas	132 530
Adana	351 660	Malatya	130 340
Bursa	275 920	Kocaeli	123 010
Eskisehir	216 330	Icel	114 300
Gaziantep	255 880	Elazig	108 340
Konya	200 760	Maras	105 200
Kayseri (Caesarea)	167 700	Adapazari	101 590
Diyarbakir	138 660	Urfa	100 230

Syria

Until the First World War, Syria was part of the Turkish Empire. Afterwards it was administered by France under mandate from the League of
Nations, until in the Second World War it received promise of independence from the Free French and was constituted a republic; in 1945
it joined the Arab League, and all foreign troops were withdrawn in
1946. In 1958 Syria and Egypt formed the United Arab Republic, and
were joined by Yemen in a union of federated Arab states; in 1961
Syria seceded from Egypt, and Egypt withdrew from the union with
Yemen. The UAR was reformed in 1964 to consist of Egypt only; in
1972 Egypt's title was changed to the Arab Republic of Egypt.

The Syrian Republic itself lies due south of Turkey in Asia, its
northern frontier being followed, for most of the way, by the course of
the Baghdad railway. On the west it has a short seaboard (about
160 km: 100 miles) along the Mediterranean, opposite Cyprus, and it
continues south on the landward side first of the Lebanese Republic,
then of Israel, as far as the southern end of the Lake of Tiberias, where
it turns east and north, marching first with Jordan and then with Iraq
back to the Turkish frontier. Within these limits is an area of
185 680 sq km (nearly 72 000 sq miles), inhabited by some 6m. people
(1971 estimate). A narrow but fertile coastal belt is backed by mountain ranges, dropping on the further side to the valley of the Orontes,
which, rising in the Lebanon, flows northwards through Syria, parallel

with the coast, till it finds an outlet to the sea in Turkey, just north of the Syrian frontier. Eastward the country merges into the Syrian Desert, though the northeast corner is crossed by the Euphrates.

Twenty per cent of the republic is classed as unproductive, and another 16 per cent is unused though potentially productive. Of the remainder nearly half is pastoral country and about half is arable. In Syria, as in Turkey, the wooded country has suffered badly from the depredations of goats, and less than 3 per cent of the republic is now classed as forested. Only two crops are grown on a large scale — wheat, covering 1.3m. ha (3.2m. acres) in 1970 but yielding so meagrely that crops range only from about 0.5m. to 1m. tons according to the season; and barley, grown on 1.1m. ha (2.7m. acres) but yielding from under 0.25m. to over 0.5m. tons. Many other crops are cultivated: both acreage and production are comparatively small, though the grape crop yields up to 250 000 tons. Cotton is of increasing importance; in 1970, as the result of extended cultivation and better yields, the crop amounted to 159 000 tons of ginned cotton. Northern Syria offers promising conditions. A widely renowned Syrian product is latakia tobacco, an ingredient of innumerable smoking mixtures; it flourishes in the coastal plains and takes its name from the port of Lattakia. Tobacco production in 1970 totalled 9 100 tons.

Livestock are a big factor in the economy: sheep number 6.2m. and goats 770 000, cattle 520 000, asses 245 000, mules 66 000, horses 65 000, camels (declining) 7 000 (1970).

There are probably mineral resources as yet undiscovered; at present oil and natural gas have been located in the Jezirah area, and prospecting continues. Syria earns considerable foreign currency from the charges she levies on the passage of oil from the fields in Iraq to the Mediterranean ports of Baniyās and Saida (Sidon).

One of the legacies of the Second World War is a system of excellent roads. A motorbus service crosses the desert from the capital, Damascus, to Baghdad. The through railway route from Europe to Egypt traverses western Syria, and in the north, near the Turkish frontier, links on to the Baghdad railway. In the south it continues into Lebanon, where the port of Beirut serves as the commercial gateway for Syria. The trouble between the Arab states and Israel has interrupted communications. On the main line to Egypt the train service is suspended between Beirut and Haifa, as well as on a narrow gauge branch line from Haifa to Damascus; but another section of this branch line is in operation from Beirut to Damascus, continuing into the Hashemite Kingdom of Jordan.

Syria has no port of outstanding importance. Lattakia (the ancient Laodicea), with a population of nearly 68 000, has only a small harbour opening into a sheltered roadstead. Baniyās (site of Caesarea Philippi), south of Lattakia, is the terminal of a 0.76 m (30 in) oil pipeline from

Iraq, which came into operation in 1952 and can carry 14m. tons a year. The chief centres of population are inland. Damascus, the capital, has a population of 790 000, and strung along the main line of railway, from north to south, are Aleppo (567 000), Hamā (196 000), and Homs (232 000), the junction for coastal and inland routes to Beirut.

At the end of 1960, the official rate of exchange for the Syrian £ (£ Syr) was about 3*s*. 3*d*., with a market rate of about 2*s*. for ordinary commercial transactions. Early in 1961 a serious adverse balance of trade led to the abolition of the free money market, and the government took over all exchange operations. A state trading company handles nationalised foreign trade.

Imports in 1969 were valued at £ Syr 1 405.4m. and exports at £ Syr 789.9m.

No single class of commodities dominates the imports, but the biggest groups comprise machinery and transport equipment, and iron and steel. Raw cotton is the leading export. Most trading is with the USSR and Italy.

Lebanon

When, after the First World War, the French took over under mandate the administration of the Turkish territories comprised in Syria, they united various districts in the mountainous southwest corner of the country to form the state of Great Lebanon. When the mandate was relinquished during the Second World War, Lebanon as well as Syria was proclaimed an independent republic. It is a small country of some 10 400 sq km (3 400 sq miles) supporting a population of 2.6m. It has a coast some 215 km (135 miles) long and extending inland for some 40 to 80 km (25 to 50 miles), it consists almost entirely of a mountain range, rising in the north to 3 000 m (10 000 ft). The height drops further south, but the railway from Beirut (about halfway along the coast) to Damascus (in Syria) crosses the mountains by a pass nearly 1 500 m (5 000 ft) above sea level.

The Jebel Libna (Lebanon), the main range, from which the country takes its name, rises in cultivated terraces from a fringe of coastal plains, and on the other side drops more abruptly, under more sterile conditions, to the fertile El Beqa valley, which divides the Jebel Libna from the Jebel esh Sharqi — a smaller edition of the range, traversed by the Syrian—Lebanese frontier. In El Beqa flow two rivers of classical fame: the Leontes (modern Litani), flowing southwards to empty itself into the Mediterranean after a comparatively short course, and the Orontes (Nahr el Asi, or 'rebellious river'), which flows north through Syria and has a course of over 320 km (200 miles).

Of the total area of the Lebanese Republic only 38 per cent is cultivated. Forest and woodland, has, as in neighbouring countries, been sadly depleted by indiscriminate felling and the ravages of goats, though there is still a cluster of the 'cedars of Lebanon' to recall one of the ancient glories of the country. In 1970 goats numbered 330 000, sheep 214 000, cattle (85 000), and donkeys (26 000). The 13 000 pigs kept in this predominantly Muslim country may be accounted for by the fact that nearly half the population is Christian.

The narrow coastal plain and terraced hill slopes produce a wide variety of crops, though with so small a country neither areas nor crops are very large. Cereals are the most widely cultivated. Wheat tops the list, followed by barley and maize. Potatoes and pulses are also grown. But the outstanding crops after cereals are grapes, olives, and citrus fruits. Bananas, sugarcane, groundnuts, rice and sesame seed are other subtropical cultivations.

Lebanon, like Syria, has a legacy of good roads from the Second World War, and a sufficient railway service from prewar days (see under Syria), as well as an excellent port in Beirut and a secondary port in Tarābulus (Tripoli). Imports and exports are of the traditional character of countries engaged in primary production, with little industrial development. But the commercial importance of Lebanon is not limited to its own supplies and needs. It is a flourishing entrepôt of trade not only with Syria, but with Jordan and Iraq; and it has on its coast the terminals of oil pipelines, two at Tarābulus coming from Iraq, and one near Saida (the ancient Sidon) coming over 1 600 km (1 000 miles) across Arabia from Ras al Mishaab on the Persian Gulf.

A notable feature of the very small foreign trade is the great disparity between imports and exports, the value of the former commonly being treble that of exports. The difference is partly made up by tourist receipts and remittances from emigrants. The wide range of imports has no predominant features. Food and live animals provide 28 per cent of the exports. Most imports come from France, West Germany, the United Kingdom and the United States. Most exports are destined for Saudi Arabia, Kuwait, Syria, Jordan and Iraq, while some go to Libya.

Table 63 — Lebanon: population of the chief towns

Beirut (capital)	600 000	Saida (Sidon)	22 000
Tarābulus (Tripoli)	150 000	Tyre	12 000

Israel

The Republic of Israel was founded in May 1948, immediately after the British government relinquished the mandate to administer Palestine which it had exercised since the breakup of the Turkish Empire in the First World War. The new republic was, and is still (1974), without demarcated frontiers. The United Nations had recommended the division of Palestine into two states, Jewish and Arab, but no agreement had been reached, and the British withdrawal was a signal for the invasion of Palestine by its neighbours. Hostilities continued till early in 1949, when Israel concluded an armistice with the bordering Arab states: Lebanon and Syria on the north, Jordan on the east, and Egypt on the southwest. The armistice laid down provisional frontiers which differed from those of the mandated area chiefly in a big 'bite' by Jordan out of Palestine, extending (north to south) from about midway between the Sea of Galilee and the Dead Sea to about midway along the west coast of the Dead Sea, and taking in westward most of the hill country of central Palestine — an area of some 6 090 sq km (2 350 sq miles). The territory occupied by Jordan included Nablus (Shechem), Hebron, Bethlehem, and part of Jerusalem, which was divided so as to leave the modern city to Israel and the ancient city to Jordan. In 1967 Israel again clashed with her Arab neighbours in the 'Six Day War' and occupied the Gaza strip, the Sinai peninsula as far west as the Suez Canal, part of West Jordan as far as the Jordan valley, and the heights east of the Sea of Galilee, including the Syrian town of Quneitra. Israel is still in control of these areas in 1973.

The area within the provisional frontiers of the 1949 armistice agreement is 20 700 sq km (7 993 sq miles). The country is long (from north to south) and narrow, and falls geographically into three longitudinal strips. Along the coast, which Israel holds uninterruptedly, is a strip of considerable fertility, enjoying a good Mediterranean climate. Then comes a strip of hill country, broken in the north by the transverse Plain of Esdraelon, running from Haifa southeast to the Jordan valley. The third strip is formed by the Jordan valley itself, the Dead Sea, and the country beyond it to the south as far as the Gulf of Aqaba — the northeast arm of the Red Sea. Much of this third strip is below sea level at its greatest depth nearly 340 m (1 300 ft) below.

The coastal plains are the principal home of orange groves and vineyards. The northern end of the country, the hills and plains of Galilee provide an area of mixed farming; at the southern end the great tract of the Negev is a desert upland, particularly barren as it approaches the Gulf of Aqaba, with limestone hills split by deep ravines, but having further north a more regular surface with soils which need only water to become productive. With the aid of irrigation water brought by pipeline from the wetter north cultivation from new village settlements peopled by immigrants has been pushed steadily southwards, especially around the expanding town of Beersheba.

Nearly 20 per cent of the total area is under arable and permanent crops; nearly 40 per cent is permanent pasture and 5 per cent forested. Barley, wheat and maize are widely grown cereals; commercially the most important crops are citrus and other fruits, especially oranges of which the production in 1970 was 910 000 tons. Cotton and sugar beet are more recent introductions. Livestock included 240 000 cattle, 195 000 sheep and 136 000 goats.

Israel has valuable deposits of potash in the Dead Sea area, copper near Eilat, oil in the Negev and natural gas at Rosh Zohar, also in the Dead Sea area.

The exodus of Arabs, estimated at 600 000 in the first year of the republic, has since been more than balanced by the unrestricted influx of Jewish immigrants, in many cases refugees from Europe. In December 1971 the total population was 2.99m., of whom 2.56m. were Jewish.

Many settled in the towns, for example in Haifa, a port with a fine modern harbour alongside the main quay, the chief shipping centre in Israel as well as being the third largest town after Tel Aviv-Jaffa and Jerusalem. The largest conurbation is Tel Aviv-Jaffa, a modern seaside town of phenomenal growth. The other commercial ports are Ashdod and Eilat.

In line with its general policy of planned economy Israel has its own mercantile marine, with 114 vessels of 1.7m. tons gross (1969).

A standard gauge (4 ft 8½ in) railway traverses the Mediterranean coastal plain, and in normal times is linked with the railways of Lebanon and Syria as part of the through route between Europe and Cairo. From Lod (Lydda) — Israel's aviation centre near Tel Aviv — branch railways connect with the coast at Tel Aviv-Jaffa and inland, through the hill country, with Jerusalem. Other lines, including the Beersheba to Dimona line which has been extended to Oran, and the new line from Manishit to Tzefa, bring up the total to 950 km (590 miles). Some of these connect with, but are no longer run in conjunction with railway services in the neighbouring Arab states. Paved roads total over 4 000 km (2 480 miles).

Israel has developed flourishing manufacturing, processing and finishing industries. A wide range of manufactured goods are produced by highly skilled workers: textiles, metal goods, leather goods, tyres, paper, plastics, glass and ceramics, scientific instruments, electrical equipment; there is processing of tobacco and foodstuffs; diamond polishing is a lucrative finishing industry. This naturally makes the export list a long one, most prominent items being fruit and vegetables, diamonds (excluding industrial), chemicals, textiles (as well as yarn and thread, including cotton and synthetics), machinery and transport equipment, and a very wide range of small manufactured articles. Main imports are manufactured goods of all types (including the diamonds for finishing) and iron and steel, machinery and transport equipment, oilseeds, and a relatively small quantity of foodstuffs: cereals, meat and its preparations, coffee, rice and tobacco. Normally most trade is with the United States, United Kingdom, West Germany and other EEC countries.

Table 64 – **Israel: population of main towns (1971)**

Tel Aviv-Jaffa	382 900	Haifa	214 500
Jerusalem (capital)	283 100	Ramat Gan	112 600

Jordan

On the breakup of the Ottoman Empire after the First World War, the status of the 'Transjordan' territories, the territories east of Jordan ('across the Jordan' from Palestine) was for a time indeterminate. In 1922 the League of Nations appointed the United Kingdom as the mandatory Power for Palestine and Transjordan, and recognised a British arrangement to establish Transjordan as an emirate under a son of the ex-king of the Hejaz. Development in the emirate proceeded along the lines of constitutional selfgovernment, and when the mandate was relinquished after the Second World War the British concluded a treaty (1946; revised 1948) with Transjordan as a sovereign independent state; the Emir took the title of king, and the country was later proclaimed the Hashemite Kingdom of Jordan. It extends eastward to the borders of Iraq and Saudi Arabia, and is also neighboured by Saudi Arabia on the south. Northward it is bounded by Syria.

Up to the time of the foregoing change of status, the western frontier followed the River Jordan down to and through the Dead Sea, and continued south along the Wadi Araba to the Gulf of Aqaba, the northeast arm of the Red Sea. The fighting between Israel and her Arab neighbours in 1948 carried the Jordanian forces west of the River Jordan, and when an armistice was concluded in 1949 they remained in occupation of a tract of about 6 090 sq km (2 350 sq miles) of Arab Palestine (see under Israel). This tract was incorporated in the Hashemite Kingdom in 1950, known as West Jordan to distinguish it from the former emirate, East Jordan. In the same year the Hashemite Kingdom, which had previously used Palestinian currency, issued its own currency, having for unit the Jordan dinar, maintained at par with the £ sterling.

As a result of the 'Six Day War' between Israel and her Arab neighbours in 1967 part of West Jordan as far as the Jordan valley was occupied by Israel and remains under her control (1973). In view of the fluidity of the political situation the statistics quoted in the following review refer only to that part of Jordan under the control of the Jordanian government.

East Jordan has an area of some 97 740 sq km (37 730 sq miles). Here are the ancient lands of Gilead, Ammon, Moab, and Edom, dividing into cross-sections the narrow strip along the eastern floor of the deep rift valley (below sea level) which carries the River Jordan and the Dead Sea, and mounting the eastern escarpment to a narrow belt of hill country with peaks of 900 to 1 500 m (3 000 to 5 000 ft), merging into a bare plateau which forms by far the largest part of Transjordan. Beduin range the plateau with their flocks of sheep and goats; cultivation is confined to the hill country and the valley floor, and even there it is only in the north that settled villages are found. Elsewhere in the cultivable zone, seminomadic tribes settle temporarily and raise crops in season as need arises. In the hill country an average rainfall of 500 mm (20 in) is spread over the months October to May, and is followed by a rainless summer. On the plateau, the annual rainfall is negligible.

Under 15 per cent of Jordan is classed as productive. In 1969 arable land was officially estimated at 1.1m. ha (2.7m. acres), pastoral at 100 000 ha (247 000 acres) and forest at 125 000 ha (309 000 acres). The wheat crop varies greatly with the season, from under 100 000 tons to nearly 250 000 tons. Smaller but substantial crops are grown of barley, sorghum, olives and grapes. Sheep number over 854 000 and goats over 468 000; there are about 49 000 cattle and 13 000 camels (1970).

The population of Jordan under government control in 1971 was estimated to be 2.4m.; in 1961 West Jordan had a population of 805 450 and East Jordan a population of 834 589, including 550 000 refugees from Palestine but excluding some 53 000 nomads (official census). At best, Jordan is not on a self-supporting basis and the maintenance of so many refugees, mostly lodged in camps, was made possible only by financial aid from United Nations funds. In addition, Jordan has had British and other grants-in-aid.

The known mineral wealth is small but phosphate deposits are worked, and there are potash salts in the Dead Sea area. There is prospecting for oil in the north. The Trans—Arabian pipeline carrying oil from the Persian Gulf to the Mediterranean at Saida (Lebanon) traverses Jordan.

The Hejaz railway (narrow gauge, 105 cm; 3 ft 5$\frac{1}{3}$ in) runs from Deraa, a few kilometres within Syria, through the eastern borders of the Jordanian hill country, serving the Jordanian capital, Amman, and continuing south to Ma'an, the halt for Petra, the famous valley of rock-carved tombs. Before the world wars the line extended to Mecca and Medina, in Saudi Arabia, but this section was later destroyed. Jordan, Arabia and Syria agreed in 1961 to spend £8m. on restoring it and the work is being undertaken by a British consortium. There are 2 110 km (over 1 300 miles) of all-weather roads, and Amman is linked with the outside world by air. The capital has grown rapidly; not long ago a smallish country town, it had an estimated population of over 583 000 (1970). In the far south, where Jordan touches the Red Sea, is its only port, Aqaba.

Jordan's major exports are natural phosphates, which provide about 25 per cent of the total followed by fruit and vegetables (especially tomatoes). Home food production is inadequate and foodstuffs such as cereals, sugar, flour, rice and tea have to be imported, as well as a wide range of manufactured articles in which machinery and transport equipment (especially tractors) and woollen yarn are important. Foreign trade is understandably very small, the value of imports being five times that of exports. Most trading is with the United Kingdom, the USA, Lebanon, West Germany, Syria and Japan, less with the USSR, Egypt and Italy.

Iraq

The republic of Iraq occupies the southeast corner of the old Ottoman Empire. It comprises the former vilayets of Mosul, Baghdad, and Basra, which Turkey surrendered, among other territories, after the First World War. The administration was entrusted, by mandate from the League of Nations, to the United Kingdom, which established a constitutional monarchy under a sovereign elected by popular vote, a son of the ex-king of the Hejaz. The mandate was relinquished in 1932, when Iraq was admitted on British recommendation to the League of Nations as an independent sovereign state. In 1958 the then king, aged twenty-three, a grandson of the first king, was assassinated in Baghdad along with other members of the royal family and his prime minister. A republican government, with Communist sympathies and affiliations, replaced the monarchy.

Habitable Iraq is essentially the ancient Mesopotamia, the Land between the Rivers, the Rivers Tigris and Euphrates: a civilisation whose roots go down to the dim and distant past. Ur of the Chaldees, Babylon, Nineveh are three of many famous centres whose past magnificence has been confirmed by modern excavations. For some years after the First World War, Iraq was commonly known as Mesopotamia, but this was never the official name of the modern state and fell into disuse as a synonym many years ago.

Physical features. The Tigris and the Euphrates both rise in the highlands of Asian Turkey and flow for considerable distances through that country as well as, in the case of the Euphrates, through Syria before they enter Iraq and eventually unite to form the Shatt al 'Arab and discharge their waters into the head of the Persian Gulf. In Iraq the 'land between the rivers' is for the most part a low-lying alluvial plain, merging in the north into the uplands around Al Mawsil (Mosul). For untold centuries the two main rivers and their lower tributaries have meandered through this plain, often changing their courses and carrying fertility now here, now there, to a soil with great potentialities but scant rainfall — about 150 mm (6 in) a year, on average. Averages in Iraq are, however, apt to be particularly misleading, and droughts are often alleviated by floods. The frontier with Iran, which follows the edge of the alluvial plain from the Persian Gulf northwards, finally turns into Kurdistan, a large slice of which, with mountains rising to 425 m (14 000 ft), forms the northeast corner of Iraq. Several left-bank tributaries of the Tigris have their sources among these mountains, and in the rains pour down their torrents to the plain, to complicate the problem of turning it to profitable use. Irrigation and flood control are the twin needs of Iraq's agricultural economy. Their neglect led to the decay of great civilisations in the past. After the First World War, various works to meet both needs were carried out; and in recent years extensive canal systems, dams and irrigation works have taken shape to extend the area of fertility.

In contrast with the conditions in the alluvial plain and in the mountainous country of the northeast, Iraq includes on its western side a vast expanse of desert, reaching to the borders of Syria, Jordan, and Saudi Arabia. Iraq's total area is 438 446 sq km (169 240 sq miles), and of this the western desert occupies nearly half. Population (1970 estimate) 9.44m.

Products of the soil. Only a fraction of even the inhabited country is productive. The Food and Agriculture Organisation of the United Nations, in its analysis of land use in Iraq, reckons 7.3m. ha (18m. acres) to be arable, 4.2m. ha (9.8m. acres) pastoral and 1.9m. ha (4.7m. acres) forested. With improved irrigation and flood control works, the land under cultivation should increase; but cultivation is on a shifting basis: even with the areas already available only parts are used in any one year, and results are as variable as the seasons and other conditions. Barley and wheat, grown in the winter season, are the principal cereal crops. In 1970 over 1m. ha (2.5m. acres) of barley yielded only 691 000 tons, a very bad harvest. Production in the period 1961–70 has fluctuated between this figure and a record 1.2m. tons in 1969. In 1970, 2m. ha (4.9m. acres) of wheat yielded 1m. tons, again a poor harvest.

Rice, a summer crop, is also widely grown, with equally variable results: 138 000 tons of paddy from about 97 000 ha (240 000 acres) in 1961, and 203 000 tons from 105 000 ha (260 000 acres) in 1970. In both years from 8 000 to 17 000 tons of cotton were obtained from between 34 000 and 67 000 ha (84 000 and 166 000 acres). Previously some of the cotton grown was of an inferior type, but the cultivation of this was prohibited in 1949, and only a good type of American cotton, in demand on world markets, is now allowed. Tobacco is grown for the home market, the production of leaf tobacco in recent years averaging about 15 000 tons. It is used for the manufacture of cigarettes as a government monopoly.

The most distinctive of Iraq's crops is found in the date plantations which abound along the Shatt al 'Arab, and upstream along the Tigris and Euphrates as far as Samarra and Ana. It is reckoned that Iraq provides about 80 per cent of dates entering world trade, the bulk being exported from Al Basrah (Basra). Experts distinguish between 350 varieties, but only five are cultivated for export. A good Iraqi crop yields 330 000 tons.

The pastoral industry plays a big part in farming. In 1970 there were some 11.6m. sheep (of the fat-tailed woolled variety), 1.78m. goats, 1.7m. cattle, 58 000 asses, 75 000 mules, and 105 000 horses. Camels number nearly 200 000, and buffaloes 200 000. Exports regularly include wool and live animals.

Oilfields. Valuable as are all these resources, and fundamental the place which they occupy in the general economy of Iraq, they have been overshadowed commercially by another product: mineral oil. Modern development began in 1925 with the grant of a concession to the Iraq Petroleum Company, representing an international group, which opened up a big oilfield around Kirkūk, among the foothills of Kurdistan, about midway between Baghdad and Al Mawsil. Other concessions to other companies followed, for the exploitation of supplies around Al Mawsil, Khanaqin (between Baghdad and Kirkūk), and Al Basrah. By 1950 the annual output was over 6m. tons, mostly from Kirkūk, but other fields were coming into production, and it was recognised that the potentialities were very much greater. By 1954 the output had increased to 30m. tons, and the companies entered into a new agreement with the government, assigning to it half the profits from the oil produced, and other benefits, and guaranteeing in 1955 onwards a minimum output of 22m. tons of crude oil a year by the Iraq and Mosul Companies, and 8m. tons a year by the Basra Company. The Basra field centres in Zubair, southwest of the port, and is connected by pipeline with Fao, at the mouth of the Shatt al 'Arab. Several pipelines connect Kirkūk with the Mediterranean coast. The line to Haifa is not working, because of the feud between Israel and its Arab neighbours, making the pipelines to Tarābulus (Tripoli) in Lebanon and to Baniyās in Syria even more important. The Khanaqin Company, a subsidiary of British Petroleum, operated an oilfield south of Khanaqin, near the Iranian border until 1958, when it was taken over by the Iraqi government. Supplies are pumped to a refinery near Khanaqin, whence they are distributed through Iraq for local requirements at low prices. A large part of the revenues from oil are assigned to a Development Board which aims at extending irrigation and flood control, and raising the general level of production.

In 1961 the government's 50 per cent share of the Iraq Petroleum Company's profit amounted to about £95m.; but the government had become dissatisfied with its agreement, so after negotiating with the

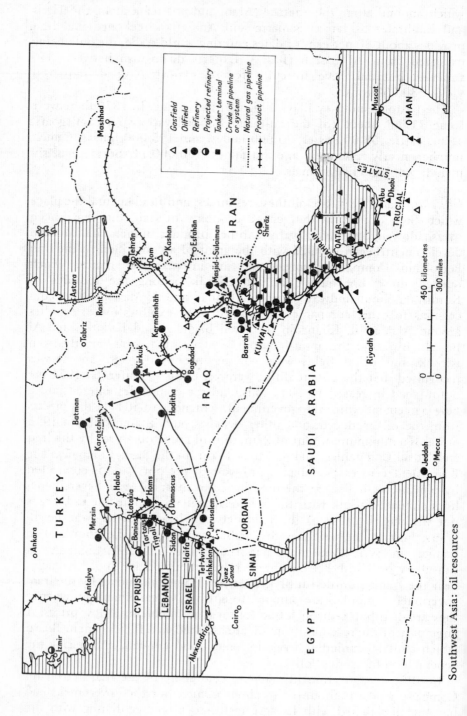

Southwest Asia: oil resources

company for three years over new demands it cancelled unilaterally in December 1961, the company's rights over oil areas which had not then been developed, and defined the area in which the company would be allowed to operate. It amounted to less than 0.5 per cent of the concessions. Output of petroleum by foreign companies was 67.7m. tons in 1966, 74.4m. tons in 1969, providing the Iraqi government with 140.8m. Iraqi dinars in the former year and 170m. in 1969.

Iraq's relationship with the oil companies is a sensitive one; she broke of diplomatic relations with the USA in 1967 and with the United Kingdom in 1971.

Trade and communications. Oil was included in the export returns in the United Nations *Yearbook of International Trade Statistics* for the first time in 1955. The exports of oil (crude petroleum) are the dominating trade factor, and are essential to a right appreciation of the position, but previously figures had not been made generally available. In 1956 they accounted for 92 per cent. The remaining 8 per cent included barley (2.9 per cent), dates (1.46 per cent), and wool (0.9 per cent). The chief import items were iron and steel and machinery (36 per cent), motorcars and parts (7.6 per cent), piece goods (7.8 per cent), sugar (6.5 per cent), and tea (6 per cent). In 1969 oil provided 94 per cent of exports, dates 2 per cent and the remaining 4 per cent was almost equally distributed among hides and skins, raw wool and cotton, barley, and very small quantities of wheat and seeds. Some light industry has been established in Iraq, but in the wide range of imports a demand for manufactured goods of all types appears. Iron and steel manufactured goods represented nearly 15 per cent in 1969, agricultural and transport equipment, with spares, 13 per cent, sugar 5 per cent, cotton piece goods 4 per cent, pharmaceuticals 4 per cent.

Most trading in 1969 was with the United Kingdom, the USA, West Germany and the USSR. France, Italy, the Netherlands, Spain, the United Kingdom and Japan take the major share of the oil exports.

The long-projected Baghdad railway, completed in 1940, follows the right bank of the Tigris between Baghdad and Al Mawsil, and connects through Syria and Turkey with the European railway system. It is of standard gauge (4 ft 8½ in) throughout, but a continuation southwards from Baghdad to Al Basrah was of metre gauge until 1964 when a standard gauge line was completed. In the reverse direction a metre-gauge line, after crossing the Tigris at Baghdad to the left bank, runs northward to Kirkūk and Erbil, with a short branch to Khanaqin. The total route mileage is about 2 350 km (1 460 miles) of which the Iraq section of the Baghdad railway accounts for about a third.

New roads are being rapidly built already. Motor vehicles registered in 1958 (1969 figures in parentheses) included 23 012 (44 229) cars,

7 059 (20 007) taxis, 3 608 (9 202) buses, 12 213 (32 496) lorries. Baghdad and Al Basrah are important airports.

Table 65 — Iraq: towns with over 100 000 people in 1965

Baghdad (capital — 1970)	2 969 000	Kirkūk	175 000
Al Basrah (Basra)	311 000	An Najaf	134 000
Al Mawsil (Mosul)	264 000	Al Hillah	85 000

Arabia

Arabia forms a vast peninsula of about 2.6m. sq km (1m. sq miles) in the southwest corner of Asia, separated from the main mass of the continent by the Arabian or Persian Gulf and the Gulf of Oman on the east, and from Africa by the Red Sea on the west. On the south it is bounded by the Gulf of Aden and the Arabian Sea. For the most part it is a desert area, and may be described as a tilted plane, raised high on the side of the Red Sea and gradually sloping eastwards to the shores of the Persian Gulf; though the eastern maritime plains are varied by another upward tilt along the Gulf of Oman. The desert conditions extend northwards into Jordan, Iraq, and Syria.

By far the larger part of Arabia is comprised in a single kingdom, Saudi Arabia, a combination of several states achieved by conquest within the lifetime of its first ruler, Abdul Aziz ibn Saud, who took the title King of Saudi Arabia in 1932. It has a long seaboard, about 1 600 km (1 000 miles), on the Red Sea, a much shorter frontage to the Arabian Gulf, and is fringed in the south by Yemen and South Yemen, Muscat and Oman. Bordering the Persian Gulf are Kuwait and Bahrain and the territories of Qatar, Abu Dhabi, as well as Muscat and Oman.

Saudi Arabia

Frontiers are ill-defined, and the area is uncertain. It has been estimated at over 2.4m. sq km (927 000 sq miles), and the population at about 6m. Its surface is apportioned among a variety of deserts, including in the south the dread Rub' al Khali, or 'Empty Quarter', which is practically devoid of inhabitants. Elsewhere conditions are not quite so desolate; nearly 40 per cent of the entire country is now classed as pastoral though only 0.4 per cent ranks as arable, and 0.78 per cent as forested. Dates are a prominent crop, while the livestock, as estimated at the half century, include 550 000 camels, 3.2m. sheep, 2m. goats, and 130 000 asses. Two other sources of wealth are of outstanding importance, and are separately associated with the two main divisions into which the modern kingdom falls. Much of the larger division is the ancestral home of the Ibn Saud dynasty, the Central Arabian state of

Nejd, which, with twentieth-century annexes, stretches across the peninsula from sea to sea. The other is the kingdom of Hejaz, occupying the northwest of Saudi Arabia; it too is a conquest of Nejd. Comprising possibly one-quarter of the total area and one-third of the total population, it is the Holy Land of Islam; pilgrims by the hundred thousand flock annually to Mecca, the birthplace of the Prophet and the cradle of the Faith, and in the past these were a major factor in the finances of Saudi Arabia.

Nejd had nothing to compare with it as a source of revenue till oil was found, in 1938, on the mainland behind the Bahrain Islands of the Persian Gulf. The exploitation of the oilfields by 'Aramco' (Arabian—American Oil Company), on the basis of an equal division of the profits with the Saudi Arabian government, brought to that government relatively fabulous wealth, enabling the late king, Ibn Saud, and his son to carry out vast schemes of development including a standard-gauge railway over 560 km (350 miles) long, from Dammam, the Gulf port for the oilfields, to Riyadh, the capital, on the inland plateau. It was opened in 1951, and there are plans for its extension to Jeddah, on the Red Sea, thus completing a Trans—Arabian railway. (See also p. 554 for the proposed rehabilitation of the Hejaz railway between Ma'an and Medina.) The possibilities of extended irrigation are also being investigated. Several areas for the settlement of nomad Wahhabis, an extreme Muslim sect closely associated with the rise of the Saud dynasty, had previously been wrested from the desert around Riyadh.

Typical of present changes, Jiddah, the port for Mecca, has been connected with that city, 72 km (45 miles) inland, by a modern asphalted highway bordered by air-conditioned villas, traversed daily in the pilgrim season by thousands of the latest types of motor vehicles, and equipped at regular intervals with concrete shelters and water taps for the use of pilgrims on foot. At one point is a flourishing government agricultural centre for growing fruit and vegetables, testing new crops, and rearing seedlings for plantations of trees. Piped water supplies have been installed at both Jiddah and Mecca, and typhoid, once endemic, has almost disappeared. At Mecca electric fans temper the heat in the colonnades of the Holy Sanctuary, a motor pump raises water from a holy well, and amplifiers transmit the Call to Prayer. The shallow port of Jiddah has been provided with a deepwater quay, and new quarantine accommodation can take 4 000 people at once. In the height of the pilgrim season, an aeroplane lands at Jiddah airport about every five minutes. Riyadh, a five days' journey by motorcar, is reached by air in three and a half hours.

The oil installations making possible these and other developments are being steadily expanded. In 1970 production reached 3m. barrels daily. Annual output was 26.6m. tons in 1950; by 1973 it was 364.1m. (13 per cent of world output). Refining capacity is growing and stood

561

at 20.6m. tons in 1973, much of it processed at the refinery at Ras Tanura. Crude oil is shipped both by sea and by 'Tapline' (Trans—Arabian Pipeline), which runs in a northwesterly direction across Saudi Arabia, Jordan, Syria, and Lebanon to the Mediterranean coast at Saida.

Estimates of the populations of the chief towns, like most of the statistics of Saudi Arabia, vary greatly: Riyadh (the capital), 300 000; Mecca, 250 000; Jiddah, 300 000; Medina, 60 000.

Yemen

This is an independent republic in the southwest corner of Arabia, fronting the Red Sea on the west, having Saudi Arabia on the north and east, and Southern Yemen (the former Aden Protectorate) on the south. It occupies the highest ground in the whole peninsula; a hot, humid coastal plain is backed by mountain ranges rising inland to over 3 000 m (10 000 ft) before dropping to the sandy wastes of the Rub' al Khali, the vast 'Empty Quarter' of southern Arabia. The total area of the republic is estimated at 195 000 sq km (75 000 sq miles), carrying a population of about 5m. It is the most fertile part of the peninsula, including most of the territory known of old as Arabia Felix. Conditions in the Maritime Range are particularly favourable to coffee, which is still grown in small quantities above 1 300 m (4 500 ft) and has long been famous under the name of the original port of shipment, Mokha (Mocha). That port has decayed, and coffee exports are now insignificant.

At higher altitudes in the Maritime Range, and in the highlands further east, as well as on a central plateau, the rainfall is regular and sufficient for the growing of grain crops, barley, wheat, and millet, while in the lowlands grapes are grown for raisins. Hillsides are carefully terraced and cultivated on intensive lines, and there is consequently usually a very small export of foodstuffs. San'a, the capital, with some 60 000 people lies in the eastern highlands at a height of over 2 100 m (7 000 ft). Ta'iz (30 000 people) at 1 400 m (4 600 ft).

Southern Yemen

In 1967 the rulers of the seventeen sultanates of the Federation of South Arabia (which had absorbed also the former British Aden Protectorate in 1963) were deposed and the Southern Yemen People's Republic proclaimed. British troops withdrew from Aden in November 1967; the name of Southern Yemen was later changed to the People's Democratic Republic of Yemen, but Southern Yemen remains in general use, to distinguish the territory from its neighbour, Yemen. The islands of Kamaran and Perim elected to remain with the new republic.

The port of Aden lies between two rocky peninsulas, extinct volcanoes, linked by a strip of low-lying sandy coast. The eastern peninsula, rising to 550 m (1 800 ft), is Aden proper; the western was known by the British as Little Aden. Offering the only good harbour on the main trade route between India and Egypt, Aden was famed as an entrepôt from early times, and the opening of the Suez Canal brought it into fresh prominence as a port of call and transhipment. It has oil refineries and an oil port dredged to 12 m (40 ft), opened in 1954. It has considerable oil-bunkering facilities as well as ship repairing yards.

The People's Democratic Republic of Yemen as a whole has an estimated area of 160 300 sq km (61 890 sq miles) with a population of about 1.5m. It is a desolate land, broken and rugged, rising to over 2 500 km (8 000 ft) on the border with Yemen. Inland a flat-topped steppe, the Hadramaut, is traversed from west to east by a great wadi of the same name. In the past the Hadramaut was largely dependent on funds supplied by emigrants who had built up fortunes in Malaysia. Most of the Southern Yemen people are engaged in agriculture which, owing to the scanty rainfall, is mainly conducted in the fertile valleys. The most important industrial crop is long-staple cotton, the growing of which was encouraged by the British government under a Development and Welfare Scheme. A tract of about 259 sq km (100 sq miles) in the Abyan district about 50 km (30 miles) east of Aden was irrigated and settled. Here, among other crops, a very high grade cotton of the Sudan type flourishes and provides a useful export. Livestock probably number over 1.2m. in total; in 1970 FAO estimated there were 90 000 cattle, 210 000 sheep, 850 000 goats, 41 000 camels and 27 000 asses. The fisheries are important to the economy, fish appearing among exports. There is usually a small surplus of other foodstuffs, especially rice, also available for export. But the main export is of petroleum products: nearly 80 per cent of the total. Main imports are textile yarns and fabrics, machinery and transport equipment and chemicals. In 1969 Kuwait, Iran and Japan provided most of the imports, while most of the exports were sent to the United Kingdom, Japan and Thailand.

Oman

Until 1970 the independent sovereign sultanate of Oman was known as the sultanate of Muscat and Oman. It occupies the eastern corner of Arabia, with a coastline of 1 600 km (1 000 miles), lying partly along he Gulf of Oman, where it is skirted by high mountainous country, and partly along the Arabian Sea, where the land is on the whole low-lying. The interior stretches back to the borders of the Rub' al Khali. The estimated area is 212 000 sq km (82 000 sq miles) and the population is about 750 000. A treaty of friendship, commerce and navigation concluded with Great Britain in 1951 reaffirmed the close ties which had existed between the two countries for some 150 years. The Kuria Muria Islands, ceded by the sultan of Muscat and Oman in 1854 to Britain for use as a cable station were returned to the sultanate in 1967.

The two chief centres of Oman, Muscat and Matrah, lie near to one another on the Gulf of Oman, where the mountains come down to the sea. Muscat (population about 6 000) lies at the head of a cove dominated by rocky heights crowned by old forts, and exposed to *shamels* (the violent northwest winds of the Gulf region). Commercially it has lost ground to Matrah (population about 14 000), which has a larger harbour, is the terminus of caravan routes to and from the interior, and now has a bigger population, though both towns are small. Beyond them, for over 240 km (150 miles) in the direction of the Persian Gulf, a narrow coastal plain, the Batinah, carries date gardens noted for the flavour and early maturity of their fruit. Inland, where the mountains rise to over 2 750 m (9 000 ft), the general aridity of the country is relieved by the green fertility of cultivated areas with sufficient rainfall for grain and other crops. Along the Arabian Sea the coast is mostly barren, but at the far western end the upland province of Dhofar is another productive area, where sugarcane is grown and cattle are reared; it is served by the small port of Murbat. Camels are extensively bred in the interior.

A survival of former expansion was the territory of Gwadur, on the opposite (north) side of the Gulf of Oman, forming an enclave about 65 km (40 miles) long and 25 km (15 miles) deep, embedded in Pakistan near the Iranian border. It had a total population of about 15 000, of whom 10 000 were congregated in Gwadur town and port, and was administered on behalf of the Sultan of Muscat and Oman until it was handed over to Pakistan in 1958.

Exploration for oil had been carried on for some years before 1964 when concessionaires announced that reserves were sufficient to be commercially exploited. Crude oil production was 16.5m. tons in 1970; the estimated figure for 1973 was 14.6m. tons. A pipeline carries the oil to the terminal at Mina al Fahl, the port lying west of the town of Muscat. Oil exploration continues offshore.

Dates, dried limes, dried fish, tobacco and frankincense are exported as well as oil, which is far more valuable. Cereals, coffee, sugar, vehicles and accessories, cement and other building materials, and cotton piece goods are the chief imports, provided mainly by the United Kingdom, India, Pakistan, Australia, Singapore and Thailand.

United Arab Emirates and Qatar

From Oman to the borders of Saudi Arabia, halfway along the shores of the Arabian Gulf, stretch some 950 km (600 miles) of coastal territory divided into various independent sheikhdoms which used to be known as the Trucial Sheikhdoms, and as such had longstanding engagements with Britain to preserve peace, suppress slavery, and abstain from entering into agreements with foreign states. Now known as the United Arab Emirates they have an area of some 93 000 sq km (36 000 sq miles) of which Qatar accounts for 10 000 sq km (4 000 sq miles) and 160 000 inhabitants. Fishing and pearling are basic industries, but much more significant is oil production. In Qatar a first shipment was made in 1949, and in 1971 output was at the rate of some 20m. tons a year. In 1964 an undersea field came into production. The state of Abu Dhabi started to ship oil in 1962. Output in 1973 was 63.5m. tons. A long-standing dispute as to the control of the fertile Buraimi oasis was settled in favour of Abu Dhabi. Production of oil in Dubai in 1971 was 6.2m. tons. Prospecting continues throughout the whole area.

Bahrain

A group of islands about halfway along the Arabian coast of the Persian Gulf, in a large bay cutting deeply into the land constitutes the independent territory of Bahrain. The islands lie about 32 km (20 miles) from the mainland (Saudi Arabia) and have treaty relations with Britain dating back to 1880. Their total area is about 598 sq km (400 sq miles) and the total population (1969 estimate), 200 000. They were renowned commercially as the headquarters of the Persian Gulf pearl fisheries, and though that industry has declined they have gained new fame as a source of oil supply.

Nearly all the area is provided by the main island, Bahrain, some 48 km (30 miles) long by 16 km (10 miles) wide. It is linked to Muharraq Island (6 km by 1.5 km: 4 miles by 1 mile) by a causeway carrying a motor road and a swing bridge spanning the deepwater channel. These islands enfold two harbours, and from a third island, Sitra, another causeway and a pipeline project eastward for nearly 5 km (3 miles) to a deepwater anchorage. Bahrain has come to appreciate the potential profit to be earned from repairing supertankers, and is building dry docks for this purpose.

Dates, citrus fruits, and lucerne are successfully grown on the main island, and it is there also that oil has been found in the neighbourhood of the highest point, a rocky crater rising some 140 m (450 ft). First developed early in the 1930s, output after the Second World War was about 1.5m. tons a year, rising lately to 3.75m. tons. This is small compared with the output in Saudi Arabia, on the mainland behind the islands, but Bahrain also possesses a well-equipped refinery, with a capacity of some 250 000 barrels a day (12 tons a year), which usefully supplements the mainland resources for refining oil. An asphalt plant has been added to the refinery, which is situated on the main island at Manama, the chief town of the group. The town has a population of about 80 000; and a piped water supply from artesian wells.

Kuwait

This independent sheikdom at the head of the Arabian Gulf, has an area of 24 280 sq km (9 375 sq miles) and a population (1971 estimate) of 1m., including over 390 000 foreign workers. Formerly under British protection, it was recognised in 1961 to be a sovereign independent state in a spirit of continued friendship with Britain, which declared itself to be still ready to assist Kuwait if asked to do so. The new agreement was welcomed by other countries, including members of the Arab League with the exception of Iraq, which claimed ownership of Kuwait and threatened to occupy it by force. Both Britain and the Arab League, to which Kuwait had been admitted as a member, supplied defence forces temporarily, and Iraq, while maintaining its claims, did not take further action.

The 'Neutral Zone', an area of 5 700 sq km (3 560 sq miles), lying south of Kuwait and bordering the Gulf, was owned and administered by Kuwait and Saudi Arabia together from 1922 to 1966. It was then divided between the two states, with an agreement that the exploitation of natural resources, especially oil, should be shared. It usually appears as a separate entity in oil statistics.

Until a few years ago Kuwait, like the other small Arabian Gulf states, was largely desert. It had an extensive harbour on which stood the capital, around it numerous date gardens and some cultivation of cereals and other foodstuffs for home consumption, a reputation for dhow-building, and a certain amount of general trade; but was chiefly notable as a pivotal point in the political geography of the Middle East. Its meteoric rise is due to its wealth of oil. Its production exceeds only that of Iran and Saudi Arabia in the Middle East. Production for export did not start till 1946, but in 1953 it surpassed that of Kuwait's giant neighbour, Saudi Arabia; and in 1971 amounted to over 147m. tons, when the Neutral Zone between Kuwait and Saudi Arabia provided over 29m. tons. Over 100 wells have been drilled in the 260 sq km (100 sq miles) of the Burgan oilfield at the back of the port of Kuwait, where the bulk of the population is concentrated. Ahmadi, the oil town and administrative headquarters of the Kuwait Oil Company, lies about 10 km (6 miles) inland at an elevation of 120 m (400 ft), and is connected by a pipeline with Mina al Ahmadi, the oil port, with berths for five supertankers at two deepwater piers. Most of the oil is shipped in crude form, though there is a refinery which has been much enlarged. Kuwait's refinery capacity in 1971 was 26m. tons.

In Kuwait proper the oil is worked by a British–American company; in the Neutral Zone between Kuwait and Saudi Arabia, by an American company; and off the coast by Japanese and Dutch companies. In 1951 the Kuwait government became entitled to a half-share of the profits, which has helped to improve living conditions in the country. Kuwait's status of sovereign independence led to other developments, including an elected national assembly in 1963.

Iran

Iran is an independent state under a constitutional sovereign, the Shah, with an area of about 1 621 860 sq km (630 000 sq miles) and a population, 1962 census, of 25.78m., 1972 estimate, 31m. It extends from the Caspian Sea to the Persian Gulf and the Gulf of Oman, and has for its neighbours on the north, Turkey and the USSR, Iraq on the west, Afghanistan and Pakistan on the east. Except at the head of the Persian Gulf, where the only navigable river, the Kārūn, finds its way to the sea, the coastal plains bordering the Caspian and the two southern Gulfs are very narrow, and the land rises rapidly to a plateau of 900 to 1 500 m (3 000 to 5 000 ft), which in turn carries mountain ranges running from northwest to southeast, with peaks of 3 000 to 4 500 m (10 000 to 15 000 ft), while in the Elburz Mountains, south of the Caspian, Mount Damavand rises to 5 670 m (18 600 ft). This mountainous plateau is characteristic of practically the whole country, not only north and south from the Caspian to the Gulfs, but east and west from frontier to frontier. Only centrally, southeastwards from Tehrān is it sundered by a wide trough in which lie the great salt deserts of Dasht-e-Kavir and Dasht-e-Luft.

Land use and agriculture. It is estimated that rather more than half the total area is waste, and another 20 per cent unused, though potentially productive. Forests cover nearly 11 per cent and pastoral land 4 per cent, leaving 7 per cent classed as arable. Much of this last category is temporarily fallow, so that very little of the total land area is under cultivation. But in a country the size of Iran even small percentages of the whole are extensive. Woods and forests cover 18m. ha (44m. acres) — half as large again as England. The pastoral country is about three-quarters the size of England, and the arable land larger than England and Wales. Wheat is easily the leading crop; it is grown throughout the country, covers over 4.7m. ha (11.6m. acres) and provides a crop of over 4m. tons. Barley is also widely grown, covering about 1m. ha (2.5m. acres) and yielding between 0.75 and 1m. tons. Other leading crops are more of a subtropical character.

The southern littoral, bordering the Gulfs, suffers from a very scanty rainfall, but it has a big asset in the date palm and is largely responsible for Iran's annual production of 290 000 tons of dates. On the other hand the coastal plain along the southern shore of the Caspian, though narrow, enjoys an abundant rainfall and a fertile soil which together make it the most productive agricultural region in Iran. Where the forests which are the natural covering of this region have been cleared,

567

it yields large crops of rice, fruit, cotton, and other products. Mulberry trees flourish, and the provinces bordering the Caspian are the centre of the silk industry. Rice is the most extensive crop after wheat and barley; in all over 1m. tons are grown on 345 000 ha (852 000 acres). Cotton is grown on 325 000 ha (803 000 acres), yielding some 135 000 tons of cotton lint. The crop of grapes averages 250 000 tons from 80 000 ha (nearly 200 000 acres) under vines. Oranges are a much smaller crop, producing about 50 000 tons. Sugar beet, a heavy crop, produces 3.4m. tons of beets from some 155 000 ha (408 000 acres). Only 17 000 ha (42 000 acres) is under tobacco, but the average crop yield is about 20 000 tons.

Livestock are a big factor in Iran's land economy. Sheep number 35m., and goats 12.6m. There are 5.8m. cattle, 2.3m. asses, 137 000 mules, 400 000 horses and 243 000 camels. Wool is an important product.

Forty-nine per cent of the total population (48 per cent of the working population) are engaged in agriculture. The land reforms and agricultural development initiated by the present Shah have had a liberating and stimulating effect on farming practices. The character of much of the country is a limiting factor, and expansion of the cultivated area is largely dependent on the spread of irrigation.

Industry. Manufactures are numerous, but mostly on a small scale. In some, such as tobacco and sugar, the government exercises a monopoly, and in some it participates; there are government cotton ginneries and textile mills. Of outstanding importance is the manufacture of carpets. Persian carpets are world-famous, and are the best known, though no longer the most valuable, of the exports; it is oil which is easily supreme.

Oil. The Anglo–Iranian Oil Company, in which the British government had a controlling interest, held a concession to work the main oilfields, near the head of the Persian Gulf. In the course of many years the company raised the output to 30m. tons of crude oil in 1950. It had also built up one of the largest oil refineries in the world at that time at Abadan, on the Shatt al 'Arab, with an annual capacity of 20m. tons. In 1951 while negotiations for giving the Iranian government a larger share of the profits were in progress, the *Majlis* (National Assembly), passed a Bill nationalising the oil industry and claimed control of the operations. The International Court of Justice at The Hague gave a provisional ruling against this unilateral action, but the Iranian government refused to recognise the court's jurisdiction. The oilfields and the refinery were abandoned by the company and export of oil practically ceased. In 1954 a settlement was reached between the Iranian government and the National Iranian Oil Company on the one hand and seventeen international oil companies (the Consortium) on the other. A new agreement was signed in 1973 when the Shah gave the National Iranian Oil Company control of the industry, a Western consortium of companies (now known as the Oil Participants) acting as contractors to the Company. Production in 1960 was 52m. tons. In 1973 it was 93m. tons, fourth in the world production of oil to the USA, USSR and Saudi Arabia.

Trade. The country is in an enviable position in that the value of her exports greatly exceeds that of her imports. Oil of course is king of the exports (crude, some refined, and petroleum products), followed by carpets and rugs, raw cotton, fruit and dried fruit, undressed hides and skins. The list of imports is long, mainly the manufactured goods of industrial nations: machinery (including electrical), iron and steel and their products, chemicals, textiles; but also foodstuffs such as sugar, wheat and tea. Most trade is with Japan, the United Kingdom, West Germany, the United States, the Netherlands and France.

Communications. Transport in Iran is not easy and the Trans—Iranian railway, opened in 1938, represents a considerable engineering feat. The line is of standard gauge and runs for 1 403 km (872 miles) from Bandar Shāh at the southeast corner of the Caspian, through Tehran to Bandar Shāpūr at the head of the Persian Gulf. From Tehran a branch runs east to Mashhad (Meshed) and another had been built to Tabrīz. An older line runs from Tabrīz northwards to Jolfā on the Soviet frontier. From Ahvās a branch line connects with Khorramshahr, where the Karūn joins the Shatt al 'Arab. A line is being laid from Kāshān to Yazd. The road system is very extensive but only about 15 per cent is surfaced or being surfaced. Tehran has a busy international airport.

Table 66 — Iran: towns with over 150 000 people (1970 estimate)

Tehrān (capital)	3 150 000	Shirāz	270 000
Esfahān	575 000	Ahvāz	206 300
Tabrīz	468 450	Kermānshāh	188 000
Mashhad	417 200	Hamadān	162 000
Abadan	273 000	Tajrīsh	157 000

Afghánistán

Afghánistán is an inland state, bordered on the north by the southern-most republics of the Soviet Union, on the west by Iran, on the south and east by Pakistan, and in the extreme northeast corner it touches China and Kashmir. It is a constitutional monarchy, member of the United Nations, with an area of some 657 500 sq km (250 000 sq miles), and a possibly exaggerated estimate of 13m. inhabitants, nearly four times the number in Norway, which is half the size. The country is extremely mountainous, an extension of the Iranian plateau and, like Iran, carrying on its basic elevation wild and lofty mountain ranges. Afghánistán may be likened to a gigantic oval pan, its main axis running from southwest to northeast, with a panhandle projecting to the north-east: the narrow Wákhán valley, 290 km (180 miles) long, bordered by the giant peaks of the Hindu Kush, soaring to 6 000 to 7 000 m (20 000 to 25 000 ft). The range extends into the heart of Afghánistán on a diminishing scale, with peaks of 4 500 to 7 000 m (15 000 to 20 000 ft) north of Kábul, the capital, itself at an elevation of nearly 2 000 m (6 000 ft); and successive ranges continue under various names to the Iranian border. Other high ranges branch off from the main range and cover most of the country, which drops to comparatively low elevations only in the desert in the southwest, and in the river valleys, notably the Amu-Dar'ya (Oxus), whose upper waters, falling to 360 m (1 200 ft), form part of the northern frontier. In the northwest the upper waters of the Hari Rūd drain the country round Herát, on their way to lose themselves in the Kara-Kum Desert of the Soviet Union. The southwest is drained by the Helmand, destined to the same fate in marshes on the Iranian border. The Kábul River, flowing east, passes into Pakistan and joins the Indus. None of these rivers is navigable in Afghánistán, but with their affluents they drain most of the country and furnish potential sources of hydroelectric power, already installed in the capital. Power stations are being built on the Kábul River and near Kandahár. Rainfall is scanty, and practically negligible in summer, but the melting mountain snow permits of irrigation. Great extremes of climate are experienced. On the plateau at over 2 000 m (7 000 ft) the winter temperature may drop to −18° C (below zero Fahrenheit), and in the Oxus valley summer temperatures of 50° C (122° F) have been recorded.

Land use and agriculture. The geographical similarity of Afghánistán to Iran is reflected in the land use of the two countries. More than half of Afghánistán is classed as waste, agriculturally, and is unused though potentially productive. Arable land covers 12 per cent of the total area, pasture over 9 per cent, forest 3 per cent. Cereal and other crops are grown in sheltered valleys and the pastoral areas support large numbers of livestock. Two harvests are common: wheat, barley and peas sown in autumn and reaped in early summer; millet, maize and in places cotton and rice are summer crops. Great quantities of fruit, such as grapes, apricots and figs, are also grown, and tobacco does well in places. In recent years 2.5m. tons of wheat were harvest from 2.2m. ha (5.4m. acres, 380 000 tons of barley from 320 000 ha (790 000 acres), 415 000 tons of rice from 210 000 ha (518 000 acres), 29 000 tons of cotton lint from 65 000 ha (160 000 acres), and 204 000 tons of grapes.

Sheep are estimated to number 21.8m., goats 3.1m., and cattle 3.6m. There are 415 000 horses, 1.3m. asses, 34 000 mules and 301 000 camels. Animal transport is still common in the absence of railways, but motor transport is on the increase as roads improve. There are two distinct classes of sheep: the fat-tailed, bred for mutton and yielding also a good though coarse wool; and karakul, whose lambs, killed at birth, have the close curly black wool known as astrakhan. Among the animal products are 30 000 tons of greasy wool annually, 16 500 tons of clean wool, and vast numbers of karakul skins for world markets.

Minerals. Afghánistán has many mineral deposits, but so far few have been seriously investigated or exploited. There are large deposits of coal in the Hindu Kush; natural gas in the north is piped to the USSR; iron ore deposits of good quality have been located about 160 km (100 miles) west of Kábul. There are known deposits of gold, silver, lapis lazuli, asbestos, mica, chrome, copper and sulphur.

Standard of living. The implications of the strategic position of Afghánistán, the 'gateway' to the Indian subcontinent, have for centuries focused attention on it. In recent times the Soviet Union and the United States have displayed their interest, and the Afghán government has not been slow to appreciate the advantages of the situation. Formerly a hermit country, deliberately cutting itself off from the outside world. Afghánistán is now willing to accept help offered, leaping from an almost medieval existence straight into the twentieth century. But this has had little effect as yet on the lives of the majority of the people. The USSR and the USA have provided substantial financial aid, members of a United Nations mission have been in the country offering technical help since 1950. The USSR has built and equipped a factory to make motor spares; a cottonseed oil extraction plant has been built by a British firm at Lashkargah, and the British are modernising a sugar factory at Baghlan; the West Germans have constructed and equipped a cotton textile factory at Gulbahar; the Chinese have provided another at Bagram. The British have a 47 per cent interest in the state insurance company.

Kábul, the capital, has a population estimated to be nearly 460 000. The only other large urban centre is Kandahár (about 125 000). Domestic water supply is a problem over much of the country and rainwater is carefully collected from the flat roofs of houses.

Power and communications. Hydroelectric power has been developed at Sarobi, Nangarhar, Naghlu and Mahipar and other hydro and thermal installations are projected; but it is the improvement of the roads that is having such a marked effect on life in Afghánistán. It is now possible to drive through the country on asphalted highways, surfaced by the Soviet Union and the United States. There are now railways but state airways operate internally and internationally. The United States is backing financially the building of an international airport at Kandahár, to match the enlargement by the USSR of the airport facilities at Kábul.

Trade. Karachi in Pakistan acts as the transit port for the very small but growing foreign trade of Afghánistán. Main exports are primary produce: karakul (sheep) skins, raw cotton, dried fruit and nuts, fresh fruit and natural gas. Main imports are manufactured goods (including machinery and transport equipment and motor vehicles), food (especially wheat and wheat flour, sugar and tea) and petroleum products. The exports are in the main destined for the USSR, the USA, the UK, India, Pakistan, West Germany and Czechoslovakia, imports coming from the USSR, the UK, India, Japan, West Germany and Pakistan.

The Indian subcontinent

India, Pakistan and Bangladesh

There is no part of the world better marked off by nature as a region by itself than the Indian subcontinent, now comprising the republics of India, Pakistan and Bangladesh. It will be convenient first to deal with the subcontinent as a whole. It is a region, indeed, full of contrast, in physical features and in climate, and one that has never been, strictly speaking, under one rule. On the north it is bounded by the Himalayas, the loftiest mountains in the world; on the west by mountains and deserts; on the east and northeast it is not only bounded by mountains, but lofty mountain chains and deep valleys spread away for great distances. For the rest the boundary is the sea.

Within the mountains a vast plain, from about 240 to nearly 500 km (150 to more than 300 miles) in width, sweeps round from the delta of the Ganga and Brahmaputra in the east to that of the Indus in the west. The peninsula to the south of these plains is mainly made up of tablelands varying in elevation for the most part from about 450 to over 750 m (1 500 to 2 500 ft). On the west this tableland advances close up to the sea, and is bounded by the mountains called the Western Ghāts, in reality the lofty edge of the plateau; but on the east its edge is generally at a greater distance from the coast and is less regular. The name of Eastern Ghāts is sometimes used generally for the whole of this eastern margin, sometimes restricted to its northern or central portion.

The dense population is for the most part confined to the plains, but is prevented by climatic and other circumstances from extending over their whole area.

Structurally the plateau of peninsular India is built up of a great mass of ancient metamorphic rocks. More than 520 000 sq km (200 000 sq miles) of these in the northwest are covered by great sheets, almost horizontal, of basaltic lava (the so-called 'Deccan Traps') which furnish a dark, almost black soil well suited to cotton. Old basins in the surface of the plateau are filled with sedimentary rocks, including the main coal-bearing strata. The great plain of the north and the coastal plains of east and west are built up of alluvium and other recent deposits, furnishing deep rich agricultural soils. The mountain wall of the north is of Tertiary or Alpine age.

Minerals. The mineral wealth of the subcontinent is tolerably abundant. Geological surveys show that both coal and iron ore are widely distributed, but of the coalfields the most productive lie in the west of Bengal and the east of Bihar. The most productive parts of the chief coalfield lie in the Damodar valley belonging to the basin of the Hooghly, where about nine-tenths of the coal raised in India is produced. Rāniganj, about 195 km (120 miles) northwest of Calcutta, was long the principal coalmining centre, but the production of this field has at last been eclipsed by that of the Jherria field, about 65 or 80 km (40 or 50 miles) further west. Still further west is Daltonganj. On the tableland three smaller coalfields are now connected with the Indian railway system. One is that at Umarīa, east of Jubbulpore; another, that of Warorā, in the Wardhā valley now in the eastern part of Bombay State; and the third that of Singareni, further south.

The total production of India reached 74.7m. tons in 1969, the production of the outlying fields representing only about 1m. tons in each case. Belonging to the Permo-Carboniferous or Gondwana deposits, these are good quality bituminous coals. Lignites and brown coals of a little importance in Assam and the Punjab, more important in Tamil Nadu, at Neyveli, where about 3.5m. tons is mined annually. It is to be noted that all the coal resources of the subcontinent, with the exception of some Punjab lignites, lie in the Republic of India.

Iron ore is widely scattered over the mountainous and hilly parts of the country, and with the profuse employment of charcoal for smelting, Indian villagers made iron of excellent quality. But this expensive mode of working was almost superseded by the import of European iron and iron wares, followed by the development of modern production methods. Of the earlier attempts to introduce the modern processes of smelting in India the most successful was that of the Bengal Iron and Steel Co. near Barākar in the north of the Rāniganj coalfield, where ores are obtainable, and a suitable coal for smelting is procured at Karharbāri or Giridhi. For many years progress was slow, but in the early years of the present century the company began to supplement the local clay ironstone ores with magnetites obtained in Chota Nagpur. Later, in 1911, a more ambitious programme was initiated by the Tata Iron and Steel Co., which obtained leases over the rich massive ore bodies of the northern part of the Mayurbhanj state of Orissa, and the Raipur district of the Central Provinces. Later even more important deposits of iron ore were discovered in the district of Singhbhūm, to the southwest, and the company obtained a concession in which, it is said, a ravine cutting across the ore range shows a continuous thickness of 215 m (700 ft) of hematite, containing more than

60 per cent of iron. Even before this last discovery, blast furnaces were started in 1911. Steel was first produced from modern rolling mills in 1933. The site chosen for the new industry was Jamshedpur where some formerly exploited ores were available. Here the Calcutta–Bombay railway (via Nagpur) has a branch to Asansol and the coalfields (about 160 km: 100 miles away), whilst the main orefields lie 75 km (45 miles) to the southwest. Limestone and manganese are within easy reach. Thus a village in the barren scrub quickly grew into a town of over 250 000 inhabitants. Jamshedpur is now with over 300 000 people a great industrial centre, producing not only a great variety of articles in iron and steel, including mill and electrical machinery, but also heavy chemicals, fertilisers, and explosives. The Tata Company is now a big factor throughout Indian industry. The large demand for tinplate by the Burmah and Anglo–Iranian Oil Companies led to the erection of plant in Bengal capable of manufacturing about 30 000 tons annually. After partition in 1947 three great new works were initiated with the help of German, Russian and British technicians.

There are abundant mineral resources, more lying in India than the other two countries. Pakistan produces oil from Khaur and other small fields in the Punjab, with refineries at Rawalpindi; and the Indian production is from several fields in Assam, notably at Digboi. Oil prospectors are at work in the Bay of Bengal. The discovery of large resources of natural gas at Sui in Pakistan whence it is piped to Karachi and Lahore and other deposits in Bangladesh are of great significance. India is the fourth or fifth largest producer of manganese ore in the world. The ores are widely distributed in the old rocks of the plateau, many are very rich, and many areas have been worked since 1901. Later Sandur in Tamil Nadu became the biggest producer. Total production in 1971 was over 650 000 tons.

Silver, though formerly the standard metal of the country, is not abundant and the output formerly credited to India was almost entirely from the Bawdwin mines of Burma; the same is true of lead. Gold is important now only in the Kolar field of Mysore, the annual production being about 3 000 kg (6 614 lb). Copper is found in the Singhbhūm district of Bihar though mining and production have been irregular, and the small deposits of the Himalayas are not now exploited. Chromite is found in many parts of India and is worked especially in Singhbhūm, Mysore, and Baluchistan. Mica, valuable as an insulator, is a characteristic Indian mineral and is obtained from the old rocks in many parts of the plateau, the huge sheets from the Nellore district of Andhra being specially famous. Monazite, ilmenite and tungsten ores take an important place in Indian minerals. Despite the existence of some famous Indian diamonds, production is unimportant.

Salt is obtained by evaporation all along the coasts (especially at Bombay and Madras) and rock salt is quarried in the Salt Range of the

Punjab (Pakistan). The extraction of saltpetre (nitrate of potash) in Punjab, Uttar Pradesh, and Bihar has declined from various causes, but chiefly in consequence of the competition of Chilean nitrate and latterly of artificial fertilisers. In India it is a natural product formed in alluvial soils from animal and vegetable refuse in a climate with alternating wet and dry seasons. In the dry season the efflorescence was collected from the soil and purified for use in lieu of soap.

Climate. The year is popularly divided into three seasons: the hot, the rainy, and the cool; but these names are appropriate only in the northeast and to some extent along the western coast. In the south, where the latitudes are low, there is no really cool season, and in the northwest, though the rains occur at the same period as in the Ganga valley, they are small in amount. The hot season is from March to May inclusive, the period that embraces the change of the monsoons from northeast to southwest, but before the 'bursting' of the southwest monsoon, that is, before the southerly winds begin to be accompanied by rain. During this period the highest temperature is in the heart of the Deccan. The rainy season lasts from June to October inclusive, and during this period the western slopes of the Western Ghāts, the hills of Assam, the slopes of the eastern Himalayas, and even the plains of the Ganga delta, are deluged with rain, and the greater part of the northeast receives a fairly abundant rainfall. The part of the Deccan immediately behind the Western Ghāts, however, has a very moderate and precarious rainfall, and so too have the plains in the northwest. A large part of the Indus valley is almost rainless. Where the rains are abundant the temperature is mitigated, but in the arid region just referred to this is naturally the hottest period of the year. The cool season, or the season of the northeast monsoons, lasts from November to February inclusive. The earlier part of this period is classed more scientifically as the period of the retreating monsoon, giving thus a fourth season. The storms of October, November and December bring rain to the southeastern plains, the moisture brought by the winds from the Bay of Bengal being condensed in consequence of the obstruction presented by the Eastern Ghāts and the mountains of Kerala. But the amount of rain that falls on these plains is only one-third or one-fourth of that which falls on the best-watered plains in the north during the rain season. The cool or winter season is naturally coolest in the northwest, where the highest altitudes are reached, and even on the plains there are genuine winter temperatures by comparison with the extreme heat of summer. In this region, in the latter half of the cool season (January to about March) there is a recurrence of rains, believed to be brought about by cyclonic disturbances originating in the Mediterranean.

Irrigation and hydroelectric power. The amount of rain that falls varies in the subcontinent, as everywhere else, from year to year; but it is an important fact that, whereas in a country like England the variations in the rainfall may increase or diminish the abundance of a crop, in a large part of the subcontinent the variation may be such that in one year there is an ample supply for a good crop, in another a rainfall wholly inadequate to produce any crop at all. It is this area of uncertain rainfall that is liable to be visited by famines and hence irrigation has to be practised not only in those parts of the country in which there is always a deficiency of rain, but also in those in which it is doubtful whether the rain may be sufficient or not. Even where the amount of the rain is sufficient for the requirements of the crops irrigation is in many cases demanded by the mode in which the rain falls. The northeast monsoon, on which the southern plains (Tamil Nadu) chiefly depend for rain, is remarkable for the fact that rain falls for the most part in bursts, and generally at night. Falls of 250 and even 280 mm (10 or 12 in) in a single night have been recorded. Accordingly Tamil Nadu and the Deccan generally are dotted with thousands of tanks or reservoirs for irrigation-water, except in the areas with the black soil.

These tanks usually contain little, if any, more than one year's supply, and hence are altogether inadequate to meet the uncertainties arising from recurring years of drought. In certain places, however, there is a natural storage of water underground that can always be made available by means of moderately deep wells. This is true of most areas of alluvium but not where ancient rocks underlie the surface. The whole of the plain along the base of the Himalayas has constant supplies of fresh water at a greater or less depth, and the middle portion of it has these supplies near enough to the surface to be easily reached. Hence, between Delhi and Varanasi (Banaras), the upper levels of the alluvial plain are riddled like a sieve with waterholes or wells 3 to 15 m (10 to 50 ft) in depth. Since electric power has become available deeper supplies are tapped by tube wells, especially important where irrigation from canals is difficult.

The greatest irrigation works are canals led from rivers. In the Indus valley the old canals for irrigation in Sind were merely laid so as to carry off the surplus water, when the melting of Himalayan snows caused a rise of the water in the main stream and its tributaries. These were known as inundation canals and were for long in operation, and, though very useful and profitable in most years, the supply of water by this method is precarious, as the rise of the rivers may be so small as to yield little water or none at all. But works of much greater magnitude have been made in the form of canals, into which is led nearly the whole body of water belonging to a river for a greater or less distance. These are known as perennial canals. On the delta of the Cauvery such canals are said to have been constructed as far back as the fourth century of the Christian era, but in the period of the British raj such works were extended to all the other deltas of the east coast and many parts of the northern plains. About 1885 the total length of canals under government supervision was above 45 000 km (28 000 miles), and the area irrigated by them was equal to that of Belgium (29 500 sq km: 11 400 sq miles). In 1919–20 the area irrigated had been increased to about 72 500 sq km (28 000 sq miles), almost the area of Scotland. In April 1914 the Upper Swat Canal, which involved the piercing of a canal through the Malakand Hills to establish a colony of nearly 1 550 sq km (600 sq miles) in extent in the northern part of the Peshāwar district, was opened. In 1922 legislative sanction was given to a project (completed in 1933) for the construction of a dam (Lloyd Barrage) across the Indus at Sukkur, which made it possible to place some 2.2m. ha (5.5m. acres) under perennial irrigation, of special importance for cotton cultivation. It is estimated that the execution of this scheme rendered about 160 000 ha (400 000 acres) available for the production of long-staple cotton similar to that of Egypt. With the view of extending irrigation into the arid tracts in Bahawalpur and districts in the southwest of Punjab, the Sutlej Valley Canals were commenced and, like the Sarda works of Uttar Pradesh, were finished shortly before the Second World War.

Later works have generally coupled irrigation with the development of hydroelectric power which can then be used to pump water from tube wells tapping underground supplies not reached by shallow hand-dug wells. In 1947, when the countries became independent, there were 148 700 sq km (57 400 sq miles) irrigated in India and 82 100 sq km (31 700 sq miles) in Pakistan. Since partition many large new works have been undertaken. In India alone the irrigated area in 1957 was nearly 22m. ha (56m. acres). The current plan is for this area to be extended to 58m. ha (143m. acres) by 1980–81. In Pakistan a huge dam on the Kābul River helps development in the northwest, dams on the upper Indus are irrigating the Thal (Indus–Jhelum Doab) and at Kotri, Hyderabad, the Indus Delta. In Bangladesh, hydroelectricity is supplied to Chittagong from the hill region and the Ganga is to be controlled. India has the comprehensive Damodar Valley scheme and benefits from a great dam on the Mahanadi. These irrigation canals serve little for navigation; indeed one of the few canals in India used primarily for this purpose is the Buckingham Canal, which, being a salt-water canal, is not available for irrigation, but forms an inland waterway from the mouth of the Godavari to Madras, and beyond.

In connection with irrigation it may be pointed out that the structure of the country, combined with the character of the climate, affords in many places, as in the Himalayas and the Western Ghāts, the opportunity of forming immense tanks or reservoirs by damming the mouths of narrow valleys, providing at once the means for irrigation and the development of water power. In one case the headwaters of the Periyar in Ketala have long been dammed and the lake thus formed drained through a tunnel to the east side of the Cardamom Hills, so as to irrigate arid plains in Tamil Nadu.

In the northwest the boundary between India and Pakistan cut across a number of important canals in such a way that it was possible for India to cut off water supplies from the land of Pakistan which depended upon them for crop production. A waters agreement was reached after many years of discussion.

Agriculture. Despite the recent developments in industry, India, Pakistan and Bangladesh remain primarily agricultural. At the census of 1881 the number of persons directly supported by agriculture and the rearing of livestock made up 72 per cent of the male inhabitants engaged in some specified occupation. There has since been little change, for the percentage in 1911 was 71; 1921 over 73; and in 1965 over 70. Holdings are mostly small, on an average about 2 ha (5 acres) each. In Bengal, the Famine Commissioners in 1880 reported that two-thirds of the peasant holdings were only about half that size. Taking the subcontinent as a whole the cropped land today represents less than 0.3 ha (0.8 acres) per head of population, compared with more than three times this area in the United States. This small area combined with low yields means that some of the population is near the starvation level, and below it in years of bad harvest, although this situation is being ameliorated by improved seeds and husbandry.

For the most part two crops are reaped in the year, but not usually from the same land. In the area of the summer monsoon rains, one crop is generally sown in the early weeks of the monsoon (June and July), and reaped in October and November; the other is sown at the end of the monsoon and reaped from January to March. The latter, accordingly, is the winter crop; and as the winter throughout the northwest is at least as cold as the summer of northern Europe, wheat, barley, and linseed are among the winter crops of the region wherever the duration of cool weather is long enough to ripen them. Although the cultivation of wheat has extended southwards to the southern limits of Bombay and Hyderabad, the chief region of production of this cereal is naturally far in the north.

Although wheat, largely in consequence of the extension of irrigation in the northwest, has been in years of plenty an export crop, it has become one of the staple food crops for home consumption in the northwest. Crops that may be described as widespread in the subcontinent are millets, pulses, and oilseeds; except on the best watered plains, suitable for ricegrowing, and in parts of the north where a stronger grain is required, millets and pulses, along with garden produce, form the bulk of the food of the agricultural population. The most extensively grown unirrigated crop is the great millet, here known as *jowar*; the millet next in importance is the smaller spiked millet, or *bajra*; the principal pulse is the chick-pea or *gram*. Grains and pulses occupy about two-thirds of the cropped land. A third of this is occupied by rice, a third by millets, with wheat, maize and barley following. The oilseeds most extensively grown are sesame, groundnuts, linseed, caster oil, mustard, and different kinds of rape. Peanuts or groundnuts with their nitrogen-fixing root bacteria have enabled poor tracts of sandy soil previously useless to be brought under cultivation.

Opium cultivation has now almost disappeared but it had its chief seats in the valley of the Ganga round Patna and Varanasi (Benares), and in central India in the region corresponding to the old kingdom of Malwa. Cotton is grown on the southern tableland, and above all in that series of fertile plains opened up by the railway that ascends the Tāpti valley: that is, the plains of Khandesh in Bombay, and of northern Berār, both lying on both sides of the Tāpti, and those of the Wardhā now in the east of Bombay State. It is likewise largely grown on many other parts of the tableland, but the finest cotton — long-stapled American varieties — is grown on irrigated land in Punjab. Regarding rice, jute, tea, lac, coffee, and indigo, nothing need be added to what will be found under these heads elsewhere in the book; and among the vegetable and animal products not mentioned in the table, reference may also be made to cinchona, silk, and pepper, all of which are likewise treated separately. Formerly the subcontinent was largely dependent on other countries, notably Java, for supplies of sugar. Sugarcane is now, however, widely cultivated in the northern plains, and sugar is also derived from palms, chiefly in southern India. Indian sugar production is now the highest in the world. With respect to the export of hides and skins, it should be explained that cattle are the chief beasts of draught and burden in most areas, but that in the wet plains of eastern Bengal and elsewhere they give place to buffaloes. Cattle include the large white humped zebu or brahmin cattle and the smaller, also humped, brown animals. The yield of milk from both cattle and buffaloes is very small, but dairy farming is developing in notably now in some areas, especially Uttar Pradesh and Bombay State.

Industries. Not only in metal-working, but also in various other branches of manufacture, the old handicrafts suffered greatly from European competition. Cheap Manchester cottons and later the products of the cotton factories of Bombay and the influx of Japanese goods, told heavily on the old hand-spinning and weaving. Even the long celebrated fine muslins of Dacca (Bangladesh) and Madras, have now almost become a thing of the past. Factories and industries are spreading, not only in cotton and jute but in other manufactures, and tremendous development took place during the Second World War at places like Kanpur (Cawnpore). The exploitation of cheap labour has been carefully controlled, especially since the Indian Factory Act, which was entirely revised in 1922 and 1923.

But silk weaving is still carried on to a large extent in Murshidābād (Bengal), Varanasi, Ahmādābad, and other old towns. Cashmere shawls are still made both in Kashmir and Punjab (Amritsar, Ludhiana, and elsewhere). Carpets and rugs are exported, and so are a variety of articles skilfully wrought in ivory, gold and silver, copper and brass; but the quality of many of these articles was greatly injured through the want of taste in European purchasers. Newer manufacturing is concerned with the making of electrical and other machinery (including vehicles), scientific instruments, aircraft, the development of glass-making, the making of sports equipment, and so on.

Communications. In the plains communication is naturally easy. The scarcity of stone in the great plains has been an obstacle to the making of good metalled roads and often the only local material available is the small concretionary nodules of 'Kankar' of the older alluvium. With the development of concrete and other all-weather motor roads, especially during the Second World War, there has been an enormous increase in lorry traffic; but the bicycle and the slow-moving bullock shuffling along are ubiquitous. The rivers of the Ganga basin furnish good water-ways, or did until the coming of the railways and the utilisation of their water for the more pressing needs of irrigation. The decrease in importance of river transport (except in the delta) led to the decay of many of the old river ports unless they also served the purpose of railway centres. The flatness of the surface greatly facilitated the construction of railways, but one must bear in mind that this very flatness creates difficulties in protecting the land adjoining the railway embankments in the rainy seasons. The number of rivers to be crossed necessitated great expense in bridging, and in the wetter regions the vigour and rapid growth of vegetation, and in the drier regions the dust storms, add to the expense of maintenance.

In the mid-Ganga basin railways at first and roads later almost superseded water carriage, even in the case of heavy goods. In the Ganga–Brahmaputra delta, which furnishes an unsurpassed system of water communications, the network of railways is not so close, and the Brahmaputra still forms the main highway to the northeast especially in Bangladesh. The Indus, owing to frequent shiftings of its bed and accumulations of sand, is difficult to navigate, and commercial traffic on it has ceased.

The first railway constructed in 'British' India was a short line out of Bombay, opened in 1853. At that time the Great Western Railway in England was using a broad gauge and under the influence of an advisory engineer from the GWR, India adopted a gauge of 1.6 m (5 ft 3 in), which thus became the standard for the subcontinent. Later the metre gauge was introduced and now there are roughly equal lengths of track in the two gauges. In addition there are also several mountain railways on narrower gauges a little over 0.75 m (2 ft 6 in) and less. Railway construction was undertaken by a number of companies incorporated in Britain and proceded apace, especially after the great famine in the subcontinent of 1878 demonstrated the need for sure and rapid transport. It was not, however, till 1900 when the track reached nearly 40 000 km (25 000 miles) that the railways, as a whole, first made a profit. Lines reached 55 772 km (34 656 miles) in 1913–14. During the First World War, rolling stock was sent to the Middle East battle areas and some branch lines taken up, and the companies were left in a difficult position. Gradually the government began to take over both ownership and management. Electrification of some lines, for example local services from Bombay, was started in 1928. By 1944 nearly all lines were government-owned. In 1947 at the time of partition there were 50 746 km (31 533 miles) of state-owned railways, 39 960 km (24 830 miles) in India, 10 785 km (6 703 miles) in Pakistan. Later the railways were regrouped into eight major systems: six in India, two in Pakistan. Total route mileage 1970, before the creation of Bangladesh, was India 60 000 km (37 000 miles), Western Pakistan 8 663 km (5 883 miles).

In Pakistan (formerly Western Pakistan) the North-Western Railway is mainly broad gauge: it has a network of lines in Punjab and two main lines to the port of Karachi. The complete separation of Pakistan and the Republic of India is not always realised: all lines across the frontier were torn up except the one from Lahore to Amritsar and even on that there is little traffic and no through long-distance trains. A line of the old North Western system was constructed to the entrance to the Khyber Pass about the beginning of the present century and continued through the Pass to the Afghan frontier in 1925.

In the peninsular portion of India the nature of the surface placed special difficulties in the way of communication between the coast and some of the richer plains or depressions of the tableland in the interior. The rivers in times of flood are too impetuous, at other seasons most of them are too scantily supplied with water to be navigable except near their mouths, and even where they are navigable higher up, their navigation is impeded by rapids occurring where they break through the mountains bordering the plateau. Not only so, but they mostly break through these mountains in gorges too narrow or country too wild to be easily traversed by roads or railways. To gain the surface of the tableland from Bombay, the railway has to cross a pass called the Thāl Ghāt, more than 580 m (1 900 ft) in height. Communication between Bombay and Madras, across the Deccan, has been effected since 1863 by means of a railway up the Bhor Ghāt, a pass about 30 m (100 ft) higher than the former, and much more difficult. The carriage road up

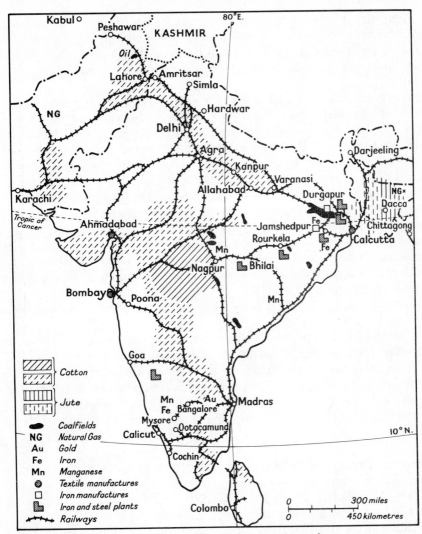

Indian subcontinent: cities, railways and chief economic products
Notice the important (continuous lines) and less important (broken lines) areas of production of cotton and of jute, and the distribution of these crops in the four countries

this pass, completed in 1830, itself a remarkable engineering achievement, formed the first good means of communication between Bombay and the interior.

The railways were thus constructed primarily through country already settled and developed. Later the influence of the railway as a pioneer in opening up remote or inaccessible regions came to be realised. A depression in the upper basin of the Mahānadi was opened up by rail in the early part of 1916, with the result that land which had

583

brought a rent of 4*d*. (2p) a unit area yielded excellent crops of cotton, groundnuts, and sugarcane, and a rent of 13*s*. (65p) a unit area. The railway, completed in 1933, from Raipur to Vizagapatam, in conjunction with the new harbour at Vizagapatam, had similar beneficial results.

In general it will be noted that the railways of India serve the hinterlands of the major ports and this is the main basis of the present grouping. The *Western* system has a main broad gauge line northwards from Bombay to Delhi and many metre gauge and narrow gauge lines. The *Central* system serves the plateau from Bombay (mainly broad gauge). The *Eastern* serves the northeastern plateau and lower Ganga valley and focuses on Howrah (Calcutta). The headquarters of the *Southern* are in Madras, the *South Central* in Secunderabad, the *South Eastern* in Calcutta. The network of lines in the fertile middle and upper Ganga, mainly broad gauge, form the *Northern* system with centre at Delhi. North of the Ganga the lines are mainly metre gauge and have been grouped as the *North Eastern* system with headquarters at Gorakhpur and the *North East Frontier* on Pandu.

Again, in Bangladesh the railways no longer connect with the Indian systems.

With the great distances involved, much use is made of the efficiently run state airlines, both internally and internationally.

The mountainous character of the northern frontiers of the subcontinent has always hampered communication between its constituent states and their neighbours; and this, combined with the lack of development in these neighbours, has concentrated trading through the seaports.

Seaports. The foreign seaborne commerce of the subcontinent is concentrated for the most part in seven seaports: Calcutta, Bombay, Madras, Visakhapatnam in India; Karāchi in Pakistan; and Chittagong, and Chalna in Bangladesh.

Calcutta, on the Hooghly, an arm of the delta of the Ganga, is the last of a succession of ports which have flourished on the same stream. The others, all of which stood higher up, have declined in consequence of silting, and the same fate is averted from Calcutta only by great engineering works. Founded in 1686, the town was made the seat of government of Bengal in 1772 and of British India in the year following. It remained the official capital of the Indian Empire till 1 October 1912, when it was replaced by Delhi.

Bombay, by far the most important seaport in the west of India and the rival of Calcutta in commerce and shipping, is both a town of modern origin and a port that has had great predecessors in the same region. The predecessors of Bombay as a seaport were Broach, near the mouth of the Narbadā, and Surat, near the mouth of the Tāpti. Their history illustrates in an interesting manner the relation between physical features and commercial development; Broach is the oldest of the three. Under the name of Barugaza it is one of the oldest Indian seaports known in commerce with the East or West. Yet it seems always to have had a poor harbour, very difficult to approach. Its difficulty of access is mentioned at least as far back as the first century AD. But in days when vessels were very small, and navigation slow, the shallowness of the river mouth and the delay in entering were of very little consequence; and the mouth of the Narbadā has the advantage of possessing high banks out of the reach of flooding, as well as being contiguous to a highly productive region. Surat shares with Broach the last-named advantage, and it has much better accommodation for shipping. The Suwāli (Swally) Roads, north of the mouth of the Tāpti, afford a safe anchorage even for large vessels from October to April, though it is dangerous for such vessels during the prevalence of the southwest monsoon. The banks of the Tāpti, on the other hand, are low and liable to inundation, a disaster which has more than once overtaken the town. The advantage of the harbour, however, began to prevail in favour of Surat in the sixteenth century, when direct commerce with Europe had begun. The Portuguese, the Dutch and the English established factories (that is, trading stations) here, and in the seventeenth and eighteenth centuries Surat was the greatest seat of foreign commerce, and towards the end of that period the most populous town in India. Bombay, built on a small island, now connected together with another larger island (Salsette) behind it with the mainland, has the immense advantage over both its predecessors of possessing a harbour safe for large ocean vessels in all weathers; but it had the misfortune to be backed by mountainous country, which cut it off from the more productive regions beyond. In 1661 Bombay Island was acquired by Charles II from the Portuguese, and in 1687 the East India Company, to which it had previously been handed over, transferred thither, from Surat, the headquarters of their possessions; but it was not till after the establishment of improved communications with the interior that Bombay rose to the commanding position it now holds in the commerce of India. Its two famous predecessors are now visited only by coasting vessels, but the inland trade of Surat is still important.

Karāchi in Pakistan, stands on a small bay west of the mouths of the Indus, and has been provided with a splendid harbour. Its wheat trade especially grew with remarkable rapidity after the planting of the extended irrigated land in the northwest, but later was replaced by cotton. In addition to its function as port it has become important in the subcontinent for its handling of air traffic from Europe.

Most of the other seaports of the west coast have only fair-weather harbours: safe in our winter months, but rendered dangerous by the heavy surf during the prevalence of the southwest monsoon. Goa (once

Portuguese) is an exception; the trade there, which had dwindled, revived after Mormugão, at the southwest extremity of the harbour, was connected by rail with the interior. In Kerala, Kozhikode (Calicut), which has an anchorage over 7 m (24 ft) deep at low water spring tides, and Cochin, which had a harbour available for ships of no more than 4.5 m (15 ft) draught, retained some importance in connection with the trade in pepper and spices, which drew the Portuguese to these ports at the end of the fifteenth century. Cochin has now been dredged to form a deepwater harbour; and following partition India developed the ports of Kandla and Okha.

The southeast coast of India, where a low plain slopes gently out under a shallow sea, did not possess a single safe natural harbour, or navigable river mouth. Ships anchored off the shore at several road-steads, and goods and passengers had to be landed in flat boats through surf. By virtue of harbour works, Madras has been made a seat of trade, but not to the extent of Bombay or Calcutta; it involves a constant struggle against natural conditions. The site of the city was ceded to the English East India Company in 1639, when Fort St George was erected there. About 100 years later Madras was already the most populous city in southern India. Down to the latter part of the nineteenth century, however, the trade was carried on in the same manner as at the other ports on this coast. In 1881 a harbour was nearly completed, when it was in great part destroyed by one of those irresistible hurricanes by which both sides of India are liable to be swept, especially about the change of the monsoons (May and October), and which on the eastern side raise the waves to a height unparalleled elsewhere. A new harbour was completed in 1895, two moles of about 1 200 m (3 900 ft) in length being run out seawards leaving an opening of 157 m (515 ft) between them; but great difficulty is experienced in keeping it dredged owing to the enormous quantities of sand drifted northwards and southwards by the monsoon currents. The completion of a fine harbour at Visakhapatnam in 1933, and the use of such lesser ports as Kakinada (Cocanada) and Tuticorin prevented undue concentration on Madras.

The voyage from Madras to Europe or the reverse is considerably lengthened by the necessity of passing round the island of Ceylon, which is nearly connected with the mainland by a string of islands and a shallow bank known as Adam's Bridge. The long-discussed proposal for connecting India with Ceylon by rail by this route was abandoned in favour of a part-rail part-steamer connection, which was established early in 1914. Only one channel, called the Pāmbam (Paumben) Passage, across this 'bridge' has been sufficiently deepened to allow of its being used by good-sized coasters, and it is doubtful whether it can ever be made navigable for large oceangoing vessels.

The partition of the subcontinent in 1947 and its aftermath. When the

British withdrew in August 1947 two separate states were set up, mainly on a religious basis: the Republic of Pakistan, primarily Muslim, and the Republic of India, primarily Hindu. Both elected to remain within the Commonwealth.

Pakistan covered about 945 000 sq km (365 000 sq miles) and in the period 1951–71 its population increased from 76m. to 127.5m. It had the disadvantage of being divided into two parts West Pakistan and East Pakistan, the two separated by 1 600 km (1 000 miles) of Indian territory. East Pakistan comprised much of the delta of the Ganga–Brahmaputra, humid, rice and jute growing land, some two-thirds of the former province of Bengal together with adjoining land formerly in Assam. West Pakistan comprised half the former province of Punjab, the North West Frontier Province, Sind, and Baluchistan, much of it arid, the chief grain crop being wheat.

The Republic of India, including Kashmir, covered the rest of the subcontinent, over 3.2m. sq km (nearly 1.3m. sq miles), and in the period 1951–71 its population increased from 357m. to 546.95m. The old provinces became known as states, and some were renamed.

These divisions obtained until the end of 1971. But it was only the tenuous link of religion that held the two widely separated and very different wings of Pakistan together, and the union endured only from the date of partition until the last months of 1971, when East Pakistan seceded from the Republic and proclaimed itself the independent Republic of Bangladesh, seeking admission to the Commonwealth. Pakistan, comprising the former West Pakistan, thereupon withdrew from the Commonwealth, in February 1972.

Foreign trade. Until the First World War one of the striking features of Indian foreign commerce was the large excess of imports of bullion and specie. This resulted in the steady accumulation of specie (formerly silver, later chiefly gold) in the country. From 1931 onwards the rise in the price of gold, expressed in terms of the Indian rupee, led to an enormous export of treasure though probably only a small part of the accumulated hoards. At the same time this points to an increased confidence in the banking system.

During the First World War the commerce of India was necessarily greatly affected by the obstacles to communication with the West, and also by the exceptionally great increase during that war and in the year or two following in the prices of the raw produce that made up the bulk of Indian exports. This latter fact is the chief explanation of the increase in the proportion by value of the goods sent to the United Kingdom from an average of 25 per cent per annum in the period 1909–14 to 31 per cent in the period 1914–19, and to 36 per cent in the year 1919–20, while the subsequent fall in prices accounts for the decline in the British share to 20 per cent in 1921–22. Later, the proportion increased again to 31.7 per cent in 1931—35, the last quin-quennium to include Burma as an Indian province. Meantime the principal advance in proportion was that of Japan, which received in the period 1909—14, 7 per cent, in the year 1919—20, 14 per cent, and in 1921—22 (after a decline to 9 per cent) 16 per cent of the value. The decline of Great Britain's share in supplying the imports from 63 per cent on the average of the years 1909—14 to 56 per cent in 1914—19, is easily understood. Her lowest percentage was in 1919—20 (51 per cent). In 1921—22 it amounted to 57 per cent, but in 1931—35 it averaged only 38.3 per cent, and later fell much lower.

In the interwar years there was abundant evidence in the trade returns that India had little to spare of agricultural produce — the export of wheat virtually ceased — whilst home manufactures in textiles, iron, and steel affected the former huge import. In 1938—39, with Burma gone, imports of foreign merchandise were valued at Rs 1 523m. (£114m.), and exports of Indian produce at Rs 1 628m. (£122m.). Imports were largely rice, mineral oils, cotton piece goods, machinery and vehicles. Chief exports were jute manufactures, raw jute, raw cotton, tea, and oilseeds (mainly groundnuts), these items making up two-thirds of the total. Britain was the best market for tea and jute, continental Europe took most of the oilseeds, and Japan much of the cotton.

As a result of partition in 1947 the bases of manufacturing industry (coal and minerals) passed to the Republic of India, while the Republic of Pakistan became well endowed with cotton, grain and jute (the latter having since passed to Bangladesh). The anomalous position of the jute industry was that the growing areas were in East Pakistan while the factories were in India; a difficulty since remedied by the building of mills in East Pakistan. In the years following partition both India and Pakistan were engrossed in becoming selfsufficient in food production while at the same time developing manufacturing industry, reflected in foreign trade.

The major imports of India, machinery and transport equipment, and food (chiefly wheat) have slowly declined. The export of textiles remains fairly steady, tea has declined mainly because of difficulties in world markets; but exports of iron and steel manufactures show a small regular rise. The main trading partners are now, in order, the United States, USSR, United Kingdom, and Japan which provides a useful export market.

In Pakistan, until 1971, the major imports, machinery and transport equipment, and, secondly, miscellaneous manufactured goods continue to grow; chemicals have increased; on the whole food has declined, especially the import of cereals, but sugar is increasing. In exports crude materials such as raw textile fibres and hides and skins have declined, while textile yarns and leather goods rise. The United States, United

Kingdom, West Germany and Japan have become the main trading partners.

Against this background the Republics of India, Pakistan and the newly constituted Bangladesh will be considered separately, in broad outline.

The Republic of India (Bharat)

India, including Jammu and Kashmir (203 000 sq km: 86 000 sq miles, population 4m.), covers an area of over 3.2m. sq km (nearly 1.3m. sq miles) with a population of 546.95m. (1971 census.)

Population. India's vast population is mainly rural, but there are eight towns with a population exceeding 1m., Bombay (5.3m.) just holding to the lead to Calcutta (5m.). They are the two main ports and both are centres of commerce and industry. The majority of the large towns, including Delhi, the capital (2.8m.) lie in the alluvial lowlands of the great northern plain. Madras (2m.), Bangalore (1.68m.) and Hyderabad (1.35m.) are notable exceptions, all lying in the peninsula. Light indus-tries have been set up in all the towns and in each there are craftsmen manufacturing merchandise in tiny workshops, often only small rooms, open and spilling on to the pathway, producing the handicrafts for which India is famous, as well as such utilitarian items as plastic, rubber-soled sandals. There is a flow of unemployed and under-employed rural workers to the towns, and when crops fail it turns into a flood. This presents Calcutta especially with seemingly insoluble problems of housing, hygiene and unemployment, with thousands of street-dwellers for whom there is little hope of work. Nearly all the bigger towns share this difficulty to some degree.

Minerals and power. India has the priceless asset of an abundance of minerals, although it must be added they are not commensurate with the size of the state and the great number of people. There are good reserves of high grade iron ore, manganese, mica, bauxite, copper and other minerals used in alloys; building stones of excellent quality and great beauty, limestone for cement, minerals suitable for atomic fission, as well as gold and some precious and semiprecious stones. Although India lies seventh in world output of coal she lacks high quality coking coal, and the main fields lie in the Damodar valley in the east corner of the peninsula. Only the major mineral deposits are indicated on p. 583.

Power is generated at thermal stations which are oustripped by hydroelectric installations. There are numerous small hydroelectric stations in association with irrigation works but major installations are in the Damodar valley, at Hirakud on the Mahanadi, at Bhakra-Nangal on the Sutlej, and on the Kosi River in Bihar. Two nuclear power stations are in operation, one at Tarappur, the other at Rana Pratap Sagar (Rajasthan); a pulsed fast reactor is being built at Kalpakham near Madras; and active research on experimental energy breeders is being undertaken at the Atomic Energy Research Centre at Trombay, near Bombay. Natural gas in Assam is harnessed at one of the largest gas-powered turbine stations in the world. There has been a marked increase in power production since 1951, a growth which must be maintained and if possible accelerated, not only for the sake of industry but for domestic consumption. There is great hydroelectric potential as yet untapped, and if electricity could only be more widely and cheaply available unrestricted tree felling and the use of dung as fuel would diminish, to the benefit of soil conservation and fertility.

Industry. Industrial development in India follows the classic pattern, being based on textiles, the powered machinery of mills taking over from domestic handlooms; but all over India the tradition of handicrafts continues. The government appreciates the appeal of such handwork in overindustrialised Western countries and is encouraging a high standard in the products of cottage industries.

The principal iron and steelworks are at Jamshedpur, inaugurated by the redoubtable and farsighted Jamshedji Tata, the great industrialist, in 1911. The works were perfectly positioned to receive all the nearby raw materials, and not far distant from the busy port and centre of commerce, Calcutta. Railways focus on Jamshedpur, where 400 000 people now live. There are also plants on the coalfields at Kulti and Burnpur in West Bengal and another at Bhadravati in Mysore. Other plants are being built with foreign aid: Rourkela in Orissa (with West German aid); Durgapur in West Bengal (British aid); while at Bhilai in Madhya Pradesh help is being given by the Soviet Union: very precisely judged to maintain India's policy of political nonalignment.

There are two main industrial areas in India. One is in the east stretching in an arc from the heavy industrial town of Jamshedpur to Calcutta, the port; the other in the west has the port of Bombay as its outlet, spreading to the south and reaching to Ahmādābād in the north. The Calcutta based area specialises in jute manufactures, engineering, paper manufacturing, chemicals, iron and steel; that based on Bombay is pre-eminently still the textile, engineering, glass-making zone. Political upheavals outside India affected industrial development in the country in its early stages. The raw jute industry developed rapidly from the time of the Crimean War when hemp supplies to Britain were cut off, and Dundee, having already conducted successful experiments, turned to Indian raw jute. The raw cotton trade received a boost when cotton supplies to Britain from America were cut off in the American Civil War. Then the opening of the Suez Canal in 1869 provided a stimulus to the establishment of jute mills in Bengal and cotton spinning mills in Bombay, the latter fed by raw cotton from the Deccan but coal imported for power from Britain, to be superseded later by hydroelectric power, now by nuclear power.

The manufacture of textiles is still important, with cotton as the leading fibre and Bombay still the main centre. Other cotton towns are Ahmādābad, Kanpur and Nagpur, as well as several towns in Tamil Nadu drawing power from the rivers of the Nilgiri hills and the River Cauvery. Many of the ancient towns of India are associated with special types of silk cloth and continue with this specialisation. Silk textiles are woven in small mills in Bengal, Punjab, in other towns of the northern plain such as Agra and Varanasi, as well as in Ahmādābad, and in southern India. Wool is mainly used in carpet-making, a widely spread industry, with concentrations in Punjab, in Kashmir and in Madhya Pradesh. Traditional metalwork is produced in small and large workshops all over India, and from it has developed a newer industry in Varanasi: the making of scientific instruments, at which the skilled metal-working craftsmen are adept. Other workers are employed in packing tea in Assam and Madras; in sugar, flour and tobacco mills in the northern plain, especially in Uttar Pradesh; in manufacturing electrical and other machinery, including vehicles, on Hooghlyside (Calcutta); in glass-making in Uttar Pradesh; in textile and chemical manufacturing in Baroda, the latter at Port Okha. Bangalore has aircraft, electrical and engineering works. All these industrial activities are located near the source of raw material, the labour supply being no problem. A factory making Lambretta scooters under licence has been planned in Uttar Pradesh and should be in production in 1974. There is a small shipyard at Vishakhapatnam.

India has the advantages of adequate natural resources, great potential in hydroelectric power from some of the rivers, and a large pool of labour. Her relatively slow industrial growth stems from the problems of feeding her vast and rapidly growing population, many of whom are conservative in their customs and way of life, and from a lack of capital. Following partition the government very wisely concentrated on trying to solve the problems of agriculture and did not leap ahead with grandiose ideas of immediately becoming an industrial power; a soundly based policy which is reaping its reward in improved output of grain crops. The human problems are great but steady progress is being made in industrialisation.

Communications. India is well supplied with railways. They are very efficiently run and much used. Highways connect the state capitals and major ports, and there is a good network of interconnecting minor roads. Bus services are good; and India is well served by international airlines, including its own national and international airline. Even today the natural physical boundaries of the subcontinent hinder land communication and contact with the outside world is easiest by air. Indeed air routes are so much used that the P and O shipping line ended its passenger services in 1969, being unable to compete with air travel and handicapped by the need to use the long sea route via the Cape as a consequence of the closure of the Suez Canal consequent on the hostilities between Egypt and Israel.

Trade. Leading exports in 1970 were machinery (other than electrical), wheat, jute manufactures, tea, raw cotton and cotton textiles and iron ore. Imports included machinery and transport equipment (including electrical machinery), manufactures of iron and steel (rods, plates, bars and so on), manufactured fertilisers and other chemicals, textile fibres including raw cotton, cereals (mainly rice) and some oil. Most trading is with the United States, followed by the United Kingdom, Japan and West Germany; there is practically none at all with Pakistan. The trade with Japan has shown a marked increase in recent years, while imports from the United Kingdom are slightly declining. Expressed per head of population the amount of foreign trade is small, simply because most of the production of India is consumed at home. At present the capacity for export is not great and India therefore is not earning foreign currency to pay for imports on any considerable scale.

Table 67 — India: population of the largest towns

According to the 1971 census in India there were eight towns which, with their suburbs, had a population exceeding 1m., ten between 500 000 and 1m., eleven between 400 000 and 500 000 and fourteen with between 300 000 and 400 000 people. The largest were:

Calcutta	7 005 000	Bangalore	1 648 000
Bombay	5 969 000	Ahmādābad	1 588 000
Delhi (inc. New Delhi)	3 630 000	Kanpur	1 273 000
Madras	2 470 000	Nagpur	866 000
Hyderabad	1 799 000	Poona	853 000

Pakistan and Bangladesh

The termination of the union of West and East Pakistan as of the Republic of Pakistan has been briefly outlined (see p. 587); but at the time of going to press the infant Republic of Bangladesh is scarcely yet functioning as a political unit. It is useful at this stage therefore to study the area historically in its context as the eastern province of the united Republic of Pakistan. In the section that follows it should be remembered that the post-1971 Republic of Pakistan comprises what used to be West Pakistan; and that Bangladesh used to be East Pakistan.

The Islamic Republic of Pakistan (1947–71)

The united Republic of Pakistan was considerably smaller than India; the total area of about 945 000 sq km (365 500 sq miles) (excluding Jammu and Kashmir) was split into West Pakistan where, in the census of 1961, 43m. people (1965 estimate: 51.4m.) were living on 803 000 sq km (310 000 sq miles), and into East Pakistan where, according to the same census, 51m. people were living on 142 000 sq km (55 000 sq miles), the official estimate for 1965 being 61m. The total population in 1965 was officially estimated to be 112.4m., and at the beginning of 1970 to be 127.5m. The reason for the marked difference in population density is obvious: West Pakistan (now Pakistan) occupied much arid and mountainous land, while East Pakistan (now Bangladesh), one of the most densely peopled areas in the world, enjoyed the fertility of rice-productive monsoon lowlands. The differences between the people and in living conditions in the two regions are in some respects as great as any to be found in the sub-continent. In the former eastern province live a homogeneous Bengali-speaking people accustomed to the warm, wet conditions of their fertile, tropical monsoon lowlands, with an abundance of fish in the waterways and where sugarcane, padi, jute are the main crops. In the former western province several languages are spoken, Urdu being understood by the majority; and life in a principally arid and harsh environment is largely dependent on irrigation, where the main crops are wheat, millet, maize and cotton (under irrigation), giving high yields where water is available. It was the common background of the Muslim faith of the majority in each province which bound the two together until 1972.

Each province had a governor, Rawalpindi in West Pakistan being the interim administrative capital (a new capital is being built at Islamabad nearby). Dacca was the legislative capital of East Pakistan (and has the same function in Bangladesh). For administrative purposes the English language continues to be used. In both West and East Pakistan there was a drift of population from rural areas to the towns, a trend which continues.

Following the partition of the subcontinent in 1947 it was the avowed intention of the government of the Republic of Pakistan to concentrate on the improvement of agriculture: to extend the area of cultivable land by irrigation, land reclamation and the introduction of modern farming techniques with the use of improved seeds, fertilisers and measures for plant protection. At the same time it aimed to increase power supplies and transport facilities, and to build up industry.

These plans were acted on and good progress was made in the twenty-four years of its existence.

In the area covered by West Pakistan food production is based on irrigation, and dams on the Kābul, Jhelum and Indus Rivers provide water not only for this purpose but for power. The availability of both has greatly helped development and there is now in some years surplus production of wheat, cotton and irrigated rice. Food production in the area of East Pakistan was also rising at the time of secession from the Republic; but the region's commercial crops, jute and tea, face an uneasy situation in world markets, the former on account of competition from manmade fibres, the latter on account of inelastic world demand combined with competition from India and Ceylon.

Minerals and power. Pakistan lacks the mineral reserves which India has in quantity, but there are chromite, gypsum, salt, manganese and possibly iron ore and mica in the northeast corner of West Pakistan, which also has the advantage of oil and natural gas fields. Natural gas from the field at Sui is piped to Karāchi, the main port, and to Multan. East Pakistan has the benefit of deposits of lignite and natural gas. The potential for hydroelectric power is great and is being developed in West Pakistan; a huge dam being built at Tarbela should be completed by 1975. The lignite deposits provide fuel for the power stations at Dacca (East Pakistan) and natural gas is piped from Titas; but these resources are as yet insufficient and coal and oil have to be imported. On the whole the rivers of this region are not well suited for the generation of hydroelectric power as they flow over the plain and over the great delta lands, but a dam at Kaptoi provides Chittagong (now the main port of Bangladesh) with abundant power.

A nuclear power station is being built with Canadian help west of Karāchi (West Pakistan); and the possibility of another, also near Karāchi, is being investigated with the aid of the United Kingdom Atomic Energy Authority. The aim is that it should serve a dual purpose, providing power for the industrial complex near Karāchi, as well as acting as a desalination plant. Salinity is a major problem of Pakistan, as in other arid zones. Another nuclear power station is being built, in this case in collaboration with a Belgian company, financed by private Belgian banks, at Roorppur (East Pakistan) and should be commissioned by 1975.

Industry. At the time of the partition of the subcontinent in 1947 industry in the Republic of Pakistan was practically non-existent. Under British economic influence commerce and industry had been most active in the great ports, all of which came to be included in the Republic of India, with the exception of Karāchi; and Karāchi, with its arid hinterland, had always been an outlier, overshadowed by the vigour of Bombay (India) with its prosperous cotton trade. Both provinces of Pakistan had been essentially primary producers, exporting their products to external markets; and a high proportion of the commerce had been in the hands of Hindus, who left the area on partition.

Lacking the resources necessary for basic heavy industry, Pakistan had to import scrap for the steel melting furnaces in Lahore (electrically fired), for the plant at Karāchi (oil fired) in West Pakistan, and for the steel works at Chittagong (East Pakistan). All the raw materials had similarly to be imported for the manufacture of pumps, agricultural machinery, small machine tools and light metal goods made in factories in West Pakistan, mostly in the Karāchi and Lahore-to-Peshawar areas.

The area covered by West Pakistan has the limestone necessary for cement, with a considerable output; and the basic salts required in the chemical industry for fertiliser production are readily available in quantity. It was the farmers of East Pakistan who could have benefited from this, but sea freight charges from Karāchi to Chittagong (the port of East Pakistan, the trade of which increased when Calcutta, the chief outlet port of the region, was incorporated in the Republic of India) were as high as those from Britain.

Despite the handicap of separation and the difficulties of communication between the two provinces, the united Republic of Pakistan developed industrially faster than agriculturally. The industrial area of the east province (now Bangladesh) was around the delta town of Dacca and around Narayanganj. Both towns now have jute mills, that at Dacca being the largest in the world. Cotton textiles are woven at Narayanganj. Sugarcane, tobacco and tea are processed in the area and there are glass-making and paper factories (using bamboo as raw material). Chittagong is the outlet port for tea and jute manufactures as well as for timber; and cement manufacture is the typical port industry.

The burgeoning industrial area included in the western province is the Lahore–Peshawar area, based on the accessibility of the mineral deposits of the Salt Range, the limestone for cement, the available oil. Lahore, with cotton and wool mills, lies in irrigated land where tobacco is grown, and it is in this town that scientific instruments are made. Peshawar lies centrally in enclosed lowland, irrigated by water from the Warsak Dam on the River Kābul, commanding the ancient route to the Khyber Pass. Cotton is grown on irrigated land of Punjab and cotton textiles are made in this famous town. A factory processes the locally grown sugarcane at Mardan, the sugar being used in canning and preserving the fruit grown in the northeast. Sialkot is an interesting town, specialising in the manufacture of sports equipment. Muslim craftsmen have long been famous for the quality of their leather goods and their skills are channelled into factories at Hyderabad in Sind. Karāchi too has new industries: oil refining, motor assembly, textile manufacture (cotton, wool, silk) and much light industry producing small consumer goods, as well as a small shipyard. It is the outlet port for all the industrial products of the region included in West Pakistan. All this industrial development is as yet on a small scale, but it must be remembered that nearly all has been built up since 1950.

Communications. East and West Pakistan lacked the web of railways enjoyed by India. The British laid their lines in the north of the sub-continent mainly for strategic reasons, in their attempt to control the northwest frontier. Traffic is led from a network in Punjab to Karāchi in the west, which well suits the present industrial development. The maze of rivers in East Pakistan greatly hampered railway development, but Dacca and Chittagong are focal points on railways. The waterways of this region provide transport routes. The united Republic concen-trated on road improvement, especially in West Pakistan; and although motor traffic is growing traditional means of transport are still employed: the bullock cart holds its own, and the camel remains a beast of burden in the dry (West) Pakistan.

At the time of partition lines of communication with India were nearly all severed: railway lines were torn up at the frontiers, roads blocked. The sea route between West and East Pakistan was long, so communication between the two was mostly by air; and Pakistan has its own international airline.

Trade. Foreign trade of the Republic of Pakistan was naturally small and displayed features common to developing countries. Exports were mainly primary produce, raw cotton and raw jute, and textiles made from these same raw fibres; while manufactured goods, machinery, iron and steel figures prominently among imports. In some years cereals, mainly wheat were imported. Most trading was with the United States, followed by the United Kingdom, West Germany, Japan and Australia. Pakistan was importing increasingly from Australia. A small amount of trade was carried on with the Soviet Union and with mainland China.

Table 68 — Pakistan and Bangladesh: population of chief towns

Pakistan (1972)		Bangladesh (1971)	
Islamabad (new capital)	77 000	Dacca (capital)	915 000
Karāchi	3 469 000	Chittagong	458 000
Lahore	2 148 000	Khulna	403 000
Lyallpur	820 000	Narayanganj	389 000
Hyderabad	624 000		
Rawalpindi	615 000		
Multan	544 000		

Bangladesh

From this brief outline it will be appreciated that Bangladesh (14 797 sq km: 55 126 sq miles, population about 69m., capital Dacca) embarks on its sovereign existence encumbered with some formidable burdens: heavy pressure of population on resources in a monsoon land; commercial crops, jute (80 per cent of world production) and tea, difficult to sell in world markets; communications hampered by rivers liable to flood; inadequate power resources; a general low level of industrial development except in the Dacca—Narayanganj and Chittagong areas. There is a lack of minerals other than coal, natural gas and possibly oil in the Bay of Bengal, and of raw materials for heavy and light engineering. On the credit side there are some coal, gas and probably oil resources; and nuclear and hydroelectric power are being developed. It has good ports in Chittagong and Chalna. Much capital investment is clearly needed.

Pakistan (post-1971)

The post-1971 Republic of Pakistan, outside the Commonwealth and without the eastern province, does not have to contend with the problem of overpopulation. Extensive irrigation schemes are alleviating the problems of its arid lands; minerals, natural gas, oil and some other minerals are available; hydroelectric and nuclear power are being developed; industrial development has made a promising start in the Lahore—Peshāwar region and in Karāchi, served by railways; and roads are being improved. As in Bangladesh there is a lack of raw materials for both heavy and light engineering industries and a need of capital investment. Population in 1971 estimated at 66m.

The countries of the Himalayas

Three countries lie remote in the Himalayas on India's border with China: Nepál, Sikkim, Bhután.

The Kingdom of Nepál

With an area of 142 000 sq km (54 600 sq miles), Nepál has a population of about 10.8m. It lies to the north of the Ganga plain, includes part of Mount Everest within its borders, and its natural regions are typical of those of the Himalayan region in general. The submontane or sub-Himalayan region lying between the broad cultivated plains of the Ganga and the mountains proper is sandy as it rises from the plains, with stones washed down from the hills. It is widely covered with tall grasses, and known as the *terai*. As the land rises, to about 1 500 m

(5 000 ft), there is a belt of damp hills covered with forest, which includes useful timber such as sal. From 1 500 m (5 000 ft) to 2 750 m (9 000 ft) there is a zone of evergreen oak forest. It was in the agreeable climate of this zone that the British in India established their hill stations. Coniferous forest takes over between 2 750 m (9 000 ft) and 3 700 m (12 000 ft); the alpine belt lies between 3 700 and 4 900 m (12 000 and 16 000 ft), and upwards all is snow.

In Nepál therefore there are valuable forests in the south, and on the northern mountain slopes medicinal herbs are grown. Cereal crops are paddy, maize and millet and wheat, reflecting climatic conditions at increasing elevation. Cattle, buffalo, sheep, goats, pigs and poultry are reared in great numbers, for there are good pastures in the valleys. With the help of the United States and of India a highway is being built to run from east to west, passing through Káthmándu, the capital, which has a population estimated to be about 195 000, but which lies in a populated valley with an estimated 415 000 people. With Chinese aid another road is issuing from Káthmándu, to the border with Tibet. The capital is also served by a road which runs to Amlekganj, from which a railway runs to Raxaul. Jayanagar is connected by rail with Janakpur and Bijulpura. Air services from Káthmándu now link Nepál with Calcutta, Patna, New Delhi and Dacca.

Hydroelectricity is being developed, and there is rudimentary industry processing jute and sugarcane from the lowlands, leather, making matches and shoes, and some chemicals. Food grains, jute, timber, oilseeds, ghee, potatoes, medicinal herbs, hides and skins and cattle are the main exports, the principal imports being machinery, refined petroleum and kerosene, sugar, salt, cement, iron and steel, tea, and a wide range of other manufactured goods including textiles, boots and shoes and medical supplies. It is all on a small scale.

Sikkim

East of Nepál is Sikkim (Denjong to the Sikkimese). About 208 600 people live on its 7 300 sq km (2 780 sq miles). An ore containing lead—zinc—copper is being mined at Photang. The country covers the Himalayan natural vegetation zones, so about a third of the land is covered with forest, as yet unexploited. Potatoes are the main cash crop, and rice, maize and millet, cardamom, oranges, pineapples and apples are grown according to elevation. Fruit is preserved in a factory at Singtam, and there is a distillery at Rangpo, but Sikkim does not as yet feel the need for other industry. There are neither railways nor airfields but the capital, Gangtok (probably 15 000) is connected by road to the Indian airport at Siliguri, via Rangpo. Indian engineers are energetically constructing a highway in North Sikkim which is opening up that area and the other strategic roads being built will have a similar effect. A small amount of trade is conducted with India.

Bhután

Bhután is in the Himalayas on Sikkim's eastern border, with an area of 46 600 sq km (18 000 sq miles), an estimated population of 1m., and the capital at Thimphu. It has an independent democratic monarchical constitution, but there is an agreement with India concerning foreign affairs. There are known to be extensive deposits of limestone and of gypsum, but they are not yet exploited; and the wide stretches of valuable forest are similarly untouched. Rice, maize and millet are the grain crops of the valleys; elephants, ponies and yaks are reared as draught and pack animals; wax and lac are collected; and cloth is woven on handlooms. Roads are being built with the help of India, with whom most of the trade of this isolated country is conducted.

Sri Lanka (Ceylon)

The Crown Colony of Ceylon attained Dominion status in 1948. In 1972 it renounced this to become the Republic of Sri Lanka – within the Commonwealth. It is a pear-shaped island, broad-based in the south and tapering in the north to where it almost links on with southern India. The greatest length is 435 km (270 miles), greatest width 225 km (140 miles), area 64 645 sq km (25 000 sq miles), population 12.75m. (1971 census).

The south has a massive central core, mountainous and jungle-clad, rising to over 2 500 m (8 300 ft) at its highest, though the most conspicuous and famous summit, Adam's Peak, revered as a place of pilgrimage throughout Asia, is 300 m (1 000 ft) lower. A comparatively narrow plain fringes the coast in this main southern area. The smaller northern part is flat and sparsely wooded. Nearly 45 per cent of the island is classed as forest country and nearly a quarter as land in agricultural use, the remaining quarter being either waste or unused.

The most populous region is the southwest, which has the benefit of rain from both the southwest and northeast monsoons. The northern plains are arid and require irrigation. For many centuries they have been scantily populated, but the remains of gigantic reservoirs and other extensive ruins show that at one time the population was much denser and formed part of a flourishing civilisation. The depopulation is probably the result of malaria and other fevers. Restoration of the old reservoirs began under British rule, many of them are again in working order, and ambitious new irrigation and settlement schemes have been undertaken.

The Sinhalese, who are mostly Buddhists account for about 59 per cent of the population; indigenous Tamils, living mainly in the north and east, number 9 per cent, and immigrant Tamils from southern India (providing labour for the tea and rubber estates) a further 8.78 per cent. The balance is made up of Ceylon and Indian Moors, Malays, Burghers (English-speaking people of Dutch and Portuguese descent), and Europeans. Only about 19 per cent of the population is urban.

A few years after the grant of independence, a law by a new government, making Sinhalese the sole official language, aroused strong opposition among the Tamils and threatened serious trouble, which was patched up in 1957. In 1966 the use of Tamil in some official purposes was given parliamentary approval. The British naval base at Trincomalee and the air base at Katunayake were taken over by Ceylon in 1957.

Economically Sri Lanka is largely dependent on her export trade; it is a weakness of her position that she relies for this trade on three main products: tea, rubber, and coconuts. As Ceylon she had previous experience of the danger that may lurk in dependence on a predominant crop. About the beginning of the nineteenth century, soon after the arrival of the British, coffee was introduced and by the middle of the century it had become the most important commercial crop. A disastrous leaf disease attacked the plants about 1870, and in little more than a decade had wiped out the entire production.

The place of coffee was taken by tea, which has become by far the most important of the island's exports. The tea gardens, occupying the higher elevations up to 1 800 m (6 000 ft), covered a cultivated area of 240 000 ha (590 000 acres) in 1970 and yielded 211 400 tons of tea, about 16.5 per cent of the world total.

Rubber first became important early in this century. The plantations cover the slopes of the foothills (below 1 000 m: about 3 000 ft) and were extensively developed during the Second World War, when Ceylon became the Allies' principal source of supply. There was extensive replanting and by 1970 Ceylon's output was 159 100 tons, over 5 per cent of the world total. The entire production is exported.

Also important as a factor in the island's economy are the products of the coconut palm: coconut oil, copra, desiccated coconut, coir fibre and yarn, and fresh coconuts. About half the production is exported. The coconut plantations lie in the plains, valleys, and lower hill terraces of the southwest, also in the extreme north, and intermittently along the coast.

Lesser agricultural exports are cocoa, cinnamon, cardamoms and other spices. Paddy (unhusked rice) is an important crop to which is devoted about 656 000 ha (1.6m. acres), a larger acreage than that of any other crop except coconuts. It grows in all but the higher parts and yields 1.5m. tons; but despite this rice has to be imported.

Livestock are chiefly of importance as an adjunct to agricultural operations. Cattle are the most numerous, over 1.5m.; and the number of buffaloes exceeds 765 000. There are more than 28 200 sheep and over 500 000 goats.

The ancient rocks lying south of the centre of the island have many minerals, those of chief commercial importance being gemstones (notably sapphires) and an almost pure graphite (containing more than 99 per cent of carbon) the latter now nearly exhausted. In the north are large deposits of limestone, worked for the manufacture of cement. Kaolin, heavy mineral sands, and quartz are also present. Geologically a detached fragment of the ancient plateau of peninsular India, Sri Lanka is unlikely to yield oil or coal.

Manufacturing industries are mainly restricted to the preparation of agricultural products.

Food usually accounts for about 40 per cent of the imports, rice and wheat preparations being the biggest items (over 21 per cent). Manufactures, including machinery and transport equipment, provide another 43 per cent. As already indicated, the major exports are tea (57 per cent), rubber (23 per cent) and coconut products (nearly 14 per cent), chiefly desiccated coconut and coconut oil. In 1969 the United Kingdom was the largest contributor (18 per cent) of the imports and the biggest buyer (20 per cent) of the exports. Other main suppliers of imports were China (11 per cent), India (8.4) the United States (8.3). After Britain (20 per cent), the only outstanding customer for the exports were China (12.8 per cent).

Internal communications are well developed both by road 18 830 km (11 700 miles) and by railway 1 500 km (932 miles). The capital and chief seaport is Colombo, which is connected by broad-gauge railways with the main centres, including the old capital and sacred Buddhist centre of Kandy. Galle, on the south coast, which was a much frequented port of call before the opening of the Suez Canal and before the completion of the fine harbour at Colombo, is now little used. Trincomalee, on the northeast coast, has one of the finest natural harbours in the world.

Table 69 — Sri Lanka: chief cities, 1971

Colombo (capital)	562 000
Dehiwala — Mount Lavinia	155 000
Jaffna	108 000
Kandy (1963)	68 200

Maldive Islands

The Maldive Islands, 640 km (400 miles) southwest of Sri Lanka consist of about 2 000 coral atolls, only about 220 of which are inhabited. They are clustered in twelve distinct groups. From 1887 to 1965 they came under the protection of Britain, but on 11 November 1968 became an independent republic. The majority of the population is Muslim, a seafaring people, estimated in 1970 to number about 115 000. Coconut palms are grown in great profusion, as well as millet, fruit and nuts; but there is much trade in dried 'Maldive fish' (*bonito*).

By an agreement made in 1956, confirmed in 1965, the Maldivian government allowed the British government to establish a Royal Air Force base on the island of Gan; and another at Hulele in the Malé atoll.

Southeast Asia

A peninsula formerly called Further India, or Indo–China, lies between the Indian subcontinent and China. To the south, linked with it by the Isthmus of Kra, is a long narrow subsidiary peninsula, the Malay peninsula. The heart of the main area and stretching southwards to include the isthmus is occupied by the independent Kingdom of Thailand. To the west lies Burma, once an independent empire or empires, later to become a province of the British Indian Empire, now since 1948 an independent republic. To the east of Thailand lie the states which as colonies or protectorates once formed French Indo–China. After the Second World War they were regrouped, within the framework of the French Union, as three states: the republic of Vietnam (uniting the territories of Tongking, Annam and Cochin–China) and the monarchies of Cambodia and Laos. Later the connection with the French Union was severed and Vietnam was split into North and South. South of Thailand, Malaya was from 1957 to 1963 a federation of nine Muslim states and two British settlements, enjoying independence within the Commonwealth, while the island of Singapore at its southern end was a separate British colony with local self-government. In 1963 the Federation of Malaya was enlarged by the inclusion of Singapore, Sarawak and Sabah to form Malaysia; but Singapore contracted out two years later and is now an independent state.

Taking the peninsula as a whole, the mountainous character of a large part of the country, especially the north to south alignment of the mountains, the existence of numerous extensive swamps in the more level tracts of the interior, and the defectiveness of the communications, go a long way to account for the low density of population, coupled with the effects of devastating wars. While Burma was in the hands of the British, there was a constant stream of settlers into the country including many immigrants from India, and population, production, and commerce rapidly increased. Similarly the development of resources in former French Indo–China, Thailand, and the Malaya peninsular led to a huge influx of Chinese.

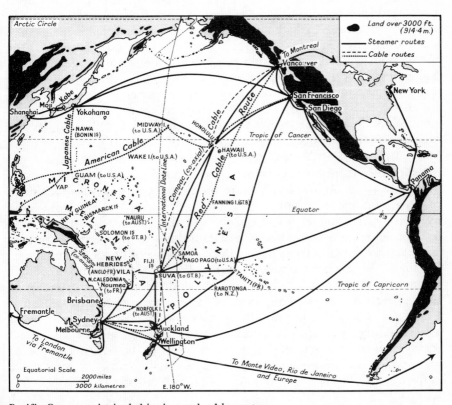

Pacific Ocean: principal shipping and cable routes

The COMPAC and SEACOM coaxial cables can carry eighty simultaneous telephone conversations, and provide teleprinter and picture transmission services.

The shortest way from Panama to Singapore is via the Atlantic, the Mediterranean, the Suez Canal and the Indian Ocean.

The International Dateline deviates from 180° longitude for political reasons. On travelling eastwards across the line successive days bear the same name; on crossing westwards the succeeding day is omitted: so a day is gained in moving from west to east, and a day lost in going from east to west.

Burma

Modern Burma has had a chequered career. Till April 1937 it was one of the provinces of the British Indian Empire; it was, in fact, the largest, having an area of 678 000 sq km (about 261 800 sq miles), but was markedly contrasted to the remainder of India in that the population of this vast area was only a little over 15m. Immigrants from the over-populated Indian subcontinent came to work on the plantations and in factories established by the British, and to act as shopkeepers. They were joined by Chinese immigrants with a keen eye for business. The population in 1971 was estimated to be in the region of 28.2m., but Indian immigrants have been squeezed out.

Burma was invaded by the Japanese in December 1941 and occupied by them until 1945. By friendly agreement and a treaty signed in London in 1947 Burma (under the title of the Union of Burma) became an independent republic, outside the Commonwealth, on 4 January 1948. Unfortunately armed strife between different racial groups and the spread of bands of dacoits or robbers halted progress. Burma can be described as an undeveloped monsoon country with great possibilities of expansion and economic activity. It is, however, cut off from India by a wall of mountains and from the thickly populated parts of China by a broad expanse of plateaus and mountains, so that almost the only approach to the country is by sea through its major port of Rangoon or by air. It is this remarkable isolation from its neighbours that left Burma in the position of a pleasant but undeveloped backwater. Until the Japanese invasion the quickest way from Assam to northern Burma, a distance of 160 or 250 km (100 or 150 miles) across the mountains in a straight line, was via Calcutta round to Rangoon, up the River Irrawaddy and so to complete the journey in about ten days. The motor roads which the British and American armies built across the mountains in the Second World War have again fallen into disuse.

Physical features. In its physical build the remarkable feature of Burma is the north to south alignment of its ranges and its principal river valleys. From west to east there is first the complicated folded mountain chain of the Arakan Yoma, between which and the sea, the Bay of Bengal, there are but small plains suitable for the support of a population, the most extensive being around the town of Akyab. At present no railway or motor road crosses these mountains. Then comes the valley of the Chindwin, somewhat narrow and sparsely populated, which is extended southwards into the valley of the lower course of the Irrawaddy. The valley of the lower Irrawaddy, through the heart of the Dry Belt, is broad and supports a considerable population, whilst the fertile delta of the Irrawaddy is also a very important part of the country. Then comes another line of mountains from north to south, much lower in the south, where it forms the forested ridge known as the Pegu Yoma; this line of mountains is breached about the centre by the Irrawaddy River. Then comes the valley of the upper course of the Irrawaddy (as far as Mandalay) and the continuation of the valley southwards now drained by a smaller stream, the Sittang; both these valley regions are important. The whole of the east of the country is occupied by a broad plateau, the Shan plateau, through which runs the deep cleft occupied by the Salween River. The Shan plateau is continued southwards into broken forested country, towards Tenasserim and the Malay peninsula.

Minerals. Structurally Burma falls into two parts: the western half with its valley plains and its folded mountains, of comparatively recent geological age, and the eastern half which consists of a great block of ancient rock, including many metamorphic rocks, tracts of limestone and other areas which are most important because of their yield of minerals. In the western half of the country, in the valley of the Chindwin and the Irrawaddy, is a succession of oilfields, so that Burma before 1941 was the rival of Trinidad as the largest producer of oil in the British Empire, with a total production then about 0.6 or 0.7 per cent of the world's total The main field was at Yenangyaung until the development of the field at Chauk. Oil was piped to the refineries at Syriam near Rangoon, but all the installations were demolished in the Second World War. Restoration of equipment has been slow and because of internal strife the field at Yenangyaung has been abandoned. The Chauk field, together with a new small local refinery, has slowly come into production and almost meets Burma's small home demands for oil; none is now available for export. Burmese oil is rich in volatile constituents and is largely refined for its yield of petrol rather than used as crude oil. There is not much possibility of the further discovery of oil in Burma, but the fields that exist have been very carefully worked. In the eastern half of the country one finds in the north the famous old Burma ruby mines, but the drop in the value of rubies and the growth in the manufacture of artificial rubies have led to the virtual disappearance of the mining of gemstones. Not far away is one of the largest silver-lead mines in the world, that of Bawdwin with its refinery or smelting works at Namtu, operated until 1952 by the Burma Corporation. The minerals produced here are sent by rail to Rangoon. Other mineral deposits are known to occur in the Shan plateau, but many of them are too inaccessible to be worked at present. In the south of the country, however, in Tenasserim particularly, there are tin and tungsten deposits, some worked in the alluvial valleys, some as lode deposits, which fluctuate in importance according to the world price of tin.

Climate. Climatically Burma has the same monsoon climate as India. The Tropic of Cancer passes through Burma in such a way that about a third of the country lies outside the tropics, the remainder within. Thus in the cool season there is a gradual decrease in temperature from the south of the country where it is really always hot and moist, towards the north, where even in the valleys frost may occur in January. The really important factor in the climate of Burma is the way in which the mountain ranges of the west and the Irrawaddy delta catch the full force of the monsoon and so in places may suffer from a rainfall of as much as 5 000 mm (200 in). Most of the great rice region of the delta has a rainfall of about 2 500 mm (100 in), which is the total received by the capital, Rangoon. In the heart of the country, sheltered from the rain by the surrounding mountains, the rainfall may drop as low as 500 mm (20 in), resulting in semidesert conditions. Thus within a limited area there is a great range of climatic conditions with corresponding vegetation and crops: from the dense equatorial type of forest in the wettest regions to the semidesert plants of the Dry Belt.

Forests and agriculture. The equatorial forest trees of commercial value are difficult to exploit because they are mixed with less valuable species; and some have been destroyed by the practice of shifting cultivation. The most valuable hardwood, teak, grows best where rainfall is between 1 000 and 2 000 mm (40 and 80 in). It used to be the second most important export, after rice, but is now of diminished and diminishing importance. The forests in which teak occurs belong to the group of the monsoon forests in which the trees lose their leaves as a protection against the great heat of the hot season. The drier parts of the country have too little rainfall for the adequate growth of forest and are covered by almost useless scrub. A yellow dye, known as *cutch*, is made from the acacia trees of the Dry Belt.

In all the wetter parts of the country paddy is the main crop, particularly in the Irrawaddy delta and the smaller delta and valley of the Sittang, together with the limited tracts of flat land along the coasts of Arakan and Tenasserim. Burmese rice used to be used in the European market more for industrial purposes than for human food. Burma was however with Thailand, Khmer (Cambodia) and Vietnam one of the great rice-exporting countries of the world before the Second World War. Rice still constitutes the largest export from Burma, but the amount is insignificant at present in world trade. Most is destined for other countries in southeast Asia: Sri Lanka, India and Pakistan. In the 1960s China was an important customer, but this rice trade ceased on the severance of diplomatic relations between Burma and China in 1966. The grain is taken by paddy-boats through the creeks or canals of the delta to the ricemills of Rangoon or Bassein.

In the Dry Belt of Burma there is a certain amount of irrigation, but much opportunity exists for more. The dry zone crops are the usual millet and sesamum, together with a certain amount of cotton and the more important groundnuts.

Industry. There is no highly developed manufacturing industry. Cotton spinning and weaving, handicrafts, the ricemills and sawmills employed Burmese and Indian labour before the Second World War. All industry is now nationalised but production appears to be low. There are cement works in operation at Thayetmyo, textiles are produced at Myingyan from home-grown and imported raw cotton. Manufactured goods constitute the major imports (mainly raw cotton and cotton textiles, followed by machinery and transport equipment) but it must be emphasised that foreign trade is on a very small scale and the present government does not encourage investment from foreign countries.

Communications. Burma suffers greatly from inadequate lines of communication. The railways are gradually being restored after wartime destruction in the 1940s. The railway system is on the metre gauge. Rangoon, the capital and chief port, is connected by rail with Prome, the port on the Irrawaddy to the west, and with Mandalay via the Sittang valley. A fine rail and road bridge across the Irrawaddy near Mandalay, destroyed during the Japanese invasion in the Second World War, was reopened in 1954, and the railway with branches now runs considerably further north. The main highway of Burma is still the River Irrawaddy, navigable for 1 600 km (1 000 miles) from its mouth. The waterways of its delta handle the rice traffic of the area, and the use of the great river as a main route into the interior is slowly being resumed. Its chief tributary, the Chindwin, is similarly used. Roads in Burma are few and poorly surfaced, and the number of road vehicles *per capita* is the lowest of southeast Asian countries. Equipment for road transport supplied by the Japanese as part of their war reparations has kept public road transport facilities going. No attempt has been made to restore external land communications destroyed in the Second World War. The Union of Burma Airways operate internal flights and since 1963 international services between Rangoon and Bangkok and Calcutta.

Cities. Rangoon (1.6m.) situated on the stream east of the Irrawaddy delta and conveniently placed for the Sittang valley route is some 34 km (21 miles) from the sea. It is the port through which the small amount of foreign trade passes. Mandalay, in the Dry Belt, was once a capital city, and is the second largest town with a population of about 317 000. The only other settlement of any size is Moulmein (157 000).

Trade. Burma is at present in an unenviable economic situation. Her agricultural output is too low to produce the surplus for export which would pay for the imports so badly needed for modernisation and for the development especially of her mineral resources; and the present government is averse to foreign interest in her affairs.

Thailand

Thailand (Land of the Free) is a constitutional monarchy in southeast Asia with an area of 514 000 sq km (198 000 sq miles) (more than twice the size of Great Britain) and a rapidly growing population of over 34.15m. (1970 census, preliminary figures). Occupying the western part of the Indo—Chinese peninsula, it lies to the southeast of Burma, just beyond the River Salween, which partly borders it on the west, while on the northeast and east are two of the three states of Indo—China formerly within the French sphere, namely Laos and Cambodia (now Khmer). Southward it reaches the Gulf of Siam, and a long southwestern arm, which for some distance divides the Malay peninsula with Burma, afterwards occupies the full width of the peninsula as far as the borders of Malaysia and looks out not only on the Gulf of Siam to the east, but on the Indian Ocean to the west. This long southern extension is for the most part a mass of jungle-clad hills covering in all some 78 000 sq km (30 000 sq miles), an area equal to that of Scotland. Thailand falls into four natural regions.

The northern region is a land of mountains through which the rivers which rise near the eastern edge of the Tibetan plateau have carved deep valleys. Dense forests which include the commercially valuable teak cover the hillsides. Where river basins widen the forest has been cleared and rice is grown under irrigation. Maize, millet and buckwheat are cultivated in the uplands.

The streams join the Menam Chao Phraya, the great river of Thailand which crosses a vast central depression, occupied by an alluvial plain, the heart of Thailand. As it flows southward the Chao Phraya breaks up into distributaries which have been connected by canals (khlongs) northeast of Bangkok, the capital. Other rivers from the mountains on the west which border Burma drain towards the delta of the Chao Phraya and all combine to form an involved deltaic network, providing highly fertile silt. Much of the great plain lies in the rainshadow of the western mountains, but the Chao Phraya River system, swollen by rain from the northern mountains, permits irrigation. Thus the central depression of Thailand, the great plain, is one of the most important rice-producing areas in the world. There is a barrage across the Chao Phraya at Muang Chainat to control the flow of water, and the River Ping has been dammed some 400 km (250 miles) northwest of Bangkok at Yan Hee both for the generation of electricity and for flood control.

Southeastwards the plain gives way to the low forest covered mountains of the Cambodian (Khmer) border.

Lying to the east of the great plain is a low arid plateau, the Khorat plateau, with porous, infertile, salt-encrusted sandy soils, cut off on its west and south by densely forested low mountains. The Khorat plateau slopes slightly eastward so its few streams drain to the Mekong River and its tributaries, the Mekong being another of the great rivers of southeast Asia, flowing through Laos, Khmer (Cambodia) and Vietnam. The plateau suffers a long dry period lasting some five months, and although rice is cultivated in the river valleys, it is an impoverished region badly in need of large-scale efficient water control.

In the fourth region, peninsular Thailand, the western mountain ranges continues southwards towards the Thailand—West Malaysian border. It is a subequatorial region, rain falling through the year, but the heavy rainfall of the southwest monsoon, falling from April to September, promotes dense forest in the mountains, where yang is the leading commercial timber; while the coastal plain of the east, which receives maximum rain from the northeast monsoon from October to March, favours paddy. This is the most efficiently organised rice-producing area in Thailand; and this is the location of Thailand's rubber plantations, as well as the main coconut palm area. Oil palms flourish but have not yet been fully exploited commercially.

Rice, covering 7.3m. ha (18m. acres), producing over 13.6m. tons in 1970, forms, as might be expected, the staple part of Thai diet; but sea and freshwater fish are important, the latter being farmed. Sugar, groundnuts, cotton, kenat and tobacco are grown and a very wide variety of fruits and vegetables is cultivated. Livestock include 5.2m. cattle and nearly 7m. buffalo, both used as draught animals.

Thailand has extensive mineral resources. There is a lignite field in the northern region near Lampang, the lignite being used mainly for power generation both locally and at Bangkok. Oil is among the minerals known to exist in the north, but present inaccessibility precludes its economic exploitation. More important is the tin of peninsular Thailand, which makes her second to Malaysia in world tin production.

Bangkok, the capital, which grew up in the well-favoured delta area of the Chao Phraya, is a spacious vigorous city with wide boulevards crowded with traffic, and high-rising office blocks and hotels contrasting with ancient temples and palaces. It is the main commercial centre, port and seat of government, with a cosmopolitan population of about 2m. The other main towns are Thonburi (540 000) west of Bangkok, and Chiang Mai (66 000) in the north.

The ratio of population to land area is not high in Thailand, but there is a marked imbalance in population distribution. The largest number of people, and the most prosperous, live in the central plain, with a great concentration on the delta area, while the rest of the country has a low population density, and the people have lower incomes. In view of its inadequate resources, the Khorat plateau is undoubtedly overpopulated. Attempts are being made to increase the incomes of those living outside the prosperous area of the great plain by village schemes for cottage industry and the encouragement of sericulture, especially in the north and east.

The number of people employed in manufacturing industries is very small, perhaps about 4 per cent of the population, and many of these are engaged in cottage industries. Home supplies of silk thread are proving inadequate to meet the needs of the successfully expanding, but small, silk textile industry, and raw silk is imported from Japan. Most of the silk textiles are exported. Most of the manufacturing industry is concentrated in the Bangkok area, where there is a modern mill producing cotton textiles; also clothing, furniture and footwear factories. Other works are concerned with the processing of primary products: rice, sugar, timber (which is floated from the mountains down river to Bangkok, although some is similarly floated down the Salween River into Burma), and the making of jute sacks, tobacco and cement. The Japanese are investing in manufacturing industry in Thailand and have laid the foundations for a motor vehicle and agricultural machinery industry. As yet there is very little mechanisation in agriculture.

The waterways of Thailand have long been the principal means of communication, and coastal shipping serves the peninsula. In the dry Khorat plateau the ox-cart takes over. The railway system was initially developed for strategic reasons but it has advanced the economic development of the country in bringing the other regions in closer contact with the central area. Extension of the railways progresses. Bangkok is connected with Chiang Mai and the lignite field at Lampang in the north, and with Padang Besar, the station on the frontier with West Malaysia, in the peninsula. Another line serves the east peninsula coast. Bangkok is connected with the Khorat plateau via Nakhon Ratsima to Nong Khai near the Laos border, and, again via Nakhon Ratsima, eastwards to Muang Ubon. An eastern line from Bangkok runs to Aranya Prathet on the Khmer (Cambodian) border. A road system has not yet been greatly developed, but trunk roads are being built with foreign aid and technical assistance, particularly in the northeast; and in Bangkok some of the khlongs have been filled in to carry metropolitan traffic. There were reputed to be about six vehicles per 1 000 head of population on the roads in 1969, about half in Bangkok.

The main towns are linked by air, and Bangkok is well served by international airlines.

Thailand has maintained steady economic growth since the end of the Second World War. Her consumption of rice has increased but so has her production, and there is still sufficient for export. Rice is in fact the principal export, followed by tin, rubber and maize. Kenaf (a jute-like fibre) is also a useful export. Main imports are motor vehicles, iron and steel, industrial machinery, petroleum products, electrical machinery. Nearly all this foreign trade passes through Bangkok. Japan easily leads as the major trading partner, supplying most of Thailand's imports, followed by the United States, West Germany, the United Kingdom and Singapore.

In general Thailand can be said to be prospering, and she does not reject foreign investment or aid. The Japanese especially are happy to provide capital.

Indo—China

Before the Second World War, Indo—China was part of France's colonial empire, comprising the colony of Cochin—China and the four protectorates of Tonkin, Annam, Cambodia and Laos, the last three ranking as kingdoms. After the war these territories were reconstituted as independent states within the French Union. Cambodia and Laos, bordering Thailand, became sovereign states with constitutional monarchies, Tonkin, Annam and Cochin—China, bordering the South China Sea, combined in a federation of North, Central and South Vietnam, with the former King of Annam as Chief of the State.

Association with France was continued through a French High Commissioner and Commander-in-Chief, with a commissioner in each state. French troops, fighting along with the national armies, were involved in a long and costly war to hold back Vietminh (Communist) forces, based on southern China. In the first half of 1954 the Vietminh forces made considerable headway, and in July an armistice was arranged by an international conference at Geneva, attended by representatives of not only France, the Associated States of Indo—China, and Vietminh, but the United Kingdom, the United States, and China. A military demarcation line drawn near 17° N latitude divided Vietnam into two roughly equal areas, leaving in Vietminh occupation the northern half, including the Red River delta, the port of Haiphong, and Hanoi the capital. Vietminh troops were to be withdrawn from southern Vietnam, Cambodia and Laos. An International Supervisory Commission, with representatives of India, Poland and Canada, was appointed to see that the terms of the armistice were kept. The future government of Vietnam, Cambodia, and Laos was made dependent on free elections to be held in 1955.

These arrangements did not come to full fruition. The armistice line was drawn, dividing the Vietminh and Vietnam forces, but the Vietnam government refused to recognise the agreement. A referendum in 1955 deposed the king of Annam as head of the state, and his successor proclaimed a republic, with himself as president. All association with France was severed, and the upshot has been the establishment of four distinct states:

1. The northern zone of Vietnam, in Communist (Vietminh) occupation as a Democratic Republic, which came to be known as North Vietnam, capital Hanoi.
2. South Vietnam, a republic, capital Saigon.
3. The kingdom of Cambodia, a republic since October 1970, and now known as the Republic of Khmer, capital Phnom Penh.
4. The kingdom of Laos, capital Vientiane.

Mountains and plateaus curve southwards through this eastern part of the peninsula, separating two main river systems: the Mekong with its vast delta lands in the south, with the outlet port of Saigon in South Vietnam; the Song Koi (Red River) in the north, with Haiphong the port of North Vietnam. Along the coastal strip small plains here and there form oases of fertile land amidst the rocky mountains. In the heart of Cambodia a great lake, the Tonle Sap, fills a low basin. Formerly an arm of the sea it was cut off by the silt of the Mekong. The major mineral deposits, coal and metalliferous minerals, are in North Vietnam. The mountains are nowhere very high; as usual the peoples who live in them are culturally different from the lowlanders.

The climate of the whole region is tropical monsoon, with a dry season during the time of the northeast monsoon and a wet season during the southwest monsoon. South Vietnam however lies in the rain-shadow of the mountains and so does not conform. Heavy rain in South Vietnam falls during the period of the northeast monsoon, and the territory is comparatively dry at the time of the southwest monsoon.

The forests of the mountains include valuable timber trees, such as teak; and padi is the main crop of the basins and deltas of the Mekong and Song Koi Rivers. Oxen and buffalo are everywhere used as draught animals.

North Vietnam

The Democratic Republic of Vietnam 158 000 sq km (61 000 sq miles) is a little larger than England and Wales. The population was assessed in 1960, based on the results of a census, at 15.9m., 1968 estimate, 18.8m. The country is mountainous, rising to over 3 500 m (11 000 ft). Two lowland areas, the Song Koi delta and a section of the littoral, support most of the inhabitants. About half the land areas is forested, and the Song Koi River system provides good padi land. Rice, the chief crop, yielded 2.5m. tons before the war, and though production dropped when the country was overrun by the Vietminh forces, it was reported to amount to 5m. tons in 1970. Sugarcane, maize, sweet potatoes and cotton are cultivated, raw silk is produced; but the most notable features of North Vietnam are its reserves of coal (anthracite, bituminous and lignite) and minerals (iron ore, manganese, titanium, chromite, bauxite and apatite). It possesses the basic resources in sufficient abundance to make it the leader in heavy industry in south-east Asia. Aid from the USSR and from China has been concentrated on advancing heavy industry and fuel and power (at the expense of agriculture); North Vietnam has the only integrated iron and steel plant in southeast Asia. It now produces its own machine tools; and food processing and textile manufacturing are growing in importance. Hanoi (about 850 000, 1968) is connected by rail to the Chinese border. Haiphong, the next largest town and port, had an estimated population in 1968 of 370 000. Culturally the people of North Vietnam are, on the whole homogeneous. About 90 per cent of the people are Kinh and inhabit the lowlands. There are many minority cultural groups, but their combined population is small and dispersed over the high land.

South Vietnam

The Republic of South Vietnam (171 665 sq km: 66 260 sq miles) had in 1959 an estimated population of 14m., which had risen to 18.3m. by 1969. The most densely settled area is the Mekong delta where the government has its seat in the conurbation of Saigon (1969 estimate: over 1.6m.).

Nearly all the cultivated land is under padi: 2.5m. ha (nearly 6.2m. acres) producing over 5.6m. tons, despite wartime difficulties. If the ambitious development scheme envisaged for the Mekong valley materialises there is no doubt that the Mekong delta, the third largest rice-exporting area in the world before the Second World War, could become an even greater producer. At present, on account of the war, much of the padi area has been abandoned and South Vietnam is now an importer of rice. Her rubber plantations have suffered defoliation in the war, but this has probably not harmed them irreparably. Tea, coffee, tobacco, cinnamon, raw silk and timber are products of the plateaus in the mountains. Maize, sugar, groundnuts and copra are also produced; pigs and poultry are the principal livestock, oxen and buffalo are draught animals. The only mineral asset is one small coalfield at Nong Son. The little manufacturing industry that exists is mostly to be found in the area of the capital, Saigon: rice and rubber mills, sawmills; fruit, fish and sugar processing, and factories producing a variety of small consumer goods. Cement is made near Hué. United States economic aid to South Vietnam during the war has in the main been centred on providing new roads and harbour facilities, as well as quantities of consumer goods. There are plans to develop the coalfield and to set up oil refining with associated petrochemical works; and an industrial estate is being developed at Da Nang (1969 estimate: 335 000).

South Vietnam lacks the general cultural homogeneity of the North: in South Vietnam Buddhists and Catholics (including refugees from the North) are not in sympathy with each other, the supporters of Vietminh (Vietcong) have gone underground, and there are many other peoples of differing cultures and beliefs.

Laos

With an area of 235 700 sq km (91 000 sq miles) and an estimated population of 2.8m., mostly concentrated on the plains near the Thai border, the hilly land of Laos was, before the Second World War, a rice-exporting country. Now, with most of the male population in the army, she is dependent on food supplied under foreign aid schemes. Her capacity for food production would be enormously increased if the Mekong Valley Scheme, by which the flow of the Mekong would be regulated, were implemented. There is one small tin mine near Thakhek, producing for export; but the high quality iron ore which is known to exist in Kieng Knouang province has not yet been exploited owing to inadequate transport facilities. Maize, tobacco, cotton, potatoes and other vegetables are cultivated; coffee is grown particularly on the Boloven plateau for export, and timber is another export commodity. The small amount of manufacturing is mainly concerned with processing primary products such as timber near Vientiane, the capital. Laos has great problems of communication. Even the Mekong rushes through narrow deep gorges on its way through the country, so does not provide a routeway. Vientiane is connected by road to Luang Prabang, but other roads are few. There is no railway in Laos but a ferry across the Mekong east of Vientiane (about 150 000) links the capital to Nong Khai on the border with Thailand, and thence by rail to Bangkok. The difficulties of land transport have encouraged the provision of air services, airports and landing strips. A valuable export from Laos, noticeably absent from export statistics, is opium, produced from the opium poppy which is widely cultivated.

Khmer Republic (Cambodia)

Two thousand years ago Cambodia was the centre of a great kingdom that extended over Laos, Thailand, Malaya and Cochin—China. The territory now covers 181 000 sq km (71 000 sq miles), with a small population of 6.5m. The monarchy ended on 9 October 1970 with the declaration of a republic and Cambodia took the name of Khmer Republic. About half the land area is covered with valuable forests. Padi is the major crop of the cultivated land (2.4m. ha: nearly 6m. acres produce over 3.8m. tons), with a surplus for export. The second commercial crop is rubber, the plantations being near the border with South

Vietnam. Other crops include maize, pepper, soybeans and a variety of vegetables. The useful Palmyra palm breaks the monotony of the padi fields; its sap produces sugar and its timber and leaves provide excellent house-building materials. Khmer's freshwater fish resources especially in Tonle Sap (Great Lake), an immense backwater of the Mekong, are the greatest in southeast Asia; but at present they are in need of careful conservation. There is high grade iron ore in the north, but lack of transportation makes it inaccessible. Industry at present is mostly concerned with the processing of agricultural products, and the manufacture of small consumer goods. There is an oil refinery at Kompong Som which meets all the needs of the country. As in Laos, lines of communication are inadequate. A highway has been built, with United States economic aid, from Phnom Penh to Kompong Som, the port on the Gulf of Siam, and extensions of roads are planned. The Mekong provides a waterway through South Vietnam; and international air services use the airport at Pochentong, near Phnom Penh.

As in all the other countries of former French Indo—China, external trade has been profoundly affected by the prolonged war. The main imports of Khmer comprise machinery and motor vehicles, mineral products and foodstuffs. Rice, rubber and maize are exported, the rubber destined for France, with whom most trade is conducted, followed by Japan, Singapore and China.

Malaysia

At the southern end of the long Kra peninsula, which stretches southwards from Burma and Thailand nearly to the equator, lies Malaysia. From 1957 to 1963 it was an independent country within the Commonwealth consisting of nine Malay states — from north to south, Perlis, Kedah, Perak, Kelantan, Trengganu, Pahang, Selangor, Negri Sembilan, and Johore — together with the two west coast settlements of Malacca and Penang, which also became states. In the same period Singapore, an island at the southern extremity of the Malay peninsula, to which it is connected by a causeway carrying road and rail, was also an independent state within the Commonwealth.

British influence in the Malay peninsula began with the acquisition of Penang in 1786 and was gradually extended over the mainland states, chiefly by treaty with the different Malay rulers, the last being with the sultan of Trengganu in 1919. After the liberation of Malaya from Japanese occupation in the Second World War, the states were federated in 1948 under a British high commissioner, with a nominated executive council, each ruler being left to govern his own state according to an agreed constitution, subject to the authority of the central government. Political aspirations increased, and in 1957 the Federation was given full independence, the 'Settlements' of Penang and Malacca being incorporated in it as additional states. The British high commissioner was withdrawn, and one of the Malay rulers was elected to be head of the state for five years. Provision was made for a senate, partly elected by each state and partly nominated by the head of the state, as well as for an elected house of representatives. British financial aid was continued against Communist terrorists in the jungle, and the state of emergency was ended in July 1960. Plans were discussed for a closer political and economic association to comprise Malaya, Singapore, British North Borneo, Brunei and Sarawak.

On 16 September 1963 independent Malaysia came into being. It consisted of the eleven states of Malaya, Singapore, together with the former British colonies of Sarawak and North Borneo (the latter name being changed to Sabah) on the island of Borneo. By mutual agreement on 9 August 1965 Singapore seceded from Malaysia, to become an independent republic. Both sovereign states remain within the Commonwealth.

It is now common practice to refer to the territories on the peninsula as West Malaysia (area 131 587 sq km: 50 806 sq miles; total population (1969) 9.12m., of which over 4.6m. are Malay, 3.3m. Chinese and 1m. Indian and Pakistani; capital Kuala Lumpur), which is separated, even by the shortest crossing, by 644 km (400 miles) of frequently stormy sea from East Malaysia, the territories on the island of Borneo (Sabah with an area of 80 520 sq km: 30 000 sq miles, the population estimate in 1969 being nearly 648 000, of whom only 106 000 were Chinese; and Sarawak with an area of nearly 122 000 sq km: 48 000 sq miles, with a mid-1969 population of nearly 956 000 of whom over 306 000 were Chinese and 168 000 Malay). West Malaysia is thus only two-thirds the size of East Malaysia, but has six times the population. Brunei, a small state with oil and natural gas resources, and considerable reserves of timber wedged in between Sabah and Sarawak on the northwest coast of Borneo, elected not to join Malaysia, and remains a dependent territory in the Commonwealth. Liquid gas is now a useful export, shipped to Japan.

Many geographers continue to use the term 'Malaya', but in the restricted sense, as referring to the Malayan peninsula and immediate offshore islands, including Singapore.

Malaysia and Singapore are unlike any other territories in southeast Asia. They have never had a large subsistence-farming population. Europeans came to what was a sparsely populated area and developed the main resources (tin-mining and rubber plantations) which gave rise to the growth of population. But it is the peoples of Malaysia and Singapore themselves who are in the process of further expanding and diversifying their economy, planting oil palms and starting manufacturing industries in their increasingly urban society; and maintaining a respectable economic growth rate in highly competitive world trade.

West Malaysia

The northern and central parts of West Malaysia, where the peninsula is at its widest, consist for the most part of jungle-clad mountainous country rising in outstanding peaks to over 2 100 m (7 000 ft), broken by the valleys of swift-flowing rivers of which the two longest, the Perak and the Pahang, on opposite sides of the peninsula, have courses of 320 km (200 miles) or more. Further south, where the peninsula tapers towards Singapore, the mountains peter out and the general level is below 180 m (600 ft); but even here are patches of the central mountain chain which traverses the peninsula from north to south. By far the greater part of the country is covered with dense tropical jungle or swamps. The official estimate of the forested area is 70 per cent of the land area; and 20.75 per cent is classified as land under permanent crops and arable. Another 6 per cent is classed as unused but potentially productive and built on or waste areas account for about 2.5 per cent.

Rubber. Commercially the peninsula is largely dependent on rubber and tin, which provide nearly 72 per cent of the exports by value, in 1969, rubber 48.5 per cent, tin 23 per cent. In spite of difficulties of rehabilitation after the Japanese occupation, Malaysian rubber production increased steadily, and Malaysia became not only the largest dollar-earner among British Dependencies but the world's largest producer of natural rubber. In 1950 Indonesia took the lead and held it for ten years with rapid development of her smallholdings, but in 1960 West Malaysia regained its position as the world's leading producer, thanks largely to its big estates, with an output of 710 500 tons — over a third of the estimated world production of 1 985 000 tons of natural rubber. In 1970 Malaysian production was 1.23m. tons, about 615 000 tons from estates, 597 000 tons from smallholdings. The world total that year was 2.9m. tons.

The yield of Malaysian rubber has been much improved in recent years by the introduction of high-yielding budded stock on the estates. While the market price remained high, many smallholders were reluctant to undertake much-needed replanting, but they too introduced improved methods and higher yielding stock. In the early days a yield of about 448 kg per ha (400 lb an acre) was considered satisfactory; now yields up to 2 242 kg per ha (2 000 lb an acre) are obtained. All possible improvements in this and other ways are especially desirable, not only to meet the drop in price which followed the postwar boom, but to compete with the synthetic product, which has become a serious rival, especially in the United States.

Rice and other crops. Apart from rubber, the main agricultural crop is rice, of which West Malaysia produces nearly 75 per cent of its own

617

requirements. Before 1939 the area under padi cultivation averaged about 304 000 ha (nearly 750 000 acres), with an average yield of 500 000 tons. After the Second World War, when rice was in very short supply in southeast Asia, the area under cultivation was increased considerably, and in 1949, a particularly favourable season, the padi crop reached 700 000 tons. In 1970 the yield from 515 000 ha (nearly 1.3m. acres) was 903 000 tons, equivalent to 1.2m. tons of milled rice, a reflection of the use of high-yielding strains.

The area under oil palms has also increased steadily since the end of the Second World War. In 1971 production of palm kernels was 98 000 tons, of palm oil 589 000 tons. The oil palm gives very high yields in Malaysia. Unlike rubber it has not attracted smallholders, cultivation being almost entirely confined to estates. On the other hand many smallholders grow coconuts. In 1971 1 025m. nuts were produced, yielding 194 000 tons of copra.

Tea is grown, mainly as an estate crop, in both highlands and lowlands. Much of it is sold locally and about one-third of the total produced is exported. Pineapples are grown throughout the peninsula, but cultivation for canning is mainly in Johore, and to a minor extent in Selangor and Perak; production in 1970 was 329 000 tons. Other products include coffee, tobacco, bananas, areca nut, tapioca and mixed tropical fruits.

Forest resources are carefully managed, and timber, rough and worked, appears among exports.

The fishing industry is also expanding, with the introduction of modern power-driven craft and up-to-date methods of fishing and marketing. Landings totalled nearly 295 000 tons in 1970.

Malaysia offers little scope to a livestock industry. There are only about 39 000 sheep, 320 000 goats, 300 000 cattle, and 678 000 pigs (1970). The rearing of buffaloes for work in ricefields is of importance, and though their numbers declined during the war they have since more than recovered lost ground, and numbered 225 000 in 1970.

Minerals. Some of the world's richest deposits of tin ore are found among the mountain ranges of the Malayan peninsula, and West Malaysia has for many years provided about one-third of the world's total output. The industry employs most of the total mining labour force in West Malaysia, the ore being smelted and the tin exported in the form of ingots, blocks, bars and slabs. In the years immediately following the Second World War demand exceeded supply and prices soared. Normally the supplies of tin available on the world's markets exceed the demand, and conditions reverted to this state of affairs in 1951, with recession of prices and other difficulties for the tin mining industry, but since then prices have soared again.

Bauxite and iron ore also appear among exports. At Prai the

Malawata integrated iron and steel works has been in production since 1967, despite all the prognostications that Malaysia, lacking coking coal, could never support heavy industry. The plant has been built and operates with the aid of experts from a consortium of Japanese companies who have in part financed it. The choice of the site was influenced by the availability of local high grade iron ore (and the ease with which ferromanganese and ferrosilicon can be imported from India and Japan), the supply of limestone flux from Ipoh, seawater for cooling, and charcoal for fuel provided from a convenient supply of rubber trees scrapped as a result of replanting. When this supply of fuel is exhausted it is planned to turn to forest timbers. The outlet for the production of the plant is at hand in the nearby industrial area at Butterworth, which has deepwater berthing facilities, and at Prai itself, where much light manufacturing and assembly work is developing.

Communications. A through railway system connects the peninsula with Singapore to the south and with Thailand to the north. The main line traverses the western coastal belt and sends out short branch lines to the western ports. The east coast line runs through the centre of the peninsula to the east coast at Tumpat on the Thai border of Kelantan. The total track, which is metre gauge, was over 1 600 km (over 1 000 miles) in 1970. There are nearly 17 500 km (11 000 miles) of roads of varying surfaces; and vehicles registered in 1970 included 231 539 private cars, 55 823 lorries and vans, 5 932 buses and over 350 000 motor cycles.

Manufacturing. Although primary production, of field and mine, is the mainstay of the economy, West Malaysia is fast developing manufacturing industry, and industrial regions are emerging. The first is in the Kuala Lumpur—Port Swettenham area, where Kuala Lumpur, the capital, has a population exceeding 317 000. Another is in Penang state opposite Penang Island, in the neighbourhood of the iron and steel plant at Prai; and small scale light industry is developing rapidly along the routeway to Singapore, through which much of West Malaysian trade passes. At present 55 per cent of the total population are engaged in agriculture, but with the upsurge in manufacturing there is a migration from the land to developing urban areas.

Trade. West Malaysia's main exports are rubber, tin, iron ore (mainly destined for Japan), palm oil and timber. The major imports are food and live animals, machinery and transport equipment, manufactured goods, chemicals and oil. The more important trading partners are Singapore (through which much of West Malaysian trade passes), Japan, the United Kingdom, the United States and — much less — Australia (which takes a considerable proportion of West Malaysia's exports).

619

Economic growth. Malaysia's economic growth is strong and steadily expanding, and the country is enjoying a steadily increasing prosperity, but with an imbalance: West Malaysia is progressing at a faster rate than East Malaysia, which lacks manufacturing industry, but exports quantities of timber.

East Malaysia

Though the major part of the great island of Borneo, the third largest island in the world if continents are excluded, is Indonesian territory, Sabah (formerly North Borneo) and Sarawak together form East Malaysia (see p. 616).

Sabah was administered by the British North Borneo Chartered Company from 1882 to 1946 when it was taken over as a colony.

The annual rainfall is 1 500 to 2 500 mm (60 to 100 in). A mountainous interior with the highest peak, Mount Kinabalu rising to over 4 100 m (13 455 ft), is bordered on the west by a long and fairly narrow coastal plain, containing the main rice and rubber producing areas, and on the east by much more extensive plains comprising both padi-growing lands and wide stretches of pastoral country. Dense forests covering most of the hills and valleys are a valuable source of timber; the other commercial products are oil palm, rubber, copra, manila hemp (abaca), tobacco, rice and sago. Rubber is cultivated mostly on small holdings of under 20 ha (50 acres) and provides only about 8 per cent of exports by value. There are also small exports of palm oil and cigarettes, but the chief export is timber, which provides 72 per cent of the total.

A metre gauge railway 187 km (116 miles) long serves the west coast region and there are over 2 900 km (1 800 miles) of roads, some metalled. The coastline, deeply indented, extends to nearly 1 600 km (1 000 miles), mostly alluvial flats, creeks and swamps. The chief towns are the ports, which in 1969 handled nearly 4.8m. tons of cargo. The main commercial centres are Kota Kinabalu (Jesselton) the capital (33 370), halfway along the west coast; Sandakan, the former capital (33 400) on the east coast, Tawau (17 500), and, on Labuan Island (formerly one of the Straits Settlements incorporated in North Borneo when the colony was constituted in 1946), Victoria (nearly 5 000).

Sarawak. For over 100 years after the Englishman, James Brooke, was invited by the people in 1841 to become their ruler, Sarawak was known as the Land of the White Rajahs. At the end of the Second World War the third Rajah Brooke ceded the country to the British Crown; and it was proclaimed a colony in 1946, exchanging the paternalistic rule which the first two rajahs and their enthusiastic officers had developed for the modernist outlook of the Colonial Office. A new constitution in 1956 provided for a council with an elected majority; and Sarawak became one of the constituent parts of East Malaysia in 1963.

Stretching southwest from Sabah, Sarawak is much the bigger territory with a larger population. A wide rampart of mountains with peaks rising to 1 800 to 2 500 m (6 000 to 8 000 ft), part of the backbone of Borneo as a whole, borders its inland frontier. The mountains drop to an extensive belt of lowlands, reaching to the sea and mostly covered, like the mountains themselves, with dense jungle and forest, which are estimated to occupy over 75 per cent of the surface. With an annual rainfall of 2 500 to 5 000 mm (100 to 200 in) the country is traversed by wide rivers, some of which are navigable for considerable distances and provide locations for some of the chief towns, well away from the coast. Kuching, the capital (estimated population 70 000) in the southwest lies about 34 km (21 miles) up the Sarawak River, and Sibu (population 40 000) more centrally situated and well known as a river port, is about 130 km (80 miles) up the Rejang.

Agriculture is the chief industry, practised mainly on a subsistence basis, but sago, rice, pepper and rubber are also commercial crops. Timber supplies over 38 per cent of all exports. An oilfield in the north, near Miri, has a small output; but petroleum products represent 33 per cent of exports. Crude and partly refined oil accounts for nearly 45 per cent of imports by value, food and live animals being the next largest category, followed by a miscellaneous collection of manufactured goods.

Manufacturing industry is not making rapid progress in East Malaysia as in West Malaysia.

Brunei

Comprising a couple of enclaves at the north end of Sarawak, Brunei, a self-governing state within the Commonwealth, has a total area of under 5 800 sq km (2 250 sq miles); 1971 population estimate 137 000. The British government is responsible for external affairs, while local authority is vested in the Sultan-in-Council. Formerly the Governor of Sarawak was High Commissioner for Brunei but in 1959 it was agreed Brunei should be administered separately from Sarawak, and the British Resident in Brunei was replaced by a resident High Commissioner. In 1963 the Brunei legislature decided not to join Malaysia, the only Malay-speaking territory to remain outside the Federation.

An oilfield at Seria in Brunei has passed peak production, but prospecting for oil and gas continues offshore in the area. Ten per cent of the working population is employed in the oil industry, and the refineries of Brunei provide nearly 96 per cent of the total exports.

Natural gas is shipped to Japan. Brunei has valuable timber resources. Sarawak takes over 97 per cent of the exports; and imports (a wide range of foodstuffs, raw materials and manufactured goods of all kinds) are provided by the United Kingdom, Singapore, Japan, West Malaysia and Australia.

Singapore

A geographical appendix to the Malayan peninsula, the island of Singapore was a British dependency, exercising internal self-government from August 1958, and ranking as a state, but with defence and foreign affairs reserved to the Crown. It is separated from the mainland by a strait only 1.2 km (0.75 mile) wide, and this is crossed by a causeway carrying both a road and a railway, the main railway north through the peninsula. The island (581 sq km: 225 sq miles) supports a population of over 2m. of whom over 76 per cent are Chinese and under 7 per cent Malays (1970). When Singapore joined the Federation of Malaysia in 1963 some difficulties stemmed from this racial structure. In Singapore the Chinese formed the major group; in the rest of the Federation Malays were more numerous and stressed the desirability of using their language. On 9 August 1965 Singapore withdrew from the Federation of Malaysia to become an independent state within the Commonwealth. Malay, Chinese, Tamil and English are all official languages, English being used for administrative purposes.

The island is low-lying (180 m: under 600 ft, at its highest point), with a few patches of the original vegetation but mostly covered with a light growth of secondary forest, plantations of economic crops (rubber, coconuts, pineapples, tobacco, pepper), market gardens, and ever-expanding urban areas. Mangrove swamps fringe the west coast and extend up the inlets; on the eastern side are low cliffs.

Singapore today is a focal point of commerce, port of call for international airlines and shipping (with facilities for handling container and bulk transport) and a leading entrepôt port for southeast Asia. The town and port of Singapore has shipyards, engineering works, sawmills, brick and cement works as well as many factories making small consumer goods; and with the new industrial estate at Jurong to the west of Singapore town (which also has shipyards and factories producing iron and steel rods, tyres, chemical and pharmaceuticals, plywood, plastics and so on) the south of the island of Singapore is developing a major industrial complex. There is a large oil refinery on Pulau Bukom, an island off the southwest coast. Singapore resembles Hong Kong in that wage rates are still low compared with those of industrial nations, and it is economic for foreign manufacturers to send small consumer goods to Singapore in component parts, there to be assembled.

Rubber, tin and other exports from West Malaysia pour along the causeway and thence to the docks at Singapore, where they join Singapore-made goods for transmission overseas. The main imports of the island of Singapore are foodstuffs (including rice, fruit and vegetables), fuel oil, machinery and transport equipment, chemicals, textile yarns and innumerable manufactures. Most trading is naturally with West Malaysia, followed by Japan, the United Kingdom, the United States, China and Thailand.

Indonesia

Forming a great arc which spans some 4 830 km (3 000 miles), the distance between London and New York, in the sea between the Malayan peninsula and Australia is a vast archipelago, the Malay Archipelago of over 13 500 islands; some are inhabited, some not, some not even named. Before the Second World War the Malay Archipelago comprised the Netherlands East Indies: it now constitutes the Republic of Indonesia. As a sovereign independent state, the republic was at first associated with the Netherlands under a statute of union which recognised the Netherlands Crown as the common head; but in 1954 Indonesia contracted out of this association. The republic includes all the island territories formerly belonging to the Netherlands. Western New Guinea or Irian was not finally transferred until 1962. The republic has a total area of 1.9m. sq km (575 500 sq miles) with a population estimated at 124m. (1971), the most densely peopled state of southeast Asia. The territory was occupied by the Japanese in the Second World War. Since gaining independence on 27 December 1949 Indonesia has been in a state of political disorder which has profoundly affected her economy. The population is predominantly Muslim but people of many different cultural backgrounds live on the islands and there is a lack of harmony between the various groups. Antagonism against Chinese Indonesians whose interests, as usual, lie mainly in commerce manifests itself openly from time to time. Indonesia has great resources and potential, and an energetic people (the population growing at a rate of 2.4 per cent per annum), but the state is still so disorganised that income *per capita* is probably as low now as it has been for some fifty years. Inflation after the Second World War went out of control and rose at a dangerously high rate, although by 1969 it had apparently begun to slow down.

The main islands in the republic are Sumatra (population about 19.7m. in 1970); Java and Madura (74m. in 1970); Sulawesi (Celebes) (7m.); Nusa Tenggara (Lesser Sunda Islands) (6.5m.); Kalimantan, the major part of the island of Borneo (4m.); and West Irian, the western half of New Guinea (700 000). The figures given are 1966 estimates

623

apart from those relating to Sumatra and Java and Madura. Java shows a striking population increase: in 1800 some 3m. to 4m. people lived on the island, by 1926 there were 36.9m., and by 1966 63m. It is now the most densely populated agricultural area in the world.

All the islands are mountainous, mainly Tertiary in age, and the older rocks of the core are rarely exposed. There is a string of active volcanoes parallel to the axis of the island arc along a line of weakness in the earth's crust, especially in Sumatra, Java and Sulawesi; and the small amount of low, flat land is mainly on the 'inner' side of the mountains in Sumatra and Java. In Kalimantan, also a mountainous land, the lowland enfolds the mountainous centre of the territory.

With the exception of east Java and the Nusa Tenggara Indonesia lies in the equatorial climatic zone and this, combined with the soft Tertiary rocks, has a profound effect on soil formation. In Java particularly volcanic rocks have been swiftly broken down in the heat and heavy rainfall to produce soils of great depth and fertility, even on the mountainsides, and to provide the rich alluvium washed down to the northern lowlands. Only the very high slopes of the peaks remain uncultivated. It is interesting to compare Java and Japan in this respect. Both have comparable geological structure, only about one-third of the land lying under 180 m (600 ft), both have about one-third of the land surface formed by volcanic rock; but Java has 80 per cent of land under cultivation, whereas, despite all her efforts, Japan has less than 20 per cent. This is mainly due to the climatic conditions prevailing in Japan which do not lead to the speedy breaking down of the volcanic rock, thin soils being the result.

The natural evergreen forest cover has been removed so that the land can be cultivated on most of the islands of Indonesia, except on the highest mountains.

Indonesia's leading mineral asset is oil, lying on the 'inner' side of the mountains in Sumatra and Java and on the east coast of Kalimantan in Borneo. The republic is the only large oil producer in southeast Asia, and undoubtedly possesses resources of oil and natural gas not yet exploited. Other mineral deposits include tin (on Bangka and Balitung (Billiton), and Singkep), bauxite (at Bintan in the Riau group), coal (Java, Sumatra, Kalimantan), iron ore (west Java, south Sumatra in the Kanggal area which is forming a basis for an iron and steel industry), manganese and nickel.

Padi is the main crop of all the lowland areas in Indonesia, and is also cultivated on carefully terraced hillsides. Other crops include maize, groundnuts and cassava (for tapioca). The Dutch established a prosperous plantation agriculture especially in Java: sugarcane and rubber on the lowlands, tea on the hillsides in the southwest; coffee on hillsides in the southeast; tobacco; coconuts (especially for copra) and oil palm.

In Sumatra plantation crops are tobacco, rubber and oil palm; food crops are padi and maize. Kalimantan is still largely forest-covered but there are rubber and coconut plantations, and padi is the chief crop. The Celebes and Moluccas (the famous Spice Islands) have rich fertile soils comparable with those of Java, but the islands are as yet undeveloped: padi, maize, and coconuts are cultivated.

By far the most important, economically and politically, is the smallest of the four main islands, Java. Though no larger than England, it has an even denser population, numbering some 74m. It contains the capital and seat of government, long famous under the Dutch as Batavia, now renamed Djakarta, and it is easily the biggest factor in production and trade. Long and narrow, traversed by a volcanic chain with peaks up to 3 700 m (12 000 ft), some of which are still active, it has rich volcanic and alluvial soils, combined with facilities for irrigation, which, together with the equatorial climate, make it unsurpassed as a forcing-house for agricultural tropical products. Like other tropical countries, it is peculiarly subject to swift fluctuations and changes if disease should sweep through the crops or if standards of efficiency be allowed to deteriorate. At one time coffee was the staple product; it was displaced by sugar, which in turn declined, and rubber came to the fore. Tea, sisal, tapioca, cinchona, and tobacco are other favoured crops; and large areas are sown to padi.

Though not to be compared with Java in their development, many of the other islands have valuable resources. Sumatra, with its backbone of volcanic mountains running down its western side, has on the east a great plain 970 km (600 miles) long and from 96 to 177 km (60 to 110 miles) wide. This plain is low-lying, marshy near the coast, and liable to flooding in the rainy season from the rivers that wander through it; but in the northeast, where the island narrows and the highlands come near to the coast, which is traversed by a railway, the conditions are more favourable to plantation crops, and various estates have been established, largely under rubber, in the neighbourhood of Medan. Sumatra has considerable mineral resources: coal among the mountains at the back of Padang, on the west coast, which is served by a railway, oil around Palembang; and tin.

Borneo has oilfields and refineries on the east coast of Kalimantan, but in the main it is richly wooded, little developed territory, with a mountain backbone and lateral ranges separated by wide expanses of lowlands. Sulawesi (Celebes) is still less developed, consisting almost wholly of jungle-clad volcanic mountain ridges, sprawling over the ocean like a giant scorpion, with long arms straggling out from a central mass; yet even here copra and spices are grown for export, notably around Manado, as the eastern end of the northernmost arm; and Macassar, in the southwest corner of the island, has made a double contribution to the English language; for not only did Macassar oil become a household word as a hairdressing in the nineteenth century but the need of some protection for upholstered backs of chairs and sofas after its use led to the introduction of antimacassars.

Some of the smaller islands are of distinctive commercial interest. The Moluccas (Spice Islands) have lost much of their medieval glamour and renown, but they still contribute to the world's supplies of the products which gave them their name: pepper, cloves, nutmegs, and other spices. Another example of this specialised commercial interest is found in one of the Lesser Sunda Islands, Soemba, otherwise known as Sandalwood Island.

Livestock are fairly numerous, if not only the size of the republic but its character be considered. The available returns, relating to the islands as a whole, showed heavy losses of cattle and buffaloes in the decade of 1939–49; but other livestock increased, and since the war there has been a general recovery. In 1970 FAO estimated that there were 7m. cattle, 2.7m. buffaloes, 3.7m. sheep, 7m. goats, 2.65m. pigs and 620 000 horses.

Such, then, briefly, are some of the natural factors governing the commercial development of Indonesia. In recent years they have been complicated by other factors which cannot be ignored in any survey of conditions and prospects. Before the Second World War, when the country was under Dutch control, a large number of estate companies carried on a highly successful plantation industry. There was also a large production, especially of food crops, from small holdings; but the commercial crops from the estates, rubber, tea, sugar, copra, tobacco, were the backbone of the export trade.

During the war the islands were occupied by the Japanese, and the owners of estates were deprived of their properties. In the Moluccas the pepper vines, which provided a large part of the world supply of black and white pepper, were nearly all destroyed, resulting in a world shortage of which the effects were felt on the opposite side of the globe. An autonomous Indonesian administration was set up, and, after the Japanese surrender, proclaimed its independence. This was contested by the Netherlands, and there was a further period of unsettlement, attended by fighting, which delayed the rehabilitation of the estates. It was the end of 1949 before the republic was accorded rights of sovereignty and entered into temporary union with the Netherlands. Indonesia had been organised on the federal system, but in 1950 it was made a unitary state, a change which was not accomplished without further disturbance. In the same year it was admitted to membership of the United Nations.

The tragedy of Indonesia at present (1970s) is that in the past the great fertility of her agricultural land, the efficient development of industrial crops and the wealth derived from their export led to an upsurge in numbers of population. This population increase continues at a reduced but still high rate, but now her production of primary products is not keeping pace. She lacks the surplus of industrial crops that used to be available for export, on which her prosperity was based, now needed more than ever to earn foreign exchange to pay for much needed raw materials for manufacturing industry, for food, and for the maintenance of equipment. Before the Second World War Indonesia led the world in rubber production (now second to Malaysia); she was the world's second largest producer of tin (now a bad fifth). She is at present fifth in production of tea and padi, fourth in palm oil; third in coconuts (after the Philippines and India), second in copra (after Philippines). Other valuable crops are pepper and spices, kapok, cinchona bark (for quinine); but of all this wealth little is now exported, and rice is imported.

Indonesia's manufacturing is mainly concerned with textiles and clothing, on little more than a cottage-industry basis, relying on imported cotton yarn. The Chinese have been pioneers in the financial management of manufacturing industry, but it is all on a very small scale. The capital, Djakarta (4.75m. in 1970) in Java has food, drink and tobacco processing factories as well as shipyards. Surabaja (over 1m.), Semarang (500 000) and Amboina also have small shipyards. In Java there are cement works and chemical plant, and there is a petro-chemical plant at Palembang (475 000); but the contribution of the manufacturing industry to the national economy is diminishing when it should be growing.

Inter-island shipping constitutes the lifeline of Indonesia's scattered territories, but with the rundown in the economy since the Second World War services and port facilities have suffered, and leave much to be desired, individual islands being forced into self-sufficiency. Java is well provided with roads and railways but some of the outer islands, which could now contribute much more to the economy, are poorly provided with means of transportation. The main port is Tandjunpriok (the port of Djakarta) but there are port facilities also at Semarang, Bandjarmasin, Balikpapan and Belawan. Indonesia's national airline, GIA, maintains services between Djakarta and Manila, Bangkok, Hong Kong, Tokyo and Amsterdam.

Foreign trade, which is slight, has been greatly depressed since the Second World War but the present government hopes to maintain the slight upward trend of the late 1960s. Rubber is the main export, followed by petroleum, a small amount of palm oil and coffee. Imports include rice, cotton and a little machinery. Most trade is with the United States, Japan, Netherlands, West Germany and Australia (who also takes most of the exports). Japan and the United States provide most imports. Indonesia undoubtedly has the natural resources, especially oil, to expand her economy once she is politically on an even keel.

Portuguese Timor

Timor, an island at the southeastern extremity of the Malay Archipelago, falls within the geographical range of Indonesia, but neither the Portuguese, who started its European occupation, nor the Dutch, who came after them, succeeded in ousting the other, and the island was divided between them till the Dutch handed over their part of it to Indonesia in 1949, leaving the Portuguese still in possession of the rest.

Timor is a long narrow island with a longitudinal axis of some 480 km (300 miles), lying northeast to southwest, and an area about half as large again as Wales. Portugal has the northeast part of the island, and an enclave on the northwest coast of the Indonesian section; altogether, some 14 925 sq km (5 672 sq miles) supporting a population of 610 541 (1970), Dili, the capital and chief port, on the northwest coast, has some 10 753 inhabitants.

The physical characteristics of Portuguese Timor are those of the whole island, which is traversed by a volcanic range, quiescent now except for a few mud geysers, with peaks up to nearly 3 000 m (10 000 ft). An interesting feature is a series of raised coral beaches at an elevation of 1 200 to 1 500 m (4 000 to 5 000 ft). Monsoon forest covers most of the country, though there are stretches of savanna suitable for livestock. The arable land is not highly cultivated. Chief exports are coffee, copra, rubber and wax. The value of imports is commonly double that of the exports.

The Philippines

The Philippine islands, forming the northern extension of the Malay Archipelago, were ruled by Spain for over 300 years after their conquest in the sixteenth century; ceded to the United States for $20m. in 1898, after the Spanish—American War of that year; granted provisional independence in 1935; occupied by Japan during the Second World War; and accorded by the United States full independence as a republic in 1946, with reciprocal trade privileges; followed in 1947 by the lease to the United States of numerous defence bases in the Philippines. Under the original constitution exploitation of natural resources was limited to Filipinos and to companies controlled by them, but the right to engage in such activities was extended after the war to American interests.

The islands range over nearly 1 900 km (1 200 miles) of ocean, between Taiwan in the north and Borneo and Sulawesi in the south, and extend some 1 200 km (750 miles) from east to west. Upwards of 7 000 islands have been charted within these limits, but under 500 exceed 2.6 sq km (1 sq mile) in extent, and eleven of these account for over nine-tenths of the total area of 299 400 sq km (115 600 sq miles), while two of the eleven comprise two-thirds of the total. The largest, **Luzon**, at the northern end of the group, has an area of 108 375 sq km (41 845 sq miles); and the second largest, Mindanao, at the southern end of the group, an area of 94 225 sq km (36 381 sq miles). The other ten main islands, namely in descending order of size, Samar, Negros, Palawan, Panay, Mindoro, Leyte, Cebu, Bohol, Masbate and Catanduanes, are all very much smaller, ranging from 13 426 sq km (5 184 sq miles) in the case of Samar to 1 510 sq km (583 sq miles) in the case of Catanduanes. The total population in 1970 (census) was 37 008 419, nearly half of them in Luzon, which includes Manila, the former capital seat of government with a population of 1.5m. With Quezon City (over 585 000), the new capital, and Pasay City, Manila forms a conurbation of over 3m. Luzon is not only the largest but much the most important island in the group, whereas Mindanao, the second largest is the wildest and least developed, and in general is thinly populated, though it has two large ports, Davao (315 300) and Zamboango (188 300).

Agriculture and forests. The islands are mountainous, rising in Mindanao to a greatest height of 2 900 m (9 500 ft), and are subject to volcanic eruptions. Except in favoured areas the soil is not highly productive, but it is officially estimated for the United Nations that only between 4 and 5 per cent of the whole is built on or waste. A much larger area, some 13 per cent, is described as unused but potentially productive. Nearly 40 per cent is under forest, and about 28 per cent as arable. Only the relatively small proportion of 13 per cent counts as permanent pasture, and the pastoral industry is inconsiderable, the number of sheep being especially small (11 000 in 1970). Livestock generally declined during the Japanese occupation, but in 1970 included 4.43m. water buffaloes, 6.6m. pigs, 1.6m. cattle, 700 000 goats and 300 000 horses.

There is a considerable trade in lumber and logs from the predominant forest lands, both for home use and for export. A wide range of forest products (gums and resins, vegetable oils, dye woods and barks, rattan and bamboo) provides a useful source of minor industries. But agriculture is the mainstay of the archipelago's economy, employing over 57 per cent of the total population. Crops fall into two main classes: subsistence and commercial. The chief food crops are rice, grown in 1970 on nearly 3.2m. ha (7.9m. acres) and yielding over 5.6m. tons of padi; maize grown on over 2.4m. ha (5.9m. acres) and yielding over 2.4m. tons; sweet potatoes, 706 000 tons; cassava, 506 000 tons; and bananas, a subsistence crop with a standing area of 58 000 ha (143 000 acres) yielding 760 000 tons in 1970. Despite these and other subsistence crops, the islands are not selfsupporting in food, no small part of the home production consisting of plantation crops grown for export. Three of the commercial products are of outstanding importance: coconut products, sugar, and abaca (manila hemp). In 1938 they provided more than three-quarters of the total value of the exports other than gold, in 1958 over two-thirds, but in 1969 only 38 per cent. Timber accounted for 27 per cent in 1969.

Before the Second World War, sugar was the biggest contributor to these commercial crops, with 8m. tons of cane yielding 1m. tons of raw sugar, and an export of 800 000 tons of centrifugal plus 29 000 tons of molasses, providing 40 per cent of the total value of the exports other than gold. The production of cane dropped during the war, but by 1956 exports had recovered the lost ground, reaching 900 000 tons of sugar and 200 000 tons of molasses. In 1969 979 500 tons of sugar were exported.

Abaca is another crop which suffered from the war and its aftermath. Known commercially as manila hemp, it is one of the 'hard' or 'leaf' fibres obtained from the tissue of the leaves and leaf-bases, as contrasted with the 'soft' or 'bast' fibres derived from the bast tissues of the stem. The latter are the true hemp, and are grown in Europe and Asia, especially the USSR. 'Soft' fibres also include sunn or Indian hemp, produced only in India. The 'hard' fibres classed in trade circles as hemp include not only manila hemp (abaca) but sisal (known in Mexico as henequen) and the New Zealand phormium. Before the war, the Philippines produced and exported a larger quantity of fibres recognised by the trade as 'hemp' than any other country. The crop averaged about 170 000 tons, nearly all of which was exported. During the Japanese occupation it fell to a very low ebb, and the export has never regained the prewar standard. Apart from the competition of manmade fibres, it has been outstripped by sisal, which even before the war had a bigger world production than manila hemp, and since has shot ahead till in 1955 it provided two-thirds of the world supply of hard hemps, with Tanzania in the position which the Philippines used to occupy as the world's leading exporter, providing 30 per cent of the total world exports. The quantity of manila hemp now exported by the Philippines is negligible: it contributes only 1.7 per cent of total exports.

It is, however, in respect of copra and other products of the coconut palm that the Philippines play their biggest part in world trade. They not only competed before the Second World War with Indonesia (then the Netherlands East Indies) for the lead over all other countries exporting such products, but since the war their lead has been unchallenged. Before the war, Indonesia exported much more copra than the Philippines but much less coconut oil. The combined products in terms of oil (taking the average oil content of copra as 63 per cent) gave Indonesia the bigger total in 1937, but the Philippines gained the lead in 1938 with exports equivalent to 376 000 tons of oil against Indonesia's 370 000 tons. The third and fourth countries in the list,

Malaya and Ceylon, came far below, with less than half the foregoing quantities. Some of the groves of coconut palms in the Philippines at the outbreak of war were not in full bearing, and with their growing maturity after the war the production of copra, so far from having to be built up again by slow degrees, almost at once took on a big increase. Total production in 1955 was over a third of the world production of 3m. tons, and exports, in terms of oil equivalent, were half of the world total, representing over 900 000 tons of copra. The coconut oil industry fell to a low ebb after the war, and the proportion of the copra crop now exported from the Philippines as oil is much less than before the war. It is to be noted that while the Philippines have gone ahead both as producers and as exporters of coconut products, their old rival, Indonesia, has lost ground. In 1970 copra production in the Philippines was 1.35m. tons, more than half the world total.

Most of the islands have their specialised crops or mineral products. Luzon is of outstanding importance. In addition to the minerals mentioned below in connection with the north of the island, the central plain north of Manila Bay is good agricultural country raising large crops of rice and sugar, while coconut groves abound in southern Luzon. Coconuts are also a feature of Leyte, sugar of Negros, abaca of Davao, rice of Panay, and maize of Cebu.

Although 53 per cent of the labour force were actively engaged in agriculture in 1967, production is insufficient for the needs of the growing population; foodstuffs have to be imported and exports of industrial crops are not expanding enough. The average size of farm is small, 3.21 ha (7.93 acres); and most farmers are either rent-paying or share-cropping tenants. Even the industrial crops are cultivated on these small farms; there are very few really large scientifically managed plantations. Many agricultural workers find it hard to make a living and are drifting to the towns.

Minerals. Mineral resources are numerous but not highly developed, and the war led to a big decline in output. Gold is found in most of the islands but is chiefly mined in north Luzon. In 1941, before the Japanese occupation of the islands, the production of gold was returned as 1.144m. fine troy ounces, and exports were valued at £17m. Since the war production has been about 0.5m. troy ounces − 376 036 ounces in 1963, when the exports of gold were valued at US $8.8m.; a little over 0.5m. in 1969, when the export was valued at US $18.44m. Copper mining is also pursued in north Luzon, with exports in 1956 of 88 000 tons of ore and concentrates, in 1968 398 000 tons, 8 per cent by value of total exports; it has since declined. At Zambales, in north Luzon, are reputedly large chromite reserves. Exports of chrome concentrates in 1970 contributed less than 1 per cent to the value of all exports. There are also known deposits of manganese, iron ore, coal, mercury (a little exported), nickel, limestone (used for cement); and uranium in Luzon.

Industry is on a small scale. Hydroelectric and thermal power plants provide power for expanding manufacturing industries in Manila. There is a small steel plant at Lanao del Norte, but the Philippines import the products of heavy industry. Much of the growing manufacturing industry is subsidised by the government. The wealthy landowners of the Philippines are reluctant to invest their capital in industry, their concern being traditionally with the land. Industry therefore depends to a large extent on Chinese initiative and foreign capital, especially from the United States. The Greater Manila area is the centre of the manufacturing industry, with a strong emphasis on the processing of foodstuffs for export (sugar mills, pineapple canning, coconut-processing). For the home market cement is made in quantity and there are textile and clothing, vehicle assembly, china and glass, pharmaceutical, and food processing works. In the smaller towns and villages there are traditional handicraft cottage industries: embroidery, handwoven textiles (cotton and raw silk) and so on.

Communications. Two of the islands are served by railways: Luzon has 940 km (585 miles) of track, Panay has 116 km (72 miles) but they are not much used. The well-surfaced roads (56 180 km: 34 830 miles) are more important for the relatively slowly increasing number of motor vehicles (303 300 registered in the mid-1960s, 305 000 by the end of the decade).

Inter-island shipping is important but services and port facilities on the whole are inadequate, and both need much capital investment for improvement. Manila is the major international port and airport.

Trade. Leading exports include logs, lumber and plywood, copra, sugar (centrifugal), abaca fibres, coconut oil, desiccated coconut, copper concentrates, iron ore and canned pineapple. Main imports are machinery and transport equipment, fuel oils, metals electrical machinery and manufactured goods such as textile fibres, foodstuffs (especially cereals, rice and wheat). Most trading is carried on with the United States (which gives a good deal of economic aid to the Philippines) and Japan, the former usually taking Philippine sugar, coconut products and abaca, the latter the copper concentrates, iron ore and timber. Japan supplies the transport equipment and base metals, the United States generally supplying the major part of the other imports. The main trading partners with the Philippines in Europe are the United Kingdom and West Germany, but the quantity of merchandise involved is insignificant.

Table 70 — Philippines: towns with population exceeding 150 000 (1968)

Manila	1 499 000	Iloilo	201 000
(former capital)		Caloocan	195 000
Quezon City	546 000	Zamboanga	177 000
(new capital)		Pasay	174 000
Davao	337 000	San Carlos	165 000
Cebu	332 000	Bacolod	157 000
Basilan	209 000		

Hong Kong

This small island (about a fifth of the size of the Isle of Wight) 146 km (91 miles) off the south coast of China southeast of Kwangchow (Canton), was ceded to the British Crown in 1841. To it was added in 1860 the peninsula of Kowloon (about 9 sq km: 3.5 sq miles) on the mainland opposite, and in 1898 a ninety-nine year lease was obtained of a further 935 sq km (360 sq miles) of the mainland and neighbouring islands. The New Territories, as the leased areas are called, are mostly wild and rugged, rising to heights of over 900 m (3 000 ft). Hong Kong's value lies in the original island and Kowloon, and more particularly in the strait between them, which forms a magnificent harbour. The total area of the colony, that is Hong Kong island and the New Territories, is 1 045.6 sq km (403.7 sq miles), including land reclaimed since 1945 on both shores of the strait. A road tunnel under the strait, opened in 1972, unites the island to the mainland.

Hong Kong island itself, within its area of some 75 sq km (30 sq miles), rises to over 550 m (1 800 ft) and boasts a cable tramway up Victoria Peak as well as an electric tramway service at lower levels. The capital city of Victoria extends along the north shore, facing the mainland, and has all the accessories of a great port. So has Kowloon, opposite, which has developed not only as a shipping centre but also industrially. It is the terminus of a standard gauge (4 ft 8½ in) railway, which, though running through British territory for only 35 km (22 miles) is continued through China to Kwangchow and Hankow. There has not been any through traffic since 1949.

Hong Kong city and port (large enough to accommodate big container vessels), together with Kowloon, is a hive of commercial and industrial activity: one of the great entrepôts of world trade. Before the Second World War the population was estimated at about 1m.; the colony suffered in many ways from the Japanese occupation and later became a place of refuge for Chinese from the adjoining territory; the urban population has risen to 3.9m., 37 per cent of whom were under fifteen at the 1971 census. Trade recovered with remarkable rapidity, and industry, which before the war had been a minor factor, acquired new importance. An outstanding example of the new industrial development was the establishment of textile manufactures which quickly became the colony's major industry. In 1957 they employed nineteen spinning mills operating over 300 000 spindles, as well as over 600 weaving, knitting and other mills. The impact of the exports, at relatively low prices, on the Lancashire cotton trade seriously affected the home industry, and after prolonged negotiations agreement was reached to limit the imports into the United Kingdom. In 1971 22 per cent of the labour force were engaged in the textile industry, which accounted for 45 per cent by value of total exports.

There are factories, large and small, producing clothes, carpets, toys, plastic goods in great variety, shoes, electrical and electronic equipment, clocks and watches, cameras, travel goods and light metal ware, while others specialise in the assembly of electrical components. It is economic for such components to be sent even from Europe to Hong Kong for assembly and export because of the skill and relative cheapness of labour available there. Heavy industry is represented by big iron foundries and steel mills; and there are efficient ship repair and building yards.

Until the turn of the half-century, trade and industry continued to go ahead. Then new troubles arose. Until then China normally had been the dominant factor in Hong Kong's trade. The outbreak of the Korean War led to growing restrictions on Hong Kong's exports to China; and the United States ceased trading with China. The volume and the value of the trade alike suffered in turn, largely because of the ban on strategic exports, but partly because of other adverse trade conditions, including the revival of Japanese competition. Despite these temporary setbacks, Hong Kong easily retained its position as the leading international trading centre in the Far East. China gradually resumed the use of Hong Kong as an outlet for her relatively small quantity of exports. Since 1970 over 42 per cent of exports from Hong Kong were destined for the United States which lifted its twenty-year embargo on trade with China in 1970, 14 per cent for the United Kingdom. Imports came from Japan (24 per cent), China (16 per cent), United States (13 per cent), United Kingdom (9 per cent), mainly consisting of textiles, foodstuffs, machinery and transport equipment.

Much use is made of air transport and the international airport, Kai Tak, with its runway jutting into the sea of Kowloon Bay, is as busy with air freight as it is with passengers. There is very little land available for farming on Hong Kong island itself, but Kowloon and the New Territories are intensively cultivated, with rice, vegetables and flowers predominating. Great numbers of poultry and pigs are reared and the disposal of manure presents commensurate problems. The farmers cannot put it all back on the land, the amount is too great; and pig manure is difficult to process for concentration and recycling. Consequently there is at present a growing problem of pollution of watercourses as the animal manure is disposed of haphazardly. It is a problem facing intensive animal farming units in many other closely settled areas in the world. The colony was for long dependent on China for its water supply, but great reservoirs have now been constructed and others are being built to make it self-sufficient. There is also plant for the desalting of seawater.

China

One of the world's most ancient empires, the Chinese empire, became a republic in 1912. The old empire had included the rich, thickly populated region of China proper, Manchuria and the huge Outer Territories lying in the heart of Asia which included Chinese Turkestan, Tibet and Mongolia. The republic, which had its capital at Nanking from 1928 to 1937, instead of at Peking, the capital of the old empire, exercised its influence only over what may be called China proper. Manchuria, declared an independent state, came under Japanese influence; Tibet was virtually independent; and Outer Mongolia became a Communist state closely linked with the Soviet Union.

In 1937—38 the Japanese invaded China and gained control of much of the country. They were finally defeated in 1945 and Manchuria and the island then known as Formosa were restored to China. Civil war followed, in which the Communists gained control of the whole country, except Formosa. Peking once again became the capital, in 1949. The Chinese Nationalist Government withdrew to Taiwan (Formosa) and set up an independent state.

When the Chinese Communist Party took over, the nation was exhausted by prolonged wars, inflation was running at a high level, and the economy of the country was collapsing.

The Communist government, supreme on the mainland, was recognised by many countries, including the United Kingdom, but not by the United States. It concluded a treaty of friendship and mutual aid with the Soviet Union, later to lapse; but in general has pursued a policy of isolation in its development programmes, with little trade with the outside world. In the United Nations applications for the recognition of the People's Republic as China's representative was for long vetoed by the United States, which recognised the Nationalist Government in Taiwan as representing the Chinese people. The People's Republic was eventually officially admitted to the United Nations in 1972. To avoid ambiguity some reference books use 'China mainland' to identify the People's Republic.

Administrative divisions. If Taiwan is included China consists of twenty-two provinces, five autonomous regions where the original population was non-Han (Inner Mongolia, Kwangsi-Chuang, Tibet, Ningsia-Hui and Sinkiang-Uighur) and three municipalities (Peking, the capital Shanghai and Tientsin). 'China proper' is a term frequently used by foreigners. Originally it referred to the ancient China protected by the Great Wall and covered eighteen provinces; it has now come to cover the twenty-two provinces as shown on p. 641. 'Manchuria' is a term no longer used by the Chinese, the territory now roughly coinciding with the three provinces of the Northeastern Region (Heilungkiang, Kirin and Liaoning).

Position, size and population. China is an enormous country which stretches from latitude 54° N to 18° N and from longitude 74° E to 135° E. The total area is given officially as 9 597 000 sq km (3 704 400 sq miles), a figure which includes Taiwan (36 000 sq km: 93 000 sq miles) which the People's Republic regards as part of China. The last census statistics available are those for 1953 which gave a total population of 601 938 035. It included 574 205 940 by 'direct census'; 7 591 298 in Taiwan; 11 743 000 Chinese resident or studying abroad; 8 397 477 in 'remote border regions'. The official estimate for the total population in 1970 was 700m.; foreign estimates for the year 1972 varied between 730m. and 786m. 'Han' is used to identify the Chinese race; about 6 per cent of the population are estimated to be non-Han.

China is the only part of the mainland of Asia, besides India and Bangladesh, with a population of high density. From the 1953 census China proper alone was supporting a population of some 520m. so that in comparison with an area smaller than Europe without the Soviet Union, China proper was supporting a much larger population.

It is able to support so dense a population largely because of the seasonal rainfall distribution. The winter temperatures are cool even in the south, and in the north and most parts of the interior, rigorous: the mean January temperature at Kwangchow (Canton), on the Tropic of Cancer is about 12.3° C (55° F), at Zikawei (Shanghai), in about 31° N, 2.8° C (37° F) and at Peking, in 40° N, 5° C (23° F). But the rains occur, as in monsoon regions generally, during the season of high temperatures and thus promote an enormous vegetable production.

The population is especially dense in much of the eastern plain, which stretches from north of Peking to south of the Yangtze Kiang, and is mostly below 180 m (600 ft); north of the Yangtze it contains only two considerable tracts of uplands, rising to 915 m (3 000 ft), and though such uplands are much more common south of the Yangtze, and the coast opposite to Taiwan is backed by a wide belt of mountainous country, both uplands and mountains are interspersed with much low-lying land. This is especially true in the far south of eastern

China, where the province of Kwantung, extending behind and on either side of Hong Kong, is largely a deltaic alluvial plain.

West of the great eastern plain, China is for the most part elevated and to a large extent mountainous, but even the elevated regions are in some places capable of supporting a numerous population. A very densely populated region, embracing parts of eastern Szechwan and northern Yunnan, is the so-called Red Basin, which, besides great mineral wealth, has a peculiar red soil of great fertility. Where that soil is found cultivation can be pursued to a great height up the mountains; and the Chinese in eastern Szechwan cultivate the hillsides wherever the slope is not above 30°, which is about the steepest a man can walk up unaided by his hands. To the west of this area an isolated level plain of somewhat more than 5 180 sq km (2 000 sq miles) in extent, formed of the bed of an old lake, has been irrigated from the waters of the Min with the utmost care for upwards of 2 000 years, and is everywhere covered with a verdure which would be monotonous were it not for the variety of shades. Towards the southeast of this plain lies the rich and populous city of Chengtu, seat of the administration in Szechwan.

The northern half of China is covered, and vast hollows to a great depth are filled, with a yellow soil known as loess, which is also of remarkable fertility, and rewards cultivation even at great heights. This soil is light and easy to work, but it has one great drawback. Its productiveness, though often very great, is very uncertain. The soil is so porous that water runs through it with great rapidity, and crops are thus liable to suffer from drought unless refreshed with frequent showers or supplied with water by irrigation; and so it happens that a region which, when rain falls with sufficient frequency, yields the most abundant crops, may in other seasons have its crops entirely destroyed, though the rainfall may have been plentiful enough for soils of another kind. Irrigation, therefore, is practised throughout this region wherever the structure of the ground admits of it. Many parts of China are, like certain parts of India, pitted with wells like a sieve, every field having one.

Contrasts between north and south China. While the general characteristics of a monsoon climate are found throughout China, there are necessarily considerable differences in a country which spreads a distance of some 4 000 km (2 500 miles) from north to south. Differences in temperature will be taken for granted, but differences in the distribution of rainfall should also be noted. In the north and south the average rainfall shows a decided culmination in the middle of summer and is very slight at the extremes of the year; but in the Yangtze valley the summer rains are more prolonged, and while the average maximum here also is in the middle of the year, there is a second period of heavy rains in September and October.

Many years ago Baron Richthofen noted the somewhat marked contrasts for the most part directly or indirectly due to climate, on opposite sides of the Chin Ling Shan (Tsinling-shan) and Funiu Shan, ranges west of the great plain and south of the 35th parallel, which form an easterly continuation of the Tibetan Kunlun Mountains and constitute a main divide. North of this line of water partings lie the great loess deposits already described, which are the result of climatic influence, inasmuch as they represent accumulations of dust brought from inner Asia by the northwest winds of the exceedingly dry winters. Filling up the hollows, these deposits give a remarkably uniform aspect to the surface features, except locally where the deposits are themselves cut by deep vertical sided gorges. On the other hand, to the south of the divide, loess is present only in isolated patches; mountains and valleys are fully formed. Loess being unfavourable to tree growth, the mountain slopes in the north are generally bare, whereas in the south they may have luxuriant trees and shrubs as well as innumerable clumps of bamboo, and expansions of the valley bottoms are filled with fertile alluvium densely peopled. The north is the land of wheat, cotton, and podfruits, the south that of rice, tea, silk, tung oil (a drying oil used for varnishing wood, expressed from the seeds of *Aleurites fordii* and *A. montana*), and sugarcane. Traditional road communication in the north is by wagon roads, in the south for the most part by narrow footpaths and tracks for pack animals. In the north, mules, horses, asses, and camels are used as beasts of burden, the first two also for draught. In the south, buffaloes work in the fields, but asses and camels are unknown, and apart from the waterways, human porterage was the chief means of transport before roads and railways were built.

Rivers and inland waterways. China's great rivers are at once her blessing and her bane: on the one hand a source of her soil fertility and a means of travel and transport, on the other, an instrument of devastation and death, overwhelming the countryside with floods and shifting channels. Three rivers of outstanding magnitude cross China from east to west. In the north is the Hwang Ho or Yellow River, so called because of the yellow tinge imparted to its waters by the loess which they carry as silt. The 4 000 km (2,500 miles) or more of its course from the Tibetan highlands to the China coast range between rapid torrents and sluggish shallows, neither of which is favourable to navigation; and the current is so heavily laden with silt that in its lower reaches the bed of the river, hemmed in by restraining dykes, has risen above the surrounding plain. So liable indeed is the river to flooding on a large scale and following a new course, often with great loss of life, that the Hwang Ho has long been known as 'China's sorrow'. Shorter by half and milder in character is the Si Kiang (2 000 km: 1 250 miles), or West River, in south China. Rising in Yunnan it crosses the province of

Kwangsi into Kwantung, where it unites with other important rivers for example the Peh Kiang and expands into a great delta, at the head of which is the city of Kwangchow (Canton), while off the coast lies the island of Hong Kong. Kwangchow is one of the great ports of China, accessible to oceangoing vessels, of which the larger find anchorage at Whampoa, 13 km (8 miles) downstream. The Si Kiang and the Peh Kiang are navigable by smaller craft for 320 km (200 miles) or more above Kwangchow.

Neither the Hwang Ho nor the Si Kiang can compare in commercial importance with the third and longest of China's great rivers, the Yangtze Kiang, which flows across central China for 5 150 km (3 200 miles) in its passage from the Tibetan plateau to the China Sea near Shanghai. In the summer months (April to October) it is navigable by large vessels as far as Hankow, 1 125 km (700 miles) upstream; and before the Second World War several lines of steamers plied between the two ports, while two British shipping companies maintained a service between Hankow and Europe. In the winter months the depth of water limits navigation to lightdraught steamers. Beyond Hankow, steamers drawing up to 4.5 m (15 ft) can ascend the river in the season of high water up to Ichang, over 1 600 km (1 000 miles) from the sea. Above that point, a succession of rapids makes navigation difficult, but Ichang is at the western edge of the plain and land travel is also difficult in the mountainous country beyond, leading to the fertile and populous Red basin of Szechwan. The need for the exchange of products between the highland provinces and the provinces of the plains is insistent, and despite the difficulties of navigation there is river traffic for another 645 km (400 miles) above Ichang, maintaining communications with Chungking, Szechwan's largest city. Specially built flat-bottomed vessels force their way up the rapids, while Chinese junks (a feature of the Yangtze all the way from the sea) are hauled up by hand along narrow tracks in the face of the precipitous gorges through which the river flows. So strong is the current that sometimes the junks have to be unloaded and the cargo carried to a point upstream to which the empty junks can be hauled. The return voyage from Chungking to Ichang, though accomplished in only a fraction of the time, is even more hazardous.

In addition to the three giant waterways thus briefly characterised, there are many rivers, minor only in a relative sense, which play an important part as vehicles of travel and transport. Canals also play their part in China's vast economy, especially in the eastern plain. One great canal, the old Imperial Canal dating from the seventh century, extends north and south for 1 125 km (700 miles). Starting in the south at Hangchow, at the head of the inlet south of the Yangtze estuary, it crosses both that river and Hwang Ho, and finishes at Tientsin, which serves as the port for Peking.

The official estimate of the length of inland waterways is 150 000 km (93 000 miles), of which 40 000 km (nearly 25 000 miles) are navigable by steamers.

Railways and roads. Communication across the mountain ridges and the wide river basins, where the rivers are always prone to flood, has made communication by land extremely difficult. There was no railway between the Yangtze basin or Central China and Kwangchow in the south until 1936.

Owing to popular prejudice against the foreigner and all his ways, railways were a late arrival in China. The first, built to connect Shanghai with its outport, Woosung, was not opened till 1876 and was bought in the following year in order that it might be torn up. Its destruction was a last despairing effort. By 1956, China had 27 350 km (17 000 miles) of railway, including what were then known as the South Manchurian line to Dairen and the Chinese Eastern railway across northern Manchuria, the Chinese section of the original Russian-built Trans—Siberian railway. These two railways extend to nearly 3 550 km (2 200 miles) and another 3 860 km (2 400 miles) are covered by a continuous sequence of lines providing communication from south to north: from Kwangchow via Hankow and Peking, to Mukden, the old Manchurian capital. There are very many new lines being planned or built, especially to the west and to the new industrial areas such as the oil centres of Lanchow, Karamai and Urumchi. Some remarkable bridges have been engineered across rivers, the mighty rail and road bridge across the Yangtze at Wuhan (a conurbation incorporating the old cities of Hankow, Wuchang and Hanyang) being especially important. China is hastening to make up for lost time: in 1947 the railway system was only a fourth of that of India at the close of the British raj; by 1957 it was half of that of India. The locomotives are coal burning.

The government of the People's Republic at first concentrated on the expansion and improvement of the railway system rather than on roads. There are probably now some 35 000 km (21 700 miles) of railway. There are officially estimated to be about 300 000 km (186 400 miles) of mainly all-weather roads and 500 000 km (310 700 miles) of secondary roads (1969); in the same year there were only 409 000 lorries, 600 000 cars and 30 000 buses. In 1959 railways carried 58.5 per cent of total freight, roads 16.7 per cent and waterways 25 per cent.

Air transport. The main cities are linked by air routes and new routes are being added. Airlines other than those from countries with a centrally controlled economy operate services in China; and the Chinese international airline has flights to a growing number of countries.

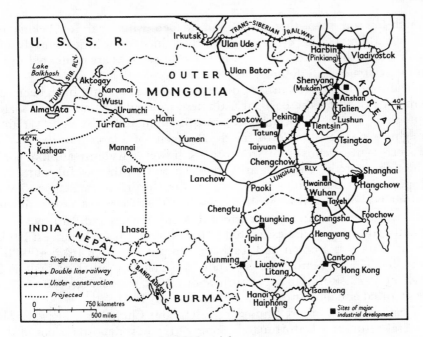

China: main railways and chief industrial areas

Minerals. Mineral wealth, though large, had been little exploited before the present regime. Coalfields are found in most of the provinces, and much of the coal is excellent; production in the war year 1944 reached 26m. tons, but in 1970 it was estimated at 400m. tons, the bulk coming from modern mines. The main fields straddle Shansi and Shensi provinces, the southern half of which, on the loess plateau (600 to 900 m: 2 000 to 3 000 ft above sea level), has enormous deposits both of anthracite and of bituminous coal. Southeast Shansi forms one of the most remarkable mineral regions in the world. The anthracite extends over an area of about 35 000 sq km (13 500 sq miles), but true anthracite occurs chiefly in two groups, and most of the deposit is only half-anthracite with from 87 to 89 per cent of carbon and much ash. While the average aggregate thickness of the coal seams is at least 12 m (40 ft), almost everywhere is to be seen a seam of from 4.5 to 6 m (15 to 20 ft), and often one of from 6 to 9 m (20 to 30 ft) in thickness. So frequently does the productive part of the coalfield crop out on the surface that along one line, about 320 km (200 miles) in length, an opening might be made direct into a seam of great thickness almost anywhere. The stratification seems to be undisturbed, and in many places it is nearly horizontal. Where the seam of from 6 to 9 m (20 to 30 ft) in thickness crops out, with an easterly slope only just sufficient for drainage, level adits could be tunnelled far to the west; so that once a railway had been constructed to the surface of the plateau the wagons

641

could be run into the mines and loaded with coal for Peking or Shanghai direct. This great coalfield rivals in size the vast Pennsylvania coalfield in the United States. China's coal reserves are estimated to lie in the region of 263 000m. tons.

The iron ores of Shansi are of very good quality, and have been for hundreds of years the basis of a Chinese iron industry on a small scale; but their mode of occurrence, mostly in nodules of very variable weight, is not favourable to the development of a large industry of the modern type. Deposits of iron ore are however widespread, like coal. The richest are at Tayeh, near Wuhan. There are other useful sources in Hopei and in Shantung, as well as in the Northeastern Region. Total output was estimated to be 46m. tons in 1969. There are large iron and steel works at Anshan (Northeastern Region), Wuhan and Paotow.

Crude oil reserves are estimated to be 5 000m. tons. The largest fields are at Karamai, Yumen and Taching. Output has risen from 400 000 tons in 1954 to 50m. tons of crude oil (including oil from shale and coal) in 1973. Refining capacity is about 40m. tons a year. Natural gas is exploited and amounted to 1 000m. cu m in 1967.

Coal, iron and oil are important assets, but China has other valuable mineral resources. Unfortunately some of the best deposits occur in the inaccessible southwest. In Yunnan, which has some of the richest tin deposits in the world, copper, tin and antimony have long been mined. Copper is fairly widespread, but the ore is not of high quality; west Szechwan seems likely to provide most in the future. China leads the world in the production of the ores of the metal tungsten (wolfram and wolframite). As with the ore antimony they occur particularly in the eastern part of the Nanling range, in Hunan. China is fortunate too in her bauxite resources, in Yunnan, Shantung, Liaonong and Kansu. There are also small reserves of a wide variety of non-ferrous minerals: zinc, lead, molybdenum, mercury, bismuth, and a very little gold.

Agriculture. Mainland China is credited with a total area of 956.1m. ha (nearly 2 362m. acres) of which 110.3m. ha (272.5m. acres) or 11.5 per cent is classed as arable land; 177m. ha (437m. acres), 18.5 per cent, as pastoral; 17.6m. ha (43.5m. acres), 8 per cent, as forested; and 592.2m. ha (1 462.7m. acres), 62 per cent, as built on or waste.

The two outstanding crops are wheat and rice. The respective areas cultivated are not available for recent years, but in the period 1961–65 the average for wheat was 25m. ha (62m. acres). The wheat output for 1970 was 30m. tons, China lying third in world output, to the USSR and the United States. The average area of padi in the years 1961–65 was 30m. ha (74m. acres) and production, 83.2m. tons, was at that time two and a half times the output of wheat. The production of rice in 1971 was 104m. tons, China being the chief world-producer.

Other food crops, even when grown on a less extensive or less productive scale, are in some cases among the leading sources of world supply of their respective products. Sweet potatoes in China yield over half the world supply. More than half the world's maize is grown in the United States, but China, though far behind, ranks second among producing countries. Before the Second World War China produced 80 per cent (9 to 10m. tons) of the world supply of soybeans, and though the United States was the largest producer in 1970 (30.9m. tons, 66.5 per cent of the world total), China was second with 11.5m. tons, nearly 25 per cent of the world's output. Some 13 per cent (2.4m. tons, unshelled weight) of the world supply of groundnuts also comes from China, a proportion exceeded only by India. Cotton is another important crop, grown on 5m. ha (12.3m. acres) yielding over 3m. tons of cottonseed and half that weight of cotton lint. The production of sugarcane in 1970 was estimated to be 29.5m. tons, and of sugar beet over 5m. tons. The tobacco crop, grown on 670 000 ha (1.65m. acres) was 811 000 tons in 1971, the largest in the world.

The livestock estimates enforce the impression of the vast size of the country. In 1970 horses numbered 7.3m., mules 1.6m., asses 11.6m., cattle 63.1m., pigs 220m. (out of a world total of 626.6m.), sheep 70.6m., goats 57m., buffaloes 29.3m., camels 16 000; and poultry 1 160m. Most of the cultivated land in the country is occupied by the three chief food grains: rice in the south where the yield is high; a mixture of rice and wheat in central China; a complete absence of rice in the north, where the food grains are wheat and millet, the latter tending to become the dominant grain where the rainfall is less than 1 000 mm (40 in) a year. There is not yet complete mechanisation of farming in China and much farm work is still undertaken manually or with the aid of small machines. The number of tractors in 1965 was estimated to be 100 000; in 1972 there were 23m.

In the south a very wide range of fruit and vegetables is cultivated, including groundnuts and citrus fruits; sugarcane flourishes and this is a silk-producing area. A quantity of short-staple cotton is grown in central China, particularly in the river basins, with heavy crops in the lower reaches of the Yangtze and the Hwang Ho. A great variety of vegetables is grown here too, and mulberry trees provide leaves to feed the silkworms. Sericulture is still a cottage industry. Ramie, a perennial plant cultivated in the Yangtze basin, provides the Chinese with an important fibre. Retted in the same way as flax, the silky fibres are woven to make the famous grass cloth, which is very strong, cool and comfortable to wear. It is generally made into table linen for export. Tobacco is grown in Honan, Anhwei, Shantung, Szechwan, Yunnan and Kweichow. The tea for which China was once famous, and which many years ago constituted the chief export, is grown particularly on the hills of the south and west. The growing of soybeans is widespread; maize, peas and beans are particularly sown in the north.

Among animals pigs are the most important and numerous. Nearly every farmer has at least one sow, and pork is the only meat consumed in any quantity in the country. Bristles, once a very valuable by-product, now have to compete with synthetic fibres, but they still form a useful export.

Neither beef nor mutton is popular in China and is very rarely eaten. Cattle are used as draught animals: oxen in the dry fields of the north and south, water buffalo in the wet padi fields. Milk is increasing in popularity, but yields are naturally low from draught cows. Sheep are reared on the highlands, particularly in the northwest, for their wool. In the drier north horses and mules are used as pack animals.

Poultry are abundant everywhere, chicken being second in popularity only to pork on the menu. Before the Second World War frozen and dried eggs were exported even as far as the United Kingdom. Ducks also form a favourite food and are reared especially in the wetter areas.

The primary aim of the government of Mao Tse-tung is to raise agricultural production. This is to be achieved by increasing the area of agricultural land, by land reclamation, by irrigation and by flood control as well as by afforestation, particularly in the northwest, where shelter belts have been planted to prevent soil erosion. The soil is to be improved by the increased use of fertilisers; improved seeds are to be sown; new farming techniques followed (such as deep ploughing and close planting); pesticides and fungicides are to be used; old simple tools are to be adapted and improved, new simple mechanical aids developed as well as farm machinery and tractors: the Green Revolution is to be achieved by 'walking on two legs', which should not be taken literally: it means that the expert and the amateur, the big and the small can mutually help each other and advance together.

The secondary aim is to disperse industry throughout China so that even the most rural areas have some industrial development: agriculture and industry too are to 'walk on two legs'.

Sixty-three per cent of the working population are engaged in agriculture; but despite their efforts the output of grain is insufficient to meet the needs of China's vast population and wheat is imported from Canada and Australia.

Forest reserves have been decimated for centuries, the timber being needed particularly for fuel. They are now being carefully husbanded and managed and there is some afforestation. The main forest areas lie in Szechwan and Yunnan in the southwest and Heilungkiang in the Northeastern Region. The most important tree is the tung, which supplied 95 000 tons of oil in 1970, mainly in Szechwan. Teak is the most valuable tree for timber.

Fisheries. The Chinese who live near water are great fishermen. The rivers and the seas washing the shores of China abound in fish. There are as yet few mechanised trawlers: most sea fishing is still conducted from the picturesque sailing junks. The Chinese have long tended fish-ponds in their villages, but fish farming is now being carried on in the south on a commercial scale.

Industry. The instability of the government in China in the nineteenth century, and several small wars, gave the western powers the oppor-tunity they had long awaited. They were able to establish footholds for trading in the treaty ports which were developed at accessible sites along the coast, where good lines of communication existed or could be easily provided. Foreign capital began to flow in and in its wake came railways, mines and industries. By the end of the nineteenth century the treaty ports were flourishing commercial centres, with Shanghai, the centre of the textile trade, pre-eminent. Impetus was given to the expansion of cotton and silk production in the Yangtze delta. Factories under foreign control were built in the treaty ports themselves and between the two world wars Shanghai became the most important manufacturing town in China, with big textile mills.

The Japanese were not slow to seize their opportunities either. When Manchuria was under their control they built up the iron and steel plant at Anshan; by 1937 South Manchuria was producing two-thirds of the iron, nine-tenths of the steel and half the coal output of the whole of China. The Japanese also dammed the rivers for the generation of electric power.

The first large scale iron and steel smelting plant to be built by the Chinese was that at Hanyang, where the River Han joins the Yangtze. It used iron ore from Tayeh and coking coal from Hunan, and came into production in the late nineteenth century. Other heavy industry was established but it was all on a very small scale.

Generally speaking this industrial development was insignificant in comparison with the size of the country, and there was no great pool of skilled industrial workers when the Communists gained control. China lacked capital too, so it was impossible for her to import industrial plant, although a certain amount of help was forthcoming from the USSR. China has had therefore to rely on agricultural production to pay for new industry. The old small family farms, often fragmented, had by 1958 given way to large communes organised on lines similar to the collectives of the USSR. Each farmer owns his own family house with a small plot of land for private use (these small plots are estimated to total between 4 and 5 per cent of the cultivated area); labour is pooled and the distribution of the wealth earned by the commune by the sale of produce is based on the amount of work accomplished by the individual. There are also state farms which teach new farming techniques and serve as models for the neighbouring communes.

This new farming system has radically affected the landscape. The old pattern was a mosaic of tiny fields, separated by dykes and ditches, hedges, and winding paths trodden by the farmer as he trudged from one small irregularly shaped field to another. His fields were often widely scattered because of the fragmentation of his holding. All this, and the hallowed graves of the ancestors with their shading trees has been swept away in the north, to be replaced by huge stretches of flattened land sown with one crop, to be worked by machine. The structure of the land has on the whole prevented similar development in the south: hilly land, terraced for padi cultivation, is unsuitable for large scale mechanisation; and the graves are left undisturbed on the rocky hillocks. Land has been reclaimed wherever possible, little fertiliser plants, mostly producing ammonium sulphate, have been widely built in association with the communes. The largest is at Kirin and there are other major works at Kwangchow, Nanking and Talien (Darien). Small local workshops produce improved agricultural implements, again alongside the communes; and they are thus able to service and repair the larger agricultural machinery. There has not been so far a concentration on the output of large agricultural machinery to the same extent as there was in the USSR.

Cotton is an important industrial crop; sugarcane from the south and sugar beet from the Sungari plain are processed at Kianmen, near Kwangchow. Oilseed production is rising and state farms are experimenting with the cultivation of tropical industrial crops, such as rubber, copra, palm oil, as well as cocoa, coffee and quinine.

The present government is aiming at the expansion, dispersal and relocation of industry over the whole country; industry is to be developed at the site of raw materials. Textile mills, for example, will no longer be concentrated in the coastal cities as formerly but will be developed in the cotton-growing areas. The 'five small industries' (iron and steel, machinery manufacture, chemicals including fertilisers and insecticides, cement manufacture) are being set up at scattered locations throughout China so that even quite small areas will be self-sufficient; and light industry is to be built up even in the most rural areas to meet local needs.

There are still the great industrial concentrations. In north China there are big iron and steel works at Taiyan in Shensi; and at Paotow near the Hwang Ho an industrial centre which has expanded rapidly since 1951. Coking coal is imported from Shansi, and the factories produce rolling stock for the railways, heavy machinery (especially textile machinery), building materials and processed food. The vast steel works were built under Soviet supervision. At Yentai City, Shantung, a new small iron and steel works has been established.

South Manchuria remains pre-eminently the industrial region of China. The former capital Changchun, is now a modern industrial town with works producing motor vehicles.

The Northwest Region is being developed for its mineral wealth, especially oil. On the Yangtze the old Hanyang iron and steel works have grown, and Wuhan is another big industrial centre. Plant in Shanghai now produces steel as well as textiles.

Industrial production as a whole in 1971 was estimated to be 10 per cent higher than in 1970 (Chinese official sources).

Foreign trade. It is extremely difficult to obtain details of foreign trade. Exports include foodstuffs, especially rice, raw materials such as minerals, textiles (cotton and silk), light metal goods, ceramics and handicrafts. Imports in the main are nearly all raw materials needed for industry (chemicals, fertilisers, rubber, metals, cotton), machinery and transport equipment, as well as food grains and some manufactured goods. There used to be much trading with the Soviet Union, but when relations between the two countries became strained it declined. It may revive, because a Sino—Soviet trade agreement was signed in November 1970. In June 1970 the United States raised its twenty-year embargo on trade with mainland China. Most foreign trade of the People's Republic of China is now carried on with Japan, followed by Hong Kong, West Germany and the United Kingdom. The rest of China's trade is with nations with a centrally controlled economy and with those states to which she is granting aid. Much of the trade with non-Communist countries passes through the great entrepôt port, Hong Kong. It has been estimated by foreign experts that the value of exports in 1970 was US $2 072m., and of imports US $2 127m.

Table 71 — China: conurbations and towns with a population exceeding 1m.
(estimates)

Shanghai	10m.	(1970)
Peking	7m.	(1970)
Tientsin	4m.	(1970)
Shenyang (Mukden)	4m.	(1965)
Lushun-Talien (Lü-ta)	3.6m.	(1965)
Wuhan	2.1m.	(1957)
Chungking	2.1m.	(1957)
Kwangchow (Canton)	1.8m.	(1957)
Changchun	1.8m.	(1965)
Harbin	1.6m.	(1965)
Sian	1.5m.	(1965)
Nanking	1.4m.	(1957)
Tsingtao	1.1m.	(1957)
Chengtu	1.1m.	(1957)
Taiyan	1.02m.	(1957)
Fushun	1.0m.	(1965)

There are probably about twenty other towns with a population exceeding 500 000

Macao

The territory of Macao, lying to the south of the delta of the Si Kiang, came into the possession of the Portuguese in 1557 and is indisputably the oldest European colony in the Far East. Although officially recognised as Portuguese by the Chinese in 1887 its boundaries have not yet been agreed. Including two small adjacent islands the province is estimated to cover 16 sq km (6 sq miles) and is said to support the incredibly large population of some 265 000, about 97 per cent of whom are Chinese, many from Communist China. It includes a port which attracts a good deal of small shipping.

Tolerated by the Chinese government, it has something of the reputation of an eastern Monaco, practising a few manufactures, principally firecrackers and matches, and having a considerable fishing industry. It has a pronounced imbalance in its external trade: the value of imports is estimated usually to be about three times that of exports. The trade, mostly transit, is in the hands of the Chinese.

Taiwan

Taiwan, to use the Chinese name for the island where the former government of China the Nationalist Government, still asserts its claim to that title and maintains an administration with United States support, lies athwart the Tropic of Cancer about 160 km (100 miles) from the mainland. It is 400 km (nearly 250 miles) long, with an average width of about one-quarter of that distance, and has an area of close on 36 000 sq km (14 000 sq miles), or about twice the size of Wales. Through its length runs a magnificent mountain range, with richly wooded slopes and peaks rising to nearly 4 000 m (13 000 ft). On the east side of the island the coastal belt is narrow and the coast rockbound, but on the west the lowlands are wider and are bordered by mudbanks, fed and extended by the silt brought down by the rivers in flood. The highlands and the east of the island are the home of people with Malayan affinities; the western lowlands have long been settled by Chinese, Taiwan having been a possession of China since 1683 except for the half-century 1895–1945, when it was held by Japan. At a census in 1957 the population was returned as 9.4m., including some 300 000 of the forces which had remained faithful to the Nationalist Government when it took refuge in Formosa. The population was estimated to total 14.68m. in January 1971.

About 64 per cent of the country is classed as forest and woodland, and 11 per cent as built on or waste. Practically the whole of the remaining 24 per cent, comprising over 867 000 ha (nearly 2.2m. acres), ranks as arable land, only 2 000 ha (5 000 acres) being occupied with permanent meadows and pastures. The arable land is extremely fertile, so much so that Taiwan used to be described, with an exaggeration which at any rate stressed its fruitfulness, as 'the granary of China'.

The main lowland area which stretches the length of the island west of the mountains provides two crops of rice a year, sweet potatoes, groundnuts and soybeans. The areas assigned to individual products in the *Yearbook* of the United Nations Food and Agriculture Organisation are thus in the aggregate, one and three-quarter times as large as all the arable land (867 000 ha: 2.2m. acres) on the island. In 1970, 3.2m. tons of rice were reaped from over 826 000 ha (2m. acres), and 3.7m. tons of sweet potatoes from 233 000 ha (575 000 acres); 95 000 ha (235 000 acres) of sugarcane produced nearly 7m. tons. Other crops include groundnuts, tea (mainly in the extreme northwest), bananas, pineapples and other tropical fruits, wheat, jute and tobacco. Cotton is cultivated experimentally, but yields are not high and raw cotton is still imported. Yields of all crops are rising as improved farming techniques and fertilisers are employed.

Livestock in 1970 included 3m. pigs, 212 000 buffaloes and 169 000 goats; as might be surmised from the small proportion of pasture, cattle and sheep are relatively few.

The timber of the natural forests which clothe the eastern half of the island was badly despoiled during the Second World War. Reafforestation has restored this resource and camphor is once again an important forest product.

Taiwan has useful mineral resources: coal in the extreme northeast (with a production of about 5m. tons a year); oil deposits in the northwest and in the west lowland area near the Tropic, and reserves of natural gas. The main oil refinery is at Kaohsiung on the west coast, a town which also supports metallurgical industry. There are small deposits of gold, silver and copper. Hydroelectric power has been developed; and a nuclear power station should be in use by 1975.

A railway encircles the island, and private lines serve the sugar estates; roads are most developed on the west and on the north of the mountains. In the north Chilung is the port of the capital, Taipei. The main airport at Sungshan is served mainly by local airlines.

Occupations include mining and the manufacture of building materials (especially cement), textile production, sugar refining, smelting, and machine assembly, but 47 per cent of the population were engaged in agriculture in 1965. The density of her population prevents Taiwan from being selfsufficient: imports of raw materials (such as iron and steel and cotton) and manufactured goods (including transport equipment) are paid for by the exports of foodstuffs, textiles and an increasing export of manufactures such as transport equipment and electrical machinery. Most trade is carried on with the United States, followed by Japan, the Republic of Vietnam, Hong Kong and West Germany.

The capital Taipei, was estimated in 1969 to have a population of 1.6m.; Kaohsuing had 720 000; Tainan 442 000; Taichung 407 000 and Chilung (Keelung) 305 000.

Mongolia

The Mongolian People's Republic comprises a vast territory lying between the USSR and the northwest of China which between 1691 and 1911 as 'Outer Mongolia' formed a Chinese province. Now, as a People's Republic, it has close links with the Soviet Union, and is a member of Comecon. 'Inner Mongolia' to the south is an autonomous state within the People's Republic of China.

The Mongolian People's Republic covers over 1.5m. sq km (nearly 605 000 sq miles) but the population numbers only 1.2m. (1970). It stretches in the southeast over the inhospitable high plateaus of the Gobi desert where rainfall is almost non-existent and differences between summer and winter temperatures are extreme. In the north mountain ranges are separated by comparatively well watered valleys and grass plains. There are gold deposits; wolfram and fluorspar which are exported to the USSR; good coal reserves near Ulaanbaatar (Ulan Bator) and Darhan which provide thermal electric power; and there is oil at Dzüünbayan in the eastern Gobi desert, not as yet fully exploited.

The Mongolian nomadic pastoralists, traditionally superb horsemen, herd their great numbers of horses, cattle, sheep, goats and camels in the north, away from the Gobi, as they have done for centuries. Collective and state farms have been established, as well as stock-breeding stations, but on the whole they have made no great difference to pastoral life. Hay is, however, being produced in the northwest. The present government is encouraging its people to settle, to become agriculturalists and industrialists, and in this it has received considerable aid from the Soviet Union, particularly in the establishment of industry and the building of railways. Factories have been set up concerned with meat canning, the making of woollen textiles and felts, leatherwork, and wood manufactures. Most are grouped in the capital, Ulaanbaatar (254 000 in 1969), an ancient centre of caravan routes, which is now linked by rail to the USSR Trans—Siberian railway to the north and to the Chinese railway system in the southeast. It is a city of great contrasts with fine modern buildings in happy juxtaposition with the simple *ger* (the traditional tent of the country, known as *yurt* in other parts of Asia). There are now hard surface roads around Ulaanbaatar and a concrete road which runs for 80 km (50 miles) towards the Soviet border. Otherwise trucks manage very well by driving at will over the country. Darhan and Choybalsan are also becoming industrial cities, with establishments producing shoes and woollen textile, and processing sheep- and goatskins.

650

Live cattle and horses, wool and hair, meat, grain, hides and skins, furs, non-ferrous and precious metals as well as butter are exported, nearly all to the Soviet Union. Imports are manufactured goods, machinery and raw materials for industry. Most trade is with the USSR; there is a little with Switzerland and Japan.

North and South Korea

Korea (the Japanese *Chosen*) occupies a long and comparatively narrow peninsula (roughly 800 to 970 km: 500 to 600 miles by 240 km: 150 miles), stretching out from mainland China (Manchuria) towards the extreme southwestern end of Japan and almost shutting off the Sea of Japan from the Yellow Sea. Under the loose suzerainty of China for centuries, though having its own sovereign, Korea became a dependency of Japan early in the present century. After the Second World War it was occupied temporarily by Allied Forces pending arrangements for establishing its independence, the northern half of the country being in Soviet occupation and the southern in American occupation, with the 38th parallel as the dividing line. Failing agreement between the Allies on the prospective arrangements, two republics, North and South, were established and the foreign troops were withdrawn. The area of democratic South Korea is about 98 000 sq km (38 000 sq miles), capital Seoul, population (1970) 31.46m. The area of Communist North Korea is about 121 000 sq km (47 000 sq miles), capital Pyongyang, population (1970) 13.9m. In 1950 South Korea was invaded by the Northern Forces; the United Nations espoused the cause of South Korea, and there was active warfare till an armistice was arranged in 1953. In 1972 the two republics began discussing 'peaceful unification'.

A thickly wooded mountain range forms the backbone of the country, bordering for the most part the east coast, but finally swinging round into the southwest corner of the peninsula. In the north, extensive fields of lava, one as much as 65 km (40 miles) long and 30 to 43 m (100 to 140 ft) thick, are evidence of ancient volcanic activity; and on the northern frontier the range reaches its greatest height in a peak of 2 600 m (8 500 ft). The east coast is rocky, with few harbours, and rivers are short and rapid; but on the western side of the peninsula the mountains drop to a fairly wide coastal plain, through which the principal rivers, many navigable for considerable distances, wind their way to the sea, here lined with mudflats and fringed with numerous islands, icebound in winter and subject at other times to very high tides, which rise as much as 12 m (40 ft). There are many ice-free natural harbours.

The climate is on the whole similar to that of north China; it may be termed a temperate monsoon climate. Practically the whole country has one month with temperatures below freezing, the area near the

Manchurian border having five; and the east coast has considerable winter snow. Most rain falls in the hot summer, but a short season of April rain in the south is useful for irrigation in the padi fields.

The natural vegetation of 70 per cent of Korea would be forest, conifers mixed with deciduous trees such as oak and walnut in the south, birch in the north, with willows and bamboo in the valleys. Much of the forest cover has however been removed, although re-afforestation is now being carried out.

On the narrow coastal strip running two-thirds of the way down the east coast from the north the main grain crop is millet, and rice wherever possible. The main occupation of the people living in this area is fishing. In the southeast region millet gives way to rice and barley, with some millet and wheat; in the southwest, the most fertile area of the whole peninsula, rice and barley predominate. This southern half of the peninsula is fortunate in being able to support two grain crops annually. As soon as the rice is harvested in October the fields are ploughed for the second grain: mostly barley, but sometimes limited areas of wheat. The severity of the winter climate of the northwest prevents the extension of this admirable procedure: this is the wheat area, with millet and soybeans, and a smaller quantity of rice. Where climatic conditions permit in Korea as a whole, maize, potatoes, tobacco, ginseng (a medical plant), cotton, a variety of vegetables, and fruit such as apples, pears, strawberries and peaches are cultivated. Sericulture is an activity of the south, particularly the southeast.

The whole peninsula is rich in wild life, especially birds; and the seas yield a variety of fish, as well as molluscs, lobsters, and shrimps.

North Korea has the advantages of the mineral wealth of the peninsula: coal in the northeast and in the west of the state (production about 27.5m. tons annually); iron ore in the west (annual production about 7.4m. tons), some fortunately placed in juxtaposition with the coal near Pyongyang, which is not only the capital but a notable metallurgical centre. Other minerals occurring in North Korea include lead, zinc, tungsten ores, nickel, manganese, graphite, gold and copper (the last two in small quantities). Oil wells came into production in 1957. The Japanese were quick to see the hydroelectric power potential when they were in occupation, and North Korea has now some 85 per cent of the total hydroelectric power output of the peninsula.

South Korea is not so fortunate in mineral assets. It has been calculated that there are reserves of hard coal totalling 1 479m. tons of which some 514m. tons could be profitably mined (output at present is about 12.4m. tons, of which 70 per cent is burnt in households); the output of iron ore is about 700 000 tons; but South Korea has one of the largest deposits of the ores of tungsten in the world at Sandong, as well as small reserves of lead, zinc, silver, gold and copper. Prospecting for oil and natural gas on the continental shelf under the Yellow Sea is in progress and there seems good hope that it may prove fruitful. South Korea imports all the vast amount of oil now used in the country, so the success of this search is of vital importance to her.

In North Korea only 20 per cent of the land is suitable for agriculture, the remainder being too mountainous, but over two-thirds of the population are engaged in farming. The cultivable area has been considerably increased in recent years by irrigation, and much attention is paid to soil conservation. Under the Communist government farming has been organised on a collective basis, and highly mechanised, with the use of large-scale machinery. State farms specialise in the rearing of livestock. The fishing fleet has been modernised and motor vessels as well as sailing craft are now in operation; it is reported that factory and refrigerator ships are being developed, and cold storage facilities ashore being extended.

North Korea is developing industrially, with an emphasis on heavy industry. A modern iron and steel plant is in operation at Kimchaek; the chemical industry (inaugurated by the Japanese) is producing quantities of fertilisers for the collective farms. Other industries founded by the Japanese continue to prosper, such as cotton spinning and textile manufacture (using cotton, silk and rayon fibres). Hamheung, Chungjin, Kanggye and Kusong are the main textile towns, and their mills are being extended. Cement is also produced in great quantity; and oil refined.

The railways were disrupted as a result of the severance of the peninsula into two states. There has been some restoration of lines within North Korea, of which 30 per cent are now electrified. North Korea has ample supplies of electricity provided by the hydroelectric power schemes developed by the Japanese and since enlarged. An international railway line running from Moscow–Pyongyang–Peking crosses the Yalu bridge to link up with Chinese railways. In view of the inadequate rail system roads are important in North Korea, but very few are metalled, and the others have poor surfaces. The main towns, Pyongyan, Hamhung and Chongjin are connected by air; and there are international air routes to Peking and Moscow.

North Korea has good ports, especially on the east coast. Nampo is the port of the capital, Pyongyang, to which it is connected by rail. Trade is carried on mostly with Communist countries, but there is some with the United Kingdom.

In South Korea only 4.6m. people are wholly engaged in agriculture, and there is a steady drift of rural population to the towns. The south and west of the state are extremely densely populated, Seoul, the capital, with over 5.5m. people and Pusan with nearly 1.9m. The population has been swollen by an influx of people from North Korea and by about 2m. Koreans repatriated from the former Japanese empire. It is a land of tiny farms, and the country was devastated in the war with North Korea. Agriculture has received a considerable amount of international aid, and the government is trying to increase farm production with a diminishing labour force. There are schemes for better irrigation systems, electrification of rural areas, increased use of fertilisers and pesticides, and the use of improved strains of seed, such as the high-yielding IR-667 strain of rice. Encouragement is being given to sericulture and livestock rearing, the latter having been almost discontinued until recently. On the whole the state of agriculture in South Korea at present is not a happy one; it is supported by financial help from the United Nations, the Colombo Plan, Food and Agriculture Organisation, the World Bank as well as from the United States, and yet quantities of foodstuffs, particularly grain, are imported. The fish catch is fortunately usually good: it was over 862 000 tons in 1969.

The emphasis in South Korea is on the development of the country as an industrial state. With the aid of the United States, in the form of raw materials, and capital amounting to some $4 000m. in the period 1963—70, many branches of manufacturing industry have been set up. They include the manufacture of textiles (based on synthetic fibres, cotton and woollen fibres), plastic products, paint, cement, plywood, paper and paper products (using Korean forestry resources), transport equipment; and motor vehicle assembly. The 1967—71 Five Year Plan aimed at the expansion of oil refineries, petrochemical works, iron and steel plant at Pohang on the east coast, and machinery manufacturing plant. South Korea suffered a severe setback when the power lines fed by hydroelectric power from the north were severed.

The railway system in South Korea is efficient, if overloaded; with international aid it has been brought up to date, with diesel locomotives outnumbering steam by over two to one. The road network has received even more attention and has been overhauled since 1960. It is used by trucks, buses and cars, totalling nearly 107 000 vehicles in 1969, of which about 14 237 were buses, 50 300 were cars, the rest trucks. Inchon and Seoul are now connected by a wide motorway, and an even wider motorway links Seoul and Pusan, a remarkable engineering feat. Other motorways are scheduled for the southwest to connect Taejon and Sonchon-ni, and Sonchon-ni with Pusan; in the east, others are planned to link Seoul to the airport at Kangnung; and Samchok to Sokcho. This programme is being financed by the World Bank.

South Korea has a small international airline with services to neighbouring Far East countries and plans to develop international air freight to Los Angeles via Tokyo and Honolulu.

Pusan and Inchon are considerable ports handling most of the trade of South Korea.

The efforts of South Korea to become an industrial nation are proving successful: in 1962 her exports were mineral products 28 per cent; manufactured goods 27 per cent; the produce of agriculture, forestry and fisheries 45 per cent. In 1969 comparable figures were 7.4 per cent, 79 per cent and 13.6 per cent: a remarkably rapid change. It must be remembered that this has been achieved largely with the help of overseas aid, especially from the United States. United States aid is about to be discontinued but South Korea hopes to maintain her industrial growth. Her major problem is that imports of raw materials for industry are very great: in 1969 the value of total imports was US $836.6m. (including 'aid'), while her total exports amounted only to US $622.5m.

A free export zone near the port of Masan on the south coast, in which Japanese industrialists are taking an interest, is being set up.

Most trading is carried on with the USA and Japan, on a much smaller scale with Taiwan, Hong Kong, West Germany, Malaysia, the Philippines; and on a much smaller scale with Australia and Canada and many European countries, as well as the Middle East.

Table 72 — Korea: population of chief towns

North Korea		
Pyongyang (capital)	1.5m.	(1970)
South Korea		
Seoul (capital)	5.5m.	(1970)
Pusan	1.88m.	(1970)
Taegu	845 000	(1966)

Japan

The island empire of Japan, 'the Land of the Rising Sun', which except for the extreme northeast corner of the Soviet Union is the most easterly country in Asia, has developed in a little over 100 years from an isolated, exclusive community, having few contacts with the western world or knowledge of its inventions, into one of the leading world powers. Breaking out from her seclusion and pursuing a policy of territorial expansion, embarking on a career of competitive industry and world trade, Japan was one of the victors in the First World War, had the reverse experience in the Second World War, was shorn of her extraneous possessions (Taiwan (Formosa), Korea, Manchuria, and various Trustee island groups in the Pacific), but was restored to the comity of nations in 1952 when peace treaties with the Western Powers became operative.

Reduced to her original island empire, Japan now comprises four principal islands strung along an arc, whose inner curve, facing Korea and the USSR, encloses the Sea of Japan, while the outer curve confronts the open Pacific Ocean; and thousands of tiny islands in the adjacent seas. Centrally situated along the arc, and forming nearly the whole of it, is the long and comparatively narrow island of Honshū, otherwise known as the mainland, which is as large as Great Britain (230 000 sq km: 89 000 sq miles) and more than half as large again as the other three islands together. To the north of it lies Hokkaidō (the old Yezo), about the size of Scotland (77 700 sq km: 30 000 sq miles); off its southwest coast, bordering and largely forming the famous Inland Sea of Japan, is the smallest of the four principal islands, Shikoku, about the size of Wales (over 18 000 sq km: 7 000 sq miles), and south of that again is Kyūshū, more than double the size of Wales (41 400 sq km: 16 000 sq miles). At the Strait of Shomoneseki the islands of Honshū and Kyūshū come close together; they have been linked by a railway tunnel since 1942 and in 1958 a road tunnel was opened which took twenty-two years to build and which runs undersea for nearly 800 m (0.5 mile). Two more tunnels connecting Honshū with the other islands are being built, both to carry rail traffic. The first, the longest in the world, will link Honshū and Hokkaidō under the Tsugaru Strait. The second will pass under the Kanmon Strait between Honshū and Kyūshū. Both should be completed by 1975.

The coasts of all the islands are much indented and have an estimated length of 16 000 km (10 000 miles), or including some of the larger of the adjacent small islands 27 400 km (17 000 miles). The total area of Japan is 369 662 sq km (142 726 sq miles) carrying at the 1970 census a population of over 103.7m., the estimate for 1972 being over 104.67m.

The whole group of islands is both mountainous and volcanic, containing upwards of fifty active, besides numerous extinct, volcanoes. The highest peak is the famous Fuji san (3 777 m: 12 390 ft) whose beautiful snowcapped cone is visible from Tokyo 97 km (60 miles) away. Like other highly volcanic regions Japan is much subject to earthquakes. The surface is extremely irregular and though the mountain passes are low relative to the height of many of the peaks the slopes are generally steep. During the rainy season the copious rains that deluge the mountain slopes cause frequent destructive floods in the numerous short rivers that descend both sides of the mountains, and make difficult the construction and maintenance of railways and roads.

Climate. Climatic conditions vary considerably, being affected by the latitudinal extent of the islands which are spread over some 15°, by their situation on the eastern side of a great land mass, and by their insular character and narrow width, fronting on the one hand the open Pacific with its warm currents and on the other the almost enclosed Sea of Japan, swept during the winter monsoon by northwest winds which beat on the flat and dangerous western coast and practically stop shipping.

The southeast winds of the summer monsoon, coming from the Pacific, drop their moisture on the mountainous uplands of Japan, which everywhere has a heavy rainfall, ranging from 1 000 mm (40 in) in the north to double that quantity in the south. There is much snow in winter, especially in the north and along the west coast; in Hokkaidō, the northernmost island, mean January temperatures are well below freezing point; southward they range up to 4.5° C (40° F) or a little more. In August the mean temperature range is from 21° C (70° F) in the north to nearly 30° C (80° F) in the south.

Agriculture. It is not surprising that in a land with these physical characteristics under 16 per cent of the whole is classed as arable country. Built on and waste areas account for nearly 13.5 per cent but the mountains are largely wooded and more than 69 per cent ranks as forest. There remains only about 2.5 per cent for open pastures; but the forests include a little over 1 per cent of 'wooded pastures' as they are called, so that about 4 per cent in all is suitable for grazing. Livestock are not a factor of prime importance in Japanese farming, though they are growing as Japan adopts western eating habits in the increased consumption of meat and milk. Cattle, the most numerous of the larger livestock, had increased from about 2m. in 1951 to 6m. in 1971; pigs, which were mostly killed off during the war, had multiplied from 513 000 to 6.9m. in 1970; sheep are now only 26 000 and goats are 160 000; horses (1971) number only 175 000.

Timber is worked on a large scale, production amounting to nearly 75m. cu m of felled timber in recent years; but agriculture plays the biggest part in rural economy. The arable land lies in many scattered areas, chiefly around the coasts. Tokyo, on the southeast coast of Honshū, lies in a fairly extensive plain, now greatly urbanised, but for the most part the tracts of low-lying land are narrow coastal belts, mostly divided into smallholdings, as also are the upland valleys, with their terraced hillsides. There are over 6m. agricultural holdings, most averaging 0.8 ha (2 acres), only 5 per cent covering over 4 ha (10 acres). These small units are intensively farmed, to produce high yields. Many operate on a cooperative basis for the sale of produce and the purchase of farm necessities. There are very many small hand controlled machines in use, especially suited to the tiny fields, and the land is intensively fertilised with home-produced and imported chemical fertilisers. Eighteen per cent of the working population in 1970 were engaged in agriculture, and of these 68 per cent were classified as being 'middle-aged and old persons', nearly 30 per cent being over the age of sixty, and very many being women. The young men are leaving the farms to work in industry, although very many work both at the factory bench and on the land at peak farming periods.

Rice is the chief grain crop, grown even as far north as Hokkaidō, where a crop is snatched from a quick-ripening variety of padi. So efficient are the methods of cultivation that Japan's rice yields are the highest in the world: nearly 14.2m. tons from 2.7m. ha (6.6m. acres) in 1971. Wheat (440 000 tons from 166 000 ha (410 000 acres)) and barley are frequently cultivated in winter in the south as second crops on the padi fields after the padi has been harvested. Wheat, barley, rye, sweet potatoes are crops of the upland farms where houses cling to the hillsides to leave the level areas of land free for cultivation. A variety of vegetables as well as apples, peaches, cherries, strawberries, small fruit and soybean are produced wherever possible. In the south tea occupies a decreasing area, while orange groves increase in importance. In 1971 production reached 3m. tons, rather more than half being Satsuma oranges, so-called after the district of that name in the extreme south of Japan; they are a loose-skinned variety akin to the mandarin orange, and were introduced many years ago into the United States, where they are now widespread in the Gulf States. Tea, prepared for export as green tea, is grown chiefly between 34° and 36° N latitude, that is, in the south of Honshū. The crop has increased from its average before the Second World War, production in 1971 being 930 000 tons from 54 000 ha (133 400 acres). Tobacco more than doubled, with a crop of 149 700 tons from 66 000 ha (163 000 acres).

Mulberry trees, grown for their leaves as silkworm feed, and planted in rows with other crops between, cover much less than their prewar acreage. Raw silk is no longer Japan's leading export, but production is usually half the world total. Japan's output in 1971 was 20 515 tons from nearly 112 000 tons of cocoons. The lacquer-tree (*Rhus vernicifera*, DC), which furnishes the material employed in lacquering, one of the most celebrated of old Japanese industries, is cultivated mainly in the northern part of Honshū, between 37° and 39° N. Camphor, extracted from the stem and roots of the camphor tree, which attains to a circumference of 15 m (50 ft), is another of the ingredients used in lacquering, and is also a minor export. The camphor tree is found mainly in the southwest of Japan.

The principal agricultural exports of Japan are now mandarin oranges, peaches and some raw silk, but together they represent less than 2 per cent of total exports.

A rise in standard of living is commonly accompanied by a change in diet, away from one predominantly based on cereals with a high carbohydrate intake to one with a greater variety of foodstuffs — fruits, vegetables and animal produce — containing a higher proportion of protein. Japan, since 1955, exemplifies this perfectly. Until recently Japan imported rice, but for the first time in her history she now has overproduction, and a surplus. This is in part due to the use of high-yielding strains and improved methods of cultivation, but it is also due to decreasing demand. There is instead an increasing consumption of high protein foods such as dairy produce, meat produces, and eggs, as well as sugar, vegetables, oils and fats, and fruit, with a consequent rising import of these commodities. Fish still plays an important part in Japanese diet. The changing food demands are affecting Japanese agriculture. Stock-rearing and dairy-farming are for the first time becoming significant; and fodder crops appear in imports, because the shortage of land rules out the extravagence of home-pasturage. Land is more productive under crops than under pasture for grazing cattle.

Fisheries. The fisheries of Japan are extremely valuable and important and provide the principal source of animal protein in the Japanese diet: Japanese consumption of fish per head of population is probably one of the highest in the world.

Fish abound in the shallow waters of the continental shelf near the coast, to make Japan one of the major fishing nations. The annual catch averages about 7m. tons, and some 612 000 Japanese are employed in the fishery industry. Coastal fishing is carried on as a small-scale enterprise by individuals; offshore fishing involves larger vessels of up to 100 tons; but the deep-sea fishing fleet is highly mechanised and organised, with mother ships processing and canning the catch at sea, and refrigerated transport vessels relieving the fishing boats of their catch to enable them to stay longer in the fishing areas. The deep-sea fleet operates far away from Japan not only in the Pacific but in the Indian Ocean, in the Atlantic off the coast of Brazil, in the South Atlantic; and in Antarctic waters for whale.

Inland waters also provide important sources of fish, and there are government measures to prevent their pollution. The Japanese have made great advances in fish farming and in the cultivation of edible seaweed as well as the raising of oysters for the cultured pearl industry.

Minerals. A wide variety of minerals occur, but they are small in quantity. There is coal in the sedimentary rocks, but it has been disturbed and is difficult to work. The principal fields are in Kyūshū (Moji and Nagasaki) and in Hokkaidō. Reserves are estimated to total about 20 800m. tons, but the coal is low grade and unsuitable for the production of high quality metallurgical coke.

Reserves of iron ore are very poor, only a little over 1m. tons being mined annually mainly from southwest Honshū; but copper resources are more cheering. The ores are widespread, high grade ore occurring at Ashio, central Honshū and the quantity mined annually (about 112 000 tons) supplies nearly a third of the industrial need. Of the other minerals required in Japanese industry lead, zinc, iron pyrites, sulphur, arsenic, bismuth, limestone, gypsum, barytes, silica stone, feldspar and dolomite occur in quantities almost sufficient to fulfil the demand. Oil occurs in two main areas, near Akita and near Niigata, but the resources are very slight and production is under 1 per cent of Japan's annual need. There is a small production of natural gas.

Japan thus lacked adequate home supplies of both coal and iron ore on which she could base her early industrial programme. Her military excursions into Manchuria and Korea were in part motivated by her need of iron ore.

Industry. The industrial revolution did not stir Japan until the end of the nineteenth century. She lacked the requisite raw materials for early industry but had the advantage of a large, industrious labour force. Her initial manufacturing industry was based on cotton and silk textiles. By the late 1930s good progress had been made, with an emphasis on light industry. The Japanese at this time had the reputation of being very quick to imitate the manufactured products of foreigners, which they were able to make at lower cost because of the plentiful supply of cheap labour, working in small workshops and factories; but these products were often not of the highest quality. After the Second World War the situation changed completely, the emphasis switching to heavy and chemical industries, based on imported coal, iron ore and oil. Before the Second World War iron ore had been imported from Japan's near neighbours. Now it comes from West Malaysia, India, Australia and North America. Since 1955 Japan's rise as an industrial power has accelerated at speed. Mass production techniques have been introduced although a number of small enterprises remain. Employers are paternalistic, operate comprehensive welfare schemes, and frequently provide housing for employees. Employees anticipate staying with the firm they enter for the whole of their working life, sacking is very rare indeed, there is outstanding team spirit and loyalty to the organisation; suggestions made from the shop floor are taken seriously by management, and there are few industrial disputes.

Spectacular progress has been made in the production of iron and steel, in heavy engineering (electrical and other machinery) and in shipbuilding. Japanese shipyards are the most up to date and productive in the world as befits an industrial nation dependent on seaborne trade. Yokohama, Nagoya, Kōbe, Hiroshima and Nagasaki are the main centres of heavy industry. Textiles are not as important as formerly, but fabrics based on cotton, rayon and silk continue to be made, with an increasing use of synthetic fibres. Osaka and Hiroshima are textile centres, drawing on female labour from the surrounding rural areas. Much more important to Japan's economy are the industries using relatively small quantities of raw materials but much technological skill, such as electrical equipment, computers, cameras, watches and clocks, television sets and precision instruments. Her manufactured products now are not only ingenious, they are of the highest quality. The output of the machine manufacturing industry increased twenty-five fold between 1950 and 1967 to take a growing share of the world's markets. By 1967 Japan was leading the world in the production of radio and television receivers, merchant ships and tankers; she was second in motor vehicles, kerosene and jet fuel, lubricating oils (the mineral oil figures exclude the USSR in their totals); third in cement, zinc, crude steel and pig iron; fourth in aluminium and refined copper; fifth in lead, cotton and wool yarns. Her production of lumber was third in the world in the same year (greater than that of Canada), but is insufficient for home needs of pulp and paper, quantities of which are imported.

In 1969 Japan's production of electric power was third in the world to the United States and the USSR. At the end of 1967 the ratio of methods of generation were: hydro − thermal − atomic: 40:60:0.4. It is estimated that schemes at present under construction should change these ratios to 28:65:7, and there will probably be even greater reliance on atomic power in the future. Only one atomic power plant is at present in use, at Tokai-mura. Oil is widely used in the thermal generating stations. Electricity charges in Japan are a little higher than those in North America, but much lower than those in most west European countries, and this plays a significant factor in her industrial costs.

Most of the industrial effort is concentrated on the belt of lowland stretching from Tokyo in the east to Nagasaki in the west, where the three great ports of Yokohama, Kōbe and Osaka as well as many smaller centres are ready to receive the imports of raw materials and the constant flow of exports.

Population. The population recorded in the census of 1965 was 98.3m., which gave an average density of nearly 266 per sq km (689 per sq mile), one of the highest in the world; but on the aggregate of the agricultural land (about 16 per cent of the total area) and the urbanised land (1 per cent), that is on the inhabited area, the density reached 1 600 per sq km (4 144 per sq mile). The total population in 1970 was 103 720 060m., the mean annual increase between 1965 and 1970 being about 1 per cent. It is officially estimate that only 31 per cent of the total land area can be regarded as habitable.

There is a constant flow of people from the rural areas to the big cities, especially to the industrial areas of Tokyo, Nagoya and Osaka−Kyoto−Kōbe. It is estimated that 40m. people are now concentrated in these major conurbations, which are spreading over the area most favourable for agriculture. The Tokyo area now houses over 11.4m. people, Osaka 2.9m., Kyoto 1.4m., Kōbe 1.3m. There are in all 135 urban centres with a population of over 100 000 squeezed into the limited areas of lowland.

So great is the pressure on land in the Tokyo area that Japan is looking towards the sea. A manmade island is being constructed in Tokyo Bay on land reclaimed near the coast at Kawasaki, Japan's second largest port, south of Tokyo. Its 4 140 000 sq m (1 020 acres) will be packed with resited factories, wharves and other port facilities, and it will be linked to the town of Kawasaki by undersea tunnels.

Communications. The main industrial belt, which stretches from Tokyo in the east to Nagasaki in the west and which may be compared with Megalopolis in the United States, is well served by an efficient rail network, as is the rest of Japan. It is much used and was a key factor in Japan's speedy industrialisation. The first railway was laid in Japan in 1872 to link Tokyo to its port, Yokohama, and construction continues today, the new tunnels already mentioned being especially important. Steam locomotives are being replaced by electric and diesel locomotives, and the fastest train in the world runs along the famous New Tokaido line which puts Tokyo within 3 hr 10 min of Osaka. The efficiency of the rail network, the shortage of land and the difficulty of terrain in mountainous areas discouraged the provision of a comparable road network; but the building of a system of highspeed highways (expressways) is in hand to cater for the 12m. motor vehicles of 1968 (twenty-eight times the number for 1950). The expressway connecting

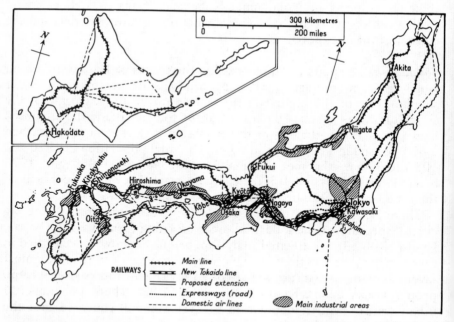

Japan: main industrial areas and communications

The plan for the construction of a super-express nationwide railway network envisages lines linking all the major cities by 1985, with trains running at 250 km per hour, and 90 per cent of the estimated population living within an hour's journey of the nearest super-express station. A suspension bridge linking Shimonoseki (Honshu to Moji (Kyushu) should be open to vehicles in 1975

Tokyo, Nagoya and Osaka is already open, and is being extended westwards.

Ferries, both long and short distance, carry passengers, cars, buses, and roll-on, roll-off cargo trucks between the islands, and in June 1970 the first international ferry route was opened for commercial service, linking Shimonoseki with Pusan, in Korea. Pusan has already been linked to Korea's capital, Seoul, by motorway, built with Japanese cooperation; and when the new motorway running through western Honshū is completed it will be possible to travel from the industrial region of Tokyo to Seoul in less than a day: an important fast route between Japan and continental Asia along which trade and tourists will surely flow.

The chief ports of Japan all serve the main industrial belt: Yokohama and Kawasaki handle the trade of the Tokyo area, while the other major ports are Nagoya, Osaka and Kōbe, which has excellent deep-water facilities. Japan has been quick to appreciate the advantages of container ships. She now has vessels of over 51 000 gross tons, holding 1 836 containers, on the Japan–Europe route, capable of making the round trip in sixty days.

The major cities of Japan are linked by air and an efficient international airline, Japan Airlines (JAL), caters for passengers and freight. There are already two international airports in the country, at Tokyo and Osaka, and work has begun on a third about 60 km (38 miles) east of Tokyo, at Narita. It will be linked by super-express railway and motorway to Tokyo.

Trade. Great changes have taken place in the foreign trade of Japan since the Second World War. Raw materials for industry and foodstuffs remain the principal imports, but petroleum and metal ores are now the dominant items, raw cotton and wool having receded to insignificance. The raw cotton comes from the United States and Mexico, raw wool from Australia. Crude oil is imported from Iran and Kuwait, coal largely from Australia and the United States, some from South Africa. The iron ore arrives from India, Malaysia and Chile, steel scrap from the United States, non-ferrous metals from Canada and the Philippines. Hides and soybeans are imported from the United States, rubber from Malaysia, lumber from Malaysia and the Philippines. Wheat is supplied by the United States and Canada, sugar by Australia. The United States, West Germany and the United Kingdom supply electrical machinery, business machines (including computers) and aircraft.

Exports illustrate the marked shift in the Japanese economy from light industry in the years prior to the Second World War to the present emphasis on the products of the heavy and chemical industries. Machinery now leads as the main export item, followed by iron and steel plates, bars, rods, etc., ships and transport equipment, and manufactures of all types and materials. Textiles make a declining contribution to the total; they are, with clothing, in the main destined for southeast Asia, the United States and Africa. Japanese machinery of all types has a world-wide distribution, much going to the United States; merchant ships are built for Liberia, Norway, the USSR and the United Kingdom. Metal products are bought by the United States and the Chinese People's Republic; while most of the processed food is destined for Europe and the United States.

As a major industrial nation Japan has a strong interest in the removal of tariff barriers. Her bounding prosperity following her economic recovery after the Second World War and her position in the Asia–Pacific region give her a leading role to play in the development of economic cooperation between the nations of the area. Undoubtedly her trade links with Australia and Malaysia particularly, as suppliers of raw materials for Japan's industries, will become even stronger in the future.

Table 73 – **Japan: towns with population over 400 000 (1970 census)**

Tokyo	8 841 000	Sendai	545 000
Osaka	2 980 000	Amagasaki	545 000
Yokohama	2 238 000	Hiroshima	542 000
Nagoya	2 036 000	Higashiosaka	500 000
Kyōto	1 419 000	Chiba	482 000
Kōbe	1 289 000	Kumamoto	440 000
Kitakyushu	1 042 000	Hamamatsu	432 000
Sapporo	1 010 000	Nagasaki	421 000
Fukuoka	853 000	Shizuoka	416 000
Kawasaki	853 000	Himeji	405 000
Sakai	594 000	Kagoshima	403 000

Ryukyu Archipelago. From Kyushu, following the same general direction as the main arc of Japanese islands, the Ryukyu Archipelago stretches as far south as 26° N. These small islands are merely the summits of a submerged mountain chain, but during the Second World War they acquired strategic importance and came into prominence when the United States occupied the largest island, Okinawa, some 112 km (70 miles) long and 5 to 16 km (3 to 10 miles) wide. After the war Japanese sovereignty over the archipelago was recognised in the San Francisco Peace Treaty; but the islands remained under American military administration, and Okinawa in particular developed into an important American base in the Pacific, containing the biggest American airfields in the Far East and providing a popular subject of anti-American criticism in Japan. In June 1971 the Okinawa Reversion Agreement was signed in which the United States agreed to relinquish control of Okinawa in 1972; and by the same Agreement Japan would reassume complete control of the Ryukyu Archipelago in the same year.

Economically the islands have a limited importance as producers of tropical crops: sugarcane (the most important), pineapples, rice, sweet potatoes, tobacco and a variety of vegetables. The population was estimated to be 945 465 in 1971, of whom 797 615 were in Okinawa. The capital, situated in Okinawa, is Naha City (276 906).

Africa

Of the six continents Africa is second in size to Asia, with an area of some 30.3m. sq km (11.7m. sq miles), and fourth in population (estimated at some 344m. in 1970). Commercially however, in relation to its size, Africa may be regarded as the least developed of the continents, though its external trade is not absolutely the lowest. Contributory factors are its relatively late political and economic development and the large areas of deficient or unreliable rainfall. The surface, as in Spain, is made up mainly of plateaus with bordering mountains, so that the interior is in most parts reached only by winds that have been deprived of the greater portion of their moisture. The only regions with fairly abundant rainfall are certain parts of the equatorial region, narrow strips on the east and southeast coast, and part of the north coast in the neighbourhood of the Atlas Mountains. There are vast regions in the north and the southwest entirely desert, or nearly so, except where capable of irrigation. The only district possessing a really high density of population is the lower Nile valley, and especially the Nile delta in the Arab Republic of Egypt.

Apart from rainfall, the soils are often far from fertile. Large areas in the Congo basin and elsewhere are covered with poor tropical red soils, including laterite, from which the valuable plant foods have been leached by rain. Improvident methods of cultivation and stock grazing have led to widespread soil erosion.

Transport difficulties have been another hindrance. Until the end of the nineteenth century Africa was mostly dependent on porters and pack animals. A camel caravan took about three months to cross the Sahara, covering from 25 to 30 km (15 to 18 miles) a day. In tropical Africa caravans of porters travelled at the rate of about 32 km (20 miles) a day, the normal load for each porter being about 22 kg (50 lb), though some carried up to 54 kg (120 lb). Except along the main routes, only narrow tracks connect the villages, but these have proved very suitable for bicycles, which are widely used. The present century has seen a big extension both of railways and of seasonal motor roads, with a more gradual increase of all-weather roads. Motor trans-

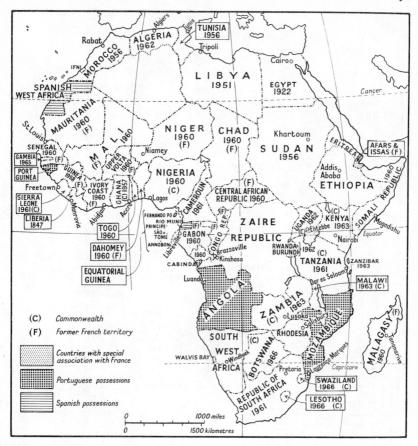

Africa: political, 1973

port can cross the Sahara in a few days, and air services are numerous. Water transport has also improved, although the rivers are interrupted by rapids and falls which destroy their value as continuous commercial highways.

Above all, fast development was limited by the paucity and backward condition of the people. Intertribal warfare, slave-raiding, famine, disease, all kept the numbers down and held up progress. The future is brighter. European control not only established law and order and brought material development, but lessened the ravages of disease to such an extent that rapid increase in the population is giving rise to economic anxiety. In general, the climate of tropical Africa has long been regarded, perhaps unjustly, as enervating and unfavourable to prolonged strenuous labour. Malaria is still prevalent in the lowlands, and even the highlands are not free from it, for although it can be contained locally it cannot yet be eradicated universally. Still more dreaded pests are the tsetse flies (various species of *Glossina*) which

The railways of Africa

carry the active agent of sleeping sickness in man and the corresponding disease, *nagana*, in cattle. They range over a large part of tropical and, in the east, subtropical Africa — between about 15° N and 17° S in the west, and between 4° N and 27½° S in the east. The disease in man can be contained where medical facilities are available, but *nagana* in cattle is widespread and it is still virtually impossible to raise domestic stock in these areas and so improve the soils by mixed farming.

In one way and another, therefore, many of the handicaps to Africa's progress, if not yet conquered, are being reduced. Population is on the increase; Africans allowed to exercise their talents are showing their capabilities; and if the continent is not one of the wealthiest or easiest to develop, it has latent resources of farm and forest products, and of mineral wealth which the various governments are eager to turn to account. Everywhere are development and welfare schemes.

An important factor in the early commercial development of Equatorial Africa was the Free Trade Zone established by the European Powers at the Berlin Conference of 1885 in connection with their recognition of the then Congo Free State (later the Democratic Republic of the Congo, now Zaire). Nominally related to the Congo Basin, this treaty zone covered an even vaster area, extending across Africa from the Atlantic to the Indian Ocean and embracing not only the former Belgian Congo and adjacent parts of former French Equatorial Africa, Portuguese West Africa, and Zambia which fall within the Congo Basin, but the whole of Kenya, Uganda, Tanganyika and Malawi, with parts of the former Anglo—Egyptian Sudan, Italian Somaliland, and Portuguese East Africa. The treaty was subject to various modifications after 1885, but the vital principle of equality of treatment among the signatories had been initiated.

Arab Republic of Egypt

Egypt was for a long period a province of the Ottoman empire. In 1882 British influence began when, at the request of the Khedive an expeditionary force was sent out to suppress a rebellion of the Egyptian army. A British protectorate was established during the First World War, when the reigning Khedive was deposed and a successor appointed with the title of Sultan, but in 1922 Egypt was recognised as an independent sovereign state, the Sultan being proclaimed king. Thirty years later, in 1952, his successor was forced to resign in favour of his infant son as the result of a military coup d'état, whose leaders announced a programme of radical reforms, including the break up of the big landed estates and their subdivision among the *fellahin*. In June 1953 a republic was proclaimed, with General Nasser as President.

An Anglo—Egyptian Treaty in 1936 had left for discussion the defence of the Canal Zone and the future of the Anglo—Egyptian Sudan. Egypt claimed the restoration of sovereignty in the Sudan, but accepted (February 1953) the decision of the Sudan in favour of self-government. Egypt pressed, however, for withdrawal of the British troops from the Canal Zone, and in October 1954, withdrawal was agreed. This was completed in June 1956. In July, disappointed in his hopes of an international loan for a gigantic rebuilding of the Aswan Dam on the Nile, the President took over the Suez Canal and announced his intention of using its revenues to rebuild the dam, subject to compensation to the Canal Company. Later in the year, Israel, fearful of Arab attacks across her frontiers, launched a campaign against Egypt in the Sinai Peninsula; an Anglo—French ultimatum to both parties was rejected by Egypt, fighting ensued, and the Canal was blocked. Britain and France withdrew in favour of a force representing the United Nations, which left in the spring of 1957, after clearing the Canal. More or less normal conditions were gradually restored. Egypt sought the hegemony of the Arab states and developed business relations with the USSR, China and their associates. In 1958 Egypt and

Syria were federated as 'the United Arab Republic'. Later the Kingdom of Yemen was included to form the 'United Arab States'. In 1961 Syria withdrew from her union with Egypt, and Egypt from the union with Yemen. The UAR as reestablished in 1964 was Egypt only. After further fighting with Israel (the Six Day War of 1967) the Canal was again blocked and has yet to be re-opened. In 1972 the name of the country was changed to the Arab Republic of Egypt.

Egypt extends from the Mediterranean Sea and the mouths of the Nile to Wadi Halfa in about latitude 22° N, a length roughly equal to the distance between the Scillies and the Shetlands. In the east it extends to the Red Sea and Israel, including the Suez Canal (p. 677), and in the west the boundary is an almost entirely straight line running north to south through the Libyan desert. The area of the country is some 1m. sq km (386 000 sq miles), but mostly it is uninhabited and uninhabitable. The settled area is about 35 000 sq km (13 500 sq miles), between 3 and 4 per cent of the whole; one-quarter the size of England — and of this some 2.4m. ha (6m. acres) — under 26 000 sq km (10 000 sq miles) — are cultivated. The settled area comprises the tract capable of being irrigated by the waters of the Nile — the Nile delta and a valley varying in width from 3 to 24 km (2 to 15 miles), lying between the deserts on either side — together with a few oases. On this area are crowded over 34.5m. people, who are dependent on agriculture, although 40 per cent are town dwellers. The overall density averages some 30 per sq km (78 per sq mile), but rises to over 900 per habitable sq km (2 331 per sq mile) — a density almost unparalleled for an agricultural community except in China. With a population which doubled between 1950 and 1970, and which will double again by 1990, there is great pressure to extend the habitable area. Irrigation schemes in the Nile valley and delta, and new artesian wells under the oases (in the 'New Valley' area from Kharga to Farafra) could add a further 1m. ha, but this will scarcely keep pace with population growth. There is increasing industrialisation, which by 1970 had made Egypt the second most industrialised nation in Africa, after the Republic of South Africa.

The Greek geographer Herodotus, 2 300 years ago, aptly called Egypt 'the gift of the Nile'. Agriculture in Egypt certainly depends for its very existence on the waters of the Nile, for the annual rainfall at Cairo is only 25 mm (1 in), and at Wadi Halfa precipitation is seldom known to occur. The annual flood of the Nile was the result of the summer monsoon rains occurring on the Abyssinian Mountains in Ethiopia. The perennial source of water in the lower Nile is the White Nile (Bahr-el-Abiad), a name which properly applies only to the main river from Khartoum to Lake No (10° N), where the Upper Nile — Bahr-el-Jebel (Mountain River) — is joined by the Bahr-el-Ghazal; but the name 'White Nile' is often loosely applied to the main river as far as the Great African Lakes. Supplementing this main supply, the annual floods are brought by the Blue Nile and the Atbara Rivers, which rise in Ethiopia.

During the floods the Blue Nile has been found to be responsible for nearly 70 per cent of the water in the Egyptian Nile, the Atbara for 17 per cent, and the White Nile for 14 per cent; but during the period of low water the White Nile provides over 80 per cent, and is thus the mainstay of the dry season flow. The Nile in Egypt began to rise about the end of June, growing turbid and red with the fertilising mud held in suspension. By the month of September it had reached the top of its banks and began to overflow, except where held in check by artificial embankments. In November and December it subsided again. This age-old seasonal pattern finally ceased with the completion of the High Dam at Aswan in 1970.

The methods employed for utilising this vast volume of water for the benefit of the crops have changed considerably. But until only about 100 years ago the sole method was that of the Pharaohs — the method described by Shakespeare in the words which he puts into the mouth of Mark Antony:

> The higher Nilus swells,
> The more it promises: as it ebbs, the seedsman
> Upon the slime and ooze scatters his grain,
> And shortly comes to harvest.

It depended on the fact that thousands of annual floods have deposited silt brought down from Ethiopia to such an extent that the Nile banks in Egypt, below Aswan, are now slightly above the level of the surrounding floor of the valley. Traditional cultivation was based on cuts made in the raised bank, and as the river level rose the water flowed through on to the fields, which are arranged in a series of basins separated by embankments. The water remained on the land, depositing its valuable load of fertile silt, for six to eight weeks and was then allowed to run back to the river, the level of which has meanwhile fallen. The seed was sown in the mud, and the crop reaped before all the moisture dried up. By this method of irrigation the soil was condemned to sterility for half the year, during which it was either under water or baked to a degree of hardness which made it impossible to grow anything. By it, too, only such crops could be grown as ripen within a short period — such as beans, clover, lentils, wheat, barley, and onions. Of far more economic importance is perennial irrigation, because it guards against the risk of a poor flood, permits of more than one crop being obtained in the year, and greatly extends the range of crops which can be grown.

Perennial irrigation of a kind has been practised from very ancient times, close to the river bank, by the use of the primitive 'shaduf', a lever device for raising water from the river. The use of dams thrown across the river to store the water for irrigation purposes dates only from the early part of the last century. Mohammed Ali Pasha built a barrage across the Nile at the head of the delta to dam up the flood-water, which could thus be used to irrigate the fields for a much longer period than would have been possible under the old basin system. These works were extended under British influence; they consist of a pair of dams with sluices on the two main arms of the delta a little below Cairo. By their use a large part of the delta and the part of Egypt to the northeast of Cairo and the south of Zagazig have been made independent of the state of the Nile. The delta sluices are closed about February or March, and little water is allowed to escape to the sea between the time of closing and the commencement of the flood season in July. Large earthen banks called *sudds* are built across the mouths to retain the water for irrigation. During the present century other barrages have been built at various localities on the river in Middle and Upper Egypt, the intention being to allow the water in basins belonging to a group in one part of the valley to be supplemented in a low flood by canals led from the next group higher up. The largest of these barriers was for long the first dam at Aswan, opened in 1902 and enlarged in 1912 and 1933. The culmination of man's attempt to make the best use of the waters of the Nile was the construction of the new Aswan High Dam opened in 1970 some 6 km (4 miles) upstream from the old dam. This was a vast irrigation and hydroelectric project which took ten years to build. The lake it created, Lake Nasser, displaced some 70 000 people, should provide a major source of fish, and stretches as far as Wadi Halfa. As a direct result of this dam the flow of the Nile is now controlled and regular; large areas have been converted from seasonal to perennial irrigation; and an additional 525 000 ha (1.3m. acres) have been irrigated for the first time (some as far away as the lower valley and in the delta). It is estimated that the project will increase the total agricultural output by 25 per cent and will double the electric power available when the grid to Lower Egypt is completed, with immense benefits to Egypt's expanding industrialisation.

Invaluable as these works are in distributing the fertilising waters of the Nile as the river flows through Egypt, the problem of supply goes beyond the confines of that country. As already noted, the sources of the Nile are far away to the south — those of the White Nile in the Great Equatorial Lakes, and those of the Blue Nile in the highlands of Ethiopia. The masses of vegetation known as the *sudd*, which obstruct the progress of the White Nile northward in its middle course through the Sudan, are another potent factor. The regulation of the Nile waters in these higher reaches of the river has long been the subject of engineering and political study, and developments are in progress. In 1949 an Anglo–Egyptian agreement provided for building a dam (opened 1954; see p. 712) at Owen Falls, Uganda, near the outlet of the

Nile from Lake Victoria, for the production of hydroelectric power and for the control of the waters of the Nile in conjunction with other important works lower down the valley. Negotiations for these other works have been started in the Sudan and in Ethiopia, as well as in Egypt, Kenya and Uganda, but the national interests of the various countries are conflicting, and the full potential of the water resources of the Equatorial Nile Control Project has yet to be exploited.

Before the introduction of perennial irrigation, the agricultural year in Egypt was divided into three parts, the season of inundation, from June to October; the season of cultivation, after the subsidence of the waters, from October to February; and the harvest season, varying with the individual crops, from February to June. Only one crop could be obtained each year from a single patch of ground. The fertility was amply maintained by the annual deposit of silt, supplemented in respect of nitrogen content by the growing of beans, lentils, and particularly the Egyptian variety of clover known as *bersim*. Under the present regime many new features have been introduced. In the first place, it is now possible to obtain two crops per annum of the old staples of Egyptian agriculture, the small cereals and pulses. The winter crops occupy the ground between October and April, and the summer crops between April and October. Increasingly an extra 'season' may be added, a quick crop of maize or millet being obtained between September and November. The following is a typical example of the succession of crops grown during a three-year period: cotton is grown from March to the end of October, and is immediately followed by clover, of which perhaps seven cuts are taken before July; in the next eighteen months two crops of maize and one of wheat may be reaped, the wheat being grown in winter and spring; the second crop of maize may be succeeded by clover, of which two cuts can be obtained before the ground is cleared once more at the beginning of March for cotton.

Secondly, crops which require a rather longer season than was to be obtained under the old system are now able to be grown; such as cotton, now the most valuable crop of all, sugarcane, rice, maize, and millet. Thirdly, the use of the water in irrigation canals instead of in floods over the fields has deprived the soil of its annual deposit of silt. This is the most serious drawback to perennial irrigation. The silt is now deposited in the river-bed and in the canals and reservoirs, and increased labour is involved in removing these deposits, which are piled up on the banks. This is of little moment, however, beside the loss of fertility which has resulted. Artificial fertilisers are used in ever-increasing quantities in order to maintain crop yields. Egypt is fortunate in having two available sources of such material, the nitrates — known as 'tafla' — of the Nile valley between Keneh and Aswan where additional power is increasing production, and the more recently discovered and far more valuable field of phosphate rock on the Red Sea coast near Safaga and

Quseir. Further deposits at Siba'iya in the upper Nile valley are the basis of a superphosphate plant.

One feature of Egyptian agriculture which has scarcely been changed by the substitution of new for old methods of water supply is its comparatively primitive character. Only recently has mechanisation been introduced to overcome the limitations imposed where over two-thirds of the holdings were less than 0.4 ha (1 acre) in extent, and were separated by mudbanks.

The principal commercial crop in Egypt is cotton. The plant was introduced into the country a little over a century ago by Mohammed Ali Pasha, the originator of perennial irrigation, and its cultivation has extended steadily, very largely owing to two factors, the high quality of the product and the increased facilities for its cultivation in areas watered by the perennial canals. There were two main varieties cultivated. The finest, called Sakellaridis (or in the trade 'Sakel') has a silky lustre and a long staple of about 38 mm (1.5 in), qualities which make it second only to the famous 'sea island' cotton (p. 177) of the West Indies. It is grown mainly in the delta, but has been supplanted by other improved strains notably Giza. Ashmouni is not so outstanding as Sakel but still a good quality fibre, and even more prolific. This is the principal variety grown in Upper Egypt.

In the quinquennium before the Second World War, the land under cotton averaged over 728 000 ha (1.8m. acres) (rather less than a third of the total cultivated area), produced a crop of some 400 000 tons of ginned cotton, and supplied from two-thirds to three-quarters of the total value of Egyptian exports. During the war, when food crops had preference, the area under cotton dropped below 300 000 ha (741 316 acres). Naturally the lands retained for that crop were the best suited to cotton, and the average yield was more than maintained, never falling below the prewar average of 5.4 quintals per ha (480 lb per acre). In the 1960s the area reached over 800 000 ha (1.9m. acres) and though the yield declined heavy crops were harvested and stocks accumulated, adding to a world glut of cotton. By 1970 the area was reduced to 685 000 ha (1.69m. acres) producing some 437 000 tons. Formerly the United States, which produces a quarter of the world's cotton, had an average yield of only about 2.5 quintals per ha (230 lb per acre), but in the past few years its average has also been above 5.5 quintals per ha (505 lb per acre). But for restricted cultivation this would swamp the world market for cotton, which is facing increased competition from other fibres. India averages 1.1 quintal per ha (100 lb per acre) and Pakistan's highest is no more than double that figure.

Egypt's other crops are mainly cereals and pulses: food crops whose wartime experience was the reverse of that of cotton; their area increased, but as the new land was not always the most naturally suited to them the average yield tended to decline. Postwar experience varied with the crop. Wheat and maize, more or less on a par, tended to increase slightly, the 1968 figures being: wheat, 550 000 ha (1.36m. acres), maize, 660 000 ha (1.6m. acres), yielding 1.7m. and 2.3m. tons respectively, the maize yield increasing with the improvement in new strains. Barley not only declined from the level of war production but fell much below the prewar average, from 110 000 to 55 000 ha (271 700 to 135 850 acres) and from 255 000 tons to little over 100 000. Sorghum on the other hand did better than before the war, increasing its prewar average of 142 000 to over 208 000 ha (350 740 to 514 000 acres) and its crop from 430 000 to 900 000 tons. Rice, though a variable crop, did better still, being grown on over 450 000 ha (1.1m. acres), treble the prewar area, and increasing prewar output tenfold to 2.57m. tons. There is a surplus of rice for export but other cereals are insufficient for home needs; wheat and maize are both imported to feed a population growing at the rate of 1m. a year.

Other major crops include sugarcane, of which 6m. tons yielding over 450 000 tons of raw sugar were produced in 1968; and broad beans, averaging over 0.25m. tons from 160 000 ha (400 000 acres). Onions are largely grown for export in a variety of forms (fresh, dehydrated, powdered, etc.), and potatoes are also exported. Animals are reared as part of the farming system and in the year 1969—70 sheep, cattle, and buffaloes each numbered between 1.7 and 2.2m., with asses 1.2m., goats 820 000, camels 190 000 and pigs a low 15 000. Fodder is available in the form of *bersim* (clover), grown universally as part of the crop rotation. In the oases, the more important of which are Siwa (far out in the desert west of El Faiyûm), Khârga (west of Isna), and Farafra (west of Asyût), the same food crops are increasingly grown under irrigation, and in addition dates, of which the production in 1971 was estimated at 350 000 tons — the largest in the world.

Apart from its crops, the tending of which occupies 55 per cent of the labour force, Egypt's natural resources are limited. There are small quantities of gold, asbestos, lead, zinc, and chromite; rather more of phosphates, iron ore and salt. There is no coal but oil has been found in the Gulf of Suez and in the Western desert. Annual production has risen from 3.2m. tons in 1960 to 16.9m. tons in 1972. With refining capacity and consumption at some 8.5m. tons in 1970 there should be increasing quantities of crude oil available for export and to support expansion of the refineries. Natural gas has also been discovered and exploited in the lower Nile delta; it is piped to the industries of Alexandria and fertiliser plants at Talkha (increasingly important with the loss of the annual replenishment of Nile silt). Hydroelectric power from the High Dam has assisted the expansion of the steel works at Helwan; fertiliser plants based on the phosphates from the Red Sea coast; and the introduction of aluminium and petrochemical plants. Other industries are of a light nature and, except for car assembly, are mainly concerned with

Table 74 – Egypt: growth of principal towns (over 200 000), 1947–66

	1947	*1966*
Cairo (El Qâhira)	2 090 654	4 220 000
Alexandria (El Iskandariya)	919 024	1 801 000
El Giza (suburb of Cairo)	150 000	571 000
Port Said (Bûr Said)	177 703	283 000
Suez (El Suweis)	107 244	264 000
Tanta	139 926	230 000
El Maehalla el Kubra	115 738	225 000

processing of local products – food, textiles, cement, carpets, tobacco, sugar, etc. The availability of electric power will make it possible to disperse these in an attempt to slow down the population drift to the larger towns. Only some 10 per cent of the labour force were employed in industry in 1970. The growth of the principal towns (over 200 000) is shown by a comparison of the 1947 and 1966 census figures: see Table 74.

Raw cotton and cotton textiles have long dominated foreign trade, although falling from 70 per cent of exports in 1956 to some 50 per cent in 1968. Total exports in 1968 were £E270m.* with rice, mineral products, fruit and vegetables making up the bulk of the balance – mainly to the USSR, Czechoslovakia, Italy and West Germany. Imports totalled £E290m., comprised of foodstuffs, machinery and transport equipment (together some 50 per cent) followed by chemicals, mining equipment and metal products from USSR, France and Romania.

Although the items of foreign trade have remained much the same since the Second World War (except for a slowly increasing self-sufficiency in oil) the pattern of trading partners has fluctuated considerably. The takeover of the Suez Canal in 1956 and its short closure in 1957 were accompanied by political realignments which had economic repercussions. For example, imports from UK and France totalled £E32m. in 1956 but fell to £E8m. in 1957, while the USSR took the lead from the USA as the main trading nation. By 1963 however imports from the UK and France had risen again to £E44m., and the USA (a source of £E109m. imports and a recipient of £10m. exports) had regained the lead from the USSR (a source of £E21m. imports and a recipient of £E44m. exports). After 1967 the pattern changed yet again to make USSR and Comecon countries the main trading partners.

The bulk of the foreign commerce is concentrated in Alexandria, the ancient port named after Alexander the Great, situated at the north-west extremity of the delta, away from the silt, which is swept east-

* Value of Egyptian (£E) in 1971; official rate £E1.13 to £1.00, free rate varies from £E1.85 to £E2.15.

wards by currents. The remainder of the trade was divided between Port Said, at the Mediterranean entrance to the Suez Canal and Suez, at the southern end; but the closure of the canal has brought their trade to minor importance. The capital, Cairo, situated on the right bank of the Nile at the head of the delta, was a natural converging point in the past for caravan routes, as it now is for rail and air routes.

Not the least valuable of Egypt's assets are the archaeological and art treasures and the agreeable climate which have long attracted tourists: 540 000 visited the country in 1965 and the numbers have increased spasmodically since then. The full potential will not be realised until the threat of war is removed. The Nile itself plays an important part in tourism, and commercially also it is not a negligible factor, though it presents difficulties for navigation. Shallow-draught vessels ply as far up as the Aswan Dam. Thereafter it is possible to proceed on Lake Nasser as far as Wadi Halfa, on the Sudan border. In 1960 work was started on the new High Dam at Aswan. This was completed in 1970 and greatly increased the size and depth of the lake and resulted in the flooding of many settlements, including Wadi Halfa. Several canals assist navigation from the Cairo district to the sea; the chief (the Mahmudia Canal) connects the western arm of the delta with the port of Alexandria; another connects Zagazig, on the eastern side of the delta, with the Suez Canal. Some 4 200 km (2 600 miles) of state railways have a gauge of 4 ft 8½ in, and there are some 1 100 km (700 miles) of narrow gauge lines (2 ft 6 in), serving the agricultural districts of the delta as feeders to the standard gauge system. Until the Suez Canal was closed, railway traffic was carried across it on a swing bridge built during the Second World War, by the British Army a few miles from El Qantara (Kantara) on the east bank.

The Suez Canal. A monument to the genius of the French engineer, Ferdinand de Lesseps, the Suez Canal was sponsored by the then Turkish viceroy of Egypt in the middle of the last century across an isthmus which had been a trading route since 2 000 BC. It was supported by France and other European countries, but not by Britain. Work was begun in 1859 and the canal was opened in 1869. In 1875 the Khedive of Egypt sold to the British government his 44 per cent holding in the enterprise, and from then onwards France and Britain developed the canal until 1956.

Including approach channels to the terminal harbours, the canal is 174 km (108 miles) long. From time to time since it was opened with a depth of 7.9 m (26 ft), it has been widened and deepened. By 1967 it had a minimum depth of 12 m (40 ft), the permitted maximum draught for ships passing through it being 11.6 m (38 ft). The general width had been increased from 61 to 152 m (200 to 500 ft), and the minimum at the standard navigable depth is 60 m (197 ft). Even at this width there is not room for vessels to pass each other, and after the Second World War a oneway convoy system was introduced with passing places at Kabret and Ballah. The traffic on the canal increased steadily from two or three vessels a day in 1870 to nearly sixty a day in 1966, by which time it was close to maximum capacity and a major factor in limiting the size of bulk tankers. The temporary closure by Egypt after the seizure of the canal in 1956 turned attention to the old trading route round the Cape of Good Hope; and hastened the introduction of giant tankers whose economy of scale could offset the longer route. The second closure in 1967 (at which time 65 000 ton tankers were the largest that could pass through the canal) gave greater impetus to this trend and orders were placed for tankers from 250 000 to 450 000 tons for the Cape route. Plans exist to enlarge the canal to accommodate 110 000 tonners in the short, and 250 000 tonners in the longer, term but their commencement must await the reopening of the canal which will then once again become a vital trade route (for all but the largest tankers) as the following comparative distances show:

Nautical miles from	Via Suez	Via Cape of Good Hope
UK to Persian Gulf	6 500	11 300
UK to Singapore	8 300	11 800
UK to Melbourne	11 000	11 900
USA to Persian Gulf	8 600	12 100
USA to Singapore	10 200	12 400

The smaller differences on the long haul to Australia contrast with the larger differences to the Persian Gulf (a matter of some twenty-five days on the return trip to Europe). The difference is far greater to seaborne trade between eastern Europe and the Gulf.

The potential loss of oil traffic from the cargoes of the largest tankers is to be in part recouped by a 340 km (210 miles) pipeline running from the Gulf of Suez to the Mediterranean coast, west of Alexandria with a planned annual capacity of 60m. tons. Before the closure of the canal some 15 per cent of the world's seaborne trade passed through. As Table 75 shows, the total trade of the canal has increased steadily since the Second World War in line with the increase in the size of vessels.

The pattern of traffic through the canal in the twentieth century has been largely dominated by oil from the Persian Gulf. Oil and its byproducts moving northward before the First World War amounted to less than 0.3m. tons a year. In 1966 they totalled 166m. tons (some 75 per cent of all canal traffic) and were responsible for the great preponderance of the northbound trade (83 per cent of the total) which also included minerals, bulk foods and fibres. The remaining 17 per cent was southbound and included manufactures, machinery and

Table 75 — Shipping passing through Suez Canal: net tonnage in thousands of tons (000 omitted)

Year	No. of vessels	Tonnage	Year	No. of vessels	Tonnage	Year	No. of vessels	Tonnage
1869	10	6.6	1901	3 699	10 824	1933	5 416	30 674
1870	486	437	1902	3 708	11 248	1934	5 651	31 736
1871	756	761	1903	3 761	11 907	1935	5 992	32 811
1872	1 082	1 161	1904	4 237	13 402	1936	5 877	32 379
1873	1 173	1 368	1905	4 116	13 134	1937	6 635	36 491
1874	1 264	1 632	1906	3 975	13 446	1938	6 171	34 418
1875	1 494	2 010	1907	4 267	14 728	1939	5 277	29 573
1876	1 457	2 097	1908	3 797	13 640	1940	2 589	13 536
1877	1 663	2 355	1909	4 241	15 418	1941	1 804	8 263
1878	1 593	2 270	1910	4 538	16 575	1942	1 646	7 028
1879	1 477	2 263	1911	4 969	18 327	1943	2 262	11 274
1880	2 026	3 057	1912	5 372	16 672	1944	3 320	18 125
1881	2 727	4 137	1913	5 085	20 034	1945	4 206	25 065
1882	3 198	5 057	1914	–	–	1946	5 057	32 732
1883	3 307	5 776	1915	3 708	15 266	1947	5 972	36 577
1884	3 284	5 872	1916	3 110	12 325	1948	8 686	55 081
1885	3 624	6 336	1917	2 353	8 369	1949	10 420	68 862
1886	3 100	5 768	1918	2 522	9 252	1950	11 751	81 796
1887	3 137	5 903	1919	3 986	16 014	1951	11 694	80 336
1888	3 440	6 641	1920	4 009	17 575	1952	12 168	86 137
1889	3 425	6 783	1921	3 976	18 260	1953	12 731	92 905
1890	3 389	6 890	1922	4 347	20 861	1954	13 215	102 493
1891	4 207	8 699	1923	4 621	22 873	1955	14 616	115 756
1892	3 559	7 712	1924	5 122	25 261	1956*	13 291	107 006
1893	3 341	7 659	1925	5 337	26 762	1957†	10 958	89 991
1894	3 352	8 039	1926	4 980	26 060	1958	17 842	154 479
1895	3 434	8 448	1927	5 543	28 965	1961	18 148	187 059
1896	3 409	8 560	1928	6 081	31 906	1962	18 518	197 837
1897	2 986	7 899	1929	6 274	33 466	1963	19 146	210 498
1898	3 503	9 239	1930	5 761	31 669	1964	19 943	227 991
1899	3 607	9 896	1931	5 352	30 031	1965	20 289	246 817
1900	3 441	9 738	1932	5 029	28 354	1966	21 250	274 466

* January–October.
† April–December.

fertilisers. The growth of the mercantile fleets sailing under 'flags of convenience' and the changing pattern of world shipping is also reflected in the changing percentage of British shipping passing through the canal. In 1913 this was 60; in 1920, 64; in 1938, 50.4; in 1952, 33.3; in 1960, 21.4; and in 1966, 17 per cent.

Sudan

After its reconquest in 1896–99 from the Mahdists, who for sixteen years had held tyrannical sway over it, the area lying between Egypt and Uganda was given the status of a condominium, or joint dominion of England and Egypt. Known as the Anglo–Egyptian Sudan, or simply 'the Sudan', it was administered under the Anglo—Egyptian Convention of 1899, by a governor-general appointed by Egypt with the assent of Britain. Its status as a condominium was reaffirmed in the Anglo—Egyptian Treaty of 1936, but in 1951 Egypt abrogated both Convention and Treaty and claimed sovereignty over the Sudan. The British government refused to recognised this unilateral action, and in February 1953 an Anglo—Egyptian Agreement assured to the Sudanese the right to decide their own future within three years of an 'Appointed Day', to be named by the governor-general after a Sudanese general election. The election was held at the end of 1953, and 9 January 1954 was named the Appointed Day. In December 1955 the House of Representatives voted unanimously for an independent sovereign state, and a republic was proclaimed by the co-domini in January 1956.

The Sudan covers an area of 2.5m. sq km (968 000 sq miles) with an estimated population (1970) of 15.8m. in two main divisions — the Arab peoples of the northern provinces, with their distinctive civilisation, and the Negro tribes of the upper Nile. Throughout the territory the Nile valley is the main artery of trade and seat of population; but there are nomadic or semi-nomadic tribes in the highlands of Darfur and the Libyan desert on the west, and in the Ethiopian foothills and the Nubian desert on the east and northeast. In the extreme northeast the territory extends to the Red Sea, which it borders for some 800 km (500 miles), forming the central section of the western shore.

Under 3 per cent of the total area is classed as arable, nearly 10 per cent as pastoral, over 36 per cent as wooded. The remaining 50 per cent is not of much account at present; 15 per cent is reckoned as potentially productive; 35 per cent is classed as 'built on, waste, and other'.

The summer rainfall, largely in thunderstorms, increases steadily from north to south. At the northern limit (22° N) is absolute desert. Khartoum, the capital (16° N), has 158 mm (6.2 in), nearly all in July and August; Lake No (10° N) has nearly 760 mm (30 in); Mongalla (5° N, a degree from the southern frontier) has nearly 1 016 mm (40 in), mainly from April to October. The seasonal character of the rainfall is responsible for the annual flooding of large areas in the south, where the topography of the vast basin of the Bahr-el-Jebel, which lies at an elevation of some 430 m (1 400 ft) above sea level, is extremely flat. On its way north the Bahr-el-Jebel is joined at the great swamp of Lake No by the Bahr-el-Ghazal, its only considerable affluent from the highlands of Darfur, and shortly afterwards by the Sobat, which collects the drainage of the Ethiopian foothills. Beyond these the Nile receives little or no water from tributaries on either side except the two great streams from the Ethiopian Mountains, the Blue Nile and — below Khartoum — the Atbara, which are responsible for the annual flooding of the Nile.

The natural vegetation of the Bahr-el-Jebel basin is savanna, or tropical grassland; trees are found along the watercourses only, lack of perennial water and the natural annual firing of the grass preventing much tree growth elsewhere. The streams themselves frequently flow through swamps, where papyrus, bulrushes, and floating weeds grow in abundance. During the flood season much of this vegetation becomes detached and floats, blocking up the water channels, causing further flooding, and hindering navigation. This floating vegetation is called *sudd*. The main stream of the Bahr-el-Jebel is regularly patrolled and kept navigable from Lake Albert to Nimule on the northern frontier of Uganda, and again, after a long stretch of rapids, from Rejaf, just south of latitude 5° N. On the Sobat and Bahr-el-Ghazal navigation is practicable only in summer, on the former to the Ethiopian town of Gambela, and on the latter to Wau. The savanna becomes drier towards the north. Acacias are the principal trees.

The southern portion of the Sudan is inhabited mainly by Negro peoples, such as the Nuer and Dinka tribes, who support life by rearing cattle, fishing, and growing crops of millet or maize after the summer rains. The region is remote and development has been hindered by poor communications and political instability. Nonetheless there is potential for cash crops of tea, coffee, sugar and tobacco, while the papyrus of the *sudd* area could be pulped for high quality paper. Northwards, where the rainfall decreases and the vegetation merges to savanna, there is cattle rearing. Dura millet (sorghum), groundnuts and sesamum are cultivated, and gum arabic (the bulk of the world's supply) is collected from the acacias in the dry months. Further north still cultivation is limited by the lower rainfall to irrigation schemes in the vicinity of the rivers, while nomadic tribes tend camels, sheep and goats. Food crops here are dates, wheat, barley, millet, lubia (a bean), and a wide range of vegetables. Fruit is grown along the Blue Nile; but the main arable area is the Gezira (see below) a profit-sharing government scheme which produced 73 per cent of the total cotton crop, 50 per cent of the wheat, 30 per cent of the lubia, 12 per cent of the dura and a sizeable proportion of other food crops.

Economically cotton is the most important crop. In 1969–70, an unusually good year, some 1.3m. bales (260 000 tons) were produced from 510 000 ha (1.26m. acres) 90 per cent for export. Some American cotton is grown during the summer rains in the Nuba Mountains of Kordofan and in the Bahr-el-Jebel region, but most of the crop is Egyptian 'sakel' cotton. This was first cultivated in the northeast, on the Gash and Baraka Rivers, around Kassala and Tokar, but since irrigation water has been available in the Gezira (the plain occupying the angle between the White and Blue Niles south of Khartoum), the latter area produces 73 per cent of the crop. It is remarkably level, with a gentle slope to the west and northwest, and grows many crops. A mighty dam at Sennar, on the Blue Nile, was completed in 1925, and almost at once 100 000 ha (0.25m. acres) of hitherto semi-arid land were brought under cultivation; further canal construction has steadily increased the area of the Gezira scheme to over 810 000 ha (2m. acres) of which 25 per cent is under cotton. The dam at Khashm el Girba (1964) on the Atbara supports 120 000 ha (300 000 acres) to take population from Wadi Halfa displaced by the Aswan High Dam scheme. The dam at Roseires on the Blue Nile (1966) is to supply the El Rahad irrigation scheme of some 162 000 ha (400 000 acres) of new arable land.

As in Egypt, livestock are everywhere important. Forage crops grown in the irrigation areas provide fodder for cattle, whilst cattle reared on the natural grasses represent the chief source of wealth for the semi-nomadic peoples. The total number of cattle is estimated at over 14m. Sheep (13m.), goats (10m.), and camels (3m.) are also reared, for milk, meat, wool, or hair, or as beasts of burden. Camel caravan routes, running across the Libyan and Nubian deserts to the Red Sea are now almost supplanted by railway and some limited motor roads; and the old market centres of El Fasher in Darfur, Berber on the Nile, and Suakin on the Red Sea coast have lost much of their former importance.

Over 5 400 km (3 350 miles) of narrow, 3 ft 6 in, railway and some 3 200 km (2 000 miles) of river-steamer routes in the flood season carry most of the trade of the Sudan. The main line of railway runs from Wadi Halfa across the great Dongola bend of the Nile to Abu Hamed, follows the river up to Atbara and Khartoum, and then goes up the Blue Nile to Sennar. From Atbara a line goes east to Port Sudan and Suakin on the Red Sea. At Sennar the line forks: one branch goes west, crossing the Nile at Kosti, to the Kordofan market centre of El Obeid and on to Wau; the other east and north through country bordering on Ethiopia and Eritrea, along the Nile—Red Sea watershed, to link up with the Port Sudan line. The railways carry 60 per cent of the passenger traffic, 75 per cent of the freight and 95 per cent of all exports.

The White Nile — using the name in its loose sense — is navigable nearly to the Uganda frontier, and the Blue Nile in summer up to Roseires. Road communication in the south, where the seasonal rains render maintenance difficult, is in its infancy, but all-season roads are available across the southern frontier into Uganda and Zaire (the Republic of the Congo (Kinshasa)). There is still, however, no permanent road linking northern and southern Sudan; the river and, more recently, the aeroplane providing the only routes. In 1970 the only all-weather, surfaced road ran from Khartoum to Wad Medani, with plans for extensions to Kosti and, via Ghedaref, to Port Sudan. There is also a project for a road to link the cotton-growing area of the Nuba Mountains (Kadugli) to El Obeid, a new venture which, unlike other projects, will not duplicate existing rail and water links. Khartoum is a regular landing-ground on the air service from London to Nairobi, and Wadi Halfa, Malakal, and Juba are landing-grounds for local services.

Khartoum, which was captured from the Mahdists, together with the large village of Omdurman, in 1898, has been rebuilt as the capital and is the administrative centre. It lies at the junction of the Blue and White Niles, in the angle between them, and has derived much importance from its focal position and from the development of cotton and other crops in the Gezira. With Khartoum North, on the far side of the Blue Nile, and Omdurman, on the far side of the White Nile, it forms a conurbation of about 400 000 people. Omdurman is essentially an overgrown African market centre, but with the continued increase of population it is beginning to develop civic character, with broad thoroughfares and a boulevard stretching for kilometres along the river front.

Under the condominium the Sudan currency was the same as the Egyptian. Since 1957 the Sudan has had its own currency, but the Sudan £ is roughly equivalent to that of Egypt. Imports in 1970 amounted to £S100m. and exports to £S104m. The chief imports were machinery and transport equipment, foodstuffs, textiles and fertilisers. The dominating exports were cotton and cottonseed (63 per cent); gum arabic (10 per cent) and groundnuts (6 per cent). Other exports included sesame, cattle and sheep, and hides and skins. Over half the imports came from the United Kingdom, India, Japan and USSR. The exports went mainly to West Germany, Italy, India, UK, USSR and China, with increasing trade to the last two.

More than 80 per cent of the foreign trade passes through Port Sudan (60 000), an artificial port constructed in 1906, when the railway reached the coast, to replace the old Arab harbour of Suakin, which was unable to accommodate large vessels.

Ethiopia

Ethiopia (Abyssinia) is an independent sovereign state, organised on feudal lines. Along with the Territory of Afars and Issas, and the Somali Republic, it forms the 'Eastern Horn' of Africa. It has an ancient civilisation with a barbaric background, which a progressive emperor is trying to modernise. It was conquered and occupied by Italy in 1936, but was restored to independence by the British in the Second World War, with an Italian legacy of improved road communications. By resolution of the United Nations the adjoining territory of Eritrea (formerly an Italian colony; see below) was federated with Ethiopia in 1952 on the basis of autonomy in local affairs. The new arrangement is important to Ethiopia as giving her access to the sea, from which she was formerly cut off. The area of Ethiopia is some 1m. sq km

683

(400 000 sq miles). Eritrea has an area of about 100 000 sq km (40 000 sq miles). The combined population is estimated officially at over 24m.

Ethiopia is a land of high mountains and plateaus, and the population is mostly resident above 1 500 m (5 000 ft). Addis Ababa, the capital (644 000), lies above 2 400 m (8 000 ft), and there are peaks rising to 4 300 m (14 000 ft). Some forests, where coffee grows wild, occur at lower levels; much of the land between 1 800 and 2 700 m (6 000 and 9 000 ft) can be used for cultivation and pasture, producing cereals and fruit of Mediterranean type while between 2 700 and 3 900 m (9 000 and 13 000 ft) there are vast areas of open pasture with grazing and barley. Cattle are numbered at 26m., sheep at 25m. and goats at 18m. Eighty-eight per cent of the labour force is engaged in agriculture; there is little industry and few minerals. Salt is produced, mainly in Eritrea, and there is gold and some potash deposits. There is great hydroelectric potential. Exploration for oil and gas (mainly along the Red Sea coast) is proceeding and there is a small oil refinery operating at Assab. Industry is rudimentary and is centred in Addis Ababa and Asmara (179 000). It is mainly concerned with textiles, footwear, foodstuffs, cement and building materials. There are two main railway lines, one (metre gauge) running 780 km (486 miles) from Addis Ababa to the port of Djibouti; and the other (95 cm gauge) 307 km (191 miles) from Massawa to Asmara and Agordat, and then on to Biskia. Air traffic between the capital and Asmara is considerable, and the country is well served with its own and other international airlines.

The Ethiopian dollar, the currency unit, had a sterling value of 17p (six to the £1) in 1968. In that year Ethiopia had imports valued at E$432m. (£72m.), and exports valued at E$258m. (£43m.). Imports were mainly machinery, manufactured goods, textiles, vehicles and chemicals from Italy, West Germany, Japan, the USA and the UK. Exports included coffee, hides and skins, pulses and oilseeds to the USA, West Germany, Saudi Arabia and Italy. The USA is the main trading partner.

Eritrea, now fully integrated with Ethiopia, is nearly as large as England. It includes a narrow coastal strip, extending for more than 800 km (500 miles) along the Red Sea from the Strait of Bab-al-Mandab northward, backed by an escarpment rising some 2 400 m (8 000 ft) to a plateau which falls away again to the west. Both the winter rains of the tropical lowlands and the summer rains of the temperate plateau are scanty and uncertain, and cultivation on a commercial scale calls for irrigation. In addition to the single narrow gauge railway from Massawa to Biskia, the roads are first class, and Asmara has regular air services to and from neighbouring countries. The small population is divided mainly between Muslims and Christians (Copts). Pearl fishing was practised along the coast, and there is a big production of salt from saltpans at Massawa (202 000 tons in 1968) and Assab, the second port. Some cotton and millet are grown, under irrigation, on the coastal strip, but the main wealth of the population is in their flocks and herds. Hides and skins are exported.

Afars and Issas

This French Territory is situated on the coast between Eritrea and the Somali Republic. It occupies a commanding position immediately south of the entrance to the Red Sea, and is the former French Somaliland with an area of 23 000 sq km (8 500 sq miles) and a population estimated at 125 000. Nearly half of these are resident in Dibouti, the capital and port of the territory, terminus of the railway to Addis Ababa. This railway, which carries much of the external trade of Ethiopia, is the Territories' chief claim to economic importance. Some hides and skins are exported, while textiles, foodstuffs and cement are imported. The bulk of external trade is with France.

Somali Republic

The Somali Republic came into existence as an independent republic on 1 July 1960 when the British Somaliland Protectorate and the Italian trusteeship territory of Somalia merged. Its total area is about 700 000 sq km (270 000 sq miles), with a population of 2.9m. The capital is Mogadiscio (Mogadishu), with 220 000 people in 1971.

The former British Somaliland lies along the northern coast of the Horn of Africa and looks across the Gulf of Aden to Aden. With an area of 195 000 sq km (75 000 sq miles) it is largely desert and occupied by nomad tribes whose wealth is in their flocks and herds. Among the limited vegetable products are frankincense and myrrh. A coastal plain is backed by plateaus rising to 2 130 m (7 000 ft) where sorghum is grown. The chief northern port, Berbera, varies seasonally in population from 15 000 to 30 000. Hargeisa (50 000) in the uplands, is the only other town of any size.

The former Italian Somaliland has an area of 505 000 sq km (195 000 sq miles) and is largely desert or semidesert, ranged by pastoral tribes. The two main water courses, the Giuba and the Uebi Scabili, are in the south, and here are extensive plantations yielding commercial crops of cotton, sugarcane and bananas.

The capital, Mogadiscio, is also the chief port but has only lighterage facilities. A new port Chisimaio (Kismayu) is under construction to the south.

There is no railway and only a limited road system in the vicinity of the capital. A new 1 000 km (620 miles) highway is planned from Beled Wein in the centre to Burao in the northwest. This will provide the first all-weather communication link between the two former colonies and will provide access to many scattered areas. Mining is little developed although there are deposits of uranium, iron ore, gypsum and columbite, and there could be reserves of oil. Industry is limited to small factories processing foodstuffs (milk, meat and fish), some leatherworks and textile workshops. Eighty-nine per cent of the labour force is engaged in agriculture and almost all are nomadic pastoralists. Livestock in 1970 totalled 2.8m. cattle, 5m. goats, 4m. sheep and 3m. camels. Exports generally cover only 60 per cent of imports, the chief exports being live animals, bananas, hides and skins.

Libya

The vast area lying between Egypt and Tunisia and Algeria was the former Turkish province of Tripoli. It was seized by Italy in 1912 and lost by her in the Second World War. It contains three provinces, of which Cyrenaica in the east, bordering Egypt, and Tripolitania in the northwest, bordering Tunisia, came temporarily under British rule, while the third, Fezzan, a desert inland territory, bordering Algeria, was administered by France, pending decision by the United Nations on the future of Libya. In accordance with the decision finally reached, Libya was constituted, in December 1951, an independent sovereign kingdom, combining the three provinces on a federal basis, with the Amir of Cyrenaica as hereditary monarch of the whole. The country became a republic in 1969. The total area is estimated at 1.76m. sq km (680 000 sq miles) (six times the size of Italy), of which Cyrenaica forms nearly half, Fezzan a third, and Tripolitania a fifth. On the other hand Tripolitania has some two-thirds of the total population (1971) of 2.16m., Cyrenaica one-third, and Fezzan less than 0.5 per cent. Tripoli and Benghazi are joint capitals, but a new capital is planned at Al Bayda.

Much of the country is rock or sand, desert or semidesert, and southwards it merges into the Sahara; but the desert is interspersed with many extensive oases — Ghudams, Ghat, Marysiq (Maryak), Al Kufrah, Wabat Jalu (Jalo), etc. In the coastal zone also are some of the richest oases in North Africa, yielding good crops of dates, oranges, olives, and other Mediterranean products. These are varied by steppe country suitable both for growing cereals and for raising livestock. Italian colonisation was especially active in the coastal region round Tripoli and in the historical granary region of Cyrenaica. Salt is obtained along the seashore, and sponge and tunny fisheries are carried on along the coast.

Date palms are estimated at 3m., yielding over 50 000 tons a year, and olive trees at 3.5m., producing 35 000 tons of olives. In Tripolitania, 220 000 ha (540 000 acres) of barley produced some 50 000 tons in 1970, and 170 000 ha (420 000 acres) of wheat some 45 000 tons. Livestock in 1970 were 2.2m. sheep, 1.2m. goats, 108 000 cattle, and 165 000 camels.

Oil was found in Fezzan in 1957, near the Algerian frontier, and though the strike was not an economic proposition it led to a big prospecting campaign by leading oil companies. A surprise discovery was an abundant freshwater supply over a wide area at a watertable level of 180 to 304 m (600 to 1 000 ft) below the surface of the desert. This could be the largest underground freshwater lake in the world and would provide irrigation for crops, cereals and cattlefeed in a hitherto largely desert area. The major oil discoveries between 1958 and 1968, however, have been in the Sirte basin and although the known reserves are not great by world standards, their rapid exploitation has completely changed the economy. The closure of the Suez Canal and the proximity to European markets gave impetus to production which rose from a nominal quantity in 1960 to 104m. tons in 1973. Of the 10.2 per cent contributed by Africa to total world production in 1973, some 4 per cent came from Libya.

Previously subsidised for the use of military and air bases, the oil industry has now made Libya independent of external assistance and provided income for an improved standard of living and for industrialisation. Imports and exports in 1965 were £114m. and £282m. (Libya £). In 1971 they were £200m. and £766m., a direct reflection of the growth in value of oil exports which accounted for over 95 per cent of all exports. Imports came mainly from Italy, USA, West Germany and UK, while exports went to the same countries together with France and the Netherlands.

Road communications are limited mainly to the coastal region and the immediate hinterland. Routes to the Fezzan are mainly tracks, although plans exist for more permanent roads to the neighbouring states of Chad and Niger. The country has moved from road to air transport without passing through the intervening phase of railway construction. International and local airlines link the airports at Tripoli and Benghazi to the world's aviation network.

Algeria

Algeria, Morocco and Tunisia form the Atlas Lands of western North Africa, so called from their chief physical feature, the Atlas Mountains. They are European rather than African in their structure and climate, Asian rather than African in their native population. They are known to the Arabs as 'Djezira-el-Maghreb' — the Island in the West — because they form a large habitable area enfolded by the Mediterranean and the Sahara. During the past 2 000 years one empire after another has conquered the area and left its mark: Carthage, Rome, the Vandals, the Byzantines, the Arabs, and the Turks. French influence dates from 1830. Algeria was proclaimed a French colony in 1834, but several decades elapsed before economic progress began; Tunisia accepted French protection in 1881, and after a long period of warfare the sultan of Morocco did likewise in 1912. The varying length of the period of French influence, and the varying proportion of African to European population, result in distinct differences of development. After the Second World War, Arab nationalist sentiment increased. Morocco and Tunisia were given independence in 1956. French diehards — 1m. settlers who had no other home — resisted Algerian independence but it was granted in 1962.

The parallel chains of the Great and Little Atlas cross northern Algeria from southwest to northeast, coming from Morocco and extending into Tunisia. The region best fitted for cultivation is a strip of lowland or land at moderate elevation between the coast and the Little Atlas, a strip known as the Tell. The region between the Great and the Little Atlas is a plateau producing little besides coarse grass for sheep-rearing and alfa (esparto). South of the Atlas is the Biled-ul-jerid, or Land of Dates. In its full extent Algeria embraces a vast tract of the Sahara — not all level sandy wastes, but broken by extensive uplands, notably the great mountain mass of Ahaggar, rising to between 1 800 and 2 100 m (6 000 and 7 000 ft). Algeria has a total area of 2.46m. sq km (950 000 sq miles) and a population of some 15.7m. Northern Algeria occupies less than a tenth of the total area but supports more than nine-tenths of the total population.

Before 1960 about a tenth of the population was French; the great majority Kabyles (Berbers — hence the 'Barbary Coast') and Arabs. Now less than 100 000 French remain though the development of the country since the Second World War has been largely due to French industry and enterprise, supported by government expenditure on public works. Roads and railways were built, harbours constructed, new lands brought under cultivation by the sinking of artesian wells. Northern Algeria has good natural resources. There are extensive fisheries, and considerable mineral wealth, chiefly iron ore (3m. tons in 1965), phosphates (400 000 tons in 1965), and oil and natural gas. The first cargo of oil left Skikda (Philippeville) for France in 1958 and production has risen steadily to 51.9m. tons in 1972, when oil represented 60 per cent of total value of exports. Algeria was one of the first countries to export natural gas in bulk, in specially constructed bulk liquid carriers at −160° C (−260° F). Early exports went to France and the east coast of USA.

Large areas of Algeria are occupied by woodlands, often of secondary growth, but including some fine forests, among which the cork-oak is the chief commercial factor. Climate and crops are similar to those of southern Italy and southern Spain. The principal cereals grown are wheat and barley — wheat with a crop of 1.5m. tons in 1970 from 2.1m. ha (5.2m. acres), barley 400 000 tons from 688 000 ha (1.7m. acres). Among Mediterranean fruits, grapes are outstanding; grown chiefly for wine, crops reach over 2m. tons from 303 500 ha (750 000 acres). The orange crop reaches over 350 000 tons, and the production of dates is around 100 000 tons. Some 10 000 tons of tobacco are also grown annually. Sheep are pre-eminent among livestock. In 1970 they numbered 7.5m., and goats over 2m. Cattle were estimated at 600 000, and camels at 250 000 in 1960. In 1970 the figures were 870 000 and 170 000; an indication of changing standards of living.

Communications are served by 18 000 km (12 000 miles) of main roads and numerous by-roads and desert routes. Nearly 4 000 km (2 500 miles) of railway link the principal centres of population in Northern Algeria and connect with the railway systems of Morocco and Tunisia, as well as sending out tentacles southwards into the fringes of the Sahara — as far as Touggourt in the east and beyond Béchar in the west. The Sahara region may also benefit from a new road which may run from El Golea to Tamanrasset and on to Mali and Niger. This could open up the copper and walfram deposits in the central Sahara and encourage cereal growing from the underground freshwater lakes.

The country suffered great unrest between 1954 and 1962 and the pattern of trade and industry was adversely affected. Since 1962 the income from oil and natural gas, and the use of hydroelectric power installations west of Algiers, have provided a base for improved conditions. In 1939 exports exceeded imports by 12 per cent; in 1956 imports exceeded exports by 80 per cent; in 1970 imports and exports balanced. The main trading partners are France, USA, West Germany and Italy.

In terms of US dollars (the local currency is the dinar) imports and exports in 1960 were $1 249m. and $389m. In 1968 they were $804m. and $820m.

Table 76 — Algeria: population of principal towns in 1970

Alger (Algiers)	943 000	Skikola (Philippeville)	85 000
Oran	328 000	Blida	85 000
Constantine	254 000	Tlemcen	80 000
Annaba (Bone)	169 000	Mostaganem	64 000
Sidi-Bel-Abbès	105 000	Bougie	63 000
Sétif	98 000	Béchar	27 000

Tunisia

A French protectorate from 1881, Tunisia was accorded internal autonomy in 1955 and independence as a sovereign state in March 1956. In July 1957 the monarchy was abolished and a prime minister was elected as president and head of a sovereign independent republic.

Though parts of a geographical whole, Morocco, Algeria and Tunisia differ in some notable respects physically as well as politically. The Great and Little Atlas extend from Algeria across northern Tunisia, but the chief area of cultivation in Tunisia is not, as in Algeria, between the coast and the Little Atlas, but between the two chains of the Atlas, where the Algerian intermediate plateau narrows and drops to the valley of the Mejerda, a river which rises on the plateau and in its lower course regularly overflows its banks during the winter rains, irrigating and fertilising the neighbouring plains. South of the Atlas a string of shallow salt lakes (*shotts*) extend from near the Gulf of Gabès inland for some 400 km (250 miles), reaching beyond the Tunisian frontier into Algeria. These lakes lie below sea level and have long obstructed the passage of caravans trading between the fertile north and the desert south. It is estimated that there are over 3m. date palms in the southern oases, and over 22m. olive trees in the Sahel, as the southeast littoral is called.

In spite of differences, Tunisia is essentially a small edition, economically and commercially, of northern Algeria. It is half the size of northern Algeria (i.e. Algeria less the Algerian Sahara) and slightly larger than England with an area of 164 000 sq km (63 400 sq miles) its population in 1970 (nearly 5m.) is less than half that of its neighbour. But it has much the same climatic conditions and resources. Twenty-seven per cent of the total area is classed as arable, nearly 20 per cent is pastoral and under 8 per cent is forested. The other 45 per cent is divided more or less equally between 'unused but potentially productive' and 'built on area, waste land, and other'. Sheep (estimated at 3.1m. in 1970) are the most numerous livestock. There are over 500 000 cattle, and more camels (280 000) than in Algeria. The chief cereal crops are wheat (up to 470 000 tons) and barley (about 170 000 tons). Fruit crops are abundant: 100 000 tons of grapes in 1970; 47 000 tons of dates; 75 000 tons of oranges. Wine is not the dominating factor in the export trade that it is in Algeria, but Tunisia has the greater production of olive oil. The output in 1970 was 160 000 tons, though in the previous year, true to the erratic nature of the olive crop, it was only 90 000 tons. Although sixth in world production, Tunisia is one of the leading exporters of olive oil.

The forests on the hill slopes north of the Mejerda are rich in cork oaks and another species of oak which has a valuable tanning bark. Supplies of esparto grass are also abundant. Other products which

Tunisia has in common with Algeria are iron ore and phosphates. The output of phosphates (3.6m. tons) is double that of iron ore.

Imports since the Second World War have regularly exceeded exports by up to 80 per cent, but the imbalance is being reduced as oil exports and tourism play an increasing role. Imports are mainly machinery and transport equipment, manufactures, foodstuffs and chemicals; exports include petroleum, phosphates, olive oil, iron ore, fruit and dates. Oil production of 4.2m. tons in 1970 was small in comparison with Algeria (and negligible in comparison with Libya) but is rising slowly. Pipelines for oil and natural gas run from the El Borma field in the south to Gabès, which is a major port and fast becoming the centre of an industrial region. There is a steel plant at Menzel Bourguiba and an oil refinery at Bizerte.

Internal transport is served by 2 200 km (1 300 miles) of railway and 9 000 km (5 600 miles) of roads, mostly main roads, bitumenised or otherwise metalled. Air services, both internal and external, and including freight, are developing. Most of the Tunisian ports were open roadsteads. Tunis itself, the capital and chief seat of foreign commerce, situated at the northeast corner of the protectorate, is at the head of a shallow lagoon, but oceangoing vessels have access to the city and to the outer port, Tunis—Coulette, on the coast. On the north coast, France established a naval station at Bizerte. Other main ports are Gabès, Sfax and Sousse (Susa).

Table 77 — Tunisia: population of chief towns, 1966 census

Tunis	642 000	Kairouan	82 000
Sfax	250 000	Gabès	76 000
Bizerte	95 000	Béja	72 000

Morocco

Morocco, an independent kingdom, occupies the northwest corner of Africa, extending from the Strait of Gibraltar eastward along the Mediterranean and southward along the Atlantic. Formerly a sultanate whose ruler exercised absolute authority, it came under European control for much of the first half of the twentieth century. In March 1912 France concluded a treaty with the sultan establishing a French protectorate over the country. In November of the same year a Franco—Spanish convention recognised a Spanish sphere of influence in northern Morocco, bordering the Mediterranean. After the First World War, France, Britain and Spain established an international zone around Tangier, and other powers, including the United States, became associated with the administration of the zone.

After the Second World War the growth of nationalism in Morocco provoked widespread opposition to French rule, and in 1955 France recalled the legitimate sultan, whom she had exiled. In March 1956 she recognised the sultan's independence; Spain followed suit in Africa by relinquishing her claims in northern Morocco; and the sultan's full authority in the Tangier zone was restored by the powers in October. The sultan set up a cabinet system with a council of ministers, and Morocco was admitted to membership of the United Nations as a sovereign independent state. In August 1957 the sultan changed his title to king, and the Shereefian empire became the Kingdom of Morocco.

Spain has retained various minor enclaves on the Mediterranean coast and held the territory of Ifni in southwest Morocco from 1860 to 1969. Spain's possessions on the Mediterranean coast of Morocco, Alhucemas, Ceuta, Chafarinas, Melilla and Peñón de Vélez, total about 3 000 ha (7 410 acres), with an estimated population of 164 000 in 1969. Though small, they have considerable commercial and strategic value. Ifni, about the size of one of the smaller English counties, has an area of some 1 500 sq km (580 sq miles), but is largely desert with a population of only about 51 000. It reverted to Morocco by treaty in June 1969. To the south is another Spanish province, Spanish Sahara, comprising two districts: Sekia El Hamra and Rio de Oro. An arid territory, with an estimated area of 266 000 sq km (100 300 sq miles) it has a resident population of some 61 000, augmented after the rains by an influx of nomads. There are rich phosphate deposits and port facilities at Villa Cisneros.

The area of Morocco is about 500 000 sq km (166 000 sq miles), with a population of about 15m. It is estimated that nearly 18 per cent of the land is under arable cultivation, 17 per cent is pastoral and over 12 per cent is forested. Another 20 per cent is classed as 'built on, waste and other'. Morocco is a mountainous land. Only in occasional tracts along the coast, nowhere reaching far inland except in the valley of Sebou does the elevation fall below 183 to 213 m (600 to 700 ft). In the north the coastal range, Er Rif, rising to heights of 1 830 to 2 130 m (6 000 to 7 000 ft), is the home of semi-independent tribes. Further south the High Atlas, whose topmost peaks rise 3 900 to 4 600 m (13 000 to 15 000 ft) run from southwest to northeast in a broad range or succession of ranges occupying most of the zone. The southeastern flanks, exposed to the dry winds of the Sahara, are generally parched and desolate; the northwestern slopes are well wooded at the lower levels. Where the mountains approach the Mediterranean they connect with the coastal range. In the angle between these ranges is a tract of uplands and lowlands stretching down to the Atlantic coast, and further south the coast is backed by plains and uplands rising to the main range. The rivers flowing through the mountains are unnavigable, and where they cross the lower country they are apt to dry up or become much reduced in volume, except when the snows are melting on the mountains; but in many places they are well adapted for irrigation and provide better facilities for hydroelectric power than are available in Algeria or Tunisia.

The Moors are a Muslim people, and until the country came under European control the government kept largely aloof from the outside world. Foreign trade was not encouraged; there were no railways, no wheeled carts. European intervention brought about great changes and although most of the French and Spanish left after independence, it is estimated that some 200 000 Europeans remain, mostly French, many of them in the towns but a large number on the land.

The natural resources of the country are much the same as in Algeria and Tunisia, though barley takes the place of wheat as the chief cereal crop, being grown on some 2m. ha (5m. acres) and yielding up to 2m. tons, against 1.9m. ha (4.7m. acres) under wheat, yielding over 1.5m. tons. Many other cereal and root crops are grown, but none of outstanding magnitude. The most important products, after wheat and barley, are fruits. The grape crop, grown mostly for wine, was 203 000 tons in 1970; oranges, 880 000 tons; grapefruit, 15 000 tons; dates, 90 000 tons. Olive crops of some 180 000 tons yield 50 000 tons of olive oil. Flax is grown, for seed only (linseed), on a reduced scale with very variable production (up to 15 000 tons). But the big feature of the farming industry in Morocco is the large numbers of its livestock, which exceed those of its neighbours. In 1970, cattle numbered 3.6m., sheep over 17m., goats over 8.8m., camels 230 000, and horses, asses and mules 1.5m., mostly asses. There are extensive forests, especially of cork oaks, which alone cover over 2 600 sq km (1 000 sq miles) to make Morocco the third largest producer after Spain and Portugal. There is an active fishing industry (tunny, sardines, etc.).

Minerals include iron ore, which has not, however, been exploited to so large an extent as in Algeria; output in 1969 was under 750 000 tons. As in Tunisia, production of phosphate rock is on a much bigger scale, amounting in 1971 to over 12m. tons. There are extensive deposits about 80 km (50 miles) inland from Safi, a port about midway between Casablanca and Agadir. The mines are connected by rail (standard gauge) both with Safi (which is also a centre of the sardine fishery) and with Casablanca, and at both these ports there are facilities for exporting the phosphates. From Casablanca also a main line connects with Rabat, Meknès and Fès (Fez), and continues eastward to the important frontier town of Oujda, where it sends out a branch southwards across the Great Atlas to link up at Béchar in the Sahara. Beyond Oujda it joins the Algerian railway system at the frontier. Altogether there are in Morocco over 1 770 km (1 100 miles) of railway, and nearly 22 600 km (14 000 miles) of main and secondary roads.

With the transfer of the French and Spanish protectorates and the

Tangier international zone to the authority of the sultan in 1956, the overseas trade of Morocco ceased to be subject to divided control and became the concern of unified sovereign state. Such changes take time and the excess of imports over exports is slowly diminishing, with increasing tourism to aid the balance. The trade of the former French zone accounts for an overwhelming proportion of the whole and France is by far the main trading partner, followed by West Germany, USA and UK. Imports are of the usual miscellaneous character, exports are mainly minerals, citrus fruits and sardines. In terms of the national currency, the dirham, imports and exports in 1961 were DH 2 257m.; DH 1 731m. In 1971 they were DH 3 533m.; DH 2 526m.

The chief towns are along the coast and between the coast and the mountains. Rabat, towards the northern end of the coast, was the official capital of the French protectorate, and usually the sultan's place of residence. It has been far outstripped by Casablanca, a little further south, which has developed as the leading commercial centre and port handling over 70 per cent of the total shipping and the focus of 50 per cent of the industrial labour force. Inland from Rabat are Meknès and Fès (Fez), the traditional northern capital; and inland from Essaouira (Mogador), which is centrally situated along the coast, is Marrakech, the traditional southern capital, though the latter is now more easily reached by rail from Casablanca.

Table 78 — Morocco: estimated populations of chief towns in 1968

Casablanca	1 250 000	Tanger (Tangier)	150 000
Rabat	410 000	Oujda	140 000
Marrakech	285 000	Kénitra (Port Lyautey)	120 000
Fès (Fez)	270 000	Safi	120 000
Meknès	225 000	Tétouan	115 000

Spanish Sahara

Among the remaining Spanish territories in northwest Africa are the small enclaves of Ceuta (88 000) and Melilla (78 000). There are two garrison towns on the Mediterranean coast of Morocco with a combined area of 33 sq km (13 sq miles); the former has an expanding tourist industry and both have small fishing fleets. Ifni, a former enclave of some 1 500 sq km (580 sq miles) on the Atlantic coast has port facilities at Sidi Ifni but no exports of any kind, and was incorporated in Morocco in June 1969. The Canary Islands (see p. 752) are provinces within Spanish national territory.

Spanish Sahara remains as Spain's only major overseas province. This is a largely desert area stretching along the Atlantic coast for 1 650 km (1 020 miles) between Morocco and Mauritania. It is divided into two districts, Sekia El Hamra in the north and Rio de Oro in the south, with a total area of 266 000 sq km (102 680 sq miles) and a population of some 60 000, 7 000 of whom are in the capital of El Aaiún. There is little arable soil and the inhabitants (apart from some 30 000 from Spain) are Arab and Berber nomads with small flocks of camels, sheep and goats. Apart from a little dried fish, there are no exports. Considerable (estimated at from 1 700m. to 10 000m. tons) reserves of phosphates have been found at Bu Croa between El Aaiún and Smara, and these will shortly be exploited. In preparation for this, port facilities are being developed at Playa de El Aaiún; and the port at Villa Cisneros (which is also the major airport) is also being improved.

South Africa

Though geographically it may be applied to a much larger region, the term South Africa is generally understood to refer to the Republic of South Africa, which withdrew from the Commonwealth on 15 March 1961. It was formed in 1910 by the union of the former self-governing colonies of the Cape of Good Hope, Natal, the Orange Free State and the Transvaal, which became provinces of the Union. Development has had to contend not only against the physical conditions of the country but against the differing outlooks of the Boer and British elements in the population. A prominent feature of Afrikaner nationalism, as developed since the Second World War, was the growing application of apartheid policy to the Africans, which led finally to the Union becoming a Republic and leaving the Commonwealth.

Apart from the Sudan, which while under Anglo–Egyptian rule was in a class by itself, the Union was for long the largest African territory of the British Commonwealth and empire, and, though slightly surpassed in size by the shortlived Federation of Rhodesia and Nyasaland, it was still easily the most important, both internationally and commercially. Its area is 1.2m. sq km (471 500 sq miles) (five times that of the United Kingdom), and its population (1970 census) 21.4m. About one in six of the population is white. Cape Town is the legislative and Pretoria the administrative capital.

The adjacent territory of South West Africa, formerly a German possession, has been administered by South Africa since the First World War. What were known as the High Commission Territories were three British dependencies, one (Basutoland) surrounded by Union territory and the other two (Swaziland and the Bechuanaland Protectorate) bordering on the Union. These three territories were administered by a British High Commissioner in South Africa until 1966 when Basutoland became independent as the Kingdom of Lesotho and Bechuanaland as the Republic of Botswana. In 1968 Swaziland also became independent. All three remained in the Commonwealth.

All round the coast, the country rises rapidly to considerable heights. From the western half of the south coast the ascent is made in well-marked terraces, the innermost of which form tablelands of 915 m (3 000 ft) or more in height. These tablelands are known by the Hottentot name of Karoos. The Little Karoo comes first, and beyond it the Great Karoo, which has a length of nearly 480 km (300 miles) from west to east and a width in many parts of up to 120 km (75 miles). On the eastern side the rise in terraces is not so well marked, or at least not so regular. Here the main feature is the Drakensberg (Dragon Mountain) Range, really the high eastern edge of the plateau. It has the highest mountains in South Africa, rising to 3 350 m (11 000 ft) and descending to plateaus of over 2 100 m (7 000 ft) in Lesotho.

Together with the physical features just described, the circumstance of most importance in determining the character of the climate of South Africa is its situation between the trade wind belts of the Indian Ocean and the South Atlantic, though a small portion in the extreme southwest receives winter rains from the westerly winds. The Karoos are subject to prolonged droughts, but they are occupied by a vegetation singularly adapted to a climate of this nature — able to survive, though in a withered condition, the want of rain for months, and even years, so that in a week or two after the occurrence of rains the surface becomes green with herbs and bushes or richly coloured with multitudes of flowering plants. In such a climate cultivation, and even the rearing of livestock are obviously precarious without irrigation.

Throughout the greater part of the northwest Cape Province the annual rainfall is altogether insignificant. Only on a narrow strip of the south coast rains are fairly equally distributed all the year round, with a predominance of summer rains in the area of Durban. In the greater part of South Africa, only the rains at the end of summer, culminating in February and March, fall with fair regularity and abundance. As this period of the year, in consequence of the high altitude and resulting rarity of the atmosphere, is immediately followed by a rigorous winter, those rains are useless for sowing. Only in a few parts sufficiently near the Drakensberg to get rains in August and September can wheat be grown without irrigation. Sown at the time of those rains it is reaped in December. Dry farming is a partial solution. Maize and a few other crops suited to warm, rainy summers can be grown more widely.

The rivers of South Africa being mostly fed only by summer rains have the characteristics of all tableland rivers in countries with alternating rainy and dry seasons. They flow in valleys deeply cut, having a width and slope varying with the nature of the rock in which they have been cut. In summer they are in flood, and in winter they are mostly reduced to a mere trickle between heaps of boulders filling a wide bed bordered by high bluffs. The Orange, though longer than the Rhine, is navigable for boats only a few kilometres up. Even the east side of

South Africa is practically without navigable rivers. Irrigation based on such rivers is a costly project.

So long as the development of South Africa was dependent on agriculture and pastoral industries the character of the climate confined the bulk of the inhabitants to the southwest and to the east. The regions first settled by Europeans lie in the southwest; the desire for further territory suitable for pastoral and agricultural development, amongst other causes, led to the great treks to the east and north. The purely British settlements of Port Elizabeth (1820) and Durban (1824) were on the south and east. In 1867 the first diamond was discovered in South Africa at Hope Town; the diamondfields of Kimberley, discovered three years later, were the cause of the first long railway line being built into the interior. A greater stimulus to railway construction was given by the discovery of the goldfields of the Rand (Witwatersrand) in the southern Transvaal and the subsequent foundation of Johannesburg in 1886. Nearby deposits of coal, easily and cheaply mined, made it possible to work the goldfields to advantage. Both the goldfields and the diamondfields attracted population. The markets which they provided stimulated, in turn, agriculture and other industries and justified expenditure on irrigation, especially for citrus fruits.

On all the railways into the interior the geographical features have necessitated steep gradients, but routes have tended in that direction, partly because of the character of the coastline. South Africa is short of good natural harbours, and the few convenient sites are at great distances from one another. In False Bay, east of the Cape Peninsula, there is a naval station at Simonstown, but it is not so situated as to be suitable for a commercial harbour. Cape Town, Port Elizabeth, East London and Durban are the main ports. Durban (Port Natal) is the premier port commercially. It has a fine sheltered harbour but a very narrow entrance exposed to the southeast trade winds. Saldanha Bay, about 1° N of Cape Town, forms an excellent natural harbour, and is linked by rail with Cape Town. A new major port is planned here to handle the bulk export of iron ore from mines in the area of Sishen, to which it will be connected by a new rail link.

In general, both railways and harbours in the Republic are state-owned. Out of 22 000 km (14 068 miles) of railway over 7 250 km (4 500 miles) have been electrified to facilitate traffic on steep gradients and sharp curves. About half the electrified mileage is in Natal, including the main line from Durban to the Transvaal and Orange Free State borders. Other districts which have benefited are around Cape Town and the Rand, including the line between Pretoria and Johannesburg. A large proportion of the Natal railways have a gradient steeper than 1 in 35. The line from Durban to Johannesburg, after ascending to about 910 m (3 000 ft), descends nearly 300 m (1 000 ft) to Maritzburg, then in 18 km (11 miles) climbs to 1 130 m (3 700 ft) and then on to 1 460 m (4 800 ft). On the Delagoa Bay line the great rise is within the Transvaal, the line rising 1 580 m (5 190 ft) in the last 180 km (112 miles) and requiring a rack as it nears Belfast.

The following particulars of the individual provinces will exemplify the general characteristics and resources of the country.

Cape Province or, more correctly, the Province of the Cape of Good Hope, formerly known popularly as Cape Colony, stretches from the Atlantic to the Indian Ocean and extends northwards to the lower reaches of the Orange River in the west, and to Losotho, and Natal in the east. It includes, as an integral part of the province (but administered as part of South West Africa), an enclave of 969 sq km (374 sq miles) around Walvis Bay, the best harbour on the coast of South West Africa and the chief port. It was formerly a whaling station.

With an area of 721 000 sq km (278 000 sq miles), the province is easily the largest in the Republic (over half the total area) and until the Second World War it had the most inhabitants, but the Transvaal has since held the lead. Though the population is about a fifth of the total for the whole country, the Cape Province is the most thinly peopled of all the provinces. As a result of the physical conditions previously described, the population is found mainly in the east, in the extreme southwest, and along a narrow strip of the south coast. Broadly, 60 per cent are Bantus, with a few Hottentots and Bushmen in the west; 20 per cent are white, mainly Dutch, Huguenot, or British descent, with English and Afrikaans (a modified Dutch) as the principal languages; and the remaining 20 per cent are mostly 'Coloured' — a mixture of European stocks with the indigenous population.

Only a small proportion of the surface is adapted for agriculture. In the western half of the province irrigation is absolutely necessary for the growing of crops, except in a small district round Cape Town, where most of the products of the Mediterranean can be grown, and whence there is a large export of the characteristic fruits of that climate. In the north, the Orange River Project, one of the largest irrigation and hydroelectric schemes in the world, will take thirty years to complete (1966—90) and will provide a great increase in the arable area. In the eastern half larger areas have a sufficient rainfall for agriculture, especially south of the Stormberg and Drakensberg, and here the Bantu grow maize (mealies) and other grain adapted to warm rainy summers.

The pastoral industry has from the first been of much more importance than the growing of crops. At first only cattle and native sheep were reared, the latter yielding excellent mutton but only a coarse kind of hair rather than wool. The merino sheep was introduced about 1812, and thereafter wool came to be an important export of the colony. The sheep are reared partly on grass on the coast strip, partly on the Karoos, where they depend chiefly on the deep-rooted bushes. In the arid western parts of the Great Karoo, some 4.8 ha (12 acres) are required on the average for the support of a single sheep, but in the eastern parts only 1.2 ha (3 acres). Besides sheep and cattle, the Angora goat has been largely reared since about 1840 and the ostrich since about 1865. Oudtshoorn, a rich irrigated district in the western part of the Little Karoo, had extensive fields of lucerne entirely devoted to the rearing of ostriches. The industry reached its zenith in 1913, when feathers were exported to the value of nearly £3m. Since the First World War, demand and exports have dwindled to trifling proportions.

The 'deep' diamondfields of Kimberley have been actively worked since about 1871. Great expansion of the industry came when the diamonds of the surface deposits were traced to their source in the hard rock, known to the miners as 'blue ground': a volcanic rock filling the round necks or pipes of ancient volcanoes. Working the hard rock and excavating to great depths necessitated the amalgamation of interests and the beginning of the great combines which dominate the world market, associated with such names as Cecil Rhodes, De Beer, Joel, and Oppenheimer. Alluvial mining is still important, particularly in Namaqualand.

Other mineral resources of the Cape Province include iron ore, copper, manganese and coal. Coal was supplied to the Kimberley mines in their early days from Molteno, Cyphergat and Indwe (in the Stormberg region), but it was of poor quality. Copper mining flourished in Namaqualand (the arid northwest of the province) in the latter half of the nineteenth century, but the industry declined with the price of copper and by 1932 all the mines had closed down. Extensive copper/zinc resources have now been discovered in the Prieska area; and there are large resources of rich iron ore (66 per cent iron) in the Sishen area of the northern Cape.

In the parts of the province beyond the Great Kei River known as the Transkeian Territories, which include Pondoland, the white population is very scanty. The Drakensberg Range hinders access to the interior, but the Territories are capable of greater development, forming one of the best parts of South Africa — fertile, well-watered, and eminently suited for pasture.

The northern extension of the Cape Province, stretching from the middle course of the Orange River up to the Molopo, includes not only Griqualand West (Kimberley), with its diamond mines, but the former Crown Colony of British Bechuanaland, with such historic centres as Kuruman, Vryburg, and Mafeking. This is not to be confused with Botswana, the former, Bechuanaland Protectorate, north of the Molopo (see p. 706).

Natal. The Province of Natal lies between the Indian Ocean and the

Drakensberg, on the far side of which its neighbours are Lesotho and the Orange Free State. Coastwise it extends from the Cape Province to Moçambique (to the north of 27° S), having also on its northern borders the Transvaal and Swaziland. Its area of 86 900 sq km (33 600 sq miles), a little larger than Ireland, is only about one-fourteenth of the Republic, but it is the most densely populated province, with 2.14m. inhabitants at the 1970 census. The land rises rapidly from the coast to the interior, and the climate changes from subtropical to temperate in the same direction. Near the coast are grown sugarcane, cotton, tea, arrowroot, black wattle (an acacia) and other tropical and subtropical products. Natal is pre-eminent in South Africa in two of these products: it is the sole seat of the sugar industry, which yields 1.5 to 2m. tons of raw sugar annually and not only supplies the country but supports a valuable export trade: and it grows most of South Africa's output of wattle (by far the most important of the minor forest products of South Africa), which supports a valuable export trade in wattle bark and tanning extract.

Further inland are grown the temperate cereals, and sheep and cattle are reared. Here also there is a large native population, mainly Zulu Kaffirs, who form the majority of the inhabitants. There are also many Indians who came originally as labourers on the tea and other plantations, and as miners; many remained and their descendants are active as market gardeners and traders. Durban is the chief seaport and largest town. It is the nearest port in the Republic to the Rand and the coalfields of Natal and the Transvaal, and, as already noted, surpasses Cape Town in the volume of its shipping and trade. Pietermaritzburg, the capital, at an altitude of 670 m (2 200 ft), is situated amid scenes of tropical beauty, but in a hollow in which the heat is oppressive. In the extreme north of the province Newcastle and Dundee rapidly increased their production of coal, which is better than that of the other provinces, and, in spite of the long haul of 482 km (300 miles) over a difficult railway route, is exported by sea and was the basis of the bunkering trade in the days of steamships.

The Orange Free State, situated between the Orange and Vaal Rivers, had a population (1970) of only 1.65m. in a country of 129 000 sq km (50 000 sq miles) (about the size of England); it is nearly as thinly populated as the Cape Province. The population is made up of Afrikaans-speaking farmers or 'Boers'. The surface is typical veld country, rolling grassy plains seamed by river beds. It has been called South Africa's prairie province. The plains vary from under 1 070 m (3 500 ft) in altitude in the west to 1 690 m (5 500 ft) in the east. Much of the country has a rainfall inadequate for agriculture without irrigation, but the northeastern districts form part of the great 'maize-triangle' where maize is grown mainly for human consumption. They lack the August—October rains, but on the other hand have abundant rains from December to March. The remainder of the country is mostly sheep-farming land, but goldfields which have sprung into fame have been discovered around Odendaalsrust, southwest of Kroonstad. Other minerals include uranium, diamonds and coal. The capital is Bloemfontein, on the direct railway route from Port Elizabeth to Johannesburg and Pretoria.

The Transvaal lies to the north of the Orange Free State: that is, beyond the Vaal River — trans-Vaal. It is second to the Cape Province in extent, first in total population, and second to Natal in density of population. With an area of 285 000 sq km (110 000 sq miles) — nearly double that of England and Wales — it had some 6.38m. inhabitants in 1970. The surface features are similar to those of the Orange Free State, but here the geological structure, and the resultant mineral wealth, is of great importance. The Transvaal may be divided into five regions: (1) The Witwatersrand, the goldfield stretching from east to west through Johannesburg. (2) The High Veld lying to the south of the Witwatersrand, composed of undulating grassy plains at an altitude of 1 430 to 1 780 m (4 700 to 5 700 ft), with very cold dry winters, but with a rainfall from January to March rendering it suitable for the cultivation, without irrigation, of maize, potatoes, and other roots, as well as of pulses. (3) The Bush Veld north of the Witwatersrand. (4) The Low Veld to the northeast. In both (3) and (4) the plains are generally below 910 m (3 000 ft) in height, and hence, being in a latitude below 26° S, not well adapted for European settlement. Both are traversed by comparatively high ranges of hills. Farmers migrate (trek) from the High Veld to the Low Veld with the dying-down of the grasses on the High Veld in the winter. (5) The Southwestern District, an arid and comparatively unproductive region.

The mineral wealth of the Transvaal is enormous in amount and varied in character. The first place belongs to gold, which is found in many parts of the country. The possibilities attracted increasing attention in the latter half of the nineteenth century. In 1872 mining was begun in the Northern Transvaal at Eersteling, since scheduled as a National Monument. Larger and more successful operations quickly followed in the Lydenburg district of the Eastern Transvaal, one of the few Transvaal districts outside the Rand where gold is still mined on a considerable scale. The next decade saw a temporary boom in the De Kaap valley, where the town of Barberton sprang up in 1886. But these ventures were rendered of minor importance by the discovery, about the same time, of the goldfields of the Rand (Witwatersrand). On the richest part of the Rand the town of Johannesburg was founded in September 1886, and at a census held in 1896 the population of the town and district was found to have grown to upwards of 100 000, of whom about half were whites. Sixty years later (1957) the population was estimated at over 1m., including nearly 400 000 whites. In 1970 it was over 1.4m.

The Rand is a ridge about 97 km (60 miles) long, rising 305 m (1 000 ft) above the adjacent country. The gold-bearing rocks are a conglomerate, in which the gold occurs in the form of minute particles more or less evenly disseminated through it. Hence powerful machinery is required for its extraction, and from the first this has been a capitalist's, not a poor man's, goldfield. Labour is the perennial difficulty. After the South African War, the introduction of Chinese coolies who were kept in compounds was much criticised, and they were gradually repatriated. African labour is now recruited from nearby Commonwealth countries, and Moçambique but their employment is strictly limited by apartheid laws.

The Transvaal is also rich in other minerals, particularly coal and iron of medium quality, and copper, of which there are large mines at Messina, on the northern border, near the Limpopo. The production of coal in 1964 approached two-thirds of the country's total output — mostly from the collieries of the Witbank district, east of Pretoria, but also from the Vereeniging mines on the northern bank of the Vaal, south of Johannesburg. Vereeniging, where the peace treaty was signed in 1902 after the South African War, is now one of the leading industrial centres in the country. It has steelworks, many engineering and other industrial works, and one of the largest steam power stations in the whole of Africa. Electric power for industrial purposes is among the cheapest in the world, and future supplies to Transvaal will come from the Cabora Bassa on the Zambezi.

Resources and trade of South Africa (and Namibia). Of the total area of South Africa it is estimated that 74 per cent of it is pastoral country, less than 10 per cent arable, 33 per cent wooded, and 12 per cent waste or built on. Small as is the percentage of arable land, it represents 11m. ha (27m. acres) and nearly a half of this is under maize, yielding a crop of over 5m. tons. Wheat is grown on 1.4m. ha (3.4m. acres), but the average yield is low and the crop about 1.6m. tons. Sugar-planting in Natal yields over 15m. tons of cane, from which 1.5 to 2m. tons of raw sugar is extracted. Viticulture is practically confined to the Cape Province, and grapes are grown mainly for wine. The total crop in 1970 was 760 000 tons, of which only a small percentage was exported as fresh fruit. Grown chiefly in the southwest of Cape Province, the crops fall into two main categories, differing according as they are grown under natural rainfall in the coastal zone below the mountains or under irrigation in the Little Karoo. Apples are also a valuable export, and fresh citrus fruits, chiefly oranges, of which the production amounts to over 0.5m. tons. Among other crops, as illustrating the variety of South

Africa's products, though on a smaller scale, are groundnuts (240 000 tons), and sunflower seed (1.2m. tons).

As might be expected from the pastoral character of most of the country, the numbers of livestock are outstanding. South Africa has the seventh largest flock of sheep (30.6m.) in the world and is the fifth largest wool producer (145 000 tons). Cattle are estimated at 12.3m. and goats at 5.5m. (1970). South Africa is poorly timbered. Forests are mostly found in comparatively small patches on the seaward slopes of the mountains behind the coastal zone. Fishing is a major industry — the catch ranging from whales to pilchards.

On balance, agriculture is of declining comparative importance in a country fast exploiting its mineral wealth and already the main industrial power in Africa. Agriculture's contribution to the gross domestic product has fallen from 21 per cent in 1911 to 10 per cent in 1969; and although 29 per cent of the total labour force is engaged (mainly Bantu subsistance farming) the 90 000 white farmers were responsible in 1970 for 90 per cent of the gross value of the agricultural products.

In 1970 South Africa was the largest producer in the non-Communist world of antimony, gold and platinum; second or third in chrome ore (75 per cent of the known world reserves), diamonds, manganese ore, uranium and vanadium; fourth in asbestos, and a major producer of iron ore, copper, coal, nickel, vermiculite and fluorspar. The only important minerals not found in economic quantities were bauxite and petroleum. Gold and diamonds have been the traditional source of mineral wealth, and although the production of gold has risen rapidly between 1957 and 1968 (from 530 000 kg to 967 000 kg: 1 168 450 lb to 2 131 870 lb) its percentage contribution to the total mining output has fallen from 61 to 57. It may well fall to less than half as the production of other minerals moves ahead.

In South Africa, as in most countries, the nominal value of the overseas trade has gone up by leaps and bounds since the Second World War, partly as a result of the changing value of money and partly from the increased processing ('beneficiation') of raw materials. In 1956 general imports were valued at R(Rand)762m. against R144m. in 1938; and national exports exclusive of gold bullion and specie at R579m. against R47m. — thirteen times as much. In 1969 the figures were R2 134m. and R1 531m. respectively. Gold exports are not included in the ordinary trade returns. According to the United Nations *Yearbook of International Trade Statistics* exports of gold in 1938 amounted to R124m. and in 1956 to R386m. By 1969 they were R779m. Four main groups made up 89 per cent of the total exports in 1964 (food and live animals, 26; crude materials, 37; manufactured goods, 22; machinery, 4). In 1969 the same groups made up 82 per cent, with the following respective percentages: 18.5, 24, 33 and 6.5. In five short years crude materials had fallen from 37 to 24 per cent, and manufactured goods had risen from 22 to 33 per cent, to reflect the increased processing of raw materials mentioned above.

Imports cover a wide range of commodities, with no very dominant item. Cars, trucks and vans, machinery and manufactured goods making up 72 per cent of the total in 1969, chemicals and petroleum products making another 15 per cent.

Over half the imports in 1956 (SA£1 = £1) were supplied by the United Kingdom (£156.5m.) and the United States (£99m.). Another quarter was made up by eight countries – Germany £32m., Canada £22.5m., Rhodesia and Nyasaland (17.5m.), Japan £12m., Saudi Arabia £11.25m., Iran £11m., Italy £10m., and Belgium £10m. Over half the exports were taken by three countries – UK £109m., Rhodesia and Nyasaland £55m., USA £29m.; and the next half-dozen principal buyers took another quarter – Belgium £21.5m., Germany £18m., Italy £16.75m., France £15.5m., Netherlands £9.5m., Japan £8.5m.

It has seemed worth while to retain these trade figures of the Union for 1956 so that a rough comparison can be made with the 1969 figures. The currency is now the rand (R1.7 = £1.00). Both imports and exports have shown a steady rise, imports from R1 529m. (1964) to R1 944m. (1969) and exports from R1 038m. to R1 391m. Imports came from UK, USA, West Germany and Japan; exports go to UK, USA, Africa, Japan and West Germany. The pattern is broadly the same (1974) with Japan playing an increased part in purchase of raw materials.

Table 79 – South Africa: population of chief towns, including suburbs (1968)

	White	Total
Johannesburg	482 600	1 408 000
Durban	244 000	874 000
Cape Town	271 300	825 700
Pretoria	308 700	571 500
Port Elizabeth	119 600	386 600
Bloemfontein	74 500	180 200
Pietermaritzburg	46 000	160 300
Germiston	101 200	139 500
East London	58 000	125 000

South West Africa (Namibia), bordering the Atlantic, extends from the Cape Province northwards to Angola, and inland to Botswana. Before the First World War it was a German colony. In 1920 the League of Nations vested the administration in the Union of South Africa. The mandate is still valid internationally but the Republic now governs independently and the apartheid laws apply. Trade returns are incorporated in those of South Africa.

With an area of 823 000 sq km (318 000 sq miles) the Territory supports (1970 census), 746 330 people, including 90 660 whites. In general, the rainfall is scanty and there is much barren desert. Only in the far north is agriculture possible, to a limited extent, without irrigation. The mainstay of the country has been the pastoral industry. Sheep predominate in the south, cattle further north. Livestock include over 4m. sheep (mostly Karakul for 'Persian' lambskins), 2.5m. cattle, 1.7m. goats. In 1962, 2.35m. Karakul pelts were exported and by 1970 the figure had risen to almost 3m. Diamonds and copper are also valuable exports. These minerals along with uranium, iron, wolfram and tin constitute the main potential commercial wealth of the Territory. There is also a fishing industry with an annual production of around 1m. tons, based largely on the inshore pilchard shoals off Cape Cross.

Windhoek, the capital, is situated in the centre of the Territory at a height of 1 680 m (5 500 ft). At the census of 1970 it had a population of 60 000, of whom over half were white. It is linked with the Cape railways by a line of South African narrow gauge (3 ft 6 in), which extends beyond Windhoek to Walvis Bay (see p. 698) and is also connected with Lüderitz Bay. There are 2 330 km (1 430 miles) of standard-gauge line.

Lesotho

The Kingdom of Lesotho, formerly Basutoland, has an area of 30 300 sq km (11 700 sq miles) and an African population of 935 000 in 1969, with probably another 110 000 in the Republic of South Africa since the main 'export' is really labour. In 1966 the country became an independent monarchy within the Commonwealth. From the western or Orange Free State border, marked by the Caledon River (tributary to the Orange), 'Lowlands' of 1 500 to 1 800 m (5 000 to 6 000 ft) rise eastward to 3 300 m (11 000 ft) in the Drakensberg, along the Natal border. The mountains form a main watershed, and Lesotho is known as the 'Switzerland' and the 'Sponge' of South Africa; on its borders rise not only the Caledon and the Orange River itself, flowing to the Atlantic, but the Tugela, flowing to the Indian Ocean. It is a pastoral country, carrying nearly 1.75m. sheep, 410 000 cattle and nearly 1m. goats. Basuto ponies, despite some deterioration, are renowned in South Africa for their hardy qualities, but sheep and goats are the factor of prime economic importance. Exports are mainly wool, mohair (Angora goats' wool) and diamonds. About one-sixth of the land is under cultivation and yields normally a sufficiency of cereal and leguminous crops. There is hydroelectric power potential in the mountainous northwest. Maseru, the capital, a township of about 18 000 people, near the Caledon, is linked by rail with the Orange Free State.

Swaziland

Swaziland, 17 400 sq km (6 705 sq miles; a little smaller than Wales) has been an independent kingdom since 1968, and has a population (1969) of 423 000, including fewer than 10 000 Europeans. Mbabane, the capital, has a population of 14 000 and Manzini (Bremersdorp), the former capital, in a less healthy situation, has a population of 16 000. The Swazis are akin to the Zulus and have suffered in the past from a welter of concessions granted recklessly to Europeans by former chiefs. North and west and south lies the Transvaal; to the east are Natal and Moçambique. From the High Veld at 1 200 m (4 000 ft) in the west the land drops through the Middle Veld to the low-lying Bush Veld. It is mixed country, with many products, but mainly pastoral; there are some 540 000 head of cattle, and 280 000 sheep and goats. The pastures are overstocked and badly eroded. A large asbestos mine has an annual output of around 43 000 tons, and since 1964 a railway (leading to Lourenço Marques) has tapped rich iron ore deposits to make iron ore the major export (production in 1969 was over 2.5m. tons). The country has a customs union with the Republic of South Africa and other main exports include sugar, meat and meat products, forest products and wood pulp and, increasing in importance, citrus fruits and pineapples. Imports are oil, machinery, transport equipment and consumer goods mainly from South Africa. Exports in 1970 exceeded imports by 20 per cent.

Botswana

Lying east of South West Africa and north of the Molopo, the Republic of Botswana (formerly Bechuanaland), is a country of 575 000 sq km (275 000 sq miles) with a population (1969) of 629 000. The distinctive feature of this land-locked country is the Kalahari Desert, which is far from being the legendary sandy waste; a modern survey encouraged hopes of ranching possibilities. There are numerous salt pans and a wide expanse of swampy country in the north, between Lake Ngami and the Zambezi. Development has been essentially on pastoral lines with up to 90 per cent of the population working on the land. In 1969 there were 1.5m. cattle and 1.6m. sheep and goats. Livestock, carcases, hides and skins have provided two-thirds of the exports. A government abattoir is an aid to the marketing of produce. There is every prospect that minerals will be more important in the future. Copper, nickel and diamonds are available for exploitation. Coal is available for power and there are light industries at the capital, Gaborone (14 000), and Francistown. Tourism is also likely to become increasingly important.

Rhodesia

Much of the territory of Rhodesia is a tableland 1 200 to 1 500 m (4 000 to 5 000 ft) above the sea, with a climate suitable for white settlers, and at the 1969 census the population of 5.1m. in a country three-quarters the size of France, included 228 600 Europeans. Grassy plains alternate with bush country and groups of hills, notably the Matopos, where Cecil Rhodes is buried. The largest towns are Salisbury, the capital, in the northeast (Mashonaland), population 384 500; and Bulawayo, in the southwest (Matabeleland), with a population of 245 600. The main line from Cape Town to the north passes through Bulawayo, whence another line runs to Salisbury and Beira, the Moçambique east coast port which is the ocean gateway to Rhodesia and Zambia. Congestion of shipping at Beira has caused many delays, and in 1955 new links were constructed between the Rhodesian and Moçambique railways, so as to provide Rhodesia with an outlet to the sea at Lourenço Marques, via Guija, on the Limpopo River. There is also a link through Botswana to the South African railway system. A total of 4 340 km (2 700 miles) in all.

With an area of 390 000 sq km (150 000 sq miles) on the African high plateau, the chief crops are maize (for home consumption), citrus fruits and tobacco in the wetter east, with cotton, sunflower seeds, sugarcane, rice, cassava and a wide range of vegetables. Cattle rearing (4m. in 1970) and sheep (0.5m.) take over where the rainfall is less, except in the tsetse area of the Zambezi lowlands.

Among a wide range of minerals, asbestos is the most valuable (eighth largest in world production) with many others including gold, copper, chrome ore, iron ore and coal. The Wankie coalfield with a reserve of over 4 000m. tons is one of the continent's major coalfields supplying all south central Africa and providing a basis for Rhodesian industrialisation. The Second World War gave impetus to the development of industry, which was further stimulated by ample electric power from the Kariba project and by the need for increased self-sufficiency after the imposition of United Nation's sanctions which followed the unilateral declaration of independence in 1965. There is an iron and steel plant at Que Que, ferrochrome smelting plants at Gwelo, an oil refinery at Umtali (with a pipeline to Beira which will eventually link up with Salisbury and Bulawayo) and a range of textile, food-processing and consumer goods factories. Rhodesia therefore has a surplus of manufactured goods which, after tobacco and asbestos, are a major export along with clothing, sugar and electrical power. Before the declaration of independence, imports came mainly from UK, South Africa and USA. Exports went to Zambia, UK, South Africa and West Germany. Political controls have since altered the natural flow of trade.

Zambia

Zambia, like Rhodesia to the south, is mostly a high plateau country, but more typically tropical. Both the Zambezi and the Congo rise on its northern borders, and most of the country falls within the Upper

Zambezi basin. The population in 1969 was 4.2m. The main urban settlements are along the line of the railway, which enters the territory over a bridge across the Zambezi, just below the Victoria Falls, and runs for 805 km (500 miles) from Livingstone, on the northern bank, northwards to the Katanga (Zaire). Lusaka, the capital (152 000), is rather more than halfway.

Zambia, as northern Rhodesia, was a member of the Federation of Rhodesia, and Nyasaland, and after the dissolution of the Federation became an independent republic within the Commonwealth in 1964. The years 1964—70 were spent in building economic independence and breaking traditional ties to the south with the politically unacceptable regimes of Rhodesia and South Africa. That she was largely successful was a direct result of the income available from the mining industry. Copper is the dominating commodity and contributes over 90 per cent of all export earnings and some 48 per cent of the countries total revenue. Income from copper and assistance from the United Nations have made possible the opening up of alternative transportation routes to the sea. A new allweather road, an oil pipeline and a new railway (the Tanzam Railway started in 1971 with aid from China) all cross the northern border near Nakonde to link with Dar es Salaam. This over-dependence on a single commodity (at the mercy of world price fluctuations) emphasised the need to diversify and also provided the means to do so. The thinly scattered rural population (1967: 35 000 working in agriculture and 51 000 in mining) in an area of 750 000 sq km (290 000 sq miles) therefore contrasts sharply with a rapidly expanding urban industrialisation. The new industries include an oil refinery at Ndola (with a pipeline to Dar es Salaam), steel works at Kafue, increased semifabrication of copper products and a variety of hydroelectric projects including a new dam on the Kafue River and a new generating station on the north side of the Kariba Dam.

In addition to general subsistence farming and limited cattle-rearing (1970: 1.3m. cattle and 0.25m. sheep and goats) there is commercial agriculture in the fertile belt along the railway line from Kalomo to Lusaka. Tobacco, dairy products, meat and vegetables are produced for the copper belt. There are also good reserves of hardwood in the extreme north; and plantation softwood and eucalyptus in the Ndola area provide materials for wood product factories at Kitwe.

The balance of trade is affected directly by the world demand for copper and Zambia's trading partners are worldwide. Exports have doubled in the first five years of independence. Imports and exports in 1965, 1968 and 1970 were: 211—380m.; 325—544m.; 311—766m. (figures in Kwacha, the new decimal currency introduced in 1968—71 value £0.53). In 1970 copper, zinc, cobalt and lead accounted for 98 per cent of exports. Imports were mainly transport equipment, machinery, manufactures, fuels and food. Exports to Japan, UK, West

Germany and South Africa; imports from UK, South Africa, USA and Rhodesia, with future trade with China likely to increase.

Malawi

Though the total area of Malawi (119 000 sq km: 46 000 sq miles) is nearly equal to that of England, nearly a quarter of it is water. Taking its name from Lake Nyasa, now Lake Malawi, Malawi (formerly Nyasaland) includes the greater part of that long expanse of water (nearly half as large again as Lake Erie) at the southern end of the Great Rift Valley. The territory itself is long and narrow: a strip between the western shore of the lake and Zambia, together with a long tongue south of the lake, thrusting into Moçambique nearly to the Zambezi River. Most of the development has been in this southern section. Through it flows the Shire River, which issues from the southern end of Lake Malawi and descends in a series of cataracts about midway in its course to provide power for hydroelectric stations at Nkula and Tedzani. The valley is bordered by highlands with a general level of 910 to 1 500 m (3 000 to 5 000 ft) and peaks rising to 2 400 to 3 000 m (8 000 to 10 000 ft). The bed of the lake is well below sea level with a depth of 700 m (2 300 ft).

Malawi became independent in 1964, and a republic in 1966. Agriculture is the predominant industry, while the only mineral resource (the bauxite of Mlanje) has yet to be exploited. Agriculture provides a livelihood for 90 per cent of the population, either subsistence or commercial crops, and 95 per cent of the exports. With a population (1971) of over 4.5m. the country is fairly densely populated, particularly in the Shire valley and highlands where the main commercial crops of sugarcane, coffee, tobacco, cotton, tea and groundnuts are grown. To ease the pressure on land in this area, efforts are being made to increase the productivity of the centre and north (rice, tobacco and groundnuts). In line with this the seat of government is moving from Zomba (20 000) to a newly constructed capital at Lilonge in the central region. Secondary industry is also being encouraged here to spread factories away from Blantyre (110 000) the traditional commercial centre. These include food processing, textiles, household goods and other light industries that will reduce the dependence on imports.

Railway communications are also concentrated in the south, the line to Beira being the traditional outlet. A new rail link to Nacala (on the coast to the north of Moçambique port) was opened in 1970 to give an alternative route to trade, and offer prospects of an eventual rail connection with both Zambia and Rhodesia should this become feasible. Plans also exist for a new Lakeshore road which would open up new tourism prospects and assist the development of the north region. The airport at Chileka (Blantyre) is already of international importance, both for visiting tourists and as an interchange point for Zambia and Rhodesia.

With agriculture as the main resource, exports are mainly raw tobacco, groundnuts, raw cotton, maize and tung oil. Imports (machinery, transport equipment, coal, oil and manufactures) are some 50 to 100 per cent in excess of exports, and international aid is still an important balancing factor — as are the sums remitted home by some 250 000 workers in South Africa. The bulk of trade is with UK and with African neighbours.

Kenya

Kenya along with Uganda and Tanzania (Tanganyika) was a member of the East African Governor's Conference between the two world wars. Later expanded with a central secretariat and executive to the East African High Commission, this common interest is still reflected by the formation in 1967 of the East African Community (and Common Market), which provides close communication, financial and trade links between the three founder members. Although not the largest, and less populous than Tanzania, Kenya has always played the leading part in this association, particularly so since independence in 1963.

A country of 583 000 sq km (225 000 sq miles) (rather larger than France), with a population of 10.9m. (census 1969), including 40 600 Europeans and 137 000 Asians, Kenya is crossed by the Equator along the northern slopes of snowclad Mount Kenya 5 193 m (17 040 ft). The greater part of it is arid, especially in the north, where it borders on Ethiopia, and in the northeast, where it borders on Somalia. Development of local industry and commercial agriculture is mostly confined to the southern part, and especially the southwest, where the Kenya Highlands provide conditions ranging from tropical to temperate as altitude increases.

This region was opened up at the end of the nineteenth century by the construction of a remarkable railway (metre gauge). Starting on Mombasa Island, which shelters one of the finest harbours (Kilindini) on the east coast of Africa, it crosses to the mainland over a causeway and ascends steadily to Kiu, 434 km (270 miles) from Mombasa, where at 1 480 m (4 860 ft) the tropical climate of the coast gives way to the more temperate conditions of the Highlands. Nairobi at 1 667 m (5 475 ft), the capital, was a collection of shanties when the line was built; now it is a city of over 500 000 (270 000 in 1962).

Beyond Nairobi the line continues to Kisumu, on Lake Victoria. There it connects with a steamship service on the lake, which is the second largest freshwater lake in the world (the third if the Caspian Sea be included), nearly as large as Scotland and not much smaller than Lake Superior. Another branch goes round the northern end of Lake

Victoria to serve Uganda, running westward to Kampala, the capital, and thence onward to Kasese, near the Congo frontier. With the Tanzania railways there is a unified system of nearly 6 400 km (4 000 miles) route miles of railway which has played a vital part in the development of the East African countries. A development now being augmented by the construction of a comprehensive road network in Kenya.

With limited mineral resources (which include small quantities of fluorspar, soda ash, graphite, asbestos and gold, together with prospects of developing lead—silver—zinc deposits north of Mombasa), the chief wealth lies in cash crops and associated industries. Although four-fifths of the country is dry or subject to marginal rainfall, some 85 per cent of the population is engaged in agriculture, the commercially important areas being the fertile and well-watered land of the Highlands and Lake Victoria basin, and the coast region of the southeast. The Highlands in particular are ideal for European-type mixed farming and for cash crops (on a plantation or cooperative basis) of semi-tropical or temperate crops and fruits according to altitude. Since independence many, but not all, of the former large estates have been resettled by small farmers. In a typical example, 4 950 ha (about 12 230 acres), previously supporting five large mixed farms producing maize, sunflower seeds and beef cattle as cash crops, is now divided among 709 individual farmers producing some crops for local markets and some, cooperatively, for export. The major commercial products are coffee, tea, sisal, cotton, and pyrethrum; with sugar, pineapples (and similar fruit capable of air shipment to European markets) and maize (of new hybrid strains) becoming increasingly important. Animal husbandry has always been a major item, and meat and meat products form a valuable export. Cattle in 1970 totalled 8.5m., sheep 3.7m. and goats 4m.

Power from the Owen Falls project, at Jinja in Uganda, supplies Nairobi and its factories; Mombasa (246 000) is supplied with power from the Pangani River in Tanzania (two examples of the inter-dependence of these three East African countries), and additional supplies from the Seven Forks scheme in Kenya will be available to the central and coastal regions. This adequate supply of power and extensive work on the all-weather road network have assisted the development of small factories, of tourism and of rural resettlement during the early years of independence, the latter being particularly important because the scale of industrialisation cannot provide employment opportunities sufficient to keep pace with population growth. Apart from oil refineries at Mombasa and Nairobi, industry is concerned mainly with food processing, beverages, textiles and household goods.

Exports cover a wide range, of which half is accounted for by coffee, tea, meat and animal products, pyrethrum (a base for insecticides), sisal and cotton. Imports are mainly machinery, transport equipment, iron and steel, petroleum and manufactured goods. The main trading partner is the UK, followed by USA, the European countries and, increasingly, Japan. Imports exceed exports by from 30 to 85 per cent, but invisible imports (international aid, private investment, tourism and transport charges, e.g. to Uganda) have more than held the balance during the 1960s.

Uganda

In 1862 the pioneer explorers, Speke and Grant, visited a country on the northwestern shores of Lake Victoria in marked contrast with the lands through which they had previously passed. The people, though living under a despotic ruler, were more intelligent than their neighbours, better clothed, more highly organised. They were the Baganda of Buganda, and have given their name to the country (Uganda). A British protectorate was proclaimed in 1894 and the country became independent in 1962.

Uganda, 236 000 sq km (94 000 sq miles) is a little larger than Great Britain although 42 400 sq km (16 380 sq miles) are lake and swamp. The total population of 9.7m. in 1970 is less than that of Kenya, and includes Asians and refugee groups from Rwanda, Sudan and Zaire (Congo Kinshasa). The country is mainly a high equatorial plateau, dropping abruptly to the western branch of the Rift valley with Lakes Albert and Edward, and to Lake Victoria in the south. High rainfall, fertile soils and a climate modified by elevation make for ideal agricultural conditions in the southern half, but decreasing rainfall gives rise to semidesert conditions in the northeast. Agriculture is therefore the mainstay, largely by small farmers in the absence of any large farm developments as was the case in Kenya. Some 90 per cent of the total labour force is engaged in agriculture; and in 1970 of the 300 000 people in paid employment over half (180 000) were in government service and 50 000 of the rest were also in farming. Coffee, cotton, tea and tobacco are the main cash crops. Sugarcane, bananas, maize, sorghum, and groundnuts are also grown. There are ample supplies of freshwater fish in the lakes and rivers (some 230 000 tons a year are landed from Lake Victoria alone, and modern trawlers could greatly enlarge this catch), and limited animal husbandry in areas free of the tsetse fly (3.9m. cattle and 1.7m. goats in 1969).

Mineral resources are small. Low grade copper ore is mined in some quantity at Kilembe on the eastern slopes of the Ruwenzori (Mountains of the Moon) and is smelted at Jinja for export. There is also limited production of tungsten, bismuth and beryllium. Hydroelectric power from the Owen Falls (on the Nile below Lake Victoria) supplied all Uganda's requirements and 40 per cent of Kenya's in 1970, but increasing demand makes additional projects essential. The topography and the ample rainfall provide opportunities for many new sites. Industry, mainly light and based on local raw produce, is concentrated in the Jinja—Lugazi—Kampala area and at Mbale and Tororo. Further growth will depend on the size of the home market, and the fact that Kenya and Tanzania are developing the same type of industries with which they wish to trade within the East African Community.

Although an agricultural country, urban growth of the major towns has been rapid since independence. The administration centre, previously at Entebbe (which is still the site of the major international airport) has moved to Kampala, the capital, where population has risen from 118 000 in 1960 to 360 000 in 1970. Mbale has increased from 13 000 to 23 000 in the same period, and Jinja the industrial centre has a population of over 50 000. Also at Kampala is Makerere college, now part of the University of East Africa, the earliest (1938) university establishment in East Africa.

Coffee and cotton however, are the twin supports of the economy. As the largest coffee producer in the Commonwealth, and fourth largest in the world, Uganda's coffee exports make up half her total exports. Cotton accounts for 20 per cent. Coffee, mainly *robusta* but with small pockets of *arabica* (the milder coffee of Kenya), is grown largely in Buganda in the south and southeast. Production in 1956 was 63 000 tons and in 1969, 207 000 tons. Other exports are copper, tea and animal feedstuffs. The USA (coffee) and the UK are the best customers, followed by Japan, West Germany and India (cotton). Imports, as with other developing countries of the area, are mainly machinery, transport equipment, iron and steel, fuel oils and manufactured goods, coming from the UK, West Germany and Japan. In the early years of independence, exports have exceeded imports by from 50 to 100 per cent, the equilibrium being dependent upon world prices for the two main products.

Tanzania

After the First World War, the mountainous northwest corner of German East Africa, comprising the Ruanda-Urundi country, about two-thirds the size of Scotland, was added to the Belgian Congo under mandate; the Kionga triangle, a tract about the size of a small English county in the extreme southeast, south of the mouth of the Rovuma River, became part of Portuguese East Africa; all the rest was mandated to Britain and renamed Tanganyika Territory after the great lake which bounds it on the west. In 1961 Tanganyika became independent, and in 1964 combined with the islands of Zanzibar and Pemba to form a United Republic which was renamed Tanzania in October 1964.

Covering some 940 000 sq km (363 000 sq miles) the new republic was four times the size of the United Kingdom, and carried about one-fifth as many people — some 13m. in 1971. It shares with its neighbours parts of the great African lakes — Victoria and Tanganyika; and within its northern border, hard by Kenya, is the highest mountain in Africa — snow-capped Kilimanjaro at 5 952 m (19 565 ft). It has a coastline of 805 km (500 miles) bordering the Indian Ocean, backed by an irregular coastal plain and low plateau, in places reaching 320 km (200 miles) and more inland. Behind this belt the land rises more rapidly, forming the escarpment to a broad plateau of woodland savanna at some 1 350 m (4 500 ft), dropping again in the west to the lake levels, which are like giant steps descending from north to south (Lake Victoria, 1 135 m: 3 724 ft; Tanganyika, 789 m: 2 590 ft; Malawi or Nyasa, 488 m: 1 600 ft). To the southwest, the highlands of the Rift valley and the Livingstone Mountains rise to 3 050 m (10 000 ft) with higher rainfall and tropical rainforests.

The Central Railway (metre gauge) bisects the country. From Dar es Salaam, the capital and chief port (population 129 000 in 1957 and 370 000 in 1970) it runs westward to Kigoma, on Lake Tanganyika, and connects with the southern end of Lake Victoria at Mwanza by a branch line running north from Tabora. The main line traverses diversified country with a wide range of products: sisal, groundnuts, cotton, rice, maize, millet in the low-lying country; millet and pulses on the plateau, where, however, there are long stretches of thornbush country, with little cultivation. Much of the plateau has a scanty rainfall and is better suited to grazing than to agriculture but only about a fifth of the whole country is stock-raising country, the rest being infested by tsetse fly. Even so there are (1970) 11m. cattle, 3m. sheep and 4.2m. goats.

In the northeast, the railway from Tanga, the second town and port, winds through rich plantation country up to Moshi at the foot of Kilimanjaro, and on to Arusha (1 410 m: 4 620 ft), on the slopes of Mount Meru, which is now the headquarters of the East African Community.

Until after the Second World War the chief commercial agricultural development was located in the northeast. Here the railway to Tanga carried sisal and copra from the lower-lying country along its route, and coffee and tea from the highlands. Tanganyika was the world's chief source of supply of sisal, which is still an important crop throughout the country. In 1963 production was 214 000 tons, roughly half the world supply, and the exports (practically all the local production) were a third of Tanganyika's total exports. Coffee and cotton have now both surpassed sisal. Most of the coffee comes from the Bukoba district, on the western shore of Lake Victoria, and is of the *robusta* type; but coffee is also grown on the slopes of Kilimanjaro and around Arusha where conditions favour the cultivation of *arabica*.

Agriculture is therefore, in independence as in colonial days, still the mainstay of the country employing 90 per cent of the population and contributing two-thirds of the export earnings. A wide range of products is grown, including tea, rice, tobacco, cashew nuts, coconuts, sugarcane, bananas, cassava, pyrethrum and rubber. Other recently independent African countries, similarly dependent on a limited range of cash crops or raw materials, have concentrated on these items to provide the basis for later development. Tanzania has by direct government action nationalised much of her services and resources, to promote diversification and improve the lot of the rural community by promoting the production of cash crops by the small farmer alongside the state farms. Both coffee and sisal come under international quota agreements (and the latter is increasingly affected by manmade substitutes) so diversification is encouraged by growing maize, sunflowers, rice, fruits, vegetables, and beef and dairy products where feasible.

Gold is mined south of Lake Victoria and near Mbeya, but following the discovery of a Kimberlite pipe at Mwadui, diamonds are the main mineral resource — accounting for 10 per cent of all exports in 1970. The future development of minerals is dependent on hydroelectric power and improved communications. The Tanzam railway started with Chinese aid in 1970 will link Dar es Salaam with Kapiri Mposhi and Lusaka. Its 1 600 km (1 000 miles) will include 147 new stations in addition to marshalling yards and repair shops, and it will open up the west and southwest of Tanzania since both it and the new all-weather Zamtan highway will promote agricultural and mineral production. Development of low grade coal deposits at Ketewaka-Mchuchuma and of the iron ore at Liganga will be feasible, and Zambia will provide a market for the agricultural produce. Although built to meet Zambia's wish to redirect her copper exports through Dar es Salaam, the railway will be of equally great importance to Tanzania. Dar es Salaam in particular will benefit, growing from a handling capacity of 500 000 tons in 1963, to 1m. tons in 1969 and an estimated 2.7m. tons in 1980 (half of which could be copper from Zambia). In line with this growth the number of major berths is to be steadily expanded from three to eleven. Hydroelectric power has yet to be extensively developed. The Panga River is the main project (with fisheries and irrigation as subsidiary developments near Tanga). There is potential for further sites, in particular at Steiglers Gorge on the Great Ruaha River.

Exports (mainly coffee, cotton, sisal, diamonds and cashew nuts to UK, Zambia and India) exceeded imports during the early years of independence; but as government plans proceeded (the construction of communications and of industries to broaden the base of the economy and eventually reduce imports) so imports have gone ahead. Imports are mainly transportation equipment, machinery, iron and steel, manufactured goods and petroleum from UK, Japan, West Germany, Iran and (increasingly) China.

Zanzibar. The islands of Zanzibar (1 658 sq km: 640 sq miles) and Pemba (984 sq km: 380 sq miles) off the coast of Tanzania have long been an Arab stronghold with close ties with Oman. Their population of 370 000 gives a density of 137 per sq km (355 per sq mile) in contrast to the 13.9 per sq km (36 per sq mile) of the mainland. On 24 June 1963 Zanzibar became an internal self-governing state, on 9 December she became independent. On 12 January the sultanate was overthrown, the sultan fled into exile. On 27 April 1964 Tanganyika and Zanzibar combined to form a united republic which assumed the name Tanzania.

Zanzibar is renowned as 'The Island of Cloves', and Pemba shares its fame. Cloves are the dominating factor in the trade of the two islands, and it has been reckoned that between them they produce four-fifths of the world's supply. Crops vary greatly from year to year, and the fluctuations in quantity, coupled with other factors affecting prices, notably disease, have caused great extremes in postwar trade. But with a virtual monopoly, Zanzibar has an income *per capita* which is among the highest in the developing world and is sufficient to ensure almost complete independence within Tanzania. Production averages 6 500 tons a year. Exports were valued at £500 000 a year in 1939. In 1962 they were £2.1m.; in 1968, £3.8m.; in 1970, nearly £7m. Prices rose from £250 a ton in 1964 to £1 600 a ton in 1969 (when production failed). At this point an export duty of £1 200 a ton was imposed — and clove smuggling to Mombasa became a lucrative trade.

Ghana

The former British colony of the Gold Coast began moving towards independence in 1951. It was joined in 1956 by British Togoland (a United Nations trust territory) and the two became the first African colony to achieve independence in 1957. The country was declared a republic within the Commonwealth on 1 July 1960 and has an area of 238 540 sq km (92 100 sq miles) and a population (1970) of 8.6m.

The coast, some 530 km (330 miles) long, is surf-bound and has, generally, a low sandy foreshore threaded by lagoons. It lacks natural harbours, though many historically famous towns are scattered along it, such as Axim, Sekondi, Elmina, Cape Coast and Winneba. The most important coastal towns today are Accra, the capital, a city of 758 000, but with limited harbour facilities; Sekondi and Takoradi, adjacent towns with a joint population of 209 000 and a deepwater harbour constructed between the two world wars, capable of accommodating the largest vessels engaged in the West African trade; and Tema the new industrial centre.

Forest comes nearly down to the coast in the west, but eastward a

716

coastal belt of rolling plains and dry scrub, with occasional isolated hills, widens out on the frontier. The coconut palm flourishes all along the coast. North of this belt the forest area extends through much of the coastal plain and the southwestern half of Ashanti. It is broken by ridges of hills and is a major source of wealth. Not only does it yield valuable timbers, but here is found the oil palm and the home of the dominant factor in Ghana's trade, the cocoa industry. This industry, which has been built up since the closing decade of the nineteenth century, has largely superseded the cultivation of the oil palm. It was threatened in the 1930s by the appearance of a new disease, Swollen Shoot, among the cocoa trees. During the Second World War the menace grew to one of the first magnitude. The only known remedy was to destroy the diseased trees, and millions were destroyed before intensified research produced control: the capsid spraying technique. Beyond the forest, in Brong-Ahafo and the Central and Northern Territories, while the rivers are mostly bordered by dense belts of trees and scrub, in between are open woodlands and parklands, orchards and plains.

The general elevation of the country is not great, under 305 m (1 000 ft), but some of the hills rise on the eastern border, to nearly 915 m (3 000 ft). On the whole the country is well-watered, though the rivers are not navigable (except by canoes) for any great distance inland; north of the forest they are apt to flood after rains and shrink to pools in the dry season. Much the biggest river is the Volta, whose two main headstreams, the Black and the White Volta, come from afar in the lands to the north. Since 1915 proposals have been under study for the building of a dam to form a great reservoir, which would serve as a source of hydroelectric power and would extend navigation nearly to the junction of the Black and White Voltas. The Akosombo Dam was finally built with international aid between 1962 and 1966, along with the new port and town (1962) of Tema.

Some 1 290 km (800 miles) of railway and 4 020 km (2 500 miles) of surfaced road link the main centres of population; Accra and Takoradi-Sekondi with Kumasi (343 000) the capital of Ashanti, Koforidou (70 000), Tamale (99 000) and Bolgatanga (93 000) in the north. Further all-weather roads are required to develop the rural areas, for the country is still dependent on agriculture which occupies 60 per cent of the labour force and produces the bulk of the exports. Tree cash crops dominate the agriculture (cocoa, rubber and oil palm). All have a long life span and reduce farming potential which is further limited by the average size of farms — a small holding of 2.4 ha (6 acres). In spite of the wide variety of crops grown, the rising population has outstripped farm production and food imports have been a major factor of the early years of independence. The vast, 8 500 sq km (3 280 sq miles) lake created by the Akosombo Dam has both hindered and helped development. The project involved resettlement of hundreds of villages and 80 000 people, but it also provided fertile new lands in the area between high and low water on the lake side; improved communications; and added 70 000 tons to the fishery catch which now totals 250 000 tons a year. Cocoa, in spite of all attempts to diversify, still dominates the economy after fifteen years of independence. Ghana is by far the world's largest producer, with a peak crop in 1964 of 580 000 tons out of a world total of 1.5m. tons, and an average crop of some 400 000 tons — 85 per cent of which comes from small holdings of less than 3 ha (7 acres) and only 15 per cent from cooperatives and estates. Cattle rearing is limited but ranches are planned which could produce 60 per cent of the country's meat in due course. Cattle, sheep and goats each totalled less than 750 000 in 1970.

Ghana has a number of minerals. Gold, which initially attracted the Europeans and gave its name to the country, is mined at Obuasi and is a major export. There are also diamonds, manganese and bauxite (yet to be exploited). Limited quantities of oil have been found, but not yet on a commercial scale. All industrial development stems from the Volta River Dam, which produces power for all Ghana's needs (through a grid covering the southern half of the country) and for export to Togo and Dahomey (the first major economic interchange between the former British and French colonies of West Africa). Industrial development includes an oil refinery and aluminium smelter at Tema (the latter taking 70 per cent of the Askombo power output in 1970 — and both processing imported raw materials), textile, sugar, timber and consumer goods factories. The prospects for the future depend on further development of power output from the Volta project, on the production of alumina from local bauxite (more lucrative than the processing of imported alumina), and on possible exploitation of petroleum.

With 60 per cent of foreign exchange dependent on cocoa (and at the mercy of fluctuations in world prices), with considerable imports of food and essential capital equipment for development, the early years of independence have not been easy ones. Imports tend to exceed exports and there has been great reliance on foreign aid to maintain the balance. In 1958 cocoa contributed 60 per cent to the total exports; gold, diamonds and manganese, 26 per cent; and timber 11 per cent. In 1969 cocoa still contributed nearly 60 per cent; timber 11 per cent; gold 7 per cent; and diamonds and manganese 5 per cent, exports going to UK, USA, West Germany, Netherlands and Japan. Imports (machinery, transport equipment, food, chemicals and petroleum) came mainly from UK, USA, West Germany and the Comecon countries. The United Kingdom was the major trading partner in 1951, providing 54 per cent of the imports and taking 41 per cent of the exports; in 1969 the respective figures were 26 and 33, the USA, EEC countries and Comecon having increased their participation.

718

Nigeria

Nigeria is the largest country in West Africa. It is roughly a square block of territory, with sides of some 1 130 km (700 miles), in the angle of the Gulf of Guinea where the general trend of the coast is east and west. The Niger River flows in from the northwest, follows a southeasterly course to near the centre, then turns and flows south to the Gulf. Its main mouth is in the centre of the coast, but the delta spreads out so far on either side and has so many channels, connecting with one another and with other rivers beyond the delta, that almost the entire seaboard is backed by a network of waterways. The rivers and creeks are separated by mangrove swamp forests, which the silt carried by the Niger is gradually extending seaward.

This coastal belt has a depth of 16 to 97 km (10 to 60 miles). Behind it lies a belt of tropical rain forest and oil palm bush, stretching north for another 80 to 160 km (50 to 100 miles). As the land rises, the forest changes to open woodlands, which in turn give place to grasslands with patches of scrub, until in the far north desert conditions are encountered on the verge of the Sahara. In the northeast corner is Lake Chad, which in its fullest extent (some 51 000 sq km: 20 000 sq miles) is second only to Lake Victoria among African lakes, and is not much smaller than Lake Michigan. But it is shallow, and fluctuates greatly in size, like Lake Ngami in the Kalahari.

Near to where the Niger turns south it is joined, at Lokoja, by its great tributary the Benue, flowing from the east and forming with the Niger itself, above the confluence, a continuous line of rivers stretching across Nigeria and dividing it into two parts, northern and southern. To the north is plateau country, generally of no great height, but rising to over 1 820 m (6 000 ft) in the Jos Plateau, which covers some 5 180 sq km (2 000 sq miles) north of the Benue and is noted for its tinfields. Elsewhere the surface is broken by scattered hills, but there is little mountainous country except along the eastern border, where the Cameroons Mountain, near the coast, rises to 4 070 m (13 350 ft). After the First World War, most of the German Cameroons was assigned to France, but the western strip was attached to Nigeria. In 1961 the northern part of this strip joined northern Nigeria; the southern part decided to join the former French Cameroun.

The total area of the Federation of Nigeria is 924 000 sq km (357 000 sq miles) — four times the size of Great Britain — with 64.5m. inhabitants (1970). It is thus the most populous country of tropical Africa and the largest in West Africa. Under the constitution of 1960 Nigeria became an independent federation, and in 1963 was declared a republic. In 1967 twelve states were formed in place of the former regions. The Northern Region was by far the largest, extending across the whole country from east to west, and from the northern boundary to the south of the Niger and the Benue. It comprised three-quarters of the total area and rather more than half the total population and is now divided into six states. The Western, Mid-West, and Eastern Regions cover most of the remaining quarter of the federation, and contain between 40 and 50 per cent of the total population.

Peoples and resources are as diversified as the geographical conditions. This diversity produces a sound basis for future development and growth. The country is a meeting-place of contrasting cultures (the Muslim, Hausa and Fulani of the northern savanna, and the Christian and pagan peoples of the south, the Yoruba and the Ibos) and the first ten years of independence were interrupted by the civil war of 1967–70. The country lies wholly within the tropics, from 4° to 14° N, and conditions vary from the tropical coast of the south to the near arid north, giving rise to many different types of farming and a wide range of crops, all produced abundantly. The coastline, mainly mangrove swamps and lagoons which yielded little beyond fishing and trading, is now the centre of petroleum production with industrial centres and many ports: Lagos (federal capital territory) 665 000, Warri, Forcades, Port Harcourt (180 000), Bonny and Calabar. Inland the forest zone produces hardwoods and oil palm (Nigeria is the world's largest producer of palm oil), rubber, cassava, banana and cocoa in the west. Nigeria is second to Ghana in world production of cocoa. As precipitation decreases northwards, crops include yams, paddy (under irrigation) millet, tobacco, groundnuts and cotton with cattle-rearing in the tsetse fly free far north. In 1970 there were 11.5m. cattle, 23.4m. goats (by far the largest flock in Africa) and 8m. sheep.

Mineral resources include one of Africa's rare coal deposits at Enugu; iron ore in Lakoja area; tin (of which Nigeria is the fifth largest producer) from alluvial deposits of limited extent around Jos; gold, tantalite and columbite. Above all there is the oil of the delta region, well placed to supply the European market. Nigeria has exported oil only since 1958 when production was 0.8m. tons. In 1969 production had reached 27.3m. tons. In 1973 production was 100m. tons and Nigeria joined the top ten largest producers. Output could well be doubled by 1980 as new wells are brought into use. Power supplies, apart from small hydroelectric plants such as those which support the tin smelters at Jos, come almost entirely from the Kainji project on the Niger. This provides all the power required by the country through a grid covering the majority of the states, and there is potential on the Niger to produce five times as much. Apart from textiles and small factories in the traditional trading centres of the north (such as Kadina and Kano) and the tin smelters at Jos, most of the industrial development is in the south – near the ports and well served by communications. Factories produce a wide range of import substitutes such as foodstuffs, beverages, textiles, footwear, cement, wood products, etc.

These are largely based on local raw materials, with plans for car assembly and petrochemical plants. Broadly the north produces the surplus food for the industrial south.

Communications suffered some neglect during the civil war, but rising oil revenues and foreign aid is rapidly rehabilitating an already extensive and well-used network. The rivers are navigable over great distances, and have been improved where dams and irrigation projects have stabilised their hitherto seasonal flow. There are rail and road networks linking all major towns (no fewer than twenty-five have a population of over 100 000) and ports, with some 3 000 km (1 870 miles) of railway and 16 000 km (10 000 miles) of surfaced roads out of a total of 80 000 km (50 000 miles) of maintained roads. Internal air services date back to 1940, and international connections will be facilitated by the construction of a new major airport at Lagos (Ikeja).

Nigeria's widely based agricultural economy makes her (some 96 per cent) self-supporting in foodstuffs. Cassava, yams and (increasingly) maize are the main food crops followed by millet (Nigeria is the world's fourth largest producer of cassava and millet/sorghum). Agriculture also provides nearly 50 per cent of all exports, although oil is rapidly becoming the overwhelming item. Main exports in 1970 were petroleum, cocoa, groundnuts (the world's largest exporter), tin, palm oil and kernels, rubber and cotton. Imports were mainly transport equipment, machinery, manufactured goods, chemicals, iron and steel, fertilisers. Exports were to the UK (48 per cent in 1960, 27 per cent in 1970), USA, Netherlands, West Germany and France. Imports came from UK (42 per cent in 1960, 29 per cent in 1970), USA, West Germany and Japan.

The early years of independence showed the usual pattern of imports exceeding exports with aid to sustain the balance. The civil war extended this pattern, but by 1970 exports moved ahead. Increasing oil revenues and the great agricultural potential should continue this trend.

Sierra Leone

The Colony and Protectorate of Sierra Leone were an outcome of the antislavery movement at the end of the eighteenth century. William Wilberforce and his fellow-workers founded a settlement for freed slaves at the foot of a lofty peninsula sheltering an excellent harbour; the land was ceded to them by the local chief, and they named the settlement Freetown. That was in 1788; today Freetown is a city of 163 000 people, the capital of an independent state (1961) covering an area of nearly 72 500 sq km (28 000 sq miles) — almost the size of Scotland. The peninsula on which the city stands follows the general direction of the coast and is really a short mountain range, rising to conical peaks of 910 m (3 000 ft). It is a notable feature of the West African coast, which is generally low-lying, and the harbour which it shelters is also outstanding on the West Coast.

Two explanations are offered of the name Sierra Leone (Lion Mountains), which was given to the peninsula by fifteenth-century Portuguese navigators. Some attribute it to the supposed resemblance of part of the mountain crest to the figure of a lion; others think that the reverberations of thunder among the mountains suggested the roaring of lions to the discoverers. Apart from the peninsula, the coast is edged with mangrove swamps and backed by rolling wooded country, varied by low ranges of hills. In the north and east the territory rises to a plateau of some 460 m (1 500 ft), with peaks of over 1 830 m (6 000 ft) near the frontier. This is bordered for the most part by the Republic of Guinea, and in the southeast by the Republic of Liberia.

In general, Sierra Leone is a country of tropical heat with torrential rains during six months of the year. Rice is the staple food of the 2.5m. inhabitants, and paddy is grown on 300 000 ha (750 000 acres) yielding nearly 500 000 tons. Cassava, sweet potatoes and groundnuts are also grown extensively for home consumption. Livestock are comparatively few, rough estimates of the numbers being 240 000 cattle, 57 000 sheep, 156 000 goats, 29 000 pigs. The country is well watered by rivers, many of which are navigable; oceangoing vessels can ascend the Sherbro River for 72 km (45 miles). Over 7 150 km (4 450 miles) of trunk roads are classed as suitable for motoring throughout the year, but there are only 643 km (400 miles) of surfaced roads. The government has built and operates over 547 km (340 miles) of narrow gauge railway. Iron ore, a high-grade haematite, is exported from the Marampa mines over a privately owned railway 91 km (57 miles) long. Freetown (Lungi) has an international airport.

Diamonds are plentiful, and after the Second World War there was much smuggling, both by Sierra Leoneans and by other Africans who flocked in from neighbouring countries. Illicit diamond dealing was officially estimated in 1958 to be 20 per cent of the national product. Both industrial diamonds and gemstones are produced, the latter including some of quite exceptional size from alluvial deposits — one of 530 carats in 1943 and another of 770 carats in 1945.

In 1970 while imports were valued at 97m. leone, exports amounted to 85m. (The leone, introduced in 1965, was valued at 50p in 1970.) The chief exports were diamonds (64 per cent), iron ore, palm kernels, coffee and cocoa. The United Kingdom took about 70 per cent, the next largest customers being the Netherlands, West Germany and USA. Between 15 and 20 per cent of the imports were for food, the rest mostly for transport equipment, machinery, and fuel oils. Nearly 30 per cent came from the United Kingdom; followed by Japan, USA and West Germany.

Gambia

The Crown Colony of Gambia was the smallest British dependency on the mainland of Africa; with an area of some 11 300 sq km (4 300 sq miles), the territory is about half the size of Wales. It is an enclave in the former French territory of Sénégal, and may be likened to a mounted thermometer, in which the tube represents 480 km (300 miles) of the River Gambia, stretching inland at right angles to the coast, and the mount a strip of territory 16 km (10 miles) wide on either side of the river. The waterway is the main artery of travel; shallow-draught river steamers of some hundreds of tons ply along practically the whole of the Gambian section of the Gambia, and ocean-going steamers ascend it for 240 km (150 miles). There is no railway, and roads are mostly dry-weather tracks. In the rains there is extensive flooding along the banks.

Just as the river is the dominating physical feature, so there is a dominating product — groundnuts. They constitute all but a minor part of the domestic exports, varying a good deal in quantity from year to year but averaging about 110 000 tons of unshelled nuts. There is also fishing (with a processing plant at Bathurst, the capital), oil palms, cotton and paddy, the latter being encouraged in order to reduce reliance on food imports. Mining for ilmenite was commenced in 1956, but ceased in 1969; no other workable mineral deposits are known. There is a very small tourist industry based on the port and airport (Yundum) at Bathurst (40 000). The total population of some 360 000 is augmented by the annual migration of 'strange farmers' from adjacent territories who assist with the groundnut harvest.

The Gambia has been fully independent since 1965 and has an overseas trade of some £8m. imports and £6m. exports, with grants of aid to maintain the economy. Exports are almost entirely groundnuts, groundnut oil and meal, and small quantities of palm kernels and fish products, 48 per cent going to UK followed by Portugal, Italy and Switzerland. Imports are chiefly manufactured goods, textiles, foodstuffs and machinery; 30 per cent from UK, followed by Japan, Burma and West Germany.

Former French West Africa

The Constitution of the Fifth Republic of France came into force on 4 October 1958 under the leadership of General de Gaulle. Under it the French Community (La Communauté) was divided into the French Republic comprising metropolitan departments, oversea departments and overseas territories on the one hand and 'member states' on the other. The countries which had previously comprised French West Africa became 'member states' or established 'special relations' with

Table 80 — Population of former French West African territories

	Square miles	Population (1960)
Republic of Ivory Coast (République de Côte d'Ivoire	124 500	3 115 000
Republic of Dahomey (République du Dahomey)	44 500	2 002 000
Republic of Upper Volta (République de Haute Volta)	106 000	4 004 000
Republic of Mali (République du Mali)	465 000	4 307 000
Islamic Republic of Mauritania (Rép. Is. de Mauritanie)	419 000	727 000
Republic of Niger (République du Niger)	459 000	2 803 000
Republic of Senegal (République du Sénégal)	76 000	2 579 000
Total	1 694 000*	19 556 000

* 4 377 000 sq km.

France, with the exception of French Guinea which declared for complete independence. The other territories became independent republics in 1960. They were previously divided into two groups. Along the coast, Sénégal, the Ivory Coast and Dahomey were three colonies comparable with those of British West Africa. Behind them lay another four territories: Mauritania, which has a stretch of desert coast; and the French Sudan, Upper Volta, and Niger Colony, which are wholly inland. This second group is practically six times as large as the first, but it merges in the Sahara and, except in the Upper Volta, is much more sparsely populated. Table 80 gives the position at the end of 1960.

These figures show that French West Africa was between three and four times as large as all the British Commonwealth in West Africa (barely 1 290 000 sq km: 500 000 sq miles); but its population was less than half as large indeed, less than half that of Nigeria alone. By 1969 the total population of these seven countries had risen to 26m.

Their geographical characteristics are typically West African. From a low-lying coastal zone, in places covered with tropical forest, elsewhere rich in oil palms, coconut palms and cultivated products, the land rises to open woodlands and savannas, which in turn give place to more or less desert country, merging to the Sahara. The importance of its river systems is partially indicated by the names of three of the territories: Sénégal, Niger and Upper Volta. The Sénégal River, over 1 610 km (1 000 miles) long, lies wholly in former French West Africa, forming in the lower half of its course the northern boundary of the country of Sénégal; crossing, higher up, a corner of the Mali Republic; and having its main source in Guinea, among the highlands of Fouta Djallon. These highlands, which rise to 1 520 m (5 000 ft) are not only the main orographical feature of former French West Africa, but a notable watershed. As well as the Sénégal, here is the source of the Gambia River (1 130 km: 700 miles) and of the Niger River at the outset of its long journey of 4 180 km (2 600 miles), during which it flows from Guinea through the Mali Republic and thence across the Niger Republic before entering the Federation of Nigeria. Both the Black Volta and the White Volta rise in the Upper Volta Republic and, with their affluents, water that territory before passing on to Ghana. These are the dominant rivers of West Africa. Many relatively minor but considerable rivers flow more directly to the coast, and though their passage down the giant steps by which the country descends from the interior plateaus to the sea renders them unnavigable except in stretches, they are an essential factor in maintaining the fertility of the soil.

Livestock are numerous, the estimated total in these seven countries in 1970 was 17m. cattle, 16m. sheep, and 19m. goats.

The value of the trade in francs is many times what it was before the Second World War; but true comparison is made difficult not only by the changing values of the franc but by the institution, after the war, of an 'African franc' equivalent to two ordinary French francs, this African franc (CFA — Colonies Françaises d'Afrique) being the monetary unit in all French Africa except North Africa and French Somaliland. Imports are mostly manufactures — largely textiles, transport equipment and machinery. Groundnuts are grown on an even more extensive scale than in Nigeria, and are the major export along with coffee and cocoa. These three products provide nearly three-quarters of the total value, with palm kernels and palm oil provided another 5 per cent. About two-thirds of the trade, as regards both imports and exports, is with France, which is followed at a distance in the inward trade by the United States, Morocco, and West Germany, and in the outward trade by the United States, the Netherlands, and Algeria.

Sénégal

Sénégal, with an area of 197 000 sq km (76 000 sq miles) and a population of 4.1m., is half as large again as England and was the premier country in French West Africa when Dakar was the colonial administrative capital. The country has a fringe of coastal mangrove swamps giving way to cultivated lands (from the River Sénégal in the north to the Casamance in the south beyond Gambia) and then to an interior sandy plateau which eventually becomes too dry to be habitable in the north and east. The country has long been, and still is, almost entirely dependent upon groundnuts which provide 70 per cent of foreign exchange earnings, occupy half of the cultivated area, and are the livelihood of 2m. of the 4.1m. inhabitants. As the world's second largest exporter, the economy is directly affected by world prices and the availability of the many alternative edible oils. Production therefore varies greatly, for example from 1m. tons in 1967 to 500 000 tons in 1970. Future plans are to recover production to 1m. tons, to encourage millet production (the second largest crop at 700 000 tons a year) and diversify to sugarcane, rice, cotton, vegetables and fishing. Livestock rearing is also important with (in 1970) 2.7m. cattle, 1.4m. sheep and 1.6m. goats.

The only important mineral resource is the phosphate deposits at Tivaouane which provide the second major export commodity. As a long settled colony (St Louis at the mouth of the Sénégal was founded in 1659) there is an adequate road and rail network supporting the industrial area of Dakar (474 000). Industry is diverse and well established; mainly cement and fertiliser works, groundnut oil plants and factories for food processing, textiles, leather and small consumer goods. Further industrialisation (as with all newly independent countries) is affected by the balance of the cost of importing the raw materials with the return from the finished product in a limited home market. Exports, mainly groundnuts and groundnut products, phosphate and fish, fall below imports – mainly machinery, manufactured goods, food and chemicals. France is by far the major trading partner, followed by West Germany, the Netherlands and African neighbours.

From serving the French West African hinterland of 20m., Sénégal has successfully readjusted to independence (1960), with a small population and limited resources. Plans for trading groups and customs unions with neighbouring countries offer prospects for development, in particular the proposed Sénégal basin community with Mauritania, Mali and Guinea.

Ivory Coast

This republic with an area of some 322 000 sq km (124 500 sq miles) and a population of 4.5m. (at least 1m. of whom are from neighbouring states) became independent in 1960 and has 'special relations' with France and various regional groupings. The country is divided by central tsetse-ridden virgin forests into a well-developed eastern region and a western region of considerable potential. It is an agricultural country with cassava and yams as the main food products; and coffee, cocoa and timber as the main cash products. The Ivory Coast is the largest producer of coffee in Africa, and third in the world (270 000 tons in 1971); it is fourth in world production of cocoa (200 000 tons in 1971), and the largest timber producer (hardwood, mahogany) by volume in Africa with a peak of 4.5m. cu m (5.9m. cu yd) in 1969. To these primary resources have been added, during the first ten years of independence, an extensive industrial development based on an 'open door' policy for foreign investment (in contrast to the nationalisation policy adopted by many other newly emergent states). As a result industry is 95 per cent foreign owned; but the country has a healthy trade balance after doubling its overseas trade during these years, has attracted workers from neighbouring states, and is now considering the development of industry for exports (fruit canning, tyres, synthetic fibres, light electronics).

Minerals include diamonds, manganese and iron ore in the Mount Nimba range (yet to be exploited). Communications and urban development are more advanced in the east around the capital, Abidjan (450 000), on the landward side of a lagoon connected by a ship canal to the sea, and Bouake (120 000) a trading and livestock centre to the north. Here there are road and rail links to Upper Volta and plans for a new coast road through to Accra and Lagos. Future development is to be concentrated in the west, with a new port complex around San Pedro. This will ease the marketing of the arable products and timber of the hinterland, will create a new industrial area, and will assist in the resettlement of the 100 000 likely to be dispossessed of their land by the flooding of the Bandama River above the new Kossou hydroelectric project. Some 280 km (174 miles) north of Abidjan, the Kossou Dam will provide a lake of some 2 000 sq km (772 sq miles) with fishing and irrigation capabilities, in addition to developing the power available throughout the country.

Exports, 76 per cent of which are coffee, cocoa and timber, are largely to France followed by the EEC countries and USA. Imports (machinery, transport equipment, textiles, chemicals and petroleum) are consistently below exports and come in the main from the same trading partners.

Dahomey

Dahomey, the smallest of the French West African colonies with an area of 112 600 sq km (44 690 sq miles) and a population of 2.6m. (1970), became an independent republic in 1960. It is a member of the regional customs and monetary unions and enjoys 'special relations' with France. A largely self-contained agricultural community, it has minimal international trade and the early years of independence were accompanied by some political uncertainty (there being eleven heads of state in one period of seven years). As with neighbouring countries, a well-watered, lagoon-fringed coastland gives way to a higher, dryer interior to the north. Oil palm, planted extensively by the old kings between the coast and the ancient capital of Abomey (42 000) some 95 km (60 miles) inland, is by far the leading commercial crop; with some coffee and coconuts in the south, and cotton and groundnuts in the dryer zones. Future plans are to foster this rural economy with equal emphasis on greater food production (vegetables, rice, cassava and livestock) and improvements in cash crop output. Industrial development is largely limited to food processing.

Of the few roads some 800 km (500 miles) are bitumenised, the main one running north to Gaya on the Niger border, accompanying the railway from Cotonou to Parakou. Power is available from the Volta Dam in Ghana. The capital, Porto Novo (75 000), and Cotonou (110 000) are the main ports. Both are on the coast lagoon which is navigable through to Lagos in Nigeria, and the latter (formerly an open roadstead but now a fine deepwater harbour constructed during the early years of independence) serves both Dahomey and the adjacent Nigerian hinterland.

Such international trade as there is, is dominated by France; followed by European and West African countries. Exports (almost entirely oil palm products with a little coffee and cotton) are approximately one-third of imports and continued French aid is essential. There is prospecting for offshore oil.

Mauritania

The Islamic Republic of Mauritania with an area of over 1m. sq km (419 000 sq miles) is almost twice the size of Sénégal, the Ivory Coast and Dahomey together, yet it has a population of only 1.2m. The country north of 19° N is true desert with occasional oases supporting date palms and a little grazing. Most of the population lives in the south where pasture is available for their 3.8m. cattle and 6m. sheep and goats. Crops are cultivated wherever water can be retained, as in the Sénégal valley (rice, guinea corn, millet, tobacco, vegetables and fruits such as gourd and melon), and gums are collected from the acacias. Fish are caught offshore and processed at Port Étienne.

There is little industry, beyond the processing of raw materials. The major resources are mineral deposits which will be the main factor in the future development of the country. In 1961 mining of the high grade iron ore deposits at Fort Gouraud began and the ore is exported from Port Étienne via a railway specially constructed in 1963. Production is some 5 to 7m. tons a year and can be considerably increased. There are also copper deposits at Akjoujt for export via Nouakchott the new capital (20 000) which has replaced the old administrative centre at St Louis. Port Étienne (15 000) has no local water supply. Previously water was brought by sea from France; it is now brought by rail from the mining area to the northeast and is also produced by local desalination plants.

Exports are almost entirely (90 per cent) iron ore with some fish (dried, smoked and salted) and animal products, and show a steadily increasing predominence over imports which are mainly machinery and manufactured goods. France is by far the major trading partner — followed by the UK, Italy, West Germany and Belgium—Luxembourg (the main recipient of the iron ore).

Mali

The Republic of Mali, independent since 1960 and still closely linked with France, is a landlocked, arid country, formerly the French Sudan. Larger than Mauritania with an area of 1.2m. sq km (465 000 sq miles) it is a pastoral community giving way to agriculture within reach of the influence of the River Niger; the animals (5m. cattle and 10m. sheep and goats) far outnumber the total population of 5.4m. (1971). The Niger is navigable for some 1 800 km (1 100 miles) within Mali from Gao upstream to the capital, Bamako, and seasonally on up to Kourroussa in Guinea. The river is also the essential source of fishing and irrigation; with schemes in the Ségou and Mopti districts and at the Sansanding Barrage, which produce good irrigated crops, including sugar and paddy. The range of dry zone products includes groundnuts, sisal and cotton. Gums are also collected.

Minerals are not exploited as yet and there is little industry. Apart from the river and air services to Bamako, the main communications are the railway from Sénégal which runs through Kayes to Bamako (282 000) and on to Koulikoro. There are plans for a rail link, to be built with aid from China, between Bamako and Kourroussa—Kankan in Guinea. The main road, some 700 km (435 miles) of which is bitumenised, is that which runs from Dakar through Mali to Niamey in Niger; again, there are plans for an all-weather road to replace the old trading route northwards to Béchar in Algeria. Timbuktu (10 000), the old terminus of the trans—Sahara caravans from the north, is now less important than Kayes and Ségou (each of 30 000) on the route to the west (and the trading partners of the regional French community).

Imports, machinery, transport equipment, and food (wheat and dairy products) greatly exceed exports as is to be expected in a subsistence economy without special resources. The few exports are mainly live animals, fish (salted and dried), cotton, groundnuts and oilseeds. Trade, although still dominated by France, is increasingly with the USSR and China, followed by West African neighbours and Egypt.

Upper Volta

Formerly the seat of the Mossi tribe who for centuries opposed the Arab invasions from the north, Upper Volta was carved out of the French colonies of Upper Sénégal and Niger in 1919. In 1932 it ceased to exist when its territory was divided between the Ivory Coast, Sudan and Niger. In 1947 it was reestablished, and in 1958 became a self-governing state. Two years later it was a fully independent republic closely linked with France. With an area of 274 000 sq km (106 000 sq miles) it is half the size of France with a population of some 5.4m. The soils are lacking in fertility and there are few natural resources; as a result there is pressure on the population and a considerable emigration of labour to the Ivory Coast and to Ghana. The high plateau of the water-shed between the Niger and the Volta has fairly good rainfall, but is rapidly drained by the many tributaries of the great rivers. Crops such as millet, sorghum, maize, cotton, paddy and groundnuts are grown however where the availability of water permits. The dryer zones support the usual large numbers of livestock (cattle 2.2m., sheep and goats 3m.).

There is no mineral production, although proved deposits of manganese and limestone should promote exports, and a basis for a thriving cement industry, in the future. Industry is limited to the local processing of raw materials. The main railway runs from Ouagadougou, the capital (115 000), through the commercial centre of Bobo-Dioulasso (70 000) to Abidjan, and much of Mali's trade with the Ivory Coast and Ghana passes through. Most road links are to the south, except for the main route linking with Bamako in the west and Niamey in the east. Both of the main urban centres are served by French airlines.

Imports (the usual manufactures, machinery and small supplementary supplies of foodstuffs) greatly exceed exports which are mainly live animals groundnuts and oilseeds and cotton. Trade is dominated by France, followed by the Ivory Coast, Mali and Ghana.

Niger

The Republic of the Niger with a present area of 1.2m. sq km (489 000 sq miles) is even larger than Mali, and is equally landlocked. A great and largely desert country with adequate rainfall along the southern regions only, it supports a population of 4.3m. and some 14m. livestock (4m. cattle, 9m. sheep and goats, and 1m. camels, horses and asses). A pastoral zone divides the northern deserts from the agricultural region of the southern fringe. Dates and gums are collected; groundnuts, millet and cassava are grown in the south, along with cotton and paddy where seasonal flooding or wetter conditions permit, particularly along the Niger in the extreme southwest and around Lake Chad in the southeast.

Minerals include tin, salt and natron as well as iron ore (as yet unexploited). Most important, however, is the uranium deposit some 320 km (280 miles) north of Agadez. This (in 1970) is the fifth largest deposit in the world and a newly constructed concentrate plant came into operation in 1970. There are no railways and a limited modern road network, although both Niamey (70 000) the capital and Zinder (40 000) are termini of the traditional trans–Sahara routes from the north. Niamey has an international airport, and there are smaller airfields at Maradi, Zinder and Agadez. There is a growing tourist (safari) trade.

Imports, mainly of manufactured goods and petroleum from France and USA, exceeded exports until uranium began to change the balance. Exports were limited almost exclusively to groundnuts, groundnut oil and live animals, to France and Nigeria respectively.

Guinea

Of the French West African colonies gaining independence in 1958–60, the Republic of Guinea alone decided not to join the French Community. There are, however, still close cultural and economic ties with France. With an area of 246 000 sq km (95 000 sq miles) the country has a population of 3.8m. (1970) and a typically West African diversity of terrain ranging from the well-watered coastal area, through the deep valleys of the Fouta Djallon highlands (where the Niger, Gambia and Sénégal Rivers all originate) to savanna lands in the north and east, and heavily forested highlands along the Liberian border. Paddy, bananas and pineapples are grown in the wetter areas, with citrus fruits, coffee and kola nuts on the valley slopes. The cattle (1.8m.) of the high plateaus are of the small Ndama breed which is resistant to the tsetse fly.

In addition to industrial diamonds and gold, there are rich deposits of bauxite (to the northeast of the capital, Conakry) and of iron ore (in the Mount Nimba range on the borders of Liberia and Ivory Coast). With a production of some 2m. tons a year, Guinea is the seventh largest producer of bauxite. Hydroelectric power from the Konkouré River supplies an alumina processing plant, and alumina is shipped from Conakry to provide some 60 per cent of all exports.

The single railway line connects Conakry (200 000) the main port on an island off the coast, with Kouroussa (head of navigation on the Niger) and Kankan (head of navigation on the Milo). There are plans to extend this line to Bamako to improve trading communications with Mali. There are some 3 500 km (2 175 miles) of all-weather road, and airports at Conakry and Kankan.

Exports (largely alumina with some iron ore and bananas) exceed imports (textiles, foodstuffs, machinery and petroleum). Trade during the early years of independence has been increasingly with USSR and China, but France, the USA, West Germany and the UK are beginning to take a larger share.

Togo

The Republic of Togo was a former German colony entrusted to British and French mandate after the First World War. The British (western) region was incorporated into the Gold Coast and became independent within the new state of Ghana. The larger eastern region voted in 1956

731

to become an autonomous republic within the French Union. In 1960 it became fully independent, but with special cooperative agreements made with France in 1963. Togo, a strip of land running north from the coast between Ghana and Dahomey, has an area of 56 000 sq km (21 000 sq miles) and is one of the smallest countries in West Africa. With a population of 1.9m. it runs from a lagoon-fringed coast with coconuts (copra) and oil palms, northwards to well-watered mountains where coffee and cocoa are grown. Further north as the rainfall dies away there is cotton and groundnuts; and finally savannas where, free of the tsetse fly, there are some hundreds of thousands of livestock.

Minerals include limestone, iron ore and bauxite; but rich phosphate deposits are the main resource with production running at over 1m. tons a year. There is a limited road system and little industry. Three short railways fan out from the capital, Lomé (195 000) for a combined distance of some 440 km (275 miles) to the centres of the oil palm, coconut, and coffee/cocoa areas respectively. The coast is surf-bound, and Lomé the main port and airport has an open roadstead.

Imports (machinery, petroleum, foodstuffs) run slightly ahead of exports (phosphates, cocoa, coffee, oil palm and groundnut products). Trade, though small, is well spread by phosphate exports. France is the main partner, followed by the European countries, Japan and Australia.

Cameroun

The former German colony of Kamerun was placed under French and British trusteeship after the First World War. The larger portion, four-fifths, became independent in 1960 and enjoys 'special relations' with France. The smaller, British, eastern region decided its future by plebiscite in 1961; the northern portion voted to join Nigeria and the southern portion joined Cameroun to form the Federal Republic of Cameroun. With an area of 475 000 sq km (183 600 sq miles) the country has a comparatively short coastline of 240 km (150 miles), but from a narrow coastal plain the land widens inland and rises steeply in great steps to a central plateau of 760 m (2 500 ft) carrying here and there mountains up to 2 100 m (7 000 ft), but falling away to the river basins of the interior; the altitude of Lake Chad, some 1 300 km (800 miles) inland, is only 300 m (1 000 ft). The southern third of the territory is a vast primeval forest opening out to the north in savannas and semidesert tracts.

The population of 5.8m. includes some 200 tribes and a great variety of languages; but varied relief and latitude give a wide range of crops and occupations, and the new federation has formed a stable community with the distinction of having both French and English as its official languages. Rubber, oil palms, cocoa, coffee (both *robusta* in the lowlands, and the more valuable *arabica* in the highlands) cotton and bananas are grown as cash crops. The dense forests are an important source of timber.

There is limestone, iron ore and bauxite but these are not greatly exploited. Industry is developing however, around Yaoundé the capital (100 000) and at Douala, the river port and rail centre (200 000). The major commercial development is between these cities at Edea (17 000) where there is a rubber processing plant and an aluminium smelter (drawing alumina from Guinea) supplied with power from the hydro-electric installation at the falls on the Sanaga River. This power supply is transmitted to the main towns, and the aluminium is exported to such West African countries as can use it. Communications, both road and rail, are limited and difficult to develop; particularly those to the Central African Republic which handles most of its trade through Douala. There is a major airport at both Yaoundé and Douala.

Exports (in the main coffee, cocoa, cotton, timber and aluminium) are in excess of imports (machinery, transport equipment, chemicals, foodstuffs and petroleum). France is by far the main trading partner, followed by West Germany, USA, Italy, Belgium—Luxembourg, and Japan for imports; and by the Netherlands, West Germany, USA and Italy for exports.

Former French Equatorial Africa

This vast territory, for which 'Equatorial' was always in part a misnomer, stretched from the heart of the Sahara in the north to beyond the equator in the south. As French Equatorial Africa it comprised the four territories of Gabun, Middle Congo, Ubangi and Chad. Under the constitution of the Fifth Republic of France these territories became autonomous members of the French Community in 1958, two years later each became an independent republic so that the four republics, each a member of United Nations, are now Gabon, Congo (République du Congo, not to be confused with Zaire (Congo, Kinshasa) which replaces the former Belgian Congo), Central African Republic and Chad. The first two have an Atlantic seaboard, the latter two are entirely inland. There are marked differences in size, but practically none in the density of the population, which varies from 1.8 to 2.7 per sq km (5 to 7 per sq mile).

Table 81 — Area and population of territories of Former French Equatorial Africa

| | Area | | Population 1968—9 |
	sq km	sq miles	
Gabon	268 000	103 000	500 000
Congo (Brazzaville)	342 000	132 000	940 000
Central African Republic	623 000	240 000	2 255 000
Chad	1 284 000	496 000	3 700 000

Gabon

The Gabon Republic was the parent colony of this agglomeration of territories. Libreville the capital (73 000) was founded in 1849 as a home for freed slaves and stands on the Gabon 'River' which, like the Comeroun 'River' is a great estuary fed by many streams. The smallest of the group, this country has great potential in its mineral riches. Virtually the entire country is covered with dense equatorial rain forest, with rivers carving deep torrential valleys as they plunge over the plateau in their westward course. One of the main resources is extensive areas of valuable timber (okoumé, mahoganies, limba and ebony) which is floated down the rivers to Libreville and Port Gentil (25 000) where there are sawmills and plywood factories.

The variety and quantity of mineral reserves could make Gabon one of the most prosperous countries of tropical Africa. There is gold, oil, natural gas, manganese, uranium and iron ore. Not all are yet worked as they must await adequate communications for full exploitation. Uranium is already mined near Franceville, and iron ore will be exported through the new deepwater port at Owendo via a new railway from Belinga. Further rich iron ore deposits await development in the inaccessible northeast. Manganese is worked in the upper Ogowé valley at Moanda near Franceville, and must be conveyed by aerial ropeway, narrow and standard gauge railways before reaching the docks at Pointe Noire in the Congo Republic. Offshore oil wells are in production around Port Gentil where there is a refinery with some 850 000 tons a year capacity. Production of crude petroleum in 1973 was some 9.1m. tons (fifth largest in Africa after Libya, Nigeria, Algeria and Egypt).

Gabon, like Libya, is almost unique in Africa in that agricultural products play a minor role in exports. With great potential in minerals, hydroelectric power sites and forest resources, the main shortage of the future could be labour. Exports (manganese, uranium, petroleum, timber and timber products (such as plywoods and veneers)) steadily move ahead of imports (machinery, transport equipment and consumer goods). France is the major trading partner, followed by West Germany, USA, the Netherlands and UK.

Congo

The People's Republic of the Congo, or Congo (Brazzaville) as it was known to distinguish it from Congo (Kinshasa) now known as Zaire, was formerly the French colony of Middle Congo. Bisected by the Equator and with only a short coastline, it is largely a landlocked country rising in a series of steep ridges from the equatorial climate of the Congo valley to dry, savanna-covered plateaus in the north. Some 50 per cent of the country is covered by equatorial forests. The northern regions are largely uninhabited, and the population of

980 000 (1971) is concentrated in the area between Brazzaville (nearly 250 000), the capital and former administrative centre of French Equatorial Africa, and Pointe Noire (nearly 150 000) which are joined by the first railway constructed in tropical Africa.

Timber is the major resource, with fine cabinet woods such as okoumé, limba and mahoganies. There are also diamonds, some potash, lead and gold, and a small offshore oilfield. Hydroelectric power has yet to be developed on a significant scale, but there is growing local industry with factories concerned with food processing, timber products (veneers) and consumer goods. The railway to Brazzaville, situated above the rapids at Stanley Pool, is a vital link with the upstream navigation of the Congo and the Ubangi since it makes Pointe Noire the focus of the Congo's function as a transit country. The port handles minerals from the Gabon, cotton and groundnuts from Chad and timber from the whole of the Congo basin.

Imports (machinery, transport equipment, petroleum and some foodstuffs such as wheat) are well in excess of exports (largely timber veneers, diamonds and sugar). France is the major trading partner, followed by West Germany, the Netherlands, UK, Italy and Israel (diamonds).

Central African Republic

Previously the French colony of Ubangi—Shari, this country is a land of high plateaus forming the watershed of the two rivers after which it was named; the former flowing into the Congo and the latter inland to Lake Chad. The state is remote and landlocked; communications with the outside world are difficult and, being on the fringe of the mountain ranges stretching northeast from Cameroun, it has long been a crossroads of migrations. Even since 1960 it has played host to refugees from South Sudan and former Congo (Kinshasa). The country has well watered plateaus, tropical forest and grassland in the south, but the north and northeast are in the dry zone. It is largely a subsistence farming community growing cassava, millet, groundnuts and maize, with coffee and cotton as cash crops, and with limited livestock.

Timber is sent to neighbouring countries, and diamonds and some uranium is worked. Lack of communications and minimal external trade both limit development. Rail links with Chad and Cameroun have been considered, but as yet have not been justified. The capital, Bangai (150 000), on the Ubangi River, is the main river port and airport. Diamonds provide 50 per cent of a limited range of exports, followed by cotton, coffee, groundnut products and some timber. Imports, which usually exceed exports include machinery, manufactures and foodstuffs. France is by far the main trading partner, followed by USA, West Germany, Israel and Italy.

Chad

The Chad Republic is the largest of the former French Equatorial colonies with a population of only 3.7m. The country is landlocked, is an area of inland drainage, and has seen many migrations. Some 9 000 years ago Lake Chad, which is shared with Niger, Nigeria and Cameroun, was a vast inland sea of some 230 000 sq km (88 800 sq miles) stretching northeastwards to include the Bodee depression. Subterranean seepage and changing climatic conditions have reduced it to 21 000 sq km (8 100 sq miles) — about the size of Wales. In spite of the surrounding conditions (the northern two-thirds of the country is true desert) the lake has very low salinity and is an important source of fish to all four countries. South of 14° N the rainfall increases and is sufficient for cultivation. In the extreme south it reaches 1 000 mm (40 in) in places to give rise to wet tropical conditions. The country is largely self-sufficient since these areas suffice to support the limited population. Cotton, grown in the southwest around the Chari (Shari) basin is the main cash crop, with livestock (in the upland savanna) second in importance. In 1970 there were 4.5m. cattle, 1.8m. sheep, and 370 000 camels.

There are no mineral resources beyond a little natron, no internal railways, and little industry. Air services are essential, with meat and cotton being flown out from the capital, Fort Lamy (132 000) and imports flown in. Surface movement is by road, largely impassable in the rainy season, and trade flows largely via Maiduguri (the nearby rail-head in Nigeria) and through Cameroun to Douala. Fort Lamy is at the confluence of the Chari and the Logone, and there are plans to divert the latter westward into the Benue for the production of hydroelectric power. The flow of all rivers is highly seasonal and the shape of Lake Chad (at most a few metres deep and encompassed by swamps, sand-banks and islands of floating vegetation) could well be affected if the work is carried out. Chad has set aside two national parks and seven large reserves for the preservation of game. The lake itself, with its extensive insect population and lush peripheral vegetation is one of the world's great staging posts for migratory birds. Bundles of papyrus stalks provide both huts and boats for the local fishermen.

With limited resources and a small population in a largely inhospitable land, the country is not well placed for economic development. Overseas trade is small. The two major exports, raw cotton (85—90 per cent of the total) and livestock (both live animals and meat) suffice to very nearly balance the standard range of imports (manufactured goods, machinery and some petroleum and foodstuff). France is by far the major trading partner; followed by USA, West Germany, Nigeria and Cameroun for imports, and by Cameroun, Nigeria, Japan and Congo (Kinshasa) for exports.

Liberia

Liberia is unique in Africa as a Negro republic founded by American philanthropists as a home for freed American slaves and constituted an independent state in 1847. Liberia is therefore the oldest independent republic in Africa, with an area of 110 000 sq km (43 000 sq miles) – a little smaller than England – and a population in 1970 of 1.3m. Rainfall, which is heavy and monsoonal in summer, gives rise to extensive marshes, lagoons and mangrove swamps backed by a well forested plateau. In spite of the large swamp area, the coastal lowlands are productive. Paddy, sugarcane, cassava, coffee, cocoa and oil palms are grown, and there are extensive rubber plantations. These plantations, owned by American companies, were started after the First World War to assist the economy, and have become a valuable source of income: the largest employs some 35 000 and covers 40 500 ha (100 000 acres).

Gold and diamonds are worked, but by far the most important mineral resource is iron ore. This is a high grade haematite and Liberia is Africa's largest producer. With an annual production of some 15m. tons the country is among the world's ten major producers, and was the third largest exporter in 1970. The ore is mined at several places: at Boni Hill northwest of Monrovia (the capital, 110 000), on the boundary with Sierra Leone at the Mano River, at Mount Nimba in the Guinea highlands and in the Bong Mountains. All these sites are served by railways either to the port at Monrovia or the new (1963) deepwater port at Buchanan, where there is a pelletizing and ore washing plant. Road communications are difficult in the hinterland, but a good highway connects Monrovia with the Guinea road system. The main international airport is Robertsfield, some 80 km (50 miles) south of the capital.

Although no ships are built in Liberia, and few are owned there, the Liberian merchant fleet is now the largest in the world thanks to the practice of registering ships, especially tankers, under 'flags of convenience' to minimise financial dues and the impact of restrictive governmental regulations. In 1970, the Liberian fleet totalled 33.3m. gross tons (see p. 92 for conversion to dwt) out of a world fleet of 227.5m. tons. Japan was second with 27m. and UK third with 25.8m. tons. The dominance in the bulk carriers is even greater. Of oil tankers within the world fleet, Liberian registrations were 19.3m. tons (of a total of 86m.) with UK second at 12m. tons. Of ore and bulk carriers, Liberian registrations were 10.1m. tons (of a total of 46.6m.) with Japan second at 7.9m. tons. This merchant fleet is not a major source of revenue, as the Liberian government exercises no control over ships flying its flag and makes only a modest charge for registration and annual fees.

There is limited industrial development, with small factories producing consumer goods, foodstuffs and beverages. Nonetheless the balance of her limited overseas trade has long been in Liberia's favour with first rubber and then iron ore as the major earner of foreign exchange. Exports are almost exclusively iron ore (76 per cent) and rubber (18 per cent) followed by industrial diamonds and some coffee and cocoa, to USA, West Germany, Italy, UK, Belgium—Luxembourg and the Netherlands. Imports mainly transport equipment, machinery foodstuffs, chemicals and petroleum come from the USA, West Germany, Japan and the UK.

Equatorial Guinea

Equatorial Guinea, with a history dating back to 1471, has been under Portuguese and Spanish control. Administered as a Spanish Overseas Province since 1904, it became independent in 1968 and comprises two provinces — the mainland territory of Rio Muni (between Cameroun and Gabon) with adjacent islets, and the islands of Fernando Póo and Annobón. With a total combined area of 28 100 sq km (10 800 sq miles) and a population of 300 000, the former accounts for 90 per cent of the area and 75 per cent of the population. Rio Muni is typically West African, rising by steps from a coastal zone of virgin tropical forest to grassy plateaus in the interior at some 1 200 m (4 000 ft). The main products are cocoa, coffee and West African timbers, with some oil palm plantations near the Benito estuary. Apart from lumbering there is no industry and few surfaced roads. There is an airport at Bata (40 000) the chief port and commercial centre.

The island of Fernando Póo (some 2 000 sq km: 780 sq miles) is, like the Cameroun Mountain, of volcanic origin with a main peak of over 2 750 m (9 000 ft). The capital of the republic, Santa Isabel (20 000) is situated on the lofty cliffs of the island, and is connected by cog-railway to a fine natural harbour, originally a deep crater. Cocoa is grown, and coffee (with the help of migrant labour from the mainland), as a plantation crop. The limited industry is confined to fish preserving and food processing. The main international airport is at Santa Isabel.

Overseas trade is limited to the export of cocoa, coffee and timber. Spain is the main trading partner, followed by the USA, the UK and West Germany. There may be reserves of oil and uranium, but these have yet to be exploited.

Zaire Republic

Founded as the Congo Free State by King Leopold II of Belgium in his individual capacity, recognised by the powers at the Berlin Conference in 1885 as a philanthropic enterprise under his personal sovereignty, but afterwards severely criticised in respect of the administration, this vast territory was taken over by Belgium in 1909. It includes all the

Congo basin save some subsidiary streams on the outskirts, and has an area of some 2.3m. sq km (895 000 sq miles) and a population (1970) of 21.6m. The country was divided into six provinces — Leopoldville, Equator, Eastern, Kivu, Katanga and Kasai. As elsewhere in Africa there was strong nationalist agitation for independence, accentuated by its attainment in neighbouring French territories. Independence (as the Democratic Republic of Congo, or Congo, Kinshasa) was declared on 30 June 1960 but the hurried departure of the Belgian administrators, teachers, doctors and professional men left the vast country unprepared to carry on normally and was the signal for an outburst of ancient tribal jealousies and new political rivalries. In particular the rich mining province of Katanga in the south began to follow a separate path. United Nations forces intervened to restore order, and it was not until these forces left in 1964 that some degree of political stability was achieved. The country was renamed the Republic of Zaire in 1971.

The northern part of the country is covered with forest, opening out in the south to parklike country. The Congo (now Zaire) basin is a vast shallow depression in the African plateau, but the headstreams flowing from distant ridges are often unnavigable. In general, however, the outstanding feature of the country lies in the long navigable stretches between rapids both on the main river and its tributaries, of which the two outstanding are the Kasai (left bank) and the Ubangi (right bank). The total length of waterways navigated by steamers is about 12 000 km (7 500 miles) or two and a half times the total length of the Congo (4 670 km: 2 900 miles). Barges up to 1 200 tons can ply on over 2 400 km (1 500 miles) of river routes. The river is the heart of the transport system — with roads and railways to feed it, and railways to bypass the rapids.

Though it can claim to be a maritime state, Zaire could scarcely have a shorter seaboard. Angola extends up to the south bank of the mouth of the Zaire River, and north of the river mouth there is Cabinda, an isolated patch of Portuguese territory which occupies the coast right up to former French Africa. Just at the river mouth, on the north side, Zaire has 38 km (24 miles) of coast, with the small seaport of Banana. Upriver is another small port, Boma, terminus of a narrow gauge railway for the export of timber, and beyond that is the chief port, Matadi. It is about 173 km (107 miles) from the open sea and is the limit of navigation for oceangoing vessels. Above it, for over 320 km (200 miles), the course of the Zaire is broken by a series of falls as the river forces its way through the Crystal Mountains. The falls are circumvented by a railway built in 1898 connecting Matadi with Kinshasa (Leopoldville), the capital on Pool Malebo (Stanley Pool). They are also connected by oil pipelines. Above Kinshasa the Zaire, sometimes kilometres wide, is navigable for over 1 770 km (1 100 miles) up to Kisangani (Stanleyville). There a railway circumvents the Stanley Falls and connects at Ponthierville with another navigable section of the river (now known as the Lualaba) extending a further 323 km (200 miles) upstream to Kindu. From Kindu another railway mounts the valley to Kabalo, and then strikes eastward to Kalemie (Albertville), on the shore of Lake Tanganyika, a notable connection because from Kigoma, on the opposite side of the lake, the Tanzania central railway gives access to the East African coast at Dar es Salaam. West of Kabalo, railway connection has been provided with Kamina, on the main line north, thus giving Katanga (now Shaba) access to East Africa. Also the mixed gauges of the Zaire railways have all been brought up to the South African standard narrow gauge of 3 ft 6 in.

Above Kabalo the Lualaba is again navigable to Bukama, once the terminus of the through railway to the south. This rail service not only links up Shaba with Cape Town, but more important commercially, provides connection with the east coast port of Beira. Northward the rail service now extends beyond Bukama to Port Francqui, on the Kasai, so that there is through communication by rail from Cape Town northwards into the heart of the Zaire basin for a distance of 5 280 km (3 288 miles). Further extension of the line to Kinshasa is contemplated; already there is connection by motor road, coming from Shaba. Meanwhile there is transport by river steamer from Port Francqui down the Kasai and the Zaire to Kinshasa (six days) and from there by rail to Matadi.

Another outlet from Shaba lies in Angola (former Portuguese West Africa) to the coast at Benguela and Lobito Bay. This service, coupled with the further service from Lubumbashi to Beira, provides through railway communication across Africa from west to east. These rail and river communications are as important as the mineral resources of the country. Indeed without them the full potential of the minerals in the remote crystalline rocks of the southeast could not be realised.

The mineral wealth of the Zaire Republic is its major resource, and the bulk of this is in the province of Shaba (Katanga). The country is the leading producer of cobalt (11 000 tons in 1969, 50 per cent of the world's total) and diamonds (15m. metric carats, two-thirds of the world's total); is sixth in the production of copper (390 000 tons in 1970) and seventh of tin. Manganese, zinc, silver, gold and uranium are also important, while there are great reserves of iron ore and bauxite yet to be exploited. Although communications are available, distances are still great and transportation is costly: the processing of mineral ores within the country is therefore encouraged. Coal for such processing in Shaba was imported from the Wankie coalfield in Rhodesia, but the Zaire River now provides hydroelectric power. Again the river offers great potential. The great flow of water (second in volume only to the Amazon) cuts a submarine canyon deep into the Atlantic, and silt from the estuary (which is over 450 m: 1 500 ft deep) is carried over 450 km (280 miles) out to sea. This fast deep flow (with minimal seasonal variations) is interrupted by rapids which make it ideal for hydroelectric projects. Apart from smaller installations in Shaba, the major project is at Inga in the Crystal Mountains below Kinshasa. This single project, if fully developed, could generate power (estimated at nearly 30 000 MW) equal to that of the whole of North America.

With ample mineral resources and power, industry is encouraged, and could in the future include iron and steel works, aluminium smelters, etc. Already towns are expanding to serve the mining interests and their subsidiary factories. Some 25 per cent of the population is now urban, with 1.5m. in greater Kinshasa and a further 1.5m. living in towns of over 100 000. There is therefore great contrast between the 'developed' areas and the rest of the country.

Much of the soil is infertile and the forests discourage settlement. The rural population is unevenly scattered in areas of rich alluvial and volcanic soils. The country is not self-sufficient in foodstuffs (even with 69 per cent of the labour force engaged in agriculture) and has only limited livestock (less than 1m. cattle, 1.6m. goats and 0.5m. sheep in Upper Shaba and on the eastern border) and limited fish resources. Both meat and fish must be imported. Cash crops are mainly coffee, cocoa, rubber and oil palms; but the exodus of Belgian plantation managers hindered development during the early years of independence.

Although there is great scope for advancement based on the mineral and hydroelectric potential, the country faces many problems. Population is sparse, communications away from river and railway are extremely difficult, agriculture suffers from soil deficiency, and political uncertainty inhibits large scale enterprises. Nonetheless overseas trade has moved steadily ahead since independence, with exports increasingly in excess of imports since 1965. The wide range of mineral products gives rise to an equally wide range of trading partners. Copper alone represents 50 per cent of all exports, production having risen from 15 tons in 1900 to 326 000 in 1968 and 390 000 in 1970 — with plans to produce over 600 000 by 1980. Minerals in aggregate (copper, diamonds, cobalt, zinc, manganese, tin, cadmium and tungsten) account for four-fifths of all exports, followed by coffee, palm oil and rubber. Imports include transport equipment, machinery, manufactured goods, foodstuffs, chemicals and petroleum. Belgium—Luxembourg is still by far the major trading partner followed by France, Italy, the UK, West Germany and the Netherlands for exports; and by the USA, Italy, France and West Germany (among many others) for imports.

Former Portuguese Africa

Portuguese Africa fell into two main provinces — Angola, or Portuguese

West Africa, and Moçambique, or Portuguese East Africa. In addition to various outlying islands (see p. 751), there was a third mainland territory, comparatively small and seldom heard of, Portuguese Guinea — now Guinea-Bissau.

Guinea-Bissau

This territory was discovered in 1446 by Nuno Tristão and was a Portuguese colony from 1879 to 1974. Bounded by Sénégal in the north and by Guinea in the east and south, it has an area of 36 000 sq km (14 000 sq miles) which includes the adjacent archipelago of Bijagós with the island of Bolamo. The population in 1970 was 530 000, some 25 000 being in the capital and chief port of Bissau. The coastline is deeply indented, the rainfall is heavy, and the country is low-lying, reaching only 180 m (600 ft), in the southeast. Agriculture is largely subsistence with paddy, coconuts and bananas in the comparatively heavily populated coastal areas; and cassava millet, groundnuts and vegetables in the dryer interior. Livestock (of all types) totals less than 500 000. The pattern has changed little since independence in 1974.

The country is at the northern limits of the oil palm; palm kernels and palm oil, along with coconuts and groundnuts, are the main cash products. Nearly all trade is with Portugal through Bissau (which is also the site of the airport), and the minor ports of Bolamo and Cocheu. There are no minerals, no railway, and only a limited road network.

Angola

Angola was Portugal's largest overseas province, with an area of 1.25m. sq km (481 350 sq miles) and a population in 1970 of 5.5m. The territory includes **Cabinda**, a small enclave (7 250 sq km: 2 800 sq miles) to the north of Zaire's short coastline at the mouth of the Congo. The country consists mainly of broad tablelands 910 to 1 520 m (3 000 to 5 000 ft) above sea level which range from a tropical luxuriance in the north to an arid south. The 1 610 km (1 000 miles) of coastline is cooled by westerly winds blowing over the cold Benguela current, and rainfall, except along the northern coast, tends to fall mainly on the higher country inland. There is therefore a marked transition along the coast from open savannas with oil palms in the north to near desert conditions at the southern boundary with South West Africa (Namibia).

Behind the coast the central plateau dips eastward down to the Zaire and Zambezi River basins. Food crops grown are mainly for subsistence and include maize, beans and manioc. There are also extensive plantations of coffee, oil palms, sisal and cotton, with ranching and mixed farming on the higher, tsetse free, plateaus. It is estimated that ivestock in the territory include 2.2m. cattle, 7.4m. sheep and goats (mostly sheep), and 0.75m. pigs. Rolling tracts of open woodlands and grassy plains are diversified by deciduous forests. This upland country is well watered, for the most part, by rivers flowing not only westward to the Atlantic Ocean (notably the Cuanza) but northwards to the Kasai and eastwards to the Zambezi. It is indeed a vast watershed, reaching in its highest points levels of 2 440 to 2 740 m (8 000 to 9 000 ft). The Serra da Chela in the southwest, where the great scarp at the back of Moçâmedes is particularly imposing, rise to over 2 130 m (7 000 ft).

Among the mineral resources, diamonds mined in the Kasai basin are the most important with an annual production of some 1.7m. metric carats (seventh largest in the world). Manganese, copper, iron ore and salt are also worked for export; and there is petroleum both in Cabinda and offshore, and in the Luanda area. Crude oil production in 1973 was 8.1m. tons (slightly more than Tunisia). There are oil refineries at Luanda and in Lobito Bay with an annual capacity of some 1m. tons. Hydro-electric power is well developed to serve Luanda, Lobito/Benguela, Nova Lisboa (the rail centre and possibly the future capital) and Matala in the southwest.

Four lines of railway from as many points on the coast have been built inland to assist in opening up the country and providing communications to the copper ore in Shaba (Katanga) and north Zambia. These lines are separate enterprises, and are not uniform gauge. The most northerly (metre gauge) runs from Luanda eastward to Malange. Luanda, founded in 1575 and capital of Angola since 1927, is by far the largest town (225 000). It comprises a lower and an upper town and has a deepwater harbour protected by an outlying island. A new capital was once proposed: Huambo (Nova Lisboa) some 300 km (185 miles) inland from Lobito at a height of 1 700 m (5 580 ft).

The most southerly line, the Mossamedes railway, is of narrow (3 ft 6 in) gauge. Starting from the little old town (Moçâmedes) from which it takes its name, which has an open roadstead for a port, it climbs the arid scarp of the Chela range to the Huila Plateau, where it has reached Serpa Pinto. Its ultimate goal is the Barotseland frontier of Zambia. In between these two railways is a third, running 100 km (62 miles) inland from Porto Amboin to hilly country, but stopping short of the final ascent to a plantation area where coffee and oil palms do particularly well.

Of far greater importance than these lines, useful as they are, is the Benguela railway, which is on the standard South African gauge and has a length of 1 343 km (835 miles) in Angola, beyond which it extends to Katanga and links up with the Rhodesian railways, incidentally providing railway communication right across the continent to Beira, in Moçambique, a through journey of 4 750 km (2 953 miles). At the Angola end the line actually starts from Lobito Bay, north of Benguela.

The bay is formed by a sandspit enclosing sheltered deep water which provides the best harbour in the territory. At Benguela — one of the oldest of the Portuguese settlements and slave marts, but with only an open roadstead, and now outstripped by Lobito in both size and trade — the line turns inland and mounts by degrees to the central plateau.

Overseas trade has long been mainly with Portugal, and exports and imports are broadly in balance. In 1960 coffee provided 35 per cent of the exports, diamonds 14 per cent, and sisal over 10 per cent. In 1969 the corresponding percentages were 34, 19 and under 3, followed by iron ore, cotton, fuel oils, food products (such as maize, fish and fish-meal), sugar and manioc. After Portugal, West Germany, the USA and the UK were the main sources of imports; while the USA, the Netherlands, West Germany and Japan followed on exports.

Moçambique

Moçambique (Mozambique), former Portuguese East Africa, is smaller than Angola with an area of some 785 000 sq km (303 000 sq miles), but with a slightly higher population: 7.5m. in 1970. The country was referred to in the past as 'the Portuguese foreshore to British South Africa'. It stretches over some 16° of latitude and straggles irregularly backwards and forwards inland. In the south, near Natal, it is a strip 80 km (50 miles) wide, while along the Zambezi it follows the river for over 1 130 km (700 miles) from the coast to form a wedge between Zambia and Rhodesia. South of the Zambezi much of the country is low-lying and under 150 m (500 ft); to the north the hilly areas rise to over 1 800 m (6 000 ft); and so provide a wide range of climatic conditions. Rainfall comes with the trade winds between December and May, to be followed by a hot dry season. The delta areas (Zambezi and Limpopo) and the coasts have mangrove swamps, coral reefs and shallows. Inland the rainfall decreases, but rises again on the higher plateaus.

Portugal's interest in this region goes back to Vasco da Gama's famous voyage to India in 1498, when the navigator touched at Moçambique Island. A settlement was formed there in 1504, and a massive fort erected which has kept the Portuguese flag flying through all the vicissitudes of the succeeding 450 years. Other settlements were formed, but Moçambique held the pre-eminence. Its position corresponds, in some ways, with that of Mombasa Island, and though it is further from the coast (about 5 km: 3 miles), the channel provides a sheltered harbour which is still a centre for the coasting trade. The town retains many of the features of early Portuguese settlement, but has not kept pace with modern developments, and not only had to give way in 1907 to Lourenço Marques as the capital city of Portuguese East Africa, but has been outstripped commercially by the port of Beira also. The country was administered until 1942 by the Mozambique Company whose charter then expired. Subsequently administered as a Portuguese Overseas Province it moved forward, along with Angola, to eventual 'statehood' and independence.

Moçambique has wealth of its own, chiefly in plantation products, but benefits greatly from transit trade with the Transvaal and the land-locked states to the west. This has given a stimulus to railway construction cutting across the territory and to the provision of modern port facilities. Both Lourenço Marques, the capital with a population of over 200 000, and Beira owe their progress in the present century largely to these circumstances. The close ties between South Africa and Moçambique are further shown by the inclusion of the latter in the South African Postal Union, and by the Moçambique Convention, which provides for the recruitment of labour in Moçambique for the South African mines, the free exchange of the products of the two countries, and the apportionment to Lourenço Marques of certain ocean traffic. Apart from the railway to the Transvaal, Lourenço Marques is the terminus of a line to Goba near the Swaziland border, and another line across the Limpopo which gives Rhodesia another access to the sea.

Beira (50 000), at the mouth of the Pungwe and Busi Rivers, south of the Zambezi, was unknown till nearly the end of the last century. It came into prominence as the coastal terminus of the Beira railway, which crosses the coastal plain and ascends the escarpment to join the Rhodesian railway system. The line was built by the Mozambique Company and Beira became 'the Gateway to Rhodesia'. From being 'the Gateway to Rhodesia' Beira went on to become also 'the Gateway to Nyasaland' (now Malawi). British railways had been built in the Shire valley to circumvent the cataracts and other obstacles to through navigation on the Shire, in its course from Lake Malawi to the Zambezi. But Nyasaland had no outlet of its own to the sea, and its railways were handicapped till in 1922 a line from Beira reached the southern bank of the Zambezi opposite to the terminus on the north bank. The bridging of the Zambezi was a formidable problem, but a bridge was finally built near Sena and the line was opened for traffic in January 1935. The bridge is one of the longest in the world, 3 677 m (over 2 miles). Another line links Malawi with Lumbo, a mainland harbour opposite Moçambique island. Lumbo is not a first-class port, and the railway has been linked up with Nacala, a port in a large natural harbour 96 km (60 miles) north which could be made a major tanker terminal.

A climate ranging from a tropical north to a temperate south encourages a wide number of agricultural products. There are extensive coconut plantations along the coast to the north of Quelimane, which give way to sisal, groundnuts and cashew nuts with cotton, tobacco and tea in the northern foothills. In the south there is paddy and fruit, particularly bananas, pineapple and citrus fruits in the Lourenço Marques area.

Mineral resources, which are limited, include coal, bauxite, gold and beryl. Industry has been stimulated by the railways, the port requirements and the transit trade in general. There are oil refineries, small steelworks, chemical and fertiliser plants with sawmills along the line to Malawi, cement works at Dondo and cotton mills at Vila Pery (inland from Beira). Hydroelectric power is available from the Revué River, but the major project is the Cabora Dam on the Zambezi some 100 km (62 miles) above Tete. This dam will be the largest in Africa and will provide power to points as far away as Nairobi, Entebbe and Johannesburg. It will more than suffice for all Moçambique's requirements and in addition will make tens of thousands of hectares of irrigated land available. The potential output from this project is, however, less than one-tenth of the potential of the Inga project on the Zaire below Kinshasa.

Moçambique earns considerable revenue from her extensive transit trade as well as from tourism and the sums sent home by migrant workers in South Africa.

Imports are somewhat in excess of visible exports which include cotton (18 per cent), cashew nuts (15 per cent), sugar, tea, refinery products, copra, coconut oil, sisal and small quantities of coal, bauxite and gold. Portugal is by far the major trading partner, followed by South Africa, the UK, West Germany, the USA, Angola and Rhodesia.

Outlying African Islands

Mauritius

Mauritius lies some 800 km (500 miles) east of Madagascar, is of volcanic origin and covers 1 865 sq km (720 sq miles). Seaward it is ringed by coral reefs; inland it rises to a central plateau of 460 m (1 500 ft), fringed with peaks up to 823 m (2 700 ft). It is a picturesque, well-watered and fertile island supporting a population of 830 000, the average density 409 per sq km (1 059 to the sq mile), exceeding that of England and Wales. Port Louis, the capital, has a population of 139 000. Mauritius, with a temperature of 22–26° C (71.6–78.8° F) throughout the year, might be a Garden of Eden but for one great drawback — it is subject to devastating cyclones. Industry and trade centre in a single product, sugar. The volcanic soils are ideal for sugarcane, which is grown extensively in the south and east of the island, and under irrigation in the rainshadow area of the north and west. Production is some 650 000 tons a year, but the quantity varies. In 1945, when three cyclones struck the island, the crop was 139 000 tons; by 1956 it was 560 000 tons. Sugar accounts for 98 per cent of all exports and 90 per cent of the cultivable area is under sugar. Most of the crop is grown and treated on big estates, though these are far outnumbered by small plantations. Apart from the sugar, and a little tea and tobacco, the main crops are cassava, potatoes and onions.

There are no mineral resources and the main industry is cane-milling. The island's pool of labour and its attractive setting are important resources however. Labour intensive industries, such as diamond polishing, watch component manufacture and wig-making are attracted by free port facilities and the existing administrative services; and tourism (largely from South Africa) is of growing significance, rising from 14 000 in 1967 to 25 000 in 1970. There are no railways, but there is an excellent road network and an international airport at Plaisance, across the island from Port Louis. Imports include foodstuffs, petroleum and manufactured goods; exports are sugar — with a little mollasses and tea. The United Kingdom is by far the major trading partner, followed by South Africa and Burma (rice imports).

The island had been under Arab, Malay, Portuguese, Dutch and French rule before it was captured during the Napoleonic wars, when it bore the name Ile de France. Mauritius still preserves much of its French character but owing to the introduction of Indian coolie labour to work the sugar estates, two-thirds of the population is now Indian (52 per cent Hindu, 17 per cent Muslim); 90 per cent of the rest are descended from African slaves. The population is increasing rapidly and has doubled in the last thirty years since malaria has been eradicated. Mauritius attained full independence in 1968.

British Islands

The Seychelles

The Seychelles and their dependencies, a numerous and widely scattered group of some ninety small islands north of Madagascar and south of the Equator, became British at the same time as Mauritius, of which they were a dependency. Since 1903 they have been a separate colony, and since 1965 have formed, with the Chagos Archipelago, Aldabra, Farquhar and Des Roches, the British Indian Ocean Territory. The total area is some 388 sq km (150 sq miles).

The Seychelles proper are in about the latitude of Mombasa. The main island, Mahé, comprises most of the total population and is the seat of the capital and chief port, Victoria. It is mountainous and exports copra, cinnamon, essential oils, patchouli, vanilla, etc. Imports are mainly food, textiles and consumer goods. Distinctive products of the colony as a whole are coco-de-mer (a double coconut) and the giant tortoise, whose special habitat is the Aldabra group. Its main trading partners are the United Kingdom, Kenya, South Africa and Hong Kong. A new airport gives an opportunity for increased tourism in the future.

St Helena

St Helena is on the opposite side of Africa, 1 930 km (1 200 miles) from the west coast in the South Atlantic. The island (122 sq km: 47 sq miles) with a population of 5 000, is a little larger than Jersey; it rises rapidly to a volcanic peak at 823 m (2 700 ft). Famous historically as the final place of exile of the Emperor Napoleon, and once an important place of call on the long sea voyage to India, it faded into comparative insignificance with the opening of the Suez Canal. It is still an occasional port of call, and its people eke out a meagre livelihood by selling specimens of their handicrafts to passengers. It is also an important cable station. The cultivation and processing of New Zealand 'flax' is the only 'industry'. The cultivated area is some 3 800 ha (8 000 acres) growing fodder and vegetables. The capital is Jamestown (1 500).

Ascension Island

Between the two world wars St Helena was given two remote dependencies — Ascension Island 1 130 km (700 miles) to the northwest and Tristan da Cunha, 2 410 km (1 500 miles) to the southwest. The former, mostly a waste of volcanic cinders, but redeemed from complete barrenness by the upper slopes of Green Mountain (854 m: 2 800 ft), has importance as a cable station and a space tracking station. In the Second World War the airstrip near Georgetown was used as a refuelling base. Large numbers of turtles are caught on the island which is a major hatching ground. Population 748; and 4 ha (10 acres) of cultivable ground.

Tristan da Cunha

Tristan da Cunha, one of the loneliest and bleakest of outposts, a volcano rising 2 060 m (6 760 ft) from the sea, was garrisoned during Napoleon's exile on St Helena, and until 1961 was inhabited by the descendants (200—300) of a party of men and women who elected to stay when the garrison was withdrawn in 1817. They were barely able to support themselves, and the island — or rather islands, for there is a group of four, though only Tristan was inhabited — remained of negligible importance till the Second World War. Then a meteorological station was established, based on South Africa. After the war an Administrator was appointed, and a South African company started crawfishing operations. The cultivated area is 12 ha (30 acres) growing potatoes and fruit.

In 1961 the volcano, long believed to be completely extinct, erupted. The inhabitants were evacuated to Britain but in 1963 the majority returned and the population in 1969 was 271.

Malagasy Republic

The island of Madagascar came under French influence in the seventeenth century and was recognised by Britain as a French protectorate in 1890. As the outcome of hostilities before and after the latter date, the native (Hova) dynasty was suppressed in 1896. Nearly 1 610 km (1 000 miles) long, with an area of 590 000 sq km (229 000 sq miles) (rather more than that of France), Madagascar is the only African island comparable in size with the mainland territories. Its population is 6.7m. and includes some eighteen ethnic groups in addition to Indians and Chinese. Much of the interior is occupied by a plateau, averaging some 1 200 m (4 000 ft) above sea level and carrying mountains up to over 2 740 m (9 000 ft). The east coast is lined with lagoons, beyond which the land rises sharply to the central plateau. The descent on the other side is more gradual, and the longest rivers flow westward to the extensive plains bordering the Moçambique Channel, which separates the island from Former Portuguese East Africa (Moçambique). The channel is deep: 386 km (240 miles) across at its narrowest, and having a depth below sea level as great as the height of the mountains above it. But Madagascar ranks definitely as an African island, linked with the continent by land in past geological ages, but with Asia in much of its history.

In 1960 Madagascar, after two years as a member state of the French community, became an independent republic (République Malgache or Malagasy) and joined the United Nations.

Tananarive, the capital, and by far the largest city (340 000), is situated on a ridge of the central plateau at a height of 1 295 m (4 250 ft). Tamatave (50 500), on the east coast, is the principal port; over a quarter of the trade of the island passes through it. Among other ports are Majunga (44 000), on the west coast; Diego Suarez (38 600), in the north; and Fort Dauphin (10 000), in the south. There are plans to develop a port and repair yard, for giant tankers using the Cape route, in the landlocked bay at Narinda (60 km: 37 miles north of Majunga).

The island has a wide range of crops (to serve the tastes of people of varying origin) and spices. Paddy is by far the most important, followed by cassava and maize. Coffee does well; and the island supplies the world with most of its vanilla — as well as cloves and essential oils. Minerals are also diverse, but small in quantity.

Madagascar leads the world in graphite production and has much mica, although neither are major items in world commerce. There is also chrome, ilmenite, zircon, beryl, phosphates and a little gold. The flora and fauna are also interesting, unique species having developed in isolation since the separation of the island from the mainland. Cattle total some 9m., and poultry exceed 14m.

Industry is mainly concerned with the processing of agricultural products, but also includes oil refining, textiles, tanneries, cement and a host of household goods. Limited development of the hydroelectric potential and a scattered population do not encourage major industrial growth, and most factories are centred around Tananarive and Tamatave. There is an adequate road system, four short railways and an international airport at Tananarive.

Exports are mainly foodstuffs (coffee, rice, vanilla, cloves, sugar), with some tobacco, sisal, graphite and mica. Imports are transportation equipment, machinery, manufactures and petroleum. France is the main trading partner, followed by the USA, West Germany and the UK; Réunion and Sénégal take a considerable share of the exports.

French Islands

Comoro Islands

The Comoro Islands, a volcanic group at the northern end of the Moçambique Channel, are an independently administered Overseas Territory within the French Community. Including Mayotte they cover nearly 2 176 sq km (840 sq miles) (rather less than the combined areas of the Orkney and Shetland Isles) and have a population of about 280 000. Plantation products include vanilla, copra, sugar, cocoa, and raw materials of perfumery (citronella, patchouli, etc.). Now forming the territory of TAAF (Terres Australes et Antarctiques Françaises) are the scattered French islands in the south of the Indian Ocean — *Nouvelle-Amsterdam, St Paul, Kerguelen, Crozet* — used as whaling and fishing stations, and the Antarctic *Terre Adélie*, south of Australia.

Réunion

Réunion, a French colony since the seventeenth century, given the status of an Overseas Department within the French Community on 1 January 1947, is 725 km (450 miles) east of Madagascar, on the way to Mauritius. It is volcanic, with an area of 2 512 sq km (970 sq miles). Opposite peaks of some 2 950 m (9 000 ft) are connected by a plateau. The population of 450 000 includes four towns — St Denis (the capital, 86 000) and St Louis, St Pierre and St Paul (each with from 25 000 to 40 000 inhabitants). Sugar provided nearly 90 per cent of the exports, the balance consisting mainly of rum, vanilla, and essential oils. Imports greatly exceed exports, and foreign trade is dominated by France and Malagasy.

Portuguese Islands

Madeira

Madeira is the principal island of a small group (total area 797 sq km: 308 sq miles) to the west of Morocco. Only one of the other islands is inhabited — Porto Santo. Madeira lies some 565 km (350 miles) off the mainland and its capital, Funchal, was a regular port of call for the mail steamers between Southampton and Cape Town. The islands which are administered as a province of Portugal, have a population of 270 000. About a third of the number live in and around Funchal.

Madeira is of volcanic origin, rugged and mountainous, rising in its highest peak to over 1 830 m (6 000 ft); but the soil is fertile and there is a rich flora, though little evidence remains of the forests which gave the island its name (*madeira*, Portuguese for *wood*). Commercially the name was given to the wines produced in the island from vineyards which largely took the place of sugar plantations after the abolition of the slave trade, and which in turn suffered from devastating attacks, first of a fungoid disease and then of the insect pest, phylloxera. Cultivable land is limited; wheat, maize, sugarcane and barley are grown. Bananas enter largely into the export trade in fruit and vegetables. Embroidery and wicker furniture, the product of local handicrafts, are also exported, while the tourist traffic, based on Madeira's attractions as a winter health resort, provides an invisible export of the first importance. Almost all trade is with Portugal.

Cape Verde Islands

This group, situated some 565 km (350 miles) west of Cape Verde in Sénégal, comprises ten islands and a few islets, with a total area of some 4 030 sq km (1 557 sq miles) (about half as large again as the Orkneys and Shetlands), the largest, São Tiago is the seat of the capital, Praia (13 000). The islands are volcanic, with peaks ranging up to 2 740 m (9 000 ft); and, coming under the influence of the harmattan winds from the Sahara, they are largely arid desert, supporting little vegetation except in the river valleys. The population (255 000) is beyond the economic capacity of the group, and normally there is a seasonal migration of labour to South America, with the striking consequence, thanks to the earnings of the men, that the value of the imports is many times the value of the exports. These last include castor oilseed, coffee and brandy, the coffee being of high quality and especially rich in caffeine. But the chief commercial importance of the group is as an oiling station for ships at Porto Grande, on São Vicente, which is largely used by vessels engaged in the South American trade.

São Tomé and Principe

São Tomé and Principe are two islands in the Gulf of Guinea, 240 km (150 miles) off the Gabon coast, the first immediately north of the Equator, the other about 145 km (90 miles) further north. They are smaller editions of Fernando Póo (p. 738), and their luxuriant vegetation and imposing mountain scenery have gained for them among the Portuguese the sobriquet 'The Pearls of the Ocean'. São Tomé (829 sq km: 320 sq miles), about half as large again as the Isle of Man, has an extinct volcano rising some 2 134 m (7 000 ft) above the sea. Principe (109 sq km: 42 sq miles), much the same size as Jersey, rises to about 914 m (3 000 ft). A total population of some 70 000 is divided between them in proportion, roughly, to their size with 6 000 in the capital, São Tomé. Their economic importance dwindled with the decline of slavery. Crops are similar to those on the adjacent mainland. Exports are cocoa, copra and coffee grown on large estates using imported labour from Angola and Moçambique.

Spanish Islands

Canary Islands

The Canary Islands lie to the northwest of the Spanish Sahara, the nearest island being about 105 km (65 miles) from Cape Juby, and the other islands stretching west for 400 km (250 miles) or more. There are seven inhabited islands, of volcanic origin, besides islets and rocks, the whole having an area of nearly 7 510 sq km (2 900 sq miles) and forming two provinces of Spain. Tenerife and Gran Canaria are easily the best known members of the archipelago. In association with their respective capitals. Santa Cruz de Tenerife and Las Palmas de Gran Canaria, they have given their names to the two groups (constituting provinces of Spain) into which the islands were divided in 1927, and between which the total population of 965 000 is shared nearly equally. The two capitals alone are the homes of nearly half the people – 170 000 in Santa Cruz and 245 000 in Las Palmas.

The high density of the population, relative to the mainland territories of Africa, is all the more remarkable in view of the mountainous character of the islands – the lowest of them reaches over 610 m (2 000 ft), while the famous Peak of Tenerife attains to over 3 660 m (12 000 ft) – and is evidence of the favourable climatic and other subtropical conditions which account for one of the chief industries of the islands, the tourist traffic. These conditions are also conducive to agricultural industry, and in the course of time there has been a succession of outstanding products – wines till disease wrought havoc in the vineyards in the middle of the last century; then cochineal, till the discovery of aniline dyes reduced the profits of the industry; and more recently, before the Second World War, fresh vegetables and fruits, especially early potatoes, tomatoes, onions and not least bananas, a smaller and finer fruit than the species mostly found on the market in Britain, and sent largely to the United States.

America

America, the New World, with an area of some 42m. sq km (over 16m. sq miles) is approximately half the size of the combined area (85m. sq km: nearly 33m. sq miles) of the three continents of the Old World: Europe, Asia and Africa. In 1965 the New World's population of 460m. was however only 16 per cent of the Old World's 2 817m.; and the population density of 11 per sq km (28 per sq mile) compared with that of 10; 10; 66 and 90 per sq km (26; 26; 171 and 233 per sq mile) respectively for Africa, USSR, Asia and Europe. Over 70 per cent of these 460m. are of European descent, with Negroes making up 10 per cent of the United States population and indigenous Indians providing a similar percentage in South America.

The outstanding feature of the commerce of the Americas is the vastness of its scale relative to the density of the population. The United States dominates the world trade of the mid-twentieth century, while still consuming internally some 90 per cent of her total production, and Canada is sixth in importance (after West Germany, United Kingdom, France and Japan). The New World's rapid development during the nineteenth and twentieth centuries (with the United States and Canada classified as 'developed', while Central and South America are still developing) has been based on the rapid exploitation of virgin lands and vast natural resources. The scale of this exploitation was given initial impetus by the Industrial Revolution of the Old World, and this impetus has been sustained by a rapidly rising population of mixed origins determined to succeed in a new land and ready to apply modern techniques and technology to the full. Industrial development has been such that the United States has now taken on the features of the Old World with a diminishing surplus of primary materials (she is already a net importer of iron and steel, of oil, natural gas and wood products) and a steady expansion of manufacturing and commerce. In a lesser degree the same is true of Canada.

Nonetheless the exports of America still include a high percentage of foodstuffs and primary minerals. In the United States they rank third in importance after machinery and transport equipment, while the US and

Canada are by far the world's largest exporters of wheat. Trade in such bulky materials depends on adequate communications for a continent situated midway between Europe and Asia. Since the opening of the Panama Canal in 1914 bulk movement of freight between the west and east coasts of North America has been as much by sea as by land; while the great circle routes from Panama northwards around the Pacific to Japan and around the North Atlantic to Europe both follow the North American seaboard as far as the major ports of San Francisco in the west and New York in the east.

The date of completion of the main railway links between the east and west coasts of North America indicates how rapid, and comparatively recent, the industrial development of the continent has been. These rail links made possible the shipment out of the great cereal harvests of the central prairies, and the exchange of the raw materials of the west for the manufactures of the east. The first transcontinental link between New York and Oakland (San Francisco) was completed in 1869 (5 295 km: 3 290 miles) to be followed by others, in particular the first Canadian link, the Canadian Pacific, from Montreal to Vancouver in 1885 (4 680 km: 2 910 miles), and later by a more northerly route, the Canadian National, from Halifax to Vancouver in 1915 (6 200 km: 3 850 miles). These distances should be compared with the sea route from Montreal to Liverpool (4 510 km: 2 800 miles) and New York to Liverpool (4 880 km: 3 030 miles). In South America without the benefit of single great political units such as the United States and Canada, and with even more difficult terrain, the transcontinental links were limited to one until 1948, that between Valparaiso and Buenos Aires being opened in 1910 (1 450 km: 883 miles).

Of the waterways of the New World, the Panama Canal and the St Lawrence — Great Lakes are the most important commercially. The tonnage of shipping passing through the Panama Canal rose rapidly until the 1920s, when it almost equalled that of the Suez Canal. Since then the tonnage has increased threefold, although always less than the Suez Canal, until the latter was closed in 1967. Apart from providing Europe with an alternative route to the Far East, the main effect of the Panama Canal has been to bring the west coast of North America closer to the Atlantic. This was important for the movement of Californian oil and timber products from Washington and British Columbia, and the larger tonnages moved from the Pacific to the Atlantic until 1957 when the trend was reversed. Although approximately the same number of vessels move in each direction, tonnages from the Atlantic to the Pacific are now twice as great as those from the Pacific to the Atlantic, a reflection of the rapidly growing industrialisation and urbanisation of the North American Pacific seaboard. The St Lawrence—Great Lakes waterway has been of outstanding importance in the shipment of the produce of the interior of the continent and in the development of industry. Both as an internal highway for the interchange of bulk cargoes of limestone, iron ore and coal and, in spite of being frozen from December to April, as an external highway for import and export into the industrial heartland of North America.

The major extension of communications since the Second World War has been in the development of the airline networks, of motor highways and of pipelines. Scheduled air services now cover an extensive network both internally and internationally and the airlines of the American continent dominate world air movement, with 68 per cent of the passenger traffic and 75 per cent of the cargo traffic. Road movement is also well developed. The United States alone has some 55 per cent of the world's vehicles and traffic movement by road vehicles has become an outstanding feature of the great urban areas. Although by 1934 the coast-to-coast highways were not metalled throughout their length, construction since the Second World War has been extensive. The Alcan or Alaska Highway was built during the war through Canada to Alaska, and other coast-to-coast highways have been completed – the latest being the Trans–Canada highway from Vancouver to St John's, Newfoundland. The great project of the Pan–American Highway from Canada to Argentina has been completed except for the stretch between Costa Rica and Ecuador.

The construction of continental pipeline networks, particularly in North America, for the bulk movement of natural gas, crude oil and petroleum products has been the other major postwar development. Natural gas is now sent from Alberta to California and Montreal; and oil products and gas from Texas to New England and the Great Lakes area. In Canada some 20 per cent of all bulk freight is carried by pipeline, and research is going ahead for the construction of long distance pipelines to carry solids, for example mineral ores and coal, etc.

The importance of communications has been stressed in these introductory paragraphs on the New World because they have been essential to the commercial development (both internally and internationally) of a 'new' and comparatively sparsely settled continent: a continent rich in resources yet with the great disadvantages of major geographical barriers and vast distances. In North America in particular the efficiency with which communications have been developed and the initiative demonstrated in the exploitation of each new advance as it came along (from railways to automobiles, aeroplanes, computers and space travel) is indicative of a highly developed, industrialised society.

North America

North America has approximately half the area (21m. sq km: over 8m. sq miles) and half the population (223m.) of the New World.

The surface is made up mainly of plains and tablelands, with great mountain chains of a more or less southerly trend. In the west mountains stretch through the entire length of the continent, with a central tableland 1 220 m (4 000 ft) or more in height which at its widest (about lat. 40°) extends over fully one-third of the breadth of the United States. The mountain chain which rises above this tableland in the east is the Rocky Mountains. There are also a great number of shorter mountain ranges, which vary the surface of the tableland, and nearly all of which trend north and south. The Cascade Mountains and the Sierra Nevada are the principal mountain chains that border the tableland in the west, in the wider part of the continent; and still further west are lower mountains, known as the Coast Range. In the narrower part of the continent in Mexico, the tableland stretches almost from sea to sea. Several railways now cross these mountains at passes varying from about 1 740 (5 300) to upwards of 2 620 m (8 000 ft) in height. The only other great mountain system of North America is that of the Appalachians or Alleghany Mountains, which extend in long parallel chains roughly in the same direction as the Atlantic coast.

A chain of magnificent lakes, Lakes Superior, Michigan, Huron, Erie, and Ontario, is drained by the St Lawrence into the Atlantic, and together with that river form an invaluable international commercial waterway. The great rivers of the central plain are, or at least have been, equally important for the internal movement of goods.

The general correspondence between the climate of the west of North America and that of western Europe, and between the climate of the eastern side of the continent and that of eastern Asia, has been referred to in the paragraphs relating to climate generally (p. 23). Here two features in that correspondence may be recalled to mind: first, the more equable climate of the temperate zone in the west than in the east, and secondly, the dearth of rain in the west, south of the parallel of 37° or 38° N; and it is only necessary to add some particulars regarding the effect of some of the great physical features on the climate of the continent.

Important climatic effects are due to the direction of the mountain chains. The western mountains, shutting off the moisture from the Pacific, cause a large part of the interior of the United States to be too dry for agriculture without irrigation. It is mainly from this cause that the greater part of the area of the United States west of 100° W, with the exception of a portion of the maritime strip, has this arid character (see p. 40). Further, the open plains and gently falling ground between these mountains and the Appalachians allow even the most southerly points of the United States, as well as the east coast of Mexico, to be swept from time to time by keen winds funnelled down from the north, so that ice forms at the mouth of the Mississippi in lat. 30° N, and even in the extreme south of Texas (lat. 26° N, about the same latitude as Patna in Bengal) as much as 14° of frost has been experienced. In some years severe frosts may seriously injure a large proportion of the trees in the orange groves of Florida. Even below St Louis (38½° N) the Mississippi navigation is partly closed by ice for thirty-three days a year on the average.

Other important effects on the climate are due to the great gulfs in the north and south, Hudson Bay and the Gulf of Mexico; and to the body of water of the Great Lakes, the aggregate area of which is larger than that of Great Britain. Besides exercising through the agency of winds an equalising effect on the temperature, they are all sources of moisture, especially during the summer months, when moisture is most needed. It is in a large measure from this cause that north and east of the arid region of the continent the plains are supplied with rain enough at least for the growth of pasture grasses and other herbage. These plains form the prairies of North America. They are for the most part treeless, except in the valleys along the water courses.

For a long period after the discovery of America by Columbus, the only important commodities furnished by North America were the precious metals derived from the West Indies and Mexico, and cod from the Grand Bank of Newfoundland. The West Indies and Mexico were entirely in Spanish hands. The West Indies from 1492 and Mexico from the conquest by Cortez in 1519–21. Though the first English voyage to America, that which set sail from Bristol under the Venetian, John Cabot, in search of a northwest passage to India, was made in 1497, and though it was in virtue of that voyage that the English afterwards laid claim to a great part of the coast of North America, the first settlements in the temperate latitudes of that continent were made by the French. The banks of the St Lawrence were explored by Jacques Cartier in 1533–43; but the most successful French settlements were due to the efforts of Samuel Champlain (1602–35). He founded

Québec in 1608, and a few years later after his death Montréal was founded in 1642. French explorations and a few isolated French settlements were made higher up, but the rapids above Montréal put a limit to continuous settlement by the French. All the territory on both banks of the St Lawrence below Montréal continued to be French till the capture of Québec by General Wolfe in 1759.

Meantime settlements were made by other countries elsewhere. The first attempted settlement of the English was a failure. It was made on Roanoke Island in Pamlico Sound at the suggestion of Sir Walter Raleigh in 1585, but the survivors of the settlement were brought back to England by Sir Francis Drake in 1586. The first successful English settlement, known as Jamestown, was made in 1607 on a promontory of the James River, at the mouth of Chesapeake Bay. This former promontory is now an island in the river, on which the relics of the settlement are carefully preserved by the government of the United States. The next English settlements were made in Massachusetts, at Plymouth in 1620, and on Massachusetts Bay in 1628–30. In 1612 the Dutch began to trade at the mouth of the Hudson, a river ascended by the English navigator of that name when in Dutch service (1609), and in 1623 the first regular colony was founded by the Dutch West India Company on Manhattan Island. This formed the nucleus of New Amsterdam, whose name was changed to New York when it was taken over by the English in 1664. Forest produce, hemp, and in the southern settlements tobacco, formed the principal articles of export trade among these communities. Early in the seventeenth century, however, furs began to reach Europe from Hudson Bay, and in 1670 this trade became a monopoly of the English Hudson Bay Company. Sugar, coffee, and cotton gradually came to be important products of the West Indies, but it was not till after the severance of the English colonies from the mother country in the American Revolution or War of Independence (1776–83) that cotton came to be extensively cultivated on the mainland. But the great commercial development of North America was that which followed the introduction of steamships and railways. By that means bulky produce of the far interior, such as grain and provisions, could for the first time be conveyed to Europe at a sufficiently low cost to allow of the growth of an immense trade in these commodities and for the subsequent industrial development of the United States and Canada.

Greenland

A dependency of Denmark, Greenland has an area of 2 175 000 sq km (840 000 sq miles) — nearly three times the size of Scandinavia; but five-sixths of it is under ice. Ninety per cent of the population of 52 000 (1971), mainly Eskimos, live on the west coast; only 4 500 are

Europeans. A Council meets at Godthåb the capital, and two representatives have seats in the Danish Parliament. Greenland has reserves of cryolite, the primary source of aluminium before bauxite came into use, and from 40 000 to 50 000 tons are still exported annually. Over 1m. tons of lead and zinc ores have been located. Fishing is also important with an annual catch of some 50 000 tons. Aviation has given strategic value to Greenland, and the United States has acquired from Denmark bases for joint defence.

Canada

Canada is situated to the north of the United States, the frontier running along the middle line of Lakes Superior, Huron, Erie and Ontario, and (west of the Lake of the Woods) along a parallel 49° N. The 21.57m. (1971) inhabitants are mainly (44 per cent) of British origin and Protestant in religion; but Roman Catholic of French origin make up more than 5.5m. of the population, chiefly in Québec where the first colonists were French. There are about 244 000 of Indian and 17 000 of Eskimo origin, a few of whom are hunters, roaming over the northern and western forest regions; the Eskimos live mainly in the far north and northeast. The islands of the Arctic Archipelago are of interest in the history of commerce from the fact that a northwest passage to eastern Asia was for centuries sought in vain among the channels that separate them. A passage was at last effected by Maclure in 1850—53, but the route is too much encumbered by ice to be of any use commercially, although the need to move oil from Alaska to the East Coast has revived interest in the possibility of using it.

Modern Canada was born in 1867, through the union of separate colonies. It has a central government and parliament for common affairs, but it has ten provinces (some of which correspond with old colonies) with separate parliaments, empowered to deal with matters of local concern. These provinces are Nova Scotia, Prince Edward Island, New Brunswick, Québec, Ontario, Manitoba, Saskatchewan, Alberta, British Columbia, and Newfoundland, the last named joining in 1949. In addition to these there is a vast area to the northwest of Hudson Bay organised as two Territories. The Yukon Territory was separated in 1898 and the Northwest Territories delineated in 1920, with three districts of Franklin, Keewatin, and Mackenzie. The seat of the government is Ottawa, in the province of Ontario.

Physical features. The extent of Canadian territory is upward of 9.8m. sq km (3.8m. sq miles), the more populous portions of this vast area are confined to the region of the St Lawrence from the city of Québec to the peninsular of land between the Great Lakes, the southern parts of the three Prairie Provinces and the southwest of British

Columbia. The whole of the more populous area lies further south than southern England.

The surface east of the Rocky Mountains is made up principally of plains and undulating lowlands. Tundra, similar to that of northern Russia and Siberia, covers large tracts in the north, descending in the east to about 58° N on the western shore of Hudson Bay, and still further east extending along the whole coast of Labrador. Southwards follows a range of vast forests, chiefly of spruce, a region that embraces the whole of the country east of Lake Winnipeg, except the tundra area and the limited agricultural area in the south. Further to the west, this forested region is succeeded in the south by the prairies, which extend furthest north on the gently sloping tablelands, immediately to the east of the Rocky Mountains. The nearly treeless prairies here extend about 3½° N of the United States frontier, and the area with less than 20 per cent of forest land reaches about 10° N of that frontier, between the Rocky Mountains and Lake Athabasca. In the development of Canada in the present century this prairie region has been of the highest importance, for it contains vast areas of rich soils and a climate admirably adapted for agriculture. In this prairie region there is a rise from east to west in the form of three prairie levels or steps. The lowest level is that of the Red River valley, some 230 m (750 ft). West of that plain the surface rises to 450 m (1 500 ft), and this terrace stretches westwards for about 400 km (250 miles). The ground then rises to about 900 m (3 000 ft), and then the rise is more gradual to the foothills of the Rocky Mountains.

In the eastern half of Canada the geological structure is of peculiar geographical importance. It is of such a nature as must for ever forbid extensive agricultural settlement. From the banks of the St Lawrence, some little distance below Québec, to the Red River valley and north-westwards to the Mackenzie River, there extends an enormous region of ancient crystalline rocks — the Canadian Shield — protruding in many places in naked masses, in other places having only a thin covering of soil supporting forests of spruce and pine. This ancient, glaciated core of the North American continent has been tilted and worked by the folding of younger structures (the Rocky Mountain System and the Appalachians) on its flanks. Long a major barrier and still inhospitable, it is now a great source of national wealth for it is rich in minerals such as iron ore, copper, nickel, lead, zinc, gold and silver; provides a vast reserve of timber for pulping and newsprint; and its lakes and escarpments have great hydroelectric potential. In addition glacial deposits in the valleys and on the southeastern periphery provide rich soils for agriculture.

Climate. The general similarity between the climate of North America and that of corresponding latitudes in Europe and Asia is noted on

p. 44, but some details should be stressed. An important difference between western Canada and Europe is due to the fact that the whole area between the Rocky Mountains and the Pacific coast is mountainous, and that the mountains run throughout parallel to the coast and nearly at right angles to the prevailing winds. Hence great contrasts, in respect of both rainfall and temperature, begin within a short distance of the Pacific. At New Westminster, at the mouth of the Fraser, the mean temperature of the coldest month of the year is 2° C (36° F), of the hottest about 17° C (63° F), and the total precipitation* is 1 650 mm (65 in); at Lillooet, higher up the Fraser valley but behind the Coast Mountains, the corresponding figures for temperature are −6° C (22° F) and 20° C (68° F), for rain and snow about 330 mm (13 in). To the east of the Rocky Mountains the total precipitation is scanty, though it begins to increase again in eastern Saskatchewan. But as affecting the cultivation of grains, two considerations must be borne in mind. First, it is important that the great bulk of the total precipitation takes place during the summer, especially the early summer, months (see p. 40). Second, throughout Canada a considerable proportion of the precipitation takes place in the form of snow, the amount of which, however, is much greater in the east than in the west. Montreal has an average annual precipitation of 3 050 mm (120 in); at Toronto, the average is 1 475 mm (58 in); and even in 42° N, in the extreme south of Ontario (the same latitude as the northern frontier of Portugal) in a district in which grapes are grown for wine-making in summer, the average of fourteen years was 1 450 mm (57 in). At Winnipeg, in Manitoba, the average of thirty years (1885−1914) was only 1 240 mm (49 in). Two advantages for wheat-growing accrue from the snowfall component in precipitation. In the east the total precipitation is ample, and is fairly equally distributed throughout the year, and there the great advantage of the snow as regards wheat culture is that it protects the ground against the severe frosts. There accordingly winter wheat (or, as it is called in America, fall wheat) can be regularly grown, whereas in all the Prairie Provinces the frost comes before the snow, and hence only spring wheat can be cultivated. But in this part of Canada it is important that the melting in spring of water frozen underground furnishes moisture just when it is wanted. In the more arid parts of the prairies, however, irrigation is necessary − in the southern parts of Saskatchewan and Alberta. The Canadian Pacific Railway Company has constructed and operated in the Province of Alberta three large projects known as the Eastern, Western, and Lethbridge sections. The water is obtained from the Bow River and the St Mary River. There are other important schemes in Alberta as well as many hundred small schemes in Saskatchewan and Alberta.

* Including both rain and snow. The meteorological office of Canada reckons 250 mm (10 in) of snow are equal to 25 mm (1 in) of rain.

In those parts in which wheat is most largely grown, it is not the total amount of the annual rainfall that determines the amount of the produce. The annual precipitation in Manitoba for example has varied from 300 to 570 mm (12 to 22.5 in), and the average yield of wheat per hectare between 620 and 1 880 kg (between 9 and 28 bushels per acre), but there is no marked correspondence between the rainfall and the yield, though the rains of May and June seem to be particularly significant. The chief disadvantage of the Canadian climate for wheat-growing, and especially in the northwest, is the liability to the occurrence of frost before harvest, but this risk is being greatly reduced by the careful selection of seed and the cultivation of hardy varieties of wheat which ripen quickly, and, as it happens, yield hard wheats of exceptionally high value. The use of these quick-maturing wheats has made possible the settlement of the Peace River area as a northern extension of the prairies. The summers that follow the cold but dry, invigorating, healthy and pleasant winters are remarkably bright as well as warm, and the whole of Canada, with the exception of near the coast in British Columbia, is favoured with more sunshine than any portion of Great Britain, Germany, Holland, or northern France. In winter the temperature in districts adjacent to the great mountain ranges is greatly mitigated by warm, dry, or moist winds, from the southeast, south or southwest, west of the Rocky Mountains, and from the southwest, west or northwest to the east of the Rocky Mountains, those in the latter case being such as are experienced in all parts of the world on the leeside of mountains exposed on the weather side to copious rains. In Canada they are known as chinook winds. In southern Alberta they cause the cold of winter to alternate with spells of bright warm weather, in which the ground is swept bare of snow and the pasture grasses are revived, and they thus help to make the rearing of livestock the characteristic industry of this part of the prairies.

Communications. The most important Canadian routeway is that of the St Lawrence River and the Great Lakes, supplemented by a number of short canals, which form a system of internal navigation for seagoing vessels unparalleled in any other continent. The first of the canals to be constructed was the Lachine Canal immediately above Montréal, opened in 1824, and other canals between Montréal and Lake Ontario were completed by 1843. The Welland Canal, which runs parallel to the Niagara River and avoids the Falls of Niagara between Lakes Erie and Ontario, was constructed in 1824–29. It has been reconstructed several times, finally as the Welland Ship Canal opened in 1931. The difference of 99 m (325 ft) in the level of the two lakes was overcome by seven locks 244 by 24 m (800 by 80 ft). In 1954 work was begun on the St Lawrence Seaway to enable vessels drawing 7.6 m (25 ft) to pass from the Great Lakes to tidal waters at Montréal. American cooperation, favoured by successive United States governments but opposed by rival commercial interests was later agreed and the project was completed in 1959. Further dredging carried out in 1968 allows vessels of 8.25 m (27 ft) draught to pass through to Thunder Bay (Fort William–Port Arthur).

The shortest but perhaps the most important of the Canadian canals is the Sault Ste Marie ('Soo') Canal between Lakes Superior and Huron, which was constructed between 1889 and 1895. It is little more than 1.6 km (1 mile) in length, and has only one lock on the Canadian side, four on the United States side; yet in the eight ice-free months each year more traffic passes through this canal alone than through the Suez, Panama and Manchester Ship Canals combined. The traffic through all these canals is in the forefront of the world's canal traffic and has doubled in the 1960s. In 1955 13.5m. tons passed through the St Lawrence and 23m. tons through the Welland Canal. In 1968 the figures were 48m. tons and 52m. tons respectively.

By this series of waterways seagoing ships may pass inland for 3 700 km (2 300 miles) from the Strait of Belle Isle in the north of Newfoundland to Lakehead Harbour on Lake Superior within only about 3 060 km (1 900 miles) by rail from Vancouver the seaport at the Pacific terminus of the CPR. On the United States side they are carried up a distance of 3 940 km (2 400 miles) to Duluth, at the very head of Lake Superior, within 3 040 km (1 890 miles) by rail of the nearest Pacific port.

The St Lawrence navigation is usually open from about the end of April to near the end of November, or even the first week in December. The route from the mouth of the St Lawrence, round the north of Newfoundland by the Strait of Belle Isle, is closed for a longer period than that by Cabot Strait, round the south of Newfoundland, which adds about 260 km (160 miles) to the distance to Liverpool. Ice breakers are used to prolong navigation on the lakes and the lights on Lake Superior, Lake Huron, Georgian Bay, Lake Erie, and Lake Ontario are kept in operation until the end of December, or later, if possible.

In addition to this main waterway, Canada possesses other less important inland waterways. The River Ottawa is continuously navigable, with the aid of a few canals, as far as the city of Ottawa; and thence there is a navigable though little used connection by the Rideau River and Canal with Kingston on Lake Ontario. Above Lake Superior, navigation can be continued with canoes and motorboats by Rainy Lake and River, Winnipeg Lake and River, and the North Saskatchewan River to near the base of the Rocky Mountains. The Assiniboine and Red River, which both belong, like the Saskatchewan, to the basin of Lake Winnipeg, are likewise navigable by very shallow draught boats, but the Nelson, the outlet of Lake Winnipeg to Hudson Bay, is too much obstructed by rapids to be of any service as a waterway. In the summer there are regular services on the Mackenzie and Yukon Rivers.

In the more populous parts of Canada there is a complete network of railways, and since November 1885, when the Canadian Pacific Railway was completed, there has been uninterrupted railway communication from ocean to ocean within Canadian territory. The Canadian Pacific has an advantage over both its older rivals, the Northern Pacific and the Union and Central Pacific, in the lower height of its passes, and the shorter length of route at high levels. The Great Northern Railway, the main line of which was completed in 1893, has however, as favourable a route on the whole as that of the Canadian Pacific. The Canadian Northern Railway, which was begun in 1896, is now part of the Canadian National system. It also extends from ocean to ocean, operating trains between Québec and Montréal in the east and Winnipeg, Edmonton, and Vancouver in the west. Between Edmonton and Vancouver it uses the Yellowhead Pass and the through line was completed in 1915. Another line runs to the Pacific port of Prince Rupert. The company got into financial difficulties, and passed under government ownership and operation in 1923.

In 1906 Canada had 2 760 km (1 713 miles) of government, as against 32 920 km (20 454 miles) of private railways. In 1964 the total was 68 560 km (42 623 miles), of which government owned well over half: the systems formerly owned by the Canadian Northern, Grand Trunk and Grand Trunk Pacific Railways. The whole group is now known as the Canadian National Railways with a total of 36 850 km (22 937 miles) in 1964. The Canadian Pacific (26 250 km: 16 278 miles) is the only important privately owned railway. There are in addition some 7 095 km (4 408 miles) of other lines, mainly single track. As with all other developed countries, the railways now face a major falling off in passenger traffic. Although freight traffic is increasingly profitable (with 'unit trains' carrying single bulk commodities such as coal and sulphur, and with 1 610 km (1 000 miles) of new track built since the Second World War) it may require government intervention to avoid the complete cessation of passenger services.

The construction of a railway direct from the grain-growing areas of Manitoba to Churchill, on Hudson Bay at the mouth of the Churchill River, was begun in 1911. By 1929 the track was laid, and in the autumn of 1931 the first shipment of grain to the United Kingdom by this route was made. The importance of this railway arises from the fact that it is the shortest route (2 936 nautical miles from Churchill to Liverpool) for the products of the Canadian Prairies to England, but its value depends in a great measure on the navigability of Hudson Bay and Hudson Strait. The difficulties of navigation are almost confined to the strait, which is 800 km (500 miles) in length, and for the greater part of the year is obstructed by ice. The strait is open, however, for at least two or three months every year which leaves little time between harvest and shipment. The route has not proved the success which was hoped, whereas the shipment of grain via the ever open Pacific port of Vancouver and the Panama Canal to Europe has greatly increased.

The main railway network was constructed between 1880 and 1915, and was essential to the opening up of the prairies and the shipment of their produce. Equally important for the development of the resources of the north and northwest have been the feeder lines built since the Second World War, for example that to Lynn Lake, Manitoba (copper and nickel) in 1953; to Schefferville, Labrador (iron ore) in 1954; to Chibougamu, Québec (copper and gold) in 1957; to Hay River on the Great Slave Lake (lead and zinc) in 1964, and to link the Athabasca tar sands region to Edmonton.

Another outstanding change in communications since the Second World War has been the construction of the oil and gas pipelines. Work started in the late 1940s and the network now totals 19 000 km (12 000 miles) of oil lines and 11 200 km (7 000 miles) of gas lines — linking the great fields of Alberta and Saskatchewan with consumer areas throughout Canada and as far afield as California and Illinois.

Minerals. In minerals Canada is the world's largest producer of nickel, zinc, asbestos and platinum; second in uranium, silver and gypsum; important also are petroleum, copper, iron ore, gold, coal, lead, natural gas, cadmium, cobalt, magnesium, palladium, selenium, titanium and tungsten; also barite, fluorspar, lithia, dolomite, quartz, salt and potash. From 1950 to 1959 the output more than doubled in value — from $1 045m. (£356m.) to $2 400m. (£819m.) and nearly $3 000m. (£1 023m.) in 1963. By 1969 it reached $4 700m. (£1 800m.).

Though Canada has coalfields which are enormous in extent, production has been declining from the peak of 19m. tons in 1950. About a third is good quality bituminous coal from the Sydney field of Nova Scotia where some of the mining involves following the seams under the sea. There are other small fields in the east in New Brunswick but it is 3 200 km (2 000 miles) from there to the vast fields of the Rocky Mountain foothills. The province of Alberta is underlaid to the extent of about 44 000 sq km (17 000 sq miles) with bituminous and semi-bituminous coal and lignites of varying quality and anthracite is known in western Alberta. Four-fifths of Canada's total proved reserves are in Alberta (coal and anthracite). In British Columbia there is a small coalfield producing coal of good quality though somewhat powdery, immediately to the west of the Crow's Nest Pass. There are some small fields along the west coast of Canada and at Nanaimo on Vancouver Island since 1840. No coal is found near the populous industrial regions of southern Ontario and Québec, hence the movement of coal across the Great Lakes from the United States and the importance of Canadian oil and gas brought in by pipeline.

766

In contrast to the declining importance of coal in competition with other power sources, most other minerals are on the upgrade. The economic position of Canada has been greatly changed by the discovery of rich oilfields and their accompanying reserves of natural gas in the Prairie Provinces — especially near Edmonton in Alberta, in the older Turner Valley field near Calgary, and also in southeastern Saskatchewan. There are even greater reserves in the tarsands of Athabasca (probably the world's largest reserve of oil) but commercial processing is still only on a limited scale. Oil output in 1973 was 102m. tons.

Iron ore is met with in many places, but for long it seemed that Canada had no resources to rival those of the United States near Lake Superior occurring in rocks which are an extension of the Canadian Shield. Despite various small deposits, no iron ore was mined in Canada from 1921 to 1936, and the iron and steel industry depended upon imported ore. Then came the opening up of the Steep Rock and other desposits near Lake Superior and the discovery of vast ore bodies (estimated at 2 000m. tons) in the Ungava region of northern Québec and Labrador. A railway from the shores of the lower St Lawrence was constructed in 1954 and there was a jump in production, when these ores were tapped, from 7m. tons in 1954 to 17m. in 1955. In 1966 it exceeded 40m. tons to become the third most important mineral resource after petroleum and nickel. Gold is obtained in largest quantity from Porcupine, Kirkland Lake and numerous newer localities in Ontario and Québec, and also in Manitoba, Saskatchewan, Nova Scotia, and in British Columbia and the Yukon. The production from the once famous alluvial deposits of the latter has dwindled to a very small figure. Since 1938, however, there has been an important mine at Yellowknife in the Northwest Territories. Of great strategic importance was the discovery and development of uranium ores in the region of Blind River and Beaverlodge Lake — 1959 peak output worth $324.5m. (£118m.). The silver production of Canada comes chiefly from the rich silver-cobalt ores of northern Ontario and from mixed ores in British Columbia. In 1963 nickel was first and copper third among metallic minerals in value, copper coming mainly from Sudbury, Ontario, new mines in the Gaspé, and from British Columbia. Ontario provides the bulk of the world's supply of nickel and cobalt, and also much palladium, platinum, selenium, and tellurium. Québec is the world's largest producer of asbestos and has a large output of other minerals. A recent development is in non-metallic minerals, notably for cement. Aluminium is another important product — based on imported bauxite and the hydroelectric power generated by the great Kitimat Scheme in British Columbia and at Arinda in Québec.

External trade. Tables 82 and 83 show the principal features of the external commerce of Canada. Wheat from the Prairies remains a great

767

staple export, but is now surpassed in value by the exports of newsprint and cars, the outstanding value of the latter (one-sixth of all Canada's exports) being a notable example of the growth of manufacturing industry. Most of the newsprint is exported to the United States. Lumber (conifer) and wood pulp are also major exports, while a range of minerals rival forest products. The exports show clearly however the rapid rise of Canada as a great manufacturing country. The high place taken by uranium, aluminium, nickel, copper, iron ore, asbestos, and petroleum shows also the great mineral resources. Relatively foodstuffs such as meats and dairy produce have declined. Of the imports, iron and steel goods, machinery and vehicles, now hold the first place. British shipping still takes the lead in the seaborne traffic of Canada, and no small portion is conveyed by the Canadian Pacific Steamship services (British registration). Canadian vessels handle over half the trade with the United States but only 3 per cent of that with other countries — together making rather under a third of the total.

The more important manufacturing industries at first were naturally those which consist in subjecting the raw materials of the country to the simplest processes, preparatory to sending the products to a home or foreign market — flour-milling, saw-milling, the manufacture of wood pulp, paper, and various articles made of wood, the making of boots and shoes, and other industries connected with leather — but in recent years there has also been a very rapid development of rubber, cotton, and woollen manufactures and other industries depending on imported raw materials and in the manufacture of agricultural implements, automobiles, machinery, and a wide variety of factory products, including aircraft and parts, electrical apparatus, and industrial machinery. At the beginning of the century about half of the manufacturing output consisted of lumber, and the processing of agricultural and fishing resources. These now account for less than one-fifth of factory shipments, about one-half now being from industries not directly related to primary resources — transport and electrical equipment, machinery, chemical products, textiles, etc. The top five manufacturing industries (in value of output) in 1967 were wood pulp and paper-making, motor vehicles, meat packing, petroleum refining and iron- and steel-mills. Manufacturing and the service industries (hotels, insurance, etc.) are now by far the leading occupations with 51 per cent of the employed population. The percentage engaged in agriculture has fallen from 40 in 1901, to 25 in 1946, and to 7.2 in 1968. With a population which is 75 per cent urban (a figure which could rise to 90 per cent by the year 2000), Canada is now as industrialised as the United States.

Three-quarters of the foreign trade of Canada is with the United States and the United Kingdom. In interwar years the exports went almost equally to the two countries, but the United States sent three times as many imports as the United Kingdom. The percentage value of the imports into Canada from the United Kingdom reached its maximum, 58.57 per cent, in 1871–72. After that year the percentage of the United States rose from 33.09 to 60.96 per cent in 1900–01. In that year, however, more than 50 per cent of the value of the imports from the United States was duty free, as against only 26.3 per cent from the United Kingdom. In 1913–14 the percentage value of the imports from the United Kingdom was 21.35 as against 64.0 from the United States. Inevitably the First World War told adversely on British imports, which in 1917–18 sank to 8.5 per cent of the total, in the following year to less than 8 per cent. In the competition the United States has these advantages amongst others: (1) that transport can be effected without break of bulk; (2) that the ports at which British goods must be transferred from ocean ships to railways or to lake steamers were, until 1959, at a great distance from the populous parts of the country (Montréal is 540 km (335 miles) from Toronto, 2 290 km (1 424 miles) from Winnipeg); (3) that the large and highly protected market of the United States greatly favours the economies of large-scale production; and (4) the similarity of tastes and needs of the two countries is favourable to mutual commercial intercourse. In 1929–30 15 per cent of the imports came from the United Kingdom, 68 per cent from the United States. Of the exports 35 per cent went to the United Kingdom, 46 per cent to the United States. The trend was strengthened inevitably during the Second World War. In 1967 only 6.3 per cent of imports came from the United Kingdom against 72.2 per cent from the United States. Of exports, 10.5 per cent went to Britain and 63.7 per cent to the United States.

Even before the Second World War Canada had become the fourth country in world export trade; but by 1968, with the postwar revival of West Germany and Japan, she occupied sixth place.

PROVINCES AND TOWNS

1. Nova Scotia ('New Scotland') is a province including both the peninsula of that name and the island of Cape Breton to the north; in all it is about two-thirds of the size of Scotland with a population of 788 960 in 1971, against Scotland's 5.2m. The fertile land, not a quarter of the whole, is mainly situated towards the west. The valleys of Annapolis and Cornwallis on the west side parallel to the coast are the most favoured districts in respect of soil and climate, and above all noted for their apple orchards. The fisheries of this province furnish a large proportion of the Canadian output of cod and lobsters. The capital, Halifax, on the east coast, is situated at the head of a fine natural harbour, which in most years is free from ice all the winter through, and is the eastern terminal of the Canadian National Railways. It is the

Table 82 — Canada: special imports fob

	Percentages of total value					
	1924	*1931–35*	*1938*	*1951*	*1963*	*1971*
Raw materials, etc.						
Coal and coke	7.9	6.6	5.5	4.4	1.5	1.1
Petroleum and gasolene	4.8	7.9	7.5	8.7	5.0	4.6
Silk and silk products	2.5	1.8	0.9	0.2	–	–
Cotton and products	7.4	5.9	4.0	4.5	1.0	0.8
(raw cotton)	(3.1)	(2.5)	(1.8)	(2.4)	–	(0.3)
Wool and products	6.0	4.0	3.4	4.0	–	–
Other textiles	1.7	4.7	4.0	3.4	3.2	4.3
Chemicals	3.1	5.7	4.8	4.7	5.4	5.4
Foodstuffs						
Fruits, nuts, vegetables	–	4.4	4.1	3.6	1.6	2.7
Alcohol	2.4	3.3	1.0	0.5	0.4	0.5
Sugar	5.3	3.7	2.8	2.1	2.0	0.6
Manufactures						
Iron and steel (raw and manufactured)	12.9	7.9	4.4	5.6	–	3.3
Machinery, non-electric	–	3.6	7.8	12.8	25.7	18.2
Electrical appliances	–	1.7	1.8	2.9	9.0	6.8
Cars	3.2	3.6	5.4	6.9	9.0	8.6
Textiles (see above)						
Total value in million $*	797	449	737	4 085†	6 559†	15 458
Countries						
United States	64.0	57.4	57.7	68.8	67.8	70.2
United Kingdom	19.0	21.4	16.2	10.3	8.0	5.3
France	2.3	1.7	0.8	0.6	0.9	1.4
Germany‡	0.9	2.1	1.3	0.8	2.2	2.7

* Par rate of exchange 1924–35 £1 = $4.867. In 1949 the £ was devalued and has since been subject to slight fluctuations. Rate of exchange in February 1959, £1 = $2.73, and in 1968 = $2.56. In 1971 = $2.40
† Merchandise only
‡ West Germany only, 1951 onwards

principal naval station of Canada and could well become a major container port for the North Atlantic trade. One of Canada's largest iron and steel works is at Sydney in Cape Breton Island, where coal of excellent quality for smelting purposes and limestone for flux are both found in abundance close beside the admirable natural harbour formed by the Bras d'Or Channel. The iron ore was obtained from Bell Island, Newfoundland, but now comes from the Labrador fields. Nova Scotia furnishes a third of Canada's output of coal, and there are paper-mills and other factories. Manufacturing and construction are by far the major industries, followed by mining and the fisheries.

2. *Prince Edward Island,* about the size of the county of Norfolk, had a population of 110 640 in 1971 and is situated in the bay of the Gulf of St Lawrence between New Brunswick and Nova Scotia. It is 16.5 km

Table 83 — Canada: special exports fob

	Percentages of total value					
	1924	*1931–35*	*1938*	*1951*	*1963*	*1971*
Raw materials						
Wood	10.2	6.4	7.1	10.6	6.7	5.0
Wood pulp	3.9	4.1	2.9	9.3	6.0	4.5
Furs	1.6	2.2	1.5	0.8	0.6	0.2
Chemicals	—	2.2	2.1	3.4	1.1	3.3
Copper ore and products	1.2	3.5	5.6	2.2	3.2	3.2
Nickel ore and products	1.0	3.5	5.6	3.5	4.9	4.2
Foodstuffs						
Wheat	23.5	21.4	9.5	11.3	11.6	4.6
Milled wheat	6.6	3.2	1.9	3.0	0.9	0.3
Whisky	—	2.2	1.1	1.4	1.3	1.1
Fishery products	3.1	3.7	2.8	3.0	2.3	0.2
Meats	2.1	2.2	3.8	1.9	—	6.3
Manufactures						
Newsprint	8.6	14.5	11.1	13.7	11.2	6.0
Cars	2.4	2.1	2.7	2.1	1.3	11.9
Total value in million $	*1 069*	*599*	*943*	*3 914*	*6 799*	*17 675*
Countries						
United States	39.1	35.3	36.7	58.7	55.4	68.3
United Kingdom	37.0	37.8	36.0	16.1	14.9	7.6
Germany*	2.3	1.3	1.9	0.9	2.5	1.8
Japan	2.1	2.4	2.2	1.9	4.4	4.4
France	1.0	2.2	1.0	1.2	0.9	0.9

* West Germany only, 1951 onwards.

(9 miles) from the nearest point of New Brunswick, with a ferry link and a loop of the Trans–Canada Highway passing through the island. The capital, Charlottetown, is on a large, deep, and well-sheltered harbour. The rich red soil is well suited to potatoes, fruits, oats, hay, and dairy farming, hence the name 'the Garden of the Gulf'. Agriculture, fishing and food processing are the main industries — with tourism rapidly increasing (there is a large National Park on the St Lawrence shore).

3. *New Brunswick,* rather less than Scotland in size and with a population of 634 557 in 1971, is very rich in forests, and also possesses valuable fisheries. The capital is Fredericton, but the largest town and chief seaport is Saint John, occupying a fine harbour on the Bay of Fundy, at the mouth of the river of the same name. The harbour is open all the year round, is safe, easy of access, and capable of accommodating vessels of 9 m (30 ft) draught, and since the port (which is the eastern terminal of the Canadian Pacific) has been connected with Montréal by the 'Short Line', a great trade in livestock, dairy produce, and bulk-handled grain has been developed. The province is fairly rich in minerals with zinc, lead, copper, coal and limestone actively mined.

Timber and wood products are the main source of wealth, followed by light industry, agriculture and mining. There are thermal and hydro-electric power plants; and studies are in hand to harness the tides in the Bay of Fundy to provide further power.

4. Québec, on both sides of the St Lawrence, mostly east of the Ottawa, is a province approximately six times the size of Great Britain, but with a population of 6.1m. in 1971, mostly in the St Lawrence lowlands. In the settled south the winter is long, snow generally covering the ground (sometimes to a depth of more than 1 m: 3 ft) from December to April; but the summer is warm enough to grow not merely the ordinary crops of the British Isles but also maize and tobacco. About four-fifths of the inhabitants of the province are of French origin and still speak French — even in the so-called Eastern Townships, on the south bank of the St Lawrence, where the bulk of the settlers were originally English. Ninety per cent of Canada's asbestos comes from great quarries at Thetford and Black Lake in Eastern Townships. Copper ores are mined in the scenic Gaspé peninsula but the spectacular development is that of iron ore on the Québec—Labrador border.

The capital of the province is Québec City, situated at the confluence of the Charles River with the St Lawrence, and the lowest point at which the river is bridged. Once the head of navigation for sailing vessels, its growth was checked by the deepening of the river above the city, and by other causes; for though trans—Atlantic passengers sometimes prefer to land or start here, freight favours water carriage without transhipment as far into the heart of a country as possible. Thus Montréal is now the chief seat of commerce in Canada. Table 84 shows the relative growth of the cities proper; the population of the metropolitan areas (cities plus suburbs) in 1971 is shown in Table 86.

Montréal, the second most important manufacturing city in Canada, stands on an island in the St Lawrence, at the confluence of the Ottawa, 290 km (180 miles) above Québec. All the improvements in the communications below the port tend to increase its shipping and population. In 1906 the ship channel up to this point had a depth of 8.4 m (27 ft 6 in), but this was increased to 9.2 m (30 ft) in 1912 and further deepening followed. There is as yet little indication that the improvment of navigation above the city (the St Lawrence Seaway) has

Table 84 — Canada: growth of Québec and Montréal

	1881	*1911*	*1921*	*1931*	*1951*	*1961*	*1971*
Québec	62 500	78 000	95 000	131 000	164 000	172 000	182 420
Montréal	141 000	470 000	619 000	819 000	1 021 500	1 191 000	1 197 750

affected this continued growth. The trade of Montréal was greatly stimulated by the freeing of the Canadian canals from tolls in 1903. In that year nearly 20 per cent of the shipments of grain from Chicago and Duluth passed through Canadian territory. It is now after Vancouver, its western rival, the greatest grain port in Canada, a situation greatly influenced by the fact that Montréal is also the focus of the Canadian Railways. The water power resources of the province are enormous and have been developed especially on the St Maurice, Saguenay, Lièvre, Ottawa, and St Lawrence Rivers. Many important storage dams have been built and in 1968 the province had 48 per cent of the total Canadian turbine capacity. As a result of this hydroelectric power development, power lines link all important centres on the St Lawrence lowlands, and Québec has become the second manufacturing province handling nearly one-third of Canadian imports and exports. A great copper smelting town has grown up at Noranda. Three Rivers, at the mouth of the St Maurice, has become a considerable town and port. The St François Dam on the river of the same name materially assisted the numerous pulp and other mills along its course; Shipshaw is even more important.

5. *Ontario,* about four and a half times the size of Great Britain and with a population of 7.7m., is the province to the west of Québec, extending along the north of the Great Lakes. The populous region, which is the St Lawrence lowlands and the Great Lakes peninsula. has a much shorter winter than that of Québec. Here wine is produced from native grapes, and a strip running eastwards from Hamilton and bordering Lake Erie is known as 'the garden of Canada', since the crops include table grapes, peaches, and other soft fruits. Despite the rapid development of the other areas Ontario still produces more than half of all fruit grown in Canada, and about one-half of the milk, cheese and butter. Forests cover huge areas of the north. Ottawa, the seat of government, stands on the river of the same name, about 144 km (90 miles) above its confluence with the St Lawrence. It is a centre of the lumber, pulp, and paper industries of the province, and has some of the largest paper-mills in Canada. The capital of the province is Toronto, near the western end of Lake Ontario, on which it has a fine harbour, and is so situated as to form the centre at which the railways running from the east, parallel to Lake Ontario, begin to diverge in different directions through the Lake peninsula. The most important manufacturing centre in Canada, the city has grown almost as rapidly as Montréal, with a metropolitan population in 1971 of over 2.6m. Steel works and other manufacturing industries are carried on at Hamilton at the western end of Lake Ontario. Hydroelectric power has been developed extensively in the province especially on the Nipigon (north of Lake Superior) and Ottawa River and above all at Niagara.

Hydroelectric stations on or near the Niagara River utilise the difference of level between Lakes Erie and Ontario (about 100 m: 328 ft) for power development. Sudbury, Timmins, and Kirkland Lake are large centre of mining and metallurgy. Thunder Bay (Fort William and Port Arthur on Lake Superior together make a great centre for the shipment o western grain. Midland, Collingwood, Goderich, and Port Golborne are now also important wheat-reception ports where the wheat of the west is received and then railed, in the form of wheat or flour, largely to Montréal. Cobalt, near Lake Temiscaming, in northern Ontario, was formerly famous for cobalt and silver. Windsor, like Detroit in the United States, is devoted to the manufacture of motorcars, and other manufacturing centres include London, Oshawa, and Ottawa. Ontario is the leading commercial province, producing over half Canada's manufactures and 40 per cent of her total exports.

6. *Manitoba*, the rich, flat farming province to the west, is nearly three times the size of Britain, with a population of 988 250 in 1971. The capital is Winnipeg, situated at the confluence of the Red River and the Assiniboine. This city is now also the place of convergence of numerous railways and has grown rapidly as the trade centre for the wheatfields of the prairies. Its population in 1881 was 8 000; in 1911, 136 000, in 1931, 219 000 and in 1971, 534 690 (metropolitan area). In 1881 the area under wheat in Manitoba was 21 000 ha (51 000 acres), in 1918, 1.21m. ha (2.98m. acres), but in 1960 it had dropped to under 1m. ha. As world prices dictate, the wheat lands are converted to more intensive forms of agriculture, including dairying. Of the 10m. ha (25m. acres) in Manitoba classed as suitable for arable farming about one-third is so used. The northern two-thirds of the Province lies on the Canadian Shield and has gold–zinc mines at Flin Flon and nickle at Lynn Lake. There has been much development in hydroelectric power. Manitoba has now its own ocean port in Churchill, on Hudson Bay, linked by rail with the wheat lands. Agriculture has for long been the major industry, but this is now overtaken by manufactures.

7. *Saskatchewan*, with a population of 926 240 in 1971 and slightly larger than Manitoba, was created a province only in 1905. It is still mainly a wheat-growing province, especially in the southern half, with over one-third of Canada's agricultural land. The northern half is a forest and mining region. In 1905 the area under wheat was 0.4m. ha (1.1m. acres), in 1929 5.8m. ha (14m. acres), spring wheat only, winter wheat trifling. Now the total area under cultivation is 8m. ha (20m. acres), three-quarters under wheat. Flax-growing has been encouraged, for both seed and fibre. Agriculture is by far the most important, and highly mechanised, industry; followed by mining, the construction industry and manufacturing. As with the other Prairie

rovinces, the acreage under wheat was greatly reduced by 1970, with diversification to feed barley, rapeseed and even summer fallow. The most important centres are the capital, Regina, Saskatoon, Moose Jaw and Prince Albert. Oilfields are now being developed and petroleum is the main mineral product, followed by potash, copper and uranium. The south has vast lignite fields and there are large supplies of natural gas associated with the oilfields.

8. *Alberta,* which lies mainly on the higher levels of the great plains but extends westwards so as to include a most beautiful part of the Rockies, is the third of the Prairie Provinces and had a population of 1.6m. in 1971. It originally owed its settlement to the advantages of cattle-ranching offered by the natural pastures to the east of the Rocky Mountains, but has attracted agricultural settlers who grow oats as well as wheat, at first largely winter wheat. Some 28m. ha (70m. acres) are classified as potentially suitable for agriculture, but less than 30 per cent of this is farmed. The area under wheat shows the same pattern as the neighbouring provinces, rising from 43 000 ha (107 000 acres) in 1905 to a peak of 2.8m. ha (7.5m. acres) in 1929 thereafter falling steadily as better husbandry, new strains and improved use of fertilisers greatly increased the crops while reducing the acreage. In the south sugar beet is grown under irrigation. The capital is Edmonton, on the Saskatchewan River, and at a point to which railways are giving increased importance. It had less than 5 000 people in 1901, in 1971, 490 810. As the oil boom town its present growth is very rapid for Alberta produces over 70 per cent of Canada's oil and natural gas. One of the world's longest pipelines runs 3 260 km (2 020 miles) from Alberta to Ontario, and another connects to the United States for eventual delivery to the west coast. The province is also rich in coal and has the enormous oil reserves of the Athabasca tarsands from which a pilot production of some 100 000 barrels a day has started. Calgary the traditional ranching centre is now a major industrial city. Canada has paid much attention to the tourist industry and in the mountains of this province are the world-famous Jasper and Banff National Parks.

9. *British Columbia* is a province four times the size of Great Britain, comprising the Rocky Mountains with high tablelands and lofty mountain ranges separated by deep and narrow valleys, but also including Vancouver Island and the coastal archipelago to the north as far as the Queen Charlotte Islands inclusive. In 1971 the population was 2.2m., 75 per cent of whom lived within 80 km (50 miles) of Vancouver. Its wealth consists chiefly in minerals, forests, and fisheries. British Columbia produces about 10 per cent of the mineral output of all Canada, a third of the forest and fishery output, and 70 per cent of the sawn timber. The discovery of gold first brought a rush of settlers here

in 1856, but the deposits then discovered were worked out. Since 1895, gold, silver, copper, lead, and zinc mining have all been carried on. Lead, silver, and zinc are or have been mined in East and West Kootenay; copper near Howe Sound (Britannia mine) and near Princeton; auriferous copper ores in the Rossland and Boundary district near the southern border of British Columbia; gold is however no longer worked in any of the once famous old localities. Coal is mined and converted into coke at Fernie in the Crow's Nest coalfield for use in the smelters, refineries, and fertiliser plants at Trail. Copper is also found on Texada Island, where there exist also deposits of iron ore. The oldest and most important coalmines of the province are those of Nanaimo on the east side of Vancouver Island, and Cumberland, further north. Coal is also mined in the Nicola valley and in the country traversed by the Tulameen and Similkameen Rivers. The province has vast water power resources second only to those of Québec. Special interest attaches to the Kitimat scheme, not only because it is creating an aluminium smelting town in what was formerly almost uninhabited forest country but also because the water is brought through a tunnel in the coast mountains. British Columbia is steadily advancing as an agricultural province with the aid of irrigation. The rich valleys and lowlands in the interior offer favourable conditions for fruit-growing and dairying. Of these the Okanagan valley contains the largest area of fruit lands in the province. Apples of excellent quality are exported in large quantities to the English and other markets, and peaches, plums, apricots, and vines are successfully grown. The forests of the Coast Mountains, composed of gigantic Douglas fir, cedar, and other trees, are among the grandest in the world. The capital of the province is Victoria, on a beautiful harbour at the southeast end of Vancouver Island. It has a considerable entrepôt trade. Esquimalt, on an excellent harbour adjacent to that of Victoria is a naval base with an arsenal and graving dock. Vancouver, whose harbour, formed by Burrard Inlet, can accommodate the largest liners alongside the wharves, and New Westminster, near the mouth of the Fraser River, are the western termini of the two great trans-continental railways. The quickest sea-and-land route from London and New York to the Far East is via Vancouver, hence the possible use of Canada as a 'land bridge' for container traffic. Since the opening of the Panama Canal Vancouver has become a centre for shipment of

Table 85 — Wheat export from Vancouver in millions of bushels

	1920–21	*1921–22*	*1922–23*	*1927–28*	*1952*
Europe	0.5	4.06	14.86 ⎫		
South America	–	–	0.33 ⎬ 79.0		117.36
Orient	–	3.44	3.83 ⎭		

prairie wheat, lumber and metals for Europe and the east of America, later also to eastern Asia (the Orient). It is now the largest grain exporting port in the world.

Vancouver was founded in 1885 and by 1891 had a population of 14 000. By 1911 this had increased to 100 000, and now the population of 'Greater Vancouver' is over 1.1m. Its mild climate, huge natural harbour and latterly the receipt of oil and gas by pipeline have encouraged many industries in the fastest-growing city in Canada. Prince Rupert, the port on Kai-En Island, is a terminus of the Canadian National Railway (formerly Grand Trunk Pacific). A large dry dock was opened here in 1921. It is about 3 860 nautical miles from Yokohama, 500 miles nearer than any other Pacific port. Recent developments include fish freezing and processing plants.

10. Newfoundland. Newfoundland was formerly a separate British Dominion, to which belonged not only the island of that name but also the inhospitable coast and a considerable inland tract of Labrador. Owing to financial difficulties the government of the United Kingdom assumed responsibility for the government and finances of Newfoundland in 1933 and later, in 1948, the country joined Canada as the tenth province. The population (522 100 in 1971) is chiefly settled on the coast and includes many fishermen. The island has very extensive forest resources. The mill at Corner Brook is the largest integrated newsprint and pulp-mill in the world and there is another very large mill at Grand Falls. There are unworked coalfields, situated in the southwest, being a continuation of those in Cape Breton Island. A railway and the Trans—Canada Highway run from St John's, the capital of the island, on the east coast, through agricultural settlements to the west coast. Iron ore of excellent quality was mined on the small island known as Bell Island in Conception Bay, near St John's. These Wabana deposits contained about 54 per cent metallic iron, free from deleterious ingredients. They pass from the island under the sea, and the amount of ore on the island has been estimated to exceed 3 000m. tons. The Ungava field is now a more economic source, and the Bell Island mines closed in 1967. Other minerals worked include lead, zinc, copper and fluorspar. The major project for the province in the 1970s will be the Churchill Falls hydroelectric station, which will be one of the largest in the world. Canadian demand will have expanded sufficiently by 1980 to take all of the output.

Northern Canada. The remainder of Canada is divided into the Northwest Territories 3.38m. sq km (1.3m. sq miles) — Franklin (the northern islands), Keewatin, and Mackenzie — and the Territory of Yukon 536 000 sq km (207 000 sq miles). They all yield fur, and the Yukon territory is rich in gold and silver. Here was discovered in 1896 the Klondike goldfield, on which Dawson City now stands. Access to the region is facilitated by a mountain railway from Skagway (South Alaska), over the White Pass, to a navigable river of the Yukon basin. The gold occurs both in alluvial deposits and in quartz, but the most easily worked deposits are exhausted, and the production has fluctuated greatly. It increased in value from £60 000 in 1896 to £4.5m. in 1900, at the time of the rush; declined to £136 000 in 1930, but reached £781 000 in 1959, only to fall to £250 000 in 1967, when the total value of mineral production in the Yukon (gold, silver, lead, etc.) was $14.7m. (£5.7m.). The population fell from 27 000 in 1901 to 4 000 in 1931, but was 18 388 in 1971 (Dawson City 881, Whitehorse, now the capital, 11 080).

The Northern Territories, with a population in 1971 of 34 000 produced in 1967 minerals valued at $115m. (£44.2m.), most of which was zinc and lead. Mining is by far the principal pursuit, followed by lumbering, fishing and trapping. Yellowknife (on the north of the Great Slave Lake) is still the centre of gold mining, with Hay River across the lake as the new railhead. Two-thirds of the population are Indian and Eskimo.

During the Second World War United States Army engineers constructed the Alcan or Alaskan Highway from the Peace River area (and so from Edmonton) to Alaska through the mountainous heart of the northern forests and across southern Yukon with spur roads to the mining areas.

Table 86 — Canadian metropolitan areas (cities and suburbs), 1971

Montréal	2 720 000	Calgary	400 500
Toronto	2 609 600	Windsor	255 170
Vancouver	1 071 080	London	284 470
Winnipeg	534 680	Halifax	220 350
Hamilton	495 860	Kitchener	224 400
Edmonton	490 811	Victoria	193 500
Québec	476 200	Regina	138 900
Ottawa	447 700	Saskatoon	125 080

St Pierre and Miquelon

A group of eight small French islands off the south coast of Newfoundland; total area 243 sq km (93 sq miles). The land is too barren for agriculture and the population (5 000) is dependent mainly on the codfishery, with fox-farming as a secondary industry. Exports are dried, smoked and frozen fish, and fishmeal.

United States

Apart from Alaska and Hawaii with a combined area of 1.5m. sq km (600 000 sq miles), the contiguous territory of the United States, between Canada and Mexico, extends over an area of about 7.8m. sq km (3m. sq miles), or more than thirty-three times the area of Great Britain. Physically this territory is a continuation of that of Canada. In the west the mountains of British Columbia are prolonged into Washington, Idaho, and Montana. In the centre the plains and prairies are similar in the two countries, and the southeastern highlands of Canada are the northern extremities of the Appalachians. Almost the entire population of the United States is of non-American origin, being composed either of immigrants or descendants of immigrants from Europe, or of descendants of African Negroes originally introduced as slaves on the southern plantations. It is in a large measure due to this cause, and to the fact that the development of the population has from the first depended in a great measure on commerce with Europe, that the density of population is still greatest in the east, and above all in the vicinity of the great seaports from Massachusetts Bay to Chesapeake Bay. There is, however, a steady movement of the centre of gravity of the population towards the west and the movement was 1° of longitude or more for each decennial census from 1810 to 1900. It is now as far west as Illinois.

No other state has had its population so steadily reinforced by a stream of foreign settlers. In the ten years 1877—86 the total number of immigrants was upwards of 4.2m., and in one year (1882) the number approached 800 000. Till near the end of the eighteenth century the United Kingdom furnished the largest contingent of immigrants from the earliest date from which statistics are obtainable, but from about the middle of the nineteenth century the German total approached and occasionally exceeded the British. In later years a change took place in the character of the immigration. In the ten years ending 30 June 1890 the United Kingdom and Germany together furnished rather more than 55 per cent of the immigrants; in the ten ending 30 June 1910, less than 14 per cent; the contingents supplied by Austria—Hungary, Italy, and Russia (including Poland) in the latter period were equal to 24.5, 23, and 18 per cent of the total respectively. In the four decades ending with 30 June 1880, 1890, 1900, and 1910, the total number of immigrants in millions was 2.8, 5.2, 3.8, and 8.8. In the last five years before the First World War, that is, the five ending with 30 June 1914, the number of immigrants was 5.2m., in the next five, 1.2m. Immigration of any nationality was restricted for fifteen months beginning 21 April 1921, to 3 per cent of the population of that nationality in the country at the census of 1910. Under the quota thus initiated the last interwar year of large immigration was 1923—24

(241 709). During the great depression with consequent unemployment which followed, immigration fell greatly — to a minimum of 23 068 in 1932—33, a figure far exceeded by the emigrants. After the Second World War there was a large influx of 'displaced persons' from Europe. In 1949—50, 249 187 alien immigrants were admitted against 27 598 leaving. Of the arrivals 58 per cent were German and Austrian, 7.5 British and Irish, 5 Italian. Between 1820 and 1960 a total number of 41 841 000 alien immigrants entered the United States. A large number of the non-European immigrants are from Canada, and hence in the first instance likewise of European origin. Chinese and Japanese were also among the immigrants during the years before the Second World War. The Negro population, though not recruited by immigration, is multiplying rapidly by natural increase (excess of births over deaths), but the small native Indian population is dwindling or becoming absorbed. In 1900 the Negro population of the United States (almost confined to the southeast) was 8.8m. In 1920 the figure was 10.5m., the rate of increase 1910—20 being 6.5 per cent. The natural increase of the white population (excluding immigrants) was 11.6 per cent for the same decade. By 1950 the total population was 151m., with 14.9m. Negroes, and in 1970 it was 203m., with 20m. Negroes. However, in the last fifty years the natural rate of population growth has been of more significance than the increase from immigration. The natural rate of growth in the late 1960s was 1.8 per cent; equivalent to an increase of some 4m. per year.

Both the history of the country and the physical features of its territory, have favoured the unity of its government. In consequence of this unity there is free trade, as in Canada, from ocean to ocean; and though the individual states have each legislative powers within certain limits, there could be no more striking illustration of the importance to commerce of the central government than the passing, in February 1887, of the Interstate Commerce Act, which may be briefly described as an Act prohibiting local and individual preferences on the great highways of commerce throughout the length and breadth of a territory four-fifths the size of Europe.

If we look at this unity of government from an historical point of view, there are several important considerations to bear in mind. The separate 'plantations' or colonies that ultimately formed the first United States grew up independently from several convenient starting-places. They grew up under English influence, and with a common language, but this would not in itself have sufficed to make them one, and it was perhaps fortunate that when they had become strong enough, they were united in a common war against the mother country; fortunate, too, that, when that war was over, the common burdens which it entailed necessitated a common government, and that the great state thus formed held such a preponderance in the middle of the

continent that it easily acquired in course of time all the present territory by settlement, purchase, or conquest. And it was likewise fortunate that, when the practice of slavery in the southern states threatened
a permanent division, the north should have been strong enough, in
virtue of its more rapid development by immigration, to conquer the
south by force of wealth and numbers (1861–65).

Physically the circumstance most favourable to unity is the great
plains of the central region, communicating freely with Atlantic plains
and lowlands in the east, and in the west sloping imperceptibly up to
the tableland which forms the base of the Rocky Mountains. This great
central plain is traversed by some of the grandest navigable rivers in the
world which provided essential north to south communication links.
These however became of less comparative importance when the railways opened up the centre and the west, and made the main communication axis an east to west one.

Communications. The Mississippi, the great waterway running north
and south through this region, is continuously navigable for steamers of
considerable size to Minneapolis on the parallel of 45°, within 4° of
the northern frontier. The river traverses a region in which the products
of temperate and subtropical climates are brought closer together than
in any other part of the world, and today it is difficult to believe that in
the year 1887 more freight was carried on the Upper Mississippi in eight
months than any of the three great trunk lines of railroads carried in a
year, and at about one-third the rate. Stern-wheelers would proceed
down the stream from Louisville, pushing thirty-seven barges with a
total cargo equal to nearly 26 000 tons, and by this system coal used to
be carried from Pittsburgh to New Orleans, a distance of 3 200 km
(2 000 miles), at the cost of about 60 cents (then worth 12½p) per ton,
equal to 0.006p per ton mile. The Cumberland and the Tennessee, on
the left of the Ohio, and the Wabash on the right, have likewise considerable stretches of navigable water. The Red River, the Arkansas, and
the Missouri, the great right-bank tributaries of the Mississippi, are also
all navigable, the Missouri for more than 3 200 km (2 000 miles). With
the advent of railways traffic on all these great rivers declined and there
has, for instance, been no commercial traffic on the Upper Missouri
since the 1890s.

The Appalachian Mountains in the east, and the Rocky Mountain
system in the west, interrupt the east–west axis of communication. The
rivers which cross them have their navigation interrupted by rapids and
are of smaller size, than those of the great plains; but it must be
remembered that some of them (the Hudson, Delaware, Susquehanna,
Potomac, and James River) are of great value to commerce in that they
provide essential routeways through the mountains and good harbours
in their estuaries.

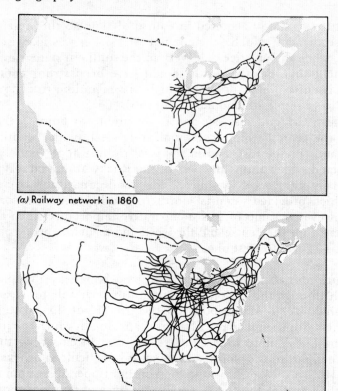

(a) Railway network in 1860

(b) Railway network in 1884

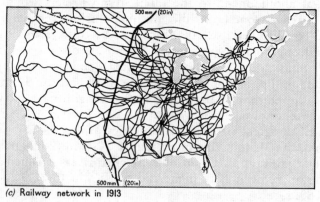

(c) Railway network in 1913

United States: development of the railroad network

Notice the comprehensive cover of the whole of the main agricultural and manu-facturing regions to the east of the 500 mm (20 in) annual rainfall line

The building of the railway network provided the essential link to open up and develop the interior and the west of the continent. The obstacles presented by the great mountain chains in the east and west were less than might have been expected from the extent and height of the mountains. The gradual slope of the ground up to the base of the Rocky Mountains facilitated the laying of railways to the foot of the passes, and several routes were found by which railways could be advantageously laid across these and other western mountains. The Appalachian Mountains in the northeast — precisely where population is densest, coal and anthracite most abundant, the connections between coast and interior most important — break up into a number of smaller mountain ranges with many gaps between them, facilitating railway and canal construction. In the southern part of the Appalachian system (Alleghany Mountains) the ranges are higher and more continuous, and there is still a stretch of nearly 480 km (300 miles) with only one railway across it. Immediately to the west of that stretch there lies one of the most sparsely peopled districts of the eastern states.

Today the great railway network is in decline. Many branch lines are being closed down and the rails taken up. Other lines now have no passenger services, being used for freight only. (Dallas, for instance, a city of 1.5m. and once served by nine railway companies, now has no passenger trains.) As in many other developed countries, nationalisation of the railways is the only solution to retaining essential public services, and in 1971 a form of state ownership was introduced to supervise the remaining minimum rail movements. In large measure this is due to road competition, reinforced by airline competition for both passengers and goods, and also pipeline competition. Even in 1939 out of all the freight moved in the United States, the railways were only handling 50 per cent compared with coastwise shipping 25 per cent, Great Lakes shipping 10 per cent, pipelines 7 per cent, highways 6 per cent, and inland waterways 2 per cent. In 1939 there were also 15 000 long distance, intercity, passenger trains a day. In recent years the railways have lost further ground and new developments are in progress, such as the movement of powdered coal suspended in water by pipeline, and the use of long conveyor belts. Air transport has gained enormously. By 1970 the long distance passenger trains were down to 190 a day and freight movement by road was of increasing importance.

There are several important canals in the Appalachian system, among others the Erie and Champlain Canals. The Erie Canal, laid through the Mohawk valley, serves to connect the navigation of the Great Lakes with New York, starting from Buffalo at the eastern end of Lake Erie, and proceeding eastwards to Troy and Albany on the Hudson. It was opened in 1825, and the fact that New York then first came to exceed Philadelphia in population, will serve to give an idea of its importance at that date. The Champlain Canal connects the eastern end of the Erie Canal (now called the New York State Barge Canal) with the head of Lake Champlain, and thus completes the waterway between New York and the St Lawrence. The Cape Cod Canal, opened in 1914, cutting across the hook-shaped peninsula in the east of Massachusetts, reduces the distance between Boston and New York from 537 to 438 km (334 to 272 miles), and enables vessels to escape the risks of the voyage round the Cape, where wrecks used to average thirty-five a year. After the construction of the Erie Canal the fertile lowlands of the Mississippi basin had the advantage of two great waterways in communication with the ocean, in competition with one another and the railways. Although the grain traffic by the old Erie Canal declined very rapidly,* this did not prevent it from having a great influence on the cost of carriage.

The physical features that favoured the construction of the two waterways from New York were of equal importance for the railway connections of that port. The Hudson and Mohawk valleys allow of railway connections with easy gradients between New York and Chicago (the 'sea level' route of the New York Central Lines), and at one time this was the only route for the great expresses between these two cities, even although in following this route one has to run for 225 km (140 miles) north before turning westwards. This route still competes easily with the more direct but more difficult route through the Alleghany Mountains. It is these physical features which no doubt have enabled New York to beat Boston in competing for the bulk of the traffic with the important hinterland of which Chicago is the centre. Boston is cut off from that hinterland by the Hoosac Mountains in the west of Massachusetts, through which there was no railway tunnel till 1875. Even now that route appears to be a difficult one, for a large part of the traffic of Boston with the west passes through New York. While the Hudson and Mohawk valleys afford an easy route between New York and the west, the Hudson, Lake Champlain, and Richelieu valleys afford an equally easy route running almost in a straight line due north between the Adirondacks and the Green Mountains to Montréal.

Climate and agriculture. In the United States, as in Canada, there are differences as well as resemblances in comparing different parts of the country with corresponding parts of Asia and Europe. The continental United States, that is exclusive of Alaska and Hawaii, may be divided into four climatic regions with characteristic products, two east and two west of the meridian of 100° W, though the boundaries must be recognised as more or less arbitrary.

The main agricultural products of the United States are mentioned under the four sections into which this vast country is divided below, but two general observations may here be introduced. Professor J. Russell Smith pointed out long ago that both in the north and south of

* In 1886 the cost of carriage of a bushel of wheat from Chicago to New York was 16.5 cents by an all-rail route, 12 cents by lake and rail, and only 8.71 cents by lake and canal. In that year upwards of 45m. bushels of grain and flour were carried through the Erie Canal. In 1900, the corresponding rates were 9.98, 5.05 and 4.42 cents, but the total movement of wheat on all the New York State Canals (of which the Erie Canal is one) declined from 37.6m. bushels in 1862 to 4.6m. in 1900.

the United States, crops like maize, cotton, and tobacco are widely grown, which unlike the prevailing European cereals, do not cover the surface, and thus leave much soil between the plants liable to be washed away. The problem of soil erosion and of the disastrous floods which result from the rapid run off from the eroded surfaces has become a matter of the most serious import in the last few decades, so that the Federal government set up a special service to deal with soil conservation. The development of agriculture in the United States during the twentieth century is in marked contrast to that in the nineteenth. In the nineteenth century there was an expansion, a movement westwards, especially after the Civil War of 1861–65. In the twentieth century the progress has been along three lines: (1) reclamation by drainage, irrigation, and other means; (2) the more active and constant use of good land already worked; but the elimination of farms established in unfavourable positions on 'submarginal' land, i.e. beyond the pioneer 'fringe'; and (3) more intensive cultivation and organisation into larger farm units on industrial lines. In the 1920s the late O. E. Baker distinguished a number of agricultural regions, now partly outdated, which may, however, be grouped roughly together in Chisholm's original four main divisions.

1. *The Northeast.* This region lies north of the Ohio and Delaware Bay (38° N), and comprises, among others, the New England States. It corresponds with the same latitudes of eastern Asia chiefly as regards extremes of temperature, for it has not the typically dry winters of the corresponding parts of Asia. In this region the inhabitants are almost all of European origin, and the products are similar to those of Europe with mixed cattle-farming and dairy products in the east; the great corn (maize) belt in the centre, and the wheatlands in the west. The northern and eastern portion is the most densely peopled part of the United States, and that in which manufacturing industries have long been most highly developed; here there is a belt of intensive vegetable or 'truck' farming along the Atlantic coast.

2. *The Southeast* is a region in which cotton, maize or corn, and tobacco are grown as staples. The climate is well adapted for maize and warm temperate or even subtropical plants, including the groundnut (peanut), the pecan nut,* and, in the far south, in spite of occasional disaster, even the orange. Here the correspondence with the same latitudes in the east of Asia as regards rainfall is closer. There is for the most part a decided preponderance of summer rains, though the winters are far from rainless. The growth of arable farming in the sandy 'pine barrens' as they are called, which occupy a large portion of the coastal plain from North Carolina to the Lower Mississippi (a process of

---

* The fruit of a species of hickory, genus *Carya*, which is closely akin to the walnut, genus *Juglans*.

reclamation facilitated, it should be mentioned, by the neighbouring supplies of phosphatic fertilisers), is a notable feature. In the extreme south, along the shore of the Gulf of Mexico and Florida, there is citrus fruit, sugarcane and paddy.

3. *The region between 100° and 120° W* (mostly tableland), comprising an area of about 1.7m. sq km (1.2m. sq miles), may be described as the arid region of the United States, inasmuch as, except in the neighbourhood of mountains and near the northern frontier, the rainfall is too scanty for agriculture without irrigation. Here, therefore, we find the majority of the irrigation schemes of the United States. This region corresponds in the north to the southern part of western Siberia, and in the south to the arid and almost rainless tracts of Asia forming Soviet Central Asia. The part of this region lying immediately east of the Rocky Mountains and sloping gently eastwards is known as 'the plains' or short grass prairies and is a cattle-rearing region. The western part, consisting of mountains and high tablelands, is rich in metallic minerals and is a sheep-rearing region.

4. *The Pacific Coast* has a climate closely corresponding to that of the same latitudes in the west and south of Europe and northern Africa. In the north the rains are very abundant west of the mountains, and the climate compares with that of northwestern Spain or France. As we pass southwards we come to a climate closely resembling that of the Mediterranean region, the summers nearly rainless, the winters mild. The difference between the coastal climate with low summer temperatures due to the prevalence of fogs, and the climate of the Great Valley of California with a lower rainfall but higher temperatures is particularly significant. Gold, which first attracted a large population to this part of the world, is still an important product, but the fine Californian valley, watered by the Sacramento in the north and the San Joaquin in the south, now teems with wheat, barley, grapes, and southern fruits, and excellent wheat is also grown on both sides of the Columbia River, and on the Snake River Plateau, as well as in the valley of the Willamette, between the Coast and Cascade Ranges. In southern California various fruits and even wheat and barley are grown by irrigation, the water for which is obtained mainly by means of canals, though some water is obtained from wells. The earliest recorded canal was opened in 1835, the first in the Anaheim district in 1856. Nearly all the oranges and other citrus fruits are grown above the valley floors, which are less liable to fogs and frosts than the low grounds. The fruits of California (oranges, grapefruit, lemons, apricots, prunes, raisins, and dried peaches) furnish, along with rice, vegetables, and wool, the great bulk of the eastward traffic of the middle and southern transcontinental railways. On the mountains the forest scenery is unique. Dense forests of giant conifers cover the slopes, and a great timber trade

has grown up round Puget Sound (Washington), at Seattle, Tacoma, Bellingham, and other ports.

Minerals. The mineral resources of the United States are enormous. Besides coal and petroleum, the United States now produce more copper, potash, uranium, natural gas and aluminium than any other country, in addition to being second or third amongst the producers of gold, silver, iron ore, zinc, and lead.

The major industrial regions have grown up for the most part away from coalfields. This trend continues. Among the significant developments associated with the Second World War has been, the continuous growth of manufacturing on the Pacific Coast. Los Angeles has grown with extreme rapidity and handles a very great variety of both heavy and light industries. Special interest attaches to the great aircraft industry of California. In the northwest Seattle has also been developing rapidly. Another area of very marked development in varied manufacture has been in the Gulf states of the South.

Coal production is mainly bituminous with a small, but important, percentage of anthracite and some lignite. The total production increased with very rapid strides during the latter part of last century. The production of 1886 was more than three times that of 1870, and more than seven times that of 1860. In the present century the output has dropped slowly owing to increased competition of oil, gas and hydroelectric power. But, so great is the total demand for power, coal output is again gaining in importance and 60 per cent of all coal produced goes to thermal power stations. The great Appalachian fields, lying in the eastern states, yield 70 per cent of the output, which reaches about 500m. tons a year (25 per cent of the world's total).

Pennsylvania produces 17 per cent of the bituminous coal and most of the anthracite. Anthracite is produced in several small fields in the east of the state, the centre of the region of production being about 320 km (200 miles) from New York and 200 km (125 miles) from Philadelphia. Access is afforded to the productive region by the valley of the Delaware, with those of its tributaries, the Schuylkill and the Lehigh, and in all of these valleys there is water communication (by canal or river), as well as, of course, abundance of railways. Bituminous coal is produced chiefly in the west of Pennsylvania around Pittsburgh which is the major coking centre of the United States. The bituminous coal region of western Pennsylvania extends into west Virginia, Kentucky and Ohio. The combined area produces 70 per cent of the total United States production. Further west another productive coal region extends from the west of Indiana through Illinois to the east of Iowa; and Illinois ranks after west Virginia and Pennsylvania in the total amount of its production.

The **iron ores** of the United States are abundant, widely distributed,

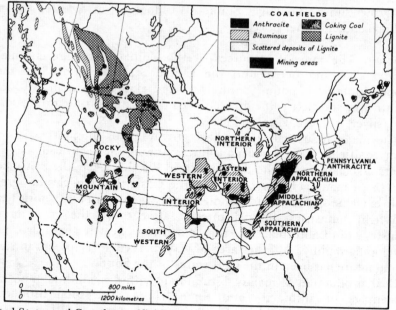

United States and Canada: coalfields
The chief coalfields are:
1 The Appalachian, subdivided into the North, Middle and South Appalachian coalfields
2 The east-central, or eastern interior, coalfield, east of the Mississippi
3 The west central, or western interior, coalfield, west of the Mississippi
The most productive are the Appalachian in Pennsylvania, Ohio, West Virginia and Kentucky

and of excellent quality; but nowhere in the country are the best steel-making ores found in proximity to smelting coal. The Lake Superior region, which yields five-sixths of the iron ore produced in the United States, is, however, conveniently situated to the Great Lakes, which facilitates cheap transport by water. The Marquette Range in Michigan has been worked since 1885. The Menominee Range, a little to the south, since 1877; the Vermilion Range in Minnesota, since 1884, and the Mesabi in Minnesota since 1892. This last discovery was the most important on account of the extraordinary facility with which the ores can here be worked. The deposits were covered merely with a skin of glacial drift and railway lines are laid to the ores, which are then dug and loaded directly into the rail trucks. There is then a short down-hill haul to the lake ports of Duluth, Superior, and Two Harbors. The development of these areas, together with that of the wheat region to the northwest, led to the huge traffic in bulk products (the returning ships bringing coal) through the Great Lakes and their canals, particularly the Sault Ste Marie canals.

Despite huge reserves the Lake Superior ores are not inexhaustible (it is estimated that at least half have already been used) and the United

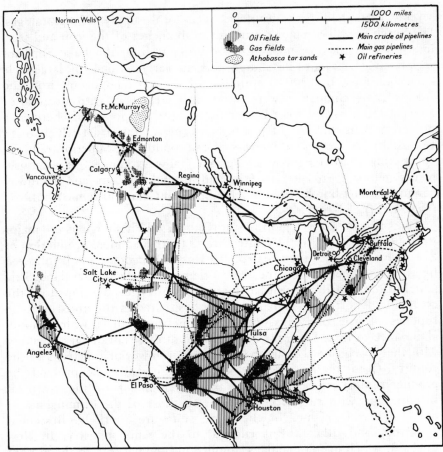

United States and Canada: oilfields, gasfields and main pipelines
The largest production of oil is from the mid-continent and Gulf Coast fields, the latter, mainly in Texas, giving over 30 per cent of the total United States production. The extensive Appalachian field produces only small quantities of oil. Rich deposits of oil were discovered in the Prudhoe Bay area in Alaska in 1969. Notice the concentration of supply lines to the northeastern states; and the important link from Texas which supplements the Californian oilfield

States is now importing increasingly from Labrador and Venezuela.

Although the general rule prevails in the United States, as elsewhere, that the ore is brought to the fuel (rather than the fuel to the ore) there are many works where both raw materials must be brought in. The great centre of the iron industry of the United States was Pittsburgh, which in the early stages of the industry had the advantage of local supplies of ore as well as coal; and also the advantage of being situated where two navigable rivers unite to form the Ohio. Local supplies of ore were long ago exhausted, but Pittsburgh still has the advantage of fuel in a higher degree than any other town in the United States. It was likewise one of the early centres of petroleum production and for several years had the advantage of a local supply of natural gas. Pittsburgh is still a major centre for all branches of the iron and steel industry but the ore must now be brought from the Lake Superior region and Labrador. Pittsburgh was an early witness of large-scale amalgamations. In 1900–1 numbers of the most important iron and steel-working companies were united in a great trust with a capital of above £230m. – the great United States Steel Corporation. There were no fewer than thirty-eight plants belonging to this trust which owns vast coalfields, extensive deposits of ore round Lake Superior, railways connecting these ranges with the lake, railways connecting establishments belonging to the trust in and around Chicago, and a railway connecting Pittsburgh with the lake ports of Conneaut (Ohio) and Erie (New York).

The Chicago–Gary region has now surpassed Pittsburgh as the major iron and steel centre of the United States (with an annual production of 27m. tons – greater than that of the United Kingdom) and is followed by the region centred on the Lake Erie ports (Toledo, Cleveland, Erie and Buffalo). In the southeast the iron industry has developed on the coalfield of northern Alabama, which is situated in the midst of large supplies of iron ore. This ore lies in limestone valleys which supply abundance of flux. From the combination of these advantages, together with that of cheaper labour than in other iron-working districts of the country, this is the district in which pig and cast iron can probably be produced most cheaply. Hence the development of the town of Birmingham, with similar associations to those of the Birmingham of older and wider fame. In the same state are Sheffield, Bessemer, Anniston, and other towns engaged in the same industry. In New England, which in colonial days supplied pig and bar iron to the mother country, the making of pig iron is almost extinct, but some of the cities still retain a reputation for their manufacture of iron and steel articles of high quality, such as tools and cutlery. It is in the Atlantic states that most of the imported iron ore (nearly all ore of high quality, notably from Spain and Algeria) is used. The principal steel-working establishments on this coast are at Sparrow Point on Chesapeake Bay, 14 km (9 miles) from Baltimore, and at South Bethlehem on the Lehigh River in Pennsylvania.

The rapid expansion of the iron and steel industry was essential to the development of the American railway system, the manufacture of machinery of all kinds (particularly agricultural machinery), and later the enormous use of structural steel in building skyscrapers. From this great industry has followed a widespread export of finished articles containing iron, such as automobiles, agricultural implements, sewing machines, typewriters, steel bridges, machinery, locomotives, etc. In the manufacture of all these articles the iron and steel manufactures have had the advantage of an enormous home market, favouring production on a large scale and by the most economic methods. In shipbuilding in which the Americans have not the same advantage, the fortunes of industry have varied. In 1900 only one steel steamship was built in the United States for the foreign trade. During the First World War American shipbuilding came to the front, but the tonnage built in 1920, 2.7m. tons showed a great decline on the figures of 1919 (4.7m. tons). In the year ending 30 June 1925 only 125 000 tons were built. With the coming of the Second World War there was an enormous rise in shipbuilding, especially of standard type welded ships, and a considerable proportion of the building took place for strategic reasons on the newly industrialised west coast. Shipbuilding has again decreased to under 5 per cent of world total with higher labour costs as a major factor.

The **precious metals** of the United States are chiefly produced in the mountains in the west; gold principally in California and Arizona, and in many of the Rocky Mountain States as well as in the Black Hills of south Dakota. Silver is principally from the Rocky Mountains, in Utah, Colorado, Montana, and Nevada. Mercury is found mainly in the Pacific coast ranges, and on the Nevada/Oregon border. Bauxite is mined only in Arkansas although aluminium is smelted throughout the States wherever ample supplies of power are available — in Washington from the Columbia River scheme, on the Gulf coast from gas-fired electrical stations, in the Tennessee valley, and near the thermal stations in the Appalachians.

Among **other metals** copper is produced largely in the peninsula of Keeweenaw, which juts northeastwards into Lake Superior (Michigan), in the southeast of Arizona, and in Montana. In this last state the copper ore is almost entirely obtained from the small district containing the mining and smelting towns of Butte and Anaconda, where metallic copper of exceptional purity is produced by the electrolytic process, which yields at the same time considerable quantities of silver as well as gold. The chief lead-producing centre of the United States is the Ozark Mountains in Missouri. Lead is also mined in the Rocky Mountains (in Idaho, Utah, and Colorado). Among other important economic minerals of the United States may be mentioned the phosphate rock of Florida and Tennessee. Natural gas occurs in the vicinity of all the major oilfields, 70 per cent coming from Texas and Louisana, and a further 8 per cent from Oklahoma and New Mexico. As early as 1901 there were 35 000 km (21 848 miles) of pipe for the supply of natural gas. By 1969 the figure was 1.38m. km (860 000 miles). In 1980 it will exceed 2.1m. km (1.3m. miles) by which time 30 per cent will be imported. The production of petroleum is considered elsewhere (pp. 267—9).

There is only one metal of importance in which the United States are almost entirely deficient, and that is tin. Hence the large import of tin and tin ores, and formerly of tinplate; the latter being a much-needed commodity in consequence of the traditional employment of 'tins' or 'cans' for American foodstuffs. The heavy import duties on tinplate first imposed in 1890, aided by the increasing facilities for the production of iron, succeeded in establishing a great tinplate industry in the United States. The production of tinplate in the country increased from next to nothing in 1891 to upwards of 399 000 tons in 1901. Meanwhile, the import of this commodity, almost entirely from the United Kingdom, sank from about 325 000 tons to less than 53 000. The import of ore and metal still continues, however, to a total of some 60 000 tons a year (47 per cent from Malaysia and Thailand). Production of 'secondary' tin, that is by recovery processes from scrap, is now a major source running at 20 000 tons a year. Some 36 per cent still goes to tinplating (now in competition with many alternative materials for the manufacture of containers) with an increasing proportion (21 per cent) to solders for the electronic industries.

Manufactures. The United States is the most developed of the industrial nations, with less than 5 per cent of the employed population engaged in agriculture. The noteworthy characteristics of the manufacturing industries are the high cost of labour, the resultant extensive use of mechanisation and a utilisation of power far greater than that of any other nation – no less than one-third of the world's total. In 1971 the United States produced 1.7m. kWh of electrical energy, of which 270 000 kWh were from hydroelectric installations. Coal, oil and gas fired plants produce over 95 per cent of this power and are spread throughout the country. Coal predominates in the east within reach of the Appalachian fields; oil on the Pacific coast and along the pipelines from Texas to the Great Lakes, and gas on the Gulf coast and in the southern plains. The present major hydroelectric sources are on the Columbia River (shared with Canada), in California, in the Tennessee valley (where an Authority has been set up to develop a regional scheme to include flood control, navigation, power generation and industrial development), and at Niagara Falls. Future developments are planned on the Colorado and Columbia Rivers, and in the Appalachians. Nuclear power will become increasingly important.

The major industrial area lies in the north and northeast of the United States, in a rectangular between Boston and Minneapolis, Baltimore and St Louis. This area which, like the nation, has developed steadily westward from the Atlantic coast, has ample communications, power supplies and a pool of skilled labour, and is the site of three-quarters of the industry and two-thirds of the commerce. The smaller manufacturing areas outside this great complex are those on the Pacific Coast (centred around Seattle, San Francisco and Los Angeles) and on the Gulf coast (centred around Houston). These two areas have expanded rapidly with the influx of the newer industries (aero-space, electronics and petrochemicals) since the Second World War, but the self-perpetuating nature of the main industrial area is so great that it still shows a growth rate only slightly less than that of California and Texas. In value of manufactures, California now ranks second to New York State — with a total commercial economy which (were it a separate nation) would place it among the top ten trading nations of the world. Lastly the comparatively isolated major cities throughout the country, such as Salt Lake City, Denver, Kansas City, Atlanta, etc., have each developed their own industrial areas which are mainly consumer orientated (for example foodstuff processing, marketing, etc.). The distribution of the great metropolitan areas of the United States, that is concentrations with over 1m. population in 1970, shows clearly the urban dominance of the main manufacturing regions

Table 87 — USA: population distribution in metropolitan areas (thousands)

Area	1920	1950	1960*	1966	1970
Northern industrial area					
New York, NY	5 600	7 835	10 604	11 400	11 500
Chicago, Ill	2 700	3 606	6 172	6 732	6 979
Philadelphia, Pa	1 800	2 065	4 289	4 690	4 818
Detroit, Mich	1 000	1 839	3 745	4 060	4 200
Boston, Mass	750	791	2 567	3 201	2 754
Washington, DC	440	798	1 969	2 615	2 861
Pittsburgh, Pa	570	674	2 396	2 376	2 401
St Louis, Mo	770	853	2 040	2 284	2 363
Cleveland, Oh	800	906	1 780	2 004	2 064
Baltimore, Md	735	940	1 706	1 980	2 071
Newark, NJ	415	438	1 676	1 862	1 857
Minneapolis–St Paul, Minn	615	826	1 107	1 629	1 814
Cincinnati, Oh	400	501	1 059	1 353	1 385
Milwaukee, Wis	460	633	1 187	1 331	1 404
Buffalo, NY	510	577	1 303	1 323	1 349
Indianapolis, Ind	315	425	690	1 027	1 110
Pacific Coast industrial areas					
Los Angeles/Long Beach, Cal	580	2 202	2 772	6 789	7 032
San Francisco/Oakland, Cal	725	1 007	1 142	2 958	3 109
Seattle, Wash	315	462	1 097	1 214	1 422
San Diego, Cal	75	321	913	1 168	1 358
Santa Ana/Anaheim, Cal	–	60	204	1 164	1 420
San Bernadino, Cal	–	63	378	1 040	1 143
Gulf Coast industrial areas					
Houston, Texas	138	594	1 235	1 740	1 985
Dallas, Texas	160	434	1 074	1 352	1 556
New Orleans, Lou	390	567	860	1 044	1 046
Other cities with over 1m.					
Atlanta, Ga	200	327	1 014	1 258	1 390
Kansas City, Mo	325	453	1 027	1 209	1 254
Denver, Col	260	413	923	1 083	1 228
Miami, Fla	75	247	918	1 081	1 268

* In 1960 the 'Outer City' areas are included for the first time, i.e. the population for the total metropolitan area is shown.

mentioned above, and the meteoric development of the Pacific coast areas (Table 87).

The continuing growth of all these great cities emphasises the outstanding characteristic of the present trend in the industrial United States, that is that 90 per cent of the population growth over the last twenty years has taken place in the urban areas. The number of 'million' cities has increased sevenfold since 1920 and, where located in reasonable proximity, their areas of influence are now interacting to form even greater urban conglomerations (megalopolis). For example, there is the region stretching from Boston through New York and Philadelphia to Baltimore; the region along the shores of Lake Michigan from Milwaukee through Chicago/Gary to Michigan City; the region on the Pacific Coast from Santa Barbara through Los Angeles to San Diego. In all of these areas the old climatic, geological and physical regions tend to be completely dominated by the all-pervasive influence of urbanised industrialisation.

The standard of living of this predominantly urban population is the highest in the world and it presents an enormous home market which is reflected in the comparative importance of the major manufacturing industries. Communications of all types, food, mechanisation and clothing are the essentials for mid-twentieth century urban man living in densely packed cities. These industries, 90 per cent of whose products are consumed within the United States, in turn dictate (as will be seen later) the 10 per cent which is available for overseas trade. It is the measure of the great industrial wealth of this country that this 10 per cent alone suffices to dominate world trade. (In 1971 the United States combined imports and exports totalled $90 000m., West Germany was second with $73 000m. and the United Kingdom third with $45 700m.). The leading industries in the United States between 1954 and 1966, based on dollar value added by manufacture, are shown on p. 795.

Of the major manufacturing cities, **New York** is of paramount importance. With a population of 7.8m. in 1970, estimated as 13m. in the metropolitan area in 1972, this is the commercial capital of the United States. A Dutch settlement in 1623, the city still has its original advantages of a deep natural harbour and a routeway to the interior through the Hudson—Mohawk gap to Montréal and to Buffalo on Lake Erie. A natural focal point for the early colonies, it grew rapidly in the nineteenth century and now handles over 40 per cent of the total overseas trade (New Orleans comes second with 7 per cent). Airports and an extensive highway system of tunnels, bridges and expressways have been developed to serve the city and its associated industries which cover a wide range. The labour force comprises a mixture of highly skilled and cheap immigrant workers, with clothing as the major industry, followed by luxury goods (furs, jewellery, cosmetics), printing

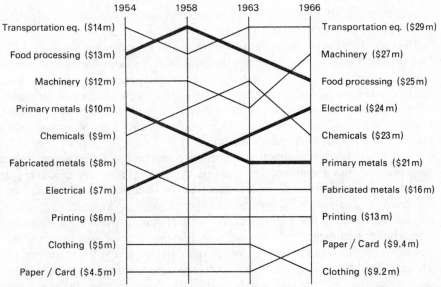

1954	1958	1963	1966

Transportation eq. ($14m) — Transportation eq. ($29m)
Food processing ($13m) — Machinery ($27m)
Machinery ($12m) — Food processing ($25m)
Primary metals ($10m) — Electrical ($24m)
Chemicals ($9m) — Chemicals ($23m)
Fabricated metals ($8m) — Primary metals ($21m)
Electrical ($7m) — Fabricated metals ($16m)
Printing ($6m) — Printing ($13m)
Clothing ($5m) — Paper / Card ($9.4m)
Paper / Card ($4.5m) — Clothing ($9.2m)

Graph of the leading industries of the United States, based on dollar value added by manufacture

and publishing, and food products. Above all it is the financial centre of the nation, and epitomises the congestion, the urban pollution and the self-regenerating nature of a great modern metropolis.

Chicago with a population approaching 7m. is the largest inland city and a clearing house between the interior and the Atlantic seaboard. Water, rail, road and air networks make Chicago a focal point for communications and this in turn makes the city a major service centre. Markets for cattle, hogs and cereals spread their influence as far as Denver and Cincinnati, and while the products of the west move to the east through Chicago so the industry of the east has moved west to Chicago. The demand for heavy engineering to build the railways, the bridges, the river boats and the agriculture machinery, which opened up the continent — all these supported the development of a major manufacturing centre, confirmed by the opening of the United States Steel Corporation steelworks at Gary in 1907, with coal coming by rail from the Appalachian fields and iron ore and limestone via the Great Lakes.

Philadelphia, with a population of some 5m. is the fourth largest city and has developed as the centre of the 'Ruhr of America' on a site carefully chosen by the original settlers as midway between Boston and Richmond. Although 160 km (100 miles) from the sea, the Delaware River provides ample facilities for handling bulk cargoes. Industrial development is based on local coal and imported materials with large steel and chemical works; oil and sugar refineries. The old colonial industries based on wool, butter and paper are still continued, much modified by the use of synthetic replacements. The area produces machinery of all kinds, rolling stock and automobiles and, as with all major urban areas, there is an extensive food processing industry.

Detroit developed on a natural harbour and routeway between Lake St Clair and Lake Erie. An early trading post, it later became a centre for the construction of river boats, wagons and steam engines and these skills are reflected today in the great automobile industry of the area, which in turn has attracted steel works and a wide range of subsidiary manufactures. There are also heavy chemicals and pharmaceutical products based on local mineral sources.

In the spectacular postwar development of the Pacific coast area, **Los Angeles** and **San Francisco** have taken the lead. The early discovery of oil in California (it still ranks third in production after Texas and Louisiana), the ample potential for hydroelectric power in the valleys of the rivers from the high plateaus, and efficient internal communications have combined to provide suitable conditions for the modern, 'footloose', industries which were decentralised to the area in the Second World War — aeroplanes, electronics, instruments, etc. The ideal climate attracted the pioneering aircraft constructors in the years between the wars, and it now attracts a steady flow of immigrants from the rest of the States and from overseas. In turn, the dynamic growth of the region has fostered a demand for food services and recreation and this expansion augments itself with yet further demands for irrigation facilities, financial and commercial businesses, and yet more power (both oil and gas are now imported into California). The isolation of the region has generated a wide range of minor industries producing goods locally that otherwise must travel from the industrial eastern regions. Heavy industries are also included, such as the iron and steel works set up at the end of the nineteenth century to supply agricultural machinery (elevators, flour mills), the oil industry (derricks, pipelines, pumps), shipyards and food processing plants. The iron and coal must travel a great distance (the coal, 1 290 km: over 800 miles, from Utah) to an industry located solely on the grounds of proximity to market; and with such expensive raw materials, great use is made of the major local resource of scrap from the urban areas.

Washington, like Canberra and Brasilia, is one of the few cities on a site deliberately planned to house a capital. It is the administrative and cultural capital, with few industries beyond printing/publishing, food preparation and tourism. **Minneapolis—St Paul** is the metropolitan centre for the wheat belt, with extensive flour-milling, lumber-mills and meat-packing industries. **Cincinnati** was, similarly, the centre for the corn belt, with hog-slaughtering and packing plants. It also has flour and beer industries, although the main centre for these has moved further west to Minneapolis, St Louis and Milwaukee. Animal and vegetable fats from the corn belt support major industry (soap, etc.) and steels from Pittsburgh are used for machinery and tool manufacture. **Houston,** likely to become the metropolis of the south, has grown as quickly as the great cities of the Pacific coast. It shares with them the advantages of a pleasant climate, an early oil boom, the impetus of the industrial decentralisation programme of the war, and rapidly expanding modern industries such as petrochemicals and space travel. With its outport of Galveston, to which it is joined by a ship canal, it is now the third busiest port in the United States (after New York, New Orleans; and ahead of San Francisco, Philadelphia, Boston, Seattle and Los Angeles). **Miami** joins the 'million' cities as a retirement, convention and tourist centre. As the standard of living has increased, Florida and California have become equally attractive for these purposes; but 'Winter in Florida' for the populous north and east, and the lack of competing industry, makes Miami the outstanding example of growth of a purely resort city both for its own attractions and as a jumping-off place for the Caribbean, South America and West Africa.

Any account of American industry based on the exploitation of minerals and the use of power ignores what is probably the greatest of all industries – the *tourist industry*. However remote they may be, the great National and State parks of special scenic beauty and interest are visited by tens of thousands annually, and it is the private automobile, as much as the freight truck, which necessitates ever-increasing road development.

Recent decades have been marked by three major changes in American manufacturing industry. The first is the shift westwards and the relative decline of New England coupled with the upsurge of the West Coast centres of Los Angeles, San Francisco and Seattle, together with the great cities of Texas. The second is the diversification of industry. Machinery, electrical apparatus, cars and aeroplanes represent almost a third of the total industrial output whereas textiles, with an emphasis on manmade fibres, and clothing have dropped, relatively, to 10 per cent. The third is the enormous increase in the export of manufactured goods (see Table 89, p. 800) and its worldwide distribution coincident with the emergence of the US as the major world power.

Foreign trade. The changing pattern of the foreign trade of the United States will be most conveniently studied in detail with reference to Tables 88 and 89. In examining these tables two considerations must be borne in mind. In the first place the foreign commerce of the country is affected from time to time by customs tariffs raised to protect home industries – a major consideration in a country whose home market consumes almost all of the total production. Secondly, it must not be inferred that because certain products are imported into the United States they could not be home-produced. The high cost of labour in the country excludes or limits the production of certain commodities, such as sugar (to some extent), tea, and raw silk, for which the climate of the United States in some part of their territory is in no way unsuited. But so great is the demand of the home market that many of the major resources must be supplemented by imports (e.g. timber, newsprint, oil, gas and certain minerals).

A study of the exports suggests that the United States remained on the whole pre-eminently an agricultural country until the First World War, and this is still largely true in that foodstuffs remain a major export, notwithstanding the immense increase in recent years in the manufacturing and mining industries. A comparison of the period 1881–85, the first after the Civil War in which figures could be obtained fairly comparable with those of other countries, with the four years 1910–14 shows that the exports of machinery, iron and steel wares, leather and cottons increased from an aggregate of 5.6 per cent of the total value of exports to 21.6 per cent. By 1926–30 manufactures had increased to 54.9 per cent, and by 1962 to 69 per cent. But the years of the Second World War (1939–45) and after emphasised that a hungry world still needed food that the United States could easily provide by a more intensive use of land. In the 1960s the United States led the world in the production of maize, beef cattle, pork and cheese; and was second only to the USSR in production of wheat, wheat flour, butter and timber. The acreage under wheat expanded rapidly between the wars and now is not far short of that of maize. In 1969 there were 23m. ha (57m. acres) under wheat as against 26m. ha (65m. acres) under maize, although the figures change yearly as world prices and government subsidies dictate. The much smaller export of maize than of wheat is due to the fact that the bulk of the former crop is employed in the feeding of swine and other animals, so that the production and export of bacon, hams, lard, cattle and beef, as well as maize, may all be regarded as representing this branch of American agriculture. The development of 'hybrid corn' in the 1930s and 1940s led to a spectacular increase in yield.

The smaller timber export takes place mainly from the Pacific states of Washington and Oregon. In the other forested areas cut now exceeds growth and large timber, although it is a renewable resource, is practically exhausted. As a result the world's largest producer is a net importer.

Cattle are most numerous in the United States east of the meridian of 100° W, especially in the states occupying the northern part of the basin of the Mississippi. With 110m. head the herd is second in the world, after India with 170m. Dairy-farming is carried on in New England and south of the Great Lakes, notably in Wisconsin; pig-rearing in the maize belt south and west of Chicago. Sheep are most numerous in the drier climate of the western states, but the total number of sheep is limited; sheep, moreover, are now being reared more for meat than

Table 88 — United States: imports fob

	Percentages of total value					
	1926–30	1931–35	1936–40	1950	1963	1967
Foodstuffs	20.8	19.0	12.7	29.0	21.8	14.4
Coffee	7.0	8.4	–	12.0	5.6	3.5
Cane sugar	5.1	6.8	–	4.2	3.6†	2.3†
Nuts and fruit	2.1	2.9	1.1	1.9	2.0	2.1
Raw materials	34.1	18.6	15.4	27.0	19.2	13.9
Silk (raw)	9.2	6.9	2.1	0.2	0.2	–
Rubber (crude)	7.1	3.6	3.9	5.0	1.1	0.7
Wood pulp	2.2	3.5	1.5	2.6	2.0	1.1
Tin	2.2	2.5	1.6	2.2	1.0	0.6
Hides and skins (raw)	2.9	2.1	1.0	1.3	0.4	0.3
Furs, and manufactures of	2.8	2.0	1.3	1.2	0.6	0.3
Woods, and manufrs. of	2.4	1.9	0.8	4.0	3.3	2.6
Copper (unmanufactured)	2.7	1.7	0.9	2.7	0.5	2.5
Petroleum	3.3	1.7	0.9	6.5	10.4	7.9
Manufactures	37.8	27.0	18.5	39.8	53.7	69.8
Printing paper	3.4	5.1	2.2	5.2	4.5	3.3
Gold, and silver, specie and unmanufactured	7.3	35.2	52.5	3.0	5.3	0.5
Total value in 1 000 million $*	4.3	2.6	5.2	9.1	17.0	26.8
Countries ‡						
Canada	11.7	11.3	14.5	22.1	22.3	27.0
Japan	9.4	8.7	6.6	2.1	8.8	11.4
United Kingdom	8.0	6.9	6.7	3.8	6.3	6.5
Brazil	4.9	5.5	4.3	8.1	3.3	2.1
Philippines	2.9	5.3	4.1	2.7	2.1	1.4
Germany	5.3	5.0	2.4	1.2	5.9	7.4
Malaya	6.1	4.7	7.6	3.5	0.5	0.7
Cuba	5.1	4.5	4.8	4.6	–	–
France	3.8	3.4	2.4	1.5	2.5	2.6
Mexico	3.1	2.3	2.3	3.6	3.5	2.9

* Par rate of exchange (1924–49) £1 = $4.866; (1949–67) = $2.80; from 1967 = $2.40.
† Including beet sugar and sugar preparations.
‡ In addition to the countries listed, imports from Venezuela, were 5.5 per cent in 1963 and 3.9 per cent in 1967.

for wool, and the flock of 22m. is tenth in the world.

Among the agricultural deficiencies of the United States which the import table reveals, attention may be drawn to two, sugar and coffee. Until the 1920s sugar had held the first place among the imports of the United States for over a century. There is now a very large home production, especially in Louisiana, of cane sugar, and beet sugar in various states such as Colorado and Michigan. Except for negligible production in Hawaii, coffee is not grown in the United States. As the Americans are essentially coffee drinkers and not tea drinkers, coffee has always been a leading import.

Fruits typical of the cooler temperate climates flourish in the United

Table 89 — United States: exports fob

	Percentages of total value					
	1926–30	*1931–35*	*1936–40*	*1950*	*1963*	*1967*
Foodstuffs	*14.9*	*10.6*	*9.1*	*12.6*	*15.4*	*12.7*
Fruits and nuts	2.6	4.3	2.3	0.9	1.2	1.1
Wheat and flour	4.9	2.0	1.7	4.5	5.7	3.5
Lard and substitutes	2.1	1.6	0.6	1.1	0.3	1.1
Raw materials, etc.	*22.5*	*25.2*	*18.6*	*17.4*	*11.3*	*10.3*
Cotton (raw)	16.2	19.0	8.7	9.5	2.5	1.5
Petroleum (refined)	10.0	9.0	10.6	4.6	1.9	1.7
Tobacco (raw)	3.1	5.2	3.4	2.3	1.7	1.9
Wood, and manufrs. of	3.2	2.8	1.9	0.7	0.7	1.4
Coal	2.5	2.4	2.1	2.6	2.0	1.5
Copper	3.0	1.7	2.7	0.8	1.1	1.0
Manufactures	*54.9*	*47.6*	*69.9*	*63.7*	*69.2*	*73.6*
Iron and steel	5.1	4.4	8.3	4.4	5.4	1.7
Cars and parts	8.5	7.1	8.4	6.7	5.8	7.9
Electric machinery and apparatus	2.2	3.1	3.3	4.0	4.8	6.6
Agricultural machinery and apparatus	2.4	1.2	2.1	1.0	2.6	1.4
Other machinery and apparatus	6.1	6.0	14.3	18.1	15.1	16.9
Cotton goods	2.6	2.3	1.9	2.4	0.8	2.2
Gold and silver, specie and unmanufactured	*5.9*	*15.0*	*0.8*	*5.0*	*4.1*	*3.4*
Total value in 1 000 million $*	*5.1*	*2.4*	*3.2*	*10.8*	*23.2*	*31.5*
Countries ‡						
United Kingdom	17.6	18.5	18.7	5.0	5.0	6.2
Canada	17.1	14.5	15.9	19.4	17.7	22.6
Japan	5.1	8.4	7.4	4.1	7.3	8.5
Germany	8.3	6.5	2.4	4.3	4.8	5.4
France	5.2	5.9	5.4	3.2	2.9	3.2
Italy	3.0	3.0	1.9	3.3	3.8	3.1
Netherlands	2.8	2.6	2.3	2.2	3.3	3.9
Belgium	2.2	2.5	2.0	2.6	2.3†	3.5†
Mexico	2.6	2.4	2.7	5.0	3.6	3.8
Cuba	2.8	2.0	2.5	4.4	—	—

* See rate * on Table 88.
† Belgium—Luxembourg.
‡ In addition to the countries listed, 2.8 per cent went to Australia in 1967.

States and are produced in sufficient abundance to leave a surplus for export, as also do the Mediterranean fruits of California and Florida. It is indeed characteristic of development in the United States that, one by one, commodities previously imported have been replaced by home production. Where home production has not proved possible substitutes have been developed, e.g. artificial rubber for natural rubber, rayon for silk, and so on. On the other hand bananas can be grown only in Hawaii and are therefore still imported in large quantities from Central and South America and the West Indies.

The bulk of the overseas trade of the United States is carried by the ships of other nations, and shipbuilding is not among the major industries. This is largely the result of high rates of pay for American crews, and even government assistance with shipbuilding incentives and regulations limiting the use of foreign lines (such as the requirements that all movement between United States ports, all exports of foreign aid and military cargoes must move in American vessels) have not greatly improved the importance of the merchant fleet. The percentage of the imports and exports of the United States carried in vessels registered in the country amounted in 1860, to 66.5; in 1870 to 35.6; in 1880 to 17.4; in 1900 to 9.3. In consequence of the expansion of shipbuilding during the First World War, the percentage rose in 1918, to 21.9. These figures have since dropped steadily to 6.4 per cent in 1968. The total amount of shipping engaged in foreign trade flying the American flag in 1914 was less than 1.6m. dwt* tons; in 1919, 8m.; in 1930, 9.14m. There was again a big rise during the Second World War. In 1951 the United States merchant marine, including ships of the reserve fleet, numbered 4 909 ships of 41m. dwt tons — nearly a third of the world total. Subsequently there has again been a decline. By 1961 over 1 900 government-owned ships were in the reserve fleets. In 1970 the fleet was down to 2 983 ships (27.7m. dwt tons), of which some 1 000 ships (9m. tons) were in reserve. The fleet is the fifth largest in the world — after Liberia, Japan, the United Kingdom and Norway — although American companies own a further 18m. tons sailing under foreign flags.

Outlying territories. In addition to the outlying territories of Alaska and the Hawaiian Archipelago, both of which became states of the Union in 1959, the United States possesses Puerto Rico, the Panama Canal zone, some of the Virgin Islands, and the small Pacific Islands of Guam and Tutuila, the latter in the Samoan group. Puerto Rico† was acquired from Spain after the Spanish—American War in 1898, and in the same year the Hawaiian Archipelago was acquired. The greater number of the Virgin Islands were purchased from Denmark in 1917.

Mexico

South of the United States is Latin America, containing twenty countries in which the dominant influence is Spanish, Portuguese, or that of some other European people, but in which the masses of the people except in the temperate south of South America are partially or wholly American Indian in blood.

* For conversion to gross tons see p. 92.
† Technically described as a 'Commonwealth associated with the United States'.

The first of these is Mexico, a land more than eight times as large as Great Britain, nearly three times the area of Texas, tapering southwards from the boundary of the United States into the tropics, and then expanding again where it embraces the peninsula of Yucatan. It is nearly 3 200 km (2 000 miles) from north to south, its frontier with the United States extends for over 2 400 km (1 500 miles), and there are 9 660 km (6 000 miles) of coastline, 7 200 km (4 480 miles) of which face the Pacific.

The population of 50.7m. (1970) is about 10 per cent of European origin and 30 per cent of pure Indian origin, the balance of 60 per cent being mestizo (mixed Indian and European). Of the total area of 1.96m. sq km (760 000 sq miles) it is estimated that 40 per cent is covered by pastures, against 12 per cent by arable land, with forests accounting for 22 per cent, potentially useful land for 4 per cent, and waste land for 22 per cent. Landed property developed in Spanish colonial days under a system of large feudal estates, *haciendas*, and many of these still survive; but more common today are the *ejidos* (communal farms or villages) for which 25m. ha (65m. acres) of land had been expropriated up to 1945 and distributed among more than 2m. families. Rather less than half the land workers are settled on these *ejidos*.

The several regions of which the country is made up are for the most part separated by mountain barriers and it is mainly the pre-eminent importance of one of the regions, the Central Plateau, which has caused the whole to form one political unit for hundreds of years, a unit physically separated from the United States by an area of desert or semidesert, in the eastern part of which the Rio Grande forms a convenient line of demarcation.

The Central Plateau, the favoured highland area about Mexico City, though only about one-sixth of the area of Mexico, contains more than half the population, and by far the larger proportion of the white population, mainly Spanish, many of them the descendants of those who, under Cortez, here overthrew the old Aztec Empire in 1519–21. It lies at the height of about 2 100 m (7 000 ft) above sea level, is bordered east and west by rugged mountains, and is made up of a number of basins separated by mountains of volcanic origin, including some cones towering to heights of eternal snow, and containing a few surviving lakes, notably in the great valley of Mexico. Although in the tropics, these basins enjoy a climate more truly temperate than that of most of the temperate zone. There is no hot summer or cold winter, but an average temperature of between 13° and 18° C (55° and 65° F), for every season of the year. Days are warm and nights cool; the sun is hot at midday, and occasionally there are frosty nights. The rainfall, on the average about 760 mm (30 in) per annum, occurring mostly between April and October, is sufficient for agriculture, though crops

uffer in dry seasons. Irrigation is practised where streams fed by the
heavier rains and melting snows of the encircling mountains reach the
basins.

Maize, the principal crop and staple food, occupies as much land as
all other crops together, a greater proportion of the crop land than in
any other large country. Other crops conspicuous in the central region
are wheat and barley, beans and potatoes, and — as fodder for cattle —
alfalfa (lucerne). Much of the pasture land is on the less fertile lower
slopes of the mountains, where the soil is apt to be dry, and on these
slopes also are grown the agaves, the most distinctive crop of the
Central Plateau, drought-resisting plants native to Mexico, with long,
sharp, fleshy leaves, of which the century plant is an example. Most of
these are raised for their sap, which is used in the making of *pulque*, a
favourite fermented beverage. A distilled beverage, *mescal*, is also made
from the root. Part of the crop is used to yield the long, strong maguey
fibre to make woven mats and other articles.

Mineral wealth, too, associated partly with the volcanic rocks, has
long been important in central Mexico. The silver and gold mines of the
Aztecs were the chief attraction for the Spanish conquerors, and
Mexico was for long the world's major producer of silver — 1 332 tons
in 1970 — the third largest producer.

Manufactures date back to the bygone civilisation, but the old
industries, the making of pottery, textiles, and other articles, have
somewhat declined since the rise of factories over 90 per cent of which
are financed by foreign capital. Cotton factories using raw material
from northern Mexico are important, as are iron and steel works, oil
refining and, increasingly petrochemicals. Tobacco factories, flour-mills,
breweries, plants for the extraction of vegetable oils, and other
establishments supplying the domestic market and having the additional
advantage of more or less raw material produced locally, are also to be
noted. Wartime conditions so stimulated industrial production that by
1947 the output of the leading industries had increased nearly fourfold
over that for 1940 and the expansion of the oil and gas industry has
continued the development since then.

Each basin of the Central Plateau has an important town as its
centre, and the most important, the city of Mexico, is the centre of the
richest of all the basins, the Valley of Mexico. With a census population
in 1970 of 7m. (and a further 1.2m. in the Valley of Mexico), this city
is not only the political capital but also the financial, commercial,
industrial, and cultural centre of the country.

The Northern Plateau is a continuation of the Central Plateau, with
similar landforms and without any marked physical breach, but
distinguished by its smaller rainfall and a consequent difference in
vegetation and distribution of the population. Without irrigation, crop
cultivation is impossible, and cattle-rearing on large ranches is the

prevailing economic feature. In the basins, dry bush and grassland furnish the fodder, especially from June to October, when the rainfall is somewhat more plentiful. Here fibre is obtained from several wild plants, chiefly two kinds of ixtle, and this region is also the source of guayule (a type of rubber). The basin known as la Laguna, at the intersection of the International and Central railways, is irrigated by the control of the floodwaters of the Rio Nazas, and in it is grown the major part of the Mexican cotton crop.

Mines are important in the Northern Plateau. The cities are mainly centres of mining areas producing, in addition to silver and gold, copper, lead, zinc, iron, and coal. These latter industries are modern, the copper production in particular being an extension of the Arizona industry into Mexico.

The state of Sonora, in the northwest of the country, slopes down to lower altitudes, and is, in the main, desert, especially where it approaches the frontier. Further south, where higher mountains promote greater rainfall, more streams descend to allow of irrigation settlements. A railway running parallel to the east shore of the Gulf of California into the United States, and several small ports along the coast, furnish outlets for the mines on the mountain slopes as well as for the irrigation settlements. Across the Gulf of California, the narrow, mountainous peninsula of Baja California (Lower California) is also desert for the most part, though there are a few patches of irrigated land. There are a few mines, notably a large copper mine on the east coast, and a little fishing.

The sierras bordering the plateaus east and west present some marked contrasts. The Sierra Madre Occidental, being on the lee side with reference to the prevailing rain-bearing winds, the trade winds, has a scantier rainfall than the eastern range, though enough to maintain green pastures below and pine forests above. Its chief wealth is in its mines. It forms a marked barrier, an unbroken wall in which the valleys are mostly narrow gorges without utility as passes.

The Sierra Madre Oriental is less high and continuous, and has several lines of valleys through which run railways to the Gulf ports. The most important of these is the series followed by the railway from Mexico City to Veracruz. The way is steep, but the valleys are flat-floored and productive, the products changing in the descent from grain to coffee and tobacco, and still lower to sugarcane, bananas, and tropical forests. On the middle slopes of the depression leading down to Veracruz the temperature is always pleasantly warm, and the rainfall in many places averages 2 540 mm (100 in) or more in a year. Here, also, manufactures are carried on. Orizaba is the centre of textile factories in Mexico.

At the foot of the Eastern Sierra is a coastal lowland, *tierra caliente*, a hot country. Most of it is unimportant at present, but in it are three places or districts of outstanding importance: the port of Veracruz with nearby refineries and petrochemical works; the petroleum fields near Tampico; and the sisal district of Yucatan.

Petroleum has been found in many parts of Mexico, but nearly all the production has been in the state of Veracruz, west and south of Tampico. Most of the petroleum is heavy and has an asphaltic base. The product of the oilfields on the northern coast of the Isthmus of Tehuantepec, the narrow waist of Mexico, is light and has a paraffin base, but the amount is small compared with the total production. The wells of the Veracruz districts in general are not exceptionally deep and include some of the largest and most sustained gushers known, but the production of the whole has dropped greatly since 1921 — from the peak of 28m. tons (25 per cent of the world's supply) in that year to 10m. tons in 1950. By 1970 production was up to 25m. tons. The industry developed in foreign hands, mainly American and British, but in 1938 the oilfields were expropriated by the state. Most of the oil is refined within the country and Mexico is again a net exporter of petroleum and petroleum products. Tampico, the chief town and port of the oilfields, has been improved so as to allow modern tankers and freighters to berth along the waterfront. A coastal lagoon with connecting canals provides a sheltered shallow waterway 137 km (85 miles) southwards to Tuxpam, another oil port, where a submarine pipeline conveys oil to tankers lying offshore.

The other important lowland area is in the northern part of the Yucatan Peninsula. The rainfall here is scanty and the dryness is accentuated by surface conditions. The soil is underlain by a highly soluble limestone, in which sink holes are numerous, and there is no surface drainage. Maize and other supply crops can be raised, and in prehistoric times the Maya Indian civilisation flourished here. Modern commerce and foreign capital have brought a new prosperity to the district. Nowhere else in the western world can sisal be grown under conditions at once so favourable to production and so accessible to the United States market. Henequen, as the fibre is here called, is grown on nearly 200 000 ha (500 000 acres) yielding a crop of over 147 000 tons, much of which is made locally into rope and twine. Railways radiating from the inland centre of Merida, supplemented by tramways running through the large plantations, convey the product to the north Yucatan port of Progreso, where a pier 2 km (1¼ miles) long, ending in a large wharf, provides berthing for vessels of moderate draught. The southern part of the peninsula is the chief source of chicle, the basis of American chewing-gum, obtained from tapping the zapote tree (*Achras Sapote*, Linn.).

The narrow lowlands on the Pacific coast east and west of the Isthmus of Tehuantepec are similar to those on the Atlantic side, moist in some places, and dry in others, wooded, slightly developed. The isthmus itself is a low, hilly area.

Southern Mexico has, for the most part, a population out of the reach of railways. More people live in the highlands than in the low-lands. The Sierra Madre del Sur is a highland region separated from the Central Plateau by the great gorge of the Rio Balsas. Round the head of the Balsas valley a ridge allows of a railway from the plateau entering the sierra, but the region is so dissected that communities within it, mostly of Indians, are isolated from each other and contribute little or nothing to world trade. Indian languages and ways of living still persist.

The highlands of Chiapas, running into Guatemala, are less dissected. There is a rather dry highland valley in which grain crops are raised and cattle and sheep pastured, and there are moist slopes below on which coffee is grown for export. The people are largely Indian and primitive in their mode of life. There is more trade with Guatemala than with other parts of Mexico, and the region forms the northernmost of the Central American highlands.

Production and trade. Table 90 gives the principal crop returns for Mexico in 1950, 1956, 1967 and 1971.

Table 90 — Mexico: crop returns (in metric tons)

Crop	1950	1956	1967	1971
Maize	3 122 000	4 515 000	9 490 000	9 500 000
Wheat	587 000	1 100 000	1 890 000	1 900 000
Barley	162 000	197 000	233 000	230 000
Dry beans	250 000	459 000	1 040 000	1 100 000
Cotton (ginned)	259 000	403 000	514 000	364 000
Sugar (raw)	705 000	1 079 000	1 980 000	2 555 000
Coffee	66 000	102 000	171 000	192 000
Rice (paddy)	187 000	235 000	454 000	383 000
Bananas	257 000	207 000	551 000	1 136 000

Methods of cultivation are often crude, and though the crop of maize is so big the yield averages only about 1 100 kg per ha (1 000 lb per acre) less than a third of what it is in the United States. The future of Mexico's agricultural development lies largely in the extension of irrigation works, increased use of fertilisers, and of new strains of seeds. Maize and wheat are now available for export and other cash crops figure largely in the foreign trade. About half the production of ginned cotton is exported; and in 1955 cotton provided for over one-quarter of the value of all exports although by 1970 the proportion had fallen to less than 15 per cent. In recent years there has been also a substantial surplus of sugar for export. Production has risen rapidly from 700 000 tons in 1950, to 1.5m. tons in 1960 and 2.2m. tons in 1970. The target 'or 1980 is an annual 4m. tons to make Mexico the fourth largest producer in the world. In 1970 sugar surpassed cotton for the first time as the main export. Among other export crops are coffee, bananas, tomatoes and citrus fruits. The importance of henequen (sisal) in Yucatan has been noted in the regional survey.

Livestock run to big numbers: 38m. cattle, 6.8m. sheep, 13.2m. goats, 10.8m. horses, mules and donkeys, 14.5m. pigs and 95m. poultry. They tend to be concentrated in the central states, and the livestock industry could well be expanded, possibly at the expense of some of the less productive land; but a discouraging factor has been widespread foot and mouth disease.

Mexico has long been the world's major producer of silver, a position now shared with Canada and Peru. Annual production is some 1 200 tons. Mining is the main industry, although 97 per cent of the mines are foreign-owned. The annual recoverable quantity of lead from ore is some 180 000 tons (fourth in the list of world supplies); and of copper 60 000 tons. Much of the lead and zinc are refined locally before being exported. There are large reserves of good coking coal and iron ore. Steel production, centred on Monterrey, was 3.4m. tons in 1969, and pig iron 2m. tons. There are ample supplies of natural gas which is exported to the USA.

The great preponderance of the trade is with the United States. The unit of currency is the peso of 100 centavos, with an exchange rate (1971) of 30 pesos to the £. In 1963, when imports amounted to 15 496m. pesos the United States' share was just on 80 per cent, while Germany, which came second on the list, supplied under 5 per cent. Exports were valued at 11 636m. pesos, with the United States taking nearly 75 per cent and Japan, the next best customer, taking under 6 per cent. In 1969 imports were valued at 25 974m. pesos and exports at 17 875m., and trading partners were unchanged except that the United States' share as a market for exports had fallen to 57 per cent and Japan took a little over 6 per cent. The United States provided 62 per cent of imports, West Germany 7.5 per cent, Japan only 4 per cent. Imports are mainly transport equipment, machinery and other manufactured goods; exports are foodstuffs (sugar, fruit and fish), cotton and minerals.

Besides the ports already mentioned, Coatzacoalcos (Puerto Mexico), the Atlantic terminus of the Tehuantepec Railway, and Salina Cruz, the Pacific terminus, handle a good deal of traffic, though inevitably much less than before the opening of the Panama Canal. The Pacific coast generally has better harbours than the Atlantic, but suffers from the lack of tributary areas with convenient means of communication. Acapulco, at the foot of the Sierra Madre del Sur, has the best natural Mexican harbour, but insignificant commerce. Even Manzanillo, the only Pacific port having direct rail connection with the Central Plateau, draws very little except local trade. Mazatlán, formerly the chief port of the Pacific coast, has lost most of its seaborne trade, being no longer a regular port of call for any shipping line, and visited by tramp steamers only when cargo is offered. Excellent air and road communications have greatly increased the tourist trade with the United States since the Second World War. Tourism is now the second largest source of foreign exchange, with a gross revenue of $520m. in 1960, rising to $1 209m. in 1969 (2m. tourists). In addition some 53m. visit the northern border towns each year.

Table 91 — Mexico: population of principal towns (1970)

Mexico City conurbation	8 206 000	León	324 000
Mexico City	3 418 000	Tijuana	323 000
Guadalajara	1 264 000	Torreón	235 000
Monterrey	955 000	Chihuahua	234 000
Ciudad Juarez	484 000	Mérida	197 000
Puebla	372 000	Veracruz	193 000

Bermuda

Bermuda is a British colony consisting of a group of some 300 coral islands (twenty or so being inhabited) lying in the warm Gulf Stream. The islands are far to the north of the West Indies (of which they are not strictly a part) 917 km (570 miles) off Cape Hatteras, NC and 1 110 km (690 miles) from New York. The main island, seat of the capital Hamilton (3 000), is 20 km long and some 1.5 km wide (14 miles by 1 mile). With a total area of 53.3 sq km (20.59 sq miles) and a population in 1971 of 56 000, the islands have an agreeable climate and tourism is important. The 300 ha (740 acres) under cultivation produce tropical and temperate fruits and vegetables (potatoes, citrus fruits, bananas, etc.). Pharmaceuticals and concentrated essences are also produced and exported.

With tourism as the major industry, imports include foodstuffs, electrical equipment, clothing and construction material from the United States, the United Kingdom, Canada and the Netherlands West Indies. Exports which did not exceed £1m. until 1969, are mainly concentrated essences and early flowers to the UK, the USA, and Canada. In 1969 imports were valued at £35.6m. and exports at £1.1m., the imbalance of visible trade being more than compensated for by invisible exports, to which tourism contributed £27.5m. Other invisible exports are income from the free port facilities and from the personnel at the naval and air base leased to the United States — the latter being also the main airport (Kindley Field).

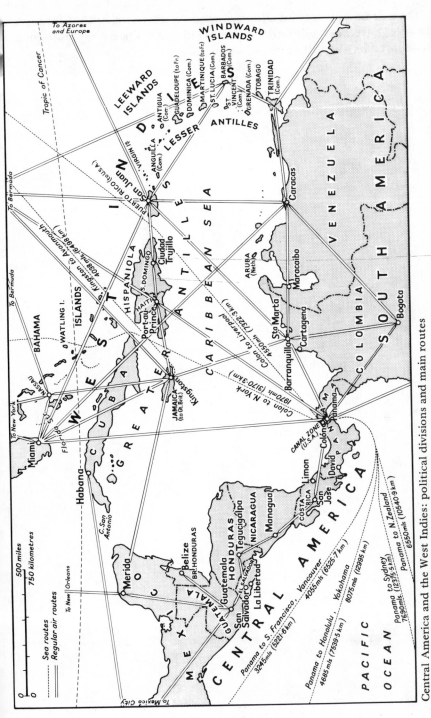

Central America and the West Indies: political divisions and main routes

Only the main shipping and air routes are shown. Notice the sea routes between the islands, the convergence of shipping routes on the Panama Canal, and how the principal towns are linked by air. (Com) indicates membership of the Commonwealth

There is no railway and a limited road system; cars, except for service vehicles, have been allowed on the islands only since 1946. Bermuda is well served by the international airlines.

The West Indies

These islands form an archipelago over 2 570 km (1 600 miles) long, curving southeastwards from near the coast of Florida to the shores of Venezuela. Enclosing the Caribbean Sea, they lie across the trade routes to the Gulf of Mexico and the Panama Canal. Together they have an area slightly larger than that of Great Britain and support a population of nearly 23m.

The four largest islands — Cuba, Hispaniola, Jamaica, and Puerto Rico — form the Greater Antilles and lie in the west of the group; they account for nine-tenths of the total area and only a slightly smaller fraction of the population. The very numerous small islands to the east and south form the Lesser Antilles, while to the north are the Bahamas, a group which is not properly within the West Indies but may conveniently be considered here.

The Bahamas are coral islands, as are some of the outer islands (Anguilla, Barbuda, Antigua, and Barbados) of the Lesser Antilles. All the other islands are part of the young fold mountains of the Americas and are mountainous. The Lesser Antilles are, in most cases, the peaks of these mountains; many of them are of volcanic origin.

The population is almost entirely descended from natives of other continents, the aboriginal Caribs (themselves the descendants of Mongolian migrants) having been almost exterminated within a short period of the discovery of the islands by Columbus. A large proportion of the inhabitants are the descendants of African slaves, and these are rapidly increasing their numbers. So are the descendants of East Indians and Chinese, who were introduced as labourers after the liberation of the Negroes, because of the unwillingness of the free Negroes to work on the plantations.

Some of the islands are today very densely peopled. Barbados, for instance, has more than 635 inhabitants to the sq km (1 640 to the sq mile), Martinique 332 (860), and Puerto Rico 306 (793). These figures contrast with much lower densities on the larger islands: Cuba 72 (186), Hispaniola 120 (311), Jamaica 180 (466). On the other hand, many of the smaller islands are inhabited either sparsely or not at all, and the lowest density of all these territories is found in the Bahamas 18 (47). In spite of much progress achieved during and since the Second World War, the living standards of the majority of the people are low, the demand for labour being to a large extent seasonal. Overcrowding and underemployment remain serious problems.

As primary producers, the islands export sugar and other commodities to Europe and North America, receiving manufactured goods in return. But the economic history of the area has been one of great fluctuations, as the price of sugar has risen and fallen on the world market. Overproduction has played its part in the story, and the competition of beet sugar has been seriously felt. The banana industry has had its own troubles, in the form of widespread disease. Hurricanes also provide a serious setback from time to time, much devastation being caused. Recovery takes perhaps a year in the case of bananas, two years or longer in the case of sugar, and as long as ten years in the case of coconuts. Irregular rainfall is another drawback in many parts, particularly in the northeast, where there is too much rain on the windward (Atlantic) side and too little on the leeward.

Many of the islands have long been dependent upon a single export commodity, so that the effects of failure or of a drop in price are felt severely. The general policy of concentrating on cash crops for export has furthermore tended to discourage the growing of food which is much needed for the rapidly increasing indigenous population. Sugar is pre-eminently a plantation crop, but apart from the large estates a good deal is also grown on small holdings, which are particularly numerous in Trinidad.

The development of close relations between the territories has always been handicapped by traditional ties with the various colonial powers, by the great number of islands involved and by the distances separating them. Lack of easy communication has caused the islands to grow up apart, each developing its own characteristics and traditions. However the introduction of air services has done something to break down the barriers of isolation and improved communications will change the situation. Shipping problems have also been aggravated by the fluctuating and varied demands of the traffic: refrigerated ships are required for the conveyance of bananas, tankers for the transport of oil, while passenger traffic, formerly seasonal, is now largely by air. Navigation, too, is sometimes rendered dangerous by hurricanes in the period from July to October, and especially in September, when the sea is at its warmest and the winds are very variable.

Political divisions. Cuba is an independent republic. Two other republics — Haiti and the Dominican Republic — share the island of Hispaniola. Puerto Rico and some of the Virgin Islands belong to the United States. The remaining islands are or have been linked with Great

Britain, France, and the Netherlands, those with British associations being by far the most numerous and important.

Most of the British islands were linked in a West Indies Federation in 1958, but this was dissolved when Jamaica and Trinidad opted out in 1962. In 1968 Antigua, Barbados, Trinidad and Tobago, together with Guyana agreed to form the Caribbean Free Trade Association (CARIFTA) aimed at improving trade between members by removing barriers, and encouraging diversification and economic growth. Dominica, Grenada, St Kitts–Nevis–Anguilla, St Lucia, St Vincent, Jamaica and Montserrat, and finally Belize (British Honduras) have since joined the association. The similarity of the members' exports and the economic dominance of Jamaica and Trinidad present difficulties, but the prospects are that increasing interdependence will be fostered between the islands for the first time.

Cuba

Cuba is almost as large as all the other islands put together, with an area of 114 200 sq km (44 164 sq miles – nearly nine-tenths the size of England) and a population in 1970 of 8.4m. It lies just within the tropics and the interior is upland and hilly, but the only important mountain range is the Sierra Maestra, rising from the south coast in the east to nearly 2 440 m (8 000 ft).

With a growing season lasting the whole year, and ample labour, Cuba is, after the USSR, the world's foremost producer of raw sugar and the largest exporter, with an annual crop of some 8–10m. tons. The cane is grown in fertile areas throughout the island, but especially in the centre and east, where less rainfall is received than in the west. In certain regions sugar gives place to tobacco, Cuba's second staple crop, the basis of a flourishing cigar industry. Other main products are fruit (chiefly citrus and pineapples), maize, rice and coffee, most of which is grown in the mountainous districts of the southeast. Extensive plains, or savannas, are characteristic of the east-central part of the island, and here cattle-ranching has been actively developed. There is extensive forest cover providing mahogany and hardwoods. Mineral deposits are both valuable and varied, but only manganese, chrome, iron, and copper have been seriously exploited to become the second major export after sugar.

Cuba has become a centre in the western world of political change under the revolutionary leader, Dr Fidel Castro. In 1953, soon after General Batista became president, Dr Castro started a campaign against labour conditions and eventually General Batista fled the country at the beginning of 1959. Dr Castro assumed dictatorial power, with government by decree, and initiated an extensive programme of land reform, including the nationalisation of all land and the formation of hundreds of cooperative farms. Private holdings are limited to 65 ha (165 acres) and 70 per cent of agricultural land is state owned. Mineral resources and many industrial companies (including over 100 sugar-mills) were also nationalised as also were all the banks except two Canadian banks which were bought out later. The legal status of the Communist Party was restored.

The United States, which had been the main economic support of Cuba, buying more than half the 5 to 6m. tons of her exports of sugar, cut her purchases, but the USSR and associates took over the surplus supplies at lower prices, with disturbance to the world's sugar market. During the 1960s a new pattern of trade has evolved, 75 per cent being with the Communist countries — mainly the USSR (55 per cent) and China.

There are plans to diversify the economy. Sugar production has again been built up to its former predominance; there is some production of crude oil processed at four small refineries; heavy industry is being established at Nipe Bay (Orient); local fisheries (lobster) are being expanded for export and there is light industry around Habana (Havana), capital and main port (1.7m.). Exports are sugar (90 per cent), minerals and tobacco (6 per cent); main imports are engineering and transport equipment, electrical goods and chemicals. All foreign trade is channelled through state monopolies.

Table 92 — Cuba: cities with a population of over 100 000 (1970)

Habana	1 700 000	Camagüey	199 000
Santiago de Cuba	260 000	Santa Clara	142 000
Holguín	230 000	Guantánamo	131 000

Haiti

The French-speaking Republic of Haiti, about a third as large again as Wales, occupies the western third (27 750 sq km: 10 700 sq miles) of Hispaniola. It was a French colony before 1804, when the slaves revolted and founded the world's first Negro republic; only a few hundred of the 5.2m. inhabitants are white, and less than 10 per cent speak French. In spite of the mountainous terrain nearly a third of the area is classed as arable or pastoral country; a fourth is forested, another fourth is potentially productive, and less than a fifth is reckoned as waste or built on. Early methods of farming led to some impoverishment of the soil, deforestation, and erosion; measures to restore productivity are now in hand but 90 per cent of the arable land is held as small farms totalling over 500 000. Coffee is the principal crop, followed by sugar, sisal and bauxite. Cocoa, cotton and bananas have dwindled. Copper, lignite and manganese are being developed. A new hydroelectric plant at Péligre Dam will provide power for an expansion of light industries for export to the United States (which is by far the major trading partner). Road and rail communications are limited and only two cities exceed 15 000 — Port-au-Prince (240 000) the capital, and Cap Haitien (30 000). There are air links with Jamaica, Puerto Rico and the United States.

The Dominican Republic

The Dominican Republic occupying the eastern two-thirds (48 400 sq km: 18 700 sq miles) of Hispaniola, was formerly under Spanish rule and has been a separate Republic since 1844. Its population in 1970 was 4.3m. The mountainous interior includes the highest ground (Pico Decarte, 3 200 m: 10 500 ft) in the West Indies. Nearly three-quarters of the whole area is forested, most of the remainder being divided between cultivated and pasture land to make agriculture the chief source of wealth. The forests, largely untouched, yield cabinet woods and dye woods. Mineral deposits await development although bauxite is exported and copper is produced. Sugar provides the bulk of the exports, followed by coffee, fruit, cocoa and tobacco. The United States supplies most of the imports and takes most of the exports. Ciudad Trujillo, the capital (650 000), has reverted to its old name, Santo Domingo. There are airlines to the USA and other West Indian islands.

Puerto Rico

Puerto Rico, with an area of 8 900 sq km (3 435 sq miles) (somewhat smaller than Devon and Cornwall), and a population, mostly of Spanish descent, of 2.7m. (double that of Devon and Cornwall), is the smallest and most easterly of the Greater Antilles. Ceded by Spain to the United States in 1898, it was given an increasing measure of self-government, subject to the approval of local legislation by the United States Congress; and even this restriction was abolished in 1952 when Puerto Rico acquired the status of a self-governing 'free commonwealth' in close association with the United States. The mountainous interior rises to over 1 220 m (4 000 ft) and is fringed by coastal plains varying up to 19 km (12 miles) in depth. Rainfall is adequate for successful agriculture in most parts of these plains, but in the south it has been necessary to develop irrigation schemes. Lands devoted to agriculture account for three-quarters of the total, equally divided between arable and pasture. Compared with many other West Indian islands Puerto Rico enjoys a high standard of living, based on its agricultural exports. Cultivation has been so intensive that the soil has become seriously deficient and is kept fertile only by imported fertilisers. Sugar forms the backbone of the economy – a supremacy gained since the beginning of the century at the expense of coffee, which is still grown on the hillsides for export. Tobacco leaf and rum are also important exports. The former forest lands were denuded during the nineteenth century and attention is now being devoted to reafforestation. Tax exemption has encouraged industrial enterprise which includes cement production and mining. Ninety per cent of all trade is with the United States. The capital, San Juan, on the north coast, in which was merged the town of Rio Piedras with its 132 000 inhabitants in 1951, has a population of 800 000. In the south the chief town is Ponce (164 000).

To the east of Puerto Rico are the fifty small islands and cays forming the **American Virgin Islands**, with an aggregate area of 360 sq km (140 sq miles). A third of this is arable and pasture land (mostly the latter), and a half is clad with forest, leaving a sixth which is barren. The islands have little rainfall and are mostly uninhabited, but the three principal islands – St Thomas, St Croix, and St John – support 60 000 people and produce rum. St Thomas was once the leading slave market and trading centre of the Antilles. It has a magnificent harbour at Charlotte Amalie (12 700), the capital of the group, which is a free port and was an important centre for fuelling and servicing ships. It is now the main tourist centre, as tourism has taken over from the sugarcane as the main industry.

Former British West Indies

The Federation of the British West Indies – agreed among the colonies themselves in 1956, enacted by the British Parliament in 1957, and coming into operation in 1958 – was short-lived. Within four years Jamaica broke away in favour of independence, and Trinidad followed suit, leaving only a handful of minor colonies, who wanted to form a federation of their own. In 1967 new constitutional arrangements were made with the 'West Indies Associated States'. Antigua, St Kitts–Nevis–Anguilla, Dominica, St Lucia, Grenada and St Vincent were given self-government, while Britain retained responsibilities for defence and external affairs. The British Virgin Islands, Caymans, Montserrat, Turks and Caicos are dependencies. In 1968 the Caribbean Free Trade Area (CARIFTA) was established – with Trinidad, Jamaica, Barbados and Guyana as additional members.

Only the Bahamas and the Virgin Islands had stood outside the original federation, which included Jamaica, Trinidad and Tobago, Leeward Islands, Windward Islands, and Barbados, totalling 20 100 sq km (8 000 sq miles) with 3.1m. people (1960 census). Admittedly the conditions were not favourable to union. The islands are widely scattered – Jamaica is 1 600 km (1 000 miles) from Barbados – and local patriotism is intense. Shipping services with the United Kingdom are limited. Canada provided an important market, but it was a dollar country and the islands belonged to the sterling area. Sterling is widely used as the legal currency, but in 1965 most of the territories (Trinidad excepted) united under the East Caribbean Currency Authority and adopted a unified currency of West Indian dollar notes.

The absence of adequate mineral resources in most of the islands — the oil of Trinidad and bauxite of Jamaica provide notable exceptions — weakens their position economically, but the possibilities of industrialisation have not been overlooked and industries are being developed in Jamaica, Barbados and Trinidad. The climate encourages winter tourist traffic, which is an important industry; there are first-class hotels in the Bahamas, Jamaica, Barbados, and Trinidad. By an arrangement made with Britain during the Second World War, the United States obtained the right to establish six bases for defence in the Bahamas, and others in Jamaica, Antigua (Leeward Islands), St Lucia (Windwards), and Trinidad, but these were mostly surrendered in 1961.

The Bahamas

The Bahamas are a chain of some thirty inhabited islands, with many hundreds of uninhabited cays and rocks, extending southeast 1 200 km (750 miles) through the Atlantic from the coast of Florida to the north of Haiti. Their area is 11 400 sq km (4 400 sq miles), equal to that of Jamaica, and their population 195 000. In 1964 they became self-governing, and in 1973 independent. One-ninetieth of the whole is cultivated; there are miles of forests, but little else of potential value, the coral soils being porous, dry, and not well suited to agriculture. Where favourable conditions exist, tomatoes, sisal hemp, pineapples, bananas, and vegetables are grown, and a small export trade is carried on, mostly with the United States and Canada. The collection of sponges, once the predominant industry, suffered from a fungus disease in the sponge beds, and these were closed, but have been reopened. Nassau, the capital, lies on the island of New Providence, where nearly half the population live. The climate of these low-lying coral islands is ideal, and tourism is by far the major single industry. Ninety per cent of the tourists arrive by air from the USA and provide 60 per cent of the annual revenue; 250 000 arrived in 1960 and spent $30m.; in 1970 the figures were 1.25m., and $234m. Any falling off of this trade has a direct effect on the economy, and attempts to diversify include the construction of a tax-assisted development area at Freeport in Great Bahama (with a supertanker terminal and a small oil refinery). Aragonite (a pure calcium carbonate sand used in cement, steel, glass, etc.) is mined from considerable reserves in Bimini Isles (east of Miami).

Jamaica

Jamaica by far the largest West Indian island in the Commonwealth, became independent in 1962, with an area of 11 500 sq km (4 400 sq miles; more than half the area of Wales) and a population of 2m. The main axis of the island runs east and west and is traversed by a mountain range culminating in the east in the Blue Mountains, which rise to over 2 140 m (7 000 ft). Indeed, the whole island is mountainous and the trade winds, striking the north and east coasts, cause a very heavy rainfall in those areas, accounting for a great contrast in vegetation and products between that side of the island and the south and west, where rainfall is often inadequate. Occasionally hurricanes bring devastation, that of 1951 having been a serious setback to postwar development. Rather more than a third of the island is devoted to agriculture but over 100 000 farms are of 1.6 ha (4 acres) or less, and Jamaica is a net importer of food.

Bananas, grown on the lower and wetter ground, supplied nearly half the exports before the Second World War; production then fell disastrously through leaf disease, but energetic research work helped to put the industry on its feet. Sugar, now the main crop, is grown in plantations away from the areas of greatest rainfall and is the basis of a thriving output of rum. Both bananas and sugar have benefited from special trade agreements, but both face increased competition (for labour and capital) from industry and mining. Tobacco (chiefly in the form of cigars), coffee (grown in the Blue Mountains), pimento, cocoa, oranges, and grapefruit are also exported. Ginger, for pharmaceuticals and flavouring, is a special (though minor) product. Jamaica, as the sole source of the best varieties of ginger, has the ability to control prices by production limitation. Market prices in 1965 were £230 a ton; in 1970 they were £1 200.

The major development since the Second World War has been the exploitation of bauxite deposits and, since independence, government aid for the diversification and expansion of industry. Jamaica has large reserves and is by far the largest producer of bauxite. Production, by American and Canadian firms, started in 1952 and reached 11m. tons in 1970; with exports to Kitimat (British Columbia) and Norway, and increasing local processing to alumina — production of which increased from 0.8m. tons in 1967 to 1.7m. in 1970. This partial processing increases earnings from royalties and taxes, promotes more foreign exchange and greatly increases employment opportunities. There is pressure to augment these advantages further by smelting the alumina locally; a development which will depend on the availability of capital and the world market for aluminium. Industry has been greatly encouraged by tax concessions and a diversity of products are now made for home consumption and export. Membership of CARIFTA doubled the potential market in 1968. Tourism is also important, although its 'invisible' income has not sufficed to counterbalance the considerable increase in imports (raw materials, machinery, foodstuffs) that has followed the rapid industrial growth. The United Kingdom has long been the major trading partner, but the exploitation of bauxite and Jamaica's membership of the Organisation of American States (1969) has shifted the balance to give North America (the United States and Canada) the dominant position. Imports are now mainly from the United States, the United Kingdom, West Germany and Japan. Exports (bauxite and alumina, sugar, rum and molasses, manufactured goods, bananas, coffee and petroleum products) are mainly to the USA, the UK, Canada and Norway.

Kingston, the capital (population 494 000), accommodates the University of the West Indies, with which was merged in October 1960 the Imperial College of Tropical Agriculture (Trinidad). The international airport is at Palisadoes, Kingston.

The Turks and Caicos Islands

The Turks and Caicos Islands, and the Cayman Islands, formally administered by the Governor of Jamaica (until 1962), are now under the British Colonial Office. The former are a group of some thirty small islands and cays to the southeast of the Bahamas with an area of 430 sq km (166 sq miles) and a population of some 6 000 in the six inhabited islands. The capital is Grand Turk (2 000) and the main products are crawfish, salt and conch shells. The three Cayman Islands to the northwest of Jamaica, have an area of 260 sq km (100 sq miles) and a population of 10 000 (3 000 in the capital at Georgetown). Exports are mainly rope, turtle and shark products. Both have air links with their neighbours and Florida.

The Leeward Islands

The Leeward Islands (which, together with the Windward Islands, make up the Lesser Antilles) form a curving arc on the northeast of the Caribbean and are made up of an inner chain of mountainous islands (the British Virgin Islands, St Christopher—Nevis and Montserrat) terminating in the French island of Guadeloupe. The outer chain of low-lying coral islands, which also lie in the path of the northeast trade winds, include Anguilla, Barbuda and Antigua. The main rainfall is on the mountainous islands and their towns are on the sheltered, westward side. The islands are British dependencies and associated states with four territorial administrators. The Virgin Islands (shared with the United States whose islands have a population of 63 000 as against the British island's 11 000) are barren and rocky. Fruit, vegetables, livestock, fish and poultry are produced and exported to the US Virgin Islands. Tourism is of increasing importance. St Christopher—Nevis (usually called St Kitts—Nevis) are federated with Anguilla and have an area of 396 sq km (153 sq miles) and a combined population of 60 000. The soils are volcanic and sugarcane is the main crop, along with sea island cotton and salt from Anguilla. Monserrat, with an area of 101 sq km (39 sq miles), has a population of some 15 000, 4 000 in the capital, Plymouth. There are active volcanoes but good soils for the production of limes, bananas, fruit and cotton. Tourism is increasing and so is the retired section of the population. Barbuda (160 sq km: 62 sq miles) and Antigua (280 sq km: 108 sq miles) together with the small island of Redonda have a population of 64 000. Antigua differs from the other islands, with their mainly rural population, in that some 25 000 live in the capital, St Johns. Chief products are, again, sugar, and cotton, with tourism making a major contribution to the economy.

The Windward Islands

The Windward Islands extend southwards from the Leeward Island towards Trinidad. Like the Leeward Islands they had a governor till 1960, now replaced by administrators. They have much more rain than the Leewards, are mountainous, volcanic, and heavily forested, and are distinguished by their great beauty. They have a combined area of 2 140 sq km (826 sq miles), of which a third is forested. Over a third is arable land, and only 4 per cent (confined to St Lucia) is classed as pastures. Over a quarter is unused, but much the greater part of this is potentially productive. Some of the islands were once French possessions, and French culture is still evident. The four major islands of the group are **Dominica** (with a population of 72 000 producing citrus fruit, coconuts, cocoa and vanilla — and with bananas as the main export), **St Lucia** (producing sugar, copra, cocoa and bananas; population 110 000; with growing tourism), **St Vincent** (main products sea island cotton of outstanding quality, copra, sweet potatoes, bananas, nutmegs, forest products, and a virtual world monopoly of arrowroot; population 93 000), and **Grenada** (cocoa, cinnamon, cloves and nutmegs).

Dominica is the largest of the islands, but the beautifully situated little port of St George's (9 000), in Grenada, is the capital. The chief town and port in Dominica is Roseau (12 500); the biggest town and port, Castries (40 000), is in St Lucia. The total population which includes the last survivors of the original Caribs, is about 350 000.

Barbados

Barbados is the most easterly of the West Indies and is closely cultivated, the soil being rendered very fertile by an admixture of volcanic dust. It is little larger (430 sq km: 166 sq miles) than the Isle of Wight, but with 240 000 people it is one of the most densely populated areas of the world at 600 per sq km (1 550 per sq mile). The interior of this coral island is nowhere mountainous, the land rising to not much more than 305 m (1 000 ft) with the result that nearly 80 per cent of it is devoted to farming. A great deal of pioneer scientific work has been done in the plantations, and the Central Sugar Cane Breeding Station for the Caribbean is located here, doing valuable work in producing varieties with a higher extraction rate, so successfully that production per hectare has doubled since 1928.

Climate and soil are ideal for the sugarcane, which has been the main-stay of the country for centuries. Production varies greatly with weather conditions: 200 000 tons were produced in 1967 and only 134 000 in 1971. Sugar, rum and molasses account for over 80 per cent of the exports. Traditional overdependence on this single crop has resulted in plans for increased diversification since independence. Fruit, cotton, vegetables and deepsea fishing are being encouraged, as are light labour-intensive industries such as textile manufacture and electronics for import substitution and for exports. Tourism is also increasing in importance as facilities are provided, 57 000 visitors in 1964 rising to 188 000 in 1971. With these various alternative outlets, labour is being attracted away from agriculture and recently it has been necessary to import labour (and to increase mechanisation) for the sugarcane harvest.

Barbados, a member of the Commonwealth since 1627, became fully independent in 1966, and joined the Organisation of American States in 1967 and the Caribbean Free Trade Association in 1968. Imports are consistently in excess of exports, and invisible exports do not yet close the gap. Trade, traditionally almost entirely with the United Kingdom, is increasingly with the United States, Canada and neighbouring countries. The UK, however, still has the major share of imports (27 per cent) and exports (40 per cent).

Bridgetown (13 000), on the leeward side of the island, is the capital. It has a new deepwater harbour opened in 1961 and a deepwater wharf extending beyond the coral reefs to eliminate lighterage. The inter-national airport at Seawell, Christchurch, is well served by the major airlines.

Trinidad and Tobago

Trinidad (4 830 sq km: 1 864 sq miles; about the size of Lancashire) and Tobago (300 sq km: 116 sq miles) are the southernmost of the West Indian islands; they support a population of 1.1m., of whom Trinidad has all but some 35 000; about a third of the total are of East Indian descent. The larger island lies opposite the mouths of the Orinoco, and is only 11 km (7 miles) from the coast of Venezuela; a continuation of the mainland coastal range runs through the north of the island. On the west coast, facing the mainland and forming one side of the almost enclosed Gulf of Paria, are the chief port and capital, Port of Spain (240 000), and good anchorage generally. Elsewhere the island is devoid of harbours and almost unapproachable by shipping, though hurricanes are almost unknown. Tobago, 32 km (20 miles) to the northeast, is geologically a part of the Antilles.

Over a third of Trinidad and Tobago is suitable for farming, and nearly half is forested; most of the balance is waste. Sugar (from the dryer western side of Trinidad) coconuts and cocoa are the principal agricultural products, but these are far surpassed in value by the island's mineral wealth. Trinidad is a considerable oil-producing territory. With an output of 8.7m. tons of crude oil in 1973 she was fourth in the Commonwealth after Canada, Nigeria and Australia. There is also the famous 42 ha (104 acres) Pitch Lake, a deposit of natural asphalt used by Drake for caulking his ships in the sixteenth century and now a source of asphalt for macadamised roads. Both the oil wells and the Pitch Lake are in the southern part of the island. Besides producing and refining its own oil, Trinidad refines crude oil imported in 1963 from Venezuela and Saudi Arabia equally, but by 1970 almost entirely from Venezuela. Production at 22m. tons in 1973 was the third largest in the Commonwealth behind Canada (89m.) and Australia (30m.). Light industry has been developed since independence in 1962, and natural resources combined with tourism have made Trinidad the richest of the West Indian nations, with increasing opportunities as a member of OAS and CARIFTA. Imports (crude oil, machinery and other manufactured goods) are from Venezuela, the United States, the United Kingdom, and Canada. Exports (80 per cent petroleum products, chemicals, sugar and asphalt) go to the USA, the UK and Canada, as well as to many other countries.

Tobago produces sugar, but only about a quarter of the island is devoted to agriculture. It is hilly and rugged, and about half the surface is clothed with forest. Scarborough, the chief town and port, has about 1 500 inhabitants.

French West Indies

The French Islands of the Caribbean are **Guadeloupe** (two islands of 1 700 sq km: 657 sq miles) and **Martinique** (1 100 sq km: 425 sq miles), with a few smaller islands and half of **St Martin** (shared with the Netherlands), all of them situated in the general area of the Leeward and Windward groups. Each of the two main islands has a population of about 330 000. Nearly 40 per cent of Guadeloupe is forested and 33 per cent is utilised for farming, the rest being waste or unused. Martinique is divided about equally in four categories: arable, pasture, forest, and waste. Sugar, rum, and bananas are the chief products, together with pineapples and vegetables. The capital of Martinique is Fort-de-France (90 000); of Guadeloupe, with a fine harbour, Pointe-à-Pitre (30 000). Martinique and Guadeloupe were raised to the status of overseas departments of France in 1946.

Netherlands West Indies

These are in two groups, with a total area of 1 000 sq km (390 sq miles) and a population of nearly 218 000. The largest islands (Curaçao, Bonaire, and Aruba) lie 65 km (40 miles) off the Venezuelan coast and have a population of 210 000 (141 000 of whom live on Curaçao). A few fragments — St Maarten (shared with France), St Eustatius, and Saba — are sandwiched among the Leeward Islands 800 km (500 miles) away to the east of Puerto Rico. Known collectively as the Netherlands Antilles, they gained local autonomy in 1954. The rainfall in the larger islands is scanty, the rocky soil permits little agriculture and only about 5 per cent of the land is cultivated. The chief importance of the islands lies in the development of Curaçao and Aruba as refining centres of crude oil from the Venezuelan oilfields; the refineries are among the largest in the world; established in 1915, over 45m. tons of the products were exported in 1973. There is mining of calcium phosphate on Curaçao, and a small fishing industry. Several factories are in operation (petrochemicals in Aruba; consumer goods, dry docks and ship repairs in Curaçao; textiles in Bonaire and rum in St Maarten) but a wide range of products must be imported. The capital, Willemstad (45 000) in Curaçao has a good harbour, a large water desalination plant, and handles approximately one-tenth of the shipping of the western hemisphere.

Central America

Southeastward from Mexico the continent tapers off in the narrowing isthmus of Central America, which has a total area less than a third of that of Mexico, and considerably less than that of Texas. There is less variety than in Mexico, and certain characteristics persist throughout. There is a backbone of highlands. The highest peaks are volcanic cones, a number of them active. Lava flows and ash deposits are widespread. Towards the Caribbean Sea the highlands are older mountains, deeply dissected, and with worndown hills. On the east coast there are broader lowlands than on the Pacific coast — swamps and alluvial lands instead of mountains sloping sharply to the sea.

The temperature of the lowlands is high all the year, with a greater range between day and night than between season and season. The average for every month is about 27° C (80° F), the result of a range from about 21° C (70° F) by night to 32° C (90° F) by day. At 914 m (3 000 ft) altitude the temperature is very agreeable, averaging about 21° C (70° F). The rainfall varies greatly from place to place in accordance with the exposure and the topographic structure. As in Mexico, the northeast trade winds are the chief rain-bearers, and on the Atlantic side, where there is direct exposure to those winds, there is no dry season and the rainfall averages above 2 500 mm (100 in). Lowlands and mountain slopes are clothed with tropical rain forest. On the Pacific coast and in the interior highlands the rainfall is considerably less; there is a dry season between December and April, when the trees in many places shed their leaves, and there is much scrubby and thorny vegetation. The ethnic groups resemble those in Mexico, but with the addition of some English-speaking Negroes on the Caribbean coast.

Almost throughout the territory there are similar resources, similar problems of development, similar people and common interests, yet the conditions are not favourable to political unity. There is no continuity of population, but rather a congeries of population groups each gathered round one chief nucleus and separated from its neighbours by almost impassable country. None of the isolated population groups is strong enough to control the others, with the result that the area is

824

divided up into six independent republics — Guatemala, El Salvador, Honduras, Nicaragua, Costa Rica, and Panama, besides a British colony, Belize (British Honduras), and the Panama Canal Zone, which is controlled by the United States. To some extent travel, even between adjacent countries, is by sea. Moreover, these population islands lack the advantage of true islands, that of being circumnavigable, so that travel from coast to coast of the same country is in some cases by a roundabout sea and land route.

These difficulties are being lessened by the spreading network of air routes, which already link all the important towns with Mexico, on the one hand, and South America on the other, while direct routes run to Florida and the West Indies. The position is also much improved by the Inter-American Highway. This great project, part of a larger scheme to link the countries of North and South America by the road system known as the Pan—American Highway in North America, involves the construction of a through route from the Texas—Mexican frontier to Panama City — a distance of more than 4 800 km (3 000 miles) — and then on to southern Chile. The work of construction was speeded during the Second World War, the countries concerned receiving aid from the United States, but later progress has been slower. By 1951, 61 per cent of the highway had been furnished and another 30 per cent though unpaved, was usable; by mid-1964 the road was usable through the Central American republics to Panama; by 1970 the road was completed except for a short stretch on the Panama—Colombia borders. Central America has been called a connecting link between North and South America; but so far it has been rather a barrier.

Agriculture is the chief industry in Central America, although less than 10 per cent of the surface is cultivated. The more advanced Indian communities were agricultural before the Spanish occupation, and in large measure still carry on the same methods and cultivate the same crops. As in Mexico, maize occupies more land than any other crop. Sugarcane, beans, and various starchy root crops are common.

In modern times certain commercial crops have become important, but the most important of all as an export commodity, coffee, occupies a very small proportion of the surface, and the exacting requirements of this crop (cf. p. 197) limit it to certain districts, the best of which are plateaus or high basins mantled with volcanic ash. The high quality of the product causes it to be in great demand in continental Europe. The industry is a Central American one, but European and United States interests have a strong hold on it.

Bananas have long been second among the exports of Central America, but the cultivation of this fruit as now carried on is of modern and foreign origin. It demanded, for its inception, large amounts of capital and a high degree of organisation. Until comparatively recent times the Caribbean coast, where all the banana estates lie, was an uninhabited wilderness. The inhabitants of the temperate highlands of this region had never tried to subdue the dense, fever-ridden forests of the rainy lowlands. Individual enterprise was helpless in the face of such obstacles. In a banana district it was necessary to build a network of railways radiating from a newly equipped port, to clear the forest, to plant and tend thousands of acres of bananas, to harvest the crop week by week in perfect condition on scheduled time, to be transported successively by man, mule, tramway, railway, and special refrigerating ocean liner to a United States or European port, and thence to be distributed by special railway cars. Thousands of Negroes were brought as labourers from the West Indies, particularly Jamaica, and these have had to be housed, supplied with their everyday needs, protected against disease, and in some cases governed and policed. English and not Spanish is the language of the banana districts. The United Fruit Company of the United States is the largest of the organisations concerned.

Other crops are sugarcane, principally for the domestic market, cacao, oilseeds, and coconuts. Cocoa is a commercial crop that has been growing in importance, particularly in Costa Rica. It replaced bananas in some of the older districts, where a banana blight, spreading uncontrollably, had infected the soil. Central America is a rather important source of supply of coconuts for the United States, being near enough to ship fresh nuts instead of the less bulky copra for oil only. Of the miles of coconut palms fringing the well-drained, well-watered beaches of the Caribbean coast, some belong to fruit companies and some to coastal Indian tribes.

Mineral industries play a minor part. Precious metals were mined in prehistoric times, and the Spaniards were mainly attracted to the mining districts; but large rich deposits are lacking, and small workings are the rule.

Forest industries are widespread, though their importance is not commensurate with the proportion of tree-covered land, which occupies about one-half of the whole area. Mahogany, Spanish cedar, rosewoods, and other less important cabinet woods, as well as dyewoods (such as logwoods), grow on the Caribbean slope, and in some relatively moist forests on the Pacific slope, but the valuable trees are widely scattered among those of little value. There are unmixed stands of pine, suitable for structural timber, on sandy ridges of the Caribbean slope, but their isolated situation does not favour easy working. Dyewood exploitation continues in dry as well as moist forests, although adversely affected by coal-tar dye competition. Rubber-gathering has declined. Chicle is gathered in forests adjacent to the Mexican chicle territory. Of the numerous other forest resources, some, such as Peruvian balsam, have been known and utilised for centuries.

Manufacturing industries have made much progress in the last two decades and are now both numerous and diverse, though they do not challenge the paramount position of agriculture. Industry in general is short of power, although the hydroelectric potential of the area is great. With the exception of factories concerned with the processing of coffee and other raw materials they are mostly confined to the production of goods for the home market, such as textiles, shoes, furniture, soap, cigarettes, and matches. Household industries survive in communities which preserve an Indian culture.

The bulk of the trade, both import and export, of the whole region is with the United States.

Guatemala

This is the most populous and productive (slightly ahead of El Salvador) of the six republics. It has a 320 km (200 mile) coastline on the Pacific and one of 113 km (70 miles) on the Caribbean, and meets at its frontiers four other countries: Mexico in the north and west, Honduras and El Salvador in the south, and Belize (British Honduras) (to which it has laid claim for over a century) in the east. Volcanic mountains rising to nearly 4 270 m (14 000 ft) occupy two-thirds of the land, other physical features being a large and undeveloped northern plain and low coastal strips. Both highlands and lowlands are densely forested, trees and jungle growth covering 49 per cent of the whole area, which extends to 109 000 sq km (42 000 sq miles) (four-fifths the size of England). Arable land and pastures occupy 23 per cent and about 28 per cent is waste or built on. The 5m. people are largely concentrated on the Pacific side, on fertile slopes 305 to 1 520 m (1 000 to 5 000 ft) above sea level, and here is situated the capital, Guatemala City, which is the home of some 650 000 people. Only small numbers are found on the Caribbean side (in spite of some important coffee and banana interests) and still fewer in the well-forested northern plain. The pure-blooded Indians, who constitute over half the population, are descendants of the Mayas and Aztecs, of whose distant civilisations there are numerous remains.

Apart from sugar (beet and cane), maize, beans and rice are grown for home consumption, the major cash crops, mainly grown on foreign owned estates, are coffee (of high grade from the cooler Pacific slopes), cotton, bananas and beef. Chicle is collected, for export to Mexico, and there is a large production of essential oils (citronella and lemon grass). Fishing produces shrimp for export to the USA.

Hydroelectric potential has yet to be fully developed and most industry consists of small factories for the home market. The mining potential is considerable, with deposits of laterite ore in the Lake Izabal area with good nickel content. Zinc and lead are also mined, and there is gold, silver, copper and manganese. A coast to coast railway joins San

Jose to Puerto Barrios, and other links connect with Mexico and El Salvador. The Pan—American Highway runs to Guatemala City, which is also well served by the international airlines.

Exports, over half of which are food products (coffee, sugar, bananas, beef and fodder), include cotton, essential oils and some manufactured goods (textiles and wood products) to the USA, West Germany and neighbouring Central American countries. Imports include machinery, transport equipment, manufactured goods, wheat, petroleum and chemicals, mainly from the USA, West Germany, El Salvador and Japan.

Belize (British Honduras)

Lying between the undeveloped northern part of Guatemala and the Caribbean, Belize is bordered on the north by the Mexican peninsula of Yucatan. The most sparsely populated political division of Central America, the territory has within its 22 900 sq km (8 870 sq miles) a little larger than Wales, some 125 000 inhabitants, a third of whom still live in the capital and chief port, Belize. Much of Belize was destroyed, with heavy loss of life, when it was struck by a hurricane ('Hattie') in 1961. A new capital, Belmopan (3 000 in 1970) is being built 80 km (50 miles) inland at the geographical centre of the country; an eventual population of 30 000 is anticipated.

Internal self-government came into force in 1964.

The coastal areas are flat and swampy and inland there is a gradual rise to a height of several thousand metres. Much of the interior is inaccessible. Officially nearly a quarter of the country is classed as agricultural, 60 per cent as forests, and the balance as built on or waste. Logging and lumbering, especially of mahogany and pine, have traditionally provided most of the exports; but sugar became the major export in 1956.

Bananas and sugarcane are cultivated in forest clearings and on the coastal plain, where citrus fruits (and fruit products) are of increasing importance. Fishing (lobsters for export to the United States) within the long coral reef, and chicle, add to the cash crops. Trade, through Belize by means of lighters, is mainly with the United Kingdom and the United States, with transport equipment, machinery and foodstuffs as the chief imports.

Honduras

An independent sovereign state since 1838, Honduras has an area of 112 000 sq km (43 000 sq miles) and is about five times as large as Belize. It is approximately the size of Guatemala but is less densely populated. The 2.5m. inhabitants (chiefly mestizos — Indians with Spanish blood) are widely scattered and live at around 1 000 m

(3 280 ft) in the higher lands; some 240 000 live in the capital, Tegucigalpa. The east—west coastline on the Caribbean is 480 km (300 miles) long and the coastal plains give way to a mountainous interior which falls southward to the Pacific coastline of less than 80 km (50 miles). Honduras was devastated by a hurricane in 1974.

There are extensive forests (40 per cent of the area) in the northeast, the interior valleys, and near the south coast, producing hardwood (mahogany, walnut and rosewood) and softwood. The arable areas (30 per cent) produce a wide range of crops (potatoes, maize, sugar, coconuts and beans), with bananas, coffee, cotton and some sugar as the main cash crops grown largely on US-owned estates. Dairy and beef cattle thrive on the Pacific slopes and fishing on the Atlantic coast provides shrimp for export.

Lead, zinc and silver are mined and there are reserves of gold, asbestos, platinum, copper and iron ore. Hydroelectric power is being developed at Rio Lindo for the central and Costa Norte regions with their range of small factories producing consumer goods. Railway and port development has been mainly to facilitate export from the banana estates, but no railway runs through the country. Tegucigalpa is connected to the Pan—American Highway by the Pacific—Atlantic road. The country is extremely airminded and this is the normal means of transport for passengers and freight, with thirty-four small airfields and two international airports (the second, La Mesa, at San Pedro Sula).

Exports are mainly bananas, coffee, timber, minerals (lead, zinc, silver), cotton and beef to the United States, West Germany, El Salvador, Guatemala. Imports are mainly manufactured goods, machinery, cereals, petroleum and chemicals from the export countries together with Costa Rica and Japan.

El Salvador

Smallest of the Central American republics with an area of 21 000 sq km (8 200 sq miles — rather less than Wales), is the most densely populated (3.4m., largely mestizo). Its frontier is confined to the Pacific — a disadvantage partly offset by an arrangement with Guatemala for free access to the Caribbean port of Puerto Barrios, with rail connection. The land is mountainous and volcanic, with most of the population in the subtropical central valleys.

Over a third of the country is forested, over another third is pastoral, and over a quarter is agricultural. High quality coffee (*arabica*) has long provided three-quarters of the exports. It still provides 45 per cent, but is now augmented by cotton (of good quality and high yield), sugar and shrimps.

Outstanding among forest products is balsam: El Salvador is the main source of world supply of this medicinal gum.

El Salvador is the most industrialised of the Central American states with a wide range of manufactured exports. Power from the Lempa River, northeast of the capital, supports steel, chemical and glass factories among others. There is an oil refinery at Acajutla. There is no mineral production and all raw materials must be imported except those for the food and textile industries. The United States is by far the major trading partner, followed by West Germany (coffee) and the other Central American states (when politics allow).

San Salvador, the capital (over 430 000) is about 32 km (nearly 20 miles) inland from its port, La Libertad. It has an international airport and railway links with neighbouring countries.

Nicaragua

Nicaragua (148 000 sq km: 57 000 sq miles) is the largest state in Central America. The volcanic Central American chain, broken in the south by a low isthmus once considered as the alternative route for the Panama Canal, divides the country so that about three-quarters drains into the Caribbean and a quarter into the Pacific. The land area of the Pacific slopes is further reduced by two large lakes with a combined area of nearly 9 060 sq km (3 500 sq miles). Yet on the Pacific side are found most of the agricultural land and nearly 70 per cent of the population (mostly mestizo) of 2m. On the shores of the smaller lake is situated the capital city of Managua (320 000), rebuilt after an earthquake in 1931, destroyed by another in 1973.

Over 36 per cent of the country is forested and a third is water and waste. Only 6.7 per cent is used for arable crops, and 7 per cent for pasturage. Much of the forest covered land of the Atlantic coast is unproductive. Cotton and coffee are the most valuable exports, followed by oilseeds, beef, sugar, coffee and shrimps. Sugar is produced on the Pacific side, but not to such an extent as the favourable climatic conditions make possible, coffee being more popular. Out of over 1.8m. cattle, the largest herds are on the Pacific side. But forestry is carried on in the east, along some of the principal rivers, though production is falling. Mineral wealth is varied, but not greatly exploited. Communication between the two coastal areas are difficult but have been aided by a road, which links up with the Inter-American Highway; before the route came into use surface travel was by way of the Panama Canal. There have been plans to link the two coasts by a waterway across the low southern isthmus, canalising the waters of the River San Juan, which separates Nicaragua from Costa Rica. This could also be the possible route for an oil pipeline.

Industry is on a small scale, but power supplies (especially from the Rio Tuma Scheme) are increasing. There is an oil refinery at the capital,

Managua. The country has considerable potential in timber, minerals, and tourism.

The United States is the major trading partner, followed by Japan, West Germany, and neighbouring Central American states.

Costa Rica

Costa Rica 51 000 sq km (19 700 sq miles), two-thirds the size of Scotland, is sandwiched between Nicaragua and Panama at a part of Central America where the mountains and coastal strips are confined to a minimum breadth of about 128 km (80 miles). The heart of the country is a warm and fertile plateau or high basin protected by volcanic peaks. Rivers are numerous on both sides of the central range and, besides feeding hydroelectric power stations, add valuable alluvial material to a soil already enriched by volcanic ash. Over 50 per cent of the country is wooded, 20 per cent is arable and 27 per cent is classified as pasture. Agriculture is mostly on the lands of smallholders and follows the familiar pattern of coffee (*arabica*) on the uplands, bananas and sugarcane on the lowlands, with the addition of abaca (manila hemp) and cocoa on the Caribbean side, rice and maize on the Pacific side. Cattle number 1.5m.

Hydroelectric power is being developed and exports from many small factories are increasing. Coffee provides nearly half of exports, followed by bananas, sugar, meat and cocoa beans. The United States supplies half the imports and takes half the exports, followed by West Germany, Japan and neighbouring Central American countries.

The Caribbean port of Limón and the Pacific port of Puntarenas share most of the trade. Both are connected by rail with the capital, San José, which lies on the central plateau and has 370 000 of the total population of 1.8m. Most of the people are of European descent.

Panama

Nearly as large as Scotland, Panama is a rugged, jungle-clad neck of land, 788 km (490 miles) long and nowhere a quarter as wide. It is crossed by the Panama Canal and adjoins the South American Republic of Colombia, from which it broke away in 1903. Of its 75 600 sq km (29 000 sq miles) only 7.5 per cent is arable and pastoral. Less than 4 per cent of the land is cultivated (rice being the main crop, with maize, cocoa and coffee), but there is a high livestock population (1.1m. cattle, 3m. poultry and 0.25m. pigs) mainly on the Pacific slopes. Forests cover over 80 per cent of the total area. Imports provide 60 per cent of the food required by the 1.4m. population; of whom 412 000 live in Panama City and a further 65 000 in Colón, the two ocean terminals of the canal. They are joined by a rail link, and are both enclaves in the Canal Zone.

831

There is a wide range of local industries and, at Colón, a refinery and a Free Zone (for the processing and storage of transit goods). The economic life of the country is dominated by the canal, however, and will be affected by further projects for the cutting of a second canal and the laying of an oil pipeline across the isthmus. There is a large adverse trade balance occasioned by the import of consumer goods for Canal Zone personnel and transients, although this is largely offset by services to the Zone. The United States has assisted in rail and road development, and in the completion of the Pan—American Highway to the Colombian border. Panama also offers shipowners the facility of a 'flag of convenience' and in 1968 there were 1 880 ships (5m. tons) under Panamanian registration.

Main exports (averaging some 35 per cent of imports) are bananas, petroleum products, fresh fish and sugar. Imports are manufactures, consumer goods, crude petroleum and chemicals. The United States (taking over 75 per cent of exports) is the main trading partner, followed by Venezuela, Japan and West Germany.

The **Panama Canal Zone** is a strip about 16 km (10 miles) wide running from northwest to southeast across the centre of the republic. It has an area of 1 676 sq km (647 sq miles) and a population of 50 000 (39 000 of whom are US citizens). Just over one-third of the area is water (including water out to the 4.8 km (3 miles limit)). The Canal Zone was granted in perpetuity by Panama to the United States in 1903 in return for a lump sum of $10m., and an annual payment now standing at $1.93m. The canal, built by the United States between 1904 and 1914, is 82 km (52.1 miles) long from deep water to deep water. The passage takes seven to eight hours; three sets of locks have to be negotiated. Government is exercised by the Canal Zone government, and commercial operation of the canal and railway is in the hands of the Panama Canal Company. The headquarters of the Company are at Balboa, at the Pacific terminal of the canal, not far from Panama City.

As with the Suez Canal, the Panama Canal changed the pattern of the world shipping routes. It has been of great importance to the trade between the Atlantic and the Pacific coasts of North America; it has shortened the voyage from New Zealand, and from the west coasts of the Americas, to Europe; and it has moved the West Indies from the periphery to the centre of the Atlantic shipping lanes. The canal was planned to take the size of modern vessels, nor to handle the volume of mid-twentieth century trade. The difference between the 0.3 m (1 ft) tide at the Caribbean end and the 3.9 m (13 ft) in the Pacific, and the canal's average height of 26 m (85 ft) above sea level, made locks essential. The triple set at Gatun limits the number of vessels which can pass through the canal each year and the maximum capacity could be reached before 1990.

By 1930 the biggest ships were already too large to pass through the locks (the largest ever to pass through was 80 260 dwt tons) and by 1970 some 1 000 ships (including all the giant oil tankers) were too big to pass through. There have therefore been plans to build a second canal of greater capacity. Alternatives have been (*a*) to the east of the present canal, near the Colombian border (a plan to cut the isthmus by controlled nuclear explosions − since abandoned); (*b*) a sea level canal along the line of the Costa Rica−Nicaragua border (of greater length than the third alternative); and (*c*) a sea level canal to take vessels up to 150 000 tons, 16 km (10 miles) west of the present canal and outside the Canal Zone, with sea gates at each end to work in tandem with the present canal. The financial and political problems make it unlikely that any new canal will be completed before 1985−90. Meanwhile the limitation on the passage of giant tankers has made it necessary to

Table 93 − **Shipping and tonnage through the Panama Canal (oceangoing traffic only; tonnages in thousands)**

Fiscal year ending 30 June	Vessels	Net tonnage* (000)	Cargo tonnage (000)	Fiscal year ending 30 June	Vessels	Net tonnage* (000)	Cargo tonnage (000)
1915	1 058	3 507	4 888	1946	3 747	17 516	14 977
1916†	724	2 212	3 093	1947	4 260	20 233	21 670
1917	1 738	5 357	7 054	1948	4 678	22 902	24 117
1918	1 989	6 072	7 525	1949	4 793	23 473	25 305
1919	1 948	5 658	6 910	1950	5 448	28 013	28 872
1920	2 393	7 898	9 372	1951	5 593	27 180	20 073
1921	2 791	10 550	11 595	1952	6 524	30 674	33 610
1923	3 908	17 206	19 566	1953	7 410	36 768	36 095
1925	4 592	21 134	23 956	1954	7 784	38 027	39 095
1927	5 293	24 245	27 733	1955	7 997	38 643	40 646
1929	6 289	27 585	30 647	1956	8 209	41 273	45 119
1931	5 370	25 690	25 065	1957	8 579	43 714	49 702
1932	4 362	21 842	19 798	1958	9 187	47 968	48 125
1933	4 162	21 094	18 161	1959	9 718	52 216	51 153
1934	5 234	26 410	24 704	1960	10 795	58 302	59 258
1935	5 180	25 720	25 309	1961	10 866	61 826	63 670
1936	5 382	25 923	26 505	1962	11 149	65 379	67 525
1937	5 387	25 430	28 108	1963	11 017	64 438	62 247
1938	5 524	25 950	27 385	1964	11 808	69 727	70 550
1939	5 903	27 170	27 866	1965	11 835	74 823	76 573
1940	5 370	24 144	27 299	1966	11 926	78 918	81 711
1941	4 727	20 642	24 950	1967‡	12 413	88 266	86 193
1942	2 688	11 010	13 607	1968	13 199	96 488	96 550
1943	1 822	8 233	10 599	1969	13 150	100 603	101 391
1944	1 562	6 073	7 003	1970	13 658	113 490	114 257
1945	1 939	8 380	8 603				

* Net tonnages based on Panama Canal measurement rules.
† Canal closed by landslides for seven months.
‡ Closure of Suez Canal.

commence the construction of a 70 km (44 mile) crude oil pipelin
across the isthmus from the Isle of Cepilo on the Pacific coast to th
Gulf of San Blas (east of the Canal Zone) to bring petroleum from
Alaska, Colombia and Ecuador to the east coast of the United States.

Table 93 shows how traffic has varied since 1914, and th
pronounced upward trend since the Second World War. Between 196(
and 1970 the number of vessels increased by 26 per cent, but thei
cargo tonnage nearly doubled. Until 1957 traffic in each direction wa
evenly balanced; but thereafter traffic to the Pacific steadily move(
ahead of traffic from the Pacific. By 1970, 74m. tons moved to th
Pacific, as against 40m. tons in the opposite direction. Vessel move
ments in each direction are almost equal — an indication of the numbe
returning to the Atlantic in ballast.

South America

This, the smaller half of the New World, has at least four-fifths of its area within the tropics, and hence yields chiefly tropical products; but here as elsewhere the temperate area, relatively to its extent, furnishes a greater abundance of commercial commodities, and it is in this part of the continent that the rate of increase in the production of such commodities and the development of means of distribution for them have been most rapid, and European immigration has been most constant in the past. The most powerful South American country until the Second World War, Argentina, lies almost wholly in temperate latitudes. Brazil, the current leader, lies within the tropics.

The lofty chains of the Andes, on the west side of the continent, form an important climatic barrier. They extend some 8 000 km (5 000 miles) throughout the entire length of South America, rising to heights of over 6 000 m (20 000 ft) and reaching their culmination at the back of Valparaiso in Mount Aconagua, which has an elevation of over 7 000 m (23 000 ft). In the latitudes in which trade winds prevail they arrest the moisture-laden winds from the Atlantic, draining the moisture out of winds that have already been partly drained in their course over the continent further east. The western slopes of these mountains, on the other hand, receive in these latitudes no rain from the Atlantic, and as far as 33° S little or none from the Pacific. On that side the tendency of the wind is to blow away from the land, and the rarefaction of the air on the narrow strip west of the Andes is not enough to counteract that tendency. There is also, flowing northwards along the west coast, the cold Humboldt or Peruvian current, which is accompanied by much upswelling of cold bottom water. The air over this current is cold and, if moving towards the land, is not likely to deposit any moisture over the warmer land surface. Hence the absolute desert, frequently entirely rainless, is along the actual sea coast. The Andes also constitute a great obstacle to communication between the east and west coasts. More than one railway reaches a height of upwards of 4 270 m (14 000 ft) before attaining the tablelands between the principal chains of the mountains.

Some of the mighty rivers to the east of the Andes form excellent waterways. The Orinoco, in the north of the continent, is navigable for steamers continuously for nearly 1 600 km (1 000 miles). The Amazon is navigable without interruption to the base of the Andes, a distance of 4 180 km (2 600 miles) from its mouth, and many more thousands of kilometres of navigation are afforded by its tributaries great and small; ocean liners of 10 000 tons regularly reach Manaus, 1 600 km (1 000 miles) from the mouth. Many of these tributaries, however, have their navigable course obstructed by falls and rapids. The value of the navigation of the Amazon is diminished by the paucity of population and products in the region through which it flows and by the similarity of the products in nearly the whole of its navigable course. The traditional article of trade is rubber. The inland waterway which is of most importance and likely to remain most useful is outside the Amazon basin; it flows from north to south in the upper Paraguay and the lower Parana, a waterway which is uninterrupted from near the source of the former river, and which, like the Mississippi, brings hot and temperate climates into direct communication. All these rivers have great hydroelectric potential.

In general the populous areas are well served by rail and air, which in some cases also provide communication between adjoining states. Travel by air is commonplace. In recent years rather more attention has been devoted to the development of roads, particularly the Inter-American Highway which runs down the west coast to Puerto Montt in south Chile. This project will undoubtedly have a considerable effect on cultural and commercial relations throughout the continent.

In the twenty years 1937—56 the population rose by more than 50 per cent, as against 10 per cent in Europe and 36 per cent in North and Central America. It is still increasing faster than any other continent; but with some 180m. in 1970 the density, in relation to the total land area, is not high. Regions favourable for settlement are few however, and the concentration in the fertile areas and in the rapidly expanding major cities is presenting major problems. European, African and some Asian (on the borders of the Caribbean) groups have intermarried with the native Indians to produce much intermixing of peoples. But the line of 60° W, agreed by Spain and Portugal as the major colonisers in 1494, is still the major divide. East of the line, the white population in Brazil is of Portuguese origin, and Portuguese is there the official language; but elsewhere, except in Guyana, the whites are mainly of Spanish descent, and Spanish is the official language.

One effect on Latin America of the Second World War was to cut off the supplies of manufactured goods on which she relied in exchange for her raw materials. In consequence, internal industries have developed. A wide range of agricultural products has also been introduced in the attempt to achieve greater economic self-sufficiency. Interstate trade within the continent and foreign investment has been increased. By 1949 British investments (totalling nearly £600m.) were only half what they were ten years earlier, and trade with Britain had also declined. Trade with the United States and Japan, on the other hand, showed a very large increase compared with prewar years. Another feature has been the restoration of trade with Germany, which is striving with some success to regain her prewar position in this respect.

Brazil

A federal republic with an area of 8.5m. sq km (3.28m. sq miles), Brazil is nearly as large as all the other states and territories of South America put together. It has frontiers with all of them except Ecuador and Chile, an Atlantic coastline of some 8 000 km (5 000 miles), and lies almost entirely within the tropics. It is the world's fifth largest country, exceeded in size only by the USSR, Canada, China, and USA. Over 60 per cent is under forest and over 20 per cent is classified as built on or waste, while only 3.5 per cent (but this is an area larger than Ecuador) is arable land, and 12.5 per cent (an area as large as Bolivia) is permanent pasture; the residue of 4 per cent (larger than the British Isles) being assessed as potentially productive though not in present use. In the north, are the broad, sparsely populated plains of the Amazon basin, crossed by the Equator and covered by the world's greatest tropical rainforest. Southward they rise to the central tablelands of ancient mineralised rocks (*campos*), 300 to 910 m (1 000 to 3 000 ft) above sea level, which cover nearly a quarter of the country with savanna vegetation. Here also the land is very thinly peopled, since the coastal ranges to the east cut off the Atlantic moisture and give little opportunity for a profitable livelihood. Southward again the plateau rises into rolling hill country culminating in ridges which reach a maximum height of over 2 700 m (9 000 ft) before dropping sharply to the sea. It is in this third area, crossed by the Tropic of Capricorn, that the centre of economic and political activity is found; in this area, comprising only about a sixth of the republic, live more than half the population of 92m. (a population which was only 9.6m. in 1870). Most of the remainder are scattered along the coastal regions to the south and north. Politically, the country is divided into five regions, comprising twenty-two states, four federal territories, and a federal district in which is situated the capital. Until 1960 the capital was the world-famous port of Rio de Janeiro; then it was replaced by a new city built for the purpose, Brasilia, in the interior, about 960 km (600 miles) northwest of Rio.

Brazil is important both as a manufacturing country and as a source of agricultural products. Although the potential (particularly in minerals and hydroelectric power) is great, the country is already a

major commercial nation. Brazil leads the world in the production o
coffee (25 per cent), cassava (30 per cent), bananas (20 per cent) and
castor beans; is second largest producer of sugarcane and citrus fruit
third in cocoa, maize, raw sugar, asbestos and manganese, fourth in
tobacco and cattle; fifth in cotton, jute, goats and beef; sixth in ground
nuts and eighth in rice (the largest producer in the western hemisphere
and coconuts. Although her industries include iron and steel, ship
building, aluminium smelting, oil refining, and paper and textile
factories, agricultural products account for over 85 per cent of all
exports. The increasing demands of industry have, however, caused a
drain on rural labour to the detriment of agriculture, and a movement
back to the land is being encouraged by opening the hitherto inacces
sible areas.

Coffee is the most important crop; it grows so luxuriantly in the
terra roxa (red soil) of the southeastern region that the production is
unsurpassed by any other country and the difficulty is one of limiting
supplies to preserve an economic price. During the 1930s a drastic
policy of burning the surplus output resulted in the destruction in all of
77m. bags.* In postwar years a state approaching equilibrium has been
maintained, but controls of an International Coffee Agreement are still
applied to safeguard against a repetition of the earlier experience. In
1960 the coffee plantations yielded a crop of 2.6m. tons from 4.2m. ha
(10.3m. acres) and provided nearly 50 per cent of the total value of the
exports. The normal annual crop is about 1.5m. tons. The southeast
devotes nearly as great an acreage to maize as to coffee, but this staple
cereal, of which Brazil is one of the leading producers, is grown not
only there but in most parts of the country as a subsistence crop, the
total yield in 1960 being 7.7m. tons from 6.1m. ha (15m. acres), and in
1971 14.3m. tons from 9.8m. ha (24.2m. acres).

Cotton, long established in the northeastern bulge of Brazil, began to
receive serious attention in the southeast when coffee slumped in the
1930s, and output in the latter area has so increased that in 1970 it
contributed more than half the total yield of 645 000 tons. Raw cotton
has become the second export commodity. Very considerable areas are
also devoted to rice, beans, cassava, sugar and wheat — all over 1.2m. ha
(3m. acres). Other products, cultivated on a smaller scale, include
cocoa, potatoes, tobacco, groundnuts, and fruit. Most of these are
grown to meet the needs of the home population, but cocoa, which
flourishes along the east coast, is fourth in the list of exports and makes
Brazil third to Ghana and Nigeria as a producer, its crop in 1971 being
197 000 tons against Ghana's 411 500 tons. There are exportable
surpluses of sugar, tobacco, sisal, rice, and fruit. Production of wheat
was greatly increased under the stimulus of war but is still far from

* Nearly 5m. tons. A bag of Brazilian coffee is reckoned as 60 kilos, so that seventeen bags are just over 1 ton.

ufficient to meet home needs; and wheat figures largely among the mports.

The pastoral industry is of special importance in the extreme south, n the region adjoining the grasslands of Uruguay, but other concentrations of livestock occur in the states of the southeast and northeast, as well as in the *campos* of the central plateau, which are used as breeding areas whence cattle are moved to the seaboard states for fattening. Cattle number over 97m., pigs 67m., sheep 24.5m., goats 14.7m., and horses 9m. (1971). Only India, the United States and the USSR have larger herds of cattle, and Brazil now ranks ahead of Argentina as a livestock producer. These great numbers of livestock, besides supplying meat and dairy produce for a growing home consumption, form the basis of a diminishing export of chilled and canned meat and hides. The wool clip, from the sheep farms in the far south, goes mostly to Brazilian textile mills.

The extensive forest lands, though furnishing many valuable commercial products, lie comparatively undeveloped, particularly in the case of Amazonia which accounts for 50 per cent of the area and only 8 per cent of the population. Some timber is floated down the Amazon to its mouth, but most of the timber supplies come from the pinewoods of the Rio Paraná. Rubber is of some importance in the Amazon region, though it no longer enjoys the world supremacy it had in 1890—1910 before the development of the Malayan and Indonesian plantations. Exports are small — carnauba wax (formerly used for gramophone records), vegetable oils, maté tea. Brazil nuts, balata gum, reptile skins, and sisal fibre are other products of the forests. New roads are making the region and its products more accessible.

The mineral deposits are of great variety and in some cases of very considerable size. (It has been estimated that iron ore deposits are 25 per cent of the world total.) Exploitation has been slow. Iron ore of good quality is mined on the surface in the southeast near Itaberá, production in 1963 being 10.8m. tons, and in 1971 23m. tons. Coal of not very good quality is mined and import of good coking coal has been necessary. Gold, manganese, bauxite, mica and diamonds are secondary minerals worked mainly in the southeast. Further north oil has been found, 8.7m. tons being produced in 1973, but petroleum must be imported for the refineries with a capacity of 39m. tons a year.

Except for engineering products, local industries now go a long way towards meeting home requirements for manufactured goods. Before the Second World War, Brazil was already the foremost manufacturing country of South America, and the disappearance of foreign competition during the war years did much to aid the consolidation and expansion of her industries. Those concerned with the processing of food and the production of cotton and woollen textiles are the most flourishing, the mills providing an important export of cotton piece goods. Iron and steel mills and rubber factories have also seen a great expansion. Steel production (4.5m. tons in 1971 and a planned expansion to 11m. tons in 1980) is the largest in Latin America. Other major industries now include chemical plants, oil refineries, shipbuilding, car assembly (and manufacture from 1974), electronics and a wide range of consumer durables. The main industrial area is in the mineral-rich state of Minas Gerais in the triangle Belo Horizonte–São Paulo–Rio de Janeiro, a region well served by communications and a multiplicity of major hydroelectric projects. Apart from the potential of the Amazon in the north (probably equal to that of the whole of North America) and Paulo Alfonso on the São Francisco, the major projects of the south are the Marimbondo and Furnas on the Rio Grande and the Urubupungá and the Sete Guedas on the Paraná. Eighty-five per cent of power is from hydroelectric sources.

In many regions capable of development, lack of communications has long been a barrier to progress. Over 38 000 km (24 000 miles) of railways provide an excellent network limited to the populous regions of the southeast and south, and in the northeast around Recife (Pernambuco). The state-owned Central Brazil Railway links up with the railways of Uruguay, Argentina, and Paraguay, but in some of the coastal areas there are only varying lengths of disconnected track and in the main central mass none at all. Distances are great and the terrain does not favour a widespread development of railways which account for only 10 per cent of the communications network (as against 50 per cent in the United States and 80 per cent in the USSR). Between 1959 and 1969 the road network increased from 460 000 km (286 000 miles) to 1.1m. km (680 000 miles), mainly in the industrial east and south. Although very little is surfaced, some 70 per cent of all internal freight movement is by road. Major new roads are now opening up the Amazon basin and the remoter north. Brasilia (once reached by air alone) now has road and rail links with the coast, and a road link to Belém in the north. Construction is going ahead on two Transamazonia Highways, from Recife on the coast through Humaitá to the Peru border, and from Santarém (the Amazon River port) southwards to Cuiabá in the Mato Grasso. Both exceed 1 500 km (930 miles) through difficult terrain.

Coastal shipping has long been of great importance and the volume of traffic shows a steady increase. There is also a great deal of regular traffic on the navigable waters of the main rivers, but these do not effectively serve the main centres of population. The growth of air transport has been as notable as in other South American countries, but the new roads are beginning to reduce the volume of air freight.

Brazil has received a steady flow of immigrants from Portugal, Italy and Spain and there is a large number of German settlers in the southern highlands. More than half the people are white. Rio de

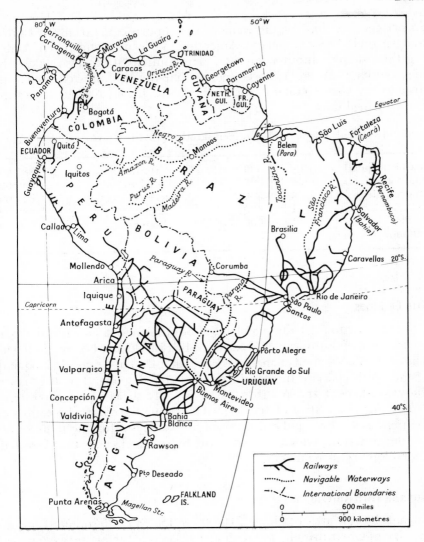

South America: principal railways and navigable waterways

Janeiro, long the capital and chief seaport, famous for the beauty of its harbour, has now been displaced both as the capital by Brasilia and as the largest city by inland São Paulo, the centre of the industrial area, and the commercial capital of the coffee industry.

With rapidly expanding industrialisation imports almost equal exports. Machinery, transport equipment, a wide range of materials, chemicals and petroleum are imported. These should be more than counterbalanced by exports in the future as the great potential of the country is developed. Meanwhile coffee accounts for between 50 and 60 per cent of the exports and agricultural products as a whole for over

841

85 per cent. A third of the value of the imports come from the United States, while West Germany, Argentina, Venezuela and Saudi Arabia together supply another quarter. The United States also takes the biggest share of the exports (nearly one-third), followed at a long distance by West Germany, the Netherlands, Japan, Argentina and the United Kingdom.

Table 94 – Brazil: populations of principal towns (1970)

Brasilia (capital)	545 000	Porto Alegre	885 000
São Paulo	5 900 000	Fortaleza	842 000
Rio de Janeiro	4 300 000	Belém	642 000
Belo Horizonte	1 233 000	Goiânia	389 000
Recife	1 080 000	Manaus	249 700
Salvador	1 000 000		

The Guianas

The only portions of the mainland of South America now remaining as possessions of European Powers since British Guiana became independent in 1966, are the Guianas — French, and Dutch — ranged along part of the north coast of the continent and extending inland till they reach the watershed of the Amazon basin. Broadly speaking, all three territories comprise a strip of fertile lowland along the coast where most of the population live, and one or more river valleys affording some access to the interior, which consists of huge blocks of the forested, undeveloped Guiana massif.

Guyana (British Guiana)

Guyana has an area of about 210 000 sq km (83 000 sq miles), nearly the size of Great Britain, and is almost as large as the other two Guianas combined. It is split into two parts by the Essequibo River, which traverses the length of the territory from south to north but is interrupted by rapids. As much as 87 per cent of the whole is forested, but less than 20 per cent of this is reasonably accessible for exploitation. Six per cent is arable and 5 per cent, though now unused, is potentially productive; the remainder is waste or swamp. Agricultural production is almost wholly confined to the lowland zone, which extends up to 48 km (30 miles) in depth along the coastline and is largely below sea level. Behind this zone a second belt, about 160 km (100 miles) deep, provides most of the territory's mineral and forest wealth. The remaining hinterland, partly mountain, partly savanna, produces hardly anything at present and lacks communications.

South America: principal roads

Sugarcane, rice, coconuts, coffee and cocoa are grown, along with tropical vegetables and fruits (mangoes, pawpaws, bananas, etc.) The livestock industry is capable of great expansion, for though the potential grazing land is extensive the number of cattle reared at the present time is less than 300 000. In the forests balata is collected and some of the timber, notably greenheart, used in underwater dock construction, is worked, providing 1 per cent of the exports in 1969. Much more valuable are the mineral products. Gold and diamonds have long been extracted from alluvial workings in the river valleys and there are deposits of manganese, iron ore, titanium, mica and quartz. Most important are the bauxite reserves. Guyana, with a production of 4.2m. tons in 1971 was the fifth largest producer in the world. The ore, with 50 to 60 per cent metal content, is a higher grade than that of Jamaica and alumina works at Mackenzie have an annual output of some 300 000 tons.

Nearly half the population of 750 000 (1971) are 'East Indians' who supply most of the labour for the sugar plantations. The others are mostly African Guyanese, working in the towns. Georgetown the capital at the mouth of the Demerara River had an estimated population of 195 000 in 1971. Guyana became independent in 1966, and a republic within the Commonwealth in 1970.

Communications are largely inadequate and electric power is mostly produced by thermal stations as hydroelectric potential has yet to be developed. Industry, somewhat boosted by joining CARIFTA as a founder member in 1968, is confined to food and timber processing, alumina production, consumer goods for the home market and, increasingly, fishing and fish processing. Exports are mainly bauxite, sugar, molasses and rum, shrimps, diamonds, alumina and timber. The importance of the processing of bauxite is shown by comparative export earnings in 1969, when 2 336 932 tons of bauxite was valued at G$62m., while 296 150 tons of alumina was worth G$39m. Imports include machinery, transport equipment, food (wheat and dairy products), chemicals and petroleum. Trade is mainly with the USA, the UK, Canada and Trinidad.

Surinam (Netherlands Guiana)

Surinam has been an autonomous territory of the Kingdom of the Netherlands since 1954. Covering an area of about 142 000 sq km (55 000 sq miles — nearly the size of England and Wales), it is similar in character to Guyana, with a corresponding low coastal zone and a rising hinterland covered with forest and jungle growth. It lacks the broad central valley that distinguishes Guyana, but has a smaller area of 'waste' — about a fifteenth of the whole. Forests cover nearly all the rest of the country. Arable and pastoral areas are estimated at only 40 000 ha (100 000 acres). The cultivated area, producing a variety of tropical products, chiefly paddy, sugarcane, bananas and citrus fruits, is in the coastal zone, where the rivers are navigable.

Bauxite, alumina and aluminium are by far the main export items, providing 75 per cent of total exports in 1971. With a production of 6.7m. tons of bauxite Surinam is third to Australia and Jamaica in world production. Exports, which include rice, fish and timber products, have moved ahead of imports since 1966. Trade is mainly with the USA, the Netherlands, Trinidad and West Germany. About half the population of 400 000 (1970) are Asians. Paramaribo, with

150 000 inhabitants is the capital and chief port, and the only large town. It lies on the Surinam River, a few kilometres from its mouth. This river and others form a convenient means of communication with parts of the interior, but navigation of the upper reaches is prevented by rapids which in turn offer hydroelectric potential.

French Guiana

French Guiana is the smallest and least developed of the three territories, with an area of about 90 000 sq km (35 000 sq miles; about a sixth the size of France) of which it is an overseas department. About 95 per cent of the territory is covered with forest; only some 3 300 ha (8 000 acres) are under crops, producing paddy, maize, manioc and sugarcane. The mineral structure includes bauxite and gold, but the deposits are widely scattered and not easily worked. Cayenne, the capital and chief port, has nearly half the total population of 51 000, almost all of whom live in the coastal area. The notorious Devil's Isle is no longer used as a penal settlement. Exports are mainly timber and shrimps, and almost all trade is with France and the United States.

Venezuela

The United States of Venezuela comprise twenty autonomous states, two territories, and a federal district, constituting a federal republic in the north of the continent, bordering Colombia in the west, Brazil in the south, and Guyana in the east. Its 3 220 km (2 000 mile) coastline looks northward, mostly to the Caribbean but also to the open Atlantic. There are four well-defined regions: the main mass of the Guyana Highlands in the southeast; the central plains, or *llanos*, occupying the basin of the Orinoco; the northern highlands, formed by the Andean and coastal ranges; and the lowlands around the great lake or lagoon of Maracaibo, in the extreme northwest corner.

The Guyana Highlands, rising towards the south to about 3 050 m (10 000 ft), occupy about half the total area of 912 000 sq km (352 000 sq miles — four times the size of Great Britain) and are heavily forested, but have been little explored or exploited. The grassy central plains cover a quarter of the country and support about 20 per cent of the population of 10.5m.; the northern highlands (reaching a height of over 4 880 m (16 000 ft) in the Andes and nearly 2 740 m (9 000 ft) along the coastal range) support about 55 per cent. Another 15 per cent of the population inhabit the Maracaibo lowlands, which are the smallest of the four regions but the chief source of the country's wealth.

Venezuela is the fifth oil producer after USA, USSR, Saudi Arabia and Iran, and it exports more crude petroleum than any other country.

The industry has grown very rapidly; the 1956 yield of 129m. tons (904m. barrels) was more than twice that of 1946, six times that of 1934, and nearly fifty times that of 1925. In 1963 the yield was 169m. tons and in 1973, 175m. Oil now provides over 90 per cent by value of all Venezuela's exports. It is found in three areas, of which the basin of Lake Maracaibo with 75 per cent is by far the most important. Some of the fields lie beneath the waters of the so-called 'lake', which is in fact a landlocked bay or lagoon of 12 950 sq km (5 000 sq miles) opening on to the Gulf of Maracaibo and navigable throughout by shallow-draught tankers. About a third of the output is refined locally, but most of it goes to the great refineries in the Netherlands West Indies. The oil companies are almost entirely foreign-owned, the Venezuelan government receiving half the profits. Another mineral of noteworthy but variable production is gold, found towards the Guyana border. Asphalt deposits occur in many places but few are worked. Iron is a comparatively recent discovery and has rapidly become a valuable export.

The agricultural picture is less spectacular but is still of great importance in the general economy — thirty years ago it was the mainstay. The trade winds blow parallel to the northern coast; rainfall is often scanty, and there are large areas of scrub in this zone. Where the rainfall is higher, sugar, cocoa, and tobacco are grown on the lowlands, and coffee in the temperate valleys, together with cotton in some drier parts. Maize, beans, and rice are widely grown; wheat, on the higher ground, to a smaller extent. Coffee and cocoa are export crops, the remainder subsistence crops. The aggregate of the arable land (over 2.4m. ha; about 6m. acres) is only one-thirtieth of the total and nearly half of it lies fallow. The attractions of urban life and growing industrialisation have caused a major rural exodus. The broad plains of the Orinoco are devoted to stock raising but the quality of the pasture is not first-class and lack of communications has retarded development. Livestock are dominated by cattle, estimated to number 6m.

Over 20 per cent of the country is forested, but its products are potential rather than actual, and large tracts of valuable woods await serious exploitation. More than half the total area is classed as built on, waste, or unknown. The key to its development lies largely in the extension of internal communications. There are less than 500 km (310 miles) of railways, including 300 km (185 miles) owned by the oil and other mining companies. Large extensions of the 'all-weather' roads are the major projects, with expressways linking the main cities. River transport offers considerable possibilities in the central area, where the Orinoco and its tributaries are navigable for about 9 600 km (6 000 miles). The main river, 22 km (14 miles) broad where it enters its low swampy delta, is navigable for 1 600 km (994 miles), and ocean-going vessels are able to make the 430 km (270 mile) journey up to

Ciudad Bolivar, which ranks as a seaport. The river is also the major factor in the development of the new industrial centre at Ciudad Guayana (previously San Tome de Guayana and Puerto Orday) at the confluence of the Caroni and the Orinoco.

The development of hydroelectric power at the Guri (with a potential of 6m. kW) and Macagua Dams on the Caroni has been essential to the planned diversification of industry away from over-dependence on oil. Steel works, iron ore enrichment, aluminium and petrochemicals are being encouraged to add to the existing oil refineries, food processing, textile, cement and leather factories. The new industrial centre of Ciudad Guayana has a population approaching 200 000 and is well placed for future expansion with ample resources of raw materials, power and communications. In addition to iron ore, there is manganese, gold, diamonds, coal and limestone, and there are further oil reserves north of the Orinoco.

The increasingly favourable balance, which has been a feature of foreign trade in the postwar years, provides a basis for the expansion of potential exporting industries. Venezuela is not as yet a member of CARIFTA or of the Andean Pact (Chile, Colombia, Peru, Bolivia, Ecuador) and trade is still largely with the United States, but decreasingly so: the United States took 68 per cent of exports in 1950; 50 in 1965; and 38 in 1970. Oil accounts for 90 to 95 per cent of all exports, followed by iron ore and a little coffee, rice and sugar destined to the United States, the Netherlands, Antilles, Canada, the United Kingdom and Trinidad. Imports are largely machinery, transport equipment, manufactured goods and wheat from the USA, West Germany, Japan, Canada and the UK.

Table 95 – Venezuela: estimated population of principal towns (1970)

Caracas	2 500 000	Valencia	290 000
Maracaibo	715 100	Maracay	209 000
Barquisimento	345 600	San Cristóbal	136 000

Colombia

This republic with an area of 1.1m. sq km (456 500 sq miles) is more than twice the size of France, and occupies the northwestern corner of South America, bordering upon Venezuela and Brazil in the east, Peru and Ecuador in the south. In the north and west its 3 220 km (2 000 mile) coastline is broken near its centre by the narrow land mass of Panama, so that one part (the longer) is washed by the Caribbean and the other by the Pacific. The chain of the Andes, following the

Pacific coast closely as it sweeps up from the south, spreads out northward into three roughly parallel ranges — the western, central and eastern cordilleras — which maintain a height of 3 000 to 4 270 m (10 000 to 14 000 ft). In the valleys between, in the adjoining coastal areas, and particularly on the healthy tablelands of the eastern cordillera, live 96 per cent of Colombia's population of 21.2m. The remainder of the people are dispersed over the greater area to the east, a broad, little-developed plain consisting of grassland in the north and tropical forest in the south.

The Equator passes through the southern extremity of the country, but because of its varied altitudes Colombia offers considerable climatic diversity, including a tropical zone (up to 1 370 m: 4 500 ft), a subtropical zone, and a temperate highland zone (above 2 280 m: 7 500 ft), while in the highest regions there is perpetual snow. Dry (*verano*: summer) and wet (*invierno*: winter) seasons usually alternate every three months, but this is not the experience everywhere. The great range of climate gives rise to a correspondingly great range of crops.

About 2.4m. ha (6m. acres), less than 2 per cent is classified as arable, the most fertile soil occurring in the Andean valleys in areas inconveniently remote from the sea, so that access is slow. In the subtropical zone and in the higher parts of the tropical zone, and especially in the Cauca valley, the most important crop is coffee, of which Colombia is the world's second largest source of supply, producing about one-half (480 000 tons) of Brazil's crop in 1968. The yield is of fine and mild quality, and the quickly recurrent seasons mean that picking can go on almost throughout the year. On the higher ground of the temperate zone wheat and other grains are common, but small farms are the rule, even for coffee production. In the lowlands, maize and rice, sugarcane, cocoa, and bananas are grown. To all these products may be added a host of others: plantains, potatoes, beans, tobacco, fibres, cotton, oilseeds, coconuts, and rubber.

Nearly a third of Colombia consists of natural grazing land and in consequence the livestock industry is important. There are over 18m. head of cattle as well as over 1m. each of sheep, pigs, and horses. But the greater part of the country (50 per cent) is covered with forests which are little developed. The mineral wealth is great, including gold, silver, copper, lead, mercury, manganese, emeralds and platinum (one of the largest deposits in the world). Petroleum is increasingly important with deposits in the north and in the south in Putomago. Pipelines have been laid across difficult country; including one of 300 km (185 miles) across the Andes (at 3 500 m: 11 500 ft) to Tumaco in the south, and another of 400 km (250 miles) from Manizales to the Caribbean. Production in 1973 was 10m. tons, the fourth largest in Latin America after Venezuela, Mexico and Argentina. Less than half is refined within the country — chiefly at Barrancabermeja.

The rivers in the populous region flow northwards to the Caribbean and form Colombia's main outlets: the Magdalena is navigable for 1 290 km (800 miles) and its tributary the Cauca for 250 km (155 miles). But in spite of the paramount importance of the Magdalena as a means of communication it is not without its disadvantages, for droughts sometimes render it unnavigable and shifting sandbanks are prevalent. In the less populous region in the east rivers flow out of the country and into the Orinoco and the Amazon. The terrain does not facilitate the development of railways and roads, and the problems are formidable in the case of lateral communications. The communities therefore tend to be isolated from one another with twenty cities having a population of over 100 000 as the centres of their regions. Some 3 500 km (2 200 miles) of railways consist to a large degree of short lines connecting highland areas with their river ports. Motor roads extend over a network of 45 000 km (28 000 miles) but are not always good, though they include three main north—south highways forming part of international systems. In one mountain area the problem of freight conveyance has been solved by an aerial cableway of 72 km (45 miles — the longest in the world). Air development has made striking progress particularly in the remote eastern region, and frequent services now link remote areas with the main centres. Bogotá, the capital, is within 5° of the Equator, but, by virtue of its situation 2 200 m (8 660 ft) above sea level, enjoys a healthy climate. It is 1 210 km (750 miles) from the Caribbean ports of Barranquilla and Cartagena and 725 km (450 miles) from the Pacific port of Buenaventura, with which it is connected by a somewhat roundabout rail route. In spite of its remote situation and indifferent communications it is the largest commercial and distribution centre.

In 1948 Colombia joined with Ecuador, Panama, and Venezuela in forming a commercial and economic union. (All four territories were formerly united in the great but shortlived Republic of Colombia founded by Simon Bolivar in 1819.) In 1970 Colombia joined Chile, Peru, Bolivia and Ecuador to form the Andean Pact with the objects of improving trade within the market of 57m. people so formed and of reducing dependence on foreign capital. The increasing use of natural gas and hydroelectric and thermal power has encouraged industrial growth which is centred mainly on mining, petroleum, assembly of imported components and processing of primary agricultural products. Foreign trade is broadly in balance, with exports of coffee (55—60 per cent), petroleum and products, bananas, sugar, cotton and some manufactures (paper and paperboard; textiles) to the USA, West Germany, the Netherlands, Spain and the UK. Imports, manufactured goods of all types, chemicals, iron and steel, come mainly from the USA, West Germany, the UK, Spain and Japan.

Table 96 – Colombia: population of principal towns (1970)

Bogotá	2 512 000	Barranquilla	640 800
Medellín	1 089 000	Cartagena	318 000
Cali	917 600	Bucaramanga	315 400

Ecuador

Ecuador is the smallest of the four republics sharing the Pacific coast of South America. It is bordered on the north by Colombia and on the east and south by Peru, with whom it had to accept a settlement in 1942 favourable to Peruvian claims in a long-standing dispute over the ownership of a large tract of territory east of the Andes – Ecuador's Region Oriental. This treaty was unilaterally denounced by Ecuador in 1961, and estimates of the area of Ecuador are extraordinarily diverse. United Nations publications give the area as 270 670 sq km (104 505 sq miles) excluding 'Oriente Province' and the Galápagos Islands. Other estimates of up to 455 000 sq km (175 000 sq miles) add to the variety of choice. The first census, taken in 1950, met with active opposition from the tribes of the interior. The returns showed a population of something over 3m. Latest estimate (1970), 6.1m.

Ecuador owes its name to the fact that its capital, Quito, is almost on the Equator, where it lies at a height of 2 830 m (9 300 ft). Bordering the Pacific are undulating plains up to 145 km (90 miles) wide and about 640 km (400 miles) long. Behind these is a highland area formed by two parallel chains of the Andes. East of these is the much disputed Oriente, now confined, according to cartographical representation of the 1942 settlement to an almost uninhabited corner of the upper Amazon basin in the far northeast of Ecuador. Of the 270 000 sq km (104 000 sq miles) credited to the republic in United Nations statistics, over 54 per cent is covered with a vast forest. Another 21 per cent though potentially productive, is not in use. Though only a small proportion is in active farming use – about 4 per cent arable and 8 per cent pastoral – agriculture is the mainstay of the republic's economy.

The two cordilleran chains, rising to over 6 000 m (20 000 ft) are separated by a valley which lies 2 400 to 3 000 m (8 000 to 10 000 ft) above sea level and is divided into ten basins or pockets by lava ridges formed by the neighbouring volcanic heights. Each of these basins is a centre of population, and between them they hold the greater part of the population. In this highland zone the main agricultural occupations are the raising of livestock and the growing of temperate cereals, fruit and vegetables for home consumption. Livestock include 2.5m. cattle; 1.9m. sheep; 1.4m. pigs and 250 000 horses (1971). The sheep are confined to the highlands, while other livestock are scattered throughout the country generally.

Tropical farming is pursued in the coastal zone and the Guayas basin with the aid of irrigation, and this region is responsible for almost all the exports. Cocoa was for long the outstanding product, but the incidence of witchbroom disease caused output to decline greatly. During the Second World War cocoa was overtaken by rice, in spite of the primitive methods of rice cultivation and the low yield; and more recently coffee and bananas have come to the fore. In recent years Ecuador has led the world in exports of bananas, though third to Brazil and India in total production.

The Ecuadorean forests are the world's principal source of supply of that extraordinarily light wood, balsa. Other forest products include rubber, kapok, hardwood logs, tagua or ivory nuts (for the manufacture of buttons and collar studs), cinchona bark (quinine) and the straw of the toquilla palm (of which Panama hats are made). The great bulk of the forest products are too remote for exploitation.

Oil is found, but output is less than 10m. tons. Refining capacity is greater than this, and crude oil is imported. Gold, silver, copper, and lead are also worked in small quantities.

Manufacturing industries are on a small scale and include — in addition to cement, textiles, sugar refining and oil refining — the making of Panama hats, so named because they reach the United States and European markets by way of Panama. It is a declining industry. There are resources of coal, iron, gold, silver, copper and kaolin, but mining is carried out on a small scale. Further industrial expansion will await development of hydroelectric power, for which the foothills of the Andes offer great opportunity to the east of the Guayas basin.

Bananas provided nearly two-thirds of the exports, coffee and cocoa 30 per cent — 90 per cent between them. The United States supplies over half the imports, followed by West Germany, Japan and the UK. Exports are to the USA, West Germany, Belgium, Colombia and Italy.

Guayaquil (680 000), the chief port, is connected with Quito (402 000), situated in one of the highland basins, by a railway which rises to 3 540 m (11 653 ft), but communications generally are not developed and there is great dependence on air movement and small airfields.

Galápagos Islands. To Ecuador belong the Galápagos (Tortoise) Islands, a group situated on the Equator about 960 km (600 miles) from the coast, with an aggregate area of some 7 800 sq km (3 000 sq miles) and a population (1967) of about 3 000. Guano and orchilla moss (for purple dyes) are exported, and the group is a centre for commercial fisheries.

Peru

Peru is third in size of the republics of South America, its 1.28m. sq km (496 000 sq miles) giving it an area over five times that of Great Britain. The 14.4m. inhabitants, of whom rather more than half are whites or mestizos, and rather less than half are Indians, are distributed unevenly: most of the whites live along the coast, where the cool Humboldt Current tempers the tropical heat, and most of the Indians inhabit the mountains of the south as they have done since the days of the Inca civilisation. The Andes here form a broad belt, 320 to 400 km (200 to 250 miles) wide, of plateaus and mountain chains dissected by deep longitudinal valleys and rising to over 6 100 m (20 000 ft) in some of the loftiest heights in South America. The main watershed, the western cordillera, rises steeply from a narrow and arid coastal strip to form an unbroken barrier which hinders communication and hardly drops below 4 300 m (14 000 ft). The steepness of the valleys adds the threat of avalanches to the periodic earthquakes which afflict the country. On the landward side the heavily forested Andean slopes give way to the hot tropical lowlands of the Amazon basin in a vast, sparsely inhabited region which covers half the country.

Forests comprise about 67 per cent of all Peru, waste and built on areas another 10 per cent. The balance of 23 per cent is suitable for farming — a little over 2 per cent for cultivated crops and 21 per cent (mostly rough grazings) for livestock. There are no broad fertile plains, and arable land is confined to strips developed along the river valleys. The dry ribbon of the coastal zone, 2 250 km (1 400 miles) by 40 to 80 km (25 to 50 miles) wide, is crossed by the courses of over fifty rivers; most of them dry up from time to time, but wherever the volume of water is sufficient irrigation is practised and the land intensively cultivated. Water is also brought by tunnel from rivers flowing eastwards to the Amazon. Production for the export trade occurs chiefly in the northern sector of this zone, where cotton, sugar, and rice are the staple crops. In the central sector, cotton is supplemented by fruit and market-garden produce, while the southern sector specialises in subsistence crops for the local Indian population. Subsistence crops — wheat, maize, barley, oats, and potatoes — are grown more extensively in some of the valleys of the *sierra*, or highland region, corresponding to the concentrations of Indian population. But with such a limited arable area, food is an important import. The pastures of the *sierra*, though of indifferent quality, support large numbers of sheep 17.1m., cattle 4.1m., llamas, alpacas, etc., 4.76m., goats 1.8m., and pigs nearly 2m. The llama is the traditional beast of burden.

Agricultural development of the trans-Andean region, or *montana*, is on a small scale, though there are extensive areas which are considered suitable for cultivation and stock raising. Difficulties of transport and the hot climate have militated against development, and the valuable timbers of the area remain largely untouched, though a great variety of useful products — rubber, balata, quinine, kapok, and medicinal plants — come from the forests of this region.

The northward flowing Humboldt Current teems with fish, which attract a prolific bird life; but the extensive deposits of guano on the islands along the coast are greatly depleted and are no longer such a great asset to Peru's agricultural industry.

The republic is exceptionally rich in mineral resources, which include petroleum in the northern extremity of the coastal zone and in newly discovered fields in Amazonas (3.6m. tons in 1973), and copper, gold, silver, lead, zinc, iron, coal, and molybdenum, often mined in remote workings high up in the Andes. Some of the copper mines have been worked for centuries, and Peru is the third largest producer of silver in the world. Minerals do not, however, challenge the leading position of agriculture in the economic life of the country, but they provide some 50 per cent of foreign trade earnings. Raw cotton and sugar remain of some importance. The bulk of the cotton is of the Tanguis variety, a long-staple type which is native to Peru and was in great demand in world markets. Total production in 1971 was 250 000 tons. Sugar production in that year amounted to 823 000 tons. Other agricultural exports are fish, fishmeal, coffee, hides, and skins, and wool. In recent years there has been a spectacular development in the fishing industry so that Peru in 1964 led even Japan in landings of fish. Peru has become the largest exporter of fishmeal in the world — 32 per cent, of total exports in 1971 (45 per cent of world total fishmeal supplies).

Cotton mills employ several thousand workers and other industrial establishments include woollen mills and rayon factories, iron and steel works, and a petroleum refinery. A number of industries produce consumer goods, nearly all of them centred in and around Lima, the capital, which lies midway along and behind the coast, close to its excellent modern harbour, Callao. Most of the imports for the whole country are brought in through Callao, but exports leave through a string of smaller ports situated nearer the centres of production, while the products of the Amazon region find their outlet through the river port of Iquitos to the Atlantic.

The seaports are linked by coastwise services which play an important part in the communications system. Because of the nature of the terrain, road and rail routes have been developed primarily to link the centres of production with the nearest ports. There is now a highway extending along the coastal zone (the Inter-American Highway), and another crosses the *sierra* to connect Lima with the navigable headwaters of the Amazon. Work started in 1965 on the Carretera Marginal de la Selva (Marginal Forest Highway) which will link the Columbian—Venezuela border with Santa Cruz, Bolivia; 2 460 km (1 529 miles) will run through Peru. The railways grouped separately in the northern, central, and southern regions and comprising 2 880 km (1 790 miles) of track, have been largely instrumental in opening up the mineral resources of the country. Two of the routes, by which the tablelands of the Andes are reached, are among the most remarkable in the world. The Lima–Oroya line attains in its passage through the western cordillera a height of 4 780 m (15 665 ft). The other Andes railway rises from the southern seaport of Mollendo by way of Arequipa to Lake Titicaca, attaining on the way an altitude of 4 480 m (14 688 ft). Lake Titicaca is the largest lake in South America and is shared between Peru and Bolivia. The railway from Mollendo is one of the chief means of access to the latter republic, which has no coast of its own, but great use is now made of air services as throughout the Andean area.

Exports are mainly minerals and metals (54 per cent — copper, iron ore, and silver), fishmeal, cotton, sugar and coffee to the United States, West Germany, Belgium–Luxembourg and the Netherlands. Imports — machinery, transport equipment, manufactured goods, wheat and chemicals — come mainly from the USA, West Germany, Japan, Argentina and the UK.

Table 97 — Peru: population of principal towns (1972 estimate)

Lima	3 317 700	Chiclayo	141 040
Callao	335 000	Cuzco	109 600
Arequipa	195 000	Huancayo	80 570
Trujillo	156 700	Iquitos	67 920

Bolivia

Bolivia, twice the size of France, is the most thinly populated of the South American republics; its 1.1m. sq km (424 000 sq miles) support about 5m. people — 4.5 to the sq km (12 to the sq mile). Up to the of the war with Chile in 1879–82 it had the advantage of a coastline on the Pacific between Arica and Antofagasta, but since then it has been wholly an inland state, hemmed in by Brazil, Paraguay, Argentina, Chile and Peru.

The western part of the country consists of a high plateau, the Altiplano, covering 16 830 sq km (6 500 sq miles) and maintaining an average height of 3 960 m (13 000 ft), flanked on either side by the two main chains of the Andes, with peaks rising to over 6 400 m (21 000 ft). In the south the plateau is semidesert; the northern part, which is better watered and contains the only substantial concentration of population, terminates in the shallow depression which holds Lake Titicaca and carries the frontier with Peru. The eastern cordillera — split by fertile valleys known as *yungas* — drops sharply beyond the plateau to the forested lowlands of the Amazon basin (with its northward-flowing rivers) and descends in a series of gently falling *sierras* to the valley of the Paraguay (with its southward-flowing rivers). These eastern lowlands, constituting about two-thirds of the whole country, are difficult of access and remain virtually undeveloped. Their tropical climate contrasts with the subtropical temperatures of the *yungas* and the cool or cold temperatures of the plateau.

Less than 3 per cent of the total area is classed as arable land, and most of that is lying fallow. Pasture occupies 10 per cent, forests over 42 per cent. On the plateau there is a limited production of potatoes and the hardier cereals; other cereals, cocoa, and coffee are grown in the *yungas*; and sugar, rice, and cotton are cultivated on the few developed patches of the eastern plains. Forest products from these plains range from balsa to tropical hardwoods and include a fluctuating yield of rubber and quinine bark. Livestock include 2.4m. cattle, and 6.8m. sheep (1970–71), as well as many llamas (used as pack animals), and alpacas (providing a small export of wool). Stock-raising is carried on in cleared areas in the Amazon basin, from which refrigerating plants send their meat to La Paz by air.

It is estimated that two-thirds of the population gain their livelihood from agriculture and less than 3 per cent from mining, but commercially the mines are the dominant factor, providing over 75 per cent of the exports. The main focus of activity is tin, which is found in the mountain area, is difficult to mine and yet provides 60 per cent of all exports. Bolivia ranks next to Malaysia as a producer of tin, supplying 29 000 tons (16 per cent) in 1968, against Malaysia's 76 000 tons (41 per cent), out of a world total of 185 000 tons, exclusive of the USSR. The government has acquired the principal mines. Silver has been mined on the plateau since the Spaniards discovered the Potosi deposits in the sixteenth century. Lead, antimony, copper, wolfram, and zinc are found in the upland districts, and the ores are enriched for export. A new tin smelter near Oruro will have a planned capacity of 20 000 tons a year, and antimony and zinc plants will follow. Petroleum and natural gas, sufficient for the countries needs are produced in the Camiri and Santa Cruz districts — with an oil pipeline across the Andes to Arica, and a planned gas pipeline to Argentina. Industrial development is small and a wide range of products must be imported. Long-term projects aim at providing new rail and road communications which will give the potentially fruitful eastern regions convenient access to the centres of population on the plateau.

Various railways, covering close on 3 520 km (2 190 miles) and attaining to heights of over 4 570 m (15 000 ft) extend from Lake Titicaca to Argentina, and link up with Chilean lines which climb steeply up the western cordillera from the ports of Arica and Antofagasta. Much of the greater part of Bolivia's foreign trade passes through these ports. Another outlet is the Peruvian port of Mollendo, reached first by steamer across Lake Titicaca and then by rail. Roads cover more than 20 000 km (12 500 miles), but not all of them are passable in wet weather. Particularly important is the new motor highway through difficult country from Cochabamba to the farming country of Santa Cruz. In the northeast lowlands are broad, navigable rivers, tributaries of the Madeira whose rapids on the Brazilian side of the frontier are bypassed by railway. In the southeast, Bolivia is reached from Buenos Aires by river steamers which follow the course of the Paraguay. Sucre, in the south of the plateau, is the legal capital, but the seat of government and virtual capital is La Paz, not far from Lake Titicaca. At some 3 800 m (12 000 ft) La Paz and its airport are the highest in the world.

Exports are chiefly ores and concentrates (tin, wolfram, copper, antimony, silver, lead, zinc, bismuth and sulphur) with a little coffee, rubber and petroleum. Almost all go to the USA (41 per cent), the UK (39 per cent) and Argentina (7 per cent). Imports include a wide range of manufactures, transport equipment, wheat and consumer goods. They are increasingly covered by exports and come in the main from the USA, Japan, West Germany, Argentina and the UK.

Table 98 — Bolivia: estimated population of principal towns (1970)

La Paz	562 000	Oruro	119 700
Cochabamba	149 000	Potosi	96 800
Santa Cruz	125 000	Sucre	84 900

Chile

The Republic of Chile comprises the whole of the Pacific coast of South America south of Peru, together with the islands that fringe the coast, including part of Tierra del Fuego and the entire length of the Strait of Magellan. It is some 4 260 km (2 650 miles) from north to south with an average width of 177 km (110 miles) — a narrow strip of territory that would just fit comfortably across the North Atlantic from Land's End to Nova Scotia. For the greater part of its length, the long frontier with Argentina follows the watershed of the Andes, whose slopes fill over half the width of the strip to an average height of 3 050 m (10 000 ft) and culminate in the northern part in peaks exceeding 6 710 m (22 000 ft). A range of lesser heights along the coast is separated from the main cordillera by a longitudinal trough. Chile also administers Easter Island and other small Pacific islands, and claims a sector of Antarctica.

The northern portion of the country is a continuation of the desert strip along the coast of Peru; this gives place in the middle portion, between Coquimbo and Concepción, to a 'Mediterranean' region which contains the bulk of the population, while further south again is a region which suffers progressively from an excess of wind and rain. The extremes of climate combine with the physical structure to render barren 42 per cent of a country which occupies 741 700 sq km (286 400 sq miles), or three times the area of the United Kingdom. Another 10 per cent, potentially productive, is still unused. About 27 per cent in the southern region forms a forest zone, and of the remainder 6 per cent is arable land and nearly 15 per cent rich permanent pasture on the sheltered Atlantic side.

The agricultural products are mainly wheat, barley, oats, potatoes, and southern fruits — similar in fact to those of Spain and California. The temperature, however, is somewhat lower, so that oranges are not grown as a commercial product. Most of the agricultural production occurs in the central zone, particularly in the longitudinal valley, and in those areas to the north where it is assisted by extensive irrigation. All irrigated farms of over 80 ha (200 acres) are being expropriated for redistribution to small holdings and cooperatives. Crops fluctuate greatly from year to year. Wheat is widely grown, and until 1930 was a major export. Recently the rising population has exceeded food production. Some two-thirds of all food is now imported — and food is 25 per cent of imports.

The livestock industry, including nearly 3m. cattle and 6.8m. sheep, is the source of small exports of fresh and frozen meat, as well as of a considerable quantity of wool, but large imports of beef cattle are made from Argentina across the passes of the Andes. The district around Valdivia, about 40° S, is largely given over to cattle, while more than half the sheep are reared in the extreme south, in Chilean Patagonia and Tierra del Fuego. Fishing is also important, and there is production and export of fishmeal.

In Chile, however, as in most other countries on the western side of South America, mineral wealth is the dominating commercial factor. Minerals, mainly from the northern provinces, provide over four-fifths of Chile's exports by value. Copper alone accounts for 75 per cent; its output of over 1m. tons in 1971 surpassed only by the USA, and the USSR. The reserves of copper ore are estimated to be about a quarter of the world total. Nitrates from the northern Atacama desert provide another 5 per cent. Early in the century Chile enjoyed a virtual monopoly of nitrate fertilisers, and though the competition of synthetic nitrogenous fertilisers has greatly reduced the dependence on Chile, the industry remains a very important one. Two-thirds of the world's iodine is produced as a byproduct of the nitrate works. Large deposits of iron ore are worked in the province of Coquimbo, while in the neighbourhood of Concepción is found one of the few South American sources of coal, with an output of 2m. tons annually. Among a great many lesser mineral products may be mentioned gold and silver, manganese, molybdenum, borax, sulphur, salt, and oil. Oil was struck in Tierra del Fuego in 1945 and in 1973 production exceeded 1.8m. tons. With a refinery capacity in excess of 5m. tons, Chile is an oil importer.

Manufacturing industries have made tremendous strides in the last few decades, strong contributing factors being the development of hydroelectric power and the diversity of raw materials. Textiles, leather goods, chemicals, flour, iron and steel goods, petrochemicals, plastics and motorcars are among the wide range of products.

Most of the internal trade is carried in coastwise shipping, which, however, suffers from a lack of good harbours in those parts where the population is most concentrated, though sheltered inlets and natural harbours are plentiful enough further south. Small bulk carriers and refrigerator ships of up to 80 000 tons are used in this trade. The railways are limited to one long central line — following the longitudinal valley and linking the centre with the north and south — with many short arms reaching out to the sea or into the mountains. Two arms extend across the Andes into Argentina, one to link Valparaiso with Buenos Aires, the other to join Antofagasta with Salta. The road system is also based on main routes following the longitudinal valley. The Inter-American Highway is paved throughout its length to the southern terminal at Puerto Montt.

The population of 9.8m. is 40 per cent European and 60 per cent mestizo. The capital, Santiago, is an inland city, and its port is Valparaiso, on a fine bay looking to the north. Here is received the great bulk of the imports, but exports are mainly from the northern ports of Antofagasta and Iquique, nearer the centres of mineral production. Punta Arenas, on the stormy Strait of Magellan, is the southernmost city in the world.

Copper, from the great opencast pits of the Andes, is now state-controlled (as are all mineral rights), and provides 70 to 80 per cent of all foreign exchange earnings; Chile is the world's leading exporter. Such dependence on a single commodity makes the economy sensitive to world price fluctuations which have proved difficult to control (either by agreement among the major producers or by control of scrap metal, which can be the source of 40 per cent of the total supply). Prices fluctuate rapidly, for example £718 per ton in 1970; £418 in 1971; £1 400 in 1974. Other exports are iron ore, chemical products, paper and pulp, and fishmeal. Copper widens the range of trading partners to the USA, the UK, the Netherlands, Japan, Italy, West Germany, Spain, Argentina and Brazil. Imports are mainly manufactured goods, food (cereals, live animals, sugar and coffee), chemicals

Table 99 — Chile: population of principal towns (1970 estimate)

Greater Santiago (1972)	3 720 000	Antofagasta	120 000
Valparaiso	296 000	Valdivia	89 500
Concepción	178 000	Talca	84 000
Viña del Mar	169 000	Punta Arenas	67 600
Talchuano	139 000		

and petroleum from the USA, West Germany, Argentina, the UK, Venezuela, Mexico and Japan.

Argentina

Argentina, or the República Argentina, comprises a territory of more than 2.7m. sq km (1m. sq miles) — nearly a sixth of the whole South American continent, whose 'tail' it shares with Chile. Extending half the length of the continent it exhibits a corresponding diversity of climate: from the tropical zone of the Chaco plains in the north, through the temperate zone of the central grasslands, or pampas, to the cool temperate zone of the Patagonian plateau (1 980 m: 6 500 ft above sea level) in the south. The frontier with Chile follows the main watershed of the Andes, which reach well over 6 100 m (20 000 ft), and give place eastwards to a broad and dry sub-Andine belt before dropping to the northern and central lowlands.

The district in which the bulk of the population of 24m. is established is the pampa region, stretching fanwise around Buenos Aires for a distance of some 640 km (400 miles) from that city. Here there is the main commercial region with a climate well suited to peoples of European stock; the soil is rich and deep. There is generally an ample rainfall in the eastern districts, but towards the interior the rainfall diminishes and irrigation becomes necessary for cultivation. To the north of this fertile and populous zone the forest-covered lowlands of the Gran Chaco, extending into Bolivia and Paraguay, form a vast, little-developed area with great potentialities. Swampy in summer, it has a dry winter season, the climate combining with the remoteness to hinder settlement. The sparse population is largely the dwindling Indian component. The undulating ground between the Chaco and the frontiers with Uruguay and Brazil has been described as a 'mesopotamian' region, from the position it occupies in the fork of the great Rivers Parana and Uruguay.

In the present century the Republic has undergone a rapid development, parallel with that in the United States and Canada. Streams of agricultural settlers have entered the country, principally from Italy and Spain. During the Second World War the numbers fell to a trickle, and though later they rose again with French immigrants from North Africa, the increase has not been stable. Economic development has been predominantly agricultural. Today just over half the total area is classed as agricultural and ranching land, permanent pastures covering 41 per cent and arable land nearly 12 per cent, while forests occupy another 32 per cent and the remaining 15 per cent is waste or built on.

Argentina stands among the great food-exporting countries of the world. It has become identified particularly with the production of meat, but the yield from crops have been hardly less important. Cereals alone contribute about a third of the value of all the exports. Wheat and maize are the main crops. Wheat is grown on over 3.75m. ha (9m. acres) in the drier parts of the pampas, the wheat lands forming a gigantic crescent from Rosario to Bahia Blanca, and the output in normal seasons is 5 to 7m. tons. Sometimes, not only wheat but crop production generally suffers a setback by reason of prolonged droughts. During such a period, around the turn of the half-century, the 1951—52 wheat crop was returned as only 2m. tons. Improved strains of wheat are reducing the area under cultivation, and the increasing self-sufficiency of former importers is affecting the traditional export pattern. Maize, which is grown in the wetter and warmer areas of the northern pampas, and before the war averaged nearly 8m. tons a year from 4m. ha (10m. acres), was reduced in 1949—50 to less than 1m. tons from 2m. ha (5m. acres). It has now recovered to 4m. ha (9.8m. acres) yielding nearly 19m. tons with the improved strains (1971). Barley, oats, and rye each produce about 500 000 tons a year. Argentina is second only to the USA in the export of feed grains.

Apart from cereals, a crop of outstanding importance is alfalfa (lucerne), which provides excellent cattle food for the livestock industry. Flax is cultivated for seed, and linseed has been one of Argentina's most valuable crops, averaging before the war nearly 1.75m. tons from nearly 2.5m. ha (6.5m. acres); but the 1955 crop was only 235 000 tons. Since then production has improved and both linseed and linseed oil are exported. While linseed has declined from its prewar eminence, sunflowerseed, which has gained in favour as a source of edible oil, has gone rapidly ahead, from an average prewar crop of 150 000 tons to over 1.3m. tons in 1971.

Olive trees flourish, notably in the Mendoza district in the west, and the vine and sugarcane are both cultivated, the vine on irrigated fields in the 'oasis' pockets of Mendoza and San Juan, near the base of the Andes, and sugar around Tucumán and Salta in the northwest. The elevation of Tucumán is only about 460 m (1 500 ft), but Salta lies nearly 1 220 m (4 000 ft) above sea level, and the canefields, although so near to the tropics, have been known to suffer damage from frost, which more frequently injures the grain crops. Argentina is the fourth largest wine producer (after Italy, France and Spain) but, with an annual consumption of 90 litres (20 gallons) per head, almost all goes to home consumption.

Cotton is grown on the edge of the Chaco lowlands, yielding about 87 000 tons of ginned cotton; and enough rice is grown in the north to meet internal needs. Potatoes come both from the pampas and the sub-Andine belt in sufficient quantities to allow, in some years, a good margin for export. From the northern forests the most important commercial product is quebracho, which yields an extract used in the tanning industry. Argentina is the world's chief source of supply of this commodity. Wood pulp is also a major product.

The cattle-rearing industry began intensive development when refrigerated sea transport was introduced in the 1880s. Imported pedigree cattle, especially shorthorns and Herefords from England, have greatly improved the stock, and to a large extent the natural pastures have been superseded by alfalfa, with its superior fattening properties. Cattle number 50m. (1971). They are concentrated in the damper parts of the pampas, within the arc formed by the wheat belt, and particularly in the 'mesopotamian' region between the Parana and the Uruguay, but to a lesser degree they are raised all over northern Argentina, where, however, harder conditions result in poorer qualities. Production of beef and veal is third in the world (after USA and USSR) but Argentina is still by far the major exporter.

The number of sheep has fallen away from 55m. to 43m. (1971). The farms extend not only over the cattle country but over the whole of the Patagonian plateau as well, where the rainfall is insufficient for cattle rearing; there are considerable numbers also in Tierra del Fuego, Lincolns and Merinos predominate, and supply both wool and meat. The wool clip formerly amounted to about a twelfth of the world's supply, and is still surpassed only by Australia, the USSR and New Zealand. But sheep-farming has declined in favour of cattle and cereals: in 1895 there were 35m. more sheep than there are today, although mutton and lamb are still a major export. Other livestock figures include 3.6m. horses, and 4.3m. pigs.

The mineral wealth of Argentina is mainly of local importance, and such deposits as exist are usually too inaccessible for economic exploitation. Petroleum is an exception. It is found at Rivadavia on the Patagonian coast, and in the northern foothills of the Andes; production in 1973 was 31.5m. tons — below the consumption. In the absence of mineral resources, and especially of adequate supplies of iron and coal, the manufacturing industries are primarily concerned with the preparation of agricultural products. Meat refrigeration (centred in Buenos Aires, but with plants as far afield as Patagonia and Tierra del Fuego) is the largest single industry, followed by flour milling. Woollen and cotton textile mills produce goods for the home market, and sugar-refining, leather-tanning and car manufacture are also active industries. Petroleum reserves appear to be limited and hydroelectric power is being developed. The El Chacon—Cerros Colorados project (1 200 km:

750 miles southwest of Buenos Aires) will double available power by 1980, and will be followed by joint projects with Paraguay and Uruguay. Resultant industrial development will include an aluminium smelter at Puerto Madryn and electrification of urban railways.

No other South American country is so well served by railways. There are over 38 000 km (24 000 miles) of them, though they suffer the disadvantage of being on four separate gauges. As in the United States, they were the means used to promote the commerce on which immigration depended. Most of the construction was carried out by British capital, but in 1948 all the British-owned railways were transferred to the Argentine government. The grasslands are particularly well served and there is through rail communication with Chile, Bolivia, Paraguay, and Uruguay. The absence of stone from the pampas has greatly hindered the making of roads, but latterly progress has been made with concrete highways and there are four spurs to the Inter-American Highway. In all, the roads make a network of over 960 000 km (600 000 miles) of which 14 per cent is metalled. The country is well served by air transport.

Among inland waterways, the Parana is navigable by seagoing vessels to Rosario (354 km: 220 miles upriver from Buenos Aires) and Santa Fé (502 km: 312 miles upstream). River steamers can ascend to above the confluence of the Paraguay as far as the limit of the Argentine frontier. On the Uruguay River, along the eastern frontier, seagoing vessels can reach the Uruguayan town of Paysandu, 483 km (300 miles) from Montevideo, and river steamers continue to the falls near the Uruguayan town of Salto. The Pilcomayo, on the northern frontier, and the Rio Negro, in the north of Patagonia, both afford some 400 km (250 miles) of navigation.

The capital of the republic is Buenos Aires, which stands on the River Plate and with a population of over 8m. is the largest city in the southern hemisphere. The Plate, formed by the combined waters of the Parana and Uruguay, is here more than 48 km (30 miles) wide and is so shallow that only continuous dredging makes the passage of large ocean vessels possible. Modern harbour works have made Buenos Aires the chief port of the country, and more than half the foreign trade passes through it. Bahia Blanca, whose fine natural harbour serves the southern pampas, vies for second place with Rosario, serving the northern pampas from its position on the Parana.

Despite her wealth of agricultural resources, Argentina's economic future is greatly dependent on the world trade in wheat, wool and meat. A policy of national self-sufficiency in a welfare state has been actively pursued. Foreign-owned railways and other public services have been expropriated and nationalised. In 1950 the whole of the livestock industry was placed under state control, from ranch to refrigerator. Four-fifths of the total meat production of 2.5m. tons is absorbed locally, and the consumption per head is the largest in the world. Argentina has had difficulty in fulfilling her contracts to supply beef to the United Kingdom, traditionally her largest customer. The prewar supply of 400 000 tons a year was nearly reached in 1956 (364 000 tons) and 1957 (399 000 tons), but fell away again to 280 000 tons in 1960. Mutual complaints of exorbitant demands on the one side and of unwillingness to pay the world rates on the other have given rise to serious disputes threatening a deadlock and significant of weakness in the commercial situation. One of the advantages enjoyed by Argentine beef before the war was that it was shipped in a chilled, not frozen condition. This was not practicable during the war, but later it was agreed to revert to the dispatch of chilled beef. The changeover was delayed, on account of technical difficulties and dispersal of the special craft, and there have since been difficulties with foot and mouth disease.

Exports which in general exceed the value of imports, are almost all of agricultural origin: cereals, meat, meat and dairy products, feed-stuffs, wool, hides and skins, vegetable oils and textiles. The United Kingdom for long the main customer, has been overtaken by Italy and the Netherlands and is followed by the United States, Brazil, Spain, West Germany and France. Imports cover a wide range of items (machinery, transport equipment, iron and steel manufactures, chemicals, petroleum and coffee) from a wide range of suppliers including the USA, Brazil, West Germany, Italy, the UK, Spain, Japan and Chile.

Table 100 — Argentina: population of principal towns (latest estimates available)

Buenos Aires	2 972 000	Mar del Plata	300 000
(with suburbs)	8 353 000	Tucumán	290 000
Rosario	800 000	Santa Fé	275 000
Córdoba	802 000	Parana	128 000
La Plata	506 000	Bahia Blanca	155 000

Uruguay

Uruguay is not only the smallest of the South American republics (roughly half as large again as England), it is also the most thickly populated and the most consistently low-lying. On the map its comparative smallness is emphasised by the fact that it is driven, wedgelike, between the two largest republics — Brazil to the northeast, Argentina to the west. From a broad base on the shores of the River Plate and the Atlantic Ocean the land frontiers converge northwards to form the tip of the wedge, the frontier with Argentina following uninterruptedly the course of the Uruguay River. The population of 2.9m. is predominantly of European origin; nearly a half live in Montevideo, the capital, which is one of the great cities of South America and has a first-class modern harbour, handling nearly all the country's foreign trade. In the interior the population presses more thickly on the cultivated belt than upon the pastoral regions. About 77 per cent of the total area of 187 000 sq km (72 000 sq miles) consists of pastures, nearly 18 per cent is arable, and only 3 per cent is forested, a remarkably low proportion for a South American country. The forests occur chiefly in riparian strips.

Lying well outside the tropics, in latitudes corresponding with those of Morocco, Uruguay is favoured with a warm and pleasant climate marking a transition between the subtropical and temperate zones. The undulating grassy terrain nowhere reaches 610 m (2 000 ft) above sea level and is ideally suited to pastoral occupations, which dominate the life of the country. Cattle-raising and sheep-raising vie with each other in claiming the greater share of the industry, and between them they usually account for about three-quarters of the exports, though the proportion rose to about 90 per cent in 1950, when wool provided as much as 60 per cent of the exports, meat 17 per cent, and hides and leather 11 per cent. By 1969, meat and meat products accounted for 31 per cent, and wool for only 21 per cent. There were about 9m. cattle, 23m. sheep and considerable numbers of horses, pigs and goats.

Normally, agricultural products (edible oils, hides and skins, etc.) add more than 20 per cent to the pastoral exports. In general the soil is not of good quality for easy crop production, and cultivation on a large scale is confined to an east—west belt behind the coastline of the River Plate. Production of wheat has been assisted by government price guarantee, and in 1971 a yield of over 460 000 tons was harvested from 350 000 ha (over 865 000 acres) — enough to meet all internal needs and give an exportable surplus. Other main crops are rice, maize, linseed, and sunflowerseed. Before the war, maize averaged 150 000 tons a year. The area planted has been maintained, but crops are very variable — 218 000 tons in 1955, 69 000 tons in 1968, and 160 000 in 1971. Flax, for linseed, has tended to decline; it is grown on variable areas — in recent years 110 000 ha (270 000 acres), yielding some 80 000 tons. The seed yields 25 to 30 per cent of its weight in oil, and practically all the crop is exported in that form. As in Argentina, sunflowerseed came rapidly into favour, rivalling linseed, but this crop also has tended to produce a variable yield (65 000 tons in 1965; 76 000 in 1967 and 49 000 in 1971).

Other crops grown on a comparatively small scale and fluctuating in yield include barley, groundnuts, alfalfa (lucerne), beans, potatoes, sugar beet, and tobacco. A great deal of excellent fruit, including grapes for the making of wine for home consumption, is also produced; oranges are especially prolific. Minerals are scanty, and coal and oil have to be imported. There are deposits of marble, granite, sand, and talcum, and gold is worked on a small scale.

Meat-packing plants are the oldest and most important of the industrial establishments, and the extent of the business has made such small towns as Fray Bentos, on the Uruguay, well known throughout Europe. In addition to preparing frozen and chilled meat, canned meat and meat extract, the factories deal with a multitude of byproducts. The dressing of hides and skins is similarly of long standing. Newer industries, mostly developed after 1939 under the impetus of wartime shortages, include the manufacture of textiles and leather goods, chemicals, cement, oil-refining and light engineering and a range of consumer goods. Not only raw wool but worsteds are among the main exports. Industries of all kinds are nursed by government controls and subsidies, and the development of electric power has been a government monopoly since 1897. A major hydroelectric project is in hand (the Salto—Grande) on the River Uruguay. Uruguay prides itself on being the most advanced welfare state in South America. In 1952 it abolished the office of President and entrusted all executive authority to a National Council, but in 1966 it returned to a presidential system.

The Uruguay River is navigable as far as Salto (see under Argentina), and also gives access to its big tributary, the Rio Negro, which flows across the country from east to west. The railways radiate from Montevideo in a standard-gauge system covering over 2 900 km (1 800 miles) most of them were British-owned until the end of 1948, when they were acquired by the state. The road network (about 40 000 km: 25 000 miles), is perhaps the best in South America.

Imports cover a wide range of goods, easily the most valuable item being crude petroleum. Motor vehicles and accessories form a distinctive group, and another is agricultural and industrial machinery. The United States, Brazil, West Germany, the United Kingdom, Kuwait and Argentina supplied, in that order, nearly two-thirds of all the imports, Venezuela having been overtaken by Kuwait, as the supplier of petroleum. The chief commodities furnishing the export trade have already been indicated. The chief buyers in 1967, taking half of the whole, were in order of their purchases, the United Kingdom, Spain, the United States, Italy, and West Germany.

Table 101 — Uruguay: population of principal towns

Montevideo	1 300 000	Salto	80 000
Paysandu	90 000	Mercedes	40 000

Paraguay

Like its northern neighbour Bolivia, Paraguay is an inland republic; its other neighbours are Argentina, on the west and south, and Brazil on the east. But, unlike Bolivia, it has no really high ground, and the only range of hills, running from north to south through the eastern part of the country, rarely exceeds a height of 610 m (2 000 ft). The Tropic of Capricorn crosses the centre of the republic, dividing it almost equally into tropical and temperate zones. A more effective division, however, is that created by the Paraguay River, which flows from north to south and forms a tangible line of demarcation between the Oriental, the habitat of over 95 per cent of the population, and the little developed Occidental, or Paraguayan Chaco. Of a total area of 407 000 sq km (157 000 sq miles) the Oriental accounts for 160 000 sq km (61 700 sq miles) (an area somewhat larger than England and Wales) and the Occidental for 247 000 sq km (95 300 sq miles) (a little larger than the whole of the United Kingdom). The total population in 1970 was 2.39m., mostly mestizo.

Half of the whole country is forested, and some 22 per cent may be classed as waste. The Chaco is flat, and large parts of it are subject to flooding in the summer months. Only about 2.3 per cent of the republic is reckoned to be arable, and 24 per cent pastoral. Rather more than 1 per cent, though unused, is potentially productive. The arable land consists for the most part of forest clearings in the Oriental, where the soil of decomposed sandstone is remarkably fertile; for stock-raising there are tracts of savanna in both the eastern and the western zones.

Stock-raising is an important industry, and in 1971 cattle were estimated at 5.8m., but these were the only large numbers of livestock; sheep were 320 000. The forests, the greater part of which are still untouched, yield excellent timbers, and a valuable source of supply of quebracho extract (produced chiefly in the Chaco where the more accessible areas have been over-exploited). Yerba maté, formerly widely famed as a strongly flavoured tea, is also a forest product as well as a plantation crop.

To a large extent, Paraguay is self-supporting in foodstuffs. Maize is a principal subsistence crop, and rice, sugar, cassava (manioc), potatoes and beans are also grown. Attempts are being made to promote wheat-growing and groundnuts. Limited mineral wealth, particularly in the form of deposits of iron ore, manganese, kaolin, and copper, has not yet been seriously exploited. Industry is also on a small scale and, with the exception of meat-canning factories, saw-mills, textiles and plants for quebracho extract, serves internal requirements only.

The chief exports in 1969 were wood, meat and meat products, tobacco, raw cotton, tung oil, coconut oil, quebracho extract. The United States, Argentina, the United Kingdom, and the Netherlands

:ook 70 per cent of the exports, while 50 per cent of the imports were
,upplied by Argentina, the United States, West Germany, and the
United Kingdom. The main imports were foodstuffs, manufactured
goods, and machinery and transport equipment.

The Parana and Paraguay Rivers, which enclose the southern part of
the country and meet at is southwestern extremity, provide the most
valuable means of communication and potential source of hydroelectric
power. Asunción, the chief port and capital, stands on the Paraguay and
is some 1 530 km (950 miles) from the sea. Asunción is also linked with
Buenos Aires by rail. The railways are government owned and total
440 km (275 miles). Roads cover about 6 260 km (3 750 miles), of
which about 645 km (400 miles) are asphalted.

Table 102 – **Paraguay: population of principal towns (1970 census)**

Asunción	437 000	Concepción	52 830
Caaguazú	73 580	Pedro J. Caballero	52 000
Coronel Oviedo	59 310		

Falkland Islands

These islands, situated 480 km (300 miles) to the east of the Strait of
Magellan, have been in continuous British occupation since 1833. They
consist of two main islands – East and West Falkland – separated by a
long channel and surrounded by numerous small islands. East Falkland
(6 730 sq km: 2 600 sq miles) is about the same size as the English
county of Devon; West Falkland is smaller by about a fifth. Both have a
deeply indented coastline and in each the highest land rises to upwards
of 610 m (2 000 ft). The climate is not a great deal colder than that of
London, with which the islands correspond in latitude, but because of
the prevalent strong winds conditions are considerably more rigorous.
Vegetation is sparse and the soft peaty soil is covered mainly with grass.
Almost the sole occupation is the rearing of sheep, which number some
629 000 and produce wool for export. Tallow, obtained by boiling the
carcases is a useful secondary product. The export of frozen mutton has
been proposed, but has not been found practicable so far. The 10 750
cattle provide hides for export. The population is almost wholly of
British descent and numbered 2 045 in 1971, of whom about half live
in Stanley, the capital, at the head of a fine harbour in East Falkland.
There are no roads apart from those in Stanley.

The colony had a number of scattered dependencies far to the south
and east: South Georgia, South Shetlands, South Orkneys, and the
South Sandwich Islands, besides a big sector of Antarctica which

includes Graham Land. Much of this territory is the subject of over-lapping claims by Argentina and Chile. Whaling is carried on by the chief maritime powers under international regulations. Over 127 000 barrels of whale and seal oil were exported in 1959. The whalers, many of which were Scandinavian and Japanese, used bases in South Georgia and the South Orkneys. Disputes have arisen over the renewal of the international regulations, and the diminution in the catch suggests that the various species of whale have been hunted almost to extinction. South Georgia is no longer used as a whaling base, and the focus of operations is shifting to the North Pacific.

In March 1962 the South Shetlands, South Orkneys and Graham Land were constituted a separate colony, British Antarctic Territory.

Australia, New Zealand
and the Pacific Islands

Australia

The vast island continent of Australia has an area of nearly 7.7m. sq km (3m. sq miles), and is accordingly almost exactly equal in extent to the United States of North America, exclusive of Alaska. A good deal more than one-third of it lies within the tropics, but the great bulk of its population is to be found in the region outside of that belt. Most of the inhabitants of this sparsely populated island are found within 320 km (200 miles) of the coast, and from the nature of the climate this can never be otherwise.

The coastline of this vast island is remarkable for its long stretches of uniform character, without inlets that can be made use of by shipping even for shelter. The principal exceptions to this character are on the eastern side, and in some parts of the northwest.

To the north of Fraser Island, on the east coast, numerous coral reefs rise to the surface of the water, making the seas dangerous to shipping, and about 1° N of the Tropic of Capricorn there begins a series of coral reefs such as are to be seen nowhere else in the world over the same extent of sea. These form the **Great Barrier Reef**, which extends for a distance of about 1 900 km (1 200 miles), advancing into the latitudes of Torres Strait, which it nearly closes. Its widest part is in the south, where it extends for about 160 km (100 miles) from east to west, and in that part also it lies furthest from the coast. At low tide the surface of the reef is just about the level of the surface of the water, and at all states of the tide the border of the reef can be distinguished by the strong breakers that wash over it. The reef, however, is not continuous. It is broken up by many deep channels which allow a choice of routes between the seaports in the east of Australia and Torres Strait. The route within the Barrier Reef has the advantage of a calm and beautiful sea owing to the protection which the reef affords. But this route, as Chisholm stressed in the early editions, is one that requires careful navigation, 'above all at night, when the reef cannot be made out a greater distance than half a mile [0.8 km]. By day it is visible at a

distance of four miles [6.4 km] from the bridge and seven mile
[11.2 km] from the rigging'.

Physical characteristics of the mainland. Australia is for the most part
fairly level, more than half consisting of a great western plateau of
ancient rocks. In the east, however, the land drops to a great saucer of
sedimentary rocks, rises to a continuous range of highlands runs at no
great distance from the coast from north to south, and then bends with
the coast westwards, terminating in the southeast of the state of South
Australia. The general name of Dividing Range is given to the whole of
this series, since it separates the low-lying coast valleys and small plains
from the big plains of the interior. In New South Wales the flat-topped
ranges west of Sydney are called the Blue Mountains. In the southeast
the Range forms a regular mountain chain, the Australian Alps, culminating in Mount Kosciusko at 2 230 m (7 313 ft). Here, in the Snowy
Mountains, there are major engineering schemes of tunnels, hydroelectric stations and dams. The Dividing Range was long the chief
obstacle in the establishment of communications with the interior and
has played its part in setting the pattern of the Australian economy —
the concentration of population and industry around the coastal fringe.

The series of highlands above described is appropriately called the
Great Dividing Range, not only on account of the contrast presented by
the surface on different sides of it, but also because of the influence
which it has upon the climate. The chief rain-bearing winds of Australia
blow more or less from the east, since the island lies in latitudes of the
southeast trade wind. The highlands on the east are therefore well
watered at all seasons of the year, but in the tropical and subtropical
latitudes chiefly in summer. The interior plains and plateaus, on the
other hand, receive less and less rain the further they are distant from
the sea, and desert conditions prevail over almost a third of the interior.
Even where the average rainfall is adequate for limited winter crops or
for livestock, it is in many parts precarious, years of flood alternating
with years of drought, leading to great variations in the yield of the
crops and the number of sheep and cattle that can be reared in a given
area. The climate, in turn, affects the rivers. Most of those which enter
the sea on the east and southeast of the Dividing Range are comparatively short, but are generally well supplied with water all the year
round. They vary greatly in their depth according as the weather is dry
or rainy, and they are in many cases apt to overflow their banks. Many
of them are navigable for a shorter or longer distance; but they bring
down so much sediment that bars are formed in many cases at their
mouths, and the entrance of large vessels is thus prevented or impeded.

All the great rivers of Australia take their rise on the inner slopes of
the tableland, and flow towards the west or southwest. Only one of
these, the Murray, enters the sea by an independent mouth. The longest

tributaries of the Murray are the Murrumbidgee, the Darling, and the Lachlan. These rivers might all be ranked among the great rivers of the world if we considered only their length (the Murray and the Darling being both much more than 2 410 km: 1 500 miles long), but the climate of the region through which they flow causes them to be very scantily supplied with water. The Darling dries up in summer into a chain of small lakes in parts of its course. Nevertheless these rivers are navigable by steamers of shallow draught for a long distance into the interior. In ordinary circumstances the Murray can be ascended to Albury, 1 930 km (1 200 miles) up, where the river is crossed by the railway from Melbourne to Sydney. A system of locks on the Murray and the Murrumbidgee assists the navigation and is the basis of the major irrigation schemes of the area.

Of the other long rivers traversing the plains in the interior, the greater number are hardly rivers at all. They are merely watercourses which may be filled at times with running water, but which are often empty except for a few days in the year. Many disappear into the porous sand or are evaporated under the heat of the sun. The most important of the streams that end in this way is the Diamantina, which enters South Australia from the southwest of Queensland. Others empty themselves into large shallow lakes, which in summer shrink greatly in dimensions. There are several such salt lakes in the lower parts of Australia, the chief being Lake Torrens and Lake Eyre, into the latter of which flows at certain seasons the Barcoo River, or Cooper's Creek, the longest of these feeders of inland lakes. In the dry period of the year this river in its lowest part creeps on more and more slowly, and in the end dries up like the Diamantina, though the course which it follows in times of flood, when it swells to a breadth of 3 km (2 miles) can still be distinguished by the grass and trees bordering it. Nonetheless the gradual slope of the plains over which these rivers flow admits of many large tracts being irrigated. The irrigated areas are mainly in the Murray Basin. In Queensland, New South Wales, Victoria, and South Australia a valuable source of water is from the underground artesian basins — especially the Great Basin and the Murray River Basin. The former, extending over 1 740 000 sq km (670 000 sq miles) and underlying two-thirds of Queensland, has been pierced by thousands of bores. The water is excellent for stock but owing to a considerable proportion of salts cannot be used for irrigation.

Vegetation. On the tableland and plains of the interior the Australian 'bush' is open and easily traversed either by horseman or by car. In some of the more arid parts, however, large stretches of ground are occupied by low bushes difficult to penetrate and difficult to destroy. Even some of the grasses, notably the well-known spinifex, have sharp pointed leaves. In tussocks this grass covers by itself vast areas in the deserts of the west. Most of the native grasses of Australia are nutritious, and among these the tall kangaroo grass is notable for its power of withstanding long drought. And even where the climate is so dry that grasses do not thrive, there are certain herbs, such as the salt-bush, which will still thrive and yield food for sheep and cattle. Owing to the variations in rainfall, the forest of the east, south and southwest coasts gives place to open forest, bush, and scrub and finally to semidesert and desert in the dry heart of the landmass. Since the continent has long been isolated there is not the difference one would except between the tropical and temperate parts owing to the highly peculiar character of both flora and fauna. The most typical trees are the eucalyptus or gum trees and species of acacia, whilst the typical animals are the marsupials, notably the kangaroo. The danger of upsetting the 'balance of nature' by introducing wild or semi-wild plants and animals into a country free from hereditary enemies was well seen in the case of the prickly pear (which has overrun thousands of hectares) and the rabbit.

People. The aboriginal Australians belong to an ancient race and probably migrated from Indonesia some 20 000 years ago. The level of their material culture is low though their social organisation is complex. They were never numerous, perhaps 300 000 when Cook landed, and their total number in 1966 was under 85 000. The majority live in the north and west. The first inhabitants sent from the British Isles to Australia were convicts, and the first ship containing convicts sailed in 1787, and arrived at Botany Bay, in New South Wales, early in 1788. Soon free settlers began to arrive. These were mainly from the British Isles, but there were also many Germans. Chinese (these nearly all men) and Polynesians were introduced into Queensland as labourers on the tropical plantations, but under subsequent legislation all Coloured labour was prohibited. Under the Pacific Island Labourers' Act no Pacific Islanders were allowed to enter Australia after 31 March 1904, or were to be allowed to remain there after the end of 1906. However, the bulk of the immigrants throughout Australian history have been British citizens attracted by the possibilities of a great new land. In 1939, 90 per cent of the population were native born, 7 per cent were immigrants from the UK and 3 per cent were immigrants of non-British origin. Since the Second World War a further 2.5m. have immigrated — three in five being of non-British origin (mainly from southern Europe) and the number of non-European immigrants has been increased under a quota system. In 1850 the European population was some 400 000. With the discovery of gold this rapidly trebled and thereafter the steamship and immigration has raised it steadily to over 12.7m. in 1971. The main settlement is in the coastal areas (90 per cent), while 85 per cent of the total live southeast of a line between Brisbane and Port Augusta in South Australia; 80 per cent live in urban areas, and no less than 8m.

of the 12.7m. live in the ten towns and cities of over 100 000; 7m. live in the five main cities — Sydney, Melbourne, Brisbane, Adelaide and Perth.

The Australian Commonwealth was constituted under an Act of the United Kingdom Parliament passed in 1900, and was proclaimed at Sydney on 1 January 1901. The six former colonies of Victoria, New South Wales, Queensland, South Australia, Tasmania, and West Australia formed the six original states of this Commonwealth. In 1911, South Australia transferred its Northern Territory to the Commonwealth as a separate 'territory', and a site was acquired at Canberra for a new capital city. The capital city is part of a 'Capital Territory' of 2 430 sq km (939 sq miles) in the southeast of New South Wales. Canberra itself stands at an elevation of 610 m (2 000 ft) above the sea. It has been connected by rail with the New South Wales system, and a railway was proposed to connect it with Jervis Bay, east-northeast of Canberra, where a further 73 sq km (28 sq miles) has been reserved as Federal Territory for a port and naval station. Most traffic however to the capital is now by air or road. The government departments were gradually moved to Canberra from Melbourne, which was the temporary seat of the general government. The Parliament Houses were opened in 1927 by the Duke of York, later King George VI. Australia also administers Papua, the trustee territory of New Guinea, and some Pacific islands.

Animal products. The native land mammals, nearly all of which belong to the same peculiar group as the kangaroo (marsupials), yield furs of comparatively small value in the aggregate, and from a commercial point of view destroy a great deal more than they produce. The same is true of the dingo, or native dog, the only large native mammal that is not a marsupial. The most valuable of the introduced animals is the sheep, wool being the major single export until 1969 when it was overtaken by minerals. The wool production of Australia coming mainly from the fine (merino) wool (see p. 164) of the treeless grassy plains with a saline soil bordering the Murray River and its tributaries in Victoria and New South Wales. Cattle are next in importance with a major export trade in meat. Exports of dairy products — especially butter, cheese and eggs — despite fluctuations, have largely recovered the ground they lost during the Second World War.

Cultivated crops. Wheat is by far the main crop and, with a small population, is a major export. Until the end of the last century South Australia was the chief wheat-exporting part of Australia, but the movement for closer settlement and the introduction of dry farming techniques has brought about a great increase in wheat cultivation in all the states extending into higher latitudes. The area under wheat in the

Table 103 — Australia: area, population and livestock

	Area in millions of square kilometres	Ratio to Great Britain	Population in thousands						Millions, 1969	
			1901	1921	1936	1954†	1961	1971†	Sheep	Cattle
Victoria	0.23	1	1 208	1 532	1 843	2 452	2 930	3 496	30	3.9
New South Wales	0.83	3.5	1 360	2 100	2 656	3 424	3 917	4 589	68	4.9
Queensland	1.73	7.5	503	756	972	1 318	1 519	1 823	20	7.7
South Australia	0.98	4.3	366	495	586	797	969	1 172	18	0.8
Western Australia	2.23	11	195	332	447	640	737	1 027	33	1.5
Tasmania	0.07	0.4	173	214	230	309	350	390	4	0.6
Northern Territory	1.35	6	–	4	5	16	27	85	0.007	1.2
Aust. Capital Territory	0.003	–	–	2.5	9	30	59	143	0.2	0.01
Commonwealth	7.69	33	3 805	5 435	6 750	8 987	10 508	12 728	174.6	20.6
Papua	0.22	1	–	–	275*	452‡	–	640¶	–	–
New Guinea (Trust Territory)	0.24	1	–	–	265*	1 286‡	–	1 800¶	–	–
New Zealand	0.27	1.14	816	1 320	1 466*	2 174§	–	2 860	59.9	8.6

* 1933.
† Census.
‡ 1956.
§ 1956 (census).
¶ 1970 estimate.

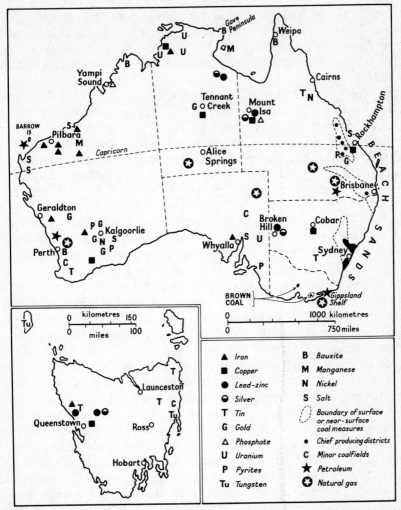

Australia: mineral resources

Valuable metallic minerals are widely distributed. The Pilbara area, a dry plateau region, has immense resources of iron ore. Coal production is substantial, partly because of demand from Australian iron and steel works, partly on account of Japanese demand.

Some important discoveries of natural gas have been made in the remote arid interior, which makes development difficult. Oil and gas are both produced in the hinterland of Brisbane; and the Gippsland Shelf area probably has the greatest oil reserves.

Commonwealth has followed a pronounced zigzag course during the present century. The area rose from 2.4m. ha (6m. acres) in 1900—01 to 5m. ha (12m. acres) in 1915—16, fell again to 2.5m. at the end of the First World War, rose in the next decade to 7.3m., declined to 3.2m. in the Second World War, was up to 5.7m. at the end of the war, fell to 3.2m. in 1956—57, and rose to a peak in 1968: 10.8m. ha (26.7m. acres). By 1971 it had fallen again to 7m. ha (17.3m. acres). These fluctuations are mainly due to Australia's recurrent droughts. There is also considerable production of barley, oats, maize and silage for fodder.

The vine, for raisins, sultanas and currants as well as for wine, is grown in Victoria and South Australia. Sugarcane is cultivated in Queensland, and a variety has been found to succeed far beyond the tropics and is grown even in the northeastern valleys of New South Wales. The fruit-growing industry is also important, with apples in the cooler parts of Victoria and Tasmania; oranges, peaches and apricots in the warmer Western Australia, South Australia and the Murray basin.

Minerals. The mineral wealth of the country is enormous. Gold was the first mineral to be exploited. It has been found in all the states, but most abundantly in the three eastern states and Western Australia. Victoria heads the list; from 1851 (when gold was first discovered in the colony) to the end of 1964, total production amounted to 42 per cent of the Commonwealth total output (5.8m. kg: 184m. fine oz). In 1851—60 Australia's production of gold totalled nearly 800 000 kg (25m. fine oz) but the alluvial deposits were rapidly worked out and the production in each of the next three decades declined. The last decade of the century witnessed the remarkable series of discoveries in Western Australia which made that state the leading producer of gold and brought up the aggregate production in 1901—10 to over 1m. kg (32m. fine oz). But the new boom, like the original, was shortlived; in the decade after the First World War production dropped to less than 200 000 kg (6m. fine oz), and though there was some revival after the devaluation of the Australian currency in 1935, output soon fell again, and in 1959 to 1964 the total annual production in the Commonwealth was little more than 30 000 kg (1m. fine oz). of which Western Australia provided 80 per cent. Current production is some 22 000 kg (700 000 fine oz) a year.

Baser metals such as copper, lead, zinc, iron ore and silver were discovered towards the end of the nineteenth century and their smelting in turn encouraged coal mining. Coal, mainly from New South Wales, is still the most valuable single mineral product with an annual output ('black' and 'brown') of 65m. tons. The New South Wales basin is the largest in the southern hemisphere and has considerable reserves of good coking coal. Lignite is worked in Victoria and is used for the generation of electricity.

Since the Second World War, and particularly since 1960, the discovery and development of new mineral resources has been the outstanding feature of the economy. Production of iron ore (reserves estimated to be fourth largest in the world), bauxite, nickel, uranium, manganese and the titaniferous minerals from beachsands (rutile, zircon, ilmenite) has increased the value of mineral exports sevenfold between 1959 and 1969. The growth is exemplified by iron ore exports which rose from 97 000 tons in 1965 to 40m. tons in 1970. In 1969 Australia was among the world's first ten producers of coal, lignite, nickel, copper, silver, tin, manganese and tungsten; was sixth in gold and uranium; third in iron ore and zinc; second in bauxite and lead; and first in rutile (titanium oxide) and ilmenite. The exploitation of minerals is developing hitherto empty lands, changing the pattern of overseas trade and attracting a flow of foreign capital for the construction of handling and processing plants (alumina/aluminium, nickel, iron and steel, and uranium in particular). Japan has provided the main market and already takes 80 per cent of the iron ore and 90 per cent of the coal exports. The search for petroleum and natural gas has also been widespread. Wells at Moonie in Queensland have been in production since 1961 and these, together with output from the Bass Strait, should provide 60 per cent of the home requirements. This will reduce crude oil imports and provide a basis for the new petrochemical industries. New discoveries of both oil and natural gas off Barrow Island and the northwest coast of Western Australia will add to that state's importance as a major primary producer. Output was 19m. tons in 1973.

Industry and commerce. Before 1901 the protective tariffs of the individual colonies and the distances between the areas of main settlement encouraged the growth of local industries. The remoteness of the country and the impact of the two world wars provided further stimulus and today no less than 28 per cent of the work force (as against 25 per cent in Japan) are engaged in manufacturing. Labour costs are high and the home market is limited, but there is a great diversity of industry solidly based on iron and steel plants, shipbuilding and heavy construction engineering. Most rapid growth is in food, clothing and textiles for a growing population and in engineering, mineral and petroleum processing. New South Wales and Victoria together employ three-quarters of this labour force, of which 80 per cent is in the two cities of Sydney and Melbourne. State policies are to reduce this overconcentration, but the pull of the capitals is still important in the location of all but the newest industries which have followed on the mineral exploitation of recent years.

International trade has long been dominated by the export of primary products. Initially agricultural and pastoral products to the United Kingdom, and later wool, wheat, beef and dairy products to other European countries. (The last of the famous sailing vessels of the Australian trade ceased to operate only in 1951.) Since the Second World War, when the links with Europe were disrupted, the pattern of trade has changed: the industrial rise of Japan and the development of

Table 104 — Australia: general imports

			Percentages of total value				
	1911–13	*1924*	*1931–35*	*1938–39*	*1951–52*	*1962–63*	*196*
Raw materials							
Petroleum	–	3.6	8.4	7.1	7.5	10.7	
Wood	4.2	3.8	1.7	2.1	2.7	1.2	
Paper and manfs.	2.5	4.5	7.2	4.3	5.2	4.4	2
Tobacco	–	2.0	1.6	1.9	1.8	1.1	
Foods							
Tea	1.7	2.4	3.1	2.5	1.1	1.2	1
Manufactures							
Machinery	6.0	8.4	7.8	13.8	12.0	13.3	18
Cars*	2.1	8.6	3.2	7.5	9.2	10.4	6
Iron and steel	9.1	2.8	2.6	3.3	7.0	2.1	2
Other metals and manufactures	–	8.6	5.8	20.5	9.2	11.5	15
Silk or synthetic silk goods	⎫		5.2	2.6	2.6 ⎫		
Cotton goods	⎬ 6.3	19.5	8.5	4.5	6.3 ⎬	6.8	8
Yarn and cordage	⎭			1.2	1.6 ⎭		
Chemicals	1.2	2.8	5.7	5.6	2.8	6.4	4
Total £A. million†	75.0	140.6	58.3	99.9	1 053.4	1 081	3 8
Countries							
United Kingdom	50.3	45.2	41.1	40.5	44.2	30.5	21
United States	13.7	24.6	31.5	14.7	10.4	21.3	24
Indonesia‡	1.2	3.3	6.2	7.1	2.4	2.7	1
India	3.4	3.4	5.7	2.9	4.5	1.7	0
Japan	1.2	2.5	5.6	4.1	4.2	6.0	14
Germany§	9.1	1.0	3.2	4.1	3.1	5.4	6
Canada	1.2	3.6	4.1	7.7	2.2	4.2	4
France	3.0	2.9	2.0	1.0	2.1	1.7	1
New Zealand	3.6	1.7	–	2.2	0.7	1.7	2

* Motorcars and other vehicles and parts.

† Values in Australian pounds, which were formerly equivalent to sterling. From 1935 £A.1 = £ sterling 0.8.

‡ Dutch East Indies till after Second World War.

§ West Germany 1951 *et seq.*

Australian mineral resources have been the dominant factors. Wool, wheat and beef are still important but wool faces increasing competition from synthetic fibres and the foodstuffs the increasing self-sufficiency of previous importers. Minerals are steadily overtaking these traditional exports; and the export of manufactures is expanding as the following table shows.

Communications were essential for the development of a continent so large and remote as Australia. Telegraph links with the rest of the world were first opened in 1872 on the completion of the overland line from Adelaide through the Northern Territory to Port Darwin and thence under the sea to Java. The cable from Vancouver to Queensland (via New Zealand, Fiji and Norfolk Island) was completed in 1902. Direct wireless links to London were established in 1927 and with North

Table 105 — Australia: general exports

	Percentages of total value						
	1911–13	*1924*	*1931–35*	*1938–39*	*1951–52*	*1962–63*	*1969–70*
Raw materials							
Wool	33.2	50.0	39.8	30.4	47.9	35.3	19.0
Hides and skins	5.5	4.8	3.3	2.9	2.5	3.6	2.1
Lead	1.9	3.0	2.5	3.1	3.8	1.6	1.9
Minerals	–	–	–	–	1.4	2.5	13.0
Foods							
Wheat	10.1	12.4	15.1	6.2	8.3	10.1	11.0
Wheat flour	–	4.7	4.0	3.2	4.9	1.5	0.8
Butter	4.9	4.4	9.2	9.2	0.8	2.3	2.1
Meat	5.4	2.3	6.9	8.4	5.3	10.5	8.3
Mutton and lamb	–	1.0	3.2	3.4	0.3	–	1.5
Beef	–	1.2	2.2	3.1	1.8	–	6.3
Sugar	–	–	2.1	3.0	1.0	4.3	3.1
Fruits	–	–	4.3	4.5	2.9	3.3	2.8
Manufactures	–	–	–	2.4	6.8	7.8	10.5
Total £A. million*	–	112.4	95.9	140.5	675	1 076	4 131
Countries							
United Kingdom	42.8	38.1	48.9	48.9	30.8	18.6	12.2
France	10.9	12.5	5.7	6.7	8.6	5.0	2.8
Japan	1.4	9.7	9.7	3.5	7.2	15.9	25.5
Germany†	8.8	3.7	5.0	1.9	3.0	3.2	2.8
Belgium	8.5	5.5	4.9	4.0	3.7	2.2	1.1
United States	2.6	6.0	2.3	13.9	11.4	12.3	14.0
Italy	–	3.9	3.2	0.9	5.6	4.1	2.7
New Zealand	3.1	4.2	2.9	4.8	5.5	6.1	5.0
India	3.2	–	–	1.4	2.5	1.7	1.0
Ceylon	6.0	–	–	0.9	1.6	0.6	0.4

* See footnote† to table on p. 878.

† West Germany 1951 *et seq.*

America in 1928. Communications are now universal by multichannel submarine cables and satellite.

Early grain and wool shipments were by sail, but rapid growth followed the opening of the Suez Canal and the introduction of refrigerated steamships. Capacity has been increased more recently by the introduction of container ships and bulk carriers. In 1970 nine container ships provided an annual capacity equal to eighty to ninety conventional cargo ships and by 1975 it is estimated that 14 per cent of the world's container fleets will serve Australia. The utilisation of bulk carriers and the construction of new ports to handle them (Port Hedland, Dampier, Darwin and Botany Bay) has been essential to the realisation of the full potential of the mineral resources. Coastal shipping still plays a major role in bulk movements between the scattered coastal industrial areas.

The efficiency of the railway network, totalling some 40 000 km (25 000 miles) has long been limited by the variety of gauges laid down by the individual colonies: narrow gauge in Western Australia and

Queensland, standard gauge in South Australia and New South Wales, and broad gauge in Victoria. Under Commonwealth standardisation agreements, however, Brisbane, Sydney and Melbourne were linked by a standard gauge, and in 1969 Sydney was linked to Perth for the first time by a single, standard gauge railway of 3 960 km (2 460 miles). Recent construction has centred on small feeder lines to carry coal, iron ore, bauxite, etc., from the mines to the coast and the processing plants. Of the road network 900 000 km (56 000 miles) some 45 per cent is surfaced and carries an increasing number of cars and trucks (in 1970 over 3.9m. and nearly 1m. respectively). International air links are extensive, as are internal air services. Light aircraft replace the car on many of the larger farms, and provide regular and essential services as that of the 'flying doctor'.

Victoria is the smallest of the states on the mainland of Australia with 3 per cent of the total area and 28 per cent of the population. The first permanent settlement on its territory was made towards the close of 1834. Till 1851 it was a dependency of New South Wales and until 1895 it had a larger population than New South Wales. The Australian Alps, with their spurs, fill the greater part of the eastern half of the state. West of these mountains the Dividing Range sinks in elevation, so that easy routes could be found for the railways laid north of Melbourne such as through the Kilmore Gap to the plains on the other side. The plains to the south of the Dividing Range (the Great Valley of Victoria), lying as they do on the moister side of the mountains, are well watered, in many places thickly covered with trees, and clothed with rich grasses, more suited for horses and cattle than for sheep. This is especially the character of Gippsland, the region to the south of the Australian Alps and where, south of the plains, rise the Gippsland Hills. This has become important dairying country. In the north there is greater dearth of rain; nevertheless, it is in this part of the state that the area under crops, especially wheat, was greatly increased after the decline of the goldfields. In some years the rainfall even here is sufficient to allow of abundant crops being grown, but when the rains fail great loss follows to the cultivators. Hence, if farming is to be carried on regularly with success in this region, it can only be by irrigation, to which great attention is given by the government. All the streams are vested in the state, which has constructed storage works for irrigation on all the more important of them. In the northwest is the district called Wimmera, formerly in the main a waterless desert, but containing a tract with an excellent soil bordering the Murray, on which large irrigation works have been carried out at Mildura and elsewhere. Among the objects of cultivation are grapes, including the raisin and currant grapes; oranges, figs, apricots, and peaches; plums, including plums for prunes; besides sorghums, tobacco, fibre plants, and other crops.

Further south large areas of the plains have been reclaimed for wheat cultivation by clearing them of what is known as the mallee scrub, that is, thickets of the *Eucalyptus dumosa*, brittle-stemmed trees growing to the height of from 4 to 6 m (12 to 20 ft), but the yield of the crops, like the rainfall is apt to be somewhat precarious. Sugar beet is cultivated at Morwell, east of Melbourne. The output of brown coal (mined only in Victoria) is being developed rapidly. In 1960 it reached 15m. tons and in 1970, 23m. tons. Ninety per cent of the state's electricity is generated from the brown coal of the Latrobe valley.

The capital and chief seaport is Melbourne, situated on the Yarra, a short distance above its mouth in Port Phillip Bay. The Yarra was navigable up to the city by vessels of considerable size, including all those engaged solely in the coastal trade; but the harbour of Melbourne for ocean liners is formed by Hobson's Bay, the upper part of Port Phillip. On this bay stands Port Melbourne, now an integral part of Melbourne itself. Port Phillip itself is a shallow sheet of water, which affords a large extent of safe anchorage, but has a narrow and difficult entrance which limits access for the largest vessels. On a western arm of this bay stands the port of Geelong, a town that has long carried on the manufacture of woollen tweeds, etc., which are supplied to all the Australian states. To the east lies Westernport Bay with a less restrictive entrance channel. This is the site of a large industrial complex which will maintain Victoria's position as supplier of one-third of Australia's manufactures. Plants include refineries, petrochemicals, fertilisers, and iron and steel works. Melbourne with over 2.4m. (1971) houses two-thirds of the state's population and 82 per cent of the workforce; it is estimated that it will expand to 3.7m. by 1985 and will expand to link with Geelong. In the interior, northwest of Melbourne, is Ballarat, the centre of the richest alluvial goldfield ever opened up, but which is to a large extent exhausted, gold being now mainly obtained not by digging but by the crushing of quartz rock. Ballarat (58 000 in 1971) is the second largest inland city after Canberra. In a more northerly direction from Melbourne lies Bendigo (Sandhurst), the chief centre of quartz-crushing. On the Murray, Wodonga, opposite the New South Wales town of Albury, is at the head of the ordinary navigation, where the river is crossed by the railway to Sydney; lower down is Echuca, where the river makes a sharp bend to the northwest, and there another railway crosses into New South Wales. Above and below Echuca, extensive tracts are irrigated from the Goulburn Weir and Lodden River works.

New South Wales was so called by Captain Cook, who was reminded of the Wales of Great Britain by the appearance of the mountains which he saw from off the coast. It was in this state that the first permanent settlement was founded in Australia in 1788, on the magnificent natural harbour of Port Jackson, the harbour of Sydney, which has few rivals in the world for either beauty or convenience. Throughout the state the Dividing Range forms a more continuous barrier between the coast lowlands and the interior plains and tablelands than it does in Victoria, and it was long before the settlers found a way across the Blue Mountains, as the part of the Dividing Range behind Sydney is called. The route at last found is now followed by the railway which crosses the mountains in a tunnel 1 130 m (3 700 ft) above sea level. North of Sydney the New England Range, trending north and south and the Liverpool Range, trending east and west, shut off a tableland known as the Liverpool Plains, which contains the headwaters of the Namoi, or Peel River, one of the tributaries of the Darling. The interior of New South Wales generally is traversed by the chief tributaries of the Murray, and the treeless plains noted for their wool lying to the north of that river are hence known as the Riverina. The population of New South Wales increased at a much more rapid rate than that of Victoria, which it now exceeds by about 1m. (in 1971, 4.589m., as against 3.496m.). It is, however, more evenly distributed because the mineral resources of the state are widely scattered and the population engaged in agriculture is similarly scattered over the large area of the interior plains where wheat and sheep farming are possible. Nonetheless, three-quarters of the population is concentrated in the coastal strip between Wollongong and Newcastle. Some of the coast strip is rather sterile, but south of Sydney is much dairying, and northwards, along the line of the Brisbane to Sydney coast railway, are lands wet enough and warm enough for sugarcane and there is much dairy farming.

New South Wales occupies some 10 per cent of the total area of Australia and has 36 per cent of the population.

The capital of the state and chief seaport of all Australia is Sydney. With suburbs, Sydney had a population (1971) of 2.8m. — over half the population of the state and providing three-quarters of its total work-force. Residential suburbs are scattered round the shores of the harbour, and Sydney has been linked since 1932 with North Sydney across the harbour by the then largest single-arch bridge in the world. At the head of the Parramatta River, which is in reality a prolongation of the inlet of Port Jackson, stands Parramatta, in a district noted for its oranges. North of Sydney, on the estuary of the Hunter River, stands Newcastle (250 000), the chief coal mining town and place of export of coal. The coal is exported not only to all the Australian states, but also to Japan and many other countries. Newcastle is the centre of important manufacturing industries — iron and steel (40 per cent of Australia's output), shipbuilding, engineering, food processing and consumer products. Another important coal port is Wollongong, to the south of Sydney, the port of the Illawarra coalfield. In this district Port Kembla is rapidly developing into a leading manufacturing city — with iron, steel, and metal refining works. The coastal strip from

Wollongong to Newcastle is the industrial hub of New South Wales. This state produces some 40 per cent of the revenue of Australia, and the coastal strip, with its new mines, ports and industries, could well double its population, to become a major complex focused on the greater Sydney region, with a third of the total Australian population. Bathurst, on the tableland behind Sydney, is the centre of the chief wheat-growing district of the state; Deniliquin, that of the pastures of the Riverina, and the starting-place of the railway by which the wool of that district is dispatched for export to Melbourne (not to Sydney); Broken Hill and Silverton, near the western frontier, are the chief towns of the Barrier Range, a silver-lead-zinc yielding area, amongst the richest in the world. The water supply of the silver-mining district was at first a difficulty, but is now obtained from local rivers. Most of the ore is conveyed to Port Pirie in South Australia, for smelting. A portion of the zinc concentrates produced is treated at Risdon, Tasmania, and the balance exported overseas.

Lord Howe Island 700 km (436 miles) to the northeast of Sydney is a dependency of New South Wales. Norfolk Island, nearer New Zealand, is administered by the Commonwealth. They both contain a small number of inhabitants, grow fruits, and are popular tourist resorts. Production of Kentia palm seeds is, however, the chief industry of Lord Howe Island (see p. 901).

Queensland, the state to the north of New South Wales, was once, like Victoria, a dependency of New South Wales, from which it was separated in 1859. The state is the second largest in Australia, with 22 per cent of the area and 15 per cent of the population. It includes all the islands in the narrowest part of Torres Strait. The surface consists mainly of land above 305 m (1 000 ft) in height, and the district in the southeast known as the Darling Downs, on which are the finest pasture grasses in the state, is about 610 m (2 000 ft) high, and thus has a comparatively cool climate for its situation, within 5° of the Tropic of Capricorn. Extending far into the tropics, Queensland has more varied products than the more southern states. Among the tropical and subtropical products are cotton, bananas, pineapples, and melons, but at present the chief is sugarcane, which is largely grown in the low river valleys on the coast. The yield of unginned cotton increased from 12 tons in 1919 to 12 000 tons in 1934; later it fell away, and in 1969 was just over 3 800 tons. The output of raw sugar in 1954—55 was then a record — 1.3m. tons; in 1971—72 it reached nearly 2.8m. tons. In the warmer, wetter parts of Queensland maize is the chief grain, wheat on the cooler lands.

Queensland has long been the most important cattle-raising state in the Commonwealth, having vast areas of some of the finest grazing lands in the world, with ample room for expansion in the production of chilled and frozen beef for export purposes. The wool industry is the most valuable of all the state's activities, practically the whole output being of fine merino wools. The state had, in 1936, 18 060 000 sheep, in 1970 the numbers had fallen to 16.4m.

Gold is found in many places, but most abundantly at Mount Morgan. Other famous fields include Charters Towers and Gympie. Tin is found in several widely separated districts. One of these is on the tableland in the extreme south of the state, in a district adjoining the New South Wales tinfield, the centre of this district being Stanthorpe. Another, which is the more productive, is at Mount Garnet, Heberton, near the east coast, in about 17½° S lat. A very rich copper district lies round Cloncurry, in the northwest of the state, south of the Gulf of Carpentaria. Here the Mount Isa mine (which produces lead, zinc and silver as well as more than half of Australia's total copper output) is the largest underground copper mine in the world; the metal is refined at Townsville on the coast. At Weipa in the York peninsula is one of the largest bauxite deposits (an estimated 2 500m. tons with 55 per cent alumina content). Production should exceed 15m. tons a year by 1975 and export contracts already exist to AD 2000. Internal shipments are made to the alumina works at Gladstone on the coast north of Brisbane. Besides metals, Queensland is very rich in coal, but it has not, like New South Wales, a coalfield accessible to oceangoing vessels. The chief collieries are in the basin of the Brisbane, Dawson and Bowen Rivers. Next to copper, bauxite and coal, Queensland's most valuable mineral product in 1962 was uranium although output varies with world demand. In the northwest, a township, Mary Kathleen, has grown up around plant for the extraction of uranium oxide. Oil was discovered at Moonie in south Queensland in 1961 and is now piped to refineries at Brisbane. Later natural gas deposits of great size were found further north at Roma. These too have been piped to Brisbane since 1969.

The capital of the state is Brisbane, 800 km (500 miles) north of Sydney, situated on both sides of the Brisbane River, at the head of navigation for large seagoing vessels. Toowoomba, on the tableland to the west of Brisbane, is the chief town on the Darling Downs. Rockhampton, close to the Tropic of Capricorn, is at the head of navigation of the Fitzroy River and is the outlet for a rich and extensive pastoral district as well as for districts producing gold and copper. Townsville, the second town in size in the state, is the outlet for several large mining fields, including that of Cloncurry, and also for a large area of pastoral country, so that it has become an important seaport. Brisbane, Rockhampton, and Townsville are the starting-points of three lines of railway which have been laid westwards for a distance of some 800 km (500 miles) to Cloncurry and Yaraka. Bowen and Gladstone have natural harbours which are two of the best on the coast. The coast towns as far north as Cairns are linked with Brisbane by rail and it has long been planned to join Darwin with Cloncurry and so with the whole Australian system. A good motor road, however, was eventually built instead during the Second World War.

South Australia was founded in 1834 by a British Act of Parliament, and was then expected ultimately to include the territory belonging to Victoria. The state has 9 per cent of the population of Australia in 12 per cent of the area. Most of the inhabitants of the state are confined to the south, chiefly the part of the state that receives a minimum of 250 mm (10 in) of rain per annum, mostly in winter. This district lies mainly to the east and west of Spencer Gulf and the Gulf of St Vincent, where it is traversed by the Mount Lofty Range and the Flinders Range of mountains. Among agricultural products wheat is the most important. The sheltered slopes of the Mount Lofty Range are well suited to the vine and the state produces three-quarters of Australia's wine. From an early date copper was its chief mineral, but the excellent iron ore obtained from Iron Knob, Magnet Mountain, and elsewhere is now the most valuable and forms the basis of the steel and shipbuilding plants at Whyalla. Irrigation is practised in the drier parts of the state, especially in the lower part of the Murray basin. At Renmark similar irrigation works to those of Mildura in Victoria have been carried out, and there is a large production of fruit (for sale fresh, and for canning and drying). The extension of sheep runs — the production of wool is of great importance — and stock rearing has been made possible over some of the drier areas by the use of water, for watering the animals, from artesian wells. The northeast of the state lies in the Great Basin. The land round Lake Eyre (11 m: 36 ft below sea level) is the lowest-lying part of Australia. Most of this 'lake' is now dry except for swamps at the southern end. This region is sparsely settled, even after the construction of the railway to Oodnadatta. In 1931 this line was extended to the more promising grassland around Stuart (Alice Springs) in the Northern Territory; later, connection (road and part rail) was made with Darwin. Since the Second World War this area has been the site of the Woomera weapon-testing range.

The war also gave impetus to the industrial development of South Australia. Cars are a major product, with smelting, steelworks, shipbuilding, saw-mills and consumer goods. There is no hydroelectric power and coal has been the main source of power until the discovery of natural gas at Gidgealpa/Moomba, east of Lake Eyre. The gas is piped some 800 km (500 miles) to Adelaide. Other important minerals are gypsum, magnesite and opals. There are extensive pine forests in the extreme southeast.

The capital of the state is Adelaide, situated near the east side of the Gulf of St Vincent. It was founded in 1837 and named after the queen-consort of William IV and laid out on spacious lines which embody many of the principles of modern town-planning. In 1971 the population was 840 000 of a total 1.2m. in the state. About 11 km (7 miles) from the city stands Port Adelaide, on a small inlet opening out of the Gulf of St Vincent. An outer harbour opened at this port in January 1908, first provided accommodation for large ocean steamers. From the completion in 1887 of the series of railways from Adelaide to Melbourne and Sydney, the port of Adelaide became the place at which all the mails were collected and landed by vessels following the south coast route. Adelaide was displaced by Fremantle after the opening of the transcontinental line from Port Augusta in South Australia to Kalgoorlie in Western Australia, a line which, along with various state lines, completes a through rail connection between Brisbane on the east and Fremantle on the west. Much of the mail landed at Fremantle is now taken by air to the eastern states, while the direct air mail from Europe comes via Darwin. Port Augusta is a wheat-port at the head, Port Pirie another on the east side, of Spencer Gulf, and Port Lincoln a third, near the south end of Eyre's peninsula.

Western Australia is the largest (33 per cent of the total area) but least populous (7 per cent of the total population) of the mainland states. The vast deserts belonging to it will always cause it to be more imposing in extent than population, and even in the principal settled area, the district in the southwest, which receives autumn and winter rains brought by the northwest winds, corresponding to the southwest winds of western Europe, the population is still sparse. This is largely owing to the character of the country. Though there is much good soil, the fertile districts are scattered, and the best land is far from what was, till the construction of the excellent harbour of Fremantle, the only good harbour of the settled district, that of King George's Sound at Albany. After the development of the goldfields, however, population rapidly increased, and all the industries for which the state offers advantages, including agriculture were stimulated. Wheat area increased from 14 000 ha (34 000 acres) in 1890—95 to 690 000 ha (1.7m. acres) in 1915—16, a wartime maximum. It is now normally close on 3m. ha (7m. acres). Fine hard timber from the moist southwest has always been an important product of this state. The most productive goldfields are those of Kalgoorlie in about 31° S, but so far in the interior that the industry was at first greatly hindered by the lack of water. A plentiful supply has, since January 1903, been pumped from a reservoir near Perth at a distance of 560 km (350 miles) from Kalgoorlie. Before the discovery of the Coolgardie goldfield in 1891 the population of Western Australia did not exceed 50 000, in 1971 it was just over 1m. The state produces 70 per cent of Australia's gold output. In the southwest, on the Collie River, are important deposits of coal, which is exported from

Bunbury, a place of export also for the hard timber of the state. In the northern parts of Western Australia pearl fisheries have long been carried on along the coast, but this industry was adversely affected by the cultured pearls of Japan. Gold also exists in the interior of this part of Western Australia, and good pasture-lands have attracted a few settlers. The chief pastures are in Kimberley District, along the banks of the Fitzroy River, which flows into King Sound, about 17½° S. This is cattle-ranch country but development is hampered by lack of communications and Western Australia has only 2m. of Australia's 20m. cattle. The capital of the state is Perth (over 701 300 in 1971) on the Swan River, about 19 km (12 miles) above its port, Fremantle (26 000), on the west coast. Albany, on King George's Sound is where the first settlement was made on West Australian territory (in 1826). Kwinana is a rapidly developing industrial centre on the coast just south of Fremantle with alumina and smelting plants.

Western Australia has some 20 per cent of Australia's sheep and until 1968—69 wool and wheat were the most valuable products. Since then mineral production has become the major factor, with iron ore (Hammersley Range and Mount Newman), bauxite, coal, nickel, manganese and beach sands. Petroleum (in Barrow Island area) and natural gas (north of Perth and off the northwest coast) are also important. New towns, new ports (Port Hedland, Dampier) and new connecting railways have followed on the mineral development during the 1960s.

Tasmania. This state consists of the island so called, together with the smaller islands adjacent with a total population (1971) of 389 000. It is separated from Victoria by Bass Strait, now the site of oil production and exploration. Like Victoria and Queensland, the state was originally a dependency of New South Wales, and the first settlement was a convict establishment in 1803. It became a separate colony in 1825 and joined the Commonwealth in 1901. The surface of the main island is mountainous. A bleak tableland, 900 m (3 000 ft) in height, occupies the middle and a large part of the western half of the island, and is crowned by mountains, and cleft by deep chasms through which issue the torrents which come to form the rivers of the west coast with great hydroelectric potential. To the east of this tableland lies a tolerably level and open district, which forms the great grazing ground of the state. Elsewhere the land is more or less heavily timbered with ample material for saw-mills, chipboard and other timber products. The climate is somewhat warmer than that of England, very suitable for all temperate crops, and specially well adapted for fruits. Copper (at Mount Lyell in the west), silver-lead (at Mount Zeehan), tin (at Mount Bischoff in the northwest and elsewhere), iron ore (transported 90 km: 56 miles as slurry to pelletising plant from Savage River) and gold are

887

important minerals; coal mines and oil-shales (the latter near Latrobe in the north) are also worked. The capital is Hobart (130 000 in 1971), at the end of the island furthest from Australia, an inconvenience which is, however, outweighed by the excellence of its harbour (formed by the estuary of the Derwent) and the introduction of roll-on, roll-off ferries. The electric power that is available has enabled several important industries to be worked such as carbide manufacture, woollen goods, etc. At George Town there are aluminium (alumina from Queensland) and manganese smelters. One of the largest electrolytic zinc treatment works in the world, at Risdon, near Hobart, treats ores sent there from other states on the mainland in addition to those from Tasmania itself. These ores, being zinc blende, contain sulphur which is used in the manufacture of sulphuric acid, and that again in converting Nauru phosphates into superphosphates. The waters of the Great Lake and other catchment areas on the Central Plateau (in particular the Gordon River) are used for generating power. Principal exports are refined metals and minerals, wool and wool products, timber and wood products, and fruit and vegetables. Tourism is becoming increasingly important.

The Northern Territory of Australia, embracing more than 1.3m. sq km (0.5m. sq miles), was separated from South Australia and transferred to the Commonwealth on 1 January 1911. In 1927 the Northern Territory was divided into North Australia (centre at Darwin) and Central Australia (centre Alice Springs), but from 1931 the whole was placed again under one administrator at Darwin. The Territory has 18 per cent of the area and 1 per cent of the population of the Commonwealth. Its southern limit being lat. 26° S, by far the greater part of the area lies within the tropics. It is only in the peninsular portion to the north that there is a copious rainfall – 1 000 mm (40 in) and upwards per annum, occurring of course, almost entirely in summer, so that conditions here resemble the 'monsoon lands' of peninsular India. Towards the interior, here as elsewhere in Australia, the precipitation becomes very scanty. The part with good rains should be well adapted for the growth of the vegetable products of the tropics, but the rainfall tends to be unreliable and soils would appear often to be naturally poor. The livestock industry has traditionally been the most important, but since 1962 mineral output has steadily taken pride of place. The main export is manganese from Groote Eylandt in the Gulf of Carpentaria, followed by copper, iron ore and gold. The McArthur River area has large deposits of lead, zinc and silver and there are uranium deposits at Rum Jungle in Western Arnheim Land. Bauxite is mined in the Gove area and converted to alumina. The search for petroleum has already revealed large reserves of natural gas at Mereenie and Palm Valley near Alice Springs. Towards the south of the Territory are some well-grassed stretches, suitable for sheep, bordering the Finke and other rivers descending from the Macdonnell Ranges (on the Tropic of Capricorn) now accessible from railhead at Alice Springs, the terminus of a narrow-gauge line from Adelaide. In the north, a similar line runs south from the coast at Darwin, the capital, to Birdum. Birdum and Alice Springs 1 030 km (640 miles) apart are linked by Stuart Highway, a wartime enterprise. Another highway connects with the Mount Isa mineral area in Queensland in lieu of a railway. During the First World War meat-preserving works were erected near Darwin, but the cattle-rearers found it easier to send their stock overland to Queensland or to Wyndham in Western Australia. Population, 1961 census (exclusive of full-blood aboriginals): Darwin, 12 458; Northern Territory, 27 139. In 1971, 35 000 and 85 000 respectively.

Table 106 — Australian capital cities (including suburbs) and principal towns in 1971

Town	State	Population	Town	State	Population
Canberra	ACT	158 450	Wollongong	NSW	198 100
Sydney	NSW	2 799 300	Hobart	Tas	153 900
Melbourne	Vic	2 497 300	Geelong	Vic	121 300
Brisbane	Qld	866 000	Townsville	Qld	69 000
Adelaide	SA	842 400	Gold Coast	Qld	68 400
Perth	WA	701 000	Launceston	Tas	62 500
Newcastle	NSW	351 010	Toowoomba	Qld	57 250

New Zealand

New Zealand, a British colony first settled in 1840 and proclaimed a Dominion in September 1907, consists mainly of two large islands situated about 1 900 km (1 200 miles) southeast of Australia. Long and mostly narrow, they lie tandemwise along a curve extending from north to southwest for over 1 600 km (1 000 miles). They are known simply as North Island (a little smaller than England) and South Island (a little larger than England), and support a population (1971) of 2.8m., nearly all of British descent. The native Maori population has risen from 42 000 in 1896 to 223 000 in 1971. Cook's Strait, separating the two islands, is not quite so wide at its narrowest as the Strait of Dover. An interesting tailpiece is Stewart Island, famous for its oyster fisheries, lying south of South Island, from which it is separated by Foveaux Strait; it is about half the size of Cornwall. The three islands have an area of 260 000 sq km (104 000 sq miles).

Besides these main islands, New Zealand jurisdiction covers several groups of small islands in the Pacific Ocean. Some of them, like the

Chatham Islands to the east and the uninhabited Auckland Islands to the south, are within the official limits of the main islands; others are dependent territories lying far to the north and east, in some cases as much as 3 000 km (2 000 miles) away. In the latter category are the important Cook Islands, Niue, the Tokelau Islands, and the Kermadec group. New Zealand also includes within her sphere the Ross Dependency of the Antarctic regions, to the south of the Dominion, while it shares with the United Kingdom and Australia responsibility for administering the United Nations Trusteeship of the phosphate island of Nauru, just south of the Equator. New Zealand also acts as the official representative of Western Samoa (since 1962 an independent sovereign state, and formerly a trustee territory) outside the Pacific islands area.

The coastline of New Zealand is in most places high and rocky, especially on the west coast. In the extreme southwest it is broken up by numerous inlets with very steep and lofty shores, resembling the fjords of Norway. Almost the whole surface is mountainous. One long succession of mountains runs through both the main islands. In the North Island, which is characterised by its volcanoes, both active and extinct, in association with innumerable hot springs and geysers, the highest peak is Ruapehu 2 797 m (9 175 ft). In the South Island, where the mountains lie for the most part close by the west coast, the central part of the range is called the Southern Alps; it includes fifteen peaks rising to over 3 000 m (10 000 ft), culminating in Mount Cook 3 764 m (12 349 ft). Like the Alps of Europe, they are crowned by perpetual snow, and have their higher valleys filled with large glaciers, their lower valleys occupied by large and picturesque lakes. So difficult are these mountains to cross, that for more than 160 km (100 miles) there is no road connecting the east and west coasts of the South Island.

The most extensive plains in New Zealand are the Canterbury Plains, which occupy the middle of South Island on the eastern side, extending for upwards of 160 km (100 miles) from north to south, with a varying breadth. Rivers in both islands are numerous, but are for the most part unfit for navigation. Those of South Island are mostly rapid torrents, fed in summer by the melting snows and glaciers of the Southern Alps. The longest is the Clutha, draining southeastwards three of the chief lakes at the base of the Southern Alps. In North Island, the chief navigable river is the Waikato which drains Lake Taupo northwards to the west coast.

Two-thirds of the total area is classified as arable or pasture land, but only a small share of this is arable land — the great bulk being natural or sown pastures which are the mainstay of the economy. Forest and woodland cover much of the remainder.

The climate of New Zealand is free of the droughts which affect so much of Australia. The winds that carry the most plentiful rains blow from the northwest, as in the southwest of Australia, so that the western slopes of the mountains and the plains at their base are plentifully supplied with rain, whereas the plains on the east have a much smaller rainfall. Hence the forests are chiefly on the west side of the mountains, and the Canterbury Plains on the east are the chief pastoral and agricultural region. For the same reason the mountains form a rough and ready division between the sheep and cattle areas. Although there is much overlapping, the main sheep country lies to the east of the mountains, the wetter cattle country to the west. This division results in a preponderance of sheep farms in South Island, where, as already noted, the mountains are close to the west coast, and in roughly equal areas for sheep and cattle in North Island, where dairy cattle predominate.

The temperature, especially in summer, resembles that of England more than that of Italy, with which New Zealand corresponds in latitude. Grapes are grown in the open air in the northern districts, but wine is rarely made from them. Wheat, oats and barley are the chief crops, but much of the oats is cut for chaff or fed-off, comparatively little being threshed. In 1961–5 (annual average) and 1971, wheat production was 248 000 and 324 000 tons; barley, 98 000 and 227 000; oats, 34 000 and 49 000 tons. In spite of the small proportion of arable land, New Zealand is practically self-supporting agriculturally; imports of foodstuffs are negligible, apart from tropical products. The average yield of wheat in New Zealand is high (over 33 kg per hectare in a good year) but it is the pastoral industry which predominates. The more abundant rain of New Zealand causes the pastures to be richer than those of Australia, and English cultivated grasses thrive remarkably well. Indeed, the area under sown grasses is nine times that of all crops combined. A further illustration of the resemblance between the climate of New Zealand and that of England is presented by the success with which the various breeds of English sheep are reared on the New Zealand pastures.

Wool became the staple export at an early stage, and though its fortunes have suffered from time to time it is still in the forefront of exports. But it was the development of refrigeration, making it possible to transport foodstuffs long distances through the tropics, that established the pattern of New Zealand's overseas trade. The first cargo of frozen meat was dispatched in 1882. As the trade in mutton increased, a change took place in the breeds of sheep employed, and today it is the dual-purpose, crossbred animals, giving both good wool and good meat (mutton and lamb), that are characteristic of New Zealand. There are Romney (meat) and Merino (wool) as well as the crossbreds in the flock of (1971) 59m. sheep, the fourth largest in the world. New Zealand lies second (to Australia) in the production of clean wool; third in greasy wool, and fourth in production of mutton and lamb.

More important still, the advent of refrigeration laid the foundations of the presentday large-scale and highly efficient dairy-farming industry, with emphasis on high grade butter and cheese; dairy produce exported is of equal importance to wool and meat. There were 8.8m. cattle (2.4m. milk cows) in 1970.

New Zealand has developed as a country of small and medium-sized farms. The few large holdings that remain are devoted to sheep raised for wool only and are found mainly in the high country. Freezing works for lamb and mutton are among the largest industrial plants in the Dominion, which is the world's largest exporter of this meat. New Zealand is also the largest exporter of dairy produce, and this industry owes much of its economic success to the fact that the cattle can mostly be grazed on open pastures the whole year round, with only a limited reliance on fodder. The butter and cheese factories are highly mechanised and operated on a cooperative ownership system. Pigs (apt to fluctuate) numbered 617 000 in 1970. The raising of stock for chilled and frozen beef is on the increase — particularly for the North American and Japanese markets.

The minerals of New Zealand are of minor importance. In the 1860s and again at the turn of the century goldmining was a booming industry, but it has since declined. The quantity of gold mined in 1969 was under 500 kg (110 lb). Coal, mostly sub-bituminous, found in limited areas in both islands, yields some 2.5m. tons a year, sufficient for home consumption. Iron ore is present in two areas, the more important being the iron sands of North Island. Of volcanic origin, this deposit of some 700m. tons of titanamagnetite can be separated magnetically to yield 58 per cent iron which provides raw material (along with local coal and scrap steel) for a continuous casting steel works at Glenbrook, Auckland; and is also exported as enriched iron ore to Japan. Nickel, copper, beach sands (South Island) and sulphur (from the geothermal region near the Bay of Plenty) exist but are not exploited. Oil has been found off the Taranaki coast of North Island, as has natural gas in the Maui field some 40 km (25 miles) offshore. Natural gas from the Kapuni field in North Island is piped to domestic users in Wellington and Auckland.

Industrial development has been limited by the small home market and by the traditional dependence on manufactured imports in exchange for primary exports. Since the Second World War, however, manufacturing industries have steadily expanded under government protection, and in 1968 manufactures (30 per cent of the labour force) took over from agriculture (14 per cent of the labour force) as the major contributor to the gross national product. Ninety per cent of the industrial plants employ less than fifty people and production is mainly concerned with a wide range of items for the home market with an increasing surplus for export. In addition to the steel works at Glenbrook, there is an aluminium smelter at Bluff (South Island) which will be among the world's largest with an annual planned output of 220 000 tons. The plant uses cheap power from Lake Manapauri and alumina from Gladstone, Australia. There are also car assembly plants (with an increasing range of locally manufactured components) organised on a rationalised basis with Australia, and an expanding range of timber products (sawn timber, newsprint, pulp, wood chips and fibre board). There is an oil refinery at Whangarei (North Island) with an annual capacity of 2.7m. tons to process crude oil imports.

The high relief and plentiful rainfall have made the development of water power an easy matter throughout the country, and hydroelectric installations provide 90 per cent of the total electric power generated. In 1945 a state Hydroelectric Department was established. In 1959 the capacity of public utility generators was 1.4m. kW and by 1970 it had increased to over 3.3m. kW. The principal source of power in North Island is the Waikato River, which drops 356 m (1 170 ft) from Lake Taupo to the sea, and will have ten power stations. With the Waikato are linked the Lake Waikaremoana and other schemes since North Island with 70 per cent of the population has the greater demand. In South Island the Lake Coleridge scheme, begun in 1911, still serves Christchurch and the Canterbury plains; but the chief source of power is the Waitaki River, Lake Manapauri, and the Clutha River. In June 1957 a government report recommended doubling the capacity of New Zealand's power stations and in 1961 it was decided to link North Island and South Island by a submarine cable across Cook Strait. There is also a small geothermal steam station in North Island.

Despite its dependence on pastoral industry, rather more than half the people of New Zealand live in 'urban areas', and just under half in the four principal cities: Wellington/Hutt (324 000) and Auckland (698 000) in North Island, Christchurch (302 000) and Dunedin (117 800) in South Island. None of the other towns can compare with these four, or has more than about 50 000 inhabitants — except Hamilton with 136 000, Napier-Hastings (96 900), Palmerston North (80 700) and Invercargill (50 700) (1971 census).

The capital, windswept Wellington, is in the south of North Island, on the slopes of an inlet from Cook Strait, forming a safe and commodious harbour (Port Nicholson). Auckland, on a narrow isthmus at the base of the long northwestern peninsula of North Island, is the largest city and the foremost commercially; it was once the seat of government. It is a calling station for steamers from San Francisco and the Panama Canal to Sydney, and as it lies on the east side of the isthmus (the west side having only a shallow harbour), vessels from Auckland bound for Sydney have to sail round the northern end of the island. Auckland is also the principal airport. Other noteworthy, though much smaller, centres in North Island include Napier, on Hawke's Bay, outlet for an extensive farming district back of the east coast; New Plymouth, on the opposite side of the island, focus of the Taranaki dairy farms; Wanganui, also on the west coast, at the mouth of the Wanganui River, a centre of education and art with offshore mooring facilities for 100 000 ton bulk carriers taking iron sand products to Japan; and inland, Palmerston North, hub of the Manawatu sheep and dairy farms, and Hamilton, capital of the Waikato dairying district.

In South Island the chief towns are Christchurch and Dunedin. Christchurch is the principal town on the Canterbury Plains. It is situated a few kilometres from the east coast, and separated by a tunnelled hill from its port, Lyttelton, on one of the inlets of Banks Peninsula. Dunedin, further south, is the port for the province of Otago and stands at the head of the long Otago Harbour. Large ocean vessels have to stop at Port Chalmers, halfway along the inlet. Invercargill is the chief town on Foveaux Strait; its port, for large vessels, is Bluff Harbour. Greymouth and Westport are the ports of the principal New Zealand coalfields, on the west side of South Island.

New Zealand's traditional overseas trade has been dominated by the products of her pastures (wool, meat, butter and cheese) and by the fact that the United Kingdom was by far the major trading partner. As the United Kingdom moved closer to the European Economic Community in the 1960s, so New Zealand sought to expand her exports to new markets in North America, Japan, Australia and South America — her coarser wools being exported as carpets; meat, particularly beef, becoming more important as the standard of living in these new markets improved; and dairy products being diversified to include powdered and condensed milk, and casein for industrial uses. In 1958 the United Kingdom took 56 per cent of exports (including almost all the meat: mutton, lamb and beef). By 1969 this figure was 39 per cent (and included only 55 per cent of the meat). Sixteen per cent went to the USA (beef and lamb), 9 per cent to Japan (mutton and timber), 7 per cent to Australia (manufactures) and 3 per cent (rapidly increasing) to Canada. In 1958 the United Kingdom took 89 per cent of all dairy products; by 1969 this figure was still 70 per cent, which represented some 40 per cent of all butter and cheese consumed in the United Kingdom. Thus the United Kingdom was still the main, though less dominant, trading partner in 1969 — particularly important for lamb, butter and cheese as it took 85, 95, and 78 per cent respectively of the total New Zealand production — although changing values reduced these to only 10 per cent of the value of total exports. In 1970 the traditional exports still held pride of place — 40 per cent were meat and meat products; 22 per cent dairy and milk products; 20 per cent wool; 5 per cent timber, fruit and fish; 3 per cent manufactures. Exports mainly to the UK, the USA, Japan, Canada and Australia and imports from the UK, Australia, the USA and Japan.

The Pacific Islands

Fiji

Formerly the premier British Crown Colony in the Pacific, Fiji became an independent Dominion within the Commonwealth in 1970. It comprises over 800 heavily wooded and volcanic islands situated more than 1 600 km (1 000 miles) to the north of New Zealand. The total land area is just over 18 000 sq km (7 000 sq miles). **Viti Levu,** the largest of the islands, has more than half of the land surface, and **Vanua Levu,** the second largest, occupies two-thirds of the remainder. The islands were ceded to Britain in 1874 by their native king, but even before that time people of European origin had arrived in search of sandalwood and had established plantations of tropical crops.

Plantation sugar was introduced soon after the start of British rule, and the Indian labourers who were brought to Fiji to work on the plantations after 1880 numbered 60 000 by 1921 and formed 38 per cent of the population; they now form 53 per cent. Sugar is the principal export, providing nearly 70 per cent of all exports. Coconut oil and copra provide 12 per cent, followed by fish, bananas and timber. The economy is overdependent on the sugar crop (subject to international quota agreements) and the copra/coconut oil production varies considerably. The banana crop goes almost exclusively to New Zealand. There is a little gold mined: less than 3 000 kg in 1969. The generally unfavourable balance of trade (imports include machinery, fuel textiles and food) is balanced by steadily increased earnings from tourists, who totalled 14 000 in 1960 and 60 000 in 1970. Exchange earnings from this source are now second only to sugar exports. Industry is limited to sugar-mills and copra-mills (coconut oil and coconut meal), and many light industries. A small oil refinery is planned on Viti Levu.

The chief towns are seaports with fine harbours protected by coral reefs. Suva, the capital (a city of 54 000 at the 1966 census) and Lautoka are both on Viti Levu; Levuka, a former capital, is on a small island east of Viti Levu. Fiji's tourist industry is based on the fact that it is an important centre of air and sea communications. A population census is taken every ten years, and in 1966 the total of 514 000 included 218 000 Fijians, 230 000 Indians and 7 000 Europeans.

Fiji joined other South Pacific islands in 1972 to discuss a common approach to customs and communications.

Nauru

Nauru is a small coral island of 21.2 sq km (8.2 sq miles) just south of the Equator in the centre of the Pacific Ocean. Formerly held by

Germany and later a trustee territory jointly administered by Great Britain, Australia and New Zealand, it became an independent republic in 1968 with special links with the Commonwealth. A barren island with steep coral reefs, it has no harbour or anchorage. The population of 6 664 (1970) is concentrated in a narrow fertile coastal strip surrounding a central plateau which is a rich deposit of high grade phosphate. Previously owned by the British Phosphate Corporation, the deposit has been owned by the Nauruans since 1970 and represents the sole export (to Australia, New Zealand and Japan) at some 2m. tons a year to make Nauru the fifth largest producer in the world. Most food, all manufactured goods and some labour for the phosphate workings must be imported; but exports exceeded imports by 500 per cent in 1968—69. Domaneab is the administrative centre and there are air links with other islands and Brisbane. It is estimated that the phosphate deposit will be exhausted before the year 2000.

The Tonga Islands

The Tonga Islands, also known as the Friendly Islands, lie 640 km (400 miles) east of Fiji and consist of some 150 islands (of which only thirty-six are inhabited) with an area of 700 sq km (270 sq miles). The islands have a constitutional monarchy and became an independent kingdom within the Commonwealth in 1970. There are three main groups; Vava'u in the north, Tongatapu in the south (mostly volcanic) and Ha'apai in the centre (coral atolls). The population in 1969 was some 80 000, half of whom live in Tongatapu where the capital, Nukualofa, is situated. Subsistence crops form the main produce, and there are no mineral resources. Exports are almost entirely bananas and copra, and imports include food, textiles and manufactures. There are air links with Fiji and Western Samoa.

Western Samoa

Western Samoa is situated midway between Honolulu and Australia. With an area of 2 840 sq km (1 097 sq miles) it consists mainly of two large volcanic islands — **Savai'i** and **Upalu**. The vegetation is lush with mangrove forests and the highest peak, in Savai'i reaches 1 860 m (6 094 ft). Formerly administered by New Zealand as a United Nations trustee territory, the island became an independent state in 1962 with external affairs still handled by New Zealand. The population (1969) was 143 000 with 29 000 in the capital, Apia. The islands are fertile with exports of bananas, cocoa and copra. Imports, which tend to exceed exports, are food and manufactured goods — with New Zealand, Australia and the United Kingdom as the main trading partners. The islands have air links with American Samoa, and thence to New

Zealand, Tahiti and Honolulu. Western Samoa has joined Fiji, Nauru, Tonga, Australia and New Zealand in talks on economic cooperation, improved communications and a common approach to civil aviation.

British Territories

The British Solomon Islands

This protectorate includes all the Solomon Islands except the most northerly, which lie within Australia's trust territory of New Guinea. Separated from Australia by the Coral Sea and dispersed over 645 000 sq km (250 000 sq miles) of ocean, the Protectorate has a land area of about 29 000 sq km (11 000 sq miles) (roughly the size of Belgium), with a population (1970) of 161 000, mostly Melanesians, with a few hundred Europeans. The islands are largely of volcanic origin and are mountainous with tropical rainforests and an average rainfall of 2 300 mm (130 in). **Guadalcanal**, the biggest, has an area of 6 000 sq km (2 500 sq miles) and three others (**Santa Isabel**, **Malaita**, and **San Cristobal**) are each in excess of 2 600 sq km (1 000 sq miles). Some of the islands saw fierce and destructive fighting in the Second World War and the work of reconstruction has been going on ever since.

The main crops are coconuts, tropical roots, rice (in which the islands are rapidly becoming self-sufficient), cocoa and sorghum. Copra, cocoa and timber are the chief exports. Timber resources are being developed but there are no minerals beyond a small bauxite deposit on Choiseul (the nearest island to Bougainville). The flood-prone rivers offer hydroelectric potential. The capital, Honiara (11 400) on Guadalcanal is also the seat of the High Commissioner for the Western Pacific (which includes the Gilbert and Ellice Islands and the New Hebrides). Imports are mainly machinery, transport equipment, manufactures and food with the United Kingdom, Australia and Japan as the main partners. There are internal air links between the islands, and with Papua (thence to Australia) and Fiji.

The New Hebrides

The New Hebrides are a condominium jointly administered by Britain and France. Like the Solomons to the northwest, they are volcanic and mountainous, and the native people, numbering 83 000 in 1969, are Melanesians. The total land area (14 700 sq km: 5 700 sq miles) of the seventy-three islands of the group is only about half the size of the British Solomons. The largest islands are **Espiritu Santo** (3 880 sq km: 1 500 sq miles), **Malekula**, and **Efate**. The fertile soil produces luxuriant vegetation and encourages agricultural industry. The main subsistence crops are yams, manioc and bananas; the commercial crops are coconuts, cocoa, coffee and cattle for beef. There is a manganese mine timber (the Kauri pine) is exploited, and there is fishing for tuna and bonito. There is no industry apart from a plant for freezing fish. Exports are copra, frozen fish, manganese ore and a little meat, cocoa, coffee and timber, mainly to France, Japan and the USA. Imports (food and manufactures) come from Australia and France. There are internal air services and links from Espiritu Santo and Port Vila, to the international airlines via Fiji and New Caledonia. Two-thirds of the small European population (5 400) are French; the largest plantations are French-operated. The seat of administration is Vila, on the island of Efate in the centre of the group.

The Gilbert and Ellice Islands

This colony is an administrative unit of some forty coral reef islands and atolls formed into five island territories and groups described below, spread out over 5m. sq km (2m. sq miles) of ocean and crossed both by the Equator and the international date line. With the single exception of Ocean Island, all the islands are low-lying atolls. Pigs and fowls are kept but there is little soil for agricultural production. Their combined areas amount to barely 1 000 sq km (400 sq miles), and nearly half of this is contributed by **Christmas Island,** the largest atoll in the Pacific. The inhabitants eke out a sometimes precarious existence on the fruit of the coconut and pandanus palms and breadfruit trees, supplementing these staple foods with fish. Total population (1969) 55 000, with 1 000 in the capital at Bairikion Tarawa Atoll.

The Gilbert Islands, forming the northwestern part of the colony, consist of sixteen atolls with a land area of 260 sq km (102 sq miles) and 44 000 inhabitants (Micronesians). Periodic droughts add to the problems of supporting so dense a population, some of whom migrate annually to the copra plantations of the Line Islands. The headquarters of the colony are on the island of Tarawa and there are limited air services to Fiji.

The Ellice Islands, to the south of the Gilberts, are nine in number, with a total area of only 24 sq km (9.5 sq miles) and a population (Polynesian) of about 6 000. Funafuti, the District Headquarters, has an air service with Tarawa.

Ocean Island is the westernmost outpost of the colony and an important source of high-grade phosphate, which is worked by the British Phosphate Commissioners, more than 500 000 tons being produced annually. This isolated patch of land, less than 6.4 sq km (2.5 sq miles) in extent, had a population at the end of 1968 of 2 192.

The Phoenix Islands lie well to the east and comprise eight atolls together making 28 sq km (11 sq miles). Formerly uninhabited, they were used between 1937 and 1964 to take part of the surplus population of the Gilberts and had well over 1 000 people. Their remote situation gave them a new importance as landing grounds for aircraft on trans-Pacific flights, a fact which was responsible for an agreement in 1939 between Britain and the USA for joint control of two of the islands — **Canton** and **Enderbury**. The introduction of long range aircraft made the airport at Canton unnecessary, and recurring droughts have closed the permanent settlements.

The Northern Line Islands, in the northeastern part of the colony, comprise the detached islands of **Fanning** 33 sq km (12.5 sq miles), **Washington** and **Christmas Islands**. Their population is only about 1 200, and some of the Gilbertese are being settled there to provide labour for the copra plantations. On Fanning is established a repeater station on the trans-Pacific cables.

Exports from the colony are almost exclusively phosphate and copra, and usually exceed the value of imports — food, textiles and manufactures. An internal air service, to the outer islands from Tarawa, was started in 1969.

Pitcairn Island, its area of 4.6 sq km (2 sq miles) making it barely larger than Gibraltar, is midway between South America and Australia. Its scanty but hardy population are descended from the *Bounty* mutineers (who occupied the island in 1790). They engage in farming and fishing and produce for export a small quantity of fruit, vegetables and curios. The uninhabited islands of Henderson, Ducie, and Oeno (from 100 to 460 km: 65 to 290 miles away) are annexed to Pitcairn. There are no air services and the population had declined to eighty in 1969.

Australian Territories

Papua and New Guinea

This single administrative unit combines two distinct regions in East New Guinea with separate status: the Australian territory of Papua (southeastern New Guinea) and the Trusteeship Territory of New Guinea (consisting of the former German possessions of northeastern New Guinea, the Bismarck Archipelago and the northernmost Solomons). It may be noted that, including the western half — a remnant of the former Netherlands East Indies which as West Irian (now Irian Barat) was handed over to Indonesia in 1962 — the island of New Guinea covers over 777 000 sq km (300 000 sq miles) and is the second largest island in the world (excluding the continents); it ranks next to Greenland. The portion administered by Australia is just over half the whole, and with the associated islands totals 460 000 sq km (178 300 sq miles) — twice the size of Great Britain. The estimated total population is 2.4m. (1969).

The surface of New Guinea is in many parts mountainous. The whole of the narrow southeastern extremity (lying mostly in Papua) is traversed by chains of mountains, known as the Owen Stanley Range, with peaks upwards of 3 990 m (13 000 ft) — above the snowline in spite of proximity to the Equator. Lying within the monsoon area, the whole island receives copious rains during about half the year, and, like other tropical countries with an abundant rainfall, is covered with dense forests, which are one of the chief causes why the interior remained so long unexplored. The rivers have hydroelectric potential and two great navigable rivers serve as highways into the interior. One of these, the Fly, forms a large delta on the western side of the Gulf of Papua; the other, the Sepik, enters the sea near the middle of the northeastern coastline. Neither of these rivers, however, served as the means of gaining much knowledge of the land beyond its banks; the exploration for minerals, often with the help of the aeroplane, has been necessary for that. Even today the full mineral resources of the island have not been adequately prospected although the search for oil and natural gas is actively pursued, and large copper deposits have been found in West Irian.

Easily cultivated food crops such as bananas, yams, sago, sugarcane, coconut and taro are grown in both Territories, though in recent years introduced crops, including coffee, rubber, tea and cocoa, have been added both for local consumption and for export. Rice and maize are also grown, and cattle are being reared for beef. Alluvial goldfields are worked in both Territories, but are now of little importance in Papua. In the Trust Territory, government-aided factories turn out 8 000 to 10 000 tons of coconut oil from copra and over 11m. sq m (40m. sq ft) of high-grade plywood and veneer. The seat of administration of the combined territories is at Port Moresby, which lies to the east of the Gulf of Papua, sheltered behind a long barrier reef that skirts the whole of this part of the coast, access to it being obtained by one of the numerous deep channels by which this reef, like the Great Barrier Reef of the neighbouring coast of Australia, is crossed.

Papua has an area of 220 000 sq km (86 100 sq miles) and a population of about 670 000 (1969). Industries at Port Moresby (56 000) cover a wide range of products for local consumption. Exports are mainly copra and rubber.

New Guinea, with its associated islands, covers 239 000 sq km (93 000 sq miles) of land, of which about three-quarters is mainland territory. The population is 1.7m. (1969). Exports are mainly coconut products, coffee, cocoa, timber and plywood. The largely undeveloped Bismarck Archipelago contributes 49 700 sq km (19 200 sq miles) to the total area and includes New Britain, New Ireland, Lavongai, and the Admiralty Islands; the population is about 280 000. The fine port of Rabaul, on New Britain, was formerly the seat of administration of the whole territory of northeastern New Guinea; and was largely destroyed in the Second World War. The principal Solomon Islands included in the territory are Bougainville (10 000 sq km – 3 880 sq miles) and Buka. The development of the Panguna valley copper mine on the former will be a major source of future income for the territories. With estimated reserves of some 900m. tons of low-grade copper, this deposit is easily worked by opencast methods and the ore (concentrated at the mine) is conveyed by a slurry pipeline to a new port at Anewa Bay. Long-term contracts have been signed by Japan, West Germany and Spain and production capacity is aimed at 29m. tons of ore annually – some 150 000 tons of copper (with 14 000 kg of gold and 30 000 kg of silver as a subsidiary product).

Norfolk Island

Norfolk Island (34 sq km – 13 sq miles), with a population of about 1 100, is over 1 400 km (900 miles) to the northeast of Sydney and is administered by the Commonwealth government. Fruit is the chief product with beef cattle and forestry being developed. Tourism is a major industry as the climate is ideal.

Lord Howe Island

Lord Howe Island (3.7 sq km – 6 sq miles) lies midway between Sydney and Norfolk Island and is a dependency of New South Wales. It exports seeds of the kentia palm and has a population of about 280 (1969).

Christmas Island

Christmas Island 360 km (224 miles) south of Java, has 3 361 (1970) inhabitants in its 135 sq km (52 sq miles), which are rich in phosphate of lime. It was administered by Singapore from 1900 till 1958, when it was transferred to Australia. Singapore received an *ex gratia* payment of M$20m. for loss of revenue. Phosphate rock is exported to Australia and New Zealand; Australia, Malaysia and Singapore take much of the phosphate dust.

Cocos and Keeling Islands

A group of small coral islands clothed with coconut palms (total area 14.2 sq km (5.5 sq miles), population about 611 in 1970) in the middle of the Indian Ocean. Long incorporated in the colony of Singapore, the group was transferred to the Commonwealth of Australia in 1955 by British and Australian Acts of Parliament, for use as a halfway house on the air route between Australia and South Africa. Groves of coconut palm yield nuts, oil and copra for export.

New Zealand Territories

The Cook Islands

The Cook Islands, lying in the central Pacific 2 570 km (1 600 miles) to the northeast of New Zealand, have a total land area of under 260 sq km (100 sq miles) and a population of about 21 000. The fifteen islands of which they are composed are in two groups, Lower and Northern, the former being the more extensive and containing the main island of Rarotonga and the administrative centre at Avarua. The islands have had internal self-government since 1965, but New Zealand is still responsible for foreign affairs. Exports are mainly fruit and vegetables (tomatoes, citrus fruit, pineapples and juices) with some clothing and copra. Almost all go to New Zealand, which also supplies two-thirds of all imports. There is a weekly air service between Rarotonga and New Zealand.

Niue

Niue, or Savage Island, 960 km (600 miles) west of Rarotonga, is an outlier of the Cook group but is separately administered. It is 260 sq km (100 sq miles) in area and has a population of about 5 300 (1970). There are small exports of bananas, copra and sugar. Almost all trade is with New Zealand.

The Kermadec Islands

The Kermadec Islands (33 sq km: 13 sq miles) are 960 km (600 miles) to the north of New Zealand. They have a meteorological and radio station and under half a score of inhabitants (the official staff) on Raoul, the larger island.

The Tokelau Islands

The Tokelau Islands, or Union Islands, over 3 200 km (2 000 miles) from New Zealand and halfway to Hawaii, are a group of three atolls with 10 sq km (4 sq miles) of land and a population of 1 745 (1969). The islands are subject to frequent hurricanes and are dependent on subsistence agriculture.

French Territories

New Caledonia

New Caledonia and its dependencies form one of the overseas territories of France. They mostly lie between the New Hebrides and Queensland, being distant from the latter by about 1 120 km (700 miles). They have an estimated area of 19 000 sq km (7 400 sq miles) including outlying groups, chiefly the Loyalty Islands (2 000 sq km: 800 sq miles) lying to the east. More remote is the Wallis Archipelago, no less than 2 100 km (1 300 miles) to the northeast. The group population is 120 000 of whom New Caledonia itself has about 101 000, the Loyalty Islands 14 000, and Wallis Archipelago 5 400. Cigar-shaped and mountainous, the main island is about 400 km long and 50 km broad (250 by 30 miles). The climate is favourable for European settlement and a third of the population are French. The native Melanesians form half the total, but their decline in number is shown by once-cultivated terraces that now lie abandoned. In France's constitutional referendum in September 1958 New Caledonia decided by an overwhelming majority (26 085 to 500) in favour of continued association with France. Coconuts (copra) and coffee are exported, other crops being bananas, yams, manioc, taro, maize, wheat, rice, and sweet potatoes. Large areas of savanna assist the pastoral industry, and there are over 100 000 head of cattle. But it is its great wealth of mineral resources for which New Caledonia is chiefly remarkable. The island is the world's second source of nickel (23 per cent in 1968, Canada 38 per cent), as well as an important source of chromium. Iron ore and manganese are plentiful, and chrome, lead, copper, gold and silver are found. Nickel ore production is some 3.5m. tons a year and emphasis is placed on local smelting and semi-fabrication with plans to produce 200 000 tons of refined nickel annually by 1975. Local industry includes food processing and subsidiary industries for mineral-processing. France is the main trading partner, but some 90 per cent of all Japan's imported nickel ore came from New Caledonia in 1968. Exports are nickel ore, processed nickel ore, iron ore, and a little cocoa and coffee.

The capital of the territory is Noumea (population 48 000), on a fine harbour in the southwest of New Caledonia — its airport is served by the international airlines. It is also the seat of the South Pacific Commission, an international advisory body formed in 1947 to promote the economic and social welfare of the island peoples. The members of the

Commission are Britain, Australia, New Zealand, the United States and France.

French Polynesia

French Polynesia comprises the remaining French possessions in the Pacific. There are some 130 islands, widely dispersed over the eastern (Polynesian) Pacific, with a total land area of about 4 000 sq km (1 550 sq miles) and a population (1969) of some 100 000. The main group is that of the **Society Islands** (the Windward and Leeward Islands), in which the chief island is **Tahiti** (1 042 sq km: 403 sq miles), with a census population of 61 520 at the end of 1967. Tahiti has a mountainous interior with a fertile littoral. It contains the French Polynesian capital, Papeete, with a population of over 22 000 and is served by the international airlines. Other groups included in French Polynesia are the **Marquezas Islands**, the **Tuamotu Group**, the **Austral** and **Rapa Group**, and the **Gambier Group**. Bananas, pineapples and oranges are grown along with other subsistence crops on these largely volcanic islands. Exports are copra, coffee, vanilla and mother-of-pearl. Exports of phosphates ceased in 1966 when the deposits were exhausted. Tourism is becoming increasingly important as an industry.

United States Territories

Guam

Guam, in the northwest of the Pacific, is 2 250 km (1 400 miles) east of the Philippines and south of Japan. Although it is the largest of the Mariana Islands (one of the group of the North Pacific Trust Territory; see below) it is under separate administration, having been an American possession and naval base since 1898. It has an area of 450 sq km (209 sq miles), and a population at the 1970 census of 87 000 (exclusive of 38 000 military personnel). The capital is Agaña (1 640) and there is a deepwater harbour at Apra. Agriculture includes maize, sweet potatoes, cassava, bananas and truck crops such as bread fruit, coconuts and sugarcane; but 90 per cent of the food and all consumer goods are imported. In 1969 imports were valued at $58m. and exports at $1m. Guam is a free port with a 1.5m. ton refinery. Tourism is increasingly important; the number of visitors rising from 1 900 in 1964 to 40 000 in 1970. The island is well served by United States airlines.

American Samoa

American Samoa is not a trusteeship territory, as is Western Samoa. It has been under American administration since 1899, when the Samoan islands were divided between Germany and the United States, the interest of the latter being in the use of the great natural harbour at Pago Pago as a naval base. There are five islands, mountainous and forested, with a total area of 197 sq km (76 sq miles) and a population of 28 000 (1970 census), the main island of Tutuila (on which is Pago Pago) accounting for more than half the area and 85 per cent of the people. Cultivation is mainly coconuts and tropical vegetables and fruits. Exports are canned tuna, copra, woven matting and handicrafts. There are air services to the USA and New Zealand via Honolulu and Fiji.

North Pacific Trust Territory

At the conclusion of the First World War the German possessions in the North Pacific were placed under Japanese mandate. Following the Second World War they have become a United Nations trusteeship terri- tory for which the United States has assumed responsibility. They cover an ocean area of 8m. sq km (3m. sq miles), and consist of over 2 000 islands and islets (of which 98 are inhabited), making a total land area of less than 1 813 sq km (700 sq miles). The combined populations number 98 000 (1969), the indigenous inhabitants being Micronesians. The islands fall into three groups: the Mariana Islands, the Carolines, and the Marshalls. Copra is the main export; imports include food and building materials. Atomic bomb experiments in the Marshalls have made famous the names of Bikini and Eniwetok.

Former Netherlands Territory

Irian Barat (Western Irian)

Irian Barat was formerly West (Dutch) New Guinea and was taken over by Indonesia in 1963. It has an area of 414 000 sq km (160 000 sq miles) and an estimated population of 1m. (less than 1 per cent of Indonesia's 118m.). It is largely mountainous, and is still little developed, but oil has been located and is beginning to be exported, and large copper deposits which could yield up to 2.5m. tons of ore annually were found in 1970. Exports are mainly forest products and crude oil.

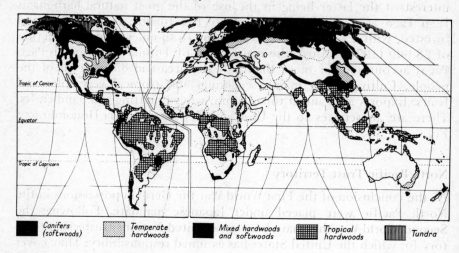

Conifers (softwoods) Temperate hardwoods Mixed hardwoods and softwoods Tropical hardwoods Tundra

The world's forests and tundra

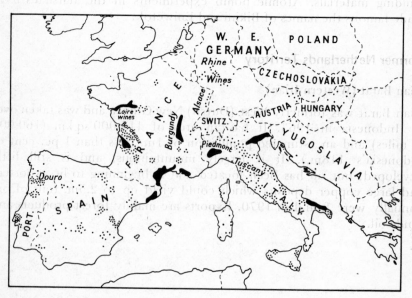

The wine lands of Europe

In 1972 18.8 million tons of grapes for wine were produced in Europe. The world total was 27.8 million

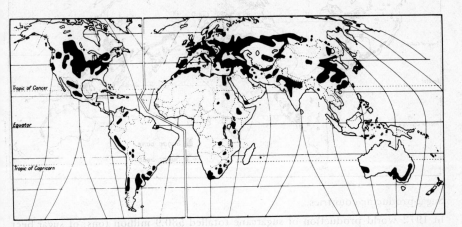

World distribution of wheat.

In 1972 world production totalled 347.6 million tons. (China estimate included)

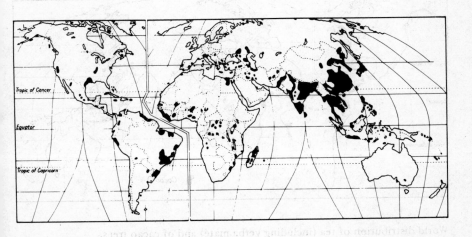

World distribution of paddy.

In 1972 world production totalled 295.4 million tons. (China estimate included)

907

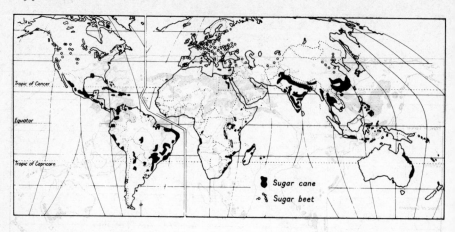

Sugar-producing countries.

In 1972 world production of sugarcane totalled 580.9 million tons; of sugar beet 240.3 million tons. Centrifugal raw sugar 73.97 million tons

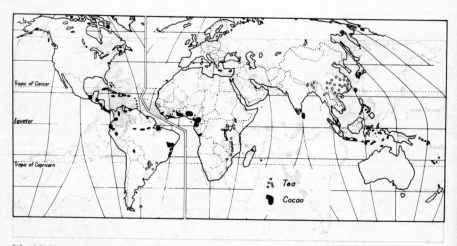

World distribution of tea (including yerba maté) and of cacao trees.

In 1972 world production of all teas totalled 1.374 million tons (China estimate included); of cocoa beans 1.48 million tons

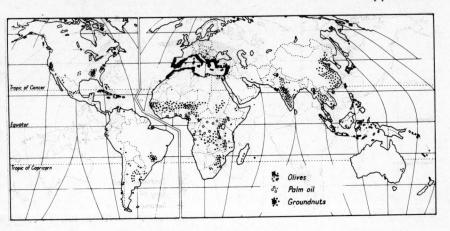

World distribution of groundnuts, olives, palm oil.

World production (1972): groundnuts in shell 16.9 million tons; total olives 7.7 million tons; olive oil 1.5 million tons; palm oil 2.4 million tons. (China estimate included)

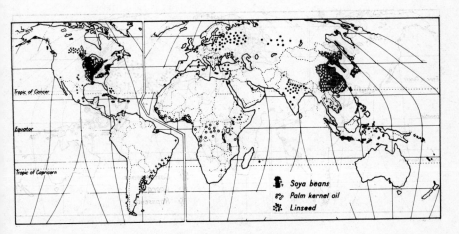

World distribution of palm kernel oil, soya beans, linseed.

World production (1972): palm kernels 1.3 million tons; soya beans 53 million tons; linseed 2.6 million tons. (China estimate included)

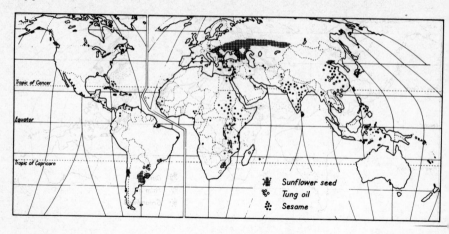

World distribution of sunflower seed, tung oil, sesame.

World production (1972): sunflower seed 9.45 million tons; tung oil 113 683 tons; sesame seed 1.9 million tons. (China estimates included)

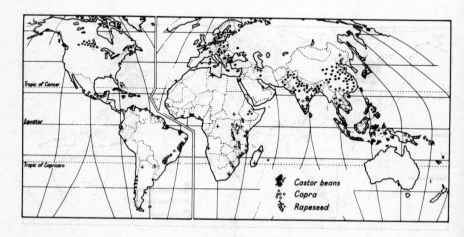

World distribution of castor beans, rapeseed, copra.

World production (1972): castor beans 810 000 tons and rapeseed 6.9 million tons. (China estimates included); coconuts 27.9 million tons; copra 4.42 million tons

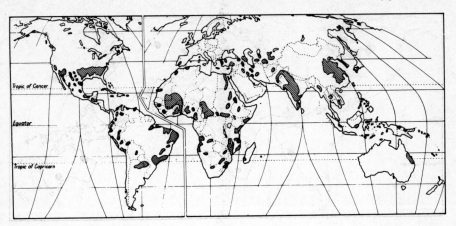

World distribution of cotton production.

In 1972 world production of cotton (lint) totalled 13.031 million tons. (China estimate included)

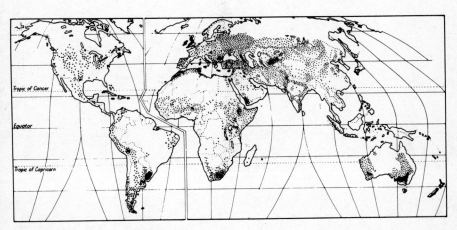

World distribution of sheep.

Australia, New Zealand, Argentina, South Africa, United Kingdom, Uruguay and France are the chief exporters of wool. Total sheep (1972): 1.065 million. (China estimate included)

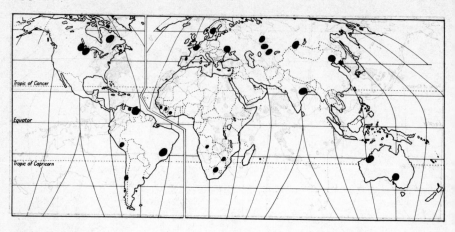

World distribution of iron ore of economic importance in 1972.

World reserves are enormous, and distribution is widespread. Total world production in 1971 was 428.73 million tons (pre-1939 annual average was about 109 million tons)

Appendix 2 Area and population of countries

The population figures are the latest available estimates. As far as possible the areas stated exclude water areas. The figures for the areas of small territories have been rounded but the exact area has been used in calculating population density. The average annual rates of increase take account of migration as well as balance between births and deaths.

Country	Area thousand km^2	Population thousands	Density of population persons per km^2	Mean annual increase % 1963–71
Afghanistan	647	17 878	27.6	2.3
Albania	29	2 286	79.5	3.0
Algeria	2 382	15 772	6.6	3.5
American Samoa	0.2	31	157.4	3.6
Andorra	0.5	19	41.9	6.6
Angola (Port.)	1 247	5 812	4.7	1.8
Antigua (U.K.)	0.4	73	165.2	2.0
Argentina	2 777	23 923	8.6	1.5
Australia	7 687	12 959	1.7	1.9
Capital Territory	2.4	158	65.4	8.4
New South Wales	801	4 663	5.8	1.6
Northern Territory	1 347	93	0.07	18.6
Queensland	1 728	1 869	1.1	1.7
South Australia	984	1 186	1.2	1.4
Tasmania	68	392	5.7	1.0
Victoria	228	3 546	15.6	1.7
Western Australia	2 527	1 053	0.42	3.9
Austria	84	7 488	89.3	0.5
Bahamas, The	14[1]	185	13.3	4.6
Bahrain	0.6[1]	224	360.1	2.9
Bangladesh	143	69 000	483.2	3.4
Barbados	0.4	240	556.8	0.1
Belgium	31	9 711	318.3	0.5
Belize (U.K.)[2]	23	128	5.6	2.8
Bermuda (U.K.)	0.05	56	1 056.6	1.8
Bhutan	47	874	18.6	2.2
Bolivia	1 099	5 195	4.7	2.6
Botswana	600	709	1.2	2.8
Brazil	8 512	98 854	11.6	2.8
British Indian Ocean Territory	0.08	2.0	25.6	–
British Solomon Is.	28[1]	174	6.1	2.6
British Virgin Is.	0.2	12	78.4	3.8
Brunei (U.K.)	5.8	142	24.6	4.6
Bulgaria	111	8 579	77.3	0.7
Burma	678	28 870	42.6	1.9
Burundi	28	3 615	129.9	2.0
Cameroun	475	5 836	12.3	2.2
Canada	9 221	22 047	2.4	1.6
Alberta	644	1 655	2.6	2.2

Country	Area thousand km²	Population thousands	Density of population persons per km²	Mean annual increase % 1963—71
British Columbia	931	2 185	2.3	3.1
Manitoba	549	992	1.8	0.5
New Brunswick	72	635	8.8	0.6
Newfoundland	370	522	1.4	1.1
Northwest Territories	3 246	35	0.01	3.9
Nova Scotia	53	794	15.0	0.9
Ontario	891	7 703	8.6	2.0
Prince Edward I.	5.7	112	19.7	0.6
Quebec	1 357	6 028	4.4	0.8
Saskatchewan	570	928	1.6	−0.6
Yukon	532	18	0.03	5.0
Cape Verde Is. (Port.)	4.0	285	70.7	2.6
Cayman Is. (U.K.)	0.3	11	42.8	1.7
Central African Republic	623	1 637	2.6	2.2
Chad	1 284	3 791	3.0	2.3
Chile	757	10 045	13.3	1.4
China[3]	9 561	700 000	73.2	1.8
Christmas Is. (Austral.)	0.1	3.0	22.5	−4.5
Cocos (Keeling) Is. (Austral.)	0.01	0.6	44.6	−2.0
Colombia	1 139	23 331	19.6	3.2
Comoro Archipelago (Fr.)	2.2	275	126.7	2.1
Congo	342	981	2.9	2.2
Cook Is. (N.Z.)	0.2	25	107.8	3.5
Costa Rica	51	1 867	36.8	3.2
Cuba	115	8 749	76.4	2.3
Cyprus	9.3	647	69.9	1.0
Czechoslovakia	128	14 562	113.9	0.4
Dahomey	113	2 869	25.5	2.5
Denmark	43	5 010	116.3	0.7
Dominica (U.K.)	0.8	73	97.2	1.7
Dominican Republic	49	4 305	88.3	2.9
Ecuador	284	6 726	23.7	3.4
Egypt[4]	1 001	34 839	34.8	2.5
El Salvador	21	3 760	175.8	3.7
Equatorial Guinea	28	293	10.4	1.4
Ethiopia	1 222	25 933	21.2	1.8
Falkland Is. (U.K.)[5]	16	2.1	0.13	−0.0
Faroe Is. (Dan.)	1.4	42	30.0	1.6
Fiji	18	545	29.8	2.5
Finland	337	4 643	13.8	0.4
France	547	52 000	95.1	0.9
French Guiana	91	56	0.61	4.6
French Polynesia	4.0	127	31.8	4.2
French Southern & Antarctic Territory	7.6	0.2	0.02	—
French Territory of the Afars and Issas	22	99	4.5	2.0

Country	Area thousand km^2	Population thousands	Density of population persons per km^2	Mean annual increase % 1963–71
Gabon	268	500	1.9	1.2
Gambia	11	383	33.9	2.1
Germany, East[6]	108	17 043	157.6	−0.1
Germany, West[6]	248	61 880	249.1	0.8
Ghana	239	9 087	38.1	3.0
Gibraltar (U.K.)	0.006	28	4 666.7	1.4
Gilbert & Ellice Is. (U.K.)	0.9	59	66.6	2.0
Greece	132	8 957	67.9	0.5
Greenland (Dan.)	2 176	52	0.02	4.2
Grenada (U.K.)	0.3	96	279.1	0.5
Guadeloupe (Fr.)	1.8	341	191.7	1.4
Guam (U.S.)	0.5	93	169.4	3.5
Guatemala	109	5 409	49.7	3.1
Guinea	246	4 109	16.7	2.2
Guyana	215	763	3.5	2.3
Haiti	28	5 073	182.8	2.0
Honduras	112	2 687	24.0	3.0
Hong Kong (U.K.)	1.0	4 077	3 942.9	2.1
Hungary	93	10 433	112.1	0.5
Iceland	103	209	2.0	1.3
India[7]	3 280	563 494	172.8	2.2
Indonesia	1 904	124 052	65.1	2.8
Iran	1 648	30 956	18.8	3.0
Iraq	435	10 074	23.2	3.2
Irish Republic (Eire)	70	3 014	42.9	0.5
Israel[8]	21	3 175	153.4	3.0
Italy	301	54 765	181.8	0.8
Ivory Coast	322	4 526	14.0	2.4
Jamaica	11	1 923	175.4	1.4
Japan[9]	372	107 561	288.9	1.1
Johnstone I. (U.S.)	0.001	1.0	1 007.0	—
Jordan[4]	98	2 467	25.2	3.4
Kenya	583	12 067	20.7	3.1
Khmer Republic (Cambodia)	181	6 800	37.6	1.6
Korea, North	121	14 680	121.8	2.8
Korea, South	98	32 848	333.6	2.2
Kuwait	18[1]	1 004	56.3	9.8
Laos	237	3 106	13.1	2.4
Lebanon	10	2 963	284.9	2.9
Lesotho	30	1 081	35.6	2.2
Liberia	111	1 571	14.1	5.3
Libya	1 760	2 161	1.2	3.7
Liechtenstein	0.2	21	133.8	1.9
Luxembourg	2.6	348	134.6	0.7
Macao (Port.)	0.02	268[10]	16 750.0	1.8
Malagasy Republic	587	6 750	11.5	2.0

Country	Area thousand km²	Population thousands	Density of population persons per km²	Mean annual increase % 1963–71
Malawi	118	4 666	39.4	2.6
Malaysia	330¹	10 910	33.1	2.6
Maldives	0.3	112	375.8	1.8
Mali	1 240	5 376	4.3	2.1
Malta	0.3	322	1 019.0	−0.1
Martinique (Fr.)	1.1	344	312.2	3.2
Mauritania	1 031	1 200	1.2	2.2
Mauritius	2.0	857	419.1	2.0
Mexico	1 973	52 641	26.7	3.2
Midway Is. (U.S.)	0.005	2.2	444.0	—
Monaco	0.002	24	16 107.4	0.8
Mongolia	1 565	1 340	0.86	2.8
Montserrat (U.K.)	0.1	13	132.7	0.2
Morocco	447	15 825	35.4	2.3
Mozambique (Port.)	783	8 508	10.9	2.7
Nauru	0.02	6.8	323.8	4.8
Nepal	141	11 467	81.4	1.8
Netherlands	34	13 439	398.6	1.2
Netherlands Antilles	1.0	230	239.3	1.4
New Caledonia (Fr.)	19	111	5.8	2.6
New Hebrides (U.K.-Fr.)	15	90	6.1	2.3
New Zealand	269	2 964	11.0	1.5
Nicaragua	130	1 988	15.3	2.7
Niger	1 267	4 356	3.4	2.7
Nigeria	924	71 262	77.1	2.5
Niue I. (N.Z.)	0.3	5.0	19.3	−0.8
Norfolk I. (Austral.)	0.04	1.7	46.8	8.9
Norway	324	3 948	12.2	0.8
Oman	212	699	3.3	3.0
Pacific Is., Trust Territory of the (U.S.)	1.8	107	60.1	2.8
Pakistan¹¹	888	66 000	74.3	3.8
Panama	76	1 524	20.1	3.0
Panama Canal Zone (U.S.)	1.4	45	31.4	0.6
Papua New Guinea	462	2 581	5.6	2.4
Paraguay	407	2 581	6.3	3.2
Peru	1 285	14 456	11.2	3.1
Philippines	300	40 423	134.7	3.0
Pitcairn I. (U.K.)	0.005	0.09	18.4	−1.2
Poland	313	33 391	106.8	0.8
Portugal¹²	92	8 590¹⁰	93.3	−0.3
Portuguese Guinea	36	479¹⁰	13.3	—
Portuguese Timor	15	626	41.9	1.7
Puerto Rico (U.S.)	8.9	2 852	320.6	1.4
Qatar	22	160	7.3	5.0
Réunion (Fr.)	2.5	466	185.7	2.6
Rhodesia	391	5 780	14.8	3.3

Country	Area thousand km²	Population thousands	Density of population persons per km²	Mean annual increase % 1963–71
Romania	238	20 769	87.4	1.1
Rwanda	26	3 896	147.9	2.9
St Helena (U.K.)[5]	0.3	6.6	20.9	4.2
St Kitts—Nevis—Anguilla (U.K.)[13]	0.3	65	182.1	1.4
St Lucia (U.K.)	0.6	115	186.7	1.6
St Pierre & Miquelon (Fr.)	0.2	5.6	23.1	5.0
St Vincent (U.K.)	0.4	91	234.5	0.8
San Marino	0.06	18	295.0	0.7
São Tomé & Príncipe (Port.)	1.0	75	77.8	1.7
Saudi Arabia	2 150	8 199	3.8	2.7
Sénégal	196	4 122	21.0	2.4
Seychelles (U.K.)	0.4	55	146.3	2.0
Sierra Leone	72	2 627	36.6	1.6
Sikkim	7.1	205	28.8	2.0
Singapore	0.6	2 185	3 760.8	2.0
Somali Republic	638	2 941	4.6	2.3
South Africa	1 221	22 987	18.8	3.1
Cape Province	721	6 722	9.3	2.2
Natal	87	4 246	48.6	3.6
Orange Free State	129	1 718	13.3	2.2
Transvaal	284	8 762	30.9	3.4
South West Africa (Namibia)	824	746	0.91	2.0
Spain[14]	505	34 494	68.3	1.1
Spanish Sahara	266	102[10]	0.38	4.2
Sri Lanka (Ceylon)	66	13 033	198.6	2.3
Sudan	2 506	16 901	6.7	2.8
Surinam (Neth.)	163	419	2.6	3.1
Svalbard & Jan Mayen (Nor.)	62	4.2	0.07	—
Swaziland	17	434	25.0	2.6
Sweden	450	8 134	18.1	0.8
Switzerland	41	6 422	155.5	1.2
Syrian Arab Republic[4]	185	6 879	37.1	3.3
Taiwan[3]	36	14 990	416.6	2.2
Tanzania	945[1]	14 372	15.2	2.6
Tanganyika	942[1]	13 969	14.8	2.6
Zanzibar	2.5[1]	403	163.8	2.0
Thailand	514	36 286	70.6	2.7
Togo	56	2 111	37.7	2.5
Tokelau Is. (N.Z.)	0.01	1.6	160.0	−2.8
Tonga	0.7	92	131.6	3.5
Trinidad & Tobago	5.1	1 043	203.4	1.4
Tunisia	164	5 509	33.8	3.2
Turkey	781	37 933	48.6	2.5
Turks & Caicos Is. (U.K.)	0.4	5.7	13.2	−0.1
Uganda	236	10 810	45.8	2.7

Country	Area thousand km²	Population thousands	Density of population persons per km²	Mean annual increase % 1963–71
U.S.S.R.	22 402	247 459	11.0	1.1
United Arab Emirates	84	203	2.4	3.0
United Kingdom	245	55 966	228.6	0.4
England and Wales	151	49 029	324.4	0.5
Scotland	79	5 210	66.1	0.0
Northern Ireland	14	1 549	109.5	0.7
Channel Is.	0.2	122	625.6	0.9
Isle of Man	0.6	56	95.2	0.7
U.S.A.	9 363	210 157	22.4	1.1
Upper Volta	274	5 611	20.5	2.1
Uruguay	178	2 956	16.7	1.2
Vatican City State	0.0004	1.0	—	—
Venezuela	912	10 969	12.0	3.5
Vietnam, North	159	22 038	138.8	2.4
Vietnam, South	174	18 809	108.2	2.6
Virgin Is. (U.S.)	0.3	67	194.8	5.0
Wake I. (U.S.)	0.008	1.6	205.9	—
Wallis & Fortuna Is. (Fr.)	0.2	10	50.0	1.5
Western Samoa	2.8	148	52.1	2.2
Yemen, North	195	6 062	31.1	2.7
Yemen, South	288	1 555	5.4	3.0
Yugoslavia	256	20 925	81.8	1.0
Zaïre	2 345	22 860	9.7	4.2
Zambia	753	4 420	5.9	2.9

[1] Area revised after new survey or inclusion of additional islands.
[2] Formerly British Honduras.
[3] China's population was estimated at 700 million in 1970 by Chinese sources. The UN estimate for 1972 was 801 million, but included Taiwan.
[4] Includes territory occupied by Israel.
[5] Includes dependencies.
[6] The sectors of Berlin are included in the relevant Germany.
[7] Including Indian held Jammu and Kashmir.
[8] Israel administers 90 000 km² of Arab territory with 1 million inhabitants.
[9] Includes Ryukyu Islands.
[10] Estimates revised from latest census reports.
[11] Includes Pakistani held Jammu and Kashmir.
[12] Includes Azores and Madeira.
[13] Anguilla is now administered separately but is still included in these figures.
[14] Includes Balearic and Canary Islands, also Alhucemas, Ceuta, Chafarinas, Melilla and Peñón de Vélez de la Gomera, previously listed as Spanish North Africa.

Sources: *UN Statistical Yearbook 1972. UN Population and Vital Statistics Report, July 1973.*

Extracted from *Geographical Digest 1974* by kind permission of George Philips and Son Ltd.

Appendix 3 International trade

The United Nations organisation publishes annually the *Yearbook of International Trade Statistics*, prepared by the Department of Economic and Social Affairs. The *Yearbook* includes tables which indicate by commodity the weight and value (converted to $US) of imports and exports of individual countries according to the Standard International Trade Classification (now Revised), i.e. SITC (Revised). The ten basic groups of the SITC (Revised) are:

Code No.

0	Food and live animals
1	Beverages and tobacco
2	Crude materials, excluding fuels
3	Mineral fuels
4	Animal and vegetable oils and fats
5	Chemicals
6	Basic manufactures (classified by materials)
7	Machinery and transport equipment
8	Miscellaneous manufactured goods
9	Goods not classified by kind (and special transactions)

Gold is excluded from these commodity statistics.

The table which follows draws on the statistics in the *Yearbook* for 1970–71 (the latest available at the time of going to press) but SITC (Revised) categories 6, 7, 8 and 9, which are essentially concerned with manufacturing, have been grouped together under the heading Manufactures (6, 7, 8, 9).

Countries whose total foreign trade exceeded 10 per cent of the total foreign trade of the United States of America, 1971 (unless indicated otherwise)

Country and total trade as % of total USA trade	Total imports, total exports (million US $)	Value of imports and of exports as percentage of the value of the country's total imports and total exports						
		SITC (Revised) Code No.						Manufactures (6, 7, 8, 9)
		0	1	2	3	4	5	
USA – 100								
Imports	45 563	12.0	2.0	7.4	8.1	0.4	3.5	66.6
Exports	43 492	10.0	1.6	10.0	3.4	1.4	8.8	64.8
Germany, W. – 82.4								
Imports	34 341	14.8	1.6	10.9	10.2	0.8	6.3	55.4
Exports	39 040	2.9	0.3	2.2	3.0	0.4	11.1	80.1

Table — *continued*

Country and total trade as % of total USA trade	Total imports, total exports (million US $)	Value of imports and of exports as percentage of the value of the country's total imports and total exports						
		SITC (Revised) Code No.						
		0	1	2	3	4	5	Manufactures (6, 7, 8, 9)
UK[1] — 52.0									
Imports	23 943	20.0	2.1	11.8	12.7	1.1	5.8	46.5
Exports	22 353	3.0	3.3	3.0	2.5	—	9.6	78.6
Japan — 49.0									
Imports	19 712	14.1	0.6	32.1	24.1	—	5.0	24.1
Exports	24 019	2.7	—	1.7	0.2	0.1	6.2	89.1
France — 46.6									
Imports	21 137	10.9	1.1	9.6	13.9	1.1	8.5	54.9
Exports	20 420	13.8	3.1	4.7	2.2	0.4	8.8	67.0
Canada[2] — 37.2									
Imports	15 458	6.6	0.5	4.8	5.9	0.3	5.4	76.5
Exports	17 675	10.4	1.4	21.3	7.1	0.2	3.3	56.3
Italy — 35.0									
Imports	15 968	18.2	0.8	14.0	16.8	1.3	7.7	41.2
Exports	15 112	6.9	1.6	2.0	5.4	0.3	7.0	76.8
Netherlands — 32.2									
Imports	14 771	11.0	1.1	7.8	13.0	1.1	7.6	58.4
Exports	13 927	20.7	1.2	5.8	12.4	1.0	12.6	46.3
USSR — 29.7 (1970)									
Imports	11 739	10.5	4.9	5.6	1.4	—	2.2	75.4
Exports	12 800	6.8	—	16.6	15.4	0.9	1.9	58.4
Belgium—Luxembourg — 28.3									
Imports	12 856	10.7	1.3	9.8	9.5	0.7	7.6	60.4
Exports	12 391	8.4	0.5	3.5	2.7	0.4	9.5	75.0
Sweden — 16.3									
Imports	7 082	8.7	1.0	4.6	12.2	0.6	8.6	64.3
Exports	7 464	2.4	0.1	18.1	0.9	0.3	4.0	74.2
Switzerland — 14.5									
Imports	7 154	10.3	2.0	4.5	6.4	0.4	10.1	66.3
Exports	5 768	4.0	2.3	1.6	—	0.1	21.2	70.8
Australia — 10.9									
Imports	4 632	3.9	1.2	5.6	4.8	0.4	10.1	74.0
Exports	5 073	36.1	0.3	28.4	6.2	0.7	5.0	23.3

[1] For detailed UK trade statistics see pp. 378—80
[2] For detailed Canadian trade statistics see pp. 770, 771

The foreign trade of some countries with a developing economy

Table — *continued*

Country and total trade as % of total USA trade	Total imports, total exports (million US $)	Value of imports and of exports as percentage of the value of the country's total imports and total exports						
		SITC (Revised) Code No.						Manufactures (6, 7, 8, 9)
		0	1	2	3	4	5	
Brazil — 6.3								
Imports	2 845	10.0	0.2	2.8	12.3	0.8	16.6	57.3
Exports	2 739	58.0	1.2	23.3	0.6	2.4	1.4	13.1
India — 5.0 (*1970*)								
Imports	2 094	18.4	—	12.2	7.7	2.2	11.2	48.3
Exports	2 012	26.7	2.1	17.1	0.8	0.4	2.3	50.6
Saudi Arabia — 3.7 (*1970*)								
Imports	692	3.5	3.4	0.9	1.1	0.5	8.1	82.5
Exports	2 423	—	—	10.2	89.8	—	—	—
Ghana — 1.0 (*1970*)								
Imports	410	19.0	1.0	2.2	5.8	1.0	15.8	55.2
Exports	433	76.4	—	14.0	0.1	—	0.1	9.4

Appendix 4 Exports of selected commodities from chief producing countries

Com-modity	World output '000 tons		Chief producing countries				
			Country	Year	Output '000 tons	Percentage of output exported	Value of export as percentage of value of total exports
Foodstuffs							
Cocoa	(a)	1 461	Ghana	(a)	396	100	75.0
	(b)	1 502		(b)	412	100	54.5
			Nigeria	(a)	300	65	17.0
				(b)	285	100	12.0
			Brazil	(a)	197	71.5	3.9
				(b)	204		
			Ivory Coast	(a)	180	89.6	24.6
				(b)	200		
			Cameroun	(a)	112	79.0	31.0
				(b)	112	85.6	28.8
Coffee	(a)	3 985	Brazil	(a)	755	100	35.85
	(b)	5 195		(b)	1 795		
			Colombia	(a)	570	67.3	63.4
				(b)	661		
			Ivory Coast	(a)	240	82.0	34.6
				(b)	268		
			Angola	(a)	204	88.5	31.8
				(b)	228		
			Ethiopia	(a)	205	34.6	61.5
				(b)	215		
Wheat	(a)	317 969	USSR	(a)	99 734	4.7	2.7
	(b)	353 269		(b)	98 760		
			USA	(a)	37 291	53.2	2.4
				(b)	44 028	36.8	2.3
			China	(a)	31 000*	n.a.	n.a.
				(b)	30 000	n.a.	n.a.
			India	(a)	20 093	nil	nil
				(b)	23 832	nil	nil
			France	(a)	12 921	26.6	1.5
				(b)	15 360	21.8	1.5
			Canada	(a)	9 689	100	4.0
				(b)	14 412	90.0	4.6

For explanation of symbols, see p. 924.

Table — *continued*

Commodity	World output '000 tons	Country	Year	Output '000 tons	Percentage of output exported	Value of export as percentage of value of total exports
Meat and meat preparations	(a) 80 128 (b) 81 548	USA	(a)	16 428[1]	n.a.	4.1
			(b)	17 126[1]	n.a.	4.4
		USSR	(a)	10 900[1]	n.a.	0.3
			(b)	11 800[1]	n.a.	
		China	(a)	11 193*[2]	n.a.	n.a.
			(b)	11 310*[2]	n.a.	n.a.
		Germany, W.	(a)	3 518[2]	n.a.	0.3
			(b)	3 712[2]	n.a.	0.3
		France	(a)	2 809*[1]	n.a.	0.9
			(b)	3 140*[1]	n.a.	1.1
		Brazil	(a)	2 635*[1]	n.a.	3.7
			(b)	2 640*[1]	n.a.	
		Argentina	(a)	2 817[1]	n.a.	24.9
			(b)	2 194[1]	n.a.	
		Australia	(a)	1 728[3]	n.a.	10.0
			(b)	2 073[3]	n.a.	11.0
Minerals Coal (bituminous only)	(a) 2 126 000 (b) 2 128 000	USA	(a)	541 562	12.0	2.3
			(b)	503 050	10.3	2.1
		USSR	(a)	432 715	5.6	2.4
			(b)	441 416		
		China	(a)	360 000*	n.a.	n.a.
			(b)	390 000*	n.a.	n.a.
		UK	(a)	144 562	3.1	0.3
			(b)	147 064	2.3	0.2
		Poland	(a)	140 101	20.6	9.6
			(b)	145 491		
		Germany, W.	(a)	111 443	24.5	2.0
			(b)	111 053	22.0	1.9
Iron ore (Fe content)	(a) 418 800 (b) 428 730	USSR	(†)			2.5
			(a)	106 058		
			(b)	110 341		
		USA	(a)	53 308	nil	nil
			(b)	48 799	nil	nil
		Australia	(a)	32 732	100	7.9
			(b)	39 588	100	9.0
		Canada	(a)	29 687	100	2.8
			(b)	27 045	100	2.3

Table — *continued*

Com- modity	World output '000 tons		Chief producing countries				
		Country	Year	Output '000 tons	Percentage of output exported	Value of export as percentage of value of total exports
Petroleum (crude oil)	(a) 2 278 400 (b) 2 401 300	USA	(a) (b)	475 346 466 704	n.a. n.a.	0.04 2.2
		USSR	(a) (b)	352 574 377 075	18.9	7.1
		Iran	(a) (b)	191 740 223 921	77.7 71.6	74.8 74.7
		Saudi Arabia	(a) (b)	176 850 223 412		83.3
		Venezuela	(a) (b)	193 873 185 776	65.8	61.8

Symbols
(†) 1969
(*a*) 1970
(*b*) 1971
*   estimate
blank not yet available
n.a.   not available
1   mainly beef and veal
2   mainly pork
3   mainly beef, but mutton and lamb 762 000 (1970), 935 000 (1971)
4   greasy wool
5   clean wool

Sources: United Nations Yearbook of International Statistics, 1970–71. FAO Production Yearbook

Appendix 5 Statistical tables from the First Edition, 1889

Average prices of British imports and exports of certain commodities in the under-mentioned years

I. Imports

Years	Wheat	Maize	Rice	Raw sugar	Refined sugar	Tea	Coffee	Unmanfd. tobacco
	per cwt.	per cwt.	per cwt.	per cwt.	per cwt.	per lb.	per cwt.	per lb.
Extreme	s.	s.	s.	s.	s.	d.	£	d.
years	9.20 to	6.29 to	9.02 to	20.29 to	28.57 to	14.61 to	2.65 to	7.33 to
1854–70	16.75	10.14	14.64	35.14	45.98	19.88	3.97	12.00
1871	11.84	7.69	10.19	25.10	36.15	16.44	3.15	8.09
1872	12.42	7.09	10.00	26.20	36.35	16.78	3.54	8.24
1873	13.01	7.06	9.92	23.97	33.84	16.67	4.42	7.72
1874	12.15	8.46	10.33	22.42	30.70	17.00	5.03	8.34
1875	10.61	7.95	8.95	21.16	30.33	16.73	4.73	8.63
1876	10.43	6.39	9.06	20.92	29.45	16.42	4.68	8.36
1877	12.49	6.47	10.55	25.73	33.79	15.98	4.83	8.05
1878	10.99	6.04	10.48	21.47	29.26	15.29	4.66	6.73
1879	10.56	5.43	10.15	20.22	27.39	14.68	4.40	7.20
1880	11.08	6.00	9.52	21.71	29.23	13.47	4.44	7.04
1881	11.04	6.22	8.64	21.72	28.93	12.82	3.87	6.85
1882	10.67	7.15	7.98	21.11	28.67	12.58	3.81	7.67
1883	9.81	6.53	8.20	20.10	27.22	12.46	3.51	7.63
1884	8.41	5.89	8.14	15.51	20.89	11.78	3.30	7.87
1885	7.83	5.39	7.82	13.89	18.15	12.06	3.19	7.92
1886	7.55	4.91	7.48	13.07	16.70	11.77	3.27	7.23

Years	Refined petroleum	Copper ore	Tin	Crude zinc	Guano	Nitrate of soda	Window glass	Rags	Esparto	Paper
	per gal.	per ton	per cwt.	per ton	per ton	per cwt.	per cwt.	per ton	per ton	per cwt.
Extreme	d.	£	£	£	£	s.	s.	£	£	s.
years	15.82 to[1]	11.44 to	4.02 to	17.62 to	9.15 to	10.96 to	14.00 to	16.77 to[2]	4.49 to[2]	51.33 to[2]
1854–70	35.91	18.93	6.87	29.74	12.58	20.08	16.29	20.92	9.66	56.15
1871	16.59	13.65	6.34	20.55	11.11	15.59	14.95	16.53	8.63	51.22
1872	16.85	17.23	6.92	20.30	10.12	15.31	17.27	16.76	7.98	56.33
1873	14.30	16.54	6.70	23.38	11.41	14.68	18.76	17.63	8.47	60.80
1874	11.10	14.91	4.91	22.21	12.00	12.00	17.45	17.06	8.42	53.09
1875	9.62	13.78	4.33	22.57	11.30	11.99	16.79	17.34	8.04	47.11
1876	13.74	12.38	3.77	22.58	11.52	11.47	15.80	16.51	8.23	48.64
1877	12.66	10.10	3.49	20.49	10.88	13.52	14.59	14.97	7.60	49.92
1878	9.70	8.65	3.13	18.64	10.16	14.88	13.71	15.19	6.93	49.51
1879	7.68	8.69	3.41	16.62	9.15	14.02	14.12	15.33	6.77	37.40
1880	8.15	9.37	4.45	18.94	10.06	15.32	14.36	15.24	7.19	36.32
1881	7.96	7.81	4.61	16.40	9.73	14.64	14.60	14.80	6.83	36.18
1882	6.92	9.73	5.23	16.93	8.64	13.27	15.73	14.31	7.09	35.29
1883	7.39	10.34	4.69	15.70	9.76	11.41	15.69	14.08	6.74	33.02
1884	7.75	11.10	4.07	14.69	9.10	9.64	13.90	13.46	6.29	30.49
1885	7.44	7.04	4.28	14.11	9.70	9.92	13.63	13.16	5.98	29.92
1886	7.04	6.85	4.81	14.32	7.81	9.94	12.58	12.45	5.51	31.21

[1] 1863 to 1870.
[2] 1861 to 1870.

Appendix 5

I. Imports — *continued*

Years	Cotton	Flax	Raw silk	Wool	Hewn wood	Hides, dry and wet
	per cwt.	per cwt.	per lb.	per lb.	per load	per cwt.
Extreme	£	s.	s.	d.	£	£
years	} 2.55 to	39.04 to	13.85 to	13.65 to	2.91 to	2.52 to
1854–70	} 9.79	60.53	26.56	18.02	4.35	4.06
1871	3.52	46.96	21.62	13.32	2.82	2.99
1872	4.24	52.28	21.43	14.51	2.91	3.42
1873	4.01	49.95	20.97	14.75	3.24	3.53
1874	3.62	48.76	16.80	14.71	3.22	3.63
1875	3.47	53.05	15.35	15.41	2.87	3.48
1876	3.02	55.29	19.18	14.54	2.90	3.13
1877	2.93	49.37	20.05	14.38	2.81	3.09
1878	2.80	48.01	17.65	13.90	2.45	2.93
1879	2.76	45.25	17.42	13.56	2.10	2.88
1880	2.94	46.13	17.04	13.66	2.47	3.12
1881	2.92	41.04	16.98	13.87	2.57	3.18
1882	2.93	38.73	16.54	12.27	2.62	3.15
1883	2.91	39.92	16.20	12.08	2.61	3.18
1884	2.85	40.73	14.79	12.09	2.39	3.19
1885	2.86	41.62	14.07	10.05	2.40	3.15
1886	2.49	41.52	13.73	9.08	2.16	2.96

II. Exports (British produce and manufactures)

Years	Alkali	Salt	Soap	Candles	Plate glass	Coals	Pig and puddled iron
	per cwt.	per ton	per cwt.	per doz. lb.	per sq. foot	per ton	per ton
Extreme	s.	s.	s.	s.	s.	s.	s.
years	} 7.58 to	8.98 to	24.71 to	7.19 to	2.04 to[1]	7.09 to	44.93 to
1840–70	} 11.04	14.94	33.19	11.87	2.67	10.18	85.05
1871	8.37	10.47	27.14	7.78	1.95	9.63	61.08
1872	11.17	14.15	26.04	7.89	2.29	15.51	100.85[2]
1873	12.32	18.77	26.45	8.04	3.01	20.49	124.65[2]
1874	10.45	16.00	25.35	8.26	3.06	16.98	94.67
1875	9.16	14.75	24.74	8.00	2.62	13.10	72.80
1876	8.15	12.35	24.58	7.60	2.22	10.80	62.47
1877	7.73	11.10	24.45	7.73	2.22	10.05	57.34
1878	7.00	12.31	24.15	7.64	1.85	9.35	53.52
1879	6.34	11.50	22.54	6.81	1.58	8.63	51.50
1880	6.96	11.49	22.47	6.80	1.62	8.76	63.94
1881	6.14	11.64	22.48	6.52	1.52	8.83	55.38
1882	6.14	11.90	22.40	6.50	1.53	8.99	56.45
1883	6.12	12.84	22.96	6.72	1.42	9.20	52.14
1884	6.37	12.91	22.99	6.66	1.45	9.18	46.40
1885	5.87	14.59	23.50	6.14	1.27	8.83	43.56
1886	5.73	14.61	20.93	5.40	1.09	8.32	43.17

[1] 1857 to 1870.

[2] Export of iron, wrought and unwrought, from the United Kingdom to the United States in thousands of tons: 1869, 735; 1870, 832; 1871, 1 064; 1872, 975; 1873, 493; 1874, 287; to Germany: 1869, 200; 1872, 440; 1873, 396; 1874, 227.

II. Exports (British produce and manufactures) — *continued*

Years	Tin, un-wrought	Tinned plates	Copper, unwrought	Lead: pig sheet, and pipe	Cement	Cotton yarn	Cotton piece goods		Wool: sheep and lamb
							Plain	Printed	
	per cwt.	per ton	per cwt.	per ton	per cwt.	per lb.	per yd.	per yd.	per lb.
Extreme	£	£	£	£	s.	d.	d.	d.	d.
years	}3.04 to	23.47 to[1]	3.73 to	17.24 to	2.43 to[2]	10.44 to	2.79 to	4.01 to	11.40 to
1840–70	}6.64	26.71	5.96	24.88	4.12	28.80	5.79	6.32	23.89
1871	6.70	24.25	3.78	19.27	2.44	18.66	3.33	4.71	16.64
1872	7.47	32.24	4.81	20.45	2.45	18.87	3.51	4.92	19.86
1873	6.83	32.77	4.68	23.75	3.04	17.76	3.45	4.78	21.18
1874	5.24	30.21	4.40	2.63	2.98	15.79	3.22	4.69	21.92
1875	4.57	26.64	4.40	23.17	2.61	14.66	3.13	4.77	21.14
1876	3.96	21.81	4.13	22.55	2.55	13.19	2.83	4.48	18.53
1877	3.68	19.80	3.78	21.49	2.58	12.85	2.83	4.31	17.73
1878	3.32	17.60	3.49	18.74	2.56	12.47	2.76	4.18	19.87
1879	3.60	17.81	3.17	15.42	2.49	12.33	2.65	3.91	14.39
1880	4.52	20.48	3.41	17.41	2.50	13.25	2.73	3.79	16.57
1881	4.80	17.11	3.28	15.72	2.37	12.39	2.65	3.68	15.26
1882	5.24	17.51	3.57	15.45	2.34	12.96	2.71	3.73	15.20
1883	4.88	17.47	3.38	14.07	2.31	12.25	2.61	3.62	12.71
1884	4.27	16.45	2.94	12.58	2.25	12.24	2.47	3.60	10.94
1885	4.43	14.84	2.40	12.25	2.20	11.58	2.33	3.47	9.55
1886	5.03	14.16	2.19	13.85	2.02	10.84	2.21	3.18	10.07

Years	Woollen and worsted yarn	Woollen cloths, etc.	Linen manufactures:		Jute manu-factures	Silk manu-factures	Boots and shoes
			Plain	Sails and sailcloth			
	per lb.	per yd.	per yd.	per yd.	per yd.	per yd.	per doz. prs.
Extreme	d.	d.	d.	d.	d.	s.	s.
years	}22.12 to	23.83 to	6.84 to	8.34 to	3.56 to[3]	3.14 to[4]	60.82 to[4]
1840–70	}41.06	40.99	8.50	14.20	6.16	4.09	75.83
1871	33.49	37.52	7.39	12.94	3.95	3.32	59.72
1872	36.91	41.19	7.43	14.29	4.22	3.15	58.54
1873	37.26	41.00	7.62	13.97	3.98	3.54	64.73
1874	38.14	39.53	7.80	14.41	3.57	3.36	67.02
1875	38.58	39.09	7.59	14.36	3.30	3.08	65.56
1876	34.36	38.25	7.14	14.37	3.09	3.29	63.35
1877	32.12	35.72	6.93	13.71	3.18	3.22	61.28
1878	30.07	34.53	7.20	12.96	3.10	3.32	61.16
1879	26.71	31.89	7.08	11.69	2.87	3.38	60.52
1880	30.33	32.34	7.38	12.15	2.95	3.26	61.03
1881	26.04	32.55	7.03	12.01	2.78	3.27	57.13
1882	25.62	34.18	6.89	12.44	2.70	3.37	58.72
1883	23.41	38.30	6.95	11.73	2.64	3.26	60.10
1884	23.78	41.42	6.62	10.95	2.43	3.26	59.92
1885	24.19	40.23	6.35	10.83	2.13	3.72	58.09
1886	23.19	39.56	5.98	11.09	2.01	3.97	58.38

[1] 1857 to 1870.
[2] 1843 to 1870.
[3] 1861 to 1870.
[4] 1862 to 1870.

United Kingdom – General imports

A. Principal articles	Average value in millions Sterling							Percentages of total value						Principal countries of origin
	1854–5	1856–60	1861–5	1866–70	1871–5	1876–80	1881–5	1856–60	1861–5	1866–70	1871–5	1876–80	1881–5	
1. Corn, total	19.63	22.46	27.85	36.47	49.96	59.70	58.66	12.3	11.2	12.5	13.8	15.6	14.7	1. U.S., Rus., Ind., B.N.A.
Wheat, also included in corn	*10.68*	*11.31*	*14.94*	*19.16*	*26.15*	*29.31*	*28.24*	*6.2*	*6.0*	*6.5*	*7.2*	*7.6*	*7.0*	U.S., Ind., B.N.A., Rus.
Wheat flour included in corn	*3.13*	*3.18*	*3.86*	*3.46*	*4.79*	*7.10*	*10.40*	*1.7*	*1.5*	*1.2*	*1.3*	*1.8*	*2.6*	U.S., A.H., Ger., B.N.A.
2. Cotton, raw	20.51	31.23	54.05	59.01	52.19	37.61	43.29	17.1	21.8	20.2	14.4	9.8	10.8	2. U.S., Ind., Eg.
3. Wool: sheep, lamb, alpaca, etc.	6.51	9.63	12.76	15.87	20.10	24.25	24.73	5.3	5.2	5.4	5.5	6.3	6.1	3. Alia, S. Af., B.E.I.
4. Sugar, raw	9.62	12.42	12.06	12.72	16.67	18.02	18.07	6.8	4.9	4.3	4.6	4.7	4.5	4. Ger., Jav., Gui., B.W.I.
5. Butter and butterine	–	2.54	5.19	6.41	7.51	10.34	11.72	1.4	2.1	2.2	2.1	2.7	2.9	5. Hol., Fr., Den.
6. Tea	5.38	5.57	9.23	10.82	12.24	12.22	10.98	3.0	3.7	3.7	3.4	3.2	2.7	6. Ch., Ben., Cey.
7. Silk manufactures	1.87	2.42	7.06	11.33	10.43	12.72	10.94	1.3	2.9	3.9	2.9	3.3	2.7	7. Fr.
8. Wood, sawn or split	4.17	4.31	6.01	6.80	9.28	10.29	9.85	2.3	2.4	2.3	2.5	2.7	2.4	8. B.N.A., Rus., Swe.
9. Wood and timber, hewn	4.27	4.03	5.44	4.24	5.86	4.89	5.00	2.2	2.2	1.5	1.6	1.2	1.2	9. B.N.A., Bur., Swe., Nor., Rus.
10. Wine	3.34	3.36	4.18	5.01	7.34	6.39	5.40	1.8	1.7	1.7	2.0	1.6	1.3	10. Fr., Port., Sp., Hol.
11. Coffee	1.63	1.89	3.65	4.63	6.49	6.80	4.38	1.0	1.5	1.6	1.8	1.7	1.1	11. Cent. Am., Mad., Cey., Braz., Fr.
12. Flax or linseed	2.54	3.08	3.52	3.74	4.43	4.56	4.52	1.7	1.4	1.3	1.2	1.2	1.1	12. Ben., Bom., Rus.
13. Jute, from 1861	–	–	1.42	1.86	3.48	3.24	3.92	–	0.6	0.6	0.9	0.8	0.9	13. Ind.
14. Hides, tanned and untanned	1.98	3.29	3.11	3.60	4.46	3.41	3.70	1.8	1.3	1.2	1.2	0.8	0.9	14. Ind., Bel., S. Af.
15. Flax, dressed and undressed	3.35	3.31	4.11	4.13	4.61	3.45	2.83	1.8	1.7	1.4	1.2	0.9	0.7	15. Rus., Bel., Hol.
16. Rice, not in the husk	1.29	1.48	1.9	2.29	3.14	3.37	3.00	0.8	0.8	0.8	0.8	0.8	0.7	16. Bur., Ben., Hol.
17. Tobacco, manufactured and unmanufactured	1.44	2.10	2.87	2.35	3.37	3.19	2.91	1.1	1.2	0.8	0.9	0.8	0.7	17. U.S., Fr., Hol.
18. Silk, raw	4.95	9.22	8.68	7.71	6.38	4.08	2.52	5.0	3.5	2.6	1.7	1.0	0.6	18. Ch., Bel., Fr.
19. Eggs	0.23	0.34	0.71	1.06	2.07	2.42	2.65	0.2	0.3	0.4	0.5	0.6	0.6	19. Fr., Ger., Bel.
20. Indigo	1.65	2.27	2.41	2.68	2.32	1.79	2.40	1.2	1.0	0.9	0.6	0.4	0.6	20. Ind., Cent. Am.
21. Caoutchouc, from 1861	–	–	0.49	1.07	1.61	1.67	2.58	–	0.2	0.4	0.4	0.4	0.6	21. Braz., Ind.
22. Paper-making materials	–	–	0.53	0.88	1.43	1.65	2.16	–	0.2	0.3	0.4	0.4	0.5	22. Alg., Sp., Trip., Bel.
23. Spirits	–	2.19	1.88	2.43	2.88	2.78	2.00	1.2	0.8	0.8	0.8	0.7	0.5	23. Fr., B.W.I., Gui.
Average total value	148.0	182.9	247.6	292.8	360.2	382.5	400.0							

United Kingdom — Exports of native produce and manufactures

A. Principal articles	Average value in millions Sterling									Percentages of the total value of the exports of British and Irish produce						Principal destinations
	1843–5	'46–50	1851–5	'56–60	1861–5	'66–70	1871–5	'76–80	1881–5	'56–60	1861–5	'66–70	1871–5	'76–80	1881–5	
1. Cotton manufactures[1]	18.07	18.75	25.02	34.98	40.07	55.92	60.20	56.06	61.16	28.1	27.7	29.7	25.1	27.8	26.3	1. Ind., Tur., Ch., Egg., Brazil, etc.
Cotton manufactures[1] *including yarn*	25.11	25.32	31.83	44.10	48.66	70.32	75.26	68.45	74.20	35.4	33.6	37.3	31.3	33.9	31.9	2. Widely scattered
Iron and steel	3.09	4.91	8.90	13.33	13.92	19.75	31.35	21.41	26.79	10.7	9.6	10.5	13.1	10.6	11.5	3. U.S., and many other countries
3. Woollen manufactures	7.56	6.97	8.82	10.84	15.70	21.18	25.87	17.16	18.83	8.7	10.8	11.2	10.8	8.5	8.1	
Woollen manufactures *including yarn*	8.48	8.01	10.41	13.85	20.13	26.58	31.52	20.95	22.46	11.1	13.8	14.0	13.1	10.3	9.6	4. Ind., Ger., Hol., Jap.
4. Cotton yarn	7.04	6.57	6.81	9.12	8.59	14.40	15.06	12.39	13.04	7.3	5.9	7.6	6.2	6.1	5.6	
5. Machinery and steam engines	0.79	0.98	1.71	3.55	4.54	4.97	8.60	7.59	11.89	2.8	3.1	2.6	3.6	3.7	5.1	5. Widely scattered
6. Coal, cinders, and fuel	0.77	1.08	1.77	3.16	3.98	5.39	10.30	7.93	10.09	2.5	2.7	2.8	4.3	3.9	4.3	6. Fr., It., Ger.
7. Apparel, slops, haberdashery, and millinery	1.47	1.86	4.57	5.90	6.79	7.13	9.16	6.85	7.42	4.7	4.7	3.8	3.8	3.4	3.1	7. Alia, S. Af., Fr.
8. Linen manufactures	2.95	3.20	4.26	4.58	6.56	7.63	7.48	5.66	5.47	3.7	4.5	4.0	3.1	2.8	2.3	8. U.S., Alia, For. W. I.
Linen manufactures *including yarn*	3.95	3.92	5.28	6.22	8.86	9.97	9.46	6.86	6.52	5.0	6.1	5.2	3.9	3.9	2.7	
9. Woollen and worsted yarn	0.92	1.04	1.59	3.01	4.43	5.40	5.65	3.79	3.63	2.4	3.0	2.8	2.3	1.8	1.5	9. Ger., Hol., U.S., etc.
10. Hardware and cutlery	2.03	2.24	3.20	3.72	3.39	3.61	4.54	3.33	3.54	3.0	2.3	1.9	1.9	1.6	1.5	10. Alia, U.S., Ger., Fr.
11. Copper, wrought and unwrought, including mixed or yellow metal	—	—	—	—	3.18	2.95	2.97	3.10	3.40	—	2.2	1.6	1.2	1.5	1.4	11. Ind., Fr., Ger., Hol.
12. Silk manufactures, from 1861	—	—	—	—	1.38	1.19	1.99	1.83	2.36	—	0.9	0.6	0.8	0.9	1.0	12. U.S., Fr., Ind.
13. Jute manufactures from 1861	—	—	—	—	0.23	0.61	1.43	1.78	2.32	—	0.1	0.3	0.6	0.8	1.0	13. U.S., Ger., Braz., A.R.
14. Earthenware and porcelain	—	—	—	1.35	1.31	1.72	1.99	1.86	2.13	1.1	0.8	0.9	0.8	0.9	0.9	14. U.S., B.N.A.
15. Herrings	—	—	—	—	0.54	0.64	1.00	1.04	1.24	—	0.4	0.3	0.4	0.5	0.5	15. Ger., Rus.
16. Linen yarn	1.00	0.72	1.02	1.64	2.30	2.34	1.98	1.20	1.05	1.3	1.6	1.2	0.8	0.6	0.4	16. Various Eur. countries
Average total value	56.95	60.89	88.87	124.2	144.4	187.8	239.5	201.4	232.3							

[1] In 1785 the estimated value of the cotton piece goods exported from the United Kingdom was 5.4 per cent of the total value of the exports, in 1815 38 per cent

Appendix 6 Conversion tables

Temperature

°F	°C	°C	°F
0	−17.8	0	32.0
32	0.0	5	41.0
40	4.4	10	50.0
50	10.0	15	59.0
60	15.6	20	68.0
70	21.1	25	77.0
75	23.9	30	86.0
80	26.7	35	95.0
85	29.4	40	104.0

To convert degrees Fahrenheit to degrees Centigrade (Celsius):

$$(°F - 32°) \times \tfrac{5}{9} = °C$$

To convert degrees Centigrade (Celsius) to degrees Fahrenheit:

$$(°C \times \tfrac{9}{5}) + 32° = °F$$

Length

1 inch = $\begin{cases} 2.54 \text{ centimetres} \\ 25.4 \text{ millimetres} \end{cases}$

1 foot = 0.3048 metre
1 yard = 0.914 metre
1 mile = 1.609 kilometres

1 millimetre = 0.0394 inches
1 centimetre = 0.394 inches

1 metre = $\begin{cases} 39.37 \text{ inches} \\ 3.28 \text{ feet} \\ 1.09 \text{ yards} \end{cases}$

1 kilometre = 0.62 mile

Approximations

10 inches =	*250 millimetres*
40 inches =	*1 000 millimetres*
10 feet =	*3 metres*
500 feet =	*150 metres*
100 yards =	*90 metres*
5 miles =	*8 kilometres*
100 miles =	*160 kilometres*

25 millimetres =	*1 inch*
1 500 millimetres =	*60 inches*
10 centimetres =	*4 inches*
100 metres =	*110 yards*
8 kilometres =	*5 miles*
250 kilometres =	*155 miles*

10 fathoms = 18.3 metres
10 nautical miles (international)
 = 11.51 statute miles
10 nautical miles (international)
 = 18.52 kilometres

10 metres = 5.5 fathoms
10 statute miles = 8.69 nautical
 miles (international)
10 kilometres = 5.40 nautical
 miles (international)

Area

1 acre	= 0.4 hectare	1 hectare	= 2.471 acres
100 acres	= 40.47 hectares	100 hectares	= 247.11 acres

1 sq. mile
= 640 acres } = 2.59 sq. kilometres

1 sq. kilometre
= 100 hectares } = 0.386 sq. miles

150 sq. miles = 388.5 sq. kilometres

150 sq. kilometres } = 57.91 sq. miles

Capacity

1 pint	= 0.568 litre	1 litre	= 1.76 pints
1 gallon (UK)	= 4.545 litres	1 hectolitre	= 22 gallons (UK)
8 gallons (UK)	= 36 litres		= 2.7 bushels (UK)
	= 1 bushel		= 2.8 bushels (US)
		1 quintal	= 3.7 bushels (UK)
			= 100 kilograms

Petroleum

1 barrel = 42 gallons (US)
= 35 gallons (UK)
= 350 lb
= 1.59 hectolitres
7 barrels = 1 metric ton (tonne) approximately
1 million barrels per day (bpd) = 50 million tons per year

Weight

1 lb	= 453.592 grams	1 kilogram	= 2.20 lb
	= 0.45 kilogram	100 kilograms	= 220.46 lb
100 lb	= 45.36 kilograms	1 tonne	= 0.98 UK (long) ton
1 long ton	= 2 240 lb		
1 metric ton (tonne) = 2 204.6 lb			= 1.1 US (short) tons
1 short ton = 2 000 lb			

Metals

1 troy oz = 480 grains
= 31.1 grams
= 0.03 kilogram
32 troy oz = 1 kilogram
35.3 avoirdupois oz = 1 kilogram

Note. All references to tons in the text are to metric tons unless otherwise stated. Shipping tons are gross tons unless otherwise stated.

Appendix 6

Yield

1 lb per acre = 1.12 kilograms per hectare
100 lb per acre = 112 kilograms *or* 1.12 quintals per hectare
1 cwt per acre = 125.54 kilograms *or* 1.3 quintals per hectare
10 bushels (UK) per acre = 9 hectolitres per hectare

1 000 kilograms per hectare = 892 lb per acre
  10 quintals per hectare   = 8 cwt per acre
    1 quintal per hectare   = 1.49 bushels (UK) per acre
  10 hectolitres per hectare = 11.1 bushels (UK) per acre

(1 quintal = 100 kilograms)

The bushel and the hectolitre are now in general use as standard units of weight, but it should be remembered that they vary for different commodities and for different countries:

Rice (@ 45 lb per bushel)

10 bushels per acre = 5 quintals per hectare
50 bushels per acre = 25.1 quintals = 2 500 kilograms
                  = 2.5 tonnes per hectare

Wheat (@ 60 lb per bushel)

10 bushels per acre = 6.7 quintals per hectare
50 bushels per acre = 33.6 quintals per hectare

Population density

  10 persons per sq. kilometre = 26 per sq. mile
  39 persons per sq. kilometre = 100 per sq. mile (approx.)
  90 persons per sq. kilometre = 250 per sq. mile (approx.)
100 persons per sq. kilometre = 259 per sq. mile
193 persons per sq. kilometre = 500 per sq. mile

Comprehensive conversion tables will be found in *Geographical Conversion Tables*, compiled and edited by D. H. K. Amiran and A. P. Schick, The Hebrew University of Jerusalem, an International Geographical Union publication, obtainable from Kümmerly and Frey, Hallerstrasse 6–8, 3 000 Berne, Switzerland.

Index

Only principal references are included, and the more important are shown in heavy type.

Free-trade, effects of, 4, 9
Freight handling, 107–10; *see also* Air
transport, Railways, Roads, Ocean
transport and vessels, Transport
bulk, 107 *et seq.*
break of bulk, 107
containers in, 108–9
costs, 107, 108
means of, 107
pallets in, 109
pipelines, 110
railbridge, by, 108
technical improvements, 107 *et seq.*
French Equatorial Africa, former,
733–6
territories, area and population, 733
French West Africa, former, 723–5
territories, area and population, 724
French Polynesia, 904
French Territories, Pacific, 903–4
Fronts, 28
Frost, 48, 49, 70
pockets, 26, 27
Fruit, citrus, 39, 149–51, 322; *see also*
Grapefruit, Lemons, Oranges
Africa, South, 702
Belize, 828
Cuba, 813
Dominica, 820
Israel, 551
Italy, 497
Moçambique, 746
oils, 228, 229
Rhodesia, 707
Surinam, 844
trade, 150
USA, 786
Fruit, deciduous, 39, 44
Canada, 769, 771, 773
Fruit, dried, 505
Fruits, Mediterranean, 39, 462
Africa, South, 698, 702
Chile, 857
Fruits, temperate zone, 149–52
tropical, 216
Fuji san, 656
Fundy, Bay of, tidal power, 772
Funtumia elastica, 218
Fur, 46, 239–40
animals yielding, 239
Canada, 240, 777
farms, 240, 470, 483–4, 518
manmade, simulated, 240
markets, 239

producing area, 239
trade, 434
USSR, 240
Fustic (*Morus tinctoria*), 235

Gabon, 733, 734
Galápagos Islands, 851
Gambia, 723
Gambier (from *Uncaria Gambier*), 301
Gambier island group, 904
Gamboge, 236
Gan, 602
Ganga, River and valley, 52, 58, 70, 74,
179, 573, 576, 581, 584
Ganister, 297
Garancine, 235
Gas, natural, 273–4
Algeria, 688
Australia, 875 (map), 877, 885, 887,
888
Bolivia, 855
Brunei, 616, 621
Canada, 766, 775, 789 (map)
Czechoslovakia, 455
Egypt, 675
France, 391
Gabon, 734
Germany, 418
Germany, W., 421
Hungary, 459
Indian subcontinent, 575, 583 (map)
Indonesia, 624
Israel, 552
Mexico, 807
Netherlands, 405
New Zealand, 892
Pakistan, 594
pipelines, 273, 274
Romania, 467
Southwest Asia, 558 (map)
transport, 273–4
USSR (map), 513, 514, 515
UK, 271, 365
USA, 789 (map), 791
Gas production, 315
Gases
production, 315
transport of, 315
uses of, 315
Gasoline, 265
Gelatine, 247
Gemstones, 605
Geographical inertia, 120, 350
Geographical momentum, 120

Hardwood, 32, 44, 47, **236—8**, 606,
  612; *see also* Timber
  America, Central, 826, 828
  cabinet, 826
  Cameroun, 733
  Canada, 237
  Congo (Brazzaville), 735
  Central African Republic, 735
  dollar shortage, and, 237
  Gabon, 734
  greenheart, 843
  Ivory Coast, 726
  temperate, 236, 906 (map)
  trade, 236, 237
  tropical, 236, 906 (map)
  types, 238
  USA, 237
  world distribution, 906 (map)
Hargreaves, 183
Harwich, 365, **370**
Hausa language, 124
Hawaii, 779, 801
Heat, 21
Heat loss, 24
Hedley, 84
Helsinki, 485
Helium, 315
Hemp (*Cannabis sativa*), and similar
  fibres, **160—1**
  conditions for growth, 161
  Italy, 496
  manila, 161
  New Zealand flax (*phormium*), 161
  products, 161
  sisal, 161
  USSR, 161
Hemp fibres, varieties of, 215
Herbertson, A. J., 27, 28, 34
Herodotus, 176
Herring, 251, 252, **254—5**
Hessian fly, 72
Hevea brasiliensis, 30, 217, 220; *see also*
  Rubber
Hides and skins, **244—5**, 247
  Africa, South, 245
  Australia, 245
  exporters, 245
  New Zealand, 245
High altitudes
  temperature, 25
Highland regions climate
  temperate, **48—9**
  tropical, **47—8**
High pressure, 21, 36, 40, 42

Highway, Pan- (Inter-) American, 825,
  829, 830, 853, 858
Himalayas, 42, 573
  countries of, 597 *et seq.*
Hindustani, 124
Hinterlands, **113—15**
  concept of, 114
Hobart, 888, 889
Hokkaidō, 656, 659; *see also* Japan
Holy Roman Empire, 408
Hominy, 142
Honduras, 825, **828—9**; *see also*
  America, Central
Honey, **229**
Hong Kong, 100, **633—5**, 641
  China, and, relations with 634
Honolulu, 101
Honshū, **655—6**; *see also* Japan
Hops, **158**
Horns and hoofs, 246
Horsehair, 246
Horses, draught, 80
Hosiery and knitwear, 167
Houston, 792, 793, 797
Houston—Galveston Canal, 88
Hudson Bay, 46
Hudson—Mohawk gap, 794
Hudson's Bay Company, 125, 240, 373,
  759
Huertas, 487
Huguenots, 174
Hull, and Humberside, 252, **367—8**
Humboldt, 48
Humboldt (Peruvian) current, 835, 852
Humus, 52, 54
Hungary, 53, **457—60**
  agriculture and crops, 458—9
  farm organisation, 458
  fish, 458
  foreign trade, 460
  manufacturing, 458, 459—60
  minerals, 459
  population, 458, 460
  surface, 458
  wine, 157
Hunterston, 369
Hurricanes, 70
Hydrocarbon products, 311
Hydroelectric power, **69**
Hydrogen, 315
Hwango Ho (Yellow River), 638

Iberian peninsula, 486, 491
Ibiza, 491